P9-DTE-811

CANADIAN OXFORD

WORLD ATLAS

NEW EDITION

Edited by Quentin H. Stanford

Toronto **OXFORD UNIVERSITY PRESS**

2 Contents

Canada, satellite images — 4·5
Latitude and longitude — 6
Map projections — 7
Understanding topographic maps — 8.9

Canada Thematic

Canada — 10·11
Pleistocene glaciation — 10
Geology — 12
Glacial effect on landforms — 12
Landforms — 13
Climate: Isotherms — 14
Temperature range — 14
Mean annual precipitation — 15
Mean annual snowfall — 15
Thunderstorms and tornadoes — 15
Air masses and winds — 15
January wind chill — 16
Growing season — 16
Sunshine — 16
Climate regions — 17
Natural vegetation, forestry — 18
Ecozones — 19
Fishing: Pacific Coast — 19
Atlantic Coast — 19
Soils — 20
Agriculture — 20
Agricultural lands — 21
Wheat production and export — 21
Endangered lands and species — 22
Water resources, electrical power — 23
Great Lakes pollution — 23

Electricity trade — 23
Nonfuel minerals — 24
Fuel minerals — 25
Production and consumption — 25
Manufacturing: Value added by manufacturing — 26·27
Southern Ontario — 26
Southern Québec — 27
Population distribution, 1991 — 28
Population distribution, 1901 — 28
Native peoples — 29
First language/ethnic origin — 29
Immigrant population — 29

Canada Topographic (Physical/Political)

Atlantic Provinces — 30·31
Nova Scotia and Prince Edward Island — 31
Québec — 32·33
Ontario — 34·35
Central Canada — 36·37
Central Ontario — 38
Manitoba — 39
Saskatchewan — 40
Alberta — 41
British Columbia — 42·43
Southwestern BC — 42
Northern Canada — 44·45

North America Urban Land Use

Vancouver, Toronto — 46
Montréal, Ottawa, Halifax — 47
Edmonton, Calgary, Winnipeg — 48
San Francisco — 49
New York — 50
Los Angeles — 51
Boston, Detroit — 52
Chicago, Pittsburgh — 53

North and South America

Relief — 54·55
Minerals, build — 55
Climate — 56·57
Land use: Agriculture — 58·59
Natural vegetation — 59
Population and communications — 60·61
Political — 61
U.S.A. — 62·63
Northeastern U.S.A. — 64·65
Mexico, Central America and the Caribbean — 66·67
Trinidad — 66
Barbados — 66
Panama Canal — 67
Jamaica — 67
South America — 68·69
Rio de Janeiro (urban land use) — 69

Europe

Relief — 70
European economic organizations — 70
Climate — 71
Land use — 72
Population and communications — 73
Europe — 74·75
Western Europe — 76·77
Ruhr (urban land use) — 76
British Isles — 78
Scandinavia and Iceland — 79
Eastern Europe — 80·81
London (urban land use) — 82
Paris, Berlin (urban land use) — 83

Asia

Relief — 84
Climate — 85
Land use — 86

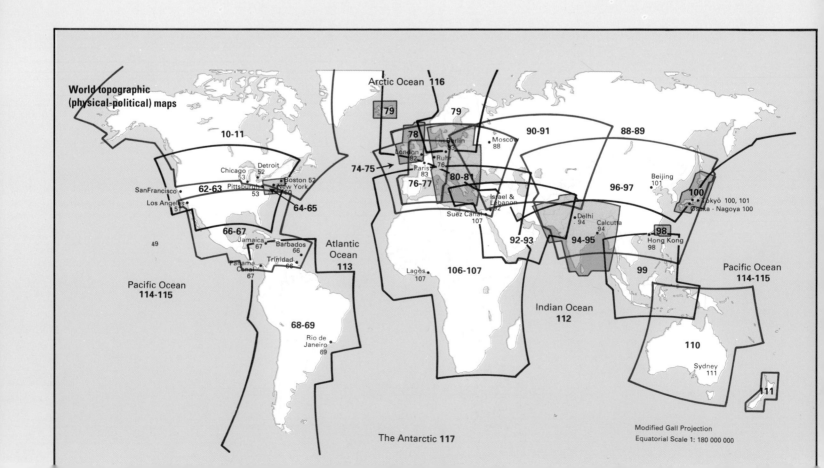

World topographic (physical-political) maps

Modified Gall Projection
Equatorial Scale 1: 180 000 000

Contents 3

Population and communications 87
Northern Eurasia 88·89
Moscow (urban land use) 88
Central Eurasia 90·91
Middle East 92·93
Israel and Lebanon 92
Southern Asia 94·95
Delhi, Calcutta (urban land use) 94
China 96·97
Taiwan, Hong Kong 98
South East Asia 99
Japan 100
Ōsaka - Nagoya area 100
Tōkyō area 100
Tōkyō, Beijing (urban land use) 101

Africa

Relief 102
Political 102
Climate 103
Land use 104
Tsetse fly 104
Population and communications 105
Africa 106·107
Suez Canal 107
Lagos (urban land use) 107

Australasia

Climate 108
Land use, population and
  communications 109
Australasia 110
Sydney (urban land use) 111
New Zealand 111

Oceans

Indian Ocean 112
Rainfall during the summer
  monsoon 112

Atlantic Ocean 113
Pacific Ocean 114·115
Fiji 114
Subregions of Oceania 114
Hawaiian Islands 115

Poles

The Arctic 116
The Antarctic 117

World

Political 118·119
Physical 120·121
Plate tectonics 120
The moving continents 120·121
Climate: Rainfall 122·123
    Temperature, ocean
      currents 122·123
    Pressure and winds 122·123
    Tropical revolving storms 123
    Air masses 123
Climate regions 124
Water 124
Natural vegetation 125
Soils 125
Natural hazards: Storms and
          floods 126
        Earthquakes and
          volcanoes 126
Environmental damage:
    Drought, fire and pests 127
    Tropical deforestation 127
Global warming 128
Atmospheric pollutants 129
Fresh water 130
Protected areas and
  endangered species 130
Nuclear 131
Military expenditure 131
Population 132·133

Quality of life: Life expectancy at birth 134
        Medical care 134
        Education 135
        Radios and TVs 135
Agriculture: Agriculture 136
        Percentage of labour
          force in agriculture 136
        Nutrition 137
        Cropland 137
        Irrigated land 137
Pacific Rim countries, trade with
  Canada 138·139
Standard Time 138
Economic development:
        Gross Domestic Product 140
        Industrialization 140
        Employment 141
        Givers and receivers of aid 141
Energy: Oil 142
    Gas 142
    Coal 143
    Electricity 143
Energy consumption 144

Gazetteer

How to use the gazetteer 145
Gazetteer of Canada 146·156
Gazetteer of the World 157·184
Glossary 216

Canada   Statistics

Land 185
Population 185·190
Agriculture 190·193
Forestry and fishing 194·195
Mining 196
Energy 197·199
Manufacturing 199·200
Transportation 200·202
Trade 202
The economy 203
Conservation and pollution 204·205
Climate 206·207

World   Statistics

Trade 208·209
Demographics 210·214
Acknowledgements, credits 215
Notes to countries and regions
  of the world statistical data 216

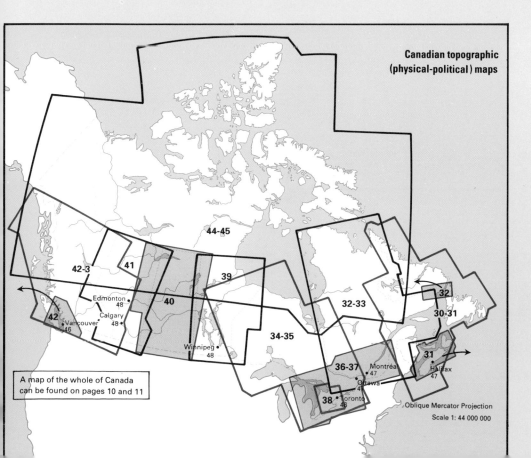

**Canadian topographic
(physical-political) maps**

44-45
42-3
41
39
40
42
Edmonton 48
Calgary 48
Vancouver 46
Winnipeg 48
32-33
34-35
32
30-31
36-37
Montréal 47
31
Halifax 47
Ottawa
38
Toronto 46
Oblique Mercator Projection
Scale 1: 44 000 000

A map of the whole of Canada
can be found on pages 10 and 11

Canada Satellite Images

These images were produced by Landsat satellites which orbit the earth 14.5 times each day at an altitude of approximately 900 km. Each image covers approximately 34 000 km²; in order to be visible, objects on the earth must be at least 30 m² in size.

The satellite does not take a photograph in the normal sense. Rather, sensors record the reflected light, heat, and radio waves from the microwave portion of the electromagnetic spectrum, through the infra-red and visible light sections, to the near ultra-violet sections. This information is digitized and sent back to earth, where it is stored on computer tapes. It is then transformed into images such as the ones shown here.

Since every object on the surface absorbs and reflects radiation differently, different surfaces such as trees, rocks, concrete, and crops can be easily recognized. For the most part, however, the colours we see on the images are "false" colours. This is because each surface reflects one part of the electromagnetic spectrum better than another. For example, green vegetation appears in various red tones since it reflects infra-red radiation more strongly; urban areas show up in blue and grey; and bare ground is seen from black to blue to white depending on the moisture and organic content of the soil. On some images, notably the one of Toronto on page 9, colours of the features have been changed to normal ones. Thus on this image vegetation is shown in green.

Scale 1:1 000 000

Southwestern British Columbia, including the cities of Vancouver and Victoria.

The Mackenzie River delta, with the town of Inuvik in the centre.

The Fraser River near Lillooet, British Columbia.

Calgary, Alberta, on the Bow River.

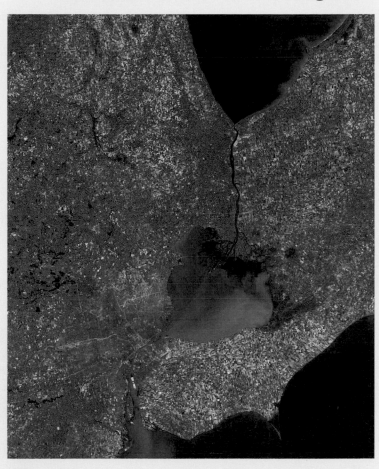

Lake Huron, Detroit-Windsor, and western Lake Erle.

The Canadian Shield, the Saguenay valley, and the cities of Chicoutimi-Jonquière.

Southern Nova Scotia, including the Annapolis Valley and Halifax-Dartmouth.

Latitude and Longitude

The earth is a small, blue planet.
Seen from space it has no right way up.

An imaginary grid is used to pinpoint the position of any place on earth.
This grid consists of two sets of lines. Those running east and west are called parallels of latitude, and those extending north and south are called meridians of longitude. Both are measured in degrees.

Latitude
Parallels of latitude are concentric circles that diminish in diameter from the equator to the poles. They are used to determine locations either north or south in relation to the equator. North of the equator parallels are designated north (N), while those south of the equator are labelled south (S). The equator is at latitude 0°. The poles are at latitudes 90°N and 90°S.

Longitude
Meridians of longitude pass through both poles intersecting all parallels of latitude at right angles. The meridian through Greenwich, England was chosen in 1884 as the Prime Meridian and given the value 0°. Meridians determine locations east (E) or west (W) of the Prime Meridian. The 180° meridian of longitude was designated the International Date Line and has a special role in the operation of Standard Time.

The equator divides the earth into halves: the Northern Hemisphere and the Southern Hemisphere. The Prime Meridian and the 180° meridian together also divide the earth into halves: the Western Hemisphere and the Eastern Hemisphere.

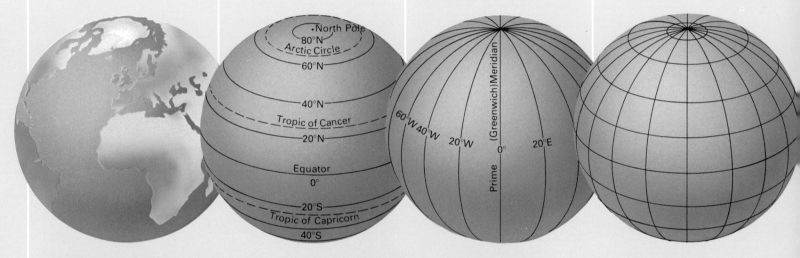

When used together, lines of latitude and longitude form a grid. The position of places on the surface of the earth can be located accurately using this grid.

To locate places really accurately, each degree of latitude and longitude can be divided into 60 minutes and each minute into 60 seconds. A location specified in degrees, minutes, and seconds (for example, 44° 25' 14" N, 80° 45' 36" W) will describe a location accurately to within a few metres.

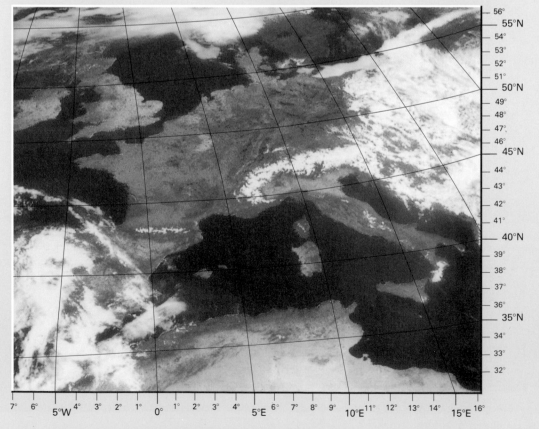

Extract from the Landsat view of Southern Nova Scotia shown on page 5.
Scale 1: 1 000 000.

Extract from a Meteosat view of Europe, 35 790 km above the equator.
(This is an enlargement of the image of the earth shown at the top of the page.)

© Oxford University Press

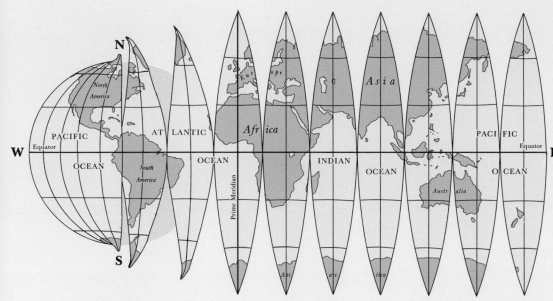

The most accurate way of looking at the earth's land and sea areas is to use a globe. For obvious reasons maps are more convenient to use than globes. One method of changing the surface of the globe into a map is to unpeel strips or gores from the globe's surface, but such a method has obvious drawbacks. Since it is impossible to flatten the curved surface of the earth without stretching or cutting part of it, it is necessary to employ other methods in order to produce an orderly system of parallels and meridians on which a map can be drawn. Such systems are referred to as **map projections**.

There are two main types of projections: **equal area projections,** where the area of any territory is shown in correct size proportion to other areas, and **conformal projections,** where the emphasis is on showing shape correctly. No map can be both equal area and conformal, though some projections are designed to minimize distortions in both area and shape.

The **Oblique Aitoff projection** is equal area. The arrangement of the land masses allows a good view of routes in the northern hemisphere. The position of North America and Asia on either side of the Arctic is shown clearly.

Mercator's projection is a conformal projection and was initially designed (1569) to be used for navigation. Any straight line on the map is a line of constant compass bearing. Straight lines are not the shortest routes, however. Shape is accurate on a Mercator projection but the size of the land masses is distorted. Land is shown larger the further away it is from the equator. (For example, Alaska is shown four times larger than its actual size.)

———— Line of constant compass bearing

- - - - Shortest route

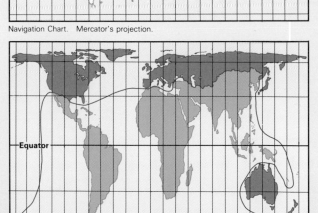

Navigation Chart. Mercator's projection.

Peters' projection is an equal area projection. The land masses are the correct size in relation to each other, but there is considerable distortion in shape. This projection has been used to emphasize the size of the poor countries of the South compared with the rich countries of the North.

———— Brandt Line

▓ Rich North.

░ Poor South.

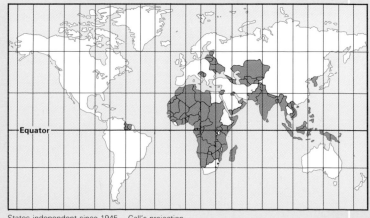

Rich North—Poor South. Peters' projection.

Gall's projection compromises between equal area and conformal. A modified version is used in this atlas as a general world map. This map shows states which have gained their independence since 1945.

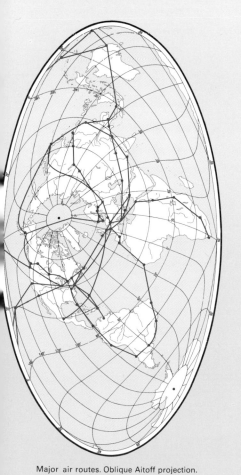

Major air routes. Oblique Aitoff projection.

▓ States independent since 1945.

States independent since 1945. Gall's projection.

Topographic maps (physical-political) show the main features of the physical and human landscape. There are small differences in the symbols and colours used for the maps of Canada and those for the rest of the World.

Canadian Maps

Boundaries

international

province, territory

region, county, district, regional municipality

national park/ provincial park

Communications

expressway/other multilane highway

other highway

winter road

railway

canal

⊕ major airport

✈ other airport

Cities and towns

◁ built-up areas

■ over 1 million inhabitants

● more than 100 000 inhabitants

• smaller urban places

Physical features

marsh

ice cap

Scale 1:5 000 000

0   50   100 km

Scale is shown by a representative fraction and a scale line.

Non-Canadian maps

Boundaries

international

disputed

internal

national park

Communications

expressway

other major road

track

railway

canal

✈ major airport

Cities and towns

◁ built-up areas

■ over 1 million inhabitants

● more than 100 000 inhabitants

• smaller towns

+ historic sites

Physical features

seasonal river/lake

marsh

salt pan

ice cap

sand dunes

coral reef

Place names

Local spellings are used. Anglicised and other common spellings are shown in brackets.

e.g. **Roma** (Rome)

This atlas has been designed for English speaking readers and so all places have been named using the Roman alphabet. Compare this extract of the map of Southern Asia with the same map printed in Bengali.

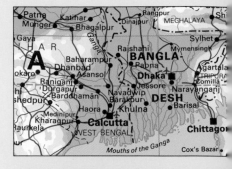

Type style

Contrasting type styles are used to show the difference between physical features, settlements, and administrative areas. Physical features (except for peaks) are shown in italics.

e.g. *Hautes Fagnes*   **Maas**

Peaks are shown in condensed type.

e.g. Hohe Acht 746

Settlement names are shown in upper and lower case.

e.g. Valkenswaard

Administrative areas are shown in capital letters.

e.g. LIÈGE

The importance of places is shown by the size of the type and whether the type face is **bold,** medium or light.

e.g. Malmédy   Bergheim   Duisburg

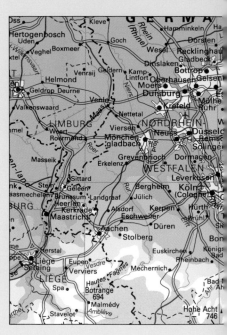

Land height

Colours on topographic maps refer only to the height of the land. They do not give information about land use or other aspects of the environment.

Sea ice

White stipple patterns over the sea colour show the seasonal extent of sea ice.

Sea Ice

unnavigable

pack ice - average fall minimum

pack ice - average spring max.

Sea depth

metres below sea level

200

3000

4000

5000

6000

sea depths shown as minus numbers

Land height

metres

5000

3000

2000

1000

500

300

200

100

sea level

land below sea level

▲ spot height in metres

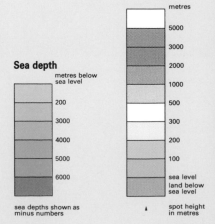

A map is a symbolic representation of the earth's surface. The amount and kind of detail shown by symbols on a map depend on the scale and purpose of the map. Satellite images, and indeed all photographs, provide a visual record of part of the earth's surface *without* symbols. Because of the complexity of such images their interpretation is usually more difficult than that of a map.

Landsat image of Metropolitan Toronto and its environs.
Scale approximately 1: 300 000

Extract from the urban land use map of Toronto, page 46. **Scale 1: 300 000**

Extract from the topographic map of Central Ontario, page 38.
Scale 1: 1 250 000

Extract from the topographic map of Ontario, page 35.
Scale 1: 5 000 000

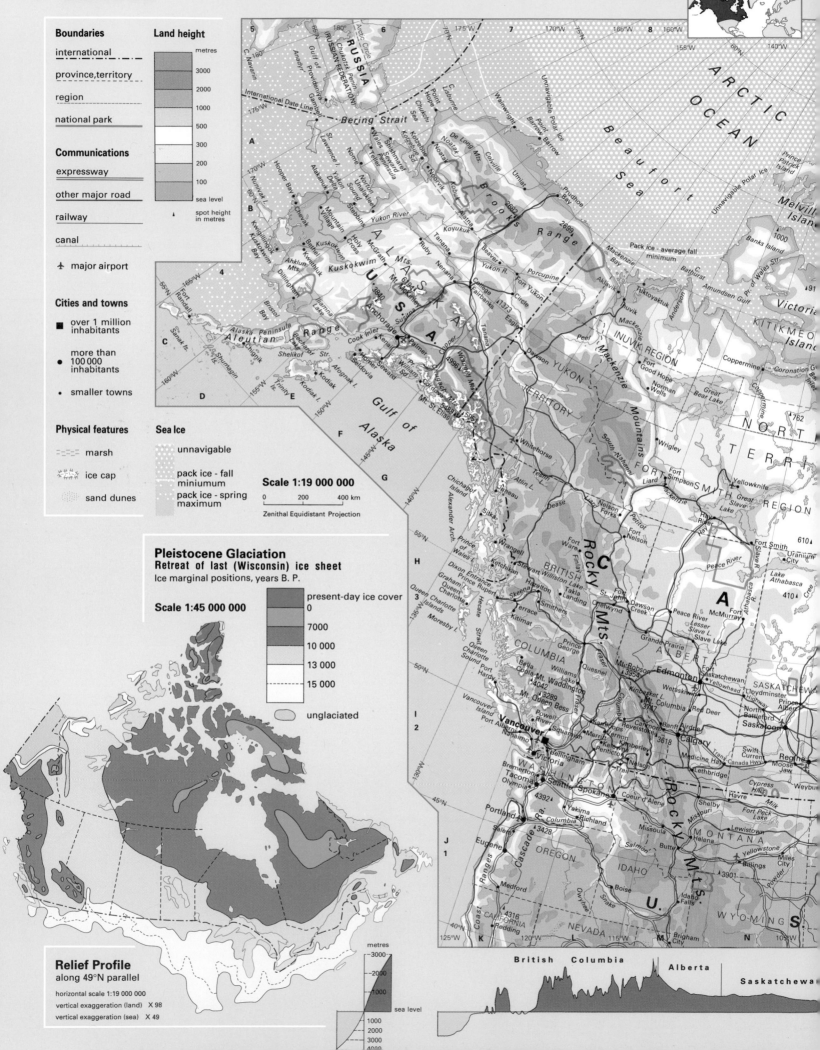

Distance chart — official highway distances, in kilometres

Calgary	Charlottetown	Edmonton	Fredericton	Halifax	Montréal	Ottawa	Québec	Regina	St. John's	Saskatoon	Thunder Bay	Toronto	Vancouver	Victoria	Whitehorse	Winnipeg	Yellowknife	
●	4917	299	4558	5042	3743	3553	4014	764	6183	620	2050	3434	1057	1123	2385	1336	1811	Calgary
	●	4949	359	232	1184	1374	945	4163	1294	4421	2878	1724	5985	6051	7034	3592	6460	Charlottetown
		●	4598	5082	3764	3574	4035	785	6212	528	2071	3455	1244	1310	2086	1357	1511	Edmonton
			●	346	834	1024	586	3813	1622	4070	2527	1373	5634	5700	6684	3241	6109	Fredericton
				●	1318	1508	912	4297	1349	4554	3011	1857	6119	6185	7168	3726	6593	Halifax
					●	190	270	2979	2448	3236	1693	539	4801	4867	5850	2408	5275	Montréal
						●	460	2789	2638	3046	1503	399	4611	4677	5660	2218	5086	Ottawa
							●	3249	2208	3507	1963	810	5071	5137	6120	2678	5546	Québec
								●	5427	257	1286	2670	1822	1888	2871	571	2297	Regina
									●	5684	4141	2987	7248	7314	8298	4855	7723	St. John's
										●	1543	2927	1677	1743	2614	829	2039	Saskatoon
											●	1384	3108	3174	4157	715	3582	Thunder Bay
												●	4492	4558	5528	2099	4966	Toronto
													●	66	2697	2232	2411	Vancouver
														●	2763	2298	2477	Victoria
															●	3524	2704	Whitehorse
																●	2868	Winnipeg
																	●	Yellowknife

© Oxford University Press

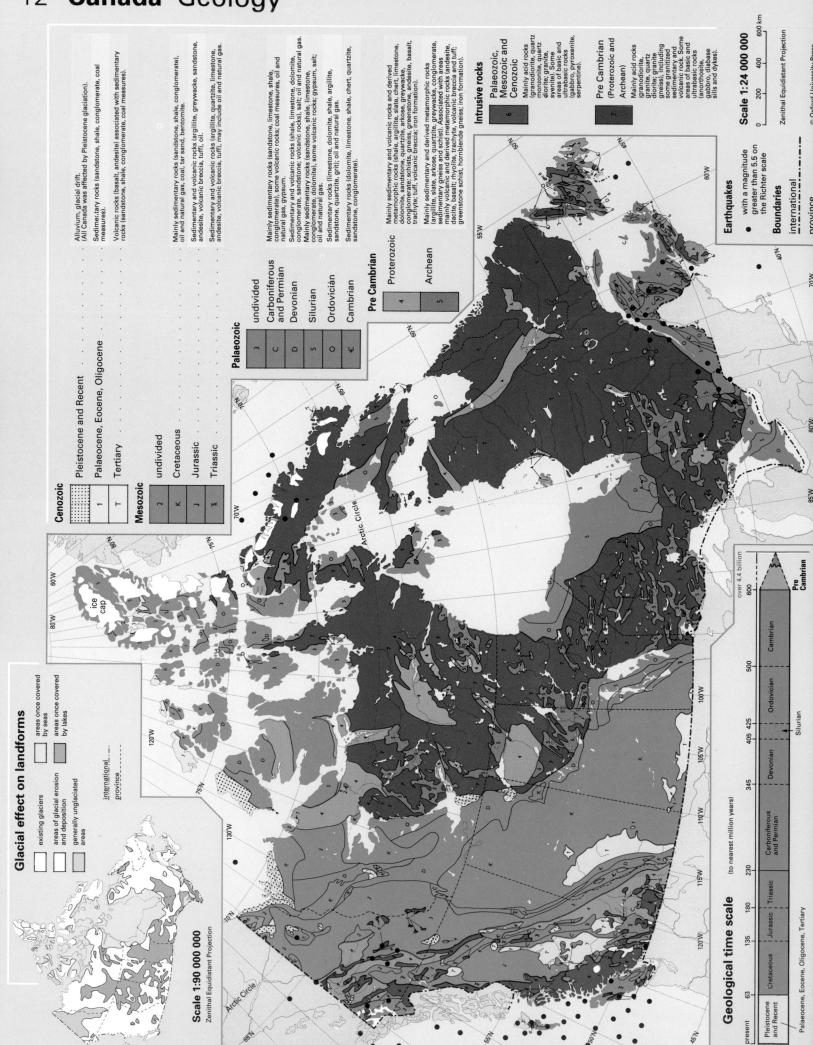

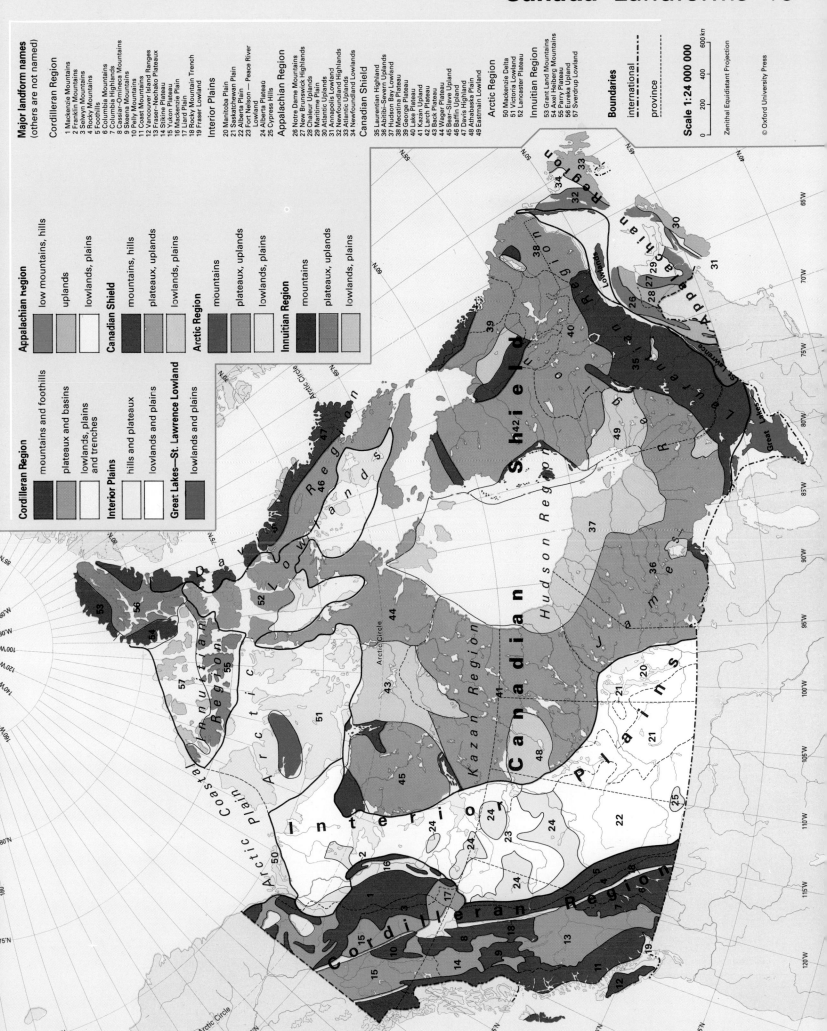

Major landform names
(others are not named)

Cordilleran Region
1 Mackenzie Mountains
2 Franklin Mountains
3 Selwyn Mountains
4 Rocky Mountains
5 Foothills
6 Columbia Mountains
7 Columbia Highlands
8 Cassiar–Omineca Mountains
9 Skeena Mountains
10 Pelly Mountains
11 Coast Mountains
12 Vancouver Island Ranges
13 Fraser–Nechako Plateaux
14 Stikine Plateau
15 Yukon Plateau
16 Mackenzie Plain
17 Liard Plain
18 Rocky Mountain Trench
19 Fraser Lowland

Interior Plains
20 Manitoba Plain
21 Saskatchewan Plain
22 Alberta Plain
23 Fort Nelson — Peace River Lowland
24 Alberta Plateau
25 Cypress Hills

Appalachian Region
26 Notre Dame Mountains
27 New Brunswick Highlands
28 Chaleur Uplands
29 Maritime Plain
30 Atlantic Lowland
31 Annapolis Lowland
32 Newfoundland Highlands
33 Atlantic Uplands
34 Newfoundland Lowlands

Canadian Shield
35 Laurentian Highland
36 Abitibi–Severn Uplands
37 Hudson Bay Lowland
38 George Plateau
39 Mecatina Plateau
40 Lake Plateau
41 Kazan Upland
42 Larch Plateau
43 Back Plateau
44 Wager Plateau
45 Bear–Slave Upland
46 Baffin Upland
47 Davis Highland
48 Athabaska Plain
49 Eastmain Lowland

Arctic Region
50 Mackenzie Delta
51 Victoria Lowland
52 Lancaster Plateau

Inuitian Region
53 Grant Land Mountains
54 Axel Heiberg Mountains
55 Parry Plateau
56 Eureka Upland
57 Sverdrup Lowland

Boundaries
international
province

Scale 1:24 000 000

0   200   400   600 km

Zenithal Equidistant Projection

© Oxford University Press

Cordilleran Region
mountains and foothills
plateaux and basins
lowlands, plains and trenches

Interior Plains
hills and plateaux
lowlands and plains

Great Lakes—St. Lawrence Lowland
lowlands and plains

Appalachian region
low mountains, hills
uplands
lowlands, plains

Canadian Shield
mountains, hills
plateaux, uplands
lowlands, plains

Arctic Region
mountains
plateaux, uplands
lowlands, plains

Inuitian Region
mountains
plateaux, uplands
lowlands, plains

Heating the Earth

The Greenhouse Effect

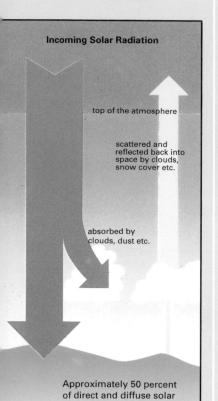

Incoming Solar Radiation

top of the atmosphere

scattered and reflected back into space by clouds, snow cover etc.

absorbed by clouds, dust etc.

Approximately 50 percent of direct and diffuse solar radiation passes through the atmosphere to heat the Earth

Outgoing Earth Radiation

top of the atmosphere

eventually all heat energy received is lost to space

Earth radiation window

absorbed by greenhouse gases* CO_2, H_2O, CH_4

radiation from land and water (also latent heat of condensation and conduction)

counter radiation

Absorbed solar radiation converts to heat (warms the air, evaporates water, melts snow and ice) used in photosynthesis, is released into the atmosphere and ultimately is lost to space

* Global warming is occurring because of additions to greenhouse gases resulting from human activity.

© Oxford University Press

Isotherms

°C
20
15
10
5
0
-10
-20
-30
-35

Permafrost

—— approximate southern limit of continuous permafrost

-- -- approximate southern limit of discontinuous permafrost

Growing degree days

Number of degrees above 5°C added together for all the days of the growing season

—— 1000
—— 1500
······ 2000

Boundaries

international

province/territory

Scale 1: 44 000 000

0   500 km

Temperature range

The difference between the average daily mean temperature in January and July

0°C
10
20
30
40
50

Boundaries

international

province/territory

Scale 1: 44 000 000

0   500 km

Zenithal Equidistant Projection

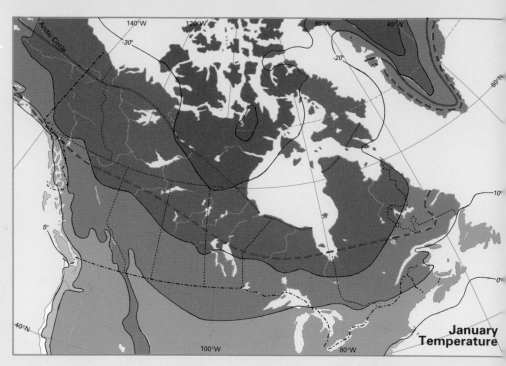

January Temperature

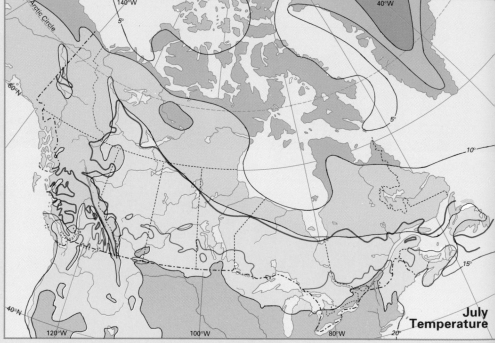

July Temperature

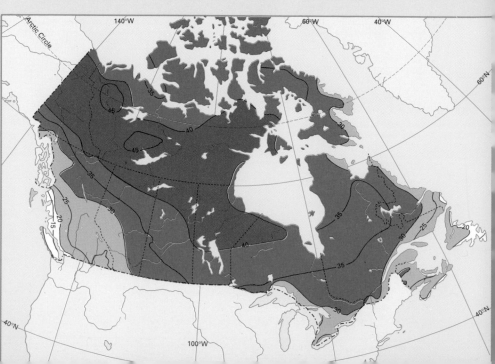

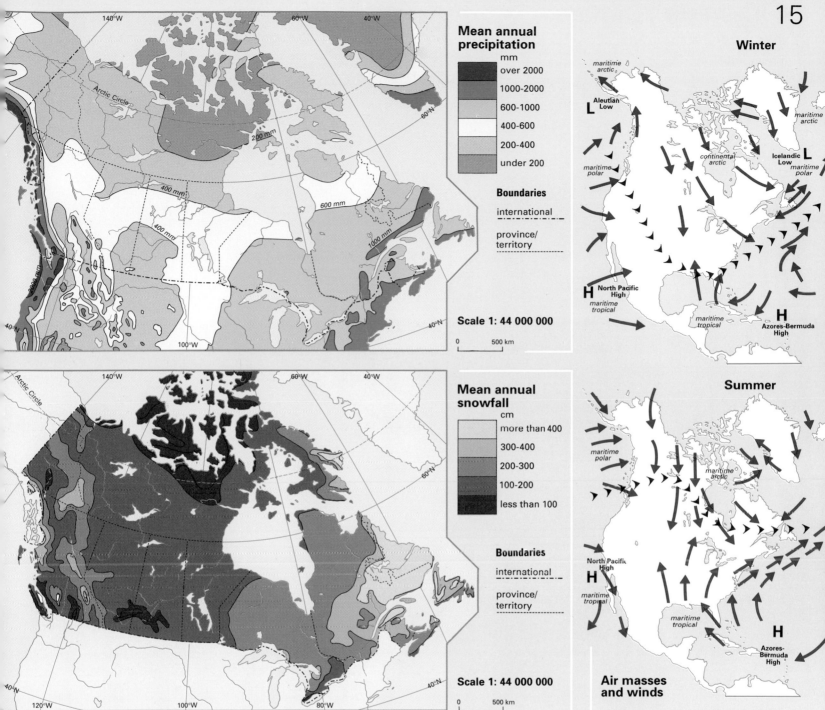

Mean annual precipitation

mm
- over 2000
- 1000-2000
- 600-1000
- 400-600
- 200-400
- under 200

Boundaries

international

province/territory

Scale 1: 44 000 000

0   500 km

Mean annual snowfall

cm
- more than 400
- 300-400
- 200-300
- 100-200
- less than 100

Boundaries

international

province/territory

Scale 1: 44 000 000

0   500 km

Thunderstorms

Average annual number of days with thunderstorms

- 5
- 10
- 20

Tornadoes

Average annual frequency of tornadoes per 10 000 km²

- more than 2.0
- 1.2-2.0
- 0.8-1.2

Scale 1: 44 000 000

0   500 km

Zenithal Equidistant Projection

Winter

maritime arctic
Aleutian Low **L**
maritime arctic
continental arctic
Icelandic Low **L**
maritime polar
maritime polar
H North Pacific High
maritime tropical
maritime tropical
H Azores-Bermuda High

Summer

maritime polar
maritime arctic
North Pacific High **H**
maritime tropical
maritime tropical
H Azores-Bermuda High

Air masses and winds

→ prevailing winds

▸▸ polar jet stream

H high ┐ semi-permanent
L low ┘ pressure

Scale 1: 108 000 000
Oblique Mercator Projection

Acid Precipitation

A pH scale measures whether a liquid is acidic or alkaline.
A pH of 7 indicates neutrality.
Lower values indicate acidity, higher values alkalinity.
"Clean" rain has a pH value of 5.6.

For a map of annual mean values of pH in precipitation in North America see page 129.

© Oxford University Press

Wind Chill

a measure of the wind's cooling effect, as felt on exposed flesh, expressed either as the **wind chill equivalent temperature** (in ° C) or as **heat loss** (in watts/m²)

Wind chill equivalent temperature

referenced to a base wind speed of 8 km per hour

	wind speed in km per hour					
	10	**20**	**30**	**40**	**50**	**60**
5	4	-2	-5	-7	-8	-9
0	-2	-8	-11	-14	-16	-17
-5	-7	-14	-18	-21	-23	-24
-10	-12	-20	-25	-28	-30	-32
-15	-18	-26	-32	-35	-38	-39
-20	-23	-32	-38	-42	-45	-47
-25	-28	-39	-45	-49	-52	-54
-30	-33	-45	-52	-56	-60	-62
-35	-39	-51	-59	-64	-67	-69
-40	-44	-57	-65	-71	-74	-77

Temperature (°C)

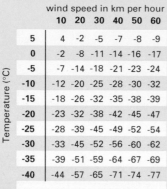

Humidex

an index showing temperature measures that allow for the added stress that results from high humidities - referred to as **effective temperature**

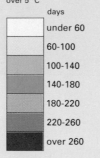

actual temperature (°C)
effective temperature (°C)
humidity (%)

Canadian weather records

highest air temperature	45°C Midale and Yellow Grass, Sask. July 5, 1937
lowest air temperature	-63°C Snag, Y.T. February 3, 1947
coldest month	-47.9°C Eureka, N.W.T February, 1979
highest sea-level pressure	107.96 kPa Dawson, Y.T. February 2, 1989
lowest sea-level pressure	94.02 kPa St.Anthony, New foundland January 20, 1977
greatest precipitation in 24 hours	489.2 mm Ucluelet Brynnor Mines, B.C. October 6, 1967
greatest precipitation in one month	2235.5 mm Swanson Bay, B.C. November 1917
greatest precipitation in one year	8122.6 mm Henderson Lake, B.C. 1931
greatest average annual precipitation	6655 mm Henderson Lake, B.C.
least annual precipitation	12,7 mm Arctic Bay, N.W.T. 1949
highest average annual number of thunderstorm days	34 days London, Ontario

January wind chill

The values on the map indicate the maximum wind chill; there is a 5% chance of having a wind chill value worse than the value shown

Wind chill equivalent temperature

	°C	heat loss watts /m²
	-70	2755
	-60	2488
	-50	2220
	-40	1953
	-30	1685
	-20	1418

Boundaries

international

province/territory

Scale 1: 44 000 000

0   500   1000 km

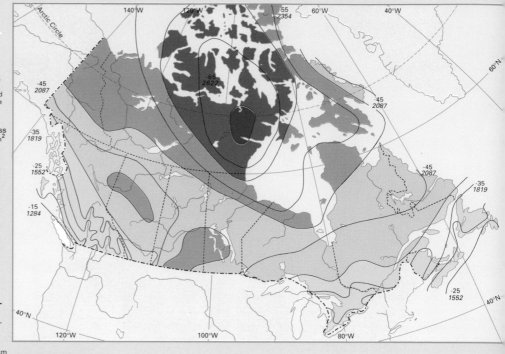

Growing season

Average number of days with an average temperature over 5 °C

days
under 60
60-100
100-140
140-180
180-220
220-260
over 260

Boundaries

international

province/territory

Scale 1: 44 000 000

0   500   1000 km

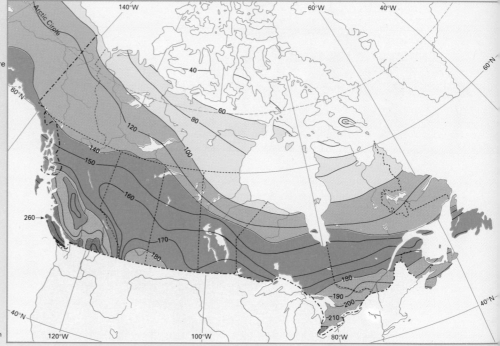

Sunshine

Average annual hours

1200
1600
2000

253 number of days with some sun

Boundaries

international

province/territory

Scale 1: 44 000 000

0   500   1000 km

Zenithal Equidistant Projection

© Oxford University Press

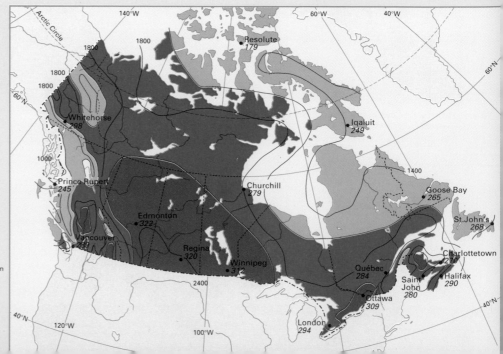

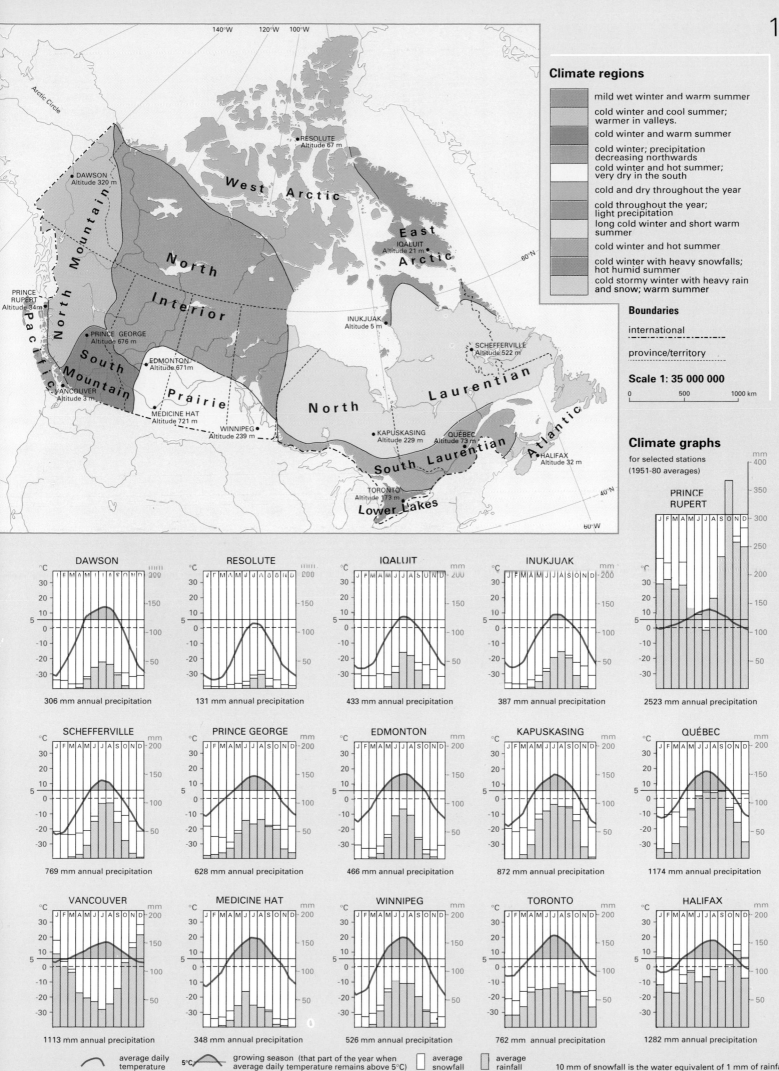

Climate regions

	mild wet winter and warm summer
	cold winter and cool summer; warmer in valleys.
	cold winter and warm summer
	cold winter; precipitation decreasing northwards
	cold winter and hot summer; very dry in the south
	cold and dry throughout the year
	cold throughout the year; light precipitation
	long cold winter and short warm summer
	cold winter and hot summer
	cold winter with heavy snowfalls; hot humid summer
	cold stormy winter with heavy rain and snow; warm summer

Boundaries

international

province/territory

Scale 1: 35 000 000

0   500   1000 km

Climate graphs

for selected stations
(1951-80 averages)

PRINCE RUPERT — 2523 mm annual precipitation

DAWSON — 306 mm annual precipitation

RESOLUTE — 131 mm annual precipitation

IQALUIT — 433 mm annual precipitation

INUKJUAK — 387 mm annual precipitation

SCHEFFERVILLE — 769 mm annual precipitation

PRINCE GEORGE — 628 mm annual precipitation

EDMONTON — 466 mm annual precipitation

KAPUSKASING — 872 mm annual precipitation

QUÉBEC — 1174 mm annual precipitation

VANCOUVER — 1113 mm annual precipitation

MEDICINE HAT — 348 mm annual precipitation

WINNIPEG — 526 mm annual precipitation

TORONTO — 762 mm annual precipitation

HALIFAX — 1282 mm annual precipitation

average daily temperature

5°C growing season (that part of the year when average daily temperature remains above 5°C)

average snowfall

average rainfall

10 mm of snowfall is the water equivalent of 1 mm of rainfall

Canada Natural Vegetation, Forestry

Zenithal Equidistant Projection
© Oxford University Press
Trembling Aspen
Sugar Maple
Red Oak
Western Hemlock
Tundra
Alpine sedges/grasses and shrubs
Dwarf shrubs/sedges/lichen/heath
Arctic stony lichen/heath
Rock desert
Vegetation regions and main tree species
Boreal (predominantly forest) — Black Spruce, White Spruce, Balsam Fir, Jack Pine, White Birch, Trembling Aspen
Boreal (forest and barren ground) — Black Spruce, White Spruce, Tamarack
Boreal (forest and grassland) — Trembling Aspen, Willow
Subalpine — Alpine Fir, Engelmann Spruce, Lodgepole Pine
Montane — Douglas Fir, Lodgepole Pine, Ponderosa Pine, Trembling Aspen
Coast — Western Red Cedar, Western Hemlock, Douglas Fir, Sitka Spruce
Columbia — Western Red Cedar, Western Hemlock, Douglas Fir
Deciduous — Beech, Sugar Maple, Black Walnut, Hickory, Red Oak
Great Lakes–St.Lawrence — Eastern White Pine, Eastern Hemlock, Red Pine, Yellow Birch, Sugar Maple, Oak
Acadian — Red Spruce, Balsam Fir, Maple, Yellow Birch
Grassland — Trembling Aspen, Willow, Bur Oak
Area of productive forest (more than 50% of total land area)
Pulp and Paper Mills
Capacity (tonnes per day)
1000–2499
500–999
less than 500
Product
pulp
paper
pulp and paper
Boundaries
international
province/territory
Scale 1: 24 000 000
0 200 400 600 km
ice cap
Arctic Circle
Prince Rupert
Campbell River
Powell River
Port Alberni
Nanaimo
Crofton
Terrace Bay
Thunder Bay
Fort Frances
La Tuque
Gatineau
Quebec
Trois-Rivières
Baie-Comeau
Dalhousie
Corner Brook
White Spruce
Jack Pine
Balsam Fir
Black Spruce
Douglas Fir
Eastern White Pine
Western Red Cedar
White Birch

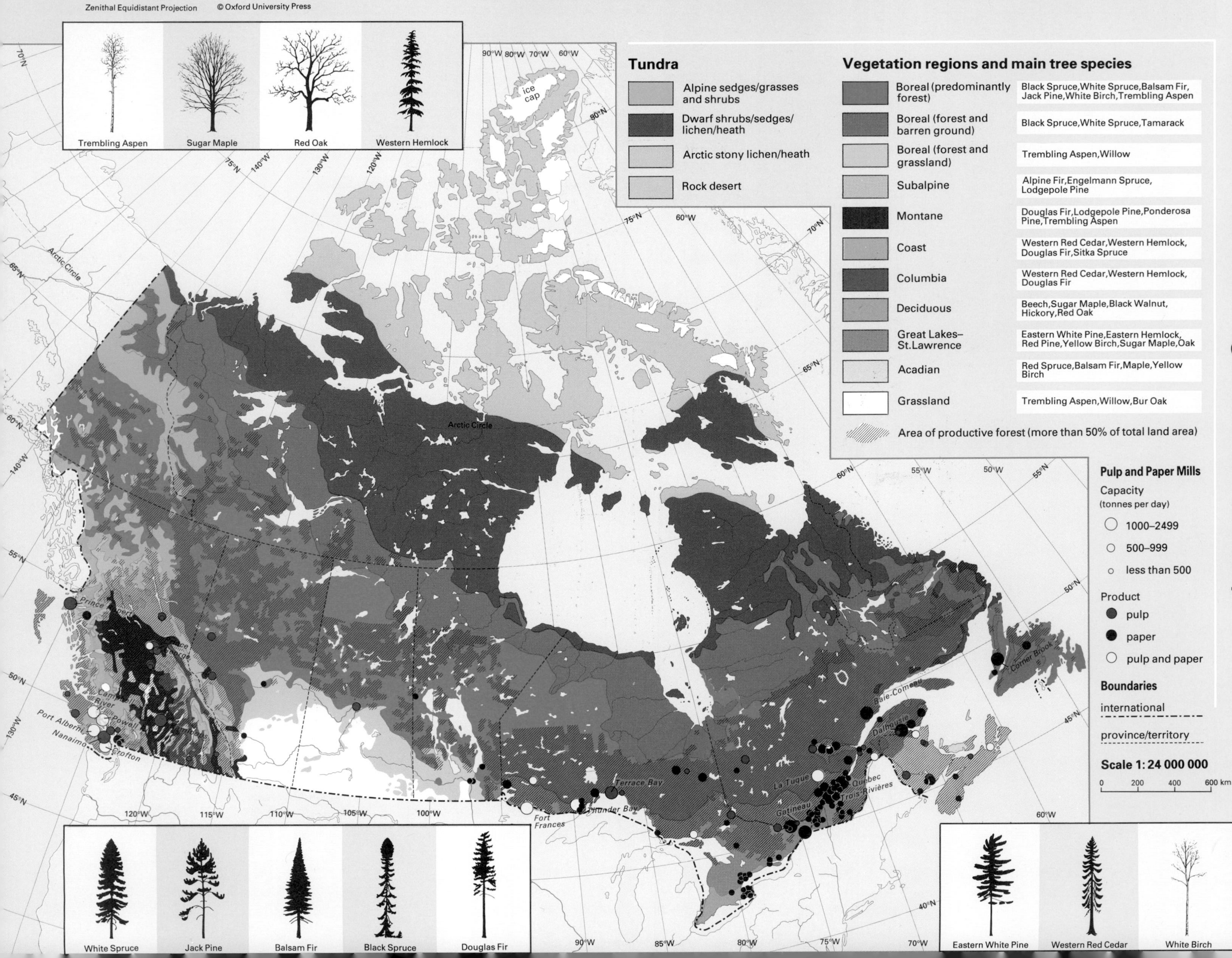

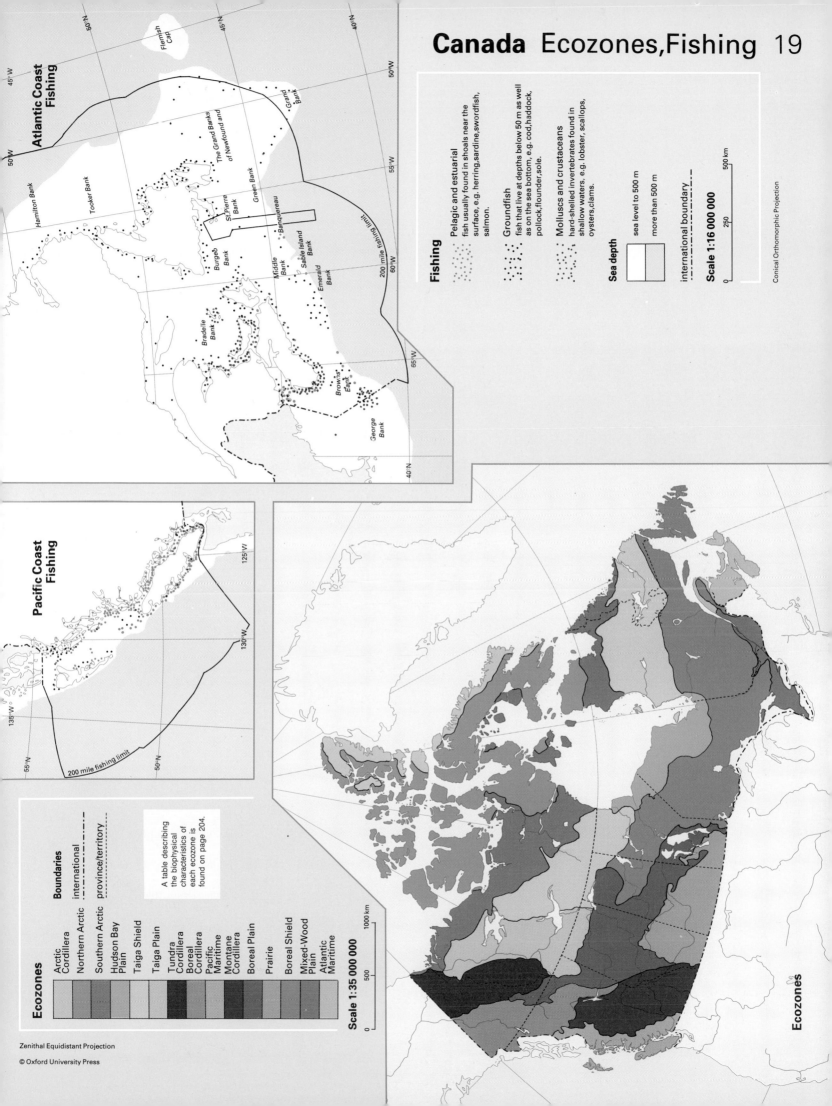

Atlantic Coast Fishing

Flemish Cap

Hamilton Bank
Tooker Bank
The Grand Banks of Newfoundland
Grand Bank
Green Bank
St. Pierre Bank
Banquereau
Sable Island Bank
Burgeo Bank
Bradelle Bank
Middle Bank
Emerald Bank
Browns Bank
George Bank

200 mile fishing limit

Pacific Coast Fishing

200 mile fishing limit

Fishing

Pelagic and estuarial fish usually found in shoals near the surface, e.g. herring, sardine, swordfish, salmon.

Groundfish fish that live at depths below 50 m as well as on the sea bottom, e.g. cod, haddock, pollock, flounder, sole.

Molluscs and crustaceans hard-shelled invertebrates found in shallow waters, e.g. lobster, scallops, oysters, clams.

Sea depth

sea level to 500 m
more than 500 m
international boundary

Scale 1:16 000 000

0   250   500 km

Conical Orthomorphic Projection

Ecozones

Arctic Cordillera
Northern Arctic
Southern Arctic
Hudson Bay Plain
Taiga Plain
Taiga Shield
Tundra Cordillera
Boreal Cordillera
Pacific Maritime
Montane Cordillera
Boreal Plain
Prairie
Boreal Shield
Mixed-Wood Plain
Atlantic Maritime

Boundaries

international
province/territory

A table describing the biophysical characteristics of each ecozone is found on page 204.

Scale 1:35 000 000

0   500   1000 km

Zenithal Equidistant Projection

Ecozones

© Oxford University Press

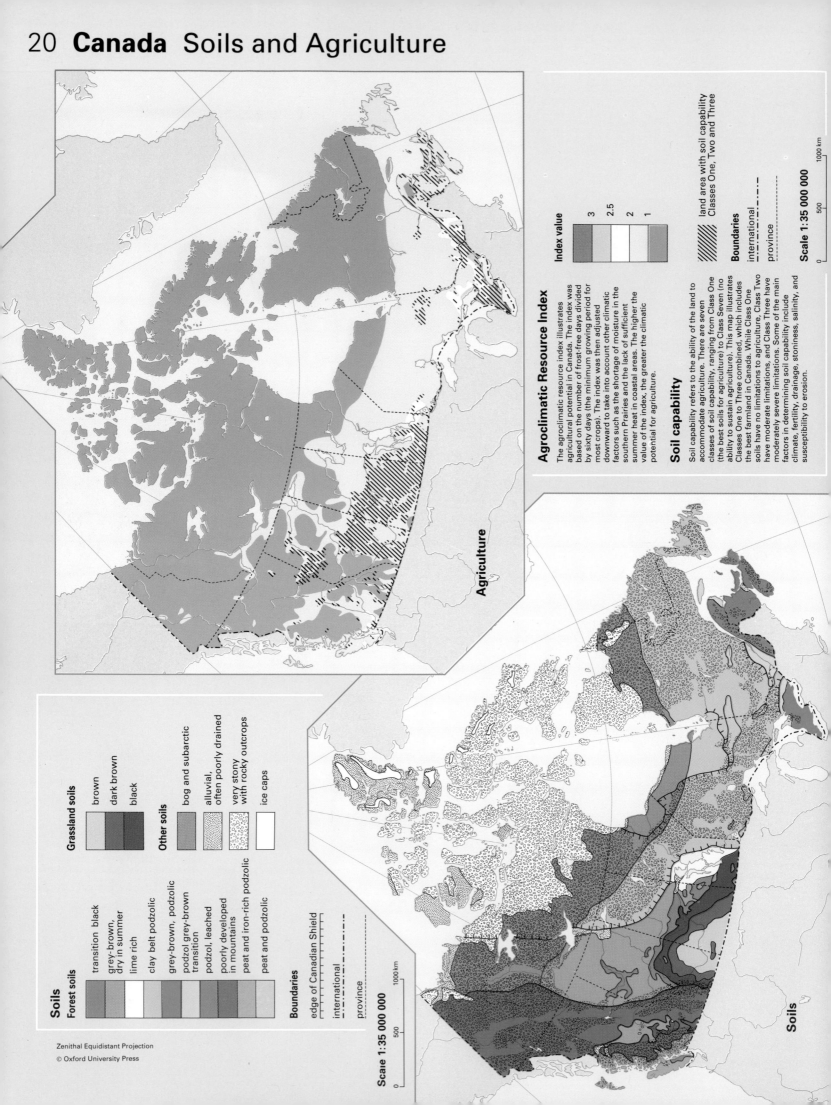

Agriculture

Agroclimatic Resource Index

The agroclimatic resource index illustrates agricultural potential in Canada. The index was based on the number of frost-free days divided by sixty days (the minimum growing period for most crops). The index was then adjusted downward to take into account other climatic factors such as the shortage of moisture in the southern Prairies and the lack of sufficient summer heat in coastal areas. The higher the value of the index, the greater the climatic potential for agriculture.

Soil capability

Soil capability refers to the ability of the land to accommodate agriculture. There are seven classes of soil capability, ranging from Class One (the best soils for agriculture) to Class Seven (no ability to sustain agriculture). This map illustrates Classes One to Three combined, which includes the best farmland in Canada. While Class One soils have no limitations to agriculture, Class Two have moderate limitations, and Class Three have moderately severe limitations. Some of the main factors in determining soil capability include climate, fertility, drainage, stoniness, salinity, and susceptibility to erosion.

Index value

| 3 | 2.5 | 2 | 1 |

land area with soil capability
Classes One, Two and Three

Boundaries

— ⋅ — international

— — — province

Scale 1:35 000 000

0   500   1000 km

Soils

Grassland soils

brown

dark brown

black

Other soils

bog and subarctic

alluvial, often poorly drained

very stony with rocky outcrops

ice caps

Forest soils

transition black

grey-brown, dry in summer

lime rich

clay belt podzolic

grey-brown, podzolic

podzol grey-brown transition

podzol, leached

poorly developed in mountains

peat and iron-rich podzolic

peat and podzolic

Boundaries

— — edge of Canadian Shield

— ⋅ — international

— — — province

Scale 1:35 000 000

0   500   1000 km

Soils

Zenithal Equidistant Projection

© Oxford University Press

Agricultural lands

land in agricultural use

Farm types

D dairy

C cattle

H hogs

P poultry

W wheat

G small grains
(oats, barley, rye, mixed grains, buckwheat, corn for grain, soybean, sunflower, rapeseed, mustard seed)

F field crops
(forage seed, potatoes, sugar beets, tobacco)

V fruits and vegetables

S miscellaneous speciality
(greenhouse and nursery products, flowers, bulbs, mushrooms, maple products, honey, beeswax, sheep, horses, fur-bearing animals, pelts, goats, goats milk)

M mixed farms
(field crops and livestock combinations)

Boundaries

international

province

Scale 1:24 000 000

0   250   500 km

Agricultural lands

Wheat production and export, 1990

Production statistics

area ('000 ha)	
yield per ha (kg)	
production ('000 t)	

Movements

→ road, rail and water transport

⟹ exports

Elevators (type)

Process (receive grain for manufacture into other products)

Transfer (transfer grain to another elevator)

Terminal (receive grain upon or after inspection; weighing and the cleaning, storing and treating of the grain before it is moved forward)

In addition to the Process, Transfer and Terminal Elevators shown on the map there are 1 860 Primary Elevators in the Prairie Provinces. These receive grain directly from the producer for storage or forwarding.

Elevators (capacity)

○ over 400 000 t

○ 200 000–400 000 t

○ 100 000–200 000 t

· 10 000–100 000 t

Boundaries

international

province

Scale 1:35 000 000

0   500   1000 km

Zenithal Equidistant Projection

Exports via

Pacific ports 60.8%

St. Lawrence ports 33.1%

Churchill 0.4%

Atlantic ports 3.3%

Thunder Bay direct 2.4%

© Oxford University Press

1989–1990 Exports through eastern ports
('000 t)

former U.S.S.R.	3497
Iran	1445
Iraq	783
Algeria	609
Cuba	434
U.S.A.	372
Italy	357
U.K.	272
Brazil	220
Venezuela	181

1989–1990 Exports through western ports
('000 t)

China	4581
Japan	1465
Philippines	360
Indonesia	336
Bangladesh	336
Others	2161

Primary Elevators: (number)

Manitoba	292
Saskatchewan	994
Alberta	560
British Columbia	14

Map labels:

Port Cartier: 5.7 / 3140.0 / 17.9

Halifax: 2.4 / 3170.0 / 7.6

Baie Comeau: 54.6 / 3110.0 / 170.0

Montréal: 3.2 / 3250.0 / 10.4

Thunder Bay: 324.2 / 4180.0 / 1355.4

Churchill: 2198.1 / 2660.0 / 5851.2

Saskatoon: 8287.8 / 2030.0 / 16846.9

Sexsmith: 3135.9 / 2110.0 / 6614.0

Prince Rupert / Vancouver: 50.6 / 2690.0 / 136.0

Québec, Sorel, Prescott, Midland, Port Colborne, Port McNicoll, Collingwood, Owen Sound, Goderich, Sarnia, Windsor, Saint John, Portier, Trois Rivières, Winnipeg, Harrowby, St. Jean, Altona, Plum Coulee, Carman, Nipawin, Moose Jaw, Lloydminster, Biggar, Medicine Hat, Lethbridge, Fort Saskatchewan, Calgary

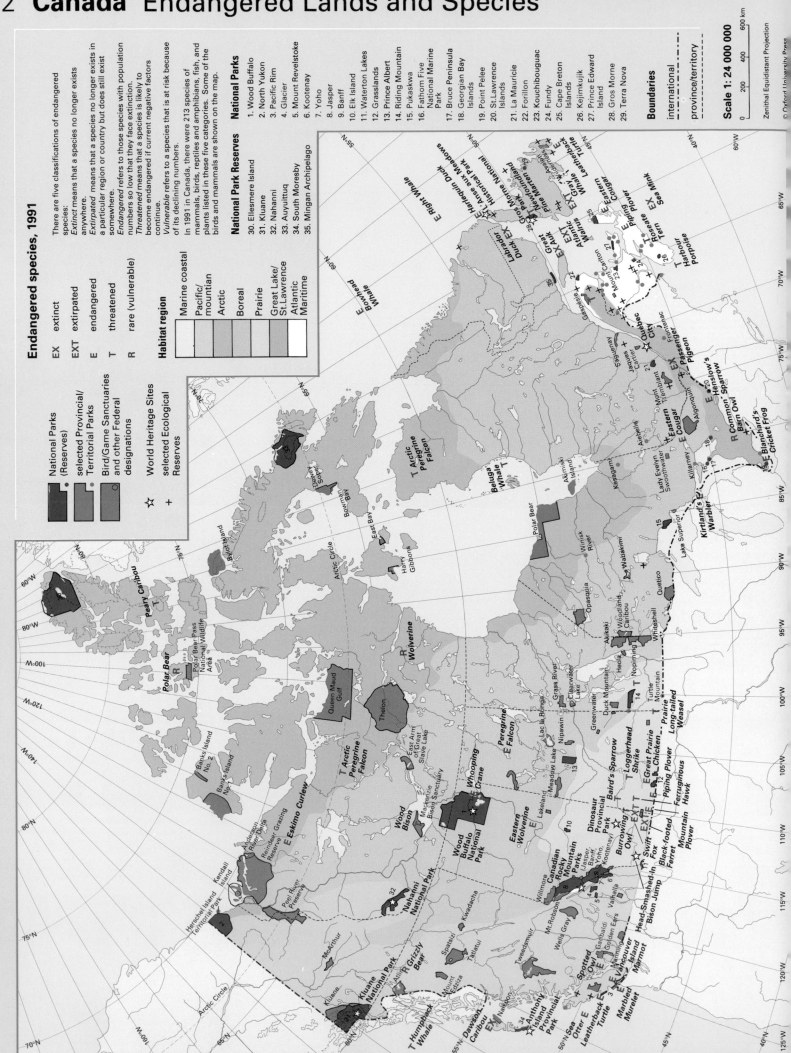

Endangered species, 1991

There are five classifications of endangered species:

Extinct means that a species no longer exists anywhere.

Extirpated means that a species no longer exists in a particular region or country but does still exist somewhere.

Endangered refers to those species with population numbers so low that they face extinction.

Threatened means that a species is likely to become endangered if current negative factors continue.

Vulnerable refers to a species that is at risk because of its declining numbers.

In 1991 in Canada, there were 213 species of mammals, birds, reptiles and amphibians, fish, and plants listed in these five categories. Some of the birds and mammals are shown on the map.

EX	extinct
EXT	extirpated
E	endangered
T	threatened
R	rare (vulnerable)

Habitat region

- Marine coastal
- Pacific/mountain
- Arctic
- Boreal
- Prairie
- Great Lake/St.Lawrence
- Atlantic Maritime

National Park Reserves
- 30. Ellesmere Island
- 31. Kluane
- 32. Nahanni
- 33. Auyuittuq
- 34. South Moresby
- 35. Mingan Archipelago

National Parks
- 1. Wood Buffalo
- 2. North Yukon
- 3. Pacific Rim
- 4. Glacier
- 5. Mount Revelstoke
- 6. Kootenay
- 7. Yoho
- 8. Jasper
- 9. Banff
- 10. Elk Island
- 11. Waterton Lakes
- 12. Grasslands
- 13. Prince Albert
- 14. Riding Mountain
- 15. Pukaskwa
- 16. Fathom Five National Marine Park
- 17. Bruce Peninsula
- 18. Georgian Bay Islands
- 19. Point Pelee
- 20. St.Lawrence Islands
- 21. La Mauricie
- 22. Forillon
- 23. Kouchibouguac
- 24. Fundy
- 25. Cape Breton Islands
- 26. Kejimkujik
- 27. Prince Edward Island
- 28. Gros Morne
- 29. Terra Nova

Boundaries

international

province/territory

Scale 1 : 24 000 000

0 200 400 600 km

Zenithal Equidistant Projection

© Oxford University Press

- National Parks (Reserves)
- selected Provincial/Territorial Parks
- Bird/Game Sanctuaries and other Federal designations
- ☆ World Heritage Sites
- + selected Ecological Reserves

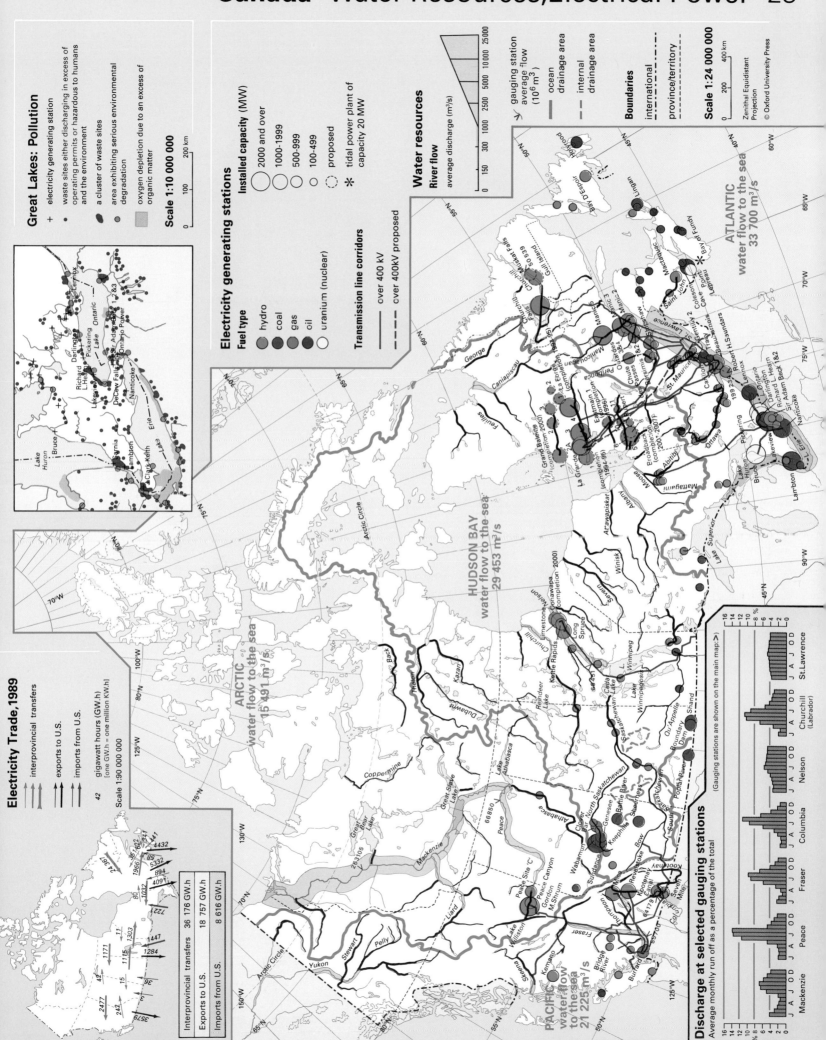

Great Lakes: Pollution

+ electricity generating station

. waste sites either discharging in excess of operating permits or hazardous to humans and the environment

● a cluster of waste sites

◗ area exhibiting serious environmental degradation

▨ oxygen depletion due to an excess of organic matter

Scale 1:10 000 000

0   100   200 km

Electricity generating stations

Installed capacity (MW)

○ 2000 and over
○ 1000-1999
○ 500-999
○ 100-499
○ proposed

✱ tidal power plant of capacity 20 MW

Fuel type

● hydro
● coal
● gas
● oil
○ uranium (nuclear)

Transmission line corridors

── over 400 kV
─·─ over 400kV proposed

Water resources

River flow

average discharge (m³/s)

150 300 500 1000 2500 5000 10000 25000

↗ gauging station average flow (10⁶ m³)

── ocean drainage area

─·─ internal drainage area

Boundaries

── international
─·─ province/territory

Scale 1:24 000 000

0   200   400 km

Zenithal Equidistant Projection

© Oxford University Press

Electricity Trade,1989

→ interprovincial transfers
→ exports to U.S.
→ imports from U.S.

42 gigawatt hours (GW.h) (one GW.h = one million KW.h)

Scale 1:90 000 000

Interprovincial transfers	36 176 GW.h
Exports to U.S.	18 757 GW.h
Imports from U.S.	8 616 GW.h

ARCTIC water flow to the sea 15 491 m³/s

HUDSON BAY water flow to the sea 29 453 m³/s

ATLANTIC water flow to the sea 33 700 m³/s

PACIFIC water flow to the sea 21 225 m³/s

Discharge at selected gauging stations

Average monthly run off as a percentage of the total

(Gauging stations are shown on the main map.)

% 16 14 12 10 8 6 4 2 0

Mackenzie   Peace   Fraser   Columbia   Nelson   Churchill (Labrador)   St.Lawrence

J A J O D

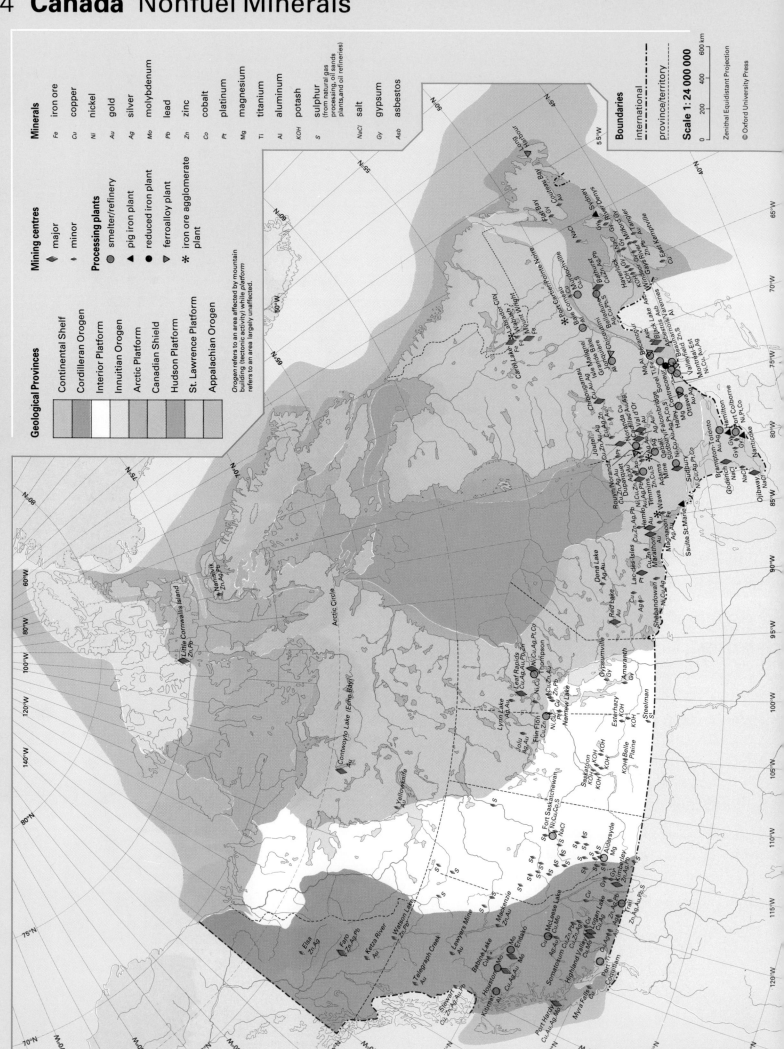

Minerals

Fe iron ore
Cu copper
Ni nickel
Au gold
Ag silver
Mo molybdenum
Pb lead
Zn zinc
Co cobalt
Pt platinum
Mg magnesium
Ti titanium
Al aluminum
KOH potash
S sulphur
   (from natural gas
   processing, oil sands
   plants, and oil refineries)
NaCl salt
Gy gypsum
Asb asbestos

Mining centres

◆ major
◇ minor

Processing plants

● smelter/refinery
▲ pig iron plant
● reduced iron plant
▽ ferroalloy plant
✳ iron ore agglomerate
   plant

Geological Provinces

Continental Shelf
Cordilleran Orogen
Interior Platform
Innuitian Orogen
Arctic Platform
Canadian Shield
Hudson Platform
St. Lawrence Platform
Appalachian Orogen

Orogen refers to an area affected by mountain building (tectonic activity) while platform refers to an area largely unaffected.

Boundaries

international
province/territory

Scale 1: 24 000 000

Zenithal Equidistant Projection

© Oxford University Press

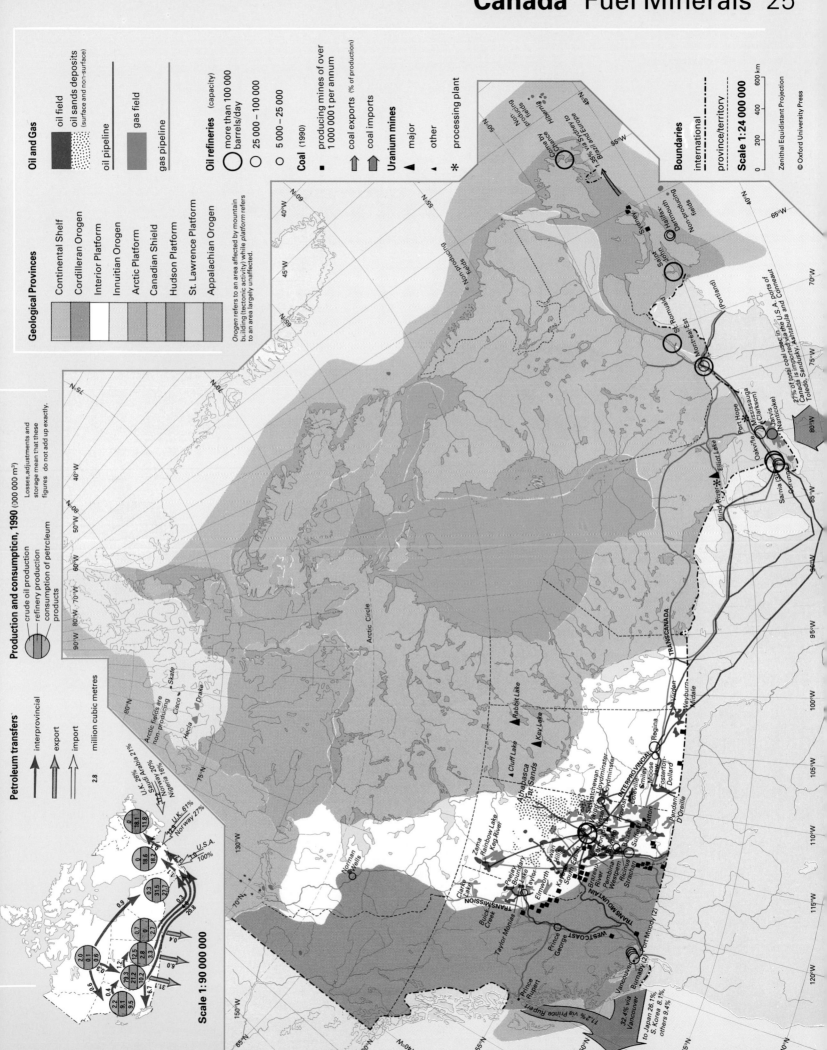

Oil and Gas

- oil field
- oil sands deposits (surface and non-surface)
- oil pipeline
- gas field
- gas pipeline

Geological Provinces

- Continental Shelf
- Cordilleran Orogen
- Interior Platform
- Innuitian Orogen
- Arctic Platform
- Canadian Shield
- Hudson Platform
- St. Lawrence Platform
- Appalachian Orogen

Orogen refers to an area affected by mountain building (tectonic activity) while platform refers to an area largely unaffected.

Oil refineries (capacity)

- ◯ more than 100 000 barrels/day
- ○ 25 000 – 100 000
- ○ 5 000 – 25 000

Coal (1990)

- ■ producing mines of over 1 000 000 t per annum
- ⬆ coal exports (% of production)
- ⬆ coal imports

Uranium mines

- ▲ major
- ▴ other
- ∗ processing plant

Boundaries

- international
- province/territory

Scale 1:24 000 000

0 200 400 600 km

Zenithal Equidistant Projection

© Oxford University Press

Production and consumption, 1990 (000 000 m³)

- crude oil production
- refinery production
- consumption of petroleum products

Losses, adjustments and storage mean that these figures do not add up exactly.

Petroleum transfers

- interprovincial
- export
- import

2.8 million cubic metres

Scale 1:90 000 000

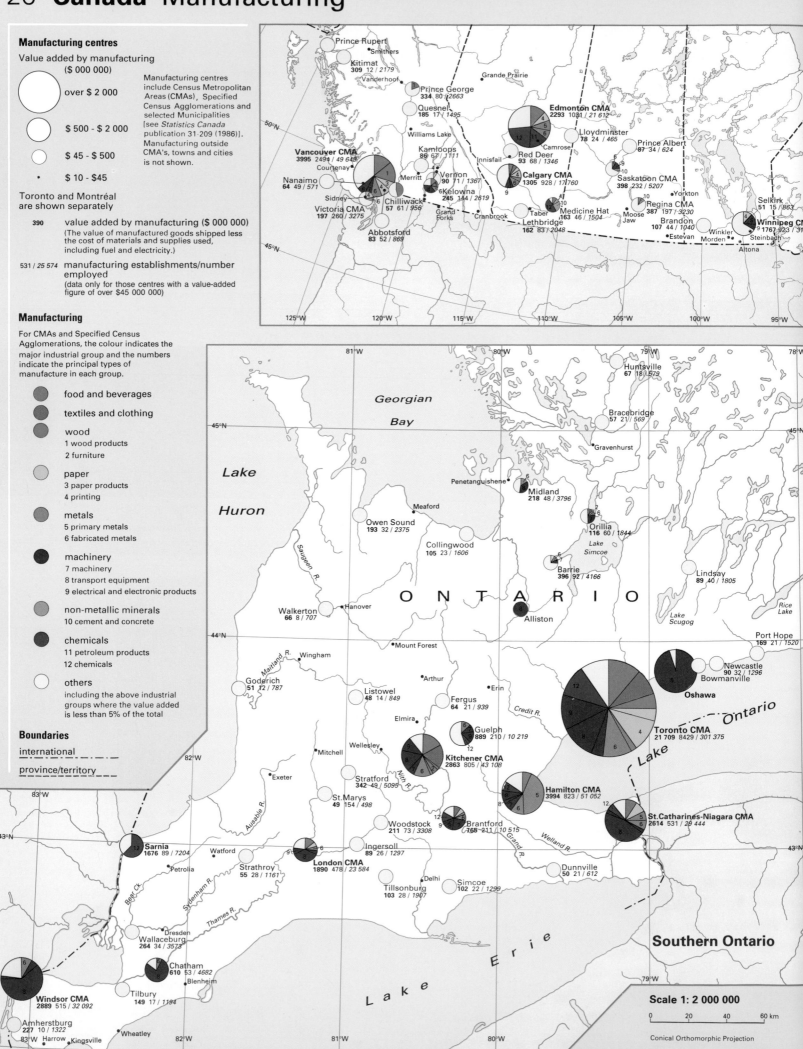

Manufacturing centres

Value added by manufacturing
($ 000 000)

○ over $ 2 000

○ $ 500 - $ 2 000

○ $ 45 - $ 500

· $ 10 - $45

Manufacturing centres include Census Metropolitan Areas (CMAs), Specified Census Agglomerations and selected Municipalities [see *Statistics Canada* publication 31-209 (1986)]. Manufacturing outside CMA's, towns and cities is not shown.

Toronto and Montréal are shown separately

390 value added by manufacturing ($ 000 000)
(The value of manufactured goods shipped less the cost of materials and supplies used, including fuel and electricity.)

531 / 25 574 manufacturing establishments/number employed
(data only for those centres with a value-added figure of over $45 000 000)

Manufacturing

For CMAs and Specified Census Agglomerations, the colour indicates the major industrial group and the numbers indicate the principal types of manufacture in each group.

● food and beverages

● textiles and clothing

● wood
1 wood products
2 furniture

● paper
3 paper products
4 printing

● metals
5 primary metals
6 fabricated metals

● machinery
7 machinery
8 transport equipment
9 electrical and electronic products

● non-metallic minerals
10 cement and concrete

● chemicals
11 petroleum products
12 chemicals

○ others
including the above industrial groups where the value added is less than 5% of the total

Boundaries

international

province/territory

Southern Ontario

Scale 1: 2 000 000

0   20   40   60 km

Conical Orthomorphic Projection

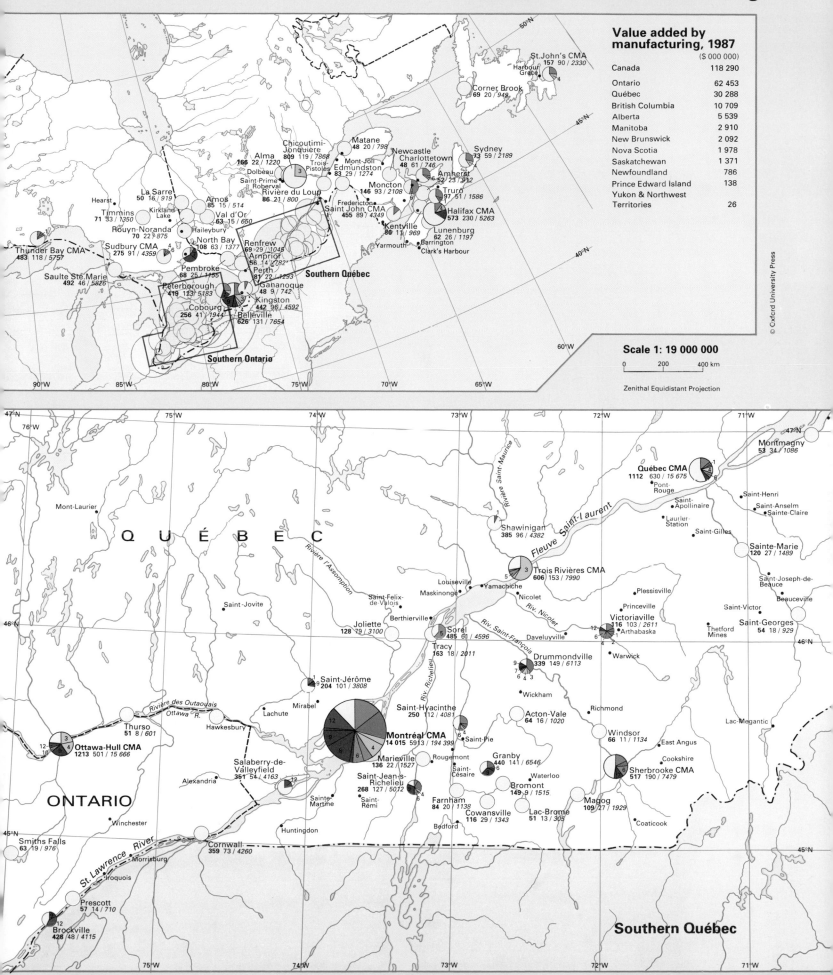

Value added by manufacturing, 1987

	($ 000 000)
Canada	118 290
Ontario	62 453
Québec	30 288
British Columbia	10 709
Alberta	5 539
Manitoba	2 910
New Brunswick	2 092
Nova Scotia	1 978
Saskatchewan	1 371
Newfoundland	786
Prince Edward Island	138
Yukon & Northwest Territories	26

© Oxford University Press

Scale 1: 19 000 000

0   200   400 km

Zenithal Equidistant Projection

Southern Québec

Scale 1: 2 000 000

0   20   40   60 km

Conical Orthomorphic Projection

Population distribution, 1901

one dot represents 1000 people

Boundaries, 1901

international

province/territory

Scale 1:45 000 000

1991 Census

Census total : 27 296 859

urban : 20 907 135 (76.6%)

rural : 6 389 724 (23.4%)

Detailed population statistics begin on page 185.

Population distribution, 1991

settled area (ecumen)

one red dot represents 1000 persons

one black dot represents 100 persons north of latitude 60°N

○ cities with more than 20 000 inhabitants

All Canadian cities with a population greater than 20 000 are shown on the map. Cities with more than 100 000 inhabitants, Census Metropolitan Areas (CMAs), are named on the map.

Boundaries

international

province/territory

Scale 1: 22 500 000

0   200   400km

Zenithal Equidistant Projection

Census Metropolitan Areas

one small square represents 50 000 people

('000 people, census 1991)

A Census Metropolitan Area (CMA) is an urban-centred region that includes a large urbanized core (with more than 100 000 people) together with adjacent urban and rural fringe areas that have a high degree of economic and social integration with that core.

3839   3127   1603   921   840   754   652   646   600   382   365   356   321

Toronto   Montréal   Vancouver   Ottawa-Hull   Edmonton   Calgary   Winnipeg   Québec   Hamilton   London   St.Catharines-Niagara   Kitchener   Halifax

288   262   240   210   192   172   161   158   139   136   125   124

Victoria   Windsor   Oshawa   Saskatoon   Regina   St.John's   Chicoutimi-Jonquière   Sudbury   Sherbrooke   Trois Rivières   Saint John   Thunder Bay

© Oxford University Press

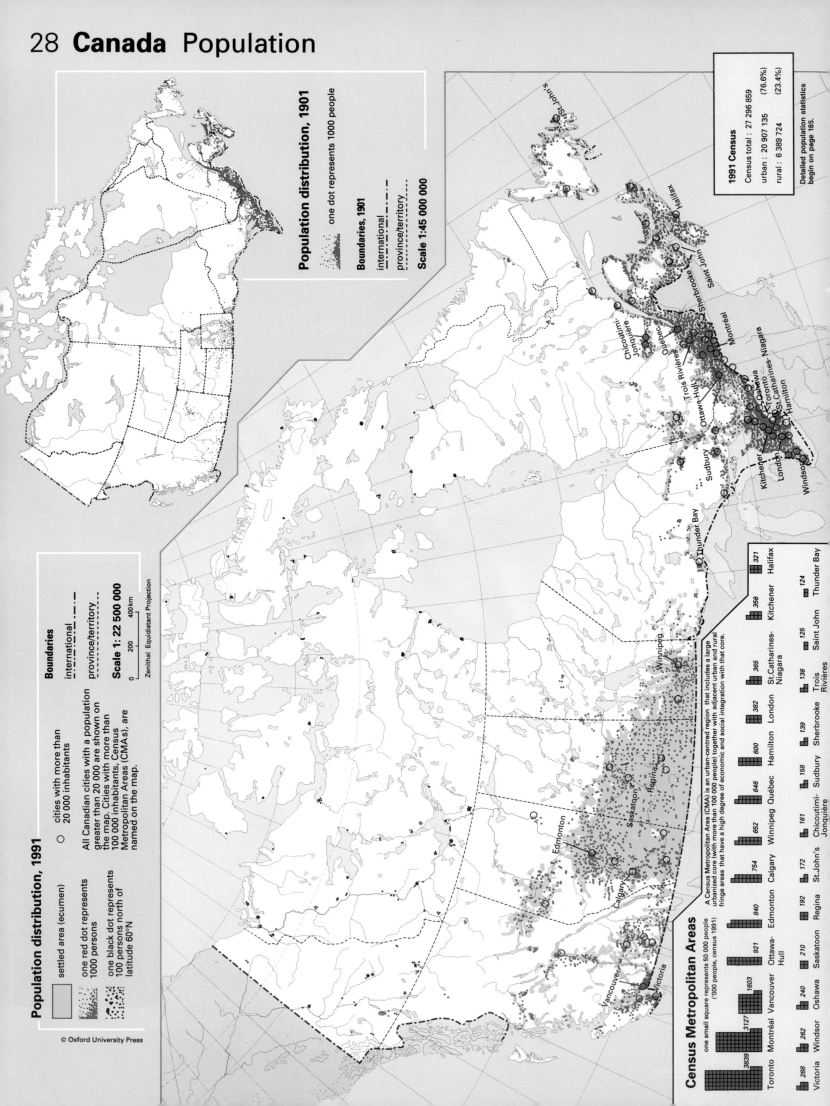

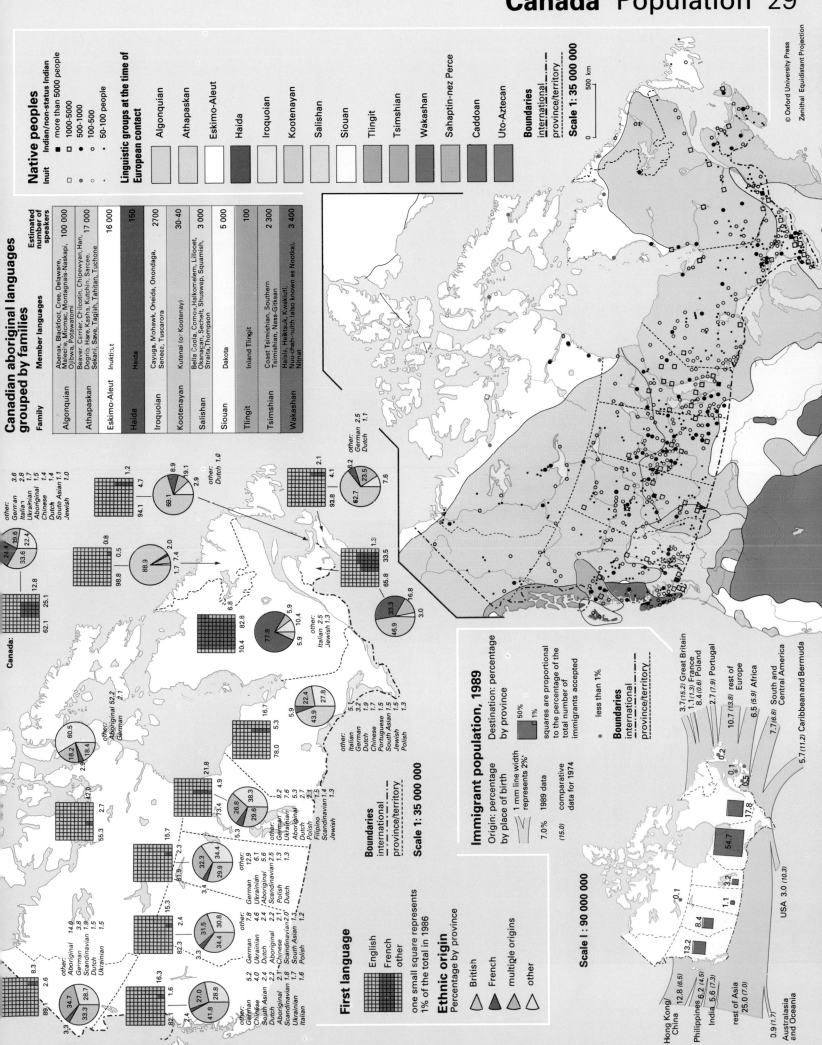

© Oxford University Press
Zenithal Equidistant Projection

Native peoples

	Inuit	Indian/non-status Indian
■	□	more than 5000 people
●	◐	1000–5000
●	●	500–1000
○	○	100–500
·	·	50–100 people

Linguistic groups at the time of European contact

Algonquian
Athapaskan
Eskimo-Aleut
Haida
Iroquoian
Kootenayan
Salishan
Siouan
Tlingit
Tsimshian
Wakashan
Sahaptin-nez Perce
Caddoan
Uto-Aztecan

Boundaries
international
province/territory

Scale 1: 35 000 000

0   500 km

Canadian aboriginal languages grouped by families

Family	Member languages	Estimated number of speakers
Algonquian	Abenak, Blackfoot, Cree, Delaware, Malecite, Micmac, Montagnais-Naskapi, Ojibwa, Potawatomi	100 000
Athapaskan	Beaver, Carrier, Chilcotin, Chipewyan, Han, Dogrib, Hare, Kasha, Kutchin, Sarcee, Sekani, Save, Tagish, Tahltan, Tuchone	17 000
Eskimo-Aleut	Inuktitut	16 000
Haida	Haida	150
Iroquoian	Cayuga, Mohawk, Oneida, Onondaga, Seneca, Tuscarora	2700
Kootenayan	Kutenai (o· Kootenay)	30–40
Salishan	Bella Coola, Comox, Halkomelem, Lillooet, Okanacan, Sechelt, Shuswap, Squamish, Straita, Thompson	3 000
Siouan	Dakota	5 000
Tlingit	Inland Tlingit	100
Tsimshian	Coast Tsimshian, Southern Tsimshian, Nass-Gitksan	2 300
Wakashan	Haisle, Heiktsuk, Kwakiutl, Nuu-chah-nulth (also known as Nootka), Nithat	3 400

First language

English
French
other

one small square represents 1% of the total in 1986

Ethnic origin

Percentage by province

△ British
▲ French
◭ multiple origins
▽ other

Boundaries
international
province/territory

Scale 1: 35 000 000

Canada:
62.1   25.1   12.8

other:
German 3.6
Italian 2.8
Ukrainian 1.7
Aboriginal 1.5
Chinese 1.4
Dutch 1.4
South Asian 1.1
Jewish 1.0

24.4   19.6
33.6   22.4

Immigrant population, 1989

Origin: percentage by place of birth

7.0%   1989 data
(15.0)   comparative data for 1974

Destination: percentage by province

[50%]
[1%]   squares are proportional to the percentage of the total number of immigrants accepted

· less than 1%

Boundaries
international
province/territory

Scale I : 90 000 000

3.7 (15.2) Great Britain
1.1 (1.3) France
8.4 (0.6) Poland
2.7 (7.9) Portugal
10.7 (13.8) rest of Europe
6.5 (5.9) Africa
7.7 (6.8) South and Central America
5.7 (11.2) Caribbean and Bermuda
USA 3.0 (10.3)
0.9 (1.7) Australasia and Oceania
25.0 (7.0) rest of Asia
India 5.6 (7.3)
Philippines 6.2 (4.5)
Hong Kong/ China 12.8 (6.5)

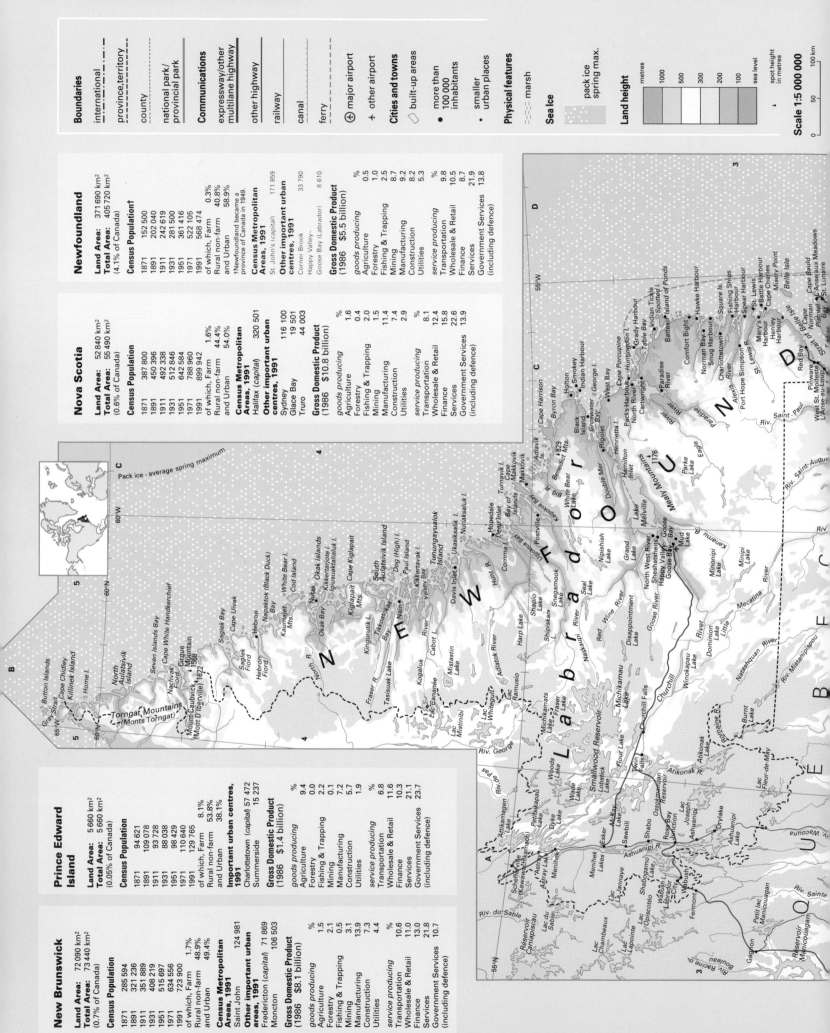

Legend

Boundaries
international
province, territory
county
national park/ provincial park

Communications
expressway/other multilane highway
other highway
railway
canal
ferry
⊕ major airport
✈ other airport

Cities and towns
◇ built-up areas
● more than 100 000 inhabitants
● smaller urban places
• smaller urban places

Physical features
marsh

Sea ice
‐‐‐‐ pack ice spring max.

Land height
metres
1000
500
300
200
100
sea level
▲ spot height in metres

Scale 1:5 000 000
0 50 100 km

New Brunswick

Land Area: 72 090 km²
Total Area: 73 440 km²
(0.7% of Canada)

Census Population

1871	285 594
1891	321 236
1911	351 889
1931	408 219
1951	515 697
1971	634 556
1991	723 900

of which, Farm	1.7%
Rural non-farm	48.9%
and Urban	49.4%

Census Metropolitan Areas, 1991
Saint John 124 981

Other important urban areas, 1991
Fredericton (capital) 71 869
Moncton 106 503

Gross Domestic Product
(1986 $8.1 billion)

goods producing	%
Agriculture	1.5
Forestry	2.1
Fishing & Trapping	0.5
Mining	3.1
Manufacturing	13.9
Construction	7.3
Utilities	4.4

service producing	%
Transportation	10.6
Wholesale & Retail	11.0
Finance	13.0
Services	21.8
Government Services (including defence)	10.7

Prince Edward Island

Land Area: 5 660 km²
Total Area: 5 660 km²
(0.05% of Canada)

Census Population

1871	94 621
1891	109 078
1911	93 728
1931	88 038
1951	98 429
1971	110 640
1991	129 765

of which, Farm	8.1%
Rural non-farm	53.8%
and Urban	38.1%

Important urban centres, 1991
Charlottetown (capital) 57 472
Summerside 15 237

Gross Domestic Product
(1986 $1.4 billion)

goods producing	%
Agriculture	9.4
Forestry	0.0
Fishing & Trapping	2.2
Mining	0.1
Manufacturing	7.2
Construction	5.7
Utilities	1.9

service producing	%
Transportation	6.8
Wholesale & Retail	11.6
Finance	10.3
Services	21.1
Government Services (including defence)	23.7

Nova Scotia

Land Area: 52 840 km²
Total Area: 55 490 km²
(0.6% of Canada)

Census Population

1871	387 800
1891	450 396
1911	492 338
1931	512 846
1951	642 584
1971	788 960
1991	899 942

of which, Farm	1.6%
Rural non-farm	44.4%
and Urban	54.0%

Census Metropolitan Areas, 1991
Halifax (capital) 320 501

Other important urban centres, 1991
Sydney 116 100
Glace Bay 19 501
Truro 44 003

Gross Domestic Product
(1986 $10.8 billion)

goods producing	%
Agriculture	1.6
Forestry	0.4
Fishing & Trapping	2.0
Mining	1.5
Manufacturing	11.4
Construction	7.4
Utilities	2.9

service producing	%
Transportation	8.1
Wholesale & Retail	12.4
Finance	15.8
Services	22.6
Government Services (including defence)	13.9

Newfoundland

Land Area: 371 690 km²
Total Area: 405 720 km²
(4.1% of Canada)

Census Population

1871	152 500
1891	202 040
1911	242 619
1931	281 500
1951	361 416
1971	522 105
1991	568 474

of which, Farm	0.3%
Rural non-farm	40.8%
and Urban	58.9%

†Newfoundland became a province of Canada in 1949.

Census Metropolitan Areas, 1991
St. John's (capital)† 171 859

Other important urban centres, 1991
Corner Brook 33 790
Happy Valley–
Goose Bay (Labrador) 8 610

Gross Domestic Product
(1986 $5.5 billion)

goods producing	%
Agriculture	0.5
Forestry	1.0
Fishing & Trapping	2.5
Mining	8.7
Manufacturing	9.2
Construction	8.2
Utilities	5.3

service producing	%
Transportation	9.8
Wholesale & Retail	10.5
Finance	8.7
Services	21.9
Government Services (including defence)	13.8

Pack ice - average spring maximum

Nova Scotia and Prince Edward Island

Scale 1:3 150 000

0   50 km

Conical Orthomorphic Projection

© Oxford University Press

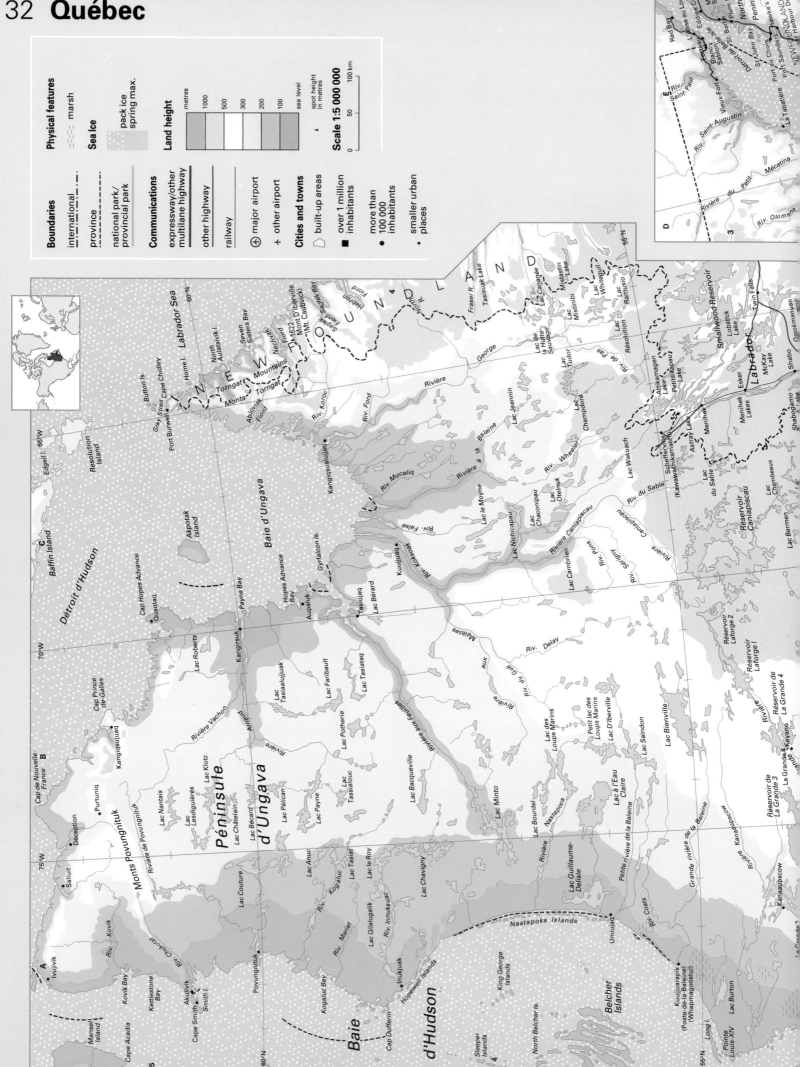

Physical features
------ marsh

Sea Ice
- - - - pack ice
spring max.

Land height

metres
1000
500
300
200
100
sea level

▲ spot height
in metres

Scale 1:5 000 000

0   50   100 km

Boundaries
— · — · — international
— · — · — province
national park/
provincial park

Communications
expressway/other
multilane highway
other highway
railway
⊕ major airport
✈ other airport

Cities and towns
⬡ built-up areas
■ over 1 million
inhabitants
● more than
100 000
● smaller urban
places

Labrador Sea

Baffin Island

Détroit d'Hudson

Baie d'Ungava

Péninsule d'Ungava

Monts Povungnituk

Baie d'Hudson

Labrador

NEWFOUNDLAND

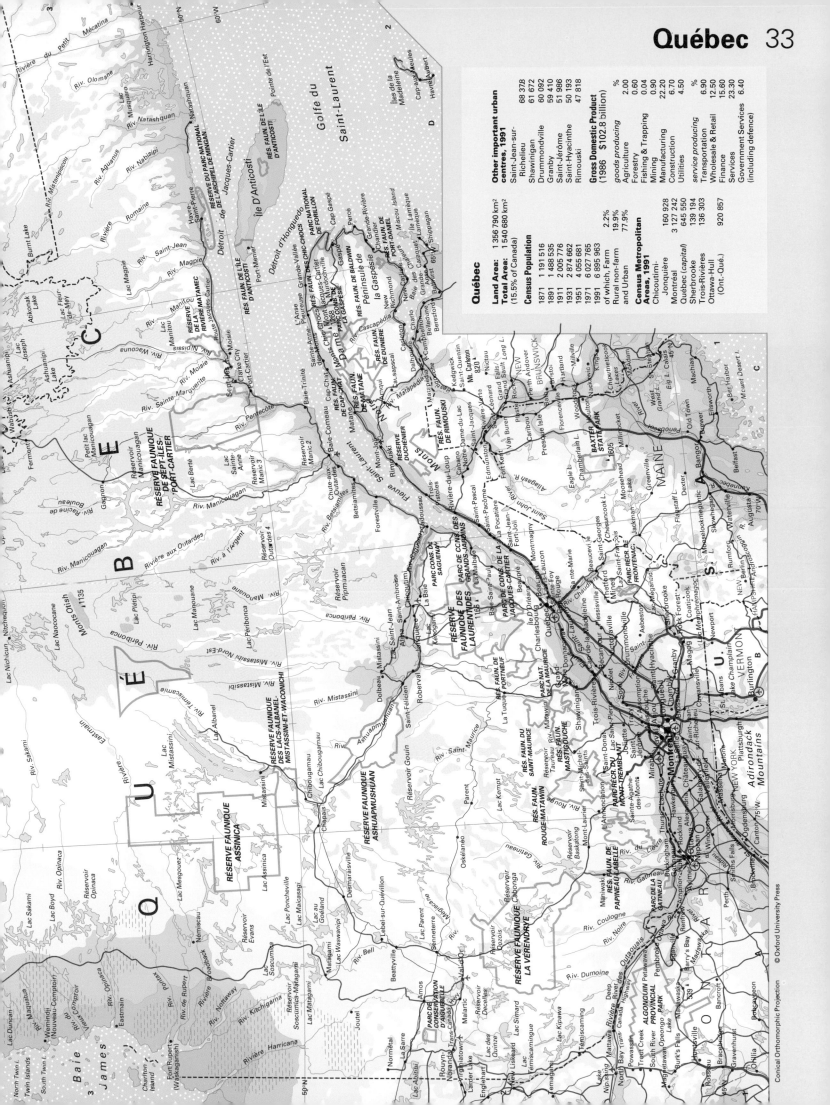

Québec

Land Area: 1 356 790 km²
Total Area: 1 540 680 km²
(15.5% of Canada)

Census Population

1871	1 191 516
1891	1 488 535
1911	2 005 776
1931	2 874 662
1951	4 055 681
1971	6 027 765
1991	6 895 963
of which, Farm	2.2%
Rural non-farm	19.9%
and Urban	77.9%

Census Metropolitan Areas, 1991

Chicoutimi-Jonquière	160 928
Montréal	3 127 242
Québec (capital)	645 550
Sherbrooke	139 194
Trois-Rivières	136 303
Ottawa-Hull (Ont.-Qué.)	920 857

Other important urban centres, 1991

Saint-Jean-sur-Richelieu	68 378
Shawinigan	61 672
Drummondville	60 092
Granby	59 410
Saint-Jérôme	51 986
Saint-Hyacinthe	50 193
Rimouski	47 818

Gross Domestic Product
(1986 $102.8 billion)

goods producing	%
Agriculture	2.00
Forestry	0.60
Fishing & Trapping	0.04
Mining	0.90
Manufacturing	22.20
Construction	6.70
Utilities	4.50

service producing	%
Transportation	6.90
Wholesale & Retail	12.50
Finance	15.60
Services	23.30
Government Services (including defence)	6.40

Conical Orthomorphic Projection

©Oxford University Press

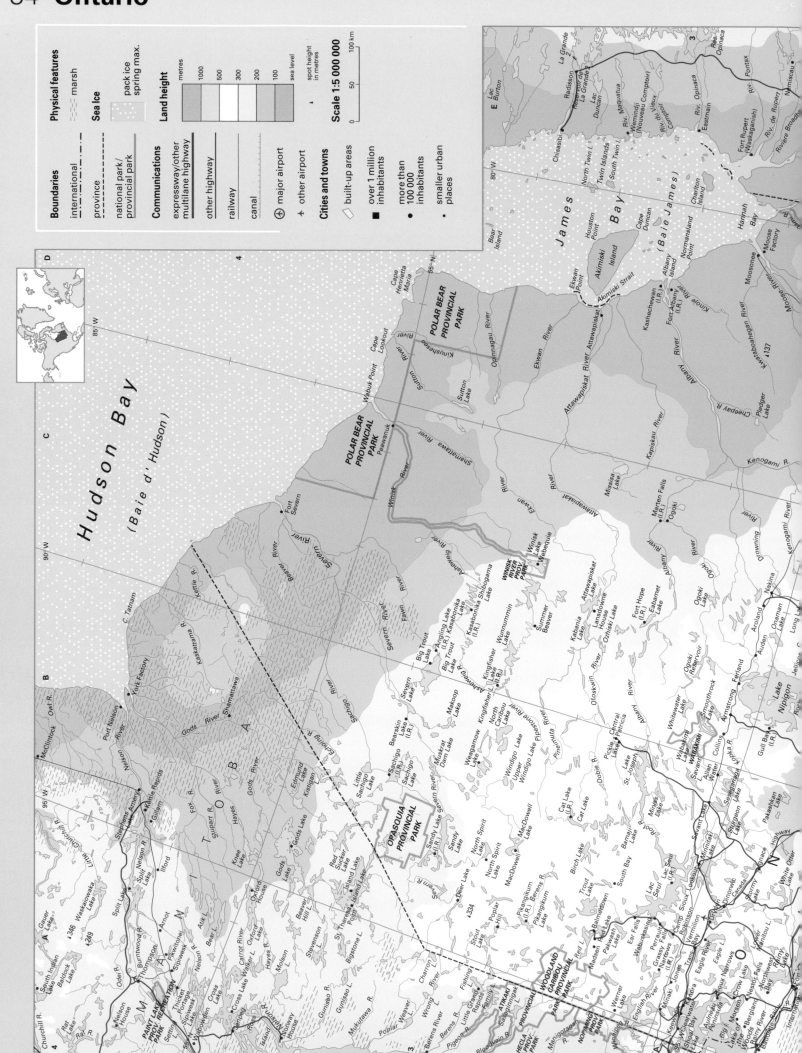

Boundaries
international
province
national park/
provincial park

Communications
expressway/other
multilane highway
other highway
railway
canal

Cities and towns
built-up areas
over 1 million inhabitants
more than 100 000 inhabitants
smaller urban places

Physical features
marsh

Sea Ice
pack ice spring max.

Land height
metres
1000
500
300
200
100
sea level

spot height in metres

Scale 1:5 000 000

major airport
other airport

0   50   100 km

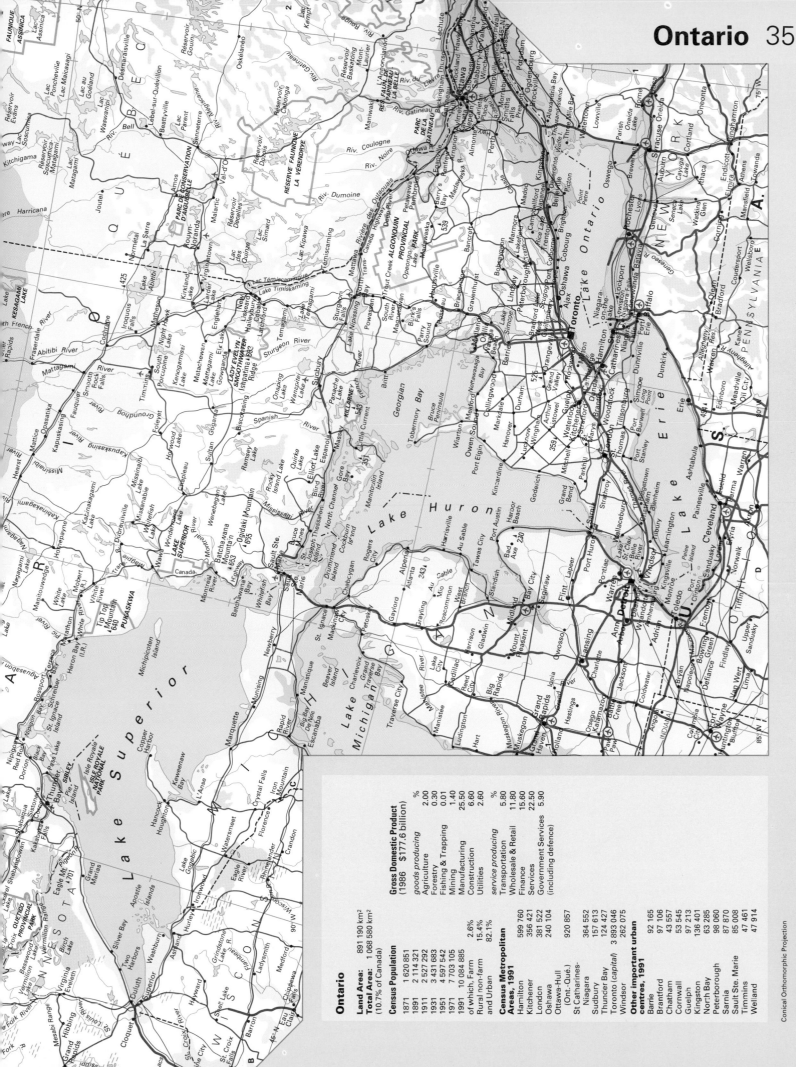

Ontario

Land Area: 891 190 km²
Total Area: 1 068 580 km²
(10.7% of Canada)

Census Population

1871	1 620 851	
1891	2 114 321	
1911	2 527 292	
1931	3 431 683	
1951	4 597 542	
1971	7 703 105	
1991	10 084 885	
of which, Farm	2.6%	
Rural non-farm	15.4%	
and Urban	82.1%	

Census Metropolitan Areas, 1991

Hamilton	599 760
Kitchener	356 421
London	381 522
Oshawa	240 104
Ottawa-Hull (Ont.-Qué.)	920 857
St Catharines-Niagara	364 552
Sudbury	157 613
Thunder Bay	124 427
Toronto (capital)	3 893 046
Windsor	262 075

Other important urban centres, 1991

Barrie	92 165
Brantford	97 106
Chatham	43 557
Cornwall	53 545
Guelph	97 213
Kingston	136 401
North Bay	63 285
Peterborough	98 060
Sarnia	87 870
Sault Ste. Marie	85 008
Timmins	47 461
Welland	47 914

Gross Domestic Product
(1986 $177,6 billion)

	%
goods producing	
Agriculture	2.00
Forestry	0.30
Fishing & Trapping	0.01
Mining	1.40
Manufacturing	25.50
Construction	6.60
Utilities	2.60
service producing	
Transportation	5.80
Wholesale & Retail	11.80
Finance	15.60
Services	22.50
Government Services (including defence)	5.90

Conical Orthomorphic Projection

© Oxford University Press

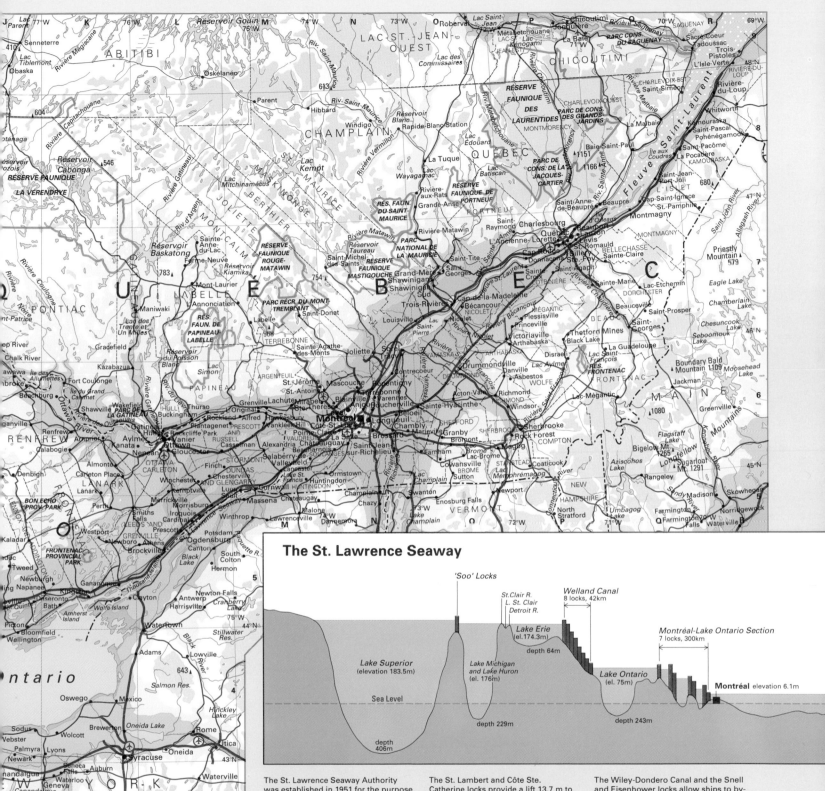

The St. Lawrence Seaway

'Soo' Locks

Welland Canal
8 locks, 42km

St.Clair R.
L. St. Clair
Detroit R.

Lake Erie
(el. 174.3m)

depth 64m

Montréal-Lake Ontario Section
7 locks, 300km

Lake Superior
(elevation 183.5m)

Lake Michigan
and Lake Huron
(el. 176m)

Lake Ontario
(el. 75m)

Montréal elevation 6.1m

Sea Level

depth 229m

depth 243m

depth
406m

The St. Lawrence Seaway Authority was established in 1951 for the purpose of constructing, operating, and maintaining a deep waterway between the Port of Montréal and Lake Erie, replacing an earlier network of shallow draught canals. Two of the seven seaway locks along the St. Lawrence River, in the United States, are operated by the U.S. St. Lawrence Seaway Development Corporation.

The St. Lawrence Seaway was officially opened in 1959. It allows navigation by ships not exceeding 222.5 m in length, 23.2 m in width, and loaded to a maximum draught of 7.9 m in a minimum water depth of 8.2 m.

Beginning at Montréal, the Seaway naturally divides into four sections:

1. The Lachine Section required the construction of the 33 km South Shore Canal, to by-pass the Lachine Rapids.

The St. Lambert and Côte Ste. Catherine locks provide a lift 13.7 m to Lake St. Louis.

2. The Soulanges Section contains the two Beauharnois locks, by-passing the Beauharnois hydro-electric plant to reach Lac Saint-François.

3. The Lac Saint-François Section extends to a point just east of Cornwall, Ontario.

4. The International Rapids Section was developed simultaneously for hydro-electric power generation and navigation. Ontario and the State of New York jointly built the Moses-Saunders Power Dam, the Long Sault and Iroquois control dams, and undertook the flooding of the river above the power dam to form Lake St. Lawrence, the 'head pond' of the generating station.

The Wiley-Dondero Canal and the Snell and Eisenhower locks allow ships to by-pass the Moses-Saunders power station. The Iroquois lock and adjacent control dam are used to adjust the level of Lake St. Lawrence to that of Lake Ontario.

The Welland Canal joins lakes Ontario and Erie and allows ships to by-pass Niagara Falls by means of eight locks. The present Welland Canal, completed in 1932, was later deepened to ensure 7.9 m draught navigation throughout the Seaway.

The final section consists of four parallel locks, the 'Soo' locks, on the St. Mary's River and connects Lake Superior to Lake Huron.

© Oxford University Press

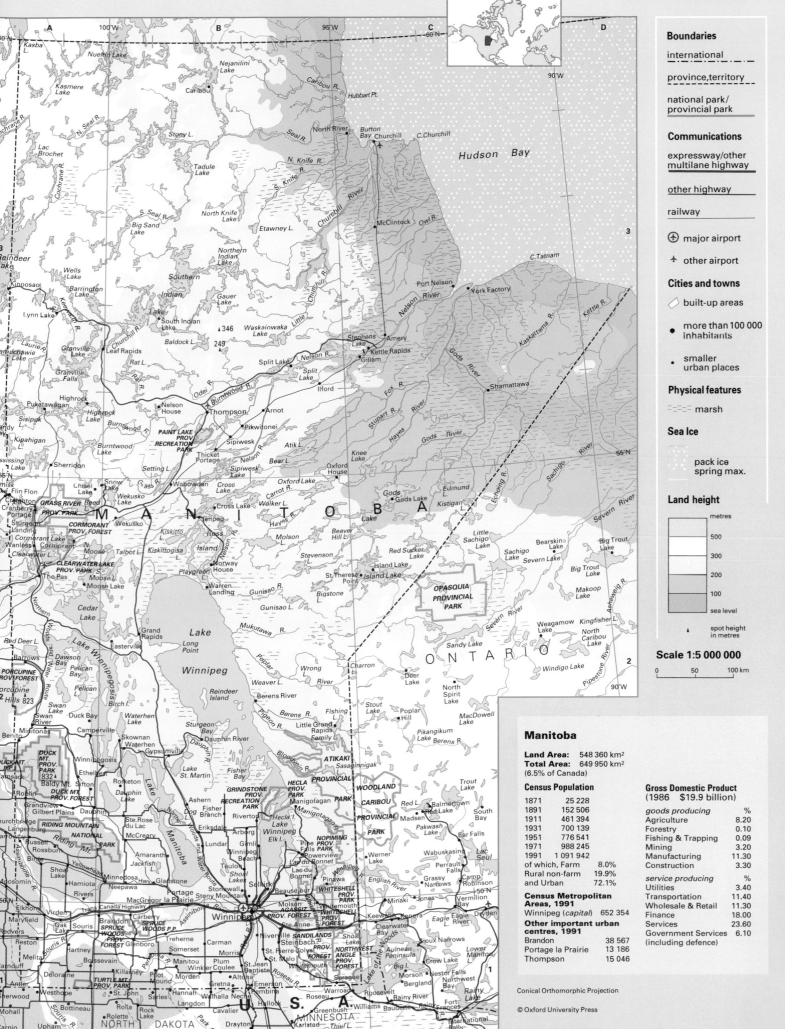

Boundaries

international

province, territory

national park/ provincial park

Communications

expressway/other multilane highway

other highway

railway

⊕ major airport

✈ other airport

Cities and towns

⬦ built-up areas

● more than 100 000 inhabitants

• smaller urban places

Physical features

--- marsh

Sea Ice

pack ice spring max.

Land height

| metres |
| 500 |
| 300 |
| 200 |
| 100 |
| sea level |

▲ spot height in metres

Scale 1:5 000 000

0   50   100 km

Conical Orthomorphic Projection

© Oxford University Press

Manitoba

Land Area: 548 360 km²
Total Area: 649 950 km²
(6.5% of Canada)

Census Population

1871	25 228
1891	152 506
1911	461 394
1931	700 139
1951	776 541
1971	988 245
1991	1 091 942
of which, Farm	8.0%
Rural non-farm	19.9%
and Urban	72.1%

Census Metropolitan Areas, 1991

Winnipeg (capital) 652 354

Other important urban centres, 1991

Brandon	38 567
Portage la Prairie	13 186
Thompson	15 046

Gross Domestic Product
(1986 $19.9 billion)

goods producing	%
Agriculture	8.20
Forestry	0.10
Fishing & Trapping	0.09
Mining	3.20
Manufacturing	11.30
Construction	3.30

service producing	%
Utilities	3.40
Transportation	11.40
Wholesale & Retail	11.30
Finance	18.00
Services	23.60
Government Services (including defence)	6.10

Boundaries

international

province, territory

national park/ provincial park

Communications

expressway/other multilane highway

other highway

railway

✈ major airport

✈ other airport

Cities and towns

built-up areas

● more than 100 000 inhabitants

· smaller urban places

Physical features

marsh

Land height

metres

1000
500
300
200
100
sea level

▲ spot height in metres

Scale 1:5 000 000

0   50   100 km

© Oxford University Press

Conical Orthomorphic Projection

Saskatchewan

Land Area: 570 700 km²
Total Area: 652 330 km²
(6.5% of Canada)

Census Population

1871	included in
1891	NWT
1911	492 432
1931	921 785
1951	831 728
1971	926 240
1991	988 928

of which, Farm 16.0%
Rural non-farm 22.6%
and Urban 61.4%

Census Metropolitan Areas, 1991

Regina (*capital*) 191 692
Saskatoon 210 023

Other important urban areas, 1991

Lloydminster 17 283
Moose Jaw 35 552
Prince Albert 41 257
Swift Current 14 815
Yorkton 18 023

Gross Domestic Product
(1986 $17.4 billion)

goods producing	%
Agriculture	12.4
Forestry	0.2
Fishing & Trapping	0.0
Mining	12.5
Manufacturing	5.7
Construction	4.3
Utilities	2.7
service producing	%
Transportation	7.7
Wholesale & Retail	9.7
Finance	17.0
Services	17.8
Government Services (including defence)	10.0

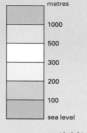

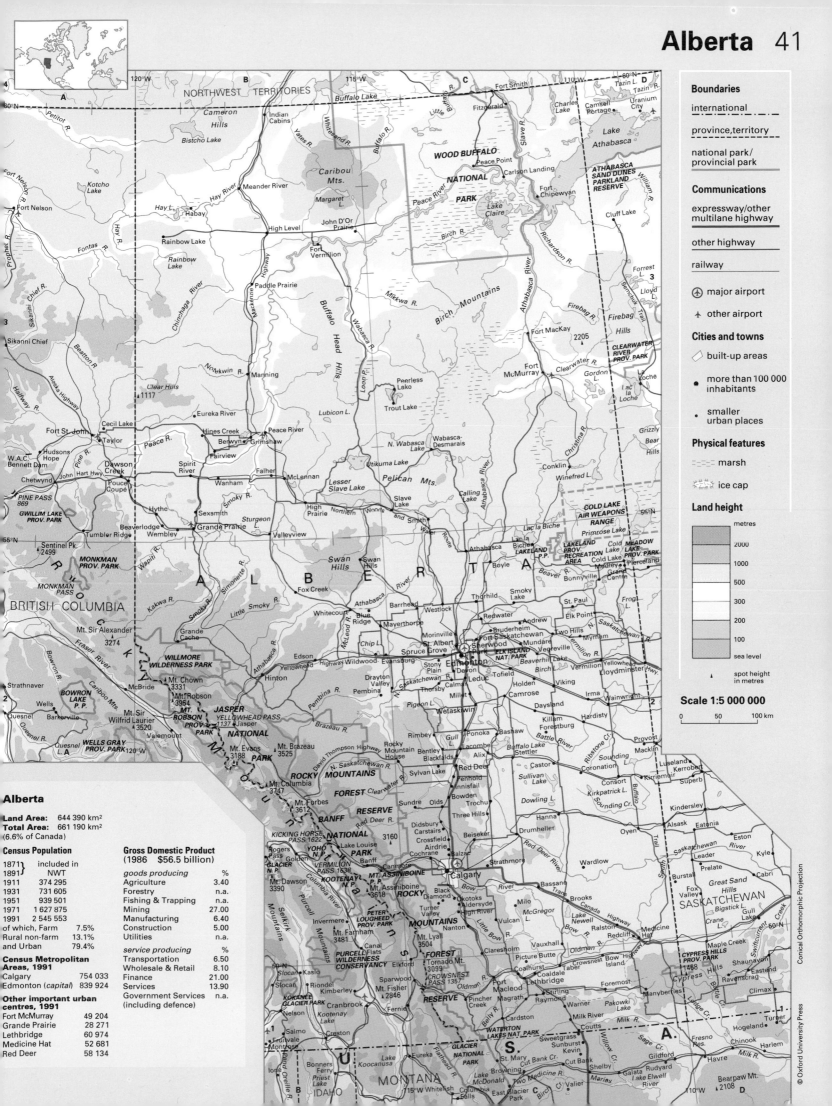

Alberta

Land Area: 644 390 km²
Total Area: 661 190 km²
(6.6% of Canada)

Census Population

1871	included in	
1891	NWT	
1911	374 295	
1931	731 605	
1951	939 501	
1971	1 627 875	
1991	2 545 553	
of which, Farm	7.5%	
Rural non-farm	13.1%	
and Urban	79.4%	

Census Metropolitan Areas, 1991

Calgary	754 033
Edmonton (*capital*)	839 924

Other important urban centres, 1991

Fort McMurray	49 204
Grande Prairie	28 271
Lethbridge	60 974
Medicine Hat	52 681
Red Deer	58 134

Gross Domestic Product
(1986 $56.5 billion)

goods producing	%
Agriculture	3.40
Forestry	n.a.
Fishing & Trapping	n.a.
Mining	27.00
Manufacturing	6.40
Construction	5.00
Utilities	n.a.

service producing	%
Transportation	6.50
Wholesale & Retail	8.10
Finance	21.00
Services	13.90
Government Services	n.a.
(including defence)	

Boundaries

international

province, territory

national park/ provincial park

Communications

expressway/other multilane highway

other highway

railway

⊕ major airport

✈ other airport

Cities and towns

◇ built-up areas

● more than 100 000 inhabitants

• smaller urban places

Physical features

marsh

ice cap

Land height

metres
2000
1000
500
300
200
100
sea level

▲ spot height in metres

Scale 1:5 000 000

0   50   100 km

Conical Orthomorphic Projection

© Oxford University Press

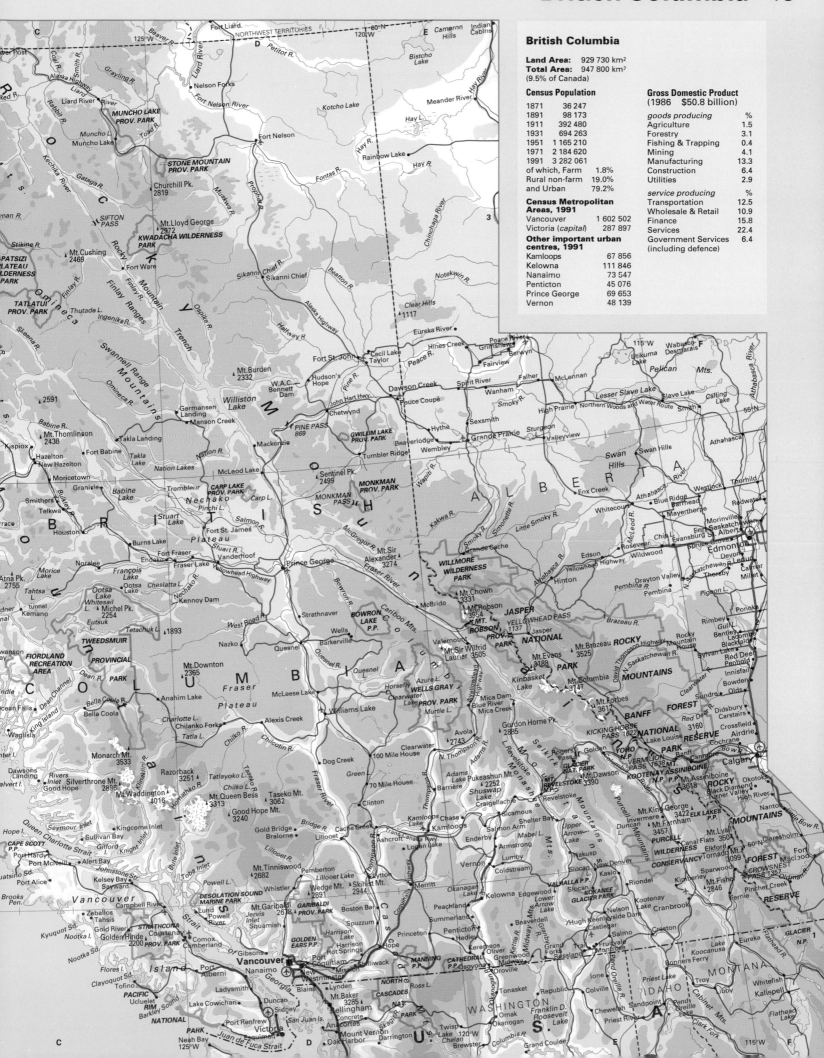

British Columbia

Land Area: 929 730 km²
Total Area: 947 800 km²
(9.5% of Canada)

Census Population

Year	Population	
1871	36 247	
1891	98 173	
1911	392 480	
1931	694 263	
1951	1 165 210	
1971	2 184 620	
1991	3 282 061	
of which, Farm	1.8%	
Rural non-farm	19.0%	
and Urban	79.2%	

Census Metropolitan Areas, 1991

Vancouver	1 602 502
Victoria (capital)	287 897

Other important urban centres, 1991

Kamloops	67 856
Kelowna	111 846
Nanaimo	73 547
Penticton	45 076
Prince George	69 653
Vernon	48 139

Gross Domestic Product

(1986 $50.8 billion)

goods producing	%
Agriculture	1.5
Forestry	3.1
Fishing & Trapping	0.4
Mining	4.1
Manufacturing	13.3
Construction	6.4
Utilities	2.9

service producing	%
Transportation	12.5
Wholesale & Retail	10.9
Finance	15.8
Services	22.4
Government Services (including defence)	6.4

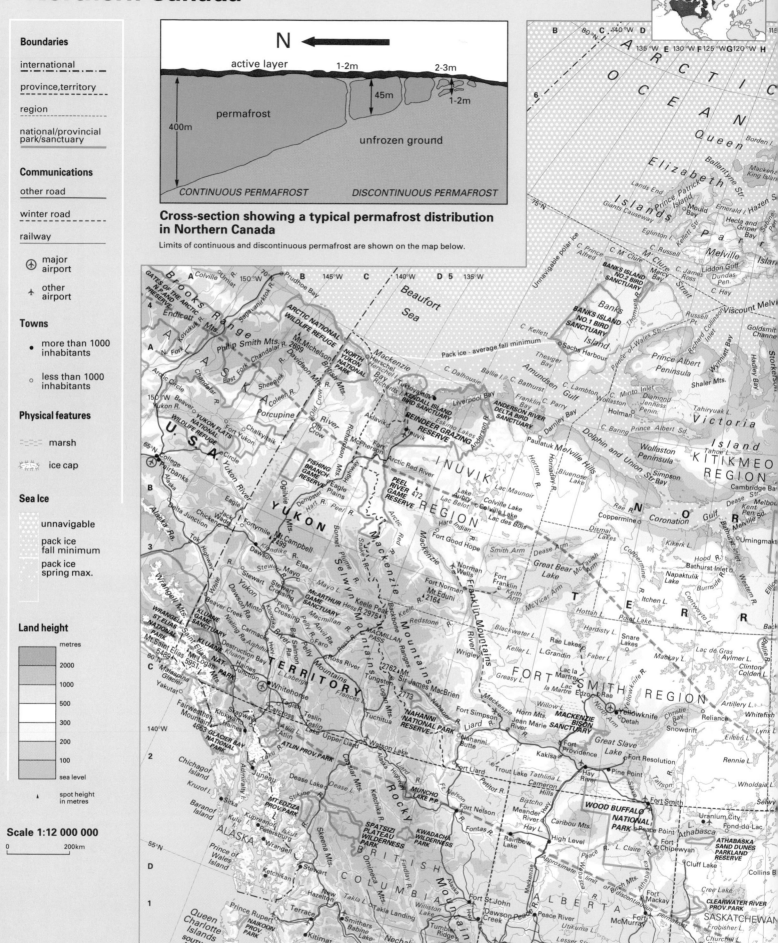

Boundaries

international

province, territory

region

national/provincial park/sanctuary

Communications

other road

winter road

railway

⊕ major airport

✈ other airport

Towns

● more than 1000 inhabitants

○ less than 1000 inhabitants

Physical features

marsh

ice cap

Sea Ice

unnavigable

pack ice fall minimum

pack ice spring max.

Land height

metres
2000
1000
500
300
200
100
sea level

▲ spot height in metres

Scale 1:12 000 000

0   200km

Cross-section showing a typical permafrost distribution in Northern Canada

Limits of continuous and discontinuous permafrost are shown on the map below.

N

active layer   1-2m   2-3m

45m

permafrost   1-2m

400m

unfrozen ground

CONTINUOUS PERMAFROST   DISCONTINUOUS PERMAFROST

Conical Orthomorphic Projection

© Oxford University Press

Yukon Territory

Land Area: 478 970 km²
Total Area: 483 450 km²
(4.8% of Canada)

Census Population

1911	8 512
1931	4 230
1951	9 096
1971	18 390
1991	27 797
of which, Farm	–
Rural non-farm	35.3%
and Urban	64.6%

Urban centres, 1991
Whitehorse
(*capital*)   17 925

Northwest Territories

Land Area: 3 293 020 km²
Total Area: 3 426 320 km²
(34.4% of Canada)

Census Population

1871	56 446*
1891	98 967*
1911	6 507
1931	9 316
1951	16 004
1971	34 805
1991	57 649
of which, Farm	–
Rural non-farm	53.6%
and Urban	46.3%

* includes Saskatchewan and Alberta

Urban centres, 1991
Yellowknife (*capital*)   15 179

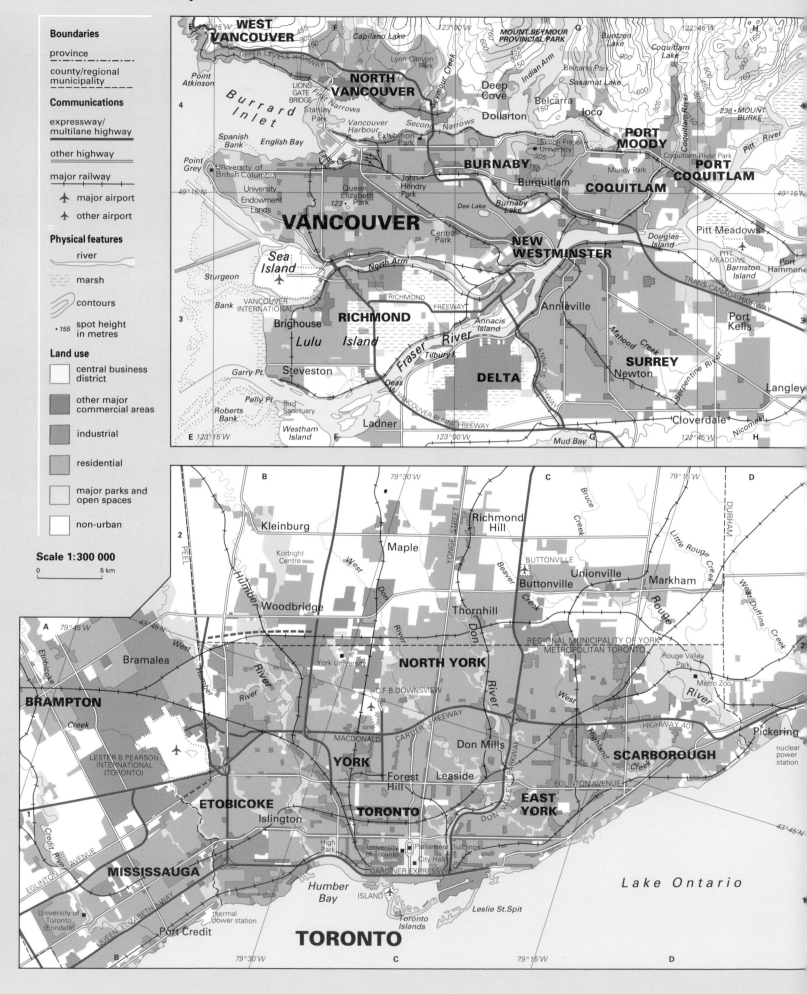

Boundaries

province

county/regional
municipality

Communications

expressway/
multilane highway

other highway

major railway

✈ major airport

✈ other airport

Physical features

river

marsh

contours

• 155   spot height
in metres

Land use

central business
district

other major
commercial areas

industrial

residential

major parks and
open spaces

non-urban

Scale 1:300 000

0   5 km

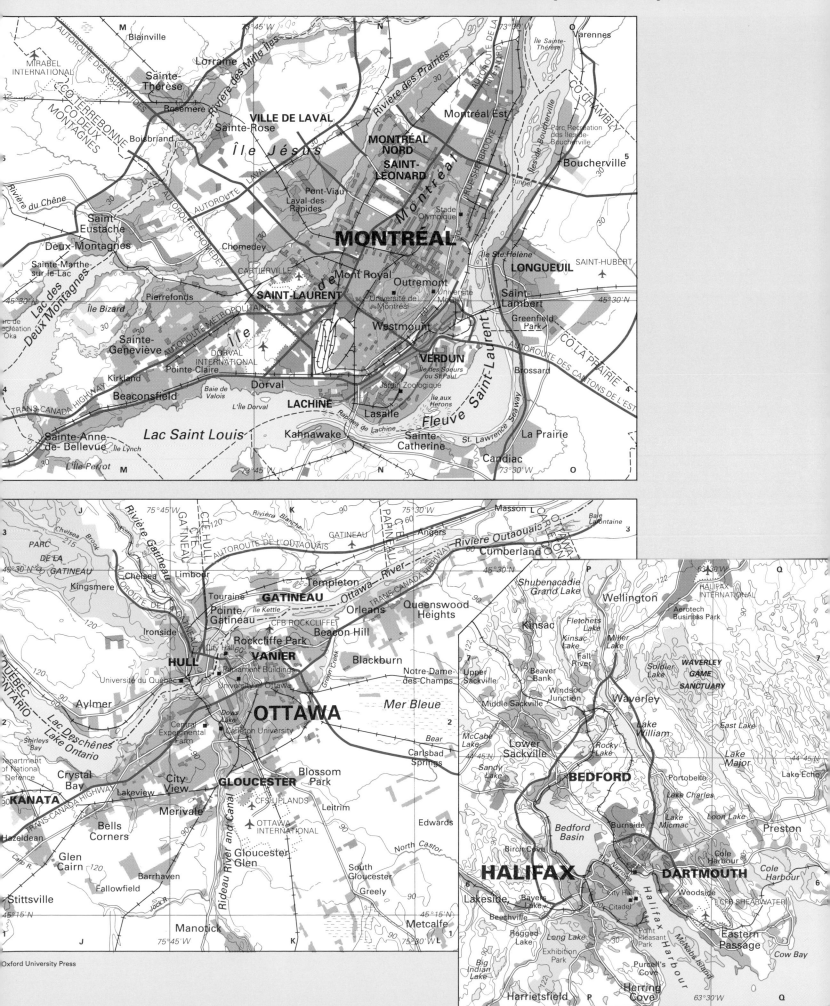

Boundaries

county/municipal/
district/city

Communications

expressway/
multilane highway

other highway

major railway

canal

✈ major airport

✈ other airport

Land use

central business district

other major commercial areas

industrial

residential

major parks and open spaces

non-urban

Physical features

river

marsh

seasonal river/lake

contours

•155 spot height in metres

Scale 1:300 000

0   5 km

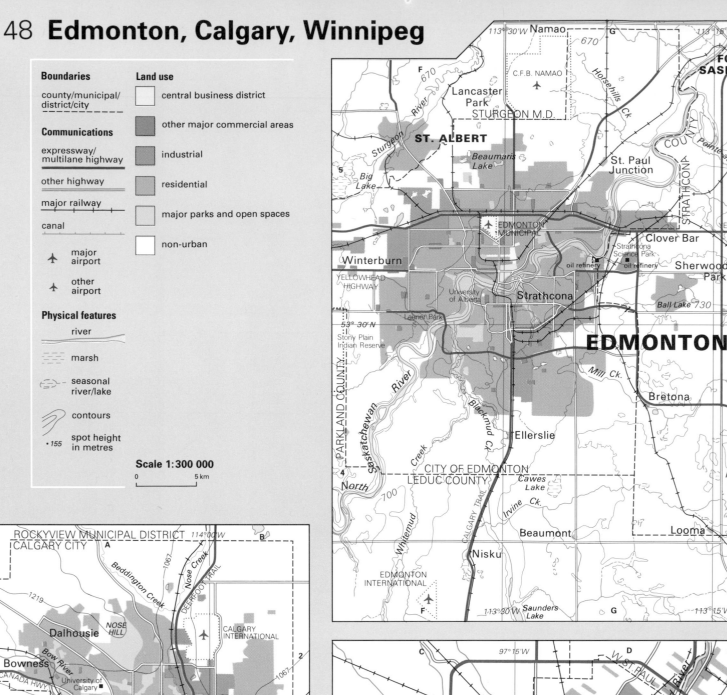

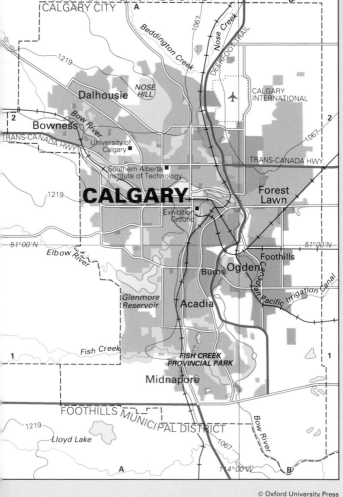

© Oxford University Press

Boundaries
county ----------

Communications
expressway
other highway
major railway
canal
✈ major airport
✈ other airport

Physical features
river
marsh
seasonal river/lake
contours
•155 spot height in metres

Land use
central business district
other major commercial areas
industrial
residential
major parks and open spaces
non-urban

Scale 1:300 000

0   5 km

NEW YORK

Atlantic Ocean

Boundaries	Communications	Land use	
state	**expressway**	central business district	major parks and open spaces
county	other major road	other major commercial areas	non-urban
Physical features	major railway	industrial	
river	canal	residential	
marsh	✈ major airport		
contours	✈ other airport		
•155 spot height in metres			

Scale 1 : 300 000

0   5 km

© Oxford University Press

San Fernando Airport

Van Norman Lake

San Fernando

Golden State Freeway

SAN GABRIEL

Big Tujunga Reservoir

MOUNTAINS

1830 ·1625 ·1569

Sunland

MOUNT LUKENS ·1853

900

ANGELES

900

Cogswell Reservoir

900 1220 1220

San Gabriel Reservoir

SAN FERNANDO VALLEY

Tujunga

1220

NATIONAL

600

900

La Crescenta

600 900

La Cañada

Mount Wilson Observatory ·1740

FOREST

Big Santa Anita Reservoir

San Gabriel Reservoir

Van Nuys

HOLLYWOOD BURBANK AIRPORT

North Hollywood

BURBANK

Brand Park

Altadena

Devils Gate Reservoir

Eaton Wash Reservoir

Sawpit Canyon Reservoir

600

Morris Reservoir

Sepulveda Dam Recreational Area

Los Angeles River

Rose Bowl

PASADENA

Arcadia

300

Azusa

Griffith Park

GLENDALE

STA. MONICA MOUNTAINS

Hollywood Reservoir

Hollywood Bowl

San Gabriel

Temple City

Santa Fe Flood Control Basin

Glendora

Stone Canyon Reservoir 397

Beverly Hills

Hollywood

Silver Lake Reservoir

ALHAMBRA

Rosemead

EL MONTE AIRPORT

El Monte

Baldwin Park

Covina

Franklin Canyon Reservoir

Hollywood Freeway

Elysian Park

LOS ANGELES

Monterey Park

West Covina

La Puente

SAN BERNARDINO FREEWAY

West Los Angeles

Santa Monica Freeway

Civic Center

East Los Angeles

Whittier Narrows Dam Reservoir Area

SANTA MONICA

SANTA MONICA AIRPORT

Culver City

Montebello

POMONA FREEWAY

Marina del Rey

Rio Hondo

Pico-Rivera

Whittier ·431

INGLEWOOD

San Gabriel River

LOS ANGELES COUNTY

ORANGE COUNTY

LOS ANGELES AIRPORT

SOUTH GATE

DOWNEY

La Habra

Hawthorne

HARBOR FREEWAY

NORWALK

SANTA ANA FREEWAY

Manhattan Beach

COMPTON

Los Angeles River

LONG BEACH FREEWAY

Gardena

COMPTON AIRPORT

Bellflower

Fullerton Reservoir

Lawndale

Brea Reservoir

FULLERTON AIRPORT

FULLERTON

TORRANCE

Redondo Beach

Carson

LAKEWOOD

Buena Park

RIVERSIDE FREEWAY

Knott's Berry Farm

ANAHEIM

TORRANCE AIRPORT

LONG BEACH AIRPORT

Coyote Creek

Disneyland

GARDEN GROVE

Orange

PALOS VERDES HILLS 396

300 150

San Pedro

Santa Ana River

LONG BEACH

Westminster

SANTA ANA

Marineland of the Pacific

San Pedro Channel

San Pedro Bay

Sunset Beach

SAN DIEGO FREEWAY

Fountain Valley

Huntington Beach

Pacific Ocean

118°15'W

A

B

118°00'W

C

© Oxford University Press

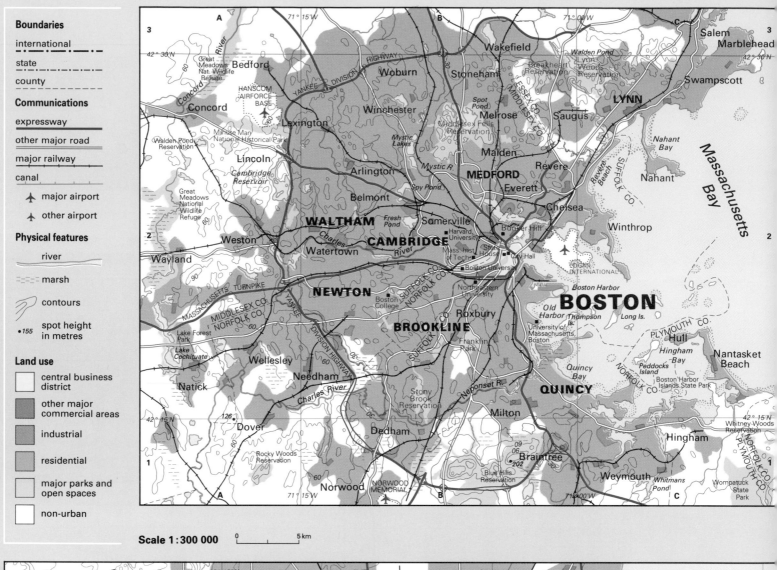

Boundaries

international

state

county

Communications

expressway

other major road

major railway

canal

✈ major airport

✦ other airport

Physical features

river

marsh

contours

•155 spot height
in metres

Land use

central business
district

other major
commercial areas

industrial

residential

major parks and
open spaces

non-urban

Scale 1:300 000   0 —— 5 km

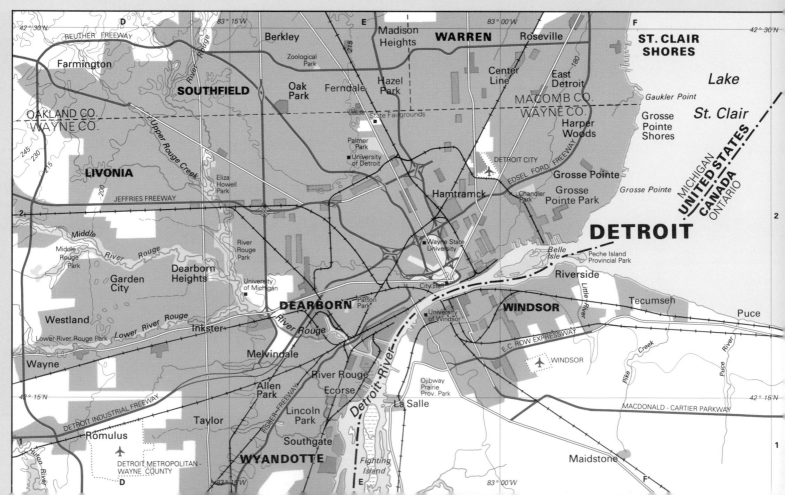

© Oxford University Press

Main map labels:

A · B · C (grid references at top)

87° 45'W · 87° 30'W · 42° 15'N · 42° 00'N · 41° 45'N

Lake Forest
Fort Sheridan
HIGHLAND PARK
•203
Deerfield
Northbrook
Glencoe
Arlington Heights
PAL-WAUKEE
Prospect Heights
Winnetka
Mount Prospect
NAVAL AIR STATION GLENVIEW
WILMETTE
Glenview
EVANSTON
SKOKIE
Des Plaines
Morton Grove
Park Ridge
Niles
Elk Grove Village •205
CHICAGO-O'HARE INTERNATIONAL
Lincolnwood
•192
COOK CO. / DU PAGE CO.
Harwood Heights
Bensenville
Franklin Park
Elmwood Park
Lincoln Park
Oak Street Beach
Chicago Harbor
Northlake
Elmhurst
Melrose Park
River Forest
OAK PARK
Humboldt Park
City Hall
Sears Tower
The Loop
Roosevelt University
Grant Park
Berkeley
Garfield Park
University of Illinois
MEIGS
Bellwood
Maywood
Douglas Park
Lake
Westchester
CICERO
BERWYN
CHICAGO
Michigan
Broadview
Illinois Institute of Technology
Oak Brook
Riverside
Stickney
Burnham Park
EAST-WEST TOLLWAY
Brookfield
Lyons
Washington Park
University of Chicago
Jackson Park
Hinsalde
La Grange
Western Springs
Summit
CHICAGO MIDWAY
ILLINOIS / INDIANA
Downers Grove
Rainbow Park
HINSDALE
Marquette Park
Calumet Harbor
Argonne Forest
Burbank
Calumet Park
Daffy Preserve
Evergreen Park
Whiting
Indiana Harbor
HOWELL
Oak Lawn
Lake Calumet Harbor
Wolf Lake State Park and Conservation Area
COOK CO. / WILL CO.
Worth
Blue Island
EAST CHICAGO
GARY
Dolton
Calumet City
GARY MUNICIPAL
Harvey
HAMMOND
Lansing
INDIANA E-W TOLLWAY
Homewood
Highland
CHICAGO-HAMMOND
Little Calumet River

Rivers/canals: Skokie River, North Branch Chicago River, Des Plaines River, EDENS EXPRESSWAY, TRI-STATE TOLLWAY, NORTH WEST TOLLWAY, Salt Creek, Chicago Sanitary and Ship Canal, Illinois and Mich. Canal, Calumet Sag Channel, Stony Creek, CHICAGO SKYWAY, Calumet R., COOK CO. / LAKE CO.

Inset map (Pittsburgh):

D · E (grid references) · 80° 00'W · 80° 30'N · 40° 30'N · 30° 00'W

New Kensington
Alison Park
Allegheny River
West View
Glenshaw
PENNSYLVANIA TURNPIKE
Etna
PITTSBURGH
Ohio River
Allegheny Observatory
Bellevue
McKees Rocks
Chartiers Creek
Highland Park
Penn Hills
W.D. Boyce Regional Park
University of Pittsburgh
Civic Arena
Carnegie Institute of Technology
Wilkinsburg
PENN-LINCOLN PKWY. EXT.
Grafton
Frick Park
Munroeville
Carnegie
tunnel
Braddock
Dormont
Munhall
Brentwood
Duquesne
Bridgeville
Mount Lebanon
McKEESPORT
White Oak Park
ALLEGHENY COUNTY
Youghiogheny River
Bethel Park
South Park
Pleasant Hills
WESTMORELAND CO.
ALLEGHENY CO. / WASHINGTON CO.
Clairton
Monongahela River

© Oxford University Press

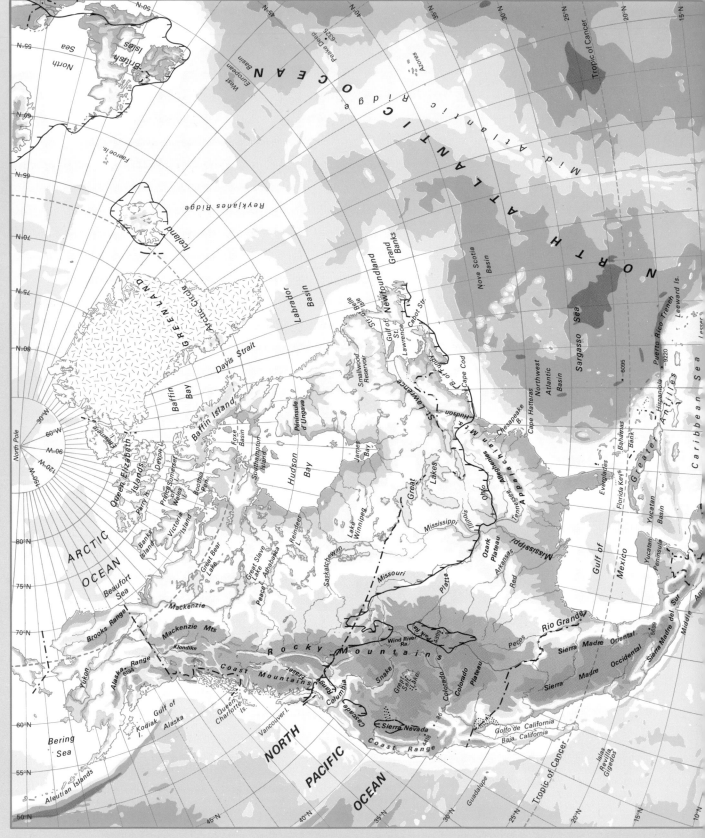

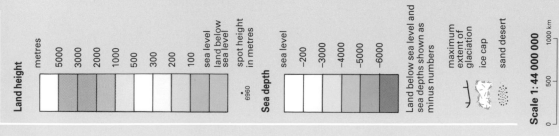

Land height

metres

5000 3000 2000 1000 500 300 200 100 sea level land below sea level | spot height in metres • 6960

Sea depth

sea level −200 −3000 −4000 −5000 −6000

Land below sea level and sea depths shown as minus numbers

maximum extent of glaciation

ice cap

sand desert

Scale 1: 44 000 000

1000 km

500

0

Oblique Mercator Projection

© Oxford University Press

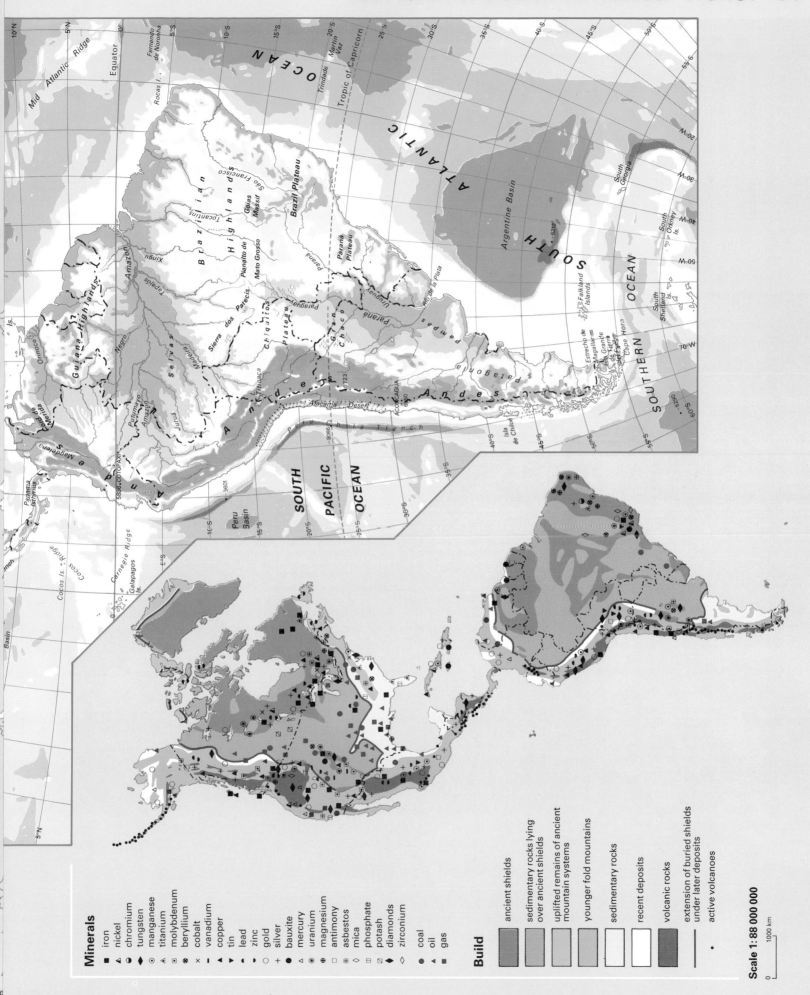

Minerals

- ■ iron
- ▲ nickel
- ◑ chromium
- ◆ tungsten
- ▲ manganese
- ◉ titanium
- ⊛ molybdenum
- × beryllium
- ◫ cobalt
- ► vanadium
- ◀ copper
- ▶ tin
- ○ lead
- ● zinc
- ◐ gold
- ◒ silver
- ⊕ bauxite
- ⊞ mercury
- ◇ uranium
- ◻ magnesium
- ◆ antimony
- ◇ asbestos
- ● mica
- ◆ phosphate
- ▲ potash
- ■ diamonds
- zirconium
- coal
- oil
- gas

Build

- ancient shields
- sedimentary rocks lying over ancient shields
- uplifted remains of ancient mountain systems
- younger fold mountains
- sedimentary rocks
- recent deposits
- volcanic rocks
- extension of buried shields under later deposits
- active volcanoes

Scale 1 : 88 000 000

0 — 1000 km

Mid Atlantic Ridge · Equator · Fernando de Noronha · Rocas I. · Tropic of Capricorn · Trindade · Martin Vaz

ATLANTIC OCEAN · SOUTH ATLANTIC · SOUTHERN OCEAN

Argentine Basin · South Georgia · South Orkney Is. · South Shetland Is. · Falkland Islands

Brazilian Highlands · São Francisco · Goiás Massif · Brazil Plateau · Tocantins · Planalto de Mato Grosso · Paraná Plateau · Xingu · Tapajós · Parecis · Sierra dos Parecis · Chiquitos Plateau · Gran Chaco · Paraná · Uruguay · Pampas · Patagonia

Guiana Highlands · Orinoco · Negro · Amazon · Selvas · Juruá · Putumayo · Amazon · COTOPAXI 5896 · Andes · Huanca · ACONCAGUA 6960 · Atacama Desert · Peru-Chile Trench · Isla de Chiloé · Estrecho de Magallanes · Isla Grande de Tierra del Fuego · Cape Horn

SOUTH PACIFIC OCEAN · Peru Basin · Galapagos Is. · Cocos Is. · Carnegie Ridge · Cocos Ridge · Panama Isthmus · Magdalena

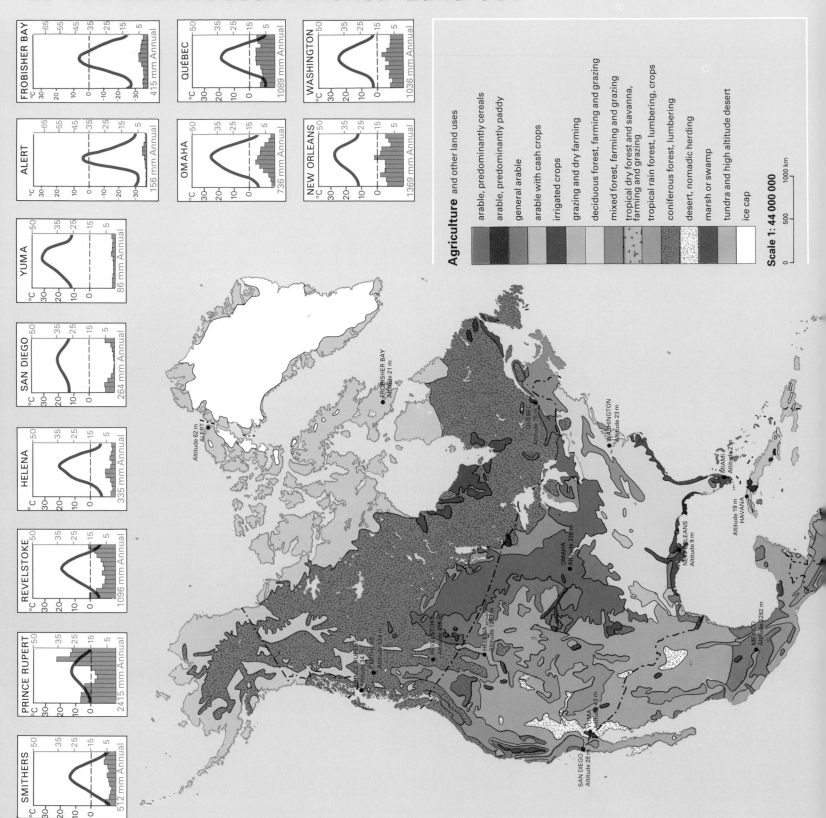

Agriculture and other land uses

arable, predominantly cereals

arable, predominantly paddy

general arable

arable with cash crops

irrigated crops

grazing and dry farming

deciduous forest, farming and grazing

mixed forest, farming and grazing

tropical dry forest and savanna, farming and grazing

tropical rain forest, lumbering, crops

coniferous forest, lumbering

desert, nomadic herding

marsh or swamp

tundra and high altitude desert

ice cap

Scale 1 : 44 000 000

0   500   1000 km

FROBISHER BAY 415 mm Annual

QUÉBEC 1089 mm Annual

WASHINGTON 1036 mm Annual

ALERT 156 mm Annual

OMAHA 736 mm Annual

NEW ORLEANS 1369 mm Annual

YUMA 86 mm Annual

SAN DIEGO 264 mm Annual

HELENA 335 mm Annual

REVELSTOKE 1096 mm Annual

PRINCE RUPERT 2415 mm Annual

SMITHERS 512 mm Annual

Oblique Mercator Projection

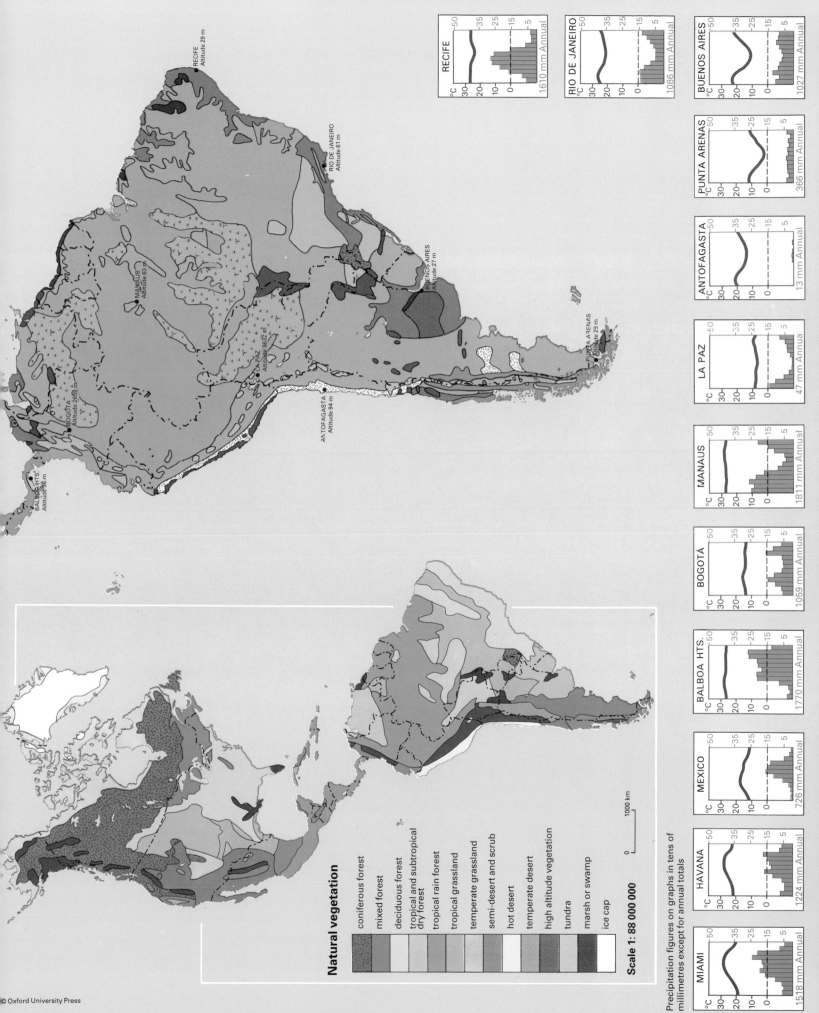

RECIFE Altitude 29 m °C 50 35 25 15 5 30 20 10 0 1610 mm Annual

RIO DE JANEIRO °C 50 35 25 15 5 30 20 10 0 1086 mm Annual

BUENOS AIRES °C 50 35 25 15 5 30 20 10 0 1027 mm Annual

PUNTA ARENAS °C 50 35 25 15 5 30 20 10 0 366 mm Annual

ANTOFAGASTA °C 50 35 25 15 5 30 20 10 0 13 mm Annual

LA PAZ °C 50 35 25 15 5 30 20 10 0 47 mm Annual

MANAUS °C 50 35 25 15 5 30 20 10 0 1811 mm Annual

BOGOTÁ °C 50 35 25 15 5 30 20 10 0 1059 mm Annual

BALBOA HTS. °C 50 35 25 15 5 30 20 10 0 1770 mm Annual

MEXICO °C 50 35 25 15 5 30 20 10 0 726 mm Annual

HAVANA °C 50 35 25 15 5 30 20 10 0 1224 mm Annual

MIAMI °C 50 35 25 15 5 30 20 10 0 1518 mm Annual

Precipitation figures on graphs in tens of millimetres except for annual totals

Natural vegetation

- coniferous forest
- mixed forest
- deciduous forest
- tropical and subtropical dry forest
- tropical rain forest
- tropical grassland
- temperate grassland
- semi-desert and scrub
- hot desert
- temperate desert
- high altitude vegetation
- tundra
- marsh or swamp
- ice cap

Scale 1 : 88 000 000

0 1000 km

RECIFE Altitude 29 m

RIO DE JANEIRO Altitude 61 m

MANAUS Altitude 83 m

LA PAZ Altitude 3632 m

BOGOTÁ Altitude 2659 m

BALBOA HTS. Altitude 36 m

ANTOFAGASTA Altitude 94 m

BUENOS AIRES Altitude 27 m

PUNTA ARENAS Altitude 23 m

© Oxford University Press

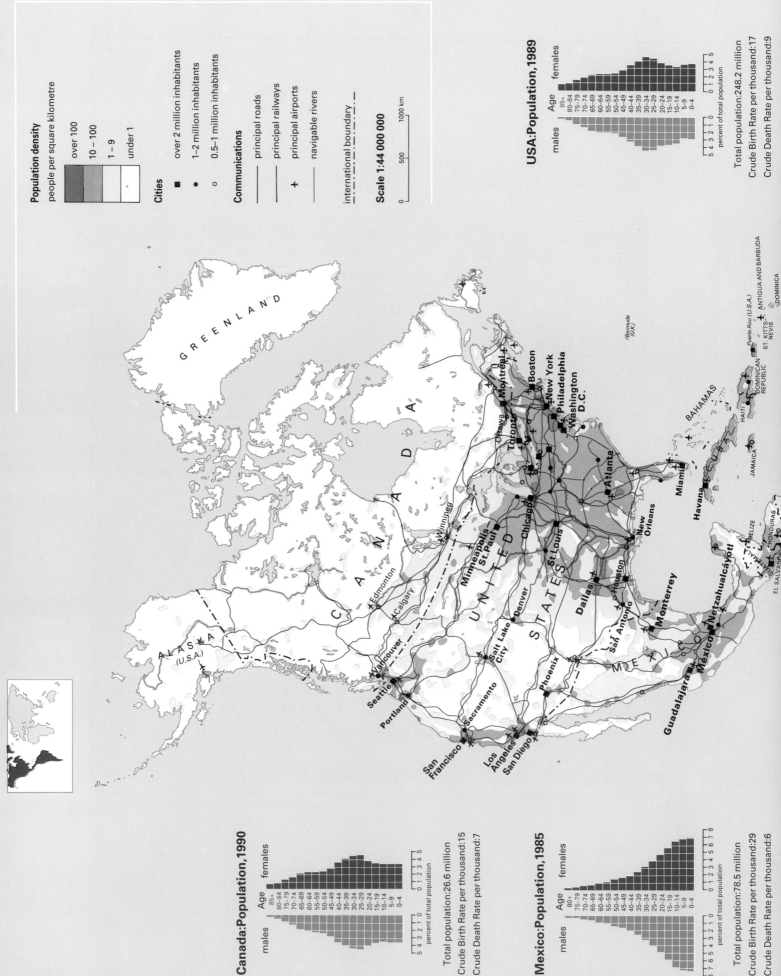

Population density
people per square kilometre
over 100
10 – 100
1 – 9
under 1

Cities
■ over 2 million inhabitants
● 1–2 million inhabitants
○ 0.5–1 million inhabitants

Communications
principal roads
principal railways
✈ principal airports
navigable rivers
─ · ─ international boundary

Scale 1:44 000 000

0   500   1000 km

USA:Population,1989

males   females
Age
85+
80–84
75–79
70–74
65–69
60–64
55–59
50–54
45–49
40–44
35–39
30–34
25–29
20–24
15–19
10–14
5–9
0–4

5 4 3 2 1 0   0 1 2 3 4 5
percent of total population

Total population:248.2 million
Crude Birth Rate per thousand:17
Crude Death Rate per thousand:9

GREENLAND

C A N A D A

ALASKA (U.S.A.)

Edmonton
Calgary
Vancouver
Seattle
Portland
Sacramento
San Francisco
Los Angeles
San Diego
Salt Lake City
Denver
Phoenix
Winnipeg
Minneapolis St.Paul
U N I T E D   S T A T E S
Chicago
St.Louis
Dallas
San Antonio
Houston
New Orleans
Atlanta
Ottawa
Montreal
Toronto
Boston
New York
Philadelphia
Washington D.C.
Miami
Havana
BAHAMAS
CUBA
JAMAICA
HAITI
DOMINICAN REPUBLIC
Puerto Rico (U.S.A.)
ST. KITTS NEVIS
ANTIGUA AND BARBUDA
DOMINICA
Bermuda (U.K.)
M E X I C O
Monterrey
Guadalajara
México
Netzahualcóyotl
BELIZE
GUATEMALA
HONDURAS
EL SALVADOR

Canada:Population,1990

males   females
Age
85+
80–84
75–79
70–74
65–69
60–64
55–59
50–54
45–49
40–44
35–39
30–34
25–29
20–24
15–19
10–14
5–9
0–4

5 4 3 2 1 0   0 1 2 3 4 5
percent of total population

Total population:26.6 million
Crude Birth Rate per thousand:15
Crude Death Rate per thousand:7

Mexico:Population,1985

males   females
Age
80+
75–79
70–74
65–69
60–64
55–59
50–54
45–49
40–44
35–39
30–34
25–29
20–24
15–19
10–14
5–9
0–4

8 7 6 5 4 3 2 1 0   0 1 2 3 4 5 6 7 8
percent of total population

Total population:78.5 million
Crude Birth Rate per thousand:29
Crude Death Rate per thousand:6

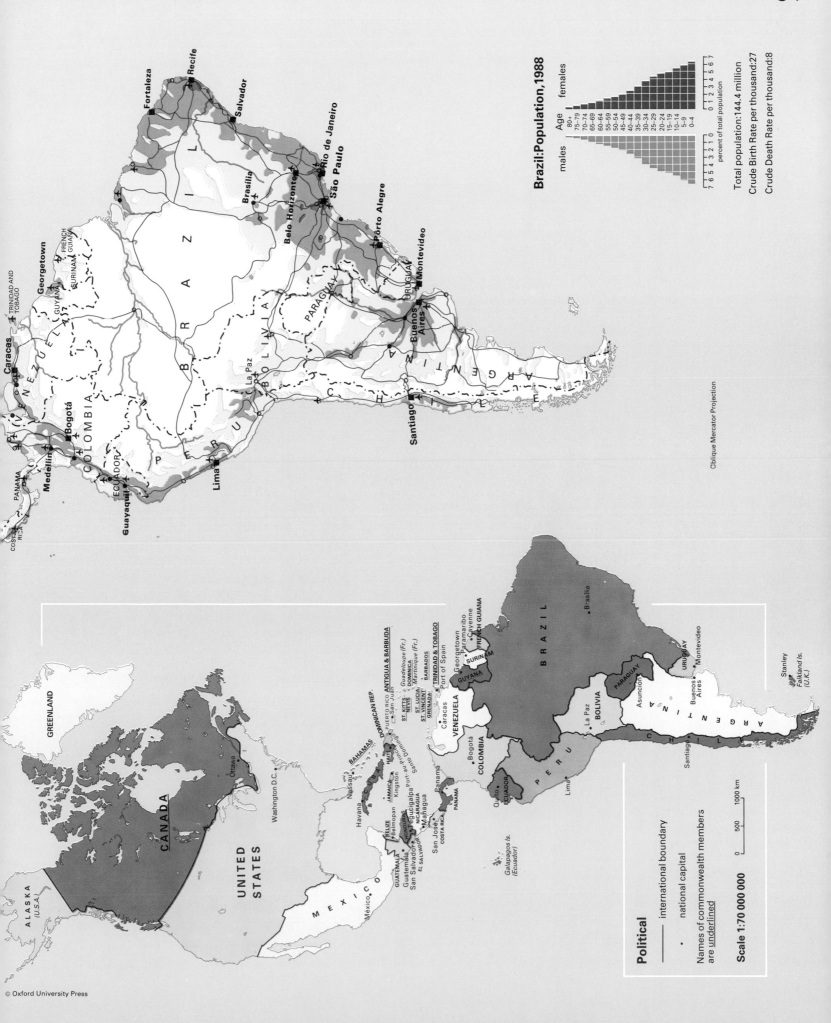

Brazil:Population,1988

males   Age   females

80+
75-79
70-74
65-69
60-64
55-59
50-54
45-49
40-44
35-39
30-34
25-29
20-24
15-19
10-14
5-9
0-4

7 6 5 4 3 2 1 0   0 1 2 3 4 5 6 7
percent of total population

Total population:144.4 million

Crude Birth Rate per thousand:27

Crude Death Rate per thousand:8

Oblique Mercator Projection

GREENLAND

ALASKA
(U.S.A.)

CANADA

Ottawa

UNITED
STATES

Washington D.C.

BAHAMAS

Nassau

CUBA

Havana

MEXICO

México

BELIZE
Belmopan

GUATEMALA
Guatemala

HONDURAS
Tegucigalpa

EL SALVADOR
San Salvador

NICARAGUA
Managua

COSTA RICA
San José

PANAMA
Panamá

JAMAICA
Kingston

HAITI
Port-au-Prince

DOMINICAN REP.
Santo Domingo

PUERTO RICO
San Juan

ANTIGUA & BARBUDA

Guadeloupe (Fr.)

ST. KITTS-
NEVIS

DOMINICA
Martinique (Fr.)

ST. LUCIA

BARBADOS

ST. VINCENT

GRENADA

TRINIDAD & TOBAGO

Port of Spain

Caracas

VENEZUELA

Bogotá

COLOMBIA

Georgetown

Paramaribo

Cayenne

GUYANA

SURINAM

FRENCH GUIANA

BRAZIL

Brasília

Quito

ECUADOR

Galapagos Is.
(Ecuador)

Lima

PERU

La Paz

BOLIVIA

PARAGUAY

Asunción

URUGUAY

Montevideo

Buenos
Aires

ARGENTINA

CHILE

Santiago

Stanley

Falkland Is.
(U.K.)

Political

—— international boundary

• national capital

Names of commonwealth members
are underlined

Scale 1:70 000 000

0   500   1000 km

Caracas

VENEZUELA

Georgetown

FRENCH GUIANA

SURINAM

GUYANA

TRINIDAD AND
TOBAGO

Bogotá

COLOMBIA

Medellín

PANAMA

COSTA
RICA

ECUADOR

Guayaquil

Quito

Lima

P E R U

La Paz

B O L I V I A

B R A Z I L

Fortaleza

Recife

Salvador

Belo Horizonte

Brasília

Rio de Janeiro

São Paulo

Pôrto Alegre

PARAGUAY

A R G E N T I N A

C H I L E

Santiago

URUGUAY

Montevideo

Buenos
Aires

© Oxford University Press

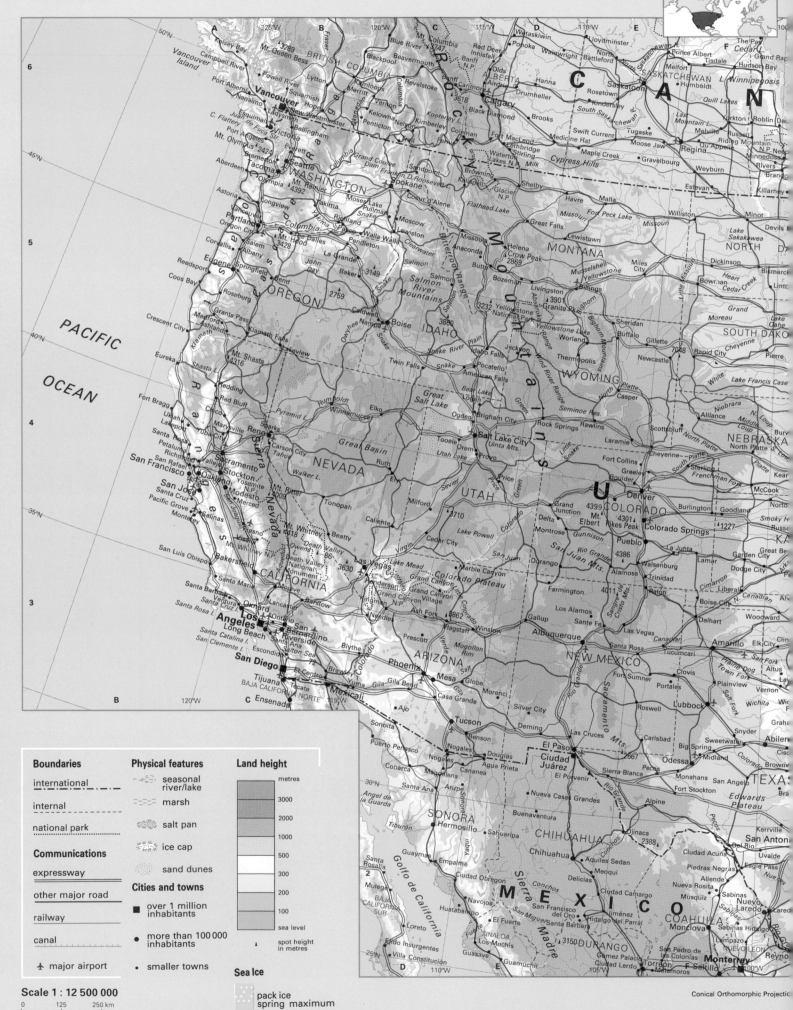

PACIFIC

OCEAN

Scale 1 : 12 500 000

0   125   250 km

Conical Orthomorphic Projection

Boundaries

international

internal

national park

Communications

expressway

other major road

railway

canal

✈ major airport

Physical features

seasonal river/lake

marsh

salt pan

ice cap

sand dunes

Cities and towns

■ over 1 million inhabitants

● more than 100 000 inhabitants

• smaller towns

▲ spot height in metres

Land height

metres

3000

2000

1000

500

300

200

100

sea level

Sea Ice

pack ice spring maximum

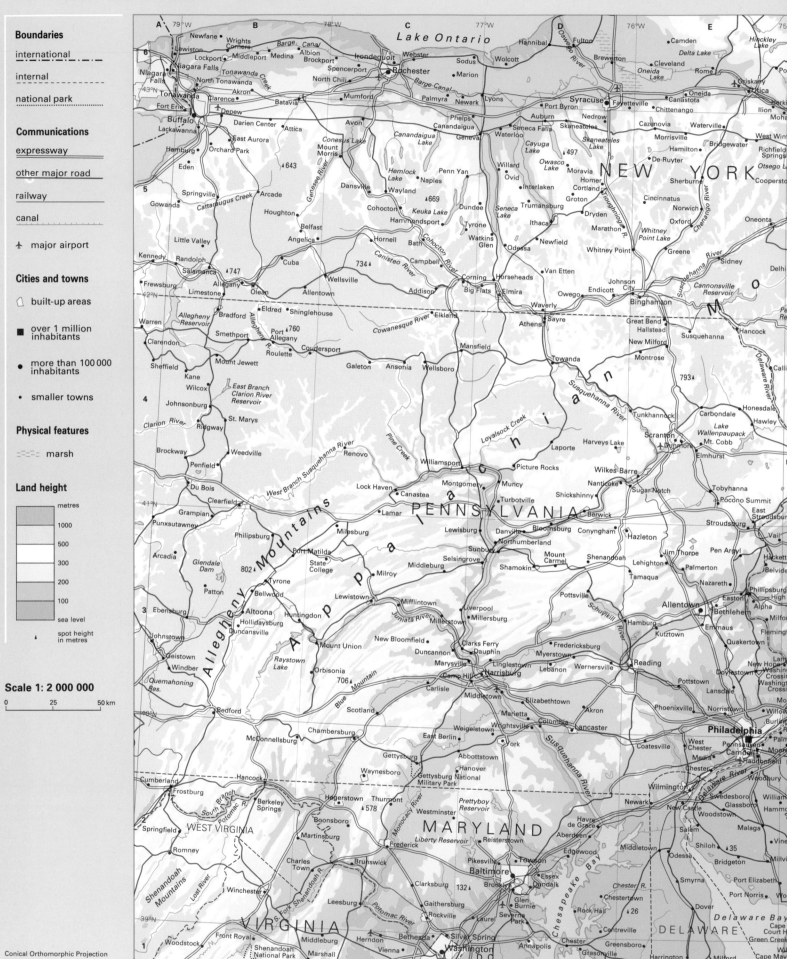

Boundaries

international

internal

national park

Communications

expressway

other major road

railway

canal

✈ major airport

Cities and towns

⬭ built-up areas

■ over 1 million inhabitants

● more than 100 000 inhabitants

• smaller towns

Physical features

marsh

Land height

metres
1000
500
300
200
100
sea level

▲ spot height in metres

Scale 1: 2 000 000

0   25   50 km

Conical Orthomorphic Projection

© Oxford University Press

ATLANTIC OCEAN

MAINE

NEW HAMPSHIRE

VERMONT

MASSACHUSETTS

CONNECTICUT

RHODE ISLAND

NEW JERSEY

Long Island Sound

Long Island

Cape Cod Bay

Cape Cod

Martha's Vineyard

Nantucket Island

Nantucket Sound

Buzzards Bay

Narragansett Bay

Block Island Sound

Montauk Point

Great Peconic Bay

New York

Boston

Providence

Hartford

Albany

Worcester

Springfield

Hudson River

Connecticut R.

Green Mountains

Catskill Mountains

Adirondack Mountains

Boundaries

international

internal

national park

Communications

expressway

other major road

track

railway

canal

✈ major airport

Cities and towns

⬭ built-up areas

■ over 1 million inhabitants

● more than 100 000 inhabitants

• smaller towns

Physical features

seasonal river/lake

marsh

sand dunes

Land height

metres

3000
2000
1000
500
300
200
100
sea level
land below sea level

▲ spot height in metres

Scale 1:16 000 000

0   200   400 km

main map only

Scale 1:1 250 000

0   25 km

Trinidad

Barbados

Scale 1:1 000 000

0   25 km

Panama Canal

Scale 1:1 500 000

0   25 km

Caribbean Sea

Portobelo

Punta Manzanillo

979

Colón
Puerto Pilón

Madden
Lake

1006

Gatún Locks

Gatún

Palmas
Bellas

Escobal

Gatún
Lake

Gamboa

Gaillard
Cut

Pedro Miguel Locks

Miraflores Locks

Panamá
Balboa

PACIFIC
OCEAN

La Chorrera

Gaillard Cut
maximum elevation 95 m

CARIBBEAN SEA

minimum depth 12 m

PACIFIC OCEAN

sea level

sea level

0   15   30   45   60   75 km

Gatún Locks
(3 pairs)
length 305 m
width 33.5 m
total lift 25.9 m

Pedro Miguel Locks
(1 pair)
length 305 m
width 33.5 m
total lift 9.1 m

Miraflores Locks
(2 pairs)
length 305 m
width 33.5 m
total lift 16.8 m

The canal, opened in 1914, is 82 km long, including approaches (actual canal 64 km). Minimum depth 12 m, minimum width 152 m (Gaillard Cut). Time of passage 8 hours. In 1990 11 941 vessels used the canal carrying 157 072 978 tonnes of cargo. In 1979 Panama assumed control of the former Canal Zone, with the USA retaining majority representation on the Panama Commission until 1989. US military forces will remain in Panama until the year 2000 and the USA will be entitled to defend the Canal's neutrality thereafter.

NORTH ATLANTIC

OCEAN

Cape Hatteras

NORTH CAROLINA

Baltimore
Washington D.C.
Annapolis
DELAWARE

Indianapolis
Dayton
Cincinnati
OHIO
WEST VIRGINIA
Parkersburg
Charleston

Louisville
Lexington
Huntington
Charleston
Lynchburg
Richmond
Charlottesville
VIRGINIA
Hampton
Newport News
Norfolk
Chesapeake
Portsmouth

KENTUCKY
Johnson City
Roanoke
Danville

Nashville
Knoxville
Asheville
Greensboro
Winston-Salem
Hickory
Raleigh
Rock Hill
Fayetteville

Chattanooga
Athens
Atlanta
Anniston
Birmingham
Augusta
Macon
Columbus
GEORGIA

SOUTH CAROLINA
Charlotte
Greenville
Columbia
Charleston

Savannah

Montgomery

Dothan
Valdosta
Albany
Flint

Pensacola
Fort Walton Beach
Tallahassee
Jacksonville

FLORIDA
Gainesville
St. Augustine
Ocala
Daytona Beach
Orlando
C. Canaveral
Melbourne

Tampa
St. Petersburg
Sarasota
Fort Myers
L. Okeechobee
West Palm Beach

Miami

Key West
Straits of Florida

New Providence
Nassau
Andros
Eleuthera
Cat I.
San Salvador

THE BAHAMAS
Great Abaco
Grand Bahama
Great Exuma
Long Island
Crooked I.
Acklins I.
Mayaguana
Caicos Passage
Great Inagua
Turks & Caicos Is. (UK)

Tropic of Cancer

Mexico

La Habana (Havana)
Matanzas
Güines
Sagua la Grande
Santa Clara
Pinar del Río
La Fé
Cienfuegos
Ciego de Ávila
Morón
Nuevitas

CUBA

Isla de la Juventud
Trinidad
Camagüey
Holguín

de Morelos
de Cozumel

Manzanillo
Bayamo
Guantánamo
2005
Santiago de Cuba

Grand Cayman (UK)

Windward Passage

Cap-Haïtien
Port-de-Paix
Santiago
San Francisco
3175
La Vega

DOMINICAN REPUBLIC

Virgin Is. (USA/UK)
St. Thomas

San Juan

Anguilla (UK)

ANTIGUA & BARBUDA
Barbuda
Codrington
St. John's
Antigua

Jérémie
Port-au-Prince
HAITI
Les Cayes
Jacmel
2680

Santo Domingo
San Pedro
La Romana
Mayagüez
Ponce

PUERTO RICO (USA)
St. Croix (USA)

Leeward Is.
Montserrat (UK)

ST. KITTS-NEVIS
Grande Terre
GUADELOUPE (Fr.)
Pointe-à-Pitre
Basse Terre

Barahona

Hispaniola

L e s s e r

DOMINICA
Roseau
1397

Montego Bay
JAMAICA
Spanish Town
Kingston

G r e a t e r   A n t i l l e s

West Indies

Martinique (Fr.)
Fort-de-France

Castries
ST. LUCIA

A n t i l l e s

St. Vincent
336
BARBADOS
Bridgetown

Caribbean   Sea

ST. VINCENT & THE GRENADINES

Kingstown

GRENADA
840
St. George's

Windward Islands

Tobago
TRINIDAD & TOBAGO
Port of Spain
Trinidad

ras
de la Bahía
La Ceiba
Laguna Caratasca
Cabo Gracias á Dios

DURAS
Pto. Cabezas
Prinzapolca

L e s s e r   A n t i l l e s

Isla Margarita
La Asunción
Porlamar
Cumaná
Carúpano
Carípito
Maturín
Barcelona
San Fernando
Guiria

Punta Gallinas

Curaçao (Neths.)
Bonaire (Neths.)
ARUBA
Willemstad

Matagalpa
NICARAGUA
Managua
Masaya
Granada
Bluefields
Laguna de Perlas
Punta del Mono
Lago de Nicaragua

Santa Marta
Riohacha
Punto Fijo
Pto. Cumarebo
Coro
Churuguara
Pto. Cabello
Maracay
CARACAS
Maiquetía
La Guaira
Los Teques
Petare
Pto. La Cruz

Barranquilla
Ciénaga
Pico Cristóbal
5800
Valledupar
Cabimas
Lagunillas
San Felipe
VALENCIA
Maracay
San Juan de los Morros
Tucupita

Cartagena
Arjona
Calamar
Sabanalarga
MARACAIBO
Lago de Maracaibo
Machiques
San Carlos del Zulia
Barquisimeto
Araure
Acarigua
Valle de la Pascua
Zaraza

COSTA
Alajuela
Limón
3432
Cartago
RICA
San José
Palmar Sur
Pto. Armuelles
Isla de Coiba

Sincelejo
Magangué
El Banco
Montería
Lorica
Golfo de

COLOMBIA

Yarumal
Bucaramanga
Cisneros

Pto. Cortés
Golfo de Mosquitos

PANAMA
Colón
Panama Canal
Balboa
Panamá
Penonomé
Santiago
Golfo de Panamá
Pen. de Azuero
David

Darién

Trujillo
San Carlos
Mérida
Cordillera
Guanare
Valera
Calabozo
El Tigre
Ciudad Bolívar
El Callao
Ciudad Guayana
Upata
Embalse de Guri
Barrancas
GUYANA
Cuyuni
Georgetown
New Amsterdam
Port Kaituma

VENEZUELA
Río Orinoco

Palmira
Blanco

Jamaica

Montego Bay
Falmouth
Lucea
Grange Hill
Brown's Town
St. Ann's Bay
Galina Point
Cambridge
Ocho Rios
Port Maria
South Negril Point
Christiana
Frankfield
Highgate
Annotto Bay
Buff Bay
Savanna la Mar
Santa Cruz
Mandeville
Chapelton
Ewarton
Linstead
Bog Walk
Port Antonio
Black River
Porus
May Pen
Spanish Town
Old Harbour Town
Old Harbour
2256
The Blue Mts
Bath
Kingston
Port Royal
Morant Point
Old Morant
Morant Bay
Great Pedro Bluff
Portland Point

nithal Equidistant Projection
Oxford University Press

Scale 1:3 000 000   0   25   50 km

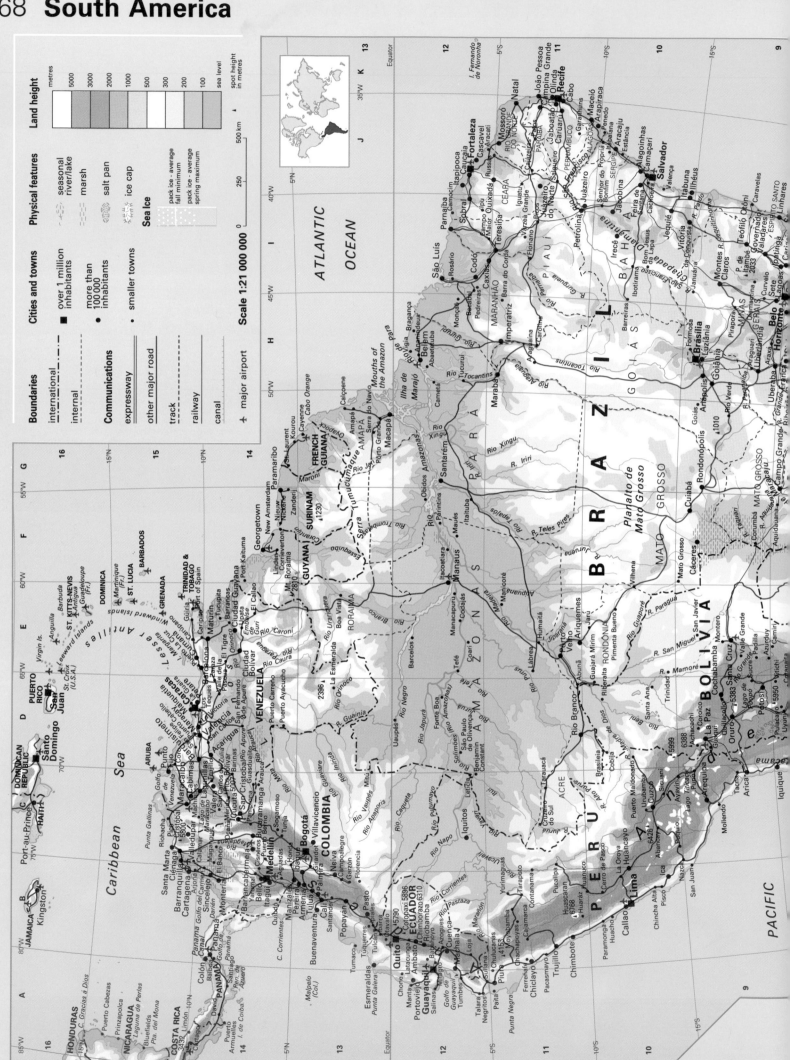

Land height

metres	
	5000
	3000
	2000
	1000
	500
	300
	200
	100
	sea level
▲	spot height in metres

Physical features

seasonal river/lake
marsh
salt pan
ice cap

Sea Ice

pack ice - average fall minimum
pack ice - average spring maximum

Cities and towns

■ over 1 million inhabitants
● more than 100 000 inhabitants
• smaller towns

Boundaries

international
internal

Communications

expressway
other major road
track
railway
canal
✈ major airport

Scale 1:21 000 000

0   250   500 km

ATLANTIC OCEAN

PACIFIC

Caribbean Sea

Equator

BRAZIL

PERU

BOLIVIA

COLOMBIA

VENEZUELA

GUYANA

SURINAM

FRENCH GUIANA

ECUADOR

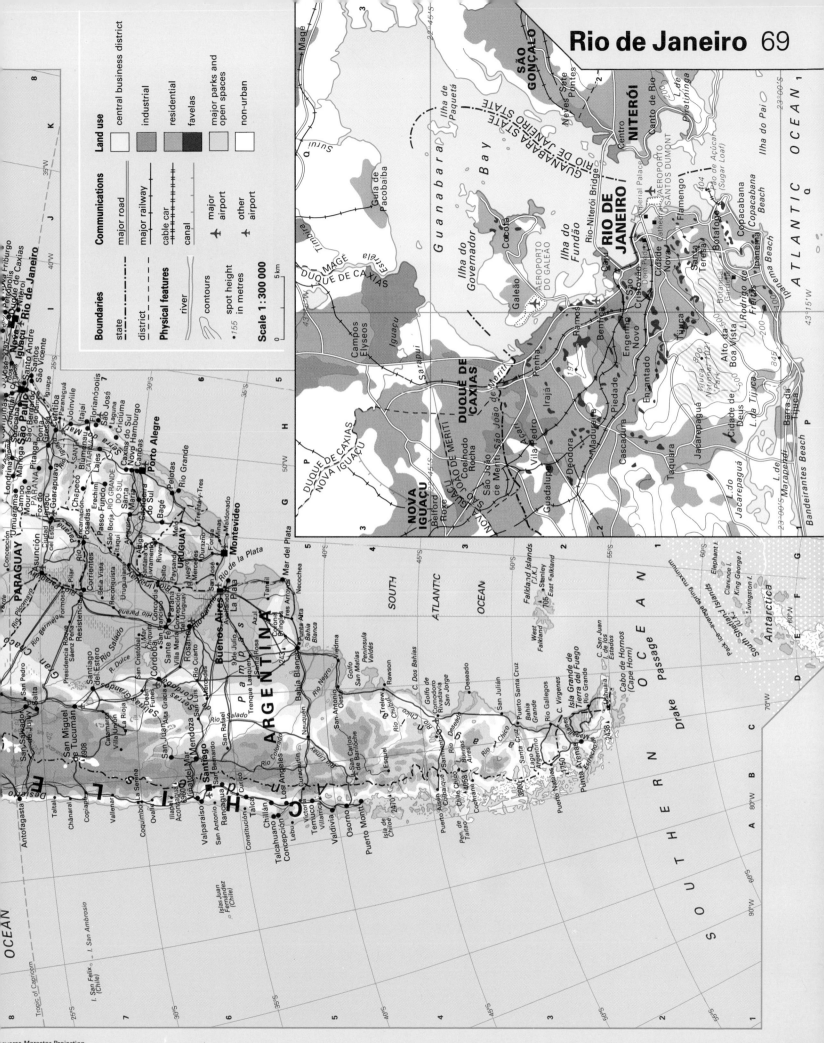

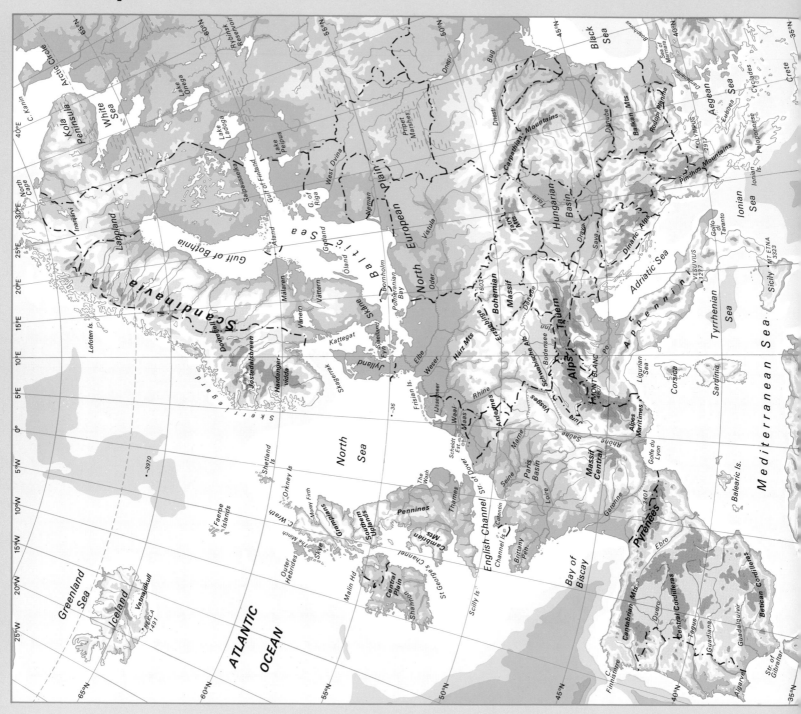

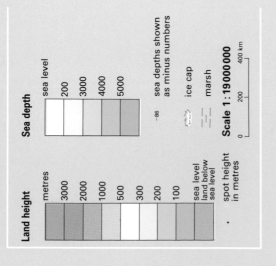

Land height

metres	
3000	
2000	
1000	
500	
300	
200	
100	
sea level land above sea level	
sea level land below sea level	

spot height in metres

Sea depth

	sea level
	200
	3000
	4000
	5000

-86 sea depths shown as minus numbers

ice cap

marsh

Scale 1 : 19 000 000

0   200   400 km

European Economic Organizations

European Community (EC) Headquarters: Brussels

European Free Trade Association (EFTA) Headquarters: Geneva

—·— international boundary

• national capital

Scale 1 : 44 000 000

0   200   400 km

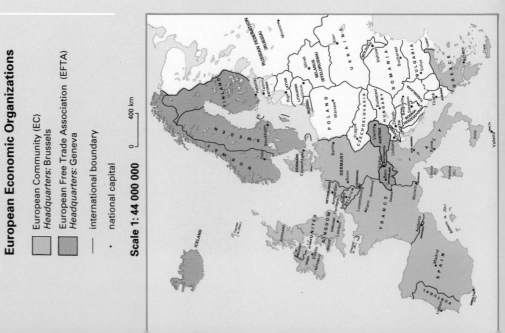

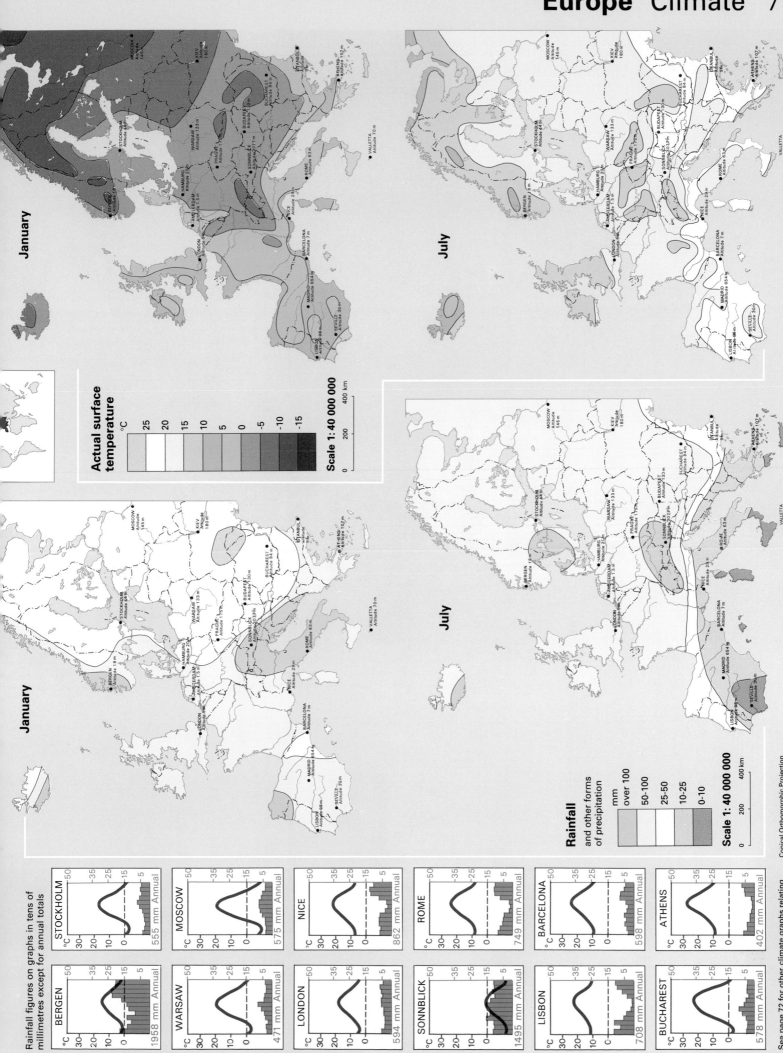

January

July

Actual surface temperature

°C
25
20
15
10
5
0
-5
-10
-15

Scale 1: 40 000 000

0   200   400 km

January

July

Rainfall
and other forms of precipitation

mm
over 100
50-100
25-50
10-25
0-10

Scale 1: 40 000 000

0   200   400 km

Conical Orthomorphic Projection

© Oxford University Press

Rainfall figures on graphs in tens of millimetres except for annual totals

STOCKHOLM — 555 mm Annual

MOSCOW — 575 mm Annual

NICE — 862 mm Annual

ROME — 749 mm Annual

BARCELONA — 598 mm Annual

ATHENS — 402 mm Annual

BERGEN — 1958 mm Annual

WARSAW — 471 mm Annual

LONDON — 594 mm Annual

SONNBLICK — 1495 mm Annual

LISBON — 708 mm Annual

BUCHAREST — 578 mm Annual

See page 72 for other climate graphs relating to climate stations shown on the maps.

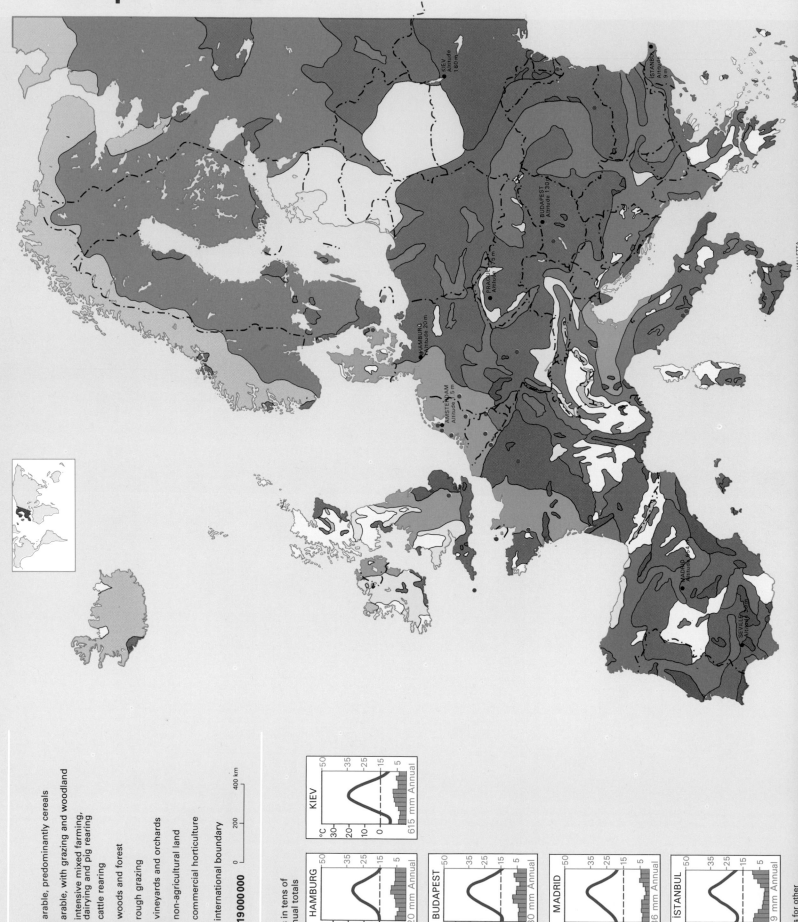

Conical Orthomorphic Projection

© Oxford University Press

arable, predominantly cereals

arable, with grazing and woodland

intensive mixed farming, dairying and pig rearing

cattle rearing

woods and forest

rough grazing

vineyards and orchards

non-agricultural land

commercial horticulture

international boundary

Scale 1 : 19 000 000

0   200   400 km

Rainfall figures on graphs in tens of
millimetres except for annual totals

KIEV
°C
30
20
10
0
50
35
25
15
5
615 mm Annual

HAMBURG
°C
30
20
10
0
50
35
25
15
5
720 mm Annual

BUDAPEST
°C
30
20
10
0
50
35
25
15
5
630 mm Annual

MADRID
°C
30
20
10
0
50
35
25
15
5
436 mm Annual

İSTANBUL
°C
30
20
10
0
50
35
25
15
5
669 mm Annual

AMSTERDAM
°C
30
20
10
0
50
35
25
15
5
787 mm Annual

PRAGUE
°C
30
20
10
0
50
35
25
15
5
508 mm Annual

SEVILLE
°C
30
20
10
0
50
35
25
15
5
559 mm Annual

VALLETTA
°C
30
20
10
0
50
35
25
15
5
516 mm Annual

See page 71 for climate graphs for other

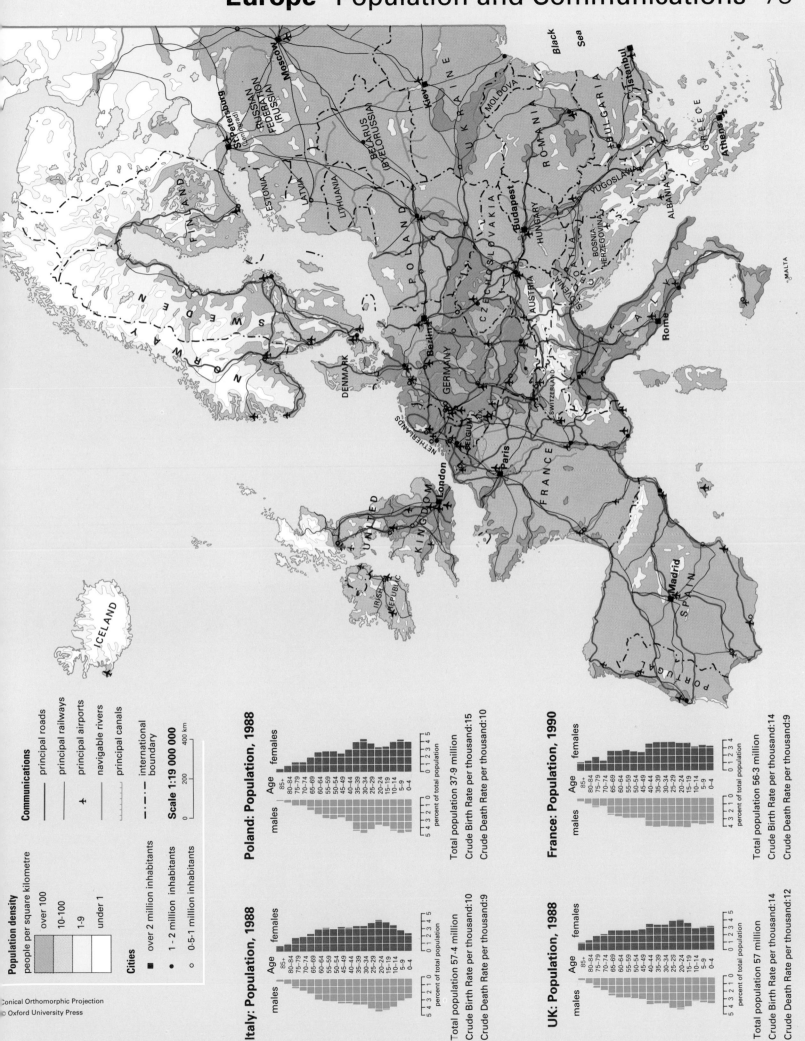

Population density

people per square kilometre

- over 100
- 10-100
- 1-9
- under 1

Cities

- ■ over 2 million inhabitants
- ● 1 - 2 million inhabitants
- ○ 0.5-1 million inhabitants

Communications

principal roads
principal railways
✈ principal airports
navigable rivers
principal canals
international boundary

Scale 1:19 000 000

0   200   400 km

Conical Orthomorphic Projection
© Oxford University Press

Italy: Population, 1988

males   Age   females
85+
80-84
75-79
70-74
65-69
60-64
55-59
50-54
45-49
40-44
35-39
30-34
25-29
20-24
15-19
10-14
5-9
0-4

5 4 3 2 1 0   0 1 2 3 4 5
percent of total population

Total population 57.4 million
Crude Birth Rate per thousand:10
Crude Death Rate per thousand:9

Poland: Population, 1988

males   Age   females
85+
80-84
75-79
70-74
65-69
60-64
55-59
50-54
45-49
40-44
35-39
30-34
25-29
20-24
15-19
10-14
5-9
0-4

5 4 3 2 1 0   0 1 2 3 4 5
percent of total population

Total population 37.9 million
Crude Birth Rate per thousand:15
Crude Death Rate per thousand:10

UK: Population, 1988

males   Age   females
85+
80-84
75-79
70-74
65-69
60-64
55-59
50-54
45-49
40-44
35-39
30-34
25-29
20-24
15-19
10-14
5-9
0-4

5 4 3 2 1 0   0 1 2 3 4 5
percent of total population

Total population 57 million
Crude Birth Rate per thousand:14
Crude Death Rate per thousand:12

France: Population, 1990

males   Age   females
85+
80-84
75-79
70-74
65-69
60-64
55-59
50-54
45-49
40-44
35-39
30-34
25-29
20-24
15-19
10-14
5-9
0-4

4 3 2 1 0   0 1 2 3 4
percent of total population

Total population 56.3 million
Crude Birth Rate per thousand:14
Crude Death Rate per thousand:9

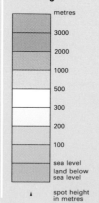

Boundaries

international

disputed

internal

Communications

expressway

other major road

railway

canal

✈ major airport

Cities and towns

■ over 1 million inhabitants

● more than 100 000 inhabitants

• smaller towns

Physical features

seasonal river/lake

marsh

salt pan

ice cap

sand dunes

Sea Ice

pack ice spring max.

Land height

metres
3000
2000
1000
500
300
200
100
sea level
land below sea level

▲ spot height in metres

Scale 1 : 12 500 000

0 125 250 km

Conical Orthomorphic Projection

© Oxford University Press

78 British Isles

Boundaries
international
internal

Land height
metres
1000
500
200
100
sea level
land below sea level
▲ spot height in metres

Communications
expressway
other major road
railway

✈ major airport

Cities and towns
⬦ major built-up areas
■ over 1 million inhabitants
● more than 100 000 inhabitants
• smaller towns

Scale 1:4 500 000
0   50   100 km

Transverse Mercator Projection
© Oxford University Press

SCOTLAND
UNITED KINGDOM
NORTHERN IRELAND
IRISH REPUBLIC
ENGLAND
WALES
FRANCE

Shetland Islands
Orkney Islands
Outer Hebrides
Inner Hebrides
Northwest Highlands
Grampian Mountains
Southern Uplands
Pennines
Cambrian Mtns.
Cheviot Hills
North York Moors
Yorkshire Wolds
Lincoln Wolds
Cotswold Hills
Chiltern Hills
Brecon Beacons
Exmoor
Dartmoor
Bodmin Moor
Mourne Mtns.
Wicklow Mtns.
Galty Mtns.
Caha Mtns.

Lewis
Harris
Skye
Rhum
Eigg
Coll
Tiree
Mull
Iona
Colonsay
Jura
Islay
Arran
Bute
Isle of Man
Anglesey
Holy I.
Lundy
Isle of Wight
Channel Islands
Isles of Scilly
Guernsey
Jersey
St. Helier
Alderney

Ben Nevis 1344
Ben Macdhui 1310
Cairngorms
Ben Wyvis 1046
1183
1009
Snowdon 1085
Scafell Pike 978
Snaefell 621
Slieve Donard 852
Carrauntoohill 1041
926
892
619
840
893
1041

Loch Ness
Loch Shin
Loch Lomond
Loch Tay
Loch Linnhe
Loch Lochy
Loch Awe
Loch Leven

The Minch
Little Minch
Sound of Jura
Firth of Lorn
Firth of Clyde
North Channel
Irish Sea
Celtic Sea
St. George's Channel
Cardigan Bay
Bristol Channel
English Channel
Strait of Dover
Moray Firth
Dornoch Firth
Pentland Firth
Solway Firth
Firth of Forth
Donegal Bay
Galway Bay
Bantry Bay
Dingle Bay
Lyme Bay
Baie de la Seine

Cape Wrath
Butt of Lewis
Duncansby Head
St. Abb's Head
Flamborough Head
Spurn Head
The Wash
The Fens
The Weald
Malin Head
Bloody Foreland
Erris Head
Slyne Head
Loop Head
Mizen Head
Cape Clear
Old Head of Kinsale
Hartland Point
Start Point
Lizard Point
Land's End
Beachy Head
North Downs
South Downs
Salisbury Plain
Mendip Hills
Sidlaw Hills
Lammermuir Hills
Fair Isle
Foula
Rona
St. Kilda

Thurso
Wick
Inverness
Elgin
Dingwall
Ullapool
Stornoway
Fort William
Oban
Mallaig
Kyle of Lochalsh
Fraserburgh
Peterhead
Aberdeen
Perth
Dundee
St. Andrews
Arbroath
Stirling
Falkirk
Alloa
Dunfermline
Kirkcaldy
Edinburgh
Glasgow
Greenock
Paisley
Clydebank
Cumbernauld
Motherwell
East Kilbride
Kilmarnock
Ayr
Campbeltown
Dumfries
Kirkcudbright
Stranraer
Berwick-upon-Tweed
Galashiels
Hawick
Holy Island

Londonderry
Coleraine
Ballymena
Larne
Newtownabbey
Bangor
Belfast
Lisburn
Lurgan
Portadown
Armagh
Newry
Omagh
Enniskillen
Dundalk
Drogheda

Donegal
Sligo
Castlebar
Westport
Galway
Athlone
Mullingar
Tullamore
Portlaoise
Naas
Dublin
Dún Laoghaire
Bray
Kells
Longford
Roscommon
Limerick
Tralee
Killarney
Kilkenny
Clonmel
Waterford
Cork
Youghal
Wexford
Rosslare

Carlisle
Penrith
Workington
Whitehaven
St. Bees
Barrow-in-Furness
Douglas
Kendal
Lancaster
Blackpool
Preston
Southport
Blackburn
Bolton
Wigan
Liverpool
Birkenhead
St. Helens
Manchester
Stockport
Oldham
Huddersfield
Bradford
Leeds
Harrogate
York
Wakefield
Sheffield
Doncaster
Rotherham
Chesterfield
Barnsley
Halifax
Scunthorpe
Grimsby
Kingston upon Hull
Lincoln
Skegness
Newcastle upon Tyne
Gateshead
Sunderland
Durham
Hartlepool
Stockton-on-Tees
Middlesbrough
Darlington
Scarborough
Blyth

Holyhead
Colwyn Bay
Caernarfon
Bangor
Wrexham
Chester
Crewe
Stoke-on-Trent
Derby
Nottingham
Stafford
Telford
Shrewsbury
Wolverhampton
Dudley
Walsall
Birmingham
Coventry
Solihull
Rugby
Leicester
Peterborough
King's Lynn
Norwich
Great Yarmouth
Lowestoft
Ipswich
Felixstowe
Harwich
Colchester
Cambridge
Bedford
Northampton
Milton Keynes
Luton
Banbury
Worcester
Hereford
Gloucester
Cheltenham
Aberystwyth
Carmarthen
Milford Haven
Fishguard
St. David's Head
Llanelli
Swansea
Neath
Merthyr Tydfil
Rhondda
Cwmbran
Pontypool
Newport
Cardiff
Barry
Bristol
Bath
Swindon
Oxford
Aylesbury
St. Albans
Watford
Slough
Reading
Basingstoke
Guildford
London
Basildon
Southend-on-Sea
Gillingham
Chelmsford
Maidstone
Canterbury
Margate
Dover
Folkestone
Hastings
Eastbourne
Brighton
Worthing
Crawley
Winchester
Salisbury
Bournemouth
Poole
Southampton
Portsmouth
Weymouth
Torbay
Exeter
Bridgwater
Taunton
Barnstaple
Plymouth
Truro
Penzance

Cherbourg
C. de la Hague
le Havre
Dieppe
le Tréport
Boulogne-sur-Mer
le Touquet–Paris–Plage
Calais
Caen
Rouen
St. Peter Port
Sark

Tay
Spey
Dee
Don
Tweed
Eden
Tyne
Tees
Ouse
Trent
Severn
Thames
Avon
Wye
Shannon
Boyne
Liffey
Suir
Nore
Barrow
Slaney

ICELAND

Grimsey, Siglufjördur, Ísafjördur, 925, reidha Fjördur, Húsavík, Vopnafjördur, Akureyri, Neskaupstadur, ykkishólmur, 65°N, Langjökull, Hofsjökull, 2000, Vatnajökull, Faxaflói, Akranes, Hekla 1491, Höfn, Reykjavík, Keflavík, Hafnarfjördur, Mýrdals-jökull, Vestmannaeyjar, Arctic Circle

Boundaries
international
internal

Communications
expressway
other major road
railway
canal
✈ major airport

Cities and towns
■ over 1 million inhabitants
● more than 100 000 inhabitants
• smaller towns

Physical features
marsh
ice cap
▲ spot height in metres

Land height
metres
2000
1000
500
300
200
100
sea level
land below sea level

Scale 1:8 500 000
100   200 km

Modified Conical
Orthomorphic Projection
© Oxford University Press

ARCTIC OCEAN

Barents Sea

Nordkapp (North Cape), Hammerfest, Søroya, Lopphavet, Porsangen, Laksefjord, Tanafjord, Berlevåg, Varangerhalvøya, Vardø, 637, Varangerfjorden, Poluostrov Rybachiy, Murmansk, Pechenga, Vanna, Ringvassøy, Alta, Lakselv, 1067, 1139, Jiesjavrre, Tenojoki, 623, 637, Tromsø, Reisa, Karasjok, Inarijärvi, Lotta, Pudushkoye More, Monchegorsk, Ozero Imandra, 1208, Apatity, Senja, Barduelv, 1144, Maanselka, Enontekiö, 807, Porttipahdan tekojärvi, 636, Kholayarvi, Kandalakshshiy Zaliv (White Sea), Langøy, Hinnøya, 1681, Lofoten Is., Vestfjorden, Narvik, 1901, Torne-träsk, Kiruna, 555, Ounasjoki, Sodankylä, Lokan tekojärvi, Ozero Pyazero, Nordfold, 2111, Stora Lulevatten, Gullivare, Kemijoki, Rovaniemi, Yli-kitka Kuusamo, Muojärvi, 431, Ozero Topozero, Bodø, 2013, 1908, 2021, Jokkmokk, Kalix älv, Torne älv, Övertornea, Kemijärvi, Kiantajärvi, Ozero Nyuk, Saltdal, 1599, 1754, 1694, Mo-i-Rana, Arctic Circle, Arjeplog, Pite älv, Boden, Tornio, Kemi, Pudasjärvi, 65°N, Ozero Kuyto, Dønna, Mosjøen, Røssvatnet 1764, Hornavan, Uddjaur, Skellefte älv, Luleå, Piteå, Oulu, Oulujoki, Kalevala, Vega, Brønnøysund, Grane, 1703, 1568, Storuman, Vindelälven, Hailuoto, Oulu järvi, Ozero Srodneye Kuyto, Kolvereid, Vikna, Folda, Namsos, Tunnsjøen, Lycksele, Vilhelmina, Skellefteå, Raahe, Pulkkila, Kajaani, 355, Ozero Leksozero, 409, Frøya, Brekstad, Smøla, Hitra, Fosna, Trondheim, Namdalen, Grong, 1337, Dragan, Hoting, Ångermanälven, Umeå, Vännäs, Kokkola, Jakobstad, Pyhäjärvi, Pielinen, Joensuu, Kristiansund, Trollheimen, Trondheimsfjorden, Stjørdal, Støren, Berkåk, 1441, 1796, Åsarna, Storsjön, Östersund, Sollefteå, Örnsköldsvik, Gulf of Bothnia, Vaasa, Lappajärvi, Lapua, Kunkka, Keitele, Varkhaus, Pytäselkä, Pyhäjärvi, Ålesund, Andalsnes, 2286, 2083, Nordfjord, Dovrefjell, Dombås, Tynset, Glama, 1277, Linsell, Ljungan, Sundsvall, Härnösand, Kaskö, Näsijärvi, Jyväskylä, Haukivesi, Puulavesi, Puruvesi, Pyhäjärvi, Floro, Jostedalsbreen, 2469, Jotunheimen, Gudbrandsdalen, Femund, 1755, Idre, Österdalälven, Ytterhogdal, Östervall, Ljusnan, Ljus, Dellen, Pori, Parkano, Tampere, Mikkeli, Saimaa, Imatra, Ladozhskoye Ozero, Sognefjorden, Laerdalsøyri, Begna, Lillehammer, 887, Voxnan, Bollnäs, Söderhamn, Rauma, Hämeenlinna, Lahti, Kouvola, Vyborg, Bergen, Voss, Valdres, Hamar, Mjøsa, Mora, Siljan, Amungen, Gävle, Åland, Turku, Pyhäjärvi, Forssa, Salpausselkä, Kronstadt, Hardangervidda, Odda, 1660, 1962, Drammen, Kløfta, Ludvika, Falun, Borlänge, Hedesunda-fjärdarna, Avesta, Mariehamn, Hangö, Salo, Hyvinkää, Vantaa, Helsinki (Helsingfors), Espoo, Gulf of Finland, St. Petersburg (Leningrad), Gatchina, Haugesund, Boknfjorden, Telemark, Oslo, Numedal, Glåma, Klarälven, Uppsala, Tallinn, Kuhtla-Järve, Tapa, Narva, Luga, Stavanger, Sira, Otra, Setesdal, Skien, Tønsberg, Moss, Sarpsborg, Karlstad, Karlskoga, Eskilstuna, Mälaren, Västerås, Nyköping, Hiiumaa, Haapsalu, Haljala, Pärnu, Ozero Chudskoye, Tartu, Ozero Pskovskoye, Pskov, Ostrov, Luga, Flekkefjord, Arendal, Kristiansand, Mandal, Uddevalla, Trollhättan, Vänern, Skövde, Katrineholm, Södertälje, Stockholm, Örebro, Vättern, Sommen, Linköping, Norrköping, Fårön, Hiiumaa, Saaremaa, Kuressaare, Võrtsjärv, Valga, Võru, Gulf of Riga, Skagerrak, Göteborg, Hjørring, Frederikshavn, Mölndal, Borås, Jönköping, Nässjö, Västervik, Visby, Gotland, Ventspils, Mazirbe, Valmiera, Rëzekne, Opochka, North Sea, Hjørring, Limfjorden, Ålborg, Lund, Halmstad, Bolmen, Växjö, Åsnen, Öland, Borgholm, Ventspils, Kuldiga, Tukums, Zap. Dvina, Daugavpils, Viborg, Randers, Herning, Århus, Helsingborg, Landskrona, Kristianstad, Karlskrona, Kalmar, Riga, Liepāja, Saldus, Jelgava, Jēkabpils, Venta, Šiauliai, Plunge, Panevėžys, Polotsk, Denmark, Horsens, Vejle, Kolding, Esbjerg, Odense, Fyn, Sjaelland, København (Copenhagen), Roskilde, Malmö, Hanöbukten, Klaipēda, Kurskiy Zaliv, Neman, Lithuania, Kaunas, Vilnius, Belarus (Byelorussia), Ukmerge, Lida, Nord-friesische Inseln, Heligoland Bight, Schleswig, Flensburg, Germany, Kiel, Rendsburg, Neumünster, Schwerin, Naestved, Lolland, Nykøbing, Sassnitz, Rügen, Mecklenburg Bay, Pomeranian Bay, Bornholm (Denmark), Baltic Sea, Gdynia, Gulf of Gdańsk, Gdańsk, Kaliningrad (Russia), Chernyakhovsk, Marijampole, Grodno, Molodechno, Minsk, Borisov, Wilhelmshaven, Bremerhaven, Bremen, Hamburg, Lübeck, Rostock, Wismar, Stralsund, Szczecin, Kolobrzeg, Koszalin, Słupsk, Netherlands, Groningen, Emden, Oldenburg, Elblag, Malbork, Olsztyn, Ełk, Tczew, Sniardwy J.

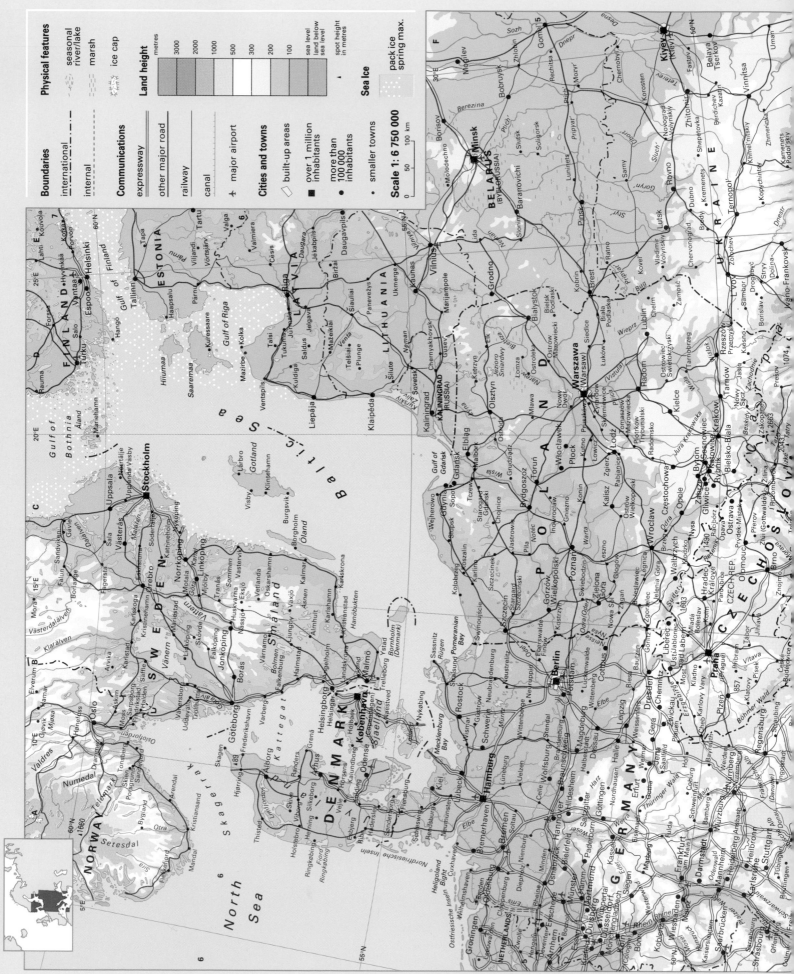

© Oxford University Press   Conical Orthomorphic Proje...

82 London

Boundaries
county

Communications
expressway

other major road

major railway

canal

✈ major airport

✈ other airport

Physical features
river

contours

•155 spot height in metres

Land use

central business district

other major commercial areas

industrial

residential

major parks and open spaces

non-urban

This image of London, United Kingdom was produced by a Landsat satellite orbiting the earth at an altitude of approximately 900 km. Other satellite images can be found on pages 4 and 5.

Scale 1:600 000

Scale 1:300 000

0   5km

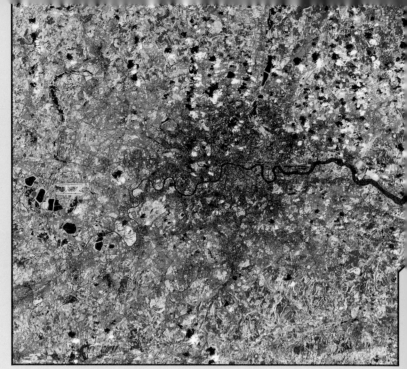

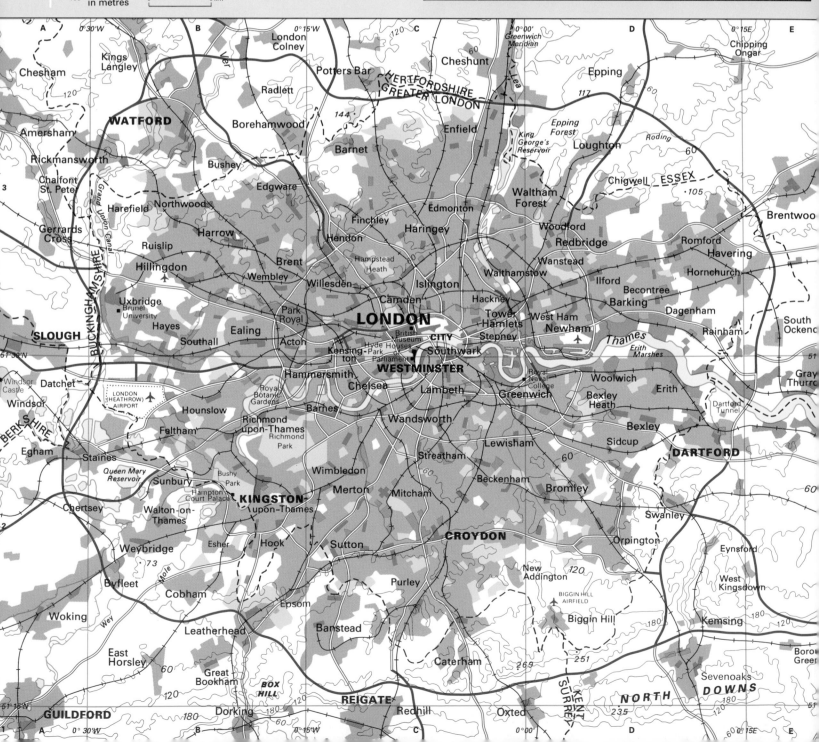

Chesham · Kings Langley · London Colney · Cheshunt · Epping · Chipping Ongar · Radlett · Potters Bar · HERTFORDSHIRE · GREATER LONDON · WATFORD · Borehamwood · Enfield · Epping Forest · Roding · Amersham · Barnet · King George's Reservoir · Loughton · Rickmansworth · Bushey · Edmonton · Woodford · Chigwell · ESSEX · Chalfont St. Peter · Edgware · Finchley · Haringey · Waltham Forest · Brentwood · Harefield · Northwood · Hendon · Redbridge · Romford · Havering · Gerrards Cross · Harrow · Hampstead Heath · Walthamstow · Wanstead · Hornchurch · Ruislip · Brent · Willesden · Islington · Ilford · Becontree · Hillingdon · Wembley · Camden · Hackney · Barking · Dagenham · Uxbridge · Brunel University · Park Royal · LONDON · Tower Hamlets · West Ham · Newham · South Ockend · SLOUGH · Hayes · Acton · CITY · Stepney · Thames · Rainham · Ealing · British Museum · Southwark · Erith Marshes · Windsor Castle · Datchet · Southall · Kensington · Hyde Park · Houses of Parliament · WESTMINSTER · Woolwich · Erith · Gray Thurro · Windsor · Hammersmith · Chelsea · Lambeth · Greenwich · Royal Naval College · Bexley Heath · BERKSHIRE · Hounslow · Barnes · Wandsworth · Woolwich · Bexley · Egham · Feltham · Richmond upon-Thames · Richmond Park · Lewisham · Sidcup · DARTFORD · Staines · Royal Botanic Gardens · Streatham · Dartford Tunnel · Queen Mary Reservoir · Bushy Park · Wimbledon · Beckenham · Bromley · Sunbury · Hampton Court Palace · KINGSTON upon-Thames · Merton · Mitcham · Swanley · Chertsey · Walton-on-Thames · Esher · Hook · Sutton · CROYDON · Orpington · Eynsford · Weybridge · Purley · New Addington · Biggin Hill Airfield · West Kingsdown · Byfleet · Cobham · Epsom · Biggin Hill · Kemsing · Woking · Leatherhead · Banstead · North Downs · Boro Greer · East Horsley · Great Bookham · BOX HILL · REIGATE · Caterham · Sevenoaks · GUILDFORD · Dorking · Redhill · Oxted · SURREY · KENT

Legend

Boundaries

département (Paris)

regierungsbezirk (Berlin)

Communications

expressway

other major road

major railway

canal

✈ major airport

✈ other airport

Physical features

river

contours

· 155 spot height in metres

Land use

central business district

other major commercial areas

industrial

residential

major parks and open spaces

non-urban

Scale 1:300 000

0 — 5 km

Paris map

Conflans-Ste-Honorine, Andrésy, Maisons-Laffitte, Poissy, St-Germain-en-Laye, Forêt de St. Germain, Sartrouville, Chatou, Nanterre, Rueil-Malmaison, St-Cloud, Vaucresson, Versailles, Château de Versailles, St-Cyr-l'École, St. Quentin-en-Yvelines, Chevreuse, St. Rémy, Saclay, Palaiseau, Orsay, les Ulis, Bièvres, Verrières, Massy, Centre d'études nucléaires, Yvelines, Essonne

Taverny, Beauchamp, Herblay, Cormeilles-en-Parisis, Argenteuil, Colombes, Gennevilliers, Asnières, Clichy, Neuilly, la Défense, Sèvres, Vanves, Montrouge, Forêt de Meudon, Meudon, Sceaux, Rungis, Thiais, Orly, Aérodrome de Villacoublay, Aéroport d'Orly, Chartres & Orléans, Lyon, Draveil

Forêt de Montmorency, Écouen, Montmorency, Sarcelles, Enghien, St-Denis, Aubervilliers, Pantin, Sacré Coeur, St-Lazare, Nord, Est, Arc de Triomphe, Opéra, Eiffel Tower, Invalides, Louvre, Notre Dame, Sorbonne, Montparnasse, Austerlitz, Boulogne-Billancourt, PARIS, Vincennes, Bois de Vincennes, St-Mandé, Ivry-s-Seine, Vitry-s-Seine, Villejuif, Choisy-le-Roi, Créteil, Villeneuve St. Georges, Montgeron, Brunoy, Juvisy-sur-Orge

Goussainville, Lille, Aéroport Charles de Gaulle, Mitry-Mory, Aéroport du Bourget, le Blanc-Mesnil, Drancy, Bobigny, Aulnay-sous-Bois, Villeparisis, le Raincy, Les Coudreaux, Noisy-le-Sec, Chelles, Neuilly Plaisance, Champs-s-Marne, Marne-la-Vallée, Champigny, St. Maur, Sucy-en-Brie, Forêt de Notre Dame, Brie-Comte-Robert, Autoroute de Nord, Canal de l'Ourcq, Seine St Denis, Val-de-Marne, Seine-et-Marne

Berlin map

Velten, Marwitz, Bötzow, Pausin, Henningsdorf, Schönwalde, Brieselang, Falkensee, Dallgow, Staaken, Charlottenburg, Spandau, Berliner Forst Spandau, Tegel, Flughafen Berlin-Gatow, Kladow, Grunewald, Berliner Forst Grunewald, Wannsee, Kleinmachnow, Potsdam, Babelsberg, Werder, Drewitz, Stahnsdorf, Teltow, Ludwigsfelde

Borgsdorf, Birkenwerder, Frohnau, Schildow, Glienicke, Hermsdorf, Berliner Forst, Reinickendorf, Flughafen Berlin-Tegel (Otto Lilienthal), Pankow, Jungfernheide, Siemensstadt, Reichstag, Brandenburger Tor, Tiergarten, Wedding, Olympiastadion, Schöneberg, Wilmersdorf, Neukölln, Tempelhof, Zentral Flughafen Berlin-Tempelhof, Steglitz, Zehlendorf, Buckow, Lichtenrade, Mahlow, Grossbeeren, Blankenfelde, Dahlewitz

Basdorf, Schönwalde, Schwanebeck, Zepernick, Bernau, Karow, Buchholz, Blankenburg, Weissensee, BERLIN, Prenzlauer Berg, Friedrichshain, Kreuzberg, Treptow, Lindenberg, Blumberg, Altlandsberg, Ahrensfelde, Hellersdorf, Lichtenberg, Karlshorst, Neuenhagen, Fredersdorf, Köpenick, Grosser Müggelsee, Berliner Stadtforst Köpenick, Schöneiche, Friedrichshagen, Rahnsdorf, Müggelheim, Erkner, Langer See, Seddin-See, Eichwalde, Königs Wusterhausen, Zernsdorf, Wildau, Flughafen Berlin-Schönefeld, Schulzendorf, Bohnsdorf, Rudow, Königsheide, Teltowkanal, Spree, Havel, Havelkanal, Tegeler See, Oder-Spree-Kanal, Zeuthener See, Berliner Ring, Schweilowsee, Schwielowsee, Werder, Potsdam, Frankfurt

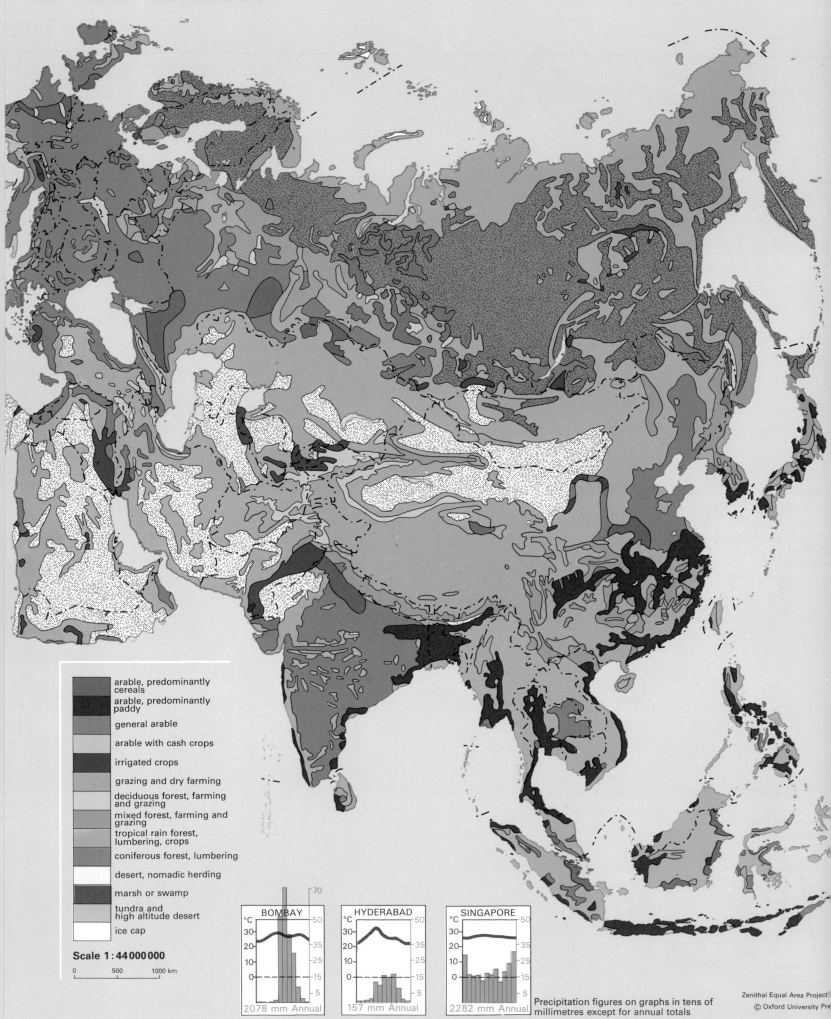

arable, predominantly cereals

arable, predominantly paddy

general arable

arable with cash crops

irrigated crops

grazing and dry farming

deciduous forest, farming and grazing

mixed forest, farming and grazing

tropical rain forest, lumbering, crops

coniferous forest, lumbering

desert, nomadic herding

marsh or swamp

tundra and high altitude desert

ice cap

Scale 1 : 44 000 000

0   500   1000 km

BOMBAY
°C
30
20
10
0
2078 mm Annual

HYDERABAD
°C
30
20
10
0
157 mm Annual

SINGAPORE
°C
30
20
10
0
2282 mm Annual

Precipitation figures on graphs in tens of millimetres except for annual totals

Zenithal Equal Area Project

© Oxford University Pr

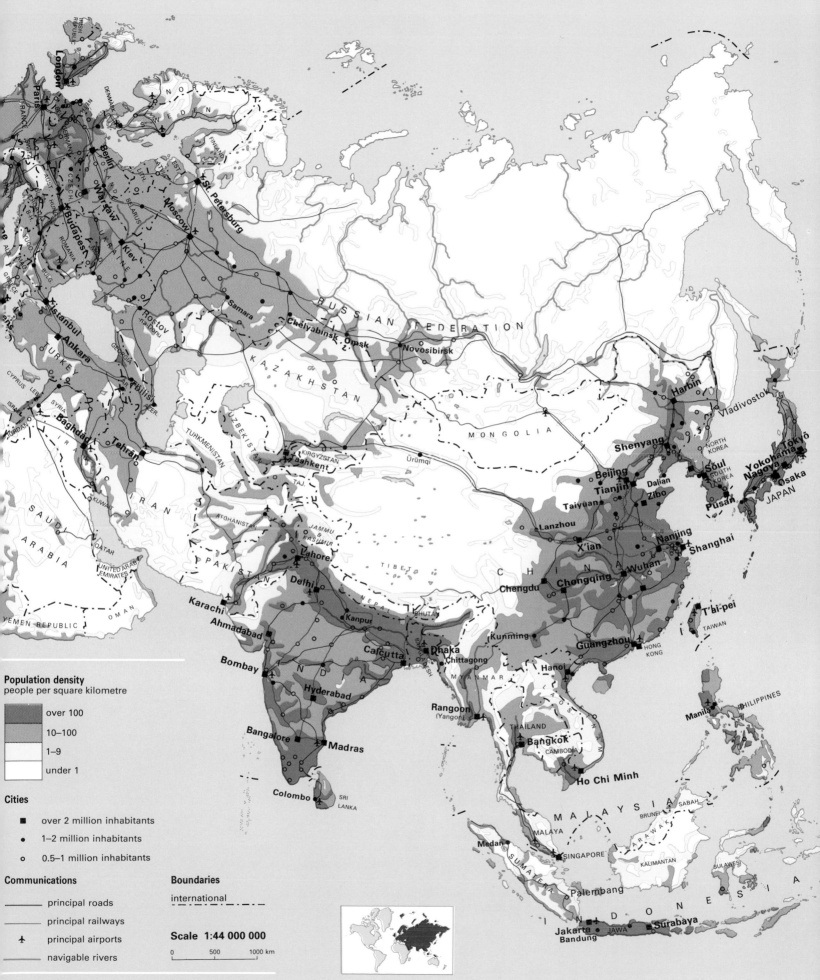

Population density
people per square kilometre

- over 100
- 10–100
- 1–9
- under 1

Cities

- ■ over 2 million inhabitants
- • 1–2 million inhabitants
- ○ 0.5–1 million inhabitants

Communications

—— principal roads

—— principal railways

✈ principal airports

—— navigable rivers

Boundaries

international

Scale 1:44 000 000

0   500   1000 km

Smithal Equal Area Projection

Oxford University Press

Boundaries

international

disputed

internal

Communications

expressway

other major road

railway

canal

✈ major airport

Cities and towns

■ over 1 million inhabitants

● more than 100 000 inhabitants

• smaller towns

Scale 1 : 25 000 000

0   250   500 km

Physical features

seasonal river/lake

marsh

salt pan

ice cap

sand dunes

Land height

metres

5000
3000
2000
1000
500
300
200
100
sea level
land below sea level

▲ spot height in metres

Sea Ice

unnavigable polar ice

pack ice - fall minimum

pack ice - spring maximum

Boundaries

city limit/oblast

Land use

central business district

other major commercial areas

industrial

residential

major parks and open spaces

non-urban

Refer to page 83 for complete legend

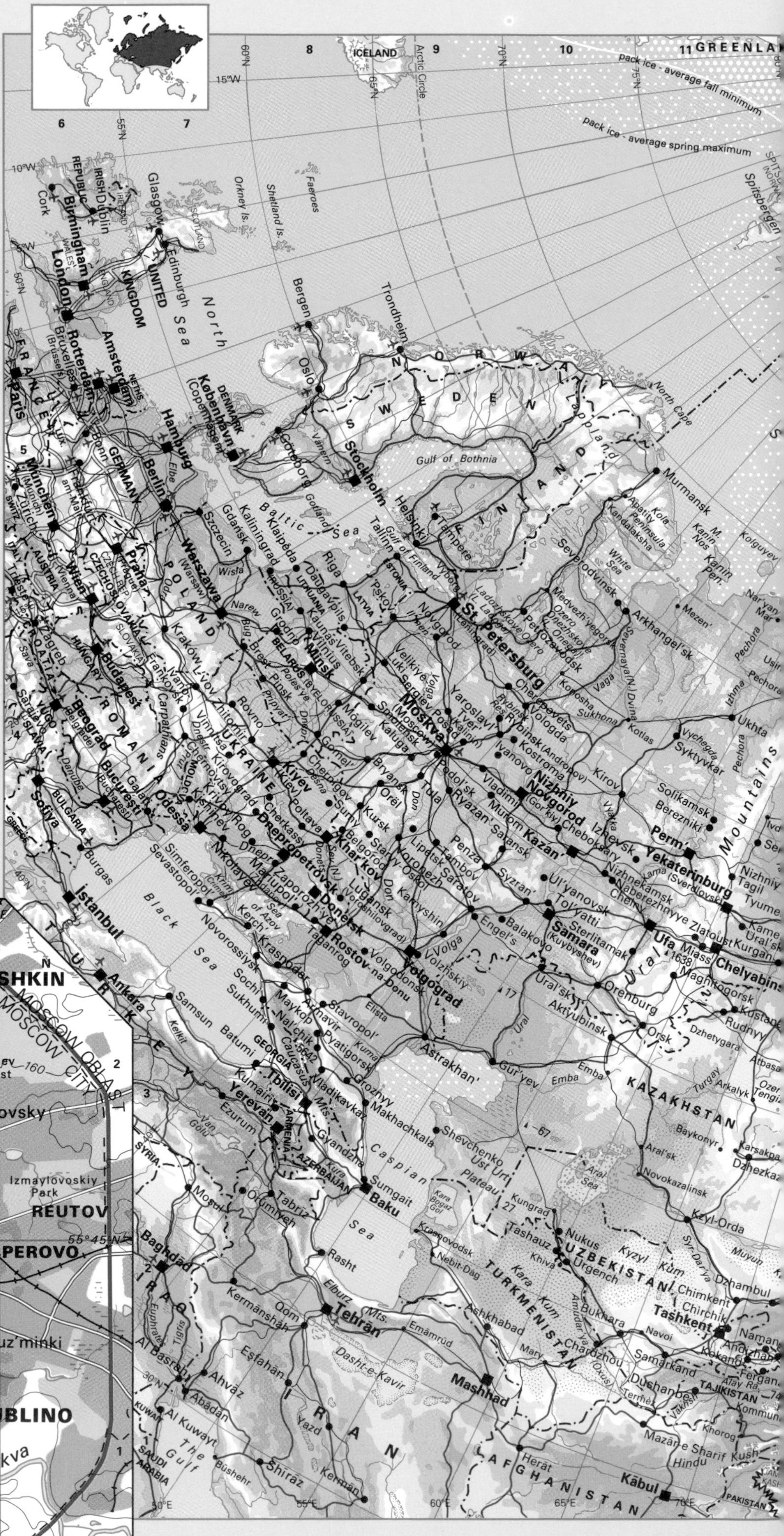

Conical Orthomorphic Project

Boundaries

international

disputed

Communications

expressway

other major road

railway

canal

✈ major airport

Cities and towns

■ over 1 million inhabitants

● more than 100 000 inhabitants

• smaller towns

Physical features

seasonal river/lake

marsh

salt pan

ice cap

sand dunes

salt lake

Sea Ice

pack ice spring max.

Land height

metres

5000
3000
2000
1000
500
300
200
100
sea level
land below sea level

▲ spot height in metres

Scale 1: 12 500 000

0   100   200   300 km

Conical Orthomorphic Projection

Map labels

SWEDEN, Gotland, Öland, Borgholm, Kalmar, Hiiumaa, FINLAND, Helsinki, Imatra, Vyborg, Petrozavodsk, Oz. Onezhskoye (L. Onega), Severnaya (N.) Dvina, Vychegda, Syktyvkar

Saaremaa, ESTONIA, Tallinn, Pärnu, Narva, Kohtla-Järve, Tartu, Pskov, St. Petersburg (Sankt Peterburg/Leningrad), Kolpino, Lodeynoye Pole, Ladozhskoye Oz. (L. Ladoga), Konosha, Kotlas, Sukhona

Gulf of Riga, Ventspils, Liepāja, Riga, LATVIA, Ozero Chudskoye, Il'men, Novgorod, Cherepovets, Vologda, Rybinskoye Vdkhr., Rybinsk (Andropov), Yaroslavl, Kostroma, Kirov, Vyatka

Zelenogradsk, Kaliningrad, KALININGRAD (RUSSIA), Sovetsk, Klaipėda, Šiauliai, LITHUANIA, Panevėžys, Kaunas, Daugava, Velikiye-Luki, Valdai Hills, Tver (Kalinin), Rzhev, Rostov, Kineshma, Ivanovo, Nizhniy Novgorod (Gor'kiy), Gor'kovskoye Vdkhr., Novocheboksarsk, Yoshkar-Ola

Gdansk, Olsztyn, Marijampole, Grodno, Vilnius, Dzerzhinsk, BELARUS (Byelorussia), Minsk (Mensk), Borisov, Berezina, Gorki, Smolensk, Moskva (Moscow), Mytishchi, Sergiev Posad (Zagorsk), Balashikha, Vladimir, Kovrov, Murom, Arzamas, Cheboksary, Nizhnekam, Kazan'

Warszawa, POLAND, Wisła, Lublin, Narew, Bug, Brest, Baranovichi, Bobruysk, Mogilev, Gomel', Bryansk, Orel, Tula, Novomoskovsk, Kaluga, Serpukhov, Podol'sk, Lyubertsy, Orekhovo-Zuyevo, Elektrostal', Kolomna, Ryazan', Tambov, Saransk, Penza, Syzran', Tol'yatti, Samara (Kuybyshev)

UKRAINE, L'vov, Rovno, Dubno, Brody, Zhitomir, Kiyev (Kiev), Chernobyl', Chernigov, Dnepr, Desna, Konotop, Sumy, Kursk, Belgorod, Voronezh, Staryy Oskol, Borisoglebsk, Balashov, Rtishchevo, Saratov, Engel's, Krasnyy Kut, Ural

MOLDOVA, Kishinev, Tiraspol, Bendery, ROMANIA, Iași, Bacău, Brașov, Buzău, Galați, Brăila, București, Shumen, Constanța, Varna, Burgas

Khmel'nitskiy, Kamenets-Podol'skiy, Chernovtsy, Vinnitsa, Belaya Tserkov', Cherkassy, Uman', Kremenchug, Kremenchugskoye Vdkhr., Poltava, Kharkov, Lozovaya, Lisichansk, Severodonetsk, Lugansk (Voroshilovgrad), Kamensk, Volgograd, Volzhskiy, Volgogradskoye Vdkhr., Volga

Kirovograd, Dnepropetrovsk, Dneprodzerzhinsk, Pavlograd, Zaporozh'ye, Krivoy Rog, Nikopol', Nikolayev, Kherson, Melitopol', Kakhovskoye Vdkhr., Dnepr, Berdyansk, Taganrog, Rostov-na-Donu, Novocherkassk, Shakhty, Novoshakhtinsk, Volgodonsk, Tsimlyanskoye Vdkhr., Akhtubinsk, Baskunchak

Kramatorsk, Konstantinovka, Gorlovka, Makeyevka, Yenakiyevo, Donetsk, Mariupol (Zhdanov), Krasnyy Luch, Sverdlovsk, Kommunarsk, Stakhanov, Andreyevka

Odessa, Belgorod-Dnestrovskiy, Karkinitskiy Zaliv, Yevpatoriya, Krim (Crimea), Sevastopol', Simferopol', Sea of Azov, Kerch', Novorossiysk, Krasnodar, Kuban', Tikhoretsk, Armavir, Maykop, Stavropol', Nevinnomyssk, Cherkessk, Pyatigorsk, Kislovodsk, Prokhladnyy, Nal'chik, Groznyy, Vladikavkaz (Ordzhonikidze), Makhachkala, Derbent

Oz. Manych Gudilo, Elista, Astrakhan', Gur'yev, Caspian Lowlands, Caspian Sea, Shevchenko, Kara-Bogaz Gol

İstanbul, Karadeniz Strait, Zonguldak, İzmit, Bursa, Adapazarı, Sakarya, İnce Burun, İnebolu, Karabük, Kastamonu, Sinop, Samsun, Ordu, Giresun, Trabzon, Black Sea, Tuapse, Sochi, Sukhumi, El'brus, Kazbek, Batumi, Poti, Kutaisi, GEORGIA, Rustavi, Tbilisi

Ankara, Kızıl Irmak, Kırıkkale, Kelkit, Erzincan, Fırat, Çoruh Dağı, Kaçkar, Bazar-Dyuzi, Babadag, Şemakha, Mingechaur, Ozero Sevan, Gyandzha (Kirovabad), AZERBAIJAN, Sumgait, Baku

TURKEY, Eskişehir, Kütahya, Afyon, Eğridir Gölü, Burdur, Antalya, Beyşehir Gölü, Konya, Karaman, Toros Dağları, CILICIAN GATES, Adana, Mersin, Tarsus, Silifke, Antakya, Kayseri, Erciyes Dağı, Sivas, Divriği, Malatya, Elâziğ, Diyarbakır, Gaziantep, Urfa, Mardin, Nusaybin, Al Hasakah, Büyük Ağrı Dağı (Mt. Ararat), Van Gölü, Erzurum, Muş, Murat, Aragats, Yerevan, ARMENIA, Nakhichevan, Araks, Tabriz, Ardabīl, Orūmīyeh, Daryācheh-ye Orūmīyeh (L. Urmia), Mīāneh, Rasht

CYPRUS, TURKISH REPUBLIC OF NORTHERN CYPRUS, Nicosia, Olympus, UN Buffer Zone, Limassol, Larnaca, LEBANON, Trâblous (Tripoli), Beyrouth (Beirut), Tartūs, Lattakia, Halab (Aleppo), Hamāh, Hims, Dimashq (Damascus), SYRIA, Ar Raqqah, Dayr az Zawr, Euphrates, Abu Kamāl, Tadmur, IRAQ, Mesopotamia, Tigris, Mosul, Arbīl, As Sulaymānīyah, Kīrkūk, Tikrit, ISRAEL, Beyrouth, ELBURZ Mountains, Qazvīn, Karaj, Tehrān, Sanandaj, Bījār, Zanjān, Qasr-e Shirin

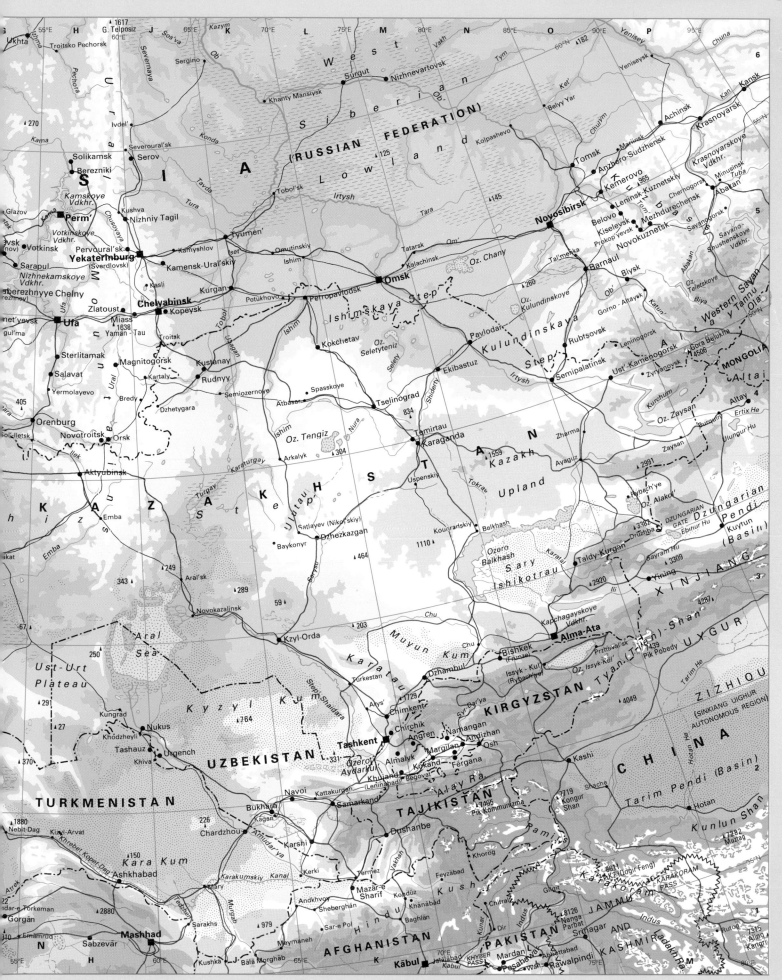

© Oxford University Press

Israel & Lebanon

Scale 1:4 000 000

0   50   100 km

Conical Orthomorphic Projection

Boundaries

international

disputed

internal

Communications

expressway

other major road

railway

canal

✈ major airport

Cities and towns

■ over 1 million
inhabitants

● more than 100 000
inhabitants

• smaller towns

+ historic sites

Physical features

seasonal
river/lake

marsh

salt pan

ice cap

sand dunes

Land height

	metres
	5000
	3000
	2000
	1000
	500
	300
	200
	100
	sea level
	land below sea level

▲ spot height in metres

© Oxford University Press

Scale 1:12 500 000

0   125   250 km

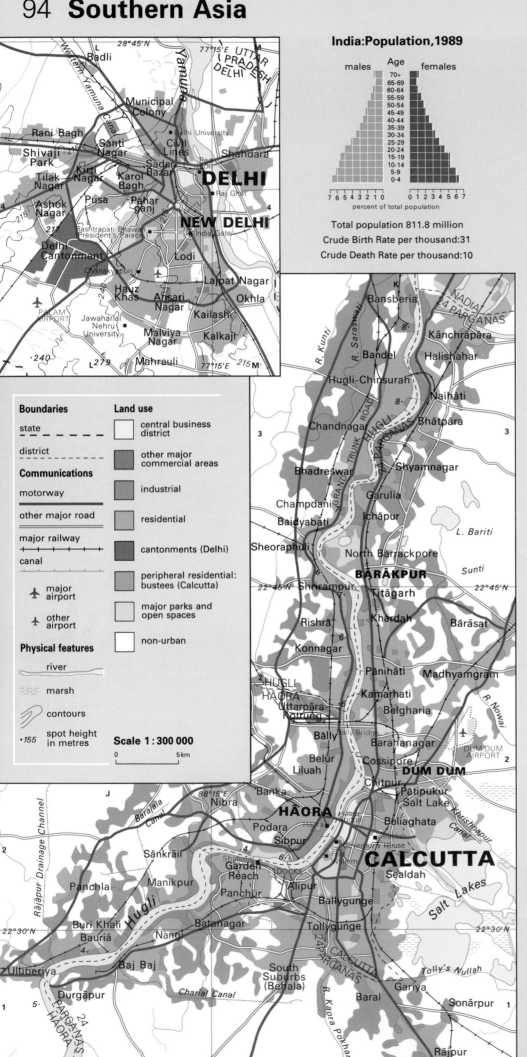

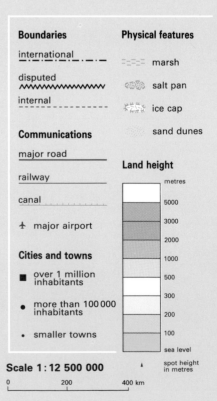

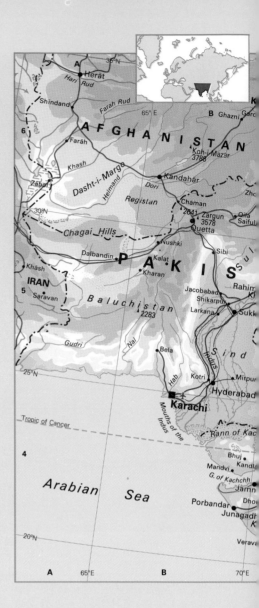

India: Population, 1989

males — Age — females

70+, 65-69, 60-64, 55-59, 50-54, 45-49, 40-44, 35-39, 30-34, 25-29, 20-24, 15-19, 10-14, 5-9, 0-4

7 6 5 4 3 2 1 0 | 0 1 2 3 4 5 6 7
percent of total population

Total population 811.8 million
Crude Birth Rate per thousand: 31
Crude Death Rate per thousand: 10

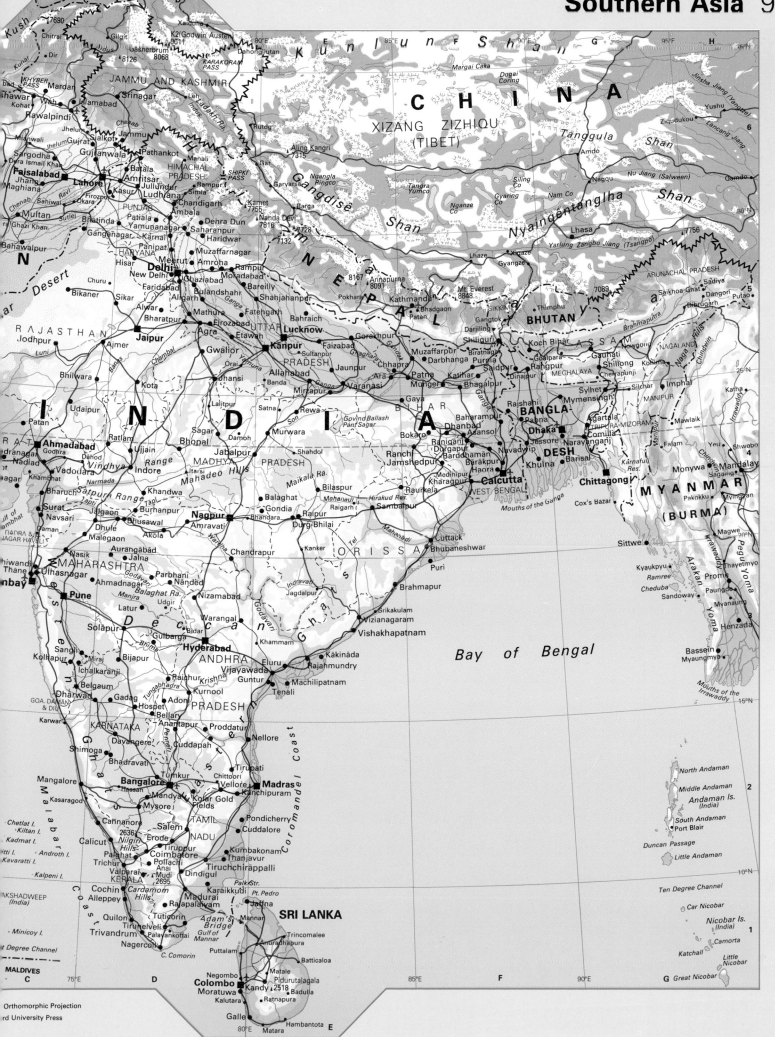

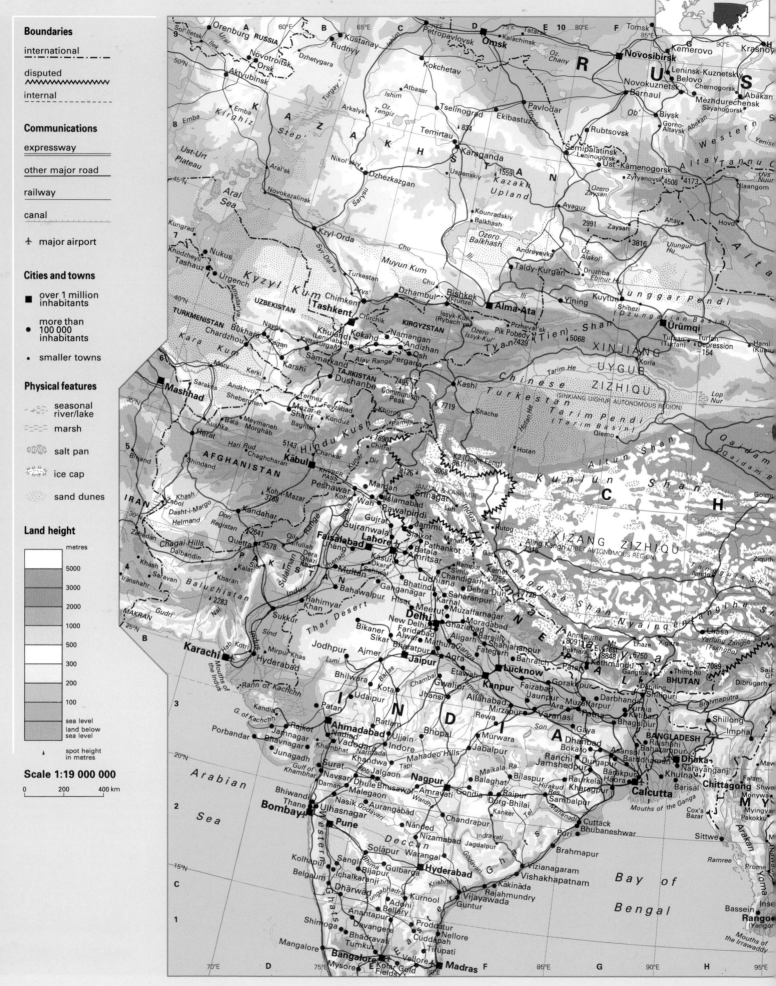

Boundaries

international ·–··–··–

disputed ~~~~~~~~~

internal –·–·–·–·

Communications

expressway

other major road

railway

canal

✈ major airport

Cities and towns

■ over 1 million
  inhabitants

● more than
  100 000
  inhabitants

· smaller towns

Physical features

seasonal
river/lake

marsh

salt pan

ice cap

sand dunes

Land height

metres

5000
3000
2000
1000
500
300
200
100
sea level
land below
sea level

▲ spot height
  in metres

Scale 1:19 000 000

0   200   400 km

Conical Orthomorphic Projec

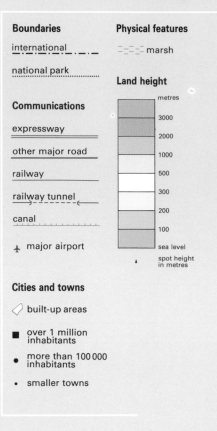

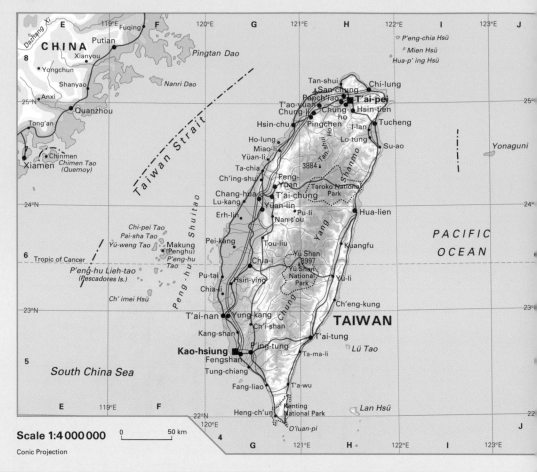

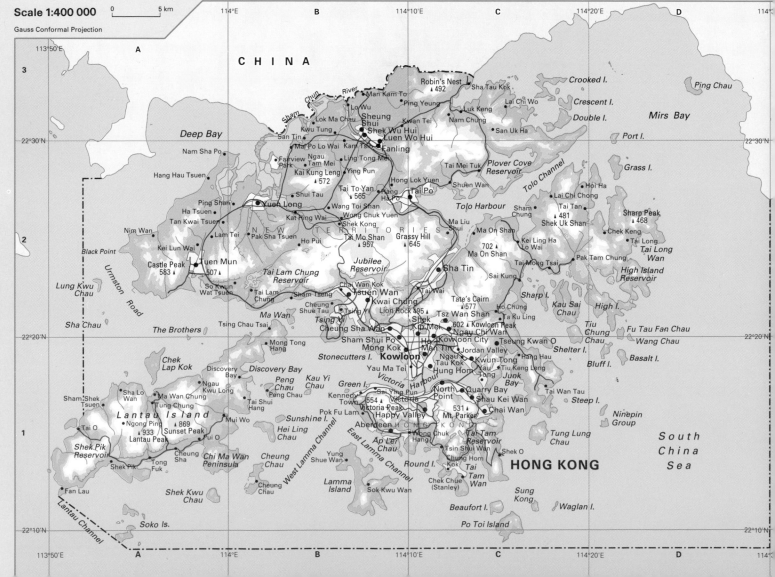

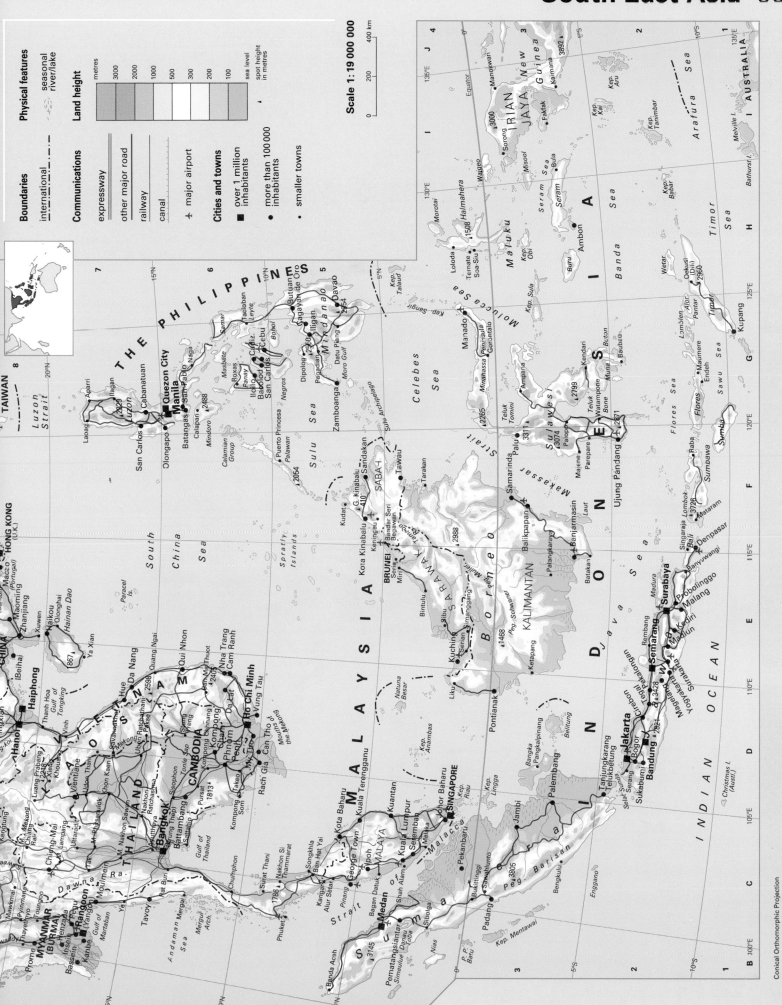

Inset map (Kansai region)

FUKUI
Wakasa-wan
Miyazu
Maizuru
Obama
Takahama
Imazu
Toyooka
Hidaka
Yōka
Wadayama
Ayabe
Miyama
833
Yura-gawa
Fukuchiyama
Hikami
Ikuno
Sannan
Nishiwaki
Sasayama
Senobe
Keihoku
KYŌTO
Kasai
Ono
Sanda
Takarazuka
Kyōto
Ōtsu
SHIGA
Biwa
Hikone
Ōmihachiman
Kusatsu
Moriyama
GIFU
Mino
Seki
Yaotsu
Gifu
Ōgaki
Ibi-gawa
Kakamigahara
Inuyama
Komaki
Kasugai
Toki
Akechi
Ena
Mizunami
Tajimi
Seto
Nagoya
AICHI
Nagahama
Maibara
Hashima
Ichinomiya
Tsushima
Asuke
Toyota
Kameoka
Takatsuki
Ibaraki
Toyonaka
Suita
Uji
Kizu-gawa
Uéno
Kuwana
Yokkaichi
Chita
Handa
Kariya
Anjō
Nishio
Okazaki
Toyoake
Tokoname
Gamagori
Toyokawa
Takasago
Miki
Akashi
Nishinomiya
Amagasaki
Higashi-Osaka
Nara
Tenri
Nabari
Suzuka-sanmyaku
Hakusan
Matsusaka
Kōbe
Ōsaka
Sakai
Yao
Kashihara
Sakurai
1038
Hisai
Tsu
MIE
Harima-nada
Awaji
Izumi takada
Yamato
NARA
Morozaki
Mikawa-wan
Tahara
Atsumi-hantō
Atsumi
Kakogawa
Kishiwada
Kawachi-Nagano
Hashimoto
Gojō
Kushida-gawa
Miya-gawa
Ise
Toba
Ise-wan
Chita-hantō
Kōka
Kino
Yoshino-Kumano
N.P.
Ise shima National Park
Shima-hantō
Ichinomiya
Sumoto
448
Awaji-shima
Tsuna
Misaki
Wakayama
Kainan
Hanazono
WAKAYAMA
Kii-sanchi
Nanto
Ago
Kii-Nagashima
Daiō-zaki
1915
PACIFIC OCEAN

Scale 1 : 2 000 000
0   25   50 km

Inset map (Kantō region)

TOCHIGI
Tomioka
Honjō
Fukuoka
Tatebayashi
Makabe
Ibaraki
Ōarai
GUMMA
Shimonita
Fukaya
Kumagaya
Koga
Shimotsuma
Ishioka
Hokota
Mamba
Yorii
Gyōda
Kuki
Iwai
Tsuchiura
Kasumiga-ura
Kita-ura
Higashi-Matsuyama
SAITAMA
Ageo
Kasukabe
Noda
Mitsukaidō
Ushiku
Aso
IBARAKI
Chichibu
Ogano
Hanno
Ōme
Kawagoe
Ōmiya
Urawa
Koshigaya
Toride
Sawara
Kashima
Arakawa
Chichibu-Tama National Park
Tokorozawa
Tachikawa
Mitaka
Musashino
Kawaguchi
Matsudo
Ichikawa
Narita
Sakura
Asahi
Yokaichiba
Chōshi
Hachiōji
Fuchū
Chofu
Tokyo
Funabashi
Hasaki
YAMANASHI
Ōtsuki
Tsuru
Sagamihara
Yamato
Atsugi
Machida
Komae
TOKYO
Chiba
Naruto
Tōgane
Mobara
Ichihara
Fuji-Hakone
Izu N.P.
1567
Hadano
Hiratsuka
KANAGAWA
Fujisawa
Kamakura
Zushi
Kawasaki
Yokohama
Kisarazu
Kimitsu
Ichihara
Kujūkuri-hama
Shizuoka
Odawara
Yokosuka
Uraga
352
Minami
Ashigara
Gotemba
Hakone
Sagami-wan
Miura
Miura-hantō
Futtsu
Tōkyō-wan
Uraga-suidō
Ōhara
Bōsō-hantō
Mishima
Numazu
Susono
Yugawara
Atami
Itō
Heda
Tsurugi-zaki
Kamogawa
Amatsukominato
Katsuura
Sagami-nada
Tateyama
Mera
Chikura
Nojima-zaki

Main map

Sea of Okhotsk
Rebun-to
Rishiri-tō
Wakkanai
Kuril Islands
Shiretoko-misaki
Kunash (RUSSI)
Shikotan
Teshio
Nayoro
Monbetsu
Abashiri
Nemuro-kaikyō
Habaro
Rumoi
Asahikawa
Asahi dake 2290
Kitami
Shikotan
Nemuro
HOKKAIDŌ
2077
Ishikari-wan
Bibai
Iwamizawa
Yūbari
Kushiro
Yoichi
Otaru
488
Sapporo
Tomakomai
Obihiro
Iwanai
1520
Uchiura-wan
Shiraoi
Mombetsu
Muroran
Mori
Urakawa
Samani
Erimo-misaki
Esashi
Okushiri-tō
Hakodate
Ōhata
Mutsu
Tsugaru-kaikyō
Tappi-zaki
Mutsu-wan
Aomori
Misawa
Hirosaki
Odate
Hachinohe
Noshiro
Nyūdō-zaki
Morioka
Miyako
Akita
Yokote
Ōu-sanmyaku
Kamaishi
2230
Ōfunato
Sakata
Shinjō
Furukawa
Ishinomaki
Tsuruoka
Yamagata
Sendai
Tobi-shima
Awa-shima
Sado-shima
Niigata
2105
Agano
Fukushima
Hegura-jima
Nagaoka
Aizu-Wakamatsu
Kōriyama
Wajima
Suzu-misaki
Kashiwazaki
Shirakawa
Iwaki
Nanao
Honshū
Nikkō
Hitachi
Takaoka
Toyama
Jōetsu
Nagano
Utsunomiya
Mito
Kanazawa
Ueda
Takasaki
Oyama
Tsuchiura
Komatsu
3180
Matsumoto
Okaya
Maebashi
Kiryū
Ashikaga
Kumagaya
Kawagoe
Urawa
Matsudo
Funabashi
Takefu
Fukui
Takayama
Iida
Kōfu
Fujisan 3776
Sagamihara
Hadano
Tokyo
Kawasaki
Chiba
Inubō-zaki
Tsuruga
Ōgaki
Gifu
Ichinomiya
Fujinomiya
Fuji
Odawara
Fujisawa
Yokosuka
Tottori
Konago
Daisen 1731
Matsue
Nagoya
Shimizu
Numazu
Nojima-zaki
Yonago
Suzuka
Toyohashi
Yaizu
755
Ō-shima
Izu-shotō
Oki
Dōgo
Dōzen
Kyōga-misaki
Wakasa-wan
Maizuru
Biwa-ko
Ōtsu
Yokkaichi
Anjō
Okazaki
Hamamatsu
Nii-jima
Kyōto
Kōbe
Amagasaki
Hirakata
Nara
Tsu
Ise
Nii-jima
Izu-shotō
Ōda
Tsuyama
Himeji
Akashi
Ōsaka
Sakai
Yao
Kishiwada
1915
Daiō-zaki
Masuda
Chūgoku
Okayama
Harima-nada
Wakayama
Tanabe
Shingū
Hamada
Kurashiki
Naruto
Shiono-misaki
1510
Hiroshima
Onomichi
Kure
Takamatsu
Tokushima
Anan
Kii-suidō
Yamaguchi
Iwakuni
Niihama
Imabari
Matsuyama
1981
Shikoku
Kōchi
Nagato
Tokuyama
Hofu
Seto Naikai
Nada
Iyo-nada
Ube
Shimonoseki
Kita-Kyūshū
Yawatahama
Uwajima
Muroto
Tosa-wan
Muroto-zaki
Higashi-suidō
Iki
Fukuoka
Saga
Kurume
Beppu
Ōita
Nakamura
Ashizuri-misaki
Tsushima
Sasebo
Ōmuta
Kuju-san 1788
Nobeoka
Nagasaki
Kumamoto
1739
Yatsushiro
Bungo-suidō
Amakusa-shotō
Minamata
1700
Miyazaki
Kyūshū
Sendai
Miyakonojō
Kagoshima
Kanoya

Sea of Japan

PACIFIC OCEAN

Legend

Boundaries
international
internal
national park

Communications
expressway
other major road
railway
canal
✈ major airport

Cities and towns
built-up areas
■ over 1 million inhabitants
● more than 100 000 inhabitants
• smaller towns

Land height
metres
3000
2000
1000
500
300
200
100
sea level
spot height in metres

Zenithal Equidistant Projection

Scale 1 : 6 250 000
0   50   100 km

© Oxford University Press

Land height

metres
5000
3000
2000
1000
500
300
200
100
sea level
land below sea level
· spot height in metres

Sea depth

sea level
200
3000
4000
5000
6000

Land below sea level and sea depths shown as minus numbers

sand desert

Scale 1 : 44 000 000

0   500   1000 km

NORTH ATLANTIC OCEAN

Iberian Peninsula

Madeira Is.

Canary Is.

Str. of Gibraltar

Haut Atlas   Atlas Saharien

4165

Grand Erg Occidental   Grand Erg Oriental

Mediterranean Sea

Adriatic Sea   Danube

Aegean Sea   Anatolian Plateau

Black   Sea

Caspian Sea

Cyprus   Zagros Mts.

Euphrates   Tigris

C. Bon   G. of Gabès

Gulf of Sirte   Libyan Desert

Nile Delta   Sinai   Dead Sea   An Nafud

Tropic of Cancer

133 Qattara Depression   Western Desert

Red Sea   Asir Mtns.   Rub'al Khali

C. Blanc

Erg Iguidi   Sahara   Desert

Tanezrouft   Hoggar   Tibe ti 3415

Kufrah Oasis

L. Nasser   Nubian Desert

Bab el Mandab   C. Guardafui

-3268   Hadramaut

Niger   Bodélé

Senegal

Fouta Djallon

C. Vert

Niger

L. Chad   Chari

Jebel Marra   4620

White Nile   Blue Nile   Atbara   Danakil

Jos Plateau

Benue   Sanaga   4095

Kainji Res.   Volta   Volta

Bight of Benin   Niger Delta

C. Palmas   Gulf of Guinea   Bight of Bonny

Guinea Depression

Adamawa Mtns.

2829

Sanga   Oubangui   Uele   Zaïre (Congo)

Sudd   Bahr el Ghazal   Ethiopian Highlands   Ogaden

Shebele

Bomu

Jub

L. Turkana

Lomami   MT. RUWENZORI 5120

Kasai   L. Mai Ndombe   Lualaba

East Rift Valley

L. Kyoga   L. Victoria   Serengeti

5895 KILIMANJARO   Equator

-534

Pemba I.   Zanzibar

INDIAN OCEAN

Ascension I.

SOUTH ATLANTIC OCEAN

Cuango   Cuilu   Lulua   Luapula

Mitumba Mts   West Rift Valley   L. Tanganyika

Aldabra Is.

St. Helena

Angola Depression

2610   Angola Plateau

L. Bangweula   L. Nyasa (L. Malawi)

Rovuma   Comoro Archipelago

Cunene   Cuito

Muchinga Mts   Zambezi

Kariba L.

Mozambique Channel   Madagascar

Namib Desert   Okavango Basin

Makgadikgadi Salt Pan

Limpopo   2658

Tropic of Capricorn

Kalahari Desert

Vaal

Namib Desert   High Veld   Drakensberg   3482

C. of Good Hope   C. Agulhas   C. St. Francis

Orange

Gt. Karoo

Zenithal Equal Area Projection

Africa: Political

— international boundary
· national capital

Names of commonwealth members are underlined

Scale 1 : 80 000 000

0   500   1000 km

CEUTA (Sp.)   Rabat   Alger   Tunis
MELILLA (Sp.)   Sale   TUNISIA
Madeira (Port.)
Canary Is. (Sp.)   MOROCCO   ALGERIA   Tarābulus (Tripoli)   Cairo
WESTERN SAHARA   LIBYA   EGYPT
CAPE VERDE IS.   MAURITANIA   Nouakchott
Praia Dakar   MALI   NIGER   CHAD   Khartoum   DJIBOUTI
THE GAMBIA   SENEGAL   Bamako   Niamey   Ndjamena   SUDAN   Djibouti   Ādīs
Banjul   BURKINA   Ouagadougou   ETHIOPIA   Ābeba
Bissau   GUINEA-BISSAU   GUINEA   NIGERIA   CENTRAL AFRICAN REPUBLIC
Conakry   CÔTE D'IVOIRE   Abuja   Bangui
Freetown   SIERRA LEONE   GHANA   Porto Novo   CAMEROON   Yaoundé   UGANDA   SOMALIA
Monrovia   LIBERIA   BENIN   Lomé   CONGO   Malabo   Yaoundé   KENYA   Mogadishu
Yamoussoukro   Accra   EQU. GUINEA   Kampala   Nairobi
São Tomé   SAO TOME AND PRINCIPE   GABON   Libreville   ZAÏRE   Kigali   RWANDA
CABINDA (Angola)   Brazzaville   Kinshasa   Bujumbura   BURUNDI   TANZANIA   Dodoma
Luanda   ANGOLA   ZAMBIA   MALAWI   Lilongwe   Aldabra Is. (Seychelles)
Lusaka   Moroni   COMOROS
ZIMBABWE   Harare   MOZAMBIQUE
Windhoek   BOTSWANA   MADAGASCAR
WALVIS BAY (S. Africa)   NAMIBIA   Gaborone   Pretoria   Maputo   Antananarivo
REPUBLIC OF   Maseru   LESOTHO   Mbabane   SWAZILAND
SOUTH AFRICA

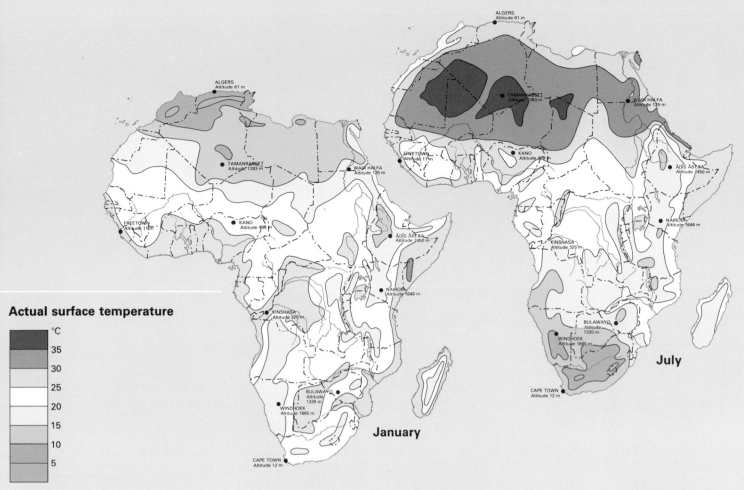

Actual surface temperature

°C
- 35
- 30
- 25
- 20
- 15
- 10
- 5

January

July

Scale 1 : 80 000 000

0   500   1000 km

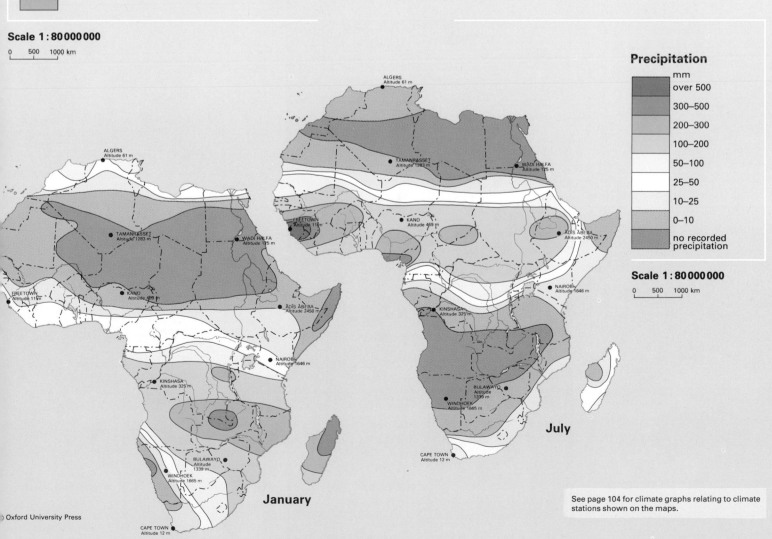

Precipitation

mm
- over 500
- 300–500
- 200–300
- 100–200
- 50–100
- 25–50
- 10–25
- 0–10
- no recorded precipitation

Scale 1 : 80 000 000

0   500   1000 km

January

July

See page 104 for climate graphs relating to climate stations shown on the maps.

© Oxford University Press

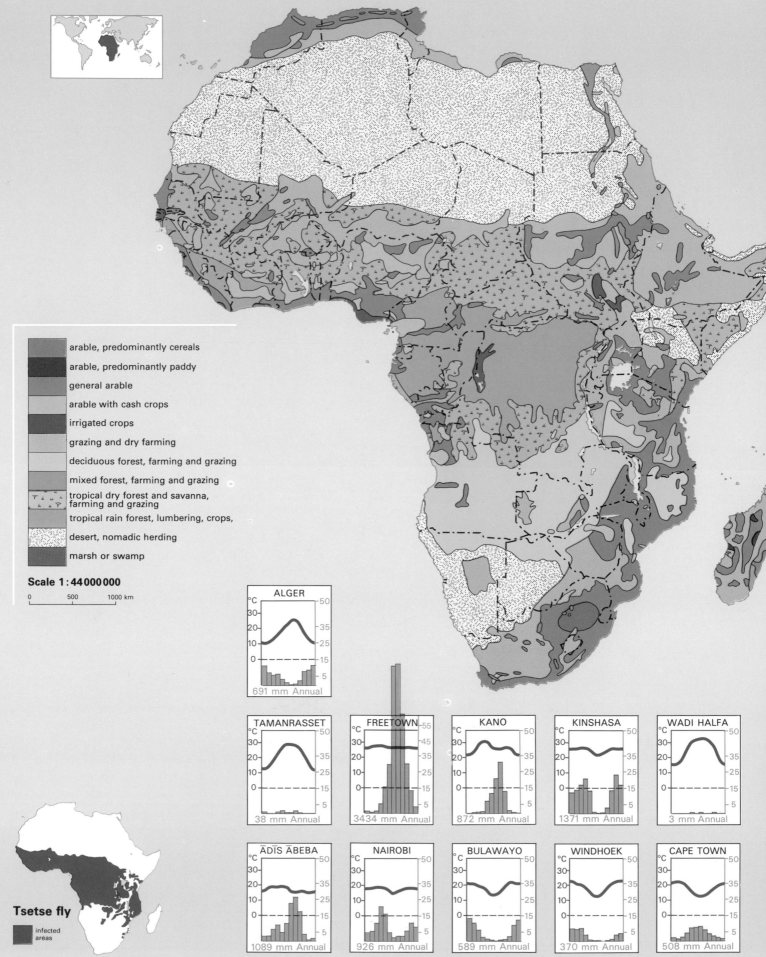

arable, predominantly cereals

arable, predominantly paddy

general arable

arable with cash crops

irrigated crops

grazing and dry farming

deciduous forest, farming and grazing

mixed forest, farming and grazing

tropical dry forest and savanna, farming and grazing

tropical rain forest, lumbering, crops,

desert, nomadic herding

marsh or swamp

Scale 1:44 000 000

0   500   1000 km

Tsetse fly

infected areas

ALGER
°C / 50
691 mm Annual

TAMANRASSET
°C / 50
38 mm Annual

FREETOWN
°C / 55
3434 mm Annual

KANO
°C / 50
872 mm Annual

KINSHASA
°C / 50
1371 mm Annual

WADI HALFA
°C / 50
3 mm Annual

ĀDĪS ĀBEBA
°C / 50
1089 mm Annual

NAIROBI
°C / 50
926 mm Annual

BULAWAYO
°C / 50
589 mm Annual

WINDHOEK
°C / 50
370 mm Annual

CAPE TOWN
°C / 50
508 mm Annual

Precipitation figures on graphs in tens of millimetres except for annual totals

Zenithal Equal Area Project

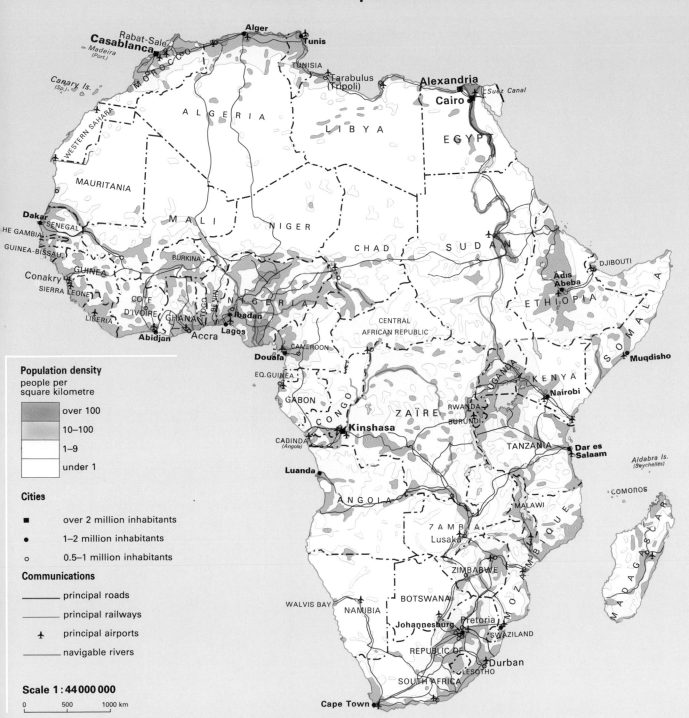

Population density
people per
square kilometre

- over 100
- 10–100
- 1–9
- under 1

Cities

- ■ over 2 million inhabitants
- ● 1–2 million inhabitants
- ○ 0.5–1 million inhabitants

Communications

- principal roads
- principal railways
- ✈ principal airports
- navigable rivers

Scale 1 : 44 000 000

0   500   1000 km

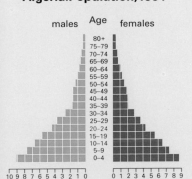

Algeria:Population,1984

males   Age   females

percent of total population

Total Population:20.8 million

Crude Birth Rate per thousand:37

Crude Death Rate per thousand:10

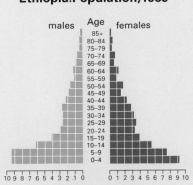

Ethiopia:Population,1989

males   Age   females

percent of total population

Total population:49.5 million

Crude Birth Rate per thousand:49

Crude Death Rate per thousand:20

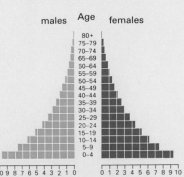

Zaïre:Population,1985

males   Age   females

percent of total population

Total population:31 million

Crude Birth Rate per thousand:46

Crude Death Rate per thousand:14

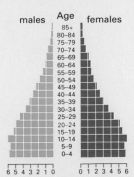

South Africa:Population,1985

males   Age   females

percent of total population

Total population:23.4 million

Crude Birth Rate per thousand:35

Crude Death Rate per thousand:8

Oxford University Press

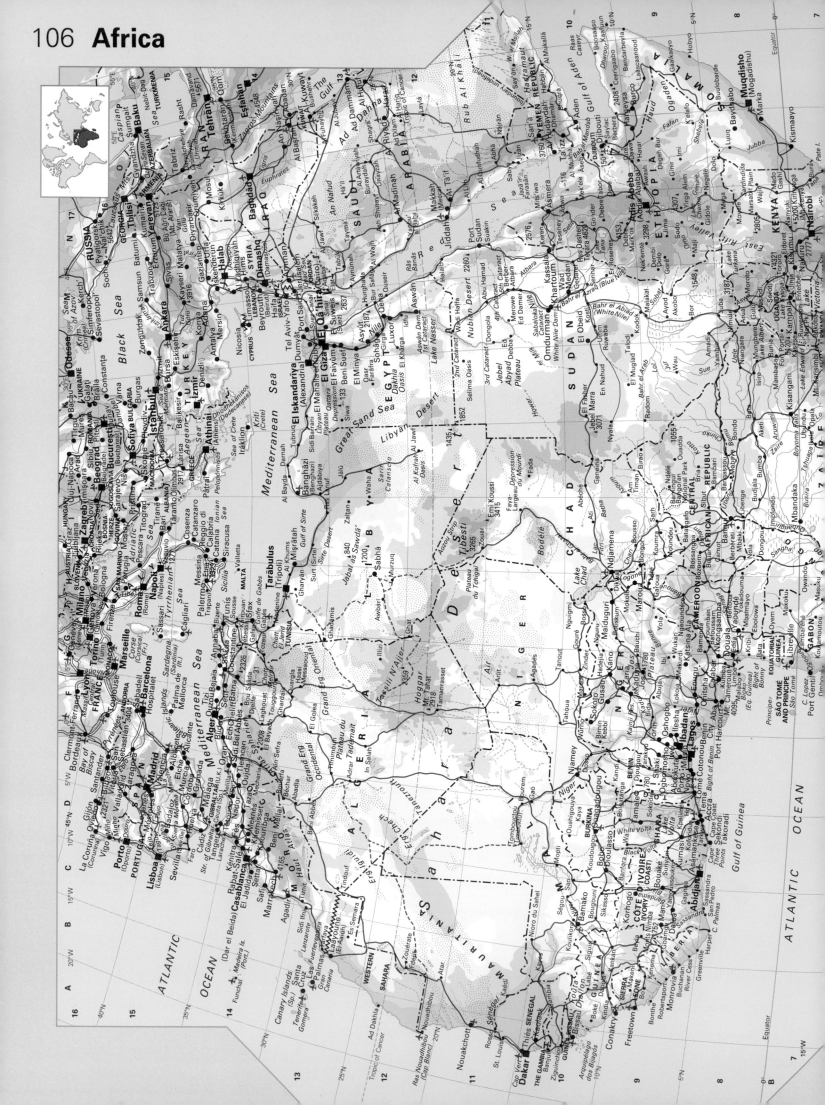

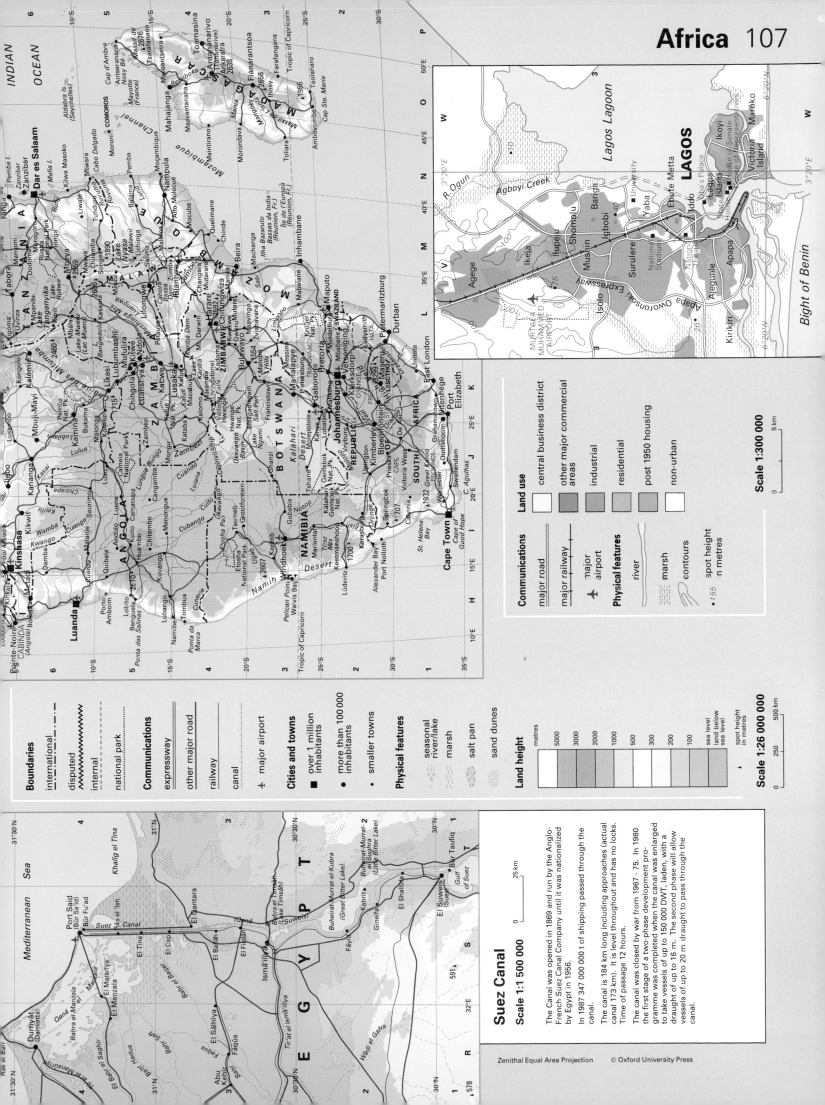

Lagos

Scale 1:300 000

Land use
- central business district
- other major commercial areas
- industrial
- residential
- post 1950 housing
- non-urban

Communications
- major road
- major railway
- ✈ major airport

Physical features
- river
- marsh
- contours
- ·155 spot height in metres

Suez Canal

Scale 1:1 500 000

The Canal was opened in 1869 and run by the Anglo-French Suez Canal Company until it was nationalized by Egypt in 1956.

In 1987 347 000 000 t of shipping passed through the canal.

The canal is 184 km long including approaches (actual canal 173 km). It is level throughout and has no locks. Time of passage 12 hours.

The canal was closed by war from 1967 - 75. In 1980 the first stage of a two-phase development pro-gramme was completed when the canal was enlarged to take vessels of up to 150 000 DWT, laden, with a draught of up to 16 m. The second phase will allow vessels of up to 20 m. draught to pass through the canal.

Boundaries
- international
- disputed
- internal
- national park

Communications
- expressway
- other major road
- railway
- canal
- ✈ major airport

Cities and towns
- ■ over 1 million inhabitants
- ● more than 100 000 inhabitants
- • smaller towns

Physical features
- seasonal river/lake
- marsh
- salt pan
- sand dunes

Land height
metres
5000
3000
2000
1000
500
300
200
100
sea level
land below sea level
spot height in metres

Scale 1:26 000 000

Zenithal Equal Area Projection   © Oxford University Press

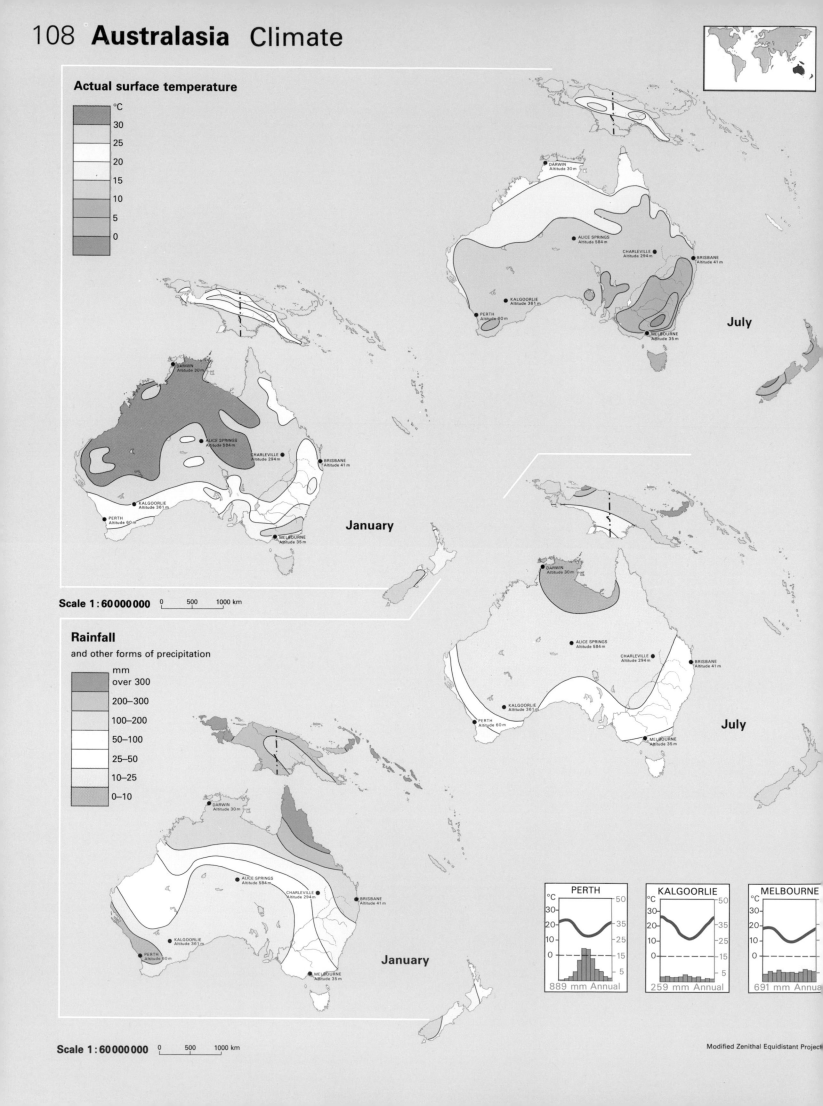

Actual surface temperature

°C
30
25
20
15
10
5
0

July

January

Scale 1 : 60 000 000   0   500   1000 km

Rainfall
and other forms of precipitation

mm
over 300
200–300
100–200
50–100
25–50
10–25
0–10

July

January

Scale 1 : 60 000 000   0   500   1000 km

DARWIN
Altitude 30 m

ALICE SPRINGS
Altitude 584 m

CHARLEVILLE
Altitude 294 m

BRISBANE
Altitude 41 m

KALGOORLIE
Altitude 361 m

PERTH
Altitude 60 m

MELBOURNE
Altitude 35 m

PERTH
°C   50
30   35
20
10   25
0   15
            5
889 mm Annual

KALGOORLIE
°C   50
30   35
20
10   25
0   15
            5
259 mm Annual

MELBOURNE
°C   50
30   35
20
10   25
0   15
            5
691 mm Annual

Modified Zenithal Equidistant Project

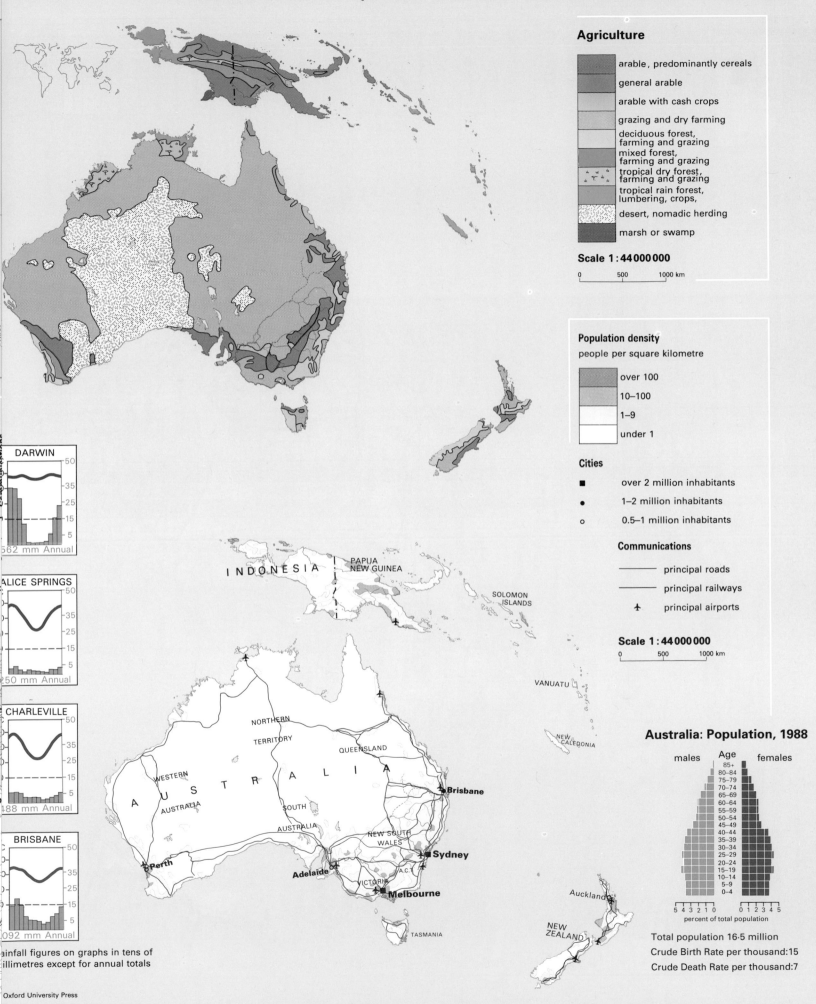

Agriculture

- arable, predominantly cereals
- general arable
- arable with cash crops
- grazing and dry farming
- deciduous forest, farming and grazing
- mixed forest, farming and grazing
- tropical dry forest, farming and grazing
- tropical rain forest, lumbering, crops,
- desert, nomadic herding
- marsh or swamp

Scale 1:44 000 000

0   500   1000 km

Population density
people per square kilometre

- over 100
- 10–100
- 1–9
- under 1

Cities

- ■ over 2 million inhabitants
- ● 1–2 million inhabitants
- ○ 0.5–1 million inhabitants

Communications

- ——— principal roads
- ——— principal railways
- ✈ principal airports

Scale 1:44 000 000

0   500   1000 km

DARWIN
1562 mm Annual

ALICE SPRINGS
250 mm Annual

CHARLEVILLE
488 mm Annual

BRISBANE
1092 mm Annual

Rainfall figures on graphs in tens of millimetres except for annual totals

INDONESIA

PAPUA
NEW GUINEA

SOLOMON
ISLANDS

VANUATU

NEW
CALEDONIA

NORTHERN
TERRITORY

QUEENSLAND

WESTERN
AUSTRALIA

A U S T R A L I A

SOUTH
AUSTRALIA

NEW SOUTH
WALES

Brisbane

Perth

Adelaide

A.C.T

Sydney

VICTORIA

Melbourne

Auckland

TASMANIA

NEW
ZEALAND

Australia: Population, 1988

males   Age   females

	85+	
	80–84	
	75–79	
	70–74	
	65–69	
	60–64	
	55–59	
	50–54	
	45–49	
	40–44	
	35–39	
	30–34	
	25–29	
	20–24	
	15–19	
	10–14	
	5–9	
	0–4	

5 4 3 2 1 0   0 1 2 3 4 5
percent of total population

Total population 16·5 million

Crude Birth Rate per thousand: 15

Crude Death Rate per thousand: 7

Oxford University Press

Boundaries

international

disputed

Cities and towns

■ over 1 million inhabitants

● more than 100 000 inhabitants

• smaller towns

national capitals are underlined

Land height

metres

5000
3000
2000
1000
500
300
200
100
sea level
land below sea level

Sea depth

metres below sea level

-200
-3000
-4000
-5000
-6000

▲ spot height in metres

sea depths shown as minus numbers

Ocean currents

→ warm

⇢ cold

Scale 1:63 000 000

0   500   1000   1500km

Modified Zenithal Equidistant Projection

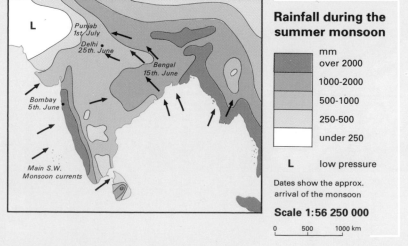

Rainfall during the summer monsoon

Punjab 1st July
Delhi 25th June
Bengal 15th June
Bombay 5th June
Main S.W. Monsoon currents

mm
over 2000
1000-2000
500-1000
250-500
under 250

L low pressure

Dates show the approx. arrival of the monsoon

Scale 1:56 250 000

0   500   1000 km

Modified Zenithal Equidistant Projection
© Oxford University Press

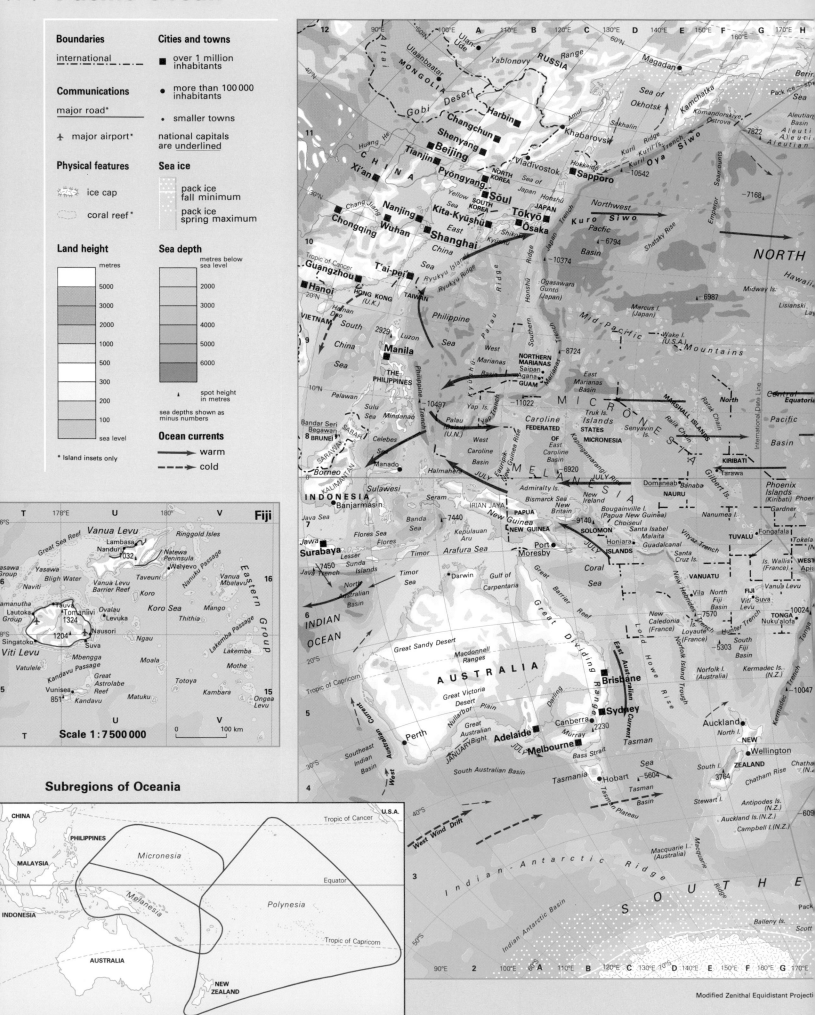

Boundaries
international

Communications
major road*

✈ major airport*

Physical features
🌨 ice cap

〰 coral reef*

Cities and towns
■ over 1 million inhabitants

● more than 100 000 inhabitants

• smaller towns

national capitals are underlined

Sea ice
pack ice fall minimum

pack ice spring maximum

Land height
metres
5000
3000
2000
1000
500
300
200
100
sea level

Sea depth
metres below sea level
2000
3000
4000
5000
6000

▲ spot height in metres

sea depths shown as minus numbers

Ocean currents
→ warm
--→ cold

* Island insets only

Fiji
Scale 1:7 500 000
0   100 km

Subregions of Oceania

Modified Zenithal Equidistant Projecti

J 160°W K 150°W L 140°W M 130°W N 120°W O 110°W P 100°W Q 90°W 60°W 80°W 70°W 13

W   X   Y   Z

Kilanea Kapaa
Kauai
Kaula
Niihau Kauai Channel Waialua Wahiawa Kahuku Pt.
Kaula Kekaha Oahu Pearl Harbor Kaneohe
          Honolulu
                    Molokai C. Halawa
          Lanai City Lanai Lahaina Wailuku Maui
          Kahoolawe Alenuihaha Channel Upolu Pt.

18   18

17 160°W X 158°W Y

Bering Strait
J
Arctic Circle
ALASKA (U.S.A.) Mt. McKinley 6194
Mt. Logan 5951
Anchorage
Gulf of Alaska
Kodiak I.
Nunivak I.
Bering Sea
ridge
Trench

Queen Charlotte Is.
Vancouver I. Vancouver
Seattle

CANADA
Rocky Mountains
Great Slave Lake
Saskatchewan
Canadian Shield
Churchill
Hudson Bay

12

Winnipeg

Minneapolis-St. Paul
Great Lakes
Toronto
Chicago 40°N

11

Gorda Rise
Mendocino Seascarp
PACIFIC OCEAN
Murray Seascarp
-6474
-6108

UNITED STATES
Salt Lake City
Mt. Elbert 4399
Colorado

San Francisco
Los Angeles
Houston
Rio Grande
New Orleans 30°N

NORTH 60°W
Tropic of Cancer
ATLANTIC OCEAN 10

10

Guadalupe (Mexico)
Roca Alijos
-5106
Is. Revillagigedo (Mexico)

MEXICO
Guadalajara México 5452
Acapulco

Gulf of Mexico
Miami
La Habana CUBA
THE BAHAMAS

North Equatorial Current

9220 Puerto Rico Trench
HAITI DOMINICAN REPUBLIC
JAMAICA Kingston PUERTO RICO (U.S.A.) Leeward Is. DOMINICA
Yucatan Basin Cayman Trench
BELIZE
Middle America Trench GUATEMALA HONDURAS
Clarion Fracture Zone
-5106 California Current

9

Islands (U.S.A.)
Nihoa Nihau
Honolulu
Hawaii
East Pacific Basin
Clarion Fracture Zone

Hawaiian Ridge

JANUARY
JULY -5298
Clipperton Fracture Zone JULY

Equatorial Counter Current

EL SALVADOR -6662 NICARAGUA
Managua Tegucigalpa
San Jose COSTA RICA
PANAMA
Panamá
Guatemala Basin
Guatemala Trench
Barranquilla Caracas
Venezuelan Basin
Caribbean Sea
Maracaibo VENEZUELA
Llanos Orinoco
BARBADOS
GRENADA
TRINIDAD & TOBAGO
Guyana Basin
Georgetown Guyana
Paramaribo SURINAM Cayenne
FRENCH GUIANA

8

Christmas Island JANUARY
Current JULY
Palmyra Atoll (U.S.A.)
Tabuaaran I. (Kiribati)
Kiritimati I. (Kiribati)
Line (Kiribati) Islands Ridge

Clipperton I. (France)
Pacific Rise
I. del Coco (Costa Rica)
Cocos Ridge
Medellín
COLOMBIA
Bogotá
Cali -5750

Equatorial Current
Equator
Malden I.
Caroline I.
-6584

Islas Galápagos (Ecuador)
Carnegie Ridge
Quito -6310
ECUADOR
Manaus Amazonas
BRAZIL

7

Marquesas Islands (France)
Palmerston Atoll (N.Z.)
Society Is. (France) Tahiti
French Polynesia
Cook Is. (N.Z.)
Tuamotu Ridge
Tuamotu Archipelago (France)
Tubuai Is. (France)
Austral Ridge
Gambier Is. Oano I. Ducie I.
Pitcairn Islands (U.K.)

East Pacific Ridge
Galápagos Rise
-5469
Peru Basin
PERU
-6768
-6601
Lima 10°S
Mato Grosso

Nasca Ridge
L. Titicaca -6388
La Paz
BOLIVIA Santa Cruz
Brasília 6

7

-144
-6584

JULY
SOUTH PACIFIC OCEAN
-1088 JULY
South West Pacific Basin
JANUARY

Easter I. (Chile)
Salay Gomez (Chile)
Easter Island Fracture Zone
I. San Felix (Chile)
Islas Juan Fernández (Chile)
-8066
-6755
Humboldt or Peru Current
Peru-Chile Trench
PARAGUAY
Gran Chaco
Asunción
Rio de Janeiro
Tropic of Capricorn
São Paulo 5

6

Eltanin Fracture Zone
Antarctic Ridge
Pacific Challenger Fracture Zone
West Wind Drift
Chile Basin
Chile Rise
Isla de Chiloé
Isla Wellington
Concepción
Valparaíso Santiago
Córdoba -6960
South East Pacific Basin

CHILE
ARGENTINA
Paraná
Rosario URUGUAY
Buenos Aires
Montevideo
Porto Alegre
Brazil Current
Rio Grande Rise 30°S 5

N

Spring maximum
Pack ice - fall minimum
Antarctic Circle

Patagonia
Pto. Santa Cruz
Isla Grande de Tierra del Fuego
C. de Hornos
Falkland Is. (U.K.)
Falkland Current
West Wind Drift
Argentine Basin
40°W 30°S 4

4

I 170°W J 160°W K 150°W L 140°W M 130°W N 120°W O 110°W P 100°W Q 90°W R 80°W S 70°W T 60°W U 50°W V 40°W W 30°W

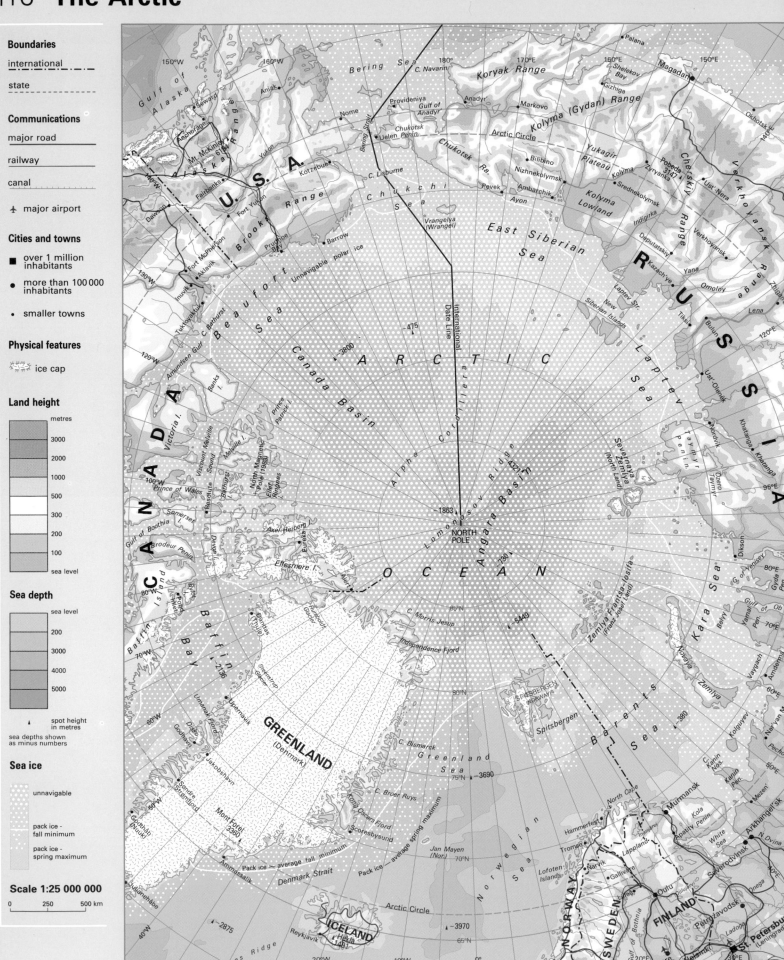

Boundaries
international
state

Communications
major road
railway
canal

✈ major airport

Cities and towns
■ over 1 million inhabitants
● more than 100 000 inhabitants
• smaller towns

Physical features
ice cap

Land height

metres
3000
2000
1000
500
300
200
100
sea level

Sea depth

sea level
200
3000
4000
5000

▲ spot height in metres
sea depths shown as minus numbers

Sea ice
unnavigable
pack ice - fall minimum
pack ice - spring maximum

Scale 1:25 000 000
0   250   500 km

Zenithal Equidistant Projection

© Oxford University Press

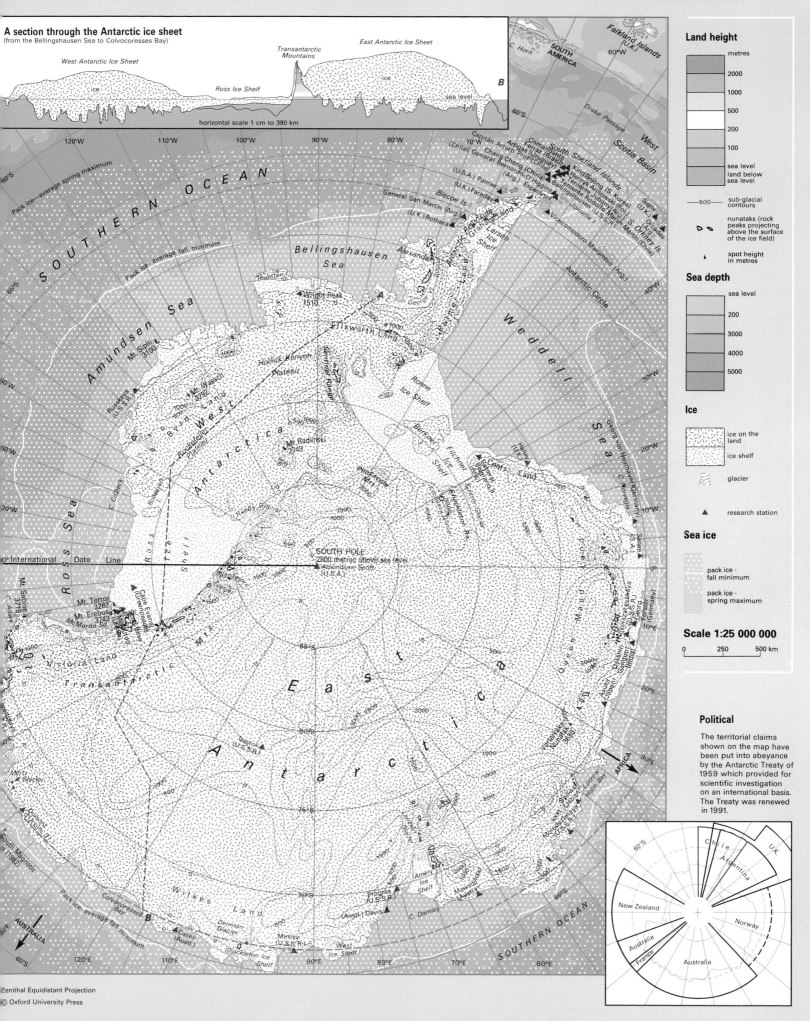

World Political

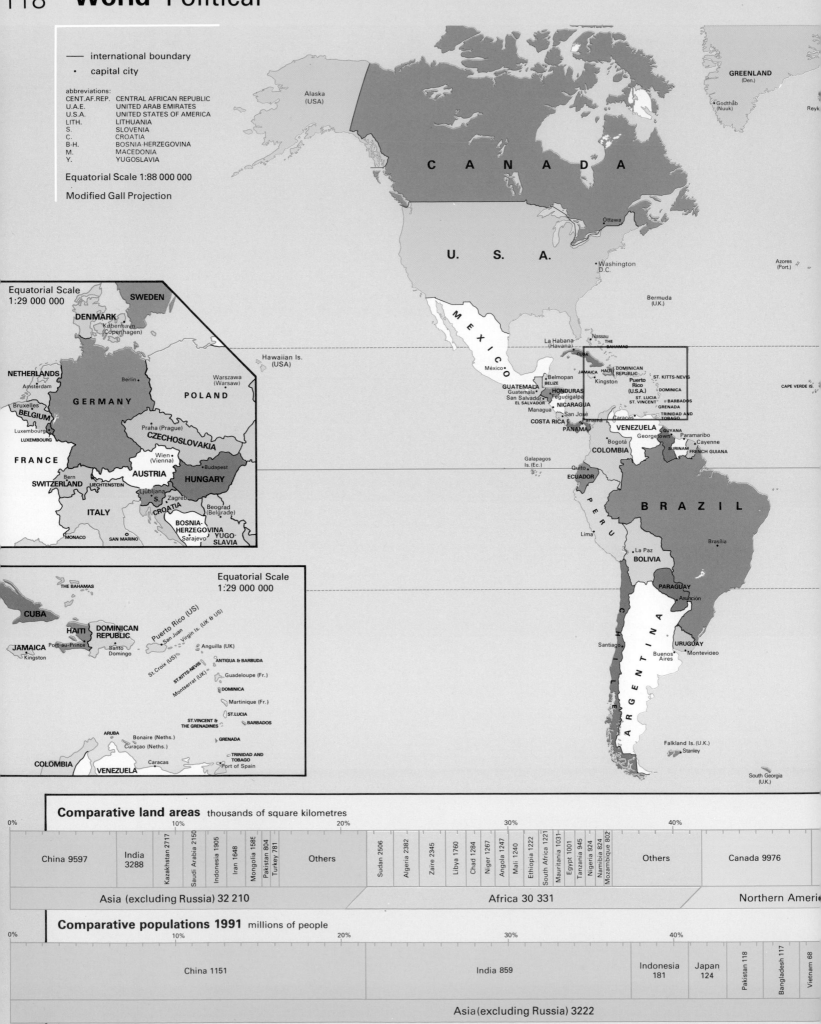

— international boundary
• capital city

abbreviations:
CENT.AF.REP. CENTRAL AFRICAN REPUBLIC
U.A.E. UNITED ARAB EMIRATES
U.S.A. UNITED STATES OF AMERICA
LITH. LITHUANIA
S. SLOVENIA
C. CROATIA
B-H. BOSNIA-HERZEGOVINA
M. MACEDONIA
Y. YUGOSLAVIA

Equatorial Scale 1:88 000 000

Modified Gall Projection

Equatorial Scale 1:29 000 000

SWEDEN
DENMARK
København (Copenhagen)
NETHERLANDS
Amsterdam
Berlin •
GERMANY
POLAND
Warszawa (Warsaw)
Bruxelles
BELGIUM
Luxembourg
LUXEMBOURG
Praha (Prague) •
CZECHOSLOVAKIA
FRANCE
Wien (Vienna) •
• Budapest
Bern •
SWITZERLAND
LIECHTENSTEIN
AUSTRIA
HUNGARY
Ljubljana
S.
Zagreb
ITALY
CROATIA
BOSNIA-HERZEGOVINA
Sarajevo •
YUGO-SLAVIA
Beograd (Belgrade)
MONACO
SAN MARINO

Equatorial Scale 1:29 000 000

THE BAHAMAS
CUBA
HAITI
Port-au-Prince
DOMINICAN REPUBLIC
Santo Domingo
Puerto Rico (US)
San Juan
Virgin Is. (UK & US)
JAMAICA
Kingston
St.Croix (US)
Anguilla (UK)
ANTIGUA & BARBUDA
ST.KITTS-NEVIS
Montserrat (UK)
Guadeloupe (Fr.)
DOMINICA
Martinique (Fr.)
ST.LUCIA
ST.VINCENT & THE GRENADINES
BARBADOS
ARUBA
Bonaire (Neths.)
Curaçao (Neths.)
GRENADA
COLOMBIA
Caracas
VENEZUELA
TRINIDAD AND TOBAGO
Port of Spain

GREENLAND (Den.)
• Godthåb (Nuuk)
• Reyk

Alaska (USA)

C A N A D A
• Ottawa

U. S. A.
• Washington D.C.

Azores (Port.)

Bermuda (U.K.)

MEXICO
• México

Hawaiian Is. (USA)

La Habana (Havana)
Nassau
THE BAHAMAS
CUBA
JAMAICA
HAITI
DOMINICAN REPUBLIC
Kingston
Puerto Rico (U.S.A.)
ST. KITTS-NEVIS
DOMINICA
ST. LUCIA
ST. VINCENT
BARBADOS
GRENADA
TRINIDAD AND TOBAGO

GUATEMALA
Guatemala •
San Salvador •
EL SALVADOR
Belmopan
BELIZE
HONDURAS
Tegucigalpa
NICARAGUA
Managua
COSTA RICA
San José •
PANAMA
Panamá •

Caracas •
VENEZUELA

Galapagos Is. (Ec.)

COLOMBIA
Bogotá •
Quito •
ECUADOR

GUYANA
Georgetown •
SURINAM
Paramaribo •
Cayenne •
FRENCH GUIANA

CAPE VERDE

P E R U
Lima •

B R A Z I L
Brasília •

La Paz •
BOLIVIA

PARAGUAY
Asunción •

C H I L E
Santiago •

A R G E N T I N A
Buenos Aires •

URUGUAY
Montevideo •

Falkland Is. (U.K.)
• Stanley

South Georgia (U.K.)

Comparative land areas thousands of square kilometres

0%		10%							20%		30%																40%	

| China 9597 | India 3288 | Kazakhstan 2717 | Saudi Arabia 2150 | Indonesia 1905 | Iran 1648 | Mongolia 1565 | Pakistan 804 | Turkey 781 | Others | Sudan 2506 | Algeria 2382 | Zaire 2345 | Libya 1760 | Chad 1284 | Niger 1267 | Angola 1247 | Mali 1240 | Ethiopia 1222 | South Africa 1221 | Mauritania 1031 | Egypt 1001 | Tanzania 945 | Nigeria 924 | Namibia 824 | Mozambique 802 | Others | Canada 9976 |

| Asia (excluding Russia) 32 210 | | | | | | | | | | Africa 30 331 | | | | | | | | | | | | | | | | | Northern Americ |

Comparative populations 1991 millions of people

0%		10%		20%		30%		40%		

| China 1151 | | | India 859 | | | Indonesia 181 | Japan 124 | Pakistan 118 | Bangladesh 117 | Vietnam 68 |

| Asia (excluding Russia) 3222 | | | | | | | | | | |

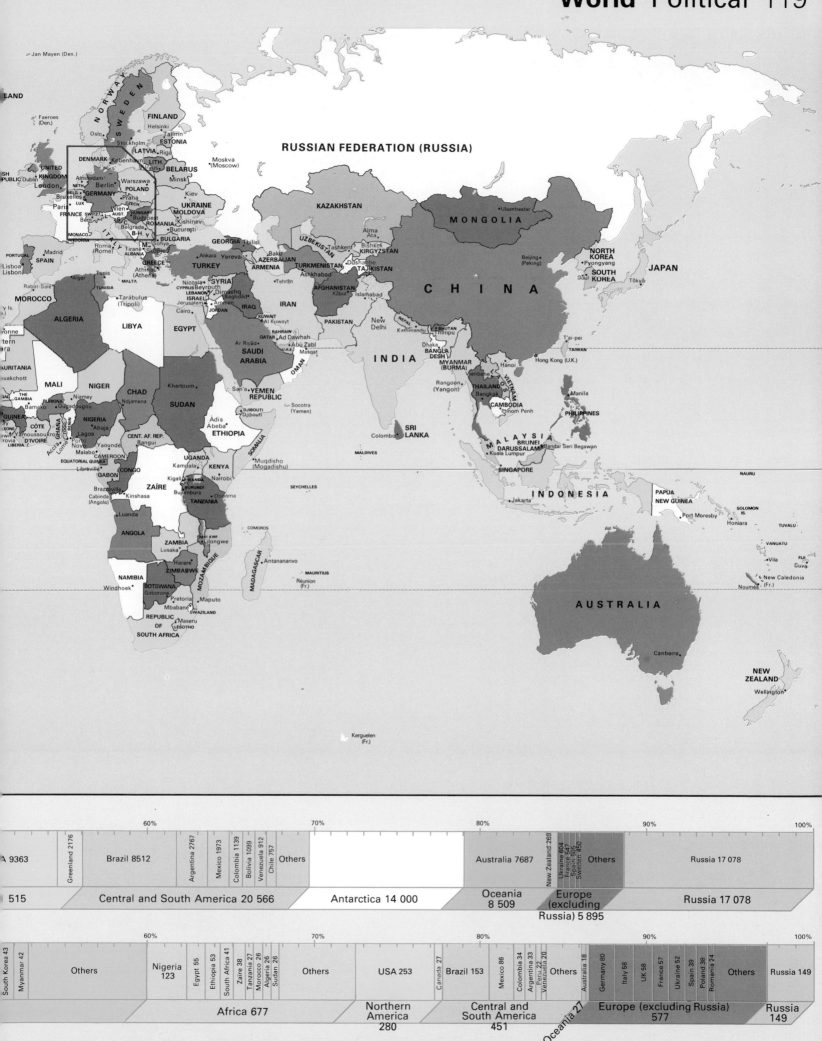

Land height and sea depth

metres

	5000
	4000
	3000
	2000
	1000
	500
	200
	sea level
	land below sea level
	200
	2000
	4000
	5000
	7000

• spot heights in metres

Land below sea level and sea depths shown as minus numbers

Equatorial Scale 1:88 000 000

Modified Gall Projection

Plate tectonics

The present positions of the major tectonic plates are shown with the white areas representing the smaller plates

Plate boundaries

▲▲ subduction zones

══ ridge zones

⟶ transform zones

➤ direction of sea-floor spreading

— major fracture zones

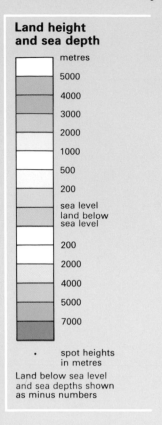

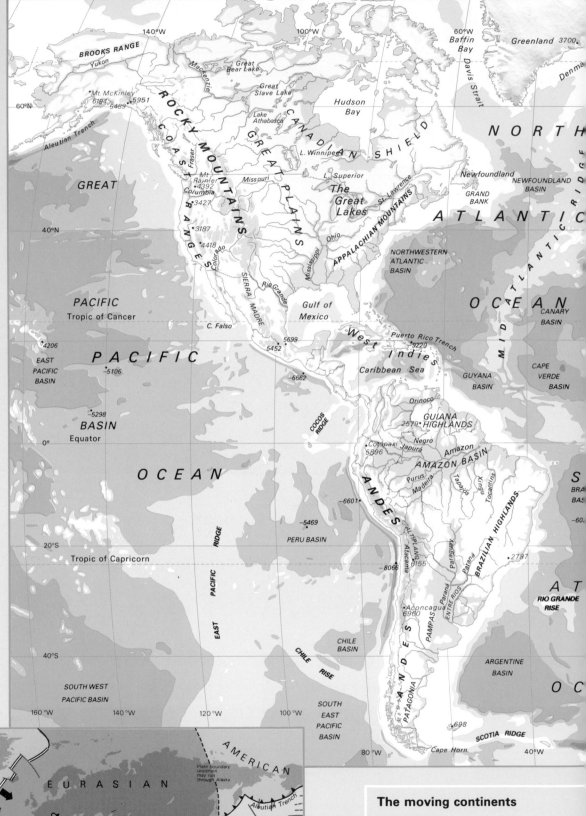

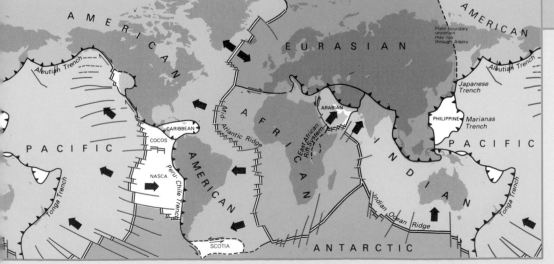

The moving continents

	land areas
	continental shelf
	sea areas
	orogenic belts

········· uncertain coastline

·········· uncertain continental shelf edge

Lines of latitude and longitude indicate position on the globe.

The graticules show how earlier positions of the continents compare with the present

Gall Projection

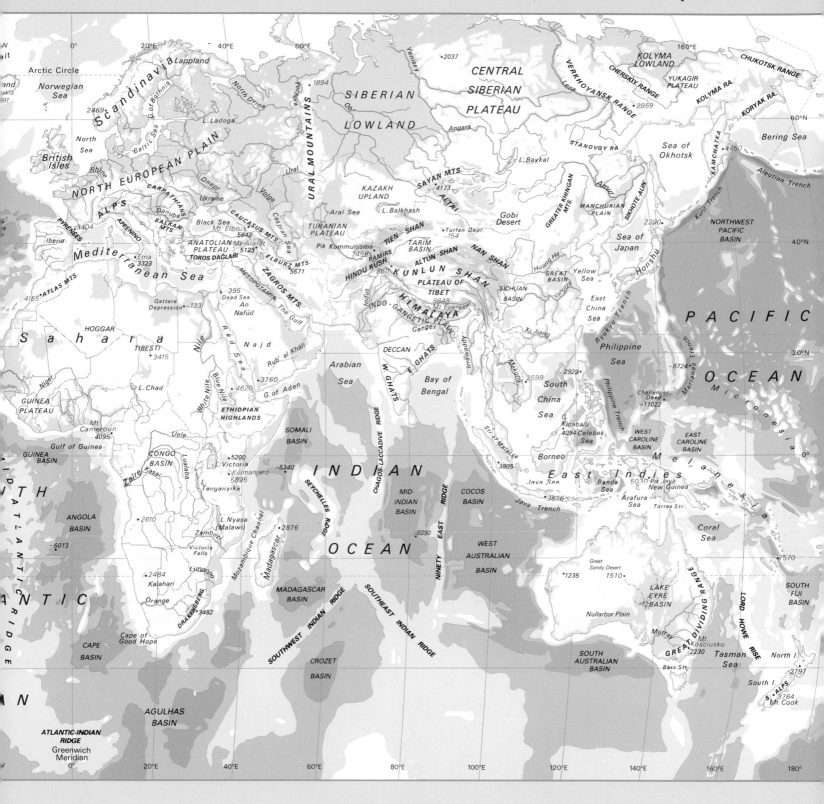

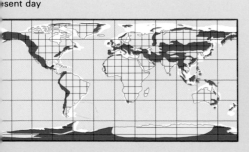

Present day

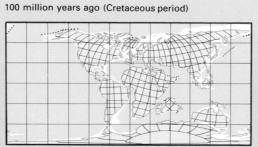

100 million years ago (Cretaceous period)

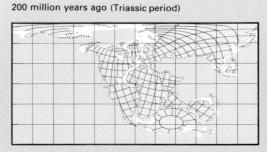

200 million years ago (Triassic period)

Oxford University Press

Rainfall
and other forms of precipitation

	mm
	over 400
	250–400
	150–250
	50–150
	25–50
	under 25

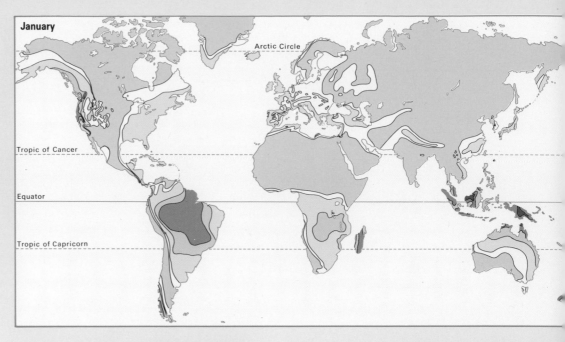

January

Arctic Circle

Tropic of Cancer

Equator

Tropic of Capricorn

Temperature, ocean currents

actual temperature °C

	32
	24
	16
	8
	0
	−8
	−16
	−24

Ocean currents

cold

warm

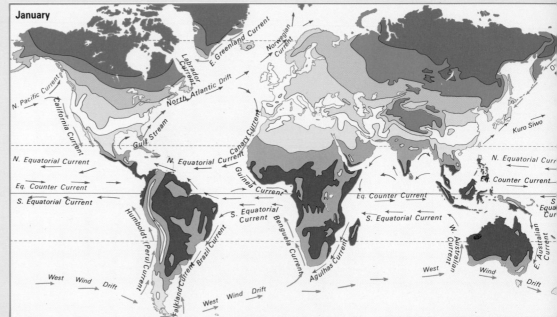

January

Pressure and winds
Pressure reduced to sea level

103.5 kilopascals
103.0
102.5
102.0
101.5
101.0
100.5
100.0
 99.5

H high pressure cell

L low pressure cell

Prevailing winds
Arrows fly with the wind:
the heavier the arrow, the
more regular ('constant')
the direction of the wind

Equatorial Scale 1:218 000 000

January

Modified Gall Projection

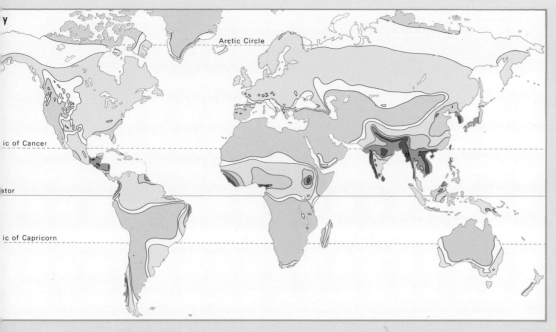

temperature 27°C and
over at mean sea level

Northern hemisphere
Maximum frequency August - September

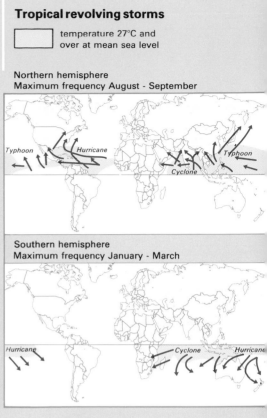

Typhoon   Hurricane   Typhoon

Cyclone

Southern hemisphere
Maximum frequency January - March

Hurricane   Cyclone   Hurricane

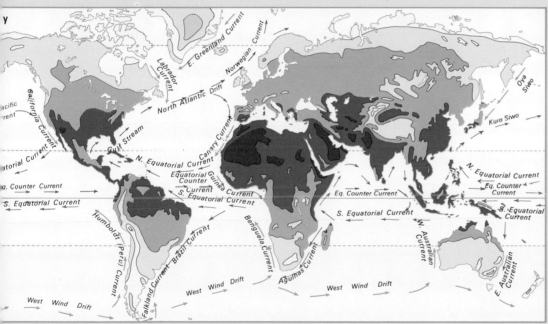

E. Greenland Current
Labrador Current
Norwegian Current
North Atlantic Drift
Oya Siwo
California Current
Gulf Stream
Kuro Siwo
Canary Current
N. Equatorial Current
Equatorial Counter Current
Guinea Current
N. Equatorial Current
Eq. Counter Current
Eq. Counter Current
S. Equatorial Current
S. Equatorial Current
S. Equatorial Current
S. Equatorial Current
Humboldt (Peru) Current
Benguela Current
Brazil Current
S. Equatorial Current
W. Australian Current
Agulhas Current
E. Australian Current
Falkland Current
West Wind Drift
West Wind Drift
West Wind Drift

Air masses

- - - fronts

Arctic

Polar

Temperate

Equatorial

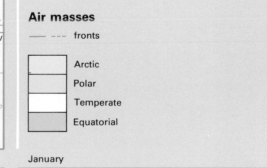

January

Pacific Arctic Front   Atlantic Arctic Front
Atlantic Polar Front
Mediterranean Front
Pacific Polar Front
Intertropical
Convergence
Polar Front
Polar Front

July

Atlantic Arctic Front   Pacific Arctic Front
Atlantic Polar Front
Convergence
Intertropical
Polar Front

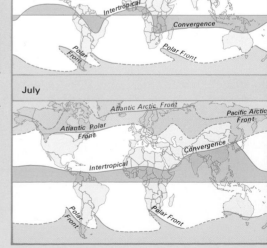

Westerlies
1015
1015
1015
L
L
1015
Westerlies
1015
1010
Westerlies
1020
L
1005
1025
H
Westerlies
1020
1015
N.E. Trades
1000
L
S.W. Monsoon
S.E. Monsoon
S.E. Trades
N.E. Trades
S.E. Trades
1010
S.E. Monsoon
S.E. Trades
1015
S.E. Trades
S.E. Monsoon
H
1020
H
H
(Roaring Forties)
Westerlies
1015
Westerlies
1010
1005

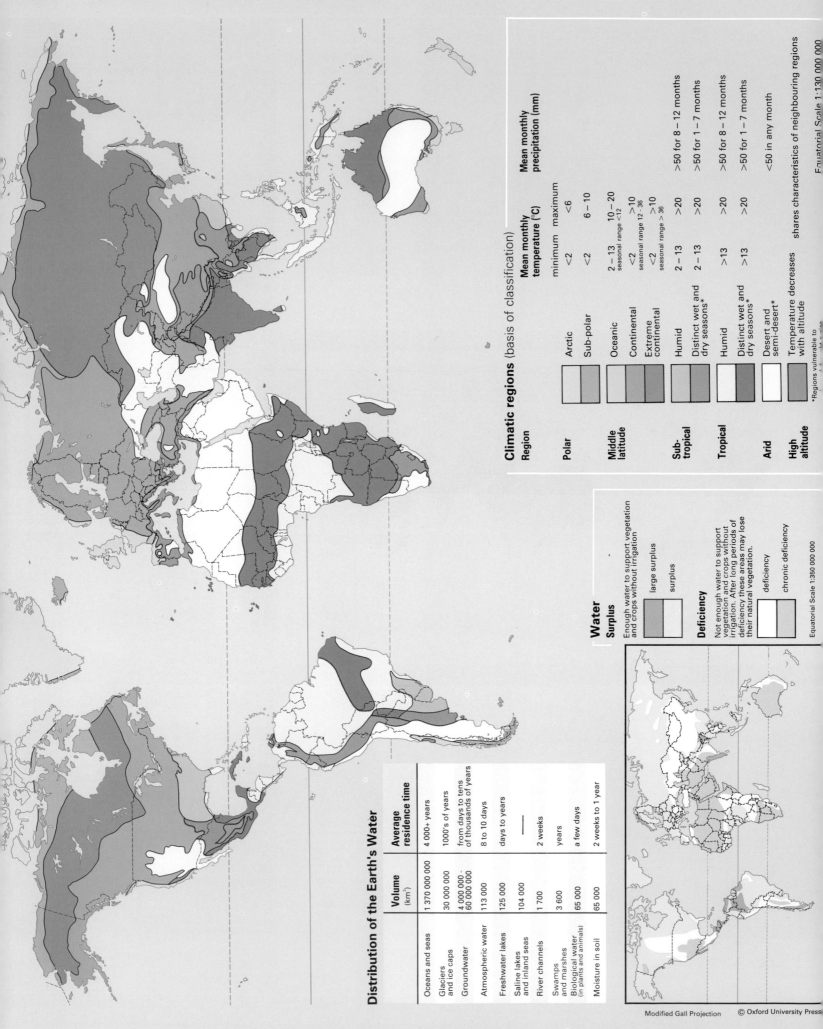

Climatic regions (basis of classification)

Region		Mean monthly temperature (°C)		Mean monthly precipitation (mm)
		minimum	maximum	
Polar	Arctic	<2	<6	
	Sub-polar	<2	6 – 10	
Middle latitude	Oceanic	2 – 13 seasonal range <12	10 – 20	
	Continental	<2 seasonal range 12 - 36	>10	
	Extreme continental	<2 seasonal range > 36	>10	
Sub-tropical	Humid	2 – 13	>20	>50 for 8 – 12 months
	Distinct wet and dry seasons*	2 – 13	>20	>50 for 1 – 7 months
Tropical	Humid	>13	>20	>50 for 8 – 12 months
	Distinct wet and dry seasons*	>13	>20	>50 for 1 – 7 months
Arid	Desert and semi-desert*			<50 in any month
High altitude	Temperature decreases with altitude		shares characteristics of neighbouring regions	

*Regions vulnerable to

Equatorial Scale 1:130 000 000

Water

Surplus

Enough water to support vegetation and crops without irrigation

large surplus

surplus

Deficiency

Not enough water to support vegetation and crops without irrigation. After long periods of deficiency these areas may lose their natural vegetation.

deficiency

chronic deficiency

Equatorial Scale 1:350 000 000

Distribution of the Earth's Water

	Volume (km³)	Average residence time
Oceans and seas	1 370 000 000	4 000+ years
Glaciers and ice caps	30 000 000	1000's of years
Groundwater	4 000 000 - 60 000 000	from days to tens of thousands of years
Atmospheric water	113 000	8 to 10 days
Freshwater lakes	125 000	days to years
Saline lakes and inland seas	104 000	—
River channels	1 700	2 weeks
Swamps and marshes	3 600	years
Biological water (in plants and animals)	65 000	a few days
Moisture in soil	65 000	2 weeks to 1 year

Modified Gall Projection   © Oxford University Press

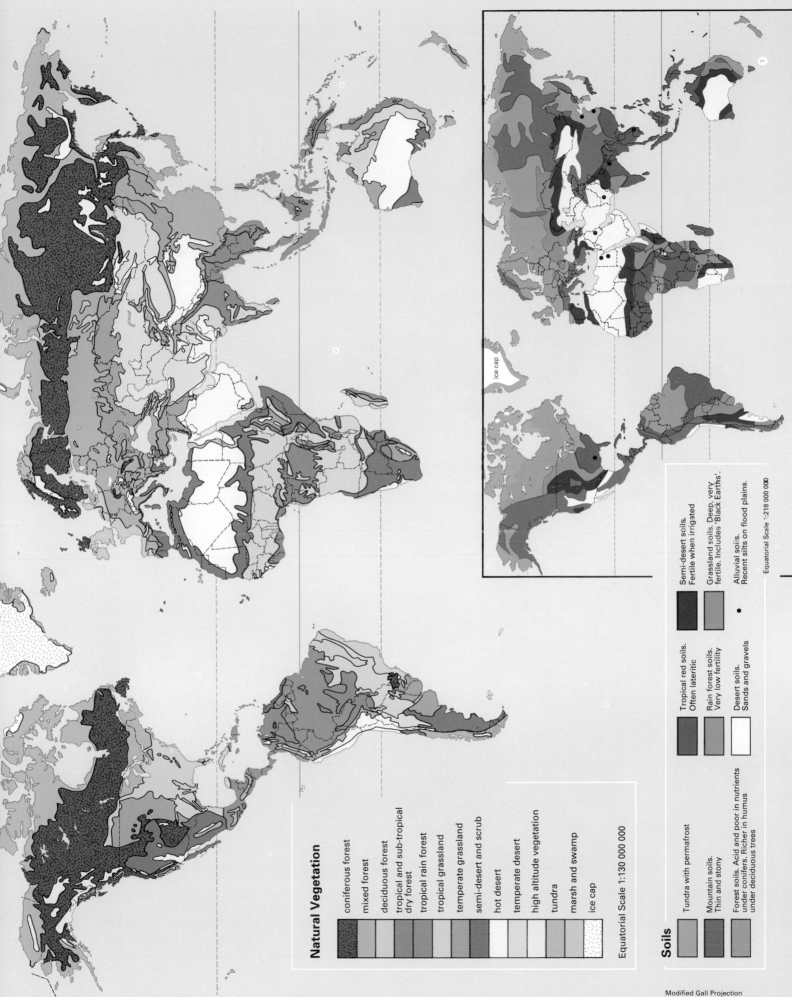

Natural Vegetation

- coniferous forest
- mixed forest
- deciduous forest
- tropical and sub-tropical dry forest
- tropical rain forest
- tropical grassland
- temperate grassland
- semi-desert and scrub
- hot desert
- temperate desert
- high altitude vegetation
- tundra
- marsh and swamp
- ice cap

Equatorial Scale 1:130 000 000

Soils

- Tundra with permafrost
- Mountain soils. Thin and stony
- Forest soils. Acid and poor in nutrients under conifers. Richer in humus under deciduous trees
- Tropical red soils. Often lateritic
- Rain forest soils. Very low fertility
- Desert soils. Sands and gravels
- Semi-desert soils. Fertile when irrigated
- Grassland soils. Deep, very fertile. Includes 'Black Earths'.
- Alluvial soils. Recent silts on flood plains.

Equatorial Scale 1:218 000 000

ice cap

Modified Gall Projection
© Oxford University Press

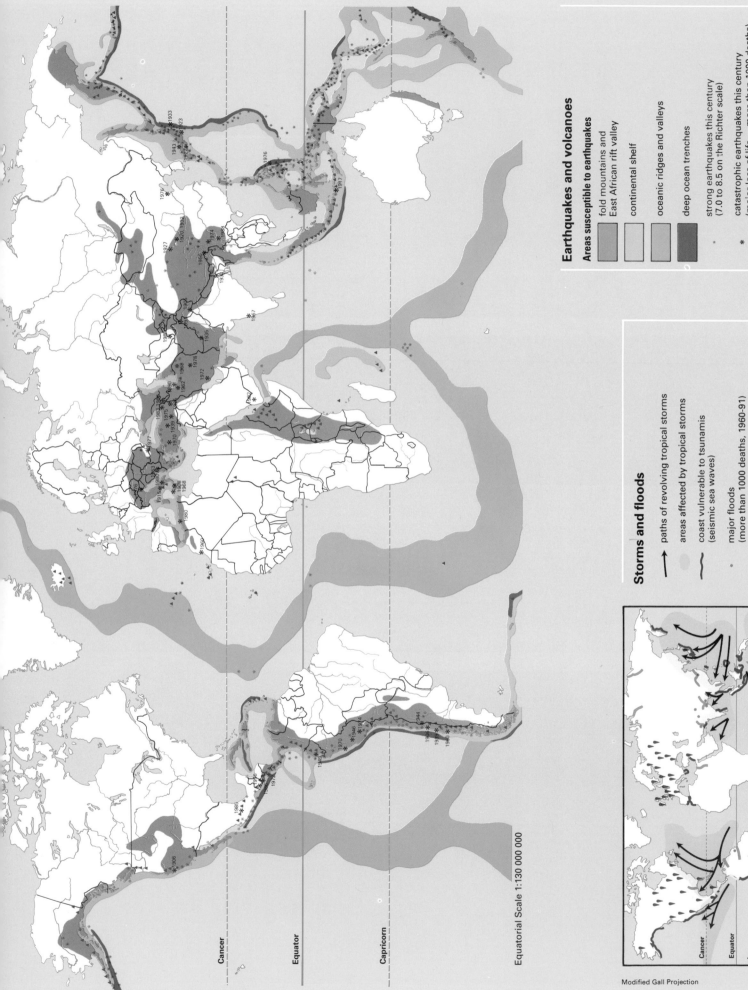

Earthquakes and volcanoes

Areas susceptible to earthquakes

fold mountains and
East African rift valley

continental shelf

oceanic ridges and valleys

deep ocean trenches

strong earthquakes this century
(7.0 to 8.5 on the Richter scale)

✳ catastrophic earthquakes this century
(major loss of life - more than 1000 deaths)

Volcanoes

▲ active volcanoes

Storms and floods

→ paths of revolving tropical storms

areas affected by tropical storms

coast vulnerable to tsunamis
(seismic sea waves)

• major floods
(more than 1000 deaths, 1960-91)

major river flood plains, some partially
controlled, which are susceptible
to flooding

▸ areas affected by tornadoes

the Tropics

Equatorial Scale 1:130 000 000

Cancer

Equator

Capricorn

Modified Gall Projection   © Oxford University Pr

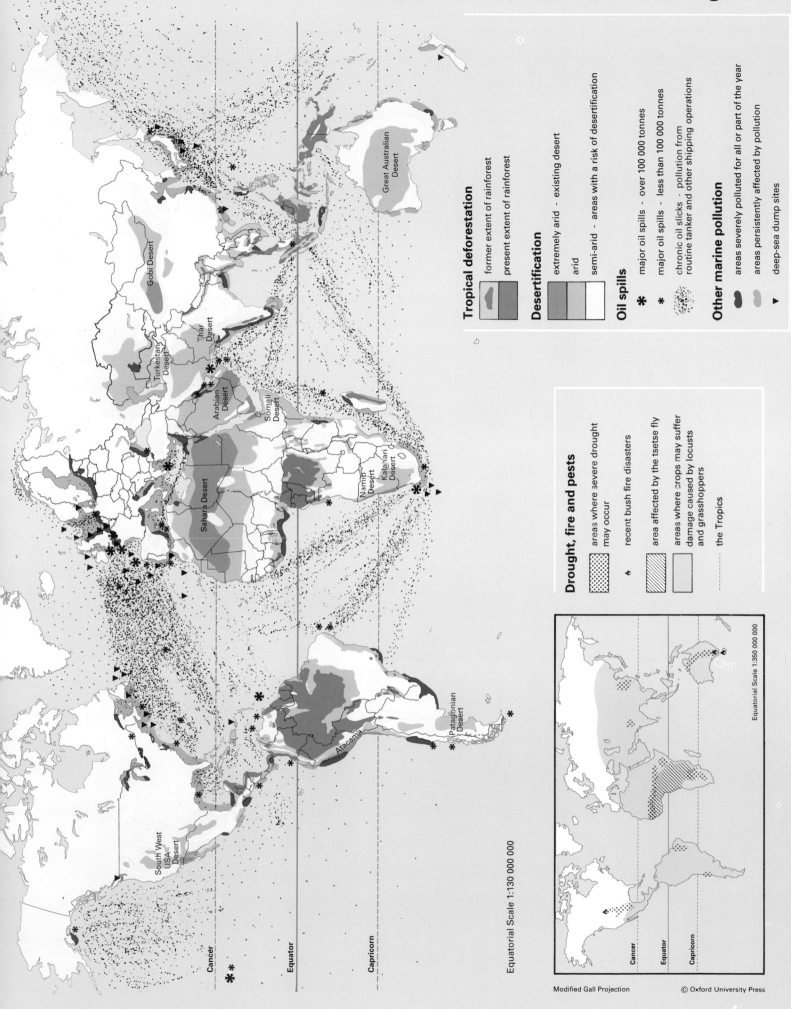

Tropical deforestation

former extent of rainforest

present extent of rainforest

Desertification

extremely arid - existing desert

arid

semi-arid - areas with a risk of desertification

Oil spills

* major oil spills - over 100 000 tonnes

* major oil spills - less than 100 000 tonnes

chronic oil slicks - pollution from routine tanker and other shipping operations

Other marine pollution

areas severely polluted for all or part of the year

areas persistently affected by pollution

▶ deep-sea dump sites

Drought, fire and pests

areas where severe drought may occur

recent bush fire disasters

area affected by the tsetse fly

areas where crops may suffer damage caused by locusts and grasshoppers

the Tropics

Equatorial Scale 1:130 000 000

Equatorial Scale 1:350 000 000

Cancer

Equator

Capricorn

Gobi Desert

Turkestan Desert

Thar Desert

Arabian Desert

Somali Desert

Sahara Desert

Namib Desert

Kalahari Desert

Great Australian Desert

Atacama

Patagonian Desert

South West USA Desert

Modified Gall Projection

© Oxford University Press

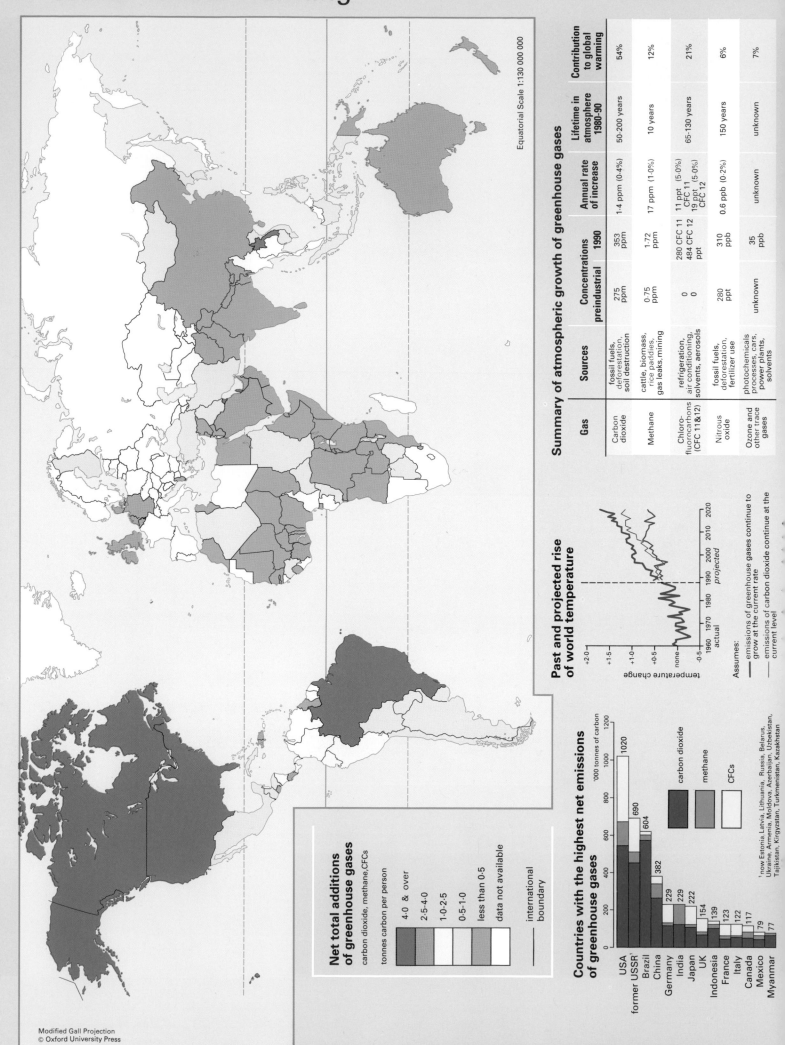

Summary of atmospheric growth of greenhouse gases

Gas	Sources	Concentrations preindustrial	Concentrations 1990	Annual rate of increase	Lifetime in atmosphere 1980-90	Contribution to global warming
Carbon dioxide	fossil fuels, deforestation, soil destruction	275 ppm	353 ppm	1·4 ppm (0·4%)	50-200 years	54%
Methane	cattle, biomass, rice paddies, gas leaks, mining	0·75 ppm	1·72 ppm	17 ppm (1·0%)	10 years	12%
Chloro-fluorocarbons (CFC 11&12)	refrigeration, air conditioning, solvents, aerosols	0 0	280 CFC 11 484 CFC 12 ppt	11 ppt (5·0%) CFC 11 19 ppt (5·0%) CFC 12	65-130 years	21%
Nitrous oxide	fossil fuels, deforestation, fertilizer use	280 ppt	310 ppb	0·6 ppb (0·2%)	150 years	6%
Ozone and other trace gases	photochemicals processes, cars, power plants, solvents	unknown	35 ppb	unknown	unknown	7%

Past and projected rise of world temperature

Assumes:
— emissions of greenhouse gases continue to grow at the current rate
— emissions of carbon dioxide continue at the current level

Net total additions of greenhouse gases

carbon dioxide, methane, CFCs

tonnes carbon per person

- 4·0 & over
- 2·5-4·0
- 1·0-2·5
- 0·5-1·0
- less than 0·5
- data not available

— international boundary

Countries with the highest net emissions of greenhouse gases

'000 tonnes of carbon

- carbon dioxide
- methane
- CFCs

USA	1020
former USSR¹	690
Brazil	604
China	382
Germany	229
India	229
Japan	222
UK	154
Indonesia	139
France	123
Italy	122
Canada	117
Mexico	79
Myanmar	77

¹now Estonia, Latvia, Lithuania, Russia, Belarus, Ukraine, Armenia, Moldova, Azerbaijan, Uzbekistan, Tajikistan, Kirgyzstan, Turkmenistan, Kazakhstan

Equatorial Scale 1:130 000 000

Modified Gall Projection
© Oxford University Press

Equatorial Scale 1:130 000 000

Air pollution (selected cities)

Sulphur Dioxide	Suspended particulate matter
number of days over 150 micrograms/m³ †	number of days over 230 micrograms/m³ †
over 75	over 200
50-74	100-199
25-49	25-99
8-24	8-24
0-7	0-7

Ozone depletion

Annual average percentage loss, 1978-88

more than 9·0	
7·5-9·0	
6·0-7·5	
4·5-6·0	
3·0-4·5	
1·5-3·0	
less than 1·5	

Polar regions
no annual readings taken in these areas, but scientists have observed massive depletions ("holes") in the ozone layer over the Poles. These "holes" vary in size depending on the time of year.

other areas where acid precipitation is becoming a problem

Acid rain

Annual mean values of pH in precipitation

	North America	Europe
	5·0	5·1
	4·5	4·5
	4·2	4·3

The pH scale

A pH scale measures the acidity of liquid. A pH of 7·0 indicates neutrality. Lower values indicate acidity, higher values indicate alkalinity. "Clean" rain water is slightly acid with a pH value of 5·6. The pH scale is logarithmic, so that a value of 4·6 is ten times as acidic as normal rain.

11·0	Ammonia
10·5	Milk of Magnesia
8·2	Baking Soda
7·0	neutral
6·6	milk
4·2	tomato juice
3·0	apple juice
2·2	vinegar
2·0	lemon juice

†World Health Organization recommends that exposure should not exceed these levels for more than 7 days per year

Modified Gall Projection
© Oxford University Press

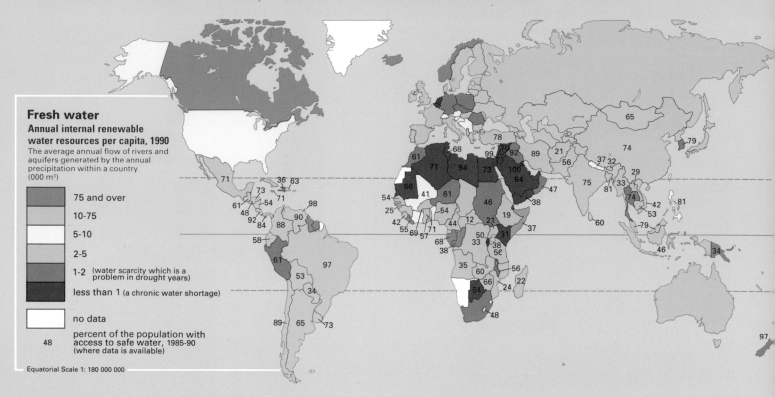

Fresh water

Annual internal renewable water resources per capita, 1990
The average annual flow of rivers and aquifers generated by the annual precipitation within a country (000 m³)

- 75 and over
- 10-75
- 5-10
- 2-5
- 1-2 (water scarcity which is a problem in drought years)
- less than 1 (a chronic water shortage)
- no data

48   percent of the population with access to safe water, 1985-90 (where data is available)

Equatorial Scale 1: 180 000 000

Protected areas

Percent of national land area protected by national protection systems, 1989
Areas of at least 1000 hectares and with partially restricted access, including scientific reserves, strict nature reserves, national parks, provincial parks, natural monuments, natural land marks, managed nature reserves, wildlife sanctuaries, and protected landscapes or seascapes (natural or cultural).

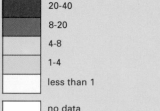

- 20-40
- 8-20
- 4-8
- 1-4
- less than 1
- no data

Estimated number of species worldwide

	Those species already identified	Estimated percentage yet to be identified
invertebrates	1 020 561	73-97
micro-organisms	5760	
plants	322 311	0-33
fish	19 056	0-17
reptiles and amphibians	10 484	5-10
mammals	4 000	
birds	9 040	0-6

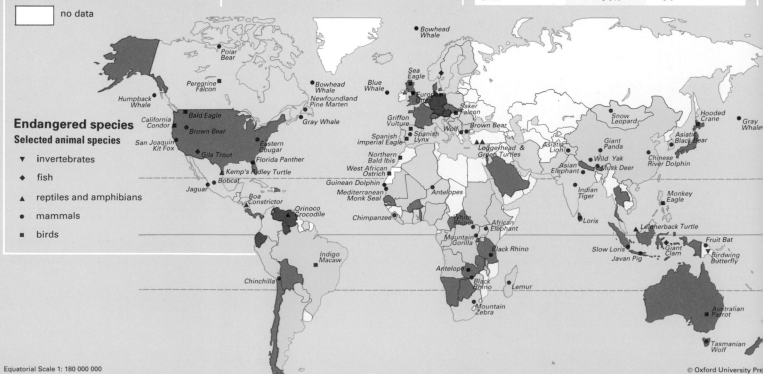

Endangered species
Selected animal species

- ▼ invertebrates
- ◆ fish
- ▲ reptiles and amphibians
- ● mammals
- ■ birds

Equatorial Scale 1: 180 000 000
Modified Gall Projection

© Oxford University Pre

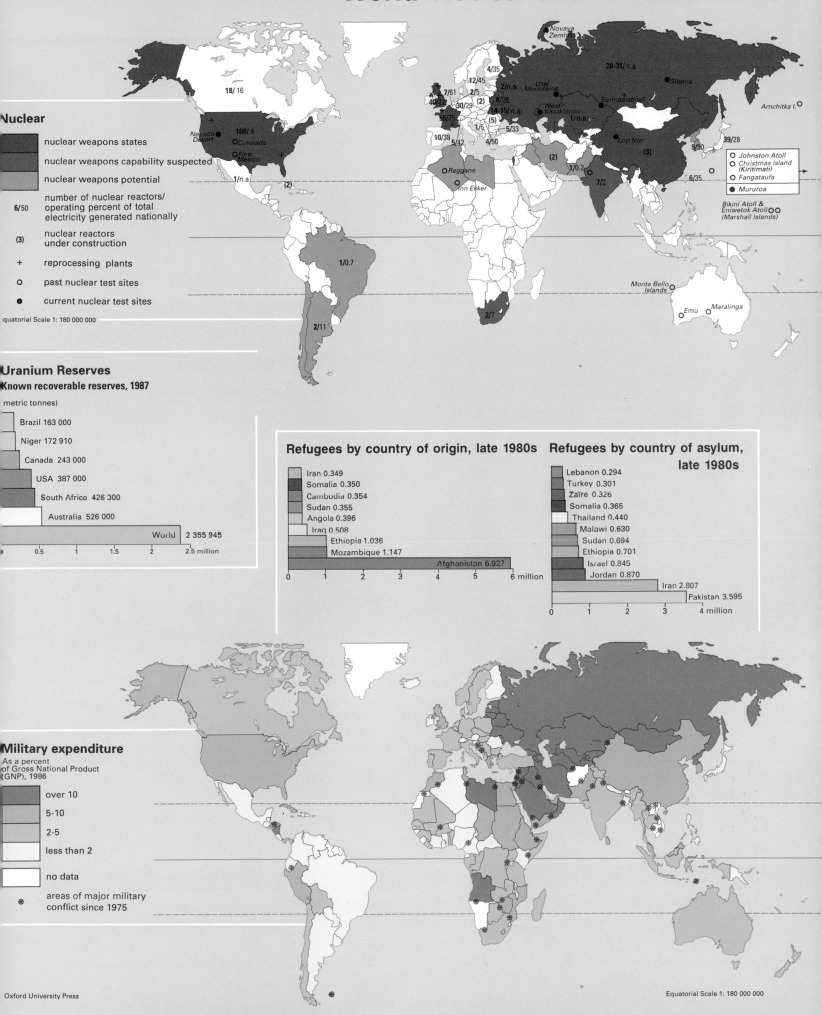

Nuclear

- nuclear weapons states
- nuclear weapons capability suspected
- nuclear weapons potential

6/50 number of nuclear reactors/ operating percent of total electricity generated nationally

(3) nuclear reactors under construction

+ reprocessing plants

○ past nuclear test sites

● current nuclear test sites

Equatorial Scale 1: 180 000 000

Uranium Reserves
Known recoverable reserves, 1987

(metric tonnes)

Brazil 163 000
Niger 172 910
Canada 243 000
USA 387 000
South Africa 426 300
Australia 526 000
World 2 355 945

0.5   1   1.5   2   2.5 million

○ Johnston Atoll
○ Christmas Island (Kiritimati)
○ Fangataufa
● Mururoa

Bikini Atoll & Eniwetok Atoll ○○ (Marshall Islands)

Novaya Zemlya
Ural Mountains
West Kazakhstan
Semipalatinsk
Siberia
Amchitka I.
Lop Nur
Nevada Desert
Colorado
New Mexico
Reggane
Inn Ekker
Monte Bello Islands
Emu   Maralinga

Refugees by country of origin, late 1980s

Iran 0.349
Somalia 0.350
Cambodia 0.354
Sudan 0.355
Angola 0.396
Iraq 0.508
Ethiopia 1.036
Mozambique 1.147
Afghanistan 5.927

0   1   2   3   4   5   6 million

Refugees by country of asylum, late 1980s

Lebanon 0.294
Turkey 0.301
Zaïre 0.326
Somalia 0.365
Thailand 0.440
Malawi 0.630
Sudan 0.694
Ethiopia 0.701
Israel 0.845
Jordan 0.870
Iran 2.807
Pakistan 3.595

0   1   2   3   4 million

Military expenditure

As a percent of Gross National Product (GNP), 1986

- over 10
- 5-10
- 2-5
- less than 2
- no data
- ✱ areas of major military conflict since 1975

Oxford University Press

Equatorial Scale 1: 180 000 000

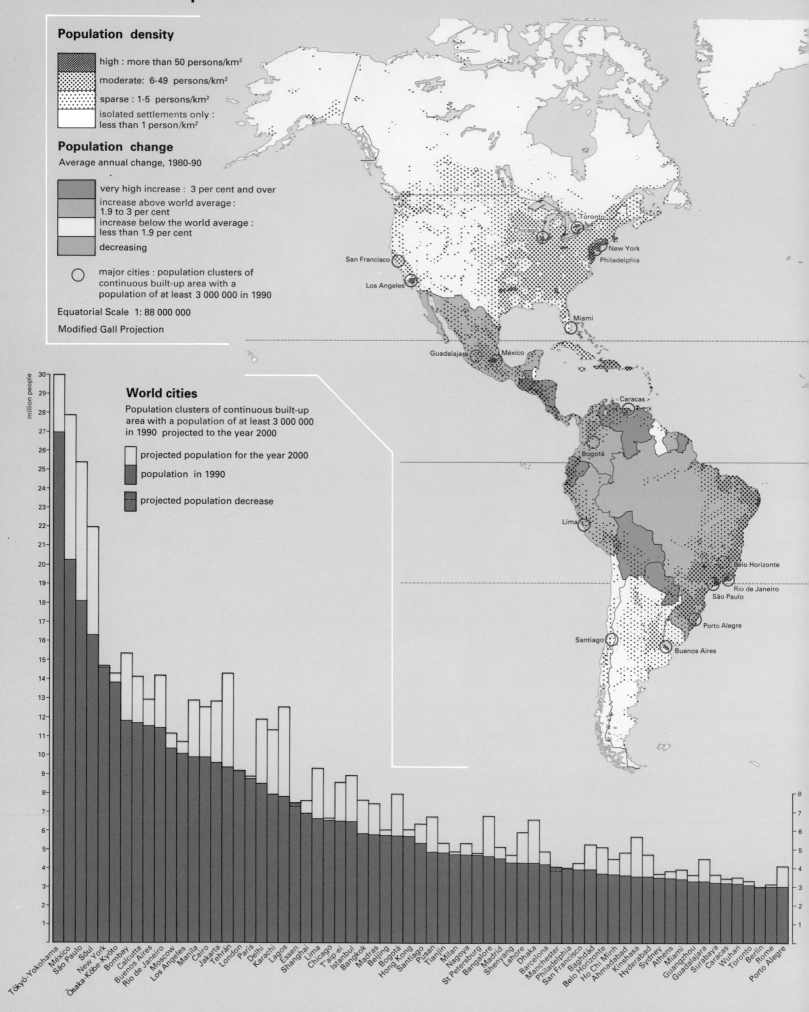

Population density

- high : more than 50 persons/km²
- moderate: 6-49 persons/km²
- sparse : 1-5 persons/km²
- isolated settlements only : less than 1 person/km²

Population change

Average annual change, 1980-90

- very high increase : 3 per cent and over
- increase above world average : 1.9 to 3 per cent
- increase below the world average : less than 1.9 per cent
- decreasing

○ major cities : population clusters of continuous built-up area with a population of at least 3 000 000 in 1990

Equatorial Scale 1: 88 000 000

Modified Gall Projection

World cities

Population clusters of continuous built-up area with a population of at least 3 000 000 in 1990 projected to the year 2000

- projected population for the year 2000
- population in 1990
- projected population decrease

million people

Tōkyō-Yokohama, México, São Paulo, Sŏul, New York, Ōsaka-Kōbe-Kyōto, Bombay, Calcutta, Buenos Aires, Rio de Janeiro, Moscow, Los Angeles, Manila, Cairo, Jakarta, Tehrān, London, Paris, Delhi, Karachi, Lagos, Essen, Shanghai, Lima, Chicago, T'ai-pei, Istanbul, Bangkok, Madras, Beijing, Bogotá, Hong Kong, Santiago, Pusan, Tianjin, Milan, Nagoya, St Petersburg, Bangalore, Madrid, Shenyang, Lahore, Dhaka, Barcelona, Manchester, Philadelphia, San Francisco, Baghdad, Belo Horizonte, Ho Chi Minh, Ahmadabad, Kinshasa, Hyderabad, Sydney, Athens, Miami, Guangzhou, Guadalajara, Surabaya, Caracas, Wuhan, Toronto, Berlin, Rome, Porto Alegre

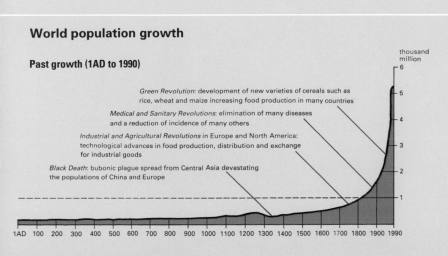

World population growth

Past growth (1AD to 1990)

Green Revolution: development of new varieties of cereals such as rice, wheat and maize increasing food production in many countries

Medical and Sanitary Revolutions: elimination of many diseases and a reduction of incidence of many others

Industrial and Agricultural Revolutions in Europe and North America: technological advances in food production, distribution and exchange for industrial goods

Black Death: bubonic plague spread from Central Asia devastating the populations of China and Europe

thousand million

1AD 100 200 300 400 500 600 700 800 900 1000 1100 1200 1300 1400 1500 1600 1700 1800 1900 1990

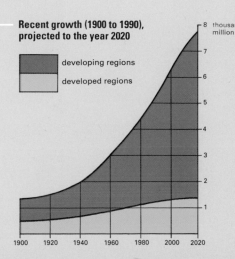

Recent growth (1900 to 1990), projected to the year 2020

thousand million

developing regions
developed regions

1900 1920 1940 1960 1980 2000 2020

Additional statistical population information for all of the countries of the world is found on pages 185-190 as well as the endpaper.

Age-sex graphs for a number of countries are found on pages 60-61, 73, 94, 105 and 109.

© Oxford University Press

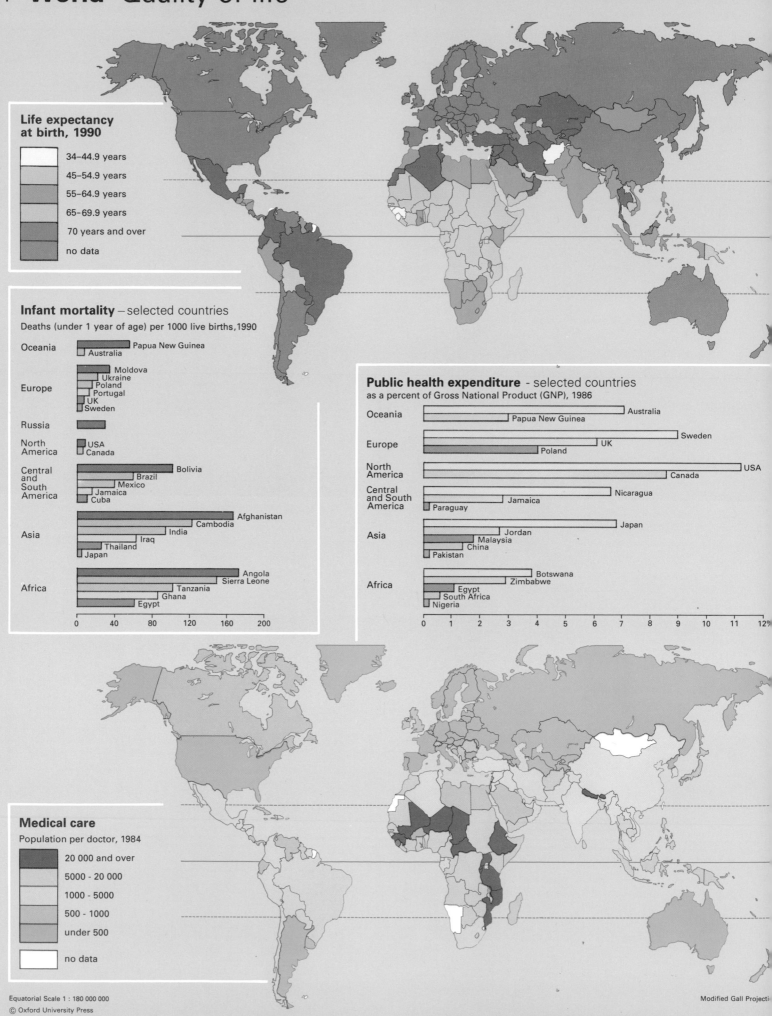

Life expectancy at birth, 1990

- 34–44.9 years
- 45–54.9 years
- 55–64.9 years
- 65–69.9 years
- 70 years and over
- no data

Infant mortality – selected countries

Deaths (under 1 year of age) per 1000 live births, 1990

Oceania
- Papua New Guinea
- Australia

Europe
- Moldova
- Ukraine
- Poland
- Portugal
- UK
- Sweden

Russia

North America
- USA
- Canada

Central and South America
- Bolivia
- Brazil
- Mexico
- Jamaica
- Cuba

Asia
- Afghanistan
- Cambodia
- India
- Iraq
- Thailand
- Japan

Africa
- Angola
- Sierra Leone
- Tanzania
- Ghana
- Egypt

(scale: 0 40 80 120 160 200)

Public health expenditure - selected countries

as a percent of Gross National Product (GNP), 1986

Oceania
- Australia
- Papua New Guinea

Europe
- Sweden
- UK
- Poland

North America
- USA
- Canada

Central and South America
- Nicaragua
- Jamaica
- Paraguay

Asia
- Japan
- Jordan
- Malaysia
- China
- Pakistan

Africa
- Botswana
- Zimbabwe
- Egypt
- South Africa
- Nigeria

(scale: 0 1 2 3 4 5 6 7 8 9 10 11 12%)

Medical care

Population per doctor, 1984

- 20 000 and over
- 5000 - 20 000
- 1000 - 5000
- 500 - 1000
- under 500
- no data

Education
Adult literacy rate, 1985

- 90% and over
- 75 - 90%
- 50 - 75%
- 25 - 50%
- 10 - 25%
- no data

58/29   male/female breakdown given for selected countries

Primary education -selected countries
Enrolment in primary school as a percentage of the population in the relevant age group, 1986-89

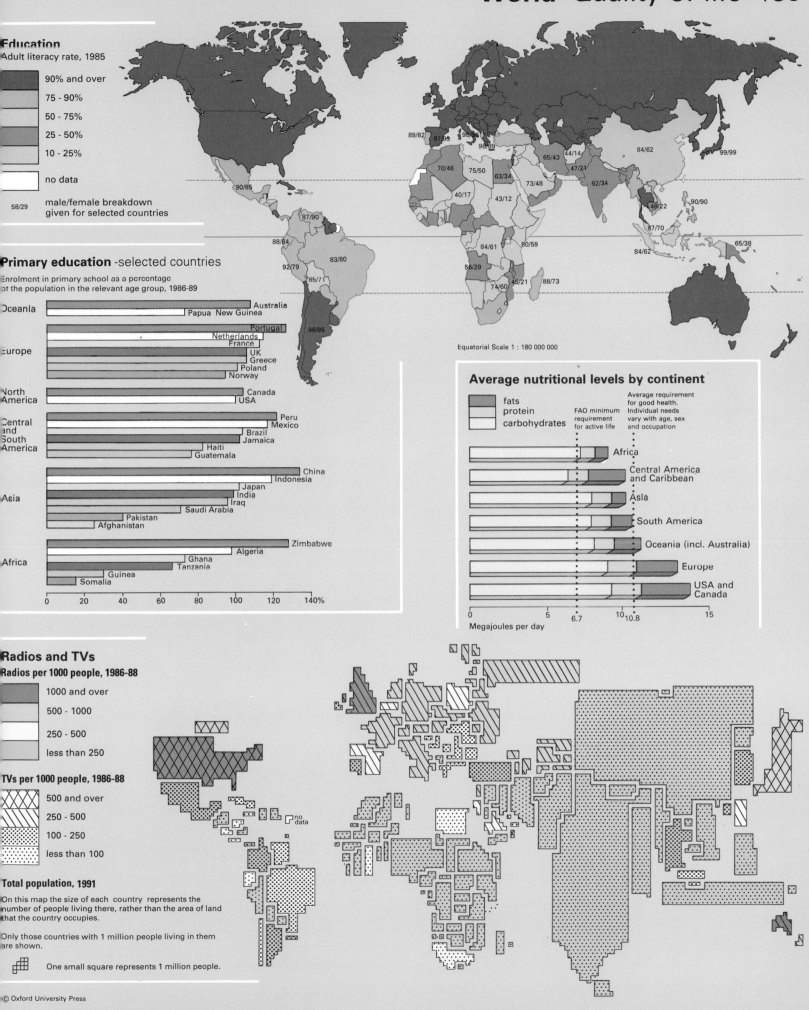

Equatorial Scale 1 : 180 000 000

Map literacy values:
89/82, 97/98, 98/96, 98/89, 65/43, 44/14, 84/62, 99/99, 70/46, 75/50, 63/34, 47/21, 62/34, 90/90, 40/17, 73/48, 43/12, 48/22, 87/70, 90/85, 87/90, 84/61, 80/59, 65/38, 88/84, 83/80, 84/62, 92/79, 56/29, 45/21, 88/73, 85/71, 74/60, 96/95

Primary education bar chart

Oceania: Australia, Papua New Guinea
Europe: Portugal, Netherlands, France, UK, Greece, Poland, Norway
North America: Canada, USA
Central and South America: Peru, Mexico, Brazil, Jamaica, Haiti, Guatemala
Asia: China, Indonesia, Japan, India, Iraq, Saudi Arabia, Pakistan, Afghanistan
Africa: Zimbabwe, Algeria, Ghana, Tanzania, Guinea, Somalia

Scale: 0, 20, 40, 60, 80, 100, 120, 140%

Average nutritional levels by continent

- fats
- protein
- carbohydrates

FAO minimum requirement for active life

Average requirement for good health. Individual needs vary with age, sex and occupation

- Africa
- Central America and Caribbean
- Asia
- South America
- Oceania (incl. Australia)
- Europe
- USA and Canada

Scale: 0, 5, 6.7, 10, 10.8, 15
Megajoules per day

Radios and TVs
Radios per 1000 people, 1986-88
- 1000 and over
- 500 - 1000
- 250 - 500
- less than 250

TVs per 1000 people, 1986-88
- 500 and over
- 250 - 500
- 100 - 250
- less than 100

no data

Total population, 1991
On this map the size of each country represents the number of people living there, rather than the area of land that the country occupies.

Only those countries with 1 million people living in them are shown.

One small square represents 1 million people.

© Oxford University Press

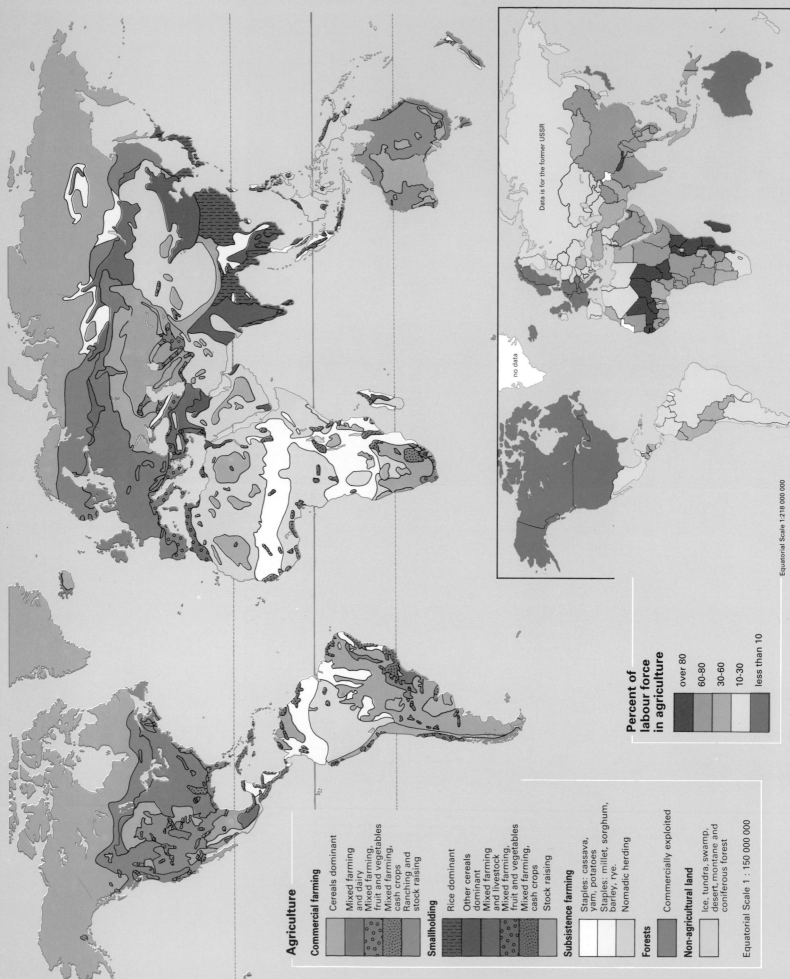

Data is for the former USSR

no data

Equatorial Scale 1:218 000 000

Percent of labour force in agriculture

- over 80
- 60-80
- 30-60
- 10-30
- less than 10

Agriculture

Commercial farming

- Cereals dominant
- Mixed farming and dairy
- Mixed farming, fruit and vegetables
- Mixed farming, cash crops
- Ranching and stock raising

Smallholding

- Rice dominant
- Other cereals dominant
- Mixed farming and livestock
- Mixed farming, fruit and vegetables
- Mixed farming, cash crops
- Stock raising

Subsistence farming

- Staples: cassava, yam, potatoes
- Staples: millet, sorghum, barley, rye.
- Nomadic herding

Forests

- Commercially exploited

Non-agricultural land

- Ice, tundra, swamp, desert, montane and coniferous forest

Equatorial Scale 1 : 150 000 000

Modified Gall Projection

© Oxford University Press

Fertilizer use -selected countries

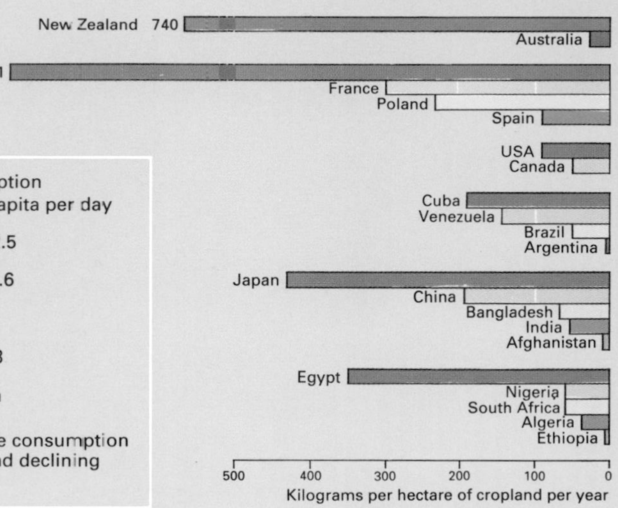
Oceania
New Zealand 740
Australia
Europe
Iceland 3061
France
Poland
Spain
North America
USA
Canada
Central and South America
Cuba
Venezuela
Brazil
Argentina
Asia
Japan
China
Bangladesh
India
Afghanistan
Africa
Egypt
Nigeria
South Africa
Algeria
Ethiopia
500
400
300
200
100
0
Kilograms per hectare of cropland per year

Nutrition

Average consumption
Megajoules per capita per day

- over 12.5
- 10.8-12.6
- 8-10.7
- under 8
- no data
- average consumption per head declining

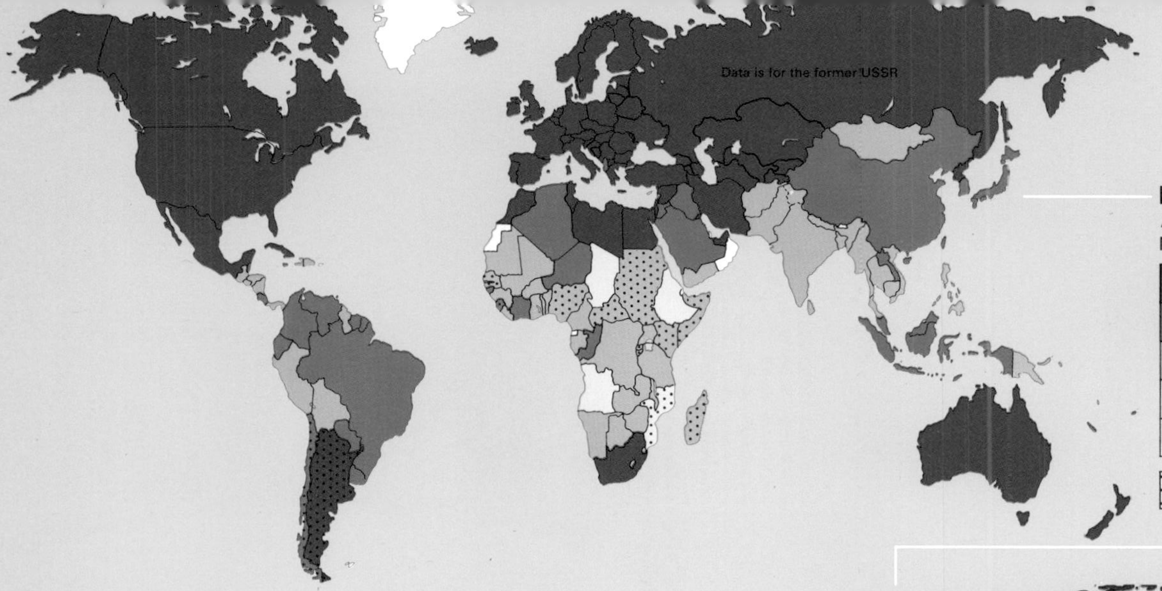
Data is for the former USSR

Cropland

Hectares per capita, 1989

- over 1.0
- 0.5-1.0
- 0.3-0.5
- 0.1-0.3
- less than 0.1

Cropland includes land under temporary and permanent crops, temporary meadows, market gardens, and temporarily fallow land

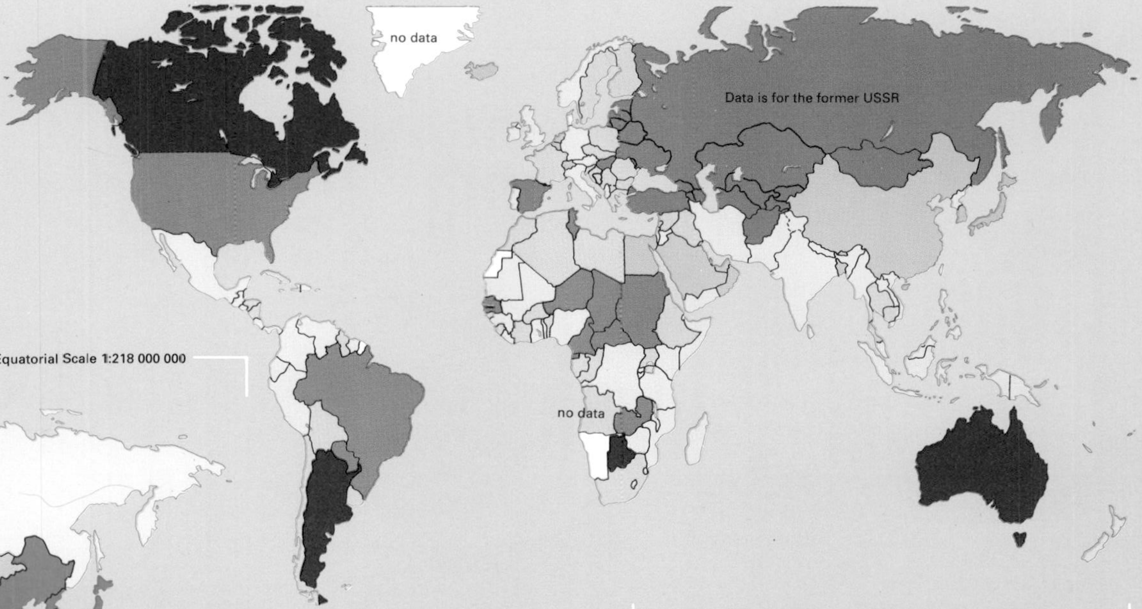
no data
Data is for the former USSR
no data

Equatorial Scale 1:218 000 000

Modified Gall Projection

© Oxford University Press

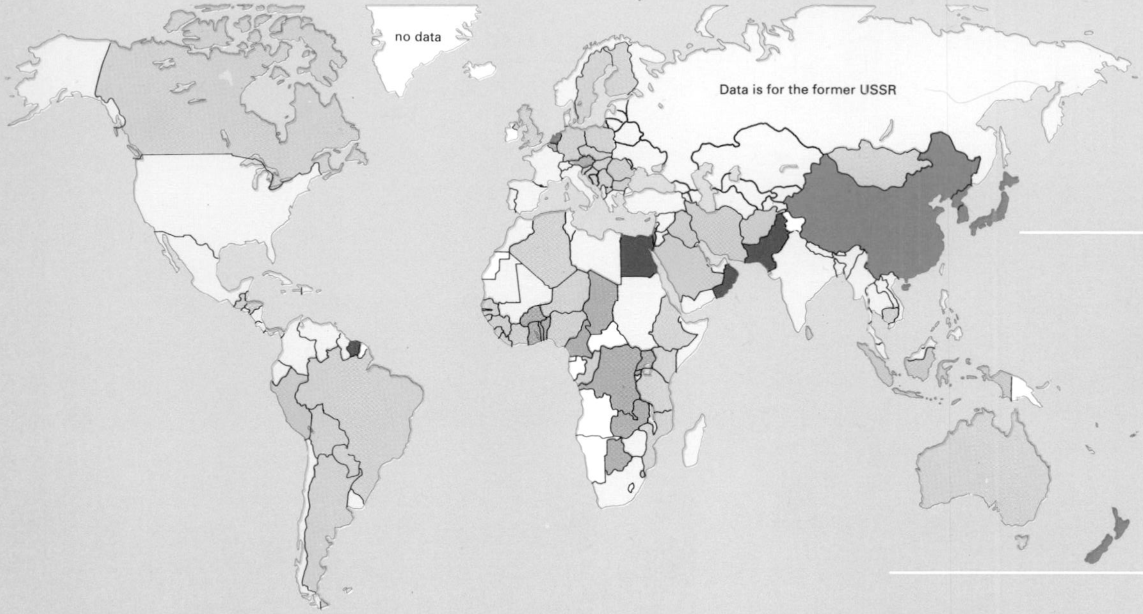
no data
Data is for the former USSR

Irrigated land

Areas permanently provided with water
As a percentage of cropland

- over 75
- 45-65
- 30-40
- 6-30
- 1-5
- less than 1

Agriculture's contribution to Gross Domestic Product (GDP)

Selected countries

GDP is the annual total value of all goods and services in a country, excluding transactions with other countries

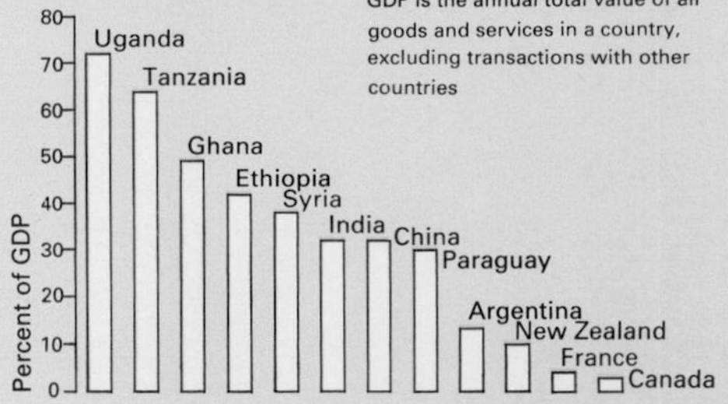
Percent of GDP
80
70
60
50
40
30
20
10
0
Uganda
Tanzania
Ghana
Ethiopia
Syria
India
China
Paraguay
Argentina
New Zealand
France
Canada

Trade with Canada, 1991

Flow lines are proportional to the volume of trade
exports

imports

exports   imports

(figures refer to each country's trade with Canada)

Each ship carries a maximum of 10 container boxes
Each container box represents $ 20 m

Each ship carries a maximum of 50 container boxes
Each container box represents $ 200 m

Major commodities
Agriculture, fishing and forestry

fish

agricultural products

cereals

pulp and paper

wood and wood products

Minerals and energy

minerals and mineral products

ores

mineral fuels and oils

Manufacturing

textiles

motor vehicles and parts

other transportation equipment

telecommunications and electronic equipment

machinery and mechanical appliances

other major manufacturing products

Others

miscellaneous products and resources

Equatorial Scale 1:70 000 000

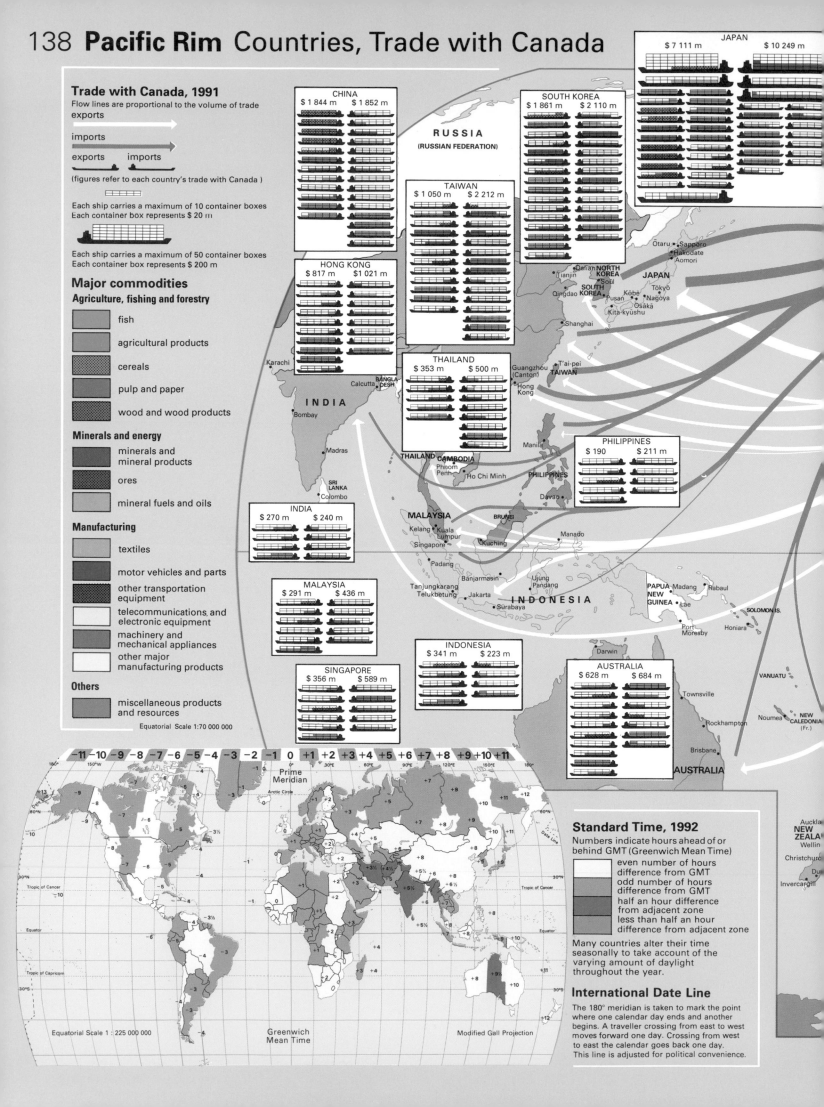

JAPAN $ 7 111 m $ 10 249 m

CHINA $ 1 844 m $ 1 852 m

SOUTH KOREA $ 1 861 m $ 2 110 m

RUSSIA (RUSSIAN FEDERATION)

TAIWAN $ 1 050 m $ 2 212 m

HONG KONG $ 817 m $ 1 021 m

THAILAND $ 353 m $ 500 m

PHILIPPINES $ 190 $ 211 m

INDIA $ 270 m $ 240 m

MALAYSIA $ 291 m $ 436 m

INDONESIA $ 341 m $ 223 m

SINGAPORE $ 356 m $ 589 m

AUSTRALIA $ 628 m $ 684 m

Otaru • Sapporo • Hakodate • Aomori

Dalian NORTH KOREA • Seoul

Tianjin

SOUTH KOREA

Qingdao Pusan Kōbe Tōkyō Nagoya Ōsaka Kita-kyūshū

JAPAN

Shanghai

Karachi

Calcutta BANGLA-DESH

INDIA

Bombay

Madras

SRI LANKA Colombo

Guangzhou (Canton) T'ai-pei TAIWAN

Hong Kong

THAILAND CAMBODIA

Phnom Penh Ho Chi Minh

PHILIPPINES

Manila

Davao

MALAYSIA BRUNEI

Kelang Kuala Lumpur Manado

Singapore Kuching

Padang

Tanjungkarang Banjarmasin Ujung Pandang

Telukbetung Jakarta

INDONESIA

Surabaya

Darwin

PAPUA NEW GUINEA Madang Rabaul

Lae

SOLOMON IS.

Honiara

Port Moresby

VANUATU

Townsville

Rockhampton Noumea NEW CALEDONIA (Fr.)

Brisbane

AUSTRALIA

Standard Time, 1992

Numbers indicate hours ahead of or behind GMT (Greenwich Mean Time)

even number of hours difference from GMT

odd number of hours difference from GMT

half an hour difference from adjacent zone

less than half an hour difference from adjacent zone

Many countries alter their time seasonally to take account of the varying amount of daylight throughout the year.

International Date Line

The 180° meridian is taken to mark the point where one calendar day ends and another begins. A traveller crossing from east to west moves forward one day. Crossing from west to east the calendar goes back one day. This line is adjusted for political convenience.

−11 −10 −9 −8 −7 −6 −5 −4 −3 −2 −1 0 +1 +2 +3 +4 +5 +6 +7 +8 +9 +10 +11

Prime Meridian

Arctic Circle

Tropic of Cancer

Equator

Tropic of Capricorn

Equatorial Scale 1 : 225 000 000

Greenwich Mean Time

Modified Gall Projection

Auckland NEW ZEALAND Wellington

Christchurch

Invercargill

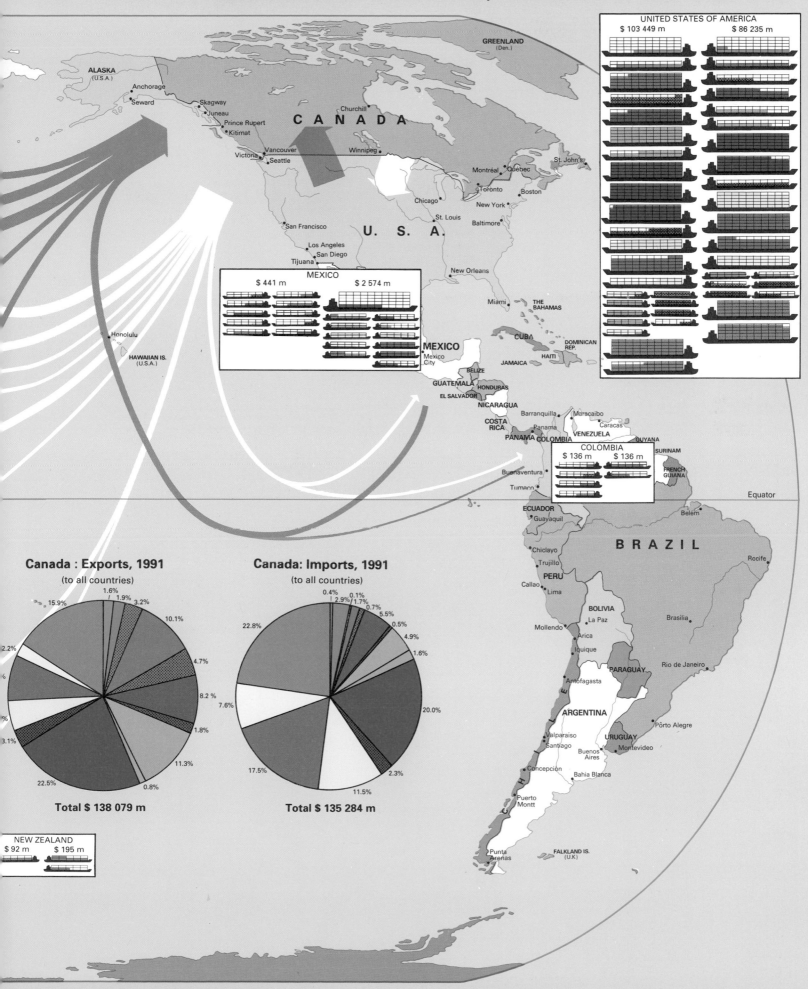

UNITED STATES OF AMERICA

$ 103 449 m $ 86 235 m

MEXICO

$ 441 m $ 2 574 m

COLOMBIA

$ 136 m $ 136 m

ALASKA (U.S.A.)
Anchorage
Seward
Skagway
Juneau
Prince Rupert
Kitimat
Churchill

CANADA

Victoria
Vancouver
Seattle
Winnipeg

Montréal
Québec
St. John's
Toronto
Boston
Chicago
New York
St. Louis
Baltimore

San Francisco

U. S. A.

Los Angeles
San Diego
Tijuana

New Orleans

Honolulu

HAWAIIAN IS. (U.S.A.)

Miami

THE BAHAMAS

CUBA
JAMAICA
HAITI
DOMINICAN REP.

MEXICO
Mexico City

BELIZE
GUATEMALA
HONDURAS
EL SALVADOR
NICARAGUA
COSTA RICA
PANAMA
COLOMBIA

Barranquilla
Maracaibo
Caracas
Panama
VENEZUELA
GUYANA
SURINAM
FRENCH GUIANA

Buenaventura
Tumaco

Equator

ECUADOR
Guayaquil

Belém

BRAZIL

Chiclayo
Trujillo
PERU
Callao
Lima

Recife

BOLIVIA
La Paz
Mollendo
Arica
Iquique
Antofagasta

Brasilia

PARAGUAY

Rio de Janeiro

ARGENTINA

Valparaíso
Santiago
Buenos Aires
Concepción
Bahía Blanca

Pôrto Alegre

URUGUAY
Montevideo

Puerto Montt

Punta Arenas

FALKLAND IS. (U.K.)

GREENLAND (Den.)

Canada : Exports, 1991
(to all countries)

15.9%
1.6%
1.9%
3.2%
10.1%
4.7%
8.2 %
1.8%
11.3%
0.8%
22.5%
3.1%
2.2%

Total $ 138 079 m

Canada: Imports, 1991
(to all countries)

22.8%
0.4%
0.1%
2.9%
1.7%
0.7%
5.5%
0.5%
4.9%
1.6%
20.0%
2.3%
11.5%
17.5%
7.6%

Total $ 135 284 m

NEW ZEALAND
$ 92 m $ 195 m

Modified Eckert IV Projection
Oxford University Press

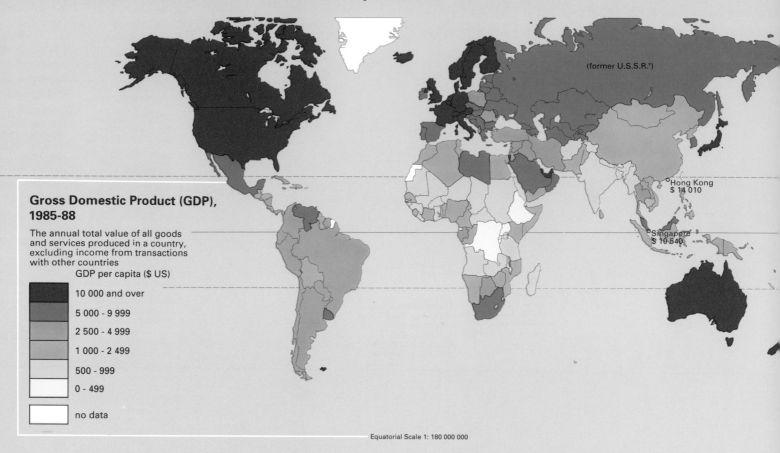

Gross Domestic Product (GDP), 1985-88

The annual total value of all goods and services produced in a country, excluding income from transactions with other countries

GDP per capita ($ US)

- 10 000 and over
- 5 000 - 9 999
- 2 500 - 4 999
- 1 000 - 2 499
- 500 - 999
- 0 - 499
- no data

(former U.S.S.R.†)

Hong Kong $ 14 010

Singapore $ 10 540

Equatorial Scale 1: 180 000 000

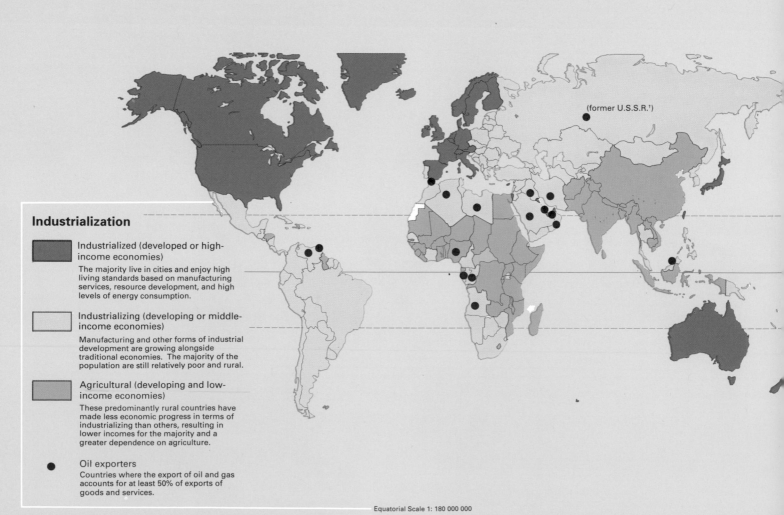

Industrialization

Industrialized (developed or high-income economies)
The majority live in cities and enjoy high living standards based on manufacturing services, resource development, and high levels of energy consumption.

Industrializing (developing or middle-income economies)
Manufacturing and other forms of industrial development are growing alongside traditional economies. The majority of the population are still relatively poor and rural.

Agricultural (developing and low-income economies)
These predominantly rural countries have made less economic progress in terms of industrializing than others, resulting in lower incomes for the majority and a greater dependence on agriculture.

● **Oil exporters**
Countries where the export of oil and gas accounts for at least 50% of exports of goods and services.

(former U.S.S.R.†)

Equatorial Scale 1: 180 000 000

Modified Gall Projection

© Oxford University Pres

Employment, 1985-88
Proportion of labour force in agriculture, industry, and service industries

services — agriculture
industry

Equatorial Scale 1: 180 000 000

(former U.S.S.R.¹)

¹Now the independent republics of Armenia, Azerbaijan, Belarus, Estonia, Georgia, Kazakhstan, Kirgyzstan, Latvia, Lithuania, Moldova, Russia, Tajikistan, Turkmenistan, Ukraine, and Uzbekistan.

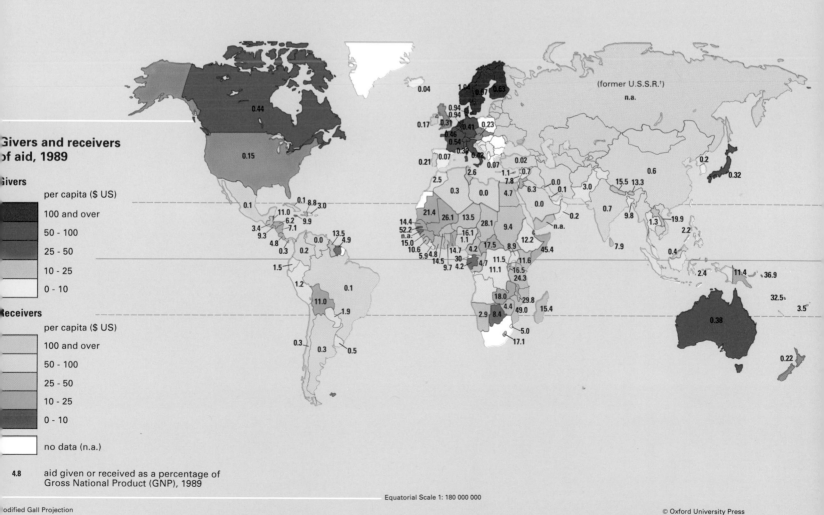

Givers and receivers of aid, 1989

Givers

per capita ($ US)

- 100 and over
- 50 - 100
- 25 - 50
- 10 - 25
- 0 - 10

Receivers

per capita ($ US)

- 100 and over
- 50 - 100
- 25 - 50
- 10 - 25
- 0 - 10

no data (n.a.)

4.8 aid given or received as a percentage of Gross National Product (GNP), 1989

(former U.S.S.R.¹)
n.a.

Equatorial Scale 1: 180 000 000

Modified Gall Projection

© Oxford University Press

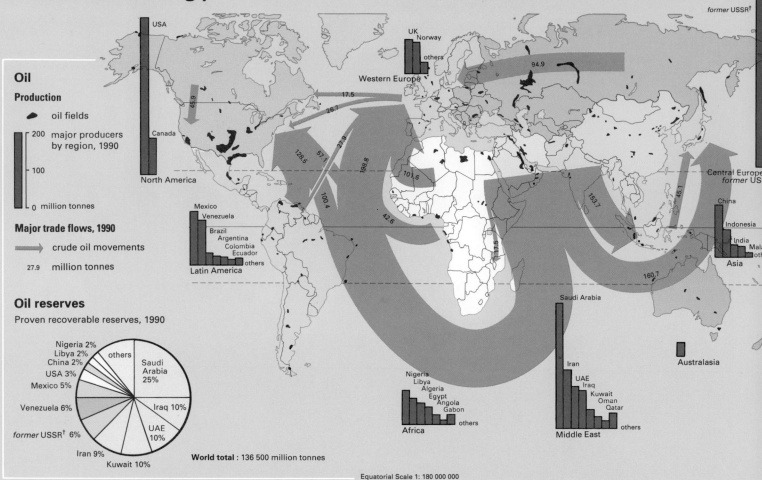

Oil

Production

🖤 oil fields

200 major producers
by region, 1990
100
0 million tonnes

Major trade flows, 1990

➡️ crude oil movements

27.9 million tonnes

Oil reserves

Proven recoverable reserves, 1990

Nigeria 2%
Libya 2%
China 2%
USA 3%
Mexico 5%
Venezuela 6%
former USSR† 6%
Iran 9%
Kuwait 10%

others
Saudi Arabia 25%
Iraq 10%
UAE 10%

World total : 136 500 million tonnes

USA
Canada
North America

UK Norway
others
Western Europe

former USSR†

94.9

45.9
17.5
26.7
27.9
128.5
57.1
27.9
198.8
100.4
42.6
101.6
11.5
153.7
45.1
160.7

Central Europe
former USSR

China
Indonesia
India
Mala
oth
Asia

Mexico
Venezuela
Brazil
Argentina
Colombia
Ecuador
others
Latin America

Nigeria
Libya
Algeria
Egypt
Angola
Gabon
others
Africa

Saudi Arabia

Iran
UAE
Iraq
Kuwait
Oman
Qatar
others
Middle East

Australasia

Equatorial Scale 1: 180 000 000

Gas

Production

🖤 gas fields

200 major producers
by region, 1990
100
0 million tonnes
of oil equivalent

Major trade flows, 1990

➡️ pipeline gas

➡️ liquified natural gas
(LNG)

45.9 thousand million m³

Gas Reserves

Proven recoverable reserves, 1990

Indonesia 2%
Nigeria 2%
Iraq 2%
Canada 2%
Venezuela 3%
Algeria 3%
Qatar 4%
USA 4%
Saudi Arabia 4%
UAE 4%

others
former USSR† 38%
Iran 14%

World total : 119 400 million m³

USA
Canada
North America

Netherlands
UK
Norway
Italy
Germany
others
Western Europe

former USSR†

40.2
16.5
2.5
64.5
45.9
39.3
3.1
3.2
3.9

Mexico
Argentina
Venezuela
others
Latin America

Algeria
others
Africa

Saudi Arabia
Iran
UAE
others
Middle East

Indonesia
Malaysia
China
Pakistan
others
Asia

Central
Europe &
former
USSR

Australasia

Equatorial Scale 1: 180 000 000

Modified Gall Projection

© Oxford University Press

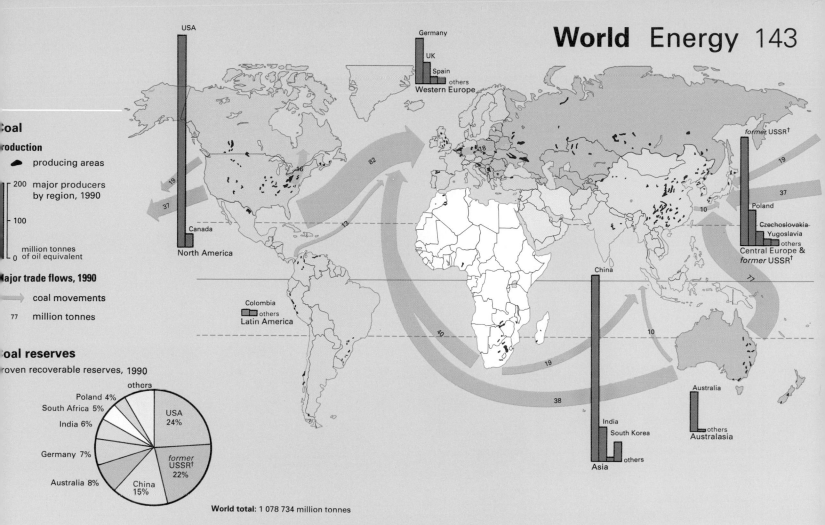

Coal

Production

⬧ producing areas

▮ major producers by region, 1990

| 200 |
| 100 |
| 0 |

million tonnes of oil equivalent

Major trade flows, 1990

➤ coal movements

77 million tonnes

Coal reserves

Proven recoverable reserves, 1990

- USA 24%
- former USSR† 22%
- China 15%
- Australia 8%
- Germany 7%
- India 6%
- South Africa 5%
- Poland 4%
- others

World total: 1 078 734 million tonnes

Equatorial Scale 1: 180 000 000

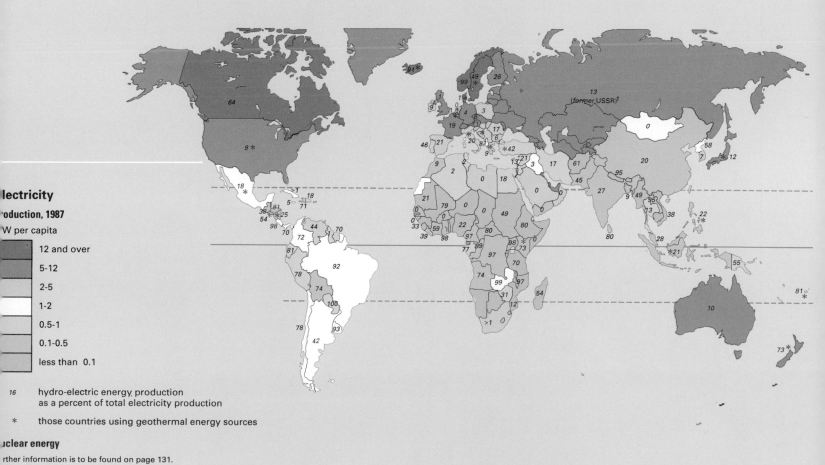

Electricity

Production, 1987

kW per capita

	12 and over
	5-12
	2-5
	1-2
	0.5-1
	0.1-0.5
	less than 0.1

16 hydro-electric energy production as a percent of total electricity production

* those countries using geothermal energy sources

Nuclear energy

Further information is to be found on page 131.

Equatorial Scale 1: 180 000 000

† Now the independent republics of Armenia, Azerbaijan, Belarus, Estonia, Georgia, Kazakhstan, Kirgyzstan, Latvia, Lithuania, Moldova, Russia, Tajikistan, Turkmenistan, Ukraine, and Uzbekistan.

Modified Gall Projection
Oxford University Press

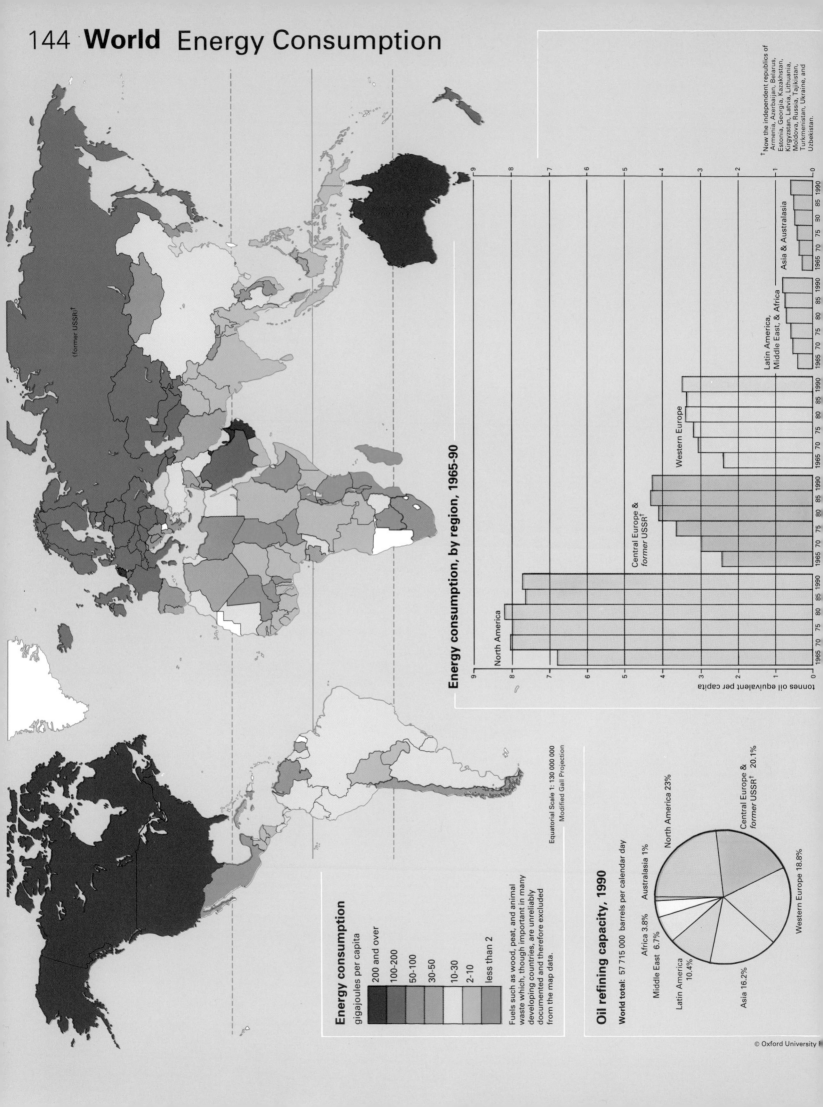

Energy consumption

gigajoules per capita

- 200 and over
- 100-200
- 50-100
- 30-50
- 10-30
- 2-10
- less than 2

Fuels such as wood, peat, and animal waste which, though important in many developing countries, are unreliably documented and therefore excluded from the map data.

(former USSR)†

Equatorial Scale 1: 130 000 000
Modified Gall Projection

Energy consumption, by region, 1965-90

tonnes oil equivalent per capita

North America

Central Europe &
former USSR†

Western Europe

Latin America,
Middle East, & Africa

Asia & Australasia

1965 70 75 80 85 1990

† Now the independent republics of Armenia, Azerbaijan, Belarus, Estonia, Georgia, Kazakhstan, Kirgyzstan, Latvia, Lithuania, Moldova, Russia, Tajikistan, Turkmenistan, Ukraine, and Uzbekistan.

Oil refining capacity, 1990

World total: 57 715 000 barrels per calendar day

- North America 23%
- Central Europe & *former* USSR† 20.1%
- Western Europe 18.8%
- Asia 16.2%
- Latin America 10.4%
- Middle East 6.7%
- Africa 3.8%
- Australasia 1%

© Oxford University

How to use the gazetteer

To find a place on an atlas map use either the grid code or latitude and longitude.

For more information on latitude and longitude look at pages 6 and 7.

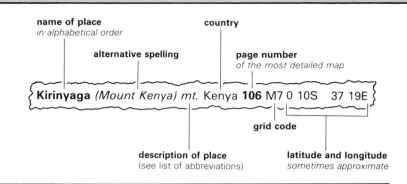

name of place *in alphabetical order*

alternative spelling

country

page number *of the most detailed map*

Kirinyaga *(Mount Kenya) mt.* Kenya **106** M7 0 10S 37 19E

grid code

description of place (see list of abbreviations)

latitude and longitude *sometimes approximate*

Grid code   Kirinyaga is in grid square M7

Kirinyaga *(Mount Kenya) mt.* Kenya **106** M7 0 10S 37 19E

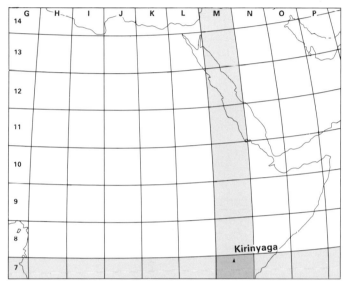

Latitude and Longitude   Kirinyaga is at latitude 0 10S longitude 37 19E

Kirinyaga *(Mount Kenya) mt.* Kenya **106** M7 0 10S 37 19E

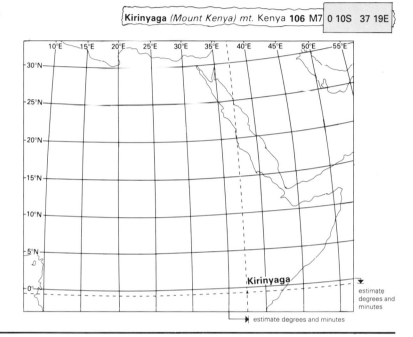

estimate degrees and minutes

Abbreviations used in the gazetteer

admin.	administrative area	mts.	mountains
A.C.T.	Australian Capital Territory	p.	peninsula
b.	bay or harbour	pk.	park
bor.	borough	plat.	plateau
c.	cape, point or headland	pn.	plain
can.	canal	pref.	prefecture
co.	county	r.	river
d.	desert	rd.	road
dep.	depression	r.s.	research station
est.	estuary	reg.	region
fj.	fjord	rep.	republic
F.R.G.	Federal Republic of Germany	res.	reservoir
g.	gulf	salt l.	salt lake
G.D.R.	German Democratic Republic	sd.	sound, strait or channel
geog. reg.	geographical region	S.S.R.	Soviet Socialist Republic
G.R.A.	Government Residential Area	sum.	summit
hist. site	historical site	tn.	town
i.	island	U.A.E.	United Arab Emirates
in.	inlet	U.K.	United Kingdom
I.R.	Indian Reservation	U.S.A.	United States of America
is.	islands	U.S.S.R.	Union of Soviet Socialist Republics
ist.	isthmus	v.	valley
l.	lake, lakes, lagoon	vol.	volcano
m.	marsh		
m.s.	manned meteorological station		
mt.	mountain		

Abbreviations used on the maps

A.C.T.	Australian Capital Territory	Peg.	Pegunungan
Ákr.	Ákra	Pen.; Penin.	Peninsula
App.	Appennino	Pl.	Planina
Arch.	Archipelago	Port.	Portugal
Arg.	Argentina	P.P.	Provincial Park
Arq.	Arquípelago	proj.	projected
Austl.	Australia	Pt.	Point
C.	Cape; Cabo; Cap	Pta.	Punta
Col.	Colombia	Pte.	Pointe
D.C.	District of Columbia	Pto.	Porto; Puerto
Den.	Denmark	R.	River; Rio
E.	East	Ra.	Range
Ec.	Ecuador	R.A.	Recreation Area
Eq.	Equatorial	Res.	Reservoir
Fj.	Fjord	Résr.	Réservoir
Fr.	France	R.M.	Regional Municipality
F.R.G.	Federal Republic of Germany	S.	South; San
G.	Gunung; Gebel	S.A.	South Africa
G.D.R.	German Democratic Republic	Sa.	Sierra
Hwy.	Highway	Sd.	Sound
I.	Island; Île; Isla; Ilha	Sev.	Severnaya
Is.	Islands; Îles; Islas; Ilhas	Sp.	Spain
J.	Jezioro	St.	Saint
Jez.	Jezero	Ste.	Sainte
Kep.	Kepulauan	Str.	Strait
M.	Muang	Terr.	Territory
Mt.	Mount; Mountain; Mont	U.A.E.	United Arab Emirates
Mte.	Monte	u/c.	under construction
Mts.	Mountains; Monts	U.K.	United Kingdom
N.	North	U.N.	United Nations
Nat. Pk.	National Park	U.S.A.	United States of America
Neths.	Netherlands	U.S.S.R.	Union of Soviet Socialist Republics
N.P.	National Park	W.	West
N.Z.	New Zealand		
Pa.	Passage		

A

Abbotsford British Columbia **42** H4 49 02N 122 18W
Aberdeen Saskatchewan **40** B2 52 20N 106 16W
Aberdeen Lake Northwest Territories **45** L3 64 30N 99 00W
Abitibi, Lake Ontario/Québec **35** E2 48 42N 79 45W
Abitibi River Ontario **35** D2 49 40N 81 20W
Abloviak Fiord Québec **32** C4 59 30N 65 25W
Acadia Alberta **41** A1 50 56N 114 03W
Acton Ontario **38** B2 43 38N 80 04W
Actonvale Québec **37** O6 45 39N 72 34W
Adair, Cape Northwest Territories **45** R5 71 32N 71 24W
Adams Lake British Columbia **43** E2 51 10N 119 30W
Adams River British Columbia **43** E2 51 23N 119 23W
Adelaide Peninsula Northwest Territories **45** M4 68 15N 97 30W
Adlatok River Newfoundland **30** B4 55 40N 62 50W
Adlavik Islands Newfoundland **30** C3 55 00N 58 40W
Admiralty Inlet Northwest Territories **45** O5 72 30N 86 00W
Admiralty Island Northwest Territories **45** M4 69 25N 101 10W
Advocate Harbour *tn.* Nova Scotia **31** F7 45 20N 64 45W
Agassiz British Columbia **42** H4 49 14N 121 52W
Agassiz Ice Cap Northwest Territories **45** Q7 80 15N 76 00W
Agassiz Provincial Forest Manitoba **39** B1 49 50N 96 20W
Aguasaban River Ontario **35** C2 48 50N 87 00W
Ailsa Craig Ontario **38** A2 43 08N 81 34W
Ainslie, Lake Nova Scotia **31** F7 46 10N 61 10W
Airdrie Alberta **41** C2 51 20N 114 00W
Air Force Island Northwest Territories **45** R4 67 58N 74 05W
Ajax Ontario **38** C2 43 48N 79 00W
Akimiski Island Northwest Territories **45** P1 52 30N 81 00W
Akimiski Island Bird Sanctuary Northwest Territories **45** P1 53 00N 81 00W
Akimiski Strait Northwest Territories/Ontario **34** D3 52 40N 82 00W
Aklavik Northwest Territories **44** E4 68 15N 135 02W
Akpatok Island Northwest Territories **32** C5 60 30N 68 00W
Akulivik Québec **32** A5 60 53N 78 15W
Albany Island Ontario **34** D3 52 15N 81 34W
Albany River Ontario **34** D3 51 40N 83 20W
Alberni Inlet *admin.* British Columbia **42** H4 49 05N 124 52W
Albert *admin.* New Brunswick **31** E7 45 40N 65 10W
Alberta *province* **41**
Alberton Prince Edward Island **31** F7 46 50N 64 08W
Albiti *admin.* Québec **37** K7 48 11N 76 48W
Aldershot Ontario **38** C2 43 17N 79 51W
Aldersyde Alberta **41** C2 50 44N 113 53W
Alert *m.s.* Northwest Territories **45** T7 80 31N 60 05W
Alert Bay *tn.* British Columbia **43** C2 50 34N 126 58W
Alexandria Ontario **37** M6 45 19N 74 38W
Alexis Creek *tn.* British Columbia **43** D2 52 05N 123 12W
Alexis River Newfoundland **30** C3 52 50N 57 60W
Alfred Ontario **37** M6 45 34N 74 53W
Alfred, Mount British Columbia **42** H5 50 13N 124 07W
Algoma *admin.* Ontario **36** C7 48 00N 84 00W
Algonquin Park *tn.* Ontario **36** H6 45 33N 78 35W
Algonquin Provincial Park Ontario **36** H6 45 50N 78 30W
Alix Alberta **41** C2 52 25N 113 11W
Allan Saskatchewan **40** B2 51 54N 106 02W
Allan Water *tn.* Ontario **34** B3 50 14N 90 12W
Alliston Ontario **38** C3 44 09N 79 51W
Alma New Brunswick **31** F7 45 36N 64 58W
Alma Québec **33** B2 48 32N 71 41W
Almonte Ontario **37** K6 45 14N 76 12W
Alouette Lake British Columbia **42** H4 49 22N 121 22W
Alsask Saskatchewan **40** B2 51 22N 110 00W
Alsek Ranges *mts.* British Columbia **42** A3 59 30N 137 30W
Altona Manitoba **39** B1 49 06N 97 35W
Alvin British Columbia **42** H4 49 25N 122 34W
Amadjuak Lake Northwest Territories **45** R3 65 00N 71 08W
Amaranthe Manitoba **39** B2 50 36N 98 43W
Amberley Ontario **38** A3 44 02N 81 44W
Amery Manitoba **39** C3 56 45N 94 00W
Amherst Nova Scotia **31** F7 45 50N 64 14W
Amherstburg Ontario **35** E1 42 06N 83 07W
Amherst Island Ontario **37** K5 44 08N 76 43W
Amisk Lake Saskatchewan **40** C2 54 30N 102 15W
Amos Québec **33** A2 48 04N 78 08W
Amund Ringnes Island Northwest Territories **45** M6 78 00N 96 00W
Amundsen Gulf Northwest Territories **44** F5 70 30N 125 00W
Anahim Lake *tn.* British Columbia **43** C2 52 25 125 18W
Ancaster Ontario **38** C2 43 13N 79 58W
Anderson Lake British Columbia **42** H5 50 38N 122 24W
Anderson River Northwest Territories **44** F4 69 42N 129 01W
Anderson River Delta Bird Sanctuary Northwest Territories **44** F4 69 50N 128 00W
Andover New Brunswick **31** A2 46 48N 67 43W
Andrew Alberta **41** C2 53 52N 112 14W
Andrew Gordon Bay Northwest Territories **45** R3 60 27N 75 30W
Angers Québec **47** L3 45 32N 75 29W
Angikuni Lake Northwest Territories **45** M3 62 00N 99 45W
Angling Lake *I.R.* Ontario **34** C3 53 50N 89 30W
Anguille, Cape Newfoundland **31** C2 47 55N 59 24W
Angus Ontario **38** C3 44 19N 79 53W
Anjou Québec **37** N6 45 37N 73 35W
Annacis Island British Columbia **46** G3 49 09N 122 57W
Annapolis *admin* Nova Scotia **31** E6 44 40N 65 20W
Annapolis Royal Nova Scotia **31** E6 44 44N 65 32W
Annieville British Columbia **46** G3 49 10N 122 54W
Anthony Island British Columbia **42** B2 52 05N 131 14W
Antigonish Nova Scotia **31** F7 45 39N 62 00W
Antigonish *admin.* Nova Scotia **31** F7 45 30N 62 10W
Anvil Range Yukon Territory **44** E3 62 25N 133 15W
Apsley Ontario **36** H5 44 45N 78 06W
Arborfield Saskatchewan **40** C2 53 06N 103 39W
Arborg Manitoba **39** B2 50 55N 97 12W
Arcola Saskatchewan **40** C1 49 38N 102 26W
Arctic Bay *tn.* Northwest Territories **45** O5 73 05N 85 20W
Arctic Red River Northwest Territories **44** E4 65 00N 125 00W
Arctic Red River *tn.* Northwest Territories **44** E4 67 27N 133 46W
Ardrossan Alberta **48** H5 53 33N 113 11W
Argenteuil *admin.* Québec **37** M6 45 50N 74 40W
Arichat Nova Scotia **31** F7 45 31N 61 00W
Aristazabal Island British Columbia **42** C2 52 40N 129 40W
Armstrong British Columbia **43** E2 50 27N 119 14W
Armstrong Ontario **34** C3 50 20N 89 02W
Arnold's Cove *tn.* Newfoundland **31** D2 47 45N 54 00W
Arnot Manitoba **39** B3 55 46N 96 42W
Arnprior Ontario **37** K6 45 26N 76 21W
Arnqui Québec **33** C2 48 30N 67 30W
Aroland Ontario **34** C3 50 14N 86 59W
Aroostook New Brunswick **31** A2 46 45N 67 40W
Arran Lake Ontario **38** A3 44 29N 81 16W
Arrowsmith, Mount British Columbia **42** H4 49 00N 124 00W
Arthabaska Québec **37** P7 46 03N 71 55W
Arthabaska *admin.* Québec **37** O6 45 58N 72 11W
Arthur Ontario **38** B2 43 50N 80 32W
Artillery Lake Northwest Territories **44** K3 63 09N 107 52W
Arviat *(Eskimo Point)* Northwest Territories **45** N3 61 10N 94 05W
Ashcroft British Columbia **43** D2 50 41N 121 17W
Ashern Manitoba **39** B2 51 10N 98 20W
Asheweig River Ontario **34** B3 53 50N 87 50W
Ashihik Lake Yukon Territory **44** D3 61 00N 135 05W
Ashnola River British Columbia **42** H4 49 13N 119 58W
Ashuanipi Newfoundland **30** A3 52 46N 66 05W
Ashuanipi Lake Newfoundland **30** A3 52 45N 66 15W
Ashuanipi River Newfoundland **30** A3 53 50N 66 50W
Aspy Bay Nova Scotia **31** F7 46 50N 60 20W
Assiniboia Saskatchewan **40** B1 49 39N 105 59W
Assiniboine Forest Manitoba **48** D2 49 51N 97 15W
Assiniboine River Manitoba/Saskatchewan **39** B1 49 40N 98 50W
Aston, Cape Northwest Territories **45** S4 70 00N 67 15W
Astray Newfoundland **30** A3 54 38N 66 42W
Astray Lake Newfoundland **30** A3 54 36N 66 30W
Athabasca Alberta **41** C2 54 44N 113 15W
Athabasca, Lake Alberta/Saskatchewan **40** B3 59 10N 109 30W
Athabasca River Alberta **41** C3 57 30N 111 40W
Athabasca Sand Dunes Parkland Reserve Saskatchewan **40** B3 59 10N 108 30W
Athens Ontario **37** L5 44 38N 75 57W
Atherley Ontario **38** C3 44 36N 79 21W
Athol Nova Scotia **31** F7 45 40N 64 10W
Atikaki Provincial Park Manitoba **39** B2 51 30N 95 30W
Atik Lake Manitoba **39** B3 55 20N 96 10W
Atikokan Ontario **34** B2 48 45N 91 38W
Atikonak Lake Newfoundland **30** B3 52 40N 64 32W
Atikonak River Newfoundland **30** B3 53 20N 64 50W
Atkinson, Point British Columbia **46** E4 49 20N 123 16W
Atlin British Columbia **42** B3 59 31N 133 41W
Atlin Lake British Columbia **42** B3 59 31N 133 41W
Atlin Provincial Park British Columbia **42** B3 59 10N 133 50W
Atna Peak British Columbia **43** C2 53 53N 128 07W
Attawapiskat Ontario **34** D3 53 00N 82 30W
Attawapiskat Lake Ontario **34** C3 52 18N 87 54W
Attawapiskat River Ontario **34** D3 53 00N 84 00W
Aubry, Lake Northwest Territories **44** F4 67 23N 126 30W
Auden Ontario **34** C3 50 14N 87 54W
Aulac New Brunswick **31** F7 45 50N 64 20W
Aulneau Peninsula Ontario **34** B2 49 23N 94 29W
Aupaluk Québec **32** C4 59 12N 69 35W
Aurora Ontario **38** C3 43 00N 79 28W
Ausable River Ontario **38** A2 43 06N 81 36W
Austin Channel Northwest Territories **45** L6 75 35N 103 25W
Auyuittuq National Park Northwest Territories **45** S4 67 00N 67 00W
Avalon Peninsula Newfoundland **31** D2 47 30N 53 30W
Avalon Wilderness Reserve Newfoundland **31** D2 47 10N 52 40W
Avola British Columbia **43** E2 51 47N 119 19W
Avon River Ontario **38** A2 43 20N 81 10W
Awenda Provincial Park Ontario **38** B2/C3 44 50N 80 00W
Axel Heiberg Island Northwest Territories **45** N7 80 00N 90 00W
Aylmer Ontario **38** B1 42 47N 80 58W
Aylmer Québec **47** J2 45 23N 75 51W
Aylmer Lake Northwest Territories **44** K3 64 05N 108 30W
Ayr Ontario **38** B2 43 17N 80 26W
Azure Lake British Columbia **43** D2 52 22N 120 07W

B

Babine Lake British Columbia **43** C2 54 45N 125 05W
Babine River British Columbia **43** C3 55 44N 127 29W
Bache Peninsula Northwest Territories **45** Q6 79 08N 76 00W
Backbone Ranges *mts.* Northwest Territories **44** F3 64 30N 130 00W
Back River Northwest Territories **45** L4 65 00N 105 00W
Baddeck Nova Scotia **31** F7 46 06N 60 45W
Badger Newfoundland **31** C2 49 00N 56 04W
Baffin *reg.* Northwest Territories **45** O5 71 30N 88 00W
Baffin Bay Northwest Territories **45** S5 72 00N 64 00W
Baffin Island Northwest Territories **45** Q5 70 00N 75 00W
Baie-Comeau *tn.* Québec **33** C2 49 12N 68 10W
Baie des Chaleurs *b.* Québec/New Brunswick **33** C2 47 59N 65 50W
Baie de Valois *b.* Québec **47** M4 45 27N 73 17W
Baie d'Hudson *(Hudson Bay)* Québec/Northwest Territories/Ontario **32** A3 58 00N 79 00W
Baie d'Ungava *(Ungava Bay)* Québec/Northwest Territories **32** C4 59 00N 67 30W
Baie James *(James Bay)* Québec/Northwest Territories Ontario **33** A3 52 00N 79 00W
Baie-St.-Paul *tn.* Québec **37** Q8 47 27N 70 30W
Baie-Trinité *tn.* Québec **33** C2 49 25N 67 20W
Baie Verte *b.* Nova Scotia **31** F7 46 00N 64 00W
Baie Verte *tn.* Newfoundland **31** C2 49 55N 56 12W
Baie Verte Peninsula Newfoundland **31** C2 49 45N 56 15W
Bailey Creek Ontario **38** C3 44 01N 79 56W
Baillie Islands Northwest Territories **44** F5 70 35N 128 10W
Baillie River Northwest Territories **44** K3 64 40N 105 50W
Baird Peninsula Northwest Territories **45** Q4 68 55N 76 04W
Baker Lake Northwest Territories **45** M3 64 00N 95 00W
Baker Lake *tn.* Northwest Territories **45** M3 64 20N 96 10W
Balcarres Saskatchewan **40** C2 50 49N 103 32W
Baldock Lake Manitoba **39** B3 56 30N 98 25W
Baldy Mountain Manitoba **39** A2 51 27N 100 45W
Balgonie Saskatchewan **40** C2 50 31N 104 15W
Ballantyre Strait Northwest Territories **44** H6 77 25N 114 20W
Ball Lake Alberta **48** G5 53 31N 113 16W
Balmertown Ontario **34** B3 51 04N 93 41W
Balsam Lake Ontario **38** D3 44 37N 78 51W
Balsam Lake Provincial Park Ontario **38** D3 44 30N 78 50W
Balzac Alberta **41** C2 51 15N 114 00W
Bamaji Lake Ontario **34** B3 51 09N 91 26W
Bancroft Ontario **36** J6 45 03N 77 51W
Banff Alberta **41** B2 51 10N 115 34W
Banff National Park Alberta **41** B2 51 00N 116 00W
Banks Island Northwest Territories **44** G5 73 15N 121 30W
Banks Island No.1 Bird Sanctuary Northwest Territories **44** G5 72 30N 124 50W
Banks Island No.2 Bird Sanctuary Northwest Territories **44** G5 73 30N 124 00W
Baring, Cape Northwest Territories **44** H5 70 02N 117 20W
Barkerville British Columbia **43** D2 53 06N 121 35W
Barkley Sound British Columbia **42** G4 48 58N 125 11W
Barnes Ice Cap Northwest Territories **45** H5 70 00N 74 00W
Barnfield British Columbia **42** G4 48 50N 125 07W
Barnston Island British Columbia **46** H3 49 11N 122 42W
Barrhaven Ontario **47** J2 45 16N 75 47W
Barrhead Alberta **41** C2 54 10N 114 22W
Barrie Ontario **38** C3 44 22N 79 42W
Barrie Island Ontario **36** D6 45 56N 82 39W
Barrière British Columbia **43** D2 51 10N 120 07W
Barrington Nova Scotia **31** E6 43 34N 65 35W
Barrington Lake Manitoba **39** B3 57 00N 99 50W
Barrow Bay Ontario **38** A3 44 58N 81 11W
Barrows Manitoba **39** A2 52 50N 101 26W
Barrow Strait Northwest Territories **45** N5 74 24N 94 10W
Barry's Bay *tn.* Ontario **36** J6 45 27N 77 41W
Bashaw Alberta **41** C2 52 35N 112 58W
Basin Lake Saskatchewan **40** B2 52 40N 105 10W
Bassano Alberta **41** C2 50 47N 112 28W
Bass Lake Ontario **38** C3 44 36N 79 31W
Bass Lake Provincial Park Ontario **38** C3 44 30N 79 40W
Bataga River British Columbia **43** C3 58 30N 126 40W
Batchawana Bay *tn.* Ontario **35** C2 46 53N 84 36W
Batchawana Mountain Ontario **35** D2 47 04N 84 24W
Bath New Brunswick **31** A2 46 30N 67 36W
Bath Ontario **37** K5 44 11N 76 47W
Bathurst New Brunswick **31** A2 47 37N 65 40W
Bathurst, Cape Northwest Territories **44** F5 70 31N 127 53W
Bathurst Inlet Northwest Territories **44** K4 66 49N 108 00W
Bathurst Inlet *tn.* Northwest Territories **44** K4 66 50N 108 01W
Bathurst Island Northwest Territories **45** L6 76 00N 100 00W
Batoche National Historic Site Saskatchewan **40** B2 52 45N 107 00W
Batteau Newfoundland **30** C3 53 24N 55 47W
Battle Creek Saskatchewan **40** B1 49 20N 109 30W
Battleford Saskatchewan **40** B2 52 45N 108 20W
Battle Harbour *tn.* Newfoundland **30** C3 52 16N 55 35W
Battle River Alberta/Saskatchewan **40** B2 52 50N 109 10W
Bauld, Cape Newfoundland **30** C3 51 40N 55 25W
Bay Bulls *tn.* Newfoundland **31** D2 47 19N 52 50W
Bay de Verde *tn.* Newfoundland **31** D2 48 03N 52 54W
Bayers Lake Nova Scotia **47** P6 44 38N 63 39W
Bayfield Ontario **38** A2 43 33N 81 41W
Bayfield River Ontario **38** A2 43 34N 81 38W
Bay of Islands Newfoundland **30** C4 55 09N 59 49W
Bay of Islands Newfoundland **31** C2 49 10N 58 14W
Bay Roberts *tn.* Newfoundland **31** D2 47 36N 53 16W
Beachburg Ontario **37** K6 45 44N 76 51W
Beacon Hill Ontario **47** K2 45 28N 75 35W
Beaconsfield Québec **47** M4 45 26N 73 52W
Beale, Cape British Columbia **42** G4 48 46N 125 10W
Beamsville Ontario **38** C2 43 10N 79 31W
Beardmore Ontario **34** C2 49 36N 87 59W
Bear Island Northwest Territories **34** E3 64 01N 83 13W
Bear Lake Manitoba **39** B3 55 10N 96 30W
Bear River Ontario **47** L2 45 22N 75 29W
Bear River *tn.* Nova Scotia **31** E6 44 34N 65 40W
Bearskin Lake *I.R.* Ontario **34** B3 53 50N 90 55W
Beatton River British Columbia **43** D3 57 18N 121 15W
Beatty Saugeen River Ontario **38** B3 44 08N 80 54W
Beattyville Québec **33** A2 48 53N 77 10W
Beauce *admin.* Québec **37** Q7 46 15N 71 00W
Beauceville Québec **37** Q7 46 12N 70 45W
Beauharnois Québec **37** N6 45 18N 73 52W
Beaufort Sea Arctic Ocean **10** E7 72 00N 140 00W
Beaumaris Lake Alberta **48** F5 53 38N 113 32W
Beaumont Alberta **48** G4 53 20N 113 28W
Beauport Québec **37** P7 46 52N 71 12W
Beaupré Québec **37** Q8 47 03N 70 56W
Beausejour Manitoba **39** B2 50 04N 96 30W
Beauval Saskatchewan **40** B3 55 09N 107 35W
Beaver Creek Ontario **46** C2 43 51N 79 23W
Beaver Creek *tn.* Yukon Territory **44** D3 60 20N 140 45W
Beaverdell British Columbia **43** E1 49 25N 119 09W
Beaverhill Lake Alberta **41** C2 53 27N 112 32W
Beaver Hill Lake Manitoba **39** B2 54 20N 95 20W
Beaverlodge Alberta **41** B3 55 13N 119 26W
Beaver River Ontario **38** B3 44 21N 80 33W
Beaver River Alberta/Saskatchewan **40** B2 52 10N 108 40W
Beaverton Ontario **38** C3 44 25N 79 10W
Beaverton River Ontario **38** C3 44 08N 79 06W
Bécancour Québec **37** O7 46 20N 72 30W
Beckwith Island Ontario **38** B3 44 53N 80 06W
Beddington Creek Alberta **48** A2 51 15N 114 11W
Bedford Nova Scotia **47** P6 44 44N 61 37W
Bedford Basin Nova Scotia **47** P6 44 41N 63 37W
Beechey Head *c.* British Columbia **42** H4 48 19 123 39W
Beechville Nova Scotia **47** P6 44 37N 63 42W
Beeton Ontario **38** C3 44 04N 79 46W
Beiseker Alberta **41** C2 51 23N 113 32W
Belcher Islands Northwest Territories **45** Q2 56 00N 79 30W
Bella Coola British Columbia **43** C2 52 30N 126 50W
Bella Coola River British Columbia **43** C2 52 22N 126 35W
Bellcarra British Columbia **46** G4 49 19N 122 56W
Belle Bay Newfoundland **31** C2 47 37N 55 18W
Bellechasse *admin.* Québec **37** Q7 46 40N 70 50W
Belledune New Brunswick **31** A2 47 50N 65 45W
Belle Isle *i.* Newfoundland **30** C3 51 57N 55 21W
Belleoram Newfoundland **31** C2 47 31N 55 25W
Belle Plaine Saskatchewan **40** B2 50 25N 105 09W
Belle River *tn.* Ontario **36** D3 42 18N 82 43W
Belleville Ontario **37** J5 44 10N 77 23W
Bell-Irving River British Columbia **42** C3 56 42N 129 40W
Bell Island Newfoundland **31** C3 50 80N 55 50W
Belle Isle, Strait of Newfoundland **30** C3 51 30N 56 30W
Bell Peninsula Northwest Territories **45** P3 63 00N 82 00W
Bells Corners Ontario **47** J2 45 19N 75 49W
Belly River Alberta **41** C1 49 10N 113 40W
Belmont Ontario **38** A1 42 52N 81 06W
Belseil Québec **37** N6 45 34N 73 15W
Belwood, Lake Ontario **38** B2 43 46N 80 20W
Benedict Mountains Newfoundland **30** C3 54 45N 58 45W
Bengough Saskatchewan **40** B1 49 25N 105 10W
Benito Manitoba **39** A2 51 55N 101 30W
Bentley Alberta **41** C2 52 28N 114 04W
Berens River Manitoba/Ontario **39** B2 52 10N 96 40W
Berens River *tn.* Manitoba **39** B2 52 22N 97 00W
Beresford New Brunswick **31** A2 47 40N 65 40W
Bergland Ontario **34** B2 48 57N 94 23W
Bernier Bay Northwest Territories **45** O5 71 05N 88 15W
Berthier *admin.* Québec **37** M8 47 40N 75 20W
Berthierville Québec **27** 46 05N 73 11W
Bertrand New Brunswick **31** A2 47 45N 65 05W
Berwick Nova Scotia **31** F7 45 03N 64 44W
Berwyn Alberta **41** B3 56 09N 117 44W
Besnard Lake Saskatchewan **40** B3 55 30N 106 10W
Bethany Ontario **38** D3 44 11N 78 34W
Betsiamites Québec **33** C2 48 56N 68 40W
Bible Hill *tn.* Nova Scotia **31** F7 45 20N 63 10W
Bienfait Saskatchewan **40** C1 49 09N 102 48W
Big Bay *tn.* British Columbia **42** G5 50 24N 125 08W
Big Creek Ontario **38** B1 42 43N 80 33W
Biggar Saskatchewan **40** B2 52 03N 107 59W
Bighead River Ontario **38** B3 44 30N 80 47W
Big Indian Lake Nova Scotia **47** P6 44 35N 63 42W
Big Island Northwest Territories **45** R3 62 43N 70 43W
Big Island Ontario **34** B2 49 10N 94 30W
Big Island Lake Alberta **48** H4 53 28N 113 12W
Big Lake Alberta **48** F5 53 37N 113 40W
Big Muddy Lake Saskatchewan **40** C1 49 10N 104 50W
Big Otter Creek Ontario **38** B1 42 46N 80 51W
Big River Newfoundland **30** C3 54 40N 59 40W
Big River *tn.* Saskatchewan **40** B2 53 50N 107 01W
Big Salmon Range *mts.* Yukon Territory **44** E3 62 40N 134 59W
Big Sand Lake Manitoba **39** B3 57 50N 99 30W
Big Silver Creek British Columbia **42** H4 49 50N 121 50W
Bigstick Lake Saskatchewan **40** B2 50 20N 109 50W
Bigstone Lake Manitoba **39** B2 53 30N 95 50W
Big Trout Lake Ontario **34** C3 53 40N 89 50W
Big Trout Lake *tn.* Ontario **34** C3 53 49N 89 54W
Birch Cove Nova Scotia **47** P6 44 40N 63 39W
Birch Hills *tn.* Saskatchewan **40** B2 53 00N 105 10W
Birch Island Manitoba **39** B2 52 20N 99 50W
Birch Lake Alberta **41** C2 53 19N 111 35W
Birch Lake Ontario **34** B3 51 20N 92 20W
Birch Mountains Alberta **41** C3 57 20N 113 55W
Birch River Alberta **41** C3 58 20N 113 20W
Birds Hill Manitoba **48** E2 49 58N 96 59W
Birken British Columbia **42** H5 50 29N 122 36W
Birkenhead Lake Provincial Park British Columbia **42** H5 50 35N 122 42W
Birtle Manitoba **39** A2 50 26N 101 04W
Biscotasing Ontario **35** D2 47 17N 82 06W
Bishop's Falls *tn.* Newfoundland **31** C2 49 01N 55 30W
Bistcho Lake Alberta **41** B3 59 45N 118 50W
Bjorne Peninsula Northwest Territories **45** M6 77 37N 87 00W
Black Bear Island Lake Saskatchewan **40** B3 55 45N 105 50W
Black Birch Lake Saskatchewan **40** B3 56 55N 107 25W
Blackburn Ontario **47** K2 45 26N 75 33W
Black Diamond Alberta **41** C2 50 45N 114 12W
Blackfalds Alberta **41** C2 52 23N 113 47W
Black Island *tn.* Newfoundland **30** C3 54 30N 58 50W
Black Lake Saskatchewan **40** C3 59 10N 104 30W
Black Lake *tn.* Québec **37** P7 46 03N 71 21W
Black Lake *tn.* Saskatchewan **40** B3 59 05N 105 35W
Blackmud Creek Alberta **48** F4 53 25N 113 33W
Black River Ontario **38** C3 44 48N 79 08W
Blacks Harbour New Brunswick **31** A2 45 03N 66 49W
Blackville New Brunswick **31** A2 46 44N 65 51W
Blackwater Lake Northwest Territories **44** G3 64 00N 123 05W
Blaine Lake *tn.* Saskatchewan **40** B2 52 50N 106 54W
Blainville Québec **47** M5 45 39N 73 52W
Blair Ontario **38** B2 43 23N 80 23W
Blanc Sablon Québec **32** E3 51 26N 57 08W
Blenheim Ontario **36** E3 42 20N 82 00W
Blind River *tn.* Ontario **36** D7 46 10N 82 58W
Bloodvein River Manitoba **39** B2 51 50N 96 40W
Bloomfield Ontario **37** J4 43 59N 77 14W
Blubber Bay *tn.* British Columbia **42** H4 49 48N 124 37W
Bluenose Lake Northwest Territories **44** G4 68 30N 119 35W
Blue Ridge *tn.* Alberta **41** B2 54 08N 115 22W
Blue River *tn.* British Columbia **43** E2 52 05N 119 09W
Blyth Ontario **38** A2 43 43N 81 26W
Blyth Brook Ontario **38** A2 43 45N 81 31W
Boag Lake Alberta **48** H5 53 31N 113 09W
Bobcaygeon Ontario **38** D3 44 32N 78 33W
Boisbriand Québec **47** M5 45 35N 73 51W
Boissevain Manitoba **39** A1 49 14N 100 02W
Bolton Ontario **38** C2 43 53N 79 44W
Bonavista Newfoundland **31** D2 48 39N 53 07W
Bonavista Bay Newfoundland **31** D2 48 45N 53 30W

Bonavista Peninsula Newfoundland **31** D2 48 60N 53 30W
Bon Echo Provincial Park Ontario **37** J5 44 55N 77 15W
Bonnet Plume River Yukon Territory **44** E4 65 25N 135 00W
Bonnyville Alberta **41** C2 54 16N 110 44W
Boothia, Gulf of Northwest Territories **45** O4 69 00N 88 00W
Boothia Peninsula Northwest Territories **45** N5 70 30N 94 30W
Borden Prince Edward Island **31** F7 46 20N 63 40W
Borden Island Northwest Territories **44** J6 78 30N 111 30W
Borden Peninsula Northwest Territories **45** P5 73 00N 82 30W
Boston Bar British Columbia **42** H4 49 52N 121 25W
Botwood Newfoundland **31** C2 49 09N 55 21W
Boucherville Québec **47** O5 45 35N 73 26W
Bouctouche New Brunswick **31** F7 46 30N 64 40W
Boundary Range *mts.* British Columbia **42** B3 58 00N 133 00W
Bourne, Cape Northwest Territories **81** 35N 91 50W
Bowden Alberta **41** C2 51 55N 114 02W
Bowen Island British Columbia **42** H4 49 23N 123 26W
Bow Island *tn.* Alberta **41** C1 49 52N 111 22W
Bowman Bay Wildlife Sanctuary Northwest Territories **45** R4 66 00N 74 00W
Bowmanville Ontario **38** D2 43 55N 78 43W
Bowmanville Creek Ontario **38** D3 44 02N 78 47N
Bowness Alberta **48** A2 51 05N 114 14W
Bow River Alberta **41** C2 50 47N 111 55W
Bowron Lake Provincial Park British Columbia **43** D2 53 00N 121 00W
Bowron River British Columbia **43** D2 53 38N 121 40W
Bowser British Columbia **42** H4 49 26N 124 41W
Boyle Alberta **41** C2 54 35N 112 49W
Boyne River Ontario **38** B3 44 07N 80 07W
Bracebridge Ontario **36** G6 45 02N 79 19W
Bradford *see* Bradford West Gwillimbury
Bradford West Gwillimbury Ontario **38** C3 44 07N 79 34W
Bralorne British Columbia **42** H5 50 46N 122 51W
Bramalea Ontario **46** B1 43 44N 79 44W
Brampton Ontario **46** A1 43 42N 79 46W
Brandon Manitoba **39** B1 49 50N 99 57W
Brant *admin.* Ontario **38** B2 43 03N 80 29W
Brantford Ontario **38** B2 43 09N 80 17W
Bras d'Or Lake Nova Scotia **31** F7 45 50N 60 50W
Brazeau, Mount Alberta **41** B2 52 33N 117 21W
Brazeau River Alberta **41** B2 52 50N 116 20W
Brechin Ontario **38** C3 44 32N 79 11W
Bremner Alberta **48** H5 53 34N 113 13W
Brent Ontario **36** H7 46 02N 78 29W
Bretona Alberta **48** G4 53 26N 113 19W
Breton, Cape Nova Scotia **31** G7 45 50N 59 50W
Breton Cove *tn.* Nova Scotia **31** F7 46 30N 60 30W
Brevoort Island Northwest Territories **45** T3 63 19N 64 08W
Bridgenorth Ontario **38** D3 44 23N 78 23W
Bridgeport Ontario **38** B2 43 29N 80 29W
Bridge River British Columbia **42** H5 50 55N 123 25W
Bridgetown Nova Scotia **31** F6 44 50N 65 20W
Bridgewater Nova Scotia **31** F6 44 23N 64 32W
Brier Island Nova Scotia **31** E6 44 20N 66 20W
Brighouse British Columbia **46** F3 49 09N 123 11W
Brighton Ontario **36** J5 44 07N 77 45W
Bristol New Brunswick **31** A2 46 28N 67 38W
Britannia Beach *tn.* British Columbia **42** H4 49 38N 123 10W
British Columbia *province* **42/43**
British Empire Range *mts.* Northwest Territories **45** P7 82 30N 78 10W
British Mountains Yukon Territory Canada/Alaska U.S.A. **44** D4 69 00N 141 00W
Britt Ontario **36** F6 45 46N 80 33W
Broadview Saskatchewan **40** C2 50 22N 102 31W
Brockville Ontario **37** L5 44 35N 75 41W
Brodeur Peninsula Northwest Territories **45** O5 72 00N 87 30W
Brome *admin.* Québec **37** O6 45 10N 72 10W
Bromont Québec **37** O6 45 18N 72 38W
Bronte Ontario **38** C2 43 23N 79 43W
Brookfield Nova Scotia **31** F7 45 15N 63 18W
Brooklyn Nova Scotia **31** F7 44 04N 64 42W
Brooks Alberta **41** C2 50 35N 111 54W
Brooks Peninsula British Columbia **43** C2 50 05N 127 45W
Brossard Québec **37** N6 45 28N 73 30W
Broughton Island *tn.* Northwest Territories **45** T4 67 40N 63 50W
Brown Lake Northwest Territories **45** M4 65 54N 91 15W
Bruce *admin.* Ontario **38** A3 44 15N 81 24W
Bruce Creek Ontario **46** C2 43 55N 79 20W
Bruce Mines *tn.* Ontario **36** C7 46 18N 83 48W
Bruce Peninsula Ontario **38** A4 45 00N 81 20W
Bruce Peninsula National Park Ontario **38** A4 45 00N 81 20W
Bruderheim Alberta **41** C2 53 47N 112 56W
Brunette Island Newfoundland **31** C2 47 16N 55 55W
Bruno Saskatchewan **40** B2 52 17N 105 31W
Brussels Ontario **38** A2 43 44N 81 15W
Bryan Channel Northwest Territories **45** K5 74 50N 105 00W
Buchan Gulf Northwest Territories **45** R5 71 47N 74 16W
Buchans Newfoundland **31** C2 48 49N 56 53W
Buckhorn Ontario **38** D3 44 33N 78 20W
Buckhorn Lake Ontario **38** D3 44 29N 78 25W
Buckingham Québec **37** L6 45 35N 75 25W
Buffalo Head Hills Alberta **41** B3 57 25N 115 55W
Buffalo Lake Alberta **41** C2 52 27N 112 54W
Buffalo Narrows *tn.* Saskatchewan **40** B3 55 52N 108 28W
Buffalo River Alberta **41** C3 59 25N 114 35W
Buffalo Trail Alberta **41** C2 51 45N 110 35W
Bulkley River British Columbia **43** C2 55 00N 127 10W
Buntzen Lake British Columbia **46** G4 49 20N 124 51W
Burden, Mount British Columbia **43** D3 56 10N 123 09W
Burford Ontario **38** B2 43 46N 80 25W
Burgeo Newfoundland **31** C2 47 37N 57 37W
Burin Newfoundland **31** C2 47 02N 55 10W
Burin Peninsula Newfoundland **31** C2 47 00N 55 40W
Burk's Falls *tn.* Ontario **36** G6 45 37N 79 25W
Burlington Ontario **38** C2 43 19N 79 48W
Burnaby British Columbia **42** H4 49 16N 122 58W
Burnaby Lake British Columbia **46** G3 49 14N 122 57W
Burns Alberta **48** A1 50 59N 114 02W
Burnside Nova Scotia **47** P6 44 41N 63 35W
Burnside River Northwest Territories **44** F4 66 20N 109 30W
Burns Lake *tn.* British Columbia **43** C2 54 14N 125 45W
Burnt Islands *tn.* Newfoundland **31** C2 47 37N 58 50W
Burnt Lake Newfoundland **30** B3 52 20N 63 40W
Burnt Lake Québec **33** D3 52 15N 63 50W
Burnt River Ontario **38** D3 44 41N 78 43W
Burntwood Lake Manitoba **39** A3 55 20N 100 10W
Burntwood River Manitoba **39** B3 55 50N 97 40W
Burquitlam British Columbia **46** G4 49 15N 122 56W
Burrard Inlet British Columbia **46** F4 49 19N 123 14W
Burstall Saskatchewan **40** B2 50 40N 109 56W
Bushell Park *tn.* Saskatchewan **40** B2 50 25N 105 30W
Bute Inlet British Columbia **42** H5 50 31N 124 59W
Buttle Lake British Columbia **42** G4 49 47N 125 30W
Button Bay Manitoba **39** C3 58 50N 94 30W
Button Islands Northwest Territories **32** D5 60 35N 64 40W
Buttonville Ontario **46** C2 43 51N 79 22W
Byam Martin Island Northwest Territories **45** L6 75 15N 104 15W
Bylot Island Northwest Territories **45** Q5 73 30N 79 00W
Bylot Island Bird Sanctuary Northwest Territories **45** Q5 73 20N 79 00W
Byron Bay Newfoundland **30** C3 54 40N 57 40W

C

Cabano Québec **33** C2 47 40N 68 56W
Cabot Head Ontario **38** A4 45 15N 81 17W
Cabot Lake Newfoundland **30** B4 56 09N 62 37W
Cabot Strait Nova Scotia/Newfoundland **31** C2 47 10N 59 30W
Cabri Saskatchewan **40** B2 50 38N 108 28W
Cache Creek *tn.* British Columbia **43** D2 50 46N 121 17W
Calabogie Ontario **37** K6 45 18N 76 43W
Calais New Brunswick **31** A2 45 10N 67 15W
Caledon East Ontario **38** C2 43 52N 79 53W
Caledonia Nova Scotia **31** E6 44 24N 65 02W
Caledonia Ontario **38** C2 43 05N 79 57W
Calgary Alberta **41** C2 51 05N 114 05W
Calgary City *admin.* Alberta **48** A2 51 10N 114 09W
Callander Ontario **36** G7 46 13N 79 22W
Calling Lake Alberta **41** C3 55 15N 113 20W
Calmar Alberta **41** C2 53 16N 113 49W
Calvert Island British Columbia **43** C2 51 30N 128 00W
Cambridge Ontario **38** B2 43 22N 80 20W
Cambridge Bay *tn.* Northwest Territories **44** L4 69 09N 105 00W
Cambridge-Narrows New Brunswick **31** A2 45 50N 65 55W
Cameron Hills Alberta **41** B3 59 48N 118 00W
Campbell Dam Saskatchewan **40** C2 53 40N 103 20W
Campbellford Ontario **36** J5 44 18N 77 48W
Campbell Lake British Columbia **42** G4 49 59N 125 30W
Campbell, Mount Yukon Territory **44** D3 64 23N 138 43W
Campbell River *tn.* British Columbia **42** G5 50 00N 125 18W
Campbellton New Brunswick **31** A2 48 00N 66 41W
Campbellton Newfoundland **31** D2 49 17N 54 50W
Campbellville Ontario **38** C2 43 29N 79 59W
Camperville Manitoba **39** A2 51 00N 100 08W
Campobello Island New Brunswick **31** A1 44 50N 66 50W
Camp Robinson Ontario **34** B3 50 08N 93 12W
Camrose Alberta **41** C2 53 01N 112 50W
Camsell Portage Saskatchewan **40** B3 59 39N 109 12W
Canal Flats *tn.* British Columbia **43** E2 50 09N 115 50W
Canal Lake Ontario **38** C3 44 34N 79 02W
Candiac Québec **47** N4 45 24N 73 31W
Candle Lake Saskatchewan **40** B2 53 55N 105 10W
Candle Lake *tn.* Saskatchewan **40** B2 53 50N 105 10W
Canmore Alberta **41** B2 51 07N 115 18W
Canning Nova Scotia **31** F7 45 10N 64 26W
Canoe Lake Saskatchewan **40** B3 55 10N 108 30W
Canora Saskatchewan **40** C2 51 38N 102 28W
Canso Nova Scotia **31** F7 45 20N 61 00W
Canso, Cape Nova Scotia **31** F7 45 19N 60 59W
Cap-aux-Meules *tn.* Québec **33** D2 47 25N 62 00W
Cap-Chat *tn.* Québec **33** C2 49 06N 66 42W
Cap-de-la-Madeleine *tn.* Québec **37** O7 46 00N 72 00W
Cap Dufferin *c.* Québec **32** A4 58 35N 78 32W
Cape Breton *admin.* Nova Scotia **31** F7 45 50N 60 00W
Cape Breton Highlands National Park Nova Scotia **31** F7 46 45N 60 40W
Cape Breton Island Nova Scotia **31** F7 46 45N 60 00W
Cape Charles *tn.* Newfoundland **30** C3 52 13N 55 38W
Cape Croker *tn.* Ontario **38** B3 44 56N 81 01W
Cape Dorset *tn.* Northwest Territories **45** Q3 64 10N 76 40W
Cape Dorset Sanctuaries Northwest Territories **45** Q3 63 50N 77 00W
Cape Dyer *m.s.* Northwest Territories **45** T4 66 37N 61 16W
Cape Le Havre Island Nova Scotia **31** F6 44 10N 64 20W
Cape North *tn.* Nova Scotia **31** F7 46 55N 60 30W
Cape Parry *m.s.* Northwest Territories **44** F5 70 08N 124 34W
Cape Sable Island Nova Scotia **31** E6 43 30N 65 40W
Cape St. George *tn.* Newfoundland **31** C2 48 28N 59 15W
Cape Scott Provincial Park British Columbia **43** C2 50 42N 128 20W
Cape Tormentine *tn.* New Brunswick **31** F7 46 08N 63 47W
Cap Gaspé *c.* Québec **33** D2 48 46N 64 10W
Cap Hopes Advance *c.* Québec **32** C5 61 00N 69 40W
Capilano Lake British Columbia **46** F4 49 22N 123 06W
Cap Pelé *tn.* New Brunswick **31** F7 46 10N 64 10W
Cap Prince-de-Galles *c.* Québec **32** C5 61 42N 71 30W
Cap Rouge *c.* Québec **37** P7 46 40N 71 32W
Cap-Saint-Ignace *c.* Québec **37** Q8 47 00N 70 29W
Capstick Nova Scotia **31** F7 47 00N 60 31W
Caramat Ontario **35** C2 49 37N 86 09W
Caraquet New Brunswick **31** B2 47 48N 64 59W
Carberry Manitoba **39** B1 49 52N 99 20W
Carbonear Newfoundland **31** D2 47 44N 53 13W
Carcross Yukon Territory **44** E3 60 11N 134 41W
Cardigan Prince Edward Island **31** F7 46 14N 62 37W
Cardinal Ontario **37** L5 44 47N 75 23W
Cardston Alberta **41** C1 49 12N 113 18W
Cariboo Mountains British Columbia **43** D2 53 20N 120 50W
Caribou Manitoba **39** B3 59 20N 97 50W
Caribou Mountains Alberta **41** B3 59 00N 115 30W
Caribou River Manitoba **39** B3 59 30N 95 30W
Carleton Québec **33** C2 48 00N 66 10W
Carleton *admin.* New Brunswick **31** A2 46 10N 67 50W
Carleton, Mount New Brunswick **31** A2 47 24N 66 52W
Carleton Place Ontario **37** K6 45 15N 75 45W
Carling Ontario **38** B4 45 24N 80 09W
Carlsbad Springs Ontario **47** L2 45 22N 75 29W
Carlson Landing Alberta **41** C3 58 59N 111 45W
Carlyle Saskatchewan **40** C1 49 39N 102 18W
Carmacks Yukon Territory **44** D3 62 04N 136 21W
Carman Manitoba **39** B1 49 32N 97 59W
Carmanville Newfoundland **31** D2 49 24N 54 18W
Carnduff Saskatchewan **40** C1 49 11N 101 50W
Carp Lake British Columbia **43** D2 54 48N 123 20W
Carp Lake Provincial Park British Columbia **43** D2 54 08N 123 30W
Carp River Ontario **47** J2 45 18N 75 55W
Carrot River Manitoba **39** B2 54 50N 96 40W
Carrot River Saskatchewan **40** C2 53 05N 104 15W
Carrot River *tn.* Saskatchewan **40** C2 53 18N 103 32W
Carstairs Alberta **41** C2 51 34N 114 06W
Cartierville Québec **47** N5 45 31N 73 43W
Cartmel, Mount British Columbia **42** C3 57 45N 129 12W
Cartwright Newfoundland **30** C3 53 42N 57 01W
Cascade Range *mts.* British Columbia **42** H4 50 48N 121 15W
Cascade Recreation Area British Columbia **42** H4 49 16N 120 56W
Cascumpec Bay Prince Edward Island **31** F7 46 45N 64 00W
Cassiar British Columbia **42** C3 59 15N 129 49W
Cassiar Highway British Columbia **42** B3 57 30N 130 10W
Cassiar Mountains British Columbia **42** B3 59 50N 131 50W
Castlegar British Columbia **43** E1 49 18N 117 41W
Castor Alberta **41** C2 52 13N 111 53W
Catalina Newfoundland **31** D2 48 31N 53 05W
Cat Arm Reservoir Newfoundland **31** C3 50 10N 56 40W
Catchacoma Lake Ontario **38** D3 44 46N 78 16W
Cathedral National Park British Columbia **42** H4 49 05N 120 11W
Cat Lake Ontario **34** B3 51 30N 91 50W
Cat Lake *I.R.* Ontario **34** B3 51 40N 91 50W
Caubvick, Mount *(Mont D'Iberville)* Newfoundland/Québec **30** B4 58 50N 64 40W
Causapscal Québec **33** C2 48 22N 67 14W
Cavendish Prince Edward Island **31** F7 46 30N 63 20W
Cawes Lake Alberta **48** G4 53 22N 113 28W
Cayoosh Creek British Columbia **42** H4 50 00N 122 00W
Cayuga Ontario **38** C1 42 57N 79 50W
Cecil Lake *tn.* British Columbia **43** D3 56 19N 120 40W
Cedar Lake Manitoba **39** A2 53 40N 100 30W
Central Butte Saskatchewan **40** B2 50 50N 106 30W
Central Patricia Ontario **34** B3 51 30N 90 09W
Centreville Newfoundland **31** D2 49 01N 53 53W
Centreville Nova Scotia **31** F7 45 10N 64 30W
Chalk River *tn.* Ontario **37** J7 46 01N 77 27W
Chambly Québec **37** N6 45 27N 73 19W
Champlain *admin.* Québec **37** N8 48 20N 74 20W
Chandler Québec **33** D2 48 21N 64 41W
Channel-Port aux Basques Newfoundland **31** C2 47 34N 59 09W
Chantrey Inlet Northwest Territories **45** M4 67 48N 96 20W
Chapais Québec **33** B2 49 47N 74 54W
Chapleau Ontario **35** D2 47 50N 83 24W
Chaplin Saskatchewan **40** B2 50 29N 106 40W
Chaplin Lake Saskatchewan **40** B2 50 25N 106 30W
Charlesbourg Québec **37** O7 46 53N 71 16W
Charles Island Northwest Territories **45** R3 62 39N 74 15W
Charles Lake Alberta **41** C3 59 50N 110 33W
Charles, Lake Nova Scotia **47** P6 44 43N 63 32W
Charlevoix-Est *admin.* Québec **37** Q8 47 50N 70 20W
Charlevoix-Ouest *admin.* Québec **37** Q8 47 57N 71 05W
Charlo New Brunswick **31** A2 47 55N 66 20W
Charlotte *admin.* New Brunswick **31** A2 45 20N 67 20W
Charlotte Lake British Columbia **43** C2 52 11N 125 19W
Charlottetown Newfoundland **30** C3 52 06N 56 07W
Charlottetown Prince Edward Island **31** F7 46 14N 63 09W
Charlton Island Northwest Territories **34** D3 52 00N 79 30W
Charron Lake Manitoba **39** B2 52 40N 95 40W
Chase British Columbia **43** E2 50 49N 119 41W
Châteauguay Québec **37** N6 45 20N 73 42W
Chatham New Brunswick **31** A2 47 02N 65 30W
Chatham Ontario **36** D3 42 24N 82 11W
Chatham Sound British Columbia **42** B2 54 30N 130 30W
Chatsworth Ontario **38** B3 44 27N 80 54W
Chedabucto Bay Nova Scotia **31** F7 45 20N 61 10W
Cheepay River Ontario **34** D3 50 50N 83 40W
Chelsea Québec **47** J2 45 29N 75 48W
Chelsea Brook Québec **47** J3 45 31N 75 51W
Chemainus British Columbia **42** H4 48 54N 123 42W
Chemainus River British Columbia **42** H4 48 58N 124 09W
Chemong Lake Ontario **38** D3 44 26N 78 22W
Cheslatta Lake British Columbia **43** C2 53 44N 125 20W
Chesley Ontario **38** A3 44 18N 81 07W
Chester Nova Scotia **31** F6 44 33N 64 16W
Chesterfield Inlet Northwest Territories **45** N3 64 00N 93 00W
Chesterfield Inlet *tn.* Northwest Territories **45** N3 63 21N 90 42W
Chesterville Ontario **37** L6 45 06N 75 14W
Cheticamp Nova Scotia **31** F7 46 39N 61 01W
Cheticamp Island Nova Scotia **31** F7 46 40N 61 05W
Chetwynd British Columbia **43** D3 55 38N 121 40W
Chibougamau Québec **33** B2 49 56N 74 24W
Chicoutimi Québec **37** P9 48 26N 71 06W
Chicoutimi *admin.* Québec **37** Q9 48 10N 71 10W
Chidley, Cape Northwest Territories **30** B4 60 23N 64 26W
Chignecto Bay Nova Scotia **31** F7 45 40N 64 40W
Chignecto, Cape Nova Scotia **31** F7 45 20N 64 55W
Chilanko Forks British Columbia **43** D2 52 04N 124 00W
Chilcotin River British Columbia **43** D2 51 54N 123 20W
Chilko Lake British Columbia **43** D2 51 15N 124 59W
Chilko River British Columbia **43** D2 51 59N 124 05W
Chilliwack British Columbia **42** H4 49 06N 121 56W
Chilliwack Lake British Columbia **42** H4 49 04N 121 22W
Chilliwack River British Columbia **42** H4 49 04N 121 52W
Chin, Cape Ontario **38** A4 45 05N 81 17W
Chinchaga River Alberta **41** B3 57 30N 119 00W
Chip Lake Alberta **41** B2 53 40N 115 23W
Chipman New Brunswick **31** A2 46 11N 65 54W
Chippawa Ontario **38** C2 43 03N 79 04W
Chiputneticook Lakes New Brunswick/U.S.A. **33** C2 45 40N 67 45W
Chisasibi *(Fort George)* Québec **32** T3 53 50N 79 01W
Chisel Lake *tn.* Manitoba **39** A2 54 50N 100 20W
Choiceland Saskatchewan **40** C2 53 30N 104 33W
Chomedey Québec **47** M5 45 32N 73 46W
Chorkbak Inlet Northwest Territories **45** R3 64 30N 74 25W
Chown, Mount Alberta **41** B2 53 24N 119 25W
Christian Island Ontario **38** B3 44 50N 80 14W
Christian Island *tn.* Ontario **38** B3 44 49N 80 10W
Christie Bay Northwest Territories **44** J3 62 32N 111 10W
Christina River Alberta **41** C3 55 50N 111 00W
Churchbridge Saskatchewan **40** C2 50 55N 101 38W
Churchill Manitoba **39** C3 58 45N 94 00W
Churchill, Cape Manitoba **39** C3 58 45N 93 00W
Churchill Falls *tn.* Newfoundland **30** A3 53 35N 64 00W
Churchill Lake Saskatchewan **40** B3 56 05N 108 15W
Churchill Peak British Columbia **43** C3 58 20N 125 02W
Churchill River Manitoba/Saskatchewan **45** M3 57 30N 96 00W
Churchill River Newfoundland **30** A3 53 20N 63 40W
Chute-aux-Outardes Québec **33** C2 49 17N 67 57W
Cirque Mountain Newfoundland **30** B4 58 56N 63 33W
City of Edmonton *admin.* Alberta **48** F4 53 23N 113 30W
City of Winnipeg *admin.* Manitoba **48** C2 49 55N 97 23W
City View Ontario **47** K2 45 21N 75 44W
Clarence Head *c.* Northwest Territories **45** Q6 76 47N 77 47W
Clarenville Newfoundland **31** D2 48 10N 53 58W
Claresholm Alberta **41** C2 50 02N 113 35W
Clarke City Québec **33** C3 50 11N 66 39W
Clark's Harbour *tn.* Nova Scotia **31** E6 43 25N 65 38W
Clarkson Ontario **38** C2 43 30N 79 38W
Clayoquot Sound British Columbia **43** C1 49 12N 126 05W
Clear Hills Alberta **41** B3 56 40N 119 30W
Clearwater British Columbia **43** D2 51 37N 120 03W
Clearwater Bay *tn.* Ontario **34** B2 49 93N 94 48W
Clearwater Lake British Columbia **43** D2 52 13N 120 20W
Clearwater Lake Manitoba **39** A2 53 50N 101 40W
Clearwater Lake Provincial Park Manitoba **39** A2 54 00N 101 00W
Clearwater River Alberta **41** B2 51 59N 115 20W
Clearwater River Alberta/Saskatchewan **40** A3 56 45N 110 59W
Clearwater River Provincial Park Saskatchewan **40** B3 57 10N 108 10W
Clifford Ontario **38** B2 43 58N 80 00W
Climax Saskatchewan **40** B1 49 12N 108 22W
Clinton British Columbia **43** D2 51 05N 121 38W
Clinton Ontario **38** A2 43 36N 81 33W
Clinton-Colden Lake Northwest Territories **44** K3 64 58N 107 27W
Close Lake Saskatchewan **40** C3 57 50N 104 40W
Clover Bar Alberta **48** G5 53 35N 113 19W
Cloverdale British Columbia **46** G3 49 05N 122 46W
Cluff Lake *tn.* Saskatchewan **40** B3 58 20N 109 35W
Clyde River *tn.* Northwest Territories **45** S5 70 30N 68 30W
Coaldale Alberta **41** C1 49 43N 112 37W
Coalhurst Alberta **41** C1 49 45N 112 56W
Coal River British Columbia **43** C3 59 56N 127 11W
Coast Mountains British Columbia **42** B3 58 10N 132 40W
Coates Creek Ontario **38** B3 44 22N 80 07W
Coaticook Québec **37** P6 45 08N 71 40W
Coats Island Northwest Territories **45** P3 63 30N 83 00W
Cobalt Ontario **35** E2 47 24N 79 41W
Cobequid Bay Nova Scotia **31** F7 45 20N 63 50W
Cobequid Mountains Nova Scotia **31** F7 45 30N 64 50W
Cobourg Ontario **35** E2 43 58N 78 11W
Cochrane Alberta **41** C2 51 11N 114 28W
Cochrane Ontario **35** D2 49 04N 81 02W
Cochrane River Manitoba/Saskatchewan **40** C3 58 50N 102 20W
Cockburn Island Ontario **36** C6 45 55N 83 22W
Codette Lake Saskatchewan **40** C2 53 15N 104 10W
Cod Island Newfoundland **30** B4 57 47N 61 47W
Colborne Ontario **36** J5 44 00N 77 53W
Colchester *admin.* Nova Scotia **31** F7 45 30N 63 30W
Cold Lake Alberta **41** C2 54 35N 110 00W
Cold Lake *tn.* Alberta **41** C2 54 28N 110 15W
Cold Lake Air Weapons Range Alberta **41** C3 55 10N 110 25W
Coldspring Head *c.* Nova Scotia **31** F7 45 55N 63 50W
Coldstream British Columbia **43** E2 50 10N 119 12W
Coldwater Ontario **38** C3 44 43N 79 39W
Cole Harbour Nova Scotia **47** Q6 44 40N 63 27W
Cole Harbour *tn.* Nova Scotia **47** Q6 44 40N 63 30W
Collingwood Ontario **38** B3 44 30N 80 14W
Collins Ontario **34** C3 50 17N 89 27W
Collins Bay *tn.* Saskatchewan **40** C3 58 10N 103 40W
Colonsay Saskatchewan **40** B2 51 59N 105 52W
Colpoys Bay Ontario **38** A3 44 48N 81 04W
Columbia, Mount British Columbia/Alberta **41** B2 52 09N 117 25W
Columbia Mountains British Columbia **43** D2 53 12N 120 49W
Columbia River British Columbia **43** E2 51 15N 116 58W
Colville Lake Northwest Territories **44** F4 67 10N 126 00W
Colville Lake *tn.* Northwest Territories **44** F4 67 02N 126 07W
Colwood British Columbia **42** H4 48 27N 123 28W
Combermere Ontario **36** J6 45 22N 77 37W
Comfort Bight *tn.* Newfoundland **30** C3 53 09N 55 48W
Comma Island Newfoundland **30** B4 55 20N 60 20W
Committee Bay Northwest Territories **45** O4 68 30N 86 30W
Comox British Columbia **42** H4 49 41N 124 56W
Comox Lake British Columbia **42** G4 49 37N 125 10W
Compton *admin.* Québec **37** P6 45 20N 71 40W
Conception Bay Newfoundland **31** D2 47 45N 53 00W
Conception Bay South *tn.* Newfoundland **31** D2 47 30N 53 00W

Conche Newfoundland **31** C3 50 53N 55 54W
Conestogo Lake Ontario **38** B2 43 47N 80 44W
Conestogo River Ontario **38** B2 43 41N 80 42W
Conklin Alberta **41** C3 55 38N 111 05W
Conne River *tn.* Newfoundland **31** C2 47 50N 55 20W
Consort Alberta **41** C2 52 01N 110 46W
Contrecoeur Québec **37** N6 45 51N 73 15W
Contwoyto Lake Northwest Territories **44** K4 65 42N 110 50W
Cook's Bay Ontario **38** C3 44 53N 79 31W
Cookshire Québec **27** 45 25N 72 09W
Cookstown Ontario **38** C3 44 12N 79 42W
Coppermine Northwest Territories **44** J4 65 00N 110 00W
Coppermine River Northwest Territories **44** J4 67 10N 115 00W
Coquihalla Highway British Columbia **42** H4 49 25N 121 20W
Coquitlam British Columbia **46** G4 49 15N 122 52W
Coquitlam Lake British Columbia **46** G4 49 21N 122 46W
Coquitlam River British Columbia **46** G4 49 17N 122 45W
Coral Harbour *tn.* Northwest Territories **45** P3 64 10N 83 15W
Cormorant Manitoba **39** A2 54 14N 100 35W
Cormorant Lake Manitoba **39** A2 54 15N 100 45W
Cormorant Provincial Forest Manitoba **39** A2 54 10N 100 50W
Corner Brook *tn.* Newfoundland **31** C2 48 58N 57 58W
Cornwall Ontario **37** M6 45 02N 74 45W
Cornwall Prince Edward Island **31** F7 46 10N 63 10W
Cornwallis Island Northwest Territories **45** N6 74 40N 97 30W
Cornwall Island Northwest Territories **45** M6/N6 77 25N 95 00W
Coronation Alberta **41** C2 52 05N 111 27W
Coronation Gulf Northwest Territories **44** J4 68 15N 112 30W
Cortes Island British Columbia **42** H5 50 07N 125 01W
Cosselman Ontario **37** L6 45 19N 78 07W
Côte-St-Luc Québec **37** N6 45 28N 73 39W
Couchiching, Lake Ontario **38** C3 44 39N 79 22W
Courtenay British Columbia **42** H4 49 40N 124 58W
Courtright Ontario **36** D3 42 49N 82 28W
Coutts Alberta **41** C1 49 00N 111 57W
Cove Island Ontario **38** A4 45 19N 81 44W
Cowansville Québec **37** O6 45 13N 72 44W
Cow Bay Nova Scotia **47** Q6 44 36N 63 26W
Cow Head *tn.* Newfoundland **31** C2 49 55N 57 48W
Cowichan Lake British Columbia **42** H4 48 50N 124 04W
Cowichan River British Columbia **42** H4 48 48N 123 58W
Cox's Cove *tn.* Newfoundland **31** C2 49 07N 58 04W
Craigellachie British Columbia **43** E2 50 59N 118 38W
Craigleith Provincial Park Ontario **38** B3 44 30N 80 15W
Craik Saskatchewan **40** B2 51 03N 105 50W
Cranberry Portage Manitoba **39** A2 54 36N 101 22W
Cranbrook British Columbia **43** E1 49 29N 115 48W
Crane Lake Saskatchewan **40** B2 50 10N 109 20W
Crane River Ontario **38** A4 45 43N 81 31W
Credit River Ontario **46** B1 43 35N 79 43W
Cree Lake Saskatchewan **40** B3 57 30N 106 30W
Creemore Ontario **38** B3 44 20N 80 07W
Cree River Saskatchewan **40** B3 58 00N 106 30W
Creighton Saskatchewan **40** C2 54 46N 101 50W
Cresswell Bay *tn.* Northwest Territories **45** N5 72 40N 93 30W
Creston British Columbia **43** E1 49 05N 116 32W
Crofton British Columbia **42** H4 48 52N 123 38W
Croker, Cape Ontario **38** A3 44 58N 80 59W
Crossfield Alberta **41** C2 51 26N 114 02W
Cross Lake Manitoba **39** B2 54 50N 97 20W
Cross Lake *tn.* Manitoba **39** B2 54 38N 97 45W
Crow Lake Ontario **34** B2 49 10N 93 56W
Crowsnest Highway Alberta **41** C1 49 50N 111 55W
Crowsnest Pass Alberta/British Columbia **43** E1 49 40N 114 41W
Crumlin Ontario **38** A2 43 01N 81 08W
Crystal Bay Ontario **47** J2 45 21N 75 51W
Crystal Beach *tn.* Ontario **38** C1 42 52N 79 03W
Crystal Lake Ontario **38** D3 44 45N 78 30W
Cub Hills, The Saskatchewan **40** C2 54 20N 104 40W
Cudworth Saskatchewan **40** B2 52 31N 105 44W
Cumberland British Columbia **42** H4 49 37N 124 59W
Cumberland Ontario **47** L3 45 31N 75 23W
Cumberland *admin.* Nova Scotia **31** F7 45 30N 64 10W
Cumberland House *tn.* Saskatchewan **40** C2 53 57N 102 20W
Cumberland Lake Saskatchewan **40** C2 54 10N 102 30W
Cumberland Peninsula Northwest Territories **45** T4 67 00N 65 00W
Cumberland Sound Northwest Territories **45** S4 65 30N 66 00W
Cupar Saskatchewan **40** C2 50 57N 104 12W
Cushing, Mount British Columbia **43** C3 57 36N 126 51W
Cut Knife Saskatchewan **40** B2 52 45N 109 01W
Cypress Hills Alberta/Saskatchewan **41** C1 49 30N 110 00W
Cypress Hills Provincial Park Alberta/Saskatchewan **41** C1 49 38N 110 00W

D

Dalhousie Alberta **48** A2 51 06N 114 10W
Dalhousie New Brunswick **31** A2 48 03N 66 22W
Dalhousie, Cape Northwest Territories **44** F5 70 14N 129 42W
Dalmeny Saskatchewan **40** B2 52 22N 106 46W
Dalrymple Lake Ontario **38** C3 44 41N 79 07W
Daniel's Harbour *tn.* Newfoundland **31** C3 50 14N 57 35W
Danville Québec **37** O6 45 48N 72 01W
D'Arcy British Columbia **42** H5 50 33N 122 28W
Darlington Provincial Park Ontario **38** D2 44 00N 78 50W
Darnley Bay Northwest Territories **44** G4 69 30N 123 30W
Dartmouth Nova Scotia **31** F6 44 40N 63 35W
Dauphin Manitoba **39** A2 51 09N 100 05W
Dauphin, Cape Nova Scotia **31** F7 46 20N 60 25W
Dauphin Lake Manitoba **39** B2 51 10N 99 30W
Dauphin River Manitoba **39** B2 51 50N 98 20W
Dauphin River *tn.* Manitoba **39** B2 51 50N 98 00W
Daveluyville Québec **27** 46 12N 72 09W
Davidson Saskatchewan **40** B2 51 15N 105 59W
David Thompson Highway Alberta **41** B2 52 15N 116 35W
Davin Lake Saskatchewan **40** C3 56 45N 103 40W
Davis Inlet *tn.* Newfoundland **30** B4 55 51N 60 52W
Davis Strait Canada/Greenland **45** T4 65 00N 57 00W
Davy Lake Saskatchewan **40** B3 58 50N 108 10W
Dawson Yukon Territory **44** D3 64 04N 139 24W
Dawson Bay Manitoba **39** A2 52 50N 100 50W
Dawson Creek *tn.* British Columbia **43** D3 55 44N 120 15W
Dawson, Mount British Columbia **43** E2 51 08N 117 26W
Dawson Range *mts.* Yukon Territory **44** D3 63 00N 139 30W
Dawsons Landing British Columbia **43** C2 51 28N 127 33W
Daysland Alberta **41** C2 52 52N 112 15W
Dean Channel British Columbia **43** C2 52 18N 127 35W
Dean River British Columbia **43** C2 52 45N 122 30W
Dease Arm *b.* Northwest Territories **44** G4 66 52N 119 37W
Dease Lake British Columbia **42** B3 58 05N 130 04W
Dease Lake *tn.* British Columbia **42** B3 58 28N 130 00W
Dease River British Columbia **42** C3 59 05N 129 40W
Dease Strait Northwest Territories **44** K4 68 40N 108 00W
Debah Northwest Territories **44** J3 62 25N 114 30W
Déception Québec **32** B5 62 10N 74 45W
Dee Lake British Columbia **46** G3 49 14N 122 59W
Deep Cove British Columbia **46** G4 49 19N 122 58W
Deep Inlet Newfoundland **30** B4 55 22N 60 14W
Deep River *tn.* Ontario **37** J7 46 06N 77 30W
Deer Island New Brunswick **31** A1 45 00N 67 00W
Deer Lake Ontario **34** B3 52 38N 94 25W
Deer Lake *tn.* Newfoundland **31** C2 49 11N 57 27W
Delhi Ontario **38** B1 42 51N 80 30W
Delisle Saskatchewan **40** B2 51 56N 107 10W
Deloraine Manitoba **39** A1 49 11N 100 30W
Delta British Columbia **42** H4 49 06N 123 01W
Dempster Highway Yukon Territory **44** D4 65 30N 138 10W
Denbigh Ontario **37** J6 45 08N 77 15W
Denman Island British Columbia **42** H4 49 32N 124 49W
Deschambault Lake Saskatchewan **40** C2 54 50N 103 50W
Deseronto Ontario **37** J5 44 12N 77 03W
Desmaraisville Québec **33** A2 49 30N 76 18W
Desolation Sound Marine Park British Columbia **42** H5 50 08N 124 45W
Destruction Bay *tn.* Yukon Territory **44** D3 61 16N 138 50W
Détroit de Jacques-Cartier *sd.* Québec **33** D3 50 10N 64 10W
Détroit d'Honguedo *sd.* Québec **33** D2 49 30N 64 20W
Détroit d'Hudson *(Hudson Strait)* Québec/Northwest Territories **32** B5 62 00N 70 00W
Detroit River Ontario Canada/U.S.A. **52** E2 42 15N 83 00W
Deux-Montagnes Québec **47** M5 45 32N 73 56W
Deux Rivieres Ontario **36** H7 46 15N 78 17W
Devil's Glen Provincial Park Ontario **38** B3 44 20N 80 30W
Devon Alberta **41** C2 53 22N 113 44W
Devon Island Northwest Territories **45** O6 75 47N 88 00W
Dewar Lakes Northwest Territories **45** R4 68 30N 71 20W
Dewey Soper Game Sanctuary Northwest Territories **45** R4 66 20N 68 50W
Diamond Jenness Peninsula Northwest Territories **44** H5 71 20N 117 00W
Dickson Peak British Columbia **42** H5 50 54N 122 59W
Didsbury Alberta **41** C2 51 40N 114 08W
Diefenbaker, Lake Saskatchewan **40** B2 51 10N 107 30W
Dieppe New Brunswick **31** F7 46 10N 64 40W
Digby Nova Scotia **31** E6 44 37N 65 47W
Digby *admin.* Nova Scotia **31** E7 44 20N 65 40W
Digby Neck *p.* Nova Scotia **31** E6 44 30N 66 00W
Dillon Saskatchewan **40** B3 55 56N 108 54W
Dingwell Nova Scotia **31** F7 46 50N 60 30W
Dinorwic Ontario **34** B2 49 41N 92 30W
Dinosaur Provincial Park Alberta **22** 50 45N 111 30W
Disappointment Lake Newfoundland **30** B3 53 49N 62 31W
Dismal Lakes Northwest Territories **44** H4 67 26N 117 07W
Disraeli Québec **37** P6 45 54N 71 22W
Dixon Entrance *sd.* British Columbia Canada/Alaska U.S.A. **42** B2 54 28N 132 50W
Doaktown New Brunswick **31** A2 46 34N 66 06W
Dobie River Ontario **34** B3 51 30N 90 50W
Dodge Lake Saskatchewan **40** B3 59 50N 105 25W
Dodsland Saskatchewan **40** B2 51 48N 108 51W
Dog Creek *tn.* British Columbia **43** D2 51 35N 122 18W
Dog (High) Island Newfoundland **30** B4 56 38N 61 10W
Dog Lake Manitoba **39** B2 51 00N 98 20W
Dog Lake Ontario **35** C2 48 50N 89 30W
Dolbeau Québec **33** B2 48 52N 72 15W
Dollarton British Columbia **46** G4 49 18N 122 58W
Dolphin and Union Strait Northwest Territories **44** H4 69 05N 114 45W
Dominion Nova Scotia **31** F7 46 14N 60 01W
Dominion Lake Newfoundland **30** B3 52 40N 61 43W
Don Mills Ontario **46** C1 43 44N 79 22W
Donnacona Québec **37** P7 46 41N 71 45W
Don River Ontario **46** C2 43 48N 79 24W
Dorcas Bay Ontario **38** A4 45 10N 81 38W
Dorchester New Brunswick **31** F7 45 54N 64 32W
Dorchester *admin.* Québec **37** Q7 46 20N 70 40W
Dorchester, Cape Northwest Territories **45** Q4 65 27N 77 27W
Doré Lake Saskatchewan **40** B2 54 50N 107 20W
Dorion Ontario **35** C2 48 49N 88 33W
Dorval Québec **47** N4 45 27N 73 44W
Double Mer *in.* Newfoundland **30** C3 54 04N 59 10W
Douglas Island British Columbia **46** G3 49 13N 122 46W
Dowling Lake Alberta **41** C2 51 44N 112 00W
Downton Lake British Columbia **42** H5 50 48N 123 10W
Downtown, Mount British Columbia **43** D2 52 45N 124 53W
Dows Lake Ontario **47** K2 45 24N 75 42W
Drayton Ontario **38** B2 43 45N 80 40W
Drayton Valley *tn.* Alberta **41** B2 53 13N 114 59W
Dresden Québec **26** 42 34N 82 11W
Drowning River Ontario **34** C3 50 30N 86 10W
Drumheller Alberta **41** C2 51 28N 112 40W
Drummond *admin.* Québec **37** O6 45 50N 72 40W
Drummondville Québec **37** O6 45 52N 72 30W
Dryden Ontario **34** B2 49 48N 92 48W
Drylake *tn.* Newfoundland **30** A3 52 38N 65 59W
Dubawnt Lake Northwest Territories **45** L3 68 15N 102 00W
Dubreuilville Ontario **35** D2 48 21N 84 32W
Duck Bay *tn.* Manitoba **39** A2 52 10N 100 10W
Duck Lake *tn.* Saskatchewan **40** B2 52 52N 106 12W
Duck Mountain Provincial Forest Manitoba **39** A2 51 20N 100 50W
Duck Mountain Provincial Park Manitoba/Saskatchewan **39** A2 51 40N 101 00W
Dufferin *admin.* Ontario **38** B3 44 00N 80 20W
Duffey Lake British Columbia **42** H5 50 24N 122 23W
Duncan British Columbia **42** H4 48 46N 123 40W
Duncan, Cape Northwest Territories **34** D3 52 40N 80 50W
Duncan Lake British Columbia **43** E2 50 23N 116 57W
Dundalk Ontario **38** B3 44 10N 80 24W
Dundas Ontario **38** C2 43 16N 79 57W
Dundas Island British Columbia **42** B2 54 33N 131 20W
Dundas Peninsula Northwest Territories **44** J5 74 50N 111 30W
Dundurn Saskatchewan **40** B2 51 49N 106 30W
Dunkirk Saskatchewan **40** B2 50 04N 105 41W
Dunnville Ontario **38** C1 42 54N 79 36W
Dunville Newfoundland **31** D2 47 16N 53 54W
Durham Ontario **38** B3 44 11N 80 49W
Durham *admin.* Ontario **38** C3 44 04N 79 11W
Durrell Newfoundland **31** D2 49 40N 54 44W
Dutton Ontario **38** A1 42 39N 81 30W
Dyer's Bay Ontario **38** A4 45 10N 81 18W
Dyer's Bay *tn.* Ontario **38** A4 45 09N 81 20W
Dyke Lake Newfoundland **30** A3 54 30N 66 18W

E

Eabamet Lake Ontario **34** C3 51 32N 87 46W
Eagle Plains *tn.* Yukon Territory **44** D4 66 30N 136 50W
Eagle River Newfoundland **30** C3 53 00N 58 30W
Eagle River Ontario **34** B2 49 50N 93 12W
Eagle River Saskatchewan **40** B2 51 35N 107 40W
Ear Falls *tn.* Ontario **34** B3 50 38N 93 13W
Earl Rowe Provincial Park Ontario **38** C3 44 15N 79 45W
East Angus Québec **27** 45 30N 71 40W
East Bay Bird Sanctuary Northwest Territories **45** P3 66 20N 74 00W
East Chezzetcook Nova Scotia **31** F6 44 34N 63 14W
Eastend Saskatchewan **40** B1 49 32N 108 50W
Eastern Passage *tn.* Nova Scotia **47** Q6 44 36N 63 29W
Easterville Manitoba **39** B2 53 00N 99 40W
East Lake Nova Scotia **47** Q7 44 46N 63 29W
Eastmain Québec **33** A3 52 10N 78 30W
East Point Prince Edward Island **31** F7 46 27N 61 59W
Eastport Newfoundland **31** D2 48 39N 53 45W
East St. Paul *admin.* Manitoba **48** D2 49 59N 97 04W
East Thurlow Island British Columbia **42** G5 50 24N 125 26W
East York *bor.* Metropolitan Toronto Ontario **46** C1 43 43N 79 20W
Eatonia Saskatchewan **40** B2 51 13N 109 22W
Echoing River Ontario **34** B3 54 30N 92 00W
Echo, Lake Nova Scotia **47** Q6 44 44N 63 24W
Eclipse Sound Northwest Territories **45** Q5 72 38N 79 00W
Ecum Secum Nova Scotia **31** F6 44 58N 62 08W
Eddies Cove *tn.* Newfoundland **30** C3 51 25N 56 27W
Edehon Lake Northwest Territories **45** N3 60 25N 97 15W
Edgewood British Columbia **43** E1 49 47N 118 08W
Edmonton Alberta **41** G4 53 34N 113 25W
Edmund Lake Manitoba **39** C2 54 50N 93 30W
Edmundston New Brunswick **31** A2 47 22N 68 20W
Edson Alberta **41** B2 53 35N 116 26W
Eduni, Mount Northwest Territories **44** F3 64 13N 128 10W
Edwards Ontario **47** L2 45 19N 75 48W
Edziza, Mount British Columbia **42** B3 57 43N 130 42W
Edzo Northwest Territories **44** H3 63 50N 116 00W
Eganville Ontario **37** J6 45 32N 77 06W
Eglington Island Northwest Territories **44** H6 75 48N 118 30W
Egmont British Columbia **42** H4 49 45N 123 55W
Egmont Bay Prince Edward Island **31** F7 46 30N 64 20W
Egmont, Cape Nova Scotia **31** F7 46 50N 60 20W
Eileen Lake Northwest Territories **44** K3 62 16N 107 37W
Ekwan Point Ontario **34** D3 53 20N 82 10W
Ekwan River Ontario **34** D3 53 30N 83 40W
Elaho River British Columbia **42** H5 50 14N 123 33W
Elbow Saskatchewan **40** B2 51 08N 106 36W
Elbow River Alberta **48** A1 50 59N 114 13W
Elgin *admin.* Ontario **38** A1 42 38N 81 36W
Elkford British Columbia **43** E2 50 02N 114 55W
Elkhorn Manitoba **39** A1 49 59N 101 14W
Elk Island Manitoba **39** B2 50 50N 96 40W
Elk Island National Park Alberta **41** C2 53 36N 112 53W
Elk Lake *tn.* Ontario **35** D2 47 44N 80 20W
Elk Lakes Provincial Park British Columbia **43** E2 50 00N 115 00W
Elk Point *tn.* Alberta **41** C2 53 54N 110 54W
Ellef Ringnes Island Northwest Territories **44** L6 78 30N 102 00W
Ellerslie Alberta **48** G4 53 24N 113 28W
Ellesmere Island Northwest Territories **45** P6 77 30N 82 30W
Ellesmere Island National Park Reserve Northwest Territories **45** R7 82 00N 72 30W
Ellice River Northwest Territories **44** L4 66 20N 105 00W
Elliot Lake *tn.* Ontario **36** D7 46 25N 82 40W
Elmira Ontario **38** B2 43 36N 80 34W
Elmvale Ontario **38** C3 44 35N 79 52W
Elora Ontario **38** B2 43 42N 80 26W
Elrose Saskatchewan **40** B2 51 12N 108 01W
Elsa Yukon Territory **44** D3 63 55N 135 29W
Elvira, Cape Northwest Territories **44** K5 73 16N 107 10W
Embree Newfoundland **31** D2 49 18N 55 02W
Emerald Island Northwest Territories **44** J6 76 48N 114 10W
Emerson Manitoba **39** B1 49 00N 97 11W
Emily Provincial Park Ontario **38** D3 44 20N 78 28W
Endako British Columbia **43** C2 54 05N 125 01W
Enderby British Columbia **43** E2 50 32N 119 10W
Enfield Nova Scotia **31** F6 44 56N 63 34W
Englee Newfoundland **31** C3 50 44N 56 06W
Englehart Ontario **35** E2 47 50N 79 52W
English Bay British Columbia **46** F4 49 17N 123 12W
English River Ontario **34** B3 50 20N 94 50W
Ennadai Lake Northwest Territories **45** L3 60 58N 101 20W
Eramosa River Ontario **38** B2 43 33N 80 11W
Erieau Ontario **36** E3 42 16N 81 56W
Erie Beach *tn.* Ontario **36** D3 42 16N 82 00W
Erie Beach *tn.* Ontario **38** D1 42 53N 78 56W
Erie, Lake Canada/USA **36** E2 42 15N 81 00W
Eriksdale Manitoba **39** B2 50 52N 98 07W
Erin Ontario **38** B2 43 48N 80 04W
Escuminac, Point New Brunswick **31** B2 47 04N 64 49W
Esker Newfoundland **30** A3 53 53N 66 25W
Eskimo Lakes Northwest Territories **44** E4 68 30N 132 30W
Eskimo Point *see* Arviat
Espanola Ontario **36** E7 46 15N 81 46W
Esquimalt British Columbia **42** H4 48 25N 123 29W
Essex Ontario **36** D3 42 10N 82 49W
Essex *admin.* Ontario **36** D3 42 10N 82 50W
Esterhazy Saskatchewan **40** C2 50 40N 102 02W
Estevan Saskatchewan **40** C1 49 09N 103 00W
Eston Saskatchewan **40** B2 51 09N 108 42W
Etawney Lake Manitoba **39** B3 57 50N 96 40W
Ethelbert Manitoba **39** A2 51 32N 100 25W
Etobicoke *bor.* Metropolitan Toronto Ontario **46** B1 43 38N 79 30W
Etobicoke Creek Ontario **46** A1 43 43N 79 47W
Eugenia Lake Ontario **38** B3 44 20N 80 30W
Eureka *m.s.* Northwest Territories **45** O6 79 59N 85 57W
Eureka River *tn.* Alberta **41** B3 56 25N 118 48W
Eutsuk Lake British Columbia **43** C2 53 12N 126 32W
Evansburg Alberta **41** B2 53 36N 115 01W
Evans, Mount Alberta **41** B2 52 26N 118 07W
Evans Strait Northwest Territories **45** P3 63 15N 82 30W
Exeter Ontario **38** A2 43 21N 81 30W
Exploits River Newfoundland **31** C2 48 40N 56 30W
Eyehill River Saskatchewan **40** B2 52 25N 109 50W

F

Faber Lake Northwest Territories **44** H3 63 56N 117 15W
Fairchild Creek Ontario **38** B2 43 13N 80 11W
Fairview Alberta **41** B3 56 03N 118 28W
Fairweather Mountain British Columbia Canada/ Alaska U.S.A. **42** A3 58 50N 137 55W
Falher Alberta **41** B3 55 44N 117 12W
Fallowfield Ontario **47** J2 45 17N 75 51W
Fall River Nova Scotia **47** P7 44 49N 63 36W
False Creek British Columbia **46** F4 49 16N 123 08W
Family Lake Manitoba **39** B2 51 50N 95 40W
Farnham Québec **37** O6 45 17N 72 59W
Farnham, Mount British Columbia **43** E2 50 27N 116 37W
Faro Yukon Territory **44** E3 62 30N 133 00W
Fathom Five National Marine Park Ontario **38** A4 54 20N 81 35W
Fauquier Ontario **35** D2 49 19N 82 02W
Fawn River Ontario **34** C3 54 20N 89 10W
Felix, Cape Northwest Territories **45** M4 69 54N 97 58W
Fenelon Falls *tn.* Ontario **38** D3 44 32N 78 45W
Fergus Ontario **38** B2 43 43N 80 24W
Ferland Ontario **34** C3 50 18N 88 25W
Ferme-Neuve Québec **37** L7 46 42N 75 28W
Fermont Québec **33** C3 52 00N 68 00W
Fernie British Columbia **43** E1 49 30N 115 00W
Ferryland Newfoundland **31** D2 47 01N 54 53W
Fife Lake Saskatchewan **40** B1 49 10N 105 45W
Fighting Island Ontario **52** E1 42 13N 83 07W
Finch Ontario **37** L6 45 08N 75 05W
Finlay Ranges *mts.* British Columbia **43** C3 57 10N 126 00W
Finlay River British Columbia **43** C3 57 20N 125 40W
Fiordland Recreation Area British Columbia **43** C2 52 00N 127 00W
Firebag Hills Saskatchewan **40** B3 57 15N 109 50W
Firebag River Alberta **41** C3 57 30N 110 40W
Fish Creek Alberta **48** A1 50 55N 114 10W
Fish Creek Provincial Park Alberta **48** A1 50 55N 114 04W
Fisher Bay Manitoba **39** B2 51 30N 97 30W
Fisher Branch *tn.* Manitoba **39** B2 51 04N 97 38W
Fisher, Mount British Columbia **43** E1 49 35N 115 20W
Fisher Strait Northwest Territories **45** P3 63 00N 84 00W
Fishing Branch Game Reserve Yukon Territory **44** D4 66 30N 139 30W
Fishing Lake Manitoba **39** B2 52 10N 95 40W
Fishing Ships Harbour *tn.* Newfoundland **30** C3 52 36N 55 47W
Fitzgerald Alberta **41** C3 59 51N 111 36W
Fitzwilliam Island Ontario **36** E6 45 29N 81 45W
Flamborough Ontario **38** C2 43 20N 79 57W
Flathead River British Columbia **43** F1 48 00N 114 00W
Flesherton Ontario **38** B3 44 16N 80 32W
Fletchers Lake Nova Scotia **47** P7 44 51N 63 35W
Fleur de Lys Newfoundland **31** C3 50 07N 56 08W
Fleuve Saint-Laurent *(St. Lawrence River)* Québec **33** C2 48 20N 69 20W
Flin Flon Manitoba **39** A2 54 50N 102 00W
Florenceville New Brunswick **31** A2 46 20N 67 20W
Flores Island British Columbia **43** C1 49 20N 126 10W
Flour Lake Newfoundland **30** A3 53 44N 64 50W
Foam Lake *tn.* Saskatchewan **40** C2 51 38N 103 31W
Foch British Columbia **42** H5 50 07N 124 31W
Fogo Newfoundland **31** D2 49 43N 54 17W
Fogo Island Newfoundland **31** D2 49 40N 54 10W
Foley Lake Alberta **48** H4 53 24N 113 13W
Foleyet Ontario **35** D2 48 05N 82 26W
Fond du Lac Saskatchewan **40** B3 59 20N 107 09W
Fond du Lac River Saskatchewan **40** C3 59 05N 104 40W
Fontas River British Columbia **43** D3 58 20N 121 25W
Fonthill Ontario **38** C2 43 02N 79 17W
Foothills Municipal District Alberta **48** A1 50 53N 114 08W
Forbes, Mount Alberta **41** B2 51 52N 116 55W
Foremost Alberta **41** C1 49 29N 111 25W
Forest Ontario **36** E4 43 06N 82 00W
Forestburg Alberta **41** C2 52 35N 112 04W
Forest Hill Ontario **46** C1 43 42N 79 25W
Forest Lawn Alberta **48** A2 51 02N 113 58W
Forestville Québec **33** C2 48 45N 69 04W
Forrest Lake Saskatchewan **40** B3 57 35N 109 10W
Fort Albany Ontario **34** D3 52 12N 81 40W
Fort Babine British Columbia **43** C3 55 20N 126 35W
Fort Chipewyan Alberta **41** C3 58 46N 111 09W
Fort Coulonge Québec **37** K6 45 51N 76 45W
Forteau Newfoundland **30** C3 51 28N 56 58W
Fort Erie Ontario **38** D1 42 55N 78 56W
Fort Frances Ontario **34** B2 48 37N 93 23W

Fort Franklin Northwest Territories **44** G4 65 11N 123 26W
Fort Fraser British Columbia **43** D2 54 03N 124 30W
Fort Garry Manitoba **48** D2 49 49N 97 10W
Fort George *see* Chisasibi
Fort Good Hope Northwest Territories **44** F4 66 16N 128 37W
Fort Hope *I.R.* Ontario **34** C3 51 37N 87 55W
Fort Langley British Columbia **42** H4 49 11N 122 38W
Fort Liard Northwest Territories **44** G3 60 14N 123 28W
Fort MacKay Alberta **41** C3 57 11N 111 37W
Fort Macleod Alberta **41** C1 49 44N 113 24W
Fort McMurray Alberta **41** C3 56 45N 111 27W
Fort McPherson Northwest Territories **44** E4 67 29N 134 50W
Fort Nelson British Columbia **43** D3 58 48N 122 44W
Fort Nelson River British Columbia **43** D3 59 20N 124 05W
Fort Norman Northwest Territories **44** F3 64 55N 125 29W
Fort Providence Northwest Territories **44** H3 61 03N 117 40W
Fort Qu'Appelle Saskatchewan **40** C2 50 46N 103 54W
Fort Resolution Northwest Territories **44** J3 61 10N 113 39W
Fort Rouge Manitoba **48** D2 49 52N 97 07W
Fort Rupert *(Waskaganish)* Québec **33** A3 51 30N 79 45W
Fort St. James British Columbia **43** D2 54 26N 124 15W
Fort St. John British Columbia **43** D3 56 14N 120 55W
Fort Saskatchewan Alberta **48** H5 53 42N 113 12W
Fort Severn Ontario **34** C4 56 00N 87 40W
Fort Simpson Northwest Territories **44** G3 61 46N 121 15W
Fort Smith Alberta **41** C3 60 00N 111 51W
Fort Smith Northwest Territories **44** J3 60 01N 111 55W
Fort Smith *reg.* Northwest Territories **44** H3 63 00N 120 00W
Fortune Newfoundland **31** C2 47 04N 55 50W
Fortune Bay Newfoundland **31** C2 47 15N 55 30W
Fort Vermilion Alberta **41** B3 58 22N 115 59W
Fort Ware British Columbia **43** C3 57 30N 125 43W
Fort Whyte Manitoba **48** D2 49 49N 97 12W
Fortymile Yukon Territory **44** C3 64 25N 140 32W
Fosheim Peninsula Northwest Territories **45** P6 80 00N 85 00W
Foster, Mount British Columbia **42** A3 59 49N 135 35W
Foster River Saskatchewan **40** B3 56 20N 105 45W
Fourchu Nova Scotia **31** F7 45 43N 60 17W
Four Mile Lake Ontario **38** D3 44 42N 78 44W
Fox Creek *tn.* Alberta **41** B2 54 24N 116 48W
Foxe Basin *b.* Northwest Territories **44** Q4 66 20N 79 00W
Foxe Channel Northwest Territories **44** Q3 65 00N 81 00W
Foxe Peninsula Northwest Territories **45** Q3 65 00N 76 00W
Fox River Manitoba **39** C3 55 50N 94 10W
Fox Valley *tn.* Saskatchewan **40** B2 50 29N 109 29W
Frances Lake Yukon Territory **44** F3 61 20N 129 30W
François Lake British Columbia **43** C2 54 00N 125 47W
Frankford Ontario **36** J5 44 12N 77 36W
Franklin Bay Northwest Territories **44** F5 69 45N 126 00W
Franklin Island Ontario **38** B4 45 25N 80 20W
Franklin Lake Northwest Territories **45** M4 66 56N 96 03W
Franklin Mountains Northwest Territories **44** G3 61 15N 123 50W
Fraserdale Ontario **35** D2 49 51N 81 37W
Fraser Lake British Columbia **43** D2 54 00N 124 50W
Fraser Lake Newfoundland **30** B3 54 24N 63 40W
Fraser Plateau British Columbia **43** D2 52 32N 124 10W
Fraser River British Columbia **43** D2 51 36N 122 25W
Fraser River Newfoundland **30** B4 56 50N 63 50W
Fredericton New Brunswick **31** A2 45 57N 66 40W
Fredericton Junction New Brunswick **31** A2 45 40N 66 38W
Freels, Cape Newfoundland **31** D2 49 15N 53 29W
Freeport Nova Scotia **31** E6 44 17N 66 19W
Frenchman River Saskatchewan **40** B1 49 30N 108 00W
Frenchman's Cove *tn.* Newfoundland **31** C2 49 04N 58 10W
French River Ontario **36** F7 46 00N 81 00W
French River *tn.* Ontario **36** F7 46 03N 80 34W
Freshwater Newfoundland **31** D2 47 15N 53 59W
Frobisher Bay Northwest Territories **45** S3 62 15N 65 00W
Frobisher Bay *tn. see* Iqaluit
Frobisher Lake Saskatchewan **40** B3 57 00N 108 00W
Frog Lake Alberta **41** C2 53 55N 110 20W
Frontenac *admin.* Ontario **37** K6 44 40N 76 45W
Frontenac *admin.* Québec **37** Q6 45 40N 70 50W
Frontenac Provincial Park Ontario **37** K5 44 32N 76 29W
Frozen Strait Northwest Territories **45** P4 66 08N 85 00W
Fruitvale British Columbia **43** E1 49 08N 117 28W
Fundy, Bay of New Brunswick/Nova Scotia **31** E6 45 00N 66 00W
Fundy National Park New Brunswick **31** E7 45 40N 65 10W
Fury and Hecla Strait Northwest Territories **45** P4 69 56N 84 00W

G

Gabarus Bay Nova Scotia **31** F7 45 50N 60 10W
Gabriola Island British Columbia **42** H4 49 10N 123 51W
Gage, Cape Prince Edward Island **31** F7 46 50N 64 20W
Gagetown New Brunswick **31** A2 45 46N 66 29W
Gagnon Québec **33** C3 51 56N 68 16W
Galiano Island British Columbia **42** H4 48 57N 123 25W
Galt Ontario **38** B2 43 21N 80 19W
Gambier Island British Columbia **42** H4 49 30N 123 25W
Gambo Newfoundland **31** D2 48 46N 54 14W
Gananoque Ontario **37** K5 44 20N 76 10W
Ganaraska River Ontario **38** D3 44 02N 78 34W
Gander Newfoundland **31** D2 48 57N 54 34W
Gander Lake Newfoundland **31** D2 48 55N 54 35W
Ganges British Columbia **42** H4 48 51N 123 31W
Gardiner Dam Saskatchewan **40** B2 51 15N 106 40W
Gardner Canal British Columbia **42** C2 53 30N 128 50W
Garibaldi Lake British Columbia **42** H4 49 55N 122 57W
Garibaldi, Mount British Columbia **42** H4 49 53N 123 00W
Garibaldi Provincial Park British Columbia **42** H4 49 58N 122 45W
Garnish Newfoundland **31** C2 47 14N 55 22W
Garry Lake Northwest Territories **45** F4 66 20N 100 00W
Garry Point British Columbia **46** F3 49 07N 123 14W
Gaspé Québec **33** D2 48 50N 64 30W
Gaspereau Lake Nova Scotia **31** F6 44 50N 64 30W
Gateshead Island Northwest Territories **45** M5 70 36N 100 26W
Gatineau Québec **37** L6 45 29N 75 40W
Gatineau *admin.* Québec **37** K7 45 47N 76 05W
Gauer Lake Manitoba **39** B3 57 10N 97 30W
Gaultois Newfoundland **31** C2 47 36N 55 54W
Geikie River Saskatchewan **40** C3 57 20N 104 40W
George, Cape Nova Scotia **31** F7 45 50N 61 50W
George Island Newfoundland **30** C3 54 16N 57 20W
Georgetown Ontario **38** C2 43 39N 79 56W
Georgetown Prince Edward Island **31** F7 46 12N 62 32W
Georgian Bay Ontario **36** E6 45 00N 81 00W
Georgian Bay Islands National Park Ontario **38** C3 44 53N 79 52W
Georgia, Strait of British Columbia **42** H4 49 39N 124 34W
Georgina Island Ontario **38** C3 44 22N 79 17W
Geraldton Ontario **34** C2 49 44N 86 59W
Germansen Landing *tn.* British Columbia **43** D3 55 47N 124 42W
Giant's Causeway *p.* Northwest Territories **44** G6 75 46N 121 11W
Giants Tomb Island Ontario **38** B3 44 55N 80 00W
Gibsons *tn.* British Columbia **42** H4 49 24N 123 30W
Gilbert, Mount British Columbia **42** H5 50 50N 124 15W
Gilbert Plains *tn.* Manitoba **39** A2 51 09N 100 28W
Gilford Island British Columbia **43** C2 50 45N 126 20W
Gil Island British Columbia **42** C2 53 10N 129 15W
Gillam Manitoba **39** C3 56 25N 94 45W
Gillies Bay *tn.* British Columbia **42** H4 49 42N 124 28W
Gimli Manitoba **39** B2 50 39N 97 00W
Gjoa Haven *tn.* Northwest Territories **45** M4 68 39N 96 09W
Glace Bay *tn.* Nova Scotia **31** F7 46 11N 59 58W
Glacial Mountain British Columbia **42** C3 58 15N 129 25W
Glacier National Park British Columbia **43** E2 51 00N 117 00W
Gladstone Manitoba **39** B2 50 14N 98 56W
Gladys Lake British Columbia **43** B3 59 50N 132 52W
Glaslyn Saskatchewan **40** B2 53 23N 108 22W
Glenboro Manitoba **39** B1 49 35N 99 20W
Glen Cairn Ontario **47** J2 45 15N 75 45W
Glencoe Ontario **38** A1 42 45N 81 44W
Glenmore Reservoir Alberta **48** A1 50 58N 114 08W
Glenwood Newfoundland **31** C2 48 59N 54 53W
Gloucester Ontario **47** K2 45 21N 75 39W
Gloucester *admin.* New Brunswick **31** A2 47 30N 65 50W
Gloucester Glen *tn.* Ontario **47** K2 45 17N 75 41W
Glover Island Newfoundland **31** C2 48 46N 57 43W
Glovertown Newfoundland **31** D2 48 41N 54 02W
Goat Island British Columbia **42** H5 50 03N 124 28W
Goderich Ontario **38** A2 43 43N 81 43W
Gods Lake Manitoba **39** C2 54 40N 94 20W
Gods Lake *tn.* Manitoba **39** C2 54 45N 94 00W
Gods Mercy, Bay of Northwest Territories **45** O3 63 30N 88 10W
Gods River Manitoba **39** C3 56 20N 92 50W
Gogama Ontario **35** D2 47 40N 81 43W
Go Home Lake Ontario **38** C4 45 01N 79 51W
Gold Bridge British Columbia **42** H5 50 51N 122 51W
Golden British Columbia **43** E2 51 19N 116 55W
Golden Ears Provincial Park British Columbia **42** H4 49 28N 122 25W
Golden Hinde *mt.* British Columbia **43** C1 49 35N 125 40W
Gold River British Columbia **43** C1 49 41N 125 59W
Goldsmith Channel Northwest Territories **45** K5 73 00N 106 00W
Golfe du Saint-Laurent *(Gulf of St. Lawrence)* Québec **33** D2 48 40N 62 40W
Goodeve Saskatchewan **40** C2 51 03N 103 11W
Good Hope British Columbia **43** C2 50 59N 124 01W
Good Hope Mountain British Columbia **43** C2 51 08N 124 10W
Goodsoil Saskatchewan **40** B2 54 24N 109 12W
Goose Bay *tn.* Newfoundland **30** A3 53 15N 60 20W
Goose River Newfoundland **30** A3 53 30N 61 50W
Gordon Horne Peak British Columbia **43** E2 51 47N 118 50W
Gordon Lake Alberta **41** C3 56 30N 110 25W
Gordon Pittock Reservoir Ontario **38** B2 43 11N 80 43W
Gordon River British Columbia **42** H4 48 38N 124 25W
Gore Bay *tn.* Ontario **36** D6 45 55N 82 28W
Goshen Nova Scotia **31** F7 45 20N 62 55W
Gott Peak British Columbia **42** H5 50 18N 122 16W
Goulbourne Ontario **47** J2 46 15N 75 54W
Goulds Newfoundland **31** D2 47 29N 52 46W
Gowganda Ontario **35** D2 47 39N 80 46W
Gracefield Québec **37** K7 46 05N 76 05W
Grady Harbour Newfoundland **30** C3 53 48N 56 25W
Graham Island British Columbia **42** B2 53 50N 132 40W
Graham Island Northwest Territories **45** M6 77 25N 90 30W
Granby Québec **37** O6 45 22N 72 43W
Granby River British Columbia **43** E1 49 27N 118 25W
Grand Bank Newfoundland **31** C2 47 06N 55 46W
Grand Bay *tn.* New Brunswick **31** A2 45 19N 66 14W
Grand Bend Ontario **38** A2 43 21N 81 45W
Grand Centre Alberta **41** C2 54 25N 110 13W
Grande-Anse New Brunswick **31** A2 47 50N 65 10W
Grande-Anse Québec **37** O8 47 05N 72 55W
Grande Cache Alberta **41** B2 53 50N 119 08W
Grande Pointe Manitoba **48** D2 49 45N 97 03W
Grande Prairie Alberta **43** E3 55 10N 118 40W
Grande-Rivière *tn.* Québec **33** D2 48 23N 64 31W
Grande rivière de la Baleine *r.* Québec **32** A4 55 08N 76 30W
Grand Étang *tn.* Nova Scotia **31** F7 46 32N 61 02W
Grande-Vallée *tn.* Québec **33** C2 49 15N 65 10W
Grand Falls *tn.* Newfoundland **31** C2 48 56N 55 40W
Grand Falls/Grand-Sault *tn.* New Brunswick **31** A2 47 02N 67 46W
Grand Forks British Columbia **43** E1 49 02N 118 30W
Grand Harbour *tn.* New Brunswick **31** E6 44 41N 66 46W
Grandin, Lake Northwest Territories **44** H3 63 50N 119 50W
Grand Jardin Newfoundland **31** C2 48 28N 59 13W
Grand Lake New Brunswick **31** A2 46 00N 66 40W
Grand Lake Newfoundland **30** A3 53 40N 60 30W
Grand Lake Newfoundland **31** C2 49 00N 57 20W
Grand Manan Island New Brunswick **31** E6 44 45N 66 40W
Grand-Mère Québec **37** O7 46 36N 72 41W
Grand Narrows *tn.* Nova Scotia **31** F7 45 55N 60 50W
Grand Prairie *tn.* Alberta **41** B3 55 10N 118 52W
Grand Rapids *tn.* Manitoba **39** B2 53 12N 99 19W
Grand River Ontario **38** C1 42 51N 79 34W
Grand Valley *tn.* Ontario **38** B2 43 54N 80 18W
Grandview Manitoba **39** A2 51 11N 100 51W
Granisle British Columbia **43** C2 54 56N 126 18W
Granite Bay *tn.* British Columbia **42** G5 50 14N 125 17W
Granite Lake Newfoundland **31** C2 48 11N 57 01W
Granville Falls Manitoba **39** A3 56 10N 100 20W
Granville Lake Manitoba **39** A3 56 00N 101 00W
Grasslands National Park Saskatchewan **40** B1 49 10N 107 30W
Grass River Manitoba **39** B2 54 50N 99 20W
Grass River Provincial Park Manitoba **39** A2 54 40N 101 40W
Grassy Narrows *I.R.* Ontario **34** B3 50 10N 93 55W
Gravelbourg Saskatchewan **40** B1 49 53N 106 33W
Gravenhurst Ontario **36** G5 44 55N 79 22W
Grayling River British Columbia **43** C3 59 43N 125 55W
Greasy Lake Northwest Territories **44** G3 62 55N 122 15W
Great Bear Lake Northwest Territories **45** G4 66 00N 120 00W
Great Central Lake British Columbia **42** G4 49 22N 125 10W
Great Harbour Deep *tn.* Newfoundland **31** C3 50 22N 56 31W
Great Cloche Island Ontario **36** E7 46 01N 81 53W
Great Plain of the Koukdjuak Northwest Territories **45** R4 66 25N 72 50W
Great Pubnico Lake Nova Scotia **31** E6 43 50N 65 30W
Great Sand Hills Saskatchewan **40** B2 50 35N 109 20W
Great Slave Lake Northwest Territories **44** J3 62 00N 114 00W
Great Village Nova Scotia **31** F7 45 25N 63 36W
Greely Ontario **47** K2 45 16N 75 33W
Greely Fiord Northwest Territories **45** P7 80 30N 85 00W
Green Creek Ontario **47** K2 45 25N 75 35W
Green Lake British Columbia **43** D2 51 26N 121 12W
Green Lake *tn.* Saskatchewan **40** B2 54 18N 107 49W
Greenville British Columbia **42** C3 55 05N 129 35W
Greenwater Provincial Park Saskatchewan **40** C2 52 35N 103 25W
Greenwood British Columbia **43** E1 49 08N 118 41W
Grenfell Saskatchewan **40** C2 50 24N 102 56W
Grenville Québec **37** M6 45 40N 74 38W
Grenville, Mount British Columbia **42** H5 50 59N 124 31W
Gretna Manitoba **39** B1 49 01N 97 34W
Grey *admin.* Ontario **38** B3 44 22N 80 33W
Grey Islands Newfoundland **31** C3 50 50N 55 35W
Grey, Point British Columbia **46** E4 49 16N 123 17W
Grey River Newfoundland **31** C2 47 50N 56 50W
Griffith Island Ontario **38** B3 44 50N 80 54W
Grimsby Ontario **38** C2 43 12N 79 35W
Grimshaw Alberta **41** B3 56 11N 117 36W
Grindstone Provincial Recreation Park Manitoba **39** B2 51 10N 96 50W
Grinnell Peninsula Northwest Territories **45** N6 76 40N 95 00W
Grise Fiord *tn.* Northwest Territories **45** P6 76 25N 82 57W
Grizzly Bear Hills Saskatchewan **40** B3 55 50N 109 30W
Groais Island Newfoundland **31** C3 50 57N 55 36W
Gros Morne *mt.* Newfoundland **31** C2 49 36N 57 47W
Gros Morne National Park Newfoundland **31** C2 49 40N 58 40W
Groswater Bay Newfoundland **30** C3 54 20N 57 40W
Groundhog River Ontario **35** D2 49 00N 82 00W
Guelph Ontario **38** B2 43 34N 80 16W
Gull Bay *I.R.* Ontario **34** C2 49 50N 89 00W
Gull Lake Alberta **41** C2 52 34N 114 00W
Gull Lake Ontario **38** D3 44 48N 78 48W
Gull Lake *tn.* Saskatchewan **40** B2 50 05N 108 30W
Gunisao Lake Manitoba **39** B2 53 30N 96 40W
Gunisao River Manitoba **39** B2 53 30N 96 50W
Guysborough Nova Scotia **31** F7 45 23N 61 30W
Guysborough *admin.* Nova Scotia **31** F7 45 20N 61 40W
Gwillim Lake Provincial Park British Columbia **43** D3 55 20N 121 20W
Gypsumville Manitoba **39** B2 51 47N 98 38W
Gyrfalcon Islands Northwest Territories **32** C4 59 05N 69 00W

H

Habay Alberta **41** B3 58 50N 118 44W
Hadley Bay Northwest Territories **44** K5 72 22N 108 30W
Haileybury Ontario **35** E2 47 27N 79 38W
Haines Junction Yukon Territory **44** D3 60 45N 137 21W
Haldimand-Norfolk *admin.* Ontario **38** B1 42 37N 80 39W
Halfway Point *tn.* Newfoundland **31** C2 48 59N 58 06W
Halfway River British Columbia **43** D3 56 42N 122 30W
Haliburton Ontario **36** G6 45 03N 78 31W
Haliburton *admin.* Ontario **38** D3 44 56N 78 42W
Halifax Nova Scotia **31** F6 44 40N 63 41W
Halifax *admin.* Nova Scotia **31** F7 45 00N 63 00W
Halifax Harbour Nova Scotia **47** P6 44 39N 63 33W
Hall Beach *tn.* Northwest Territories **45** P4 68 46N 81 12W
Hall Peninsula Northwest Territories **45** S3 68 40N 66 00W
Halls Harbour Nova Scotia **31** F7 45 12N 64 37W
Halton *admin.* Ontario **38** C2 43 26N 79 57W
Hamilton Ontario **38** C2 43 15N 79 50W
Hamilton Harbour Ontario **38** B2 43 16N 80 50W
Hamilton Inlet Newfoundland **30** C3 54 18N 57 30W
Hamilton Sound Newfoundland **31** D2 49 30N 54 15W
Hamilton-Wentworth *admin.* Ontario **38** B2/C2 43 14N 80 09W
Hamiota Manitoba **39** A2 50 11N 100 38W
Hampden Newfoundland **31** C2 49 33N 56 51W
Hampton New Brunswick **31** E7 45 30N 65 50W
Hanna Alberta **41** C2 51 38N 111 56W
Hannah Bay Ontario **34** D3 51 20N 80 00W
Hanover Ontario **38** A3 44 10N 81 03W
Hanson Lake Road Saskatchewan **40** C2 54 20N 104 35W
Hants *admin.* Nova Scotia **31** F7 45 10N 63 40W
Hantsport Nova Scotia **31** F7 45 04N 64 12W
Happy Valley-Goose Bay Newfoundland **30** A3 53 18N 60 16W
Harbour Breton *tn.* Newfoundland **31** C2 47 29N 55 50W
Harbour Grace *tn.* Newfoundland **31** D2 47 42N 53 13W
Harcourt New Brunswick **31** A2 46 29N 65 18W
Hardisty Alberta **41** C2 52 40N 111 18W
Hardisty Lake Northwest Territories **44** H3 64 30N 117 45W
Hare Bay Newfoundland **31** C3 51 15N 55 45W
Hare Bay *tn.* Newfoundland **31** D2 48 51N 54 00W
Hare Indian River Northwest Territories **44** F4 66 40N 128 00W
Haro Strait British Columbia **42** H4 48 36N 123 17W
Harp Lake Newfoundland **30** B4 55 05N 61 50W
Harrietsfield Nova Scotia **47** P6 44 34N 63 39W
Harrington Harbour *tn.* Québec **33** E3 50 31N 59 30W
Harrison, Cape Newfoundland **30** C3 54 57N 57 57W
Harrison Hot Springs *tn.* British Columbia **42** H4 49 17N 121 47W
Harrison Lake British Columbia **42** H4 49 30N 122 10W
Harriston Ontario **38** B2 43 54N 80 52W
Harrow Ontario **36** D3 42 02N 82 55W
Harrowby Manitoba **39** A2 50 45N 101 28W
Harry Gibbons Bird Sanctuary Northwest Territories **45** O3 63 50N 86 00W
Hartland New Brunswick **31** A2 46 18N 67 31W
Hartney Manitoba **39** A1 49 29N 100 31W
Hart River Yukon Territory **44** D4 65 40N 137 10W
Hastings Ontario **36** J5 44 18N 77 57W
Hastings *admin.* Ontario **36** J5 44 45N 77 40W
Hatchet Lake Saskatchewan **40** C3 58 50N 103 30W
Haultain River Saskatchewan **40** B3 56 20N 106 20W
Havelock Ontario **36** J5 44 26N 77 53W
Havre-Aubert Québec **33** D2 47 15N 61 51W
Havre-Saint-Pierre Québec **33** D3 50 20N 63 38W
Hawke Harbour *tn.* Newfoundland **30** C3 53 03N 55 49W
Hawkes Bay *tn.* Newfoundland **31** C3 50 36N 57 10W
Hawkesbury Ontario **37** M6 45 36N 74 37W
Hay, Cape Northwest Territories **44** J5 74 25N 113 00W
Hayes River Manitoba **39** C3 55 20N 94 10W
Hay Lake Alberta **41** B3 58 52N 119 20W
Hay River Alberta/Northwest Territories **41** B3 58 00N 118 00W
Hay River *tn.* Northwest Territories **44** H3 60 51N 115 42W
Hazeldean Ontario **47** J2 45 18N 75 55W
Hazelton British Columbia **43** C3 55 17N 127 42W
Hazen Strait Northwest Territories **44** K6 77 00N 110 00W
Head Lake Ontario **38** D3 44 45N 78 54W
Head of Bay d'Espoir *tn.* Newfoundland **31** C2 47 56N 55 45W
Head-Smashed-In Bison Jump Alberta **22** 49 43N 113 40W
Hearst Ontario **35** D2 49 42N 83 40W
Heart's Content Newfoundland **31** D2 47 53N 53 22W
Hebron Newfoundland **30** B4 58 12N 62 38W
Hebron Nova Scotia **31** E6 43 57N 66 03W
Hebron Fiord *in.* Newfoundland **30** B4 58 09N 62 45W
Hecate Strait British Columbia **42** B2 53 40N 131 10W
Hecla and Griper Bay Northwest Territories **44** J6 76 25N 113 00W
Hecla Island Manitoba **39** B2 51 00N 96 30W
Hecla Provincial Park Manitoba **39** B2 51 10N 96 30W
Hedley British Columbia **43** D1 49 21N 120 02W
Henley Harbour *tn.* Newfoundland **30** C3 51 59N 55 51W
Henrietta Island Newfoundland **30** C3 54 05N 58 28W
Henrietta Maria, Cape Ontario **34** D4 55 00N 82 30W
Henry Kater Peninsula Northwest Territories **45** S4 69 20N 67 20W
Hensall Ontario **38** A2 43 26N 81 31W
Hepworth Ontario **38** A3 44 37N 81 09W
Herbert Saskatchewan **40** B2 50 26N 107 12W
Heriot Bay *tn.* British Columbia **42** G5 50 06N 125 12W
Hermitage-Sandyville Newfoundland **31** C2 47 33N 55 56W
Heron Bay *I.R.* Ontario **35** C2 48 40N 86 17W
Herring Cove *tn.* Nova Scotia **47** P6 44 34N 63 34W
Herschel Yukon Territory **44** D4 69 34N 139 00W
Herschel Island Yukon Territory **44** D4 69 34N 139 00W
Hespeler Ontario **38** B2 43 26N 80 20W
Hess River Yukon Territory **44** E3 63 25N 133 50W
Hibbard Québec **37** M8 47 53N 74 03W
Hickman, Mount British Columbia **42** B3 57 15N 131 07W
High Level *tn.* Alberta **41** B3 58 10N 117 20W
High Prairie *tn.* Alberta **41** B3 55 26N 116 29W
High River *tn.* Alberta **41** C2 50 35N 113 52W
Highrock Manitoba **39** A3 55 50N 100 22W
Highrock Lake Manitoba **39** A3 55 45N 100 20W
Highrock Lake Saskatchewan **40** B3 57 00N 105 20W
Hillsborough New Brunswick **31** F7 45 56N 64 40W
Hillsborough Bay Prince Edward Island **31** F7 46 10N 63 20W
Hillsburgh Ontario **38** B2 43 46N 80 10W
Hinds Lake Reservoir Newfoundland **31** C2 49 00N 56 00W
Hines Creek *tn.* Alberta **41** B3 56 15N 118 36W
Hinton Alberta **41** B2 53 25N 117 34W
Hoare Bay Northwest Territories **45** T4 65 17N 62 55W
Hodgeville Saskatchewan **40** B2 50 07N 106 58W
Hog Island Prince Edward Island **31** F7 46 35N 63 50W
Holden Alberta **41** C2 53 14N 112 14W
Holdfast Saskatchewan **40** B2 50 58N 105 28W
Holland Landing Ontario **38** C3 44 05N 79 29W
Holland River Ontario **38** C3 44 01N 79 39W
Holman Northwest Territories **44** H5 70 44N 117 44W
Holton Newfoundland **30** C3 54 35N 57 16W
Holyrood Newfoundland **31** D2 47 23N 53 08W
Homathko River British Columbia **43** C2 51 00N 125 05W
Home Bay Northwest Territories **45** S4 69 00N 67 00W
Home Island Newfoundland **30** B5 60 10N 64 14W
Honey Harbour *tn.* Ontario **38** C3 44 51N 79 48W
Hope British Columbia **42** H4 49 21N 121 28W
Hope Bay Ontario **38** A3 44 55N 81 14W
Hopedale Newfoundland **30** B4 55 28N 60 13W
Hope Island British Columbia **43** C2 50 55N 127 55W
Hope Island Ontario **38** B3 44 54N 80 11W
Hopes Advance Bay Québec **32** C4 59 20N 69 40W
Hopewell Nova Scotia **31** F7 45 29N 62 41W
Hornaday River Northwest Territories **44** G4 69 00N 123 00W
Hornby Island British Columbia **42** H4 49 31N 124 40W
Hornepayne Ontario **35** D2 49 13N 84 47W
Horner Creek Ontario **38** B2 43 12N 80 35W

Horn Mountains Northwest Territories **44** H3 62 15N 119 15W
Horsefly Lake British Columbia **43** D2 52 25N 121 00W
Horsehills Creek Alberta **48** G5 53 45N 113 23W
Horse Islands Newfoundland **31** C3 50 13N 55 48W
Horseshoe Bay *tn.* British Columbia **42** H4 49 22N 123 17W
Horton River Northwest Territories **44** G4 68 50N 123 50W
Horwood Lake Ontario **35** D2 48 00N 82 20W
Hottah Lake Northwest Territories **44** H4 65 04N 118 30W
Houston British Columbia **43** C2 54 24N 126 39W
Houston Point Northwest Territories **34** D3 58 20N 81 00W
Howe Sound British Columbia **42** H4 49 30N 123 25W
Howley Newfoundland **31** C2 49 10N 57 07W
Hubbards Nova Scotia **31** F6 44 38N 64 03W
Hubbart Point Manitoba **39** C3 59 21N 94 41W
Hudson Bay *(Baie d'Hudson)* Northwest Territories/Ontario/Québec **11** R5 60 00N 89 00W
Hudson Bay *tn.* Saskatchewan **40** C2 52 45N 102 45W
Hudson's Hope British Columbia **43** D3 56 00N 121 59W
Hudson Strait Northwest Territories **45** R3 62 00N 70 00W
Hugh Keenleyside Dam British Columbia **43** E1 49 33N 118 00W
Hull Québec **39** J2 45 26N 75 45W
Hull *admin.* Québec **37** L6 45 40N 75 40W
Humber Bay Ontario **46** C1 43 36N 79 27W
Humber River Ontario **46** B2 43 48N 79 37W
Humboldt Saskatchewan **40** B2 52 12N 105 07W
Hunter Island British Columbia **43** C2 51 57N 128 05W
Hunter River *tn.* Prince Edward Island **31** F7 46 20N 63 20W
Huntingdon Québec **37** M6 45 05N 74 11W
Huntingdon *admin.* Québec **37** M6 45 00N 74 20W
Huntingdon Island Newfoundland **30** C3 53 47N 56 55W
Hunt River Newfoundland **30** B4 55 20N 61 10W
Huntsville Ontario **36** G6 45 20N 79 13W
Hurd, Cape Ontario **38** A4 45 14N 81 44W
Huron *admin.* Ontario **38** A2 43 27N 81 35W
Huron, Lake Canada/U.S.A. **36** D5 45 00N 83 00W
Hyde Park Ontario **38** A2 43 00N 81 20W
Hythe Alberta **41** B3 55 18N 119 33W

I

Igiusuaktalialuk Island Newfoundland **30** B4 57 20N 61 30W
Igloolik Northwest Territories **45** P4 69 23N 81 46W
Ignace Ontario **34** B2 49 26N 91 40W
Île-à-la-Crosse *tn.* Saskatchewan **40** B3 55 28N 107 53W
Île aux Coudres *i.* Québec **37** Q8 47 23N 70 20W
Île aux Herons *i.* Québec **47** N4 45 26N 73 35W
Île Bizard *i.* Québec **47** M4 45 29N 73 54W
Île D'Anticosti *i.* Québec **33** D2 49 20N 62 30W
Île de Montréal *i.* Québec **47** M4 45 30N 73 43W
Île des Allumettes *i.* Québec **37** J6 45 55N 77 08W
Ile des Chenes Manitoba **48** D2 49 41N 96 58W
Île des Soeurs *(Île des Soeurs ou St. Paul)* Québec **47** N4 45 28N 73 33W
Île des Soeurs ou St. Paul *(Île des Soeurs) i.* Québec **47** N4 45 28N 73 33W
Île d'Orléans *i.* Québec **37** Q7 46 55N 71 00W
Île du Grand Calumet Québec **37** K6 45 30N 76 35W
Île Jésus *i.* Québec **47** N5 45 35N 73 45W
Île Kettle *i.* Québec **47** K2 45 28N 75 39W
Île Lamèque *i.* New Brunswick **31** B2 47 50N 64 40W
Île Lynch *i.* Québec **47** M4 45 25N 73 54W
Île Ste. Hélène *i.* Québec **47** N5 45 31N 73 32W
Île Sainte-Thérèse *i.* Québec **47** O5 45 39N 73 30W
Îles-de-Boucherville *is.* Québec **47** N5 45 36N 73 28W
Îles de la Madeleine *is.* Québec **33** D2 47 40N 61 50W
Ilford Manitoba **39** B3 56 04N 95 40W
Indian Arm *b.* British Columbia **46** G4 49 19N 122 55W
Indian Cabins Alberta **41** B3 59 52N 117 02W
Indian Harbour *tn.* Newfoundland **30** C3 54 27N 57 13W
Indian Head *tn.* Saskatchewan **40** C2 50 35N 103 37W
Indian Tickle Newfoundland **30** C3 53 34N 56 02W
Ingenika River British Columbia **43** C3 56 48N 126 11W
Ingersoll Ontario **38** B2 43 03N 80 53W
Ingonish Nova Scotia **31** F7 46 42N 60 22W
Inklin River British Columbia **42** B3 58 54N 132 50W
Inner Bay Ontario **38** B1 42 35N 80 26W
Innisfail Alberta **41** C2 52 01N 113 59W
Inside Passage British Columbia **42** C2 53 38N 129 40W
Inukjuak Québec **32** A4 58 40N 78 15W
Inuvik Northwest Territories **44** E4 68 16N 133 40W
Inuvik *reg.* Northwest Territories **44** E4 68 21N 133 43W
Inverhuron Provincial Park Ontario **38** A3 44 20N 81 30W
Invermere British Columbia **43** E2 50 30N 116 00W
Inverness Nova Scotia **31** F7 46 14N 61 19W
Inverness *admin.* Nova Scotia **31** F7 46 00N 61 30W
Iqaluit *(Frobisher Bay)* Northwest Territories **45** S3 60 00N 65 00W
Irma Alberta **41** C2 52 55N 111 14W
Iron Bridge *tn.* Ontario **36** C7 46 17N 83 14W
Irondale Ontario **38** D3 44 53N 78 30W
Ironside Québec **47** J2 45 27N 75 46W
Iroquois Ontario **37** L5 44 51N 75 19W
Iroquois Falls *tn.* Ontario **35** D2 48 47N 80 41W
Irvine Creek Alberta **48** G4 53 20N 113 29W
Irvines Landing British Columbia **42** H4 49 37N 124 02W
Isachsen Northwest Territories **45** L6 78 47N 103 30W
Ishpatina Ridge Ontario **35** D2 47 19N 80 44W
Iskut River British Columbia **42** B3 56 45N 131 10W
Island Falls Dam Saskatchewan **40** C3 55 30N 102 20W
Island Lake Manitoba **39** C2 53 50N 94 00W
Island Lake *tn.* Manitoba **39** C2 53 50N 94 00W
Island of Ponds *tn.* Newfoundland **30** C3 53 20N 55 50W
Isle aux Morts *tn.* Newfoundland **31** C2 47 35N 58 59W
Isle Madame *i.* Nova Scotia **31** F7 45 30N 60 50W
Isle Royale Ontario **35** C2 48 10N 88 30W
Isle Royale National Park Ontario **35** C2 48 10N 88 30W
Islington Ontario **46** B1 43 38N 79 32W
Issac Lake Ontario **38** A3 44 46N 81 13W
Itchen Lake Northwest Territories **44** J4 65 33N 112 50W
Ituna Saskatchewan **40** C2 51 09N 103 24W
Ivujivik Québec **32** A5 62 25N 77 54W

J

Jackfish Lake Manitoba **39** B2 50 30N 99 20W
Jackson's Arm *tn.* Newfoundland **31** C2 49 53N 56 47W
Jacksons Point *tn.* Ontario **38** C3 44 18N 79 22W
James Bay *(Baie James)* Ontario/Northwest Territories Québec **34** D3 53 45N 81 00W
James Bay Preserve Ontario/Northwest Territories Québec **45** P1 53 00N 81 00W
James Ross, Cape Northwest Territories **44** G5 74 40N 114 25W
James Ross Strait Northwest Territories **45** M4 69 40N 96 00W
Jarvis Ontario **38** B1 42 52N 80 08W
Jasper Alberta **41** B2 52 55N 118 05W
Jasper National Park Alberta **41** B2 53 00N 118 00W
Jean Marie River *tn.* Northwest Territories **44** G3 61 32N 120 38W
Jellicoe Ontario **34** C2 49 41N 87 31W
Jennings River British Columbia **42** B3 59 33N 131 40W
Jenpeg Manitoba **39** B2 54 30N 98 00W
Jervis Inlet British Columbia **42** H4 49 47N 124 04W
Jock River Ontario **47** J2 45 15N 75 46W
Joggins Nova Scotia **31** F7 45 42N 64 27W
John D'Or Prairie Alberta **41** B3 58 30N 115 08W
John Hart Highway British Columbia **43** D3 55 40N 121 38W
Johnstone Strait British Columbia **43** C2 50 23N 126 30W
Joliette Québec **37** N7 46 02N 73 27W
Joliette *admin.* Québec **37** L8 47 40N 75 40W
Jones Ontario **34** B2 49 59N 94 05W
Jones Sound Northwest Territories **45** P6 76 00N 88 00W
Jonquière Québec **37** P9 48 25N 71 16W
Jordan Lake Nova Scotia **31** E6 44 05N 65 20W
Jordan River *tn.* British Columbia **42** H4 48 26N 123 59W
Joseph, Lake Ontario **38** C4 45 11N 79 44W
Joutel Québec **33** A2 49 28N 78 28W
Juan de Fuca Strait British Columbia **42** H4 48 30N 124 31W
Judique Nova Scotia **31** F7 45 55N 61 30W

K

Kabania Lake Ontario **34** C3 52 12N 88 20W
Kabinakagami, Lake Ontario **35** D2 48 54N 84 25W
Kabinakagami River Ontario **35** D2 49 10N 84 10W
Kagawong Ontario **36** D6 45 54N 82 15W
Kahnawake Québec **47** N4 45 25N 73 42W
Kahshe Lake Ontario **38** C3 44 51N 79 17W
Kaipokok Bay Newfoundland **30** C3 55 00N 59 35W
Kakabeka Falls *tn.* Ontario **35** C2 48 24N 89 40W
Kakisa Northwest Territories **44** H3 60 58N 117 30W
Kakwa River Alberta **41** B2 54 15N 119 45W
Kaladar Ontario **37** J5 44 39N 77 07W
Kamilukuak Lake Northwest Territories **45** L3 62 22N 101 40W
Kaminak Lake Northwest Territories **45** N3 62 10N 95 00W
Kamloops British Columbia **43** D2 50 39N 120 24W
Kamloops Lake British Columbia **43** D2 50 45N 120 40W
Kamouraska Québec **37** R8 47 34N 69 51W
Kamouraska *admin.* Québec **37** R8 47 10N 69 50W
Kamsack Saskatchewan **40** C2 51 34N 101 51W
Kamuchawie Lake Manitoba/Saskatchewan **40** C3 56 20N 102 20W
Kanaaupscow Québec **32** A3 54 00N 76 40W
Kanata Ontario **47** J2 45 20N 75 53W
Kangiqsualujjuaq Québec **32** C4 58 48N 66 08W
Kangiqsujuaq Québec **32** B5 61 40N 71 59W
Kangirsuk Québec **32** B5 60 00N 70 00W
Kapiskau River Ontario **34** D3 52 00N 89 50W
Kapuskasing Ontario **35** D2 49 25N 82 26W
Kapuskasing River Ontario **35** D2 48 40N 82 50W
Kasabonika *I.R.* Ontario **34** C3 53 32N 88 37W
Kasabonika Lake Ontario **34** C3 53 35N 88 35W
Kasba Lake Northwest Territories **45** L3 60 18N 102 07W
Kashechewan *I.R.* Ontario **34** D3 52 18N 81 37W
Kaskattama River Manitoba **39** C3 56 25N 91 10W
Kaslo British Columbia **43** E1 49 54N 116 57W
Kasmere Lake Manitoba **39** A3 59 30N 101 10W
Kates Needle *mt.* British Columbia **42** B3 57 02N 132 05W
Kaumajet Mountains Newfoundland **30** B4 57 48N 61 51W
Kawawachikamach *see* Schefferville
Kayano Québec **32** B3 53 52N 73 30W
Kazabazua Québec **37** K6 45 56N 76 01W
Kearney Ontario **36** G6 45 35N 79 17W
Kechika River British Columbia **43** C3 58 44N 127 25W
Kedgwick New Brunswick **31** A2 47 38N 67 21W
Keefers British Columbia **42** H5 50 03N 121 32W
Keele Peak Yukon Territory **44** E3 63 25N 130 17W
Keele River Northwest Territories **44** F3 64 15N 126 00W
Keewatin Ontario **34** B2 49 47N 94 30W
Keewatin *reg.* Northwest Territories **45** M3 63 30N 98 00W
Keewatin River Manitoba **39** A3 56 59N 100 59W
Keith Arm *b.* Northwest Territories **44** G4 65 20N 122 15W
Kejimkujik National Park Nova Scotia **31** E6 44 20N 65 20W
Keller Lake Northwest Territories **44** G3 64 00N 121 30W
Kellett, Cape Northwest Territories **44** F5 71 59N 126 00W
Kellett Strait Northwest Territories **44** H6 75 45N 117 30W
Kelliher Saskatchewan **40** C2 51 15N 103 41W
Kelowna British Columbia **43** E1 49 50N 119 29W
Kelsey Bay *tn.* British Columbia **43** C2 50 22N 125 29W
Kelvington Saskatchewan **40** C2 52 10N 103 30W
Kemano British Columbia **43** C2 53 39N 127 58W
Kempenfelt Bay Ontario **38** C3 44 22N 79 39W
Kemptville Ontario **37** L6 45 01N 75 38W
Kenamu River Newfoundland **30** B3 52 50N 60 20W
Kenaston Saskatchewan **40** B2 51 30N 106 15W
Kendall Island Bird Sanctuary Northwest Territories **44** D4 69 30N 135 00W
Kennebecasis River New Brunswick **31** E7 45 30N 65 55W
Kennedy Saskatchewan **40** C2 50 01N 102 21W
Kennedy Lake British Columbia **42** G4 49 12N 125 32W
Kennetcook Nova Scotia **31** F7 45 10N 63 43W
Kenney Dam British Columbia **43** D2 53 38N 124 59W
Kenogami River Ontario **34** D3 50 50N 84 30W
Kenogamissi Lake Ontario **35** D2 48 15N 81 33W
Kenora Ontario **34** B2 49 47N 94 26W
Kensington Prince Edward Island **31** F7 46 26N 63 39W
Kent *admin.* New Brunswick **31** A2 46 30N 65 20W
Kent *admin.* Ontario **36** D3 42 25N 82 10W
Kent Peninsula Northwest Territories **44** K4 68 30N 106 00W
Kentville Nova Scotia **31** F7 45 04N 64 30W
Keremeos British Columbia **43** E1 49 12N 119 50W
Kerrobert Saskatchewan **40** B2 51 56N 109 09W
Kesagami Lake Ontario **35** D3 50 00N 80 00W
Kesagami River Ontario **35** D3 50 30N 80 10W
Keswick Ontario **38** C3 44 15N 79 28W
Kettle Creek Ontario **38** A1 42 47N 81 13W
Kettle Rapids *tn.* Manitoba **39** C3 56 25N 94 30W
Kettle River British Columbia **43** E1 49 10N 119 02W
Kettle River Manitoba **39** D3 56 40N 89 50W
Key Lake Mine *tn.* Saskatchewan **40** B3 57 10N 105 30W
Kicking Horse Pass Alberta/British Columbia **43** E2 51 28N 116 23W
Kiglapait, Cape Newfoundland **30** B4 57 06N 61 22W
Kiglapait Mountains Newfoundland **30** B4 57 06N 61 35W
Kikerk Lake Northwest Territories **44** J4 66 55N 113 20W
Kikkertarjote Island Newfoundland **30** B4 57 30N 61 28W
Kikkertavak Island Newfoundland **30** B4 56 22N 61 35W
Kikona Park Manitoba **48** D2 49 56N 97 03W
Kildonan Park Manitoba **48** D2 49 57N 97 07W
Killam Alberta **41** C2 52 47N 111 51W
Killarney Manitoba **39** B1 49 12N 99 40W
Killarney Ontario **36** E6 45 59N 81 30W
Killarney Provincial Park Ontario **36** E7 46 00N 81 00W
Killbear Provincial Park Ontario **35** B4 45 22N 80 13W
Killinek Island Newfoundland/Northwest Territories **30** B4 60 24N 64 31W
Kimberley British Columbia **43** E1 49 40N 115 58W
Kinbasket Lake British Columbia **43** E2 51 57N 118 02W
Kincardine Ontario **38** A3 44 11N 81 38W
Kincolith British Columbia **42** C3 55 00N 129 57W
Kincora Prince Edward Island **31** F7 46 20N 63 40W
Kindersley Saskatchewan **40** B2 51 27N 109 08W
King Christian Island Northwest Territories **45** L6 77 45N 102 00W
Kingcome Inlet *tn.* British Columbia **43** C2 50 58N 125 15W
Kingfisher Lake Ontario **34** C3 53 05N 89 49W
Kingfisher Lake *I.R.* Ontario **34** C3 53 02N 89 50W
King George, Mount British Columbia **43** E2 50 36N 115 26W
King Island British Columbia **43** C2 52 10N 127 35W
Kings *admin.* New Brunswick **31** E7 45 30N 65 40W
Kings *admin.* Nova Scotia **31** F6 44 50N 64 50W
Kings *admin.* Prince Edward Island **31** F7 46 20N 62 40W
Kingsburg Nova Scotia **31** F6 44 20N 64 10W
Kings Landing New Brunswick **31** A2 45 50N 67 00W
Kingsmere Québec **47** J2 45 29N 75 50W
Kingston Ontario **37** K5 44 14N 76 30W
Kingsville Ontario **36** D3 42 02N 82 45W
Kingurutik Lake Newfoundland **30** B4 56 49N 62 20W
King William Island Northwest Territories **45** M4 69 00N 97 30W
Kinistino Saskatchewan **40** B2 52 58N 105 01W
Kinnoosao Saskatchewan **40** B3 57 06N 102 02W
Kinoje River Ontario **34** D3 51 40N 81 50W
Kinsac Nova Scotia **47** P7 44 51N 63 39W
Kinsac Lake Nova Scotia **47** P7 44 50N 63 38W
Kinusheseo River Ontario **34** D3 54 30N 83 50W
Kiosk Ontario **36** H7 46 05N 78 53W
Kipahigan Lake Manitoba **39** A3 55 20N 101 50W
Kipawa Québec **36** G7 46 47N 79 00W
Kipling Saskatchewan **40** C2 50 08N 102 40W
Kirkfield Lift Lock National Park Ontario **38** D3 44 30N 79 00W
Kirkland Québec **47** M4 45 27N 73 53W
Kirkland Lake Ontario **35** D2 48 10N 80 02W
Kirkpatrick Lake Alberta **41** C2 51 52N 111 18W
Kirriemuir Alberta **41** C2 51 56N 110 18W
Kiskittogisa Lake Manitoba **39** B2 54 10N 98 50W
Kiskitto Lake Manitoba **39** B2 54 20N 98 50W
Kispiox British Columbia **43** C3 55 21N 127 41W
Kississing Lake Manitoba **39** A3 55 10N 101 30W
Kistigan Lake Manitoba **39** C2 54 50N 92 40W
Kitchener Ontario **38** B2 43 27N 80 30W
Kitikmeot *reg.* Northwest Territories **44** K4 69 50N 107 30W
Kitimat British Columbia **42** C2 54 05N 128 38W
Klappan River British Columbia **42** C3 57 50N 129 40W
Kleinburg Ontario **46** B2 43 50N 79 36W
Klinaklini River British Columbia **43** C2 51 18N 125 45W
Klondike Highway Yukon Territory **44** D3 62 55N 136 10W
Klondike River Yukon Territory **44** D3 64 20N 138 50W
Kluane Game Sanctuary Yukon Territory **44** D3 61 30N 139 50W
Kluane Lake Yukon Territory **44** D3 62 20N 139 00W
Kluane National Park Yukon Territory **44** D3 60 30N 139 00W
Knee Lake Manitoba **39** C3 55 10N 94 40W
Knight Inlet British Columbia **42** G5 50 45N 125 36W
Knox, Cape British Columbia **42** B2 54 09N 133 05W
Koch Island Northwest Territories **45** Q4 69 38N 78 15W
Kogaluc Bay Québec **32** A4 59 00N 78 00W
Kogaluk River Newfoundland **30** B4 56 10N 63 30W
Kokanee Glacier Park British Columbia **43** E1 49 45N 117 10W
Komoka Ontario **38** A1 42 56N 81 26W
Kootenay Lake British Columbia **43** E1 49 35N 116 30W
Kootenay National Park British Columbia **43** E2 51 15N 116 25W
Kopka River Ontario **34** C3 50 00N 90 00W
Kotcho Lake British Columbia **43** D3 59 05N 121 10W
Kouchibouguac National Park New Brunswick **31** F7 46 45N 64 50W
Koukdjuak Northwest Territories **45** R4 66 50N 72 50W
Kunghit Island British Columbia **42** B2 52 02N 131 02W
Kuujjuaq Québec **32** C4 58 25N 68 55W
Kuujjuarapik *(Poste-de-la-Baleine, Whapmagoostui)* Québec **32** A4 55 15N 77 41W
Kwadacha Wilderness Park British Columbia **43** C3 57 50N 125 00W
Kwataboahegan River Ontario **34** D3 51 10N 82 30W
Kyle Saskatchewan **40** B2 50 50N 108 02W
Kyuquot Sound British Columbia **43** C1 50 02N 127 22W

L

La Baie Québec **37** Q9 48 20N 70 55W
La Barrière Park Manitoba **48** D1 49 43N 97 09W
Labelle Québec **37** M7 46 17N 74 45W
Labelle *admin.* Québec **37** L7 46 30N 75 40W
Laberge, Lake Yukon Territory **44** E3 61 10N 134 59W
Labrador *geog. reg.* Newfoundland **30** B3 54 00N 64 00W
Labrador City Newfoundland **30** A3 52 57N 66 55W
Labrador Sea Canada/Greenland **11** V3 52 54N 66 50W
Lac Abitibi *l.* Québec **33** A2 48 40N 79 40W
Lac Albanel *l.* Québec **33** B3 51 00N 73 20W
Lac à l'Eau Claire *l.* Québec **32** B4 56 20N 74 30W
Lac Anuc *l.* Québec **32** A4 59 15N 75 10W
Lac Assinica *l.* Québec **33** A3 50 20N 75 12W
Lac au Goéland *l.* Québec **33** A2 49 45N 76 55W
Lac Aylmer *l.* Québec **37** P6 45 50N 71 20W
Lac Bacqueville *l.* Québec **32** B4 58 05N 74 00W
Lac Batiscan *l.* Québec **37** P8 47 23N 71 53W
Lac Bécard *l.* Québec **32** B5 60 05N 73 45W
Lac Belot *l.* Northwest Territories **44** F4 66 53N 126 16W
Lac Bérard *l.* Québec **32** B4 58 25N 70 05W
Lac Bermen *l.* Québec **32** C3 53 40N 69 00W
Lac Berté *l.* Québec **33** C3 50 52N 68 35W
Lac Bienville *l.* Québec **32** B4 55 30N 73 00W
Lac Bourdel *l.* Québec **32** B4 56 42N 74 15W
Lac Boyd *l.* Québec **33** A3 52 45N 76 45W
Lac Brochet *l.* Manitoba **39** A3 58 40N 101 20W
Lac Brome *l.* Québec **37** O6 45 15N 72 30W
Lac Brome *tn.* Québec **37** O6 45 13N 72 30W
Lac Burton *l.* Québec **32** A3 54 45N 79 25W
Lac Cambrien *l.* Québec **32** C4 56 30N 69 22W
Lac Cananée *l.* Québec **32** D4 56 05N 64 05W
Lac Chaconipau *l.* Québec **32** C4 56 20N 68 45W
Lac Champdoré *l.* Québec **32** C4 56 50N 66 20W
Lac Champlain *(Lake Champlain) l.* Québec Canada/U.S.A. **37** N6 45 08N 73 08W
Lac Châtelain *l.* Québec **32** B5 60 20N 74 20W
Lac Chavigny *l.* Québec **32** A4 58 10N 75 10W
Lac Chibougamau *l.* Québec **33** B2 49 55N 74 20W
Lac Couture *l.* Québec **32** A5 60 00N 75 20W
Lac de Gras *l.* Northwest Territories **44** K3 64 10N 109 00W
Lac de la Hutte Sauvage *l.* Québec **32** D4 56 18N 65 00W
Lac des Bois *l.* Northwest Territories **44** F4 67 00N 126 00W
Lac Deschênes *(Lake Ontario)* Ontario/Québec **47** J2 45 22N 75 50W
Lac des Commissaires *l.* Québec **37** O9 48 09N 72 13W
Lac des Deux Montagnes *l.* Québec **47** M4 45 30N 73 58W
Lac des Loups Marins *l.* Québec **32** B4 56 30N 73 30W
Lac des Mille Lacs *l.* Ontario **34** B2 48 53N 90 22W
Lac des Quinze *l.* Québec **33** A2 47 45N 79 15W
Lac des Trente et Un Milles *l.* Québec **37** L7 46 18N 75 43W
Lac D'Iberville *l.* Québec **32** B4 55 55N 73 25W
Lac du Bonnet *l.* Manitoba **39** B2 50 30N 95 50W
Lac du Bonnet *tn.* Manitoba **39** B2 50 16N 96 03W
Lac Dumoine *l.* Québec **36** H7 46 07N 78 58W
Lac Duncan *l.* Québec **33** A3 53 25N 78 00W
Lac du Sable *l.* Québec **32** C3 54 25N 67 55W
Lac Édouard *l.* Québec **37** O8 47 40N 72 16W
Lac-Etchemin *tn.* Québec **37** Q7 46 23N 70 32W
Lac Faribault *l.* Québec **32** B4 59 10N 72 00W
Lac-Fleur-de-May *l.* Newfoundland **30** B3 52 00N 65 02W
Lac Gaotanaga *l.* Québec **37** J8 47 42N 77 28W
Lac Guillaume-Delisle *l.* Québec **32** A4 56 15N 77 20W
Lachine Québec **47** N4 45 26N 73 42W
Lachute Québec **37** M6 51 00N 71 00W
Lac Île-à-la-Crosse *l.* Saskatchewan **40** B3 55 40N 107 30W
Lac Jeannin *l.* Québec **32** C4 56 25N 66 30W
Lac Joseph *l.* Newfoundland **30** A3 52 45N 65 18W
Lac Kempt *l.* Québec **37** M8 47 28N 74 08W
Lac Kénogami *l.* Québec **33** B2 48 22N 71 25W
Lac Kipawa Québec **36** G7 46 55N 79 06W
Lac Klotz *l.* Québec **32** B5 60 30N 73 30W
Lac la Biche *l.* Alberta **41** C2 54 55N 112 58W
Lac la Biche *tn.* Alberta **41** C2 54 46N 111 58W
Lac la Croix *l.* Ontario **35** B2 48 21N 92 09W
Lac la Loche *l.* Saskatchewan **40** B3 56 30N 109 40W
Lac la Martre *l.* Northwest Territories **44** H3 63 20N 118 30W
Lac la Martre *tn.* Northwest Territories **44** H3 63 00N 117 30W
Lac la Plonge *l.* Saskatchewan **40** B3 55 05N 107 00W
Lac la Ronge *l.* Saskatchewan **40** B3/C3 55 10N 105 00W
Lac la Ronge Provincial Park Saskatchewan **40** C3 55 20N 104 45W
Lac le Moyne *l.* Québec **32** C4 57 10N 68 33W
Lac le Roy *l.* Québec **32** A4 58 35N 75 25W
Lac Lesdiguières *l.* Québec **32** B5 60 00N 74 20W
Lac Magpie *l.* Québec **33** D3 51 00N 64 40W
Lac Maicasagi *l.* Québec **33** A3 50 00N 76 45W
Lac Manitou *l.* Québec **33** C3 50 50N 65 20W
Lac Manouane *l.* Québec **33** B3 50 45N 70 45W
Lac Matagami *l.* Québec **33** A2 49 55N 77 50W
Lac Maunoir *l.* Northwest Territories **44** G4 67 30N 124 55W
Lac-Mégantic *tn.* Québec **37** Q6 45 34N 70 53W
Lac Memphrémagog *l.* Québec **37** O6 45 05N 72 13W
Lac Mesgouez *l.* Québec **33** A3 51 25N 75 00W
Lac Minto *l.* Québec **32** B4 57 35N 75 00W
Lac Mistassini *l.* Québec **33** B3 51 00N 73 20W
Lac Mistinibi *l.* Québec **32** D4 55 50N 64 20W
Lac Mitchinamécus *l.* Québec **37** M8 47 20N 75 00W
Lac Musquaro *l.* Québec **33** D3 50 50N 60 50W
Lac Nantais *l.* Québec **32** B5 61 10N 74 20W
Lac Naococane *l.* Québec **33** B3 52 53N 70 40W
Lac Nichicapau *l.* Québec **32** C4 56 42N 68 28W
Lac Nichicun *l.* Québec **33** B3 53 05N 71 05W
Lacombe Alberta **41** C2 52 28N 113 44W
Lac Opiscotéo *l.* Québec **33** C3 53 15N 68 20W
Lac Otelnuk *l.* Québec **32** C4 56 10N 68 20W
Lac Parent *l.* Québec **37** J9 48 30N 77 08W
Lac Payne *l.* Québec **32** B4 59 25N 74 25W
Lac Pélican *l.* Québec **32** B4 59 57N 73 40W
Lac Péribonca *l.* Québec **33** B3 50 10N 71 23W
Lac Plétipi *l.* Québec **33** B3 51 50N 70 10W
Lac Poncheville *l.* Québec **33** A3 50 12N 77 00W
Lac Potherie *l.* Québec **32** B4 58 50N 72 25W
Lac Qilalugalik *l.* Québec **32** A4 58 35N 76 00W
Lac Ramusio *l.* Québec **32** D4 55 10N 63 59W
Lac Résolution *l.* Québec **32** D4 55 15N 64 40W
Lac Roberts *l.* Québec **32** B5 60 25N 70 25W
Lac Saindon *l.* Québec **32** B4 55 35N 73 30W
Lac Sainte-Anne *l.* Québec **33** C3 50 15N 68 00W
Lac Saint-François *l.* Québec **37** P6 45 56N 71 08W

Lac Saint-Jean *l.* Québec **33** B2 48 35N 72 00W
Lac-St.-Jean-Est *admin.* Québec **37** P9 48 20N 71 40W
Lac-St.-Jean-Ouest *admin.* Québec **37** O9 48 20N 72 20W
Lac St. Joseph *l.* Ontario **34** B3 51 30N 91 40W
Lac Saint-Louis *l.* Québec **47** M4 45 25N 73 49W
Lac Saint-Patrice *l.* Québec **37** J7 46 20N 77 30W
Lac Saint-Pierre *l.* Québec **37** O7 46 12N 72 49W
Lac Sakami *l.* Québec **33** A3 53 20N 76 50W
Lac Seul *l.* Ontario **34** B3 50 20N 92 00W
Lac Seul *I.R.* Ontario **34** B3 50 15N 92 15W
Lac Simard *l.* Québec **33** A2 47 40N 78 50W
Lac Simon *l.* Québec **37** L6 45 55N 75 05W
Lac Soscumica *l.* Québec **33** A3 50 15N 77 35W
Lac Tasiaalujjuak *l.* Québec **32** B4 59 35N 71 59W
Lac Tasiat *l.* Québec **32** A4 59 05N 75 25W
Lac Tasiataq *l.* Québec **32** B4 58 40N 71 40W
Lac Tassialouc *l.* Québec **32** B4 58 59N 74 00W
Lac Témiscamingue *(Lake Timiskaming)* Québec **33** A2 47 28N 79 30W
Lac Tiblemont *l.* Québec **37** J9 48 17N 77 20W
Lac Tudor *l.* Québec **32** C4 55 58N 65 30W
Lac Wakuach *l.* Québec **32** C4 55 35N 67 40W
Lac Waswanipi *l.* Québec **33** A2 49 35N 76 36W
Lac Wayagamac *l.* Québec **37** O8 47 23N 72 35W
Lac Whitegull *l.* Québec **32** D4 55 25N 65 05W
Lady Evelyn-Smoothwater *provincial park* Ontario **35** D2 47 20N 80 30W
Ladysmith British Columbia **42** H4 48 57N 123 50W
Laflèche Saskatchewan **40** B1 49 44N 106 32W
Lagoon City Ontario **38** C3 44 31N 79 11W
La Grande 2 *dam* Québec **32** A3 53 45N 77 38W
La Grande 3 *dam* Québec **32** A3 53 40N 76 09W
La Grande 4 *dam* Québec **32** B3 53 59N 72 50W
La Grande Rivière *r.* Québec **32** B3 53 34N 74 36W
La Guadeloupe Québec **37** Q6 45 58N 70 57W
Lake Cowichan *tn.* British Columbia **42** H4 48 50N 124 04W
Lakefield Ontario **36** H5 44 26N 78 16W
Lake Harbour *tn.* Northwest Territories **45** S3 62 50N 69 50W
Lakeland Provincial Park Alberta **41** C2 54 45N 112 25W
Lakeland Provincial Recreation Area Alberta **41** C2 54 45N 111 15W
Lake of Bays *tn.* Ontario **36** G6 45 00N 79 00W
Lake of the Rivers Saskatchewan **40** B1 49 50N 105 30W
Lakeside Nova Scotia **47** P6 44 38N 63 42W
Lakeview Newfoundland **31** D2 47 20N 54 10W
Lakeview Ontario **47** J2 45 20N 75 48W
La Loche Saskatchewan **40** B3 56 31N 109 27W
La Malbaie Québec **37** Q8 47 39N 70 11W
Lamaline Newfoundland **31** C2 46 52N 55 49W
Lambeth Ontario **38** A1 42 54N 81 20W
Lambton *admin.* Ontario **36** D3 42 45N 82 05W
Lambton, Cape Northwest Territories **44** G5 71 05N 123 09W
Lamèque New Brunswick **31** B2 47 45N 64 40W
Lampman Saskatchewan **40** C1 49 23N 102 48W
Lanark Ontario **37** K6 45 01N 74 30W
Lanark *admin.* Ontario **37** K6 45 05N 76 20W
Lancaster Ontario **37** M6 45 08N 74 30W
Lancaster Park Alberta **48** F5 53 41N 113 33W
Lancaster Sound Northwest Territories **45** O5 74 00N 87 30W
L'Ancienne Lorette Québec **37** P7 46 48N 71 20W
Land's End Northwest Territories **44** G6 76 22N 122 33W
Langenburg Saskatchewan **40** C2 50 50N 101 42W
Langham Saskatchewan **40** B2 52 22N 106 55W
Langley British Columbia **42** H4 49 06N 122 38W
Lanigan Saskatchewan **40** B2 51 50N 105 01W
L'Annonciation Québec **37** M7 46 24N 74 52W
Lansdowne House *tn.* Ontario **34** C3 52 05N 88 00W
L'Anse-au-Loup Newfoundland **30** C3 51 31N 56 45W
L'Anse aux Meadows Newfoundland **30** C3 51 36N 55 32W
L'Anse Pleureuse Québec **33** C2 49 15N 65 40W
Lantzville British Columbia **42** H4 49 15N 124 05W
La Pocatière Québec **37** Q8 47 22N 70 03W
La Poile Newfoundland **31** C2 47 41N 58 24W
La Prairie Québec **47** O4 45 25N 73 29W
Larder Lake Ontario **35** E2 48 05N 79 38W
L'Ardoise Nova Scotia **31** F7 45 37N 60 46W
Lark Harbour *tn.* Newfoundland **31** C2 49 06N 58 23W
La Ronge Saskatchewan **40** B3 55 07N 105 18W
Larrys River *tn.* Nova Scotia **31** F7 45 15N 61 25W
La Salle Manitoba **48** C1 49 41N 97 04W
La Salle Québec **47** N4 45 26N 73 40W
La Salle River Manitoba **48** C1 49 42N 97 16W
La Sarre Québec **33** A2 48 50N 79 20W
La Scie Newfoundland **31** C2 49 57N 55 36W
Lashburn Saskatchewan **40** B2 53 08N 109 36W
Lasqueti Island British Columbia **42** H4 49 28N 124 20W
Last Mountain Lake Saskatchewan **40** B2 51 40N 106 55W
La Tabatière Québec **32** E3 50 50N 58 57W
Latchford Ontario **35** E2 47 20N 79 49W
La Tuque Québec **37** O8 47 26N 72 47W
Laurie River Manitoba **39** A3 56 30N 101 30W
Laurier-Station Québec **27** 46 33N 71 37W
Lauzon Québec **37** P7 46 49N 71 10W
Laval, (Ville de) Québec **37** N6 45 38N 73 45W
Laval-des-Rapides Québec **47** N5 45 33N 73 42W
Lawn Newfoundland **31** C2 46 57N 55 32W
Lawrencetown Nova Scotia **31** E6 44 54N 65 10W
Leader Saskatchewan **40** B2 50 55N 109 31W
Leading Tickles Newfoundland **31** C2 49 30N 55 28W
Leaf Rapids *tn.* Manitoba **39** A3 56 30N 100 00W
Leamington Ontario **36** D3 42 03N 82 36W
Leaside Ontario **46** C1 43 44N 79 15W
Lebel-sur-Quévillon Québec **33** A2 49 05N 77 08W
Leduc Alberta **41** C2 53 17N 113 30W
Leduc County Alberta **48** F4 53 19N 113 32W
Leeds and Grenville *admin.* Ontario **37** L6 44 35N 76 00W
Le Havre River Nova Scotia **31** F6 44 30N 64 30W
Leitrim Ontario **47** K2 45 20N 75 35W
Lemieux Islands Northwest Territories **45** T3 63 40N 64 20W
Lennox and Addington *admin.* Ontario **37** J5 44 30N 77 00W
Lenore Lake Saskatchewan **40** C2 52 30N 105 00W
Leoville Saskatchewan **40** B2 53 39N 107 33W
Leslie Street Spit Ontario **46** C1 43 38N 79 19W
Lesser Slave Lake Alberta **41** B3 55 25N 115 25W
Lethbridge Alberta **41** C1 49 43N 112 48W
Level Mountain British Columbia **42** B3 58 33N 131 25W
Lévis Québec **37** P7 46 47N 71 12W
Lewis Hill *mt.* Newfoundland **31** C2 49 48N 58 30W
Lewisporte Newfoundland **31** C2 49 15N 55 03W
Llard River Northwest Territories **44** G3 60 00N 120 00W
Liard River *tn.* British Columbia **43** C3 59 28N 126 18W
Liddon Gulf Northwest Territories **44** J6 75 03N 113 00W
L'Île Dorval *i.* Québec **47** N4 45 26N 73 44W
L'Île-Perrot *i.* Québec **47** M4 45 24N 73 55W
Lillooet British Columbia **43** D2 50 41N 121 59W
Lillooet Lake British Columbia **42** H5 50 15N 122 38W
Lillooet River British Columbia **42** H4 49 59N 122 25W
Limbour Québec **47** K2 45 29N 75 44W
Lindsay Ontario **38** D3 44 21N 78 44W
Linzee, Cape Nova Scotia **31** F7 46 00N 61 30W
Lions Bay *tn.* British Columbia **42** H4 49 28N 123 13W
Lion's Head *tn.* Ontario **38** A3 44 59N 81 16W
Lipton Saskatchewan **40** C2 50 55N 103 49W
L'Islet *admin.* Québec **37** Q8 47 00N 70 20W
L'Isle-Verte Québec **37** R9 48 00N 69 21W
Lismore Nova Scotia **31** F7 45 42N 62 16W
Listowel Ontario **38** B2 43 44N 80 57W
Little Bow River Alberta **41** C2 50 20N 113 40W
Little Buffalo River Alberta **41** C3 59 45 113 30W
Little Churchill River Manitoba **39** B3 56 40N 96 10W
Little Current *tn.* Ontario **36** E6 45 58N 81 56W
Little Dover Nova Scotia **31** F7 45 20N 61 05W
Little Grand Rapids *tn.* Manitoba **39** B2 52 10N 95 30W
Little Maitland River Ontario **38** A2 43 48N 81 10W
Little Mecatina River *(Rivière du Petit Mécatina)* Newfoundland **30** B3 52 40N 61 50W
Little Narrows *tn.* Nova Scotia **31** F7 45 59N 61 00W
Little River Ontario **52** F2 42 19N 82 55W
Little Rouge Creek Ontario **46** C2 43 54N 79 15W
Little Sachigo Lake Ontario **34** B3 54 09N 92 11W
Little Smoky River Alberta **41** B2 54 05N 117 45W
Little White River Ontario **36** C7 46 23N 83 20W
Liverpool Nova Scotia **31** F6 44 03N 64 43W
Liverpool Bay Northwest Territories **44** E4 69 45N 130 00W
Livingstone Cove *tn.* Nova Scotia **31** F7 45 52N 61 58W
Lloyd George, Mount British Columbia **43** D3 57 50N 124 58W
Lloyd Lake Alberta **48** A1 50 52N 114 10W
Lloyd Lake Saskatchewan **40** B3 57 20N 108 40W
Lloydminster Alberta/Saskatchewan **40** B2 53 18N 110 00W
Lobstick Lake Newfoundland **30** A3 54 00N 65 00W
Lockport Nova Scotia **31** E6 43 40N 65 10W
Lodge Creek Canada/U.S.A. **41** C1/D1 49 15N 110 05W
Logan Lake Ontario **38** D3 44 57N 78 59W
Logan Lake *tn.* British Columbia **43** D2 50 28N 120 50W
Logan, Mount Yukon Territory **44** D3 60 34N 140 25W
Logan Mountains Yukon Territory **44** F3 60 30N 128 30W
London Ontario **38** A1 42 58N 81 15W
Long Beach *tn.* Ontario **38** C1 42 51N 79 23W
Long Cove *tn.* Newfoundland **31** D2 47 34N 53 40W
Long Creek Saskatchewan **40** C1 49 20N 103 55W
Long Harbour *tn.* Newfoundland **31** D2 47 26N 53 48W
Long Island Northwest Territories **45** G1 54 00N 79 00W
Long Island Nova Scotia **31** E6 44 20N 66 15W
Longlac Ontario **34** C2 49 47N 86 34W
Long Lake New Brunswick **31** A2 47 00N 66 50W
Long Lake Nova Scotia **47** P6 44 37N 63 37W
Long Lake Ontario **34** C2 49 00N 87 00W
Long Lake *I.R.* Ontario **34** C2 49 45N 86 32W
Long Point Manitoba **39** B2 52 50N 98 20W
Long Point Ontario **38** B1 42 33N 80 04W
Long Point *tn.* Ontario **38** B1 42 34N 80 15W
Long Point Bay Ontario **38** B1 42 40N 80 14W
Long Point Provincial Park Ontario **38** B1 42 40N 80 15W
Long Pond Newfoundland **31** C2 48 00N 55 52W
Long Range Mountains Newfoundland **31** C2 50 00N 57 00W
Long Sault Ontario **37** M6 45 02N 74 53W
Longueuil Québec **37** N6 45 32N 73 31W
Looking Back Lake Alberta **48** H4 53 18N 113 10W
Lookout, Cape Ontario **34** D4 55 18N 83 56W
Looma Alberta **48** G4 53 20N 113 15W
Loon Lake Nova Scotia **47** P6 44 42N 63 30W
Loon Lake *tn.* Saskatchewan **40** B2 54 00N 109 10W
Loon River Alberta **41** B3 56 40N 115 20W
L'Original Ontario **37** M6 45 37N 74 42W
Loring Ontario **36** F6 45 56N 80 00W
Lorne Park *tn.* Ontario **38** C2 43 31N 79 36W
Lorraine Québec **47** M5 45 38N 73 47W
Lotbinière *admin.* Québec **37** P7 46 20N 71 65W
Loughborough Inlet British Columbia **42** G5 50 35N 125 32W
Lougheed Island Northwest Territories **45** K6 77 26N 105 06W
Louisbourg Nova Scotia **31** G7 45 56N 59 58W
Louise Island British Columbia **42** B2 52 59N 131 50W
Louise, Lake Alberta **41** B2 51 25N 116 14W
Louiseville Québec **37** O7 46 16N 72 56W
Lourdes Newfoundland **31** C2 48 39N 59 00W
Low, Cape Northwest Territories **45** O3 63 07N 85 18W
Lower Arrow Lake British Columbia **43** E1 49 40N 118 09W
Lower Foster Lake Saskatchewan **40** B3 56 30N 105 10W
Lower Manitou Lake Ontario **34** B2 49 15N 93 00W
Lower Post British Columbia **43** C3 59 56N 128 09W
Lower Sackville Nova Scotia **31** F6 44 45N 63 40W
Lubicon Lake Alberta **41** B3 56 23N 115 56W
Lucan Ontario **38** A2 43 11N 81 24W
Lucknow Ontario **38** A2 43 58N 81 31W
Lucky Lake *tn.* Saskatchewan **40** B2 50 59N 107 10W
Lulu Island British Columbia **46** F3 49 09N 123 09W
Lumby British Columbia **43** E2 50 15N 118 58W
Lumsden Saskatchewan **40** C2 50 39N 104 52W
Lund British Columbia **42** H4 49 59N 124 46W
Lundar Manitoba **39** B2 50 41N 98 01W
Lunenburg Nova Scotia **31** F6 44 23N 64 21W
Lunenburg *admin.* Nova Scotia **31** F6 44 35N 64 30W
Luseland Saskatchewan **40** B2 52 06N 109 24W
Luther Lake Ontario **38** B2 43 52N 80 26W
Lyall, Mount Alberta/British Columbia **41** C2 50 05N 114 42W
Lyell Islands British Columbia **42** B2 52 00N 131 00W
Lyndonville Ontario **38** D2 43 30N 78 45W
Lynn Lake *tn.* Manitoba **39** A3 56 51N 101 01W
Lynx Lake Northwest Territories **44** L3 62 25N 106 15W
Lytton British Columbia **43** D2 50 12N 121 34W

M

Maaset British Columbia **42** B2 54 00N 132 01W
Mabel Lake British Columbia **43** E2 50 35N 118 40W
Mabou Nova Scotia **31** F7 46 04N 61 22W
McAdam New Brunswick **31** A2 45 34N 67 20W
MacAlpine Lake Northwest Territories **45** L4 66 45N 130 00W
McArthur Game Sanctuary Yukon Territory **44** D3 62 25N 135 50W
McBride British Columbia **43** D2 53 21N 120 19W
McBrien Yukon Territory **44** F3 60 00N 130 00W
McCabe Lake Nova Scotia **47** P7 44 47N 63 43W
Maccan Nova Scotia **31** F7 45 43N 64 16W
McClintock Manitoba **39** C3 57 50N 94 10W
M'Clintock Channel Northwest Territories **45** L5 73 00N 104 00W
M'Clure, Cape Northwest Territories **44** G5 74 32N 121 19W
M'Clure Strait Northwest Territories **44** F5 74 59N 120 10W
McConnell River Bird Sanctuary Northwest Territories **45** N3 60 30N 94 00W
McCreary Manitoba **39** B2 50 45N 99 30W
Macdonald *admin.* Manitoba **48** C2 49 48N 97 18W
MacDowell Ontario **34** B3 52 10N 92 40W
MacDowell Lake Ontario **34** B3 52 15N 92 42W
McFarlane River Saskatchewan **40** B3 57 50N 107 55W
McGivney New Brunswick **31** A2 46 22N 66 34W
MacGregor Manitoba **39** B1 49 57N 98 48W
McGregor Lake Alberta **41** C2 50 25N 112 52W
McGregor River British Columbia **43** D2 54 10N 121 20W
McKay Lake Newfoundland **30** A3 53 44N 65 37W
Mackay Lake Northwest Territories **44** J3 63 55N 110 25W
McKeller Ontario **36** G6 45 30N 79 00W
Mackenzie British Columbia **43** D3 55 18N 123 10W
Mackenzie Bay Yukon Territory **44** D4 69 00N 137 30W
Mackenzie Bison Sanctuary Northwest Territories **44** H3 61 30N 116 30W
McKenzie Creek Ontario **38** B2 43 02N 80 17W
Mackenzie Highway Alberta **41** B3 57 55N 117 40W
Mackenzie King Island Northwest Territories **44** J6 77 45N 111 00W
Mackenzie Mountains Yukon Territory/Northwest Territories **44** F3 66 00N 132 00W
Mackenzie River Northwest Territories **44** F4 66 20N 125 55W
Mackey Ontario **36** J7 46 10N 77 49W
Macklin Saskatchewan **40** B2 52 20N 109 58W
Maclean Strait Northwest Territories **45** L6 77 30N 102 30W
McLennan Alberta **41** B3 55 42N 116 54W
McLeod Lake *tn.* British Columbia **43** D2 55 00N 123 00W
McLeod River Alberta **41** B2 53 40N 116 20W
Macmillan Pass Yukon Territory **44** E3 63 25N 130 00W
Macmillan River Yukon Territory **44** E3 63 00N 134 00W
McNabs Island Nova Scotia **47** P6 44 37N 63 31W
McNutt Island Nova Scotia **31** E6 43 40N 65 20W
Macoun Lake Saskatchewan **40** C3 56 30N 103 40W
Macrae Point Provincial Park Ontario **38** C3 44 30N 79 10W
McTavish Arm *b.* Northwest Territories **44** H4 66 06N 118 04W
MacTier Ontario **36** G6 45 08N 79 47W
McVicar Arm *b.* Northwest Territories **44** G3 65 20N 120 10W
Madawaska Ontario **36** J6 45 30N 77 59W
Madawaska *admin.* New Brunswick **31** A2 47 30N 68 00W
Madawaska River Ontario **35** E2 45 10N 77 30W
Madoc Ontario **37** J5 44 30N 77 29W
Mad River Ontario **38** B3 44 18N 80 02W
Madsen Ontario **34** B3 50 58N 93 55W
Maelpaeg Reservoir Newfoundland **31** C2 48 20N 56 40W
Magnetawan Ontario **36** G6 45 40N 79 39W
Magnetawan River Ontario **36** F6 45 46N 80 37W
Magog Québec **37** O6 45 16N 72 09W
Magpie River Ontario **35** D2 48 00N 84 50W
Magrath Alberta **41** C1 49 27N 112 52W
Maguse Lake Northwest Territories **45** N3 61 40N 95 10W
Mahone Bay Nova Scotia **31** F6 44 25N 64 15W
Mahone Bay *tn.* Nova Scotia **31** F6 44 27N 64 24W
Mahood Creek British Columbia **46** G3 49 09N 122 50W
Maidstone Ontario **52** F1 42 12N 82 56W
Maidstone Saskatchewan **40** B2 53 06N 109 18W
Main Brook *tn.* Newfoundland **31** C3 51 11N 56 01W
Main Channel Ontario **36** E6 45 00N 82 00W
Maitland River Ontario **38** A2 43 50N 81 28W
Major, Lake Nova Scotia **47** Q6 44 45N 63 30W
Makkovik Newfoundland **30** C4 55 05N 59 11W
Makkovik, Cape Newfoundland **30** C4 55 14N 59 09W
Makoop Lake Ontario **34** B3 53 24N 90 50W
Malartic Québec **33** A2 48 09N 78 09W
Malaspina Strait British Columbia **42** H4 49 47N 124 30W
Mallet River Ontario **38** B2 43 51N 80 42W
Malpeque Bay Prince Edward Island **31** F7 46 35N 63 50W
Malton Ontario **38** C2 43 42N 79 38W
Manigotagan Manitoba **39** B2 51 06N 96 18W
Manigotagan River Manitoba **39** B2 51 00N 96 10W
Manitoba *province* **39**
Manitoba, Lake Manitoba **39** B2 50 30N 98 15W
Manito Lake Saskatchewan **40** B2 52 40N 109 20W
Manitou Manitoba **39** B1 49 15N 98 32W
Manitou Lake Ontario **36** E6 45 48N 82 00W
Manitoulin *admin.* Ontario **36** C6 45 45N 82 30W
Manitoulin Island Ontario **36** D6 45 50N 82 20W
Manitouwadge Ontario **35** C2 49 10N 85 55W
Maniwaki Québec **37** K7 46 22N 75 58W
Manning Alberta **41** B3 56 55N 117 37W
Manning Provincial Park British Columbia **42** H4 49 09N 120 50W
Manotick Ontario **47** K1 45 14N 75 43W
Mansel Island Northwest Territories **45** Q3 62 00N 80 00W
Manson Creek *tn.* British Columbia **43** D3 55 40N 124 32W
Manyberries Alberta **41** C1 49 24N 110 42W
Maple Ontario **46** B1 43 50N 79 30W
Maple Creek *tn.* Saskatchewan **40** B1 49 55N 109 28W
Maple Grove Park Manitoba **48** D2 49 47N 97 06W
Maple Ridge British Columbia **42** H4 49 13N 122 36W
Mara Provincial Park Ontario **38** C3 44 30N 79 15W
Marathon Ontario **35** C2 48 44N 86 23W
Margaree Forks Nova Scotia **31** F7 46 20N 61 10W
Margaret Lake Alberta **41** B3 58 56N 115 25W
Margaretville Nova Scotia **31** E7 45 05N 65 05W
Marieville Québec **37** N6 45 27N 73 08W
Markdale Ontario **38** B3 44 19N 80 39W
Markham Ontario **46** C2 43 54N 79 16W
Markham Bay Northwest Territories **45** R3 63 02N 72 00W
Marmora Ontario **36** J5 44 29N 77 41W
Marten Falls *I.R.* Ontario **34** C3 51 40N 85 55W
Martensville Saskatchewan **40** B2 52 10N 106 30W
Maryfield Saskatchewan **40** C1 49 50N 101 30W
Mary's Harbour *tn.* Newfoundland **30** D3 52 19N 55 50W
Marystown Newfoundland **31** C2 47 10N 55 09W
Marysville New Brunswick **31** A2 45 58N 66 35W
Mascouche Québec **37** N6 45 47N 73 49W
Maskinongé Québec **27** 46 14N 73 01W
Maskinongé *admin.* Québec **37** M8 47 40N 74 50W
Masset British Columbia **42** B2 54 00N 132 09W
Massey Ontario **36** C7 46 12N 82 05W
Massey Sound Northwest Territories **45** N6 74 00N 94 59W
Masson Québec **47** L3 45 33N 75 24W
Matachewan Ontario **35** D2 47 56N 80 39W
Matagami Québec **33** A2 49 40N 77 40W
Matane Québec **33** C2 48 50N 67 31W
Matheson Ontario **35** D2 48 32N 80 28W
Matsqui British Columbia **42** H4 49 05N 122 22W
Mattagami Québec **33** A2 49 42N 77 35W
Mattagami Lake Ontario **35** D2 47 54N 81 35W
Mattagami River Ontario **35** D2 49 50N 81 50W
Mattawa Ontario **35** E2 46 19N 78 42W
Mattice Ontario **35** D2 49 36N 83 16W
Maurelle Island British Columbia **42** G5 50 16N 125 11W
Maxwell Ontario **38** B3 44 18N 80 23W
Mayerthorpe Alberta **41** B2 53 57N 115 08W
Mayne Island British Columbia **42** H4 48 50N 123 18W
Maynooth Ontario **36** H6 45 14N 77 57W
Mayo Yukon Territory **44** D3 63 34N 135 52W
Mayo Lake Yukon Territory **44** D3 135 00N 63 50W
Mayson Lake Saskatchewan **40** B3 57 50N 107 30W
Meadow Lake *tn.* Saskatchewan **40** B2 54 09N 108 26W
Meadow Lake Provincial Park Saskatchewan **40** B2 54 30N 108 00W
Meadowvale West Ontario **38** C2 43 35N 79 45W
Meaford Ontario **38** B3 44 36N 80 35W
Meaghers Grant Nova Scotia **31** F6 44 57N 63 15W
Mealy Mountains Newfoundland **30** C3 53 10N 60 00W
Meander River *tn.* Alberta **41** B3 59 02N 117 42W
Meath Park *tn.* Saskatchewan **40** B2 53 27N 105 22W
Medicine Hat Alberta **41** C2 50 03N 110 41W
Medley Alberta **41** C2 54 25N 110 16W
Meductic New Brunswick **31** A2 45 55N 67 30W
Medway Creek Ontario **38** A2 43 07N 81 18W
Medway River Nova Scotia **31** F6 44 15N 64 50W
Mégantic *admin.* Québec **37** P7 46 10N 71 40W
Meighen Island Northwest Territories **45** M7 80 00N 99 30W
Melbourne Island Northwest Territories **44** K4 68 30N 104 45W
Meldrum Bay *tn.* Ontario **36** C6 45 56N 83 06W
Melfort Saskatchewan **40** C2 52 52N 104 38W
Melita Manitoba **39** A1 49 16N 101 00W
Melville Saskatchewan **40** C2 50 57N 102 49W
Melville Hills Northwest Territories **44** G4 69 00N 121 00W
Melville Island Northwest Territories **44** J6 75 30N 112 00W
Melville, Lake Newfoundland **30** C3 53 45N 59 00W
Melville Peninsula Northwest Territories **45** P4 68 00N 84 00W
Melville Sound Northwest Territories **44** K4 68 05N 107 30W
Melville Sound Ontario **38** A3 43 00N 81 04W
Menihek Newfoundland **30** A3 54 28N 66 36W
Menihek Lakes Newfoundland **30** A3 53 50N 66 50W
Mer Bleue *m.* Ontario **47** K2 45 24N 75 31W
Mercy Bay Northwest Territories **44** H5 74 05N 119 00W
Merigomish Nova Scotia **31** F7 45 37N 62 25W
Merivale Ontario **47** K2 45 19N 75 44W
Merrickville Ontario **37** L5 44 55N 75 50W
Merritt British Columbia **43** D1 50 09N 120 49W
Mersey River Nova Scotia **31** E6 44 10N 65 00W
Metabetchouane Québec **37** P9 48 26N 71 52W
Meta Incognita Peninsula Northwest Territories **45** S3 63 30N 70 00W
Metcalfe Ontario **47** K1 45 14N 75 29W
Metchosin British Columbia **42** H4 48 22N 123 32W
Meteghan Nova Scotia **31** E6 44 12N 66 10W
Metropolitan Toronto *admin.* Ontario **46** C2 43 44N 79 16W
Mica Creek *tn.* British Columbia **43** E2 52 00N 118 28W
Mica Dam British Columbia **43** E2 52 04N 118 28W
Michaud Point Nova Scotia **31** F7 45 35N 60 40W
Michel Peak British Columbia **43** C2 53 30N 126 25W
Michikamats Lake Newfoundland **30** B3 54 38N 64 19W
Michikamau Lake Newfoundland **30** B3 54 15N 64 00W
Michipicoten Island Ontario **35** C2 47 45N 85 45W
Micmac, Lake Nova Scotia **47** P6 44 41N 63 32W
Midale Saskatchewan **40** C1 49 23N 103 21W
Middle Arm *tn.* Newfoundland **31** C2 49 42N 56 06W
Middle Maitland River Ontario **38** A2 43 43N 81 11W
Middle Ridge Newfoundland **31** C2 48 20N 55 15W
Middle Sackville Nova Scotia **47** P7 44 47N 63 41W
Middlesex *admin.* Ontario **38** A1 42 46N 81 46W
Middleton Nova Scotia **31** E6 44 56N 65 04W
Midhurst Ontario **38** C3 44 26N 79 45W
Midland Ontario **38** C3 44 45N 79 53W
Midnapore Alberta **48** A1 50 55N 114 05W
Midway British Columbia **43** E1 49 02N 118 45W
Midway Mountains British Columbia **43** E1 49 25N 118 45W
Mikkwa River Alberta **41** C3 57 40N 114 08W
Mildmay Ontario **38** A3 44 03N 81 08W
Milestone Saskatchewan **40** C1 49 59N 104 31W
Milk River Alberta **41** C1 49 10N 110 05W
Milk River *tn.* Alberta **41** C1 49 09N 112 05W
Millbrook Ontario **38** D3 44 09N 78 29W
Mill Creek Alberta **48** G4 53 27N 113 23W
Miller Lake Nova Scotia **47** P7 44 49N 63 35W

Millet Alberta 41 C2 53 06N 113 28W
Mill Island Northwest Territories 45 Q3 64 00N 78 00W
Milltown Newfoundland 31 C2 47 54N 55 46W
Mill Village Nova Scotia 31 F6 44 10N 64 40W
Millville New Brunswick 31 A2 46 08N 67 12W
Milo Alberta 41 C2 50 34N 112 53W
Milton Nova Scotia 31 F6 44 04N 64 44W
Milton Ontario 38 C2 43 31N 79 53W
Milton Prince Edward Island 31 F7 46 20N 63 10W
Milverton Ontario 38 B2 43 34N 80 55W
Minaki Ontario 34 B2 50 00N 94 40W
Minas Basin Nova Scotia 31 F7 45 15N 64 15W
Minas Channel Nova Scotia 31 F7 45 10N 64 50W
Minden Ontario 36 H5 44 56N 78 44W
Minipi Lake Newfoundland 30 B3 52 25N 60 45W
Miniss Lake Ontario 34 B3 50 48N 90 50W
Minitonas Manitoba 39 A2 52 04N 101 02W
Minnedosa Manitoba 39 B1 50 14N 99 50W
Minnitaki Lake Ontario 34 B3 49 58N 92 00W
Minonipi Lake Newfoundland 30 B3 52 50N 60 50W
Minto New Brunswick 31 A2 46 05N 66 05W
Minto Yukon Territory 44 D3 62 34N 136 50W
Minto Inlet Northwest Territories 44 H5 71 20N 117 00W
Mira Bay Nova Scotia 31 G7 46 05N 59 50W
Mirabel Québec 37 M6 45 41N 74 20W
Miramichi Bay New Brunswick 31 A2 47 05N 65 00W
Mira River Nova Scotia 31 F7 46 00N 60 10W
Miscouche Prince Edward Island 31 F7 46 26N 63 52W
Miscou Island New Brunswick 31 B2 47 50N 64 30W
Misery Point Newfoundland 30 C3 52 01N 55 18W
Missanabie Ontario 35 D2 48 19N 84 05W
Missinaibi Lake Ontario 35 D2 48 23N 83 40W
Missinaibi River Ontario 35 D2 49 30N 83 20W
Mission British Columbia 42 H4 49 08N 122 20W
Missisa Lake Ontario 34 D3 52 18N 85 12W
Mississagi River Ontario 36 C7 46 10N 83 01W
Mississauga Ontario 46 B1 43 38N 79 36W
Mississauga Lake Ontario 38 D3 44 43N 78 17W
Missouri Coteau *hills* Saskatchewan 40 B2 50 40N 106 30W
Mistassini Québec 33 B2 48 54N 72 13W
Mistastin Lake Newfoundland 30 B4 55 50N 63 00W
Mitchell Ontario 38 A2 43 27N 81 13W
Mitchells Brook *tn.* Newfoundland 31 D2 47 08N 53 31W
Mobert *I.R.* Ontario 35 C2 48 40N 85 40W
Moisie Québec 33 C3 50 12N 66 06W
Molson Manitoba 39 B2 50 02N 96 19W
Molson Lake Manitoba 39 B2 54 20N 96 50W
Monarch Mountain British Columbia 43 C2 51 55N 125 57W
Monashee Mountains British Columbia 43 E2 51 30N 118 50W
Moncton New Brunswick 31 F7 46 04N 64 50W
Monkman Pass British Columbia 43 D2 54 30N 121 10W
Monkman Provincial Park British Columbia 43 D2 54 00N 121 10W
Mono Mills Ontario 38 C2 43 55N 79 57W
Montague Prince Edward Island 31 F7 46 10N 62 39W
Montcalm admin. Québec 37 L8 47 40N 76 15W
Mont D'Iberville *(Mount Caubvick)* Québec/Newfoundland 30 B4 58 50N 64 40W
Montgomery Québec 37 Q7 46 58N 70 34W
Mont Jacques-Cartier *mt.* Québec 33 C2 49 00N 66 00W
Mont-Joli *tn.* Québec 33 C2 48 36N 68 14W
Mont-Laurier *tn.* Québec 36 L7 46 33N 75 31W
Montmagny Québec 33 B2 46 50N 70 33W
Montmagny *admin.* Québec 37 Q7 46 50N 70 20W
Montmartre Saskatchewan 40 C2 50 14N 103 24W
Montmorency *admin.* Québec 37 P8 47 34N 71 20W
Montréal Québec 37 N6 45 32N 73 36W
Montréal Est Québec 47 N5 45 37N 73 32W
Montreal Lake Saskatchewan 40 B2 54 15N 105 30W
Montreal Lake *tn.* Saskatchewan 40 B2 54 03N 105 49W
Montréal Nord Québec 47 N5 45 35N 73 36W
Montreal River Ontario 35 D2 47 20N 84 20W
Montreal River Saskatchewan 40 B2 54 50N 105 30W
Montreal River *tn.* Ontario 35 D2 47 14N 84 39W
Montrose British Columbia 43 E1 49 06N 117 30W
Mont Royal *mt.* Québec 47 N5 45 31N 73 40W
Monts Chic-Chocs *mts.* Québec 33 C2 49 00N 66 40W
Monts Notre Dame *mts.* Québec 33 C2 47 59N 69 00W
Monts Otish *mts.* Québec 33 B3 52 30N 70 20W
Monts Povungnituk *mts.* Québec 32 A5 61 30N 75 59W
Monts Torngat *(Torngat Mountains)* Québec/Newfoundland 32 D5 59 00N 64 15W
Moon River Ontario 38 C4 45 05N 79 51W
Moose Factory Ontario 34 D3 51 16N 80 37W
Moose Jaw Saskatchewan 40 B2 50 23N 105 35W
Moosejaw River Saskatchewan 40 B2 50 15N 105 10W
Moose Lake *tn.* Manitoba 39 A2 53 43N 100 20W
Moose Mountain Creek Saskatchewan 40 C2 50 15N 103 25W
Moose Mountain Provincial Park Saskatchewan 40 C1 49 50N 102 20W
Moose River Ontario 34 D3 50 00N 82 00W
Moose River *tn.* Ontario 34 D3 50 48N 81 18W
Moosomin Saskatchewan 40 C2 50 09N 101 41W
Moosonee Ontario 34 D3 51 18N 80 39W
Morden Manitoba 39 B1 49 12N 98 05W
Morell Prince Edward Island 31 F7 46 25N 62 42W
Moresby Island British Columbia 42 B2 53 00N 132 00W
Morice Lake British Columbia 43 C2 53 55N 127 30W
Moricetown British Columbia 43 C3 55 02N 127 20W
Morinville Alberta 41 C2 53 48N 113 39W
Morris Manitoba 39 B1 49 22N 97 21W
Morrisburg Ontario 37 L5 44 54N 75 11W
Morse Saskatchewan 40 B2 50 24N 107 00W
Morson Ontario 34 B2 49 03N 94 19W
Moser River *tn.* Nova Scotia 31 F6 44 58N 62 18W
Mostoos Hills Saskatchewan 40 B3 55 20N 109 30W
Mould Bay *m.s.* Northwest Territories 44 H6 76 14N 119 20W
Mountain Lake Ontario 38 A3 44 42N 81 02W
Mount Albert *tn.* Ontario 38 C3 44 07N 79 18W
Mount Brydges *tn.* Ontario 38 A1 42 54N 81 30W
Mount Burke British Columbia 46 H4 49 18N 122 42W
Mount Carleton Provincial Park New Brunswick 31 A2 47 20N 66 30W
Mount Edziza Provincial Park British Columbia 42 B3 57 40N 131 40W
Mount Forest *tn.* Ontario 38 B2 43 58N 80 44W
Mount Hope *tn.* Ontario 38 C2 43 09N 79 54W
Mount Revelstoke National Park British Columbia 43 E2 50 40N 118 00W
Mount Robson Provincial Park British Columbia 43 E2 52 50N 118 40W
Mount Seymour Provincial Park British Columbia 46 G4 49 22N 122 56W
Mount Stewart *tn.* Prince Edward Island 31 F7 46 22N 62 52W
Mount Uniacke *tn.* Nova Scotia 31 F6 44 54N 63 50W
Mud Bay British Columbia 46 G3 49 04N 122 53W
Mudjatik River Saskatchewan 40 B3 56 40N 107 10W
Mud Lake *tn.* Newfoundland 30 B3 53 19N 60 10W
Mukutawa River Manitoba 39 B2 53 10N 97 10W
Mulgrave Nova Scotia 31 F7 45 36N 61 25W
Muncho Lake British Columbia 43 C3 59 05N 125 47W
Muncho Lake *tn.* British Columbia 43 C3 59 00N 125 46W
Muncho Lake Provincial Park British Columbia 43 C3 58 50N 125 40W
Mundare Alberta 41 C2 53 36N 112 20W
Murdochville Québec 33 C2 48 57N 65 30W
Murray Harbour *tn.* Prince Edward Island 31 F7 46 00N 62 32W
Murray River *tn.* Prince Edward Island 31 F7 46 00N 62 38W
Murtle Lake British Columbia 43 E2 52 09N 119 40W
Musgrave Harbour *tn.* Newfoundland 31 D2 49 27N 53 58W
Musgravetown Newfoundland 31 D2 48 24N 53 53W
Muskawa River British Columbia 43 D3 58 30N 123 20W
Muskoka *admin.* Ontario 38 C3 44 57N 79 53W
Muskoka Falls *tn.* Ontario 36 G5 44 59N 79 16W
Muskrat Dam Lake Ontario 34 B3 53 25N 91 40W
Musquodoboit Harbour *tn.* Nova Scotia 31 F6 44 48N 63 10W
Muzon, Cape British Columbia 42 B2 54 41N 132 40W
Myles Bay Ontario 38 A3 44 56N 81 23W
Myrnam Alberta 41 C2 53 40N 111 14W

N

Nachvak Fiord *in.* Newfoundland 30 B4 59 03N 63 45W
Nackawic New Brunswick 31 A2 46 00N 67 15W
Nagagami Lake Ontario 35 C2 49 25N 85 01W
Nagagami River Ontario 35 D2 49 30N 84 50W
Nahanni Butte *tn.* Northwest Territories 44 G3 61 30N 123 20W
Nahanni National Park Reserve Northwest Territories 44 F3 61 30N 126 00W
Nahatlatch River British Columbia 42 H4 49 55N 121 59W
Nahlin River British Columbia 42 B3 58 58N 131 30W
Naicam Saskatchewan 40 C2 52 26N 104 31W
Naikoon Provincial Park British Columbia 42 B2 53 59N 131 35W
Nain Newfoundland 30 B4 56 32N 61 41W
Nakina Ontario 34 C3 50 11N 86 43W
Nakina River British Columbia 42 B3 59 07N 132 59W
Nakusp British Columbia 43 E2 50 15N 117 45W
Namao Alberta 48 G5 53 41N 113 28W
Nanaimo British Columbia 42 H4 49 08N 123 58W
Nanaimo River British Columbia 42 H4 49 08N 123 54W
Nanisivik Northwest Territories 45 P5 73 00N 79 58W
Nansen Sound Northwest Territories 45 O7 81 00N 90 35W
Nanticoke Ontario 38 B1 42 48N 80 04W
Nanticoke Creek Ontario 38 B1 42 56N 80 16W
Nanton Alberta 41 C2 50 21N 113 46W
Napaktok (Black Duck) Bay Newfoundland 30 B4 58 01N 62 19W
Napaktulik Lake Northwest Territories 44 J4 66 30N 112 50W
Napanee Ontario 37 K5 44 15N 76 57W
Napishish Lake Newfoundland 30 B3 54 10N 60 30W
Nares Strait Canada/Greenland 11 U8 78 30N 72 30W
Narrows, The *sd.* Nova Scotia 47 P6 44 40N 63 35W
Naskaupi River Newfoundland 30 B3 54 20N 62 40W
Nass River British Columbia 42 C3 55 10N 129 20W
Natashquan Québec 33 D3 50 10N 61 50W
Natashquan River *(Rivière Natashquan)* Newfoundland 30 B3 52 30N 62 50W
Nation Lakes British Columbia 43 C3 55 08N 125 15W
Nation River British Columbia 43 D3 55 11N 124 25W
Nauwigewauk New Brunswick 31 E7 45 28N 65 53W
Nazko British Columbia 43 D2 53 00N 123 37W
Nechako Plateau British Columbia 43 D2 54 40N 124 40W
Nechako River British Columbia 43 D2 53 35N 124 50W
Neeb Saskatchewan 40 B2 54 00N 107 50W
Neepawa Manitoba 39 B2 50 14N 99 29W
Neguac New Brunswick 31 A2 47 14N 65 03W
Nejanilini Lake Manitoba 39 B3 59 50N 97 20W
Nelson British Columbia 43 E1 49 29N 117 17W
Nelson Forks British Columbia 43 D3 59 30N 124 00W
Nelson House *tn.* Manitoba 39 B3 55 49N 98 51W
Nelson Island British Columbia 42 H4 49 43N 124 03W
Nelson-Miramichi New Brunswick 31 A2 46 55N 65 35W
Nelson River Manitoba 39 C3 56 50N 93 40W
Némiscau Québec 33 A3 51 20N 77 01W
Nepean Ontario 37 L6 45 16N 75 48W
Nepewassi Lake Ontario 36 F7 46 22N 80 38W
Nepisiguit River New Brunswick 31 A2 47 20N 66 30W
Nesselrode, Mount British Columbia 42 B3 58 55N 134 20W
Nestor Falls *tn.* Ontario 34 B2 49 06N 93 55W
Nettilling Lake Northwest Territories 45 S4 66 30N 71 10W
Neudorf Saskatchewan 40 C2 50 43N 103 00W
Neustadt Ontario 38 A3 44 04N 81 00W
Newboro' Ontario 37 K5 44 39N 76 19W
New Brunswick *province* 31 A2
Newburgh Ontario 37 K5 44 19N 76 52W
New Carlisle Québec 33 C2 48 00N 65 22W
Newcastle New Brunswick 31 A2 47 01N 65 36W
Newcastle Ontario 38 D2 43 55N 78 35W
New Denver British Columbia 43 E1 49 59N 117 22W
Newell, Lake Alberta 41 C2 50 26N 111 55W
Newfoundland *i.* Newfoundland 31 C2 48 30N 57 56W
Newfoundland *province* 31
New Germany Nova Scotia 31 F6 44 34N 64 44W
New Glasgow Nova Scotia 31 F7 45 36N 62 38W
New Hazelton British Columbia 43 C3 55 15N 127 30W
New Liskeard Ontario 35 E2 47 31N 79 41W
Newmarket Ontario 38 C3 44 03N 79 27W
New Minas Nova Scotia 31 F7 45 00N 64 30W
New Richmond Québec 33 C2 48 12N 65 52W
New Ross Nova Scotia 31 F6 44 44N 64 27W
Newton British Columbia 46 G3 49 07N 122 50W
Newtown Newfoundland 31 D2 49 12N 53 31W
New Waterford Nova Scotia 31 F7 46 17N 60 05W
New Westminster British Columbia 42 H4 49 10N 122 58W
Niagara *admin.* Ontario 38 C2 43 02N 79 34W
Niagara Escarpment Ontario 38 C2 43 00N 79 00W
Niagara Falls *tn.* Ontario 38 C2 43 05N 79 06W
Niagara-on-the-Lake Ontario 38 C2 43 14N 79 16W
Nicolet Québec 37 O7 46 14N 72 36W
Nicolet *admin.* Québec 37 O7 46 00N 72 30W
Nicomekl River British Columbia 46 H3 49 05N 122 43W
Nictau New Brunswick 31 A2 47 16N 67 11W
Night Hawk Lake Ontario 35 D2 48 28N 80 58W
Nipawin Saskatchewan 40 C2 53 23N 104 01W
Nipawin Provincial Park Saskatchewan 40 C2 54 10N 103 30W
Nipigon Ontario 35 C2 49 02N 88 26W
Nipigon Bay Ontario 35 C2 48 50N 88 10W
Nipigon, Lake Ontario 34 C2 49 50N 88 30W
Nipissing Ontario 36 G7 46 05N 79 31W
Nipissing *admin.* Ontario 36 G7 46 00N 79 00W
Nipissing, Lake Ontario 36 F7 46 17N 80 00W
Nisku Alberta 48 F4 53 18N 113 32W
Nisling Range *mts.* Yukon Territory 44 D3 62 00N 138 40W
Nitchequon Québec 33 B3 53 10N 70 58W
Nith River Ontario 38 B2 43 12N 80 22W
Nitinat Lake British Columbia 42 H4 48 45N 124 42W
Nitinat River British Columbia 42 H4 49 06N 124 35W
Niverville Manitoba 39 B1 49 39N 97 03W
Nobleton Ontario 38 C2 43 53N 79 39W
Nogies Creek Ontario 38 D3 44 43N 78 31W
Nogies Creek *tn.* Ontario 38 D3 44 19N 78 30W
Nokomis Saskatchewan 40 B2 51 30N 105 00W
Nokomis Lake Saskatchewan 40 C3 56 55N 103 00W
Nootka Island British Columbia 43 C1 49 45N 126 50W
Nootka Sound British Columbia 43 C1 49 34N 126 39W
Nopiming Provincial Park Manitoba 39 B2 50 40N 95 10W
Noralee British Columbia 43 C2 53 59N 126 26W
Norman Bay *tn.* Newfoundland 30 C3 52 55N 56 10W
Norman, Cape Newfoundland 30 C3 51 38N 55 54W
Normandale Ontario 38 B1 42 41N 80 19W
Normansland Point Ontario 34 D3 52 00N 81 00W
Norman Wells *tn.* Northwest Territories 44 F4 65 19N 126 46W
Normétal Québec 33 A2 48 59N 79 53W
Norquay Saskatchewan 40 C2 51 52N 102 00W
Norris Arm *tn.* Newfoundland 31 C2 49 05N 55 15W
Norris Point *tn.* Newfoundland 31 C2 49 31N 57 53W
North Arm *b.* Northwest Territories 44 H3 62 05N 114 40W
North Arm *r.* British Columbia 46 F3 49 12N 123 05W
North Aulatsivik Island Newfoundland 30 B4 59 46N 64 05W
North Battleford Saskatchewan 40 B2 52 47N 108 19W
North Bay *tn.* Ontario 36 G7 46 20N 79 28W
North Cape Nova Scotia 31 F7 47 10N 60 00W
North, Cape Prince Edward Island 31 F7 47 10N 64 00W
North Caribou Lake Ontario 34 B3 52 50N 90 40W
North Castor River Ontario 47 K2 45 18N 75 31W
North Channel Ontario 36 C7 46 00N 83 00W
Northern Indian Lake Manitoba 39 B3 57 30N 97 30W
Northern Peninsula Newfoundland 31 C3 50 30N 57 00W
Northern Woods and Water Route Alberta/Manitoba/Saskatchewan 40 B2 54 10N 107 20W
North French River Ontario 35 D3 50 20N 81 00W
North Head *tn.* New Brunswick 31 E6 44 46N 66 45W
North Kent Island Northwest Territories 45 M6 76 40N 90 14W
North Knife Lake Manitoba 39 B3 58 10N 96 40W
North Knife River Manitoba 39 B3 58 40N 95 50W
North Magnetic Pole (1992) Northwest Territories 45 L6 78 02N 103 07W
North Moose Lake Manitoba 39 A2 54 00N 100 10W
North Pender Island British Columbia 42 H4 48 49N 123 17W
North River Newfoundland 30 B4 57 30N 63 20W
North River Ontario 38 C3 44 47N 79 35W
North River *tn.* Manitoba 39 C3 58 55N 94 30W
North River Bridge *tn.* Nova Scotia 31 F7 46 19N 60 40W
North Rustico Prince Edward Island 31 F7 46 26N 63 20W
North Saskatchewan River Alberta/Saskatchewan 40 B2 52 40N 106 40W
North Saugeen River Ontario 38 A3 44 18N 81 10W
North Seal River Manitoba 39 A3 59 00N 100 30W
North Spirit Lake Ontario 34 B3 52 31N 92 55W
North Spirit Lake *tn.* Ontario 34 B3 52 31N 93 01W
North Sydney Nova Scotia 31 F7 46 13N 60 15W
North Thames River Ontario 38 A2 43 02N 81 14W
North Thompson River British Columbia 43 E2 51 32N 120 00W
North Twin Islands Northwest Territories 34 E3 53 20N 80 00W
Northumberland *admin.* New Brunswick 31 A2 47 10N 66 30W
Northumberland Strait Atlantic Provinces 31 F7 46 30N 64 30W
North Vancouver British Columbia 42 H4 49 21N 123 05W
North Wabasca Lake Alberta 41 C3 56 10N 114 40W
Northwest Angle Provincial Forest Manitoba 39 B1 49 20N 95 30W
Northwest Bay *tn.* Ontario 34 B2 48 50N 93 38W
Northwest Gander River Newfoundland 31 C2 48 30N 55 40W
North West River *tn.* Newfoundland 30 A3 53 32N 60 08W
Northwest Territories *territory* 44/45
North York *bor.* Metropolitan Toronto Ontario 46 C2 43 44N 79 26W
North Yukon National Park Yukon Territory 44 D4 69 20N 139 30W
Norton New Brunswick 31 E7 45 38N 65 43W
Norway House *tn.* Manitoba 39 B2 53 59N 97 50W
Norwich Ontario 38 B1 42 59N 80 36W
Nose Creek Alberta 48 A2 51 08N 114 02W
Nose Hill Alberta 48 A2 51 06N 114 07W
Notekwin River Alberta 41 B3 56 55N 118 20W
Notre Dame Bay Newfoundland 31 C2 49 45N 55 00W
Notre-Dame-des-Champs Ontario 47 L2 45 25N 75 28W
Nottawasaga Bay Ontario 38 B3 44 40N 80 30W
Nottawasaga River Ontario 38 C3 44 27N 79 53W
Nottingham Island Northwest Territories 45 Q3 63 05N 78 00W
Nouveau-Comptoir *see* Wemindji
Nova Scotia *province* 31 F7 45 30N 63 00W
Nueltin Lake Manitoba/Northwest Territories 45 L3 60 30N 99 00W
Nunaksaluk Island Newfoundland 30 B4 55 49N 60 20W
Nutak Newfoundland 30 B4 57 28N 61 52W
Nut Mountain Saskatchewan 40 C2 52 20N 102 50W
Nut Mountain *tn.* Saskatchewan 40 C2 52 08N 103 21W

O

Oak Bay British Columbia 42 H4 48 27N 123 18W
Oak Bluff Manitoba 48 C2 49 46N 97 18W
Oak Lake *tn.* Manitoba 39 A1 49 40N 100 45W
Oakville Ontario 38 C2 43 27N 79 41W
Oakwood Ontario 38 D3 44 20N 78 52W
Oban Saskatchewan 40 B2 52 09N 108 09W
Obaska Québec 37 J9 48 12N 77 22W
Observatory Inlet British Columbia 42 C3 55 05N 129 59W
Ocean Falls *tn.* British Columbia 43 C2 52 24N 127 42W
Oder River Manitoba 39 B3 55 50N 98 00W
Ogden Alberta 48 A1 50 59N 114 00W
Ogidaki Mountain Ontario 35 D2 46 57N 83 59W
Ogilvie Mountains Yukon Territory 44 D4 65 05N 139 00W
Ogoki Ontario 34 C3 51 38N 85 57W
Ogoki Lake Ontario 34 C3 50 50N 87 10W
Ogoki Reservoir Ontario 34 C3 50 48N 88 18W
Ogoki River Ontario 34 C3 50 50N 86 50W
Oil Springs *tn.* Ontario 36 D3 42 47N 82 07W
Ojibway Prairie Provincial Park Ontario 52 E1 42 14N 83 03W
Okak Bay Newfoundland 30 B4 57 28N 62 20W
Okak Islands Newfoundland 30 B4 57 30N 61 50W
Okanagan Lake British Columbia 43 E1 49 45N 119 32W
Okotoks Alberta 41 C2 50 44N 113 59W
Olcott Ontario 38 D2 43 20N 78 40W
Old Crow Yukon Territory 44 D4 67 34N 139 43W
Old Crow River Yukon Territory 44 D4 68 00N 140 00W
Oldman River Alberta 41 C1 49 50N 112 05W
Old Perlican Newfoundland 31 D2 48 05N 53 01W
Olds Alberta 41 C2 51 50N 114 06W
Old Wives Lake Saskatchewan 40 B2 50 15N 106 40W
O'Leary Prince Edward Island 31 F7 46 43N 64 15W
Oliphant Ontario 38 A3 44 44N 81 16W
Oliver British Columbia 43 E1 49 10N 119 37W
Omemee Ontario 38 D3 44 19N 78 33W
Omineca Mountains British Columbia 43 C3 57 15N 127 50W
Omineca River British Columbia 43 C3 56 02N 126 00W
Onaman Lake Ontario 34 C3 50 00N 87 26W
Onaping Lake Ontario 35 D2 46 57N 81 30W
100 Mile House British Columbia 43 D2 51 36N 121 18W
Ontario *province* 34/35
Ontario, Lake Canada/U.S.A. 36 H4 43 45N 78 00W
Ontario, Lake *(Lac Deschênes)* Ontario/Québec 47 J2 45 22N 75 50W
Ootsa Lake British Columbia 43 C2 53 40N 126 30W
Ootsa Lake *tn.* British Columbia 43 C2 53 42N 125 56W
Opasatika Ontario 35 D2 49 32N 82 52W
Opasquia Provincial Park Ontario 34 B3 53 30N 93 10W
Opeongo Lake Ontario 35 E2 45 42N 78 23W
Opinnagau River Ontario 34 D3 53 30N 83 50W
Orangeville Ontario 38 B2 43 55N 80 06W
Orient Bay *tn.* Ontario 34 C2 49 23N 88 08W
Orillia Ontario 38 C3 44 36N 79 26W
Orleans Ontario 47 K2 45 28N 75 34W
Ormstown Québec 37 M6 45 08N 74 02W
Oromocto New Brunswick 31 A2 45 50N 66 28W
Orono Ontario 38 D2 43 59N 78 36W
Oshawa Ontario 38 D2 43 53N 78 51W
Oskélanéo Québec 37 L9 48 07N 75 14W
Osoyoos British Columbia 43 E1 49 00N 119 29W
Ospika River British Columbia 43 D3 56 55N 124 10W
Ossokmanuan Reservoir Newfoundland 30 A3 53 25N 65 00W
Otoskwin River Ontario 34 C3 51 50N 89 40W
Ottawa Ontario 47 K2 45 24N 75 38W
Ottawa-Carleton *admin.* Ontario 37 L6 45 31N 75 22W
Ottawa Islands Northwest Territories 45 P2 59 10N 80 25W
Ottawa River *(Rivière des Outaouais)* Ontario/Québec 37 K6 45 34N 76 30W
Otter Lake Saskatchewan 40 C3 55 35N 104 30W
Otter Rapids *tn.* Ontario 35 D3 50 12N 81 40W
Outlook Saskatchewan 40 B2 51 30N 107 03W
Outremont Québec 47 N5 45 31N 73 36W
Owen Sound Ontario 38 B3 44 34N 80 56W
Owen Sound *tn.* Ontario 38 B3 44 34N 80 56W
Owl River Manitoba 39 C3 57 50N 93 20W
Oxbow Saskatchewan 40 C1 49 16N 102 12W
Oxford Nova Scotia 31 F7 45 43N 63 52W
Oxford *admin.* Ontario 38 B2 43 06N 80 59W
Oxford House *tn.* Manitoba 39 B2 54 58N 95 17W
Oxford Lake Manitoba 39 B2 54 40N 95 50W
Oyen Alberta 41 C2 51 22N 110 28W
Oyster River British Columbia 42 G4 49 50N 125 24W
Ozhiski Lake Ontario 34 C3 52 01N 88 30W

P

Pacific Rim National Park British Columbia 42 G4 48 52N 125 35W
Packs Harbour *tn.* Newfoundland 30 C3 53 51N 56 59W
Pacquet Newfoundland 31 C2 49 59N 55 53W
Paddle Prairie *tn.* Alberta 41 B3 57 57N 117 29W
Paint Lake Provincial Recreation Park Manitoba 39 B3 55 30N 97 00W
Paisley Ontario 38 A3 44 17N 81 16W
Pakashkan Lake Ontario 34 B2 49 21N 90 15W
Pakowki Lake Alberta 41 C1 49 20N 111 55W
Pakwash Lake Ontario 34 B3 50 45N 93 30W
Palmerston Ontario 38 B2 43 50N 80 50W
Panache, Lake Ontario 36 E7 46 15N 81 20W
Pangnirtung Northwest Territories 45 S4 66 05N 65 45W
Panmure Island Prince Edward Island 31 F7 46 10N 62 30W
Papineau *admin.* Québec 37 L6 45 40N 75 30W
Paradise Hill *tn.* Saskatchewan 40 B2 53 32N 109 26W
Paradise River Newfoundland 30 C3 52 50N 57 50W
Paradise River *tn.* Newfoundland 30 C3 53 27N 57 17W
Parc de Conservation d'Aiguebelle Québec 33 A2 48 30N 78 50W
Parc de Conservation de la Gaspésie Québec 33 C2 48 52N 65 57W

Parc de Conservation de la Jacques-Cartier Québec 37 P8 47 23N 71 30W
Parc de Conservation des Grands-Jardins Québec 37 Q8 47 47N 70 59W
Parc de Conservation du Saguenay Québec 37 Q9 48 15N 70 45W
Parc de la Gatineau Québec 47 J3 45 31N 75 53W
Parc de Récréation des Îles-de-Boucherville Québec 47 N5 45 36N 73 27W
Parc de Récréation D'Oka Québec 47 M4 45 24N 73 58W
Parc de Récréation du Mont-Tremblant Québec 37 M7 46 20N 74 43W
Parc National de Forillon Québec 33 D2 49 00N 64 00W
Parc National de la Mauricie Québec 37 N7 46 50N 73 05W
Parent Québec 37 M8 47 55N 74 36W
Paris Ontario 38 B2 43 12N 80 25W
Parke Lake Newfoundland 30 C3 53 10N 58 50W
Parkhill Ontario 38 A2 43 10N 81 41W
Parkland County Alberta 48 F4 53 40N 113 30W
Parksville British Columbia 42 H4 49 20N 124 19W
Parrsboro Nova Scotia 31 F7 45 25N 64 21W
Parry Island Ontario 38 B4 45 17N 80 11W
Parry Islands Northwest Territories 44 J6 75 15N 109 00W
Parry Sound Ontario 38 B4 45 21N 80 08W
Parry Sound *admin.* Ontario 36 G6 45 22N 80 08W
Parry Sound *tn.* Ontario 38 B4 45 21N 80 03W
Parson's Pond *tn.* Newfoundland 31 C3 50 02N 57 43W
Pasadena Newfoundland 31 C2 49 01N 57 36W
Pasfield Lake Saskatchewan 40 B3 58 20N 105 45W
Pasquia Hills Saskatchewan 40 C2 53 10N 103 00W
Pass Lake Ontario 34 C2 48 34N 88 44W
Pattullo, Mount British Columbia 42 C3 56 15N 129 43W
Paudash Ontario 36 J5 44 56N 78 04W
Paulatuk Northwest Territories 44 G4 69 49N 123 59W
Paul Island Newfoundland 30 B4 56 30N 61 25W
Payne Bay Québec 32 C4 60 00N 70 01W
Peace Point *tn.* Alberta 41 C3 59 07N 112 27W
Peace River Alberta 41 B3 58 40N 114 30W
Peace River *tn.* Alberta 41 B3 56 15N 117 18W
Peachland British Columbia 43 E1 49 49N 119 48W
Peary Channel Northwest Territories 45 L6 79 40N 101 30W
Peawanuck Ontario 34 C4 55 00N 85 30W
Peche Island Provincial Park Ontario 52 F2 42 20N 82 55W
Peel *admin.* Ontario 38 C2 43 49N 79 57W
Peel County Ontario 46 B2 43 48N 79 41W
Peel River Yukon Territory 44 D4 66 05N 136 00W
Peel River Game Reserve Northwest Territories 44 E4 66 30N 134 00W
Peel Sound Northwest Territories 45 M5 73 15N 96 30W
Peerless Lake Alberta 41 C3 56 40N 114 35W
Pefferlaw Brook Ontario 38 C3 44 10N 79 15W
Peggys Cove *tn.* Nova Scotia 31 F6 44 30N 63 50W
Pelee Island Ontario 36 D2 41 47N 82 40W
Pelee Point Ontario 36 D2 41 45N 82 39W
Pelham Ontario 38 C2 43 02N 79 19W
Pelican Bay Manitoba 39 A2 52 40N 100 30W
Pelican Lake Manitoba 39 A2 52 30N 100 30W
Pelican Mountains Alberta 41 C3 55 35N 114 00W
Pelican Narrows *tn.* Saskatchewan 40 C3 55 12N 102 55W
Pelly Bay Northwest Territories 45 N4 68 53N 89 51W
Pelly Bay *tn.* Northwest Territories 45 O4 68 32N 89 48W
Pelly Crossing Yukon Territory 44 D3 62 48N 136 30W
Pelly Mountains Yukon Territory 44 E3 62 10N 134 10W
Pelly Point British Columbia 46 F3 49 06N 123 13W
Pelly River Yukon Territory 44 E3 62 50N 134 50W
Pemberton British Columbia 42 H5 50 19N 122 49W
Pembina Alberta 41 B2 53 08N 115 09W
Pembina River Alberta 41 B2 53 15N 116 05W
Pembina River Manitoba 39 B1 49 10N 99 10W
Pembroke Ontario 38 D2 45 49N 77 08W
Penetanguishene Ontario 38 C3 44 47N 79 56W
Penhold Alberta 41 C2 52 08N 113 52W
Péninsule de la Gaspésie *p.* Québec 33 C2 48 30N 65 30W
Péninsule d'Ungava *p.* Québec 32 A5/B5 60 50N 76 00W
Penticton British Columbia 43 E1 49 49N 119 38W
Percé Québec 33 D2 48 32N 64 14W
Percé, Cape Nova Scotia 31 G7 46 10N 59 40W
Perdue Saskatchewan 40 B2 52 05N 107 33W
Perkinsfield Ontario 38 C3 44 41N 79 58W
Perrault Falls *tn.* Ontario 34 B3 50 20N 93 08W
Perry Island *tn.* Northwest Territories 45 L4 67 48N 102 33W
Perth-Andover New Brunswick 31 A2 46 45N 67 42W
Perth Ontario 37 K5 44 54N 76 15W
Perth *admin.* Ontario 38 A2 43 22N 81 10W
Petawana Ontario 35 E2 45 54N 77 18W
Petawawa Ontario 37 J6 45 54N 77 17W
Peterborough Ontario 38 D3 44 19N 78 20W
Peterborough *admin.* Ontario 38 D3 44 14N 78 32W
Peter Pond Lake Saskatchewan 40 B3 55 50N 108 50W
Petitcodiac New Brunswick 31 E7 45 57N 65 11W
Petite Rivière *tn.* Nova Scotia 31 F6 44 15N 64 25W
Petite Rivière de la Baleine *r.* Québec 32 A4 55 05N 76 28W
Petit Étang *tn.* Nova Scotia 31 F7 46 39N 61 00W
Petit lac des Loups Marins *l.* Québec 32 B4 56 30N 73 30W
Petit lac Manicouagan *l.* Québec 33 C3 52 10N 67 40W
Petitot River British Columbia 43 D3 59 55N 122 15W
Petitsikapau Lake Newfoundland 30 A3 54 37N 66 25W
Petre, Point Ontario 35 E1 43 50N 77 09W
Petrolia Ontario 36 D3 42 52N 82 09W
Phelps Lake Saskatchewan 40 C3 59 20N 102 55W
Philpots Island Northwest Territories 45 Q5 74 57N 79 58W
Pickerel Lake Ontario 35 B2 48 37N 91 19W
Pickering Ontario 46 D2 43 48N 79 11W
Pickering Village Ontario 38 C2 43 51N 79 02W
Pickle Lake *tn.* Ontario 34 B3 51 28N 90 12W
Pic River Ontario 35 C2 48 50N 86 20W
Picton Ontario 37 J5 44 00N 77 07W
Pictou Nova Scotia 31 F7 45 41N 62 42W
Pictou *admin.* Nova Scotia 31 F7 45 30N 62 40W
Pictou Island Nova Scotia 31 F7 45 41N 62 42W
Picture Butte *tn.* Alberta 41 C1 49 53N 112 47W
Pie Island Ontario 35 C2 48 15N 89 06W
Pierceland Saskatchewan 40 B2 54 20N 109 40W
Pierrefords Québec 47 M5 45 30N 73 50W
Pigeon Lake Alberta 41 C2 53 01N 114 02W
Pigeon Lake Ontario 38 D3 44 27N 78 30W
Pigeon River Manitoba 39 B2 52 10N 96 50W
Pigeon River Ontario 38 D3 44 13N 78 42W
Pikangikum *I.R.* Ontario 34 B3 51 48N 93 59W
Pikangikum Lake Ontario 34 B3 51 48N 94 00W
Pike Creek Ontario 52 F2 41 15N 82 53W
Pikwitonei Manitoba 39 B3 55 35N 97 11W
Pilot Butte *tn.* Saskatchewan 40 C2 50 29N 104 28W
Pilot Mound *tn.* Manitoba 39 B1 49 13N 98 52W
Pinawa Manitoba 39 B2 50 13N 95 56W
Pincher Creek *tn.* Alberta 41 C1 49 29N 113 57W
Pinchi Lake British Columbia 43 D2 54 36N 124 25W
Pine, Cape Newfoundland 31 D2 46 38N 53 35W
Pine Falls *tn.* Manitoba 39 B2 50 33N 96 14W
Pinehouse Lake Saskatchewan 40 B3 55 35N 106 50W
Pineimuta River Ontario 34 B3 52 10N 90 40W
Pine Pass British Columbia 43 D3 55 30N 122 25W
Pine Point Northwest Territories 44 J3 60 50N 114 28W
Pine River British Columbia 43 D3 55 50N 121 50W
Pine River Ontario 38 B3 44 18N 80 06W
Pinery Provincial Park Ontario 36 D4 43 16N 81 50W
Pinto Butte *mt.* Saskatchewan 40 B1 49 21N 107 25W
Pinware Newfoundland 30 C3 51 37N 56 42W
Pipestone River Ontario 34 B3 52 20N 90 40W
Pistolet Bay Newfoundland 30 C3 51 35N 55 45W
Pit Island British Columbia 42 C2 53 38N 129 59W
Pitman River British Columbia 43 C3 58 00N 128 15W
Pitt Lake British Columbia 42 H4 49 25N 122 33W
Pitt Meadows *tn.* British Columbia 42 H4 49 13N 122 42W
Pitt River British Columbia 42 H4 49 42N 122 40W
Placentia Newfoundland 31 D2 47 14N 53 58W
Placentia Bay Newfoundland 31 D2 47 00N 54 30W
Plantagenet Ontario 37 L6 45 32N 75 00W
Plaster Rock *tn.* New Brunswick 31 A2 46 55N 67 24W
Playgreen Lake Manitoba 39 B2 53 50N 98 10W
Pleasant Bay *tn.* Nova Scotia 31 F7 46 50N 60 48W
Pledger Lake Ontario 34 D3 50 53N 83 42W
Plessisville Québec 37 P7 46 14N 71 46W
Plum Coulee Manitoba 39 B1 49 12N 97 45W
Plum Point *tn.* Newfoundland 31 C3 51 04N 56 53W
Pohénégamook Québec 37 R8 47 28N 69 17W
Pointe au Baril *tn.* Ontario 38 B4 45 36N 80 23W
Pointe au Baril Station *tn.* Ontario 36 F6 45 36N 80 22W
Pointe aux Pins Ontario 36 D3 42 29N 84 28W
Pointe-aux-Pins Creek Alberta 48 G5 53 39N 113 16W
Pointe-Claire *tn.* Québec 37 N6 45 27N 73 50W
Pointe de l'Est *c.* Québec 33 D2 49 00N 64 00W
Pointe-Gatineau *tn.* Québec 47 K2 45 27N 75 42W
Pointe Jacques-Cartier *c.* Québec 33 C3 50 20N 66 00W
Pointe Louis-XIV *c.* Québec 32 A3 54 38N 79 45W
Point Lake Northwest Territories 44 J4 65 15N 113 04W
Point Pelee National Park Ontario 36 D2 41 57N 82 31W
Point Pleasant Park Nova Scotia 47 P6 44 37N 63 33W
Polar Bear Provincial Park Ontario 34 D3 54 50N 83 40W
Pomquet Nova Scotia 31 F7 45 34N 61 50W
Pond Inlet Northwest Territories 45 Q5 72 41N 78 00W
Pond Inlet *tn.* Northwest Territories 45 Q5 42 40N 77 59W
Ponhook Lake Nova Scotia 31 F6 44 50N 64 10W
Ponoka Alberta 41 C2 52 42N 113 33W
Ponteaix Saskatchewan 40 B1 49 45N 107 20W
Pontiac *admin.* Québec 36 J7 46 28N 77 40W
Pont-Rouge Québec 27 46 45N 71 43W
Pont-Viau Québec 47 N5 45 33N 73 41W
Poplar Hills *tn.* Ontario 34 B3 52 05N 94 18W
Poplar River Manitoba 39 B2 52 50N 97 00W
Porcher Island British Columbia 42 B2 54 00N 130 30W
Porcupine, Cape Newfoundland 30 C3 53 56N 57 08W
Porcupine Hills Manitoba/Saskatchewan 40 C2 52 30N 101 40W
Porcupine Plain *tn.* Saskatchewan 40 C2 52 36N 103 15W
Porcupine Provincial Forest Manitoba 39 A2 52 30N 101 20W
Portabello Nova Scotia 47 P6 44 44N 63 32W
Portage la Prairie Manitoba 39 B1 49 58N 98 20W
Port Alberni British Columbia 42 H4 49 11N 124 49W
Port Alice British Columbia 43 C2 50 23N 127 24W
Port au Choix Newfoundland 31 C3 50 43N 57 22W
Port au Port Peninsula Newfoundland 31 C2 48 35N 59 00W
Port Bickerton Nova Scotia 31 F7 45 10N 61 40W
Port Blandford Newfoundland 31 D2 48 21N 54 10W
Port Bruce Ontario 38 A1 42 40N 81 00W
Port Bruce Provincial Park Ontario 38 B1 42 40N 81 00W
Port Burwell Northwest Territories 45 D5 60 30N 64 50W
Port Burwell Ontario 38 B1 42 39N 80 47W
Port Burwell Provincial Park Ontario 38 B1 42 40N 80 45W
Port Carling Ontario 36 G6 45 07N 79 35W
Port-Cartier Québec 33 C3 50 02N 66 58W
Port Clements British Columbia 42 B2 53 41N 132 11W
Port Colborne Ontario 38 C1 42 53N 79 16W
Port Coquitlam British Columbia 42 H4 49 16N 122 45W
Port Credit Ontario 46 B1 43 33N 79 36W
Port Dover Ontario 38 B1 42 47N 80 12W
Port Edward British Columbia 42 B2 54 11N 130 16W
Port Elgin Ontario 38 A3 44 25N 81 23W
Port Elgin New Brunswick 31 F7 46 03N 64 08W
Porter Lake Saskatchewan 40 B3 56 20N 107 10W
Port Essington British Columbia 42 C2 54 08N 129 59W
Port Hammond British Columbia 46 H3 49 12N 122 40W
Port Hardy British Columbia 43 C2 50 43N 127 15W
Port Hawkesbury Nova Scotia 31 F7 45 36N 61 22W
Port Hood Nova Scotia 31 F7 46 00N 61 32W
Port Hope Ontario 35 F1 43 58N 78 18W
Port Hope Simpson Newfoundland 30 C3 52 33N 56 18W
Port Kells British Columbia 46 H3 49 09N 122 43W
Portland Inlet British Columbia 42 B2 54 40N 130 30W
Port Lorne Nova Scotia 31 E6 44 50N 65 20W
Port McNeill British Columbia 43 C2 50 30N 127 01W
Port McNicoll Ontario 38 C3 44 44N 79 49W
Port Maitland Ontario 38 C1 42 51N 79 33W
Port Maitland Nova Scotia 31 E6 43 59N 66 04W
Port Mellon British Columbia 42 H4 49 31N 123 30W
Port-Menier Québec 33 D2 49 50N 64 20W
Port Moody British Columbia 42 H4 49 13N 122 57W
Port Mouton Nova Scotia 31 F6 43 58N 64 50W
Port Nelson Manitoba 39 C3 57 10N 92 35W
Portneuf *admin.* Québec 37 O7 46 50N 72 20W
Port Perry Ontario 38 D3 44 06N 78 58W
Port Renfrew British Columbia 42 H4 48 33N 124 25W
Port Rowan Ontario 38 B1 42 38N 80 27W
Port Royal Nova Scotia 31 E6 44 45N 65 40W
Port Saunders Newfoundland 31 C3 50 39N 57 18W
Port Simpson British Columbia 42 B2 54 32N 130 25W
Port Stanley Ontario 38 A1 42 40N 81 14W
Portuniq Québec 32 B5 2N 74 00W
Poste-de-la-Baleine *see* Kuujjuarapik
Postville Newfoundland 30 C3 54 54N 59 47W
Pouce Coupé British Columbia 43 D3 55 40N 120 08W
Pouch Cove *tn.* Newfoundland 31 D2 47 46N 52 46W
Povungnituk Québec 32 A5 59 45N 77 20W
Powassan Ontario 36 G7 46 05N 79 22W
Powell Lake British Columbia 42 H5 50 08N 124 26W
Powell River *tn.* British Columbia 42 H4 49 54N 124 34W
Powerview Manitoba 39 B2 50 30N 96 10W
Preeceville Saskatchewan 40 C2 51 58N 102 40W
Prelate Saskatchewan 40 B2 50 52N 109 22W
Prescott Ontario 37 L5 44 43N 75 33W
Prescott and Russell *admin.* Ontario 37 M6 45 30N 74 45W
Preston Nova Scotia 47 Q6 44 41N 63 26W
Preston Ontario 38 B2 43 23N 80 21W
Price Island British Columbia 42 C2 52 25N 128 40W
Prim, Point *c.* Prince Edward Island 31 F7 46 10N 63 00W
Primrose Lake Saskatchewan 40 B2 54 50N 109 30W
Primrose Lake Air Weapons Range Saskatchewan 40 B3 55 00N 109 00W
Prince *admin.* Prince Edward Island 31 F7 46 30N 64 00W
Prince Albert Saskatchewan 40 B2 53 13N 105 45W
Prince Albert National Park Saskatchewan 40 B2 54 00N 106 00W
Prince Albert Peninsula Northwest Territories 44 J5 72 30N 117 00W
Prince Albert Sound Northwest Territories 44 H5 70 15N 117 30W
Prince Alfred, Cape Northwest Territories 44 F5 74 20N 124 46W
Prince Charles Island Northwest Territories 45 Q4 67 40N 77 00W
Prince Edward Island *province* 31 F7 46 30N 63 00W
Prince Edward National Park Prince Edward Island 31 F7 46 10N 63 10W
Prince George British Columbia 43 D2 53 55N 122 49W
Prince Gustaf Adolf Sea Northwest Territories 45 K6 78 30N 107 00W
Prince of Wales Island Northwest Territories 45 M5 73 00N 98 00W
Prince of Wales Strait Northwest Territories 44 H5 71 00N 119 50W
Prince Patrick Island Northwest Territories 44 H6 77 00N 120 00W
Prince Regent Inlet Northwest Territories 44 H6 72 40N 91 00W
Prince Rupert British Columbia 42 B2 54 09N 130 20W
Princess Margaret Range *mts.* Northwest Territories 45 N7 81 00N 92 30W
Princess Royal Island British Columbia 42 C2 53 04N 129 00W
Princeton British Columbia 43 D1 49 25N 120 35W
Princeville Québec 37 P7 46 10N 71 52W
Prophet River British Columbia 43 D3 58 20N 122 50W
Provost Alberta 41 C2 52 21N 110 16W
Pubnico Nova Scotia 31 E6 43 42N 65 48W
Puce Ontario 52 F2 42 18N 82 46W
Puce River Ontario 52 F2 42 15N 82 47W
Pugwash Nova Scotia 31 F7 45 52N 63 40W
Pukaskwa Ontario 35 C2 48 20N 85 40W
Pukatawagan Manitoba 39 A3 55 46N 101 14W
Pukeashun Mountain British Columbia 43 E2 51 12N 119 14W
Purcell Mountains British Columbia 43 E2 50 58N 116 59W
Purcell's Cove *tn.* Nova Scotia 47 P6 44 35N 63 33W
Purcell Wilderness Conservancy British Columbia 43 E2 50 00N 116 00W

Q

Quadra Island British Columbia 42 G5 50 11N 125 20W
Qualicum Beach *tn.* British Columbia 42 H4 49 21N 124 27W
Qu'Appelle Saskatchewan 40 C2 50 33N 103 54W
Qu'Appelle Dam Saskatchewan 40 B2 50 55N 106 20W
Qu'Appelle River Saskatchewan 40 C2 50 30N 102 20W
Quaqtaq Québec 32 C5 61 00N 69 40W
Quathiaski Cove *tn.* British Columbia 42 G5 50 03N 125 11W
Quatsino Sound British Columbia 43 C2 50 25N 128 55W
Québec Québec 37 P7 46 50N 71 15W
Québec *admin.* Québec 37 O8 47 50N 72 30W
Québec *province* 32/33
Queen Bess, Mount British Columbia 43 D2 51 13N 124 35W
Queen Charlotte British Columbia 42 B2 53 18N 132 04W
Queen Charlotte Islands British Columbia 42 B2 53 30N 131 50W
Queen Charlotte Sound British Columbia 42 C2 51 48N 129 25W
Queen Charlotte Strait British Columbia 43 C2 51 00N 127 55W
Queen Elizabeth Foreland Northwest Territories 45 T3 62 23N 64 28W
Queen Elizabeth Islands Northwest Territories 44 H6 77 30N 105 00W
Queen Maud Bird Sanctuary Northwest Territories 45 L4 67 30N 103 20W
Queen Maud Gulf Northwest Territories 45 L4 68 00N 101 00W
Queens *admin.* New Brunswick 31 A2 45 50N 65 50W
Queens *admin.* Nova Scotia 31 E6 44 10N 65 10W
Queens *admin.* Prince Edward Island 31 F7 46 20N 63 10W
Queenston Ontario 38 C2 43 09N 79 03W
Queenswood Heights Ontario 47 L2 45 28N 75 29W
Quesnel British Columbia 43 D2 53 03N 122 31W
Quesnel Lake British Columbia 43 D2 52 30N 121 20W
Quesnel River British Columbia 43 D2 52 58N 122 29W
Quetico Provincial Park Ontario 35 B2 48 30N 91 30W
Quill Lake *tn.* Saskatchewan 40 C2 52 03N 104 12W
Quill Lakes Saskatchewan 40 C2 52 03N 104 12W
Quince, Bay of Ontario 37 J5 44 07N 77 32W
Quirke Lake Ontario 35 D2 46 28N 82 33W
Quispamsis New Brunswick 31 E7 45 25N 65 55W
Quoich River Northwest Territories 45 N3 64 50N 94 40W

R

Raanes Peninsula Northwest Territories 45 P6 78 30N 85 45W
Rabbit River British Columbia 43 C3 59 20N 127 20W
Radisson Québec 32 A3 53 43N 77 46W
Radisson Saskatchewan 40 B2 52 27N 107 24W
Radville Saskatchewan 40 C1 49 28N 104 19W
Rae Northwest Territories 44 H3 62 50N 116 03W
Rae Lakes *tn.* Northwest Territories 44 H3 64 10N 117 20W
Rae River Northwest Territories 44 H4 68 10N 116 50W
Ragged Lake Nova Scotia 47 P6 44 37N 63 39W
Rainbow Lake Alberta 41 B3 58 17N 119 16W
Rainbow Lake *tn.* Alberta 41 B3 58 30N 119 23W
Rainy Lake Ontario 34 B2 48 00N 93 00W
Rainy River Ontario 34 B2 48 40N 94 10W
Rainy River *tn.* Ontario 34 B2 48 44N 94 33W
Ralston Alberta 41 C2 50 15N 111 10W
Ralz, Mount British Columbia 42 B3 57 24N 132 19W
Ramea Newfoundland 31 C2 47 31N 57 23W
Ramea Islands Newfoundland 31 C2 47 31N 57 22W
Ramsey Lake Ontario 35 D2 47 13N 82 15W
Rankin Inlet Northwest Territories 45 N3 62 45N 92 05W
Rankin Inlet *tn.* Northwest Territories 45 N3 62 49N 92 05W
Rapide-Blanc-Station Québec 37 N8 47 41N 73 03W
Rapides de Lachine *rapids* Québec 47 N4 45 26N 73 39W
Rat Lake Manitoba 39 B3 56 10N 99 40W
Rat River Manitoba 39 B3 56 10N 99 20W
Ray, Cape Newfoundland 31 C2 47 37N 59 19W
Raymond Alberta 41 C1 49 27N 112 39W
Raymore Saskatchewan 40 C2 51 24N 104 32W
Razorback *mt.* British Columbia 43 D2 51 28N 124 35W
Read Island British Columbia 42 G5 50 11N 125 05W
Red Bay *tn.* Newfoundland 30 C3 51 44N 56 25W
Redberry Lake Saskatchewan 40 B2 52 45N 107 20W
Redcliff Alberta 41 C2 50 05N 110 47W
Red Deer Alberta 41 C2 52 15N 113 48W
Red Deer Lake Manitoba 39 A2 52 50N 101 30W
Red Deer River Alberta 41 C2 51 20N 112 35W
Red Deer River Saskatchewan 40 C2 52 50N 103 05W
Red Indian Lake Newfoundland 31 C2 48 40N 57 10W
Red Lake Ontario 34 B3 51 50N 93 40W
Red Lake *tn.* Ontario 34 B3 51 01N 93 50W
Redonda Island British Columbia 42 H5 50 15N 124 50W
Red River British Columbia 43 C3 59 23N 128 14W
Red River Manitoba 39 B1 49 30N 97 20W
Red Rock Ontario 35 C2 48 55N 88 15W
Redstone River Northwest Territories 44 F3 63 47N 128 00W
Red Sucker Lake Manitoba 39 C2 54 10N 94 10W
Redvers Saskatchewan 40 C1 49 34N 101 42W
Redwater Alberta 41 C2 53 57N 113 06W
Red Wine River Newfoundland 30 B3 54 10N 62 10W
Reed Lake Manitoba 39 A2 54 30N 100 10W
Refuge Cove *tn.* British Columbia 42 H5 50 07N 124 51W
Regina Saskatchewan 40 C2 50 30N 104 38W
Reindeer Grazing Reserve Northwest Territories 44 E4 69 00N 132 00W
Reindeer Island Manitoba 39 B2 52 30N 98 20W
Reindeer Lake Saskatchewan/Manitoba 40 C3 57 30N 102 30W
Reindeer River Saskatchewan 40 C3 56 10N 103 10W
Reliance Northwest Territories 44 K3 62 42N 109 08W
Renews Newfoundland 31 D2 46 56N 52 56W
Renfrew Ontario 37 K6 45 28N 76 44W
Renfrew *admin.* Ontario 37 J6 45 28N 76 41W
Rennie Lake Northwest Territories 44 K3 61 32N 105 35W
Repentigny Québec 37 N6 45 29N 73 46W
Repulse Bay *tn.* Northwest Territories 45 O4 66 32N 86 15W
Réserve de la Rivière Matamec *reserve* Québec 33 C3 50 30N 65 30W
Réserve Duchénier *reserve* Québec 33 C2 48 08N 68 40W
Réserve du Parc National de l'Archipel de Mingan *reserve* Québec 33 D3 50 10N 62 30W
Réserve Faunique Ashuapmushuan *reserve* Québec 33 B2 49 00N 73 30W
Réserve Faunique Assinica *reserve* Québec 33 A3 50 48N 75 40W
Réserve Faunique de Baldwin *reserve* Québec 33 C2 48 40N 66 10W
Réserve Faunique de Dunière *reserve* Québec 33 C2 48 30N 66 40W
Réserve Faunique de l'Île D'Anticosti *reserve* Québec 33 D2 49 25N 62 58W
Réserve Faunique de Papineau-Labelle *reserve* Québec 37 L7 46 20N 75 21W
Réserve Faunique de Port-Daniel *reserve* Québec 33 D2 48 13N 65 00W
Réserve Faunique de Portneuf *reserve* Québec 37 O8 47 15N 72 30W
Réserve Faunique de Rimouski *reserve* Québec 33 C2 48 00N 68 20W
Réserve Faunique des Chic-Chocs *reserve* Québec 33 C2 49 10N 65 10W
Réserve Faunique de Sept-Îles-Port-Cartier *reserve* Québec 33 C3 50 30N 67 30W
Réserve Faunique des Lacs-Albanel-Mistassini-et-Waconichi *reserve* Québec 33 B3 50 10N 74 20W
Réserve Faunique des Laurentides *reserve* Québec 37 P8 47 50N 71 47W
Réserve Faunique de Cap-Chat *reserve* Québec 33 C2 48 50N 66 50W
Réserve Faunique du Saint-Maurice *reserve* Québec 37 N8 47 08N 73 18W
Réserve Faunique la Vérendrye *reserve* Québec 37 J8 47 08N 73 18W
Réserve Faunique Mastigouche *reserve* Québec 37 N7 46 35N 73 47W
Réserve Faunique Rouge-Matawin *reserve* Québec 37 M7 46 52N 74 35W
Réserve Frontenac *reserve* Québec 37 P6 45 52N 71 17W
Réservoir Baskatong *res.* Québec 37 L7 47 00N 76 00W
Réservoir Blanc *res.* Québec 37 N8 47 49N 73 06W
Réservoir Cabonga *res.* Québec 37 K8 47 31N 76 45W
Réservoir Caniapiscau *res.* Québec 32 C3 54 10N 69 10W

Réservoir de La Grande 2 res. Québec 33 A3 53 38N 78 40W
Réservoir de La Grande 3 res. Québec 32 A3 54 10N 72 30W
Réservoir de La Grande 4 res. Québec 32 B3 53 59N 72 50W
Réservoir Dozois res. Québec 37 J8 47 30N 77 26W
Réservoir du Poisson Blanc res. Québec 37 L7 46 05N 75 50W
Réservoir Evans res. Québec 33 A3 50 45N 76 50W
Réservoir Gavin res. Québec 37 L9 48 35N 75 15W
Réservoir Gouin res. Québec 33 B2 48 30N 74 00W
Réservoir Laforge 1 res .Québec 32 B3 54 20N 71 50W
Réservoir Laforge 2 res. Québec 32 B3 54 30N 71 20W
Réservoir Manic 2 res. Québec 33 C2 49 30N 68 25W
Réservoir Manic 3 res. Québec 33 C3 51 30N 67 58W
Réservoir Manicouagan res. Québec 33 C3 51 00N 58 00W
Réservoir Opinaca res. Québec 33 A3 52 30N 75 30W
Réservoir Outardes 4 res. Québec 33 C3 50 20N 69 20W
Réservoir Pipmuacan res. Québec 33 B2 49 30N 70 10W
Réservoir Soscumica-Matagami res. Québec 33 A3 50 10N 77 32W
Réservoir Taureau res. Québec 37 N7 46 47N 73 47W
Resolute Northwest Territories 45 N5 74 40N 95 00W
Resolution Island Northwest Territories 45 T3 61 18N 64 53W
Restigouche admin. New Brunswick 31 A2 47 40N 67 10W
Restigouche River New Brunswick 31 A2 47 35N 67 30W
Reston Manitoba 39 A1 49 33N 101 05W
Revelstoke British Columbia 43 E2 51 02N 118 12W
Revelstoke, Lake British Columbia 43 E2 51 32N 118 40W
Rexton New Brunswick 31 F7 46 41N 64 56W
Ribstone Creek Alberta 41 C2 52 10N 111 55W
Rice Lake Ontario 36 H5 44 12N 78 10W
Richard Collinson Inlet Northwest Territories 44 J5 72 45N 113 55W
Richards Island Northwest Territories 44 E4 69 20N 134 30W
Richardson Mountains Yukon Territory/Northwest Territories 44 D4 67 50N 137 00W
Richardson River Alberta 41 C3 58 15N 110 W
Rich, Cape Ontario 38 B3 44 43N 80 39W
Richibucto New Brunswick 31 F7 46 42N 64 54W
Richmond British Columbia 42 H4 49 09N 123 09W
Richmond Québec 37 O6 45 40N 72 10W
Richmond admin. Nova Scotia 31 F7 45 40N 60 40W
Richmond admin. Québec 37 O6 45 30N 72 10W
Richmond Hill tn. Ontario 46 C2 43 53N 79 26W
Rideau River Ontario 35 F1 44 50N 76 10W
Rideau River and Canal Ontario 47 K2 45 16N 75 43W
Ridgetown Ontario 36 E3 42 26N 81 54W
Riding Mountain Manitoba 39 A2 50 40N 100 40W
Riding Mountain National Park Manitoba 39 A2 50 50N 100 30W
Rigolet Newfoundland 30 C3 54 11N 58 26W
Rimbey Alberta 41 C2 52 38N 114 14W
Rimouski Québec 33 C2 48 27N 68 32W
Riondel British Columbia 43 E1 49 46N 116 51W
Riou Lake Saskatchewan 40 B3 59 00N 106 30W
Ripley Ontario 38 A3 44 04N 81 34W
Ritchot admin. Manitoba 48 D1 49 44N 97 07W
River Herbert tn. Nova Scotia 31 F7 45 42N 64 25W
River John tn. Nova Scotia 31 F7 45 44N 63 03W
Rivers tn. Manitoba 39 A2 50 02N 100 14W
Riverside Ontario 52 F2 42 20N 82 56W
Riverside-Albert New Brunswick 31 F7 45 40N 64 40W
Rivers Inlet British Columbia 43 C2 51 30N 127 30W
Riverton Manitoba 39 B2 51 00N 97 00W
Rivière Aguanus r. Québec 33 D3 51 05N 62 02W
Rivière à la Baleine r. Québec 32 C4 57 54N 67 40W
Rivière Arnaud r. Québec 32 B4 59 37N 72 55W
Rivière Ashuapmushuan r. Québec 33 B2 49 22N 73 25W
Rivière aux Feuilles r. Québec 32 B4 57 45N 73 00W
Rivière aux Mélèzes r. Québec 32 B4 56 50N 72 45W
Rivière aux Outardes r. Québec 33 C3 51 38N 69 55W
Rivière-aux-Rats tn. Québec 37 O8 47 11N 72 52W
Rivière Bécancour r. Québec 37 O7 46 15N 72 20W
Rivière Bell r. Québec 33 A2 49 30N 77 30W
Rivière Betsiamites r. Québec 33 C2 49 27N 69 30W
Rivière Blanche r. Québec 47 K3 45 32N 75 38W
Rivière Broadback r. Québec 33 A3 51 15N 77 42W
Rivière Caniapiscau r. Québec 32 C4 56 38N 69 15W
Rivière Capitachouane r. Québec 37 K8 47 42N 76 49W
Rivière Casapédia r. Québec 33 C2 48 45N 66 20Wc
Rivière Chaudière r. Québec 37 P7 46 30N 71 10W
Rivière Chicoutimi r. Québec 37 P9 48 11N 71 29W
Rivière Chukotat r. Québec 32 A5 61 02N 77 15W
Rivière Coats r. Québec 32 A4 55 30N 77 10W
Rivière Coulonge r. Québec 37 J7 46 44N 77 10W
Rivière d'Argent r. Québec 37 L7 46 59N 75 00W
Rivière Delay r. Québec 32 B4 56 50N 71 10W
Rivière de Pas r. Québec 32 C4 55 12N 65 35W
Rivière de Rupert r. Québec 33 A3 51 22N 78 30W
Rivière des Mille Îles r. Québec 47 M5 45 37N 73 47W
Rivière des Outaouais (Ottawa River) Ontario/Québec 36 K6 45 35N 76 30W
Rivière des Prairies r. Québec 47 N5 45 36N 73 37W
Rivière du Chêne r. Québec 47 M5 45 34N 73 59W
Rivière du Gué r. Québec 32 B4 56 48N 72 05W
Rivière du Lièvre r. Québec 37 L6 45 50N 75 39W
Rivière-du-Loup admin. Québec 37 R8 47 50N 69 20W
Rivière-du-Loup tn. Québec 37 R8 47 49N 69 32W
Rivière Dumoine r. Québec 36 H7 46 20N 77 52W
Rivière du Petit Mécatina (Little Mecatina River) Québec 36 H7 46 20N 77 52W
Rivière du Sable r. Québec 32 C4 55 28N 68 20W
Rivière du Vieux Comptoir r. Québec 33 A3 52 33N 78 40W
Rivière Eastmain r. Québec 33 B3 52 20N 77 52W
Rivière False r. Québec 32 C4 57 40N 68 30W
Rivière Ford r. Québec 32 C4 58 40N 58 20W
Rivière Gatineau r. Québec 37 L6 45 58N 75 52W
Rivière George r. Québec 32 C4 57 50N 65 30W
Rivière Harricana r. Québec 33 A3 50 40N 79 20W
Rivière Innuksuac r. Québec 32 A4 58 40N 77 50W
Rivière Kanaaupscow r. Québec 33 A3 54 20N 76 10W
Rivière Kitchigama r. Québec 33 A3 50 50N 78 30W
Rivière Kogaluc r. Québec 32 A4 59 33N 77 18W
Rivière Koksoak r. Québec 32 C4 57 50N 69 10W
Rivière Koroc r. Québec 32 C4 58 40N 65 20W
Rivière Kovik r. Québec 32 A5 61 50N 77 20W
Rivière Magpie r. Québec 33 D3 50 42N 64 25W
Rivière Malbaie r. Québec 37 Q9 48 01N 70 40W
Rivière Manicouagan r. Québec 33 C3 50 51N 68 55W
Rivière Manitou r. Québec 33 C3 51 08N 65 20W
Rivière Manouane r. Québec 33 B2 49 45N 70 59W
Rivière Maquatua r. Québec 33 A3 53 05N 78 40W
Rivière Mariet r. Québec 32 A4 59 05N 77 30W
Rivière Matapédia r. Québec 33 C2 48 30N 67 30W
Rivière Matawin r. Québec 37 N7 46 55N 73 39W
Rivière-Matawin tn. Québec 37 O7 46 54N 72 55W
Rivière Mégiscane r. Québec 33 A2 48 17N 76 50W
Rivière Métabetchouane r. Québec 37 O8 47 59N 72 05W
Rivière Mistassibi r. Québec 33 B3 50 20N 72 15W
Rivière Mistassibi Nord-Est r. Québec 33 B3 50 01N 71 59W
Rivière Mistassini r. Québec 33 B2 49 50N 72 40W
Rivière Moisie r. Québec 33 C3 50 52N 66 33W
Rivière Montmorency r. Québec 37 P8 47 19N 71 12W
Rivière Mucaliq r. Québec 32 C4 58 15N 67 30W
Rivière Nabisipi r. Québec 33 D3 50 59N 62 32W
Rivière Nastapoca r. Québec 32 A4 56 52N 76 10W
Rivière Natashquan (Natashquan River) Québec 33 D3 51 12N 61 35W
Rivière Nicolet r. Québec 37 O7 46 14N 72 35W
Rivière Nipissis r. Québec 33 C3 50 30N 66 05W
Rivière Noire r. Québec 37 J7 46 40N 77 23W
Rivière Nottaway r. Québec 33 A3 51 05N 77 35W
Rivière Olomane r. Québec 33 D3 50 58N 60 35W
Rivière Opinaca r. Québec 33 A3 52 20N 78 00W
Rivière Pentecôte r. Québec 33 C3 50 18N 67 35W
Rivière Péribonca r. Québec 33 B2 48 58N 71 30W
Rivière Pons r. Québec 32 C4 55 05N 69 50W
Rivière Pontax r. Québec 33 A3 51 35N 78 05W
Rivière Racine de Bouleau r. Québec 33 C3 52 00N 68 40W
Rivière Richelieu r. Québec 37 N6 45 03N 73 25W
Rivière Romaine r. Québec 33 D3 51 40N 63 40W
Rivière Saguenay r. Québec 33 B2 48 20N 70 43W
Rivière Saint-Augustin r. Québec 32 E3 51 58N 60 10W
Rivière Sainte-Anne r. Québec 37 O7 46 40N 72 11W
Rivière Sainte-Anne r. Québec 37 Q8 47 05N 70 05W
Rivière Saint-François r. Québec 37 O6 45 52N 72 21W
Rivière Saint-Jean r. Québec 33 D3 51 08N 64 08W
Rivière Saint-Marguerite r. Québec 33 C3 51 20N 56 59W
Rivière Saint-Maurice r. Québec 33 B2 47 55N 73 46W
Rivière Saint-Paul r. Québec 32 E3 51 55N 57 59W
Rivière Sakami r. Québec 33 B3 53 05N 74 05W
Rivière Sérigny r. Québec 32 C4 55 30N 69 59W
Rivière Témiscamie r. Québec 33 B3 51 15N 72 40W
Rivière Vachon r. Québec 32 B5 60 40N 72 25W
Rivière Vermillon r. Québec 37 N8 47 19N 73 22W
Rivière-Verte tn. New Brunswick 31 A2 47 19N 68 09W
Rivière Wacouna r. Québec 33 C3 50 57N 66 05W
Rivière Wheeler r. Québec 32 C4 56 25N 67 35W
Rivière Yamaska r. Québec 37 N6 45 40N 73 00W
Robert's Arm tn. Newfoundland 31 C2 49 29N 55 49W
Roberts Bank Superport British Columbia 42 H4 49 04N 123 28W
Roberts Creek tn. British Columbia 42 H4 49 25N 123 37W
Roberval Québec 37 O9 48 31N 72 16W
Roblin Manitoba 39 A2 51 15N 101 20W
Robson, Mount British Columbia 43 E2 53 08N 118 18W
Rock Bay tn. British Columbia 42 G5 50 18N 125 31W
Rockcliffe Park Ontario 47 K2 45 27N 75 39W
Rock Forest tn. Québec 37 O6 45 22N 72 00W
Rockglen Saskatchewan 40 B1 49 11N 105 57W
Rockland Ontario 37 L6 45 33N 75 18W
Rock Point Provincial Park Ontario 38 C1 42 50N 79 30W
Rockwood Ontario 38 B2 43 37N 80 10W
Rocky Bay I.R. Ontario 34 C2 49 26N 88 08W
Rocky Harbour tn. Newfoundland 31 C2 49 39N 57 55W
Rocky Island Lake Ontario 35 D2 46 55N 83 04W
Rocky Lake Nova Scotia 47 P7 44 45N 63 36W
Rocky Mountain House Alberta 41 C2 52 24N 114 52W
Rocky Mountains Canada/U.S.A. 10 K4/N1
Rocky Mountains Forest Reserve Alberta 41 B2 52 30N 116 30W
Rocky Mountain Trench British Columbia 43 C3 57 50N 126 00W
Rocky Saugeen River Ontario 38 B3 44 13N 80 52W
Roddickton Newfoundland 31 C3 50 52N 56 08W
Rodney Ontario 36 E3 42 34N 81 41W
Roes Welcome Sound Northwest Territories 45 O3 63 30N 87 30W
Rogers Pass British Columbia 43 E2 51 23N 117 23W
Rogersville New Brunswick 31 A2 46 44N 65 28W
Romaine River Newfoundland 30 B3 52 30N 64 10W
Rondeau Provincial Park Ontario 36 E3 42 17N 81 51W
Root River Ontario 34 B3 50 50N 91 40W
Rorketon Manitoba 39 B2 51 24N 99 35W
Roseau River Manitoba 39 B1 49 10N 96 50W
Rose Blanche Newfoundland 31 C2 47 37N 58 41W
Rosedale Ontario 38 D3 44 34N 78 47W
Rose Point British Columbia 42 B2 54 11N 131 39W
Rosetown Saskatchewan 40 B2 51 34N 107 59W
Rose Valley tn. Saskatchewan 40 C2 52 19N 103 49W
Ross Bay Junction tn. Newfoundland 30 A3 53 03N 66 12W
Rossburn Manitoba 39 A2 50 40N 100 49W
Rosseau Ontario 36 G6 45 16N 79 39W
Rosseau, Lake Ontario 36 G6 45 10N 79 35W
Rossignol, Lake Nova Scotia 31 E6 44 10N 65 20W
Ross Island Manitoba 39 B2 54 20N 97 50W
Rossland British Columbia 43 E1 49 05N 117 48W
Rossport Ontario 35 C2 48 50N 87 31W
Ross River tn. Yukon Territory 44 E3 62 02N 132 28W
Rosswood British Columbia 42 C2 54 49N 128 42W
Rosthern Saskatchewan 40 B2 52 40N 106 20W
Rothesay New Brunswick 31 E7 45 23N 66 00W
Rougemont Québec 27 45 26N 73 03W
Rouge River Ontario 46 D2 43 52N 79 15W
Rouge Valley Park Ontario 46 D2 43 50N 79 13W
Rouleau Saskatchewan 40 C2 50 12N 104 56W
Round Pond Newfoundland 31 C2 48 10N 55 50W
Rouyn-Noranda Québec 33 A2 48 15N 79 00W
Rowley Island Northwest Territories 45 Q4 69 06N 77 52W
Russell Manitoba 39 A2 50 47N 101 17W
Russell, Cape Northwest Territories 44 H6 75 15N 117 35W
Russell Point c. Northwest Territories 44 J5 73 30N 115 00W

S

Saanich British Columbia 42 H4 48 28N 123 22W
Sabine Peninsula Northwest Territories 44 K6 76 20N 109 30W
Sable, Cape Nova Scotia 31 A1 43 23N 65 37W
Sable Island Nova Scotia 11 X1 43 57N 60 00W
Sable River tn. Nova Scotia 31 E6 43 50N 65 05W
Sachigo I.R. Ontario 34 B3 53 50N 92 10W
Sachigo Lake Ontario 34 B3 53 49N 92 08W
Sachigo River Ontario 34 B3 54 50N 90 50W
Sachs Harbour tn. Northwest Territories 44 F5 71 59N 125 13W
Sackville New Brunswick 31 F7 45 54N 64 23W
Sacré-Coeur Québec 37 R9 48 26N 68 35W
Saglek Bay Newfoundland 30 B4 58 30N 63 00W
Saglek Fiord Newfoundland 30 B4 58 29N 63 15W
Saguenay admin. Québec 37 R9 48 20N 70 00W
Saint-Agapit Québec 37 P7 46 34N 71 26W
St. Albans Newfoundland 31 C2 47 52N 55 51W
St. Albert Alberta 48 F5 53 38N 113 38W
Saint-Ambroise Québec 33 B2 48 33N 71 20W
St. Andrews New Brunswick 31 A2 45 05N 67 04W
Saint-Anselm Québec 27 46 37N 70 58W
St. Anthony Newfoundland 30 C3 51 22N 55 35W
Saint-Antoine New Brunswick 31 F7 46 20N 64 50W
St. Antoine Québec 37 M6 45 47N 74 01W
Saint-Apollinaire Québec 27 46 37N 71 29W
St. Barbe Newfoundland 31 C3 51 13N 56 45 W
St. Bernard's Newfoundland 31 D2 47 32N 54 47W
St. Boniface Manitoba 48 D2 49 53N 97 06W
St. Bride's Newfoundland 31 D2 46 55N 54 10W
St. Catharines Ontario 38 C2 43 10N 79 15W
Saint-Césaire Québec 27 45 25N 73 01W
St. Charles Manitoba 48 C2 49 53N 97 17W
St. Clair, Lake Ontario Canada/Michigan U.S.A. 36 D3 42 28N 82 40W
St. Croix River New Brunswick 31 A2 45 30N 67 40W
Saint-Donat Québec 37 M7 46 19N 74 15W
Ste. Agathe des Monts Québec 37 M7 46 03N 74 19W
Ste. Anne Manitoba 39 B1 49 40N 96 40W
Ste. Anne de Beaupré Québec 37 Q8 47 02N 70 58W
Sainte-Anne-de-Bellevue Québec 47 M4 45 25N 73 56W
Sainte-Anne-des-Monts Québec 33 C2 49 07N 66 29W
Sainte-Anne-du-Lac Québec 37 L7 46 54N 75 20W
Sainte-Catherine Québec 47 N4 45 25N 73 35W
Sainte-Claire Québec 37 Q7 46 37N 70 51W
Sainte-Croix Québec 37 P7 46 38N 71 43W
Sainte-Eustache Québec 47 M5 45 33N 73 54W
Ste.-Foy Québec 37 P7 46 47N 71 18W
Sainte-Geneviève Québec 47 M4 45 28N 73 54W
St. Eleanors Prince Edward Island 31 F7 46 30N 63 50W
Saint Elias Mountains Yukon Territory Canada/Alaska U.S.A. 44 D3 60 12N 140 57W
Sainte-Marie Québec 37 P7 46 26N 71 00W
Sainte-Rose Québec 47 M5 45 36N 73 47W
Ste. Rose du Lac Manitoba 39 B2 51 04N 99 31W
Sainte-Thérèse Québec 47 M5 45 38N 73 50W
St.-Félicien Québec 33 B2 48 38N 72 29W
Saint-Felix-de-Valois Québec 27 46 10N 73 26W
St. Francis Harbour tn. Nova Scotia 31 F7 45 30N 61 20W
St. George New Brunswick 31 A2 45 08N 66 50W
St. George's Newfoundland 31 C2 48 26N 58 29W
Saint-Georges Québec 37 O7 46 38N 72 35W
St.-Georges Québec 37 Q7 46 08N 70 40W
St. Georges Bay Newfoundland 31 C2 48 28N 59 16W
St. Georges Bay Nova Scotia 31 F7 45 40N 61 40W
St. Germain Manitoba 48 D2 49 46N
Saint-Gilles Québec 27 46 29N 71 23W
Saint-Henri Québec 27 46 42N 71 04W
Saint-Hubert Québec 47 O5 45 31N 73 25W
Saint-Hyacinthe Québec 37 O6 45 38N 72 57W
St. Ignace Island Ontario 35 C2 48 45N 87 55W
St. Jacobs Ontario 38 B2 43 32N 80 33W
Saint-Jacques New Brunswick 31 A2 47 20N 68 28W
St. James, Cape British Columbia 42 B2 51 58N 131 00W
St. Jean Baptiste Manitoba 39 B1 49 15N 97 20W
Saint-Jean-Port-Joli Québec 37 Q8 47 13N 70 16W
Saint-Jean-sur-Richelieu Québec 37 N6 45 18N 73 18W
St.-Jerôme Québec 37 M6 45 47N 74 01W
Saint John New Brunswick 31 E7 45 16N 66 03W
Saint John admin. New Brunswick 31 E7 45 20N 65 50W
St. John r. New Brunswick 31 A2 47 00N 68 00W
St. John Bay Newfoundland 31 C3 50 55N 57 09W
St. John, Cape Newfoundland 31 C2 50 00N 55 32W
St. John, Lake Ontario 38 C3 44 38N 79 19W
St. John's Newfoundland 31 D2 47 34N 52 43W
St. Joseph New Brunswick 31 F7 45 59N 64 30W
St-Joseph-de-la-Beauce Québec 27 46 19N 70 52W
St. Joseph Island Ontario 37 C7 46 13N 83 57W
St. Joseph, Lake Ontario 34 B3 51 05N 90 35W
Saint-Jovite Québec 27 46 07N 74 36W
Saint-Lambert Québec 47 O5 45 30N 73 29W
Saint-Laurent Québec 47 N5 45 30N 73 43W
St. Lawrence, Cape Nova Scotia 31 F7 47 10N 60 40W
St. Lawrence Seaway Canada/U.S.A. 37 L5/M5 44 38N 78 34W
St. Lawrence River (Fleuve Saint-Laurent) Québec 31 C2 46 55N 55 24W
St. Léonard New Brunswick 31 A1 47 10N 67 55W
Saint-Léonard Québec 47 N5 45 34N 73 36W
St. Lewis Newfoundland 30 C3 52 22N 55 41W
St. Lewis River Newfoundland 30 C3 52 20N 56 50W
Saint-Louis-de-Kent New Brunswick 31 E7 46 50N 65 00W
St. Lunaire Newfoundland 30 C3 51 30N 55 29W
St. Malo Manitoba 39 B1 49 20N 96 55W
St. Margarets Bay Nova Scotia 31 F6 44 30N 64 50W
St. Martin, Lake Manitoba 39 B2 51 40N 98 20W
St. Martins New Brunswick 31 E7 45 20N 65 30W
St. Marys Ontario 38 A2 43 15N 81 09W
St. Mary, Cape Nova Scotia 31 E6 44 10N 66 10W
St. Mary's Newfoundland 31 D2 46 55N 53 34W
St. Mary's Bay Newfoundland 31 D2 46 50N 53 45W
St. Mary's Bay Nova Scotia 31 E6 44 20N 66 10W
St. Mary's River Nova Scotia 31 F7 45 20N 62 30W
St.-Maurice admin. Québec 37 M8 47 40N 74 30W
Saint-Michel-des-Saints Québec 37 N7 46 40N 73 55W
St. Norbert Manitoba 48 D2 49 46N 97 12W
Saint-Pacôme Québec 37 R8 47 24N 69 58W
St.-Pamphile Québec 37 R7 46 58N 69 48W
Saint-Pascal Québec 37 R8 47 32N 69 48W
St. Paul Alberta 41 C2 53 59N 111 17W
St. Paul Junction Alberta 48 G5 53 37N 113 20W
St. Peters Nova Scotia 31 F7 45 40N 60 53W
St. Peters Prince Edward Island 31 F7 46 26N 62 35W
Saint-Pie Québec 27 45 31N 72 55W
St. Pierre-Jolys Manitoba 39 B1 49 28N 96 58W
Saint-Prosper Québec 37 Q7 46 12N 70 29W
Saint-Quentin New Brunswick 31 A2 47 30N 67 20W
Saint-Raymond Québec 37 P7 46 54N 71 50W
Saint-Rémi Québec 27 45 15N 73 37W
St.-Romauld Québec 37 P7 46 52N 71 49W
Saint-Siméon Québec 37 R8 47 50N 69 55W
St. Stephen New Brunswick 31 A2 45 12N 67 18W
St. Stephens Newfoundland 31 D2 46 47N 53 37W
St. Theresa Point tn. Manitoba 39 C2 53 45N 94 50W
St. Thomas Ontario 38 A1 42 46N 81 12W
Saint-Tite Québec 37 O7 46 44N 72 34W
Saint-Victor Québec 27 46 09N 70 55W
St. Walburg Saskatchewan 40 B2 53 38N 109 12W
Sakami Québec 33 A3 53 50N 76 10W
Salaberry-de-Valleyfield Québec 37 M6 45 16N 74 11W
Salisbury New Brunswick 31 F7 46 02N 65 03W
Salisbury Island Northwest Territories 45 Q3 63 10N 77 20W
Salluit Québec 32 A5 62 20N 75 40W
Salmo British Columbia 43 E1 49 11N 117 16W
Salmon Arm tn. British Columbia 43 E2 50 41N 119 18W
Salmon Inlet British Columbia 42 H4 49 39N 123 47W
Salmon River British Columbia 42 H4 50 27N 123 34W
Salmon River New Brunswick 31 A2 46 10N 65 50W
Salmon River tn. Nova Scotia 31 E6 44 10N 66 10W
Saltcoats Saskatchewan 40 C2 51 03N 102 12W
Saltspring Island British Columbia 42 H4 48 50N 123 30W
Sambro, Cape Nova Scotia 31 F6 44 30N 63 30W
Sandilands Provincial Forest Manitoba 39 B1 49 30N 96 00W
Sandspit British Columbia 42 B2 53 14N 131 50W
Sandy Bay tn. Saskatchewan 40 C3 55 30N 102 10W
Sandy Lake Newfoundland 31 C2 49 20N 56 50W
Sandy Lake Nova Scotia 47 P6 44 44N 63 40W
Sandy Lake Ontario 34 B3 53 02N 93 00W
Sandy Lake I.R. Ontario 34 B3 53 04N 93 20W
Sanikiluaq Northwest Territories 45 Q2 56 32N 79 14W
San Juan River British Columbia 42 H4 48 37N 124 20W
Sardis British Columbia 42 H4 49 07N 121 57W
Sarnia Ontario 36 D3 42 58N 82 23W
Sasaginnigak Lake Manitoba 39 B2 51 30N 95 30W
Sasamat Lake British Columbia 46 G4 49 19N 122 52W
Saskatchewan province 40
Saskatchewan River Manitoba/Saskatchewan 40 C2 53 50N 103 10W
Saskatoon Saskatchewan 40 B2 52 10N 106 40W
Saturna Island British Columbia 42 H4 48 47N 123 07W
Sauble Falls Provincial Park Ontario 38 A3 44 40N 81 15W
Sauble River Ontario 38 A3 44 36N 81 09W
Saugeen River Ontario 38 A3 44 23N 81 18W
Sault Ste. Marie Ontario 36 B7 46 31N 84 20W
Saunders Lake Alberta 48 G4 53 18N 113 29W
Savant Lake Ontario 34 B3 50 30N 90 25W
Savant Lake tn. Ontario 34 B3 50 14N 90 43W
Sawbill Newfoundland 30 A3 53 37N 66 21W
Sayward British Columbia 43 C2 50 19N 125 58W
Scarborough bor. Metropolitan Toronto Ontario 46 D2 43 44N 79 16W
Scaterie Island Nova Scotia 31 G7 46 00N 59 40W
Schefferville (Kawawachikamach) Québec 32 C3 54 50N 67 00W
Schreiber Ontario 35 C2 48 48N 87 17W
Schultz Lake Northwest Territories 45 M3 64 45N 97 30W
Scotsburn Nova Scotia 31 F7 45 40N 62 51W
Scott Island British Columbia 42 C2 50 48N 128 38W
Scott Lake Saskatchewan 40 B3 59 50N 106 30W
Scugog Island Ontario 38 D3 44 10N 78 52W
Scugog, Lake Ontario 38 D3 44 10N 78 51W
Scugog River Ontario 38 D3 44 16N 78 46W
Seaforth Ontario 38 A2 43 03N 81 24W
Sea Island British Columbia 46 F3 49 11N 123 11W
Seal Cove tn. Newfoundland 31 C2 47 30N 56 00W
Seal Cove tn. Newfoundland 31 C2 49 56N 56 23W
Seal Cove tn. Nova Scotia 31 E6 44 38N 66 52W
Seal Harbour tn. New Brunswick 31 F7 45 10N 61 30W
Seal Lake Newfoundland 30 B3 54 20N 61 40W
Seal River Manitoba 39 B3 58 50N 97 00W
Sechelt British Columbia 42 H4 49 28N 123 46W
Sechelt Peninsula British Columbia 42 H4 49 45N 123 58W
Seine River Manitoba 48 D2 49 46N 97 02W
Selkirk Manitoba 39 B2 50 10N 96 52W
Selkirk Mountains British Columbia 43 E2 51 40N 118 20W
Selkirk Provincial Park Ontario 38 C1 42 50N 80 00W
Selwyn Lake Northwest Territories 44 L3 60 05N 104 25W
Selwyn Mountains Yukon Territory 44 E3 64 30N 134 50W
Semchuck Trail Saskatchewan 40 B3 57 35N 109 20W
Senneterre Québec 37 J9 48 24N 77 16W
Sentinel Peak British Columbia 43 D2 54 56N 121 59W
Sept-Îles tn. Québec 33 C3 50 10N 66 00W
Serpentine British Columbia 46 G3 49 06N 122 46W
Seseganaga Lake Ontario 34 B3 50 00N 90 28W
Setting Lake Manitoba 39 B3 55 10N 98 50W
Seven Islands Bay Newfoundland 30 B4 59 25N 63 45W
70 Mile House British Columbia 43 D2 51 21N 121 25W
Severn Bridge tn. Ontario 38 C3 44 46N 79 20W
Severn Lake Ontario 34 B3 53 54N 90 48W
Severn River Ontario 34 C4 55 30N 88 30W
Severn Sound Ontario 38 C3 44 47N 79 51W
Sexsmith Alberta 41 B3 55 21N 118 47W
Seymour Creek British Columbia 46 F4 49 18N 123 01W
Seymour Inlet British Columbia 43 C2 51 03N 127 05W
Shabaqua Ontario 35 C2 48 35N 89 54W
Shabo Newfoundland 30 A3 53 19N 66 12W
Shabogamo Lake Newfoundland 30 A3 53 15N 66 30W
Shag Harbour tn. Nova Scotia 31 E6 43 30N 65 40W
Shakespeare Ontario 38 B2 43 22N 80 50W
Shaler Mountains Northwest Territories 44 J5 72 10N 111 00W
Shallow Lake tn. Ontario 38 A3 44 38N 81 06W
Shamattawa Manitoba 39 C3 55 51N 92 05W
Shamattawa River Ontario 34 C3 54 05N 85 50W
Shapio Lake Newfoundland 30 B3 55 00N 61 18W
Sharon Ontario 38 C3 44 06N 79 26W
Shaunavon Saskatchewan 40 B1 49 40N 108 25W
Shawanaga Ontario 38 B4 45 32N 81 18W
Shawanaga Inlet Ontario 38 B4 45 26N 80 24W

Shawanaga Island Ontario **38** B4 45 16N 80 33W
Shawinigan Québec **37** O7 46 33N 72 45W
Shawinigan Sud Québec **37** O7 46 33N 72 45W
Shawnigan Lake *tn.* British Columbia **42** H4 48 38N 123 39W
Shawville Québec **37** K6 45 36N 76 30W
Shebandowan Ontario **35** B2 48 38N 90 04W
Shediac New Brunswick **31** F7 46 13N 64 35W
Sheet Harbour *tn.* Nova Scotia **31** F6 44 56N 62 31W
Shefford *admin.* Québec **37** O6 45 30N 72 45W
Shelburne Nova Scotia **31** F6 43 37N 65 20W
Shelburne Ontario **38** B3 44 05N 80 13W
Shelburne *admin.* Nova Scotia **31** E6 43 50N 65 30W
Sheldon Creek Ontario **38** B3 44 05N 80 06W
Shellbrook Saskatchewan **40** B2 53 14N 106 24W
Shelsey River British Columbia **42** B3 58 33N 132 02W
Shelter Bay *tn.* British Columbia **43** E2 50 38N 117 59W
Shepherd Bay Northwest Territories **45** N4 65 00N 90 00W
Sherbrooke Nova Scotia **31** F7 45 10N 61 58W
Sherbrooke Québec **37** P6 45 24N 71 54W
Sherbrooke *admin.* Québec **37** O6 45 20N 72 10W
Sherbrooke Lake Nova Scotia **31** F6 44 40N 64 40W
Sherridon Manitoba **39** A3 55 07N 101 05W
Sherwood Park *tn.* Alberta **48** G5 53 31N 113 19W
Sheshatsheits Newfoundland **30** B3 53 30N 60 10W
Shibogama Lake Ontario **34** C3 53 35N 88 15W
Shipiskan Lake Newfoundland **30** B3 54 39N 62 19W
Shippagan New Brunswick **31** B2 47 45N 64 44W
Shirleys Bay Ontario **47** J2 45 22N 75 54W
Shoal Bay *tn.* Newfoundland **31** D2 49 41N 54 12W
Shoal Harbour *tn.* Newfoundland **31** D2 48 11N 53 59W
Shoal Lake Ontario/Manitoba **34** B2 49 33N 95 01W
Shoal Lake *tn.* Manitoba **39** A2 50 28N 100 35W
Shubenacadie Nova Scotia **31** F7 45 05N 63 25W
Shubenacadie Grand Lake Nova Scotia **47** P7 44 53N 63 37W
Shubenacadie River Nova Scotia **31** F7 45 20N 63 30W
Shunacadie Nova Scotia **31** F7 46 00N 60 40W
Shuswap Lake British Columbia **43** E2 51 00N 119 00W
Sibbald Point Provincial Park Ontario **38** C3 44 15N 79 20W
Sibley *p.p.* Ontario **35** C2 48 10N 88 50W
Sicamous British Columbia **43** E2 50 50N 119 00W
Sidney British Columbia **42** H4 48 39N 123 25W
Sidney Bay Ontario **38** A3 44 55N 81 04W
Sifton Manitoba **39** A2 51 21N 100 09W
Sifton Pass British Columbia **43** C3 57 51N 126 17W
Sikanni Chief British Columbia **43** D3 57 11N 122 43W
Sikanni Chief River British Columbia **43** D3 57 16N 123 25W
Sillery Québec **37** P7 46 46N 71 15W
Silverthrone Mountain British Columbia **43** C2 51 30N 126 03W
Silvertip Mountain British Columbia **42** H4 49 09N 121 12W
Simcoe Ontario **38** B1 42 50N 80 19W
Simcoe *admin.* Ontario **38** C3 44 32N 79 54W
Simcoe, Lake Ontario **38** C3 44 23N 79 18W
Similkameen River British Columbia **42** H4 48 55N 119 25W
Simonette River Alberta **41** B2 54 25N 118 20W
Simpson Bay Northwest Territories **44** J4 69 00N 113 40W
Simpson Peninsula Northwest Territories **45** O4 68 34N 88 45W
Simpson Strait Northwest Territories **45** M4 68 27N 97 45W
Sioux Lookout Ontario **34** B3 50 07N 91 54W
Sioux Narrows Ontario **34** B2 49 23N 94 08W
Sipiwesk Manitoba **39** B3 55 27N 97 24W
Sipiwesk Lake Manitoba **39** B3 55 10N 98 50W
Sir Alexander, Mount British Columbia **43** D2 53 52N 120 25W
Sir James McBrien, Mount Yukon Territory **44** E3 62 15N 128 01W
Sir Wilfred Laurier, Mount British Columbia **43** E2 52 45N 119 40W
Sisipuk Lake Manitoba **39** A3 55 30N 101 40W
Sistonens Corners *tn.* Ontario **35** C2 48 35N 89 40W
Six Mile Lake Provincial Park Ontario **38** C3 44 50N 79 50W
Skagit Valley Recreation Area British Columbia **42** H4 49 06N 121 09W
Skeena Mountains British Columbia **42** C3 57 30N 129 59W
Skeena River British Columbia **42** C2 54 15N 129 15W
Skidegate British Columbia **42** B2 53 13N 132 02W
Skihist Mountain British Columbia **42** H5 50 12N 122 53W
Skownan Manitoba **39** B2 51 58N 99 35W
Slave Lake *tn.* Alberta **41** C3 55 17N 114 43W
Slave River Alberta/Northwest Territories **44** J3 60 30N 112 50W
Slocan British Columbia **43** E1 49 46N 117 28W
Slocan Lake British Columbia **43** E1 49 50N 117 20W
Smallwood Reservoir Alberta/Newfoundland **30** B3 54 10N 63 50W
Smeaton Saskatchewan **40** C2 53 30N 104 50W
Smith Alberta **41** C3 55 10N 114 02W
Smith Arm *b.* Northwest Territories **44** G4 66 15N 124 00W
Smith Bay Northwest Territories **45** Q6 77 12N 78 50W
Smithers British Columbia **43** C2 54 45N 127 10W
Smith Point Nova Scotia **31** F7 45 52N 63 25W
Smith River British Columbia **43** C3 59 56N 126 28W
Smiths Falls *tn.* Ontario **37** K5 44 45N 76 01W
Smithville Ontario **38** C2 43 06N 79 32W
Smokey Newfoundland **30** C3 54 28N 57 14W
Smoky, Cape Nova Scotia **31** F7 46 40N 60 20W
Smoky Lake *tn.* Alberta **41** C2 54 07N 112 28W
Smoky River Alberta **41** B3 55 30N 117 59W
Smooth Rock Falls *tn.* Ontario **35** D2 49 17N 81 38W
Smoothrock Lake Ontario **34** C3 50 30N 89 30W
Smoothstone Lake Saskatchewan **40** B2 54 40N 106 30W
Snake Creek Ontario **38** A3 44 23N 81 16W
Snake River Yukon Territory **44** E4 65 20N 133 30W
Snare Lakes *tn.* Northwest Territories **44** J3 64 10N 114 20W
Snegamook Lake Newfoundland **30** B3 54 33N 61 27W
Snowbird Lake Northwest Territories **45** L3 60 41N 102 56W
Snowdrift Northwest Territories **44** J3 62 24N 110 44W
Snow Lake *tn.* Manitoba **39** A2 54 56N 100 00W
Snug Harbour *tn.* Newfoundland **30** C3 52 53N 55 52W
Snug Harbour *tn.* Ontario **38** B4 45 22N 80 17W
Soldier Lake Nova Scotia **47** P7 44 49N 63 33W
Somerset Manitoba **39** B1 49 26N 98 39W
Somerset Island Northwest Territories **45** N5 73 15N 93 30W
Sonora Island British Columbia **42** G5 50 21N 125 13W
Sooke British Columbia **42** H4 48 20N 123 42W
Sorel Québec **37** N7 46 03N 73 06W
Soulanges *admin.* Québec **37** M6 45 15N 74 20W
Sounding Creek Alberta **41** C2 51 40N 111 05W
Sounding Lake Alberta **41** C2 52 08N 110 29W
Souris Manitoba **39** A1 49 38N 100 17W
Souris Prince Edward Island **31** F7 46 22N 62 16W
Souris River Manitoba/North Dakota U.S.A. **39** A1 49 30N 100 50W
Souris River Saskatchewan **40** C1 49 20N 103 30W
Southampton Ontario **38** A3 44 29N 81 22W
Southampton Island Northwest Territories **45** P3 64 50N 85 00W
South Aulatsivik Island Newfoundland **30** B4 56 46N 61 30W
South Bay *tn.* Ontario **34** B3 51 03N 92 45W
South Brookfield Nova Scotia **31** E6 44 23N 65 58W
Southend Saskatchewan **40** C3 56 20N 103 14W
Southern Indian Lake Manitoba **39** B3 57 00N 98 00W
Southey Saskatchewan **40** C2 50 57N 104 33W
Southgate River British Columbia **42** H5 50 54N 124 42W
South Gloucester Ontario **47** K2 45 17N 75 34W
South Henik Lake Northwest Territories **45** M3 61 30N 97 30W
South Knife River Manitoba **39** B3 58 20N 96 10W
South Maitland River Ontario **38** A2 43 39N 81 27W
South Moose Lake Manitoba **39** A2 53 40N 100 10W
South Moresby National Park Reserve British Columbia **42** B2 52 30N 130 40W
South Nahanni River Northwest Territories **44** F3 61 30N 123 22W
South Porcupine Ontario **35** D2 48 28W 81 13W
Southport Prince Edward Island **31** F7 46 10N 63 05W
South River *tn.* Ontario **36** G6 45 50N 79 23W
South Saskatchewan River Saskatchewan **40** A2 50 50N 110 00W
South Saugeen River Ontario **38** B3 44 00N 80 45W
South Seal River Manitoba **39** B3 58 00N 99 10W
South Twin Island Northwest Territories **34** E3 53 10N 79 50W
Southwest Miramichi River New Brunswick **31** A2 46 30N 66 50W
Spanish Ontario **36** D7 46 12N 82 12W
Spanish River Ontario **36** E7 46 32N 81 57W
Sparrow Lake Ontario **38** C3 44 47N 79 23W
Sparwood British Columbia **43** F1 49 55N 114 53W
Spatsizi Plateau Wilderness Park British Columbia **43** C3 57 30N 128 30W
Spear Harbour *tn.* Newfoundland **30** C3 52 25N 55 42W
Speed River Ontario **38** B2 43 29N 80 17W
Speers Saskatchewan **40** B2 52 43N 107 32W
Spence Bay *tn.* Northwest Territories **45** N4 69 30N 93 20W
Spicer Islands Northwest Territories **45** Q4 63 19N 71 52W
Spirit River *tn.* Alberta **41** B3 55 46N 118 51W
Spiritwood Saskatchewan **40** B2 53 24N 107 33W
Split, Cape Nova Scotia **31** F7 45 20N 64 30W
Split Lake Manitoba **39** B3 56 10N 95 50W
Split Lake *tn.* Manitoba **39** B3 56 16N 96 08W
Spotted Island Newfoundland **30** C3 53 31N 55 47W
Sprague Manitoba **39** B1 49 02N 95 36W
Springdale Newfoundland **31** C2 49 30N 56 04W
Springfield Nova Scotia **31** F6 44 37N 64 52W
Springfield Ontario **38** B1 42 49N 80 57W
Springfield *admin.* Manitoba **48** E2 49 48N 96 57W
Springhill Nova Scotia **31** F7 45 40N 64 04W
Spring Water Provincial Park Ontario **38** C3 44 30N 79 45W
Sproat Lake British Columbia **42** G4 49 16N 125 05W
Spruce Grove Alberta **41** C2 53 32N 113 55W
Spruce Woods Provincial Forest Manitoba **39** B1 49 40N 99 40W
Spruce Woods Provincial Park Manitoba **39** B1 49 40N 99 10W
Spry Harbour *tn.* Nova Scotia **31** F6 44 50N 62 45W
Spuzzum British Columbia **42** H4 49 40N 121 25W
Squamish British Columbia **42** H4 49 41N 123 11W
Squamish River British Columbia **42** H4 49 42N 123 11W
Square Island Newfoundland **30** C3 52 45N 55 52W
Stanley New Brunswick **31** A2 46 17N 66 45W
Stanstead *admin.* Québec **37** O6 45 10N 72 10W
Star City Saskatchewan **40** C2 52 52N 104 20W
Stave Lake British Columbia **42** H4 49 21N 122 19W
Stayner Ontario **38** B3 44 25N 80 06W
Stefansson Island Northwest Territories **45** L5 73 20N 105 45W
Steinbach Manitoba **39** B1 49 32N 96 40W
Stellarton Nova Scotia **31** F7 45 34N 62 40W
Stephens Lake Manitoba **39** B3 56 30N 95 00W
Stephenville Newfoundland **31** C2 48 33N 57 32W
Stephenville Crossing Newfoundland **31** C2 48 30N 58 26W
Stettler Alberta **41** C2 52 19N 112 43W
Stevenson Lake Manitoba **39** B2 53 50N 95 50W
Stewart British Columbia **42** C3 55 07N 129 58W
Stewart Yukon Territory **44** D3 63 15N 139 15W
Stewart Crossing Yukon Territory **44** D3 60 37N 128 37W
Stewart River Yukon Territory **44** D3 63 40N 138 20W
Stewiacke Nova Scotia **31** F7 45 09N 63 22W
Stikine British Columbia **42** B2 56 42N 131 45W
Stikine Ranges *mts.* British Columbia **42** B3 57 00N 127 20W
Stikine River British Columbia/Alaska U.S.A. **42** C3 57 00N 132 00W
Stikine River Recreation Area British Columbia **42** C3 58 07N 129 35W
Stillwater British Columbia **42** H4 49 46N 124 19W
Stirling Alberta **41** C1 49 34N 112 30W
Stirling Ontario **37** J5 44 18N 77 33W
Stittsville Ontario **47** J2 45 16N 75 54W
Stokes Bay Ontario **38** A3 45 00N 81 23W
Stone Mountain Provincial Park British Columbia **43** D3 58 35N 124 40W
Stonewall Manitoba **39** B2 50 08N 97 20W
Stoney Creek *tn.* Ontario **38** C2 43 13N 79 46W
Stony Lake Manitoba **39** B3 58 50N 98 30W
Stony Lake Ontario **36** H5 44 33N 78 06W
Stony Mountain *tn.* Manitoba **39** B2 50 04N 97 17W
Stony Plain *tn.* Alberta **41** C2 53 32N 114 00W
Stony Rapids *tn.* Saskatchewan **40** B3 59 14N 105 48W
Storkerson Peninsula Northwest Territories **44** K5 72 30N 106 30W
Stormont, Dundas and Glengarry *admin.* Ontario **37** M6 45 10N 75 00W
Stormy Lake Ontario **34** B2 49 23N 92 18W
Stouffville Ontario **38** C2 43 59N 79 15W
Stoughton Saskatchewan **40** C1 49 40N 103 00W
Stout Lake Ontario **34** B3 52 08N 94 35W
Strasbourg Saskatchewan **40** C2 51 05N 104 58W
Stratford Ontario **38** B2 43 07N 81 00W
Strathcona Alberta **48** G5 53 31N 113 29W
Strathcona County Alberta **48** G5 53 33N 113 16W
Strathcona Provincial Park British Columbia **42** G4 49 40N 125 30W
Strathmore Alberta **41** C2 51 03N 113 23W
Strathnaver British Columbia **43** D2 53 21N 122 32W
Strathroy Ontario **38** A1 42 57N 81 40W
Streetsville Ontario **38** C2 43 25N 79 44W
Stuart Island *tn.* British Columbia **42** G5 50 22N 125 09W
Stuart Lake British Columbia **43** D2 54 35N 124 40W
Stuart River British Columbia **43** D2 54 10N 124 05W
Stupart River Manitoba **39** C3 55 30N 94 30W
Sturgeon Bay Manitoba **39** B2 51 50N 98 00W
Sturgeon Creek Manitoba **48** C2 49 56N 97 25W
Sturgeon Falls *tn.* Ontario **36** G7 46 22N 79 57W
Sturgeon Lake Alberta **41** B3 55 06N 117 32W
Sturgeon Lake Ontario **38** D3 50 00N 91 00W
Sturgeon Landing Saskatchewan **40** C2 54 18N 101 49W
Sturgeon Municipal District Alberta **48** F5 53 38N 113 30W
Sturgeon Point *tn.* Ontario **38** D3 44 28N 78 42W
Sturgeon River Alberta **48** F5 53 38N 113 38W
Sturgeon River Ontario **35** D2 47 00N 80 30W
Sturgeon River Ontario **38** C3 44 36N 79 46W
Sturgeon River Saskatchewan **40** B2 53 30N 106 20W
Sturgis Saskatchewan **40** C2 51 58N 102 32W
Styx River Ontario **38** B3 44 15N 80 58W
Sudbury Ontario **36** E7 46 30N 81 01W
Sudbury *admin.* Ontario **36** E7 47 10N 82 00W
Sudbury, Regional Municipality of Ontario **36** E7 46 32N 81 00W
Suggi Lake Saskatchewan **40** C2 54 20N 103 10W
Sullivan Bay *tn.* British Columbia **43** C2 50 55N 126 52W
Sullivan Lake Alberta **41** C2 52 00N 112 00W
Sultan Ontario **35** D2 47 36N 82 45W
Summer Beaver Ontario **34** C3 52 50N 88 30W
Summerford Newfoundland **31** D2 49 29N 54 47W
Summerland British Columbia **43** E1 49 35N 119 41W
Summerside Prince Edward Island **31** F7 46 24N 63 46W
Summerville Newfoundland **31** D2 48 27N 53 33W
Sunbury *admin.* New Brunswick **31** A2 45 50N 66 40W
Sundre Alberta **41** C2 51 48N 114 38W
Sundridge Ontario **36** G6 45 46N 79 24W
Sunnyside Newfoundland **31** D2 47 51N 53 55W
Superb Mountain British Columbia **42** H5 50 48N 124 41W
Superior, Lake Canada/U.S.A. **35** B2 48 00N 88 00W
Surrey British Columbia **42** H4 49 08N 122 50W
Sussex New Brunswick **31** E7 45 43N 65 32W
Sussex Corner New Brunswick **31** E7 45 40N 65 30W
Sutherland Saskatchewan **40** B2 52 10N 106 35W
Sutton Ontario **38** C3 44 18N 79 22W
Sutton Québec **37** O6 45 05N 72 36W
Sutton Lake Ontario **34** D3 54 15N 84 44W
Sutton River Ontario **34** D3 54 50N 84 30W
Svendsen Peninsula Northwest Territories **45** P6 77 45N 84 00W
Sverdrup Islands Northwest Territories **45** M6 79 00N 96 00W
Swan Hills Alberta **41** B2 54 45N 115 45W
Swan Hills *tn.* Alberta **41** B2 54 43N 115 24W
Swan Lake Manitoba **39** A2 52 20N 100 50W
Swannell Range *mts.* British Columbia **43** C3 56 38N 126 10W
Swan River *tn.* Manitoba **39** A2 52 06N 101 17W
Swift Current *tn.* Saskatchewan **40** B2 50 17N 107 49W
Swift Current Creek Saskatchewan **40** B1 49 40N 108 30W
Swinburne, Cape Northwest Territories **45** M5 71 13N 98 33W
Swindle Island British Columbia **42** C2 52 33N 128 25W
Sydenham River Ontario **36** D3 42 40N 82 20W
Sydney Nova Scotia **31** F7 46 10N 60 10W
Sydney Mines *tn.* Nova Scotia **31** F7 46 16N 60 15W
Sylvan Lake *tn.* Alberta **41** C2 52 19N 114 05W

T

Taber Alberta **41** C1 49 48N 112 09W
Table Bay Newfoundland **30** C3 53 40N 56 25W
Tache *admin.* Manitoba **48** E2 49 47N 96 43W
Tadoussac Québec **37** R9 48 09N 69 43W
Tadule Lake Manitoba **39** B3 58 30N 98 50W
Tagish Lake British Columbia **42** B3 59 50N 134 33W
Tahiryuak Lake Northwest Territories **44** J5 70 56N 112 15W
Tahoe Lake Northwest Territories **44** K4 70 15N 108 45W
Tahsis British Columbia **43** C1 49 50N 126 39W
Tahtsa Lake British Columbia **43** C2 53 41N 127 30W
Takla Lake British Columbia **43** C3 55 12N 125 45W
Takla Landing British Columbia **43** C3 55 27N 125 59W
Taku Arm *l.* British Columbia **42** B4 60 10N 134 05W
Taku River British Columbia **42** B3 58 43N 133 20W
Talbot Lake Manitoba **39** B2 54 00N 99 40W
Taltson River Northwest Territories **44** J3 60 40N 111 30W
Taseko Mountain British Columbia **43** D2 51 12N 123 07W
Taseko River British Columbia **43** D2 51 35N 123 40W
Tasisuak Lake Newfoundland **30** B4 56 45N 62 46W
Tasiujaq Québec **32** B4 58 40N 70 00W
Tatamagouche Nova Scotia **31** F7 45 43N 63 19W
Tatamagouche Bay Nova Scotia **31** F7 45 45N 63 15W
Tathlina Lake Northwest Territories **44** H3 60 33N 117 39W
Tatla Lake British Columbia **43** D2 51 59N 124 25W
Tatlatui Provincial Park British Columbia **43** C3 57 00N 127 20W
Tatlayoko Lake British Columbia **43** D2 51 39N 124 23W
Tatnam, Cape Manitoba **39** C3 57 25N 91 00W
Tatshenshini River British Columbia **42** A3 59 30N 137 30W
Tavistock Ontario **38** B2 43 19N 80 50W
Taylor British Columbia **43** D3 56 09N 120 40W
Taylor Head *c.* Nova Scotia **31** F6 44 40N 62 30W
Tazin Lake Saskatchewan **40** B3 59 50N 109 10W
Tazin River Saskatchewan **40** B3 59 50N 109 30W
Tecumseh Ontario **52** F2 42 01N 82 45W
Teeswater Ontario **38** A2 43 59N 81 18W
Teeswater River Ontario **38** A3 44 07N 81 22W
Tehek Lake Northwest Territories **45** N3 64 55N 95 38W
Telegraph Creek *tn.* British Columbia **42** B3 57 56N 131 11W
Telkwa British Columbia **43** C2 54 44N 127 05W
Temagami Ontario **35** E2 47 04N 79 47W
Temagami, Lake Ontario **36** F7 47 00N 80 05W
Témiscaming Québec **36** G7 46 44N 79 05W
Témiscamingue *admin.* Québec **36** G7 46 44N 79 06W
Templeton Québec **47** K2 45 29N 75 36W
Terence Bay Nova Scotia **31** F6 44 20N 63 40W
Terrace British Columbia **43** C2 54 31N 128 32W
Terra Cotta Ontario **38** C2 43 42N 79 55W
Terra Nova National Park Newfoundland **31** D2 48 40N 54 20W
Terrebonne Québec **37** N6 45 42N 73 37W
Terrebonne *admin.* Québec **37** M7 46 00N 74 30W
Terrence Bay *tn.* Ontario **35** C2 48 47N 87 06W
Terrenceville Newfoundland **31** D2 47 40N 54 44W
Teslin Yukon Territory **44** E3 60 10N 132 42W
Teslin Lake British Columbia/Yukon Territory **44** E3 59 50N 132 25W
Teslin River British Columbia **42** B3 59 20N 131 50W
Tetachuck Lake British Columbia **43** C2 53 20N 126 00W
Teulon Manitoba **39** B2 50 26N 97 18W
Texada Island British Columbia **42** H4 49 30N 124 30W
Thamesford Ontario **38** A2 43 03N 81 00W
Thames River Ontario **36** E3 42 19N 82 27W
Thelon River Northwest Territories **44** L3 64 40N 102 30W
Thelon River Game Sanctuary Northwest Territories **45** L3 64 30N 103 00W
The Pas Manitoba **39** A2 53 49N 101 14W
Thesiger Bay Northwest Territories **44** F5 71 30N 124 05W
Thessalon Ontario **37** C7 46 15N 83 34W
Thetford Mines *tn.* Québec **37** P7 46 06N 71 18W
Thicket Portage Manitoba **39** B3 55 20N 97 42W
Thirty Thousand Islands Ontario **36** F6 45 56N 80 57W
Thlewiaza River Northwest Territories **45** M3 60 50N 98 00W
Thompson Manitoba **39** B3 55 45N 97 54W
Thompson River British Columbia **43** D2 50 12N 121 30W
Thomsen River Northwest Territories **44** H5 73 00N 119 50W
Thorah Island Ontario **38** C3 44 27N 79 13W
Thorhild Alberta **41** C2 54 10N 113 07W
Thornbury Ontario **38** B3 44 34N 80 27W
Thornhill *tn.* Ontario **46** C2 43 49N 79 26W
Thorold Ontario **38** C2 43 08N 79 14W
Thorsby Alberta **41** C2 53 14N 114 03W
Thousand Islands Ontario **37** K5 44 22N 75 55W
Three Hills *tn.* Alberta **41** C2 51 42N 113 16W
Three Mile Plains *tn.* Nova Scotia **31** F6 44 55N 64 10W
Thunder Bay *tn.* Ontario **35** C2 48 27N 89 12W
Thurso Québec **37** L6 45 38N 75 19W
Thutade Lake British Columbia **43** C3 56 59N 126 40W
Tide Head *tn.* New Brunswick **31** A2 47 58N 66 49W
Tignish Prince Edward Island **31** F7 46 58N 64 03W
Tikkoatokak Bay Newfoundland **30** B4 56 42N 62 12W
Tilbury Ontario **36** D3 42 16N 82 26W
Tilbury Island British Columbia **46** F3 49 08N 123 02W
Tilden Lake *tn.* Ontario **36** G7 46 37N 79 39W
Tillsonburg Ontario **38** B1 42 53N 80 44W
Timberlea Nova Scotia **31** F6 44 40N 63 45W
Timiskaming, Lake *(Lac Témiscamingue)* Ontario **35** E2 46 52N 79 15W
Timmins Ontario **35** D2 48 30N 81 20W
Tinniswood, Mount British Columbia **42** H5 50 19N 123 47W
Tip Top Mountain Ontario **35** C2 48 16N 85 59W
Tisdale Saskatchewan **40** C2 52 51N 104 01W
Tiverton Ontario **38** A3 44 15N 81 33W
Toad River *tn.* British Columbia **43** C3 58 50N 125 12W
Toba Inlet British Columbia **42** H5 50 25N 124 30W
Toba River British Columbia **42** H5 50 31N 124 18W
Tobermory Ontario **38** A4 45 15N 81 39W
Tobin Lake Saskatchewan **40** C2 53 30N 103 30W
Tofield Alberta **41** C2 53 22N 112 40W
Tofino British Columbia **43** C1 49 05N 125 51W
Tomlinson, Mount British Columbia **43** C3 55 30N 127 30W
Torbay Newfoundland **31** D2 47 40N 52 44W
Tor Bay Nova Scotia **31** F7 45 15N 61 15W
Torch River Saskatchewan **40** C2 53 40N 103 50W
Tornado Mountain Alberta/British Columbia **43** F1 49 57N 114 35W
Torngat Mountains *(Monts Torngat)* Newfoundland/Québec **30** B4 59 00N 63 40W
Toronto Ontario **46** C1 43 42N 79 46W
Toronto Islands Ontario **46** C1 43 42N 79 25W
Tottenham Ontario **38** C3 44 02N 79 48W
Touraine Québec **47** K2 45 29N 75 42W
Tracadie New Brunswick **31** B2 47 32N 64 57W
Tracadie Nova Scotia **31** F7 45 38N 61 40W
Tracy New Brunswick **31** A2 45 41N 66 42W
Tracy Québec **37** N7 45 59N 73 04W
Trail British Columbia **43** E1 49 04N 117 39W
Tramping Lake Saskatchewan **40** B2 52 10N 109 10W
Trans-Canada Highway **10** N3 50 00N 109 00W
Transcona Manitoba **48** D2 49 54N 97 01W
Treherne Manitoba **39** B1 49 39N 98 41W
Trembleur Lake British Columbia **43** D2 54 50N 124 55W
Trent Canal Ontario **38** C3 44 13N 79 23W
Trenton Nova Scotia **31** F7 45 37N 62 38W
Trenton Ontario **36** J5 44 07N 77 34W
Trepassey Newfoundland **31** D2 46 45N 53 20W
Trinity Bay Newfoundland **31** D2 47 50N 53 40W
Trinity East Newfoundland **31** D2 48 23N 53 20W
Triton Newfoundland **31** C2 49 30N 55 30W
Trochu Alberta **41** C2 51 50N 113 13W
Trois-Pistoles Québec **37** R9 48 08N 69 10W
Trois-Rivières *tn.* Québec **37** O7 46 21N 72 34W
Trout Creek *tn.* Ontario **36** G6 45 59N 79 22W
Trout Lake Ontario **34** B3 51 20N 93 20W
Trout Lake *tn.* Alberta **41** B3 56 30N 114 32W
Trout Lake *tn.* Northwest Territories **44** G3 61 00N 121 30W

Trout River *tn.* Newfoundland **31** C2 49 29N 58 08W
Troy Nova Scotia **31** F7 45 40N 61 30W
Truro Nova Scotia **31** F7 45 24N 63 18W
Tuchitua Yukon Territory **44** F3 61 20N 129 00W
Tuktoyaktuk Northwest Territories **44** E4 69 24N 133 01W
Tulameen River British Columbia **42** H4 49 30N 120 58W
Tulemalu Lake Northwest Territories **45** M3 62 58N 99 25W
Tumbler Ridge *tn.* British Columbia **43** D3 55 10N 121 01W
Tungsten Northwest Territories **44** F3 61 59N 128 09W
Tunungayualok Island Newfoundland **30** B4 56 05N 61 05W
Turkey Point Ontario **38** B1 42 37N 80 20W
Turkey Point *tn.* Ontario **38** B1 43 41N 80 20W
Turkey Point Provincial Park Ontario **38** B1 42 45N 80 20W
Turnagain River British Columbia **42** C3 58 25N 129 08W
Turnavik Island Newfoundland **30** C4 55 18N 59 21W
Turner Valley *tn.* Alberta **41** C2 50 40N 114 17W
Turnor Lake Saskatchewan **40** B3 56 35N 109 10W
Turnor Lake *tn.* Saskatchewan **40** B3 56 25N 108 40W
Turtleford Saskatchewan **40** B2 53 25N 108 58W
Turtle Mountain Provincial Park Manitoba **39** A1 49 00N 100 10W
Tusket Nova Scotia **31** E6 43 53N 65 58W
Tuxedo Manitoba **48** D2 49 51N 97 13W
Tuya River British Columbia **42** B3 58 46N 130 50W
Tweed Ontario **37** J5 44 29N 77 19W
Tweedsmuir Provincial Park British Columbia **43** C2 52 50N 126 20W
Twelve Mile Bay Ontario **38** B4 45 05N 80 00W
Twenty Mile Creek Ontario **38** C2 43 09N 79 48W
Twillingate Newfoundland **31** D2 49 39N 54 46W
Twin Falls *tn.* Newfoundland **30** A3 53 30N 64 32W
Twin Islands Northwest Territories **34** E3 53 20N 80 10W
Two Hills *tn.* Alberta **41** C2 53 43N 111 45W
Tyne Valley *tn.* Prince Edward Island **31** F7 46 36N 63 57W

U
Ucluelet British Columbia **42** G4 48 55N 125 34W
Ugjoktok Bay Newfoundland **30** B3 55 08N 60 30W
Uivak, Cape Newfoundland **30** B4 58 29N 62 34W
Ukasiksalik Island Newfoundland **30** B4 55 55N 60 47W
Umingmaktok Northwest Territories **44** K4 67 48N 108 00W
Umiujaq Québec **32** A4 56 00N 76 44W
Ungava Bay *(Baie d'Ungava)* Northwest Territories/Québec **45** S2 58 00N 72 30W
Unionville Ontario **46** C2 43 51N 79 19W
United States Range *mts.* Northwest Territories **45** R7 82 25N 68 00W
Unity Saskatchewan **40** B2 52 27N 109 10W
Upper Arrow Lake British Columbia **43** E2 50 25N 117 56W
Upper Campbell Lake British Columbia **42** G4 49 57N 125 36W
Upper Foster Lake Saskatchewan **40** B3 56 40N 105 35W
Upper Liard Yukon Territory **44** F3 60 00N 129 20W
Upper Musquodoboit Nova Scotia **31** F7 45 10N 62 58W
Upper Sackville Nova Scotia **47** P7 44 48N 63 42W
Upper Salmon Reservoir Newfoundland **31** C2 48 20N 55 30W
Upper Windigo Lake Ontario **34** B3 52 30N 91 35W
Uranium City Saskatchewan **40** B3 59 32N 108 43W
Utikuma Lake Alberta **41** B3 55 50N 115 25W
Uxbridge Ontario **38** C3 44 07N 79 09W

V
Valdes Island British Columbia **42** H4 49 05N 123 40W
Val-d'Or *tn.* Québec **33** A2 48 07N 77 47W
Valemount British Columbia **43** E2 52 50N 119 15W
Valhalla Provincial Park British Columbia **43** E1 49 00N 118 00W
Valleyview Alberta **41** B3 55 04N 117 17W
Val Marie Saskatchewan **40** B1 49 15N 107 44W
Vancouver British Columbia **42** H4 49 13N 123 06W
Vancouver Island British Columbia **42** G4 48 55N 124 33W
Vanderhoof British Columbia **43** D2 54 00N 124 00W
Vanier Ontario **47** K2 45 27N 75 40W
Vankleek Hill Ontario **37** M6 45 31N 74 39W
Vanscoy Saskatchewan **40** B2 52 01N 106 59W
Vansittart Island Northwest Territories **45** P4 65 50N 84 00W
Varennes Québec **47** O6 45 39N 73 26W
Vaudreuil *admin.* Québec **37** M6 45 20N 74 20W
Vaughan Ontario **38** C2 43 39N 79 25W
Vauxhall Alberta **41** C2 50 04N 112 07W
Vegreville Alberta **41** C2 53 30N 112 03W
Verdun Québec **47** N4 45 28N 73 34W
Vermilion Alberta **41** C2 53 22N 110 51W
Vermilion Bay *tn.* Ontario **34** B2 49 51N 93 21W
Vermilion Pass Alberta/British Columbia **41** B2 51 14N 116 03W
Vermilion River Alberta **41** C2 53 40N 111 25W
Vernon British Columbia **43** E2 50 17N 119 19W
Victoria British Columbia **42** H4 48 26N 123 20W
Victoria Newfoundland **31** D2 47 46N 53 14W
Victoria Prince Edward Island **31** F7 46 10N 63 30W
Victoria *admin.* New Brunswick **31** A2 47 10N 67 30W
Victoria *admin.* Nova Scotia **31** F7 46 30N 60 30W
Victoria *admin.* Ontario **38** C3 44 45N 79 03W
Victoria Bridge *tn.* Nova Scotia **31** F7 45 50N 60 20W
Victoria Harbour Ontario **38** C3 44 45N 79 45W
Victoria Island Northwest Territories **44** J5 70 45N 115 00W
Victoria Lake Newfoundland **31** C2 48 18N 57 20W
Victoria River Newfoundland **31** C2 48 30N 57 50W
Victoriaville Québec **37** P7 46 04N 71 57W
Vienna Ontario **38** B1 42 39N 80 47W
Vieux-Fort Québec **33** E3 51 59N 57 59W
Viking Alberta **41** C2 53 06N 111 46W
Virden Manitoba **39** A1 49 50N 100 57W
Virgil Ontario **38** C2 43 13N 79 07W
Virginiatown Ontario **35** E2 48 08N 79 35W
Viscount Melville Sound Northwest Territories **44** J5 74 10N 105 00W
Voisey Bay Newfoundland **30** B4 56 15N 61 50W
Vulcan Alberta **41** C2 50 24N 113 15W

W
Wabakimi *provincial park* Ontario **34** B3 50 30N 90 50W
Wabakimi Lake Ontario **34** B3 50 38N 89 45W
Wabana Newfoundland **31** D2 47 38N 52 57W
Wabasca-Desmarais Alberta **41** C3 55 59N 113 50W
Wabasca River Alberta **41** B3 57 30N 115 15W
Wabowden Manitoba **39** B2 54 57N 98 38W
Wabuk Point Ontario **34** C4 55 20N 85 05W
Wabush Newfoundland **30** A3 52 55N 66 52W
Wabush Lake Newfoundland **30** A3 53 05N 66 52W
Wabuskasing Ontario **34** B3 50 20N 93 10W
W.A.C. Bennet Dam British Columbia **43** D3 55 00N 122 11W
Waddington, Mount British Columbia **43** C2 51 22N 125 14W
Wade Lake Newfoundland **30** A3 54 20N 65 38W
Wadena Saskatchewan **40** C2 51 57N 103 58W
Wager Bay Northwest Territories **45** F4 66 00N 89 00W
Waglisla British Columbia **43** C2 52 05N 128 10W
Wainfleet Ontario **38** C1 42 52N 79 22W
Wainwright Alberta **41** C2 52 49N 110 52W
Wakaw Saskatchewan **40** B2 52 40N 105 45W
Wakefield Québec **37** L6 45 38N 75 56W
Waldheim Saskatchewan **40** B2 52 39N 106 40W
Wales Island Northwest Territories **45** O4 68 01N 86 40W
Walker Lake Manitoba **39** B2 54 40N 96 40W
Walkerton Ontario **38** A3 44 08N 81 10W
Wallace Nova Scotia **31** F7 45 48N 63 26W
Wallaceburg Ontario **36** D3 42 34N 82 22W
Walton Nova Scotia **31** F7 45 14N 64 00W
Wanapitei Lake Ontario **36** E7 46 45N 80 45W
Wanham Alberta **41** B3 55 44N 118 24W
Wanless Manitoba **39** A2 54 11N 101 21W
Wapawekka Hills Saskatchewan **40** C2 54 50N 104 30W
Wapawekka Lake Saskatchewan **40** C3 55 00N 104 30W
Wapella Saskatchewan **40** C1 50 16N 101 59W
Wapiti River Alberta **41** B2 54 40N 119 50W
Wardlow Alberta **41** C2 50 54N 111 33W
Wardsville Ontario **36** E3 42 39N 81 45W
Warman Saskatchewan **40** B2 52 19N 104 34W
Warner Alberta **41** C1 49 17N 112 12W
Warrender, Cape Northwest Territories **45** P5 74 28N 81 46W
Warren Landing *tn.* Manitoba **39** B2 53 42N 97 54W
Warwick Québec **27** 45 57N 71 59W
Wasaga Beach *tn.* Ontario **38** B3 44 31N 80 02W
Wasaga Beach Provincial Park Ontario **38** B3 44 30N 80 05W
Wascana Creek Saskatchewan **40** C2 50 20N 104 20W
Wasekamio Lake Saskatchewan **40** B3 56 50N 108 30W
Washago Ontario **38** C3 44 45N 79 20W
Waskaiowaka Lake Manitoba **39** B3 56 40N 96 40W
Waskesiu Lake *tn.* Saskatchewan **40** B2 53 55N 106 00W
Waterbury Lake Saskatchewan **40** C3 58 10N 104 55W
Waterdown Ontario **38** C2 43 20N 79 54W
Waterford Ontario **38** B1 42 55N 80 19W
Waterhen Manitoba **39** B2 51 50N 99 30W
Waterhen Lake Manitoba **39** B2 52 00N 99 20W
Waterhen River Saskatchewan **40** B2 54 25N 108 50W
Waterloo Ontario **38** B2 43 28N 80 32W
Waterloo Québec **27** 45 21N 72 31W
Waterloo *admin.* Ontario **38** B2 43 30N 80 46W
Waterton Lakes National Park Alberta **41** C1 49 00N 114 45W
Watford Ontario **36** E3 42 57N 81 53W
Wathaman Lake Saskatchewan **40** C3 57 00N 104 10W
Wathaman River Saskatchewan **40** C3 56 50N 104 50W
Watrous Saskatchewan **40** B2 51 40N 105 29W
Watson Saskatchewan **40** C2 52 09N 104 31W
Watson Lake *tn.* Yukon Territory **44** F3 60 07N 128 49W
Waubuno Channel Ontario **38** B4 45 11N 80 16W
Waverley Nova Scotia **31** F6 44 48N 63 38W
Waverley Game Sanctuary Nova Scotia **47** P7 44 49N 63 31W
Wawa Ontario **35** D2 48 04N 84 49W
Wawota Saskatchewan **40** C1 49 56N 102 00W
Weagamow Lake *tn.* Ontario **34** B3 52 53N 91 22W
Weaver Lake Manitoba **39** B2 52 40N 96 40W
Webbwood Ontario **36** E7 46 16N 81 53W
Webequie Ontario **34** C3 52 59N 87 21W
Wedge Mountain British Columbia **42** H5 50 07N 122 49W
Wedgeport Nova Scotia **31** E6 43 44N 66 00W
Wekusko Manitoba **39** B2 54 31N 99 45W
Wekusko Lake Manitoba **39** B2 54 30N 99 40W
Weldon Saskatchewan **40** B2 53 00N 105 08W
Welland Ontario **38** C1 42 59N 79 14W
Welland Canal Ontario **38** C2 43 14N 79 13W
Welland River Ontario **38** C2 43 05N 79 46W
Wellesley Ontario **38** B2 43 27N 80 46W
Wellington Nova Scotia **31** F6 44 50N 63 35W
Wellington Ontario **37** J4 43 57N 77 21W
Wellington *admin.* Ontario **38** B2 43 46N 80 41W
Wellington Channel Northwest Territories **45** N6 75 00N 93 00W
Wells British Columbia **43** D2 53 00N 121 30W
Wells Gray Provincial Park British Columbia **43** D2 52 00N 120 00W
Wells Lake Manitoba **39** A3 57 10N 100 30W
Wembley Alberta **41** B3 55 09N 119 08W
Wemindji *(Nouveau-Comptoir)* Québec **33** A3 52 59N 78 50W
Wenebegon Lake Ontario **35** D2 47 23N 83 06W
Wentworth Nova Scotia **31** F7 45 39N 63 35W
Werner Lake Ontario **34** B3 50 27N 94 54W
Wesleyville Newfoundland **31** D2 49 09N 53 34W
West Bay *tn.* Newfoundland **30** C3 54 08N 57 26W
West Bay *tn.* Nova Scotia **31** F7 45 40N 61 10W
West Don River Ontario **46** B2 43 49N 79 31W
West Duffins Creek Ontario **46** D2 43 53N 79 10W
Western River Northwest Territories **44** K4 66 40N 107 00W
Westham Island British Columbia **46** F3 49 05N 123 10W
West Highland Creek Ontario **46** C2 43 46N 79 15W
West Humber River Ontario **46** B2 43 48N 79 43W
Westlock Alberta **41** C2 54 09N 113 52W
West Lorne Ontario **38** A1 42 36N 81 35W
Westmorland *admin.* New Brunswick **31** F7 46 10N 64 50W
Westmount Nova Scotia **31** F7 46 10N 60 10W
Westmount Québec **47** N4 45 29N 73 37W
West Point Prince Edward Island **31** F7 46 38N 64 26W
Westport Nova Scotia **31** E6 44 20N 66 20W
Westport Ontario **37** K5 44 41N 76 24W
West Road River British Columbia **43** D2 53 12N 123 50W
West St. Modeste Newfoundland **30** C3 51 36N 56 42W
West St. Paul *admin.* Manitoba **48** D2 49 59N 97 08W
West Thurlow Island British Columbia **42** G5 50 27N 125 35W
West Vancouver British Columbia **42** H4 49 22N 123 11W
Westville Nova Scotia **31** F7 45 34N 62 44W
Wetaskiwin Alberta **41** C2 52 57N 113 20W
Weyburn Saskatchewan **40** C1 49 39N 103 51W
Weymouth Nova Scotia **31** E6 44 26N 66 00W
Whale Cove *tn.* Northwest Territories **45** N3 62 10N 92 36W
Whaletown British Columbia **42** G5 50 06N 125 02W
Whapmagoostui *see* Kuujjuarapik
Wheatley Ontario **36** D3 42 06N 82 27W
Wheeler River Saskatchewan **40** B3 57 30N 105 10W
Whippoorwill Bay Ontario **38** A4 45 01N 81 15W
Whirl Creek Ontario **38** A2 43 29N 81 07W
Whistler British Columbia **42** H5 50 08N 122 58W
Whitby Ontario **38** D2 43 52N 78 56W
White Bay Newfoundland **31** C3 50 00N 56 32W
White Bear Island Newfoundland **30** B4 57 54N 61 42W
White Bear Lake Newfoundland **30** C3 54 32N 59 30W
Whitecap Mountain British Columbia **42** H5 50 44N 122 30W
White City Saskatchewan **40** C2 50 35N 104 20W
Whitecourt Alberta **41** B2 54 10N 115 41W
Whitefish Ontario **36** E7 46 23N 81 22W
Whitefish Bay Ontario **35** D2 46 38N 84 33W
Whitefish Lake Northwest Territories **44** K3 62 30N 106 40W
Whitefish Lake Ontario **35** D2 48 05N 84 10W
Whitefox River Saskatchewan **40** C2 53 25N 104 55W
White Handkerchief, Cape Newfoundland **30** B4 59 17N 63 23W
Whitehorse Yukon Territory **44** E3 60 41N 135 08W
White Lake Ontario **35** C2 48 50N 85 30W
Whitemouth Manitoba **39** B1 49 58N 95 59W
Whitemouth Lake Manitoba **39** B1 49 10N 96 00W
Whitemouth River Manitoba **39** B1 49 50N 97 10W
Whitemud Creek Alberta **48** F4 53 18N 113 38W
White Otter Lake Ontario **34** B2 49 07N 91 52W
White Pass British Columbia **42** A3 59 37N 135 07W
White River Ontario **35** C2 48 30N 86 20W
White River *tn.* Ontario **35** C2 48 35N 85 16W
White River Yukon Territory **44** D3 62 25N 140 05W
White Rock British Columbia **42** H4 49 02N 122 50W
Whitesail Lake British Columbia **43** C2 53 25N 127 10W
Whitesand River Alberta **41** B3 59 00N 115 00W
Whiteshell Provincial Forest Manitoba **39** B1 49 50N 95 40W
Whiteshell Provincial Park Manitoba **39** B2 50 00N 95 20W
Whitewater Lake Ontario **34** C3 50 40N 89 30W
Whitewood Saskatchewan **40** C2 50 19N 102 16W
Whitney Ontario **36** H6 45 29N 78 15W
Whitworth Québec **37** R8 47 42N 69 17W
Wholdaia Lake Northwest Territories **44** L3 60 43N 104 10W
Whycocomagh Nova Scotia **31** F7 45 58N 61 08W
Wiarton Ontario **38** A3 44 44N 81 19W
Wickham Québec **27** 45 45N 72 31W
Wildcat Hill Wilderness Area Saskatchewan **40** C2 53 20N 102 20W
Wildwood Alberta **41** B2 53 37N 115 14W
Wilkie Saskatchewan **40** B2 52 27N 108 42W
William, Lake Nova Scotia **47** P7 44 46N 63 34W
William River Saskatchewan **40** B3 58 50N 108 55W
Williams Lake *tn.* British Columbia **43** D2 52 08N 122 07W
Williston Lake British Columbia **43** D3 56 00N 124 00W
Willmore Wilderness Park Alberta **41** B2 53 40N 119 30W
Will, Mount British Columbia **42** C3 57 30N 128 44W
Willowbunch Lake Saskatchewan **40** B1 49 20N 105 50W
Willow Lake Northwest Territories **44** H3 60 00N 115 00W
Wilson Ontario **38** D2 43 15N 78 50W
Winchester Ontario **37** L6 45 06N 75 21W
Windermere Lake Ontario **35** D2 47 58N 83 47W
Windigo Québec **37** N8 47 45N 73 22W
Windigo Lake Ontario **34** B3 52 35N 91 32W
Windsor Newfoundland **31** C2 48 57N 55 40W
Windsor Nova Scotia **38** C2 43 12N 79 38W
Windsor Ontario **36** D3 42 18N 83 00W
Windsor Québec **37** O6 45 35N 72 01W
Windsor Junction Nova Scotia **47** P7 44 48N 63 38W
Winefred Lake Alberta **41** C3 55 30N 110 31W
Wingham Ontario **38** A2 43 54N 81 19W
Winisk Lake Ontario **34** C3 52 55N 87 22W
Winisk River Ontario **34** C3 54 50N 87 00W
Winisk River Provincial Park Ontario **34** C3 52 50N 87 30W
Winkler Manitoba **39** B1 49 12N 97 55W
Winnipeg Manitoba **39** B1 53 49N 97 10W
Winnipeg Beach *tn.* Manitoba **39** B2 50 30N 97 00W
Winnipeg, Lake Manitoba **39** B2 53 00N 97 00W
Winnipegosis Manitoba **39** B2 51 40N 99 59W
Winnipegosis, Lake Manitoba **39** A2 52 10N 100 00W
Winnipeg River Manitoba **39** B2 50 20N 95 30W
Winokapau Lake Newfoundland **30** B3 53 10N 62 52W
Winona Ontario **38** C2 43 12N 79 38W
Winterburn Alberta **48** F5 53 33N 113 41W
Witless Bay *tn.* Newfoundland **31** D2 47 16N 52 50W
Wolfe *admin.* Québec **37** P6 45 40N 71 40W
Wolfe Island Ontario **37** K5 44 31N 75 59W
Wolfville Nova Scotia **31** F7 45 06N 64 22W
Wollaston, Cape Northwest Territories **44** H5 71 06N 118 04W
Wollaston Lake Saskatchewan **40** C3 58 20N 103 00W
Wollaston Lake *tn.* Saskatchewan **40** C3 58 05N 103 38W
Wollaston Peninsula Northwest Territories **44** J4 70 00N 115 00W
Wolseley Saskatchewan **40** C2 50 25N 103 15W
Woodbridge Ontario **46** B2 43 47N 79 36W
Wood Buffalo National Park Alberta/Northwest Territories **42** J2 59 00N 112 30W
Woodfibre British Columbia **42** H4 49 36N 123 00W
Wood Islands *tn.* Prince Edward Island **31** F7 45 50N 62 40W
Woodland Caribou Provincial Park Ontario **34** B3 51 10N 94 20W
Wood Mountain Saskatchewan **40** B1 49 15N 106 20W
Woodside Nova Scotia **47** P6 44 39N 63 31W
Woods Lake Newfoundland **30** B3 54 30N 65 13W
Woods, Lake of the Ontario **34** B2 49 15N 94 45W
Woodstock New Brunswick **31** A2 46 10N 67 36W
Woodstock Ontario **38** B2 43 07N 80 46W
Woodville Ontario **38** D3 44 24N 78 44W
Wright Corners Ontario **38** D2 43 10N 78 45W
Wrigley Northwest Territories **44** G3 63 16N 123 39W
Wrong Lake Manitoba **39** B2 52 40N 96 10W
Wunnummin Lake Ontario **34** C3 52 55N 89 10W
Wyebridge Ontario **38** C3 44 41N 79 53W
Wynniatt Bay Northwest Territories **44** J5 72 45N 110 30W
Wynyard Saskatchewan **40** C2 51 50N 104 10W

Y
Yale British Columbia **42** H4 49 31N 121 29W
Yamachiche Québec **27** 46 17N 72 50W
Yamaska *admin.* Québec **37** O7 46 00N 72 50W
Yarmouth Nova Scotia **31** E6 43 50N 66 08W
Yarmouth *admin.* Nova Scotia **31** E6 44 50N 65 40W
Yates River Alberta **41** B3 59 40N 116 25W
Yathkyed Lake Northwest Territories **45** M3 62 40N 98 00W
Yellow Grass Saskatchewan **40** C1 49 49N 104 11W
Yellowhead Highway **10** N3 54 00N 109 00W
Yellowhead Pass Alberta/British Columbia **41** B2 52 53N 118 28W
Yellowhead River Alberta **41** C2 53 20N 110 45W
Yellowknife Northwest Territories **44** J3 62 30N 114 29W
Yellowknife River Northwest Territories **44** J3 62 35N 114 10W
Yoho National Park British Columbia **43** E2 51 00N 116 00W
York New Brunswick **31** A2 46 10N 66 50W
York *admin.* Ontario **38** C2 43 57N 79 39W
York *bor.* Metropolitan Toronto Ontario **46** C2 43 41N 79 28W
York, Cape Northwest Territories **45** O5 73 48N 87 00W
York Factory Manitoba **39** C3 57 08N 92 25W
Yorkton Saskatchewan **40** C2 51 12N 102 29W
Youbou British Columbia **42** H4 48 52N 124 12W
Young Saskatchewan **40** B2 51 45N 105 45W
Yukon River Yukon Territory Canada/Alaska U.S.A. **44** D3 63 00N 138 50W
Yukon Territory *territory* **44**

Z
Zeballos British Columbia **43** C1 49 57N 126 10W
Zürich Ontario **38** A2 43 25N 81 37W

A

Aachen Germany **76** C5 50 46N 6 06E
Aaper Wald *hills* Germany **76** H2 51 17N 6 50E
Aba Nigeria **106** G9 5 06N 7 21E
Ābādān Iran **93** G5 30 20N 48 15E
Abadla Algeria **106** E14 31 01N 2 45W
Abaetetuba Brazil **68** H12 1 45S 48 54W
Abakan Russia **91** P5 53 43N 91 25E
Abakan *r.* Russia **91** O5 52 00N 88 00E
Abancay Peru **68** C10 13 37S 72 52W
Abashiri Japan **100** D3 44 02N 144 17E
Abbeville France **76** C4 50 06N 1 51E
Abbotstown Pennsylvania U.S.A. **64** C2 39 54N 77 00W
Ābd al Kūrī *i.* Socotra **93** H1 11 55N 52 20E
Abéché Chad **106** J10 13 49N 20 49E
Abeokuta Nigeria **106** E9 7 10N 3 26E
Aberdeen Hong Kong U.K. **98** B1 22 14N 114 09E
Aberdeen Maryland U.S.A. **64** D2 39 31N 76 10W
Aberdeen Scotland **78** I9 57 10N 2 04W
Aberdeen South Dakota U.S.A. **63** G6 45 28N 98 30W
Aberdeen Washington U.S.A. **62** B6 46 58N 123 49W
Aberystwyth Wales **78** G4 52 25N 4 05W
Abhā Saudi Arabia **92** F2 18 14N 42 31E
Abidjan Côte d'Ivoire **106** E9 5 19N 4 01W
Abilene Texas U.S.A. **62** G3 32 27N 99 45W
Absaroka Range *mts.* U.S.A. **62** D6 45 00N 110 00W
Abu Dhabi *see* Abū Zabī
Abu Durba Egypt **92** N9 28 29N 33 20E
Abu Hamed Sudan **92** D2 19 32N 33 20E
Abuja Nigeria **106** G9 9 10N 7 11E
Abu Kamal Syria **92** F5 34 29N 40 56E
Abu Kebîr Egypt **107** R3 30 44N 31 48E
Abunã Brazil **68** D11 9 41S 65 20W
Abu Tig Egypt **92** D4 27 06N 31 17E
Abū Zabī *(Abu Dhabi)* United Arab Emirates **93** H3 24 28N 54 25E
Acambaro Mexico **66** D4 20 01N 100 42W
Acaponeta Mexico **66** C4 22 30N 105 25W
Acapulco Mexico **66** E3 16 51N 99 56W
Açari *r.* Brazil **69** P2 22 50S 43 22W
Acarigua Venezuela **68** D14 9 35N 69 12W
Acatlán Mexico **66** E3 18 12N 98 02W
Acayucán Mexico **66** E3 17 59N 94 58W
Accra Ghana **106** E9 5 33N 0 15W
Achacachi Bolivia **68** D9 16 01S 68 44W
Achill Island Irish Republic **78** A5 53 55N 10 05W
Achinsk Russia **91** P6 56 20N 90 33E
Acklins Island The Bahamas **67** J4 22 30N 74 30W
Aconcagua *mt.* Argentina **69** C6 32 40S 70 02W
Acre *admin.* Brazil **68** C11 8 30S 71 30W
Acton England **82** B3 51 31N 0 17W
Ada Oklhoma U.S.A. **63** G3 34 47N 96 41W
Adachi Japan **101** C4 35 46N 139 48E
Adaga *r.* Spain **77** B3 40 45N 4 45W
Adamawa Mountains *mts.* Africa **102** 7 00N 13 00E
Adams Massachusetts U.S.A. **65** G5 42 38N 73 08W
Adam's Bridge India/Sri Lanka **95** D1 9 10N 79 30E
Adana Turkey **92** E6 37 00N 35 19E
Adapazarl Turkey **92** D7 40 45N 30 23E
Adare, Cape Antarctica **117** 71 30S 170 24E
Ad Dahna *geog. reg.* Saudi Arabia **106** O13 26 00N 47 00E
Ad Dakhla Western Sahara **106** B12 23 50N 15 58W
Ad Dammām Saudi Arabia **93** H4 26 25N 50 06E
Ad Dawḥah *(Doha)* Qatar **93** H4 25 15N 51 36E
Ad Dilam Saudi Arabia **93** G3 23 59N 47 06E
Ad Dir'īyah Saudi Arabia **93** G3 24 45N 46 32E
Addis Ababa *see* Ādīs Ābeba
Addison New York U.S.A. **64** C5 42 07N 77 16W
Ad Dīwānīyah Iraq **92** F5 32 00N 44 57E
Adelaide Australia **110** F3 34 56S 138 36E
Aden Yemen Republic **93** G1 12 50N 45 03E
Aden, Gulf of **93** G1 12 30N 47 30E
Adirondack Mountains New York U.S.A. **65** F6 43 15N 74 40W
Ādīs Ābeba *(Addis Ababa)* Ethiopia **106** M9 9 03N 38 42E
Admiralty Island Alaska U.S.A. **42** B3 52 45N 134 30W
Admiralty Islands Papua New Guinea **110** H9 2 30S 147 00E
Adoni India **95** D3 15 38N 77 16E
Adra Spain **77** B2 36 45N 3 01W
Adrar Algeria **106** E13 27 51N 0 19W
Adrian Michigan U.S.A. **36** C2 41 55N 84 01W
Adriatic Sea Mediterranean Sea **81** B3/C3 43 00N 15 00E
Adwa Ethiopia **92** E1 14 12N 38 56E
Aegean Sea Mediterranean Sea **81** D2 39 00N 24 00E
AFGHANISTAN **93** J5
Afognak Island Alaska U.S.A. **10** E4 58 10N 152 50W
Afyon Turkey **92** D6 38 46N 30 32E
Agadès Niger **106** G11 17 00N 7 56E
Agadir Morocco **106** D14 30 30N 9 40W
Agalega Islands Seychelles **112** E5 10 00S 56 00E
Agana Guam **114** E9 13 28N 144 45E
Agano *r.* Japan **100** C2 37 50N 139 30E
Agartala India **95** G4 23 49N 91 15E
Agboyi Creek *r.* Nigeria **107** V3 6 37N 3 30E
Agege Nigeria **107** V3 6 41N 3 24E
Agen France **77** C3 44 12N 0 38E
Ageo Japan **100** L2 35 57N 139 36E
Ago Japan **100** H1 34 20N 136 50E
Agout *r.* France **77** C3 43 50N 1 50E
Agra India **95** D5 27 09N 78 00E
Agram *see* Zagreb
Agri *r.* Italy **81** C3 40 00N 16 00E
Agrigento Italy **81** B2 37 19N 13 35E
Agrinion Greece **81** D2 38 38N 21 25E
Aguadas Colombia **68** B14 5 36N 75 30W
Aguadilla Puerto Rico **67** K3 18 27N 67 08W
Agua Prieta Mexico **66** C6 31 20N 109 32W
Aguascalientes Mexico **66** D4 21 51N 102 18W
Agueda *r.* Spain **77** A3 40 50N 6 50W
Aguilas Spain **77** B2 37 25N 1 35W
Agulhas Basin Indian Ocean **112** A2 45 00S 20 00E
Agulhas, Cape Republic of South Africa **107** J1 34 50S 20 00E
Ahklun Mountains Alaska U.S.A. **10** C4 60 00N 161 00W
Ahmadabad India **95** C4 23 03N 72 40E
Ahmadnagar India **95** C3 19 08N 74 48E
Ahrensfelde Germany **83** G2 52 35N 13 35E
Ahuachapán El Salvador **66** G2 13 57N 89 49W
Ahvāz Iran **93** G5 31 17N 48 43E
Aichi *pref.* Japan **100** J2 35 00N 137 15E
Ain *r.* France **77** D4 46 30N 5 30E
Aïn Beïda Algeria **77** D2 35 44N 7 22E
Aïn Sefra Algeria **106** E14 32 45N 0 35W
Aïn Temouchent Algeria **77** B2 35 18N 1 09W
Aïr *mts.* Niger **106** G11 19 10N 8 20E
Aire *r.* England **78** J5 53 40N 1 00W
Aiviekste *r.* Latvia **79** F2 57 00N 26 40E
Aix-en-Provence France **77** D3 43 31N 5 27E
Aiyion Greece **81** D2 38 15N 22 05E
Aizu-Wakamatsu Japan **100** C2 37 30N 139 58E
Ajaccio Corsica **77** D3 41 55N 8 43E
Ajdābiyā Libya **106** J14 30 46N 20 14E
Ajegunle Nigeria **107** V3 6 24N 3 24E
Ajlūn Jordan **92** O11 32 20N 35 45E
Ajmer India **95** C5 26 29N 74 40E
Akabira Japan **100** D3 43 40N 141 55E
Akaroa New Zealand **111** B2 43 50S 172 59E
Akashi Japan **100** F1 34 39N 135 00E
Akechi Japan **100** J2 35 19N 137 22E
Aketi Zaïre **106** J8 2 42N 23 51E
Akhelóös *r.* Greece **81** D2 39 00N 21 00E
Akhisar Turkey **68** E2 38 54N 27 50E
Akhtubinsk Russia **90** F4 48 20N 46 10E
Akita Japan **100** D2 39 44N 140 05E
'Akko Israel **92** O11 32 55N 35 04E
Akobo Sudan **106** L9 7 50N 33 05E
Akola India **95** D4 20 40N 77 05E
Ak'ordat Ethiopia **92** E2 15 26N 37 45E
Ákra Akrítas *c.* Greece **81** D2 36 43N 21 52E
Ákra Kafirévs *c.* Greece **81** D2 38 10N 24 35E
Ákra Maléa *c.* Greece **81** D2 36 27N 23 12E
Akranes Iceland **79** H6 64 19N 22 05W
Ákra Taínaron *c.* Greece **81** D2 36 23N 22 29E
Akron New York U.S.A. **64** B6 43 02N 78 30W
Akron Ohio U.S.A. **63** J5 41 04N 81 31W
Akron Pennsylvania U.S.A. **64** D3 40 09N 76 12W
Aksum Ethiopia **92** E1 14 10N 38 45E
Aktyubinsk Kazakhstan **91** H5 50 16N 57 13E
Akureyri Iceland **79** I7 65 41N 18 04W
Alabama *r.* Alabama U.S.A. **63** I3 31 00N 88 00W
Alabama *state.* U.S.A. **63** I3 32 00N 87 00W
Alagoas *admin.* Brazil **68** J11 9 30S 37 00W
Alagoinhas Brazil **68** J10 12 09S 38 21W
Alagón *r.* Spain **77** A3 40 00N 6 30W
Alajuela Costa Rica **67** H2 10 00N 84 12W
Alakanuk Alaska U.S.A. **10** C5 62 39N 164 48W
Al'Amārah Iraq **93** G5 31 51N 47 10E
Alameda California U.S.A. **49** B3 37 44N 122 14W
Alameda County California U.S.A. **49** C2 37 35N 122 11W
Alameda Creek California U.S.A. **49** C2 37 35N 122 03W
Alamo California U.S.A. **49** C3 37 51N 122 03W
Alamosa Colorado U.S.A. **62** E4 37 28N 105 54W
Åland *i.* Finland **79** D3 60 15N 20 00E
Alanya Turkey **92** D6 36 32N 32 02E
Al Artāwī yah Saudi Arabia **93** G4 26 31N 45 21E
Ala Shan *mts.* China **97** K7/K6 40 00N 102 30E
Alaska *state* U.S.A. **10** D5 63 10N 157 30W
Alaska, Gulf of Alaska U.S.A. **44** F4 58 00N 147 00W
Alaska Peninsula Alaska U.S.A. **10** D4 50 30N 159 00W
Alaska Range *mts.* Alaska U.S.A. **44** B3/C3 62 30N 152 30W
Alatna Alaska U.S.A. **10** E6 66 33N 152 49W
Al'Ayn United Arab Emirates **93** I3 24 10N 55 43E
Alay Range *mts.* Kirgyzstan/Tajikistan **91** L2 39 30N 72 00E
Albacete Spain **77** B2 39 00N 1 52W
Alba Iulia Romania **81** D4 46 04N 23 33E
ALBANIA **81** C3
Albany California U.S.A. **49** B3 37 53N 122 17W
Albany Georgia U.S.A. **63** J3 31 37N 84 10W
Albany New York U.S.A. **65** G5 42 40N 73 49W
Albany Oregon U.S.A. **62** B5 44 38N 123 07W
Al Başrah Iraq **93** G5 30 30N 47 50E
Al Baydā' Libya **106** J14 32 00N 21 30E
Albert, Lake Uganda/Zaïre **106** L8 2 00N 31 00E
Albert Lea Minnesota U.S.A. **63** H5 43 38N 93 16W
Albi France **77** C3 43 56N 2 08E
Albion Michigan U.S.A. **36** B3 42 14N 84 45W
Albion New York U.S.A. **64** B6 43 14N 78 12W
Al Bi'r Saudi Arabia **92** P9 28 50N 36 16E
Ålborg Denmark **80** A6 57 05N 9 50E
Albuquerque New Mexico U.S.A. **62** E4 35 05N 106 38W
Al Buraymī Oman **93** I3 24 16N 55 48E
Albury Australia **110** H2 36 03S 146 53E
Alcalá de Henares Spain **77** B3 40 28N 3 22W
Alcamo Italy **81** B2 37 58N 12 58E
Alcañiz Spain **77** B3 41 03N 0 09W
Alcatraz Island California U.S.A. **49** B3 37 50N 122 26W
Alcázar de San Juan Spain **77** B2 39 24N 3 12W
Alcira Spain **77** B2 39 10N 0 27W
Alcoy Spain **77** B2 38 42N 0 29W
Alcudia Balearic Islands **77** C2 39 51N 3 06E
Aldabra Islands Indian Ocean **107** O6 9 00S 46 00E
Aldama Mexico **66** E4 22 54N 98 05W
Aldan Russia **89** O7 58 44N 124 22E
Aldan *r.* Russia **89** P7 59 00N 132 30E
Alderney *i.* Channel Islands British Isles **78** I1 49 43N 2 12W
Alegrete Brazil **69** F7 29 45S 55 40W
Aleksandrovsk-Sakhalinskiy Russia **89** Q6 50 55N 142 12E
Alençon France **76** C4 48 25N 0 05E
Alenuihaha Channel Hawaiian Islands **115** Y18 20 20N 156 20W
Aleppo *see* Halab
Alès France **77** C3 44 08N 4 05E
Alessándria Italy **81** A3 44 55N 8 37E
Ålesund Norway **79** B3 62 28N 6 11E
Aleutian Basin Pacific Ocean **114** I13 54 00N 178 00W
Aleutian Range *mts.* Alaska U.S.A. **10** D4 56 30N 159 00W
Aleutian Ridge Pacific Ocean **114/115** I13 53 55N 178 00W
Aleutian Trench Pacific Ocean **114/115** I13 50 55N 178 00W
Alexander Archipelago *is.* Alaska U.S.A. **10** H4 57 00N 137 30W
Alexander Bay *tn.* Republic of South Africa **107** I2 28 40S 16 30E
Alexander Island Antarctica **117** 71 00S 70 00W
Alexandra New Zealand **111** A1 45 14S 169 26E
Alexandria *(El Iskandarîya)* Egypt **92** C5 31 13N 29 55E
Alexandria Louisiana U.S.A. **63** H3 31 19N 92 29W
Alexandria Romania **81** E3 43 59N 25 19E
Alexandroúpolis Greece **81** E3 40 51N 25 53E
Alfambra *r.* Spain **77** B3 40 35N 1 00W
Alfiós *r.* Greece **81** D2 37 00N 22 00E
Al Fuḥayḥīl Kuwait **93** Q4 29 07N 47 02E
Algeciras Spain **77** A2 36 08N 5 27W
Alger *(Algiers)* Algeria **106** F15 36 50N 3 00E
ALGERIA **106** E13
Alghero Italy **81** A3 40 34N 8 19E
Algiers *see* Alger
Al Ḥadīthah Iraq **92** F5 34 06N 42 25E
Alhambra California U.S.A. **51** B3 34 05N 118 10W
Al Hariq Saudi Arabia **93** G3 23 34N 46 35E
Al Hasakah Syria **92** F6 36 32N 40 44E
Al Hillah Iraq **92** F5 32 28N 44 29E
Al Hoceima Morocco **77** B2 35 14N 3 56W
Al Hudaydah Yemen Republic **92** F1 14 50N 42 58E
Al Hufūf Saudi Arabia **93** G4 25 20N 49 34E
Aliákmon *r.* Greece **81** D3 40 00N 22 00E
Alicante Spain **77** B2 38 21N 0 29W
Alice Texas U.S.A. **63** G2 27 45N 98 06W
Alice Springs Australia **110** E5 23 42S 133 52E
Aligarh India **95** D5 27 54N 78 04E
Aling Kangri *mt.* China **96** F5 32 51N 81 03E
Alipur India **94** K2 22 32N 88 19E
Alison Park Pennsylvania U.S.A. **53** E3 40 30N 79 45W
Alivérion Greece **81** D2 38 24N 24 02E
Al Jahrah Kuwait **93** G4 29 22N 47 40E
Al Jawf Libya **106** J12 24 12N 23 18E
Al Jawf Saudi Arabia **92** E4 29 49N 39 52E
Al Jubayl Saudi Arabia **93** G4 26 59N 49 40E
Aljustrel Portugal **77** A2 37 52N 8 10W
Al Khums Libya **106** H14 32 39N 14 16E
Alkmaar Netherlands **76** C5 52 38N 4 44E
Al Kufrah Oasis Libya **106** J12 24 10N 23 15E
Al Kuwayt Kuwait **93** G4 29 20N 48 00E
Al Kūt Iraq **93** G5 32 30N 45 51E
Al Lādhiqīyah Syria **92** E6 35 31N 35 47E
Allagash River Maine U.S.A. **37** R7 46 45N 69 20W
Allahabad India **95** E5 25 27N 81 50E
Allantown New York U.S.A. **64** B5 42 05N 78 05W
Allegany New York U.S.A. **64** B5 42 06N 78 30W
Alleghenies *see* Allegheny Mountains
Allegheny Mountains Pennsylvania U.S.A. **64** B3 40 30N 78 30W
Allegheny Reservoir U.S.A. **64** B4 41 00N 79 00W
Allegheny River Pennsylvania U.S.A. **64** B4 41 57N 78 26W
Allegheny County Pennsylvania U.S.A. **53** D1 40 18N 80 06W
Allende Mexico **66** D5 28 22N 100 50W
Allen Park Michigan U.S.A. **52** E2 42 14N 83 11W
Allentown Pennsylvania U.S.A. **64** E3 40 37N 75 30W
Alleppey India **95** D1 9 30N 76 22E
Alliance Nebraska U.S.A. **62** F5 42 08N 102 54W
Alliance Ohio U.S.A. **36** E1 40 56N 81 06W
Allier *r.* France **77** C4 46 40N 3 00E
Al Līth Saudi Arabia **92** F3 20 10N 40 20E
Alloa Scotland **78** H8 56 07N 3 49W
Alma Michigan U.S.A. **36** B4 43 23N 84 40W
Alma-Ata Kazakhstan **91** M3 43 19N 76 55E
Almada Portugal **77** A2 38 40N 9 09W
Almadén Spain **77** B2 38 47N 4 50W
Al Madīnah Saudi Arabia **92** E3 24 30N 39 35E
Almalyk Uzbekistan **91** K3 40 50N 69 40E
Al Manāmah Bahrain **93** H4 26 12N 50 38E
Almansa Spain **77** B2 38 52N 1 06W
Almanzora *r.* Spain **77** B2 37 15N 2 10W
Al Mayādīn Syria **92** F6 35 01N 40 28E
Almería Spain **77** B2 36 50N 2 26W
Al'met'yevsk Russia **90** G5 54 50N 52 22E
Älmhult Sweden **79** C2 56 32N 14 10E
Al Miqdādīyah Iraq **92** F5 33 58N 44 58E
Almodôvar Portugal **77** A2 37 31N 8 03W
Al Mubarraz Saudi Arabia **93** G4 25 26N 49 37E
Al Mukallā Yemen Republic **93** G1 14 34N 49 09E
Al Mukhā Yemen Republic **92** F1 13 20N 43 16E
Alor *i.* Indonesia **99** G2 8 00S 124 30E
Alpena Michigan U.S.A. **36** C6 45 04N 83 27W
Alpes Maritimes *mts.* France/Italy **77** D3 44 15N 6 45E
Alpha New Jersey U.S.A. **64** E3 40 40N 75 11W
Alpha Cordillera *ridge* Arctic Ocean **116** 85 00N 120 00W
Alpi Carniche *mts.* Europe **81** B4 46 00N 13 00E
Alpi Dolomitiche *mts.* Italy **81** B4 46 00N 12 00E
Alpi Lepontine *mts.* Switzerland **77** D4 46 26N 8 30E
Alpine Texas U.S.A. **62** F3 30 22N 103 40W
Alpi Pennine *mts.* Switzerland/Italy **77** D4 45 55N 7 30E
Alpi Retiche *mts.* Switzerland **77** D4/5 46 25N 9 45E
Alps *mts.* Europe **77** D4 46 00N 7 30E
Al Qunfudhah Saudi Arabia **92** F2 19 09N 41 07E
Alstead New Hampshire U.S.A. **65** H6 43 10N 72 24W
Alta Norway **79** E4 69 57N 23 10E
Altadena California U.S.A. **51** B3 34 12N 118 08W
Altaelv *r.* Norway **79** E4 69 50N 23 30E
Alta Gracia Argentina **69** E6 31 42S 64 25W
Altai *mts.* Mongolia **96** H8 47 00N 92 30E
Altamaha *r.* Georgia U.S.A. **63** J3 32 00N 82 00W
Altamura Italy **81** C3 40 49N 16 34E
Altay China **96** G8 47 48N 88 07E
Altay *mts.* Russia **91** O5 51 00N 89 00E
Altenessen Germany **76** J2 51 29N 7 02E
Altiplano *plat.* South America **68** D9 17 00S 67 00W
Altlandsberg Germany **83** G2 52 34N 13 45E
Alto da Boa Vista Brazil **69** P2 22 58S 43 17W
Alto Molocue Mozambique **107** M4 15 38S 37 42E
Altoona Pennsylvania U.S.A. **64** B3 40 32N 78 23W
Altun Shan *mts.* China **96** G6 37 30N 86 00E
Altus Oklahoma U.S.A. **62** G3 34 39N 99 21W
Alur Setar Malaysia **99** C5 6 06N 100 23E
Alva Oklahoma U.S.A. **62** G4 36 48N 98 40W
Alvarado California U.S.A. **49** C2 37 36N 122 05W
Al Wajh Saudi Arabia **92** E4 26 16N 36 28E
Alwar India **95** D5 27 32N 76 35E
Alyat Azerbaijan **90** F2 39 57N 49 25E
Amadeus, Lake Australia **110** E5 24 00S 132 30E
Amadi Sudan **106** L9 5 32N 30 20E
Amagansett New York U.S.A. **65** H3 40 59N 72 09W
Amagasaki Japan **100** G1 34 42N 135 23E
Amakusa-shotō *is.* Japan **100** A1 32 50N 130 05E
Amapá Brazil **68** G13 2 00N 50 50W
Amapá *admin.* Brazil **68** G13 2 00N 52 30W
Amarillo Texas U.S.A. **62** F4 35 14N 101 50W
Amatsukominato Japan **100** M2 35 08N 140 14E
Amazon *see* Rio Amazonas
Amazonas *admin.* Brazil **68** D12/F12 4 30S 65 00W
Amazon, Mouths of the Brazil **68** H13 1 00N 50 00W
Ambala India **95** D6 30 19N 76 49E
Ambarchik Russia **89** S9 69 39N 162 27E
Ambato Ecuador **68** B12 1 18S 78 39W
Ambon Indonesia **99** H3 3 41S 128 10E
Ambovombe Madagascar **107** O2 25 10S 46 06E
Amderma Russia **89** I9 66 44N 61 35E
Amdo China **96** H5 32 22N 91 07E
Ameca Mexico **66** D4 20 34N 104 03W
American Falls *tn.* Idaho U.S.A. **62** D5 42 47N 112 50W
American Samoa Pacific Ocean **115** J6 15 00S 170 00W
Amersham England **82** A3 51 40N 0 38W
Amery Ice Shelf Antarctica **117** 70 00S 70 00E
Amesbury Massachusetts U.S.A. **65** K5 42 50N 70 56W
Amfipolis Greece **81** D3 40 48N 23 52E
Amga Russia **89** P8 61 51N 131 59E
Amga *r.* Russia **89** P8 60 00N 130 00E
Amgun' *r.* Russia **89** P6 52 00N 137 00E
Amherst Massachusetts U.S.A. **65** H5 42 23N 72 31W
Amherst New Hampshire U.S.A. **65** J5 42 52N 71 36W
Amiens France **76** C4 49 54N 2 18E
Amirante Islands Seychelles **112** E6 5 00S 55 00E
Amman Jordan **92** O10 31 57N 35 56E
Amne Machin Shan *mts.* China **84** 35 00N 100 00E
Ampana Indonesia **99** G3 0 54S 121 35E
Amravati India **95** D4 20 58N 77 50E
Amritsar India **95** D6 31 35N 74 56E
Amroha India **95** D5 28 54N 78 29E
Amsterdam Netherlands **76** C5 52 22N 4 54E
Amsterdam New York U.S.A. **65** F5 42 56N 74 12W
Amstetten Austria **81** B4 48 08N 14 52E
Am Timan Chad **106** J10 10 59N 20 18E
Amudar'ya *(Oxus) r.* Asia **91** J2 39 00N 64 00E
Amundsen-Scott *r.s.* South Pole Antarctica **117** 90 00S
Amundsen Sea Southern Ocean **117** 72 00S 130 00W
Amungen *l.* Sweden **79** D3 61 10N 15 35E
Amur *(Heilong Jiang) r.* Asia **97** P9 52 30N 126 30E
Amursk Russia **89** P6 50 16N 136 55E
Anabar *r.* Russia **89** N10 71 30N 113 00E
Anaconda Montana U.S.A. **62** D6 46 09N 112 56W
Anacortes Washington U.S.A. **42** H4 48 30N 122 42W
Anadyr' Russia **89** T8 64 50N 178 00E
Anadyr' *r.* Russia **89** T9 65 00N 175 00E
Anadyr', Gulf of Russia **89** U8 65 00N 178 00W
Anaheim California U.S.A. **51** C2 33 50N 117 56W
Anai Mudi *mt.* India **95** D2 10 20N 77 15E
Anan Japan **100** B1 33 54N 134 40E
Ananindeua Brazil **68** H12 1 22S 48 20W
Anantapur India **95** D2 14 42N 77 05E
Anápolis Brazil **68** H9 16 19S 48 58W
Anatolian Plateau Turkey **84** 39 00N 39 00E
Anatom *i.* Vanuatu **110** L5 20 10S 169 50E
Anchorage Alaska U.S.A. **10** F5 61 10N 150 00W
Ancona Italy **81** B3 43 37N 13 31E
Anda China **97** P8 46 25N 125 20E
Andalsnes Norway **79** B3 62 33N 7 43E
Andaman Islands India **95** G2 12 00N 94 00E
Andaman Sea Indian Ocean **99** B6 12 30N 97 00E
Anderson Indiana U.S.A. **63** I5 40 05N 85 41W
Anderson South Carolina U.S.A. **63** J3 34 30N 82 39W
Andes *mts.* South America **68/69** B13/C5
Andhra Pradesh *admin.* India **95** D3 16 00N 79 00E
Andizhan Uzbekistan **91** L3 40 40N 72 12E
Andkhvoy Afghanistan **93** K6 36 58N 65 00E
ANDORRA **77** C3
Andorra la Vella Andorra **77** C3 42 30N 1 30E
Andover New Jersey U.S.A. **65** F3 40 58N 74 45W
Andrésy France **83** A2 48 59N 2 03E
Andreyevka Kazakhstan **96** F8 45 50N 80 34E
Andreyevka Ukraine **90** D4 49 34N 36 38E
Andropov *see* Rybinsk
Ándros *i.* Greece **81** D2 37 49N 24 54E
Andros *i.* The Bahamas **67** I4 24 00N 78 00W
Androscoggin River Maine U.S.A. **33** B1 44 00N 71 00W
Androth Island India **95** C2 10 51N 73 41E
Andújar Spain **77** B2 38 02N 4 03W
Andulo Angola **107** I5 11 29S 16 43E
Angara *r.* Russia **89** L7 58 00N 96 00E
Angara Basin Arctic Ocean **116** 80 00N
Angarsk Russia **89** M6 52 31N 103 55E
Angel de la Guarda *i.* Mexico **66** B5 29 00N 113 30W
Angeles National Forest California U.S.A. **51** B4 34 15N 118 10W
Angelholm Sweden **80** B6 56 15N 12 50E
Angelica New York U.S.A. **64** B5 42 18N 78 02W
Angel Island California U.S.A. **49** B3 37 51N 122 26W
Angel Island State Park California U.S.A. **49** B3 37 51N 122 24W
Ångermanälvern *r.* Sweden **79** D3 64 30N 16 15E
Angers France **77** B4 47 29N 0 32W
Anglesey *i.* Wales **78** G5 53 18N 4 25W
ANGOLA **107** I5
Angola Indiana U.S.A. **36** A2 41 38N 85 01W
Angola Basin Atlantic Ocean **113** I5 15 00S 3 00E
Angola Plateau Africa **102** 14 00S 17 00E
Angoon Alaska U.S.A. **42** B3 57 30N 133 35W
Angoulême France **77** C4 45 40N 0 10E
Angren Uzbekistan **91** L3 41 01N 70 10E
Anguilla *i.* Leeward Islands **67** L3 18 14N 63 05W
Anjŏ Japan **100** J1 34 56N 137 05E
Ankaratra *mt.* Madagascar **107** O4 19 25S 47 12E
'Annaba Algeria **106** G15 36 55N 7 47E
An Nabk Saudi Arabia **92** E5 31 21N 37 20E
An Nabk Syria **92** E5 34 02N 36 43E
An Nafud *d.* Saudi Arabia **92** F4 28 20N 40 30E
An Najaf Iraq **92** F5 31 59N 44 19E
Annam Range *hills* Asia **84** 15 00N 107 00E
Annapolis Maryland U.S.A. **64** D1 38 59N 76 30W
Annapurna *mt.* Nepal **95** E5 28 34N 83 50E
Ann Arbor Michigan U.S.A. **36** C3 42 18N 83 43W
An Nāsirīyah Iraq **93** G5 31 04N 46 17E
Annecy France **77** D4 45 54N 6 07E
Annette Island Alaska U.S.A. **42** B3 55 5N 131 30W
Anniston Alabama U.S.A. **63** I3 33 38N 85 50W
Annotto Bay *tn.* Jamaica **67** R8 18 16N 76 47W
Anqing China **97** N5 30 46N 119 40E
Ansari Nagar India **94** L4 28 33N 77 12E

Ansbach Germany **76** E5 49 18N 10 36E
Anshan China **97** O7 41 05N 122 58E
Anshun China **97** L4 26 15N 105 51E
Ansonia Connecticut U.S.A. **65** G4 41 21N 73 05W
Ansonia Pennsylvania U.S.A. **64** C4 41 44N 77 26W
Antakya Turkey **92** E6 36 12N 36 10E
Antalya Turkey **92** D6 36 53N 30 42E
Antananarivo *(Tananarive)* Madagascar **107** O4 18 52S 47 30E
Antarctica **117**
Antarctic Peninsula Antarctica **117** 68 00S 65 00W
Antequera Spain **77** B2 37 01N 4 34W
Anthony Chabot Regional Park California U.S.A. **49** C3 37 36N 122 07W
Antibes France **77** D3 43 35N 7 07E
Antigua Guatemala **66** F2 14 33N 90 42W
Antigua *i.* Antigua & Barbuda **67** L3 17 09N 61 49W
ANTIGUA & BARBUDA **67** L3
Antipodes Islands Southern Ocean **114** H3 49 42S 178 50E
Antler North Dakota U.S.A. **40** C1 48 58N 101 18W
Antofagasta Chile **69** C8 23 40S 70 23W
Antrim New Hampshire U.S.A. **65** J6 43 02N 71 57W
Antrim Mountains Northern Ireland **78** E6 55 00N 6 10W
Antseranana Madagascar **107** N5 12 19S 49 17E
Antwerp Ohio U.S.A. **36** B2 41 10N 84 44W
Antwerpen *(Anvers)* Belgium **76** C5 51 13N 4 25E
Anuradhapura Sri Lanka **95** E1 8 20N 80 25E
Anvers *see* Antwerpen
Anxi China **97** J7 40 32N 95 57E
Anxi China **98** E8 25 03N 118 13E
Anyang China **97** M6 36 04N 114 20E
Anzhero-Sudzhensk Russia **91** O6 56 10N 86 01E
Aomori Japan **100** D3 40 50N 140 43E
Aosta Italy **81** A4 45 43N 7 19E
Aozou Strip Chad **106** I12 23 00N 17 00E
Apapa Nigeria **107** V3 6 22N 3 25E
Aparri The Philippines **99** G7 18 22N 121 40E
Apatity Russia **88** F9 67 32N 33 21E
Apatzingán Mexico **66** D3 19 05N 102 20W
Apennines *see* Appennini
Apia Western Samoa **114** I6 13 48S 171 45W
Ap Lei Chau *i.* Hong Kong U.K. **98** B1 22 10N 114 00E
Apostle Islands Wisconsin U.S.A. **35** B2 47 00N 90 00W
Appalachian Mountains U.S.A. **63** J4 37 00N 82 00W
Appennini *(Apennines) mts.* Italy **81** B3
Appennino Abruzzese *mts.* Italy **81** B3 42 00N 14 00E
Appennino Ligure *mts.* Italy **81** A3 44 00N 9 00E
Appennino Lucano *mts.* Italy **81** C3 40 00N 15 00E
Appennino Tosco-Emiliano *mts.* Italy **81** B3 44 00N 12 00E
Appleton Wisconsin U.S.A. **63** I5 44 17N 88 24W
'Aqaba Jordan **92** O9 29 32N 35 00E
'Aqaba, Gulf of Middle East **92** O9 28 40N 34 40E
Aquidauana Brazil **68** F8 20 27S 55 45W
Ara India **95** E5 25 34N 84 40E
Ara *r.* Japan **101** C3 35 39N 139 51E
Arabian Basin Indian Ocean **112** F7/8 10 00N 65 00E
Arabian Sea Indian Ocean **93** J2 17 00N 60 00E
Aracaju Brazil **68** J10 10 54S 37 07W
Arad Romania **81** D4 46 10N 21 19E
Arafura Sea Australia/Indonesia **110** E8/F8 10 00S 135 00E
Aragón *r.* Spain **77** B3 42 15N 1 40W
Araguaina Brazil **68** H11 7 16S 48 18W
Araguari Brazil **68** H9 18 38S 48 13W
Arāk Iran **93** G5 34 05N 49 42E
Arakan Yoma *mts.* Myanmar **96** H3 18 00N 94 00E
Arakawa Japan **100** L2 35 58N 139 03E
Araks *(Aras, Araxes) r.* Armenia/Azerbaijan **90** F2 39 30N 45 00E
Aral Sea Kazakhstan/Uzbekistan **91** J4 45 00N 60 00E
Aral'sk Kazakhstan **91** J4 46 56N 61 43E
Aranda de Duero Spain **77** B3 41 40N 3 41W
Aranjuez Spain **77** B3 40 02N 3 37W
Aran Island Irish Republic **78** C6 55 00N 8 30W
Aran Islands Irish Republic **78** B5 53 10N 9 50W
Arapiraca Brazil **68** J11 9 45S 36 40W
Ar'ar Saudi Arabia **92** F5 30 58N 41 03E
Araraquara Brazil **69** H8 21 46S 48 08W
Ararat, Mount *see* Bü Ağri Daği
Aras *(Araks, Araxes) r.* Turkey **92** F7 40 00N 43 30E
Arauca Colombia **68** C14 7 04N 70 41W
Araure Venezuela **67** K1 9 36N 69 15W
Araxá Brazil **68** H9 19 37S 46 50W
Araxes *(Araks, Aras) r.* Iran **93** G6 38 40N 46 30E
Arbil Iraq **92** F6 36 12N 44 01E
Arbroath Scotland **78** I8 56 34N 2 35W
Arcachon France **77** B3 44 40N 1 11W
Arcade New York U.S.A. **64** B5 42 32N 78 25W
Arcadia California U.S.A. **51** B3 34 09N 118 00W
Arcadia Pennsylvania U.S.A. **64** B3 40 46N 78 50W
Arcati Brazil **68** J12 4 32S 37 45W
Archipelago Dehalak *is.* Ethiopia **92** F2 15 45N 40 12E
Arctic National Wildlife Refuge Alaska U.S.A. **44** C4 68 30N 145 00W
Arctic Ocean **116**
Arda *r.* Bulgaria **81** E3 41 30N 26 00E
Ardabīl Iran **88** G6 38 15N 48 18E
Ardennes *mts.* Belgium **76** D5 50 10N 5 45E
Ardila *r.* Spain **77** A2 38 15N 6 50W
Ardmore Oklahoma U.S.A. **63** G3 34 11N 97 08W
Arendal Norway **79** B2 58 27N 8 56E
Arequipa Peru **68** C9 16 25S 71 32W
Arezzo Italy **81** B3 43 28N 11 53E
Argentan France **76** C4 48 45N 0 01W
Argenteuil France **83** A2 48 57N 2 14E
ARGENTINA **69** D5
Argentine Basin Atlantic Ocean **113** D2 42 00S 45 00W
Arges *r.* Romania **81** E3 44 00N 26 00E
Argonne Forest Illinois U.S.A. **53** A1 41 43N 87 53W
Argun *(Ergun He) r.* Asia **97** N9 52 00N 120 00E
Argyle Minnesota U.S.A. **39** B1 48 10N 96 50W
Argyle, Lake Australia **110** D6 17 00S 128 30E
Århus Denmark **80** B6 56 15N 10 10E
Arica Chile **68** C9 18 30S 70 20W
Arima Trinidad and Tobago **66** T10 10 38N 61 17W
Aripuanã *r.* Brazil **68** E11 7 00S 60 30W
Ariquemes Brazil **68** E11 9 55S 63 06W
Arizona *state* U.S.A. **62** D3 34 00N 112 00W
Arizpe Mexico **66** B6 30 20N 110 11W
Arjeplog Sweden **79** D4 66 04N 18 00E
Arjona Colombia **68** B15 10 14N 75 22W
Arkalyk Kazakhstan **91** K5 50 17N 66 51E
Arkansas *r.* U.S.A. **63** H4 35 00N 93 00W
Arkansas *state* U.S.A. **63** H3 34 00N 93 00W
Arkansas City Kansas U.S.A. **63** G4 37 03N 97 02W
Arkhangel'sk Russia **88** G8 64 32N 40 40E
Arlanza *r.* Spain **77** B3 42 00N 3 30W
Arlanzón *r.* Spain **77** B3 42 00N 4 00W
Arles France **77** C3 43 41N 4 38E
Arlington Massachusetts U.S.A. **52** B2 42 23N 71 09W
Arlington Vermont U.S.A. **65** G6 43 04N 73 09W
Arlington Washington U.S.A. **42** H4 42 12N 122 09W
Arlington Heights Illinois U.S.A. **53** A3 42 06N 87 59W
Arlit Niger **106** G11 18 50N 7 00E
Arlon Belgium **76** D4 49 41N 5 49E
Armagh Northern Ireland **78** E6 54 21N 6 39W
Armavir Russia **90** E3 44 59N 41 10E
ARMENIA **90** E4/F4
Armenia Colombia **68** B13 4 32N 75 40W
Armenia New York U.S.A. **65** G4 41 51N 73 33W
Armidale Australia **110** I3 30 32S 151 40E
Arnhem Netherlands **76** D5 52 00N 5 53E
Arnhem Land *geog. reg.* Australia **110** E7 13 00S 133 00E
Arno *r.* Italy **81** B3 43 00N 10 00E
Arquipélago dos Bijagós *is.* Guinea-Bissau **106** B10 11 20N 16 40W
Ar Ramādī Iraq **92** F5 33 27N 43 19E
Ar Ramlah Jordan **92** O9 29 28N 35 58E
Arran *i.* Scotland **78** F7 55 35N 5 15W
Ar Raqqah Syria **92** E6 35 57N 39 03E
Ar Riyād Saudi Arabia **93** G3 24 39N 46 46E
Arta Greece **81** D2 39 10N 20 59E
Arthur's Pass New Zealand **111** B2 42 55S 171 34E
Artigas Uruguay **69** F6 30 25S 56 28W
Artigas *r.s.* Antarctica **117** 62 11S 58 51W
Arua Uganda **106** L8 3 02N 30 56E
ARUBA **68** D15 12 30N 70 00W
Arun *r.* England **78** K2 51 00N 0 30W
Arunachal Pradesh *admin.* India **95** H5 28 00N 95 00E
Arusha Tanzania **106** M7 3 23S 36 40E
Aruwimi *r.* Zaïre **106** J8 2 00N 25 00E
Arvika Sweden **79** C2 59 41N 12 38E
Arys' Kazakhstan **91** K3 42 26N 68 49E
Arzamas Russia **90** E6 55 24N 43 48E
Arzew Algeria **77** B2 35 50N 0 19W
Asahi Japan **100** M2 35 43N 140 38E
Asahi-dake *mt.* Japan **100** D3 43 42N 142 54E
Asahikawa Japan **100** D3 43 46N 142 23E
Asaka Japan **101** B4 35 47N 139 37E
Asamankese Ghana **106** E9 5 45N 0 45W
Asansol India **95** F4 23 40N 86 59E
Åsarna Sweden **79** C3 62 40N 14 20E
Asbury Park New Jersey U.S.A. **65** F3 40 14N 74 00W
Ascension Island Atlantic Ocean **113** G6 7 57S 14 22W
Ascoli Piceno Italy **81** B3 42 52N 13 35E
Aseb Ethiopia **92** F1 13 01N 42 47E
Asenovgrad Bulgaria **81** D3 42 00N 24 53E
Ashburton New Zealand **111** B2 43 54S 171 46E
Ashburton *r.* Australia **110** B5 22 30S 116 00E
Ashdod Israel **92** O10 31 48N 34 48E
Åshen *l.* Sweden **79** C2 56 45N 14 40E
Asheville North Carolina U.S.A. **63** J4 35 35N 82 35W
Ashfield Australia **111** G2 33 53S 151 07E
Ash Fork Arizona U.S.A. **62** D4 35 13N 112 29W
Ashikaga Japan **100** C2 36 21N 139 26E
Ashina Japan **101** B1 35 13N 139 36E
Ashizuri-misaki *c.* Japan **100** B1 32 42N 133 00E
Ashkhabad Turkmenistan **91** H2 37 58N 58 24E
Ashland Kentucky U.S.A. **63** J4 38 28N 82 40W
Ashland Ohio U.S.A. **36** D1 40 52N 82 19W
Ashland Oregon U.S.A. **62** B5 42 14N 122 44W
Ashland Wisconsin U.S.A. **35** B2 46 34N 90 54W
Ashokan Reservoir New York U.S.A. **65** F4 42 00N 74 15W
Ashok Nagar India **94** L4 28 38N 77 07E
Ashqelon Israel **92** O10 31 40N 34 35E
Ash Shāriqah United Arab Emirates **93** I4 25 20N 55 20E
Ash Shurayf Saudi Arabia **92** E4 25 50N 39 00E
Ashtabula Ohio U.S.A. **36** F2 41 53N 80 47W
Asilah Morocco **77** A2 35 32N 6 04W
Asir Mountains Saudi Arabia **102** 18 00N 44 00E
Askim Norway **80** B6 59 15N 11 10E
Asmera Ethiopia **92** E2 15 20N 38 58E
Asnières France **83** B2 48 55N 2 17E
Asō Japan **100** M3 36 00N 141 29E
Aspiring, Mount New Zealand **111** A2 44 23S 168 46E
Asquith Australia **111** G3 33 41S 151 07E
Assam *admin.* India **95** G5 26 20N 92 00E
As Samawah Iraq **93** G5 31 18N 45 18E
Assis Brazil **69** G8 22 37S 50 25W
Assisi Italy **81** B3 43 04N 12 37E
As Suq Saudi Arabia **92** F3 21 55N 42 02E
As Suwaydā' Syria **92** P11 32 43N 36 33E
Astārā Azerbaijan **93** G6 38 27N 48 53E
Asti Italy **81** A3 44 54N 8 13E
Astipálaia *i.* Greece **81** E2 36 00N 26 00E
Astoria Oregon U.S.A. **62** B6 46 12N 123 50W
Astrakhan' Russia **90** F4 46 22N 48 04E
Asuka *r.s.* Antarctica **117** 71 32S 24 08E
Asuke Japan **100** J2 35 08N 137 19E
Asunción Paraguay **69** F7 25 15S 57 40W
Aswa *r.* Uganda **106** L8 3 30N 32 30E
Aswân Egypt **92** D3 24 05N 32 56E
Aswân Dam Egypt **92** D3 23 40N 31 50E
Asyût Egypt **92** D4 27 14N 31 07E
Atacama Desert *see* Desierto de Atacama
Atami Japan **100** L2 35 07N 139 04E
Atar Mauritania **106** C12 20 32N 13 08W
Atbara Sudan **92** D2 17 42N 34 00E
Atbara *r.* Sudan **92** D2 17 28N 34 30E
Atbasar Kazakhstan **91** K5 51 49N 68 18E
Atchison Kansas U.S.A. **63** G4 39 33N 95 09W
Athambra *r.* California U.S.A. **49** C3 37 57N 122 07W
Athens Georgia U.S.A. **63** J3 33 57N 83 24W
Athens Greece *see* Athínai
Athens Pennsylvania U.S.A. **64** D4 41 57N 76 31W
Atherton California U.S.A. **49** C1 37 28N 122 11W
Athínai *(Athens)* Greece **81** D2 38 00N 23 44E
Athlone Irish Republic **78** E6 53 25N 7 56W
Athol Massachusetts U.S.A. **65** H5 42 36N 72 14W
Athol Springs *tn.* New York U.S.A. **38** D1 42 45N 78 51W
Áthos *mt.* Greece **81** D3 40 10N 24 19E
Ati Chad **106** I10 13 11N 18 20E
Atlanta Georgia U.S.A. **63** J3 33 45N 84 23W
Atlanta Michigan U.S.A. **35** D1 45 00N 84 07W
Atlantic City New Jersey U.S.A. **65** F2 39 23N 74 27W
Atlantic Ocean **113**
Atlantic-Indian Range Atlantic Ocean **113** I1 53 00S 3 00E
Atlas Saharien *mts.* Algeria **106** E14 33 30N 1 00E
Atrek *r.* Asia **93** H6 37 00N 54 50E
Atsugi Japan **100** L2 35 28N 139 22E
Atsumi Japan **100** J1 34 37N 137 06E
Atsumi-hantō *p.* Japan **100** J1 34 40N 137 15E
At Tā'if Saudi Arabia **92** F3 21 15N 40 21E
Attica New York U.S.A. **64** B5 42 52N 78 16W
Attleboro Massachusetts U.S.A. **65** J4 41 57N 71 16W
Aubagne France **77** D3 43 17N 5 35E
Aubenas France **76** C3 44 37N 4 24E
Aubervilliers France **83** B2 48 55N 2 22E
Auburn Indiana U.S.A. **36** A2 41 22N 85 02W
Auburn Maine U.S.A. **63** L5 44 04N 70 27W
Auburn Massachusetts U.S.A. **65** J5 42 13N 71 50W
Auburn New York U.S.A. **64** D5 42 57N 76 34W
Auch France **77** C3 43 40N 0 36E
Auckland New Zealand **111** B3 36 55S 174 47E
Auckland Islands Southern Ocean **114** G2 50 35S 116 00E
Au Gres Michigan U.S.A. **36** C5 44 03N 83 40W
Augsburg Germany **76** E5 48 21N 10 54E
Augusta Australia **110** B3 34 19S 115 09E
Augusta Georgia U.S.A. **63** J3 33 29N 82 00W
Augusta Maine U.S.A. **63** M5 44 17N 69 50W
Aulnay-sous-Bois France **83** C2 48 57N 2 31E
Aulne *r.* France **76** B4 48 10N 4 00W
Aurangābād India **95** D3 19 52N 75 22E
Aurillac France **77** C3 44 56N 2 26E
Au Sable Michigan U.S.A. **36** C5 44 25N 83 20W
Au Sable River Michigan U.S.A. **36** B5 44 40N 84 00W
Austin Texas U.S.A. **63** G3 30 18N 97 47W
AUSTRALIA **110**
Australian Capital Territory *(A.C.T.) admin.* Australia **110** H2 35 00S 144 00E
Austral Ridge Pacific Ocean **115** K5 24 00S 155 30W
AUSTRIA **81** B4
Autlān Mexico **66** D3 19 48N 104 20W
Autun France **77** C4 46 58N 4 18E
Auxerre France **77** C4 47 48N 3 35E
Avallon France **77** C4 47 30N 3 54E
Avalon New Jersey U.S.A. **65** F2 39 06N 74 43W
Aveiro Portugal **77** A3 40 38N 8 40W
Avellaneda Argentina **69** F6 34 40S 58 20W
Avesta Sweden **79** D3 60 09N 16 10E
Aveyron *r.* France **77** C3 44 30N 2 05E
Avezzano Italy **81** B3 42 02N 13 26E
Avignon France **77** C3 43 56N 4 48E
Avila Spain **77** B3 40 39N 4 42W
Avilés Spain **77** A3 43 33N 5 55W
Avon Connecticut U.S.A. **65** H4 41 47N 72 51W
Avon New York U.S.A. **64** C5 42 55N 77 44W
Avon *r.* England **78** J3 51 27N 1 40W
Avon Lake *tn.* Ohio U.S.A. **36** D2 41 31N 82 01W
Avranches France **76** B4 48 42N 1 21W
Awaji Japan **100** G1 34 35N 135 00E
Awaji-shima *l.* Japan **100** F1 34 30N 135 45E
Awali *r.* Lebanon **92** O11 33 35N 35 32E
Awash Ethiopia **106** N9 9 01N 41 10E
Awbārī Libya **106** H13 26 35N 12 46E
Ayabe Japan **100** G2 35 19N 135 16E
Ayaguz Kazakhstan **91** N4 47 59N 80 27E
Ayamonte Spain **77** A2 37 13N 7 24W
Ayan Russia **89** P7 56 29N 138 07E
Ayaviri Peru **68** C10 14 53S 70 35W
Aydin Turkey **80** E2 37 51N 27 51E
Ayios Nikólaos Greece **81** E2 35 11N 25 43E
Ayod Sudan **106** L9 8 08N 31 24E
Ayon *i.* Russia **89** S9 69 55N 168 10E
'Aynūnah Saudi Arabia **92** O9 28 06N 35 08E
Ayr Scotland **78** G7 55 28N 4 38W
Ayres Rock *mt.* Australia **110** E4 25 18S 131 18E
Ayutthaya Thailand **99** C6 14 20N 100 35E
AZERBAIJAN **90** F3
Aziscohos Lake Maine U.S.A. **37** Q6 45 00N 71 00W
Azogues Ecuador **68** B12 2 46S 78 56W
Azores *is.* Atlantic Ocean **113** F10 38 30N 28 00W
Azoum *r.* Chad **106** J10 12 00N 21 00E
Azuero, Peninsula de Panama **67** H1 7 40N 81 00W
Azul Argentina **69** F5 36 46S 59 50W
Azurduy Bolivia **68** E9 20 00S 64 29W
Azusa California U.S.A. **51** C3 34 08N 117 54W
Az Zabadānī Syria **92** P11 33 42N 36 03E
Az Zahrān *(Dhahran)* Saudi Arabia **93** H4 26 13N 50 02E

B

Baalbek Lebanon **92** P12 34 00N 36 12E
Babahoyo Ecuador **68** B12 1 53S 79 31W
Babar, Kepulauan *is.* Indonesia **99** H2 8 00S 129 30E
Babatang China **97** J5 30 02N 99 01E
Bab el Mandab *sd.* Red Sea **106** N10 12 30N 47 00E
Babelsberg Germany **83** E1 52 23N 13 05E
Babushkin Russia **88** M2 55 55N 37 44E
Babylon New York U.S.A. **65** G3 40 42N 73 20W
Babylon *hist. site* Iraq **92** F5 32 33N 44 25E
Bacabal Brazil **68** I12 4 15S 44 45W
Bacău Romania **81** E4 46 33N 26 58E
Bacolod The Philippines **99** G6 10 38N 122 58E
Badajoz Spain **77** A2 38 53N 6 58W
Badalona Spain **77** C3 41 27N 2 15E
Bad Axe Michigan U.S.A. **36** D4 43 49N 82 59W
Baden Austria **81** C4 48 01N 16 14E
Badli India **94** L4 28 44N 77 09E
Badulla Sri Lanka **95** E1 6 59N 81 03E
Bafoussam Cameroon **106** H9 5 31N 10 25E
Bāfq Iran **93** I5 31 35N 55 21E
Bagé Brazil **69** G6 31 22S 54 06W
Bagenalstown *see* Muinebeag
Baghdād Iraq **92** F5 33 20N 44 26E
Baghlān Afghanistan **93** K6 36 11N 68 44E
Bahamas Bank Atlantic Ocean **54** 24 00N 77 00W
BAHAMAS, THE **67** I4
Baharampur India **95** F4 24 00N 88 30E
Bahawalpur Pakistan **95** C5 29 24N 71 47E
Bahia *admin.* Brazil **68** I10 12 00S 42 30W
Bahía Blanca Argentina **69** E5 38 45S 62 15W
Bahı́a Blanca *b.* Argentina **69** E5 39 00S 61 00W
Bahía de Campeche *b.* Mexico **66** E4/F4 20 00N 95 00W
Bahía, Grande *b.* Argentina **69** D2 51 30S 68 00W
Bahra el Manzala *l.* Egypt **107** R4 31 18N 31 54E
Bahra el Timsâh *(Lake Timsâh)* Egypt **107** S3 30 34N 32 18E
Bahraich India **95** E5 27 35N 81 36E
BAHRAIN **93** H4
Bahrain, Gulf of The Gulf **93** H4 25 55N 50 30E
Bahr el Abiad *(White Nile) r.* Sudan **92** D1 14 00N 32 20E
Bahr el Arab *r.* Sudan **106** K10 10 00N 27 30E
Bahr el Azraq *(Blue Nile) r.* Sudan **92** D1 13 30N 33 45E
Bahr el Baqar *r.* Egypt **107** S3 30 54N 32 02E
Bahr el Ghazal *r.* Chad **106** I10 14 00N 16 00E
Bahr Faqus *r.* Egypt **107** R3 30 42N 31 42E
Bahr Hadus *r.* Egypt **107** R4 31 01N 31 43E
Bahr Saft *r.* Egypt **107** R3 30 57N 31 48E
Baia Mare Romania **81** D4 47 39N 23 36E
Baicheng China **97** O8 45 37N 122 48E
Baidyabati India **94** K3 22 48N 88 20E
Baie de la Seine *b.* France **76** B4 49 40N 0 30W
Baiwanzhuang China **100** G1 39 55N 116 18E
Baja Hungary **81** C4 46 11N 18 58E
Baja California *p.* Mexico **66** B5 27 30N 113 00W
Baj Baj India **94** J1 22 28N 88 10E
Baker Oregon U.S.A. **62** C5 44 46N 117 50W
Baker Island Alaska U.S.A. **42** B3 55 30N 133 30W
Baker, Mount Washington U.S.A. **42** H4 48 48N 121 50W
Baker River Washington U.S.A. **42** H4 48 40N 121 35W
Baku Azerbaijan **90** F3 40 22N 49 53E
Balaghat India **95** E4 21 48N 80 16E
Balaghat Range *mts.* India **95** D3 18 45N 77 00E
Balakovo Russia **90** F5 52 04N 47 46E
Bala, Lake *see* Tegid, Llyn
Balama Mozambique **107** M5 13 19S 38 35E
Bālā Morghāb Afghanistan **93** J6 35 34N 63 20E
Balashikha Russia **90** D6 55 47N 37 59E
Balashov Russia **90** E5 51 31N 43 10E
Balassagyarmat Hungary **81** C4 48 06N 19 17E
Balaton *l.* Hungary **81** C4 47 00N 17 30E
Balboa Panama **67** Y2 8 57N 79 33W
Balclutha New Zealand **111** A1 46 16S 169 46E
Baldeney-see *l.* Germany **76** J2 51 24N 7 02E
Baldwin Park *tn.* California U.S.A. **51** C3 34 05N 117 59W
Balearic Islands Mediterranean Sea **77** E4
Balgowlah Australia **111** H2 33 48S 151 16E
Bali *i.* Indonesia **99** E2/F2 8 00S 115 00E
Balikesir Turkey **92** C6 39 37N 27 51E
Balikpapan Indonesia **99** F3 1 15S 116 50E
Balkham Hills Australia **111** F2 33 46S 150 58E
Balkhash Kazakhstan **91** L4 46 50N 74 57E
Balkhash, Lake *see* Ozero Balkhash
Ballarat Australia **110** G2 37 36S 143 58E
Balleny Islands Southern Ocean **114** H1 66 30S 164E
Ballston Spa New York U.S.A. **65** G6 43 00N 73 49W
Bally India **94** K2 22 38N 88 20E
Ballygunge India **94** K2 22 31N 88 20E
Ballymena Northern Ireland **78** E6 54 52N 6 17W
Balmain Australia **111** G2 33 51S 151 11E
Balsas Mexico **66** E3 18 00N 99 44W
Balta Ukraine **81** E4 47 58N 29 39E
Baltic Sea Europe **79** D2 55 15N 17 00E
Baltimore Maryland U.S.A. **64** D2 39 18N 76 38W
Baluchistan *geog. reg.* Pakistan **94** A5/B5 27 30N 65 00E
Bam Iran **93** I4 29 07N 58 20E
Bamako Mali **106** D10 12 40N 7 59W
Bambari Central African Republic **106** J9 5 40N 20 37E
Bamberg Germany **76** E5 49 54N 10 54E
Bamenda Cameroon **106** H9 5 55N 10 09E
Bamingui Bangoran National Park Central African Republic **106** I9 8 00N 20 00E
Banaba *i.* Nauru **114** G7 1 00S 167 00E
Banas *r.* India **95** D5 26 00N 75 00E
Banbury England **78** J4 52 04N 1 20W
Banda India **95** E5 25 28N 80 20E
Banda Aceh Indonesia **99** B5 5 30N 95 20E
Bandama Blanc *r.* Cote d'Ivoire **106** D9 8 00N 5 45W
Bandar Abbās Iran **93** I4 27 12N 56 15E
Bandar-e Lengeh Iran **93** H4 26 34N 54 52E
Bandar-e Torkeman Iran **93** H6 36 55N 54 01E
Bandar Khomeynī Iran **93** G5 30 40N 49 08E
Bandar Seri Begawan Brunei **99** F4 4 56N 114 58E
Bandarbeyla Somalia **106** P9 9 30N 50 50E
Banda Sea Indonesia **99** H2 6 00S 127 00E
Bandeirantes Beach Brazil **69** P2 23 01S 43 23W
Bandel India **94** K3 22 55N 88 23E
Bandirma Turkey **92** C7 40 21N 27 58E
Bandundu Zaïre **107** I7 3 20S 17 24E
Bandung Indonesia **99** D2 6 57S 107 34E
Banfora Burkina **106** E10 10 36N 4 45W
Bangalore India **95** D2 12 58N 77 35E
Bangassou Central African Republic **106** J8 4 41N 22 48E
Banghāzī *(Benghazi)* Libya **106** J14 32 07N 20 04E
Bangka *i.* Indonesia **99** D3 2 00S 106 30E
Bangkok *(Krung Thep)* Thailand **99** C6 13 44N 100 30E
BANGLADESH **95** F/G4
Bangor Maine U.S.A. **63** M5 44 49N 68 47W
Bangor Northern Ireland **78** F6 54 40N 5 40W
Bangor Wales **78** G5 53 13N 4 08W
Bangui Central African Republic **106** I8 4 23N 18 37E
Bangweulu, Lake Zambia **107** K5 11 15S 29 45E
Ban Hat Yai Thailand **99** C5 7 00N 100 28E
Banja Luka Bosnia-Herzegovina **81** C3 44 47N 17 11E
Banjarmasin Indonesia **99** E3 3 22S 114 33E
Banjul The Gambia **106** B10 13 28N 16 39W
Banka India **94** K2 22 36N 88 17E
Banks, Cape Australia **111** G1 34 00S 151 15E
Banks Islands Vanuatu **110** L7 13 40S 167 30E
Banks Peninsula New Zealand **111** B2 43 50S 173 10E
Bankstown Australia **111** G2 33 55S 151 02E
Ban Me Thuot Vietnam **99** D6 12 41N 108 02E
Bann *r.* Northern Ireland **78** E7 54 20N 6 10W
Bannu Pakistan **93** L5 33 00N 70 40E
Bansberia India **94** K3 22 57N 88 23E
Banská Bystrica Czechoslovakia **80** C4 48 44N 19 10E
Banstead England **82** C2 51 19N 0 12W
Bantry Bay Irish Republic **78** B3 51 35N 9 40W
Banyuwangi Indonesia **99** E2 8 12S 114 22E
Baoding China **97** N6 38 54N 115 26E
Baoji China **97** L5 34 23N 107 16E
Baotou China **97** M7 40 38N 109 59E
Ba'qūbah Iraq **92** F5 33 45N 44 40E
Baracaldo Spain **77** B3 43 17N 2 59W
Barahanagar India **94** K2 22 38N 88 23E

Barahona Dominican Republic **67** J3 18 13N 71 07W
Barajala Canal India **94** J2 22 35N 88 12E
Bārākpur India **94** K3 22 45N 88 22E
Baral India **94** K1 22 27N 88 22E
Baranof Alaska U.S.A. **42** B3 57 05N 134 50W
Baranof Island Alaska U.S.A. **42** A3 57 30N 135 00W
Baranovichi Belarus **90** B5 53 09N 26 00E
Bārāsat India **94** K2 22 43N 88 26E
Barbacena Brazil **69** I8 21 13S 43 47W
BARBADOS **66** V12
Barbastro Spain **77** C3 42 02N 0 07E
Barbuda *i.* Antigua & Barbuda **67** L3 17 41N 61 48W
Barcaldine Australia **110** H5 23 31S 145 15E
Barcellona Italy **81** C2 38 10N 15 15E
Barcelona Spain **77** C3 41 25N 2 10E
Barcelona Venezuela **68** E15 10 08N 64 43W
Barcelonette France **76** D3 44 24N 6 40E
Barcelos Brazil **68** E12 0 59S 62 58W
Barcoo *r.* Australia **110** G5 23 30S 144 00E
Barcs Hungary **81** C4 45 58N 17 30E
Barddhamān India **95** F4 23 20N 88 00E
Barduelv *r.* Norway **79** D4 68 48N 18 22E
Bareilly India **95** D5 28 20N 79 24E
Barents Sea Arctic Ocean **116** 75 00N 40 00E
Barga China **95** E6 30 51N 81 20E
Barge Canal New York U.S.A. **64** C6 43 07N 77 27W
Bari Italy **68** C3 41 07N 16 52E
Bariga Nigeria **107** V3 6 32N 3 28E
Barinas Venezuela **68** C14 8 36N 70 15W
Barisal Bangladesh **95** G4 22 41N 90 20E
Bariti, Lake India **94** K3 22 48N 88 26E
Barking *bor.* Greater London England **82** D3 51 33N 0 06E
Barkly Tableland Australia **110** F6 17 30S 137 00E
Bar-le-Duc France **76** D4 48 46N 5 10E
Barlee, Lake Australia **110** B4 28 30S 120 00E
Barletta Italy **81** C3 41 20N 16 17E
Barnaul Russia **91** N5 53 21N 83 45E
Barnes England **82** C2 51 28N 0 15W
Barnet *bor.* Greater London England **82** C3 51 39N 0 12W
Barnstable Massachusetts U.S.A. **66** K4 41 00N 70 00W
Barnstaple Devon England **78** G3 51 05N 4 04W
Barquisimeto Venezuela **68** D15 10 03N 69 18W
Barra *i.* Scotland **78** D8 57 00N 7 25W
Barra da Tijuca Brazil **69** P1 23 00S 43 20W
Barra do Corda Brazil **68** H11 5 30S 45 12W
Barrancabermeja Colombia **68** C14 7 06N 73 54W
Barrancas Venezuela **68** E14 8 45N 62 13W
Barrancones Point Trinidad and Tobago **66** T10 10 30N 61 28W
Barranjoey Head *c.* Australia **111** H3 33 35S 151 20E
Barranquilla Colombia **68** C15 11 10N 74 50W
Barre Massachusetts U.S.A. **65** H5 42 25N 72 07W
Barre Vermont U.S.A. **63** L5 44 13N 72 31W
Barreiras Brazil **68** I10 12 09S 44 58W
Barreiro Portugal **77** A2 38 40N 9 05W
Barron Wisconsin U.S.A. **35** B2 45 24N 91 50W
Barrow Alaska U.S.A. **10** D7 71 16N 156 50W
Barrow *r.* Irish Republic **78** D4 52 55N 7 00W
Barrow-in-Furness England **78** H6 54 07N 3 14W
Barrow Island Australia **110** B5 21 00S 115 00E
Barrow, Point Alaska U.S.A. **10** D7 71 05N 156 00W
Barry Wales **78** H3 51 24N 3 10W
Bartlesville Oklahoma U.S.A. **63** G4 36 44N 95 59W
Bartolome, Cape Alaska U.S.A. **42** B3 55 15N 133 39W
Basalt Island Hong Kong U.K. **98** D1 22 19N 114 21E
Basdorf Germany **83** F2 52 44N 13 27E
Basel Switzerland **77** D4 47 33N 7 36E
Basildon England **78** L3 51 34N 0 25E
Basingstoke England **78** J3 51 16N 1 05W
Baskunchak Russia **90** F4 48 14N 46 44E
Bassas da India *i.* Mozambique Channel **107** M3 22 00S 40 00E
Bassein Myanmar **96** H2 16 46N 94 45E
Basse Terre Trinidad and Tobago **66** T9 10 07N 61 17W
Basse Terre *i.* Lesser Antilles **67** L3 16 00N 61 20W
Bass Strait Australia **110** H2 40 00S 145 00E
Basswood Lake Canada/U.S.A. **35** B2 48 04N 91 34W
Bastia Corsica France **77** D3 42 14N 9 26E
Bastogne Belgium **76** D4 50 00N 5 43E
Bastrop Louisiana U.S.A. **63** H3 32 49N 91 54W
Bata Equatorial Guinea **106** G8 1 51N 9 49E
Batakan Indonesia **99** E3 4 03S 114 39E
Batala India **95** D6 31 48N 75 17E
Batanagar India **94** K2 22 30N 88 14E
Batan Datuk Malaysia **99** C4 3 58N 100 47E
Batangafo Central African Republic **106** I9 7 27N 18 11E
Batangas The Philippines **99** G6 13 46N 121 01E
Batavia New York U.S.A. **64** B5 43 00N 73 11W
Bate Bay Australia **111** G1 34 03S 151 11E
Bath England **78** I3 51 23N 2 22W
Bath Jamaica **67** R7 17 57N 76 22W
Bath New York U.S.A. **64** C5 42 21N 77 19W
Batha *r.* Chad **106** I10 13 00N 19 00E
Bathsheba Barbados **66** V12 13 12N 59 32W
Bathurst Australia **110** H3 33 27S 149 35E
Bathurst Island Australia **110** E7 12 00S 130 00E
Batna Algeria **106** G15 35 34N 6 10E
Baton Rouge Louisiana U.S.A. **63** G3 30 30N 91 10W
Batroûn Lebanon **92** O12 36 16N 35 40E
Battambang Cambodia **99** C6 13 06N 103 13E
Batticaloa Sri Lanka **95** E1 7 43N 81 42E
Battle Creek *tn.* Michigan U.S.A. **63** J5 42 20N 85 21W
Batumi Georgia **90** E3 41 37N 41 36E
Bat Yam Israel **92** O10 32 01N 34 45E
Baubau Indonesia **99** G2 5 30S 122 37E
Bauchi Nigeria **106** G10 10 16N 9 50E
Baudette Minnesota U.S.A. **39** B1 48 40N 95 40W
Bauriā India **94** J1 22 29N 88 09E
Bauru Brazil **69** H8 22 19S 49 07W
Bautzen Germany **76** E5 51 11N 14 29E
Baxter State Park Maine U.S.A. **33** C2 46 00N 69 00W
Bayamo Cuba **67** I4 20 23N 76 39W
Bayan Ha Shan *mts.* China **84** 34 00N 100 00E
Bay City Michigan U.S.A. **63** J5 43 35N 83 52W
Bay City Texas U.S.A. **63** G2 28 59N 96 00W
Baydhabo Somalia **106** N8 3 08N 43 34E
Bayerische Alpen *mts.* Germany **77** E4 47 00N 11 00E
Bayeux France **76** B4 49 16N 0 42W
Bayfield Barbados **66** W12 13 10N 59 25W
Baykal, Lake *see* Ozero Baykal
Baykonyr Kazakhstan **91** K4 47 50N 66 03E
Bayonne France **77** B3 43 30N 1 28W
Bayonne New Jersey U.S.A. **50** B1 40 39N 74 07W
Bayreuth Germany **76** E5 49 27N 11 35E
Bay Ridge *tn.* New York U.S.A. **50** C1 40 37N 74 02W
Bay Shore New York U.S.A. **65** G3 40 43N 73 15W
Baytown Texas U.S.A. **63** H2 29 43N 94 59W
Baza Spain **77** B2 37 30N 2 45W
Bcharre Lebanon **92** P12 34 15N 36 00E
Beachy Head *c.* England **78** L2 50 44N 0 16E
Beacon New York U.S.A. **65** G4 41 31N 73 59W
Beardmore Glacier Antarctica **117** 84 00S 170 00E
Bear Lake U.S.A. **62** D5 42 00N 111 20W
Bearpaw Mountain Montana U.S.A. **41** D1 48 09N 109 39W
Beatrice Nebraska U.S.A. **63** G5 40 17N 96 45W
Beatty Nevada U.S.A. **62** C4 36 54N 116 45W
Beauchamp France **83** A3 49 00N 2 12E
Beaufort South Carolina U.S.A. **63** J3 32 26N 80 40W
Beaufort Island Hong Kong U.K. **98** C1 22 11N 114 15E
Beaufort Sea Arctic Ocean **116** 72 00N 135 00W
Beaumont Texas U.S.A. **63** H3 30 04N 94 06W
Beaune France **77** C4 47 02N 4 50E
Beauvais France **76** C4 49 26N 2 05E
Beaver Alaska U.S.A. **44** B4 66 22N 147 30W
Beaver Island Michigan U.S.A. **36** A6 45 40N 85 30W
Béchar Algeria **106** E14 31 35N 2 17W
Becharof Lake Alaska U.S.A. **10** D4 58 00N 156 30W
Beckenham England **82** C2 51 24N 0 01W
Beckley West Virginia U.S.A. **63** J4 37 46N 81 12W
Becontree England **82** D3 51 34N 0 10E
Bedford England **78** K4 52 08N 0 29W
Bedford Massachusetts U.S.A. **52** A2 42 28N 71 17W
Bedford Pennsylvania U.S.A. **64** B3 40 02N 78 31W
Beersheba Israel **92** O10 31 15N 34 47E
Beeville Texas U.S.A. **63** G2 28 25N 97 47W
Begna *r.* Norway **79** B3 61 00N 9 00E
Behala *see* South Suburbs
Behbehān Iran **93** H5 30 34N 50 18E
Behm Canal *sd.* Alaska U.S.A. **42** B3 56 00N 131 00W
Beht *r.* Morocco **77** A1 34 30N 5 50W
Bei'an China **97** P8 48 16N 126 36E
Beihai China **97** L3 21 29N 109 10E
Beihai *l.* China **101** G1 39 57N 116 22E
Beijing *(Peking)* China **97** N7 39 55N 116 26E
Beira Mozambique **107** L4 19 49S 34 52E
Beirut *see* Beyrouth
Beiyuan China **101** G2 40 02N 116 25E
Beja Portugal **77** A2 38 01N 7 52W
Bejaïa Algeria **106** G15 36 49N 5 03E
Békes Hungary **81** D4 46 45N 21 09E
Bela Pakistan **94** B5 26 12N 66 20E
BELARUS *(BYELORUSSIA)* **90** B5
Belaya Tserkov Ukraine **90** C4 49 49N 30 10E
Belchertown Massachusetts U.S.A. **65** H5 42 17N 72 25W
Belém Brazil **68** H12 1 27S 48 29W
Belfast Maine U.S.A. **33** C1 44 26N 69 01W
Belfast New York U.S.A. **64** B5 42 21N 78 08W
Belfast Northern Ireland **78** F6 54 35N 5 55W
Belford Roxe Brazil **69** P2 22 45S 43 24W
Belfort France **77** D4 47 38N 6 52E
Belgaum India **95** C3 15 54N 74 36E
Belgharia India **94** K2 22 39N 88 23E
BELGIUM **76** D2
Belgorod Russia **90** D5 50 38N 36 36E
Belgorod Dnestrovskiy Ukraine **90** C4 46 10N 30 19E
Belgrade *see* Beograd
Beliaghata India **94** K2 22 34N 88 23E
Belitung *i.* Indonesia **99** D3 2 30S 108 00E
BELIZE **66** G3
Belize Belize **66** G3 17 29N 88 10W
Bellaire Michigan U.S.A. **36** A5 44 59N 85 12W
Bellary India **95** D3 15 11N 76 54E
Bella Vista Argentina **69** F7 28 31S 59 00W
Belle-Île *i.* France **77** B4 47 20N 3 10W
Belle Island Michigan U.S.A. **52** F2 42 21N 82 59W
Belleplaine Barbados **66** V12 13 14N 59 35W
Bellevue Ohio U.S.A. **36** D2 41 16N 82 51W
Bellevue Pennsylvania U.S.A. **53** D1 40 32N 80 08W
Bellflower California U.S.A. **51** B2 33 53N 118 08W
Bellingham Washington U.S.A. **62** B6 48 45N 122 29W
Bellingshausen *r.s.* Antarctica **117** 62 12S 58 58W
Bellingshausen Sea Southern Ocean **117** 71 00S 85 00W
Bello Colombia **68** B14 6 20N 75 41W
Belluno Italy **81** B4 46 08N 12 13E
Bellwood Illinois U.S.A. **53** A2 41 51N 87 52W
Bellwood Pennsylvania U.S.A. **64** B3 40 36N 78 21W
Belmont California U.S.A. **49** B2 37 34N 122 20W
Belmont Massachusetts U.S.A. **52** B2 42 22N 71 11W
Belmopan Belize **66** G3 17 13N 88 48W
Belogorsk Russia **89** O6 50 55N 128 26E
Belo Horizonte Brazil **69** I9 19 54S 43 54W
Belovo Russia **91** O5 54 27N 86 19E
Bel'tsy Moldova **90** B4 47 44N 27 41E
Belur India **94** K2 22 37N 88 20E
Belvidere New Jersey U.S.A. **64** E3 40 50N 75 05W
Belyy *i.* Russia **89** J10 73 00N 70 00E
Belyy Yar Russia **91** O6 58 28N 85 03E
Bembézar *r.* Spain **77** A2 38 00N 5 15W
Bemidji Minnesota U.S.A. **63** H6 47 29N 94 52W
Benavente Spain **77** A3 42 00N 5 40W
Benbecula *i.* Scotland **78** D9 57 25N 7 20W
Bend Oregon U.S.A. **62** B5 44 04N 121 20W
Bendery Moldova **90** B4 46 50N 29 29E
Bendigo Australia **110** G2 36 48S 144 21E
Benevento Italy **81** B3 41 08N 14 46E
Benfica Brazil **69** P2 22 52S 43 16W
Bengal, Bay of Indian Ocean **95** F3/G3 17 00N 88 00E
Bengbu China **97** N5 32 56N 117 27E
Benghazi *see* Banghāzī
Bengkulu Indonesia **99** C3 3 46S 102 16E
Benguela Angola **107** H5 12 34S 13 24E
Beni Abbès Algeria **106** E14 30 11N 2 14W
Benicarló Spain **77** C3 40 25N 0 25E
Beni Mellal Morocco **106** D14 32 22N 6 29W
BENIN **106** F10
Benin, Bight of W. Africa **106** F9 5 05N 2 30E
Benin City Nigeria **106** G9 6 19N 5 41E
Beni, Rio *r.* Bolivia **68** D10 13 00S 67 30W
Beni Saf Algeria **77** B2 35 28N 1 22W
Beni Suef Egypt **92** D4 29 05N 31 05E
Benjamin Constant Brazil **68** C12 4 23S 69 59W
Ben Macdui *mt.* Scotland **78** H9 57 04N 3 40W
Benmore, Lake New Zealand **111** B2 44 10S 170 20E
Ben Nevis *mt.* Scotland **78** G8 56 40N 5 00W
Bennington Vermont U.S.A. **65** G5 42 54N 73 12W
Bénoué *(Benue) r.* Cameroon **106** H9 8 10N 13 50E
Benson Arizona U.S.A. **62** D3 31 58N 110 19W
Bentham's Barbados **66** V13 13 18N 59 40W
Benton Harbor *tn.* Michigan U.S.A. **63** I5 42 07N 86 27W
Benue *(Bénoué) r.* Nigeria **106** H9 8 00N 7 40E
Ben Wyvis *mt.* Scotland **78** G9 57 40N 4 35W
Benxi China **97** O7 41 21N 123 45E
Beograd *(Belgrade)* Serbia Yugoslavia **81** D3 44 50N 20 30E
Beppu Japan **100** B1 33 18N 131 30E
Berat Albania **81** D3 40 43N 19 46E
Berber Sudan **92** D2 18 01N 34 00E
Berbera Somalia **106** O10 10 28N 45 02E
Berbérati Central African Republic **106** I8 4 19N 15 51E
Berck France **76** C5 50 24N 1 35E
Berdichev Ukraine **90** B4 49 54N 28 39E
Berdyansk Ukraine **90** D4 46 45N 36 47E
Beregovo Ukraine **81** D4 48 13N 22 39E
Berezina *r.* Belarus **90** B5 54 00N 29 00E
Berezniki Russia **91** H6 59 26N 56 49E
Berezovo Russia **89** I8 63 58N 65 00E
Bergama Turkey **80** E2 39 08N 27 10E
Bérgamo Italy **81** A4 45 42N 9 40E
Bergen Norway **79** B3 60 23N 5 20E
Bergenfield New Jersey U.S.A. **50** C2 40 56N 74 00W
Bergerac France **77** C3 44 50N 0 29E
Bering Sea Pacific Ocean **114** H13/I13 60 00N 175 00W
Berkåk Norway **79** C3 62 48N 10 03E
Berkakit Russia **89** O7 56 36N 124 49E
Berkeley California U.S.A. **49** B3 37 53N 122 17W
Berkeley Illinois U.S.A. **53** A2 41 53N 87 56W
Berkeley Springs *tn.* West Virginia U.S.A. **64** B2 39 38N 78 14W
Berkley Michigan U.S.A. **52** E2 42 31N 83 12W
Berkner Island Antarctica **117** 80 00S 45 00W
Berkshire *co.* England **82** A2 51 28N 1 00W
Berlevåg Norway **79** F5 70 50N 29 09E
Berlin Germany **76** E5 52 32N 13 25E
Berlin New Hampshire U.S.A. **63** L5 44 27N 71 13W
Berliner Forst *pk.* Germany **83** F2 52 38N 13 16E
Berliner Forst Düppel *pk.* Germany **83** E1 52 24N 13 07E
Berliner Forst Grunewald *pk.* Germany **83** E1 52 28N 13 13E
Berliner Forst Spandau *pk.* Germany **83** E2 52 35N 13 10E
Berliner Stadtforst *pk.* Germany **83** G1 52 28N 13 24E
Berliner Stadtforst Köpenick *pk.* Germany **83** G1 52 24N 13 37E
Berlin Lake *res.* Ohio U.S.A. **36** E1 40 57N 81 06W
Bermuda *i.* Atlantic Ocean **113** B10 32 50N 64 20W
Bern Switzerland **77** D4 46 57N 7 26E
Bernardston Massachusetts U.S.A. **65** H5 42 39N 72 35W
Bernardsville New Jersey U.S.A. **65** F3 40 43N 74 35W
Bernau Germany **83** G2 52 41N 13 36E
Berner Alpen *mts.* Switzerland **77** D4 46 25N 7 30E
Berowra Australia **111** G3 33 37S 151 09E
Berthold North Dakota U.S.A. **40** C1 48 20N 101 44W
Bertoua Cameroon **106** H8 4 34N 13 42E
Berwick Maine U.S.A. **65** K6 43 17N 70 54W
Berwick Pennsylvania U.S.A. **64** D4 41 04N 76 13W
Berwick-upon-Tweed England **78** I7 55 46N 2 00W
Berwyn Illinois U.S.A. **53** A2 41 49N 87 52W
Besançon France **77** D4 47 14N 6 02E
Besenville Illinois U.S.A. **53** A2 41 56N 87 59W
Beskidy Zachodnie *mts.* Poland **80** D4 50 00N 20 00E
Beskudnikovo Russia **88** M2 55 54N 37 38E
Bethal Park Pennsylvania U.S.A. **53** D1 40 19N 80 03W
Bethel Alaska U.S.A. **10** C5 60 49N 161 49W
Bethesda Maryland U.S.A. **64** C1 39 00N 77 05W
Bethlehem Jordan **92** O10 31 42N 35 12E
Bethlehem Pennsylvania U.S.A. **64** E3 40 36N 75 22W
Béthune France **76** C5 50 32N 2 38E
Betsiboka *r.* Madagascar **107** O4 17 00S 46 30E
Beverley Massachusetts U.S.A. **65** K5 42 35N 70 52W
Beverly Hills California U.S.A. **51** A3 34 03N 118 22W
Bexley *bor.* Greater London England **82** D2 51 27N 0 09E
Bexley Heath England **82** D2 51 28N 0 05E
Beyla Guinea **106** D9 8 42N 8 39W
Beyrouth *(Beirut)* Lebanon **92** O11 33 52N 35 30E
Beyşehir Gölü *l.* Turkey **92** D6 37 40N 31 43E
Béziers France **77** C3 43 21N 3 13E
Bhadgaon Nepal **95** F5 27 41N 85 26E
Bhadravati India **95** D2 13 54N 75 38E
Bhadreswar India **94** K3 22 50N 88 20E
Bhagalpur India **95** F5 25 14N 86 59E
Bhandara India **95** D4 21 10N 79 41E
Bharatpur India **95** D5 27 14N 77 29E
Bharuch India **95** C4 21 40N 73 02E
Bhatinda India **95** C6 30 10N 74 58E
Bhātpāra India **94** K3 22 52N 88 25E
Bhavnagar India **95** C4 21 46N 72 14E
Bhilwara India **95** C5 25 23N 74 39E
Bhima *r.* India **95** D3 17 00N 77 00E
Bhiwandi India **95** C3 19 21N 73 08E
Bhopal India **95** D4 23 17N 77 28E
Bhubaneshwar India **95** F4 20 13N 85 50E
Bhuj India **94** B4 23 12N 69 54E
Bhusawal India **95** D4 21 01N 75 50E
BHUTAN **95** F/G5
Biała Podlaska Poland **80** D5 52 03N 23 05E
Białystok Poland **80** D5 53 09N 23 10E
Biarritz France **77** B3 43 29N 1 33W
Bibai Japan **100** D3 43 21N 141 53E
Biche Trinidad and Tobago **66** T9 10 26N 61 07W
Bida Nigeria **106** G9 9 06N 5 59E
Bidar India **95** D3 17 56N 77 35E
Biddeford Maine U.S.A. **63** L5 43 29N 70 27W
Biebrza *r.* Poland **80** D5 53 00N 22 00E
Biel Switzerland **77** D4 46 27N 8 13E
Bielefeld Germany **76** D5 52 02N 8 32E
Biella Italy **81** A4 45 34N 8 04E
Bielsko-Biała Poland **80** C4 49 50N 19 00E
Bielsk Podlaski Poland **80** D5 52 47N 23 11E
Bièvres France **83** A2 48 45N 2 11E
Biferno *r.* Italy **81** B3 41 00N 14 00E
Biğa Turkey **80** E3 40 13N 27 14E
Big Bay De Noc Michigan U.S.A. **35** C2 45 50N 86 30W
Big Black *r.* Mississippi U.S.A. **63** H3 33 00N 90 00W
Bigelow Mountain Maine U.S.A. **37** Q6 45 10N 70 18W
Big Flats New York U.S.A. **64** D5 42 08N 76 57W
Big Fork River Minnesota U.S.A. **35** B2 48 00N 93 45W
Biggin Hill *tn.* England **82** D2 51 18N 0 04E
Bighorn *r.* U.S.A. **62** E6 45 00N 108 00W
Bighorn Mountains U.S.A. **62** E5 44 00N 108 00W
Big Lake Maine U.S.A. **31** A2 45 10N 67 45W
Big Muddy Creek Montana U.S.A. **40** C1 48 40N 104 50W
Big Rapids *tn.* Michigan U.S.A. **36** A4 43 42N 85 31W
Big Santa Anita Reservoir California U.S.A. **51** B3 34 11N 118 01W
Big Sioux *r.* Minnesota/South Dakota U.S.A. **63** G5 44 00N 96 00W
Big Spring *tn.* Texas U.S.A. **62** F3 32 15N 101 30W
Big Tujunga Reservoir California U.S.A. **51** B4 34 19N 118 11W
Bihac Bosnia-Herzegovina **81** C3 44 49N 15 53E
Bihar *admin.* India **95** F4 24 40N 86 00E
Bijapur India **95** D3 16 47N 75 48E
Bījar Iran **93** G6 35 52N 47 39E
Bikaner India **95** C5 28 01N 73 22E
Bilaspur India **95** E4 27 51N 82 00E
Bilbao Spain **77** B3 43 15N 2 56W
Bilibino Russia **89** S9 68 00N 166 15E
Billings Montana U.S.A. **62** E6 45 47N 108 30W
Biloxi Mississippi U.S.A. **63** I3 30 24N 88 55W
Binghamton New York U.S.A. **64** E5 42 06N 75 55W
Bintulu Malaysia **99** E4 3 12N 113 01E
Bioko *i.* Equatorial Guinea **106** G8 3 00N 8 20E
Birao Central African Republic **106** J10 10 11N 22 49E
Biratnagar Nepal **95** F5 26 27N 87 17E
Birch Creek Montana U.S.A. **41** C1 48 20N 112 50W
Birch Lake Minnesota U.S.A. **35** B2 47 45N 91 48W
Birdsville Australia **110** F4 25 50S 139 20E
Bīrjand Iran **93** I5 32 55N 59 10E
Birkenhead England **78** H5 53 24N 3 02W
Birkenwerder Germany **83** F2 52 42N 13 17E
Bîrlad Romania **81** E4 46 14N 27 40E
Birmingham Alabama U.S.A. **63** I3 33 30N 86 55W
Birmingham England **78** J4 52 30N 1 50W
Birnin Kebbi Nigeria **106** F10 12 30N 4 11E
Birobidzhan Russia **89** P5 48 49N 132 54E
Biscay, Bay of Atlantic Ocean **77** B4 45 30N 2 50W
Biscoe Islands Antarctica **117** 66 00S 67 00W
Bishkek *(Frunze)* Kirgyzstan **91** L3 42 53N 74 46E
Bismarck North Dakota U.S.A. **62** F6 46 50N 100 48W
Bismarck Archipelago Papua New Guinea **110** H9/I9 2 30S 149 00E
Bismarck, Cape Greenland **116** 77 00N 18 00W
Bismarck Sea Papua New Guinea **110** H9 4 00S 147 30E
Bissau Guinea-Bissau **106** B10 11 52N 15 39W
Bistrita Romania **81** D4 47 08N 24 30E
Bistrita *r.* Romania **81** E4 47 00N 25 00E
Bitola Macedonia **81** D3 41 01N 21 21E
Bitterroot Range *mts.* U.S.A. **62** D6 46 00N 114 00W
Biwa-ko *l.* Japan **100** H2 35 10N 136 00E
Biya *r.* Russia **91** O5 51 00N 88 00E
Biysk Russia **91** O5 52 35N 85 16E
Bizerte Tunisia **106** G15 37 18N 9 52E
Blackall Australia **110** H5 24 23S 145 27E
Blackburn England **78** I5 53 45N 2 29W
Black Forest *see* Schwarzwald
Black Lake Michigan U.S.A. **36** B6 45 30N 84 20W
Black Mountains Wales **78** H3 51 55N 3 10W
Black Point Hong Kong U.K. **98** A2 22 24N 113 54E
Blackpool England **78** H5 53 50N 3 03W
Black River Michigan U.S.A. **36** D4 43 25N 82 35W
Black River *tn.* Jamaica **67** Q8 18 02N 77 52W
Black Sea Eurasia **90** C3 43 00N 35 00E
Black Volta *r.* Ghana **106** E10 9 00N 2 40W
Blackwater *r.* Irish Republic **78** C4 52 10N 9 05W
Blackwell Oklahoma U.S.A. **63** G4 36 47N 97 18W
Blagoevgrad Bulgaria **81** D3 41 01N 23 05E
Blagoveshchensk Russia **89** O6 50 19N 127 30E
Blaine Washington U.S.A. **42** H4 49 00N 122 44W
Blair Island California U.S.A. **49** C2 37 31N 122 13W
Blanc, Cape *see* Ras Nouadhidbou
Blanchisseuse Trinidad and Tobago **66** T10 10 47N 61 20W
Blankenburg Germany **83** F2 52 35N 13 26E
Blankenfelde Germany **83** F1 52 19N 13 24E
Blantyre Malawi **107** L4 15 46S 35 00E
Blenheim New Zealand **111** B2 41 32S 173 58E
Bligh Water *sd.* Fiji **114** T16 17 00S 178 00E
Block Island Rhode Island U.S.A. **65** J4 41 10N 71 34W
Block Island Sound New York U.S.A. **65** H4 41 08N 72 00W
Bloemfontein Republic of South Africa **107** K2 29 07S 26 14E
Bloody Foreland *c.* Irish Republic **78** C7 55 10N 8 15W
Bloomington Illinois U.S.A. **63** I5 40 29N 89 00W
Bloomington Indiana U.S.A. **63** I4 39 10N 86 31W
Bloomfield New Jersey U.S.A. **50** B2 40 49N 74 10W
Bloomfield New York U.S.A. **50** B1 40 37N 74 10W
Bloomsburg Pennsylvania U.S.A. **64** D3 40 59N 76 27W
Bluefield West Virginia U.S.A. **63** J4 37 14N 81 17W
Bluefields Nicaragua **67** H2 12 00N 83 49W
Blue Hills Reservation Massachusetts U.S.A. **52** B1 42 13N 71 05W
Blue Island Illinois U.S.A. **53** B1 41 40N 87 42W
Blue Mountain Pennsylvania U.S.A. **64** C3 40 10N 77 45W
Blue Mountains, The Jamaica **67** R8 18 00N 76 30W
Blue Nile *see* Bahr el Azraq
Bluff New Zealand **111** A1 46 38S 168 21E
Bluff Island Hong Kong U.K. **98** D1 22 19N 114 21E
Bluffton Indiana U.S.A. **35** C1 40 44N 85 11W
Blumberg Germany **83** G2 52 37N 13 28E
Blumenau Brazil **69** H7 26 55N 49 07W
Blyth England **78** J7 55 07N 1 30W
Bo Sierra Leone **106** C9 7 58N 11 45W
Boa Vista Brazil **68** E13 3 23S 55 30W
Bobigny France **83** B2 48 55N 2 28E
Bobo Dioulasso Burkina **106** E10 11 11N 4 18W
Bobruysk Belarus **90** B5 53 08N 29 10E
Bocas del Dragons *(The Dragon's Mouths) sd.* Venezuela **66** S10 10 47N 61 18W
Bocholt Germany **76** D5 51 49N 6 37E
Bochum Germany **76** J2 51 28N 7 11E
Bodélé *dep.* Chad **106** I11 17 00N 17 50E
Boden Sweden **79** E4 65 50N 21 44E
Bodensee *l.* Switzerland **77** D4 47 40N 9 30E
Bodmin Moor England **78** G2 50 35N 4 40W

Bodø Norway **79** C4 67 18N 14 26E
Bogalusa Louisiana U.S.A. **63** I3 30 56N 89 53W
Bogor Indonesia **99** D2 6 34S 106 45E
Bogotá Colombia **68** C13 4 38N 74 05W
Bog Walk Jamaica **67** Q8 18 06N 77 01W
Bo Hai *b.* China **97** N6 38 30N 118 30E
Bohnsdorf Germany **83** G1 52 23N 13 33E
Bohol *i.* The Philippines **99** G5 10 00N 124 00E
Bois Blanc Island Michigan U.S.A. **36** B6 45 45N 84 30W
Boise Idaho U.S.A. **62** C5 43 38N 116 12W
Boise City Oklahoma U.S.A. **62** F4 36 44N 102 31W
Bokaro India **95** F4 23 46N 85 55E
Boké Guinea **106** C10 10 57N 14 13W
Boknafjorden *fj.* Norway **79** B2 59 20N 6 00E
Bolesławiec Poland **80** C5 51 16N 34E
Bolgatanga Ghana **106** E10 10 44N 0 53W
Bolgrad Ukraine **90** B4 45 42N 28 35E
Bolivar, Pico *mt.* Venezuela **68** C14 8 33N 71 03W
BOLIVIA **68** E9
Bollnäs Sweden **79** D3 61 20N 16 25E
Bolmen *l.* Sweden **80** B6 57 00N 13 30E
Bologna Italy **81** B3 44 30N 11 20E
Bolton England **78** I5 53 35N 2 26W
Bolzano Italy **81** B4 46 30N 11 22E
Boma Zaïre **107** H6 5 50S 13 03E
Bombay India **95** C3 18 56N 72 51E
Bom Jesus da Lapa Brazil **68** I10 13 16S 43 23W
Bomu *r.* Central Africa **106** J8 4 50N 24 00E
Bonaire *i.* Lesser Antilles **67** K2 12 15N 68 27W
Bonaparte Archipelago Australia **110** D7 19 00S 126 00E
Bonasse Trinidad and Tobago **66** S9 10 05N 61 52W
Bondi Beach Australia **111** H2 33 45S 151 17E
Bondo Zaïre **106** J8 1 22S 23 54E
Bongor Chad **106** I10 10 18N 15 20E
Bonifacio Corsica **77** D3 41 23N 9 10E
Bonifacio, Strait of Corsica/Sardinia **77** D3 41 20N 8 45E
Bonita, Point California U.S.A. **49** A3 37 49N 122 32W
Bonn Germany **76** D5 50 44N 7 06E
Bonners Ferry Idaho U.S.A. **43** E1 48 41N 116 20W
Bonny, Bight of *b.* West Africa **106** G8 2 10N 7 30E
Bonthe Sierra Leone **106** C9 7 32N 12 30W
Boonsboro Maryland U.S.A. **64** C2 39 31N 77 39W
Boonton New Jersey U.S.A. **65** F3 40 55N 74 24W
Boosaaso Somalia **106** O10 11 18N 49 10E
Bor Sudan **106** L9 6 18N 31 34E
Borås Sweden **80** B6 57 44N 12 55E
Bordeaux France **77** B3 44 50N 0 34W
Borehamwood *tn.* England **82** B3 51 40N 0 16W
Borgholm Sweden **79** D2 56 51N 16 40E
Borgsdorf Germany **83** F2 52 44N 13 17E
Borislav Ukraine **80** D4 49 18N 23 28E
Borisoglebsk Russia **90** E5 51 23N 42 02E
Borisov Belarus **90** B5 54 09N 28 30E
Borlänge Sweden **79** D3 60 29N 15 25E
Borneo *i.* Asia **99** E4 0 00 114 00E
Bornholm *i.* Denmark **80** B6 55 02N 15 00E
Borough Green England **82** E2 51 17N 0 19E
Borūjerd Iran **93** G5 33 55N 48 48E
Borzya Russia **89** N6 50 24N 116 35E
Bosna *r.* Bosnia-Herzegovina **81** C3 45 00N 18 00E
BOSNIA-HERZEGOVINA **81** C3
Bossangoa Central African Republic **106** I9 6 27N 17 21E
Bosso Niger **106** H10 13 43N 13 19E
Boston England **78** K4 52 59N 0 01W
Boston Massachusetts U.S.A. **65** K5 42 20N 71 05W
Boston Harbor Massachusetts U.S.A. **52** C2 42 20N 71 00W
Boston Harbor Island State Park Massachusetts U.S.A. **52** C2 42 16N 70 54W
Boston Mountains Arkansas U.S.A. **63** H4 36 00N 94 00W
Botafogo Brazil **69** Q2 22 57S 43 11W
Botany Australia **111** G1 33 58S 151 12E
Botany Bay Australia **111** G1 34 04S 151 08E
Bothnia, Gulf of Sweden/Finland **79** D3 61 00N 19 10E
Botoşani Romania **81** E4 47 44N 26 41E
BOTSWANA **107** J3
Bottineau North Dakota U.S.A. **39** A1 48 30N 100 28W
Bottrop Germany **76** H3 51 31N 6 55E
Bötzow Germany **83** E2 52 40N 13 07E
Bouaké Côte d'Ivoire **106** D9 7 42N 5 00W
Bouar Central African Republic **106** I9 5 58N 15 35E
Bouârfa Morocco **106** E14 32 30N 1 59W
Boufarik Algeria **77** C2 36 36N 2 54E
Bougainville Island Papua New Guinea **110** J8 6 50S 155 00E
Bougouni Mali **106** D10 11 25N 7 28W
Bougzoul Algeria **77** C2 35 42N 2 51E
Boulder Colarado U.S.A. **62** E5 40 02N 105 16W
Boulogne-Billancourt France **83** B2 48 50N 2 15E
Boulogne-sur-Mer France **76** C5 50 43N 1 37E
Boundary Bald Mountain Maine U.S.A. **37** Q6 45 45N 70 14W
Bourem Mali **106** E11 16 59N 0 20W
Bourges France **77** C4 47 05N 2 23E
Bourke Australia **110** H3 30 09S 145 59E
Bournemouth England **78** J2 50 43N 1 54W
Bou Saâda Algeria **106** F15 35 10N 4 09E
Bousso Chad **106** I10 10 32N 16 45E
Bouvet Island Southern Ocean **113** I1 54 26S 3 24E
Bowbells North Dakota U.S.A. **40** C1 48 48N 102 14W
Bowen Australia **110** H6 20 00S 148 10E
Bowling Green Kentucky U.S.A. **63** I4 37 00N 86 29W
Bowling Green Missouri U.S.A. **63** H4 39 21N 91 11W
Bowling Green Ohio U.S.A. **36** C2 41 22N 83 40W
Bowman North Dakota U.S.A. **62** F6 46 11N 103 26W
Box Hill England **82** B2 51 16N 0 13W
Boyne *r.* Irish Republic **78** E5 53 40N 6 35W
Boyne City Michigan U.S.A. **36** A6 45 13N 85 00W
Boyoma Falls Zaïre **106** K8 0 18N 25 30E
Bozeman Montana U.S.A. **62** D6 45 40N 111 00W
Bozoum Central African Republic **106** I9 6 16N 16 22E
Bōsō-hantō *p.* Japan **100** M2 35 15N 140 05E
Brač *i.* Croatia **81** C3 43 00N 16 00E
Braddock Pennsylvania U.S.A. **53** E1 40 24N 79 53W
Bradford Pennsylvania U.S.A. **64** B4 41 57N 78 39W
Bradford England **78** J5 53 48N 1 45W
Brady Texas U.S.A. **62** G3 31 08N 99 22W
Braga Portugal **77** A3 41 32N 8 26W
Bragança Brazil **68** H12 1 02S 46 46W
Bragança Portugal **77** A3 41 47N 6 46W
Brahmapur India **95** E3 19 21N 84 51E
Brahmaputra *r.* India **95** G5 26 40N 93 00E
Brăila Romania **81** E4 45 17N 27 58E
Brainerd Minnesota U.S.A. **63** H6 46 20N 94 10W
Braintree Massachusetts U.S.A. **52** B1 42 14N 71 00W
Brandenburg Germany **76** E5 52 25N 12 34E
Branford Connecticut U.S.A. **65** H4 41 17N 72 48W
Brasileia Brazil **68** D10 10 59S 68 45W
Brásilia Brazil **68** H9 15 45S 47 57W
Braşov Romania **81** E4 45 39N 25 35E
Bratislava Czechoslovakia **81** C4 48 10N 17 10E
Bratsk Russia **89** M7 56 20N 101 50E
Bratsk Reservoir Russia **89** M7 56 00N 102 00E
Brattleboro Vermont U.S.A. **65** H5 42 51N 72 36W
Braunschweig Germany **76** E5 52 15N 10 30E
Bray Irish Republic **78** E5 53 12N 6 06W
BRAZIL **68** G10
Brazil Basin Atlantic Ocean **113** F5 10 00S 26 00W
Brazilian Highlands Brazil **55** 10 00S 50 00W
Brazil Plateau Brazil **55** 20 00S 45 00W
Brazos *r.* Texas U.S.A. **63** G3 32 00N 97 00W
Brazzaville Congo **107** I7 4 14S 15 14E
Breakheart Reservation Massachusetts U.S.A. **52** B2 42 29N 71 02W
Brea Reservoir California U.S.A. **51** C2 33 54N 117 56W
Brecon Beacons National Park Wales **78** H3 51 53N 3 30W
Breda Netherlands **76** C5 51 35N 4 46E
Bredy Russia **91** J5 52 23N 60 16E
Breidha Fjördur *b.* Iceland **79** H7 65 15N 23 00W
Brekstad Norway **79** B3 63 50N 9 50E
Bremen Germany **76** D5 53 05N 8 48E
Bremerhaven Germany **76** D5 53 33N 8 35E
Bremerton Washington U.S.A. **62** B6 47 34N 122 40W
Brenham Texas U.S.A. **63** G3 30 09N 96 24W
Brenner Pass Austria/Italy **81** B2 47 02N 11 32E
Brent *bor.* Greater London England **82** B3 51 34N 0 17W
Brentwood England **82** E3 51 38N 0 18E
Brentwood New York U.S.A. **65** G3 40 47N 73 14W
Brentwood Pennsylvania U.S.A. **53** E1 40 22N 79 59W
Brescia Italy **81** B4 45 33N 10 13E
Brest Belarus **90** A5 52 08N 23 40E
Brest France **76** B4 48 23N 4 30W
Brewer Maine U.S.A. **33** C1 44 52N 68 01W
Brewerton New York U.S.A. **64** D6 43 15N 76 09W
Brewster Massachusetts U.S.A. **65** K4 41 46N 70 05W
Brewster New York U.S.A. **65** G4 41 24N 73 37W
Brewster Washington U.S.A. **42** J4 48 05N 119 50W
Brezhnev *see* Naberezhnyye Chelny
Bria Central African Republic **106** J9 67 32N 22 00E
Briançon France **77** D3 44 53N 6 39E
Brick New Jersey U.S.A. **65** F3 40 04N 74 08W
Brickfield Trinidad and Tobago **66** T9 10 20N 61 16W
Bridgeport Connecticut U.S.A. **65** G4 41 12N 73 12W
Bridgeton New Jersey U.S.A. **64** E2 39 26N 75 14W
Bridgetown Barbados **66** V12 13 06N 59 37W
Bridgeville Pennsylvania U.S.A. **53** D1 40 20N 80 08W
Bridgewater New York U.S.A. **64** E5 42 52N 75 16W
Bridgwater England **78** H3 51 08N 3 00W
Brie-Comte-Robert France **83** C1 48 41N 2 37E
Brieselang Germany **83** E2 52 36N 13 00E
Briey France **76** D4 49 15N 5 57E
Brigantine New Jersey U.S.A. **65** F2 39 24N 74 22W
Brigham City Utah U.S.A. **62** D5 41 30N 112 02W
Brighton England **78** K2 50 50N 0 10W
Brighton Beach *tn.* New York U.S.A. **50** C1 40 34N 73 58W
Brindisi Italy **81** C3 40 37N 17 57E
Briones Reservoir California U.S.A. **49** C3 37 55N 122 12W
Brisbane Australia **110** I4 27 30S 153 00E
Brisbane California U.S.A. **49** B2 37 41N 122 24W
Bristol England **78** I3 51 27N 2 35W
Bristol Connecticut U.S.A. **65** H4 41 41N 72 57W
Bristol Rhode Island U.S.A. **65** J4 41 41N 71 12W
Bristol Bay Alaska U.S.A. **10** D4 57 30N 159 00W
Bristol Channel England/Wales **78** H3 51 20N 3 50W
British Isles Atlantic Ocean **54** 55 00N 2 00W
British Mountains Canada/U.S.A. **44** D4 69 00N 141 00W
Brno Czechoslovakia **80** C4 49 13N 16 40E
Broadview Illinois U.S.A. **53** A2 41 50N 87 51W
Brockport New York U.S.A. **64** C6 43 13N 77 56W
Brockton Massachusetts U.S.A. **65** J5 42 06N 71 01W
Brockway Pennsylvania U.S.A. **64** B4 41 15N 78 48W
Brody Ukraine **90** B5 50 05N 25 08E
Broer Ruys, Cape Greenland **116** 73 30N 20 20W
Broken Hill *tn.* Australia **110** G3 31 57S 141 30E
Broken Ridge Indian Ocean **112** H3 30 00S 93 00E
Bromley *bor.* Greater London England **82** D2 51 31N 0 01W
Brønnøysund Norway **79** C4 65 38N 12 15E
Bronx New York U.S.A. **65** G3 40 50N 73 52W
Brookfield Illinois U.S.A. **53** A2 41 48N 87 51W
Brookings South Dakota U.S.A. **63** G5 44 19N 96 47W
Brookline Massachusetts U.S.A. **52** B2 42 20N 71 07W
Brooklyn Connecticut U.S.A. **65** J4 41 47N 71 57W
Brooklyn Maryland U.S.A. **64** D2 39 14N 76 38W
Brooklyn New York U.S.A. **50** C1 40 41N 73 57W
Brooks Island California U.S.A. **49** B3 37 53N 122 21W
Brooks Range *mts.* Alaska U.S.A. **44** A3/B3 67 55N 155 00W
Brookvale Australia **111** H2 33 46S 151 16E
Broome Australia **110** C6 17 58S 122 15E
Browning Montana U.S.A. **62** D6 48 33N 113 00W
Brown's Town Jamaica **67** Q8 18 28N 77 22W
Brownsville Texas U.S.A. **63** G2 25 54N 97 30W
Browntown New Jersey U.S.A. **65** F3 40 25N 74 20W
Brownwood Texas U.S.A. **62** G3 31 42N 98 59W
Bruay-en-Artois France **76** C5 50 29N 2 33E
Bruges *see* Brugge
Brugge *(Bruges)* Belgium **76** C5 51 13N 3 14E
BRUNEI **99** E4
Brunoy France **83** C1 48 40N 2 31E
Brunswick Georgia U.S.A. **63** J3 31 09N 81 30W
Brunswick Maryland U.S.A. **64** C2 39 19N 77 37W
Brussel *see* Bruxelles
Brussels *see* Bruxelles
Bruxelles *(Brussel, Brussels)* Belgium **76** C5 50 50N 4 21E
Bryan Ohio U.S.A. **36** B2 41 30N 84 34W
Bryan Texas U.S.A. **63** G3 30 41N 96 24W
Bryansk Russia **90** C5 53 15N 34 09E
Brzeg Poland **80** C5 50 52N 17 27E
Bü Ağri Daği *(Mt. Ararat)* Turkey **92** F6 39 44N 44 15E
Bucaramanga Colombia **68** C14 7 08N 73 10W
Buchanan Liberia **106** C9 5 57N 10 02W
Bucharest *see* Bucureşti
Buchholz Germany **83** F2 52 37N 13 24E
Bucholz Germany **76** H2 51 25N 6 45E
Buckinghamshire *co.* England **82** B3 51 50N 0 50W
Buckow Germany **83** F1 52 24N 13 24E
Bucureşti *(Bucharest)* Romania **81** E3 44 25N 26 07E
Budapest Hungary **81** C4 47 30N 19 03E
Budd Lake *tn.* New Jersey U.S.A. **65** F3 40 52N 74 44W
Büderich Germany **76** G1 51 15N 6 20E
Budjala Zaïre **106** I8 2 38N 19 48E
Buena Park *tn.* California U.S.A. **51** B2 33 52N 118 02W
Buenaventura Mexico **66** C5 29 50N 107 30W
Buenos Aires Argentina **69** F6 34 40S 58 30W
Buenos Aires, Lake Argentina/Chile **69** C3 47 00S 72 00W
Buer Germany **76** J3 51 35N 7 05E
Buffalo New York U.S.A. **38** D1 42 52N 78 55W
Buffalo Wyoming U.S.A. **62** E5 44 21N 106 40W
Buff Bay *tn.* Jamaica **67** R8 18 18N 76 40W
Bugul'ma Russia **91** G5 54 32N 52 46E
Buheirat-Murrat-el-Kubra *(Great Bitter Lake)* Egypt **107** S2 30 22N 32 22E
Buheirat-Murrat-el-Sughra *(Little Bitter Lake)* Egypt **107** T2 30 14N 32 33E
Bujumbura Burundi **107** K7 3 22S 29 19E
Bukachacha Russia **89** N6 53 00N 116 58E
Bukama Zaïre **107** K6 9 13S 25 52E
Bukavu Zaïre **106** K7 2 30S 28 50E
Bukhara Uzbekistan **91** J2 39 47N 64 26E
Bukittinggi Indonesia **99** C3 0 18S 100 20E
Bukoba Tanzania **106** L7 1 19S 31 49E
Bula Indonesia **99** I3 3 07S 130 27E
Bulandshahr India **95** D5 28 30N 77 49E
Bulawayo Zimbabwe **107** K3 20 10S 28 43E
BULGARIA **81** D3
Buller *r.* New Zealand **111** B2 41 50S 172 20E
Bull Shoals Lake U.S.A. **63** H4 36 00N 93 00W
Bulun Russia **89** O10 70 45N 127 20E
Bumba Zaïre **106** J8 2 10N 22 30E
Bunbury Australia **110** B3 33 20S 115 34E
Bundaberg Australia **110** I5 24 50S 152 21E
Bundeena Australia **111** G1 34 06S 151 07E
Bungo-suidō *sd.* Japan **100** B1 33 00N 132 30E
Bunia Zaïre **106** L8 1 33N 30 13E
Bura Kenya **106** M7 1 06S 39 58E
Buraydah Saudi Arabia **92** F4 26 20N 43 59E
Burbank California U.S.A. **51** A3 34 10N 118 25W
Burbank Illinois U.S.A. **53** A2 41 45N 87 48W
Burco Somalia **106** O9 9 31N 45 33E
Burdur Turkey **92** D6 37 44N 30 17E
Bure *r.* England **78** L4 52 47N 1 20E
Bureya *r.* Russia **89** P6 52 00N 133 00E
Bûr Fu'ad Egypt **107** S4 31 50N 32 19E
Burgas Bulgaria **81** E3 42 30N 27 29E
Burgos Spain **77** B3 42 21N 3 41W
Burgsvik Sweden **80** C6 57 03N 18 19E
Burhanpur India **95** D4 21 18N 76 08E
Buri Khali India **94** J2 22 30N 88 10E
BURKINA **106** E10
Burlingame California U.S.A. **49** B2 37 35N 122 25W
Burlington Colorado U.S.A. **62** F4 39 17N 102 17W
Burlington Iowa U.S.A. **63** H5 40 50N 91 07W
Burlington Massachusetts U.S.A. **65** J5 42 29N 71 12W
Burlington New Jersey U.S.A. **64** F3 40 05N 74 51W
Burlington Vermont U.S.A. **63** L5 44 28N 73 14W
Burlington Washington U.S.A. **42** H4 48 28N 122 20W
BURMA *see* MYANMAR
Burnham Park Illinois U.S.A. **53** B2 41 49N 87 35W
Burnie Australia **110** H1 41 03S 145 55E
Bursa Turkey **92** C7 40 12N 29 04E
Bûr Sa'îd *see* Port Said
Bûr Safâga Egypt **92** D4 25 43N 33 55E
Bûr Taufiq Egypt **107** T1 29 57N 32 34E
Burt Lake Michigan U.S.A. **36** B6 45 30N 84 40W
Buru *i.* Indonesia **99** 3 20S 126 30E
BURUNDI **107** L7
Burwell Nebraska U.S.A. **62** G5 41 48N 99 09W
Būshehr Iran **93** H4 28 57N 50 52E
Bushey England **82** B3 51 39N 0 22W
Bushy Park England **82** B2 51 25N 0 11W
Busira *r.* Zaïre **106** I7 1 00S 20 00E
Busto Arsizio Italy **81** A4 43 37N 8 51E
Buta Zaïre **106** K8 2 49N 24 50E
Butare Rwanda **106** K7 2 35S 29 44E
Bute *i.* Scotland **78** F7 55 50N 5 05W
Buton *i.* Indonesia **99** G3 5 00S 122 40E
Butovo Russia **88** M1 55 30N 37 32E
Butte Montana U.S.A. **62** D6 46 00N 112 31W
Butt of Lewis *c.* Scotland **78** E10 58 30N 6 20W
Butuan The Philippines **99** H5 8 56N 125 31E
Buulobarde Somalia **106** O8 3 50N 45 33E
Buzău Romania **81** E4 45 09N 26 49E
Buzzards Bay Massachusetts U.S.A. **65** K4 41 35N 70 50W
Buzzards Bay *tn.* Massachusetts U.S.A. **65** K4 41 45N 70 37W
Bydgoszcz Poland **80** C5 53 16N 18 00E
BYELORUSSIA see BELARUS
Byfleet England **82** B2 51 21N 0 29W
Bygland Norway **79** B2 58 50N 7 49E
Byrd Land *geog. reg.* Antarctica **117** 77 00S 130 00W
Byrranga Mountains Russia **89** L10 75 00N 100 00E
Bytom Poland **80** C5 50 21N 18 51E

C

Cabanatuan The Philippines **99** G7 15 30N 120 58E
Cabimas Venezuela **68** C15 10 26N 71 27W
Cabinda *admin.* Angola **107** H6 5 30S 12 20E
Cabinet Mountains Montana U.S.A. **43** E1 48 15N 115 45W
Cabo Brazil **68** J11 8 16S 35 00W
Cabo Blanco *c.* Costa Rica **67** G1 9 36N 85 06W
Cabo Catoche *c.* Mexico **67** G4 21 38N 87 08W
Cabo Corrientes *c.* Colombia **68** B14 5 29N 77 36W
Cabo Corrientes *c.* Mexico **66** C4 20 25N 105 42W
Cabo de Creus *c.* Spain **77** C3 42 19N 3 19E
Cabo de Gata *c.* Spain **77** B2 36 44N 2 10W
Cabo de Hornos *(Cape Horn)* Chile **69** D1 56 00S 67 15W
Cabo de la Nao *c.* Spain **77** C2 38 44N 0 14E
Cabo Delgado *c.* Mozambique **107** N5 10 45S 40 45E
Cabo de Palos *c.* Spain **77** B2 37 38N 0 40W
Cabo de Peñas *c.* Spain **77** A3 43 39N 5 50W
Cabo de São Vicente *c.* Portugal **77** A2 37 01N 8 59W
Cabo de Tortosa *c.* Spain **77** C3 40 44N 0 54E
Cabo Dos Bahías *c.* Argentina **69** D4 45 00S 65 30W
Cabo Espichel *c.* Portugal **77** A2 38 24N 9 13W
Cabo Falso *c.* Mexico **66** B4 22 50N 110 00W
Cabo Finisterre *c.* Spain **77** A3 42 52N 9 16W
Cabo Gracias à Dios *c.* Nicaragua **67** H3 15 00N 83 10W
Cabo Orange *c.* Brazil **68** G13 4 25N 51 32W
Cabo Ortegal *c.* Spain **77** A3 43 46N 7 54W
Cabora Bassa Dam Mozambique **107** L4 16 00S 33 00E
Caborca Mexico **66** B6 30 42N 112 10W
Cabo San Juan *c.* Argentina **69** E2 54 45S 63 46W
Cabo Santa Elena *c.* Costa Rica **67** G2 10 54N 85 56W
Cabo Virgenes *c.* Argentina **69** D2 52 20S 68 00W
Cabrera *i.* Balearic Islands **77** C2 39 00N 2 59E
Cabriel *r.* Spain **77** B2 39 20N 1 15W
Čačak Serbia Yugoslavia **81** D3 43 54N 20 22E
Cáceres Brazil **68** F9 16 05S 57 40W
Cáceres Spain **77** A2 39 29N 6 23W
Cachoeira Brazil **68** J10 12 35S 38 59W
Cachoeira do Sul Brazil **69** G6 30 03S 52 52W
Cachoeiro de Itapemirim Brazil **69** I8 20 51N 41 07W
Cadillac Michigan U.S.A. **36** A5 44 15N 85 23W
Cádiz Spain **77** A2 36 32N 6 18W
Cadiz The Philippines **99** G6 10 57N 123 18E
Cádiz, Gulf of Spain **77** A2 36 30N 7 15W
Caen France **76** B4 49 11N 0 22W
Caernarfon Wales **78** G5 53 08N 4 16W
Cagayan de Oro The Philippines **99** G5 8 29N 124 40E
Cágliari Italy **81** A2 39 13N 9 08E
Caguas Puerto Rico **67** K3 18 41N 66 04W
Caha Mountains Irish Republic **78** B3 51 40N 9 40W
Cahors France **77** C3 44 28N 0 26E
Caicos Passage *sd.* West Indies **67** J4 22 20N 72 30W
Cairngorms *mts.* Scotland **78** H9 57 10N 3 30W
Cairns Australia **110** H6 16 51S 145 43E
Cairo *(El Qâ'hira)* Egypt **92** D5 30 03N 31 15E
Cairo Illinois U.S.A. **63** I4 37 01N 89 09W
Cajamarca Peru **68** B11 7 09S 78 32W
Cajàzeiras Brazil **68** J11 6 52S 38 31W
Caju Brazil **69** Q2 22 53S 43 13W
Cakovec Croatia **81** C4 46 24N 16 26E
Calabar Nigeria **106** G8 4 56N 8 22E
Calabozo Venezuela **67** K1 8 58N 67 28W
Calahorra Spain **77** B3 49 19N 1 58W
Calais France **76** C5 50 57N 1 52E
Calama Chile **69** D8 22 30S 68 55W
Calamar Colombia **68** C15 10 16N 74 55W
Calamian Group *is.* The Philippines **99** F6 12 00N 120 00E
Calapan The Philippines **99** G6 13 23N 121 10E
Calatayud Spain **77** B3 41 21N 1 39W
Calçoene Brazil **68** G13 2 30N 50 55W
Calcutta India **94** K2 22 30N 88 20E
Caldwell Idaho U.S.A. **62** C5 43 39N 116 40W
Caldwell New Jersey U.S.A. **50** A2 40 49N 74 16W
Cali Colombia **68** B13 3 24N 76 30W
Calicut India **95** D2 11 15N 75 45E
Caliente Nevada U.S.A. **62** D4 37 36N 114 31W
California *state* U.S.A. **62** C4
California Trinidad and Tobago **66** T9 10 24N 61 28W
Callicoon New York U.S.A. **64** E4 41 46N 75 03W
Calmut Harbor Indiana U.S.A. **53** C1 41 44N 87 30W
Caltanissetta Italy **81** B2 37 29N 14 04E
Calumet City Illinois U.S.A. **53** B1 41 36N 87 32W
Calumet Park Indiana U.S.A. **53** B1 41 43N 87 30W
Calumet River Illinios U.S.A. **53** B1 41 40N 87 33W
Calumet Sag Channel Illinois U.S.A. **53** A1 41 41N 87 52W
Calvi Corsica **77** D3 42 34N 8 44E
Calvinia Republic of South Africa **107** I1 31 25S 19 47E
Camaçari Brazil **68** J10 12 44S 38 16W
Camacupa Angola **107** I5 12 03S 17 50E
Camagüey Cuba **67** I4 21 25N 77 55W
CAMBODIA *(KAMPUCHEA)* **99** C6
Cambrian Mountains Wales **78** H4 52 15N 3 45W
Cambridge England **78** L4 52 12N 0 07E
Cambridge Jamaica **67** Q8 18 18N 77 54W
Cambridge Maryland U.S.A. **63** K4 38 34N 76 04W
Cambridge Massachusetts U.S.A. **52** B2 42 22N 71 06W
Cambridge New Zealand **111** C3 37 53S 175 29E
Cambridge Reservoir Massachusetts U.S.A. **52** A2 42 25N 71 16W
Camden *bor.* Greater London England **82** C3 51 33N 0 10W
Camden New Jersey U.S.A. **64** E2 39 57N 75 06W
Camden New York U.S.A. **64** E6 43 21N 75 45W
Cameia National Park Angola **107** I5 12 00S 22 00E
CAMEROON **106** H9
Cametá Brazil **68** H12 2 12S 49 30W
Camiri Bolivia **68** E8 20 08S 63 33W
Camocim Brazil **68** I12 2 55S 40 50W
Camorta *i.* Nicobar Islands **95** G1 7 30N 93 30E
Campbell New York U.S.A. **64** C5 42 14N 77 11W
Campbell Island Southern Ocean **114** G2 52 30S 169 10E
Campbeltown Scotland **78** F7 55 26N 5 36W
Campeche Mexico **66** F3 19 50N 90 30W
Camp Hill *tn.* Pennsylvania U.S.A **64** D3 40 14N 76 56W
Campina Grande Brazil **68** J11 7 15S 35 50W
Campinas Brazil **69** H8 22 54S 47 06W
Campine *see* Kempen Land
Campoalegre Colombia **68** B13 2 49N 75 19W
Campobasso Italy **81** B3 41 33N 14 39E
Campo Grande Brazil **68** G8 20 24S 54 35W
Campo Maior Brazil **68** I12 4 50S 42 12W
Campo Mourão Brazil **69** G8 24 01S 52 24W
Campos Brazil **69** I8 21 46S 41 21W
Campos Elyseos Brazil **69** P3 22 42S 43 16W
Cam Ranh Vietnam **99** C6 11 54N 109 14E
Canaan Connecticut U.S.A. **65** G5 42 02N 73 20W
Canada Basin Arctic Ocean **116** 80 00N 140 00W
Canadaigua New York U.S.A. **64** C5 42 00N 77 00W
Canadian *r.* U.S.A. **62** F4 35 00N 104 00W
Canajoharie New York U.S.A. **65** F5 42 54N 74 37W
Canakkale Turkey **92** C7 40 09N 26 25E
Canal de l'Ourcq France **83** C2 48 55N 2 32E
Canal du Midi France **77** C3 43 20N 2 00E
Canandaigua Lake New York U.S.A. **64** C5 42 50N 77 20W
Cananea Mexico **66** B6 30 59N 110 20W
Canary Basin Atlantic Ocean **113** F9 26 20N 30 00W
Canary Islands Spain **106** B13 28 30N 15 10W

Canastea Pennsylvania U.S.A. **64** C4 41 07N 77 27W
Canastota New York U.S.A. **64** E6 43 04N 75 47W
Canaveral, Cape Florida U.S.A. **63** J2 28 28N 80 28W
Canberra Australia **110** H2 35 18S 149 08E
Candlestick Point California U.S.A. **49** B2 37 42N 122 22W
Candlewood Lake Connecticut U.S.A. **65** G4 41 30N 73 30W
Cando North Dakota U.S.A. **39** B1 48 30N 99 11W
Canfield Ohio U.S.A. **36** F2 41 02N 80 47W
Cangamba Angola **107** I5 13 40S 19 47E
Cangrejos Point Trinidad and Tobago **66** T9 10 25N 61 29W
Cangzhou China **97** N6 38 19N 116 54E
Canisteo River New York U.S.A. **64** C5 42 15N 77 30W
Cannanore India **95** D2 11 53N 75 23E
Cannes France **77** D3 43 33N 7 00E
Cannonsville Reservoir New York U.S.A. **64** E5 42 05N 75 20W
Canôas Brazil **69** G7 28 55S 51 10W
Cantabrian Mountains *see* Cordillera Cantabrica
Cantaro Trinidad and Tobago **66** T10 10 42N 61 28W
Canterbury Australia **111** G2 33 55S 151 07E
Canterbury England **78** M3 51 17N 1 05E
Canterbury Bight *b.* New Zealand **111** B2 44 00S 172 30E
Canterbury Plains New Zealand **111** B2 43 30S 172 00E
Can Tho Vietnam **99** D6 10 03N 105 46E
Canto de Rio Brazil **69** Q2 22 55S 43 06W
Canton *see* Guangzhou
Caparo Trinidad and Tobago **66** T9 10 27N 61 19W
Caparo *r.* Trinidad and Tobago **66** T10 10 31N 61 25W
Cap Blanc *see* Ras Nouâdhibou
Cap Bon *c.* Tunisia **81** B2 37 08N 11 00E
Cap Corse *c.* Corsica **77** D3 43 00N 9 21E
Cap d'Ambre *c.* Madagascar **107** N5 12 00S 49 15E
Cap de la Hague *c.* France **76** B4 49 44N 1 56W
Cap des Trois Fourches *c.* Morocco **77** B2 35 26N 2 57W
Cape Basin Atlantic Ocean **113** I3 36 00S 6 00E
Cape Coast *tn.* Ghana **106** E9 5 10N 1 13W
Cape Cod Bay U.S.A. **65** K4 41 55N 70 20W
Cape Cod Canal Massachusetts U.S.A. **65** K4 41 45N 70 30W
Cape Girardeau *tn.* Missouri U.S.A. **63** I4 37 19N 89 31W
Cape Evans *r.s.* Antarctica **117** 77 38S 166 24E
Cape May *tn.* New Jersey U.S.A. **64** F1 38 56N 74 54W
Cape May Court House *tn.* New Jersey U.S.A. **64** F2 39 05N 74 50W
Cape Province *admin.* Republic of South Africa **107** J1 31 00S 22 00E
Cape Rise Indian Ocean **113** J3 42 00S 11 00E
Cape Town Republic of South Africa **107** I1 33 56S 18 28E
Cape Verde Basin Atlantic Ocean **113** E8 11 00N 35 00W
CAPE VERDE ISLANDS Atlantic Ocean **113** F8 16 00N 24 00W
Cape York Peninsula Australia **110** G7 12 30S 142 30E
Cap-Haïtien Haiti **67** J3 19 47N 72 17W
Capitán Arturo Prat *r.s.* Antarctica **117** 62 30S 59 41W
Capo Carbonara *c.* Italy **81** A2 39 07N 9 33E
Capo Passero *c.* Italy **81** C2 36 42N 15 08E
Capo Santa Maria di Leuca *c.* Italy **81** C2 39 47N 18 22E
Capo San Vito *c.* Italy **81** B2 38 12N 12 43E
Capri *i.* Italy **81** B3 40 33N 14 15E
Capricorn Channel Australia **110** I5 23 00S 152 30E
Caprivi Strip Namibia **107** J4 17 30S 27 50E
Cap Ste. Marie *c.* Madagascar **107** O2 25 34S 45 10E
Cap Vert *c.* Senegal **106** B10 14 43N 17 33W
Caracal Romania **81** D3 44 07N 24 18E
Caracas Venezuela **68** D15 10 35N 66 56W
Caratinga Brazil **68** I9 19 50S 42 06W
Caravelas Brazil **68** J9 17 45S 39 15W
Carbondale Pennsylvania U.S.A. **64** E4 41 35N 75 31W
Carcassonne France **77** C3 43 13N 2 21E
Cardamon Hills India **95** D1 9 50N 77 00E
Cárdenas Mexico **66** E4 22 00N 99 41W
Cardiff Wales **78** H3 51 30N 3 13W
Cardigan Bay Wales **78** G4 52 30N 4 30W
Carei Romania **81** D4 47 40N 22 28E
Cargados Carajos Shoals Indian Ocean **112** E5 16 00S 60 00E
Cariacica Brazil **68** I8 20 15S 40 23W
Caribbean Sea Central America **67** I3 15 00N 75 00W
Caribou Maine U.S.A. **33** C2 46 52N 68 01W
Caringbah Australia **111** G1 34 03S 151 07E
Caripito Venezuela **68** E15 10 07N 63 07W
Carlisle England **78** I6 54 54N 2 55W
Carlisle Pennsylvania U.S.A. **64** C3 40 12N 77 12W
Carlisle Bay Barbados **66** V12 13 05N 59 37W
Carlsbad New Mexico U.S.A. **62** F3 32 25N 104 14W
Carlsberg Ridge Indian Ocean **112** E7/F6 5 00N 65 00E
Carlton Washington U.S.A. **42** H4 48 14N 120 05W
Carmarthen Wales **78** G3 51 51N 4 20W
Carmel New York U.S.A. **65** G4 41 25N 73 40W
Carmen Colombia **68** B14 9 46N 75 06W
Carnarvon Australia **110** A5 24 51S 113 45E
Carnegie Pennsylvania U.S.A. **53** D1 40 24N 80 06W
Carnegie, Lake Australia **110** C4 27 00S 124 00E
Carnegie Ridge Pacific Ocean **115** R7 1 30S 95 00W
Car Nicobar *i.* Nicobar Islands **95** G1 9 00N 93 00E
Carnot Central African Republic **106** I8 4 59N 15 56E
Carnsore Point Irish Republic **78** E4 52 10N 6 22W
Caro Michigan U.S.A. **36** C4 43 29N 83 24W
Carolina Brazil **68** H11 7 20S 47 25W
Caroline Island Pacific Ocean **115** L7 10 00S 150 00W
Caroline Islands Pacific Ocean **114** E8 8 00N 148 00E
Caroni Trinidad and Tobago **66** T10 10 36N 61 22W
Caroni *r.* Trinidad and Tobago **66** T10 10 35N 61 20W
Carpaţii Meridionali *mts.* Romania **81** D4 45 00N 24 00E
Carpentaria, Gulf of Australia **110** F7 13 30S 138 00E
Carpentras France **77** D3 44 03N 5 03E
Carpio North Dakota U.S.A. **40** C1 48 25N 101 34W
Carrauntoohill *mt.* Irish Republic **78** B3 52 00N 9 45W
Carrion *r.* Spain **77** B3 42 30N 4 45W
Carson California U.S.A. **51** A2 33 49N 118 16W
Carson City Nevada U.S.A. **62** C4 39 10N 119 46W
Cartagena Colombia **68** B15 10 24N 75 33W
Cartagena Spain **77** B2 37 36N 0 59W
Cartago Costa Rica **67** H1 9 50N 83 52W
Carteret New Jersey U.S.A. **50** B1 40 34N 74 13W
Caruarú Brazil **68** J11 8 15S 35 55W
Carúpano Venezuela **68** E15 10 39N 63 14W
Casablanca *(Dar el Beida)* Morocco **106** D14 33 39N 7 35W
Casa Grande Arizona U.S.A. **62** D3 32 52N 111 46W
Cascade Range *mts.* North America **62** B6 48 00N 121 00W
Cascadura Brazil **69** P2 22 53S 43 21W
Cascais Portugal **77** A2 38 41N 9 25W
Cascavel Brazil **68** J12 4 10S 38 15W
Caserta Italy **81** B3 41 04N 14 20E
Casey *r.s.* Antarctica **117** 66 17S 77 58E
Casper Wyoming U.S.A. **62** E5 42 50N 106 20W
Caspian Lowlands *geog. reg.* Kazakhstan **90** F4 48 00N 50 00E
Caspian Sea Eurasia **90** G3 42 30N 50 00E
Cassino Italy **81** B3 41 29N 13 50E
Cass River Michigan U.S.A. **36** C4 43 30N 83 30W
Castellane France **77** D3 43 50N 6 30E
Castellón de la Plana Spain **77** B2 39 59N 0 03W
Castelo Branco Portugal **77** A2 39 50N 7 30W
Castle Hill Australia **111** F3 33 44S 150 59E
Castlebar Irish Republic **78** B5 53 52N 9 17W
Castle Peak Hong Kong U.K. **98** A2 22 23N 113 57E
Castleton on Hudson New York U.S.A. **65** G5 42 31N 73 45W
Castres France **77** C3 43 36N 2 14E
Castries St. Lucia **67** L2 14 02N 60 59W
Castrop-Rauxel Germany **76** K3 51 33N 7 18E
Castro Valley California U.S.A. **49** C2 37 42N 122 03W
Castrovillari Italy **81** C2 39 48N 16 12E
Catamarca Argentina **69** D7 28 28S 65 46W
Catánia Italy **81** C2 37 31N 15 06E
Catanzaro Italy **81** C2 38 54N 16 36E
Cataract, 1st *(R. Nile)* Egypt **92** D3 24 00N 32 45E
Cataract, 2nd *(R.Nile)* Sudan **92** D3 21 40N 31 12E
Cataract, 3rd *(R.Nile)* Sudan **92** D2 19 45N 30 25E
Cataract, 4th *(R.Nile)* Sudan **92** D2 18 40N 32 10E
Cataract, 5th *(R.Nile)* Sudan **92** D2 18 25N 33 52E
Caterham England **82** C2 51 17N 0 04W
Cat Island The Bahamas **67** I4 24 30N 75 30W
Catskill New York U.S.A. **65** G5 42 14N 73 52W
Catskill Mountains New York U.S.A. **65** F5 42 10N 74 20W
Cattaraugus Creek New York U.S.A. **64** B5 42 30N 78 40W
Caucaia Brazil **68** J12 3 44S 38 45W
Caucasus Mountains Eurasia **90** E3 42 30N 45 00E
Cavalier North Dakota U.S.A. **39** B1 48 48N 97 48W
Caxias Brazil **68** I12 4 53N 43 20W
Caxias do Sul Brazil **69** G7 29 14S 51 10W
Cayenne French Guiana **68** G13 4 55N 52 18W
Cayman Trench Caribbean Sea **115** R9 15 00N 80 00W
Cayuga Lake New York U.S.A. **64** D5 42 40N 76 45W
Cazenovia New York U.S.A. **64** E5 42 54N 75 51W
Ceara *admin.* Brazil **68** I11/J11 5 30S 40 00W
Cebu The Philippines **99** G6 10 17N 123 56E
Cebu *i.* The Philippines **84** 10 30N 123 30E
Cedar *r.* Iowa U.S.A. **63** H5 42 00N 92 00W
Cedar City Utah U.S.A. **62** D4 37 40N 113 04W
Cedar Creek *r.* North Dakota U.S.A. **62** F6 46 00N 102 00W
Cedar Grove New Jersey U.S.A. **50** B2 40 51N 74 14W
Cedar Rapids Iowa U.S.A. **63** H5 41 59N 91 39W
Cedros *i.* Mexico **66** A5 28 00N 115 00W
Cedros Bay Trinidad and Tobago **66** S9 10 08N 61 50W
Cedros Point Trinidad and Tobago **66** S9 10 07N 61 49W
Ceduna Australia **110** E3 32 07S 133 42E
Ceerigaabo Somalia **106** O10 10 40N 47 20E
Cegléd Hungary **81** C4 47 10N 19 47E
Celaya Mexico **66** D4 20 32N 100 48W
Celebes *see* Sulawesi
Celebes Sea Indonesia **99** G4 3 00N 122 30E
Celje Slovenia **81** C4 46 15N 15 16E
Celle Germany **76** E5 52 37N 10 05E
Celtic Sea British Isles **78** E3 51 00N 7 00W
Center Line Michigan U.S.A. **52** E2 42 28N 83 01W
Center Moriches New York U.S.A. **65** H3 40 48N 72 47W
Centerport New York U.S.A. **65** G3 40 54N 73 22W
Centerville Massachusetts U.S.A. **65** K4 41 39N 70 22W
CENTRAL AFRICAN REPUBLIC 106 I9
Central Pacific Basin Pacific Ocean **114** I9 10 00N 177 00W
Central Plain Ireland **70** 53 30N 8 00W
Central Russian Uplands Europe **84** 55 00N 35 00E
Central Siberian Plateau Russia **89** M9/N8 65 00N 110 00E
Centreville Maryland U.S.A. **64** D2 39 02N 76 05W
Centro Brazil **69** Q2 22 53S 43 07W
Cerro de Pasco Peru **68** B10 10 43S 76 15W
České Budějovice Czechoslovakia **80** B4 48 58N 14 29E
Ceuta *territory* Spain **77** A2 35 53N 5 19W
Cévennes *mts.* France **77** C3 44 20N 3 30E
Ceyhan *r.* Turkey **92** E6 37 45N 36 45E
Cèze *r.* France **77** C3 44 30N 4 00E
Chacachacare *i.* Trinidad and Tobago **66** S10 10 41N 61 45W
Chachapoyas Peru **68** B11 6 13S 77 54W
CHAD 106 I10
Chad, Lake West Africa **106** H10 13 50N 14 00E
Chagai Hills Afghanistan/Pakistan **93** J5 29 30N 63 00E
Chaghcharān Afghanistan **93** K5 34 31N 65 15E
Chagos Archipelago *(British Indian Ocean Territory)* Indian Ocean **112** G6 6 00S 73 00E
Chagos-Laccadive Ridge Indian Ocean **112** G6/G7
Chaguanas Trinidad and Tobago **66** T10 10 31N 61 25W
Chaguaramas Trinidad and Tobago **66** S10 10 41N 61 38W
Chāh Bahār Iran **93** J4 25 16N 60 41E
Chaine des Mitumba *(Mitumba Mountains)* Zaïre **107** K5 7 30S 27 30E
Chai Wan Hong Kong U.K. **98** C1 22 15N 114 14E
Chai Wan Kok Hong Kong U.K. **98** B2 22 23N 114 06E
Chalfont St. Peter England **82** A3 51 37N 0 33W
Chalkyitsik Alaska U.S.A. **44** C4 66 38N 143 49W
Challenger Fracture Zone Pacific Ocean **115** Q4 33 30S 100 00W
Chalon-sur-Saône France **77** C4 46 47N 4 51E
Châlons-sur-Marne France **76** C4 48 58N 4 22E
Chaman Pakistan **94** B6 30 55N 66 27N
Chambal India **95** D5 26 00N 77 00E
Chamberlain Lake Maine U.S.A. **37** R7 46 15N 69 20W
Chambersburg Pennsylvania U.S.A. **64** C2 39 57N 77 40W
Chambéry France **77** D4 45 34N 5 55E
Chamo, Lake Ethiopia **106** M9 5 55N 37 35E
Champaign Illinois U.S.A. **63** I5 40 07N 88 14W
Champdani India **94** K3 22 48N 88 21E
Champigny France **83** C2 48 49N 2 32E
Champlain, Lake *(Lac Champlain)* Canada/U.S.A. **33** B1 44 00N 73 00W
Champotón Mexico **66** F3 19 20N 90 43W
Champs-sur-Marne France **83** C2 48 51N 2 35E
Chañaral Chile **69** C7 26 23S 70 40W
Chandalar *r.* Alaska U.S.A. **44** B4 67 00N 149 00W
Chandigarh India **95** D6 30 44N 76 54E
Chandle Park Michigan U.S.A. **52** F2 42 23N 82 58W
Chandnagar India **94** K3 22 52N 88 22E
Chandrapur India **95** D3 19 58N 79 21E
Changara Mozambique **107** L4 16 50S 33 17E
Chang Cheng *r.s.* Antarctica **117** 62 13S 58 58W
Changchun China **97** P7 43 50N 125 20E
Changde China **97** M4 29 03N 111 35E
Chang-hua Taiwan **98** G7 24 06N 120 31E
Chang Jiang *(Yangtze) r.* China **97** L5/M5 31 00N 110 00E
Changsha China **97** M4 28 10N 113 00E
Changxindian China **101** F1 39 50N 116 12E
Changzhi China **97** M6 36 05N 113 12E
Changzhou China **97** N5 31 39N 120 45E
Channel Islands British Isles **78** I6 49 30N 2 30W
Chaouèn Morocco **77** A2 35 15N 5 15W
Chaoyang China **97** O7 41 36N 120 25E
Chaozhou China **97** N3 23 42N 116 36E
Chapada Diamantina *mts.* Brazil **68** I10 12 30S 42 30W
Chapecó Brazil **69** G7 27 14S 52 41W
Chapelton Jamaica **67** Q8 18 05N 77 16W
Chardzhou Turkmenistan **91** J2 39 09N 63 34E
Chari *r.* Chad **106** I10 11 00N 16 00E
Chārīkār Afghanistan **93** K5 35 01N 69 11E
Charleroi Belgium **76** C5 50 25N 4 27E
Charles *r.* Massachusetts U.S.A. **52** A2 42 15N 71 16W
Charleston South Carolina U.S.A. **63** K3 32 48N 79 58W
Charleston West Virginia U.S.A. **63** J4 38 23N 81 40W
Charlestown New Hampshire U.S.A. **65** H6 43 14N 72 25W
Charlestown Rhode Island U.S.A. **65** J4 41 24N 71 38W
Charles Town West Virginia U.S.A. **64** C2 39 18N 77 54W
Charleville Australia **110** H4 26 25S 146 13E
Charleville *see* Rath Luirc
Charleville-Mézières France **76** C4 49 46N 4 43E
Charlevoix Michigan U.S.A. **36** A6 45 19N 85 16W
Charlotte Michigan U.S.A. **36** B3 42 33N 84 50W
Charlotte North Carolina U.S.A. **63** J4 35 03N 80 50W
Charlottenburg Germany **83** E2 52 32N 13 18E
Charlottesville Virginia U.S.A. **63** K4 38 02N 78 29W
Charters Towers Australia **110** H5 20 02S 146 20E
Chartiers Creek Pennsylvania U.S.A. **53** D1 40 27N 80 05W
Chartres France **76** C4 48 27N 1 30E
Châteaubriant France **77** B4 47 43N 1 22W
Châteauroux France **77** C4 46 49N 1 41E
Château-Thierry France **76** C4 49 03N 3 24E
Châtellerault France **77** C3 49 49N 0 33E
Chatham Alaska U.S.A. **42** A3 57 30N 135 00W
Chatham Massachusetts U.S.A. **65** K4 41 40N 69 57W
Chatham Islands Pacific Ocean **114** I3 44 00S 176 30W
Chatham Rise Pacific Ocean **114** H3 45 00S 175 00E
Chatham Strait Alaska U.S.A. **42** B3 57 45N 134 50W
Chatou France **83** A2 48 54N 2 10E
Chatswood Australia **111** G2 33 48S 151 11E
Chattanooga Tennessee U.S.A. **63** I4 35 02N 85 18W
Chaumont France **76** D4 48 07N 5 08E
Cheb Czechoslovakia **80** B5 50 08N 12 28E
Cheboksary Russia **90** F6 56 08N 47 12E
Cheboygan Michigan U.S.A. **36** B6 45 40N 84 28W
Cheduba *i.* Myanmar **95** G3 18 52N 93 44E
Cheju do *(Quelpart) i.* South Korea **97** P5 33 00N 126 30E
Chek Chue *(Stanley)* Hong Kong U.K. **98** C1 22 12N 114 12E
Chek Keng Hong Kong U.K. **98** D2 22 25N 114 21E
Chek Lap Kok *i.* Hong Kong U.K. **98** A1 22 18N 113 56E
Chelan, Lake Washington U.S.A. **42** H4 48 10N 120 32W
Chelan National Recreation Area Washington U.S.A. **42** H4 48 20N 120 40W
Chélif *r.* Algeria **77** C2 36 00N 0 30E
Chelles France **83** C2 48 53N 2 53E
Chełm Poland **80** D5 51 08N 23 29E
Chelmsford England **78** L3 51 44N 0 28E
Chelsea England **82** C2 51 29N 0 10W
Chelsea Massachusetts U.S.A. **52** B2 42 24N 71 02W
Chelsea Michigan U.S.A. **36** B3 42 19N 84 01W
Cheltenham England **78** I3 51 54N 2 04W
Chelyabinsk Russia **91** J6 55 12N 61 25E
Chemnitz *(Karl-Marx-Stadt)* Germany **76** E5 50 50N 12 55E
Chenab *r.* Pakistan **95** C6 30 30N 71 30E
Chenango River New York U.S.A. **64** E5 42 30N 75 30W
Chengde China **97** N7 40 59N 117 52E
Chengdu China **97** K5 30 37N 104 06E
Ch'eng-kung Taiwan **98** H6 23 06N 121 22E
Cher *r.* France **77** C4 47 17N 0 50E
Cherbourg France **76** B4 49 38N 1 37W
Cherchell Algeria **77** C2 36 36N 2 11E
Cheremkhovo Russia **89** M6 53 08N 103 01E
Cheremushki Russia **88** M1 55 38N 37 38E
Cherepovets Russia **90** D6 59 09N 37 50E
Cherkassy Ukraine **90** C4 49 27N 32 04E
Cherkessk Russia **90** E3 44 14N 42 05E
Cherkizovsky Russia **88** M2 55 50N 37 44E
Chernigov Ukraine **90** C5 51 30N 31 18E
Chernobyl' Ukraine **90** C5 51 17N 30 15E
Chernogorsk Russia **91** P5 53 48N 91 16E
Chernovtsy Ukraine **90** B4 48 19N 25 52E
Chernyakhovsk Russia **80** D5 54 36N 21 48E
Cherokee Iowa U.S.A. **63** G5 42 45N 95 32W
Cherrapunji India **95** G5 25 16N 91 42E
Cherskiy Range *mts.* Russia **89** P9/Q8 66 30N 140 00E
Chertanovo Russia **88** M1 55 34N 37 35E
Chertsey England **82** A2 51 23N 0 30W
Chervonograd Ukraine **80** D5 50 25N 24 10E
Chesaning Michigan U.S.A. **36** B4 43 12N 84 08W
Chesapeake Virginia U.S.A. **63** K4 36 45N 76 15W
Chesapeake Bay U.S.A. **64** D2 39 00N 76 20W
Chesham England **82** A3 51 43N 0 38W
Cheshunt England **82** C3 51 43N 0 02W
Chester England **78** I5 53 12N 2 54W
Chester Connecticut U.S.A. **65** H4 41 24N 72 26W
Chester Maryland U.S.A. **64** D1 38 59N 76 16W
Chester Massachusetts U.S.A. **65** G5 42 17N 72 59W
Chester New Jersey U.S.A. **65** F3 40 47N 74 42W
Chester Pennsylvania U.S.A. **64** E2 39 50N 75 23W
Chester Vermont U.S.A. **65** H6 43 16N 72 38W
Chesterfield England **78** J5 53 15N 1 25W
Chestertown Maryland U.S.A. **64** D2 39 13N 76 04W
Chesuncook Lake Maine U.S.A. **37** R7 46 00N 69 22W
Chetlat Island India **95** C2 11 46N 72 50E
Chetumal Mexico **66** G3 18 30N 88 17W
Cheung Chau *i.* Hong Kong U.K. **98** B1 22 13N 114 01E
Cheung Sha Hong Kong U.K. **98** A1 22 14N 113 57E
Cheung Sha Wan Hong Kong U.K. **98** B2 22 20N 114 08E
Cheung Shue Tau Hong Kong U.K. **98** B2 22 22N 114 05E
Chevak Alaska U.S.A. **10** B5 63 33N 165 36W
Cheviot Hills England **78** I7 55 25N 2 20W
Chevreuse France **83** A1 48 43N 2 05E
Chewack River Washington U.S.A. **42** H4 48 40N 120 10W
Chewelah Washington U.S.A. **43** E1 48 17N 117 44W
Cheyenne Wyoming U.S.A. **62** F5 41 08N 104 50W
Cheyenne *r.* U.S.A. **62** F5 44 00N 102 00W
Chhapra India **95** E5 25 46N 84 44E
Chia-i Taiwan **98** G6 23 38N 120 27E
Chia-li Taiwan **98** H7 23 09N 120 11E
Chiang Rai Thailand **99** B7 19 56N 99 51E
Chiba Japan **100** M2 35 38N 140 07E
Chiba *pref.* Japan **100** M2 35 30N 140 15E
Chicago Illinois U.S.A. **63** I5 41 50N 87 45W
Chicago Harbor Illinois U.S.A. **53** B2 41 53N 87 35W
Chicago Sanitary and Ship Canal Illinois U.S.A. **53** A2 41 45N 87 52W
Chicapa *r.* Angola/Zaïre **107** J6 8 00S 20 30E
Chichagof Island Alaska U.S.A. **42** A3 57 40N 136 00W
Chichibu Japan **100** L2 35 59N 139 08E
Chichibu-Tama National Park Japan **100** K2 35 50N 138 50E
Chickasha Oklahoma U.S.A. **63** G4 35 03N 97 57W
Chicken Alaska U.S.A. **44** C3 64 04N 142 00W
Chiclayo Peru **68** B11 6 47S 79 47W
Chieng-Mai Thailand **99** B7 18 48N 98 59E
Chienti *r.* Italy **81** B3 43 00N 14 00E
Chieti Italy **81** B3 42 21N 14 10E
Chignik Alaska U.S.A. **10** D4 56 18N 158 27W
Chigwell England **82** D3 51 37N 0 05E
Chihuahua Mexico **66** C5 28 40N 106 06W
Chikura Japan **100** L1 34 57N 139 58E
CHILE 69 D6
Chile Basin Pacific Ocean **115** R4 36 00S 84 00W
Chile Chico Chile **69** C3 46 34S 71 44W
Chile Rise Pacific Ocean **115** Q4 40 00S 92 00W
Chillán Chile **69** C5 36 37S 72 10W
Chilpancingo Mexico **66** E3 17 33N 99 30W
Chiltern Hills England **78** K3 51 40N 1 00W
Chilumba Malawi **107** L5 10 25S 34 18E
Chi-lung Taiwan **98** J3 25 10N 121 43E
Chi Ma Wan Peninsula Hong Kong U.K. **98** A1 22 14N 113 58E
Chimborazo *mt.* Ecuador **68** B12 1 29S 78 52W
Chimbote Peru **68** B11 9 04S 78 34W
Ch'imei Hsü *i.* Taiwan **98** F6 23 11N 119 25E
Chimen Tao *(Quemoy) i.* Taiwan **98** E8 24 26N 118 24E
Chimkent Kazakhstan **91** K3 42 16N 69 05E
CHINA 96/97 G6/M6
Chinandega Nicaragua **66** G2 12 35N 87 10W
Chincha Alta Peru **68** B10 13 25S 76 07W
Chinchilla Australia **110** I4 26 42S 150 35E
Chinde Mozambique **107** M4 18 35S 36 28E
Chindwin *r.* Myanmar **95** H5 26 00N 95 30E
Chinese Turkestan *geog. reg.* China **96** E7/F7 40 00N 80 00E
Ch'ing-shui Taiwan **98** G7 24 12N 120 33E
Chingola Zambia **107** K5 12 31S 27 53E
Chin Hills Asia **84** 21 00N 94 00E
Chinju South Korea **97** P6 35 10N 128 06E
Chinko *r.* Central African Republic **106** J9 5 00N 24 00E
Chinmen Taiwan **98** E8 24 30N 118 20E
Chinook Montana U.S.A. **41** D1 48 35N 109 14W
Chi-pei Tao *i.* Taiwan **98** F6 23 44N 119 36E
Chippewa Falls Wisconsin U.S.A. **35** B2 44 56N 91 25W
Chippewa River Michigan U.S.A. **36** B4 43 36N 84 45W
Chipping Norton, Lake Australia **111** F2 33 54S 150 56E
Chipping Ongar England **82** E3 51 43N 0 15E
Chiputneticook Lakes U.S.A./Canada **33** C2 45 40N 67 45W
Chiquimula Guatemala **66** G2 14 48N 89 32W
Chiquitos Plateau South America **55** 17 00S 63 00W
Chirchik Uzbekistan **91** K3 41 28N 69 31E
Chiryu Japan **100** J2 35 01N 137 04E
Ch'i-shan Taiwan **98** G5 22 44N 120 31E
Chita Japan **100** H1 35 00N 136 51E
Chita Russia **89** N6 52 03N 113 35E
Chita-hantō *p.* Japan **100** H1 34 45N 136 53E
Chitembo Angola **107** I5 13 33S 16 47E
Chitpur India **94** K2 22 36N 88 23E
Chitral Pakistan **95** C7 35 52N 71 58E
Chittagong Bangladesh **95** G4 22 20N 91 48E
Chittenango New York U.S.A. **64** E6 43 02N 75 52W
Chittoor India **95** D2 13 13N 79 06E
Chitungwiza Zimbabwe **107** L4 18 00S 31 06E
Chōfu Japan **101** B3 35 39N 139 34E
Chōgo Japan **101** A2 35 24N 139 29E
Choiseul *i.* Solomon Islands **110** J8 7 00S 157 00E
Choisy-le-Roi France **83** B2 48 47N 2 29E
Chojnice Poland **80** C5 53 42N 17 32E
Cholet France **77** B4 47 04N 0 53W
Choluteca Honduras **66** G2 13 15N 87 10W
Chone Ecuador **68** A12 0 44S 80 04W
Ch'ŏngjin North Korea **97** P7 41 50N 129 55E
Ch'ŏngju South Korea **97** P6 36 39N 127 27E
Chōshi Japan **100** M2 35 43N 140 51E
Chŏnju South Korea **97** P6 35 50N 127 05E
Chongqing China **97** L4 29 30N 106 35E
Chott el Hodna *salt l.* Algeria **77** C2 35 30N 4 30E
Chott El Jerid *salt l.* Tunisia **106** G14 30 00N 9 00E
Chott Melrhir *salt l.* Algeria **106** G14 33 30N 6 10E
Choybalsan Mongolia **97** M8 48 02N 114 32E
Christchurch New Zealand **111** F2 33 35S 172 40E
Christiana Jamaica **67** Q8 18 13N 77 29W
Christmas Island Indian Ocean **99** D1 10 30S 105 40E
Chu Kazakhstan **91** L3 43 34N 73 44E
Chu *r.* Kazakhstan/Kirgyzstan **91** L3 44 30N 72 00E

Chugach Mountains Alaska U.S.A. **10** G5 61 40N 145 00W
Chūgoku-sanchi *mts.* Japan **100** B2 35 00N 133 00E
Chukchi Sea Arctic Ocean **116** 70 00N 170 00W
Chukotsk Peninsula Russia **89** U9 66 00N 175 00W
Chukotsk Range *mts.* Russia **89** T9 68 00N 175 00E
Chulucanas Peru **68** A11 5 08S 80 10W
Chulym *r.* Russia **91** O6 57 00N 87 00E
Chumphon Thailand **99** B6 10 30N 99 11E
Chuna *r.* Russia **91** Q6 57 30N 95 00E
Ch'unch'ŏn South Korea **97** P6 37 56N 127 40E
Chung-ho Taiwan **98** H7 25 00N 121 00E
Chung Hom Kok Hong Kong U.K. **98** C1 22 13N 114 12E
Chung-li Taiwan **98** H7 24 55N 121 08E
Chung Yang Shanmo *mts.* Taiwan **98** G6/H7 23 00N 120 00E
Chunya *r.* Russia **89** M8 62 00N 101 00E
Chupara Point Trinidad and Tobago **66** T10 10 48N 61 22W
Chur Switzerland **77** D4 46 52N 9 32E
Churu India **95** C5 28 18N 75 00E
Churuguara Venezuela **67** K2 10 52N 69 35W
Chusovaya *r.* Russia **91** H6 58 00N 59 00E
Chu'ungju South Korea **97** P6 36 59N 127 53E
Cicero Illinois U.S.A. **53** A2 41 50N 87 46W
Cidade de Deus Brazil **69** P2 22 58S 43 20W
Cidade Nova Brazil **69** Q2 22 55S 43 12W
Ciego de Avila Cuba **67** I4 21 51N 78 47W
Ciénaga Colombia **68** C15 11 01N 74 15W
Cienfuegos Cuba **67** H4 22 10N 80 27W
Cilician Gates *pass* Turkey **92** D6 37 17N 34 46E
Cimarron *r.* U.S.A. **62** F4 37 00N 103 00W
Cîmpina Romania **81** E4 45 08N 25 44E
Cinca *r.* Spain **77** C3 41 45N 0 15E
Cincinnati Ohio U.S.A. **63** J4 39 10N 83 30W
Cincinnatus New York U.S.A. **64** E5 42 33N 75 55W
Cine Turkey **80** E2 37 37N 28 03E
Circle Alaska U.S.A. **44** C4 65 50N 144 11W
Cirebon Indonesia **99** D2 6 46S 108 33E
C.I.S. *see* Commonwealth of Independent States
Cisco Texas U.S.A. **62** G3 32 23N 98 59W
Cisneros Colombia **68** B14 6 32N 75 04W
Citlaltépetl *mt.* Mexico **66** E3 19 00N 97 18W
City Island New York U.S.A. **50** C2 40 51N 73 48W
Ciucea Romania **81** D4 46 58N 22 50E
Ciudad Acuña Mexico **66** D5 29 20N 100 58W
Ciudad Bolívar Venezuela **68** E14 8 06N 63 36W
Ciudad Camargo Mexico **66** C5 27 41N 105 10W
Ciudad del Carmen Mexico **66** F3 18 38N 91 50W
Ciudad del Este *(Presidente Stroessner)* Paraguay **69** G7 25 32S 54 34W
Ciudadela Balearic Islands **77** C2 40 00N 3 50E
Ciudad Guayana Venezuela **68** E14 8 22N 62 37W
Ciudad Juárez Mexico **66** C6 31 42N 106 29W
Ciudad Lerdo Mexico **66** D5 25 34N 103 30W
Ciudad Madero Mexico **66** E4 22 19N 97 50W
Ciudad Manté Mexico **66** E4 22 44N 98 59W
Ciudad Obregón Mexico **66** C5 27 28N 109 59W
Ciudad Real Spain **77** B2 38 59N 3 55W
Ciudad Rodrigo Spain **77** A3 40 36N 6 33W
Ciudad Victoria Mexico **66** E4 23 43N 99 10W
Civil Lines India **94** L4 28 40N 77 13E
Civitavecchia Italy **81** B3 42 05N 11 47E
Cizre Turkey **92** F6 37 21N 42 11E
Clairton Pennsylvania U.S.A. **53** E1 40 17N 79 56W
Clare *r.* Irish Republic **78** C5 53 25N 8 55W
Clare Michigan U.S.A. **36** B4 43 49N 84 47W
Claremont New Hampshire U.S.A. **65** H6 43 23N 72 21W
Clarence New York U.S.A. **64** B5 42 59N 78 36W
Clarence Island South Shetland Islands **69** G0 61 10S 54 00W
Clarence Strait Alaska U.S.A. **42** B3 56 00N 133 30W
Clarendon Pennsylvania U.S.A. **64** A4 41 46N 79 06W
Clarion Fracture Zone Pacific Ocean **115** M9 18 00N 130 00W
Clarion River Pennsylvania U.S.A. **64** A4 41 22N 79 00W
Clark Fork *r.* Montana U.S.A. **43** E1 43 00N 115 55W
Clark Hill Lake U.S.A. **63** J3 33 00N 82 00W
Clarksburg Maryland U.S.A. **64** C2 39 14N 77 15W
Clarksburg West Virginia U.S.A. **63** J4 39 16N 80 22W
Clarks Ferry Pennsylvania U.S.A. **64** D3 40 23N 77 00W
Clarksville Tennessee U.S.A. **63** I4 36 31N 87 21W
Clear, Cape Irish Republic **78** B3 51 30N 9 30W
Clearfield Pennsylvania U.S.A. **64** B4 41 02N 78 27W
Clearwater Florida U.S.A. **63** J2 27 57N 82 48W
Clearwater *r.* Idaho U.S.A. **62** C6 46 00N 116 00W
Clermont-Ferrand France **77** C4 45 47N 3 05E
Cleveland New York U.S.A. **64** D6 43 15N 75 50W
Cleveland Peninsula Alaska U.S.A. **42** B3 55 30N 132 00W
Clichy France **83** B2 48 54N 2 19E
Clifton New Jersey U.S.A. **50** B2 40 52N 74 08W
Clinton Connecticut U.S.A. **65** H4 41 16N 72 32W
Clinton Iowa U.S.A. **63** H5 41 51N 90 12W
Clinton Massachusetts U.S.A. **65** J5 42 25N 71 41W
Clinton Oklahoma U.S.A. **62** G4 35 32N 98 59W
Clipperton Fracture Zone Pacific Ocean **115** N8 10 00N 120 00W
Clipperton Island Pacific Ocean **115** P9 10 20N 109 13W
Cloncurry Australia **110** G5 20 41S 140 30E
Clonmel Irish Republic **78** D4 52 21N 7 42W
Cloppenburg Germany **76** D5 52 52N 8 02E
Cloquet Massachusetts U.S.A. **35** B2 46 39N 92 27W
Clovis New Mexico U.S.A. **62** F3 34 14N 103 13W
Cluj-Napoca Romania **81** D4 46 47N 23 37E
Clutha *r.* New Zealand **111** A1 46 30S 169 20E
Clyde Ohio U.S.A. **36** D2 41 59N 82 18W
Clyde *r.* Scotland **78** G7 55 50N 4 25W
Clydebank Scotland **78** G7 55 54N 4 24W
Coari Brazil **68** E12 4 08S 63 07W
Coast Range *mts.* U.S.A. **62** B5/C3
Coatepec Mexico **66** E3 19 29N 96 59W
Coatesville Pennsylvania U.S.A. **64** E2 39 59N 75 50W
Coats Land *geog. reg.* Antarctica **117** 77 00S 25 00W
Coatzacoalcos *(Puerto Mexico)* Mexico **66** E3 18 10N 94 25W
Cobán Guatemala **66** F3 15 28N 90 20W
Cobar Australia **110** H3 31 32S 145 51E
Cobham England **82** B2 51 20N 0 24W
Cobija Bolivia **68** D10 11 01S 68 45W
Coburg Germany **76** E5 50 15N 10 58E
Cochabamba Bolivia **68** D9 17 26S 66 10W
Cochin India **95** D1 9 56N 76 15E
Cochituate, Lake Massachusetts U.S.A. **52** A2 42 17N 71 22W
Cochrane Chile **69** C3 47 16S 72 33W
Cochranton Pennsylvania U.S.A. **36** F2 41 32N 80 03W
Cocos Basin Indian Ocean **112** I6 5 00S 96 00E
Cocos Bay Trinidad and Tobago **66** T9 10 25N 61 05W
Cocos Island *see* Isla del Coco
Cocos Islands Indian Ocean **112** I5 12 30S 97 00E
Cocos Ridge Pacific Ocean **115** R8 4 00N 90 00W
Cocota Brazil **69** Q2 22 48S 43 11W
Codajás Brazil **68** E12 3 55S 62 00W
Cod, Cape Massachusetts U.S.A. **65** K5 42 05N 70 12W
Codó Brazil **68** I12 4 28S 43 51W
Codrington Antigua & Barbuda **67** L3 17 43N 61 49W
Coelhodo Rocha Brazil **69** P2 22 46S 43 21W
Coeur d'Alene Idaho U.S.A. **62** C6 47 40N 116 46W
Cognac France **77** B4 45 42N 0 19W
Cogswell Reservoir California U.S.A. **51** C3 34 14N 117 59W
Cohocton New York U.S.A. **64** C5 42 30N 77 30W
Cohocton River New York U.S.A. **64** C5 42 20N 77 20W
Coihaique Chile **69** C3 45 35S 72 08W
Coimbatore India **95** D2 11 00N 76 57E
Coimbra Portugal **77** A3 40 12N 8 25W
Colbeck, Cape Antarctica **117** 77 00S 158 00W
Colchester Connecticut U.S.A. **65** H4 41 35N 72 19W
Colchester England **78** L3 51 54N 0 54E
Coldwater Michigan U.S.A. **36** A2 41 57N 85 01W
Coleen *r.* Alaska U.S.A. **44** C4 67 30N 142 30W
Coleraine Northern Ireland **78** E7 55 08N 6 40W
Colima Mexico **66** D3 19 14N 103 41W
Coll *i.* Scotland **78** E8 56 40N 6 35W
College Alaska U.S.A. **44** B3 64 54N 147 55W
Collie Australia **110** B3 33 20S 116 06E
Collingwood New Zealand **111** B2 40 41S 172 41E
Collinsville Connecticut U.S.A. **65** H4 41 49N 72 55W
Colma California U.S.A. **49** B2 37 42N 122 29W
Colmar France **76** D4 48 05N 7 21E
Cologne *see* Köln
Colombes France **83** B2 48 55N 2 15E
COLOMBIA **68** C13
Colombo Sri Lanka **95** D1 6 55N 79 52E
Colón Panama **67** Y2 9 21N 79 54W
Colonsay *i.* Scotland **78** E8 56 05N 6 15W
Colorado *r.* North America **62** D3 33 00N 114 00W
Colorado *state* U.S.A. **62** E4 39 00N 106 00W
Colorado Plateau Arizona U.S.A. **62** D4 36 00N 111 00W
Colorado Springs *tn.* Colorado U.S.A. **62** F4 38 50N 104 50W
Columbia Missouri U.S.A. **63** H4 38 58N 92 20W
Columbia Pennsylvania U.S.A. **64** D3 40 02N 76 30W
Columbia *r.* North America **62** B6 46 00N 120 00W
Columbia South Carolina U.S.A. **63** J3 34 00N 81 00W
Columbia City Indiana U.S.A. **35** C1 41 09N 85 20W
Columbia Falls *tn.* Montana U.S.A. **41** C1 48 24N 114 11W
Columbus Georgia U.S.A. **63** J3 32 28N 84 59W
Columbus Indiana U.S.A. **63** I4 39 12N 85 57W
Columbus Mississippi U.S.A. **63** I3 33 30N 88 27W
Columbus Nebraska U.S.A. **63** G5 41 27N 97 21W
Columbus Ohio U.S.A. **63** J5 39 59N 83 03W
Columbus Channel Trinidad and Tobago/Venezuela **66** S9 10 00N 61 45W
Colville *r.* Alaska U.S.A. **44** A4 69 00N 158 00W
Colville Washington U.S.A. **43** E1 48 33N 117 55W
Colvocorresses Bay Antarctica **117** 66 00S 120 00E
Colwyn Bay *tn.* Wales **78** H5 53 18N 3 43W
Comandante Ferraz *r.s.* Antarctica **117** 62 05S 58 23W
Comilla Bangladesh **95** G4 23 28N 91 10E
Comitán Mexico **66** F3 16 18N 92 09W
Commonwealth of Independent States *see individual member countries:* ARMENIA, AZERBAIJAN BELARUS, KAZAKHSTAN KIRGYZSTAN MOLDOVA, RUSSIA,TAJIKISTAN TURKMENISTAN UKRAINE, UZBEKISTAN
Como Italy **81** A4 45 48N 9 05E
Comodoro Rivadavia Argentina **69** D3 45 50S 67 30W
Comorin, Cape India **95** D1 8 04N 77 35E
Comoro Archipelago *is.* Indian Ocean **102** 12 00S 44 00E
COMOROS **107** N5
Compiègne France **76** C4 49 25N 2 50E
Compton California U.S.A. **51** B2 33 55N 118 14W
Conakry Guinea **106** C9 9 30N 13 43W
Concepción Chile **69** C5 36 50S 73 03W
Concepción Mexico **66** D4 24 38N 101 25W
Concepción Paraguay **69** F8 23 22S 57 26W
Concepción del Uruguay Argentina **69** F6 32 30S 58 15W
Conchos *r.* Mexico **66** C5 27 30N 107 00W
Concord California U.S.A. **49** C3 37 59N 122 04W
Concord Massachusetts U.S.A. **52** A2 42 28N 71 15W
Concord New Hampshire U.S.A. **65** J6 43 13N 71 34W
Concordia Argentina **69** F6 31 25S 58 00W
Concordia Kansas U.S.A. **63** G4 39 35N 97 39W
Concord River Massachusetts U.S.A. **52** A2 42 28N 71 21W
Concrete Washington U.S.A. **42** H4 48 32N 121 46W
Condom France **77** C3 43 58N 0 23E
Conduit *r.* Israel **92** O11 32 25N 35 00E
Conecuh *r.* Alabama U.S.A. **63** I3 31 00N 87 00W
Conesus Lake New York U.S.A. **64** C5 42 46N 77 43W
Coney Island New York U.S.A. **50** C1 40 34N 74 00W
Conflans-Ste. Honorine France **83** A3 49 01N 2 09E
CONGO **106** I7
Congo *(Zaïre) r.* Congo **106** I7 2 00S 17 00E
Conneaut Ohio U.S.A. **36** F2 41 58N 80 34W
Connecticut *state* U.S.A. **65** H4 41 00N 73 00W
Connecticut River U.S.A. **65** H5 42 10N 72 35W
Conset Bay Barbados **66** W12 13 10N 59 25W
Constanța Romania **81** E3 44 12N 28 40E
Constantine Algeria **106** H15 36 22N 6 40E
Constitución Chile **69** C5 31 05S 57 51W
Contanama Peru **68** B11 7 19S 75 04W
Contra Costa Canal California U.S.A. **49** C3 37 58N 122 05W
Contra Costa County California U.S.A. **49** B3 37 58N 122 26W
Conyngham Pennsylvania U.S.A. **64** D3 40 59N 76 04W
Cook County Illinois U.S.A. **53** A1 41 39N 87 59W
Cook Inlet Alaska U.S.A. **10** E5 60 00N 152 30W
Cook Islands Pacific Ocean **115** K6 19 30S 159 50W
Cook, Mount New Zealand **111** B2 43 37S 170 08E
Cook Strait New Zealand **111** B2 41 00S 174 30E
Cooktown Australia **110** H6 15 29S 145 15E
Coolgardie Australia **110** C3 31 01S 121 12E
Cooper Creek *r.* Australia **110** F4 28 00S 138 00E
Cooperstown New York U.S.A. **64** F5 42 43N 74 56W
Coosa *r.* U.S.A. **63** I3 33 00N 86 00W
Coos Bay *tn.* Oregon U.S.A. **62** B5 43 23N 124 12W
Copacabana Brazil **69** Q2 22 58S 43 11W
Copacabana Beach Brazil **69** Q2 22 59S 43 11W
Copenhagen *see* København
Copiapó Chile **69** C7 27 20S 70 23W
Copper *r.* Alaska U.S.A. **10** F5 60 30N 144 50W
Copper Harbor Michigan U.S.A. **63** I6 47 28N 87 54W
Coquet *r.* England **78** J7 55 20N 1 50W
Coquimbo Chile **69** C7 29 57S 71 25W
Coral Sea Islands Territory *admin.* Australia **110** H6/I6 17 00S 150 00E
Coral Sea Pacific Ocean **110** I7 15 00S 154 00E
Corantijn *(Courantyne) r.* Surinam **68** F13 4 30N 57 30W
Cordillera Cantabrica *(Cantabrian Mountains)* Spain **77** A3 43 00N 5 30W
Cordillera de Mérida *mts.* Venezuela **67** J1 8 00N 72 00W
Córdoba Argentina **69** E6 31 25S 64 11W
Córdoba Mexico **66** E3 18 55N 96 55W
Córdoba Spain **77** B2 37 53N 4 46W
Cordova Alaska U.S.A. **10** F5 60 29N 145 52W
Corfu *see* Kérkira
Corinth Mississippi U.S.A. **63** I3 34 58N 88 30W
Cork Irish Republic **78** C3 51 54N 8 28W
Çorlu Turkey **80** E3 41 11N 27 48E
Cormeilles-en-Parisis France **83** A2 48 58N 2 11E
Corning New York U.S.A. **64** C5 42 10N 77 04W
Cornwall Bridge Connecticut U.S.A. **65** G4 41 49N 73 23W
Coro Venezuela **68** D15 11 20N 70 00W
Coroico Bolivia **68** D9 16 19S 67 45W
Coromandel Coast India **95** D2 12 30N 81 30E
Coromandel Peninsula New Zealand **111** C3 36 30S 175 45E
Corona Arena Dam Trinidad and Tobago **66** T10 10 32N 61 12W
Coronation Island Alaska U.S.A. **42** B3 55 50N 134 15W
Coronel Pringles Argentina **69** E5 37 56S 61 25W
Corpus Christi Texas U.S.A. **63** G2 27 47N 97 26W
Corrientes Argentina **69** F7 27 30S 58 48W
Corrieverton Guyana **68** F14 5 53N 57 10W
Corse *(Corsica) i.* France **77** D3 42 00N 9 00E
Corsica *see* Corse
Corte Corsica **77** D3 42 18N 9 08E
Cortland New York U.S.A. **64** D5 42 36N 76 10W
Çoruh *r.* Turkey **92** F7 40 45N 40 45E
Corumbá Brazil **68** F9 19 00S 57 35W
Corunna Michigan U.S.A. **36** B3 42 58N 84 05W
Corunna *see* La Coruña
Corvallis Oregon U.S.A. **62** B5 44 34N 123 16W
Cosenza Italy **81** C2 39 17N 16 16E
Cossipore India **94** K2 22 37N 88 23E
Costa Blanca *geog. reg.* Spain **77** B2 38 15N 0 20W
Costa Brava *geog. reg.* Spain **77** C3 41 40N 3 50E
Costa del Sol *geog. reg.* Spain **77** B2 36 40N 4 40W
COSTA RICA **67** H1/2
Cotagaita Bolivia **68** D8 20 47S 65 40W
Côte D'Azur France **77** D3 43 00N 7 00E
CÔTE D'IVOIRE **106** D9
Cotonou Benin **106** F9 6 24N 2 31E
Cotopaxi *mt.* Ecuador **68** B12 0 40S 78 28W
Cotswold Hills England **78** I3 51 40N 2 10W
Cottbus Germany **76** E5 51 43N 14 21E
Coudersport Pennsylvania U.S.A. **35** E1 41 46N 78 03W
Council Bluffs Iowa U.S.A. **63** G5 41 14N 95 54W
Coupeville Washington U.S.A. **42** H4 48 14N 122 40W
Courtrai *see* Kortrijk
Couva *r.* Trinidad and Tobago **66** T9 10 25N 61 24W
Coventry Rhode Island U.S.A. **65** J4 41 45N 71 38W
Coventry England **78** J4 52 25N 1 30W
Covilhã Portugal **77** A3 40 17N 7 30W
Covina California U.S.A. **51** C3 34 04N 117 53W
Covington Kentucky U.S.A. **63** J4 39 04N 84 30W
Cowan Creek Australia **111** G3 33 36S 151 13E
Cowanesque River Pennsylvania U.S.A. **64** C4 41 55N 77 30W
Cox's Bazar Bangladesh **95** G4 21 25N 91 59E
Coyote Creek *r.* California U.S.A. **51** B2 33 50N 118 05W
Coyote Hills Regional Park California U.S.A. **49** C2 37 34N 122 06W
Craig Alaska U.S.A. **42** B3 55 29N 133 06W
Craiova Romania **81** D3 44 18N 23 47E
Crandon Wisconsin U.S.A. **35** C2 45 34N 88 54W
Cranston Rhode Island U.S.A. **65** J4 41 47N 71 27W
Crawley England **78** K3 51 07N 0 12W
Cremona Italy **81** B4 45 08N 10 01E
Cres *i.* Croatia **81** B3 45 00N 14 00E
Crescent Island Hong Kong U.K. **98** C3 22 32N 114 19E
Creston Iowa U.S.A. **63** H5 41 04N 94 20W
Crete *see* Kriti
Créteil France **83** B2 48 47N 2 28E
Crete, Sea of Mediterranean Sea **81** D2 36 00N 25 00E
Crewe England **78** I5 53 05N 2 27W
Criciúma Brazil **69** H7 28 45S 49 25W
Crimea *see* Krim
CROATIA **81** C4
Cromwell New Zealand **111** A1 45 03S 169 14E
Cronulla Australia **111** G1 34 04S 151 09E
Crooked Island Hong Kong U.K. **98** C3 22 33N 114 18E
Crooked Island The Bahamas **67** J4 22 45N 74 10W
Crookston Minnesota U.S.A. **63** G6 47 47N 96 36W
Crosby North Dakota U.S.A. **40** C1 48 56N 103 20W
Cross Sound Alaska U.S.A. **42** A3 58 00N 137 00W
Crotone Italy **81** C2 39 05N 17 08E
Crow Peak *mt.* Montana U.S.A. **62** D6 46 19N 111 56W
Crows Nest Australia **111** G2 33 50S 151 12E
Croydon Australia **110** G6 18 10S 142 15E
Croydon *bor.* Greater London England **82** C2 51 23N 0 06W
Crozet Basin Indian Ocean **112** E3/F3 40 00S 55 00E
Cruzeiro do Sul Brazil **68** C11 7 40S 72 39W
Cuando *r.* Southern Africa **107** J4 16 00S 21 30E
Cuango *r.* Angola **107** I6 9 00S 18 30E
Cuanza *r.* Angola **107** H6 9 40S 15 00E
CUBA **67** I4
Cuba New York U.S.A. **64** B5 42 13N 78 16W
Cubango *r.* Angola **107** I4 17 00S 18 00E
Cúcuta Colombia **68** C14 7 55N 73 31W
Cuddalore India **95** D2 11 43N 79 46E
Cuddapah India **95** D2 14 30N 78 50E
Cuenca Ecuador **68** B12 2 54S 79 00W
Cuenca Spain **77** B3 40 04N 2 07W
Cuernavaca Mexico **66** E3 18 57N 99 15W
Cuiabá Brazil **68** F9 15 32S 56 05W
Cuito *r.* Angola **107** I4 17 30S 19 30E
Culiacán Mexico **66** C4 24 50N 107 23W
Cull Creek California U.S.A. **49** C3 37 45N 122 04W
Culver City California U.S.A. **51** A3 34 01N 118 24W
Cumaná Venezuela **68** E15 10 29N 64 12W
Cumberland Maryland U.S.A. **64** B2 39 40N 78 47W
Cumbernauld Scotland **78** H7 55 57N 4 00W
Cumbrian Mountains England **78** H6 54 30N 3 00W
Cumuta Trinidad and Tobago **66** T10 10 35N 61 12W
Cunene *r.* Angola/Namibia **107** H4 17 00S 13 30E
Cuneo Italy **81** A3 44 24N 7 33E
Cunnamula Australia **110** H4 28 04S 145 40E
Cunupia Trinidad and Tobago **66** T10 10 32N 61 22W
Cuova Trinidad and Tobago **66** T9 10 25N 61 27W
Curaçao *i.* Lesser Antilles **67** K2 12 20N 68 20W
Curacautin Chile **69** C5 38 28S 71 52W
Curicó Chile **69** C5 35 00S 71 15W
Curitiba Brazil **69** H7 25 25S 49 25W
Curvelo Brazil **68** I9 18 45S 44 27W
Cut Bank Montana U.S.A. **41** C1 48 38N 112 20W
Cut Bank Creek Montana U.S.A. **41** C1 48 38N 112 20W
Cuttack India **95** F4 20 26N 85 56E
Cuxhaven Germany **76** D5 53 52N 8 42E
Cuyahoga Falls *tn.* Ohio U.S.A. **36** E2 41 08N 81 27W
Cuyahoga River Ohio U.S.A. **36** E2 41 20N 81 35W
Cuzcu Peru **68** C10 13 32S 71 57W
Cwmbran Wales **78** H3 51 39N 3 00W
Cyclades *see* Kikládhes
CYPRUS **92** D5
CZECHOSLOVAKIA **80** C4
Czech Republic *admin.* Czechoslovakia **80** C4
Częstochowa Poland **80** C5 50 49N 19 07E

D

Dabola Guinea **106** C10 10 48N 11 02W
Dadra & Nagar Haveli *admin.* India **95** C4 20 00N 73 00E
Dagenham England **82** D3 51 33N 0 08E
Da Hinggan Ling *(Greater Khingan Range) mts.* China **97** O8/O9 50 00N 122 00E
Dahlewitz Germany **83** F1 52 19N 13 27E
Dāhod India **95** C4 22 48N 74 18E
Dahongliutan Kashmir **95** D7 35 55N 79 10E
Dahuk Iraq **94** F6 36 58N 43 01E
Daiō-zaki *c.* Japan **100** H1 34 16N 136 55E
Dairût Egypt **92** D4 27 34N 30 48E
Daisen *mt.* Japan **100** B2 35 23N 133 34E
Dakar Senegal **106** B10 14 38N 17 27W
Dakhla Oasis Egypt **106** K13 26 00N 28 00E
Dakshin Gangotri *r.s.* Antarctica **117** 70 05S 12 00E
Dalälven *r.* Sweden **80** C7 60 30N 17 00E
Da Lat Vietnam **99** D6 11 56N 108 25E
Dalbandin Pakistan **94** A5 28 56N 64 30E
Dalby Australia **110** I4 27 11S 151 12E
Dalhart Texas U.S.A. **62** F4 36 05N 102 32W
Dalian China **97** O6 38 53N 121 37E
Dallas Texas U.S.A. **63** G3 32 47N 96 48W
Dallgow Germany **83** E2 52 32N 13 03E
Dall Island Alaska U.S.A. **42** B2 55 00N 133 00W
Daloa Côte d'Ivoire **106** D9 6 56N 6 28W
Dalton Georgia U.S.A. **63** J3 34 46N 84 59W
Dalton Massachusetts U.S.A. **65** G5 42 28N 73 10W
Daly *r.* Australia **110** E7 14 00S 132 00E
Daly City California U.S.A. **49** B2 37 42N 122 28W
Daly Waters *tn.* Australia **110** E6 16 13S 133 20E
Daman India **95** C4 20 15N 72 58E
Damanhûr Egypt **92** D5 31 03N 30 28E
Damascus *see* Dimashq
Damāvand Iran **93** H6 35 47N 52 04E
Damāvand *mt.* Iran **93** H6 35 56N 52 08E
Damba Angola **107** I6 6 44S 15 20E
Damietta *see* Dumyât
Damoh India **95** D4 23 50N 79 30E
Dampier Australia **110** B5 20 45S 116 48E
Danakil *geog. reg.* Africa **102** 14 00N 40 00E
Da Nang Vietnam **99** D7 16 04N 108 14E
Danau Toba *l.* Indonesia **99** B4 2 40N 98 50E
Danbury Connecticut U.S.A. **65** G4 41 24N 73 26W
Danforth Maine U.S.A. **31** A2 45 42N 67 52W
Dangori India **95** H5 27 40N 95 35E
Danielson Connecticut U.S.A. **65** J4 41 48N 71 53W
Danlí Honduras **67** G2 14 02N 86 30W
Dannevirke New Zealand **111** C2 40 12S 176 08E
Dansville New York U.S.A. **64** C5 42 34N 77 41W
Danube *see* Donau, Duna, Dunarea, Dunav
Danvers Massachusetts U.S.A. **65** K5 42 35N 70 58W
Danville Illinois U.S.A. **63** I5 40 09N 87 37W
Danville Pennsylvania U.S.A. **64** D3 40 57N 76 36W
Danville Virginia U.S.A. **63** K4 36 34N 79 25W
Dar'ā Syria **92** P11 32 37N 36 06E
Darbhanga India **95** F5 26 10N 85 54E
Dardanelles *sd.* Turkey **92** C6 40 08N 26 10E
Dar el Beida *see* Casablanca
Dar es Salaam Tanzania **107** M6 6 51S 39 18E
Dargaville New Zealand **111** B3 35 57S 173 53E
Darien Connecticut U.S.A. **65** G4 41 05N 73 28W
Darien Center New York U.S.A. **64** B5 42 53N 78 22W
Darjiling India **95** F5 27 02N 88 20E
Darling *r.* Australia **110** G3 31 30S 144 00E
Darling Downs *mts.* Australia **110** H4 28 00S 148 30E
Darlington England **78** J6 54 31N 1 34W
Darmstadt Germany **76** D5 49 52N 8 39E
Darnah Libya **106** J14 32 46N 22 39E
Darnley, Cape Antarctica **117** 67 16S 69 53E
Daroca Spain **77** B3 41 07N 1 25W
Darrington Washington U.S.A. **42** H4 48 15N 121 37W
Dartford England **82** D2 51 27N 0 13E
Dartmoor National Park England **78** H2 50 35 3 50W
Daru Papua New Guinea **110** G8 9 05S 143 10E
Darwin Australia **110** E7 12 23S 130 44E
Daryācheh-ye Orūmīyeh *(L. Urmia) l.* Iran **93** G6 37 20N 45 55E
Dasht-e-Kavir *geog. reg.* Iran **93** H5 34 30N 54 30E
Dasht-e-Lut *geog. reg.* Iran **93** I5 32 00N 57 00E
Dasht-i-Margo *d.* Afghanistan **93** J5 30 30N 62 30E
Datchet England **82** A2 51 30N 0 35W
Datong China **97** M7 40 02N 113 33E
Datong He *r.* China **97** K6 37 30N 102 00E

Datong Shan *mts.* China **97** J6 38 00N 99 00E
Datu Piang The Philippines **99** G5 7 02N 124 30E
Daugavpils Latvia **79** E7 55 52N 26 31E
Dauphin Pennsylvania U.S.A. **64** D3 40 23N 76 56W
Davangere India **95** D2 14 30N 75 52E
Davao The Philippines **99** H5 7 05N 125 38E
Davenport Iowa U.S.A. **63** H5 41 32N 90 36W
David Panama **67** H1 8 26N 82 26W
Davidson Mountains Alaska U.S.A. **44** C4 68 00N 144 00W
Davis *r.s.* Antarctica **117** 68 17S 77 58E
Davison Michigan U.S.A. **36** C4 43 02N 83 30W
Davos Switzerland **77** D4 46 47N 9 50E
Dawna Range *mts.* Thailand **99** B7 17 30N 98 00E
Dax France **77** B3 43 43N 1 03W
Dayr az Zawr Syria **92** F6 35 20N 40 02E
Dayton Ohio U.S.A. **63** J4 39 45N 84 10W
Daytona Beach *tn.* Florida U.S.A. **63** J2 29 11N 81 01W
Dayville Connecticut U.S.A. **65** J4 41 51N 71 54W
Dazhang Xi *r.* China **98** E8 25 00N 118 00E
De Aar Republic of South Africa **107** J1 30 40S 24 01E
Dead Sea Israel/Jordan **92** O10 31 35N 35 30E
Dean Funes Argentina **69** E6 30 25S 64 22W
Dearborn Michigan U.S.A. **52** E2 42 18N 83 14W
Dearborn Heights Michigan U.S.A. **52** D2 42 15N 83 15W
Death Valley National Monument California/Nevada U.S.A. **66** A7 37 30N 117 30W
Débé Trinidad and Tobago **66** T9 10 12N 61 27W
Debrecen Hungary **81** D4 47 30N 21 37E
Debre Mark'os Ethiopia **106** M10 10 19N 37 41E
Debre Tabor Ethiopia **106** M10 11 50N 38 06E
Debreta-Turnu-Severin Romania **81** D3 44 36N 22 39E
Decatur Alabama U.S.A. **63** I3 34 36N 87 00W
Decatur Illinois U.S.A. **63** I4 39 51N 88 57W
Decatur Indiana U.S.A. **36** B1 40 50N 84 57W
Deccan *plat.* India **95** D3 18 00N 78 00E
Dedham Massachusetts U.S.A. **52** B1 42 15N 71 10W
Dee *r.* Scotland **78** G7 54 55N 4 00W
Dee *r.* Scotland **78** I9 57 05N 2 10W
Dee *r.* Wales/England **78** I4 53 16N 3 10W
Deep Bay Hong Kong U.K. **98** A3 22 30N 113 55E
Deerfield Illinois U.S.A. **53** A3 42 09N 87 50W
Dee Why Australia **111** H2 33 45S 151 17E
Defiance Ohio U.S.A. **36** B2 41 17N 84 21W
Degeh Bur Ethiopia **106** N9 8 11N 43 31E
Dehra Dun India **95** D6 30 19N 78 03E
Dej Romania **81** D4 47 08N 23 55E
Dekese Zaïre **107** J7 3 28S 21 24E
Delaware *state* U.S.A. **64** E2 39 00N 75 00W
Delaware Bay U.S.A. **64** E2 39 10N 75 10W
Delaware River U.S.A. **64** E2 39 40N 75 30W
Delhi India **94** L4 28 40N 77 14E
Delhi Cantonment India **94** L4 28 35N 77 08E
Dellen *l.* Sweden **79** D3 61 50N 16 45E
Dellys Algeria **77** C2 36 57N 3 55E
De Long Mountains Alaska U.S.A. **10** C6 68 30N 162 00W
Delphos Ohio U.S.A. **36** B1 40 50N 84 21W
Del Rio Texas U.S.A. **62** F2 29 23N 100 56W
Delta Colorado U.S.A. **62** F4 38 42N 108 04W
Delta Junction Alaska U.S.A. **44** B3 63 30N 146 00W
Delta Lake *res.* New York U.S.A. **64** E6 43 17N 75 26W
Dembī Dolo Ethiopia **106** L9 8 34N 34 50E
Deming New Mexico U.S.A. **62** E3 32 17N 107 46W
Deming Washington U.S.A. **42** H4 48 50N 122 14W
Denain France **76** C5 50 19N 3 24E
Den Haag *(The Hague) see* 's-Gravenhage
Den Helder Netherlands **76** C5 52 58N 4 46E
Denison Texas U.S.A. **63** G3 33 47N 96 34W
Denizli Turkey **92** C6 37 46N 29 05E
Denman Glacier Antarctica **117** 67 00S 100 00E
DENMARK **80** A6/B6
Denpasar Indonesia **99** F2 8 40S 115 14E
Denton Texas U.S.A. **63** G3 33 14N 97 18W
D'Entrecasteaux Islands Papua New Guinea **110** I8 9 30S 150 30E
Denver Colorado U.S.A. **62** E4 39 45N 105 00W
Deodora Brazil **69** P2 22 51S 43 22W
Depew New York U.S.A. **64** B5 42 54N 78 00W
Dépression du Mourdi *dep.* Chad **106** J11 17 00N 22 41E
Deputatskiy Russia **89** P9 69 15N 139 59E
Dera Ghazi Khan Pakistan **95** C6 30 05N 70 44E
Dera Ismail Khan Pakistan **95** C6 31 51N 70 56E
Derbent Russia **90** F3 42 03N 48 18E
Derby Australia **110** C6 17 19S 123 38E
Derby Connecticut U.S.A. **65** G4 41 19N 73 05W
Derby England **78** J4 52 55N 1 30W
Derry New Hampshire U.S.A. **65** J5 42 00N 71 00W
De-Ruyter New York U.S.A. **64** E5 42 46N 75 54W
Deseado Argentina **69** D3 47 44S 65 56W
Desē Ethiopia **106** M10 11 05N 39 40E
Desierto de Atacama *(Atacama Desert) d.* Chile **68/69** C8 22 30S 70 00W
Des Moines Iowa U.S.A. **63** H5 41 35N 93 35W
Des Moines *r.* Iowa U.S.A. **63** H5 41 00N 92 00W
Desna *r.* Russia/Ukraine **90** C5 51 00N 30 30E
Des Plaines Illinois U.S.A. **53** A3 42 02N 87 54W
Des Plaines River Illinois U.S.A. **53** A1 41 30N 87 45W
Dessau Germany **76** E5 51 51N 12 15E
Detroit Michigan U.S.A. **63** J5 42 23N 83 05W
Detroit River Canada/U.S.A. **52** E2 42 15N 83 00W
Deva Romania **81** D4 45 53N 22 55E
Deventer Netherlands **76** D5 52 15N 6 10E
Deveron *r.* Scotland **78** I9 57 25N 3 03W
Devils Gate Reservoir California U.S.A. **51** B3 34 11N 118 10W
Devonport Australia **110** H1 41 09S 146 16E
Dexter Maine U.S.A. **33** C2 45 01N 69 19W
Dezfūl Iran **93** G5 32 23N 48 28E
Dezhou China **97** N6 37 29N 116 11E
Dhahran *see* Az Zahrān
Dhaka Bangladesh **95** G4 23 42N 90 22E
Dhamār Yemen Republic **92** F1 14 33N 44 30E
Dhanbad India **95** F4 23 47N 86 32E
Dharoor *r.* Somalia **106** O10 10 00N 54 00E
Dhārwād India **95** D3 15 30N 75 04E
Dhodhekánisos *(Dodecanese) is.* Greece **81** E2 37 00N 26 00E
Dhoraji India **94** C4 21 42N 70 32E
Dhule India **95** C4 20 52N 74 50E
Diablo Lake Washington U.S.A. **42** H4 48 45N 121 05W
Diamantina Brazil **68** I9 18 17S 43 37W
Diamantina *r.* Australia **110** G5 24 00S 142 00E
Diamantina Fracture Zone Indian Ocean **112** J3/K3
Dibrugarh India **95** G5 27 29N 94 56E
Dickinson North Dakota U.S.A. **62** F6 46 54N 102 48W
Diego Martin Trinidad and Tobago **66** S10 10 48N 61 34W
Diepholz Germany **76** D5 52 37N 8 22E
Dieppe France **76** C4 49 55N 1 05E
Digne France **77** D3 44 05N 6 14E
Dijon France **77** D4 47 20N 5 02E
Dikson Russia **89** K10 73 32N 80 39E
Dikwa Nigeria **106** H10 12 01N 13 55E
Dili *see* Oekusi
Dillingham Alaska U.S.A. **10** D4 59 03N 158 30W
Dimashq *(Damascus)* Syria **92** P11 33 30N 36 19E
Dimitrovgrad Bulgaria **81** E3 42 03N 25 34E
Dimitrovgrad Russia **90** F5 54 14N 49 37E
Dinajpur Bangladesh **95** F5 25 38N 88 44E
Dinan France **76** B4 48 27N 2 02W
Dinant Belgium **76** C5 50 16N 4 55E
Dinara Planina *(Dinaric Alps) mts.* Europe **81** C3 44 00N 17 00E
Dinaric Alps *see* Dinara Planina
Dindigul India **95** D2 10 23N 78 00E
Dingle Bay Irish Republic **78** A4 52 05N 10 15W
Dingwall Scotland **78** G9 57 35N 4 29W
Dinslaken Germany **76** G3 51 34N 6 43E
Dipolog The Philippines **99** G5 8 34N 123 23E
Dir Pakistan **95** C7 35 12N 71 54E
Dirē Dawa Ethiopia **106** N9 9 35N 41 50E
Disappointment, Lake Australia **110** C5 23 00S 123 00E
Discovery Bay Hong Kong U.K. **98** B1 22 18N 114 02E
Discovery Bay *tn.* Hong Kong U.K. **98** B1 22 18N 114 01E
Disko Bugt *b.* Greenland **45** V4 69 00N 54 00W
Disko Island Greenland **45** V4 70 00N 54 00W
Distins Barbados **66** V12 13 04N 59 35W
Distins Bay Barbados **66** V12 13 03N 59 34W
Ditan China **101** G1 39 58N 116 24E
Diu India **94** C4 20 41N 71 03E
Divinopólis Brazil **68** I8 20 08S 44 55W
Divriği Turkey **92** E6 39 23N 38 06E
Dixon Entrance *sd.* Canada/U.S.A. **42** B2 54 28N 132 50W
Diyarbakir Turkey **92** F6 37 55N 40 14E
Djambala Congo **106** H7 2 32S 14 43E
Djelfa Algeria **106** F14 34 43N 3 14E
DJIBOUTI **92** F1
Djibouti Djibouti **92** F1 11 35N 43 11E
Djougou Benin **106** F9 9 40N 1 47E
Dnepr *r.* Belarus/Ukraine **90** C4 48 00N 35 00E
Dneprodzerzhinsk Ukraine **90** C4 48 30N 34 37E
Dnepropetrovsk Ukraine **90** C4 48 29N 35 00E
Dnestr *r.* Moldova/Ukraine **90** A4 49 30N 24 30E
Dobrich *(Tolbukhin)* Bulgaria **81** E3 43 34N 27 51E
Dobrogea *geog. reg.* Romania **81** E3 44 00N 29 00E
Dodecanese *see* Dhodhekánisos
Dodge City Kansas U.S.A. **62** F4 37 45N 100 02W
Dodoma Tanzania **107** M6 6 10S 35 40E
Dodson Montana U.S.A. **40** B1 48 25N 108 16W
Dogai Coring *l.* China **95** F6 34 30N 89 00E
Dōgo *i.* Japan **100** B2 36 20N 133 15E
Doha *see* Ad Dawhah
Dolgeville New York U.S.A. **65** F6 43 08N 74 46W
Dolina Ukraine **80** D4 49 00N 23 59E
Dolo Ethiopia **106** N8 4 11N 42 03E
Dolton Illinois U.S.A. **53** B1 41 36N 87 36W
Domaneab Nauru **114** G7 0 35S 166 40E
Dombas Norway **79** B3 62 05N 9 07E
DOMINICA **67** L3
DOMINICAN REPUBLIC **67** K3
Don *r.* England **78** J5 53 37N 1 02W
Don *r.* Russia **90** E4 50 00N 41 00E
Don *r.* Scotland **78** I9 57 15N 2 55W
Donau *(Danube) r.* Germany/Austria **76** E4 48 00N 16 00E
Don Benito Spain **77** A2 38 57N 5 52W
Doncaster England **78** J5 53 32N 1 07W
Donegal Irish Republic **78** C6 54 39N 8 07W
Donegal Bay Irish Republic **78** C6 54 30N 8 30W
Donegal Mountains Irish Republic **78** C6/D7 55 00N 8 05W
Donetsk Ukraine **90** D4 48 00N 37 50E
Dongba China **101** H1 39 58N 116 35E
Dongchuan China **97** K4 26 07N 103 05E
Dong Hoi Vietnam **97** L2 17 32N 106 35E
Dongola Sudan **92** D2 19 10N 30 27E
Dongou Congo **106** I8 2 02N 18 02E
Dønna *i.* Norway **79** C4 66 05N 12 30E
Donting Hu *l.* China **97** M4 29 00N 112 30E
Devils Lake *tn.* North Dakota U.S.A. **62** G6 48 08N 98 50W
Door Peninsula Wisconsin U.S.A. **63** I6 45 00N 87 00W
Dordogne *r.* France **77** C3 44 55N 0 30E
Dordrecht Netherlands **76** C5 51 48N 4 40E
Dori *r.* Afghanistan **93** K5 31 20N 65 00E
Dorking England **82** B1 51 14N 0 20W
Dormont Pennsylvania U.S.A. **53** D1 40 23N 80 03W
Dornbirn Austria **81** A4 47 25N 9 45E
Dornoch Firth *est.* Scotland **78** H9 57 55N 3 55W
Dortmund Germany **76** E5 51 32N 7 27E
Dortmund-Ems-Kanal *can.* Germany **76** K3 51 40N 7 20E
Dosso Niger **106** F10 13 03N 3 10E
Dothan Alabama U.S.A. **63** I3 31 12N 85 25W
Douai France **76** C5 50 22N 3 05E
Douala Cameroon **106** H8 4 04N 9 43E
Douarnenez France **77** B4 48 05N 4 20W
Double Island Hong Kong U.K. **98** C3 22 31N 114 08E
Doubs *r.* France **77** D4 47 20N 6 25E
Douglas Alaska U.S.A. **44** D3 58 15N 134 24W
Douglas Arizona U.S.A. **62** E3 31 21N 109 34W
Douglas Isle of Man British Isles **78** G6 54 09N 4 29W
Douglas Park Illinois U.S.A. **53** B2 41 51N 87 43W
Dourados Brazil **69** G8 22 09S 54 52W
Douro *r.* Portugal **77** A3 41 00N 8 30W
Dover Delaware U.S.A. **64** E2 39 10N 75 32W
Dover England **78** M3 51 08N 1 19E
Dover Massachusetts U.S.A. **52** A1 42 15N 71 17W
Dover New Hampshire U.S.A. **65** K6 43 12N 70 55W
Dover, Strait of English Channel **78** M3 51 00N 1 20E
Dovrefjell *mts.* Norway **79** B3 62 15N 9 10E
Downers Grove Illinois U.S.A. **53** A2 41 47N 87 59W
Downey California U.S.A. **51** B2 33 56N 118 25W
Doylestown Pennsylvania U.S.A. **64** E3 40 18N 75 08W
Dōzen *is.* Japan **100** B2 36 05N 133 00E
Dragan *l.* Sweden **79** D3 64 05N 15 20E
Dragon's Mouths, The *(Bocas del Dragons) sd.* Trinidad and Tobago **66** S10 10 37N 61 50W
Draguignan France **77** D3 43 32N 6 28E
Drakensberg *mts.* Republic of South Africa **107** K1 30 00S 28 00E
Drake Passage *sd.* Southern Ocean **69** C1/E1 58 00S 66 00W
Dráma Greece **81** D3 41 10N 24 11E
Drammen Norway **79** C2 59 45N 10 15E
Drancy France **83** B2 48 55N 2 28E
Drau *r.* Austria **81** B4 46 00N 14 00E
Drayton North Dakota U.S.A. **39** B1 48 35N 97 11W
Dresden Germany **76** E5 51 03N 13 45E
Dreux France **76** C4 48 44N 1 23E
Drewitz Germany **83** E1 52 20N 13 08E
Drin *r.* Albania **81** D3 42 00N 20 00E
Drina *r.* Europe **81** C3 43 30N 15 19E
Drogheda Irish Republic **78** E5 53 43N 6 21W
Drogobyč Ukraine **80** D4 49 22N 23 33E
Drôme *r.* France **77** D3 44 50N 5 00E
Drummond Island Michigan U.S.A. **36** C7 46 00N 83 40W
Drummoyne Australia **111** G2 33 51S 151 09E
Druzhba Kazakhstan **91** N4 45 18N 82 29E
Dryden New York U.S.A. **64** D5 42 29N 76 17W
Dubayy United Arab Emirates **93** I4 25 14N 55 17E
Dubbo Australia **110** H3 32 16S 148 41E
Dublin Georgia U.S.A. **63** J3 32 31N 82 54W
Dublin Irish Republic **78** E5 53 20N 6 15W
Dubno Ukraine **90** B5 50 28N 25 40E
Du Bois Pennsylvania U.S.A. **64** B4 41 06N 78 46W
Dubrovnik Croatia **81** C3 42 40N 18 07E
Dubuque Iowa U.S.A. **63** H5 42 31N 90 41W
Ducie Island Pitcairn Islands **115** N5 24 40S 124 48W
Dudinka Russia **89** K9 69 27N 86 13E
Dudley Massachusetts U.S.A. **65** J5 42 03N 71 55W
Dudley England **78** I4 52 30N 2 05W
Duero *(Douro) r.* Spain/Portugal **77** A3 41 25N 6 30W
Duffy Preserve Illinois U.S.A. **53** A1 41 39N 87 55W
Dugi Otok *i.* Croatia **81** C3 44 00N 15 00E
Duisberg Germany **76** H2 51 26N 6 45E
Duke Island Alaska U.S.A. **42** B2 54 50N 131 30W
Duluth Minnesota U.S.A. **63** H6 46 45N 92 10W
Dum Dum India **94** K2 22 37N 88 24E
Dumfries Scotland **78** H7 55 04N 3 37W
Dumont d'Urville *r.s.* Antarctica **117** 66 40S 140 01E
Dümpten Germany **76** H2 51 28N 6 50E
Dumyât *(Damietta)* Egypt **107** R4 31 26N 31 48E
Duna *(Danube) r.* Hungary **81** C4 46 00N 19 00E
Dunarea *(Danube) r.* Romania **81** E3 44 00N 28 00E
Dunaújváros Hungary **81** C4 47 00N 18 55E
Dunav *(Danube) r.* Serbia/Bulgaria **81** D3 45 00N 20 00E
Duncan Oklahoma U.S.A. **63** G3 34 30N 97 57W
Duncan Passage *sd.* Andaman Islands **95** G2 11 00N 93 00E
Duncannon Pennsylvania U.S.A. **64** C3 40 24N 77 03W
Duncansby Head *c.* Scotland **78** H10 58 39N 3 02W
Duncansville Pennsylvania U.S.A. **64** B3 40 27N 78 25W
Dundalk Irish Republic **78** E6 54 01N 6 25W
Dundalk Maryland U.S.A. **64** D2 39 15N 76 31W
Dundas *(Uummannaq)* Greenland **45** S6 76 30N 68 58W
Dundee Scotland **78** I8 56 28N 3 00W
Dunedin New Zealand **111** B1 45 52S 170 30E
Dunfermline Scotland **78** H8 56 04N 3 29W
Dungeness Washington U.S.A. **42** H4 48 08N 123 07W
Dunkerque *(Dunkirk)* France **76** C5 51 02N 2 23E
Dunkirk *see* Dunkerque
Dunkirk New York U.S.A. **63** K5 42 29N 79 21W
Dún Laoghaire Irish Republic **78** E5 53 17N 6 08W
Dunmore Pennsylvania U.S.A. **64** E4 41 25N 75 38W
Du Page County Illinois U.S.A. **53** A2 41 59N 87 59W
Duque de Caxias Brazil **69** P2 22 46S 43 18W
Duquesne Pennsylvania U.S.A. **53** E1 40 23N 79 53W
Dural Australia **111** G3 33 41S 151 02E
Durance *r.* France **77** D3 43 50N 5 15E
Durand Michigan U.S.A. **36** C3 42 55N 83 58W
Durango Colorado U.S.A. **62** E4 37 16N 107 53W
Durango Mexico **66** D4 24 01N 104 40W
Durant Oklahoma U.S.A. **63** G3 33 59N 96 24W
Durazno Uruguay **69** F6 33 22S 56 31W
Durban Republic of South Africa **107** L2 29 53S 31 00E
Durgapur India **95** J1 22 47N 87 44E
Durgāpur India **95** J1 22 27N 88 08E
Durg-Bhilai India **95** E4 21 12N 81 20E
Durham England **78** J6 54 47N 1 34W
Durham New Hampshire U.S.A. **65** K6 43 10N 70 52W
Durham North Carolina U.S.A. **63** K4 36 00N 78 54W
Durrës Albania **81** C3 41 18N 19 28E
Dushanbe Tajikistan **91** K2 38 38N 68 51E
Düssel *r.* Germany **76** H1 51 13N 6 55E
Düsseldorf Germany **76** H1 51 13N 6 47E
Duxbury Massachusetts U.S.A. **65** K5 42 02N 70 40W
Duyun China **97** L4 26 16N 107 29E
Dvina, North *see* Severnaya Dvina
Dzerzhinsk Belarus **90** B5 55 40N 27 01E
Dzhambul Kazakhstan **91** L3 42 50N 71 25E
Dzhetygara Kazakhstan **91** J5 52 14N 61 10E
Dzhezkazgan Kazakhstan **91** K4 47 44N 67 42E
Dzhugdzhur Range *mts.* Russia **89** P7 57 00N 137 00E
Dzungurian Basin *see* Junggar Pendi

E

Eagle Alaska U.S.A. **44** G5 64 46N 141 20W
Eagle Lake Maine U.S.A. **37** R7 46 25N 69 20W
Eagle Mountains Minnesota U.S.A. **35** B2 47 55N 90 30W
Eagle Pass *tn.* Texas U.S.A. **62** F2 28 44N 100 31W
Eagle River *tn.* Wisconsin U.S.A. **35** C2 45 56N 89 15W
Ealing *bor.* Greater London England **82** B3 51 31N 0 18W
East Antarctica *geog. reg.* Antarctica **117**
East Aurora New York U.S.A. **64** B5 42 45N 78 36W
East Berlin Pennsylvania U.S.A. **64** C2 39 58N 77 00W
Eastbourne England **78** L2 50 46N 0 17E
East Branch Clarion River Reservoir Pennsylvania U.S.A. **64** B4 41 35N 78 35W
East Branch Delaware River New York U.S.A. **65** F5 42 15N 74 35W
East Cape New Zealand **111** C3 37 42S 178 35E
East Caroline Basin Pacific Ocean **114** E8 4 00N 148 00E
East Chicago Indiana U.S.A. **53** C1 41 38N 87 27W
East China Sea China/Japan **97** P5 32 00N 126 00E
East Detroit Michigan U.S.A. **52** F2 42 29N 82 57W
Easter Island Pacific Ocean **115** P5 27 05S 109 20W
Easter Island Fracture Zone Pacific Ocean **115** Q5 24 00S 100 00W
Eastern Ghats *mts.* India **95** D2/E2 15 00N 80 00E
Eastern Group *is.* Fiji **114** V16 17 40S 178 30W
Eastern Sayan *mts.* Russia **89** L6 53 00N 97 30E
East Falkland *i.* Falkland Islands **69** F2 52 00S 58 50W
East Fishkill New York U.S.A. **65** G4 41 33N 73 47W
East Fork Chandalar *r.* Alaska U.S.A. **44** B4 66 50N 147 00W
East Frisian Islands *see* Ostfriesische Inseln
East Glacier Park *tn.* Montana U.S.A. **41** C1 48 25N 113 35W
East Haddam Connecticut U.S.A. **65** H4 41 27N 72 28W
Easthampton Massachusetts U.S.A. **65** H5 42 16N 72 40W
East Hills Australia **111** G2 33 58S 150 59E
East Horsley England **82** B2 51 16N 0 26W
East Kilbride Scotland **78** G7 55 46N 4 10W
East Lamma Channel Hong Kong U.K. **98** B1 22 14N 114 08E
East London Republic of South Africa **107** K1 33 00S 27 54E
East Los Angeles California U.S.A. **51** B3 34 02N 118 12W
East Marianas Basin Pacific Ocean **114** F9 13 00N 153 00E
Easton Pennsylvania U.S.A. **64** E3 40 41N 75 13W
East Pacific Basin Pacific Ocean **115** K9 16 00N 153 00E
East Pacific Ridge Pacific Ocean **115** O5 20 00S 113 00W
East Pacific Rise Pacific Ocean **115** P9 13 00N 103 00W
Eastport Maine U.S.A. **31** A1 44 55N 67 01W
Eastport New York U.S.A. **65** H3 40 49N 72 44W
East Rift Valley East Africa **106** M8 6 00N 37 00E
East Siberian Sea Arctic Ocean **116** 72 00N 165 00E
Eastsound Washington U.S.A. **42** H4 48 41N 122 54W
East Stroudsburg Pennsylvania U.S.A. **64** E4 41 00N 75 00W
Eastwood Australia **111** G2 33 48S 151 05E
Eaton Rapids *tn.* Michigan U.S.A. **36** B3 42 30N 85 40W
Eatontown New Jersey U.S.A. **65** F3 40 18N 74 06W
Eaton Wash Reservoir California U.S.A. **51** B3 34 10N 118 05W
Eau Claire *tn.* Wisconsin U.S.A. **63** H5 44 50N 91 30W
Eauripik-New Guinea Rise Pacific Ocean **114** E8 2 00N 142 00E
Ebensburg Pennsylvania U.S.A. **64** B3 40 28N 78 45W
Eberswalde-Finow Germany **76** E5 52 50N 13 53E
Ebinur Hu *l.* China **96** F7/6 45 00N 83 00E
Ebolowa Cameroon **106** H8 2 56N 11 11E
Ebro *r.* Spain **77** C3 41 00N 0 30E
Ebute Metta Nigeria **107** V3 6 27N 3 28E
Ech Cheliff Algeria **106** F15 36 05N 1 15E
Ecija Spain **77** A2 37 33N 5 04W
Ecorse Michigan U.S.A. **52** E2 42 16N 83 09W
Écouen France **83** B3 49 01N 2 22E
ECUADOR **68** B12
Ed Damer Sudan **92** D2 17 37N 33 59E
Ed Debba Sudan **106** L11 18 02N 30 56E
Edéa Cameroon **106** H8 3 47N 10 13E
Eden New York U.S.A. **64** B5 42 39N 78 56W
Eden North Carolina U.S.A. **63** K4 37 30N 79 46W
Eden *r.* England **78** I6 54 50N 2 45W
Eden, Mount California U.S.A. **49** C2 37 38N 122 09W
Eder *r.* Germany **76** D5 51 00N 9 00E
Edgartown Massachusetts U.S.A. **65** K4 41 24N 70 31W
Edgecombe, Cape Alaska U.S.A. **42** A3 57 00N 135 45W
Edgewood Maryland U.S.A. **64** D2 39 25N 76 18W
Edgware England **82** B3 51 36N 0 16W
Édhessa Greece **81** D3 40 48N 22 03E
Edinboro Pennsylvania U.S.A. **36** F2 41 53N 80 08W
Edinburgh Scotland **78** H7 55 57N 3 13W
Edirne Turkey **80** E3 41 40N 26 34E
Edison New Jersey U.S.A. **65** F3 40 31N 74 24W
Edmonton England **82** C3 51 37N 0 04W
Edo *r.* Japan **101** C3 35 38N 139 53E
Edogawa Japan **101** C3 35 41N 139 51E
Edremit Turkey **80** E2 39 34N 27 01E
Edward, Lake Zaïre/Uganda **106** K7 0 30S 29 00E
Edwards Plateau Texas U.S.A. **62** F3 31 20N 100 00W
Eems *(Ems) est.* Netherlands **76** D5 53 25N 6 55E
Éfaté *i.* Vanuatu **110** L5 17 30S 168 00E
Eger Hungary **81** D4 47 53N 20 28E
Egham England **82** A2 51 26N 0 34W
Egmont, Cape New Zealand **111** B3 39 15S 173 46E
Egmont, Mount New Zealand **111** B3 39 18S 174 05E
Egridir Gölü Turkey **92** D6 37 52N 30 51E
EGYPT **92** D4
Eichwalde Germany **83** G1 52 23N 13 37E
Eifel *plat.* Germany **76** D5 50 00N 7 00E
Eigg *i.* Scotland **78** E8 56 55N 6 10W
Eight Degree Channel Indian Ocean **95** C1 8 00N 73 30E
Eighty Mile Beach Australia **110** C6 19 00S 121 00E
Eindhoven Netherlands **76** D5 51 26N 5 30E
Eisenach Germany **76** E5 50 59N 10 19E
Ekibastuz Kazakhstan **91** M5 51 50N 75 10E
Eksjö Sweden **80** B6 57 40N 15 00E
EL SALVADOR **66** G2
El Aaiún *see* Laayoune
El Arco Mexico **66** B5 28 00N 113 25W
El'Arîsh Egypt **92** N10 31 08N 33 48E
Elat Israel **92** O9 29 33N 34 57E
Elâziğ Turkey **92** E6 38 41N 39 14E
El Bahr el Saghîr Egypt **107** R4 31 38N 31 39E
El Ballâh Egypt **107** S3 30 47N 32 19E
El Banco Colombia **68** C14 9 04N 73 59W
Elbasan Albania **81** D3 41 07N 20 05E
El Bayadh Algeria **77** C2 36 35N 1 18E
El Bayadh Algeria **106** F14 33 40N 1 00E
Elbe *(Labe) r.* Europe **76** D5 53 00N 9 00E
Elbert, Mount Colorado U.S.A. **62** E4 39 05N 106 27W
Elblag Poland **80** C5 54 10N 19 25E
Elburz Mountains Iran **93** H6 36 15N 51 00E
El Cerro del Aripo *mt.* Trinidad and Tobago **66** T10 10 49N 61 14W
Elche Spain **77** B2 38 16N 0 41W
Elda Spain **77** B2 38 29N 0 47W
Eldoret Kenya **106** M8 0 31N 35 17E
Eldred Pennsylvania U.S.A. **64** B4 41 57N 78 23W

El Dorado Arkansas U.S.A. **63** H3 33 12N 92 40W
El Dorado Kansas U.S.A. **63** G4 37 51N 96 52W
Elektrostal' Russia **90** D6 55 46N 38 30E
Elephant Island South Shetland Islands **69** G0 62 00S 55 00W
El Eulma Algeria **77** D2 36 00N 5 30E
Eleuthera *i.* The Bahamas **67** I5 25 05N 76 30W
El Faiyûm Egypt **92** D4 29 19N 30 50E
El Fasher Sudan **106** K10 13 37N 25 22E
El Ferrol del Caudillo Spain **77** A3 43 29N 8 14W
El Firdân Egypt **107** S3 30 42N 32 20E
El Fuerte Mexico **66** C5 26 28N 108 35W
Elgin Scotland **78** H9 57 39N 3 20W
El Gîza Egypt **92** D5 30 01N 31 12E
El Golea Algeria **106** F14 30 35N 2 51E
El Granada California U.S.A. **49** B2 37 31N 122 28W
El Harrach Algeria **77** C2 36 45N 4 00E
El Iskandarîya *see* Alexandria
Elista Russia **90** E4 46 18N 44 14E
Eliza Howell Park Michigan U.S.A. **52** D2 42 29N 83 57W
Elizabeth Australia **110** F3 34 45S 138 39E
Elizabeth New Jersey U.S.A. **50** B1 40 39N 74 13W
Elizabeth City North Carolina U.S.A. **63** K4 36 18N 76 16W
Elizabeth Islands Massachusetts U.S.A. **65** K4 41 00N 70 00W
Elizabethtown Pennsylvania U.S.A. **64** D3 40 10N 76 38W
El Jafr Jordan **92** P10 30 16N 36 11E
Ełk Poland **80** D5 53 51N 22 20E
Elk City Oklahoma U.S.A. **62** G4 34 25N 99 26W
Elk Grove Village Illinois U.S.A. **53** A3 42 00N 87 58W
El Khârga Egypt **92** D4 25 27N 30 32E
Elkhart Indiana U.S.A. **63** I5 41 52N 85 56W
Elkhorn *r.* Nebraska U.S.A. **63** G5 42 00N 98 00W
Elkland Pennsylvania U.S.A. **64** C4 42 00N 77 20W
Elko Nevada U.S.A. **62** C5 40 50N 115 46W
Ellenville New York U.S.A. **65** F4 41 43N 74 23W
Ellis Island New Jersey U.S.A. **50** B1 40 42N 74 02W
Ellsworth Land *geog. reg.* Antarctica **117** 75 00S 80 00W
Ellsworth Maine U.S.A. **33** C1 44 34N 68 24W
El Mahalla El Kubra Egypt **92** D5 30 59N 31 10E
El Manzala Egypt **107** S4 31 09N 31 57E
El Matarîya Egypt **107** S4 31 10N 32 02E
El Médano Mexico **66** B4 24 35N 111 29W
Elmhurst Illinois U.S.A. **53** A2 41 54N 87 56W
Elmhurst Pennsylvania U.S.A. **64** E4 41 20N 75 32W
el Milk *r.* Sudan **106** K11 17 00N 29 00E
El Minya Egypt **92** D4 28 06N 30 45E
Elmira New York U.S.A. **64** D5 42 06N 76 50W
El Monte California U.S.A. **51** B3 34 04N 118 01W
El Muglad Sudan **106** K10 11 01N 27 50E
Elmwood Park Illinois U.S.A. **53** A2 41 54N 87 49W
El Obeid Sudan **106** L10 13 11N 30 10E
El Paso Texas U.S.A. **62** E3 31 45N 106 30W
El Porvenir Mexico **66** C6 31 15N 105 48W
El Puerto de Sta. Maria Spain **77** A2 36 36N 6 14W
El Qantara Egypt **107** S3 30 53N 32 20E
El Qâ'hira *see* Cairo
El Qunaytirah Syria **92** O11 33 08N 35 49E
El Reno Oklahoma U.S.A. **63** G4 35 32N 97 57W
El Sâlhîya Egypt **107** R3 30 47N 31 59E
El Salto Mexico **66** C4 23 47N 105 22W
El Shallûfa Egypt **107** T2 30 06N 32 33E
El Sobrante California U.S.A. **49** B3 37 59N 122 18W
El Sueco Mexico **66** C5 29 54N 106 22W
El Suweis *(Suez)* Egypt **107** T1 29 59N 32 33E
Eltanin Fracture Zone Pacific Ocean **115** M2 52 00S 135 00W
El Tigre Venezuela **68** E14 8 44N 64 18W
El Tina Egypt **107** S4 31 03N 32 19E
El Tucuche *mt.* Trinidad and Tobago **66** T10 10 44N 61 25W
El Tûr Egypt **92** N9 28 14N 33 37E
Eluru India **95** E3 16 45N 81 10E
Elvas Portugal **77** A2 38 53N 7 10W
Elverum Norway **80** B7 60 54N 11 33E
Elwell, Lake Montana U.S.A. **41** C1 48 25N 111 58W
Ely Nevada U.S.A. **62** D4 39 15N 114 53W
Elyria Ohio U.S.A. **63** J5 41 22N 82 06W
Emāmrūd Iran **93** H6 36 15N 54 59E
Emba Kazakhstan **91** H4 48 47N 58 05E
Emba *r.* Kazakhstan **91** H4 47 30N 56 00E
Embalse de Guri *l.* Venezuela **68** E14 7 30N 62 30W
Emden Germany **76** D5 53 23N 7 13E
Emerald Australia **110** H5 23 30S 148 08E
Emeryville California U.S.A. **49** B3 37 50N 122 19W
Emi Koussi *mt.* Chad **106** I11 19 52N 18 31E
Emmaus Pennsylvania U.S.A. **64** E3 40 32N 75 30W
Empalme Mexico **66** B5 28 00N 110 49W
Emperor Seamounts Pacific Ocean **114** G12 42 00N 169 00E
Ems *r.* Germany **76** D5 53 00N 7 00E
Emscher *r.* Germany **76** K3 51 35N 7 25E
Ena Japan **100** J2 35 28N 137 25E
Encantado Brazil **69** P2 22 54S 43 18W
Encarnación Paraguay **69** F7 27 20S 55 50W
Endeh Indonesia **99** G2 8 51S 121 40E
Endicott New York U.S.A. **64** D5 42 06N 76 03W
Endicott Mountains Alaska U.S.A. **44** A4 67 35N 154 00W
Enfield *bor.* Greater London England **82** C3 51 39N 0 05W
Engel's Russia **90** F5 51 30N 46 07E
Engenno Novo Brazil **69** P2 22 54S 43 16W
Enggano *i.* Indonesia **99** C2 5 10S 102 40E
Enghien France **83** B2 48 58N 2 19E
England United Kingdom **78** I5
Englewood New Jersey U.S.A. **50** C2 40 53N 73 58W
English Channel *(La Manche)* U.K./France **76** B4/5 50 00N 2 30W
Enna Italy **81** B2 37 34N 14 16E
En Nahud Sudan **106** K10 12 41N 28 28E
Enniskillen Northern Ireland **78** D6 54 21N 7 38W
Enns *r.* Austria **81** B4 48 00N 14 00E
Enontekiö Finland **79** E4 68 25N 23 40E
Enosburg Falls *tn.* Vermont U.S.A. **37** O5 44 55N 72 49W
Enschede Netherlands **76** D5 52 13N 6 55E
Ensenada Mexico **66** A6 31 53N 116 38W
Entebbe Uganda **106** L8 0 04N 32 27E
Enugu Nigeria **106** G9 6 20N 7 29E
Épernay France **76** C4 49 02N 3 58E
Épinal France **76** D4 48 10N 6 28E
Epping Australia **111** G2 33 46S 151 05E
Epping England **82** D3 51 42N 0 08E
Epping Forest England **82** D3 51 40N 0 04E
Epsom England **82** B2 51 20N 0 16W
EQUATORIAL GUINEA **106** G8/H8
Erebus, Mount Antarctica **117** 77 40S 167 20E
Erechim Brazil **69** G7 27 35S 52 15W
Erenhot China **97** M7 43 50N 112 00E
Erfurt Germany **76** E5 50 58N 11 02E
Erg Chech *geog. reg.* Algeria **106** E12 24 30N 3 00W
Ergene *r.* Turkey **80** E3 41 00N 27 00E
Erg Iguidi *geog. reg.* Algeria **106** D13 26 00N 6 00W
Ergun He *see* Argun
Erh-lin Taiwan **98** G6 23 52N 120 18E
Erie Pennsylvania U.S.A. **63** J5 42 07N 80 05W
Erie, Lake Canada/U.S.A. **36** E2 42 15N 81 00W
Erimo-misaki *c.* Japan **100** D3 41 55N 143 13E
Erin Point Trinidad and Tobago **66** S9 10 03N 61 39W
Erith England **82** D2 51 29N 0 11E
Erith Marshes England **82** D3 51 30N 0 08E
Eritrea *see* Ertra
Erkner Germany **83** H1 52 25N 13 46E
Erkrath Germany **76** H1 51 13N 6 54E
Erne *r.* Irish Republic **78** D5 53 50N 7 30W
Erode India **95** D2 11 21N 77 43E
Erris Head *c.* Irish Republic **78** A6 54 20N 10 00W
Erromango *i.* Vanuatu **110** L6 19 00S 169 00E
Er Roseires Sudan **106** L10 11 52N 34 23E
Ertra *(Eritrea) admin.* Ethiopia **92** F1 14 40N 40 15E
Erzgebirge *(Krušnéhory) mts.* Europe **76** E5 50 00N 13 00E
Erzincan Turkey **92** E6 39 44N 39 30E
Erzurum Turkey **92** F6 39 57N 41 17E
Esashi Japan **100** D3 41 54N 140 09E
Esbjerg Denmark **80** A6 55 20N 8 20E
Escanaba Michigan U.S.A. **63** I6 45 47N 87 04W
Escobal Panama **67** Y2 9 11N 79 59W
Esfahān Iran **93** H5 32 41N 51 41E
Esher England **82** B2 51 22N 0 22W
Eskilstuna Sweden **79** D2 59 22N 16 31E
Eskişehir Turkey **92** D6 39 46N 30 30E
Esmeraldas Ecuador **68** B13 0 56N 79 40W
Esperance Australia **110** C3 33 49S 121 52E
Esperanza *r.s.* Antarctica **117** 63 24S 56 59W
Espirito Santo *admin.* Brazil **68** J9 18 40S 40 00W
Espiritu Santo *i.* Vanuatu **110** L6 15 10S 167 00E
Espoo Finland **79** E3 60 10N 24 40E
Esquel Argentina **69** C4 42 55S 71 20W
Es Semara Western Sahara **106** C13 26 25N 11 30W
Essen Germany **76** J2 51 27N 6 57E
Essequibo *r.* Guyana **68** F13 2 30N 58 00W
Essex Connecticut U.S.A. **65** H4 41 21N 72 23W
Essex Maryland U.S.A. **64** D2 39 00N 76 00W
Essex *co.* England **82** D3 51 46N 0 30E
Essex County Massachusetts U.S.A. **52** B2 42 28N 71 04W
Estância Brazil **68** J10 11 15S 37 28W
ESTONIA **79** F2
Estrecho de Magallanes *sd.* Chile **69** C2 53 00S 71 00W
Estrêla *r.* Brazil **69** Q3 22 42S 43 14W
Etawah India **95** D5 26 46N 79 01E
ETHIOPIA **106** M9
Ethiopian Highlands Africa **102** 8 00N 37 00E
Etna Pennsylvania U.S.A. **53** E3 40 31N 79 57W
Etna *mt.* Italy **81** C2 37 45N 15 00E
Etolin Island Alaska U.S.A. **42** B3 56 10N 132 30W
Etosha National Park Namibia **107** I4 18 30S 16 00E
Etosha Pan *salt l.* Namibia **107** I4 18 30S 16 30E
Euboea *see* Evvoia
Eucla Australia **110** D3 31 40S 128 51E
Euclid Ohio U.S.A. **36** E2 41 34N 81 33W
Eugene Oregon U.S.A. **62** B5 44 03N 123 04W
Euphrates *r.* Iraq **93** F5 34 40N 42 00E
Eureka Montana U.S.A. **43** B1 48 52N 115 04W
Evanston Illinois U.S.A. **53** B3 42 02N 87 41W
Evansville Indiana U.S.A. **63** I4 38 00N 87 33W
Eveleth Minnesota U.S.A. **35** B2 47 29N 92 46W
Everest, Mount China/Nepal **95** F5 27 59N 86 56E
Everett Massachusetts U.S.A. **52** B2 42 23N 71 03W
Everett Washington U.S.A. **62** B6 47 59N 122 14W
Everett Lake New Hampshire U.S.A. **65** J6 43 05N 71 40W
Evergreen Park Illinois U.S.A. **53** B1 41 43N 87 43W
Evora Portugal **77** A2 38 46N 7 41W
Evreux France **76** C4 49 03N 1 11E
Evvoia *(Euboea) i.* Greece **81** D2 38 00N 24 00E
Ewarton Jamaica **67** Q8 18 11N 77 06W
Exe *r.* England **78** H2 50 55N 3 32W
Exeter England **78** H2 50 43N 3 31W
Exeter New Hampshire U.S.A. **65** K5 42 59N 70 56W
Exmoor National Park England **78** H3 51 08N 3 40W
Exmouth Australia **110** A5 21 54S 114 10E
Eyasi, Lake Tanzania **107** L7 4 00S 35 00E
Eynsford England **82** D2 51 22N 0 13E
Eyre Creek *r.* Australia **110** F4 26 00S 138 00E
Eyre, Lake Australia **110** F4 28 00S 136 00E
Eyre Peninsula Australia **110** F3 34 00S 136 00E

F

Fada Chad **106** J11 17 14N 21 32E
Faeroe Islands *(Faroes)* Europe **70** 62 00N 7 00W
Faeroes *see* Faeroe Islands
Fafan *r.* Ethiopia **106** N9 7 30N 44 00E
Fagersta Sweden **80** C6 59 59N 15 49E
Fairbanks Alaska U.S.A. **44** B3 64 50N 147 50W
Fairfax Virginia U.S.A. **64** C1 38 51N 77 19W
Fairfield Australia **111** F2 33 52S 150 57E
Fair Isle *i.* Scotland **78** J11 59 32N 1 38W
Fair Lawn New Jersey U.S.A. **50** B2 40 57N 74 06W
Fairmont West Virginia U.S.A. **63** J4 39 28N 80 08W
Fairview Park Hong Kong U.K. **98** B2 22 29N 114 03E
Fairweather Mountain Canada/U.S.A. **42** A3 58 50N 137 55W
Faisalabad Pakistan **95** C6 31 25N 73 09E
Faizabad India **95** E5 26 46N 82 08E
Fakfak Indonesia **99** I3 2 55S 132 17E
Falam Myanmar **96** H3 22 58N 93 45E
Falfurrias Texas U.S.A. **63** G2 27 17N 98 10W
Falkenburg Sweden **80** B6 56 55N 12 30E
Falkensee *l.* Germany **83** E2 52 35N 13 08E
Falkirk Scotland **78** H8 55 59N 3 48W
Falkland Islands South Atlantic Ocean **69** E2/F2 52 30S 60 00W
Falköping Sweden **80** B6 58 10N 13 32E
Fall River Massachusetts U.S.A. **65** J4 41 00N 71 00W
Fall River *tn.* Massachusetts U.S.A. **65** J4 41 42N 71 08W
Falmouth Jamaica **67** Q8 18 29N 77 39W
Falmouth Massachusetts U.S.A. **65** K4 41 33N 70 37W
Falun Sweden **79** D3 60 37N 15 40E
Famagusta Cyprus **92** D6 35 07N 33 57E
Fang-liao Taiwan **98** G5 22 22N 120 36E
Fan Lau Hong Kong U.K. **98** A1 22 12N 113 51E
Fanling Hong Kong U.K. **98** B2 22 29N 114 07E
Fâqûs Egypt **107** R3 30 44N 31 48E
Faraday *r.s.* Antarctica **117** 65 15S 64 16W
Farafangana Madagascar **107** L3 22 50S 47 50E
Farāh Afghanistan **93** J5 32 22N 62 07E
Farah Rud *r.* Afghanistan **93** J5 32 00N 62 00E
Farewell Spit New Zealand **111** B2 40 40S 173 00E
Fargo North Dakota U.S.A. **63** G6 46 52N 96 49W
Faridabad India **95** D5 28 24N 77 18E
Farmington Maine U.S.A. **37** Q5 44 41N 70 11W
Farmington Michigan U.S.A. **52** D2 42 29N 83 22W
Farmington New Hampshire U.S.A. **65** J6 43 23N 71 06W
Farmington New Mexico U.S.A. **62** E4 36 43N 108 12W
Farmington Falls *tn.* Maine U.S.A. **37** Q5 44 36N 70 05W
Farnham New York U.S.A. **38** C1 42 36N 79 06W
Faro Portugal **77** A2 37 01N 7 56W
Fåron *i.* Sweden **79** D2 58 00N 19 10E
Farquhar Islands Seychelles **112** E5 9 00N 50 00E
Fastov Ukraine **80** E5 50 08N 29 59E
Fatehgarh India **95** D5 27 22N 79 38E
Faxaflói *b.* Iceland **79** H6 64 20N 23 00W
Faya-Largeau Chad **106** I11 17 58N 19 06E
Fayetteville Arkansas U.S.A. **63** H4 36 03N 94 10W
Fayetteville New York U.S.A. **64** D6 43 01N 76 02W
Fayetteville North Carolina U.S.A. **63** K4 35 03N 78 53W
Fâyid Egypt **107** S2 30 18N 31 19E
Fderik Mauritania **106** C12 22 30N 12 30W
Fécamp France **76** C4 49 45N 0 23E
FEDERATED STATES OF MICRONESIA **114** E8
Feilding New Zealand **111** C2 40 12S 175 37E
Feira de Santana Brazil **68** J10 12 17S 38 53W
Felixstowe England **78** M3 51 58N 1 20E
Feltham England **82** B2 51 27N 0 25W
Femund *l.* Norway **79** C3 62 30N 11 50E
Fengfeng China **97** M6 37 00N 114 00E
Feng-shan Taiwan **98** G5 22 38N 120 21E
Fengtai China **101** G1 39 51N 116 17E
Feng-Yüan Taiwan **98** G7 24 15N 120 43E
Fens, The *geog. reg.* England **78** K4/L4 52 45N 0 05E
Fenton Michigan U.S.A. **36** C3 42 48N 83 42W
Fergana Uzbekistan **91** L3 40 23N 71 19E
Fergus Falls *tn.* Minnesota U.S.A. **63** G6 46 18N 96 07W
Ferndale Michigan U.S.A. **52** E2 42 26N 83 08W
Ferndale Washington U.S.A. **42** H4 48 51N 122 36W
Ferrara Italy **81** B3 44 50N 11 38E
Ferreñafe Peru **68** B11 6 42S 79 45W
Fès Morocco **106** D14 34 05N 5 00W
Fethiye Turkey **92** C6 36 37N 29 06E
Fetlar *i.* Scotland **78** K12 60 37N 0 52W
Feyzābad Afghanistan **93** L6 37 06N 70 34E
Fianarantsoa Madagascar **107** L3 21 27S 47 05E
Fier Albania **81** C3 40 44N 19 33E
Figeac France **77** C3 44 32N 2 01E
Figueira da Foz Portugal **77** A3 40 09N 8 51W
Figueras Spain **77** C3 42 16N 2 57E
FIJI **114** H6
Filchner Ice Shelf Antarctica **117** 80 00S 37 00W
Finchley England **82** C3 51 36N 0 10W
Findlay Ohio U.S.A. **36** C2 41 02N 83 40W
FINLAND **79** E3
Finland, Gulf of Finland/Russia **79** E2 59 40N 23 30E
Fiordland *geog. reg.* New Zealand **111** A1 45 30S 167 30E
Firat *r.* Turkey **92** E6 37 30N 38 00E
Fire Island New York U.S.A. **65** G3 40 20N 73 00W
Firenze Italy **81** B3 43 47N 11 15E
Firozabad India **95** D5 27 09N 78 24E
Firozpur India **95** C6 30 55N 74 38E
Firth of Clyde *est.* Scotland **78** F7 55 45N 5 00W
Firth of Forth *est.* Scotland **78** I8 56 05N 3 00W
Firth of Lorn *est.* Scotland **78** E8 56 15N 6 00W
Fish *r.* Namibia **107** I2 26 30S 17 30E
Fishers Island New York U.S.A. **65** J4 41 16N 72 00W
Fishguard Wales **78** G3 51 59N 4 59W
Fitchburg Massachusetts U.S.A. **65** J5 42 35N 71 50W
Fitzroy *r.* Australia **110** C6 18 00S 124 00E
Flagstaff Arizona U.S.A. **62** D4 35 12N 111 38W
Flagstaff Lake Maine U.S.A. **37** Q6 45 14N 70 20W
Flambeau River Wisconsin U.S.A. **35** B2 45 30N 91 00W
Flamborough Head England **78** K6 54 06N 0 04W
Flamengo Brazil **69** Q2 22 56S 43 10W
Flatbush New York U.S.A. **50** C1 40 38N 73 56W
Flathead Lake Montana U.S.A. **62** D6 47 55N 114 05W
Flathead River Montana U.S.A. **43** F1 48 55N 114 30W
Flatlands New York U.S.A. **50** C1 40 37N 73 54W
Flattery, Cape Washington U.S.A. **62** B6 48 24N 124 43W
Flekkefjord Norway **79** B2 58 17N 6 40E
Flemington New Jersey U.S.A. **64** F3 40 31N 74 52W
Flensburg Germany **80** A5 54 47N 9 27E
Flers France **76** B4 48 45N 0 34W
Fletcher Pond Michigan U.S.A. **36** C5 45 00N 83 53W
Flinders *r.* Australia **110** G6 19 00S 141 30E
Flinders Range *mts.* Australia **110** F3 32 00S 138 00E
Flint Michigan U.S.A. **63** J5 43 03N 83 40W
Flint *r.* Georgia U.S.A. **63** J3 31 00N 84 00W
Flint River Michigan U.S.A. **36** C4 43 12N 83 50W
Florence Alabama U.S.A. **63** I3 34 48N 87 40W
Florence South Carolina U.S.A. **63** K3 34 12N 79 44W
Florence Wisconsin U.S.A. **35** C2 45 55N 88 14W
Florencia Colombia **68** B13 1 37N 75 37W
Flores Guatemala **66** G3 16 58N 89 50W
Flores *i.* Indonesia **99** G2 8 00S 121 00E
Flores Sea Indonesia **99** G2 7 30S 121 00E
Floriano Brazil **68** I11 6 45S 43 00W
Florianópolis Brazil **69** H7 27 35S 48 31W
Florida Uruguay **69** F6 34 04S 56 14W
Florida *state* U.S.A. **63** J2 28 00N 82 00W
Florida Bay Florida U.S.A. **63** J2 25 00N 81 00W
Florida Keys *is.* Florida U.S.A. **63** J1 25 00N 80 00W
Florida, Straits of U.S.A./Cuba **67** H4 24 00N 81 00W
Flórina Greece **81** D3 40 48N 21 26E
Florissant Missouri U.S.A. **63** H4 38 49N 90 24W
Florø Norway **79** B3 61 36N 5 04E
Flushing New York U.S.A. **50** C2 40 45N 73 49W
Focşani Romania **81** E4 45 41N 27 12E
Fóggia Italy **81** C3 41 28N 15 33E
Fohnsdorf Austria **81** B4 47 13N 14 40E
Foix France **77** C3 42 57N 1 35E
Folda *sd.* Norway **79** C3 64 42N 10 30E
Foligno Italy **81** B3 42 57N 12 43E
Folkestone England **78** M3 51 05N 1 11E
Fonda New York U.S.A. **65** F5 42 57N 74 24W
Fond du Lac Wisconsin U.S.A. **63** I5 43 48N 88 27W
Fongafala Tuvalu **114** H7 8 00S 178 30E
Fontainebleau France **76** C3 48 24N 2 42E
Fonte Boa Brazil **68** D12 2 33S 65 59W
Forest Hills New York U.S.A. **50** C1 40 43N 73 51W
Forêt de Montmorency France **83** B3 49 01N 2 18E
Forlì Italy **81** B3 44 13N 12 02E
Formentera *i.* Balearic Islands **77** C2 38 41N 1 30E
Formosa Argentina **69** F7 26 07S 58 14W
Formosa Brazil **68** H9 15 30S 47 22W
Forrest Australia **110** D3 30 49S 128 03E
Forssa Finland **79** E3 60 49N 23 40E
Fortaleza Brazil **68** J12 3 45S 38 35W
Fort Collins Colorado U.S.A. **62** E5 40 35N 105 05W
Fort-de-France Lesser Antilles **67** L2 14 36N 61 05W
Fort Dodge Iowa U.S.A. **63** H5 42 31N 94 10W
Fort Edward New York U.S.A. **65** G6 43 17N 73 36W
Fortescue *r.* Australia **110** B5 23 00S 117 30E
Forth *r.* Scotland **78** G8 56 00N 3 30W
Fort Kent Maine U.S.A. **33** C2 47 15N 68 35W
Fort Lauderdale Florida U.S.A. **63** J2 26 08N 80 08W
Fort Myers Florida U.S.A. **63** J2 26 39N 81 51W
Fort Peck Lake Montana U.S.A. **62** E6 48 01N 106 28W
Fort Pierce Florida U.S.A. **63** J2 27 28N 80 20W
Fort Plain New York U.S.A. **65** F5 42 56N 74 39W
Fort Portal Uganda **106** L8 0 40N 30 17E
Fort Randall Alaska U.S.A. **10** C4 55 10N 162 47W
Fort Scott Kansas U.S.A. **63** G4 37 52N 94 43W
Fort Smith Arkansas U.S.A. **63** H4 35 22N 94 27W
Fort Stockton Texas U.S.A. **62** F3 30 54N 102 54W
Fort Sumner New Mexico U.S.A. **62** F3 34 27N 104 16W
Fortuna North Dakota U.S.A. **40** C1 48 55N 103 47W
Fort Walton Beach *tn.* Florida U.S.A. **63** I3 30 25N 86 38W
Fort Wayne Indiana U.S.A. **63** I5 41 05N 85 08W
Fort William Scotland **78** F8 56 49N 5 07W
Fort Worth Texas U.S.A. **63** G3 32 45N 97 20W
Fort Yukon Alaska U.S.A. **44** B4 66 35N 145 20W
Foshan China **97** M3 23 03N 113 08E
Fosna *geog. reg.* Norway **79** C3 64 00N 10 30E
Foster City California U.S.A. **49** C2 37 30N 122 15W
Fougères France **76** B4 48 21N 1 12W
Foula *i.* Scotland **78** I12 60 08N 2 05W
Foulwind, Cape New Zealand **111** B2 41 45S 171 26E
Foumban Cameroon **106** H9 5 43N 10 50E
Fountain Valley *tn.* California U.S.A. **51** C1 33 41N 117 58W
Four Roads *tn.* Trinidad and Tobago **66** S10 10 42N 61 33W
Fouta Djallon *geog. reg.* Guinea **106** C10 12 00N 13 10W
Foveaux Strait New Zealand **111** A1 47 00S 148 00E
Foxboro Massachusetts U.S.A. **65** J5 42 05N 71 15W
Foyle Northern Ireland **78** D6 54 40N 7 30W
Foz do Iguaçú Argentina **69** G7 25 33S 54 31W
Framingham Massachusetts U.S.A. **65** J5 42 18N 71 25W
Franca Brazil **68** H8 20 33S 47 27W
FRANCE **76/77**
Francis Case, Lake South Dakota U.S.A. **62** G5 43 00N 99 00W
Francistown Botswana **107** K3 21 11S 27 32E
Frankenmuth Michigan U.S.A. **36** C4 43 19N 83 44W
Frankfield Jamaica **67** Q8 18 08N 77 22W
Frankfort Kentucky U.S.A. **63** J4 38 11N 84 53W
Frankfurt *bor.* Germany **83** F2 52 41N 13 12E
Frankfurt am Main Germany **76** D5 50 06N 8 41E
Fränkische Alb *mts.* Germany **76** E4 49 00N 11 00E
Franklin New Jersey U.S.A. **65** F4 41 07N 74 35W
Franklin Pennsylvania U.S.A. **36** G2 41 24N 79 49W
Franklin Canyon Reservoir California U.S.A. **51** A3 34 05N 118 25W
Franklin D. Roosevelt Lake Washington U.S.A. **62** C6 48 05N 118 15W
Franklin Park Illinois U.S.A. **53** A2 41 50N 87 52W
Franklin Park Massachusetts U.S.A. **52** B2 42 18N 71 06W
Franz Josef Land *see* Zemlya Frantsa-Iosifa
Fraserburgh Scotland **78** I9 57 42N 2 00W
Frederick Maryland U.S.A. **64** C2 39 25N 77 25W
Fredericksburg Pennsylvania U.S.A. **64** D3 40 27N 76 26W
Fredericksburg Virginia U.S.A. **63** K4 38 18N 77 30W
Frederikshåb Greenland **11** Z5 62 05N 49 30W
Frederick Sound Alaska U.S.A. **42** B3 57 00N 134 00W
Frederikshavn Denmark **80** B6 57 28N 10 33E
Fredersdorf Germany **83** G2 52 31N 13 44E
Fredrikstad Norway **79** C2 59 20N 10 50E
Freehold New Jersey U.S.A. **65** F3 40 16N 74 16W
Freemantle Australia **110** B3 32 07S 115 44E
Freeport New York U.S.A. **65** G3 40 40N 73 35W
Freeport Texas U.S.A. **63** G2 28 56N 95 20W
Freetown Sierra Leone **106** C9 8 30N 13 17W
Freewood Acres New Jersey U.S.A. **65** F3 40 10N 74 16W
Freiburg im Breisgau Germany **76** D4 48 00N 7 52E
Fréjus France **77** D3 43 26N 6 44E
Fremont Ohio U.S.A. **36** C2 41 21N 83 08W
French Creek Pennsylvania U.S.A. **36** F2 41 40N 80 10W
French Guiana *territory* France **68** G13 5 00N 53 00W
Frenchman Fork *r.* U.S.A. **62** F5 40 00N 103 00W
French Polynesia Pacific Ocean **115** L5 21 00S 150 00W
French's Forest *tn.* Australia **111** G3 33 45S 151 14E
Fresh Pond Massachusetts U.S.A. **52** B2 42 23N 71 09W
Fresnillo Mexico **66** D4 23 10N 102 54W
Fresno Reservoir Montana U.S.A. **41** C1 48 40N 110 00W
Frewsburg New York U.S.A. **64** A5 42 03N 79 11W
Frick Park Pennsylvania U.S.A. **53** E1 40 25N 79 55W
Friday Harbor Washington U.S.A. **42** H4 48 33N 123 04W

Friedrichshagen Germany 83 G1 52 27N 13 38E
Friedrichshain Germany 83 F2 52 32N 13 26E
Frohavet *sd.* Norway 79 B3 63 55N 9 10E
Frohnau Germany 83 F2 52 38N 13 19E
Frontera Mexico 66 F3 18 32N 92 39W
Front Royal Virginia U.S.A. 64 B1 38 56N 78 13W
Frosinone Italy 81 B3 41 38N 13 22E
Frostburg Maryland U.S.A. 64 B2 39 39N 78 56W
Frøya *i.* Norway 79 B3 63 45N 8 45E
Frunze *see* Bishkek
Fuchū Japan 101 A3 35 40N 139 29E
Fuerteventura *i.* Canary Islands 106 C13 28 25N 14 00W
Fuji Japan 100 C2 35 10N 138 37E
Fuji-Hakone-Izu National Park Japan 100 K2 35 28N 138 47E
Fujinomiya Japan 100 C2 35 16N 138 33E
Fujioka Japan 100 L3 36 15N 139 03E
Fuji-san *mt.* Japan 100 C2 35 23N 138 42E
Fujisawa Japan 101 A2 35 22N 139 29E
Fukaya Japan 100 L3 36 12N 139 17E
Fukuchiyama Japan 100 G2 35 19N 135 08E
Fukui Japan 100 C2 36 04N 136 12E
Fukui *pref.* Japan 100 G3 35 30N 135 40E
Fukuoka Japan 100 B1 33 39N 130 21E
Fukushima Japan 100 D2 37 44N 140 28E
Fukuyama Japan 100 B1 34 29N 133 21E
Fulda Germany 76 D5 50 33N 9 41E
Fullarton Trinidad and Tobago 66 S9 10 05N 61 54 W
Fullerton California U.S.A. 51 C2 33 53N 117 55W
Fullerton Reservoir California U.S.A. 51 C2 33 54N 117 54W
Fulton New York U.S.A. 64 D6 43 20N 76 26W
Funabashi Japan 100 L2 35 42N 139 59E
Funakoshi Japan 101 B2 35 18N 139 34E
Funchal Madeira 106 B14 32 40N 16 55W
Fuqing China 98 F8 25 43N 119 21E
Furneaux Group *is.* Australia 110 H1 45 00S 148 00E
Furukawa Japan 100 D2 38 34N 140 56E
Fushun China 97 O7 41 50N 123 54E
Fustic Barbados 66 V13 13 18N 59 43W
Fu Tau Fan Chau Hong Kong U.K. 98 D2 22 20N 114 21E
Futtsu Japan 100 L2 35 13N 139 53E
Fuxin China 97 O7 42 04N 121 39E
Fuzhou China 97 N4 26 09N 119 17E

G
Gaalkacyo Somalia 106 O9 6 47N 47 21E
Gabès Tunisia 106 H14 33 52N 10 06E
GABON 106 H7
Gaborone Botswana 107 K3 24 45S 25 55E
Gabrovo Bulgaria 81 E3 42 52N 25 19E
Gadag India 95 D3 15 26N 75 42E
Gadsden Alabama U.S.A. 63 I3 34 00N 86 00W
Gaeta Italy 81 B3 41 13N 13 36E
Gafsa Tunisia 106 G14 34 28N 8 43E
Gagarin Russia 88 L1 55 40N 37 27E
Gagnoa Côte d'Ivoire 106 D9 6 04N 5 55W
Gaillard Cut Panama 67 Y2 9 05N 79 47W
Gainesville Florida U.S.A. 63 J2 29 37N 82 21W
Gainesville Texas U.S.A. 63 G3 33 09N 97 38W
Gairdner, Lake Australia 110 F3 32 50S 136 00E
Gaithersburg Maryland U.S.A. 64 C2 39 08N 77 13W
Galana *r.* Kenya 106 M7 3 30S 34 30E
Galapagos Islands *see* Islas Galapagos
Galapagos Rise Pacific Ocean 115 R6 12 00S 87 00W
Galashiels Scotland 78 I7 55 37N 2 49W
Galata Montana U.S.A. 41 C1 48 29N 111 20W
Galaţi Romania 81 E4 45 27N 20 02E
Galeão Brazil 69 Q2 22 49S 43 14W
Galeda Point Trinidad and Tobago 66 U9 10 09N 60 00W
Galera Point Trinidad and Tobago 66 U10 10 49N 60 54W
Galesburg Illinois U.S.A. 63 H5 40 58N 90 22W
Galeton Pennsylvania U.S.A. 64 C4 41 43N 77 39W
Galilee, Sea of *see* Tiberias, Lake
Galina Point Jamaica 67 R8 18 24N 76 58W
Galle Sri Lanka 95 E1 6 01N 80 13E
Gallego *r.* Spain 77 B3 41 55N 0 56W
Gallipoli Italy 81 C3 40 03N 17 59E
Gallipoli Turkey *see* Gelibolu
Gallup New Mexico U.S.A. 62 E4 32 32N 108 46W
Galston Australia 111 G3 33 39S 151 03E
Galty Mountains Irish Republic 78 C4 52 20N 8 10W
Galveston Texas U.S.A. 63 H2 29 17N 94 48W
Galway Bay Irish Republic 78 B5 53 15N 9 15W
Galway Irish Republic 78 B5 53 16N 9 03W
Gamagōri Japan 100 J1 34 49N 137 15E
Gambell Alaska U.S.A. 10 A5 63 46N 171 45W
Gambia *r.* Senegal 106 C10 13 45N 13 15W
GAMBIA, THE 106 B10
Gambier Islands Pitcairn Islands 115 N5 23 10S 135 00W
Gamboa Panama 67 Y2 9 08N 79 42W
Gand *see* Gent
Gandak *r.* India 95 E5 26 30N 84 30E
Ganga *(Ganges) r.* India 95 E4 25 30N 82 00E
Ganga, Mouths of the *est.* India/Bangladesh 95 F4 21 30N 89 00E
Ganganagar India 95 C5 29 54N 73 56E
Gangdisê Shan *mts.* China 96 F5 31 00N 82 30E
Ganges *see* Ganga
Gangtok India 95 F5 27 20N 88 39E
Ganzhou China 97 M4 25 52N 114 51E
Gao Mali 106 E11 16 19N 0 09W
Gap France 77 D3 44 33N 6 05E
Garanhuns Brazil 68 J11 8 53S 36 28W
Gard *r.* France 77 C3 44 05N 4 20E
Gardena California U.S.A. 51 A2 33 53N 118 19W
Garden City Kansas U.S.A. 62 F4 37 57N 100 54W
Garden City Michigan U.S.A. 52 D2 42 18N 83 20W
Garden City New York U.S.A. 50 D1 40 43N 73 39W
Garden Grove California U.S.A. 51 C2 33 48N 117 52W
Garden Reach India 94 K2 22 32N 88 16E
Gardēz Afghanistan 93 K5 33 37N 69 07E
Gardner Massachusetts U.S.A. 65 J5 42 33N 71 59W
Gardner Island Pacific Ocean 114 I7 4 40S 174 32W
Garfield New Jersey U.S.A. 50 B2 40 52N 74 05W
Garfield Park Illinois U.S.A. 53 B2 41 52N 87 43W
Gariya India 94 K1 22 27N 88 23E
Garland Texas U.S.A. 63 G3 32 55N 96 37W
Garonne *r.* France 77 C3 44 45N 0 15E
Garoua Cameroon 106 H9 9 17N 13 22E
Garulia India 94 K3 22 49N 88 23E
Gary Indiana U.S.A. 53 C1 41 34 87 20W
Garyarsa China 95 E6 31 46N 80 21E
Garzón Colombia 68 B13 2 14N 75 37W
Gascoyne *r.* Australia 110 A5 25 00S 114 00E
Gasherbrum *mts.* Kashmir 95 D7 35 46N 76 38E
Gaspar Grande Trinidad and Tobago 66 S10 10 40N 61 39W
Gastonia North Carolina U.S.A. 63 J4 35 14N 81 12W
Gata, Cape Cyprus 92 N12 34 40N 33 01E
Gateshead England 78 J6 54 58N 1 35W
Gates of the Arctic National Park and Preserve Alaska U.S.A. 44 A4 67 00N 153 00W
Gatún Panama 67 Y2 9 16N 79 55W
Gatún Lake Panama 67 Y2 9 15N 79 50W
Gatún Locks Panama 67 Y2 9 16N 79 55W
Gauhati India 95 G5 26 10N 91 45E
Gaukler Point Michigan U.S.A. 52 F2 42 27N 82 51W
Gávdhos *i.* Greece 81 D1 34 00N 24 00E
Gävle Sweden 80 C7 60 41N 17 10E
Gaya India 95 F4 24 48N 85 00E
Gaylord Michigan U.S.A. 36 B6 45 02N 84 41W
Gaza Israel 92 O10 31 30N 34 28E
Gaza Strip *territory* Israel 92 O10 31 28N 34 05E
Gaziantep Turkey 92 E6 37 04N 37 21E
Gbarnga Liberia 106 D9 7 02N 9 26W
Gdańsk Poland 80 C5 54 22N 18 41E
Gdańsk, Gulf of Baltic Sea 80 C5 54 00N 19 00E
Gdynia Poland 80 C5 54 31N 18 30E
Gebel el Tih *p.* Egypt 92 N9 29 30N 33 45E
Gebel Katherina *hill* Egypt 92 O9 28 30N 33 57E
Gebel Mûsa *(Mount Sinai) mt.* Egypt 92 N9 28 32N 33 59E
Gedaref Sudan 92 E1 14 01N 35 24E
Gediz *r.* Turkey 92 C6 38 40N 27 30E
Geelong Australia 110 G2 38 10S 144 26E
Geistown Pennsylvania U.S.A. 64 B3 40 17N 78 52W
Gejiu China 97 K3 23 25N 103 05E
Gela Italy 81 B2 37 04N 14 15E
Gelibolu *(Gallipoli)* Turkey 80 E3 40 25N 26 41E
Gelsenkirchen Germany 76 J3 51 30N 7 05E
Gemsbok National Park Botswana 107 J2 26 00S 21 00E
Genalé *r.* Ethiopia 106 M9 6 00N 40 00E
Geneina Sudan 106 J10 13 27N 22 30E
General Belgrano II *r.s.* Antarctica 117 77 52S 34 37W
General Bernardo O'Higgins *r.s.* Antarctica 117 63 19S 57 54W
General San Martin *r.s.* Antarctica 117 68 08S 67 04W
Genesee River New York U.S.A. 64 B5 42 40N 78 00W
Geneva New York U.S.A. 64 D5 42 53N 76 59W
Geneva Ohio U.S.A. 36 F2 41 48N 80 57W
Geneva *see* Genève
Geneva, Lake *see* Lac Léman
Genève *(Geneva)* Switzerland 77 D4 46 13N 6 09E
Genil *r.* Spain 77 B2 37 20N 4 45W
Genk Belgium 76 D5 50 58N 5 30E
Gennevilliers France 83 B2 48 56N 2 17E
Genoa *see* Genova
Genova *(Genoa)* Italy 81 A3 44 24N 0 50E
Gent *(Gand)* Belgium 76 C5 51 02N 3 42E
George VI Sound Antarctica 117 72 00S 67 00W
Georges River Australia 111 F2 33 57S 150 57E
Georgetown Guyana 68 F14 6 46N 58 10W
George Town Malaysia 99 C5 5 30N 100 28E
Georgetown South Carolina U.S.A. 63 K3 33 23N 79 18W
Georg Forster *r.s.* Antarctica 117 70 46S 11 50E
GEORGIA 90 E3
Georgia *state* U.S.A. 63 J3 33 00N 83 00W
Georgina *r.* Australia 110 F5 22 00S 137 00E
Georg von Neumayer *r.s.* Antarctica 117 70 37S 08 22W
Gera Germany 76 E5 50 51N 12 11E
Geraldton Australia 110 A4 28 49S 114 36E
GERMANY 76
Gerona Spain 77 C3 41 59N 2 49E
Gerrards Cross England 82 A3 51 35N 0 34W
Getafe Spain 77 B3 40 18N 3 44W
Gettysburg Pennsylvania U.S.A. 64 C2 39 50N 77 16W
Gettysburg National Military Park Pennsylvania U.S.A. 64 C2 39 57N 77 15W
Ghadāmis Libya 106 G14 30 08N 9 30E
Ghaghara *r.* India 95 E4 26 20N 83 30E
GHANA 106 E9
Ghanzi Botswana 107 J3 21 42S 21 39E
Ghardaïa Algeria 106 F14 32 20N 3 40E
Gharyān Libya 106 H14 32 10N 13 01E
Ghāt Libya 106 H12 24 58N 10 11E
Ghaziabad India 95 D5 28 39N 77 26E
Ghazni Afghanistan 93 K5 33 33N 68 26E
Ghent New York U.S.A. 65 G5 42 19N 73 37W
Gheorghe Gheorghiu-Dej Romania 81 E4 46 17N 26 45E
Ghisonaccia Corsica 77 D3 42 01N 9 24E
Gibraltar *territory* U.K. 77 A2 36 09N 5 21W
Gibraltar, Strait of Spain/Morocco 77 A2 35 58N 5 30W
Gibson Desert Australia 110 C5 25 00S 123 00E
Gīdolē Ethiopia 106 M9 5 38N 37 28E
Gifu Japan 100 H2 35 27N 136 46E
Gifu *pref.* Japan 100 H2 35 30N 136 50E
Gigüela *r.* Spain 77 B2 39 40N 3 15W
Gijón Spain 77 A3 43 32N 5 40W
Gila *r.* U.S.A. 62 D3 33 00N 114 00W
Gila Bend Arizona U.S.A. 62 D3 32 56N 112 42W
Gilbert *r.* Australia 110 G6 17 00S 142 30E
Gilbert Islands Pacific Ocean 114 H7 0 00 173 00E
Gildford Montana U.S.A. 41 C1 48 35N 110 15W
Gilgit Kashmir 95 C7 35 54N 74 20E
Gillette Wyoming U.S.A. 62 E5 44 18N 105 30W
Gillingham England 78 L3 51 24N 0 33E
Gineifa Egypt 107 S2 30 12N 32 26E
Gīnīr Ethiopia 106 N9 7 06N 40 40E
Gippsland *geog. reg.* Australia 110 H2 37 30S 147 00E
Girard Pennsylvania U.S.A. 36 F3 42 01N 80 20W
Girardot Colombia 68 C13 4 19N 74 47W
Girga Egypt 92 D4 26 17N 31 58E
Gironde *r.* France 77 B4 45 30N 0 45W
Gisborne New Zealand 111 C3 38 41S 178 02E
Giurgiu Romania 81 E3 43 53N 25 58E
Gizhiga Russia 89 S8 62 00N 160 34E
Gjirokastër Albania 81 D3 40 05N 20 10E
Gjøvik Norway 80 B7 60 47N 10 41E
Glacier Washington U.S.A. 42 H4 48 53N 121 57W
Glacier Bay Alaska U.S.A. 42 A3 58 50N 136 30W
Glacier Bay National Park Alaska U.S.A. 42 A3 58 45N 136 30W
Glacier National Park Montana U.S.A. 62 D6 48 50N 114 00W
Gladbeck Germany 76 H3 51 34N 6 59E
Gladesville Australia 111 G2 33 50S 151 08E
Gladstone Australia 110 I5 23 52S 151 16E
Glåma *r.* Norway 79 C3 60 15N 12 00E
Glasgow Scotland 78 G7 55 53N 4 15W
Glassboro New Jersey U.S.A. 64 E2 39 42N 75 07W
Glazov Russia 91 G6 58 09N 52 42E
Glen Burnie Maryland U.S.A. 64 D2 39 10N 76 37W
Glencoe Illinois U.S.A. 53 B3 42 07N 87 45W
Glendale California U.S.A. 51 B3 34 09N 118 20W
Glendale Dam Pennsylvania U.S.A. 64 B3 40 19N 78 37W
Glendora California U.S.A. 51 C3 34 07N 117 53W
Glen Grove *tn.* New York U.S.A. 50 D2 40 52N 73 38W
Glen Ridge New Jersey U.S.A. 50 B2 40 47N 74 13W
Glens Falls *tn.* New York U.S.A. 65 G6 43 17N 73 41W
Glenshaw Pennsylvania U.S.A. 53 E2 40 32N 79 57W
Glenview Illinois U.S.A. 53 A3 42 05N 87 49W
Glienicke Germany 83 F2 52 39N 13 19E
Gliwice Poland 80 C5 50 20N 18 40E
Globe Arizona U.S.A. 62 D3 33 23N 110 48W
Głogów Poland 80 C5 51 40N 16 06E
Gloucester England 78 I3 51 53N 2 14W
Gloucester Massachusetts U.S.A. 65 K5 42 37N 70 41W
Gloversville New York U.S.A. 65 F6 43 03N 74 19W
Gniezno Poland 80 C5 52 32N 17 32E
Goa, Damān & Diu *admin.* India 95 C3 15 00N 74 00E
Gobabis Namibia 107 I3 22 30S 18 58E
Godāvari *r.* India 95 D3/E3 19 00N 80 00E
Gobi Desert Mongolia 96/97 J7/L7 48 30N 100 00E
Godhavn *see* Qeqertarsuaq
Godhra India 95 C4 22 49N 73 40E
Godthåb *(Nuuk)* Greenland 45 V4 64 10N 51 40W
Godwin Austen *see* K2
Goiânia Brazil 68 H9 16 43S 49 18W
Goiás Brazil 68 G9 15 57S 50 07W
Goiás *admin.* Brazil 68 H10 12 30S 48 00W
Goias Massif *hills* South America 55 15 00S 53 00W
Gojō Japan 100 G1 34 21N 135 42E
Gökçeada *i.* Turkey 80 E3 40 00N 25 00E
Golan Heights *territory* Israel 92 O11 33 00N 35 50E
Gold Coast *tn.* Australia 110 I4 27 59S 153 22E
Golden Bay New Zealand 111 B2 40 40S 173 00E
Golden Gate *sd.* California U.S.A. 49 A3 37 48N 122 30W
Golden Gate National Recreation Area California U.S.A. 49 A3 37 49N 122 32W
Golden Gate Park California U.S.A. 49 B3 37 46N 122 30W
Goldsboro North Carolina U.S.A. 63 K4 35 23N 78 00W
Goldsworthy Australia 110 B5 20 20S 119 31E
Golfe de Gabès *g.* Tunisia 106 H14 34 20N 10 30E
Golfe de St-Malo *g.* France 76 B4 48 55N 2 30W
Golfe du Lion *g.* France 77 C3 43 10N 4 00E
Golfo de California *g.* Mexico 66 B5 27 00N 111 00W
Golfo de Guayaquil *g.* Ecuador 68 A12 3 00S 81 30W
Golfo de Honduras *g.* Caribbean Sea 66/67 G3 17 00N 87 30W
Golfo del Darién *g.* Panamá/Colombia 67 I1 9 00N 77 00W
Golfo de Panamá *g.* Panama 67 I1 8 00N 79 00W
Golfo de San Jorge *g.* Argentina 69 D3 47 00S 66 00W
Golfo de Tehuantepec *g.* Mexico 66 E3/F3 15 30N 95 00W
Golfo de Venezuela *g.* Venezuela 68 C15 12 00N 71 30W
Golfo di Càgliari Italy 81 A2 39 00N 9 00E
Golfo di Catania Italy 81 C2 37 30N 15 20E
Golfo di Gaeta *g.* Italy 81 B3 41 00N 13 00E
Golfo di Genova *g.* Italy 81 A3 44 00N 9 00E
Golfo di Squillace *g.* Italy 81 C2 38 30N 17 00E
Golfo di Tàranto *g.* Italy 81 C3 40 00N 17 00E
Golfo di Venèzia Adriatic Sea 81 B4 45 00N 13 00E
Golfo San Matías *g.* Argentina 69 E4 42 00S 64 00W
Golmud China 96 H6 36 22N 94 55E
Gomel' Belarus 90 C5 52 25N 31 00E
Gomera *i.* Canary Islands 106 B13 28 08 17 14W
Gómez Palacio Mexico 66 D5 25 39N 103 30W
Gonder Ethiopia 106 M10 12 39N 37 29E
Gondia India 95 E4 21 23N 80 14E
Gonesse France 83 B2 48 59N 2 27E
Good Hope, Cape of Republic of South Africa 107 I1 34 30S 19 00E
Goodland Kansas U.S.A. 62 F4 39 20N 101 43W
Goondiwindi Australia 110 I4 28 30S 150 17E
Gora Kamen' *mt.* Russia 89 L9 69 06N 94 59E
Gorakhpur India 95 E5 26 45N 83 23E
Gora Narodnaya *mt.* Russia 89 I9 65 02N 60 01E
Gora Pobeda *mt.* Russia 89 Q9 65 10N 146 00E
Gorda Rise Pacific Ocean 115 M12 43 00N 130 00W
Gordon Australia 111 G2 33 46S 151 09E
Gorē Ethiopia 106 M9 8 10N 35 29E
Gore New Zealand 111 A1 46 06S 168 58E
Gorgān Iran 93 H6 36 50N 54 29E
Gorizia Italy 81 B4 45 57N 13 37E
Gorki Belarus 90 C5 54 17N 30 59E
Gor'kiy *see* Nizhniy Novgorod
Görlitz Germany 76 F5 51 09N 15 00E
Gorlovka Ukraine 90 D4 48 17N 38 05E
Gorno-Altaysk Russia 91 O5 51 59N 85 56E
Goroka Papua New Guinea 110 H8 6 02S 145 22E
Gorontalo Indonesia 99 G4 0 33N 123 05E
Goryn' *r.* Ukraine 80 E5 51 00N 26 00E
Gorzów Wielkopolski Poland 80 C5 52 42N 15 12E
Gostivar Macedonia Yugoslavia 81 D3 41 47N 20 55E
Göta älv *r.* Sweden 79 C2 58 00N 12 00E
Göta Kanal *can.* Sweden 80 C6 58 30N 15 00E
Göteborg Sweden 79 C2 57 45N 12 00E
Gotemba Japan 100 K2 35 20N 138 58E
Gotha Germany 76 E5 50 57N 10 43E
Gotland *i.* Sweden 79 D2 57 30N 18 40E
Göttingen Germany 76 E5 51 32N 9 57E
Gottwaldov *see* Zlúi
Gough Island Atlantic Ocean 113 H2 40 20S 10 00W
Goulburn Australia 110 H3 34 47S 149 43E
Gourde, Point Trinidad and Tobago 66 S10 10 40N 61 36W
Gourdon France 77 C3 44 45N 1 22E
Gouré Niger 106 G10 13 59N 10 15E
Goussainville France 83 B3 49 02N 2 28E
Governador Valadares Brazil 68 I9 18 51S 41 57W
Gowanda New York U.S.A. 64 B5 42 28N 78 57W
Gozo *i.* Malta 81 B2 35 00N 14 00E
Grafton Australia 110 I4 29 40S 152 56E
Grafton North Dakota U.S.A. 39 B1 48 28N 97 25W
Grafton Pennsylvania U.S.A. 53 D1 40 26N 80 03W
Graham Texas U.S.A. 62 G3 33 07N 98 36W
Graham Land *geog. reg.* Antarctica 117 67 00S 64 00W
Grahamstown Republic of South Africa 107 K1 33 18S 26 32E
Grampian Pennsylvania U.S.A. 64 B3 40 58N 78 37W
Grampian Mountains Scotland 78 G8/H8 56 45N 4 00W
Granada Nicaragua 67 G2 11 58N 85 59W
Granada Spain 77 B2 37 10N 3 35W
Granby Connecticut U.S.A. 65 H4 41 57N 72 47W
Gran Canaria *i.* Canary Islands 106 B13 28 00N 15 35W
Gran Chaco *geog. reg.* Argentina 69 E8 25 00S 62 30W
Gran Couva Trinidad and Tobago 66 T9 10 24N 61 23W
Grand *r.* South Dakota U.S.A. 62 F6 46 00N 102 00W
Grand Bahama *i.* The Bahamas 67 I5 27 00N 78 00W
Grand Banks Atlantic Ocean 54 47 00N 47 00W
Grand Canyon U.S.A. 62 D4 36 04N 112 07W
Grand Canyon National Park Arizona/Nevada U.S.A. 62 D4 34 00N 114 00W
Grand Canyon Village Arizona U.S.A. 62 D4 36 02N 112 09W
Grand Cayman *i.* Caribbean Sea 67 H3 19 20N 81 15W
Grand Coulee Washington U.S.A. 43 E1 47 58N 119 00W
Grand Coulee Dam Washington U.S.A. 62 C6 47 59N 118 58W
Grand Erg Occidental *geog. reg.* Algeria 106 E14 30 35N 0 30E
Grand Erg Oriental *geog. reg.* Algeria 106 F13 30 15N 6 45E
Grande Terre *i.* Lesser Antilles 67 L3 17 00N 61 40W
Grand Forks North Dakota U.S.A. 63 G6 47 57N 97 05W
Grand Gorge *tn.* New York U.S.A. 65 F5 42 22N 74 30W
Grand Island New York U.S.A. 38 D2 43 02N 79 00W
Grand Island *tn.* Nebraska U.S.A. 63 G5 40 56N 98 21W
Grand Junction Colorado U.S.A. 62 E4 39 04N 108 33W
Grand Ledge Michigan U.S.A. 36 B3 42 45N 85 44W
Grand Marias Minnesota U.S.A. 35 B2 47 45N 90 20W
Grand Rapids *tn.* Michigan U.S.A. 63 I5 42 57N 86 40W
Grand Rapids *tn.* Minnesota U.S.A. 63 H6 47 13N 93 31W
Grand Rapids *tn.* Ohio U.S.A. 36 C2 41 23N 83 52W
Grand River Michigan U.S.A. 36 A2 42 55N 85 15W
Grand River Ohio U.S.A. 36 F2 41 25N 80 57W
Grand Riviere *tn.* Trinidad and Tobago 66 T10 10 50N 61 03W
Grand Traverse Bay Michigan U.S.A. 36 A6 45 00N 85 30W
Grand Union Canal England 82 B3 51 37N 0 29W
Grandyle New York U.S.A. 38 D2 43 00N 78 57W
Grane Norway 79 C4 65 35N 13 25E
Grange Hill *tn.* Jamaica 67 P8 18 19N 78 11W
Granite Peak Montana U.S.A. 62 E6 45 10N 109 50W
Grant Park Illinois U.S.A. 53 B2 41 52N 87 35W
Grants Pass Oregon U.S.A. 62 B5 42 26N 123 20W
Granville New York U.S.A. 65 G6 43 24N 73 16W
Grasonville Maryland U.S.A. 64 D1 38 58N 76 12W
Grasse France 77 D3 43 40N 6 56E
Grass Island Hong Kong U.K. 98 D2 22 29N 114 22E
Grassy Hill Hong Kong U.K. 98 B2 22 25N 114 10E
Gravesend New York U.S.A. 50 C1 40 36N 73 58W
Gravina Island Alaska U.S.A. 42 B3 55 25N 131 45W
Grayling Michigan U.S.A. 36 B5 44 40N 84 43W
Grays Thurrock England 82 E2 51 29N 0 20E
Graz Austria 81 C4 47 05N 15 22E
Great Abaco *i.* The Bahamas 67 I5 26 40N 77 00W
Great Astrolabe Reef Fiji 114 U15 18 45S 178 50E
Great Australian Bight Australia 110 D3 33 00S 130 00E
Great Barrier Island New Zealand 111 C3 35 00S 175 00E
Great Barrier Reef Australia 110 G7/H6 15 00S 146 00E
Great Barrington Massachusetts U.S.A. 65 G5 42 12N 73 22W
Great Basin Nevada U.S.A. 62 C4 40 00N 117 00W
Great Bay New Hampshire U.S.A. 65 K6 43 05N 70 53W
Great Bay New Jersey U.S.A. 65 F2 39 30N 74 20W
Great Bend Kansas U.S.A. 62 G4 38 22N 98 47W
Great Bend Pennsylvania U.S.A. 64 E4 41 58N 75 45W
Great Bitter Lake *see* Buheirat-Murrat-el-Kubra
Great Bookham England 82 B2 51 16N 0 21W
Great Britain *i.* Europe 70
Great Dividing Range *mts.* Australia 110 G7/H2
Great Egg Harbor River New Jersey U.S.A. 64 F2 39 35N 74 55W
Greater Antilles *is.* West Indies 67 H4/K3
Greater Khingan Range *see* Da Hinggan Ling
Greater London *admin.* England 67 C4 51 30N 0 10W
Great Exuma *i.* The Bahamas 67 I4 23 30N 76 00W
Great Falls *tn.* Montana U.S.A. 62 D6 47 30N 111 16W
Great Inagua *i.* The Bahamas 67 J4 21 40N 73 00W
Great Karoo *mts.* Republic of South Africa 107 J1 32 30S 22 30E
Great Lakes North America 54 45 00N 85 00W
Great Meadows National Wildlife Refuge Massachusetts U.S.A. 52 A2 42 24N 71 22W
Great Neck New York U.S.A. 50 D2 40 48N 72 44W
Great Nicobar *i.* Nicobar Islands 95 G1 6 30N 94 00E
Great Oasis, The *geog. reg.* Egypt 92 D3 25 00N 30 30E
Great Ouse *r.* England 78 K4 52 30N 0 20E
Great Peconic Bay New York U.S.A. 65 H3 40 55N 72 30W
Great Pedro Bluff *c.* Jamaica 67 Q7 17 51N 77 45W
Great Sacandaga Lake *res.* New York U.S.A. 65 F6 43 10N 74 10W
Great Salt Lake Utah U.S.A. 62 D5 41 10N 112 40W
Great Sand Sea Sahara Desert 106 J13 27 00N 25 00E
Great Sandy Desert Australia 110 C5 21 00S 124 00E
Great Sea Reef Fiji 114 T16 16 30S 178 00E
Great Victoria Desert Australia 110 D4/E4 28 00S 130 00E
Great Wall China 97 M6 40 00N 111 00E
Great Yarmouth England 78 M4 52 37N 1 44E
GREECE 81 D2
Greely Colorado U.S.A. 62 F5 40 26N 104 43W
Green *r.* U.S.A. 62 D5 42 00N 110 00W
Green *r.* Utah U.S.A. 62 E4 39 00N 110 10W

Green Bay Wisconsin U.S.A. **63** I6 45 00N 87 00W
Green Bay *tn.* Wisconsin U.S.A. **63** I5 44 32N 88 00W
Greenbush Minnesota U.S.A. **39** B1 48 42N 96 10W
Green Creek *tn.* New Jersey U.S.A. **65** F2 39 03N 74 54W
Greenfield Massachusetts U.S.A. **65** H5 42 36N 72 37W
Green Island Hong Kong U.K. **98** B1 22 17N 114 06E
Green Islands Papua New Guinea **110** I9 4 50S 154 50E
GREENLAND 116 Z7
Greenland Basin Arctic Ocean **113** H14 72 00N 0 00
Greenland Sea Arctic Ocean **116** 76 00N 5 00W
Green Mountains Vermont U.S.A. **65** H5 43 00N 73 00W
Greenock Scotland **78** G7 55 57N 4 45W
Greensboro Maryland U.S.A. **64** E1 38 58N 75 49W
Greensboro North Carolina U.S.A. **63** K4 36 03N 79 50W
Greenville Liberia **106** D9 5 01N 9 03W
Greenville Maine U.S.A. **37** R6 45 28N 69 36W
Greenville Mississippi U.S.A. **63** H3 33 23N 91 03W
Greenville Rhode Island U.S.A. **65** J4 41 51N 71 34W
Greenville South Carolina U.S.A. **63** J3 34 52N 82 25W
Greenville Texas U.S.A. **63** G3 33 09N 96 07W
Greenwich *bor.* England **82** C2 51 29N 0 00
Greenwich Connecticut U.S.A. **65** G4 41 00N 73 00W
Greenwood Mississippi U.S.A. **63** H3 33 31N 90 10W
Greenwood Lake New York U.S.A. **65** F4 41 13N 74 17W
Grenå Denmark **80** B6 56 25N 10 53E
GRENADA 67 L2
Grenoble France **77** D4 45 11N 5 43E
Greymouth New Zealand **111** B2 42 28S 171 12E
Grey Range *mts.* Australia **110** G4 27 00S 144 00E
Griffin Georgia U.S.A. **63** J3 33 15N 84 17W
Grimsby England **78** K5 53 35N 0 05W
Grimsey *i.* Iceland **79** I7 66 33N 18 00W
Grindstone Lake Wisconsin U.S.A. **35** B2 45 55N 91 23W
Grodno Belarus **90** A5 53 40N 23 50E
Groningen Netherlands **76** D5 53 13N 6 35E
Grønnedal Greenland **11** Z5 61 20N 48 00W
Groote Eylandt *i.* Australia **110** F7 14 00S 137 00E
Grootfontein Namibia **107** I4 19 32S 18 05E
Grosbeeren Germany **83** F1 52 20N 13 19E
Grosse Pointe Michigan U.S.A. **52** F2 42 23N 82 59W
Grosse Pointe *c.* Michigan U.S.A. **52** F2 42 23N 82 54W
Grosse Pointe Park Michigan U.S.A. **52** F2 42 23N 82 56W
Grosse Pointe Shores Michigan U.S.A. **52** F2 42 25N 82 08W
Grosser Müggelsee *l.* Germany **83** G1 52 26N 13 39E
Grosser Zernsee *l.* Germany **83** D1 52 22N 12 57E
Grosseto Italy **81** B3 42 46N 11 07E
Gross Glockner *mt.* Austria **81** B4 47 05N 12 44E
Groton Connecticut U.S.A. **65** H4 41 22N 72 05W
Groton New York U.S.A. **64** D5 42 36N 76 23W
Groznyy Russia **90** F3 43 21N 45 42E
Grudziadz Poland **80** C5 53 29N 18 45E
Guadalajara Mexico **66** D4 20 40N 103 20W
Guadalajara Spain **77** B3 40 37N 3 10W
Guadalcanal *i.* Solomon Islands **110** J8 9 30S 160 00E
Guadalope *r.* Spain **77** B3 40 50N 0 30W
Guadalquivir *r.* Spain **77** A2 37 45N 5 30W
Guadalupe Brazil **69** P2 22 50S 43 23W
Guadalupe *i.* Mexico **66** A5 29 00N 118 24W
Guadeloupe *i.* Lesser Antilles **67** L3 16 30N 61 30W
Guadiana *r.* Portugal **77** A2 38 30N 7 30W
Guadix Spain **77** B2 37 19N 3 08W
Guaito Trinidad and Tobago **66** T10 10 35N 61 09W
Guajará Mirim Brazil **68** D10 10 50S 65 21W
GUAM Pacific Ocean **114** E9 13 30N 144 40E
Guamúchil Mexico **66** C5 25 28N 108 10W
Guanabara Bay Brazil **69** Q2 22 45S 43 10W
Guanare Venezuela **67** K1 9 04N 69 45W
Guangzhou *(Canton)* China **97** M3 23 08N 113 20E
Guantánamo Cuba **67** I4 20 09N 75 14W
Guapo Bay Trinidad and Tobago **66** S9 10 12N 61 40W
Guaqui Bolivia **68** D9 16 38S 68 50W
Guarapuava Brazil **69** G7 25 22S 51 28W
Guarda Portugal **77** A3 40 32N 7 17W
Guardafui, Cape *see* Raas Caseyr
Guardiana *r.* Spain **77** B2 39 00N 4 00W
Guasdualito Venezuela **68** C14 7 15N 70 40W
GUATEMALA 66 F3
Guatemala Guatemala **66** F2 14 38N 90 22W
Guatemala Basin Pacific Ocean **115** Q9 12 00N 95 00W
Guatuara Point Trinidad and Tobago **66** U9 10 20N 60 58W
Guayaguayare Trinidad and Tobago **66** T9 10 09N 61 01W
Guayaguayare Bay Trinidad and Tobago **66** T9 10 07N 61 03W
Guayaquil Ecuador **68** A12 2 13S 79 54W
Guaymas Mexico **66** B5 27 59N 110 54W
Gudbrandsdalen *v.* Norway **79** B3 62 00N 58 50E
Guelma Algeria **77** D2 36 29N 7 25E
Guéret France **77** C4 46 10N 1 52E
Guernsey *i.* Channel Islands British Isles **78** I6 49 27N 2 35W
Guiana Highlands South America **55** 4 00N 60 00W
Guilderland New York U.S.A. **65** G5 42 42N 73 54W
Guildford England **82** A2 51 14N 0 35W
Guilford Connecticut U.S.A. **65** H4 41 16N 72 41W
Guilin China **97** M4 25 21N 110 11E
Guimarães Portugal **77** A3 41 26N 8 19W
GUINEA 106 C10
Guinea Basin Atlantic Ocean **113** H7 1 00N 8 00W
GUINEA-BISSAU 106 B10
Guinea, Gulf of 106 E9 3 50N 3 00W
Güines Cuba **67** H4 22 50N 82 02W
Güiria Venezuela **68** E15 10 37N 62 21W
Guiyand China **97** L4 26 35N 106 40E
Gujarat *admin.* India **95** C4 23 20N 72 00E
Gujranwala Pakistan **95** C6 32 06N 74 11E
Gujrat Pakistan **95** C6 32 35N 74 06E
Gula de Pacobaiba Brazil **69** Q3 22 42S 43 10W
Gulbarga India **95** D3 17 22N 76 47E
Gulfport Mississippi U.S.A. **63** I3 30 21N 80 08W
Gulf, The Middle East **93** H4 27 20N 51 00E
Gulian *see* Mohe
Gullivare Sweden **79** E4 67 08N 20 25E
Gulu Uganda **106** L8 2 46N 32 21E
Gumma *pref.* Japan **100** K3 36 10N 138 27E
Gunnison *r.* Colorado U.S.A. **62** E4 38 00N 107 00W
Guntersville Lake Alabama U.S.A. **63** I3 34 00N 86 00W
Guntur India **95** E3 16 20N 80 27E
Gunung Kinabalu *mt.* Malaysia **99** F5 6 03N 116 32E
Gur'yev Kazakhstan **90** G4 47 08N 51 59E
Gusau Nigeria **106** G10 12 12N 6 40E
Gusev Russia **80** D5 54 32N 22 12E
Güstrow Germany **76** E5 53 48N 12 11E
Guthrie Oklahoma U.S.A. **63** G4 35 53N 97 26W
GUYANA 68 F13
Guyana Basin Atlantic Ocean **113** D7 8 00N 50 00W
Gwalior India **95** D5 26 12N 78 09E
Gweru Zimbabwe **107** K4 19 27S 29 49E
Gyandzha *(Kirovabad)* Azerbaijan **90** F3 40 39N 46 20E
Gyangze China **95** F5 28 53N 89 35E
Gyaring Co *l.* China **95** F6 31 05N 88 00E
Gydan Range *see* Kolyma Range
Gyda Peninsula Russia **89** J10 70 00N 77 30E
Gympie Australia **110** I4 26 10S 152 35E
Gyöngyös Hungary **81** C4 47 46N 20 00E
Györ Hungary **81** C4 47 41N 17 40E
Gyōda Japan **100** L3 36 10N 139 27E

H

Haapsalu Estonia **79** E2 58 58N 23 32E
Haarlem Netherlands **76** C5 52 23N 4 39E
Haast Pass New Zealand **111** A2 44 07S 169 22E
Hab *r.* Pakistan **94** B5 25 00N 67 00E
Habbān Yemen Republic **93** G1 14 21N 47 04E
Haboro Japan **100** D3 44 23N 141 43E
Hachinohe Japan **100** D3 40 30N 141 30E
Hachioji Japan **100** L2 35 40N 139 20E
Hackensack New Jersey U.S.A. **50** B2 40 53N 74 03W
Hackensack River New Jersey U.S.A. **50** B2 40 47N 74 06W
Hackettstown New Jersey U.S.A. **64** F3 40 52N 74 50W
Hackney *bor.* Greater London England **82** C3 51 33N 0 03W
Hadano Japan **100** L2 35 22N 139 10E
Haddonfield New Jersey U.S.A. **64** E2 39 53N 75 01W
Hadejia Nigeria **106** G10 12 30N 10 03E
Hadera Israel **92** O11 32 26N 34 55E
Haderslev Denmark **80** A6 55 15N 9 30E
Ḥadhramaut *admin.* Yemen Republic **93** G2 15 40N 47 30E
Hadiboh Socotra **93** H1 12 36N 53 59E
Haeju North Korea **97** P6 38 04N 125 40E
Hafnafjördur Iceland **79** H6 64 04N 21 58W
Hagerstown Maryland U.S.A. **64** C2 39 39N 77 44W
Ha Giang China **97** L3 23 00N 105 00W
Hague, The *(Den Haag) see* 's-Gravenhage
Haidian China **101** G1 39 59N 116 21E
Haifa Israel **92** O11 32 49N 34 59E
Haikou China **97** M2 20 05N 110 25E
Hā'il Saudi Arabia **92** F4 27 31N 41 45E
Hailar China **97** N8 49 15N 119 41E
Hailuoto *i.* Finland **79** E3 65 01N 24 45E
Hainan Dao *i.* China **97** M2 18 50N 109 50E
Haines Alaska U.S.A. **42** A3 59 11N 135 23W
Haiphong Vietnam **99** L3 20 50N 106 41E
HAITI 67 J3
Hakodate Japan **100** D3 41 46N 140 44E
Hakusan Japan **100** H1 34 38N 136 20E
Halab *(Aleppo)* Syria **92** E6 36 14N 37 10E
Halaib Sudan **92** E3 22 12N 36 35E
Halawa, Cape Hawaiian Islands **115** Y18 21 09N 157 15W
Halba Lebanon **92** P12 34 33N 36 04E
Halberstadt Germany **76** E5 51 54N 11 04E
Halden Norway **80** B6 59 08N 11 13E
Half Moon Bay California U.S.A. **49** B1 37 35N 122 28W
Half Moon Bay *tn.* California U.S.A. **49** B1 37 37N 122 29W
Halishahar India **94** K3 22 55N 88 25E
Halle Germany **76** E5 51 28N 11 58E
Halley *r.s.* Antarctica **117** 75 35S 68 07W
Hallock Minnesota U.S.A. **39** B1 48 48N 96 56W
Halls Creek *tn.* Australia **110** D6 18 17S 127 38E
Hallstead Pennsylvania U.S.A. **64** E4 41 57N 75 45W
Halmahera *i.* Indonesia **99** H4 2 00N 127 30E
Halmstad Sweden **80** B6 56 41N 12 55E
Hamada Japan **100** B1 34 56N 132 04E
Hamadān Iran **93** G5 34 46N 48 35E
Hamamatsu Japan **100** C1 34 42N 137 42E
Hamar Norway **80** B7 60 57N 10 55E
Hamāh Syria **92** E6 35 10N 36 45E
Hambantota Sri Lanka **95** E1 6 07N 81 07E
Hamborn Germany **76** G2 51 29N 6 45E
Hamburg Germany **76** E5 53 33N 10 00E
Hamburg New York U.S.A. **64** B6 43 44N 78 50W
Hamburg Pennsylvania U.S.A. **64** E3 40 33N 75 59W
Hamden Connecticut U.S.A. **65** H4 41 23N 72 55W
Hämeenlinna Finland **79** E3 61 00N 24 25E
Hamersley Range *mts.* Australia **110** B5 22 00S 117 00E
Hamhŭng North Korea **97** P7 39 54N 127 35E
Hami *(Kumul)* China **96** H7 42 37N 93 32E
Hamilton New York U.S.A. **64** E5 42 50N 75 33W
Hamilton New Zealand **111** C3 37 46S 175 18E
Hamilton Ohio U.S.A. **63** J4 39 23N 84 33W
Hamm Germany **76** D5 51 40N 7 49E
Hammerdal Sweden **79** D3 63 35N 15 20E
Hammerfest Norway **79** E5 70 40N 23 44E
Hammersmith *bor.* Greater London England **82** B2 51 30N 0 14W
Hammond Indiana U.S.A. **53** C1 41 36N 87 30W
Hammondsport New York U.S.A. **64** C5 42 24N 77 15W
Hammonton New Jersey U.S.A. **64** F2 39 38N 74 49W
Hampstead Heath England **82** C3 51 34N 0 10W
Hampton New Hampshire U.S.A. **65** K5 42 56N 70 51W
Hampton Virginia U.S.A. **63** K4 37 02N 76 23W
Hamtramck Michigan U.S.A. **52** E2 42 26N 83 02W
Hanazono Japan **100** G1 34 09N 135 31E
Hancock Maryland U.S.A. **64** B2 39 42N 78 13W
Hancock Michigan U.S.A. **35** C2 47 08N 88 34W
Hancock New York U.S.A. **64** E4 41 58N 75 17W
Handa Japan **100** H1 34 52N 136 57E
Handan China **97** M6 36 35N 114 31E
Hang Ha Po Hong Kong U.K. **98** B2 22 27N 114 08E
Hang Hau Hong Kong U.K. **98** C1 22 18N 114 16E
Hang Hau Tsuen Hong Kong U.K. **98** A2 22 28N 113 59E
Hangö Finland **79** E2 59 50N 22 50E
Hangzhou China **97** N5 30 18N 120 07E
Hannah North Dakota U.S.A. **39** B1 48 59N 98 40W
Hannibal New York U.S.A. **64** D6 43 16N 76 35W
Hannibal Missouri U.S.A. **63** H4 39 41N 91 20W
Hanno Japan **100** L2 35 52N 139 19E
Hannover Germany **76** D5 52 23N 9 44E
Hanöbukten *b.* Sweden **79** C2 55 50N 14 30E
Hanoi Vietnam **99** D8 21 01N 105 52E
Hanover Massachusetts U.S.A. **65** K5 42 07N 70 54W
Hanover Pennsylvania U.S.A. **64** D2 39 47N 76 59W
Haora India **94** K2 22 35N 88 19E
Happy Valley Hong Kong U.K. **98** C1 22 16N 114 11E
Haql Saudi Arabia **92** O9 29 14N 34 56E
Ḥaraḍ Saudi Arabia **93** G3 24 12N 49 12E
Harare Zimbabwe **107** L4 17 50S 31 03E
Harbin China **97** P8 45 45N 126 41E
Harbor Beach *tn.* Michigan U.S.A. **36** D4 43 51N 82 40W
Harbor Springs Michigan U.S.A. **36** B6 45 25N 84 59W
Hardangerfjorden *fj.* Norway **79** B2 59 45N 5 20E
Hardangervidda *plat.* Norway **79** B3 60 10N 7 00E
Harefield England **82** B3 51 36N 0 28W
Härer Ethiopia **106** N9 9 20N 42 10E
Hargeysa Somalia **106** N9 9 31N 44 02E
Haridwar India **95** D5 29 58N 78 09E
Harima-nada *sea* Japan **100** B1 34 30N 134 30E
Haringey *bor.* Greater London England **82** C3 51 35N 0 07W
Hari Rud *r.* Afghanistan **93** J5 34 00N 64 00E
Harlem Montana U.S.A. **41** D1 48 33N 108 47W
Harlem New York U.S.A. **50** C2 40 48N 73 56W
Harlingen Texas U.S.A. **63** G2 26 12N 97 43W
Härnösand Sweden **79** D3 62 37N 17 55E
Harper Liberia **106** D9 4 25N 7 43W
Harper Woods Michigan U.S.A. **52** F2 42 25N 82 57W
Harriman Reservoir Vermont U.S.A. **65** H5 42 58N 72 42W
Harrington Delaware U.S.A. **64** E1 38 55N 75 35W
Harris *i.* Scotland **78** D9 57 50N 6 55W
Harrisburg Pennsylvania U.S.A. **64** D3 40 17N 76 54W
Harrison New York U.S.A. **65** G3 40 58N 73 43W
Harrisonburg Virginia U.S.A. **63** K4 38 27N 78 54W
Harrisville Michigan U.S.A. **36** C5 44 41N 83 19W
Harrogate England **78** J6 54 00N 1 33W
Harrow *bor.* Greater London England **82** B3 51 34N 0 20W
Hartford Connecticut U.S.A. **65** H4 41 00N 72 00W
Hartland Point England **78** G3 51 02N 4 31W
Hartlepool England **78** J6 54 41N 1 13W
Harveys Lake *tn.* Pennsylvania U.S.A. **64** D4 41 22N 76 04W
Harwich England **78** M3 51 57N 1 17E
Harwood Heights Illinois U.S.A. **53** A2 41 58N 87 48W
Haryana *admin.* India **95** D5 29 20N 75 30E
Hasaki Japan **100** M2 35 46N 140 50E
Hashima Japan **100** H2 35 19N 136 43E
Hashimoto Japan **100** G1 34 19N 135 33E
Hassan India **95** D2 13 01N 76 03E
Hasselt Belgium **76** C5 50 56N 5 20E
Hassi Messaoud Algeria **106** G14 31 52N 5 43E
Hastings Barbados **66** V12 13 05N 59 36W
Hastings England **78** L2 50 51N 0 36E
Hastings Michigan U.S.A. **36** A3 42 38N 85 17W
Hastings Nebraska U.S.A. **63** G5 40 37N 98 22W
Hastings New Zealand **111** C3 39 39S 176 52E
Ha Tsuen Hong Kong U.K. **98** A2 22 26N 113 59E
Hatteras, Cape North Carolina U.S.A. **63** K4 35 14N 75 31W
Hattiesburg Mississippi U.S.A. **63** I3 31 20N 89 19W
Hattingen Germany **76** J2 51 24N 7 10E
Haud *geog. reg.* Africa **106** N9 8 00N 50 00E
Haugesund Norway **79** B2 59 25N 5 16E
Haukivesi *l.* Finland **79** F3 62 10N 28 30E
Hauraki Gulf New Zealand **111** C3 36 40S 175 00E
Haut Atlas *mts.* Morocco **106** D14 30 45N 6 50W
Hauz Khas India **94** L4 28 34N 77 11E
Havana *see* La Habana
Havel *r.* Germany **83** E2 52 35N 13 13E
Havelkanal *can.* Germany **83** E2 52 38N 13 02E
Haverhill Massachusetts U.S.A. **65** J5 42 47N 71 07W
Havering *bor.* Greater London England **82** D3 51 34N 0 14E
Havey Illinois U.S.A. **53** B1 41 36N 87 40W
Havre Montana U.S.A. **62** E6 48 34N 109 40W
Havre de Grace Maryland U.S.A. **64** D2 39 33N 76 06W
Hawaii *i.* Hawaiian Islands **115** Z17 19 50N 157 50W
Hawaiian Islands Pacific Ocean **115** J10 25 00N 166 00W
Hawaiian Ridge Pacific Ocean **115** J10 23 00N 166 00W
Hawea, Lake New Zealand **111** A2 44 20S 169 20E
Hawera New Zealand **111** B3 39 35S 174 19E
Hawick Scotland **78** I7 55 25N 2 47W
Hawke Bay New Zealand **111** C3 39 10S 175 30E
Hawley Pennsylvania U.S.A. **64** E4 41 28N 75 11W
Hawthorne California U.S.A. **51** A2 33 54N 118 21W
Hawthorne New Jersey U.S.A. **50** B2 40 57N 74 10W
Hawthorne New York U.S.A. **65** G4 41 06N 73 47W
Hayama Japan **101** B2 35 16N 139 35E
Hayes England **82** B3 51 31N 0 25W
Hayes Halvø *p.* Greenland **45** S6 76 00N 67 30W
Hayward California U.S.A. **49** C2 37 40N 122 07W
Hayward Wisconsin U.S.A. **35** B2 46 02N 91 26W
Hazel Park Michigan U.S.A. **52** E2 42 27N 83 05W
Hazleton Pennsylvania U.S.A. **64** E3 40 58N 75 59W
Heard Island Indian Ocean **112** G1 53 07S 73 20E
Heart *r.* North Dakota U.S.A. **62** F7 47 00N 102 00W
Heathcote Australia **111** G1 34 05S 151 00E
Hebi China **97** M6 35 57N 114 08E
Hebron Jordan **92** O10 31 32N 35 06E
Heceta Island Alaska U.S.A. **42** B3 55 45N 134 30W
Hechuan China **97** L5 30 02N 106 15E
Heda Japan **100** K1 34 58N 138 46E
Hedesundafjärdarna *l.* Sweden **79** D3 60 20N 17 00E
Heerlen Netherlands **76** D5 50 53N 5 59E
Hefei China **96/97** N5 31 55N 117 18E
Hegang China **97** Q8 47 36N 130 30E
Hegura-jima *i.* Japan **100** C2 37 52N 136 56E
Heidelberg Germany **76** D5 49 25N 8 42E
Heilbronn Germany **76** D5 49 08N 9 14E
Heiligenhaus Germany **76** H2 52 20N 6 49E
Heilong Jiang *see* Amur
Hei Ling Chau *i.* Hong Kong U.K. **98** B1 22 15N 114 02E
Hekla *mt.* Iceland **79** I6 64 00N 19 41W
Hekou China **97** K3 22 30N 103 54E
Helan Shan *mts.* China **97** L6 38 00N 106 00E
Helena Montana U.S.A. **62** D6 46 35N 112 00W
Helgeland *geog. reg.* Norway **79** C4 64 45N 13 00E
Heligoland Bight *b.* Germany **76** D5 54 00N 8 00E
Hellersdorf Germany **83** G2 52 32N 13 35E
Hellín Spain **77** B2 38 31N 1 43W
Helmand *r.* Afghanistan **93** H5 30 00N 62 30E
Helsingborg Sweden **79** C2 56 03N 12 43E
Helsingfors *see* Helsinki
Helsingør Denmark **80** B6 56 03N 12 38E
Helsinki *(Helsingfors)* Finland **79** E3 60 08N 25 00E
Hemlock Lake New York U.S.A. **64** C5 42 45N 77 37W
Hempstead New York U.S.A. **50** D1 40 41N 73 39W
Henares *r.* Spain **77** B3 40 45N 3 10W
Henderson Nevada U.S.A. **62** D4 36 01N 115 00W
Hendon England **82** C3 51 35N 0 14W
Heng-ch'un Taiwan **98** G5 22 03N 120 45E
Hengelo Netherlands **76** D5 52 16N 6 46E
Hengyang China **97** M4 26 58N 112 31E
Henniker New Hampshire U.S.A. **65** J6 43 10N 71 50W
Henningsdorf *admin.* Germany **83** E2 52 39N 13 08E
Henryetta Oklahoma U.S.A. **63** G4 35 27N 96 00W
Henryk Arctowski *r.s.* Antarctica **117** 62 09S 58 28W
Henzada Myanmar **99** B7 17 36N 95 26E
Herāt Afghanistan **93** J5 34 20N 62 12E
Hérault *r.* France **77** C3 43 50N 3 30E
Hereford England **78** I4 52 04N 2 43W
Herkimer New York U.S.A. **64** F6 43 02N 74 59W
Hermel Lebanon **92** P12 34 25N 36 23E
Hermon, Mount Lebanon/Syria **92** O11 33 24N 35 50E
Hermosillo Mexico **66** B5 29 15N 110 59W
Herndon Virginia U.S.A. **64** C1 38 59N 77 26W
Herne Germany **76** J3 51 32N 7 12E
Herning Denmark **80** A6 56 08N 8 59E
Hernodorf Germany **83** F2 52 38N 13 18E
Herten Germany **76** J3 51 36N 7 08E
Hertfordshire *co.* England **82** C3 51 50N 0 05W
Hibbing Minnesota U.S.A. **35** B2 47 25N 92 55W
Hickory North Carolina U.S.A. **63** J4 35 44N 81 23W
Hicksville Ohio U.S.A. **36** B2 41 18N 84 45W
Hidaka Japan **100** F2 35 29N 134 44E
Hidalgo Mexico **66** E4 24 16N 99 28W
Hidalgo del Parral Mexico **66** C5 26 58N 105 40W
Higashi-Matsuyama Japan **100** L3 36 02N 139 25E
Higashi-Murayama Japan **101** A4 35 46N 139 28E
Higashi-Ōsaka Japan **100** G1 34 40N 135 35E
Higashi-suidō *sd.* Japan **100** A1 34 10N 130 00E
Higganum Connecticut U.S.A. **65** H4 41 30N 72 34W
High Bridge New Jersey U.S.A. **64** F3 40 42N 74 53W
Highgate Jamaica **67** R8 18 16N 76 53W
High Island Hong Kong U.K. **98** D2 22 21N 114 21E
High Island Reservoir Hong Kong U.K. **98** D2 22 22N 114 20E
Highland Indiana U.S.A. **53** C1 41 33N 87 27W
Highland Park Illinois U.S.A. **53** A3 42 10N 87 45W
Highland Park Michigan U.S.A. **52** E2 42 23N 83 09W
Highland Park Pennsylvania U.S.A. **53** E1 40 28N 79 55W
High Point *tn.* North Carolina U.S.A. **63** K4 35 58N 80 00W
Highlands New Jersey U.S.A. **65** F3 40 24N 74 59W
High Veld *mts.* Republic of South Africa **107** K2 28 00S 28 00E
Hikami Japan **100** F2 35 12N 135 00E
Hikone Japan **100** H2 35 17N 136 13E
Hildesheim Germany **76** E5 52 09N 9 58E
Hillaby, Mount Barbados **66** V12 13 12N 59 35W
Hillingdon *bor.* Greater London England **82** B3 51 32N 0 27W
Hillsboro New Hampshire U.S.A. **65** J6 43 07N 71 54W
Hillsdale Michigan U.S.A. **36** B2 41 56N 84 37W
Hilo Hawaiian Islands **115** Z17 19 42N 155 04W
Hilversum Netherlands **76** C5 52 14N 5 10E
Himachal Pradesh *admin.* India **95** D6 32 00N 77 30E
Himalaya *mts.* Asia **95** D6/G5
Himeji Japan **100** B1 34 50N 134 40E
Ḥimṣ Syria **92** P12 34 42N 36 40E
Hinckley Lake *res.* New York U.S.A. **64** E6 43 20N 75 05W
Hindu Kush *mts.* Afghanistan **93** K6 35 00N 70 00E
Hingham Massachusetts U.S.A. **52** C1 42 15N 70 53W
Hingham Bay Massachusetts U.S.A. **52** C2 42 18N 70 55W
Hinnøya *i.* Norway **79** D4 68 35N 15 50E
Hinsdale Illinois U.S.A. **53** A2 41 48N 87 55W
Hirakata Japan **100** G1 34 49N 135 39E
Hirakud Reservoir India **95** E4 21 40N 83 40E
Hiratsuka Japan **100** L2 35 20N 139 19E
Hirosaki Japan **100** D3 40 34N 140 28E
Hiroshima Japan **100** B1 34 23N 132 27E
Hisai Japan **100** H1 34 42N 136 28E
Hisar India **95** D5 29 10N 75 45E
Hispaniola *i.* West Indies **67** J3 18 00N 70 00W
Hitachi Japan **100** D2 36 35N 140 40E
Hitra *i.* Norway **79** B3 63 37N 8 46E
Hjørring Denmark **80** A6 57 28N 9 59E
Ho Ghana **106** E9 6 38N 0 38E
Hobart Australia **110** H1 42 54S 147 18E
Hoboken New Jersey U.S.A. **50** B1 40 44N 74 02W
Hobyo Somalia **106** O9 5 20N 48 30E
Ho Chi Minh Vietnam **99** D6 10 46N 106 43E
Ho Chung Hong Kong U.K. **98** C2 22 22N 114 14E
Hódmezovásárhely Hungary **81** D4 46 26N 20 21E
Hodogaya Japan **101** B2 35 26N 139 36E
Hof Germany **76** E5 50 19N 11 56E
Hoffmeister New York U.S.A. **65** F6 43 22N 74 42W
Höfn Iceland **79** I6 64 16N 15 10W
Hofsjökull *ice cap* Iceland **79** I6 64 45N 18 45W
Hofu Japan **100** B1 34 02N 131 34E
Hogeland Montana U.S.A. **41** D1 48 51N 108 39W
Hohhot China **97** M7 40 49N 111 37E
Hoi Ha Hong Kong U.K. **98** C2 22 28N 114 20E
Hokitika New Zealand **111** B2 42 42S 170 59E
Hokkaidō *i.* Japan **100** D3 43 30N 143 00E
Hokota Japan **100** M3 36 10N 141 30E
Holbaek Denmark **80** B6 56 33N 10 19E
Holetown Barbados **66** V12 13 11N 59 38W
Holguín Cuba **67** I4 20 54N 76 15W
Hollick-Kenyon Plateau Antarctica **117** 77 00S 100 00W
Hollidaysburg Pennsylvania U.S.A. **64** B3 40 26N 78 24W
Hollis Reservoir Trinidad and Tobago **66** T10 10 42N 61 11W
Holly Michigan U.S.A. **36** C3 42 48N 83 37W
Hollywood California U.S.A. **51** A3 34 05N 118 21W
Hollywood Reservoir California U.S.A. **51** A3 34 07N 118 20W
Holstebro Denmark **80** A6 56 22N 8 38E
Holsteinsborg Greenland **45** V4 66 55N 53 30W

Holston *r.* U.S.A. **63** J4 37 00N 82 00W
Ho-lung Taiwan **98** G7 24 37N 120 46E
Holy Cross Alaska U.S.A. **10** D5 62 10N 159 53W
Holyhead Wales **78** G5 53 19N 4 38W
Holy Island Wales **78** G5 53 16N 4 39W
Holy Island England **78** J7 55 41N 1 48W
Holyoke Massachusetts U.S.A. **65** H5 42 12N 72 37W
Ho Man Tin Hong Kong U.K. **98** C1 22 19N 114 10E
Homberg Germany **76** G2 51 27N 6 41E
Homer Alaska U.S.A. **10** E4 59 40N 151 37W
Homer New York U.S.A. **64** D5 42 38N 76 12W
Homestead Florida U.S.A. **63** J2 25 29N 80 29W
Homewood Illinois U.S.A. **53** B1 41 42N 87 18W
Honda Colombia **68** C14 5 15N 74 50W
HONDURAS 66/67 G2
Hønefoss Norway **80** B7 60 10N 10 16E
Honesdale Pennsylvania U.S.A. **64** E4 41 34N 75 15W
Hong Kong *i.* Hong Kong U.K. **98** C1 22 10N 114 10E
Hong Kong *territory* U.K. **97**
Hong Lok Yuen Hong Kong U.K. **98** B2 22 27N 114 09E
Honiara Solomon Islands **110** J8 9 28S 159 57E
Honjō Japan **100** L3 36 16N 139 09E
Honokaa Hawaiian Islands **115** Z18 20 04N 155 27W
Honolulu Hawaiian Islands **115** Y18 21 19N 157 50W
Honshū *i.* Japan **100** C2 37 15N 139 00E
Hood, Mount Oregon U.S.A. **62** B6 45 24N 121 41W
Hook England **82** B2 51 17N 0 58W
Hooksett New Hampshire U.S.A. **65** J6 43 05N 71 25W
Hoolehua Hawaiian Islands **115** Y18 21 11N 157 06W
Hoonah Alaska U.S.A. **42** A3 58 06N 135 25W
Hooper Bay *tn.* Alaska U.S.A. **10** B5 61 29N 166 10W
Hoosic River U.S.A. **65** G5 42 50N 73 20W
Hoosick Falls *tn.* New York U.S.A. **65** G5 42 54N 73 22W
Hope Barbados **66** V13 13 20N 59 36W
Hope Valley *tn.* Rhode Island U.S.A. **65** J4 41 30N 71 42W
Hopkinsville Kentucky U.S.A. **63** I4 36 50N 87 30W
Hopkinton Lake New Hampshire U.S.A. **65** J6 43 10N 71 45W
Ho Pui Hong Kong U.K. **98** B2 22 24N 114 04E
Hörde Germany **76** K2 51 29N 7 31E
Hormuz, Strait of The Gulf **93** I4 26 35N 56 30E
Hornavan *l.* Sweden **79** D4 66 15N 17 40E
Horn, Cape *see* Cabo de Hornos
Hornchurch England **82** D3 51 34N 0 13E
Hornell New York U.S.A. **64** C5 42 19N 77 39W
Hornsby Australia **111** G3 33 42S 151 06E
Horseheads New York U.S.A. **64** D5 42 11N 76 51W
Horsens Denmark **80** A6 55 53N 9 53E
Horsham Australia **110** G2 36 45S 142 15E
Hospet India **95** D3 15 16N 76 20E
Hospitalet Spain **77** C3 41 21N 2 06E
Hotan China **96** E6 37 07N 79 57E
Hotan He *r.* China **96** F6 37 07N 79 57E
Hoting Sweden **79** D3 64 08N 16 15E
Hot Springs *tn.* Arkansas U.S.A. **63** H3 34 30N 93 02W
Houghton Michigan U.S.A. **35** C2 47 06N 88 34W
Houghton New York U.S.A. **64** B5 42 27N 78 10W
Houghton Lake Michigan U.S.A. **36** B5 44 20N 84 45W
Houghton Lake *tn.* Michigan U.S.A. **36** B5 44 17N 84 45W
Houlton Maine U.S.A. **33** C2 46 09N 67 50W
Houma China **97** M6 35 36N 111 15E
Houma Louisiana U.S.A. **63** H2 29 35N 90 44W
Hounslow *bor.* Greater London England **82** B2 51 28N 0 21W
Housatonic River Connecticut/Massachusetts U.S.A. **65** G4 41 00N 73 00W
Houston Texas U.S.A. **63** G2 29 45N 95 25W
Hovd Mongolia **96** H8 48 00N 91 43E
Hövsgöl Nuur *l.* Mongolia **97** K9 51 00N 100 00E
Howar *r.* Sudan **106** K11 17 00N 25 00E
Howe, Cape Australia **110** H2 37 20S 149 59E
Howell Illinois U.S.A. **53** A1 41 39N 87 46W
Hoy *i.* Scotland **78** H10 58 48N 3 20W
Hoya Japan **101** B3 35 44N 139 34E
Hradec Králové Czechoslovakia **80** C5 50 13N 15 50E
Hron *r.* Czechoslovakia **81** C4 48 00N 18 00E
Hsin-chu Taiwan **98** G7 24 48N 120 59E
Hsin-tien Taiwan **98** H7 24 57N 121 32E
Hsin-ying Taiwan **98** G6 23 18N 120 18E
Huacho Peru **68** B10 11 05S 77 36W
Huaide China **97** N7 43 30N 124 48E
Huainan China **97** N5 32 41N 117 06E
Huajuápan de León Mexico **66** E3 17 50N 97 48W
Hua-lien Taiwan **98** H6 23 58N 121 35E
Huambo Angola **107** I5 12 44S 15 47E
Huancayo Peru **68** B10 12 05S 75 12W
Huang Hai *see* Yellow Sea
Huang He *r.* China **97** K6/M6 38 00N 111 00E
Huangshi China **97** N5 30 13N 115 05E
Huanuco Peru **68** B11 9 55S 76 11W
Hua-p'ing Hsü *i.* Taiwan **98** H8 25 26N 121 57E
Huaráz Peru **68** B11 9 33S 77 31W
Huascaran *mt.* Peru **68** B11 9 08S 77 36W
Huashixia China **97** J6 35 13N 99 12E
Hubbard Lake Michigan U.S.A. **36** C5 44 50N 83 30W
Huckarde Germany **76** K3 51 33N 7 25E
Huddart Park California U.S.A. **49** B1 37 26N 122 19W
Huddersfield England **78** J5 53 39N 1 47W
Hudson New Hampshire U.S.A. **65** J5 42 44N 71 26W
Hudson New York U.S.A. **65** G5 42 14N 73 48W
Hudson River New York U.S.A. **65** G5 42 00N 73 55W
Hue Vietnam **99** D7 16 28N 107 35E
Huelva Spain **77** A2 37 15N 6 56W
Huesca Spain **77** B3 42 08N 0 25W
Huevos *i.* Trinidad and Tobago **66** S10 10 47N 61 11W
Hughenden Australia **110** G5 20 50S 144 10E
Hugli *r.* India **94** J2 22 30N 88 12E
Hugli-Chinsurah India **94** K3 22 54N 88 23E
Hugo Oklahoma U.S.A. **63** G3 34 01N 95 31W
Huixtla Mexico **66** F3 15 09N 92 30W
Huizhou China **97** M3 23 08N 114 28E
Hull Massachusetts U.S.A. **52** C2 42 19N 70 54W
Humaitá Brazil **68** E11 7 33S 63 01W
Humber *r.* England **78** K5 53 40N 0 10W
Humboldt *r.* Nevada U.S.A. **62** C5 41 00N 118 00W
Humboldt Glacier Greenland **116** 79 40N 64 00W
Humbolt Park Illinois U.S.A. **53** B2 41 41N 87 51W
HUNGARY 81 C4
Hung Hom Hong Kong U.K. **98** C1 22 18N 114 11E
Hüngnam North Korea **97** P6 39 49N 127 40E
Hunjiang China **97** P7 41 54N 126 23E
Hunter Trench Pacific Ocean **114** H5 23 00S 175 00E
Hunters Point California U.S.A. **49** B2 37 43N 122 21W
Huntingdon Indiana U.S.A. **35** C1 40 54N 85 30W
Huntingdon Pennsylvania U.S.A. **64** B3 40 31N 78 02W
Huntington Indiana U.S.A. **35** C1 40 54N 85 30W
Huntington Massachusetts U.S.A. **65** H5 42 37N 72 44W
Huntington West Virginia U.S.A. **63** J4 38 24N 82 26W
Huntington Beach *tn.* California U.S.A. **51** B1 33 40N 118 00W
Huntly New Zealand **87** C3 37 35S 175 10E
Huntsville Alabama U.S.A. **63** I3 34 44N 86 35W
Huntsville Texas U.S.A. **63** G3 30 43N 95 34W
Hurghada Egypt **92** D4 27 17N 33 47E
Hurley New York U.S.A. **65** F4 41 56N 74 03W
Hurley Wisconsin U.S.A. **35** B2 46 25N 90 15W
Huron River Michigan U.S.A. **36** C3 42 10N 83 15W
Huron, Lake Canada/U.S.A. **36** D5 45 00N 83 00W
Hurstville Australia **111** G2 33 58S 151 06E
Húsavík Iceland **79** I7 66 03N 17 17W
Huskvarna Sweden **80** B6 57 47N 14 15E
Husn Jordan **92** O11 32 29N 35 53E
Hutchinson Kansas U.S.A. **63** G4 38 03N 97 56W
Huzhou China **97** N5 30 56N 120 04E
Hvar *i.* Croatia **81** C3 43 00N 17 00E
Hwange Zimbabwe **107** K4 18 22S 26 29E
Hwange National Park Zimbabwe **107** K4 19 00S 26 00E
Hyde Park Greater London England **82** C3 51 31N 0 10W
Hyder Alaska U.S.A. **42** B3 55 54N 130 10W
Hyderabad India **95** D3 17 22N 78 26E
Hyderabad Pakistan **94** B5 25 23N 68 24E
Hyōgo *pref.* Japan **100** F2 35 00N 135 00E
Hyvinkää Finland **79** E3 60 37N 24 50E

I

Ialomiţa *r.* Romania **81** E3 44 00N 27 00E
Iaşi Romania **81** E4 47 09N 27 38E
Ibadan Nigeria **106** F9 7 23N 3 56E
Ibagué Colombia **68** B13 4 25N 75 20W
Ibaraki Japan **100** G1 34 50N 135 34E
Ibaraki Japan **100** M3 36 17N 140 25E
Ibaraki *pref.* Japan **100** M3 36 10N 140 00E
Ibarra Ecuador **68** B13 0 23N 78 05W
Ibb Yemen Republic **92** F1 14 03N 44 10E
Iberian Peninsula Europe **102** 40 00N 15 00W
Ibi Nigeria **106** G9 8 11N 9 44E
Ibigawa Japan **100** H2 35 32N 136 31E
Ibi-gawa *r.* Japan **100** H2 35 34N 136 30E
Ibiza Balearic Islands **77** C2 38 54N 1 26E
Ibiza *i.* Balearic Islands **77** C2 39 00N 1 20E
Ibotirama Brazil **68** I10 12 13S 43 12W
Ibrī Oman **93** I3 23 15N 56 35E
Ica Peru **68** B10 14 02S 75 48W
Icacos Trinidad and Tobago **66** S9 10 04N 61 55W
Icacos Point Trinidad and Tobago **66** S9 10 41N 61 42W
ICELAND 79 I6
Ichalkaranji India **95** C3 16 40N 74 33E
Ichāpur India **94** K3 22 48N 88 22E
Ichihara Japan **100** M2 35 32N 140 04E
Ichikawa Japan **100** L2 35 45N 139 55E
Ichinomiya Japan **100** F1 34 25N 134 47E
Ichinomiya Japan **100** H2 35 18N 136 48E
Icy Strait Alaska U.S.A. **42** A3 58 20N 135 45W
Idaho *state* U.S.A. **62** D5 44 00N 115 00W
Idaho Falls *tn.* Idaho U.S.A. **62** D5 43 30N 112 01W
Iddo Nigeria **107** V3 6 25N 3 27E
Idfu Egypt **92** D3 24 58N 32 50E
Idre Sweden **79** C3 61 52N 12 45E
Igarka Russia **89** K9 67 31N 86 33E
Igbobi Nigeria **107** V3 6 32N 3 27E
Iglesias Italy **81** A2 39 19N 8 32E
Iguaçu *r.* Brazil **69** P3 22 44S 43 16W
Iguala Mexico **66** E3 18 21N 99 31W
Iguape Brazil **69** G8 24 37S 47 30W
Iguatu Brazil **68** J11 6 22S 39 20W
Ihosy Madagascar **107** I3 22 23S 46 09E
Iisalmi Finland **79** F3 63 34N 27 08E
IJsselmeer *l.* Netherlands **76** D5 52 50N 5 15E
Ikaria *i.* Greece **81** E2 37 00N 26 00E
Ikeja Nigeria **107** V3 6 37N 3 25E
Ikela Zaïre **106** J7 1 06S 23 06E
Iki *i.* Japan **100** A1 33 50N 129 40E
Ikoyi Nigeria **107** W3 6 23N 3 32E
Ikuno Japan **100** F2 35 12N 134 46E
Ikuta Japan **101** B3 35 36N 139 34E
Ilagan The Philippines **99** G7 17 07N 121 53E
I-lan Taiwan **98** H7 24 45N 121 44E
Île Amsterdam *i.* Indian Ocean **112** G3 37 56S 77 40E
Ilebo Zaïre **107** J7 4 20S 20 35E
Île de l'Europa *i.* Mozambique Channel **95** H3 22 20S 40 20E
Île de Ré *i.* France **77** B4 46 10N 1 26W
Île d'Oléron *i.* France **77** B4 45 55N 1 16W
Île d'Ouessant *i.* France **76** A4 48 28N 5 05W
Île d'Yeu *i.* France **77** B4 46 43N 2 20W
Ilek *r.* Kazakhstan/Russia **91** H5 51 00N 57 00E
Ilesha Nigeria **106** F9 7 39N 4 38E
Île St. Paul *i.* Indian Ocean **112** G3 38 44S 77 30E
Îles Chesterfield *is.* Pacific Ocean **110** J6 19 00S 158 30E
Îles Crozet *is.* Indian Ocean **112** E2 46 27S 52 00E
Îles d'Hyères *is.* France **77** D3 43 01N 6 25E
Îles Kerguelen *is.* Indian Ocean **112** F2 49 30S 69 30E
Îles Kerkenah *is.* Tunisia **81** B1 34 50N 11 30E
Îles Loyauté *is.* Pacific Ocean **110** L5/L6 21 00S 167 00E
Iles Wallis *is.* Pacific Ocean **114** I6 13 16S 176 15W
Ilford England **82** D3 51 33N 0 06E
Ilha Bazaruto *i.* Mozambique **107** M3 21 40S 35 30E
Ilha de Marajó *i.* Brazil **68** G12/H12 1 30S 50 00W
Ilha de Paquetá *i.* Brazil **69** Q2 22 46S 43 07W
Ilha do Fundão *i.* Brazil **69** Q2 22 52S 43 13W
Ilha do Governador *i.* Brazil **69** Q2 22 47S 43 13W
Ilha do Pai *i.* Brazil **69** Q2 22 59S 43 05W
Ilha Fernando de Noronha *i.* Brazil **68** K12 3 50S 32 25W
Ilhéus Brazil **68** J10 14 50S 39 06W
Ili *r.* Asia **89** J4 44 00N 78 00E
Iliamna Lake Alaska U.S.A. **10** D4 59 30N 155 30W
Iligan The Philippines **99** G5 8 12N 124 13E
Ilikurangi *mt.* New Zealand **111** C3 37 57S 178 00E
Ilion New York U.S.A. **64** E6 43 01N 75 04W
Illapel Chile **69** C6 31 40S 71 13W
Illinois *state* U.S.A. **63** I5 40 00N 89 00W
Illinois and Michigan Canal Illinois U.S.A. **53** A2 41 45N 87 50W
Illizi Algeria **106** G13 26 45N 8 30E
Iloilo The Philippines **99** G6 10 41N 122 33E
Ilorin Nigeria **106** F9 8 32N 4 34E
Ilupeju Nigeria **107** V3 6 35N 3 25E
Imabari Japan **100** B1 34 04N 132 59E
Imatra Finland **79** B7 61 14N 28 50E
Imazu Japan **100** H2 35 25N 136 01E
Īmī Ethiopia **106** N9 6 28N 42 10E
Imperatriz Brazil **68** H11 5 32S 47 28W
Imperia Italy **81** A3 43 53N 8 03E
Impfondo Congo **106** I8 1 36N 18 00E
Imphal India **95** G4 24 47N 93 55E
Inarijärvi *l.* Finland **79** F4 69 15N 27 30E
In Salah Algeria **106** F13 27 20N 2 03E
Inca Balearic Islands **77** C2 39 43N 2 54E
Inch'ŏn South Korea **97** P6 37 30N 126 38E
Indalsälven *r.* Sweden **79** D3 63 00N 16 30E
Independence Fjord Greenland **116** 82 00N 30 00W
INDIA 94/95 B4/F4
Indiana *state* U.S.A. **63** I5 40 00N 86 00W
Indian Antarctic Basin Southern Ocean **114** B2 57 00S 113 00E
Indian-Antarctic Ridge Southern Ocean **114** C2 51 00S 124 00E
Indianapolis Indiana U.S.A. **63** I4 39 45N 86 10W
Indian Creek Illinois U.S.A. **53** A3 42 13N 87 59W
Indiana Harbor Indiana U.S.A. **53** C1 41 41N 87 27W
Indian Ocean 112
Indigirka *r.* Russia **89** Q9 70 00N 147 30E
INDONESIA 99 C3/H3
Indore India **95** D4 22 42N 75 54E
Indravati *r.* India **95** E3 19 00N 81 30E
Indre *r.* France **77** C4 46 50N 1 25E
Indus *r.* Pakistan **94/95** B5/C6 26 00N 68 00E
Indus, Mouths of the *est.* Pakistan **94** B4 24 00N 67 00E
Ingham Australia **110** H6 18 35S 146 12E
Inglewood California U.S.A. **51** A2 33 58N 118 22W
Ingolstadt Germany **76** E4 48 46N 11 27E
Inhambane Mozambique **107** M3 23 51S 35 29E
Inkster Michigan U.S.A. **52** D2 42 16N 83 18W
Inn *r.* Europe **81** B4 48 00N 12 00E
Inner Hebrides *is.* Scotland **78** E8 56 45N 6 45W
Inner Mongolia Autonomous Region *see* Nei Mongol Zizhiqu
Innherad *geog. reg.* Norway **79** C3 63 50N 12 00E
Innisfail Australia **110** H6 17 30S 146 00E
Innsbruck Austria **81** B4 47 17N 11 25E
Inongo Zaïre **106** I7 1 55S 18 20E
Inowrocław Poland **80** C5 52 49N 18 12E
Insein Myanmar **97** J2 16 54N 96 08E
Inta Russia **89** I9 66 04N 60 01E
Interlaken New York U.S.A. **64** D5 42 37N 76 44W
International Falls *tn.* Minnesota U.S.A. **39** C1 48 38N 93 26W
Inubō-zaki *c.* Japan **100** D2 35 41N 140 52E
Inuyama Japan **100** H2 35 22N 136 56E
Invercargill New Zealand **111** A1 46 26S 168 21E
Inverness Scotland **78** G9 57 27N 4 15W
Ioánnina Greece **81** D2 39 40N 20 51E
Iona *i.* Scotland **78** E8 56 19N 6 25W
Ione Washington U.S.A. **43** E1 48 45N 117 25W
Ionia Michigan U.S.A. **36** A3 42 58N 85 06W
Ionian Islands *see* Iónioi Nísoi
Ionian Sea Mediterranean Sea **81** C2 37 00N 18 00E
Iónioi Nísoi *(Ionian Islands) is.* Greece **81** C2 39 00N 20 00E
Íos *i.* Greece **81** E2 36 00N 25 00E
Iowa *state* U.S.A. **63** H5 42 00N 94 00W
Iowa City Iowa U.S.A. **63** H5 41 39N 91 31W
Ipanema Brazil **69** Q2 22 59S 43 13W
Ipanema Beach Brazil **69** Q2 23 00S 43 14W
Ipatinga Brazil **68** I9 19 32S 42 30W
Ipiales Colombia **68** B13 0 52N 77 38W
Ipoh Malaysia **99** C4 4 36N 101 02E
Ipswich Massachusetts U.S.A. **65** K5 42 41N 70 51W
Ipswich England **78** M4 52 04N 1 10E
Ipu Brazil **68** I12 4 23S 40 44W
Iquique Chile **68** C8 20 15S 70 08W
Iquitos Peru **68** C12 3 51S 73 13W
Irago-suidō *sd.* Japan **100** H1 34 27N 137 00E
Irajá Brazil **69** P2 22 50S 43 19W
Iráklion Greece **81** E2 35 20N 25 08E
IRAN 93 H5
Irapuato Mexico **66** D4 20 40N 101 30W
IRAQ 92 F5
Irecê Brazil **68** I10 11 22S 41 51W
Irian Jaya *admin.* Indonesia **110** F9 4 00S 137 50E
Iringa Tanzania **107** M6 7 49S 35 39E
Iriri *r.* Brazil **68** G11 7 00S 53 30W
IRISH REPUBLIC 78
Irish Sea British Isles **78** F5 53 30N 5 30W
Irkutsk Russia **89** M6 52 18N 104 15E
Irois Bay Trinidad and Tobago **66** S9 10 09N 61 45W
Irondequoit New York U.S.A. **64** C6 43 10N 77 38W
Iron Gate *see* Portile de Fier
Iron Knob Australia **110** F3 32 44S 137 08E
Iron Mountain *tn.* Michigan U.S.A. **35** C2 45 51N 88 03W
Ironwood Michigan U.S.A. **35** B2 46 25N 90 08W
Irrawaddy *r.* Myanmar **96** J2 20 00N 95 00E
Irrawaddy, Mouths of the *est.* Myanmar **95** G3 15 30N 94 30E
Irtysh *r.* Kazakhstan/Russia **91** L6 57 30N 72 30E
Irún Spain **77** B3 43 20N 1 48W
Irving Texas U.S.A. **63** G3 32 49N 96 57W
Irvington New Jersey U.S.A. **50** B1 40 44N 74 15W
Ísafjördur Iceland **79** H7 66 05N 23 08W
Ise Japan **100** H1 34 29N 136 41E
Isère *r.* France **77** D4 45 17N 5 47E
Ise shima National Park Japan **100** H1 34 25N 136 50E
Iset' *r.* Russia **91** K6 56 30N 65 00E
Ise-wan *b.* Japan **100** H1 34 50N 136 40E
Ishikan *r.* Japan **100** D3 43 20N 141 45E
Ishikari-wan *b.* Japan **100** D3 43 30N 141 00E
Ishim Russia **91** K6 56 21N 69 30E
Ishim *r.* Russia **91** K5 54 00N 68 00E
Ishimskaya Step' *geog. reg.* Russia **91** L5 54 00N 71 00E
Ishinomaki Japan **100** D2 38 25N 141 18E
Ishioka Japan **100** M3 36 11N 140 16E
Isiro Zaïre **106** J8 2 50N 27 40E
Iskŭr *r.* Bulgaria **81** D3 43 30N 24 00E
Isla Asinara *i.* Italy **81** A3 41 00N 8 00E
Isla de Chiloé *i.* Chile **69** C4 42 30S 74 00W
Isla de Coiba *i.* Panama **67** H1 7 40N 82 00W
Isla de Cozumel *i.* Mexico **67** G4 20 30N 87 00W
Isla d'Elba *i.* Italy **81** B3 42 00N 10 00E
Isla de la Juventud *i.* Cuba **67** H4 22 00N 82 30W
Isla del Coco *(Cocos Island)* Costa Rica **115** R8 5 33N 87 00W
Isla de los Estados *i.* Argentina **69** D2 55 00S 64 00W
Isla de Patos *i.* Venezuela **66** S10 10 38N 61 51W
Isla Grande de Tierra del Fuego *i.* Chile/Argentina **69** D2 54 00S 67 30W
Islamabad Pakistan **95** C6 33 40N 73 08E
Isla Margarita *i.* Venezuela **68** E15 11 30N 64 00W
Island Beach New Jersey U.S.A. **65** F2 39 55N 74 05W
Island Park *tn.* New York U.S.A. **50** D1 40 36N 73 39W
Isla San Ambrosio *i.* Chile **69** B7 26 28S 79 53W
Isla San Felix *i.* Chile **69** A7 26 23S 80 05W
Islas de la Bahia *is.* Honduras **67** G3 16 40N 86 00W
Islas Galapagos *is.* Pacific Ocean **115** Q7 0 05S 90 00W
Islas Juan Fernández *is.* Chile **69** B6 33 30S 78 00W
Islas Marias *is.* Mexico **66** C4 22 00N 107 00W
Islas Revillagigedo *is.* Pacific Ocean **115** O9 19 00N 112 30W
Isla Wellington *i.* Chile **115** S3 48 50S 79 00W
Islay *i.* Scotland **78** E7 55 48N 6 12W
Isle of Man British Isles **78** G6 54 15N 4 30W
Isle of Wight *co.* England **78** J2 50 40N 1 20W
Islington *bor.* Greater London England **82** C3 51 33N 0 06W
Ismâ'ilîya Egypt **107** S3 30 36N 32 16E
Isogo Japan **101** B2 35 23N 139 37E
Isole Lipari *is.* Italy **81** B2 38 00N 14 00E
Isolo Nigeria **107** V3 6 32N 3 23E
Issyk-Kul' *(Rybach'ye)* Kirgyzstan **91** M3 42 28N 76 09E
Istmo de Tehuantepec *ist.* Mexico **66** F3 17 20N 93 10W
Itabaiana Brazil **68** J10 10 42S 37 37W
Itabashi Japan **101** B4 35 46N 139 39E
Itabuna Brazil **68** J10 14 48S 39 18W
Itacoatiara Brazil **68** F12 3 06S 58 22W
Itagüí Colombia **68** B14 6 13N 75 40W
Itaituba Brazil **68** F12 4 15S 55 56W
Itajaí Brazil **69** H7 26 50S 48 39W
Itako Japan **100** M2 35 57N 140 31E
ITALY 81 B3
Itapipoca Brazil **68** J12 3 29S 39 35W
Itaqui Brazil **69** F7 29 10S 56 30W
Itarsi India **95** D4 22 39N 77 48E
Ithaca New York U.S.A. **64** D5 42 26N 76 30W
Itō Japan **100** L2 34 58N 139 04E
Itui *r.* Brazil **68** C11 5 30S 71 00W
Ivano-Frankovsk Ukraine **90** A4 48 40N 24 40E
Ivanovo Russia **90** E6 57 00N 41 00E
Ivdel' Russia **91** J7 60 45N 60 30E
Ivry-sur-Seine France **83** B2 48 48N 2 24E
Iwai Japan **100** L3 36 02N 139 53E
Iwaki Japan **100** D2 37 03N 140 58E
Iwakuni Japan **100** B1 34 10N 132 09E
Iwamizawa Japan **100** D3 43 12N 141 47E
Iwanai Japan **100** D3 43 01N 140 32E
Iwo Nigeria **106** F9 7 38N 4 11E
Ixtaccihuati *mt.* Mexico **66** E3 19 11N 98 38W
Ixtepec Mexico **66** E3 16 32N 95 10W
Iyo-nada *b.* Japan **100** B1 33 50N 132 00E
Izhevsk Russia **91** G6 56 49N 53 11E
Izhma *r.* Russia **91** G7 64 00N 54 00E
Izmail Ukraine **81** E4 45 20N 28 48E
Izumi Japan **100** G1 34 29N 135 25E
Izu-shotō *is.* Japan **100** C1 34 20N 139 20E

J

Jabal Akhdar *mts.* Oman **93** I3 23 10N 57 25E
Jābal as Sawdā' *mts.* Libya **106** H13 29 00N 15 00E
Jabalpur India **95** D4 23 10N 79 59E
Jablonec Czechoslovakia **80** C5 50 44N 15 10E
Jaboatão Brazil **68** J11 8 05S 35 00W
Jacarepaguá Brazil **69** P2 22 57S 43 21W
Jackman Maine U.S.A. **37** Q6 45 37N 70 16W
Jack Mountain Washington U.S.A. **42** H4 48 47N 120 58W
Jackson Barbados **66** V12 13 09N 59 40W
Jackson Michigan U.S.A. **36** B3 42 15N 84 24W
Jackson Mississippi U.S.A. **63** H3 32 20N 90 11W
Jackson Tennessee U.S.A. **63** I4 35 37N 88 50W
Jackson Wyoming U.S.A. **62** D5 43 28N 110 45W
Jackson Head New Zealand **111** A2 43 58S 168 38E
Jackson Heights New York U.S.A. **50** C2 40 45N 73 52W
Jackson Park Illinois U.S.A. **53** B2 41 47N 87 34W
Jacksonville Florida U.S.A. **63** J3 30 20N 81 40W
Jacksonville North Carolina U.S.A. **63** K3 34 45N 77 26W
Jacksonville Beach *tn.* Florida U.S.A. **63** J3 30 18N 81 24W
Jack Wade Alaska U.S.A. **44** C3 64 05N 141 35W
Jacmel Haiti **67** J3 18 18N 72 32W
Jacobabad Pakistan **94** B5 28 16N 68 30E
Jacobina Brazil **68** I10 11 13S 40 30W
Jaén Spain **77** B2 37 46N 3 48W
Jaffna Sri Lanka **95** D1 9 40N 80 01E
Jaffrey New Hampshire U.S.A. **65** H5 42 00N 72 00W
Jagdalpur India **95** E3 19 04N 82 05E
Jahrom Iran **93** H4 28 29N 53 32E
Jaipur India **95** D5 26 53N 75 50E
Jaisalmer India **93** L4 26 52N 70 55E
Jakarta Indonesia **99** D2 6 08S 106 45E
Jakobstad Finland **79** E3 63 40N 22 42E
Jalālābād Afghanistan **93** L5 34 26N 70 28E
Jalapa Enriquez Mexico **66** E3 19 32N 96 56W
Jalgaon India **95** D4 21 01N 75 39E
Jalna India **95** D3 19 50N 75 58E
Jalón *r.* Spain **77** B3 41 30N 1 35W
Jālū Libya **106** J13 29 02N 21 33E
JAMAICA 67 Q8
Jamaica New York U.S.A. **50** C1 40 42N 73 48W
Jamaica Bay New York U.S.A. **50** C1 40 37N 73 50W
Jamana, Mount Trinidad and Tobago **66** T9 10 27N 61 14W
Jambi Indonesia **99** C3 2 00S 103 30E
James *r.* U.S.A. **63** G6 47 00N 98 00W
James *r.* Virginia U.S.A. **63** K4 37 00N 77 00W
Jamestown New York U.S.A. **63** K5 42 05N 79 15W
Jamestown North Dakota U.S.A. **63** G6 46 54N 98 42W
Jamestown Rhode Island U.S.A. **65** J4 41 30N 71 23W
Jamiltepec Mexico **66** E3 16 18N 97 51W
Jammu India **95** D6 32 43N 74 54E
Jammu & Kashmir *state* Southern Asia **95** D6 29 40N 76 30E
Jamnagar India **95** C4 22 28N 70 06E

Jamshedpur India **95** F4 22 47N 86 12E
Janesville Wisconsin U.S.A. **63** I5 42 42N 89 02W
Jan Mayen *i.* Arctic Ocean **116** 71 00N 9 00W
Januária Brazil **68** H9 15 28S 44 23W
JAPAN 100
Japan Trench Pacific Ocean **114** E11 35 00N 143 00E
Japan, Sea of 100 C2 39 00N 136 00E
Jarú Brazil **68** E10 10 24S 62 45W
Jāsk Iran **93** I4 25 40N 57 46E
Jastrowie Poland **80** C5 53 25N 16 50E
Jasło Poland **80** D4 49 45N 21 28E
Jaunpur India **95** E5 25 44N 82 41E
Java Sea Indonesia **99** E2 6 00S 113 00E
Java Trench Indian Ocean **112** J6 10 00S 110 00E
Jawa *i.* Indonesia **99** D2/E2 2 30S 110 00E
Jayapura Indonesia **110** G9 2 37S 140 39E
Jazā'ir Farasān *is.* Saudi Arabia **92** F2 16 45N 42 10E
Jebel Abyad Plateau Sudan **106** K11 18 00N 28 00E
Jebel Marra *mts.* Sudan **106** J10 13 00N 24 00E
Jefferson Ohio U.S.A. **36** F2 41 44N 80 46W
Jēkabpils Latvia **79** F2 56 22N 25 50E
Jelenia Góra Poland **80** C5 50 55N 15 45E
Jelgava Latvia **79** E2 56 39N 23 40E
Jena Germany **76** E5 50 56N 11 35E
Jenin Jordan **92** O11 32 28N 35 18E
Jequié Brazil **68** I10 13 52S 40 06W
Jérémie Haiti **67** J3 18 40N 74 09W
Jerez de la Frontera Spain **77** A2 36 41N 6 08W
Jerez de los Caballeros Spain **77** A2 38 20N 6 45W
Jericho Jordan **92** O10 31 51N 35 27E
Jersey *i.* Channel Islands British Isles **78** I6 49 13N 2 07W
Jersey City New Jersey U.S.A. **50** B1 40 44N 74 06W
Jerusalem Israel/Jordan **92** O10 31 47N 35 13E
Jessore Bangladesh **95** F4 23 10N 89 12E
Jevisy-sur-Orge France **83** B1 48 42N 2 22E
Jewett City Connecticut U.S.A. **65** J4 41 37N 71 59W
Jezioro Sniardwy *l.* Poland **80** D5 53 00N 21 00E
Jhang Mghiana Pakistan **95** C6 31 19N 72 22E
Jhansi India **95** D5 25 27N 78 34E
Jhelum Pakistan **95** C6 32 58N 73 45E
Jhelum *r.* Pakistan **95** C6 32 30N 72 30E
Ji'an China **97** M4 27 08N 115 00E
Jiangmen China **97** M3 22 40N 113 05E
Jiamusi China **97** Q8 46 59N 130 29E
Jiaxing China **97** O5 30 15N 120 52E
Jiayuguan China **97** J6 39 47N 98 14E
Jiddah Saudi Arabia **92** E3 21 30N 39 10E
Ješjavrre *l.* Norway **79** E4 69 40N 24 10E
Jihlavà Czechoslovakia **80** C4 49 24N 15 34E
Jijel Algeria **77** D2 36 45N 5 45E
Jilin China **97** P7 43 53N 126 35E
Jiloca *r.* Spain **77** B3 41 08N 1 45W
Jīma Ethiopia **106** M9 7 39N 36 47E
Jim Thorpe Pennsylvania U.S.A. **64** E3 40 52N 75 43W
Jinan China **97** N6 36 41N 117 00E
Jingdezhen China **97** N4 29 17N 117 12E
Jin He *r.* China **101** G1 39 58N 116 16E
Jinhua China **97** N4 29 06N 119 40E
Jining China **97** M7 40 58N 113 01E
Jining China **97** N6 35 25N 116 40E
Jinja Uganda **106** L8 0 27N 33 14E
Jinsha Jiang *(Yangtze) r.* China **97** K4 27 30N 103 00E
Jinxi China **97** O7 40 46N 120 47E
Jinzhou China **97** O7 41 07N 121 06E
Jiparaná *r.* Brazil **68** E11 8 00S 62 30W
Jiujiang China **97** N4 29 41N 116 03E
Jiul *r.* Romania **81** D3 44 00N 24 00E
Jiuxiaqiao China **101** H1 39 59N 116 30E
Jixi China **97** Q8 45 17N 131 00E
Jīzān Saudi Arabia **92** F2 16 56N 42 33E
João Pessoa Brazil **68** J11 7 06S 34 53W
Jodhpur India **95** C5 26 18N 73 08E
Joensuu Finland **79** F3 62 35N 29 46E
Johannesburg Republic of South Africa **107** K2 26 10S 28 02E
John Day *r.* Oregon U.S.A. **62** B5 45 00N 120 00W
John H. Kerr Reservoir U.S.A. **63** K4 36 31N 78 18W
Johnsonburg Pennsylvania U.S.A. **64** B4 41 00N 78 00W
Johnson City New York U.S.A. **64** E5 42 06N 75 57W
Johnson City Tennessee U.S.A. **63** J4 36 20N 82 23W
Johnstown New York U.S.A. **65** F6 43 00N 74 00W
Johnstown Pennsylvania U.S.A. **64** B3 40 20N 78 56W
Johor Baharu Malaysia **99** C4 1 29N 103 44E
Joinville Brazil **69** H7 26 20S 48 55W
Joinville Island Antarctica **117** 63 00S 56 00W
Jokkmokk Sweden **79** D4 66 37N 19 50E
Jonesboro Arkansas U.S.A. **63** H4 35 50N 90 41W
Jonesville Michigan U.S.A. **36** B2 41 59N 84 39W
Jönköping Sweden **79** C2 57 45N 14 10E
Jefferson City Missouri U.S.A. **63** H4 38 33N 92 10W
Joplin Missouri U.S.A. **63** H4 37 04N 94 31W
JORDAN 92 E5
Jordan *r.* Middle East **92** O11 32 15N 32 10E
Jordan Valley *tn.* Hong Kong U.K. **98** C1 22 19N 114 13E
Jos Nigeria **106** G9 9 54N 8 53E
Joseph Bonaparte Gulf Australia **110** D7 14 00S 128 30E
Jos Plateau Nigeria **106** G10 9 30N 8 55E
Jostedalsbreen *glacier* Norway **79** B3 61 40N 7 00E
Jotunheimen *mts.* Norway **79** B3 61 40N 8 00E
Jõunié Lebanon **92** O11 33 58N 35 38E
Juan de Fuca Strait North America **62** B6 48 00N 124 00W
Juàzeiro Brazil **68** I11 9 25S 40 30W
Juàzeiro do Norte Brazil **68** J11 7 10S 39 18W
Juba Sudan **106** L8 4 50N 31 35E
Jubba *r.* Somalia **106** N8 3 00N 42 30E
Jubilee Reservoir Hong Kong U.K. **98** B2 22 24N 114 08E
Júcar *r.* Spain **77** B2 39 08N 1 50W
Juchitán Mexico **66** E3 16 27N 95 05W
Juiz de Fora Brazil **69** I8 21 47S 43 23W
Julijske Alpe *mts.* Europe **81** B4 46 00N 13 00E
Jullundur India **95** D6 31 18N 75 40E
Junagadh India **94** C4 21 32N 70 32E
Junction City Kansas U.S.A. **63** G4 39 02N 96 51W
Jundiaí Brazil **69** H8 23 10S 46 54W
Juneau Alaska U.S.A. **42** B3 58 20N 134 20W
Junggar Pendi *(Dzungarian Basin)* China **96** G7 44 00N 87 30E
Juniata River Pennsylvania U.S.A. **64** C3 40 30N 77 20W
Junk Bay Hong Kong U.K. **98** C1 22 18N 114 15E
Junsele Sweden **79** D3 63 40N 16 55E
Jur *r.* Sudan **106** K9 8 00N 28 00E
Jura *mts.* France/Switzerland **77** D4 46 30N 6 00E
Jura Krakowska *mts.* Poland **80** C5 50 00N 20 00E
Jylland *p.* Denmark **80** A6 55 00N 9 00E
Jyväskylä Finland **79** F3 62 16N 25 50E

K

K2 *(Qogir Feng, Godwin Austen) mt.* China/India **96** E6 35 47N 76 30E
Kabrit Egypt **107** S2 30 16N 32 29E
Kābul Afghanistan **93** K5 34 31N 69 12E
Kabul *r.* Afghanistan **93** K5 34 00N 69 30E
Kabwe Zambia **107** K5 14 29S 28 25E
Kachchh, Gulf of India **94** B4 22 40N 69 30E
Kadmat Island India **95** C2 11 08N 72 46E
Kadoma Zimbabwe **107** K4 18 21N 29 55E
Kaduna Nigeria **106** G10 10 28N 7 25E
Kaduna *r.* Nigeria **106** G9 10 00N 6 30E
Kaédi Mauritania **106** C11 16 12N 13 32W
Kaesŏng South Korea **97** P6 37 59N 126 30E
Kafue Zambia **107** K4 15 44S 28 10E
Kafue *r.* Zambia **107** K4 16 00S 27 00E
Kafue National Park Zambia **107** K5 15 00S 25 30E
Kagan Uzbekistan **90** J2 39 45N 64 32E
Kagoshima Japan **100** B1 31 37N 130 32E
Kahoolawe *i.* Hawaiian Islands **115** Y18 20 30N 156 40W
Kahuku Point Hawaiian Islands **115** Y18 21 42N 158 00W
Kaiapoi New Zealand **111** B2 43 24S 172 40E
Kaifeng China **97** M5 34 47N 114 20E
Kaikohe New Zealand **111** B3 35 25S 173 49E
Kaikoura New Zealand **111** B2 42 24S 173 41E
Kai Kung Leng *mt.* Hong Kong U.K. **98** B2 22 27N 114 04E
Kailash India **94** L4 28 33N 77 15E
Kailua Hawaiian Islands **115** Z17 19 43N 155 59W
Kainan Japan **100** G1 34 09N 135 12E
Kainji Reservoir Nigeria **106** F10 10 25N 4 56E
Kaipara Harbour New Zealand **111** B3 36 40S 174 00E
Kairouan Tunisia **106** H15 35 42N 10 01E
Kaiserslautern Germany **76** D4 49 27N 7 47E
Kaitaia New Zealand **111** B3 35 08S 173 18E
Kaiwi Channel Hawaiian Islands **115** Y18 21 20N 157 30W
Kajaani Finland **79** F3 64 14N 27 37E
Kakamigahara Japan **100** H2 35 23N 136 52E
Kakhovskoye Vodokhranilishche *res.* Ukraine **90** C4 47 30N 35 00E
Kākināda India **95** E3 16 59N 82 20E
Kakogawa Japan **100** F1 34 49N 134 52E
Kalachinsk Russia **91** L6 55 02N 74 40E
Kalae *(South Cape)* Hawaiian Islands **115** Z17 18 58N 155 24W
Kalahari Desert Southern Africa **107** J3 23 30S 23 00E
Kalahari Gemsbok National Park Republic of South Africa **107** I2 26 00S 20 30E
Kalámai Greece **81** D2 37 02N 22 07E
Kalamazoo Michigan U.S.A. **35** C1 42 17N 85 36W
Kalat Pakistan **94** B5 29 01N 66 38E
Kalémié Zaïre **107** K6 5 57S 29 10E
Kalevala Russia **79** G4 65 15N 31 08E
Kalgoorlie Australia **110** C3 30 49S 121 29E
Kaliavesi *l.* Finland **79** F3 63 00N 27 20E
Kalimantan *admin.* Indonesia **99** E3 2 00S 112 00E
Kálimnos *i.* Greece **81** E2 37 00N 26 00E
Kalinin *see* Tver'
Kaliningrad *reg.* Russia **80** D5 54 40N 21 00E
Kaliningrad Russia **80** D5 54 40N 20 30E
Kaliningrad Russia **90** D6 55 56N 37 55E
Kalin Kovichi Belarus **90** B5 52 10N 29 13E
Kalispell Montana U.S.A. **62** D6 48 12N 114 19W
Kalisz Poland **80** C5 51 46N 18 02E
Kalix älv *r.* Sweden **79** E4 66 40N 22 30E
Kalkajl India **94** M4 28 32N 77 16E
Kallsjön *l.* Sweden **79** C3 63 30N 13 05E
Kalmar Sweden **80** C6 56 39N 16 20E
Kalomo Zambia **107** K4 17 02S 26 29E
Kalpeni Island India **95** C2 10 05N 73 15E
Kaluga Russia **90** D5 54 31N 36 16E
Kalundborg Denmark **80** B6 55 42N 11 06E
Kalutara Sri Lanka **95** D1 6 35N 79 59E
Kama *r.* Russia **91** H6 57 00N 55 00E
Kamaishi Japan **100** D2 39 18N 141 52E
Kamakura Japan **101** B2 35 19N 139 33E
Kamarān *i.* Yemen Republic **92** F2 15 21N 42 40E
Kamarhati India **94** K2 22 40N 88 22E
Kambara *i.* Fiji **114** V15 18 57S 178 58W
Kamchatka *p.* Russia **89** R7 57 30N 160 00E
Kamchatka Bay Russia **89** S7 55 00N 164 00E
Kamchiya *r.* Bulgaria **81** E3 43 00N 27 00E
Kamenets Podol'skiy Ukraine **90** B4 48 40N 26 36E
Kamensk-Ural'skiy Russia **91** J6 56 29N 61 49E
Kameoka Japan **100** G2 35 02N 135 35E
Kamet *mt.* India **95** D6 30 55N 79 36E
Kamina Zaïre **107** K6 8 46S 25 00E
Kamogawa Japan **100** M2 35 06N 140 09E
Kampala Uganda **106** L8 0 19N 32 35E
KAMPUCHEA *see* CAMBODIA
Kamskoye Vodokhranilishche *res.* Russia **91** H6 58 30N 56 00E
Kam Tsin Hong Kong U.K. **98** B3 22 30N 114 07E
Kamyshin Russia **90** F5 50 05N 45 24E
Kamyshlov Russia **91** J6 56 55N 62 41E
Kan *r.* Russia **91** P6 56 30N 94 00E
Kanagawa Japan **101** B2 35 29N 139 38E
Kanagawa *pref.* Japan **100** L2 35 25N 139 20E
Kananga Zaïre **107** J6 5 53S 22 26E
Kanazawa Japan **100** C2 36 35N 136 38E
Kanazawa Japan **101** B2 35 20W 139 37E
Kanbe Myanmar **99** B7 16 15N 95 40E
Kanchipuram India **95** D2 12 50N 79 44E
Kānchrāpāra India **94** K3 22 56N 88 26E
Kandahār Afghanistan **93** K5 31 35N 65 45E
Kandalaksha Russia **88** F9 67 09N 32 31E
Kandavu *i.* Fiji **114** U15 19 10S 178 30E
Kandavu Passage *sd.* Fiji **114** U15 18 50S 178 00E
Kandi Benin **106** F10 11 05N 2 59E
Kandla India **94** B4 23 03N 70 11E
Kandy Sri Lanka **95** E1 7 17N 80 40E
Kane Pennsylvania U.S.A. **64** B4 41 40N 78 48W
Kaneohe Hawaiian Islands **115** Y18 21 25N 157 48W
Kaneya Japan **100** B1 31 22N 130 50E
Kangan Iran **93** H4 27 51N 52 07E
Kangar Malaysia **99** C5 6 28N 100 10E
Kangaroo Island Australia **110** F2 35 50S 137 50E
Kangerlussuaq *(Søndre Strømfjord)* Greenland **45** V4 67 00N 50 59W
Kangnŭng South Korea **97** P6 37 48N 127 52E
Kang-shan Taiwan **98** G5 22 45N 120 18E
Kanin Peninsula Russia **88** G9 68 00N 45 00E
Kankakee Illinois U.S.A. **63** I5 41 08N 87 52W
Kankan Guinea **106** D10 10 22N 9 11W
Kanker India **95** E4 20 17N 81 30E
Kannapolis North Carolina U.S.A. **63** J4 35 30N 80 36W
Kano Nigeria **106** G10 12 00N 8 31E
Kanpur India **95** E5 26 27N 80 14E
Kansas *state* U.S.A. **62/63** G4 38 00N 98 00W
Kansas City Missouri U.S.A. **63** H4 39 02N 94 33W
Kansk Russia **91** P6 56 11N 95 48E
Kanye Botswana **107** J3 24 59S 25 19E
Kao-hsiung Taiwan **98** G5 22 36N 120 17E
Kaolack Senegal **106** B10 14 09N 16 08W
Kapaa Hawaiian Islands **115** X19 22 04N 159 20W
Kapfenberg Austria **81** C4 47 27N 15 18E
Kapingamarangi Rise Pacific Ocean **114** F8 3 00N 154 00E
Kaposvár Hungary **81** C4 46 21N 17 49E
Kapsukas *see* Marijampole
Karabük Turkey **92** D7 41 12N 32 36E
Karachi Pakistan **94** B4 24 51N 67 02E
Karaganda Kazakhstan **91** L4 49 53N 73 07E
Karaginskiy *i.* Russia **89** S7 58 00N 164 00E
Karaikkudi India **95** D2 10 04N 78 46E
Karaj Iran **93** H6 35 48N 50 58E
Karak Jordan **92** O10 31 11N 35 42E
Karakoram *mts.* Asia **84** 36 00N 76 00E
Karakoram Pass Kashmir/China **95** D7 35 33N 77 51E
Kara Kum *geog. reg.* Turkmenistan **91** H2/E2 40 00N 60 00E
Karakumskiy Kanal *can.* Turkmenistan **91** J2 37 30N 62 30E
Karama Jordan **92** O10 31 58N 35 34E
Karasburg Namibia **107** I2 28 00S 18 43E
Kara Sea Russia **89** I11/J10 75 00N 70 00E
Karasjok Norway **79** F4 69 27N 25 30E
Karatal *r.* Kazakhstan **91** M4 45 00N 78 00E
Karatau *mts.* Kazakhstan **91** K3 43 00N 70 00E
Karaturgay *r.* Kazakhstan **91** J5 50 00N 65 00E
Karbalā' Iraq **92** F5 32 37N 44 03E
Karcag Hungary **81** D4 47 19N 20 53E
Kariba Dam Zambia/Zimbabwe **107** K4 16 31S 28 50E
Kariba, Lake Zambia/Zimbabwe **107** K4 17 00S 28 00E
Karibib Namibia **107** I3 21 59S 15 51E
Karisimbi, Mount Rwanda/Zaïre **106** K7 1 32S 29 27E
Kariya Japan **100** J1 35 00N 137 00E
Karkinitskiy Zaliv *g.* Ukraine **90** C4 46 00N 32 50E
Karl-Marx-Stadt *see* Chemnitz
Karlino Poland **80** C5 54 02N 15 52E
Karlovac Croatia **81** C4 45 30N 15 34E
Karlovy Vary Czechoslovakia **80** B5 50 13N 12 52E
Karlshamn Sweden **80** B6 56 10N 14 50E
Karlshorst Germany **83** G1 52 28N 13 32E
Karlsruhe Germany **76** D4 49 00N 8 24E
Karlstad Minnesota U.S.A. **39** B1 48 35N 96 31W
Karnafuli Reservoir Bangladesh **95** G4 22 30N 92 20E
Karnal India **95** D5 29 41N 76 58E
Karnataka *admin.* India **95** D2 14 40N 75 30E
Karol Bagh India **94** L4 28 39N 77 11E
Karow Germany **83** F2 52 38N 13 28E
Kárpathos *i.* Greece **81** E2 35 30N 27 12E
Karpenísion Greece **81** D2 38 55N 21 47E
Kars Turkey **92** F7 40 35N 43 05E
Karsakpay Kazakhstan **88** I5 47 47N 66 43E
Karshi Uzbekistan **91** K2 38 53N 65 45E
Kartaly Russia **91** J5 53 06N 60 37E
Karwar India **95** C2 14 50N 74 09E
Kasai Japan **100** F1 34 56N 134 50E
Kasai *r.* Angola/Zaïre **107** I7 4 00S 19 00E
Kasama Zambia **107** L5 10 10S 31 11E
Kasaragod India **95** C2 12 30N 74 59E
Kasese Uganda **106** L8 0 10N 30 06E
Kāshān Iran **93** H5 33 59N 51 35E
Kashi China **96** E6 39 29N 76 02E
Kashihara Japan **100** G1 34 28N 135 46E
Kashima Japan **100** M2 35 58N 140 39E
Kashiwa Japan **100** L2 35 51N 139 58E
Kashiwazaki Japan **100** C2 37 22N 138 33E
Kaskö Finland **79** E3 62 23N 21 10E
Kasli Russia **91** J6 55 54N 60 45E
Kásos *i.* Greece **81** E2 35 00N 28 00E
Kassala Sudan **92** E2 15 24N 36 30E
Kassel Germany **76** E5 51 18N 9 30E
Kasserine Tunisia **81** B2 35 13N 8 43E
Kastoria Greece **81** D3 40 33N 21 15E
Kasugai Japan **100** H2 35 15N 136 57E
Kasukabe Japan **100** L2 35 59N 139 45E
Kasumiga-ura *l.* Japan **100** M3 36 03N 140 20E
Kaśur Pakistan **95** C6 31 07N 74 30E
Kataba Zambia **107** K4 16 02S 25 03E
Katase Japan **101** A2 35 18N 139 30E
Katchall *i.* Nicobar Is. **95** G1 7 30N 93 30E
Kateríni Greece **81** D3 40 15N 22 30E
Katha Myanmar **96** J3 24 11N 96 20E
Katherine Australia **110** E7 14 29S 132 20E
Kathiawar *p.* India **94/95** C4 21 10N 71 00E
Kat Hing Wai Hong Kong U.K. **98** B2 22 26N 114 03E
Kathmandu Nepal **95** F5 27 42N 85 19E
Katihar India **95** F5 25 33N 87 34E
Katowice Poland **80** C5 50 15N 18 59E
Katrineholm Sweden **79** D2 58 59N 16 15E
Katsina Ala Nigeria **106** G9 7 10N 9 30E
Katsuura Japan **100** M2 35 10N 140 20E
Kattakurgan Uzbekistan **91** K2 39 54N 66 13E
Kattegat *sd.* Denmark/Sweden **79** C2 57 00N 11 00E
Katun' *r.* Russia **91** O5 51 30N 86 00E
Kauai *i.* Hawaiian Islands **115** X18 22 00N 159 30W
Kauai Channel Hawaiian Islands **115** X18 21 45N 158 50W
Kaula *i.* Hawaiian Islands **115** W18 21 35N 160 40W
Kaulakahi Channel Hawaiian Islands **115** X18 21 58N 159 50W
Kaulsdorf Germany **83** G1 52 29N 13 34E
Kaunas Lithuania **80** D5 54 52N 23 55E
Kau Sai Chau *i.* Hong Kong U.K. **98** C2 22 22N 114 19E
Kau Yi Chau *i.* Hong Kong U.K. **98** B1 22 17N 114 04E
Kavajë Albania **81** C3 41 11N 19 33E
Kavála Greece **81** D3 40 56N 24 25E
Kavaratti Island India **95** C2 10 32N 72 43E
Kawachi-Nagano Japan **100** G1 34 24N 135 32E
Kawagoe Japan **100** L2 35 55N 139 30E
Kawaguchi Japan **101** B4 35 47N 139 44E
Kawaihae Hawaiian Islands **115** Z18 20 02N 155 50W
Kawasaki Japan **101** C3 35 30N 139 45E
Kawawa Japan **101** B3 35 31N 139 32E
Kawerau New Zealand **111** C3 38 03S 176 43E
Kaya Burkina **106** E10 13 04N 1 09W
Kayes Mali **106** C10 14 26N 11 28W
Kayseri Turkey **92** E6 38 42N 35 28E
Kazach'ye Russia **89** P10 70 46N 136 15E
KAZAKHSTAN 91 H4/N4
Kazakh Upland Kazakhstan **91** M4 47 00N 75 00E
Kazan' Russia **90** F6 55 45N 49 10E
Kazanlŭk Bulgaria **81** E3 42 37N 25 23E
Kazatin Ukraine **80** E4 49 41N 28 49E
Kāzerūn Iran **93** H4 29 35N 51 40E
Kazym *r.* Russia **91** K7 63 00N 67 30E
Kéa *i.* Greece **81** D2 37 00N 24 00E
Keansburg New Jersey U.S.A. **65** F3 40 27N 74 08W
Kearney Nebraska U.S.A. **62** G5 40 42N 99 04W
Kearny New Jersey U.S.A. **50** B2 40 45N 74 07W
Kecskemét Hungary **81** C4 46 56N 19 43E
Kediri Indonesia **99** E2 7 45S 112 01E
Keene New Hampshire U.S.A. **65** H5 42 55N 72 17W
Keetmanshoop Namibia **107** I2 26 36S 18 08E
Kefallinía *i.* Greece **81** D2 38 00N 20 00E
Keflavík Iceland **79** H6 64 01N 22 35W
Keihoku Japan **100** G2 35 09N 135 37E
Kei Ling Ha Lo Wai Hong Kong U.K. **98** C2 22 25N 114 16E
Kei Lun Wai Hong Kong U.K. **98** A2 22 24N 113 58E
Keitele *l.* Finland **79** F3 63 10N 26 24E
K'elafo Ethiopia **106** N9 5 37N 44 10E
Kelkit *r.* Turkey **92** E7 40 20N 37 40E
Kells Irish Republic **78** E5 53 44N 6 53W
Kemerovo Russia **91** O6 55 25N 86 05E
Kemi Finland **79** E4 65 46N 24 34E
Kemijärvi *l.* Finland **79** F4 66 42N 27 30E
Kemijöki *r.* Finland **79** F4 66 00N 25 00E
Kempten Germany **76** E4 47 44N 10 19E
Kemsing England **82** D2 51 18N 0 14E
Kenai Alaska U.S.A. **10** E5 60 35N 151 19W
Kendal England **78** I6 54 20N 2 45W
Kendari Indonesia **99** G3 3 57S 122 36E
Kenema Sierra Leone **106** C9 7 57N 11 11W
Kengtung Myanmar **97** J3 21 16N 99 39E
Keningau Malaysia **99** F5 5 21N 116 11E
Kénitra Morocco **106** D14 34 20N 6 34W
Kenmare North Dakota U.S.A. **40** C1 48 40N 102 05W
Kennebec River Maine U.S.A. **33** B1 44 00N 69 00W
Kennebunk Maine U.S.A. **65** K6 43 24N 70 33W
Kennedy New York U.S.A. **64** A5 42 10N 79 07W
Kennedy Town Hong Kong U.K. **98** B1 22 17N 114 07E
Kennobec River Maine U.S.A. **37** R6 45 20N 70 00W
Kenosha Wisconsin U.S.A. **63** I5 42 34N 87 50W
Kensington *bor.* Inner London England **82** C3 51 29N 0 10W
Kent Connecticut U.S.A. **65** G4 41 43N 73 28W
Kent *co.* England **82** D2 51 10N 0 00E
Kenthurst Australia **111** F3 33 40S 151 01E
Kenting National Park Taiwan **98** G5 22 00N 120 50E
Kentucky *state* U.S.A. **63** I4 37 00N 85 00W
KENYA 106 M8
Kenya, Mount *see* Kirinyaga
Kepulauan Anambas *is.* Indonesia **99** D4 3 00N 106 40E
Kepulauan Aru *is.* Indonesia **99** I2 7 00S 134 00E
Kepulauan Kai *is.* Indonesia **99** I2 5 30S 133 00E
Kepulauan Lingga *is.* Indonesia **99** C3 0 30S 104 00E
Kepulauan Mentawai *is.* Indonesia **99** B3 2 00S 99 00E
Kepulauan Obi *is.* Indonesia **99** H3 1 40S 127 30E
Kepulauan Riau *is.* Indonesia **99** C4 1 00N 104 20E
Kepulauan Sangir *is.* Indonesia **99** H4 2 30N 125 20E
Kepulauan Sula *is.* Indonesia **99** G3/H3 2 00S 125 00E
Kepulauan Talaud *is.* Indonesia **99** H4 4 00N 126 50E
Kepulauan Tanimbar *is.* Indonesia **99** I2 7 30S 132 00E
Kerala *admin.* India **95** D2 10 10N 76 30E
Kerch' Ukraine **90** D4 45 22N 36 27E
Kerema Papua New Guinea **110** H8 7 59S 145 46E
Keren Ethiopia **92** E2 15 46N 38 30E
Kerguelen Plateau Indian Ocean **112** G1/H1 55 00S 80 00E
Kerikeri New Zealand **111** B3 35 12S 173 59E
Kerki Turkmenistan **91** K2 37 53N 65 10E
Kérkira *(Corfu) i.* Greece **81** C2 39 00N 19 00E
Kérkira Greece **81** C2 39 38N 19 55E
Kermadec Islands Pacific Ocean **114** I5 30 00S 178 30W
Kermadec Trench Pacific Ocean **114** I4 33 00S 177 00W
Kermān Iran **93** I5 30 18N 57 05E
Kermānshāh Iran **93** G5 34 19N 47 04E
Kerme Körfezi *b.* Turkey **80** E2 37 00N 27 00E
Kerrville Texas U.S.A. **62** G3 30 03N 99 09W
Kert *r.* Morocco **77** B2 35 00N 3 30W
Kerulen *r.* Mongolia **97** M8 47 30N 112 30E
Keşan Turkey **80** E3 40 52N 26 37E
Ket' *r.* Russia **91** O6 58 30N 86 30E
Ketapang Indonesia **99** E3 1 50S 109 59E
Ketchikan Alaska U.S.A. **42** B3 55 25N 131 40W
Ketrzyn Poland **80** D5 54 05N 21 24E
Kettwig Germany **76** H2 51 22N 6 55E
Keuka Lake New York U.S.A. **64** C5 42 30N 77 10W
Kevin Montana U.S.A. **41** C1 48 44N 111 58W
Keweenaw Bay Michigan U.S.A. **35** C2 46 50N 88 20W
Keweenaw Peninsula Michigan U.S.A. **63** I6 47 00N 88 00W
Khabarovsk Russia **89** P5 48 32N 135 08E
Khairpur Pakistan **93** K4 27 30N 68 50E
Khalīg el Tîna Egypt **107** T4 31 08N 32 36E
Khalkidhikí *p.* Greece **81** D3 40 30N 23 00E
Khalkis Greece **81** D2 38 28N 23 36E
Khambhat India **95** C4 22 19N 72 39E
Khambhat, Gulf of India **95** C4 20 30N 72 00E
Khamman India **95** E3 17 16N 80 13E
Khānābad Afghanistan **93** K6 36 42N 69 08E
Khānaqīn Iraq **93** G5 34 22N 45 22E
Khandwa India **95** D4 21 49N 76 23E
Khaniá Greece **81** D2 35 31N 24 01E
Khanty-Mansiysk Russia **89** I8 61 01N 69 00E
Khān Yūnis Israel **92** O10 31 21N 34 18E
Kharagpur India **95** F4 22 23N 87 22E
Kharan Pakistan **94** B5 28 32N 65 26E
Khardah India **94** K2 22 43N 88 23E
Khārg Island Iran **93** H4 29 14N 50 20E

Khar'kov Ukraine 90 D5 50 00N 36 15E
Khartoum Sudan 92 D2 15 33N 32 35E
Khash Iran 93 J4 28 14N 61 15E
Khash *r.* Afghanistan 93 J5 31 30N 62 30E
Khashm el Girba Sudan 92 E1 14 59N 35 59E
Khaskovo Bulgaria 81 E3 41 57N 25 32E
Khatanga Russia 89 M10 71 59N 102 31E
Khatanga *r.* Russia 89 M10 72 30N 102 30E
Khemisset Morocco 106 D14 33 50N 6 03W
Khenchela Algeria 77 D2 35 22N 7 09E
Kherson Ukraine 90 C4 46 39N 32 38E
Kheta *r.* Russia 89 L10 71 30N 95 00E
Khilok *r.* Russia 89 M6 51 00N 107 30E
Khimki Russia 88 L2 55 56N 37 26E
Khimki-Khovrino Russia 88 L2 55 56N 37 30E
Khimki Reservoir Russia 88 L2 55 54N 37 28E
Khíos Greece 81 E2 38 23N 26 07E
Khíos *i.* Greece 81 E2 38 00N 26 00E
Khiva Uzbekistan 91 J3 41 25N 60 49E
Khmel'nitskiy Ukraine 90 B4 49 25N 26 59E
Khodzheyli Uzbekistan 91 H3 42 25N 59 25E
Kholmsk Russia 89 Q5 47 02N 142 03E
Khon Kaen Thailand 99 C7 16 25N 102 50E
Khoper *r.* Russia 90 E5 50 00N 40 00E
Khorochevo Russia 88 L2 55 47N 37 30E
Khorog Tajikistan 91 L2 37 22N 71 32E
Khorramābād Iran 93 G5 33 29N 48 21E
Khorramshahr Iran 93 G5 30 25N 48 09E
Khotin Ukraine 80 E4 48 30N 26 31E
Khouribga Morocco 106 D14 32 54N 6 57W
Khrebet Kopet-Dag' *can.* Iran/Turkmenistan 91 H2 38 30N 57 00E
Khrishnapur Canal India 94 K2 22 34N 88 27E
Khujand *(Leninabad)* Tadjikistan 91 K3 40 14N 69 40E
Khulna Bangladesh 95 F4 22 49N 89 34E
Khyber Pass Afghanistan/Pakistan 93 L5 34 06N 71 05E
Kiantajärvi *l.* Finland 79 F4 65 02N 29 00E
Kibombo Zaïre 107 K7 3 58S 25 54E
Kiel Germany 76 E5 54 20N 10 08E
Kielce Poland 80 D5 50 51N 20 39E
Kieta Papua New Guinea 110 J8 6 16S 155 37E
Kiev *see* Kiyev
Kigali Rwanda 106 L7 1 56S 30 04E
Kigoma Tanzania 107 K7 4 52S 29 36E
Kii-Nagashima Japan 100 H1 34 11N 136 19E
Kii-sanchi *mts.* Japan 100 G1 34 15N 135 50E
Kii-suidō *sd.* Japan 100 B1 34 00N 134 45E
Kikinda Serbia Yugoslavia 81 D4 45 50N 20 30E
Kikori Papua New Guinea 110 G8 7 25S 144 13E
Kikwit Zaïre 107 I6 5 02S 18 51E
Kilanea Hawaiian Islands 115 X19 22 05N 159 35W
Kilimanjaro *mt.* Tanzania 106 M7 3 04S 37 22E
Kilkenny Kilkenny Irish Republic 78 D4 52 39N 7 15W
Kilkís Greece 81 D3 40 59N 22 52E
Killarney Kerry Irish Republic 78 B4 52 03N 9 30W
Killeen Texas U.S.A. 63 G3 31 08N 97 44W
Kilmarnock Strathclyde Scotland 78 G7 55 36N 4 30W
Kiltan Island India 95 C2 11 30N 73 00E
Kilwa Masoko Tanzania 107 M6 8 55S 39 31E
Kilyos Turkey 80 E3 41 14N 29 02E
Kimberley Republic of South Africa 107 J2 28 45S 24 46E
Kimberley Plateau Australia 110 D6 17 30S 126 00E
Kimitsu Japan 100 L2 35 19N 139 53E
Kindia Guinea 106 C10 10 03N 12 49W
Kindu Zaïre 107 K7 3 00S 25 56E
Kineshma Russia 90 E6 57 28N 42 08E
King George Island South Shetland Islands 69 F0 62 00S 58 00W
King George's Reservoir Essex England 82 C3 51 39N 0 01W
King Island Australia 110 G2 40 00S 144 00E
Kingissepp *see* Kuressaare
Kingman Arizona U.S.A. 62 D4 35 12N 114 02W
King Sejong *r.s.* Antarctica 117 62 13S 58 45W
Kingsgrove Australia 111 G2 33 57S 151 06E
Kings Langley Hertfordshire England 82 B3 51 43N 0 28W
King's Lynn Norfolk England 78 L4 52 45N 0 24E
King Sound Australia 110 C6 16 00S 123 00E
Kings Point *tn.* New York U.S.A. 50 C2 40 49N 73 45W
Kingsport Tennessee U.S.A. 63 J4 36 33N 82 34W
Kingston Jamaica 67 R7 17 58N 76 48W
Kingston Massachusetts U.S.A. 65 K4 42 00N 70 44W
Kingston New Hampshire U.S.A. 65 J5 42 55N 71 02W
Kingston New York U.S.A. 65 G4 41 55N 74 00W
Kingston upon Hull Humberside England 78 K5 53 45N 0 20W
Kingstonupon Thames *bor.* Greater London England 82 B2 51 25N 0 18W
Kingstown St. Vincent & The Grenadines 67 L2 13 12N 61 14W
Kingsville Texas U.S.A. 63 G2 27 32N 97 53W
Kinkala Congo 107 H7 4 18S 14 49E
Kino *r.* Japan 100 G1 34 15N 135 30E
Kinshasa Zaïre 107 I7 4 18S 15 18E
Kiparissiakós Kólpos *g.* Greece 81 D2 37 00N 21 00E
Kipili Tanzania 107 L6 7 30S 30 39E
Kirchhörde Germany 76 K2 51 27N 7 27E
Kirensk Russia 89 M7 57 45N 108 02E
KIRGHIZIA *see* KIRGYZSTAN
Kirghiz Step' *geog. reg.* Kazakhstan 90/1 H4 49 00N 55 00E
KIRGYZSTAN *(KIRGHIZIA)* 91 L3/M3
KIRIBATI Pacific Ocean 114 H8
Kirikiri Nigeria 107 V3 6 22N 3 22E
Kirikkale Turkey 92 D6 39 51N 33 32E
Kirinyaga *(Mount Kenya)* *mt.* Kenya 106 M7 0 10S 37 19E
Kiritimati Island Kiribati 115 K8 2 10N 157 00W
Kirkağaç Turkey 80 E2 39 06N 27 40E
Kirkcaldy Fife Scotland 78 H8 56 07N 3 10W
Kirkcudbright Dumfries and Galloway Scotland 78 G6 54 50N 4 03W
Kirkládhes *(Cyclades)* *is.* Greece 81 D2 37 00N 25 00E
Kirklareli Turkey 80 E3 41 45N 27 12E
Kirkūk Iraq 92 F6 35 28N 44 26E
Kirkwall Orkney Islands Scotland 78 H10 58 59N 2 58W
Kirov Russia 90 F6 58 00N 49 38E
Kirovabad *see* Gyandzha
Kirovakan Armenia 90 E3 40 49N 44 30E
Kirovo-Chepetsk *r.* Russia 90 G6 58 30N 51 00E
Kirovograd Ukraine 90 C4 48 31N 32 15E
Kirti Nagar India 94 L4 28 39N 77 09E
Kiruna Sweden 79 E4 67 53N 20 15E
Kiryū Japan 100 C2 36 26N 130 18E
Kisangani Zaïre 106 K8 0 33N 25 14E
Kisarazu Japan 101 C2 35 22N 139 55E
Kiselevsk' Russia 91 O5 54 01N 86 41E
Kishinev Moldova 90 B4 47 00N 28 50E
Kishiwada Japan 100 G1 34 28N 135 22E
Kiskunfélegyháza Hungary 81 C4 46 42N 19 52E
Kiskunhalas Hungary 81 C4 46 26N 19 29E
Kislovodsk Russia 90 E3 43 56N 42 44E
Kismaayo Somalia 106 N7 0 25S 42 31E
Kisumu Kenya 106 L7 0 08S 34 47E
Kita Japan 101 B4 35 46N 139 43E
Kita-Kyūshū Japan 100 B1 33 52N 130 49E
Kitami Japan 100 D3 43 51N 143 54E
Kita-ura *l.* Japan 100 M3 36 02N 140 33E
Kíthira *i.* Greece 81 D2 36 00N 23 00E
Kíthnos *i.* Greece 81 D2 37 00N 24 00E
Kitridge Point Barbados 66 W12 13 08N 59 22W
Kittery Maine U.S.A. 65 K6 43 05N 70 45W
Kitwe Zambia 107 K5 0 08S 30 30E
Kitzbühel Austria 81 B4 47 27N 12 23E
Kivu, Lake Zaïre/Rwanda 106 K7 2 00S 29 00E
Kiyev *(Kiev)* Ukraine 90 C5 50 25N 30 30E
Kiyose Japan 101 B4 35 46N 139 32E
Kızıl Irmak *r.* Turkey 92 D7 40 30N 34 00E
Kizlyar Russia 90 F3 43 51N 46 43E
Kizyl Arvat Turkmenistan 91 H2 39 00N 56 23E
Kladno Czechoslovakia 80 B5 50 10N 14 07E
Kladow Germany 83 E1 52 27N 13 08E
Klagenfurt Austria 81 B4 46 38N 14 20E
Klaipėda Lithuania 80 D8 55 43N 21 07E
Klamath *r.* U.S.A. 62 B5 42 00N 123 00W
Klamath Falls *tn.* Oregon U.S.A. 62 B5 42 14N 121 47W
Klarälven *r.* Sweden 79 C3 60 45N 13 00E
Klatovy Czechoslovakia 80 B4 49 24N 13 17E
Kleine Emscher *can.* Germany 76 G3 51 35N 6 45E
Kleinmachnow Germany 83 E1 52 24N 13 13E
Klerksdorp Republic of South Africa 107 K2 26 52S 26 39E
Klintehamn Sweden 80 C6 57 24N 18 14E
Kłodzko Poland 80 C5 50 28N 16 40E
Klöfta Norway 79 C3 60 04N 11 06E
Klyazma *r.* Russia 90 E6 56 00N 42 00E
Klyuchevskaya Sopka *mt.* Russia 89 S7 56 03N 160 38E
Knokke-Heist Belgium 76 C5 51 21N 3 19E
Knossós *hist. site* Greece 92 C6 35 18N 25 10E
Knoxville Tennessee U.S.A. 63 J4 36 00N 83 57W
Kōbe Japan 100 G1 34 40N 135 12E
København *(Copenhagen)* Denmark 80 B6 55 43N 12 34E
Koblenz Germany 76 D5 50 21N 7 36E
Kobrin Belarus 90 A5 52 16N 24 22E
Kobuk *r.* Alaska U.S.A. 10 D6 67 00N 157 30W
Koca *r.* Turkey 80 E2 39 00N 27 00E
Koch Bihār India 95 F5 26 18N 89 32E
Kōchi Japan 100 B1 33 33N 133 32E
Kochubey Russia 90 F3 44 25N 46 33E
Kodaira Japan 101 A3 35 44N 139 28E
Kodiak Alaska U.S.A. 10 E4 57 49N 152 30W
Kodiak Island Alaska U.S.A. 10 E4 57 20N 153 40W
Kodok Sudan 106 L9 9 51N 32 07E
Koforidua Ghana 106 E9 6 01N 0 12W
Kofu Japan 100 C2 35 42N 138 34E
Koga Japan 100 L3 36 12N 139 42E
Koganei Japan 101 D3 35 42N 139 30E
Kohat Pakistan 95 C6 33 37N 71 30E
Koh-i-Mazar *mt.* Afghanistan 93 K5 32 30N 66 23E
Kohoku Japan 101 B3 35 30N 139 39E
Kohtla-Järve Estonia 79 F2 59 28N 27 20E
Kokand Uzbekistan 91 L3 40 33N 70 55E
Kokawa Japan 100 G1 34 16N 135 24E
Kokchetav Kazakhstan 91 K5 53 18N 69 25E
Kokkola Finland 79 E3 62 45N 30 06E
Kokomo Indiana U.S.A. 63 I5 40 30N 86 09W
Kola Peninsula Russia 88 F9 67 30N 37 30E
Kolar Gold Fields *tn.* India 95 D2 12 54N 78 16E
Kolding Denmark 67 B2 55 29N 9 30E
Kolguyev *i.* Russia 88 G9 69 00N 49 30E
Kolhapur India 95 C3 16 40N 74 20E
Kolin Czechoslovakia 80 C5 50 02N 15 11E
Köln *(Cologne)* Germany 76 D5 50 56N 6 57E
Kołobrzeg Poland 80 C5 54 10N 15 35E
Kolomna Russia 90 D6 55 05N 38 45E
Kolomyya Ukraine 80 E4 48 31N 25 00E
Kolpashevo Russia 91 N6 58 21N 82 59E
Kolpino Russia 90 C6 59 44N 30 39E
Kolvereid Norway 79 C3 64 53N 11 35E
Kolwezi Zaïre 107 K5 10 45S 25 25E
Kolyma *r.* Russia 89 R9 66 30N 152 00E
Kolyma *(Gydan)* **Range** *mts.* Russia 89 R8 63 00N 160 00E
Kolyma Lowland Russia 89 R9 69 00N 155 00E
Komae Japan 101 B3 35 38N 139 36E
Komaki Japan 100 H2 35 18N 136 54E
Komandorskiye Ostrova *is.* Russia 114 G13 55 00N 166 30E
Komárno Czechoslovakia 81 C4 47 46N 18 05E
Komatsu Japan 100 C2 36 25N 136 27E
Kommunarsk Ukraine 90 D4 48 30N 38 47E
Komotiní Greece 81 E3 41 06N 25 25E
Kompong Cham Cambodia 99 D6 11 59N 105 26E
Kompong Chhnang Cambodia 99 C6 12 16N 104 39E
Kompong Som Cambodia 99 C6 11 03N 103 41E
Komsomol'sk-na-Amure Russia 89 P6 50 32N 136 59E
Konda *r.* Russia 91 J7 60 00N 65 00E
Kondūz Afghanistan 93 K6 36 45N 68 51E
Kongola Zaïre 107 K6 5 20S 27 00E
Königsheide Germany 83 F1 52 27N 13 28E
Königs Wusterhausen Germany 83 G1 52 18N 13 37E
Konin Poland 80 C5 52 12N 18 12E
Konnagar India 94 K2 22 42N 88 20E
Konosha Russia 90 E7 60 58N 40 08E
Konotop Ukraine 90 C5 51 15N 33 14E
Konstantinovka Ukraine 90 D4 48 33N 37 45E
Konstanz Germany 77 D4 47 40N 9 10E
Konya Turkey 92 D6 37 51N 32 30E
Koocanusa, Lake Montana U.S.A. 43 E1 48 55N 115 10W
Köpenick Germany 83 G1 52 27N 13 36E
Koper Slovenia 81 B4 45 31N 13 44E
Kopeysk Russia 91 J6 55 08N 61 39E
Kopychintsy Ukraine 80 E4 49 10N 25 58E
Korçë Albania 81 D3 40 38N 20 44E
Korčula *i.* Croatia 81 C3 43 00N 17 00E
Korea Bay China/North Korea 97 N6 39 00N 124 00E
Korea Strait South Korea/Japan 97 P5/Q5 33 00N 129 00E
Korhogo Côte d'Ivoire 106 D9 9 22N 5 31W
Korinthiakós Kólpos *g.* Greece 81 D2 38 00N 22 00E
Kórinthos Greece 81 D2 37 56N 22 55E
Kōriyama Japan 100 D2 37 23N 140 22E
Korla China 96 G7 41 48N 86 10E
Koro *i.* Fiji 114 U16 17 20S 179 25E
Koro Sea Fiji 114 U16 17 35S 180 00E
Korosten Ukraine 90 B5 51 00N 28 30E
Korsakov Russia 89 Q5 46 36N 142 50E
Kortrijk *(Courtrai)* Belgium 76 C5 50 50N 3 17E
Koryak Range *mts.* Russia 89 T8 62 00N 170 00E
Kos *i.* Greece 81 E2 36 00N 27 00E
Kosciusko Island Alaska U.S.A. 42 B3 56 00N 133 45W
Kosciusko, Mount Australia 110 H2 36 28S 148 17E
Koshigaya Japan 100 L2 35 54N 139 47E
Kosti Sudan 92 D1 13 11N 32 28E
Kostroma Russia 90 E6 57 46N 40 59E
Kostrzyn Poland 80 B5 52 35N 14 40E
Koszalin Poland 80 C5 54 10N 16 10E
Košice Czechoslovakia 80 D4 48 44N 21 15E
Kota India 95 D5 25 11N 75 58E
Kota Baharu Malaysia 99 C5 6 07N 102 15E
Kota Kinabalu Malaysia 99 F5 5 59N 116 04E
Kotka Finland 79 F3 60 26N 26 55E
Kotlas Russia 90 F7 61 15N 46 35E
Kōtō Japan 101 C3 35 40N 139 49E
Kotri Pakistan 94 B5 25 22N 68 18E
Kotto *r.* Central African Republic 106 J9 7 00N 22 30E
Kotuy *r.* Russia 89 M9 67 30N 102 00E
Kotzebue Alaska U.S.A. 10 C6 66 51N 162 40W
Kotzebue Sound Alaska U.S.A. 10 C6 66 40N 162 20W
Koudougou Burkina 106 E10 12 15N 2 23W
Koulamoutou Gabon 106 H7 1 12S 12 29E
Koulikoro Mali 106 D10 12 55N 7 31W
Koumra Chad 106 I9 8 56N 17 32E
Kounradskiy Kazakhstan 91 L4 46 58N 74 59E
Kourou French Guiana 68 G14 5 08N 52 37W
Kouvola Finland 79 F3 60 54N 26 45E
Kovel' Ukraine 90 A5 51 12N 24 48E
Kovrov Russia 90 E6 56 23N 41 21E
Kovzha *r.* Russia 90 D7 61 00N 37 00E
Kowloon Hong Kong U.K. 98 C1 22 19N 114 11E
Kowloon City Hong Kong U.K. 98 C2 22 20N 114 11E
Kowloon Peak Hong Kong U.K. 98 C2 22 20N 114 13E
Koyukuk *r.* Alaska U.S.A. 44 A4 66 00N 154 00W
Kozáni Greece 81 D3 40 18N 21 48E
Kpalimé Togo 106 E9 6 55N 0 44E
Kragujevac Serbia Yugoslavia 81 D3 44 01N 20 55E
Kra, Isthmus of Asia 84 10 00N 104 00E
Kraków Poland 80 C5 50 03N 19 55E
Kraljevo Serbia Yugoslavia 81 D3 43 44N 20 41E
Kramatorsk Ukraine 90 D4 48 43N 37 33E
Kranj Slovenia 81 B4 46 15N 14 20E
Krasnodar Russia 90 D4 45 02N 39 00E
Krasnovodsk Turkmenistan 90 G3 40 01N 53 00E
Krasnoyarsk Russia 91 P6 56 05N 92 46E
Krasnoyarskoye Vodokhranilishche *res.* Russia 91 P5 55 00N 91 00E
Krasny Stroitel Russia 88 M1 55 31N 37 08E
Krasnyy Kut Russia 90 F5 50 58N 47 00E
Krasnyy Luch Ukraine 90 D4 48 10N 39 00E
Kremenchug Ukraine 90 C4 49 03N 33 25E
Kremenchugskoye Vodokranilishche *res.* Ukraine 90 C4 49 30N 32 30E
Kremenets Ukraine 80 E5 50 05N 25 48E
Krems Austria 81 C4 48 25N 15 36E
Kreuzberg Germany 83 F2 52 30N 13 24E
Kribi Cameroon 106 H8 2 56N 9 56E
Krim *(Crimea)* *p.* Ukraine 90 C4 46 00N 34 00E
Krishna *r.* India 95 D3 16 00N 79 00E
Kristiansand Norway 79 B2 58 08N 8 01E
Kristianstad Sweden 79 C2 56 02N 14 10E
Kristiansund Norway 79 B3 63 06N 7 58E
Kristinehamn Sweden 80 B6 59 17N 14 09E
Kríti *(Crete)* *i.* Greece 81 D1 35 00N 25 00E
Krivoy Rog Ukraine 90 C4 47 55N 33 24E
Krk *i.* Croatia 81 B4 45 00N 14 00E
Krosno Poland 80 D4 49 40N 21 46E
Kruger National Park Republic of South Africa 107 L3 24 00S 32 00E
Krung Thep *see* Bangkok
Kruševac Serbia Yugoslavia 81 D3 43 34N 21 20E
Krušnéhory *see* Erzgebirge
Kruzof Island Alaska U.S.A. 42 A3 57 15N 135 40W
Ksar-el-Kebir Morocco 77 A2 35 04N 5 56W
Kuala Lumpur Malaysia 99 C4 3 08N 101 42E
Kuala Terengganu Malaysia 99 C5 5 30N 103 07E
Kuangfu Taiwan 98 H6 23 40N 121 25E
Kuantan Malaysia 99 C4 3 50N 103 19E
Kuban' *r.* Russia 90 E4 45 00N 41 00E
Kubiri Japan 101 B1 35 13N 139 42E
Kuching Malaysia 99 E4 1 32N 110 20E
Kudat Malaysia 99 F5 6 54N 116 47E
Kuhumo Finland 79 F3 64 04N 29 30E
Kuito Angola 107 I5 12 25S 16 56E
Kuiu Island Alaska U.S.A. 42 B3 56 45N 134 00W
Kujūkuri-hama *beach* Japan 100 M2 35 30N 140 30E
Kujū-san *mt.* Japan 100 B1 33 07N 131 14E
Kukës Albania 81 D3 42 05N 20 24E
Kuki Japan 100 L3 36 03N 139 41E
Kuldiga Latvia 79 E2 56 58N 21 58E
Kulundinskaya Step' *geog. reg.* Russia 91 M5 52 00N 80 00E
Kuma *r.* Russia 90 E4 45 00N 45 00E
Kumagaya Japan 100 C2 36 09N 139 22E
Kumairi *(Leninakan)* Armenia 90 E3 40 47N 43 49E
Kumamoto Japan 100 B1 32 50N 130 42E
Kumanovo Macedonia Yugoslavia 81 D3 42 07N 21 40E
Kumasi Ghana 106 E9 6 45N 1 35W
Kumba Cameroon 106 G8 4 39N 9 26E
Kumbakonam India 95 D2 10 59N 79 24E
Kumukahi, Cape Hawaiian Islands 115 Z17 19 30N 154 50W
Kumul *see* Hami
Kunar *r.* Asia 93 L5 35 30N 71 20E
Kunashir *i.* Russia 100 E3 44 30N 146 20E
Kungrad Uzbekistan 91 H3 43 06N 58 54E
Kunlun Shan *mts.* China 96 F6/G6 36 30N 85 00E
Kunming China 97 K4 25 04N 102 41E
Kunming Hu *l.* China 101 G2 40 00N 116 15E
Kunsan South Korea 97 P6 35 57N 126 42E
Kuntsevo Russia 88 L1 55 43N 37 25E
Kununurra Australia 110 D6 15 42S 128 50E
Kuopio Finland 79 F3 62 54N 27 40E
Kupa *r.* Croatia 81 C4 45 30N 15 00E
Kupang Indonesia 99 G1 10 13S 123 38E
Kupferdreh Germany 76 J2 51 24N 7 06E
Kupreanof Island Alaska U.S.A. 42 B3 56 50N 133 30W
Kura *r.* Azerbaijan 88 G4 41 00N 47 30E
Kurashiki Japan 100 B1 34 36N 133 43E
Kurchum *r.* Kazakhstan 91 N4 49 00N 85 00E
Kure Japan 100 B1 34 14N 132 32E
Kuressaare *(Kingissepp)* Estonia 79 E2 59 22N 28 40E
Kureyka *r.* Russia 89 L9 67 30N 91 00E
Kurgan Russia 91 K6 55 30N 65 20E
Kuria Muria Islands Oman 93 I2 17 30N 56 00E
Kurihama Japan 101 B1 35 12N 139 41E
Kurikka Finland 79 E3 62 36N 22 25E
Kuril Islands Russia 89 R5/R6 50 00N 155 00E
Kuril Ridge Pacific Ocean 114 F12 47 50N 152 00E
Kuril Trench Pacific Ocean 114 F12 45 40N 154 00E
Ku-ring-gai Chase National Park Australia 111 G3 33 40S 151 00E
Kurnell Australia 111 G1 34 01S 151 12E
Kurnool India 95 D3 15 51N 78 01E
Kursk Russia 90 D5 51 45N 36 14E
Kurskiy Zaliv *g.* Russia 80 D6 55 00N 21 00E
Kurume Japan 100 B1 33 20N 130 29E
Kusatsu Japan 100 G2 35 02N 135 59E
Kushida-gawa *r.* Japan 100 H1 34 23N 136 15E
Kushiro Japan 100 D3 42 58N 144 24E
Kushka Afghanistan 93 J6 35 14N 62 15E
Kushva Russia 91 H6 58 20N 59 48E
Kuskokwim *r.* Alaska U.S.A. 10 C5 61 30N 160 45W
Kuskokwim Bay Alaska U.S.A. 10 C4 58 50N 164 00W
Kuskokwim Mountains Alaska U.S.A. 10 D5 62 00N 158 00W
Kustanay Kazakhstan 91 J5 53 15N 63 40E
Kütahya Turkey 92 C6 39 25N 29 56E
Kutaisi Georgia 90 E3 42 15N 42 44E
Kutno Poland 80 C5 52 13N 19 20E
Kutztown Pennsylvania U.S.A. 64 E3 40 32N 74 46W
Kuusamo Finland 79 F4 65 57N 29 15E
Kuvango Angola 107 I5 14 27S 16 20E
KUWAIT 93 G4
Kuwana Japan 100 H2 35 04N 136 40E
Kuybyshev *see* Samara
Kuytun China 96 F7 44 30N 85 00E
Kuzbass *geog. reg.* Russia 91 O5/6 55 00N 87 00E
Kuzey Anadolu Dağlari *mts.* Turkey 92 E7 41 15N 36 20E
Kuz'minki Russia 88 N1 55 41N 37 45E
Kwai Chung Hong Kong U.K. 98 B2 22 22N 114 07E
Kwangju South Korea 96 P6 35 07N 126 52E
Kwango *r.* Zaïre 107 I6 6 00S 17 00E
Kwan Tei Hong Kong U.K. 98 B3 22 31N 114 09E
Kwekwe *(Que Que)* Zimbabwe 107 K4 18 55S 29 49E
Kwethluk Alaska U.S.A. 10 C5 60 46N 161 34W
Kwigillingok Alaska U.S.A. 10 C4 59 50N 163 10W
Kwilu *r.* Zaïre 107 I6 6 00S 19 00E
Kwun Tong Hong Kong U.K. 98 C1 22 18N 114 13E
Kwu Tung Hong Kong U.K. 98 B3 22 30N 114 06E
Kyaukpyu Myanmar 95 G3 19 27N 93 33E
Kyle of Lochalsh Scotland 78 F9 57 17N 5 43W
Kyoga, Lake Uganda 106 L8 2 00N 34 00E
Kyoga-misaki *c.* Japan 100 C2 35 48N 135 12E
Kyōto Japan 100 G2 35 02N 135 45E
Kyronjöki *r.* Finland 79 E3 63 00N 21 30E
Kyūshū *i.* Japan 100 B1 32 20N 131 00E
Kyūshū-Palau Ridge Pacific Ocean 114 D9 15 00N 135 00E
Kyustendil Bulgaria 81 D3 42 16N 22 40E
Kyzyl Russia 89 L6 51 45N 94 28E
Kyzyl Kum *desert* Kazakhstan/Uzbekistan 91 J3 43 00N 65 00E
Kzyl-Orda Kazakhstan 91 K3 44 25N 65 28E

L

Laascaanood Somalia 106 O9 8 35N 46 55E
La Asunción Venezuela 67 L2 11 06 N 63 53W
Laayoune *(El Aaiún)* Western Sahara 106 C13 27 10N 13 11W
la Baule-Escoublac France 77 B4 47 18N 2 22W
Labé Guinea 106 C10 11 17N 12 11W
Labe *see* Elbe
Labrador Basin Atlantic Ocean 113 C12 58 00N 50 00W
Lábrea Brazil 68 E11 7 20S 64 46W
La Brea Trinidad and Tobago 66 S9 10 14N 61 37W
Labytnangi Russia 89 I9 66 43N 66 28E
La Canada California U.S.A. 51 B3 34 12N 118 12W
La Ceiba Honduras 67 G3 15 45N 86 45W
Lac Fitri *l.* Chad 106 I10 13 00N 17 30E
Lachlan *r.* Australia 110 H3 33 30S 145 30E
La Chorrera Panama 67 Y1 8 51N 79 46W
Lackawack New York U.S.A. 65 F4 41 48N 74 25W
Lackawanna New York U.S.A. 64 F4 42 49N 78 49W
Lac Léman *(Lake Geneva)* *l.* Switzerland 77 D4 46 20N 6 20E
Lac Mai-Ndombe *l.* Zaïre 106 I7 2 00S 18 20E
Lac Moero *see* Mweru
La Coruña *(Corunna)* Spain 77 A3 43 22N 8 24W
La Cresenta California U.S.A. 51 B3 34 13N 118 14W
La Crosse Wisconsin U.S.A. 63 H5 43 48N 91 04W
Lacul Razelm *l.* Romania 81 E3 45 00N 29 00E
Ladakh Range *mts.* Kashmir 95 D6 34 30N 78 30E
la Défense France 83 A2 48 53N 2 14E
Ladozhskoye Ozero *(Lake Ladoga)* *l.* Russia 90 C7 61 00N 30 00E
Ladysmith Republic of South Africa 107 K2 28 34S 29 47E
Ladysmith Wisconsin U.S.A. 35 B2 45 27N 91 07W
Lae Papua New Guinea 110 H8 6 45S 147 00E
Laedalsøyri Norway 79 B3 61 05N 7 15E
La Esmeralda Venezuela 68 D13 3 11N 65 33W
Lafayette California U.S.A. 49 C3 37 53N 122 08W
Lafayette Indiana U.S.A. 63 I5 40 25N 86 54W
Lafayette Louisiana U.S.A. 63 G3 30 12N 92 18W
Lafayette Reservoir California U.S.A. 49 C3 37 52N 122 08W
La Fé Cuba 67 H4 22 02N 84 15W
Lågen *r.* Norway 79 B3 61 40N 9 45E
Laghouat Algeria 106 F14 33 49N 2 55E
Lago Argentino *l.* Argentina 69 C2 50 10S 72 30W
Lago da Tijuca *l.* Brazil 69 P2 22 59S 43 22W

Lago de Chapala *l.* Mexico **66** D4 20 05N 103 00W
Lago de Maracaibo *l.* Venezuela **68** C14 9 50N 71 30W
Lago de Nicaragua *l.* Nicaragua **67** G2 11 50N 86 00W
Lago de Piratininga *l.* Brazil **69** Q2 22 57S 43 05W
Lago de Poopó *l.* Bolivia **68** D9 18 30S 67 20W
Lago di Bolsena *l.* Italy **81** B3 42 00N 12 00E
Lago di Como *l.* Italy **81** A4 46 00N 9 00E
Lago di Garda *l.* Italy **81** B4 45 00N 10 00E
Lago do Jacarepaguá *l.* Brazil **69** P2 22 58S 43 23W
Lago Maggiore *l.* Italy **81** A4 46 00N 8 00E
Lago Rodrigo de Freitas *l.* Brazil **69** Q2 22 58S 43 13W
Lagos Nigeria **107** V3 6 27N 3 28E
Lagos Portugal **77** A2 37 05N 8 40W
Lagos Island *tn.* Nigeria **107** V3 6 24N 3 28E
Lagos Lagoon Nigeria **107** W3 6 30N 3 33E
Lago Titicaca *l.* Peru/Bolivia **68** C9/D9 16 00S 69 30W
La Grande Oregon U.S.A. **62** C6 45 21N 118 05W
La Grange Georgia U.S.A. **63** I3 33 02N 85 02W
La Grange Illinois U.S.A. **53** A2 41 47N 87 53W
La Guaira Venezuela **68** D15 10 38N 66 55W
Laguna Brazil **69** H7 28 29S 48 45W
Laguna Caratasca *l.* Honduras **67** H3 15 05N 84 00W
Laguna de Perlas *l.* Nicaragua **67** H2 12 30N 83 30W
Laguna Mar Chiquita *l.* Argentina **69** E6 30 30S 62 30W
Lagunillas Venezuela **68** C15 10 07N 71 16W
Lagøy *i.* Norway **79** C4 68 45N 15 00E
La Habana *(Havana)* Cuba **67** H4 23 07N 82 25W
La Habra California U.S.A. **51** C2 33 56N 117 59W
Lahaina Hawaiian Islands **115** Y18 20 23N 156 40W
Lahore Pakistan **95** C6 31 34N 74 22E
Lahti Finland **79** F3 61 00N 25 40E
Lai Chi Chong Hong Kong U.K. **98** C2 22 27N 114 17E
Lai Chi Wo Hong Kong U.K. **98** B3 22 32N 114 15E
Lajes Brazil **69** G7 27 48S 50 20W
Lajpat Nagar India **94** M4 28 34N 77 15E
La Junta Colorado U.S.A. **62** F4 37 59N 103 34W
Lake Calumet Harbor Illinois U.S.A. **53** B1 41 41N 87 35W
Lake Chabot California U.S.A. **49** C2 37 43N 122 06W
Lake Charles *tn.* Louisiana U.S.A. **63** H3 30 13N 93 13W
Lake City Michigan U.S.A. **35** C1 44 22N 85 12W
Lake Forest *tn.* Illinois U.S.A. **53** A4 42 15N 87 50W
Lake Forest Park Massachusetts U.S.A. **52** A2 42 18N 71 22W
Lake George New York U.S.A. **65** G6 43 27N 73 40W
Lakehurst New Jersey U.S.A. **65** F3 40 01N 74 19W
Lakeland Florida U.S.A. **63** J2 28 02N 81 59W
Lake Luzerne *tn.* New York U.S.A. **65** G6 43 19N 73 50W
Lakemba *i.* Fiji **114** V15 18 10S 178 49W
Lakemba Passage *sd.* Fiji **114** V15 18 10S 179 00W
Lake Merced California U.S.A. **49** B2 37 43N 122 29W
Lake Merritt California U.S.A. **49** B3 37 48N 122 15W
Lake Orion *tn.* Michigan U.S.A. **36** C3 42 47N 83 13W
Lakeview Oregon U.S.A. **62** B5 42 13N 120 21W
Lake View *tn.* New York U.S.A. **38** D1 42 42N 78 55W
Lake Wallenpaupack Pennsylvania U.S.A. **64** E4 41 25N 75 15W
Lakewood California U.S.A. **51** B2 33 49N 118 08W
Lakewood New Jersey U.S.A. **65** F3 40 00N 74 00W
Laksefjord *fj.* Norway **79** F5 70 40N 26 30E
Lakselv Norway **79** E5 70 03N 24 55E
Lakshadweep *admin.* India **95** C1 9 30N 73 00E
La Línea de la Concepción Spain **77** A2 36 10N 5 21W
Lalitpur India **95** D4 24 42N 78 24E
La Mancha *admin.* Spain **77** B2 39 10N 2 45W
La Manche *see* English Channel
Lamar Colorado U.S.A. **62** F4 38 04N 102 37W
Lamar Pennsylvania U.S.A. **64** C4 41 01N 77 33W
Lambaréné Gabon **106** H7 0 41S 10 13E
Lambasa Fiji **114** U16 16 25S 179 24E
Lambert Glacier Antarctica **117** 73 00S 70 00E
Lambertville New Jersey U.S.A. **64** F3 40 22N 74 57W
Lambeth *bor.* Greater London England **82** C2 51 30N 0 07W
Lamego Portugal **77** A3 41 05N 7 49W
Lamía Greece **81** D2 38 55N 22 26E
Lamma Island Hong Kong U.K. **98** B1 22 12N 114 08E
Lammermuir Hills Scotland **78** I7 55 50N 2 45W
Lampazos Mexico **66** D5 27 00N 100 30W
Lampedusa *i.* Italy **81** B2 35 00N 12 00E
Lam Tei Hong Kong U.K. **98** A2 22 25N 113 59E
Lamu Kenya **106** N7 2 17S 40 54E
Lanai *i.* Hawaiian Islands **115** Y18 20 50N 156 55W
Lanai City Hawaiian Islands **115** Y18 20 50N 156 56W
Lancang Jiang *r.* China **97** J5/K3 30 00N 98 00E
Lancaster England **78** I6 54 03N 2 48W
Lancaster Ohio U.S.A. **63** J4 39 43N 82 37W
Lancaster Pennsylvania U.S.A. **64** D3 40 01N 76 19W
Landes *geog. reg.* France **77** B3 44 15N 1 00E
Landianchang China **101** G1 39 58N 116 17E
Land's End *c.* England **78** F2 50 03N 5 44W
Landshut Germany **76** E4 48 31N 12 10E
Landskrona Sweden **79** C2 55 53N 12 50E
Langdon North Dakota U.S.A. **39** B1 48 46N 98 21W
Langer See *l.* Germany **83** G1 52 24N 13 36E
Langjökull *ice cap* Iceland **79** H6 64 45N 20 00W
Langon France **77** B3 44 33N 0 14W
Langres France **77** D4 47 53N 5 20E
Lan Hsü Taiwan **98** H5 22 04N 121 32E
Lannion France **76** B4 48 44N 3 27W
Lansdale Pennsylvania U.S.A. **64** E3 40 14N 75 17W
L'Anse Michigan U.S.A. **35** C2 46 45N 88 27W
Lansing Illinois U.S.A. **53** B1 41 33N 87 33W
Lansing Michigan U.S.A. **63** J5 42 44N 85 34W
Lantau Channel Hong Kong U.K. **98** A1 22 11N 113 52E
Lantau Island Hong Kong U.K. **98** A1 22 15N 113 56E
Lantau Peak Hong Kong U.K. **98** A1 22 15N 113 55E
Lanzarote *i.* Canary Islands **106** C13 29 00N 13 38W
Lanzhou China **97** K6 36 01N 103 45E
Laoag The Philippines **99** G7 18 14N 120 36E
Lao Cai Vietnam **97** K3 22 30N 103 57E
Laon France **76** C4 49 34N 3 37E
La Oroya Peru **68** B10 11 36S 75 54W
LAOS **99** C7
La Paz Bolivia **68** D9 16 30S 68 10W
La Paz Mexico **66** B4 24 10N 110 17W
Lapeer Michigan U.S.A. **36** C4 43 03N 83 09W
Laporte Pennsylvania U.S.A. **64** D4 41 25N 76 29W
Lappajärvi *l.* Finland **79** E3 63 13N 23 40E
Lappland *geog. reg.* Sweden/Finland **79** E4 67 30N 20 05E
La Perouse Australia **111** G2 33 59S 151 14E
La Pesca Mexico **66** E4 23 46N 97 47W
La Plata Argentina **69** F5 34 52S 57 55W
Laptev Sea Arctic Ocean **89** O11 76 00N 125 00E
Laptev Strait Russia **89** Q10 73 00N 141 00E
Lapua Finland **79** E3 62 57N 23 00E
La Puente California U.S.A. **51** C3 34 01N 117 58W
L'Aquila Italy **81** B3 42 22N 13 24E
Lär Iran **93** H4 27 42N 54 19E
Larache Morocco **106** D15 35 12N 6 10W
Laramie Wyoming U.S.A. **62** E5 41 20N 105 38W
Lärbro Sweden **80** C6 57 47N 18 50E
Laredo Texas U.S.A. **62** G2 27 32N 99 22W
La Rioja Argentina **69** D7 29 26S 66 50W
Lárisa Greece **81** D2 39 38N 22 25E
Larkana Pakistan **94** B5 27 32N 68 18E
Larnaca Cyprus **92** D5 34 54N 33 29E
Larne Northern Ireland **78** F6 54 51N 5 49W
la Rochelle France **77** B4 46 10N 1 10W
la Roche-sur-Yon France **77** B4 46 40N 1 25W
La Romana Dominican Republic **67** K3 18 27N 68 57W
Larsen Ice Shelf Antarctica **117** 67 00S 62 00W
Las Cruces New Mexico U.S.A. **62** E3 32 18N 106 47W
La Serena Chile **69** C7 29 54S 71 18W
la Seyne-sur-Mer France **77** D3 43 06N 5 53E
Lashio Myanmar **97** J3 22 58N 97 48E
Las Marismas *geog.reg.* Spain **77** A2 36 55N 6 00W
Las Palmas Canary Islands **106** B13 28 08N 15 27W
La Spezia Italy **81** A3 44 07N 9 48E
Las Vegas Nevada U.S.A. **62** C4 36 10N 115 10W
Las Vegas New Mexico U.S.A. **62** E4 35 36N 105 15W
Latacunga Ecuador **68** B12 0 58S 78 36W
Latina Italy **81** B3 41 28N 12 53E
Latur India **95** D3 18 24N 76 34E
LATVIA **79** E2
Launceston Australia **110** H1 41 25S 147 07E
Laurel Maryland U.S.A. **64** D2 39 06N 76 51W
Laurel Mississippi U.S.A. **63** I1 31 41N 89 09W
Laurence Harbor New Jersey U.S.A. **65** F3 40 27N 74 16W
Lausanne Switzerland **77** D4 46 32N 6 39E
Laut *i.* Indonesia **99** F3 4 00S 116 40E
Lautoka Fiji **114** T16 17 36S 177 28E
Laval France **77** B4 48 04N 0 45W
La Vega Dominican Republic **67** J3 19 15N 70 33W
Laverton Australia **110** C4 28 49S 122 25E
La Victoria Venezuela **68** D15 10 16N 67 21W
Lawndale California U.S.A. **51** A2 33 52N 118 21W
Lawrence Kansas U.S.A. **63** G4 38 58N 95 15W
Lawrence Massachusetts U.S.A. **65** J5 42 00N 71 00W
Lawrence Park *tn.* Pennsylvania U.S.A. **36** F3 42 08N 80 02W
Lawton Oklahoma U.S.A. **62** G3 34 36N 98 25W
Laylá Saudi Arabia **93** G3 22 16N 46 45E
Laysan *i.* Hawaiian Islands **114** I10 25 46N 171 44W
Lea *r.* England **78** K3 51 40N 0 20W
Leatherhead England **82** B2 51 18N 0 20W
LEBANON **92** D5
Lebanon Missouri U.S.A. **63** H4 37 40N 92 40W
Lebanon Pennsylvania U.S.A. **64** D3 40 21N 76 25W
Lebanon, Mount Pennsylvania U.S.A. **53** D1 40 21N 80 03W
le Blanc-Mesnil France **83** B2 48 56N 2 28E
Lebu Chile **69** C5 37 38S 73 43W
Lecce Italy **81** C3 40 21N 18 11E
Lee Massachusetts U.S.A. **65** G5 42 19N 73 15W
Lee *r.* Irish Republic **78** C3 51 50N 8 50W
Leeds England **78** J5 53 50N 1 35W
Leesburg Virginia U.S.A. **64** C2 39 00N 77 00W
Leeuwin, Cape Australia **110** B3 34 24S 115 09E
Leeward Islands Lesser Antilles **67** L3 17 30N 64 00W
Legnica Poland **80** C5 51 12N 16 10E
Leh Kashmir **95** D6 34 09N 77 35E
le Havre France **76** C4 49 30N 0 06E
Lehighton Pennsylvania U.S.A. **64** E3 40 50N 75 42W
Leicester England **78** J4 52 38N 1 05W
Leichhardt Australia **111** G2 33 53S 151 09E
Leiden Netherlands **76** C5 52 10N 4 30E
Leipzig Germany **76** E5 51 20N 12 25E
Leiria Portugal **77** A2 39 45N 8 49W
Leizhou Bandao *p.* China **97** M3 21 00N 110 00E
Lekkous *r.* Morocco **77** A1/2 35 00N 5 40W
le Mans France **77** C4 48 00N 0 12E
Lena *r.* Russia **89** O9 70 00N 125 00E
Leninabad *see* Khujand
Leninakan *see* Kumairi
Leningrad *see* St. Petersburg
Leningradskaya *r.s.* Antarctica **117** 69 30S 159 23E
Lenino Russia **88** M1 55 35N 37 10E
Leninogorsk Kazakhstan **91** N5 50 23N 83 32E
Leninsk-Kuznetskiy Russia **91** O5 54 44N 86 13E
Lenkoran' Azerbaijan **90** F2 38 45N 48 50E
Lenkoran' Russia **93** G6 38 45N 48 50E
Lens France **76** C5 50 26N 2 50E
Lensk Russia **89** N8 60 48N 114 55E
Leoben Austria **81** C4 47 23N 15 06E
Leominster Massachusetts U.S.A. **65** J5 42 31N 71 45W
Leon *r.* Texas U.S.A. **63** G3 32 00N 98 00W
León Spain **77** A3 42 35N 5 34W
Leonora Australia **110** C4 28 54S 121 20E
le Puy France **77** C3 45 03N 3 53E
le Raincy France **83** C2 48 54N 2 32E
Léré Chad **106** H9 9 41N 14 17E
Lérida *(Lleida)* Spain **77** C3 41 37N 0 38E
Lerwick Scotland **78** J12 60 09N 1 09W
Les Cayes Haiti **67** J3 18 15N 73 46W
Les Coudreaux France **83** C2 48 54N 2 36E
Leskovac Serbia Yugoslavia **81** D3 43 00N 43 21 57E
LESOTHO **107** K2
Lesser Antilles *is.* West Indies **67** K2/L3
Lesser Sunda Islands Indonesia **85** 8 00S 120 00E
les Sables-d'Olonne France **77** B4 46 30N 1 47W
les Ulis France **83** A1 48 41N 2 11E
Lésvos *i.* Greece **81** E2 39 00N 26 00E
Leszno Poland **80** C5 51 51N 16 35E
Leticia Colombia **68** C12 4 09S 69 57W
le Tréport France **76** C5 50 04N 1 22E
Leuven *(Louvain)* Belgium **76** C5 50 53N 4 42E
Levádhia Greece **81** D2 38 26N 22 53E
Lévêque, Cape Australia **110** C6 16 25S 122 55E
Levice Czechoslovakia **81** C4 48 14N 18 35E
Levin New Zealand **111** C2 40 37S 175 18E
Levkás *i.* Greece **81** D2 38 00N 20 00E
Levuka Fiji **114** U16 17 42N 178 50E
Lewis *i.* Scotland **78** E10 58 15N 6 30W
Lewisburg Pennsylvania U.S.A. **64** D3 40 58N 76 55W
Lewisham *bor.* Greater London England **82** C2 51 27N 0 00
Lewis Pass New Zealand **111** B2 42 22S 172 27E
Lewiston Idaho U.S.A. **62** C6 46 25N 117 00W
Lewiston Maine U.S.A. **63** L5 44 08N 70 14W
Lewiston New York U.S.A. **64** A6 43 11N 79 03W
Lewistown Montana U.S.A. **62** E6 47 04N 109 26W
Lewistown Pennsylvania U.S.A. **64** C3 40 37N 77 36W
Lexington Kentucky U.S.A. **63** J4 38 02N 84 30W
Lexington Massachusetts U.S.A. **52** A2 42 26N 71 58W
Lexington Heights *tn.* Michigan U.S.A. **36** D4 43 15N 82 32W
Leyte *i.* The Philippines **99** G6 11 00N 124 50E
Lezhë Albania **81** C3 41 47N 19 39E
Lhasa China **96** H4 29 41N 91 10E
Lhazê China **96** G4 29 08N 87 43E
Lianyungang China **97** N5 34 37N 119 10E
Liao *r.* China **84** 44 00N 121 00E
Liaoyang China **97** O7 41 16N 123 12E
Liaoyuan China **97** P7 42 53N 125 10E
Libby Montana U.S.A. **43** E1 48 25N 115 33W
Libenge Zaïre **106** I8 3 39N 18 39E
Liberal Kansas U.S.A. **62** F4 37 03N 100 56W
Liberec Czechoslovakia **80** C5 50 48N 15 05E
LIBERIA **106** D9
Liberty New York U.S.A. **65** F4 41 47N 74 46W
Liberty Reservoir Maryland U.S.A. **64** D2 39 25N 76 55W
Libourne France **77** B3 44 55N 0 14W
Libreville Gabon **106** G8 0 30N 9 25E
LIBYA **106** H13
Libyan Desert North Africa **106** J13 25 00N 25 00E
Libyan Plateau Egypt **106** J14 31 00N 26 00E
Lichinga Mozambique **107** M5 13 19S 35 13E
Lichtenberg Germany **83** G2 52 32N 13 30E
Lichtenrade Germany **83** F1 52 23N 13 22E
Lida Belarus **90** B5 53 05N 25 19E
Lidcombe Australia **111** G2 33 52S 151 03E
Lidköping Sweden **80** B6 58 30N 13 10E
LIECHTENSTEIN **81** A4
Liège Belgium **76** D5 50 38N 5 35E
Lienz Austria **81** B4 46 51N 12 50E
Liepāja Latvia **79** E2 56 30N 21 00E
Lifou *i.* Îles Loyauté Pacific Ocean **110** L5 21 00S 167 00E
Ligurian Sea Mediterranean Sea **77** D3 44 00N 9 00E
Lihue Hawaiian Islands **115** X18 21 59N 159 23W
Likasi Zaïre **107** K5 10 58S 26 47E
Liku Indonesia **99** D4 1 47N 109 19E
Lille France **76** C5 50 39N 3 05E
Lillehammer Norway **79** C3 61 06N 10 27E
Lilongwe Malawi **107** L5 13 58S 33 49E
Liluah India **94** K2 22 37N 88 20E
Lim *r.* Europe **81** C3 43 00N 19 00E
Lima Ohio U.S.A. **63** J5 40 43N 84 06W
Lima Peru **68** B10 12 06S 8 40W
Lima *r.* Portugal **77** A3 42 00N 8 30W
Limassol Cyprus **92** D5 34 04N 33 03E
Limay *r.* Argentina **69** D5 39 30S 69 30W
Limbe Cameroon **106** G8 3 58N 9 10E
Limeira Brazil **69** H8 22 34S 47 25W
Limerick Irish Republic **78** C4 52 04N 8 38W
Limestone New York U.S.A. **64** B5 42 02N 78 39W
Limfjorden *sd.* Denmark **80** A6 57 00N 8 50E
Límnos *i.* Greece **81** E2 39 00N 25 00E
Limoges France **77** C4 45 50N 1 15E
Limón Costa Rica **67** H2 10 00N 83 01W
Limoux France **77** C3 43 03N 2 13E
Limpopo *r.* Southern Africa **107** L3 22 30S 32 00E
Linares Mexico **66** E3 24 54N 99 38W
Linares Spain **77** B2 38 05N 3 38W
Lincoln England **78** K5 53 14N 0 33W
Lincoln Massachusetts U.S.A. **52** A2 42 24N 71 18W
Lincoln Nebraska U.S.A. **63** G5 40 49N 96 41W
Lincoln Park California U.S.A. **49** A3 37 47N 122 30W
Lincoln Park Illinois U.S.A. **53** B2 41 56N 87 37W
Lincoln Park Michigan U.S.A. **52** E1 42 13N 83 10W
Lincoln Wolds *hills* England **78** K5 53 25N 0 05W
Lincolnwood Illinois U.S.A. **53** B3 42 01N 87 44W
Linda Mar California U.S.A. **49** B2 37 35N 122 29W
Linden Guyana **68** F14 5 59N 58 19W
Linden New Jersey U.S.A. **50** B1 40 37N 74 13W
Lindenberg Germany **83** G2 52 37N 13 31E
Lindfield Australia **111** G2 33 47S 151 10E
Lindis Pass New Zealand **111** A2 44 33S 169 43E
Line Islands Kiribati **115** K7 0 00 160 00W
Linglestown Pennsylvania U.S.A. **64** D3 40 20N 76 50W
Ling Tong Mei Hong Kong U.K. **98** B2 22 29N 114 06E
Linhares Brazil **68** J9 19 22S 40 04W
Linköping Sweden **79** D2 58 25N 15 35E
Linsell Sweden **79** C3 62 10N 13 50E
Linstead Jamaica **67** Q8 18 08N 77 02W
Linton North Dakota U.S.A. **62** F6 46 17N 100 14W
Linxia China **97** K6 35 31N 103 08E
Linz Austria **81** B4 48 19N 14 18E
Lion Rock *mt.* Hong Kong U.K. **98** C2 22 21N 114 11E
Lipetsk Russia **90** D5 52 37N 39 36E
Lisas, Point Trinidad and Tobago **66** T9 10 22N 61 37W
Lisboa *(Lisbon)* Portugal **77** A2 38 44N 9 08W
Lisbon *see* Lisboa
Lisburn Northern Ireland **78** E6 54 31N 6 03W
Lisburn, Cape Alaska U.S.A. **10** B6 68 54N 166 18W
Lisianski *i.* Hawaiian Islands **114** I10 26 04N 173 58W
Lisichansk Ukraine **90** D4 48 53N 38 25E
Lisieux France **76** C4 49 09N 0 14E
Lismore Australia **110** I4 28 48S 153 17E
Litani *r.* Lebanon **92** O11 33 35N 35 40E
Lithgow Australia **110** I3 33 30S 150 09E
LITHUANIA **80** D6
Little Aden Yemen Republic **93** F1 12 47N 44 55E
Little Andaman *i.* Andaman Islands **95** G2 10 30N 92 40E
Little Bitter Lake *see* Buheirat-Murrat-el-Sughra
Little Calumet River Indiana U.S.A. **53** C1 42 19N 87 26W
Little Colorado *r.* Arizona U.S.A. **62** D4 36 00N 111 00W
Little Falls *tn.* Minnesota U.S.A. **63** H6 45 58N 94 20W
Little Fork River Minnesota U.S.A. **35** B2 48 00N 93 30W
Little Minch *sd.* Scotland **78** E9 57 45N 6 30W
Little Missouri *r.* U.S.A. **62** F6 46 00N 104 00W
Little Nicobar *i.* Nicobar Islands **95** G1 7 00N 94 00E
Little Rock Kansas U.S.A. **63** H3 34 42N 92 17W
Little Sioux *r.* U.S.A. **63** G5 42 00N 96 00W
Little Snake *r.* U.S.A. **62** E5 41 00N 108 00W
Little Traverse Bay Michigan U.S.A. **36** A6 45 25N 85 00W
Little Valley *tn.* New York U.S.A. **64** B5 42 15N 78 47W
Liuzhou China **97** L3 24 17N 109 15E
Liverpool Australia **111** F2 33 56S 150 55E
Liverpool England **78** I5 53 25N 2 55W
Liverpool Pennsylvania U.S.A. **64** C3 40 34N 77 01W
Livingston Montana U.S.A. **62** D6 45 40N 110 33W
Livingstone *see* Maramba
Livingston Island South Shetland Islands **69** E0 62 38S 60 30W
Livonia Michigan U.S.A. **52** D2 42 25N 83 23W
Livorno Italy **81** B3 43 33N 10 18E
Liwale Tanzania **107** M6 9 47S 38 00E
Lizard Point England **78** F1 49 56N 5 13W
Ljubljana Slovenia **81** B4 46 04N 14 30E
Ljungan *r.* Sweden **79** D3 62 35N 16 00E
Ljungby Sweden **80** B6 56 49N 13 55E
Ljus Sweden **79** D3 61 57N 16 05E
Ljusnan *r.* Sweden **79** D3 62 05N 15 10E
Llanelli Wales **78** G3 51 42N 4 10W
Lleida *see* Lérida
Lobatse Botswana **107** K2 25 11S 25 40E
Lobito Angola **107** H5 12 20S 13 34E
Lobos, Point California U.S.A. **49** A3 37 47N 122 31W
Loch Linnhe *b.* Scotland **78** F8 56 35N 5 25W
Loch Lomond *l.* Scotland **78** G8 56 10N 4 35W
Loch Ness *l.* Scotland **78** G9 57 02N 4 30W
Loch Shin *l.* Scotland **78** G10 58 05N 4 30W
Loch Tay *l.* Scotland **78** G8 56 31N 4 10W
Lockhart Texas U.S.A. **63** G2 29 54N 97 41W
Lock Haven Pennsylvania U.S.A. **64** C4 41 00N 77 00W
Lockport New York U.S.A. **64** B6 43 11N 78 39W
Lod Israel **92** O10 31 57N 34 54E
Lodeynoye Pole Russia **90** C7 60 43N 33 30E
Lodge Creek Canada/U.S.A. **41** C1 49 15N 110 05W
Lodi India **94** L4 28 35N 77 13E
Łódź Poland **80** C5 51 49N 19 28E
Lofoten Islands Norway **79** C4 68 30N 15 00E
Logan Utah U.S.A. **62** D5 41 45N 111 50W
Logan, Mount Washington U.S.A. **42** H4 48 33N 120 55W
Logone *r.* Chad **106** H10 11 00N 15 00E
Logroño Spain **77** B3 42 28N 2 26W
Loir *r.* France **77** C4 46 45N 0 35E
Loire *r.* France **77** C4 47 20N 1 20W
Loja Ecuador **68** B12 3 59S 79 16W
Loja Spain **77** B2 37 10N 4 09W
Lokan tekojärvi *l.* Finland **79** F4 68 00N 27 30E
Lok Ma Chau Hong Kong U.K. **98** B3 22 31N 114 05E
Lokoja Nigeria **106** G9 7 49N 6 44E
Lol *r.* Sudan **106** K9 9 00N 28 00E
Lolland *i.* Denmark **80** B5 54 45N 12 20E
Loloda Indonesia **99** H4 1 39N 127 37E
Lomblen *i.* Indonesia **99** G2 8 00S 123 30E
Lombok *i.* Indonesia **99** F2 8 29S 116 40E
Lomé Togo **106** F9 6 10N 1 21E
Lomela Zaïre **106** J7 2 19S 23 15E
Lomela *r.* Zaïre **106** J7 3 00S 23 00E
Lomonosov Ridge Arctic Ocean **116** 87 00N 60 00W
Łomza Poland **80** D5 53 11N 22 04E
London England **78** K3 51 30N 0 10W
London Colney England **82** B3 51 44N 0 18W
Londonderry Northern Ireland **78** D6 54 59N 7 19W
Londrina Brazil **69** G8 23 18S 51 13W
Long Bay Barbados **66** W12 13 05N 59 30W
Long Beach *beach* New Jersey U.S.A. **65** G3 40 35N 73 40W
Long Beach *tn.* California U.S.A. **51** B2 33 47N 118 15W
Long Beach *tn.* New York U.S.A. **50** D1 40 35N 73 40W
Long Beach Island New York U.S.A. **65** F2 39 40N 74 10W
Long Branch New Jersey U.S.A. **65** F3 40 17N 73 59W
Longfellow Mountains Maine U.S.A. **37** Q6 45 10N 70 00W
Longford Irish Republic **78** D5 53 44N 7 47W
Long Island The Bahamas **67** J4 23 20N 75 00W
Long Island Massachusetts U.S.A. **52** C2 42 20N 70 58W
Long Island New York U.S.A. **65** G3 40 50N 73 00W
Long Island City New York U.S.A. **50** C2 40 46N 73 55W
Long Island Sound New York/Connecticut U.S.A **65** G4 41 50N 73 00W
Longreach Australia **110** G5 23 30S 144 15E
Longview Texas U.S.A. **63** H3 32 20N 94 45W
Longwy France **76** D4 49 32N 5 46E
Loop Head *c.* Irish Republic **78** B4 52 30N 9 55W
Lopez, Cape Gabon **106** G7 0 36S 8 45E
Lopez Island Washington U.S.A. **42** H4 48 30N 122 54W
Lop Nur *l.* China **96** H7 40 15N 90 20E
Lopphavet *sd.* Norway **79** E5 70 30N 21 00E
Lorain Ohio U.S.A. **63** J5 41 28N 82 11W
Lorca Spain **77** B2 37 40N 1 41W
Lord Howe Rise Pacific Ocean **114** G5 27 30S 162 00E
Lorica Colombia **67** I1 9 14N 75 50W
Lorient France **77** B4 47 45N 3 21W
Los Alamos Mexico U.S.A. **62** E4 35 52N 106 19W
Los Altos California U.S.A. **49** C1 37 24N 122 07W
Los Angeles California U.S.A. **51** A3 34 00N 118 15W
Los Angeles Chile **69** C5 37 28S 72 23W
Los Angeles River California U.S.A. **51** B2 33 50N 118 13W
Los Mochis Mexico **66** C5 25 48N 109 00W
Los Teques Venezuela **68** D15 10 25N 67 01W
Lost River West Virginia U.S.A. **64** B2 39 10N 78 35W
Lot *r.* France **77** C3 44 35N 1 10E
Lo-tung Taiwan **98** H7 24 00N 121 00E
Loubomo Congo **107** H7 4 09S 12 47E
Loudéac France **76** B4 48 11N 2 45W
Lough Allen *l.* Irish Republic **78** C6 54 15N 8 00W
Lough Conn *l.* Irish Republic **78** B6 54 05N 9 10W
Lough Corrib *l.* Irish Republic **78** B5 53 10N 9 10W
Lough Derg *l.* Irish Republic **78** C4 54 35N 7 55W
Lough Foyle *b.* Ireland **78** D7 55 10N 7 10W
Lough Mask *l.* Irish Republic **78** B5 53 40N 9 30W
Lough Neagh *l.* Northern Ireland **78** E6 54 35N 6 30W
Lough Ree *l.* Irish Republic **78** D5 53 35N 8 00W
Loughton England **82** D3 51 39N 0 03E
Louisiade Archipelago *is.* Papua New Guinea **110** I7 12 00S 153 00E
Louisiana *state* U.S.A. **63** H3 32 00N 92 00W
Louisville Kentucky U.S.A. **64** I4 38 13N 85 48W
Lourdes France **77** B3 43 06N 0 02W

Louvain *see* Leuven
Lowell Massachusetts U.S.A. 65 J5 42 38N 71 19W
Lower Bay New York U.S.A. 50 B1 40 32N 74 04W
Lower Crystal Springs Reservoir California U.S.A. 49 B2 37 32N 122 24W
Lower Hutt New Zealand 111 B2 41 12S 174 54E
Lower Lough Erne *l.* Northern Ireland 78 D6 54 25N 7 45W
Lower Red Lake Minnesota U.S.A. 63 H6 48 00N 95 00W
Lower River Rouge Michigan U.S.A. 52 D2 42 17N 83 22W
Lower River Rouge Park Michigan U.S.A. 52 D2 42 17N 83 22W
Lower Tunguska *see* Nizhnyaya Tunguska
Lowestoft England 78 M4 52 29N 1 45E
Łowicz Poland 80 C5 52 06N 19 55E
Lo Wu Hong Kong U.K. 98 B3 22 32N 114 06E
Loyalsock Creek Pennsylvania U.S.A. 64 D4 41 25N 76 50W
Lualaba *r.* Zaïre 107 K7 4 00S 26 30E
Luanda Angola 107 H6 8 50S 13 15E
Luang Prabang Laos 99 C7 19 53N 102 10E
Luangwa *r.* Zambia 107 L5 12 00S 32 30E
Luanshya Zambia 107 K5 13 09S 28 24E
Luarca Spain 77 A3 43 33N 6 31W
Luau Angola 107 J5 10 42S 22 12E
Lubango Angola 107 H5 14 55S 13 30E
Lubbock Texas U.S.A. 62 F3 33 35N 101 53W
Lübeck Germany 76 E5 53 52N 10 40E
Lubilash *r.* Zaïre 107 J6 4 00S 24 00E
Lublin Poland 80 D5 51 18N 22 31E
Lubumbashi Zaïre 107 K5 11 41S 27 29E
Lucea Jamaica 67 P8 18 26N 78 11W
Lucena Spain 77 B2 37 25N 4 29W
Luckenwalde Germany 76 E5 52 05N 13 11E
Lucknow India 95 E5 26 50N 80 54E
Lüderitz Namibia 107 I2 26 38S 15 10E
Ludhiana India 95 D6 30 56N 75 52E
Ludington Michigan U.S.A. 35 C1 43 58N 86 27W
Ludlow Vermont U.S.A. 65 I6 43 22N 72 39W
Ludvika Sweden 79 D3 60 08N 15 14E
Ludwigsfelde Germany 83 F1 52 18N 13 16E
Luena Angola 107 I5 11 47S 19 52E
Luen Wo Hui Hong Kong U.K. 98 B3 22 30N 114 08E
Lufkin Texas U.S.A. 63 H3 31 21N 94 47W
Lugansk *(Voroshilovgrad)* Ukraine 90 D4 48 35N 39 20E
Lugo Spain 77 A3 43 00N 7 33W
Lugoj Romania 81 D4 45 41N 21 57E
Luguoqiao China 101 F1 39 51N 116 13E
Luiana *r.* Angola 107 J4 17 00S 21 00E
Lu-kang Taiwan 98 G7 24 04N 120 23E
Lukens, Mount California U.S.A. 51 B1 34 16N 118 14W
Luk Keng Hong Kong U.K. 98 B3 22 32N 114 13E
Łuków Poland 80 D5 51 57N 22 21E
Luleå Sweden 79 E4 65 35N 22 10E
Lule älv *r.* Sweden 79 E4 66 15N 20 30E
Lüleburgaz Turkey 80 E3 41 26N 27 22E
Lulua *r.* Zaïre 107 J6 9 00S 22 00E
Lumberton North Carolina U.S.A. 63 K3 34 37N 79 03W
Lummi Island Washington U.S.A. 42 H4 48 42N 122 40W
Lund Sweden 79 C2 55 42N 13 10E
Lundy *i.* England 78 G3 51 11N 4 40W
Lune *r.* England 78 I6 54 07N 2 40W
Lüneburg Germany 76 E5 53 15N 10 24E
Lünen Germany 76 K3 51 38N 7 31E
Lunéville France 76 D4 48 35N 6 30E
Lung Kwu Chau *i.* Hong Kong U.K. 98 A2 22 23N 113 53E
Lungue Bungo *r.* Angola/Zambia 107 J5 13 00S 22 00E
Luni *r.* India 95 C5 26 00N 73 00E
Luninets Belarus 80 E5 52 18N 26 50E
Luoshan China 97 M5 31 12N 114 30E
Luoyang China 97 M5 34 47N 112 26E
Lurgan Northern Ireland 78 E6 54 28N 6 20W
Lurio *r.* Mozambique 107 M5 14 00S 39 00E
Lusaka Zambia 107 K4 15 26S 28 20E
Lusambo Zaïre 107 J7 4 59S 23 26E
Lushun China 97 O6 38 46N 121 15E
Lü Tao *i.* Taiwan 98 H5 22 38N 121 30E
Luton England 78 K3 51 53N 0 25W
Lutsk Ukraine 80 E5 50 42N 25 15E
Lützow-Holm Bay Antarctica 117 69 00S 38 00E
Luuq Somalia 106 M8 2 52N 42 34E
LUXEMBOURG 76 D4
Luxembourg Luxembourg 76 D4 49 37N 6 08E
Luxor Egypt 92 D4 25 41N 32 24E
Luzern Switzerland 77 D4 47 03N 8 17E
Luzhou China 97 L4 28 55N 105 25E
Luziânia Brazil 68 H9 16 16S 47 57W
Luzon *i.* The Philippines 99 G7 16 30N 121 30E
Luzon Strait China/Philippines 99 G8 20 00N 121 30E
L'vov Ukraine 90 A4 49 50N 24 00E
Lycksele Sweden 79 D3 64 34N 18 40E
Lyme Bay England 78 H2 50 40N 2 55W
Łyna *r.* Poland 80 D5 54 00N 20 00E
Lynchburg Virginia U.S.A. 63 K4 37 24N 79 09W
Lynden Washington U.S.A. 42 H4 48 56N 122 28W
Lynn Massachusetts U.S.A. 52 C2 42 29N 70 57W
Lynn Canal *sd.* Alaska U.S.A. 42 A3 58 50N 135 05W
Lynn Woods Reservation Massachusetts U.S.A. 52 C2 42 29N 70 59W
Lyon France 77 C4 45 46N 4 50E
Lyons Illinois U.S.A. 53 A2 41 48N 87 49W
Lyons New York U.S.A. 64 D6 43 04N 76 59W
Lyttelton New Zealand 111 B2 43 36S 172 42E
Lyubertsy Russia 90 D6 55 38N 37 58E
Lyublino Russia 88 M1 55 38N 37 44E

M

Ma'ān Jordan 92 O10 30 11N 35 43E
Maanselka *geog. reg.* Finland 79 F4 68 45N 25 10E
Ma'anshan China 97 N5 31 49N 118 32E
Maastricht Netherlands 76 C5 50 51N 5 42E
Mabalane Mozambique 107 L3 23 51S 32 38E
Mabashi Japan 101 C4 35 48N 139 55E
McAlester Oklahoma U.S.A. 63 G3 34 56N 95 46W
McAllen Texas U.S.A. 63 G2 26 13N 98 15W
Macao *territory* Portugal 97 M3 22 10N 113 40E
Macapá Brazil 68 G13 0 04N 51 04W
McComb Mississippi U.S.A. 63 H3 31 13N 90 29W
McConnellsburg Pennsylvania U.S.A. 64 B2 39 00N 78 00W
McCook Nebraska U.S.A. 62 F5 40 13N 100 35W
McDonald, Lake Montana U.S.A. 41 C1 48 40N 113 50W
Macdonnell Ranges *mts.* Australia 110 E5 24 00S 132 30E
Macedonia Yugoslavia 81 D3
Maceió Brazil 68 J11 9 40S 35 44W
Macerata Italy 81 B3 43 18N 13 27E
McGrath Alaska U.S.A. 10 D5 62 58N 155 40W
Machala Ecuador 68 B12 3 20S 79 57W
Machanga Mozambique 107 L3 20 58N 35 01E
Machias Maine U.S.A. 33 C1 44 00N 67 00W
Machida Japan 101 A3 35 32N 139 27E
Machilipatnam India 95 E3 16 12N 81 11E
Machiques Venezuela 68 C15 10 04N 72 37W
Mackay Australia 110 H5 21 10S 149 10E
Mackay, Lake Australia 110 D5 22 30S 128 00E
McKee City New Jersey U.S.A. 65 F2 39 26N 74 40W
McKeesport Pennsylvania U.S.A. 53 E1 40 21N 79 52W
McKees Rocks Pennsylvania U.S.A. 53 D1 40 29N 80 29W
Mackinac, Straits of Michigan U.S.A. 36 B6 45 48N 84 43W
Mackinaw City Michigan U.S.A. 63 J6 45 47N 84 43W
McKinley, Mount Alaska U.S.A. 10 E5 62 02N 151 01W
McKinney Texas U.S.A. 63 G3 33 14N 96 37W
McLaren Park California U.S.A. 49 B2 37 43N 122 25W
Macleod, Lake Australia 110 A5 24 00S 113 30E
McMurdo *r.s.* Antarctica 117 77 51S 166 40E
McMurdo Sound Antarctica 117 75 00S 165 00E
Macomb County Michigan U.S.A. 52 F2 42 27N 82 59W
Mâcon France 77 C4 46 18N 4 50E
Macon Georgia U.S.A. 63 J3 32 49N 83 37W
McPherson Kansas U.S.A. 63 G4 38 22N 97 41W
Macquarie Island Southern Ocean 114 F2 54 29S 158 58E
Macquarie Ridge Southern Ocean 114 F2 55 00S 160 00E
Macuro Venezuela 66 S10 10 38N 61 55W
Mādāba Jordan 92 O10 31 44N 35 48E
MADAGASCAR 107 O3
Madagascar Basin Indian Ocean 112 E4 25 00S 55 00E
Madagascar Ridge Indian Ocean 112 D3/4 30 00S 45 00E
Madang Papua New Guinea 110 H8 5 14S 145 45E
Madden Lake Panama 67 Y2 9 15N 79 35W
Madeira Islands Atlantic Ocean 106 B14 32 45N 17 00W
Madhya *admin.* India 95 D4 23 00N 78 30E
Madhyamgrām India 94 K2 22 41N 88 27E
Madīnat ash Sha'b Yemen Republic 93 F1 12 50N 44 56E
Madison Maine U.S.A. 37 R5 44 48N 69 53W
Madison Wisconsin U.S.A. 63 I5 43 04N 89 22W
Madison Heights Michigan U.S.A. 52 E2 42 29N 83 05W
Madium Indonesia 99 E2 7 37S 111 33E
Mado Gashi Kenya 106 M8 0 45N 39 11E
Madras India 95 E2 13 05N 80 18E
Madrid Spain 77 B3 40 25N 3 43W
Madura *i.* Indonesia 99 E2 7 10S 113 30E
Madurai India 95 D1 9 55N 78 07E
Madureira Brazil 69 P2 22 52S 43 21W
Maebashi Japan 100 C2 36 24N 139 04E
Mae Nam Mun *r.* Thailand 97 K2 15 10N 102 05E
Mae Nam Ping *r.* Thailand 97 J2 18 00N 104 00E
Mae Sot Thailand 97 J2 16 44N 98 32E
Maevantanana Madagascar 107 O4 16 57S 46 50E
Mafia Island Tanzania 107 M6 7 00S 39 00E
Mafikeng Republic of South Africa 107 K2 25 53S 25 39E
Mafraq Jordan 92 P11 32 20N 36 12E
Magadan Russia 89 R7 59 38N 150 50E
Magangué Colombia 68 C14 9 14N 74 46W
Magdalena Mexico 66 B6 30 38N 110 59W
Magdeburg Germany 76 E5 52 08N 11 37E
Magelang Indonesia 99 E2 7 28S 110 11E
Maghâgha Egypt 92 D4 28 39N 30 50E
Magnitogorsk Russia 91 H5 53 28N 59 06E
Magwe Myanmar 96 J2 20 08N 94 55E
Mahadeo Hills India 95 D4 22 30N 78 30E
Mahajanga Madagascar 107 O4 15 40S 46 20E
Mahalapye Botswana 107 K3 23 05S 26 52E
Mahanadi *r.* India 95 E4 21 00N 84 00E
Maharashtra *admin.* India 95 C3/D3 19 30N 75 00E
Maha Sarakham Thailand 97 K2 16 12N 103 16E
Mahdia Tunisia 81 B2 35 29N 11 03E
Mahia Peninsula New Zealand 111 C3 39 10S 138 00E
Mahlow Germany 83 F1 52 22N 13 24E
Mahón Balearic Islands 77 C2 39 54N 4 15E
Mahoning River Ohio U.S.A. 36 F2 41 05N 80 40W
Mahrauli India 94 L4 28 30N 77 11E
Maidstone England 78 L3 51 17N 0 32E
Maiduguri Nigeria 106 H10 11 53N 13 16E
Maikala Range *mts.* India 95 E4 22 30N 81 30E
Maila The Philippines 99 G6 14 37N 120 58E
Main *r.* Germany 76 E5 50 00N 8 00E
Maine *state* U.S.A. 63 M6 45 00N 70 00W
Mainland *i.* Scotland 78 H11 59 00N 3 15W
Mainland *i.* Scotland 78 J12 60 15N 1 20W
Maintirano Madagascar 107 N4 18 01S 44 03E
Mainz Germany 76 D5 50 00N 8 16E
Mai Po Lo Wai Hong Kong U.K. 98 B2 22 29N 114 03E
Maiquetía Venezuela 68 D15 10 38N 66 59W
Maisons-Laffitte France 83 A2 48 57N 2 09E
Maitland Australia 110 I3 32 33S 151 33E
Maizuru Japan 100 G2 35 30N 135 20E
Majene Indonesia 99 F3 3 33S 118 59E
Maji Ethiopia 106 M9 6 12N 35 32E
Majiuqiao China 101 H1 39 45N 116 33E
Majorca *see* Mallorca
Makabe Japan 100 M3 36 15N 140 05E
Makassar Strait Indonesia 99 F3/F4 2 00S 117 30E
Makat Kazakhstan 91 G4 47 38N 53 16E
Makeni Sierra Leone 106 C9 8 57N 12 02W
Makeyevka Ukraine 90 D4 48 01N 38 00E
Makgadikgadi Salt Pan Botswana 107 K3 21 00S 26 00E
Makhachkala Russia 90 F3 42 59N 47 30E
Makkah *(Mecca)* Saudi Arabia 92 E3 21 26N 39 49E
Makó Hungary 81 D4 46 11N 20 30E
Makoku Gabon 106 H8 0 38N 12 47E
Makran *geog. reg.* Iran/Pakistan 93 J4 25 55N 61 30E
Makung *(Penghu)* Taiwan 98 F6 23 35N 119 33E
Makurdi Nigeria 106 G9 7 44N 8 35E
Malabar Coast India 95 C2/D1 12 00N 74 00E
Malabo Equatorial Guinea 106 G8 3 45N 8 48E
Malacca, Strait of Indonesia/Malaysia 99 B5/C4
Malaga New Jersey U.S.A. 64 E2 39 34N 75 03W
Málaga Spain 77 B2 3 43N 4 25W
Malaita *i.* Solomon Islands 110 K8 9 00S 161 00E
Malakal Sudan 106 L9 9 31N 31 40E
Malang Indonesia 99 E2 7 59S 112 45E
Malanje Angola 107 I6 9 32S 16 20E
Mälar, Lake *see* Mälaren
Mälaren *(Lake Mälar) l.* Sweden 79 D2 59 30N 17 00E
Malatya Turkey 92 E6 38 22N 38 18E
MALAWI 107 L5
Malawi, Lake *see* Nyasa Lake
Malaya *admin.* Malaysia 99 C4 4 00N 102 30E
Malay Peninsula Asia 84 5 00N 102 00E
MALAYSIA 99 C5/E5
Malbork Poland 80 C5 54 02N 19 01E
Malden Massachusetts U.S.A. 52 B2 42 24N 71 04W
Malden Island Pacific Ocean 115 K7 4 03S 154 59W
Maldive Archipelago *is.* Indian Ocean 84 5 00N 73 00E
MALDIVES 95 C1
Maldonado Uruguay 69 G6 34 57S 54 59W
Malegaon India 95 C4 20 32N 74 38E
Malekula *i.* Vanuatu 110 L6 16 30S 167 20E
Malema Mozambique 107 M5 14 57S 37 25E
MALI 106 D10
Malines *see* Mechelen
Malin Head *c.* Irish Republic 78 D7 55 30N 7 20W
Ma Liu Shui Hong Kong U.K. 98 C2 22 25N 114 12E
Mallaig Scotland 78 F9 57 00N 5 50W
Mallawi Egypt 92 D4 27 44N 30 50E
Mallorca *(Majorca) i.* Balearic Islands 77 C2 39 50N 2 30E
Malmédy Belgium 76 D5 50 26N 6 02E
Malmö Sweden 79 C2 55 35N 13 00E
Malonga Zaïre 107 J5 10 26S 23 10E
Måløy Norway 79 B3 61 57N 5 06E
Malpelo *i.* Colombia 68 A13 4 00N 81 35W
MALTA 81 B2
Malta Montana U.S.A. 62 E6 48 22N 107 51W
Malta *i.* Mediterranean Sea 81 B2 35 00N 14 00E
Maluku *is.* Indonesia 99 H3 1 00S 127 00E
Malviya Nagar India 94 L4 28 32N 77 12E
Mamanutha Group *is.* Fiji 114 T16 17 40S 177 00E
Mamaroneck New York U.S.A. 50 D2 40 57N 73 43W
Mamba Japan 100 K3 36 07N 138 54E
Mambasa Zaïre 106 K8 1 20N 29 05E
Man Côte d'Ivoire 106 D9 7 31N 7 37W
Manacapuru Brazil 68 E12 3 16S 60 37W
Manacor Balearic Islands 77 C2 39 35N 3 12E
Manado Indonesia 99 G4 1 32N 124 55E
Managua Nicaragua 67 G2 12 06N 86 18W
Manali India 95 D6 32 12N 77 06E
Manasquan New Jersey U.S.A. 65 F3 40 07N 74 02W
Manaus Brazil 68 F12 3 06S 60 00W
Manchester Connecticut U.S.A. 65 H4 41 47N 72 31W
Manchester England 78 I5 53 30N 2 15W
Manchester Massachusetts U.S.A. 65 K5 42 34N 70 46W
Manchester Michigan U.S.A. 36 B3 42 10N 84 01W
Manchester New Hampshire U.S.A. 65 J5 42 59N 71 28W
Manchester Tennessee U.S.A. 63 I4 35 29N 86 04W
Manchester Center Vermont U.S.A. 65 G6 43 11N 73 03W
Mandal Norway 79 B2 58 02N 7 30E
Mandalay Myanmar 96 J3 21 57N 96 04E
Mandeville Jamaica 67 Q8 18 02N 77 31W
Mandvi India 94 B4 22 50N 69 25E
Mandya India 95 D2 12 34N 76 55E
Manfredonia Italy 81 C3 41 37N 15 55E
Mangalore India 95 C2 12 54N 74 51E
Mango *i.* Fiji 114 V16 17 20S 179 20W
Mangoky *r.* Madagascar 107 N3 22 00S 45 00E
Mangui China 97 O9 52 05N 122 17E
Manhasset New York U.S.A. 50 D2 40 48N 73 41W
Manhattan Kansas U.S.A. 63 G4 39 11N 96 35W
Manhattan New York U.S.A. 50 C2 40 48N 73 58W
Manhattan Beach *tn.* California U.S.A. 51 A2 33 53N 118 24W
Mania *r.* Madagascar 107 N4 19 30S 50 30E
Manica Mozambique 107 L4 18 56S 32 52E
Manicoré Brazil 68 E11 5 48S 61 16W
Manikpur India 94 J2 22 32N 88 12E
Manipur *admin.* India 95 G4 24 30N 94 00E
Manipur *r.* Myanmar/India 95 G4 23 30N 93 00E
Manisa Turkey 80 E2 38 36N 27 29E
Manistee Michigan U.S.A. 35 C1 44 14N 86 20W
Manistee River Michigan U.S.A. 35 C1 44 20N 85 50W
Manistique Michigan U.S.A. 35 C2 45 58N 86 17W
Manistique Lake Michigan U.S.A. 36 A7 46 15N 85 50W
Manitowoc Wisconsin U.S.A. 63 I5 44 04N 87 40W
Manizales Colombia 68 B13 5 03N 75 32W
Manjra *r.* India 95 D3 18 30N 76 00E
Man Kam To Hong Kong U.K. 98 B3 22 32N 114 07E
Mankato Minnesota U.S.A. 63 H5 44 10N 94 00W
Manly Australia 111 H2 33 48S 151 17E
Mannar Sri Lanka 95 D1 8 58N 79 54E
Mannar, Gulf of India/Sri Lanka 95 D1 8 30N 79 00E
Mannheim Germany 76 D5 49 30N 8 28E
Manokwari Indonesia 99 I3 0 53S 134 05E
Manresa Spain 77 C3 41 43N 1 50E
Mansfield Massachusetts U.S.A. 65 J5 42 02N 71 12W
Mansfield Ohio U.S.A. 63 J5 40 46N 82 31W
Mansfield Pennsylvania U.S.A. 64 C4 41 47N 77 05W
Manta Ecuador 68 B12 0 59S 80 44W
Mantes-la-Jolie France 76 C4 48 59N 1 43E
Mantova Italy 81 B4 45 10N 10 47E
Manukau Harbour New Zealand 111 B3 37 00S 174 30E
Manyoni Tanzania 107 L6 5 46S 34 50E
Manzanares Spain 77 B2 39 00N 3 23W
Manzanilla Bay Trinidad and Tobago 66 T10 10 40N 61 55W
Manzanilla Point Trinidad and Tobago 66 T10 10 31N 61 01W
Manzanillo Cuba 67 I4 20 21N 77 21W
Manzanillo Mexico 66 D3 19 00N 104 20W
Maoming China 97 M3 21 50N 110 56E
Ma On Shan Hong Kong U.K. 98 C2 22 26N 114 13E
Ma On Shan *mt.* Hong Kong U.K. 98 C2 22 24N 114 16E
Maple Heights *tn.* Ohio U.S.A. 36 E2 41 24N 81 35W
Maputo Mozambique 107 L2 25 58S 32 35E
Marabá Brazil 68 H11 5 23S 49 10W
Maracaibo Venezuela 68 C15 10 44N 71 37W
Maracay Venezuela 68 D15 10 20N 67 28W
Maradi Niger 106 G10 13 29N 7 10E
Maramba *(Livingstone)* Zambia 107 K4 17 50S 25 53E
Maranhão *admin.* Brazil 68 H11 5 20S 46 00W
Marathon New York U.S.A. 64 D5 42 25N 76 04W
Maraval Trinidad and Tobago 66 T10 10 42N 61 31W
Marbella Spain 77 B2 36 31N 4 53W
Marble Bar *tn.* Australia 110 B5 21 16S 119 45E
Marble Canyon *tn.* Arizona U.S.A. 62 D4 36 50N 111 38W
Marblehead Massachusetts U.S.A. 52 C3 42 30N 70 50W
Marburg Germany 76 D5 50 49N 8 36E
Marchfield Barbados 66 W12 13 07N 59 129W
Marcus Island Pacific Ocean 114 F10 24 30N 157 30E
Mardan Pakistan 95 C6 34 14N 72 05E
Mar del Plata Argentina 69 F5 38 00S 57 32W
Mardin Turkey 92 F6 37 19N 40 43E
Mare *i.* Îles Loyauté 110 L5 22 00S 167 30E
Margai Caka *l.* China 95 F7 35 00N 87 00E
Margate England 78 M3 51 24N 1 24E
Margilan Uzbekistan 91 L3 40 30N 71 45E
Maria Elena Chile 69 D8 22 18S 69 40W
Marianas Trench Pacific Ocean 114 E9 16 00N 147 30E
Marias River Montana U.S.A. 41 C1 48 25N 111 50W
Maria van Diemen, Cape New Zealand 111 B4 34 29S 117 39E
Maribor Slovenia 81 C4 46 34N 15 38E
Mariehamn Finland 79 D3 60 05N 19 55E
Mariental Namibia 107 I3 24 36S 17 59E
Mariestad Sweden 80 B6 58 44N 13 50E
Marietta Pennsylvania U.S.A. 64 D3 40 04N 76 33W
Mariinsk Russia 91 O6 56 14N 87 45E
Marijampole *(Kapsukas)* Lithuania 80 D6 54 31N 23 20E
Marília Brazil 69 G8 22 13S 49 58W
Marina del Rey California U.S.A. 51 A2 33 58N 118 28W
Marin City California U.S.A. 49 A3 37 52N 122 31W
Marin County California U.S.A. 49 B3 37 55N 122 26W
Maringá Brazil 69 G8 23 26S 52 02W
Marin Peninsula California U.S.A. 49 A3 37 52N 122 33W
Marion New York U.S.A. 64 C6 43 09N 77 11W
Marion Ohio U.S.A. 63 J5 40 35N 83 08W
Marion, Lake South Carolina U.S.A. 63 J3 33 00N 80 00W
Mariscal Estigarribia Paraguay 69 E8 22 03S 60 35W
Mariupol' *(Zhdanov)* Ukraine 90 D4 47 05N 37 34E
Marjayoun Lebanon 92 O11 33 22N 35 34E
Marka Somalia 106 N8 1 42N 44 47E
Markha *r.* Russia 89 N8 64 00N 12 30E
Markovo Russia 89 T8 64 40N 170 24E
Marlborough Massachusetts U.S.A. 65 J5 42 21N 71 33W
Marlette Michigan U.S.A. 36 C4 43 20N 83 04W
Marlton New Jersey U.S.A. 64 F2 39 55N 74 55W
Marly-le-Roi France 83 A2 48 52N 2 05E
Marmara, Sea of Turkey 92 C7 15 40N 28 10E
Maroantsetra Madagascar 107 O4 15 23S 49 44E
Maroko Nigeria 107 W3 6 21N 3 32E
Maroni *r.* Surinam 68 G13 4 00N 54 30W
Maroua Cameroon 106 H10 10 35N 14 20E
Maroubra Australia 111 G2 33 57S 151 15E
Marquesas Islands Pacific Ocean 115 M7 10 00S 137 00W
Marquette Michigan U.S.A. 63 I6 46 33N 87 23W
Marquette Park Illinois U.S.A. 53 B2 41 46N 87 43W
Marrakech Morocco 106 D14 31 49N 8 00W
Marrickville Australia 111 G2 33 55S 151 09E
Marsabit Kenya 106 M8 2 20N 37 59E
Marsala Italy 81 B2 37 48N 12 27E
Marseille France 77 D3 43 18N 5 22E
Marshall Michigan U.S.A. 36 B3 42 16N 84 57W
Marshall Virginia U.S.A. 64 C1 38 53N 77 52W
MARSHALL ISLANDS 114 G8
Martaban, Gulf of Myanmar 96/97 J1 16 00N 97 00E
Martha's Vineyard *i.* Massachusetts U.S.A. 65 K4 41 00N 70 00W
Martinique *i.* Lesser Antilles 67 L2 14 30N 61 00W
Martin Lake Alabama U.S.A. 63 I3 33 00N 86 00W
Martinsburg West Virginia U.S.A. 64 C2 39 28N 77 59W
Martinsville Virginia U.S.A. 63 K4 36 43N 79 53W
Martin Vaz *i.* Atlantic Ocean 115 F4 21 00S 27 30W
Marton New Zealand 111 C2 40 04S 175 25E
Marwitz Germany 83 E2 52 44N 13 08E
Mary Turkmenistan 91 J2 37 42N 61 54E
Maryborough Australia 110 I4 25 32S 152 36E
Maryland *state* U.S.A. 63 K4 39 00N 77 00W
Marysville Pennsylvania U.S.A. 64 D3 40 00N 76 00W
Masada *see* Mezada
Masan South Korea 97 P6 35 10N 128 35E
Masaya Nicaragua 67 G2 11 59N 86 03W
Masbate *i.* The Philippines 99 G6 12 21N 123 36E
Mascara Algeria 77 C2 35 20N 0 09E
Mascarene Basin Indian Ocean 112 E5 15 00S 55 00E
Mascot Australia 111 G2 33 56S 151 12E
Maseru Lesotho 107 K2 29 19S 27 29E
Mashhad Iran 93 I6 36 16N 59 34E
Masindi Uganda 106 L8 1 41N 31 45E
Maşīrah *i.* Oman 93 I3 20 25N 58 40E
Mason Michigan U.S.A. 36 B3 42 34N 85 27W
Mason City Iowa U.S.A. 63 H5 43 10N 93 10W
Masqat Oman 93 I3 23 37N 58 38E
Massabesic, Lake New Hampshire U.S.A. 65 J5 42 00N 71 00W
Massachusetts *state* U.S.A. 65 H5 42 00N 72 00W
Massachusetts Bay Massachusetts U.S.A. 52 C2 42 26N 70 54W
Massif Central *mts.* France 77 C3/4 45 00N 3 30E
Massif de l'Ouarsenis *mts.* Algeria 77 C2 36 00N 2 00E
Massif de L'Isola *mts.* Madagascar 107 N3 23 00S 45 00E
Massif de Tsaratanana *mts.* Madagascar 107 N5 14 00S 49 00E
Massillon Ohio U.S.A. 36 E1 40 48N 81 32W
Massy France 83 B1 48 44N 2 17E
Masterton New Zealand 111 C2 40 57S 175 39E
Masuda Japan 100 B1 34 42N 131 51E
Masuku Gabon 106 H7 1 40S 13 31E
Masvingo Zimbabwe 107 L3 20 05S 30 50E
Matachel *r.* Spain 77 A2 38 40N 6 00W
Matadi Zaïre 107 H6 5 50S 13 32E
Matagalpa Nicaragua 67 G2 12 52N 85 58W
Matale Sri Lanka 95 E1 7 28N 80 37E
Matamoras Pennsylvania U.S.A. 65 F4 41 23N 74 43W
Matamoros Mexico 66 D5 25 33N 103 15W
Matamoros Mexico 66 E5 25 50N 97 31W
Matanzas Cuba 67 H4 23 04N 81 35W
Matara Sri Lanka 95 E1 5 57N 80 32E
Mataram Indonesia 99 F2 8 36S 116 07E

Mataró Spain **77** C3 41 32N 2 27E
Mataura New Zealand **111** A1 46 10S 168 53E
Mataura *r.* New Zealand **111** A1 46 40S 168 50E
Matehuala Mexico **66** D4 23 40N 100 40W
Matelot Trinidad and Tobago **66** T10 10 49N 61 07W
Matera Italy **81** C3 40 40N 16 37E
Mateur Tunisia **81** A2 37 03N 9 40E
Mathura India **95** D5 27 30N 77 42E
Mato Grosso *admin.* Brazil **68** F10 14 00S 56 00W
Mato Grosso *tn.* Brazil **68** F9 15 05S 59 57W
Mato Grosso do Sul *admin.* Brazil **68** F8/9 20 00S 55 00W
Matopo Hills Zimbabwe **107** K3 21 00S 28 30E
Matosinhos Portugal **77** A3 41 08N 8 45W
Maṭraḥ Oman **93** I3 23 31N 58 18E
Matsudo Japan **101** C4 35 46N 139 54E
Matsue Japan **100** B2 35 29N 133 04E
Matsumoto Japan **100** C2 36 18N 137 58E
Matsusaka Japan **100** H1 34 33N 136 31E
Matsuyama Japan **100** B1 33 50N 132 47E
Matterhorn *mt.* Switzerland **77** D4 45 59N 7 39E
Matuku *i.* Fiji **114** V15 19 11S 179 45E
Matura Trinidad and Tobago **66** T10 10 40N 61 04W
Matura Bay Trinidad and Tobago **66** T10 10 40N 61 04W
Maturin Venezuela **68** E14 9 45N 63 10W
Matveyevskoye Russia **88** L1 55 42N 37 30E
Maubeuge France **76** C5 50 17N 3 58E
Maués Brazil **68** F12 3 22S 57 38W
Maui *i.* Hawaiian Islands U.S.A. **119** Y18 20 55N 156 20W
Maumee River Ohio U.S.A. **36** C2 41 30N 83 50W
Maumere Indonesia **99** G2 8 35S 122 13E
Mauna Kea *mt.* Hawaiian Islands **115** Z17 19 50N 155 25W
Mauna Loa *vol.* Hawaiian Islands **115** Z17 19 28N 155 35W
MAURITANIA 106 C11
MAURITIUS 112 E4 20 15S 57 30E
Ma Wan *i.* Hong Kong U.K. **98** B2 22 21N 114 03E
Ma Wan Chung Hong Kong U.K. **98** A1 22 17N 113 56E
Mawkmai Myanmar **99** B8 20 12N 97 37E
Mawlaik Myanmar **96** H3 23 40N 94 26E
Mawson *r.s.* Antarctica **117** 67 36S 62 52E
Mayaguana *i.* The Bahamas **67** J4 22 30N 72 40W
Mayagüez Puerto Rico **67** K3 18 13N 67 09W
Mayaro Bay Trinidad and Tobago **66** U9 10 07N 61 00W
Mayenne *r.* France **77** B4 47 45N 0 50W
Mayfield New York U.S.A. **65** F6 43 07N 74 17W
Maykop Russia **90** E3 44 37N 40 48E
Mayotte *i.* Indian Ocean **107** N5 13 00S 45 00E
May Pen Jamaica **67** Q7 17 58N 77 15W
Mays Landing New Jersey U.S.A. **65** F2 39 27N 74 44W
Mayumba Gabon **107** H7 3 23S 10 38E
Maywood Illinois U.S.A. **53** A2 41 51N 87 48W
Mazabuka Zambia **107** K4 15 50S 27 47E
Mazama Washington U.S.A. **42** H4 48 37N 120 25W
Mazatenango Guatemala **66** F2 14 31N 91 30W
Mazār-e Sharīf Afghanistan **93** K6 36 42N 67 06E
Mazirbe Latvia **79** E2 57 40N 22 21E
Mbabane Swaziland **107** L2 26 20S 31 08E
Mbaiki Central African Republic **106** I8 3 53N 18 01E
Mbala Zambia **107** L6 8 50S 31 24E
Mbalmayo Cameroon **106** H8 3 30N 11 31E
Mbandaka Zaïre **106** I7 0 03N 18 28E
Mbengga *i.* Fiji **114** U15 18 24S 178 09E
Mbeya Tanzania **107** L6 8 54S 33 29E
Mbuji-Mayi Zaïre **107** J6 6 10S 23 39E
Mead, Lake U.S.A. **62** D4 36 10N 114 25W
Meadville Pennsylvania U.S.A. **63** J5 41 38N 80 10W
Meaux France **76** C4 48 58N 2 54E
Mecca *see* Makkah
Mechelen *(Malines)* Belgium **76** C5 51 02N 4 29E
Mecheria Algeria **106** E14 33 31N 0 20W
Mecklenburg Bay Europe **76** E5 54 00N 12 00E
Medan Indonesia **99** B4 3 35N 98 39E
Médéa Algeria **77** C2 36 15N 2 48E
Medellín Colombia **68** B14 6 15N 75 36W
Medenine Tunisia **106** H14 33 24N 10 25E
Medford Massachusetts U.S.A. **52** B2 42 25N 71 05W
Medford New York U.S.A. **65** G3 40 49N 73 00W
Medford Oregon U.S.A. **62** B5 42 20N 122 52W
Medford Wisconsin U.S.A. **35** B2 45 08N 90 22W
Media Pennsylvania U.S.A. **64** E2 39 56N 75 23W
Medicine Lake Montana U.S.A. **40** C1 48 30N 104 10W
Medina New York U.S.A. **64** B6 43 14N 78 23W
Medina Ohio U.S.A. **36** E2 41 07N 81 51W
Medina del Campo Spain **77** B3 41 18N 4 55W
Medinipur India **95** F4 22 25N 87 24E
Mediterranean Sea 74/75
Medvedkovo Russia **88** M2 55 6N 37 08E
Medvezh'yegorsk Russia **88** F8 62 56N 34 28E
Medway *r.* England **78** L3 51 24N 0 40E
Meekatharra Australia **110** B4 26 30S 118 30E
Meerut India **95** D5 29 00N 77 42E
Mēga Ethiopia **106** M8 4 02N 38 19E
Meghalaya *admin.* India **95** G5 25 30N 91 00E
Meguro Japan **101** B3 35 36N 139 43E
Mei Xian China **97** N3 24 19N 116 13E
Mejerda *r.* Tunisia **81** A2 36 30N 9 00E
Mek'elē Ethiopia **106** M10 13 32N 39 33E
Meknès Morocco **106** D14 33 53N 5 37W
Mekong *r.* South East Asia **99** C7/D6 16 30N 105 00E
Mekong, Mouths of the Vietnam **99** D5 9 00N 107 00E
Melaka Malaysia **99** C4 2 14N 102 14E
Melanesia *geog. reg.* Pacific Ocean **114** F7
Melbourne Australia **110** H2 37 45S 144 58E
Melbourne Florida U.S.A. **63** J2 28 04N 80 38W
Melilla *territory* Spain **77** B2 35 17N 2 57W
Melitopol' Ukraine **90** D4 46 51N 35 22E
Mellégue *r.* Tunisia **77** D2 36 00N 8 00E
Melo Uruguay **69** G6 32 22S 54 10W
Melrose Massachusetts U.S.A. **52** B2 42 26N 71 04W
Melrose Park Illinois U.S.A. **53** A2 41 52N 87 51W
Melun France **76** C4 48 32N 2 40E
Melville Bugt *b.* Greenland **45** T6 75 30N 62 30W
Melville, Cape Australia **110** G7 14 08S 144 31E
Melville Island Australia **110** E7 11 30S 131 00E
Melvindale Michigan U.S.A. **52** E2 42 16N 83 14W
Memmingen Germany **76** E4 47 59N 10 11E
Memphis Tennessee U.S.A. **63** I4 35 10N 90 00W
Memphis *hist. site* Egypt **92** D4 29 52N 31 12E
Menai Australia **111** G1 34 01S 151 01E
Mende France **77** C3 44 32N 3 30E
Menderes *r.* Turkey **92** C6 37 50N 28 10E
Mendi Papua New Guinea **110** G8 6 13S 143 39E
Mendip Hills England **78** I3 51 18N 2 45W
Mendocino Seascarp Pacific Ocean **115** L12 41 00N 145 00W
Mendoza Argentina **69** D6 32 48S 68 52W
Mengdingjie China **97** J3 23 30N 99 03E
Menlo Park California U.S.A. **49** C1 37 26N 122 13W
Menongue Angola **107** I5 14 36S 17 48E
Menorca *(Minorca) i.* Balearic Islands **77** C2 39 45N 4 15E
Mensk *see* Minsk
Mentawai Islands Indonesia **112** I7 2 00N 99 00E
Mentor Ohio U.S.A. **63** J5 41 42N 81 22W
Mera Japan **100** L1 34 56N 139 50E
Merauke Indonesia **110** G8 8 30S 140 22E
Mercedes Argentina **69** D6 33 41S 65 28W
Mercedes Uruguay **69** F6 34 15S 58 02W
Mercerville New Jersey U.S.A. **65** F3 40 14N 74 42W
Mergui Myanmar **99** B6 12 26N 98 34E
Mergui Archipelago *is.* Myanmar **99** B6 12 00N 98 00E
Mérida Mexico **66** G4 20 59N 89 39W
Mérida Spain **77** A2 38 55N 6 20W
Mérida Venezuela **68** C14 8 24N 71 08W
Meriden Connecticut U.S.A. **65** H4 41 32N 72 48W
Meridian Mississippi U.S.A. **63** I3 32 21N 88 42W
Merowe Sudan **92** D2 18 30N 31 49E
Merrimack New Hampshire U.S.A. **65** J5 42 50N 71 30W
Merrimack River U.S.A. **65** J5 42 40N 71 15W
Merrylands Australia **111** F2 33 50S 150 59E
Mersey *r.* England **78** I5 53 20N 2 53W
Mersin Turkey **92** D6 36 47N 34 37E
Merthyr Tydfil Wales **78** H3 51 46N 3 23W
Merton *bor.* Greater London England **82** C2 51 25N 0 12W
Mertz Glacier Antarctica **117** 68 00S 145 00E
Mesa Arizona U.S.A. **62** D3 33 25N 115 50W
Mesabi Range Minnesota U.S.A. **35** B2 47 30N 93 00W
Mesolóngion Greece **81** D2 38 21N 21 26E
Messina Italy **81** C2 38 13N 15 33E
Messina Republic of South Africa **107** K3 22 23S 30 00E
Methow River Washington U.S.A. **42** H4 48 35N 120 25W
Metlakatla Alaska U.S.A. **42** B3 55 09N 131 35W
Metz France **76** D4 49 07N 6 11E
Meudon France **83** A2 48 48N 2 15E
Meuse *r.* Belgium/France **76** C5 50 03N 4 40E
Mexicali Mexico **66** A5 32 36 N 115 30W
MEXICO 66 D4
México Mexico **66** E3 19 25N 99 10W
Mexico, Gulf of Mexico **66/67** F4/G4 25 00N 90 00W
Meymaneh Afghanistan **93** J6 35 55N 64 47E
Mezada *(Masada) hist. site* Israel **92** O10 31 17N 35 20E
Mezen' Russia **88** G9 65 50N 44 20E
Mezhdurechensk Russia **91** O5 53 43N 88 11E
Miami Florida U.S.A. **63** J2 25 45N 80 15W
Miami Oklahoma U.S.A. **63** H4 36 53N 94 54W
Mīāneh Iran **93** G6 37 23N 47 45E
Mianwali Pakistan **95** C6 32 32N 71 33E
Miao-li Taiwan **98** G7 24 37N 120 49E
Miass Russia **91** J6 55 00N 60 08E
Michelson, Mount Alaska U.S.A. **44** C4 69 19N 144 20W
Michigan *state* U.S.A. **63** I6 45 00N 85 00W
Michurinsk Russia **90** E5 52 54N 40 30E
Micronesia *geog. reg.* Pacific Ocean **114** G8
Mid-Atlantic Ridge Atlantic Ocean **113** E10/G4
Middle America Trench Pacific Ocean **115** Q9 16 30N 99 00W
Middle Andaman *i.* Andaman Islands **95** G2 12 30N 93 00E
Middleboro Massachusetts U.S.A. **65** K4 41 54N 70 55W
Middleburg Pennsylvania U.S.A. **64** C3 40 47N 77 03W
Middleburg Republic of South Africa **107** K2 31 28S 25 01E
Middleburg Virginia U.S.A. **64** C1 38 58N 77 46W
Middleburg Heights *tn.* Ohio U.S.A. **36** E2 41 20N 81 49W
Middle Harbour Australia **111** G2 33 48S 151 14E
Middle Loup *r.* Nebraska U.S.A. **62** F5 42 00N 101 00W
Middleport New York U.S.A. **64** B6 43 13N 78 28W
Middle River Rouge Michigan U.S.A. **52** D2 42 23N 83 21W
Middle Rouge Park Michigan U.S.A. **52** D2 42 23N 83 21W
Middlesbrough England **78** J6 54 35N 1 14W
Middlesex County Massachusetts U.S.A. **52** A2 42 19N 71 20W
Middlesex Fells Reservation Massachusetts U.S.A. **52** B2 42 26N 71 07W
Middletown Connecticut U.S.A. **65** H4 41 34N 72 39W
Middletown Delaware U.S.A. **64** E2 39 27N 75 44W
Middletown New York U.S.A. **65** F4 41 26N 74 26W
Middletown Pennsylvania U.S.A. **64** D3 40 12N 76 44W
Mid-Indian Basin Indian Ocean **112** H6 10 00S 80 00E
Mid-Indian Ridge Indian Ocean **112** F5/G3
Midland Michigan U.S.A. **36** B4 43 38N 84 14W
Midland Texas U.S.A. **62** F3 32 00N 102 09W
Midland Beach New York U.S.A. **50** B1 40 33N 74 07W
Midori Japan **101** B3 35 33N 139 39E
Mid-Pacific Mountains Pacific Ocean **114** F10 21 00N 160 00E
Midway Islands Pacific Ocean **114** I10 28 15N 177 25W
Mie *pref.* Japan **100** H1 34 35N 136 20E
Mien Hsü *i.* Taiwan **98** I8 25 31N 122 07E
Mieres Spain **77** A3 43 15N 5 46W
Mifflintown Pennsylvania U.S.A. **64** C3 40 34N 77 24W
Mijares *r.* Spain **77** B3 40 03N 0 30W
Mikawa-wan *b.* Japan **100** J1 34 42N 137 10E
Mikhaylovgrad Bulgaria **81** D3 43 25N 23 11E
Miki Japan **100** F1 34 50N 134 59E
Mikkeli Finland **79** F3 61 44N 27 15E
Milagra Valley California U.S.A. **49** B2 37 28N 122 28W
Milagro Ecuador **68** B12 2 11S 79 36W
Milan *see* Milano
Milano *(Milan)* Italy **81** A4 45 28N 9 12E
Milâs Turkey **80** E2 37 19N 27 48E
Mildura Australia **110** G3 34 14S 142 13E
Milesburg Pennsylvania U.S.A. **64** C3 40 57N 77 49W
Miles City Montana U.S.A. **62** E6 46 24N 105 48W
Milford Delaware U.S.A. **64** E1 38 54N 75 25W
Milford Massachusetts U.S.A. **65** J5 42 09N 71 31W
Milford New Hampshire U.S.A. **65** J5 42 50N 71 40W
Milford New Jersey U.S.A. **64** E3 40 34N 75 06W
Milford Pennsylvania U.S.A. **65** F4 41 19N 74 48W
Milford Utah U.S.A. **62** D4 38 22N 113 00W
Milford Haven Wales **78** F3 51 44N 5 02W
Milford Sound New Zealand **111** A2 44 41S 167 56E
Miliana Algeria **77** C2 36 20N 2 15E
Millau France **77** C3 44 06N 3 05E
Mill Creek Michigan U.S.A. **36** C4 43 10N 83 00W
Mille Lacs Lake Minnesota U.S.A. **35** B2 46 00N 94 00W
Millersburg Pennsylvania U.S.A. **64** D3 40 32N 76 57W
Millerstown Pennsylvania U.S.A. **64** C3 40 32N 77 08W
Millerton New York U.S.A. **65** G4 41 57N 73 31W
Millinocket Maine U.S.A. **33** C2 45 42N 68 43W
Mill Valley California U.S.A. **49** A3 37 54N 122 32W
Millville New Jersey U.S.A. **64** E2 39 24N 75 02W
Milos *i.* Greece **81** D2 36 00N 24 00E
Milroy Pennsylvania U.S.A. **64** C3 40 44N 77 35W
Milton Massachusetts U.S.A. **52** B2 42 16N 71 05W
Milton New Zealand **111** A1 46 08S 169 59E
Milton Keynes England **78** K4 52 02N 0 42W
Milton, Lake Ohio U.S.A. **36** E2 41 05N 81 00W
Midland Michigan U.S.A. **63** J5 43 38N 84 14W
Milwaukee Wisconsin U.S.A. **63** I5 43 03N 87 56W
Mimizan France **77** B3 44 12N 1 14W
Mina *r.* Algeria **77** C2 35 30N 1 00E
Minahassa Peninsula Indonesia **99** G4 0 30N 122 30E
Minamata Japan **100** B1 32 13N 130 23E
Minami-Ashigara Japan **100** L2 35 20N 139 06E
Minas Uruguay **69** F6 34 20S 55 15W
Minas Gerais *admin.* Brazil **68** I9 17 30S 45 00W
Minatitlán Mexico **66** F3 17 59N 94 32W
Minch, The *sd.* **78** F10 58 00N 6 00W
Mindanao *i.* The Philippines **99** G5/H5 7 30N 124 00E
Minden Germany **76** D5 52 18N 8 54E
Minden Louisiana U.S.A. **63** H3 32 26N 93 17W
Mindoro *i.* The Philippines **99** G6 13 20N 121 30E
Mingechaur Azerbaijan **90** F3 40 45N 47 03E
Minho *see* Miño
Minicoy Island India **95** C1 8 29N 73 01E
Minneapolis Minnesota U.S.A. **63** H5 45 00N 93 15W
Minnesota *state* U.S.A. **63** H6 47 00N 95 00W
Minnesota *r.* Minnesota U.S.A. **63** G5 44 00N 95 00W
Mino Japan **100** H2 35 34N 136 56E
Mino-Kamo Japan **100** J2 35 29N 137 01E
Minorca *see* Menorca
Minot North Dakota U.S.A. **62** F6 48 16N 101 19W
Minsk *(Mensk)* Belarus **90** B5 53 51N 27 30E
Minusinsk Russia **91** P5 53 43N 91 45E
Minute Man National Historical Park Massachusetts U.S.A. **52** A2 42 26N 71 26W
Miño *(Minho) r.* Spain/Portugal **77** A3 42 00N 8 40W
Mio Michigan U.S.A. **35** D1 44 40N 84 09W
Miraflores Locks Panama **67** Z1 8 59N 79 36W
Miraj India **95** C3 16 51N 74 42E
Miram Shah Pakistan **93** L5 33 00N 70 05E
Miranda de Ebro Spain **77** B3 42 41N 2 57W
Miri Malaysia **99** E4 4 28N 114 00E
Mirnyy *r.s.* Antarctica **117** 66 33S 93 01E
Mirnyy Russia **89** N8 62 30N 113 58E
Mirpur Khas Pakistan **94** A6 25 33N 69 05E
Mirs Bay Hong Kong U.K. **98** D3 22 33N 114 24E
Mirtoan Sea Greece **81** D2 37 00N 23 00E
Mirzapur India **95** E5 25 09N 82 34E
Misaki Japan **100** G1 34 19N 135 09E
Misawa Japan **100** D3 40 42N 141 26E
Misfaq Egypt **92** N19 31 01N 33 11E
Mishima Japan **100** K2 35 08N 138 54E
Miskolc Hungary **81** D4 48 07N 20 47E
Misool *i.* Indonesia **99** I3 2 00S 130 00E
Miṣrātah Libya **106** H14 32 23N 15 06E
Mississippi *r.* U.S.A. **63** H3 35 00N 90 00W
Mississippi *state* U.S.A. **63** H3 32 00N 90 00W
Mississippi Delta Louisiana U.S.A. **63** I2 30 00N 90 00W
Missoula Montana U.S.A. **62** D6 46 52N 114 00W
Missouri *r.* U.S.A. **63** H4 39 00N 93 00W
Missouri *state* U.S.A. **63** H4 38 00N 93 00W
Mitaka Japan **101** B3 35 41N 139 35E
Mitcham England **82** C2 51 24N 0 09W
Mitchell Australia **110** H4 26 30S 147 56E
Mitchell South Dakota U.S.A. **63** G5 43 40N 98 01W
Mitchell *r.* Australia **110** G6 17 00S 142 30E
Mitilíni Greece **81** E2 39 06N 26 34E
Mitino Russia **88** L2 55 53N 37 24E
Mitkof Island Alaska U.S.A. **42** B3 56 40N 132 45W
Mito Japan **100** D2 36 22N 140 29E
Mitry-Mory France **83** C2 48 58N 2 38E
Mits'iwa Ethiopia **92** E2 15 42N 39 25E
Mitsukaidō Japan **100** L3 36 03N 139 59E
Mitú Columbia **68** C13 1 07N 70 05W
Mitumba Mountains *see* Chaine des Mitumba
Miura Japan **100** L2 35 08N 139 37E
Miura-hantō *p.* Japan **100** L2 35 14N 139 40E
Miya-gawa *r.* Japan **100** H1 34 20N 136 16E
Miyako Japan **100** D2 39 38N 141 59E
Miyakonojō Japan **100** B1 31 43N 131 02E
Miyama Japan **100** G2 35 17N 135 32E
Miyazaki Japan **100** B1 31 56N 131 27E
Miyazu Japan **100** G2 35 33N 135 12E
Mizen Head *c.* Irish Republic **78** B3 51 30N 9 50W
Mizunami Japan **100** J2 35 25N 137 16E
Mjölby Sweden **80** C6 58 19N 15 10E
Mjøsa *l.* Norway **79** C3 60 40N 10 40E
Mladá Boleslav Czechoslovakia **80** B5 50 26N 14 55E
Mława Poland **80** D5 53 08N 20 20E
Mnevniki Russia **88** L2 55 46N 37 29E
Moala *i.* Fiji **114** U15 18 34S 179 56E
Mobara Japan **100** M2 35 26N 140 20E
Mobaye Central African Republic **106** J8 4 19N 21 11E
Mobile Alabama U.S.A. **63** I3 30 40N 88 05W
Moçambique Mozambique **107** N5 15 03S 40 45E
Mocuba Mozambique **107** M4 16 52S 36 57E
Módena Italy **81** B3 44 39N 10 55E
Moe-Yallourn Australia **110** H2 38 09S 146 22E
Mogadishu *see* Muqdisho
Mogilev Belarus **90** C5 53 54N 30 20E
Mogil'ev Podol'skiy Ukraine **90** B4 48 29N 27 49E
Mogocha Russia **89** N6 53 44N 119 45E
Mogollon Rim *plat.* Arizona U.S.A. **62** D3 34 00N 111 00W
Mohall North Dakota U.S.A. **40** C1 48 47N 101 31W
Mohammadia Algeria **77** C2 35 35N 0 05E
Mohawk New York U.S.A. **64** E6 43 00N 75 00W
Mohawk River New York U.S.A. **65** F6 43 00N 74 40W
Mohe *(Gulian)* China **97** N9 52 55N 122 20E
Mo-i-Rana Norway **79** C4 66 18N 14 00E
Mokolo Cameroon **106** H10 10 49N 13 54E
Mokp'o South Korea **97** P5 34 50N 126 25E
Moksha *r.* Russia **90** E5 50 00N 43 00E
Molango Mexico **66** E4 20 48N 98 44W
MOLDAVIA *see* MOLDOVA
MOLDOVA *(MOLDAVIA)* **90** B4
Moldova *r.* Romania **81** E4 47 00N 26 00E
Mole *r.* England **82** B2 51 15N 0 20W
Molepolole Botswana **107** K3 24 25S 25 30E
Mollendo Peru **68** C9 17 00S 72 00W
Mölndal Sweden **79** C2 57 40N 12 00E
Molodechno Belarus **80** F5 54 16N 26 50E
Molodezhnaya *r.s.* Antarctica **117** 67 40S 45 50E
Molokai *i.* Hawaiian Islands **115** Y18 21 40N 155 55W
Molopo *r.* Southern Africa **107** J2 26 30S 22 30E
Molucca Sea Indonesia **99** G3/H4 0 00 125 00E
Mombasa Kenya **107** L7 4 04S 39 40E
Mombetsu Japan **100** D3 42 28N 142 10E
Monacacy River Maryland U.S.A. **64** C2 39 30N 77 20W
MONACO 77 D3
Monadhliath Mountains Scotland **78** G9 57 10N 4 00W
Monahans Texas U.S.A. **62** F3 31 35N 102 54W
Monastir Tunisia **81** B2 35 46N 10 59E
Mona Vale Australia **111** H3 33 41S 151 18E
Monbetsu Japan **100** D3 44 23N 143 22E
Monçaó Brazil **68** H12 3 30S 45 15W
Mönchengladbach Germany **76** D5 51 12N 6 25E
Monclova Mexico **66** D5 26 55N 101 25W
Mondego *r.* Portugal **77** A3 40 30N 8 15W
Mondovi Italy **81** A3 44 23N 7 49E
Monemvasia Greece **81** D2 36 41N 23 03E
Mong Kok Hong Kong U.K. **98** B1 22 09N 114 09E
MONGOLIA 96/97 J7/M7
Mong Tong Hang Hong Kong U.K. **98** B1 22 20N 114 02E
Mongu Zambia **107** J4 15 13S 23 09E
Monomoy Island Massachusetts U.S.A. **65** K4 41 35N 70 00W
Monongahela River Pennsylvania U.S.A. **53** E1 40 19N 79 54W
Monopoli Italy **81** C3 40 57N 17 18E
Monos *i.* Trinidad and Tobago **66** S10 10 42N 61 42W
Monroe Louisiana U.S.A. **63** H3 32 31N 92 06W
Monroe Michigan U.S.A. **36** C2 41 56N 83 21W
Monroe New York U.S.A. **65** F4 41 20N 74 12W
Monroeville Pennsylvania U.S.A. **53** E1 40 25N 79 47W
Monrovia Liberia **106** C9 6 20N 10 46W
Montana *state* U.S.A. **62** D6 47 00N 111 00W
Montañas de León *mts.* Spain **77** A3 42 30N 6 15E
Montara California U.S.A. **49** B2 37 32N 122 31W
Montara Mountain California U.S.A. **49** B2 37 34N 122 29W
Montara Point California U.S.A. **49** A2 37 32N 122 33W
Montargis France **77** C4 48 00N 2 44E
Montauban France **77** B3 44 01N 1 20E
Montauk New York U.S.A. **65** J4 41 02N 71 57W
Montauk Point New York U.S.A. **65** J4 41 04N 71 51W
Montbéliard France **77** D4 47 31N 6 48E
Mont Blanc *mt.* France/Italy **77** D4 45 50N 6 52E
Mont Cameroun *mt.* Cameroon **106** G8 4 13N 9 10E
Montclair New Jersey U.S.A. **50** B2 40 48N 74 12W
Mont-de-Marsan France **77** B3 43 54N 0 30W
Montebello California U.S.A. **51** B3 34 01N 118 07W
Monte Cinto *mt.* Corsica **77** D3 42 23N 8 57E
Montego Bay *tn.* Jamaica **67** Q8 18 27N 77 56W
Montélimar France **77** C3 44 33N 4 45E
Montenegro *admin* Yugoslavia **81** C3
Monterey Park *tn.* California U.S.A. **51** B3 34 03N 118 08W
Montería Colombia **68** B14 8 45N 75 54W
Montero Bolivia **68** E9 17 20S 63 15W
Monte Roraima *mt.* South America **68** E14 5 14N 60 44W
Monterrey Mexico **66** D5 25 40N 100 20W
Montes Claros *tn.* Brazil **68** I9 16 45S 43 52W
Montes de Toledo *mts.* Spain **77** B2 39 35N 4 30W
Montevideo Uruguay **69** F6 34 55S 56 10W
Montgeron France **83** B1 48 42N 2 27E
Montgomery Alabama U.S.A. **63** I3 32 22N 86 20W
Montgomery Pennsylvania U.S.A. **64** D4 41 09N 76 54W
Monticello New York U.S.A. **65** F4 41 39N 74 41W
Monti del Gennargentu *mts.* Sardinia Italy **81** A2 40 00N 9 30E
Monti Nebrodi *mts.* Italy **81** B2 37 00N 14 00E
Montluçon France **77** C4 46 20N 2 36E
Montmorency France **83** B2 48 59N 2 19E
Monto Australia **110** I5 24 53N 151 06E
Montpelier Ohio U.S.A. **36** B2 41 35N 84 35W
Montpellier France **77** C3 43 36N 3 53E
Montreux Switzerland **77** D4 46 27N 6 55E
Montrose Colorado U.S.A. **62** E4 38 29N 107 53W
Montrose Pennsylvania U.S.A. **64** E4 41 49N 75 53W
Montrouge France **83** B2 48 49N 2 19E
Monts d'Auvergne *mts.* France **77** C4 45 30N 2 50E
Monts de Medjerda *mts.* Algeria/Tunisia **77** D2 36 50N 8 00E
Monts de Tébessa *mts.* Algeria/Tunisia **77** D2 35 00N 8 00E
Monts du Hodna *mts.* Algeria **77** C2 36 00N 4 00E
Montserrat *i.* Lesser Antilles **67** L3 16 45N 62 14W
Monts Nimba *mts.* Guinea/Liberia **106** D9 7 39N 8 30W
Monywa Myanmar **96** J3 22 05N 95 12E
Monza Italy **81** A4 45 35N 9 16E
Moora Australia **110** B3 30 40S 116 01E
Moorhead Minnesota U.S.A. **63** G6 46 51N 96 44W
Moore, Lake Australia **110** B4 30 00S 117 30E
Moorestown New Jersey U.S.A. **64** F2 39 58N 74 54W
Moosehead Lake Maine U.S.A. **37** R6 45 40N 69 40W
Moosup Connecticut U.S.A. **65** J4 41 43N 71 53W
Mopti Mali **106** E10 14 29N 4 10W
Mora Sweden **79** C3 61 00N 14 30E
Moradabad India **95** D5 28 50N 78 45E
Moraga California U.S.A. **49** C3 37 49N 122 08W
Morant Bay *tn.* Jamaica **67** R7 17 53N 76 25W
Morant Point *c.* Jamaica **67** R7 17 55N 76 12W
Moratuwa Sri Lanka **95** D1 6 47N 79 53E
Morava *r.* Europe **80** C4 48 00N 17 00E
Morava *r.* Yugoslavia **81** D3 43 00N 22 00E
Moravia New York U.S.A. **64** D5 42 43N 76 26W
Moray Firth *est.* Scotland **78** H9 57 45N 3 45W
Morbi India **93** L3 22 50N 70 52E
Moreau *r.* South Dakota U.S.A. **62** F6 45 00N 102 00W
Moree Australia **110** H4 29 29S 149 53E
Morenci Arizona U.S.A. **62** E3 33 05N 109 22W
Morgantown West Virginia U.S.A. **63** K4 39 38N 79 57W
Mori Japan **100** D3 42 07N 140 33E
Morioka Japan **100** D2 39 43N 141 08E

Moriyama Japan **100** G2 35 05N 135 59E
Morlaix France **76** B4 48 35N 3 50W
MOROCCO 106 D14
Morogoro Tanzania **107** M6 6 49S 37 40E
Moro Gulf The Philippines **99** G5 7 00N 122 40E
Morón Cuba **67** I4 22 08N 78 39W
Morondava Madagascar **107** N3 20 19S 44 17E
Moroni Comoros **107** N5 11 40S 43 16E
Morotai *i.* Indonesia **99** H4 2 30N 128 00E
Moroto Uganda **106** L8 2 32N 34 41E
Morozaki Japan **100** H1 34 41N 136 58E
Morrinsville New Zealand **111** C3 37 40S 175 33E
Morris Jesup, Cape Greenland **116** 83 20N 33 00W
Morris Reservoir California U.S.A. **51** C3 33 11N 117 53W
Morristown New Jersey U.S.A. **65** F3 40 48N 74 29W
Morrisville New York U.S.A. **64** E5 42 54N 75 40W
Morton Grove Illinois U.S.A. **53** A3 42 02N 87 46W
Moruga Trinidad and Tobago **66** T9 10 06N 61 17W
Moruga *r.* Trinidad and Tobago **66** T9 10 06N 61 15 W
Moscow Idaho U.S.A. **62** C6 46 44N 117 00W
Moscow *see* Moskva
Mosel *r.* Germany **76** D5 50 00N 7 00E
Moses Lake *tn.* Washington U.S.A. **62** C6 47 09N 119 20W
Mosgiel New Zealand **111** B1 45 54S 170 21E
Moshi Tanzania **106** M7 3 21S 37 19E
Mosjøen Norway **79** C4 65 50N 13 10E
Moskva *(Moscow)* Russia **90** D6 55 45N 37 42E
Moskva *r.* Russia **88** M1 55 36N 37 45E
Mosman Australia **111** G2 33 50S 151 14E
Mosquito Creek Lake *res.* Ohio U.S.A. **36** F2 41 20N 80 45W
Moss Norway **79** C2 59 26N 10 41E
Moss Beach California U.S.A. **49** B2 37 36N 122 30W
Mossoró Brazil **68** J11 5 10S 37 18W
Most Czechoslovakia **80** B5 50 31N 13 39E
Mostaganem Algeria **77** C2 35 45N 0 05E
Mostar Bosnia-Herzegovina **81** C3 43 20N 17 50E
Móstoles Spain **77** B3 40 19N 3 53W
Mosul Iraq **92** F6 36 21N 43 08E
Motala Sweden **80** C6 58 34N 15 05E
Mothe *i.* Fiji **114** V15 18 39S 178 32W
Motherwell Scotland **78** G7 55 48N 3 59W
Motril Spain **77** B2 36 45N 3 31W
Motueka New Zealand **111** B2 41 08S 173 01E
Mouila Gabon **106** H7 1 50S 11 02E
Moulins France **77** C4 47 00N 3 48E
Moulmein Myanmar **97** J2 16 30N 97 39E
Moulouya *r.* Morocco **77** B1 34 50N 3 00W
Moundou Chad **106** I9 8 35N 16 01E
Mountain View California U.S.A. **49** C1 37 23N 122 25W
Mountain Village Alaska U.S.A. **10** C5 62 09N 163 49W
Mount Carmel *tn.* Pennsylvania U.S.A. **64** D3 40 48N 76 25W
Mount Cobb *tn.* Pennsylvania U.S.A. **64** E4 41 24N 75 32W
Mount Darwin *tn.* Zimbabwe **107** L4 16 45S 31 39E
Mount Gambier *tn.* Australia **110** G2 37 51S 140 50E
Mount Hagen *tn.* Papua New Guinea **110** G8 5 54S 144 13E
Mount Holly *tn.* New Jersey U.S.A. **65** F2 40 00N 74 47W
Mount Isa *tn.* Australia **110** F5 20 50 S 139 29E
Mount Jewell *tn.* Pennsylvania U.S.A. **64** B4 41 44N 78 38W
Mount Magnet *tn.* Australia **110** B4 28 06S 117 50E
Mount Morgan *tn.* Australia **110** I5 23 40S 150 25E
Mount Morris *tn.* New York U.S.A. **64** C5 42 44N 77 51W
Mount Pleasant *tn.* Michigan U.S.A. **36** B4 43 36N 84 46W
Mount Prospect *tn.* Illinois U.S.A. **53** A3 42 01N 87 47W
Mount Union *tn.* Pennsylvania U.S.A. **64** C3 40 23N 77 54W
Mount Vernon *tn.* New York U.S.A. **50** C2 40 55N 73 51W
Mount Vernon *tn.* Illinois U.S.A. **63** I4 38 19N 88 52W
Mount Vernon *tn.* Washington U.S.A. **42** H4 48 25N 122 20W
Mourne Mountains Northern Ireland **78** E6 54 05N 6 05W
Moy *r.* Irish Republic **78** C5 53 55N 8 55W
Moyale Kenya **106** M8 3 31N 39 04E
Moyobamba Peru **68** B11 6 04S 76 56W
MOZAMBIQUE 107 L4
Mozambique Channel Mozambique/Madagascar **107** N4 18 00S 42 00E
Mozambique Depression Indian Ocean **102** 35 00S 40 00E
Mozyr' Belarus **80** E5 52 02N 29 10E
Mpanda Tanzania **107** L6 6 21S 31 01E
M'Sila Algeria **77** C2 35 40N 4 31E
Mtwara Tanzania **107** N5 10 17S 40 11E
Muang Lampang Thailand **99** B7 18 16N 99 30E
Muang Nakhon Sawan Thailand **99** C7 15 42N 100 04E
Muang Phitsanulok Thailand **99** C7 16 50N 100 15E
Muchinga Mountains Zambia **107** L5 12 30S 32 30E
Mudanjiang China **97** P7 44 36N 129 42E
Mud Lake Minnesota U.S.A. **39** B1 48 20N 95 50W
Mufulira Zamiba **107** K5 12 30S 28 12E
Müggelheim Germany **83** G1 52 24N 13 40E
Muğla Turkey **92** C6 37 13N 28 22E
Muhammad Qol Sudan **92** E3 20 53N 37 09E
Mui Wo Hong Kong U.K. **98** A1 22 16N 113 59E
Mukachevo Ukraine **81** D4 48 26N 22 45E
Mulegé Mexico **66** B5 26 54N 112 00W
Mulhacén *mt.* Spain **77** B2 37 04N 3 19W
Mülheim an der Ruhr Germany **76** H2 51 25N 6 50E
Mulhouse France **77** D4 47 45N 7 21E
Mull *i.* Scotland **78** F8 56 25N 6 00W
Mullet Lake Michigan U.S.A. **36** B6 45 30N 84 30W
Mullingar Irish Republic **78** D5 53 32N 7 20W
Mull of Galloway *c.* Scotland **78** G6 54 38N 4 50W
Mull of Kintyre *c.* Scotland **78** F7 55 17N 5 55W
Multan Pakistan **95** C6 30 10N 71 36E
Mumford New York U.S.A. **64** C6 42 57N 77 50W
Muna *i.* Indonesia **99** G3 5 00S 122 30E
München *(Munich)* Germany **76** E4 48 08N 11 35E
Muncie Indiana U.S.A. **63** I5 40 11N 85 22W
Muncy Pennsylvania U.S.A. **64** D4 41 12N 76 47W
Mundo *r.* Spain **77** B2 38 30N 2 00W
Mungbere Zaïre **106** K8 2 40N 28 25E
Munger India **95** F5 25 24N 86 29E
Munhall Pennsylvania U.S.A. **53** E1 40 24N 79 54W
Munich *see* München
Municipal Colony Dehli India **94** L4 28 42N 77 12E
Munising Michigan U.S.A. **35** C2 46 24N 86 40W
Münster Germany **76** D5 51 58N 7 37E
Muojärvi *l.* Finland **79** F4 65 52N 29 30E
Muonio älv *r.* Sweden/Finland **79** E4 68 20N 22 00E
Muqdisho *(Mogadishu)* Somalia **106** O8 2 02N 45 21E
Mur *r.* Europe **81** B4 47 00N 14 00E
Murat *r.* Turkey **92** F6 38 50N 40 20E
Murchison *r.* Australia **110** B4 26 00S 117 00E
Murcia Spain **77** B2 37 59N 1 08W
Mureș *r.* Romania **81** D4 46 00N 22 00E
Murfreesboro Tennessee U.S.A. **63** I4 35 50N 86 25W
Murgab *r.* Asia **93** J6 37 00N 62 30E
Müritz *l.* Germany **76** E5 53 00N 12 00E
Murmansk Russia **88** F9 68 59N 33 08E
Murom Russia **90** E6 55 34N 42 04E
Muroran Japan **100** D3 42 21N 140 59E
Muroto-zaki *c.* Japan **100** B1 33 13N 134 11E
Murray *r.* Australia **110** G2/G3 34 00S 142 00E
Murray Bridge *tn.* Australia **110** F2 35 10S 139 17E
Murray Seascarp Pacific Ocean **115** M11 32 00N 138 00W
Murrumbidgee *r.* Australia **110** H3 34 30S 146 30E
Murwara India **95** E4 23 49N 80 28E
Murzuq Libya **106** H13 25 55N 13 55E
Muş Turkey **92** F6 38 45N 41 30E
Musashino Japan **101** B3 35 43N 139 35E
Musgrave Ranges *mts.* Australia **110** E4 26 00S 132 00E
Mushin Nigeria **107** V3 6 33N 3 25E
Musin Nigeria **106** F9 6 30N 3 15E
Muskeget Channel Massachusetts U.S.A. **65** K4 41 20N 70 25W
Muskegon Michigan U.S.A. **35** C1 43 13N 86 15W
Muskegon River Michigan U.S.A. **36** A4 44 00N 85 05W
Muskogee Oklahoma U.S.A. **63** G4 35 45N 95 21W
Musselshell *r.* Montana U.S.A. **62** E6 47 00N 108 00W
Mustafa Kemalpaşa Turkey **68** E2 40 03N 28 52E
Mutarara Mozambique **107** M4 17 30S 35 06E
Mutare Zimbabwe **107** L4 18 58N 32 40E
Mutsu Japan **100** D3 41 18N 141 15E
Mutsu-wan *b.* Japan **100** D3 41 05N 140 40E
Muyun Kum *d.* Kazakhstan **91** L3 44 00N 70 00E
Muzaffarnagar India **95** D5 29 28N 77 42E
Muzaffarpur India **95** F5 26 07N 85 23E
Muzon, Cape Alaska U.S.A. **42** B2 54 41N 132 40W
Mwanza Tanzania **106** L7 2 31S 32 56E
Mwaya Tanzania **107** L6 9 33S 33 56E
Mweru, Lake *(Lac Moero)* Zaïre/Zambia **107** K6 8 30S 28 30E
Myanaung Myanmar **95** H3 18 17N 95 19E
MYANMAR *(BURMA)* **96/97** H3
Myaungmya Myanmar **95** G3 16 33N 94 55E
Myerstown Pennsylvania U.S.A. **64** D3 40 23N 76 18W
Myingyan Myanmar **96** E2 21 25N 95 20E
Myitkyina Myanmar **97** J4 25 24N 97 25E
Mymensingh Bangladesh **95** G4 24 45N 90 23E
Mýrdalsjökull *ice cap* Iceland **79** I6 63 40N 19 00W
Mys Chelyuskin *c.* Russia **89** M11 77 44N 103 55E
Mys Kanin Nos *c.* Russia **88** G9 68 38N 43 20E
Mys Navarin *c.* Russia **89** T8 62 17N 179 13E
Mys Olyutorskiy *c.* Russia **89** T7 59 58N 170 25E
Mysore India **95** D2 12 18N 76 37E
Mystic Connecticut U.S.A. **65** J4 41 21N 71 58W
Mystic Lakes Massachusetts U.S.A. **52** B2 42 26N 71 09W
Mystic River Massachusetts U.S.A. **52** B2 42 25N 71 08W
Mys Tolstoy *c.* Russia **89** R7 59 00N 155 00E
My Tho Vietnam **99** D6 10 21N 106 21E
Mytishchi Russia **90** D6 55 54N 37 47E
Mzuzu Malawi **107** L5 11 31S 34 00E

N

9 de Julio *(Nueve de Julio) tn.* Argentina **69** E5 35 28S 60 58W
Naas Irish Republic **78** E5 53 13N 6 39W
Nabari Japan **100** H1 34 37N 136 05E
Naberezhnyye Chelny *(Brezhnev)* Russia **91** G6 55 42N 52 19E
Nabeul Tunisia **81** B2 36 30N 10 44E
Nablus Jordan **92** O11 32 13N 35 16E
Nabq Egypt **92** O9 28 04N 34 26E
Nacogdoches Texas U.S.A. **63** H3 31 36N 94 40W
Nadiad India **95** C4 22 42N 72 55E
Nador Morocco **106** E14 35 10N 3 00W
Nadym Russia **89** J9 65 25N 72 40E
Naestved Denmark **80** B6 55 14N 11 47E
Naga The Philippines **99** G6 13 36N 123 12E
Naga Hills India **95** G5/H5 26 00N 95 00E
Nagahama Japan **100** H2 35 25N 136 16E
Nagai Japan **101** B1 35 11N 139 37E
Nagaland *admin.* India **95** G5 26 00N 94 30E
Nagano Japan **100** C2 36 39N 138 10E
Nagaoka Japan **100** C2 37 27N 138 50E
Nagasaki Japan **100** A1 32 45N 129 52E
Nagato Japan **100** B1 34 22N 131 11E
Nagatsuda Japan **101** B3 35 31N 139 30E
Nagercoil India **95** D1 8 11N 77 30E
Nagornyy Russia **89** O7 55 57N 124 54E
Nagoya Japan **100** H2 35 08N 136 53E
Nagpur India **95** D4 21 10N 79 12E
Nagqu China **95** G6 31 30N 91 57E
Nagykanizsa Hungary **81** C4 46 27N 17 00E
Nahant Massachusetts U.S.A. **52** C2 42 24N 70 55W
Nahant Bay Massachusetts U.S.A. **52** C2 42 26N 70 56W
Nahariya Israel **92** O11 33 01N 35 05E
Naihati India **94** K3 22 53N 88 27E
Nairobi Kenya **106** L7 1 17S 36 50E
Najd *geog. reg.* Saudi Arabia **92** F4 25 40N 42 30E
Najrān Saudi Arabia **92** F2 17 37N 44 40E
Naka Japan **101** B2 35 25N 139 38E
Nakahara Japan **101** B3 35 34N 139 39E
Nakamura Japan **100** B1 33 02N 132 58E
Nakano Japan **101** B3 35 42N 139 40E
Nakatsu Japan **100** B1 33 37N 131 11E
Nakhichevan' Azerbaijan **90** F2 39 12N 45 24E
Nakhodka Russia **89** P4 42 53N 132 54E
Nakhon Ratchasima Thailand **99** C6 15 00N 102 06E
Nakhon Si Thammarat Thailand **99** B5 8 24N 99 58E
Nakuru Kenya **106** M7 0 16S 36 05E
Nal *r.* Pakistan **94** B5 26 10N 65 30E
Nal'chik Russia **90** E3 43 31N 43 38E
Namangan Uzbekistan **91** L3 40 59N 71 41E
Nam Chung Hong Kong U.K. **98** B3 22 31N 114 12E
Nam Co *l.* China **95** G6 30 50N 90 30E
Namdalen *geog. reg.* Norway **79** C3 64 40N 12 00E
Nam Dinh Vietnam **97** L3 20 14N 106 00E
Namib Desert Namibia **107** H3 22 00S 14 00E
Namibe Angola **107** H5 15 10S 12 09E
NAMIBIA 107 I3
Nampa Idaho U.S.A. **62** C5 43 35N 116 34W
Nampula Mozambique **107** M4 15 09S 39 14E
Nam Sha Po Hong Kong U.K. **98** A2 22 29N 113 59E
Namsos Norway **79** C3 64 28N 11 30E
Namtu Myanmar **97** J3 23 04N 97 26E
Namur Belgium **76** C5 50 28N 4 52E
Nan Thailand **97** K2 18 50N 100 50E
Nanao Japan **100** C2 37 03N 136 58E
Nanchang China **97** N4 28 33N 115 58E
Nanchong China **97** L5 30 54N 106 06E
Nancy France **76** D4 48 42N 6 12E
Nanda Devi *mt.* India **95** E6 30 21N 79 58E
Nānded India **95** D3 19 11N 77 21E
Nanduri Fiji **114** U16 16 26S 179 08E
Nangi India **94** J1 22 30N 88 13E
Nanhai *l.* China **101** G1 39 55N 116 22E
Nanjing China **97** N5 32 03N 118 47E
Nan Ling *mts.* China **97** M3/M4 25 00N 112 00E
Nanning China **97** L3 22 50N 108 19E
Nanpan Jiang *r.* China **97** L3 25 00N 106 00E
Nanping China **97** N4 26 40N 118 07E
Nanri Dao *i.* Taiwan **98** F8 25 13N 119 29E
Nansei-shoto *see* Ryukyu Islands
Nan Shan *mts.* China **84** 38 00N 103 00E
Nantasket Beach Massachusetts U.S.A. **52** C2 42 17N 70 52W
Nanterre France **83** A2 48 53N 2 12E
Nantes France **77** B4 47 14N 1 35W
Nanticoke Pennsylvania U.S.A. **64** D4 41 13N 76 00W
Nantong China **97** O5 32 06N 121 04E
Nantō Japan **100** H1 34 17N 136 30E
Nan-t'ou Taiwan **98** G6 23 54N 120 42E
Nantucket Massachusetts U.S.A. **65** K4 41 17N 70 05W
Nantucket Island Massachusetts U.S.A. **65** K4 41 15N 70 05W
Nantucket Sound Massachusetts U.S.A. **65** K4 41 20N 70 15W
Nanuku Passage *sd.* Fiji **114** V16 16 40S 179 25W
Nanumea Island Pacific Ocean **114** H7 5 30S 175 40E
Nanyang China **97** M5 33 06N 112 31E
Nanyuan China **101** G1 39 48N 116 23E
Nanyuki Kenya **106** M8 0 01N 37 05E
Napier New Zealand **111** C3 39 29S 176 58E
Naples Florida U.S.A. **63** J2 26 09N 81 48W
Naples New York U.S.A. **64** C5 42 36N 77 25W
Naples *see* Napoli
Napoleon Ohio U.S.A. **35** D1 41 24N 84 09W
Napoli *(Naples)* Italy **81** B3 40 50N 14 15E
Napoopoo Hawaiian Islands **115** Z17 19 29N 155 55W
Nara Japan **100** G1 34 41N 135 49E
Nara *pref.* Japan **100** G1 34 25N 135 50E
Narayanganj Bangladesh **95** G4 23 36N 90 28E
Narbonne France **77** C3 43 11N 3 00E
Nares Deep Atlantic Ocean **113** C9 26 00N 61 10W
Narew *r.* Europe **81** D5 53 00N 21 00E
Narita Japan **100** M2 35 46N 140 20E
Narmada *r.* India **95** C4/D4 22 00N 75 00E
Narrabeen Australia **111** H3 33 43S 151 18E
Narragansett Pier *tn.* Rhode Island U.S.A. **65** J4 41 26N 71 27W
Narrogin Australia **110** B3 32 57S 117 07E
Narutō Japan **100** M2 35 37N 140 20E
Narva Estonia **79** F2 59 22N 28 17E
Narvik Norway **79** D4 68 26N 17 25E
Nar'yan Mar Russia **88** H9 67 37N 53 02E
Nasca Ridge Pacific Ocean **115** R5 20 00S 81 00W
Nashua New Hampshire U.S.A. **65** J5 42 44N 71 28W
Nashua River Massachusetts U.S.A. **65** J5 42 40N 71 35W
Nashville Tennessee U.S.A. **63** I4 36 10N 86 50W
Näsijärvi *l.* Finland **79** E3 61 45N 24 00E
Nasik India **95** C3 20 00N 73 52E
Nassau The Bahamas **67** I5 25 05N 77 20W
Nasser, Lake Egypt **92** D3 22 35N 31 40E
Nässjö Sweden **79** C2 57 40N 14 40E
Natal Brazil **68** J11 5 46S 35 15W
Natal *province* Republic of South Africa **107** L2 29 00S 31 00E
Natashō Japan **100** G2 35 23N 135 39E
Natchez Mississippi U.S.A. **63** H3 31 32N 91 24W
Natewa Peninsula Fiji **114** V16 16 40S 180 00
Natick Massachusetts U.S.A. **52** A2 42 17N 71 21W
Natron, Lake Tanzania **106** M7 2 00S 36 00E
Natuna Besar *i.* Indonesia **99** D4 4 00N 108 00E
Naturaliste, Cape Australia **110** B3 33 32S 115 01E
Naugatuck Connecticut U.S.A. **65** G4 41 30N 73 04W
NAURU 114 G7
Nausori Fiji **114** U15 18 01S 178 31E
Navadwīp India **95** F4 23 24N 88 23E
Navet Trinidad and Tobago **66** T9 10 15N 61 10W
Navet *r.* Trinidad and Tobago **66** T9 10 16N 61 10W
Navet Dam Trinidad and Tobago **66** T9 10 26N 61 12W
Navia *r.* Spain **77** A3 43 10N 7 05W
Naviti *i.* Fiji **114** T16 17 08S 177 15E
Navoi Uzbekistan **91** K3 40 04N 65 20E
Navojoa Mexico **66** C5 7 04N 109 28W
Návplion Greece **81** D2 37 34N 22 48E
Navsari India **95** C4 20 58N 73 01E
Náxos *i.* Greece **81** E2 37 00N 25 00E
Nayoro Japan **100** D3 44 21N 142 30E
Nazareth Israel **92** O11 32 41N 35 16E
Nazareth Pennsylvania U.S.A. **64** E3 40 44N 75 18W
Nazca Peru **68** C9 14 53S 74 54W
Nazilli Turkey **80** E2 37 55N 28 20E
Nazwá Oman **93** I3 22 56N 57 33E
Ndélé Central African Republic **106** J9 8 25N 20 38E
Ndjamena Chad **106** I10 12 10N 14 59E
Ndola Zambia **107** K5 13 00S 28 39E
Neah Bay *tn.* Washington U.S.A. **42** H4 48 22N 124 36W
Néapolis Greece **81** D2 36 31N 23 03E
Neath Wales **78** H3 51 40N 3 48W
Nebit-Dag Turkmenistan **91** G2 39 31N 54 24E
Nebraska *state* U.S.A. **62** F5 42 00N 102 00W
Neche North Dakota U.S.A. **39** B1 48 59N 97 34W
Neckei *i.* Hawaiian Islands **115** J10 23 25N 164 42W
Necochea Argentina **69** F5 38 31S 58 46W
Nedrow New York U.S.A. **64** D5 42 57N 76 11W
Needham Massachusetts U.S.A. **52** B2 42 17N 71 14W
Negelē Ethiopia **106** M9 5 20N 39 35E
Negev *d.* Israel **92** O10 30 50N 30 45E
Negombo Sri Lanka **95** D1 7 13N 79 51E
Negritos Peru **68** A2 4 42S 81 18W
Negros *i.* The Philippines **99** G5 10 00N 123 00E
Neijiang China **97** L4 29 32N 105 03E
Nei Mongol Zizhiqu *(Inner Mongolia Autonomous Region) admin.* China **97** L7/N2 42 30N 112 30E
Neisse *(Nysa) r.* Germany **80** B5 52 00N 14 00E
Neiva Colombia **68** B13 2 58N 75 15W
Nek'emtē Ethiopia **106** M9 9 04N 36 30E
Nellore India **95** D2 14 29N 80 00E
Nelson New Zealand **111** B2 41 18S 173 17E
Nelson Reservoir Montana U.S.A. **40** B1 48 30N 107 40W
Neman *r.* Lithuania/Russia **80** D5/6 55 00N 22 00E
Nemuro Japan **100** E3 43 22N 145 36E
Nemuro-kaikyō *sd.* Japan **100** E3 44 00N 146 00E
Nenana Alaska U.S.A. **10** F5 64 35N 149 20W
Nene *r.* England **78** K4 52 25N 0 05E
Nenjiang China **97** P8 49 10N 125 15E
Nen Jiang *r.* China **97** P9 50 00N 125 00E
NEPAL 95 E5
Neponset River Massachusetts U.S.A. **52** B2 42 16N 71 06W
Nerchinsk Russia **89** N6 52 02N 116 38E
Neretva *r.* Bosnia-Herzegovina **81** C3 43 30N 15 18E
Nerva Spain **77** A2 37 41N 6 33W
Neryungri Russia **89** O7 56 39N 124 38E
Neskaupstadur Iceland **79** J7 65 10N 13 43W
Nestor Trinidad and Tobago **66** T10 10 31N 61 09W
Netanya Israel **92** O11 32 20N 34 51E
Netcong New Jersey U.S.A. **65** F3 40 54N 74 43W
NETHERLANDS 76 C5/D5
Neubrandenburg Germany **76** E5 53 33N 13 16E
Neuchâtel Switzerland **77** D4 46 55N 6 56E
Neuenhagen Germany **83** G2 52 32N 13 41E
Neufchâtel-en-Bray France **76** C4 49 44N 1 26E
Neuilly France **83** B2 48 53N 2 17E
Neuilly Plaisance France **83** C2 48 51N 2 31E
Neukölln Germany **83** F1 52 29N 13 28E
Neumünster Germany **76** D5 54 05N 9 59E
Neuquén Argentina **69** D5 38 55N 68 05W
Neuruppin Germany **76** E5 52 56N 12 49E
Neusiedler See *l.* Austria **81** C4 48 00N 16 00E
Neuss Germany **76** G1 51 12N 6 42E
Neustrelitz Germany **76** E5 53 22N 13 05E
Nevada *state* U.S.A. **62** C4 39 00N 118 00W
Nevers France **77** C4 47 00N 3 09E
Neversink Reservoir New York U.S.A. **65** F4 41 50N 74 40W
Neves Brazil **69** Q2 22 51S 43 05W
Nevinnomyssk Russia **90** E3 44 38N 41 59E
Neviot Egypt **92** O9 28 58N 34 38E
New *r.* U.S.A. **63** J4 37 00N 81 00W
New Addington England **82** C2 51 21N 0 01E
New Albany Indiana U.S.A. **63** I4 38 17N 85 50W
New Amsterdam Guyana **68** F14 6 10N 57 30W
Newark California U.S.A. **49** C2 37 31N 122 03W
Newark Delaware U.S.A. **64** E2 39 42N 75 45W
Newark New Jersey U.S.A. **65** F3 40 44N 74 12W
Newark New York U.S.A. **64** C6 43 03N 77 06W
Newark Ohio U.S.A. **63** J5 40 03N 82 25W
Newark Bay New Jersey U.S.A. **50** B1 40 40N 74 08W
New Bedford Massachusetts U.S.A. **65** K4 41 38N 70 56W
New Bern North Carolina U.S.A. **63** K4 35 05N 77 04W
Newberry Michigan U.S.A. **35** C2 46 22N 85 30W
New Bloomfield Pennsylvania U.S.A. **64** D3 40 25N 76 13W
New Braunfels Texas U.S.A. **63** G2 29 43N 98 09W
New Britain Connecticut U.S.A. **65** H4 41 40N 72 47W
New Britain *i.* Papua New Guinea **110** I8 6 10S 150 00E
New Brunswick New Jersey U.S.A. **65** F3 40 29N 74 27W
Newburgh New York U.S.A. **65** F4 41 30N 74 00W
Newburyport Massachusetts U.S.A. **65** K5 42 47N 70 53W
New Caledonia *i.* Pacific Ocean **110** K5/L5 22 00S 165 00E
New Canaan Connecticut U.S.A. **65** G4 41 09N 73 30W
Newcastle Australia **110** I3 32 55S 151 46E
New Castle Delaware U.S.A. **64** E2 39 40N 75 34W
Newcastle upon Tyne England **78** J7 54 59N 1 35W
New City New York U.S.A. **65** F4 41 08N 74 00W
New Croton Reservoir New York U.S.A. **65** G4 41 15N 73 45W
New Delhi India **94** M4 28 37N 77 14E
New Dorp New York U.S.A. **50** B1 40 34N 74 06W
Newfane New York U.S.A. **64** B6 43 17N 78 42W
Newfane Vermont U.S.A. **65** H5 42 59N 72 40W
Newfield New York U.S.A. **64** D5 42 22N 76 36W
Newfoundland Basin Atlantic Ocean **113** D11 44 00N 40 00W
New Georgia Islands Solomon Islands **110** J8 8 00S 157 00E
New Grant Trinidad and Tobago **66** T9 10 17N 61 19W
New Guinea *i.* Pacific Ocean **110** G8 6 00S 142 00E
Newhalem Washington U.S.A. **42** H4 48 41N 121 15W
Newham *bor.* Greater London England **82** D3 51 30N 0 02E
New Hampshire *state* U.S.A. **65** H4 43 00N 72 00W
New Hartford Connecticut U.S.A. **65** H4 41 52N 72 58W
New Haven Connecticut U.S.A. **65** H4 41 18N 72 55W
New Hebrides Trench Pacific Ocean **114** G6 15 00S 169 00E
New Hope Pennsylvania U.S.A. **64** E3 40 22N 74 56W
New Hyde Park New York U.S.A. **50** D1 40 44N 73 42W
New Iberia Louisiana U.S.A. **63** H2 30 00N 91 51W
New Ireland *i.* Papua New Guinea **110** I9 3 00S 152 00E
New Jersey *state* U.S.A **64/65** E2/F2 40 00N 75 00W
New Kensington Pennsylvania U.S.A. **53** E2 40 34N 79 46W
New Lebanon New York U.S.A. **65** G5 42 27N 73 24W
New London Connecticut U.S.A. **65** H4 41 21N 72 06W
New London New Hampshire U.S.A. **65** J6 43 25N 71 58W
New London Ohio U.S.A. **36** D2 41 05N 82 24W
Newman Australia **110** B5 23 20S 119 34E
New Mexico *state* U.S.A. **62** E3 35 00N 107 00W
New Milford Connecticut U.S.A. **65** G4 41 35N 73 25W
New Milford Pennsylvania U.S.A. **64** E4 41 52N 75 44W
New Orleans Louisiana U.S.A. **63** H2 30 00N 90 03W
New Paltz New York U.S.A. **65** F4 41 45N 74 05W
New Plymouth New Zealand **111** B3 39 03S 174 04E

Newport Australia **111** H3 33 39S 151 19E
Newport Wales **78** H3 51 35N 3 00W
Newport New Hampshire U.S.A. **65** H6 43 22N 72 11W
Newport Rhode Island U.S.A. **65** J4 41 30N 71 19W
Newport Vermont U.S.A. **33** B1 44 56N 72 13W
Newport News Virginia U.S.A. **63** K4 36 59N 76 26W
New Providence *i.* The Bahamas **67** I5 25 00N 77 30W
New Rochelle New York U.S.A. **50** C2 40 55N 73 46W
Newry Northern Ireland **78** E6 54 11N 6 20W
New Siberian Islands Russia **89** Q10 75 00N 145 00E
New South Wales *state* Australia **110** G3/G4 32 00S 145 00E
New Springville New York U.S.A. **50** B1 40 35N 74 10W
New Territories *admin.* Hong Kong U.K. **98** B2 22 20N 114 00E
Newton Massachusetts U.S.A. **52** B2 42 20N 71 13W
Newton New Jersey U.S.A. **65** E4 41 03N 74 45W
Newtown Connecticut U.S.A. **65** G4 41 25N 73 19W
Newtownabbey Northern Ireland **78** F6 54 40N 5 54W
New Ulm Minnesota U.S.A. **63** H5 44 19N 94 28W
New York New York U.S.A. **65** G3 40 40N 73 50W
New York *state* U.S.A. **63** K5 43 00N 76 00W
NEW ZEALAND **111**
Neyagawa Japan **100** G1 34 45N 135 36E
Neyrīz Iran **93** H4 29 14N 54 18E
Neyshābūr Iran **93** I6 36 13N 58 49E
Ngami, Lake Botswana **107** J3 21 00S 23 00E
Ngangla Ringco *l.* China **95** E6 31 40N 83 00E
Nganze Co *l.* China **95** F6 31 00N 87 00E
Ngaoundéré Cameroon **106** H9 7 20N 13 35E
Ngau *i.* Fiji **114** U15 18 00S 179 16E
Ngau Chi Wan Hong Kong U.K. **98** C2 22 25N 114 10E
Ngau Kwu Long Hong Kong U.K. **98** A1 22 18N 113 58E
Ngauruhoe *mt.* New Zealand **111** C3 39 10S 175 40E
Ngau Tam Mei Hong Kong U.K. **98** B2 22 28N 114 04E
Ngau Tau Kok Hong Kong U.K. **98** C1 22 19N 114 13E
Ngong Ping Hong Kong U.K. **98** A1 22 15N 113 54E
Nguigmi Niger **106** H10 14 19N 13 06E
Nguru Nigeria **106** H10 12 53N 10 30E
Nha Trang Vietnam **99** C6 12 15N 109 10E
Nhulunbuy Australia **110** F7 12 30S 136 56E
Niagara Falls *tn.* New York U.S.A. **64** A6 43 06N 79 04W
Niagara River New York U.S.A. **38** C2 43 15N 79 04W
Niamey Niger **106** F10 13 32N 2 05E
Niangara Zaïre **106** K8 3 45N 27 54E
Niantic Connecticut U.S.A. **65** H4 41 20N 72 12W
Nias *i.* Indonesia **99** B4 1 30N 97 30E
Nibra India **94** K2 22 35N 88 15E
NICARAGUA **67** G2
Nice France **77** D3 43 42N 7 16E
Nicobar Islands India **95** G1 8 30N 94 00E
Nicosia Cyprus **92** D6 35 11N 33 23E
Nidd *r.* England **78** J6 54 02N 1 30W
Niedere Tauern *mts.* Austria **81** B4 47 00N 14 00E
Nienburg Germany **76** D5 52 38N 9 13E
Nieuw Nickerie Surinam **68** F14 5 52N 57 00W
NIGER **106** G11
Niger *r.* Nigeria **106** G9 5 30N 6 15E
Niger Delta Nigeria **102** 5 00N 7 00E
NIGERIA **106** G10
Niigata Japan **100** C2 37 58N 139 02E
Niihama Japan **100** B1 33 57N 133 15E
Niihau *i.* Hawaiian Islands **115** W18 21 50N 160 11W
Nii-jima *i.* Japan **100** C1 34 20N 139 15E
Niiza Japan **101** B4 35 48N 139 35E
Nijmegen Netherlands **76** D5 51 50N 5 52E
Nikko Japan **100** C2 36 45N 139 37E
Nikolayev Ukraine **90** C4 46 57N 32 00E
Nikolayevsk-na-Amure Russia **89** Q6 53 10N 140 44E
Nikol'skiy *see* Satlayev
Nikopol Ukraine **90** C4 45 34N 34 25E
Nikšić Montenegro Yugoslavia **81** C3 42 48N 18 56E
Nile *r.* Egypt **92** D4 28 30N 30 40E
Nile Delta Egypt **102** 31 00N 31 00E
Niles Illinois U.S.A. **53** A3 42 00N 87 48W
Nilgri Hills India **95** D2 11 00N 76 30E
Nimes France **77** C3 43 50N 4 21E
Nimule Sudan **106** L8 3 35N 32 03E
Nim Wan Hong Kong U.K. **98** A2 22 25N 113 56E
Ninepin Group *is.* Hong Kong U.K. **98** D1 22 15N 114 20E
Ninety East Ridge Indian Ocean **112** H4/H6
Ninety Mile Beach New Zealand **111** B4 34 50S 173 00E
Nineveh *hist. site* Iraq **92** F6 36 24N 43 08E
Ningbo China **97** O4 29 54N 121 33E
Ninh Binh Vietnam **97** L3 20 14N 106 00E
Niobrara *r.* U.S.A. **62** F5 42 00N 102 00W
Nioro du Sahel Mali **106** D11 15 12N 9 35W
Niort France **77** B4 46 19N 0 27W
Niš Serbia Yugoslavia **81** D3 43 20N 21 54E
Nishi Japan **101** B2 35 26N 139 37E
Nishinomiya Japan **100** G1 34 44N 135 22E
Nishio Japan **100** J1 34 52N 137 02E
Nishiwaki Japan **100** F2 35 00N 134 58E
Nitra Czechoslovakia **80** C4 48 19N 18 04E
Niue *i.* Pacific Ocean **115** J6 19 02S 169 55W
Nizamabad India **95** D3 18 40N 78 05E
Nizhiy Tagil Russia **91** H6 58 00N 59 58E
Nizhneangarsk Russia **89** M7 55 48N 109 35E
Nizhnekamsk Russia **90** G6 55 38N 51 49E
Nizhnekamskoye Vodokhranilishche *res.* Russia **91** G6 56 00N 53 30E
Nizhnenkolymsk Russia **89** S9 68 34N 160 58E
Nizhnevartovsk Russia **91** M7 60 57N 76 40E
Nizhniy Novgorod *(Gor'kiy)* Russia **90** E6 56 20N 44 00E
Nizhniy Novgorod *(Gor'kovskoye)* **Vodokhranilishche** *res.* Russia **90** E6 57 00N 43 30E
Nizhnyaya *(Lower)* **Tunguska** *r.* Russia **89** L8/M8 64 00N 94 00E
Nizké Tatry *mts.* Czechoslovakia **80** C4 49 00N 19 00E
Nkongsamba Cameroon **106** G9 4 59N 9 53E
Noatak Alaska U.S.A. **10** C6 67 33N 163 10W
Noatak *r.* Alaska U.S.A. **10** C6 67 33N 163 10W
Nobeoka Japan **100** B1 32 36N 131 40E
Nobi Japan **101** B1 35 11N 139 41E
Noda Japan **100** L2 35 57N 139 52E
Nogales Arizona U.S.A. **62** D3 31 20N 110 56W
Nogales Mexico **66** B6 31 20N 111 00W
Nogent France **83** C2 48 50N 2 30E
Noisy-le-Sec France **83** B2 48 53N 2 27E
Nojima-zaki *c.* Japan **100** L1 34 54N 139 54E
Nola Central African Republic **106** I8 3 28N 16 08E
Nome Alaska U.S.A. **10** B5 64 30N 165 30W
Nong Khai Laos **97** K2 18 00N 102 40E
Noorvik Alaska U.S.A. **10** C6 66 50N 161 14W
Nordfjord *fj.* Norway **79** B3 62 00N 5 15E
Nordfold Norway **79** D4 67 48N 15 20E
Nordfriesische Inseln *(North Frisian Islands) is.* Germany **80** A5 54 00N 8 00E
Nordhausen Germany **76** E5 51 31N 10 48E
Nordkapp *(North Cape) c.* Norway **79** E5 71 11N 25 40E
Nordvik Russia **89** N10 74 01N 111 30E
Nore *r.* Irish Republic **78** D4 52 25N 7 02W
Norfolk Nebraska U.S.A. **63** G5 42 01N 97 25W
Norfolk Virginia U.S.A. **63** K4 36 54N 76 18W
Norfolk County Massachusetts U.S.A. **52** A2 42 20N 71 08W
Norfolk Island Pacific Ocean **114** G5 29 05S 167 59E
Norfolk Island Trough Pacific Ocean **114** G5 27 30S 166 00E
Norfolk Lake Arkansas U.S.A. **63** H4 36 00N 92 00W
Noril'sk Russia **89** K9 69 21N 88 02E
Normanton Australia **110** G6 17 40S 141 05E
Norridgewock Maine U.S.A. **37** R5 44 43N 69 48W
Norris Lake Tennessee U.S.A. **63** J4 36 00N 84 00W
Norristown Pennsylvania U.S.A. **64** E3 40 07N 75 20W
Norrköping Sweden **79** D2 58 35N 16 10E
Norrtälje Sweden **80** C6 59 46N 18 42E
Norseman Australia **110** C3 32 15S 121 47E
North Adams Massachusetts U.S.A. **65** G5 42 42N 73 07W
Northam Australia **110** B3 31 40S 116 40E
North American Basin Atlantic Ocean **113** C10 34 00N 55 00W
Northampton Australia **110** A4 28 27S 114 37E
Northampton England **78** K4 52 14N 0 54W
Northampton Massachusetts U.S.A. **65** H2 42 19N 72 38W
North Andaman *i.* Andaman Islands **95** G2 13 00N 93 00E
North Australian Basin Indian Ocean **112** K5 14 00S 115 00E
North Baltimore Ohio U.S.A. **36** C2 41 12N 83 43W
North Barrackpore India **94** K3 22 46N 88 21E
North Bergen New Jersey U.S.A. **50** B2 40 46N 74 02W
North Branch New Hampshire U.S.A. **65** J6 43 05N 71 59W
North Branch Chicago River Illinois U.S.A. **53** A3 42 09N 87 50W
Northbrook Illinois U.S.A. **53** A3 42 07N 87 49W
North Canadian *r.* U.S.A. **62** F4 36 00N 100 00W
North Cape New Zealand **111** B4 34 23S 173 04E
North Cape *see* Nordkapp
North Carolina *state* U.S.A. **63** K4 36 00N 80 00W
North Cascades National Park Washington U.S.A. **42** H4 48 45N 121 20W
North Channel British Isles **78** F7 55 20N 5 50W
North Chili New York U.S.A. **64** C6 43 06N 77 52W
North Collins New York U.S.A. **38** D1 42 36N 78 57W
North Dakota *state* U.S.A. **62** F6 47 00N 102 00W
North Dartmouth Massachusetts U.S.A. **65** K4 41 37N 70 59W
North Downs *hills* England **82** D2 51 13N 0 30W
North East Pennsylvania U.S.A. **36** G3 42 13N 79 15W
Northern Cyprus *admin.* Cyprus **92** D6 35 15N 33 00E
Northern Ireland United Kingdom **78** D6
NORTHERN MARIANAS **114** E9
Northern Range *mts.* Trinidad and Tobago **66** T10 10 47N 61 27W
Northern Territory *territory* Australia **110** E5/E6 19 00S 132 00E
North Esk *r.* Scotland **78** I8 56 50N 2 50W
North European Plain Europe **70** 54 00N 20 00E
North Fiji Basin Pacific Ocean **114** H6 18 00S 173 00E
North Fork *r.* Alaska U.S.A. **44** A4 67 30N 152 00W
North Frisian Islands *see* Nordfriesische Inseln
North Haven Connecticut U.S.A. **65** H4 41 00N 72 00W
North Head Australia **111** H2 33 49S 151 18E
North Hollywood California U.S.A. **51** A3 34 10N 118 22W
North Island New Zealand **111** C3 36 40S 177 00E
NORTH KOREA **97** P6/7
Northlake Illinois U.S.A. **53** A2 41 52N 87 56W
North Land *see* Severnaya Zemlya
North Little Rock Arkansas U.S.A. **63** H3 34 46N 92 16W
North Loup *r.* Nebraska U.S.A. **62** F5 42 00N 100 00W
North Platte Nebraska U.S.A. **62** F5 41 09N 100 45W
North Platte *r.* U.S.A. **62** F5 42 00N 103 00W
North Point Barbados **66** V13 13 20N 59 37W
North Point *tn.* Hong Kong U.K. **98** C1 22 18N 114 12E
North Pole Arctic Ocean **116** 90 00N
Northport New York U.S.A. **65** G3 40 55N 73 21W
North Reading Massachusetts U.S.A. **65** J5 42 35N 71 06W
North Scituate Rhode Island U.S.A. **65** J4 41 49N 71 35W
North Sea Europe **70** 55 00N 3 00E
North Stratford New Hampshire U.S.A. **37** P5 44 46N 71 36W
North Tonawanda New York U.S.A. **64** B6 43 02N 78 54W
North Uist *i.* Scotland **78** D9 57 04N 7 15W
Northumberland Pennsylvania U.S.A. **64** D3 40 54N 76 49W
Northville New York U.S.A. **65** F6 43 14N 74 12W
North West Cape Australia **110** A5 21 48S 114 10E
North West Christmas Island Ridge Pacific Ocean **115** J8 9 30N 170 00W
Northwestern Atlantic Basin Atlantic Ocean **113** B10 33 00N 70 00W
Northwest Highlands Scotland **78** F8/G10
Northwest Pacific Basin Pacific Ocean **114** F11 35 00N 150 00E
Northwood England **82** B3 51 36N 0 25W
North York Moors National Park England **78** K6 55 22N 0 45W
Norton Kansas U.S.A. **62** G4 39 51N 99 53W
Norton Sound Alaska U.S.A. **10** C5 64 00N 162 30W
Norvegia, Cape Antarctica **117** 71 28S 122 25W
Norwalk California U.S.A. **51** B2 33 56N 118 04W
Norwalk Connecticut U.S.A. **65** G4 41 07N 73 25W
Norwalk Ohio U.S.A. **36** D2 41 14N 82 37W
NORWAY **79** B3
Norwegian Basin Arctic Ocean **113** H13 67 00N 0 00
Norwegian Sea Arctic Ocean **116** 70 00N 5 00E
Norwich Connecticut U.S.A. **65** H4 41 32N 72 05W
Norwich England **78** M4 52 38N 1 18E
Norwich New York U.S.A. **64** E5 42 32N 75 32W
Norwood Massachusetts U.S.A. **52** B1 42 12N 71 13W
Noshiro Japan **100** D3 40 13N 140 00E
Nosop *r.* Southern Africa **107** I3 25 00S 20 30E
Nosy Bé *i.* Madagascar **107** N5 13 00S 47 00E
Notéc *r.* Poland **80** C5 53 00N 17 00E
Nottingham England **78** J4 52 58N 1 10W
Nouadhibou Mauritania **106** B12 20 54N 17 01W
Nouakchott Mauritania **106** A11 18 09N 15 58W
Nouméa New Caledonia **110** L5 22 16S 166 26E
Nova Friburgo Brazil **69** I8 22 16S 42 34W
Nova Iguaçu Brazil **69** P2 22 46S 43 23W
Novara Italy **81** A4 45 27N 8 37E
Nova Scotia Basin Atlantic Ocean **113** C19 39 00N 55 00W
Novaya Zemlya *is.* Russia **89** H10 74 00N 55 00E
Novgorod Russia **90** C6 58 30N 31 20E
Novi Pazar Serbia Yugoslavia **81** D3 43 09N 20 29E
Novi Sad SerbiaYugoslavia **81** C4 45 15N 19 51E
Novocheboksarsk Russia **90** F6 56 05N 47 27E
Novocherkassk Russia **90** E4 47 25N 40 05E
Novo Hamburgo Brazil **69** G7 29 37S 51 07W
Novokazalinsk Kazakhstan **91** J4 45 48N 62 06E
Novokuybyshevsk Russia **90** F5 53 05N 49 59E
Novokuznetsk Russia **91** O5 53 45N 87 12E
Novolazarevskaya *r.s.* Antarctica **117** 70 46S 11 50E
Novomoskovsk Russia **90** D5 54 06N 38 15E
Novorossiysk Russia **90** D3 44 44N 37 46E
Novoshakhtinsk Russia **90** D4 47 46N 39 55E
Novosibirsk Russia **91** N6 55 04N 83 05E
Novotroitsk Russia **91** H5 51 11N 58 16E
Novyy Port Russia **89** J9 67 38N 72 33E
Novyy Urengoy Russia **89** J9 66 00N 77 20E
Nowai *r.* India **94** K2 22 39N 88 28E
Nowa Sól Poland **80** C5 51 49N 15 41E
Nowgong India **95** G5 26 20N 92 41E
Nowy Dwor Poland **80** D5 52 27N 20 41E
Nowy Sącz Poland **80** D4 49 39N 20 40E
Noyes Island Alaska U.S.A. **42** B3 56 30N 133 45W
Nubian Desert Sudan **92** D3 21 00N 33 00E
Nueces *r.* Texas U.S.A. **62** G2 28 00N 99 00W
Nueva Rosita Mexico **66** D5 27 58N 101 11W
Nueva San Salvador El Salvador **66** G2 13 40N 89 18W
Nuevitas Cuba **67** I4 21 34N 77 18W
Nuevo Casa Grandes Mexico **66** C6 30 22N 107 53W
Nuevo Laredo Mexico **66** E5 27 39N 99 30W
Nu Jiang *(Salween) r.* China **95** G6 31 30N 94 00E
Nuku'alofa Tonga **114** I5 21 09S 175 14W
Nukus Uzbekistan **91** H3 42 28N 59 07E
Nullarbor Plain Australia **110** D3 32 00S 128 00E
Numazu Japan **100** K2 35 08N 138 50E
Numedal *geog. reg.* Norway **79** B3 60 40N 9 00E
Nunivak Island Alaska U.S.A. **10** B5 60 00N 166 00W
Nura *r.* Kazakhstan **91** L5 51 00N 71 00E
Nuremberg *see* Nürnberg
Nürnberg *(Nuremberg)* Germany **76** E4 49 27N 11 05E
Nuseybin Turkey **92** F6 37 05N 41 11E
Nushki Pakistan **94** B5 29 33N 66 01E
Nuthe *r.* Germany **83** E1 52 21N 13 07E
Nuussuaq *p.* Greenland **11** Y7 70 50N 53 00W
Nyainqêntanglha Shan *mts.* China **96** G4/J5 30 00N 90 00E
Nyala Sudan **106** J10 12 01N 24 50E
Nyasa, Lake *(Lake Malawi)* Southern Africa **107** L5 12 00S 35 00E
Nyíregyháza Hungary **81** D4 47 57N 21 43E
Nykøbing Denmark **80** B5 54 47N 11 53E
Nyköping Sweden **79** D2 58 45N 17 03E
Nyngan Australia **110** H3 31 34S 147 14E
Nyons France **77** D3 44 22N 5 08E
Nysa Poland **80** C5 50 30N 17 20E
Nysa *(Neisse) r.* Poland **80** B5 52 00N 14 00E
Nyū dō-zaki *c.* Japan **100** C2 40 00N 139 42E

O

Oahe, Lake U.S.A. **62** F6 45 00N 100 00W
Oahu *i.* Hawaiian Islands **115** X18 21 30N 158 10W
Oak Bluffs Massachusetts U.S.A. **65** K4 41 28N 70 33W
Oak Brook Illinois U.S.A. **53** A2 41 50N 87 59W
Oak Harbor Ohio U.S.A. **36** C2 41 31N 83 10W
Oak Harbor Washington U.S.A. **42** H4 48 17N 122 38W
Oakland California U.S.A. **49** B3 37 50N 122 15W
Oakland County Michigan U.S.A. **52** D2 42 26N 83 27W
Oakland Inner Harbor California U.S.A. **49** B3 37 47N 122 19W
Oak Lawn Illinois U.S.A. **53** A1 41 42N 87 45W
Oak Park Illinois U.S.A. **53** A2 41 52N 87 47W
Oak Park Michigan U.S.A. **52** E2 42 26N 83 09W
Oak Ridge *tn.* Tennessee U.S.A. **63** J4 36 02N 84 12W
Oak Street Beach Illinois U.S.A. **53** B2 41 54N 87 36W
Oamaru New Zealand **111** B1 45 07S 170 58E
Oano Island Pitcairn Islands **115** N5 23 32S 125 00W
Ōarai Japan **100** M3 36 18N 140 35E
Oaxaca Mexico **66** E3 17 05N 96 41W
Ob' *r.* Russia **91** K7 65 30N 66 00E
Ob', Gulf of Russia **89** J9 68 00N 74 00E
Obama Japan **100** G2 35 25N 135 45E
Oban Scotland **78** F8 56 25N 5 29W
Oberhausen Germany **76** H2 51 27N 6 50E
Oberlin Ohio U.S.A. **36** D2 41 17N 82 14W
Obidos Brazil **68** F12 1 52S 55 30W
Obihiro Japan **100** D3 42 56N 143 10E
Obitsu *r.* Japan **101** C2 35 25N 139 53E
Ocala Florida U.S.A. **63** J2 29 11N 82 09W
Ocaña Colombia **68** C14 8 16N 73 21W
Ocatlán Mexico **66** D4 20 21N 102 42W
Ocean City New Jersey U.S.A. **65** F2 39 16N 74 35W
Ochakovo Russia **88** L1 55 39N 37 30E
Ocho Rios Jamaica **67** Q8 18 24N 77 06W
Ōda Japan **100** B2 35 10N 132 29E
Ōdate Japan **100** D3 40 18N 140 32E
Odawara Japan **100** L2 35 15N 139 08E
Odda Norway **79** B3 60 03N 6 34E
Ödemiş Turkey **80** E2 38 11N 27 58E
Odense Denmark **80** B6 55 24N 10 25E
Odenwald *mts.* Germany **76** D4 49 00N 9 00E
Oder *(Odra) r.* Europe **80** C5 52 39 27N 75 40W
Odessa New York U.S.A. **64** D5 42 21N 76 46W
Odessa Texas U.S.A. **62** F3 31 50N 102 23W
Odessa Ukraine **90** C4 46 30N 30 46E
Odiel *r.* Spain **77** A2 37 32N 7 00W
Odra *(Oder) r.* Europe **80** C5 52 00N 15 00E
Oekusi *(Dili)* Indonesia **99** H2 8 35S 125 35E
Ofanto *r.* Italy **81** C3 41 00N 15 00E
Ofuna Japan **101** B2 53 21N 139 32E
Ofunato Japan **100** D2 39 04N 141 43E
Ogaden *geog. reg* Africa **106** O9 7 00N 51 00E
Ōgaki Japan **100** H2 35 25N 136 36E
Ogano Japan **100** L2 35 55N 139 11E
Ogasawara Guntō *i.* Pacific Ocean **114** E10 27 30N 43 00E
Ogawa Japan **101** A3 35 43N 135 29E
Ogbomosho Nigeria **106** F9 8 05N 4 11E
Ogden Utah U.S.A. **62** D5 41 14N 111 59W
Ogooué *r.* Gabon **106** G7 0 50S 9 50E
Ogun *r.* Nigeria **107** V3 6 42N 3 29E
Ogunquit Maine U.S.A. **65** K6 43 16N 70 37W
Ōhara Japan **100** M2 35 16N 140 22E
Ōhata Japan **100** D3 41 22N 141 11E
Ohio *state* U.S.A. **63** J5 40 00N 83 00W
Ohio River Pennsylvania U.S.A. **53** D1 40 30N 80 05W
Ohridsko ezero *l.* Europe **81** D3 41 00N 21 00E
Oil City Pennsylvania U.S.A. **36** G2 41 26N 79 44W
Oise *r.* France **76** C4 49 10N 2 10E
Ōita Japan **100** B1 33 15N 131 36E
Ojinaga Mexico **66** D5 29 35N 104 26W
Oka *r.* Russia **90** E6 55 00N 42 00E
Okanogan Washington U.S.A. **42** J4 48 22N 119 35W
Okanogan River Washington U.S.A. **42** J4 48 40N 119 30W
Okara Pakistan **95** C6 30 49N 73 31E
Okavango *r.* Southern Africa **107** I4 17 50S 20 00E
Okavango Basin Botswana **107** J4 19 00S 23 00E
Okaya Japan **100** C2 36 03N 138 00E
Okayama Japan **100** B1 34 40N 133 54E
Okazaki Japan **100** J1 34 58N 137 10E
Okeechobee, Lake Florida U.S.A. **63** J2 27 00N 81 00W
Okha Russia **89** Q6 53 35N 143 01E
Okhla India **94** M4 28 33N 77 16E
Okhotsk Russia **89** Q7 59 20N 143 15E
Okhotsk, Sea of Russia **89** Q7 55 00N 148 00E
Oki *is.* Japan **100** B2 36 05N 133 00E
Okinawa *i.* Japan **97** P4 26 30N 128 00E
Oklahoma *state* U.S.A. **63** G4 36 00N 98 00W
Oklahoma City Oklahoma U.S.A. **63** G4 35 28N 97 33W
Oktyabr'skiy Russia **89** R6 52 43N 156 14E
Okushiri-tō *i.* Japan **100** C3 42 15N 139 30E
Öland *i.* Sweden **79** D2 56 45N 51 50E
Olbia Italy **81** A3 40 56N 9 30E
Old Bridge New Jersey U.S.A. **65** F3 40 27N 74 23W
Oldenburg Germany **76** D5 53 08N 8 13E
Oldham England **78** I5 53 33N 2 07W
Old Harbor Massachusetts U.S.A. **52** B2 42 19N 71 02W
Old Harbour Jamaica **67** Q7 17 56N 77 07W
Old Harbour Bay *tn.* Jamaica **67** Q7 17 54N 77 06W
Old Head of Kinsale *c.* Irish Republic **78** C3 51 40N 8 30W
Old Saybrook Connecticut U.S.A. **65** H4 41 18N 72 22W
Old Town Maine U.S.A. **33** C1 44 55N 68 41W
Olean New York U.S.A. **64** B5 42 05N 78 26W
Olekma *r.* Russia **89** O7 59 00N 121 00E
Olekminsk Russia **89** O8 60 25N 120 25E
Olenëk Russia **89** N9 68 28N 112 18E
Olenëk *r.* Russia **89** O10 72 00N 122 00E
Olga Washington U.S.A. **42** H4 48 36N 122 50W
Olhão Portugal **77** A2 37 01N 7 50W
Ólimbos *(Olympus) mt.* Greece **81** D3 40 05N 22 21E
Olinda Brazil **68** J11 8 00S 34 51W
Olomouc Czechoslovakia **80** C4 49 38N 17 15E
Olongapo The Philippines **99** G6 14 49N 120 17E
Olsztyn Poland **80** D5 53 48N 20 29E
Olt *r.* Romania **81** D3 44 00N 24 00E
O'luan-pi *c.* Taiwan **98** G4 21 54N 120 53E
Olympia Washington U.S.A. **62** B6 47 03N 122 53W
Olympus *see* Ólimbos
Olympus, Mount Washington U.S.A. **62** B6 47 49N 123 42W
Olympus Mountain Cyprus **92** D5 34 55N 32 52E
Om' *r.* Russia **91** M6 55 00N 79 00E
Omaha Nebraska U.S.A. **63** G5 41 15N 96 00W
Omagh Northern Ireland **78** D6 54 36N 7 18W
Omak Washington U.S.A. **43** E1 48 25N 119 30W
OMAN **93** I2
Oman, Gulf of Iran/Oman **93** I3 24 30N 58 30E
Omboué Gabon **106** G7 1 38S 9 20E
Omdurman Sudan **92** D2 15 37N 32 29E
Ome Japan **100** L2 35 48N 139 17E
Omihachiman Japan **100** H2 35 08N 136 04E
Ōmiya Japan **100** L2 35 54N 139 39E
Ommaney, Cape Alaska U.S.A. **42** B3 56 10N 134 40W
Omo *r.* Ethiopia **106** M9 7 00N 37 00E
Omolon *r.* Russia **89** R9 65 00N 160 00E
Omoloy *r.* Russia **89** P9 69 00N 132 00E
Omsk Russia **91** L6 55 00N 73 22E
Ōmuta Japan **100** B1 33 02N 130 26E
Omutinskiy Russia **91** K6 56 30N 67 40E
Onaway Michigan U.S.A. **36** B6 45 23N 84 14W
Oneida New York U.S.A. **64** E6 43 04N 75 40W
Oneida Lake New York U.S.A. **64** E6 43 10N 75 55W
Oneonta New York U.S.A. **64** E5 42 56N 75 04W
Ongea Levu *i.* Fiji **114** V15 19 11S 178 28W
Onitsha Nigeria **106** G9 6 10N 6 47E
Ono Japan **100** F1 34 52N 134 55E
Onomichi Japan **100** B1 34 25N 33 11E
Onon *r.* Mongolia/Russia **97** M9 51 00N 114 00E
Onslow Australia **110** B5 21 41S 115 12E
Ontario, Lake Canada/U.S.A. **36** H4 43 45N 78 00W
Ontonagon Michigan U.S.A. **63** I6 46 52N 89 18W
Oostende Belgium **76** C5 51 13N 2 55E
Opala Zaïre **106** J7 0 40S 24 20E
Opava Czechoslovakia **80** C4 49 58N 17 55E
Opheim Montana U.S.A. **40** B1 48 54N 106 25W
Opole Poland **80** C5 50 40N 17 56E
Oporto *see* Porto
Opotiki New Zealand **87** C3 38 00S 117 18E
Oradea Romania **81** D4 47 03N 21 55E
Oradell Reservoir New Jersey U.S.A. **50** B2 40 58N 74 00W
Oran Algeria **106** E15 35 45N 0 38W
Orán Argentina **69** E8 23 07S 64 16W
Orange Australia **110** H3 33 19S 149 10E
Orange California U.S.A. **51** C2 33 43N 117 54W
Orange France **77** C3 44 08N 4 48E
Orange Massachusetts U.S.A. **65** H5 42 35N 72 20W
Orange New Jersey U.S.A. **50** B2 40 45N 74 14W
Orange Texas U.S.A. **63** H3 30 05N 93 43W
Orange *r.* Southern Africa **107** I2 28 30S 17 30E
Orangeburg South Carolina U.S.A. **63** J3 33 28N 80 53W

Orange Free State *admin.* Republic of South Africa 107 K2 27 30S 27 30E
Oravita Romania 81 D4 45 02N 21 43E
Orbigo *r.* Spain 77 A3 42 15N 5 45W
Orbisonia Pennsylvania U.S.A. 64 C3 40 15N 77 55W
Orcadas *r.s.* Antarctica 117 60 40S 44 44W
Orcas Island Washington U.S.A. 42 H4 48 40N 122 55W
Orchard Park New York U.S.A. 64 B5 42 46N 78 45W
Orcia *r.* Italy 81 B3 42 00N 11 00E
Ordzhonikidze *see* Vladikavkaz
Örebro Sweden 79 D2 59 17N 15 13E
Oregon *state* U.S.A. 62 B5 44 00N 120 00W
Oregon City Oregon U.S.A. 62 B6 45 21N 122 36W
Orekhovo Zuyevo Russia 90 D6 55 47N 39 00E
Orël Russia 90 D5 52 58N 36 04E
Orem Utah U.S.A. 62 D5 40 20N 111 45W
Orenburg Russia 91 H5 51 50N 55 00E
Orense Spain 77 A3 42 20N 7 52W
Orient New York U.S.A. 65 H4 41 09N 72 18W
Orient Point New York U.S.A. 65 H4 41 10N 72 13W
Orihuela Spain 77 B2 38 05N 0 56W
Orinda California U.S.A. 49 C3 37 42N 122 10W
Oriskany New York U.S.A. 64 E6 43 08N 75 19W
Orissa *admin.* India 95 E4 20 20N 83 00E
Oristano Italy 81 A2 39 54N 8 36E
Orizaba Mexico 66 E3 18 51N 97 08W
Orkney Islands *is.* Scotland 78 H11 59 00N 3 00W
Orlando Florida U.S.A. 63 J2 28 33N 81 21W
Orléans France 77 C4 47 54N 1 54E
Orleans Massachusetts U.S.A. 65 K4 41 47N 70 00W
Orly France 83 B1 48 44N 2 24E
Örnsköldsvik Sweden 79 D3 63 19N 18 45E
Oropuche *r.* Trinidad and Tobago 66 T10 10 36N 61 05W
Oroville Washington U.S.A. 43 E1 48 57N 119 27W
Orpington England 82 D2 51 23N 0 05E
Orsay France 83 A1 48 42N 2 11E
Orsha Belarus 90 C5 54 30N 30 23E
Orsk Russia 91 H5 51 13N 58 35E
Ortigueira Spain 77 A3 43 43N 8 13W
Orūmīyeh Iran 92 F6 37 40N 45 00E
Oruro Bolivia 68 D9 17 59S 67 08W
Ōsaka Japan 100 G1 34 40N 135 30E
Ōsaka *pref.* Japan 100 G1 34 30N 135 10E
Ōsaka-wan *b.* Japan 100 G1 34 30N 135 10E
Osh Kirgyzstan 91 L3 40 37N 72 49E
Ō-shima *i.* Japan 100 C1 34 45N 139 25E
Oshkosh Wisconsin U.S.A. 63 I5 44 01N 88 32W
Oshogbo Nigeria 106 F9 7 50N 4 35E
Osijek Croatia 81 C4 45 33N 18 41E
Oskarshamn Sweden 80 C6 57 16N 16 25E
Oslo Norway 79 C2 59 56N 10 45E
Oslofjorden *fj.* Norway 79 C2 59 20N 10 37E
Osmaniye Turkey 92 E6 37 04N 36 15E
Osnabrück Germany 76 D5 52 17N 8 03E
Osorno Chile 69 C4 40 35S 73 14W
Ossa, Mount Australia 110 H1 41 52S 146 04E
Ossining New York U.S.A. 65 G4 41 10N 73 52W
Ostankino Russia 88 M2 55 50N 37 37E
Österdalälven *r.* Sweden 79 C3 61 40N 13 30E
Østerdalen *geog. reg.* Norway 79 C3 62 00N 10 30E
Östersund Sweden 79 C3 63 10N 14 40E
Östervall Sweden 79 D3 62 20N 15 20E
Ostfriesische Inseln *(East Frisian Islands) is.* Germany 76 D5 53 00N 7 00E
Ostrowiec Świętokrzyski Poland 80 D5 50 58N 21 22E
Ostrava Czechoslovakia 80 C4 49 50N 18 15E
Ostróda Poland 80 D5 53 42N 19 59E
Ostrołęka Poland 80 D5 53 05N 21 32E
Ostrów Mazowiecki Poland 80 D5 52 50N 21 51E
Ostrów Wielkopolski Poland 80 C5 51 39N 17 50E
Oswego River New York U.S.A. 64 D6 43 20N 76 25W
Ōta Japan 101 B3 35 34N 139 42E
Otaheite Bay Trinidad and Tobago 66 S9 10 15N 61 30W
Otaki New Zealand 111 C2 40 45S 175 09E
Otaru Japan 100 D3 43 14N 140 59E
Otavalo Ecuador 68 B13 0 13N 78 15W
Otra *r.* Norway 79 B2 56 17N 7 30E
Otranto Italy 81 C3 40 08N 18 30E
Otranto, Strait of Adriatic Sea 81 C3 40 00N 19 00E
Otsego Michigan U.S.A. 35 C1 42 26N 85 42W
Otsego Lake New York U.S.A. 64 F5 42 45N 74 55W
Ōtsu Japan 100 G2 35 00N 135 50E
Otsuki Japan 100 K2 35 38N 138 53E
Ottawa Kansas U.S.A. 63 G4 38 35N 95 16W
Ottawa Ohio U.S.A. 36 B2 41 02N 84 03W
Ottumwa Iowa U.S.A. 63 H5 41 02N 92 26W
Ouachita *r.* U.S.A. 63 H3 34 00N 93 00W
Ouachita Mountains U.S.A. 63 G3 34 00N 95 00W
Ouadda Central African Republic 106 J9 8 09N 22 20E
Ouagadougou Burkina 106 E10 12 20N 1 40W
Ouahigouya Burkina 106 E10 13 31N 2 20W
Ouargla Algeria 106 G14 32 00N 5 16E
Ouassel *r.* Algeria 77 C2 35 30N 2 00E
Oudtshoorn Republic of South Africa 107 J1 33 35S 22 12E
Ouerrha *r.* Morocco 77 A1 34 00N 6 00W
Ouezzane Morocco 77 A1 34 25N 5 35W
Ouham *r.* Central African Republic 106 I9 7 00N 17 30E
Oujda Morocco 106 E14 34 41N 1 45W
Oulu Finland 79 F3 65 02N 25 27E
Oulujärvi *l.* Finland 79 F3 64 20N 27 00E
Oulujoki *r.* Finland 79 F3 64 50N 26 00E
Oum El Bouaghi Algeria 77 D2 35 45N 7 00E
Ounasjoki *r.* Finland 79 F4 67 00N 25 00E
Ou-sanmyaku *mts.* Japan 100 D2 39 20N 141 00E
Ouse *r.* England 78 J5 53 40N 1 00W
Oust *r.* France 77 B4 47 50N 2 30W
Outer Hebrides *is.* Scotland 78 D9 58 00N 7 00W
Ovalau *i.* Fiji 114 U16 17 40S 178 47E
Ovalle Chile 69 C6 30 33S 71 16W
Övertorneå Sweden 79 E4 66 22N 23 40E
Ovid New York U.S.A. 64 D5 42 40N 76 49W
Oviedo Spain 77 A3 43 21N 5 50W
Owando Congo 106 I7 0 27S 15 44E
Owasco Lake New York U.S.A. 64 D5 42 50N 76 30W
Owego New York U.S.A. 64 D5 42 06N 76 16W
Owen Fracture Zone Indian Ocean 112 E7/8 10 00N 55 00E
Owen, Mount New Zealand 111 B2 41 33S 172 33E
Owensboro Kentucky U.S.A. 63 I4 37 45N 87 05W
Owen Stanley Range *mts.* Papua New Guinea 110 H8 8 00S 147 30E
Owosso Michigan U.S.A. 36 B4 43 00N 84 11W
Owyhee *r.* U.S.A. 62 C5 43 00N 117 00W
Oxford England 78 J3 51 46N 1 15W
Oxford Massachusetts U.S.A. 65 J5 42 08N 71 52W
Oxford New York U.S.A. 64 E5 42 26N 75 36W
Oxted England 82 C1 51 15N 0 01W
Oxus *see* Amudar'ya
Oyama Japan 100 C2 36 18N 139 48E
Oyapock *r.* Brazil 68 G13 3 00N 52 30W
Oyem Gabon 106 H8 1 34N 11 31E
Oyster Point California U.S.A. 49 B2 37 39N 122 22W
Ozarks, Lake of the Missouri U.S.A. 63 H4 38 00N 93 00W
Ozark Plateau Missouri U.S.A. 63 H4 37 00N 93 00W
Ozero Alakol' *salt l.* Kazakhstan 91 N4 46 00N 82 00E
Ozero Aydarkul' *l.* Kazakhstan 91 K3 41 00N 68 00E
Ozero Balkhash *(Lake Balkhash) salt l.* Kazakhstan 91 M4 46 00N 75 00E
Ozero Baykal *(Lake Baykal)* Russia 89 M6 54 00N 109 00E
Ozero Chany *salt l.* Russia 91 M5 55 00N 77 30E
Ozero Chudskoye *(Lake Peipus) l.* Estonia/Russia 79 F2 58 40N 27 30E
Ozero Il'men' *l.* Russia 90 C6 58 00N 31 30E
Ozero Issyk-Kul' *salt l.* Kirgyzstan 91 M3 42 30N 77 30E
Ozero Khanka *l.* Asia 89 P5 45 00N 132 30E
Ozero Kulundinskoye *l.* Russia 91 M5 53 00N 80 00E
Ozero Manych Gudilo *l.* Russia 90 E4 46 30N 43 00E
Ozero Onezhskoye *(Lake Onega) l.* Russia 90 D7 62 00N 40 00E
Ozero Pskovskoye *l.* Estonia/Russia 79 F2 58 00N 28 00E
Ozero Seletyteniz *l.* Russia 91 L5 53 30N 73 00E
Ozero Sevan *l.* Armenia 90 F3 40 35N 45 00E
Ozero Taymyr Russia 89 M10 74 00N 102 30E
Ozero Teletskoye *l.* Russia 91 O5 52 00N 88 00E
Ozero Tengiz *salt l.* Russia 91 K5 51 00N 69 00E
Ozero Zaysan *l.* Kazakhstan 91 N4 48 00N 84 00E

P

Pabianice Poland 80 C5 51 40N 19 20E
Pabna Bangladesh 95 F4 24 00N 89 15E
Pacasmayo Peru 68 B11 7 27S 79 33W
Pachuca Mexico 66 E4 20 10N 98 44W
Pacifica California U.S.A. 49 B2 37 37N 122 29W
Pacific-Antarctic Ridge Pacific Ocean 115 M2 55 00S 135 00W
Pacific Ocean 114/115
Padang Indonesia 99 C3 1 00S 100 21E
Paderborn Germany 76 D5 51 43N 8 44E
Padilla Bolivia 68 E9 19 18S 64 20W
Padova Italy 81 B4 45 24N 11 53E
Paducah Kentucky U.S.A. 63 I4 37 03N 88 36W
Paeroa New Zealand 111 C3 37 21S 175 41E
Pag *i.* Croatia 81 B3 44 00N 15 00E
Pagadian The Philippines 99 G5 7 50N 123 30E
Pahala Hawaiian Islands 115 Z17 19 12N 155 28W
Paharganj India 94 L4 28 38N 77 12E
Päijänne *l.* Finland 79 F3 61 30N 25 25E
Painesville Ohio U.S.A. 35 E2 41 43N 81 15W
Pai-sha Tao *i.* Taiwan 98 F6 23 40N 119 33E
Paisley Scotland 78 G7 55 50N 4 26W
Paita Peru 68 A11 5 11S 81 09W
PAKISTAN 94/95 A5/C5
Pakokku Myanmar 96 J3 21 20E 95 05E
Pakse Laos 99 D6 14 09N 105 50E
Pak Sha Tsuen Hong Kong U.K. 98 B2 22 25N 114 01E
Pak Tam Chung Hong Kong U.K. 98 C2 22 24N 114 19E
Palaiseau France 83 A1 48 43N 2 15E
Palana Russia 89 R7 59 05N 159 59E
Palangkaraya Indonesia 99 E3 2 06S 113 55E
Palatine Bridge New York U.S.A. 65 F5 42 55N 74 36W
Palau *(Belau) i.* Pacific Ocean 114 D8 7 30N 134 30E
Palawan *i.* The Philippines 99 F5/F6 9 00N 114 00E
Palayankottai India 95 D1 8 42N 77 46E
Palembang Indonesia 99 C3 2 59S 104 45E
Palencia Spain 77 B3 41 01N 4 32W
Palermo Italy 81 B2 38 08N 13 23E
Palestine Texas U.S.A. 63 G3 31 45N 95 39W
Palghat India 95 D2 10 46N 76 42E
Palk Strait India 95 D2 10 00N 80 00E
Palliser, Cape New Zealand 111 C2 41 37S 175 16E
Palma de Mallorca Balearic Islands 77 C2 39 35N 2 39E
Palmar Sur Costa Rica 67 H1 8 57N 83 28W
Palmas Bellas Panama 67 X2 9 16N 80 05W
Palmas, Cape Liberia 106 D9 4 25N 7 50W
Palm Beach Australia 111 H3 33 36S 151 19E
Palmer Alaska U.S.A. 10 F5 61 35N 149 10W
Palmer Massachusetts U.S.A. 65 H5 42 10N 72 19W
Palmer *r.s.* Antarctica 117 64 46S 83 55W
Palmer Land *geog. reg.* Antarctica 117 72 00S 62 00W
Palmer Park Michigan U.S.A. 52 E2 42 25N 83 08W
Palmerston Atoll *i.* Pacific Ocean 115 J6 18 04S 163 10W
Palmerston North New Zealand 111 C2 40 20S 175 39E
Palmerton Pennsylvania U.S.A. 64 E3 40 46N 75 32W
Palmira Colombia 68 B13 3 33N 76 17W
Palmyra New Jersey U.S.A. 64 E3 40 00N 75 01W
Palmyra New York U.S.A. 64 C6 43 03N 77 14W
Palmyra Atoll *ii.* Pacific Ocean 115 K8 5 52N 162 05W
Palo Alto California U.S.A. 49 C1 37 26N 122 10W
Palo Seco Trinidad and Tobago 66 S9 10 06N 61 36W
Palomares Mexico 66 E3 17 10N 95 04W
Palopo Indonesia 99 G3 3 01S 120 12E
Palos Verdes Hills California U.S.A. 51 A2 33 46N 118 23W
Palu Indonesia 99 F3 0 54S 119 52E
Pamiers France 77 C3 43 07N 1 36E
Pamirs *mts.* Tajikistan 91 L2 38 00N 74 00E
Pamlico Sound North Carolina U.S.A. 63 K4 35 00N 76 00W
Pampas *geog. reg.* Argentina 69 E5 36 00S 63 00W
Pamplona Colombia 68 C14 7 24N 72 38W
Pamplona Spain 77 B3 42 49N 1 39W
PANAMA 67 H1
Panamá Panama 67 Y1 8 57N 79 30W
Panama Canal Panama 67 Y2 9 00N 80 00W
Panama City Florida U.S.A. 63 I3 30 10N 85 41W
Panama Isthmus Central America 55 9 00N 80 00W
Panay *i.* The Philippines 99 G6 11 20N 122 30E
Pančevo Serbia Yugoslavia 81 D3 44 52N 20 40E
Panch'iao Taiwan 98 H8 25 01N 121 27E
Panchla India 94 J2 22 32N 88 08E
Panchur India 94 K2 22 31N 88 15E
Panevežys Lithuania 80 D6 55 44N 24 24E
Pangkalpinang Indonesia 99 D3 2 05S 106 09E
Pānihāti India 94 K2 22 41N 88 23E
Panipat India 95 D5 29 24N 76 58E
Panke *r.* Germany 83 F2 52 38N 13 27E
Pankow Germany 83 F2 52 35N 13 25E
Pantar *i.* Indonesia 99 G2 8 00S 124 00E
Pantelleria *i.* Italy 81 B2 36 00N 12 00E
Pao de Açúcar *(Sugar Loaf) mt.* Brazil 69 Q2 22 57S 43 09W
Papa Hawaiian Islands 115 Z17 19 12N 155 53W
Pápa Hungary 81 C4 47 20N 17 29E
Papantla Mexico 66 E4 20 30N 97 21W
Papua, Gulf of Papua New Guinea 110 H8 8 30S 145 00E
PAPUA NEW GUINEA 110 H8
Pará *admin.* Brazil 68 G12 4 30S 52 30W
Paraburdoo Australia 110 B5 23 15S 117 45E
Paracel Islands South China Sea 99 E7 16 40N 112 00E
PARAGUAY 68/69 F8
Paraiba *admin.* Brazil 68 J11 7 20S 37 10W
Parakou Benin 106 F9 9 23N 2 40E
Paramaribo Surinam 68 F14 5 52N 55 14W
Paramonga Peru 68 B10 10 42S 77 50W
Paramus New Jersey U.S.A. 50 B2 40 55N 74 03W
Paraná Argentina 69 E6 31 45S 60 30W
Parana *admin.* Brazil 69 G8 24 30S 53 00W
Paraná Plateau Brazil 55 25 00S 50 00W
Paranguá Brazil 69 H7 25 32S 48 36W
Parbhani India 95 D3 19 16N 76 51E
Pardubice Czechoslovakia 80 C4 50 03N 15 45E
Parepare Indonesia 99 F3 4 00S 119 40E
Parkersburg West Virginia U.S.A. 63 J4 39 17N 81 33W
Paria, Gulf of Trinidad and Tobago/Venezuela 66 S9 10 30N 61 45W
Parintins Brazil 68 F12 2 38S 56 45W
Paris France 77 C4 48 52N 2 20E
Paris Texas U.S.A. 63 G3 33 41N 95 33W
Paris Basin France 70 48 00N 2 30E
Parish New York U.S.A. 35 E1 43 24N 76 07W
Parkano Finland 79 E3 62 03N 23 00E
Parker, Mount Hong Kong U.K. 98 C1 22 16N 114 13E
Parkertown New Jersey U.S.A. 65 F2 39 37N 74 19W
Park Ridge Illinois U.S.A. 53 A3 42 01N 87 50W
Park River North Dakota U.S.A. 39 B1 48 30N 97 50W
Park Royal England 82 B3 51 32N 0 17W
Parma Italy 81 B3 44 48N 10 19E
Parma Ohio U.S.A. 36 E2 41 24N 81 44W
Parnaíba Brazil 68 I12 2 58S 41 46W
Parnassós *mt.* Greece 81 D2 38 30N 22 37E
Pärnu Estonia 79 E2 58 28N 24 30E
Paroo *r.* Australia 110 G4 27 00S 144 00E
Páros *i.* Greece 81 E2 37 00N 25 00E
Parramatta Australia 111 G2 33 50S 151 00E
Parramatta River Australia 111 G2 33 49S 151 05E
Parras Mexico 66 D5 25 30N 102 11W
Parsippany New Jersey U.S.A. 65 F3 40 50N 74 26W
Pasadena California U.S.A. 51 B3 34 10N 118 09W
Pasadena Texas U.S.A. 63 G2 29 42N 95 14W
Pascagoula Mississippi U.S.A. 63 I3 30 21N 88 32W
Pasco Washington U.S.A. 63 C6 46 15N 119 07W
Pascoag Rhode Island U.S.A. 65 J4 41 57N 71 42W
Passaic New Jersey U.S.A. 50 B2 40 50N 74 08W
Passaic River New Jersey U.S.A. 50 B2 40 46N 74 09W
Passau Germany 76 E4 48 35N 13 28E
Passo Fundo Brazil 69 G7 28 16S 52 20W
Pasto Colombia 68 B13 1 12N 77 17W
Patagonia *geog. reg.* Argentina 69 C2/D4 48 00S 70 00W
Patan India 95 C4 23 51N 72 11E
Patan Nepal 95 F5 27 40N 85 20E
Patchogue New York U.S.A. 65 G3 40 46N 73 01W
Patea New Zealand 111 C3 39 45S 174 29E
Pate Island Kenya 106 N7 2 05S 41 05E
Paterson New Jersey U.S.A. 50 B2 40 55N 74 08W
Pathankot India 95 D6 32 16N 75 43E
Patiala India 95 D6 30 21N 76 27E
Pātipukur India 94 K2 22 36N 88 24E
Patna India 95 F5 25 37N 85 12E
Patos Brazil 68 J11 6 55S 37 15W
Pátrai Greece 81 D2 38 14N 21 44E
Patton Pennsylvania U.S.A. 64 B3 40 38N 78 38W
Patton Park Michigan U.S.A. 52 E2 42 19N 83 07W
Pau France 77 B3 43 18N 0 22W
Paulding Ohio U.S.A. 36 B2 41 10N 84 37W
Paungde Myanmar 95 H3 18 30N 95 30E
Pausin Germany 83 E2 52 39N 13 04E
Pavia Italy 81 A4 45 12N 9 09E
Pavlodar Kazakhstan 91 M5 52 21N 76 59E
Pavlograd Ukraine 90 D4 48 34N 35 50E
Paw Paw Michigan U.S.A. 35 C1 42 13N 85 55W
Pawtucket Massachusetts U.S.A. 65 J4 41 53N 71 23W
Paysandú Uruguay 69 F6 32 21S 58 05W
Pazardzhik Bulgaria 81 D3 42 10N 24 20E
Peake Deep Atlantic Ocean 113 F11 43 00N 20 05W
Pearl *r.* Mississippi U.S.A. 63 H3 32 00N 90 00W
Pearl Harbour Hawaiian Islands 115 X18 21 22N 158 00W
Pearl River *tn.* New York U.S.A. 65 F4 41 03N 74 02W
Peč Serbia Yugoslavia 81 D3 42 40N 20 19E
Pechora Russia 88 H9 65 14N 57 18E
Pechora *r.* Russia 91 H7 60 00N 55 00E
Pecos Texas U.S.A. 62 F3 31 25N 103 30W
Pecos *r.* U.S.A. 62 F3 30 00N 102 00W
Pécs Hungary 81 C4 46 04N 18 15E
Peddocks Island Massachusetts U.S.A. 52 C2 42 17N 70 55W
Pedreiras Brazil 68 I11 4 32S 44 40W
Pedro Juan Caballero Paraguay 69 F8 22 30S 55 44W
Pedro Miguel Locks Panama 67 Y2 9 01N 79 36W
Peekskill New York U.S.A. 65 G4 41 18N 73 56W
Pegasus Bay New Zealand 111 B2 43 00S 173 00E
Pegu Myanmar 97 J2 17 18N 96 31E
Pegu Yoma *mts.* Myanmar 96 J2 19 00N 96 00E
Pegunungan Van Rees *mts.* Indonesia 110 F9 2 30S 138 00E
Pei-kang Taiwan 98 G6 23 38N 120 18E
Peipus, Lake *see* Ozero Chudskoye
Peking *see* Beijing
Pelican Point Namibia 107 H3 22 54S 14 25E
Pelješac *i.* Croatia 81 C3 43 00N 17 00E
Peloponnese *see* Pelopónnisos
Pelopónnisos *(Peloponnese) geog. reg.* Greece 81 D2 37 00N 22 00E
Pelotas Brazil 69 G6 31 45S 52 20W
Pematangsiantar Indonesia 99 B4 2 59N 99 01E
Pemba Mozambique 107 N5 13 00S 40 30E
Pemba Island Tanzania 107 M6 5 30S 39 50E
Pemba National Park Zaïre 107 K6 9 00S 26 30E
Pembina North Dakota U.S.A. 39 B1 48 59N 97 16W
Penal Trinidad and Tobago 66 T9 10 10N 61 28W
Pen Argyl Pennsylvania U.S.A. 64 E3 40 52N 75 25W
Peñarroya-Pueblonuevo Spain 77 A2 38 19N 5 16W
Pendleton Oregon U.S.A. 62 C6 45 40N 118 46W
Pend Oreille Lake Idaho U.S.A. 43 E1 48 10N 116 20W
Pend Oreille River Washington U.S.A. 43 E1 48 50N 117 25W
Penfield Pennsylvania U.S.A. 64 B4 41 13N 78 36W
Peng Chau Hong Kong U.K. 98 B1 22 17N 114 02E
Peng Chau *i.* Hong Kong U.K. 98 B1 22 17N 114 02E
P'eng-chia Hsü *i.* Taiwan 98 I8 25 38N 122 02E
P'eng-hu Lieh-tao *(Pescadores Islands) is.* Taiwan 98 F6 23 30N 119 30E
Peng-hu Shuitao *sd.* Taiwan 98 F6 23 30N 119 30E
P'eng-hu Tao *i.* Taiwan 98 F6 23 34N 119 35E
Penha Brazil 69 P2 22 49S 43 17W
Peninsula de Paria *p.* Venezuela 66 S10 10 44N 61 52W
Peninsula de Taitao *p.* Chile 69 C3 46 30S 75 00W
Pennant Hills Australia 111 G3 33 44S 151 04E
Penner *r.* India 95 D2 14 30N 77 30E
Penn Hills Pennsylvania U.S.A. 53 E1 40 28N 79 49W
Pennines *hills* England 78 I6
Pennsauken New Jersey U.S.A. 64 E2 39 58N 75 03W
Pennsylvania *state* U.S.A. 63 K5 41 00N 78 00W
Penn Yan New York U.S.A. 64 C5 42 41N 77 03W
Penobscot River Maine U.S.A. 33 C2 45 00N 68 40W
Penonomé Panama 67 H1 8 30N 80 20W
Penrith England 78 I6 54 40N 2 44W
Pensacola Florida U.S.A. 63 I3 30 26N 87 12W
Pensacola Mountains Antarctica 117 84 00S 60 00W
Pentland Firth *sd.* Scotland 78 H10 58 45N 3 10W
Penza Russia 90 F5 53 11N 45 00E
Penzance England 78 F2 50 07N 5 33W
Peoria Illinois U.S.A. 63 I5 40 43N 89 38W
Pepacton Reservoir New York U.S.A. 64 F5 42 05N 74 55W
Pereira Colombia 68 B13 4 47N 75 46W
Pergunungan Maoke *mts.* Indonesia 110 F9 4 00S 137 30E
Pergunungan Van Rees *mts.* Indonesia 110 F9 2 30S 137 30E
Perhojöki *r.* Finland 79 E3 63 30N 24 00E
Périgueux France 77 C4 45 12N 0 44E
Perm' Russia 91 H6 58 01N 56 10E
Pernambuco *admin.* Brazil 68 J11 8 00S 37 30W
Pernik Bulgaria 81 D3 42 36N 23 03E
Perovo Russia 88 N1 55 44N 37 46E
Perpignan France 77 C3 42 42N 2 54E
Perrysburg Ohio U.S.A. 36 C2 41 33N 83 39W
Perth Australia 110 B3 31 58N 115 49E
Perth Scotland 78 H8 56 42N 3 28W
Perth Amboy New Jersey U.S.A. 50 A1 40 31N 74 17W
PERU 68 B10
Peru Basin Pacific Ocean 115 Q6 18 00S 95 00W
Peru-Chile Trench Pacific Ocean 115 S6 13 00S 87 00W
Perugia Italy 81 B3 43 07N 12 23E
Pervoural'sk Russia 91 H6 56 59N 59 58E
Pesaro Italy 81 B3 43 54N 12 54E
Pescara Italy 81 B3 42 27N 14 13E
Peshawar Pakistan 95 C6 34 01N 71 40E
Petah Tiqwa Israel 92 O11 32 05N 34 53E
Petare Venezuela 68 D15 10 31N 66 50W
Petauke Zambia 107 L5 14 15S 31 20E
Peterborough Australia 110 F3 33 00S 138 51E
Peterborough England 78 K4 52 35N 0 15W
Peterborough New Hampshire U.S.A. 65 J5 42 53N 71 57W
Peterhead Scotland 78 J9 57 30N 1 46W
Petersburg Alaska U.S.A. 42 B3 56 49N 132 58W
Petoskey Michigan U.S.A. 36 B6 45 22N 84 59W
Petra *hist. site* Jordan 92 O10 30 19N 35 26E
Petrolina Brazil 68 I11 9 22S 40 30W
Petropavlovsk Kazakhstan 91 K5 54 53N 69 13E
Petropavlovsk-Kamchatskiy Russia 89 R6 53 03N 158 43E
Petrópolis Brazil 69 I8 22 30S 43 06W
Petroşeni Romania 81 D4 45 25N 23 22E
Petrozavodsk Russia 90 C7 61 46N 34 19E
Petukhovo Russia 91 K6 55 05N 67 55E
Peubla Mexico 66 E3 19 03N 98 10W
Pevek Russia 89 T9 64 41N 170 19E
Pfälzer Wald *mts.* Germany 76 D4 49 00N 8 00E
Phelps New York U.S.A. 64 C5 42 57N 77 03W
Phenix City Alabama U.S.A. 63 I3 32 8N 85 01W
Philadelphia Pennsylvania U.S.A. 64 E3 40 00N 75 10W
Philippine Sea Pacific Ocean 114 C10 21 00N 130 00E
PHILIPPINES, THE 99 G7/H5
Philippine Trench Pacific Ocean 114 C9 12 00N 127 00E
Philipsburg Pennsylvania U.S.A. 64 B3 40 54N 78 14W
Philip Smith Mountains Alaska U.S.A. 44 B4 68 00N 148 00W
Phillipsburg New Jersey U.S.A. 64 E3 40 41N 75 12W
Phnom Penh Cambodia 99 C6 11 35N 104 55E
Phoenix Arizona U.S.A. 62 D3 33 30N 112 03W
Phoenix Island Pacific Ocean 114 I7 3 30S 174 30W
Phoenix Islands Kiribati 114 I7 4 40S 177 30W
Phoenixville Pennsylvania U.S.A. 64 E3 40 07N 75 31W
Phongsali Laos 97 K3 21 40N 102 06E
Phrae Thailand 97 K2 18 07N 100 09E
Phuket Thailand 99 F5 7 52N 98 22E
Piacenza Italy 81 A3 45 03N 9 41E
Piatra Neamt Romania 81 E4 46 53N 26 23E
Piauí *admin.* Brazil 68 I11 7 30S 43 00W
Pico Cristóbal *mt.* Colombia 68 C15 10 53N 73 48W
Pico de Itambé *mt.* Brazil 68 I9 18 23S 43 21W
Pico-Rivera California U.S.A. 51 B2 33 59N 118 06W
Picos Brazil 68 I11 7 05S 41 24W
Picton New Zealand 111 B2 14 17S 174 02E
Picture Rocks Pennsylvania U.S.A. 64 D4 41 17N 76 40W
Pidurutalagala *mt.* Sri Lanka 95 E1 7 01N 80 45E
Piedade Brazil 69 P2 22 53N 43 19W
Piedmont California U.S.A. 49 C3 37 49N 122 13W
Piedras Negras Mexico 66 D5 28 40N 100 32W
Pielinen *l.* Finland 79 F3 63 20N 29 40E
Pierre South Dakota U.S.A. 62 F5 44 23N 100 20W
Pierreville Trinidad and Tobago 66 T9 10 17N 61 01W

Pietermaritzburg Republic of South Africa **107** L2 29 36S 30 24E
Pietersburg Republic of South Africa **107** K3 23 54N 29 23E
Pigeon Michigan U.S.A. **36** C4 43 50N 83 15W
Pijijiapan Mexico **66** F3 15 42N 93 12W
Pikes Peak Colorado U.S.A. **62** E4 38 50N 105 03W
Pikesville Maryland U.S.A. **64** D2 39 23N 76 44W
Pik Kommunizma *mt.* Tajikistan **88** J3 38 59N 72 01E
Pik Pobedy *mt.* Kirgyzstan **89** J4 42 25N 80 15E
Piła Poland **80** C5 53 09N 16 44E
Pilar Paraguay **69** F7 26 51S 58 20W
Pilarcitos Creek California U.S.A. **49** B1 37 28N 122 25W
Pilarcitos Lake California U.S.A. **49** B2 37 33N 122 25W
Pilica *r.* Poland **80** D5 52 00N 21 00E
Pillar Point California U.S.A. **49** B2 37 30N 122 30W
Pimenta Bueno Brazil **68** E10 11 40S 61 14W
Pinang *i.* Malaysia **99** C5 5 30N 100 20E
Pinar del Río Cuba **67** H4 22 24N 83 42W
Pindhos *mts.* Greece **81** D2 40 00N 21 00E
Pine Bluff Arkansas U.S.A. **63** H3 34 13N 92 00W
Pine City Minnesota U.S.A. **35** B2 45 59N 92 59W
Pine Creek Pennsylvania U.S.A. **64** C4 41 20N 77 30W
Pine River Michigan U.S.A. **36** B4 43 23N 84 40W
Ping Chau *i.* Hong Kong U.K. **98** D3 22 33N 114 26E
Pingchen Taiwan **98** H7 24 57N 121 12E
Pingdingshan China **97** M5 33 50N 113 20E
Ping Shan Hong Kong U.K. **98** B2 22 27N 114 00E
Pingtan Dao *i.* China **98** F8 25 00N 119 00E
P'ing-tung Taiwan **98** G5 22 40N 120 30E
Pingxiang China **96** M4 27 35N 113 46E
Ping Yeung Hong Kong U.K. **98** B3 22 32N 114 09E
Piniós *r.* Greece **81** D2 39 00N 22 00E
Pinsk Belarus **90** B5 52 08N 26 01E
Piombino Italy **81** B3 42 56N 10 32E
Pioneer Ohio U.S.A. **36** B2 41 42N 84 33W
Piotrków Trybunalski Poland **80** C5 51 27N 19 40E
Piraiévs Greece **81** D2 37 57N 23 42E
Pirapora Brazil **68** I9 17 20S 44 54W
Pírgos Greece **81** D2 37 40N 21 27E
Pírgos Greece **81** E2 35 00N 25 10E
Pirineos *(Pyrénées) mts.* Spain/France **77** B3 C3 42 50N 0 30E
Pirin Planina *mts.* Bulgaria **81** D3 41 00N 23 00E
Pisa Italy **81** B3 43 43N 10 24E
Piscataway New Jersey U.S.A. **65** F3 40 33N 74 30W
Pisco Peru **68** B10 13 46S 76 12W
Písek Czechoslovakia **80** B4 49 18N 14 10E
Pistoia Italy **81** B3 43 56N 10 55E
Pitanga Brazil **69** G8 24 45S 51 43W
Pitcairn Islands Pacific Ocean **115** N5 25 04S 130 06W
Pitch Point Trinidad and Tobago **66** S9 10 15N 61 37W
Piteå Sweden **79** E4 65 19N 21 30E
Pite älv *r.* Sweden **79** D4 66 45N 17 20E
Piteşti Romania **81** D3 44 51N 24 51E
Pitti Island India **95** C2 11 00N 73 00E
Pittsburgh Pennsylvania U.S.A. **63** K5 40 26N 80 00W
Pittsfield Massachusetts U.S.A. **65** G5 42 27N 73 15W
Pittsfield New Hampshire U.S.A. **65** J6 43 18N 71 20W
Pitt Water Australia **111** H3 33 37S 151 19E
Piura Peru **68** A11 5 15S 80 38W
Pjórsá *r.* Iceland **79** I6 64 15N 19 00W
Plainfield Connecticut U.S.A. **65** J4 41 42N 71 55W
Plainfield New Jersey U.S.A. **65** F3 40 37N 74 25W
Plainview Texas U.S.A. **62** F3 34 12N 101 43W
Planalto de Mato Grosso *geog. reg.* Brazil **68** F10 13 00S 56 00W
Plasencia Spain **77** A3 40 02N 6 05W
Plateau de Langres *hills* France **77** C4 47 40N 4 55E
Plateau du Tademaït *plat.* Algeria **106** F13 8 45N 2 00E
Plateau du Tchigaï *plat.* Chad/Niger **106** H12 21 30N 15 00E
Plateaux du Limousin *hills* France **77** C4 45 45N 1 15E
Platte *r.* U.S.A. **62** F5 41 00N 100 00W
Plattsburgh New York U.S.A. **63** L5 44 42N 73 29W
Plauen Germany **76** E5 50 29N 12 08E
Playa Azul Mexico **66** D3 18 00N 102 24W
Pleasant Hill California U.S.A. **49** C3 37 58N 122 04W
Pleasant Hills Pennsylvania U.S.A. **53** E1 40 19N 79 57W
Pleasantville New Jersey U.S.A. **65** F2 39 23N 74 32W
Plenty, Bay of New Zealand **111** C3 37 30S 117 00E
Plentywood Montana U.S.A. **40** C1 48 46N 104 32W
Pleven Bulgaria **81** D3 43 25N 24 40E
Płock Poland **80** C5 52 32N 19 40E
Ploieşti Romania **81** E3 44 57N 26 01E
Plover Cove Reservoir Hong Kong U.K. **98** C2 22 28N 114 15E
Plovdiv Bulgaria **81** D3 42 08N 24 45E
Plunge Lithuania **80** D6 55 52N 21 49E
Plymouth England **78** G2 50 23N 4 10W
Plymouth Massachusetts U.S.A. **65** K4 41 58N 70 40W
Plymouth County Massachusetts U.S.A. **52** C2 42 18N 70 55W
Plzeň Czechoslovakia **80** B4 49 45N 13 25E
Po *r.* Italy **81** B4 45 00N 11 00E
Pocatello Idaho U.S.A. **62** D5 42 35N 112 26W
Pochutla Mexico **66** E3 15 45N 96 30W
Pocono Summit Pennsylvania U.S.A. **64** E4 41 06N 75 25W
Podara India **94** K2 22 34N 88 17E
Podkamennaya *(Stony)* **Tunguska** *r.* Russia **89** L8/M8 62 00N 95 00E
Podol'sk Russia **90** D6 55 23N 37 32E
P'ohang South Korea **97** P6 36 00N 129 26E
Point-à-Pitre Guadeloupe Lesser Antilles **67** L3 16 14N 61 32W
Pointe-à-Pierre *tn.* Trinidad and Tobago **66** T9 10 20N 61 26W
Point Fortin *tn.* Trinidad and Tobago **66** S9 10 21N 61 41W
Point Hope *tn.* Alaska U.S.A. **10** B6 68 20N 166 50W
Point-Noire *tn.* Congo **107** H5 4 46S 11 53E
Point Pedro *c.* Sri Lanka **95** E1 9 49N 80 14E
Point Pleasant *tn.* New Jersey U.S.A. **65** F3 40 06N 74 02W
Point San Pedro California U.S.A. **49** A2 37 33N 122 33W
Poissy France **83** A2 48 56N 2 03E
Poitiers France **77** C4 46 35N 0 20E
Pok Fu Lam Hong Kong U.K. **98** B1 22 15N 114 08E
Pokhara Nepal **95** E5 28 14N 83 58E
POLAND **80** C5
Poland New York U.S.A. **64** E6 43 13N 75 05W
Poles'ye Pripyat' *(Pripet Marshes) marsh* Belarus **90** B5 52 00N 27 00E
Poliyiros Greece **81** D3 40 23N 23 25E
Pollachi India **95** D2 10 38N 77 00E
Poltava Ukraine **90** C4 49 35N 34 35E
Polynesia *geog. reg.* Pacific Ocean **115** J/L9
Pomeranian Bay Baltic Sea **80** B5 54 00N 14 00E
Ponca City Oklahoma U.S.A. **63** G4 36 41N 97 04W
Ponce Puerto Rico **67** K3 18 01N 66 36W
Pondicherry India **95** D2 11 59N 79 50E
Ponferrada Spain **77** A3 42 33N 6 35W
Ponta da Marca *c.* Angola **107** H4 16 33S 11 43E
Ponta Grossa Brazil **69** G7 25 07S 50 09W
Ponta Porã Brazil **69** F8 22 27S 55 39W
Pontas das Salinas *c.* Angola **107** H5 12 50S 12 54E
Pontchartrain, Lake Louisiana U.S.A. **63** H3 30 00N 90 00W
Pontevedra Spain **77** A3 42 25N 8 39W
Pontiac Michigan U.S.A. **36** C3 42 39N 83 18W
Pontianak Indonesia **99** D3 0 05S 109 16E
Pontivy France **77** B4 48 04N 2 58W
Poole England **78** I2 50 43N 1 59W
Poole *r.* Trinidad and Tobago **66** T9 10 02N 61 11W
Pool Malebo *l.* Zaïre **107** I7 5 00S 17 00E
Popocatepetl *mt.* Mexico **66** E3 19 02N 98 38W
Popayán Colombia **68** B13 2 27N 76 32W
Poplar Bluff *tn.* Missouri U.S.A. **63** H4 36 16N 90 25W
Poplar River Montana U.S.A. **40** B1 48 50N 105 30W
Popondetta Papua New Guinea **110** H8 8 45S 148 15E
Poquetanuck Connecticut U.S.A. **65** H4 41 29N 72 02W
Porbandar India **94** B4 21 04N 69 40E
Porcupine *r.* Alaska U.S.A. **44** C4 67 00N 143 30W
Porcupine Creek Montana U.S.A. **40** B1 48 50N 106 30W
Pordenone Italy **81** B4 45 58N 12 39E
Pori Finland **79** E3 61 28N 21 45E
Porirua New Zealand **111** B2 41 08S 174 52E
Porlamar Venezuela **67** L2 11 01N 63 54W
Poronaysk Russia **89** Q5 49 13N 143 05E
Porsangen *fj.* Norway **79** F5 70 40N 25 30E
Porsgrunn Norway **79** B2 59 10N 9 40E
Portadown Northern Ireland **78** E6 54 26N 6 27W
Portal North Dakota U.S.A. **40** C1 48 00N 102 32W
Portalegre Portugal **77** A2 39 17N 7 25W
Portales New Mexico U.S.A. **62** F3 34 12N 103 20W
Port Alexander Alaska U.S.A. **42** B3 56 13N 134 40W
Port Allegany *tn.* Pennsylvania U.S.A. **64** B4 41 48N 78 18W
Port Angeles Washington U.S.A. **62** B6 48 06N 123 26W
Port Antonio Jamaica **67** R8 18 10N 76 27W
Port Arthur Texas U.S.A. **63** H2 29 55N 93 56W
Port Augusta Australia **110** F3 32 30S 137 27E
Port-au-Prince Haiti **67** J3 18 33N 72 20W
Port Austin Michigan U.S.A. **36** C5 44 04N 82 59W
Port Blair Andaman Islands **95** G2 11 40N 92 44E
Port Byron New York U.S.A. **64** D6 43 03N 76 38W
Port Chalmers New Zealand **111** B1 45 48S 170 38E
Port Clinton Ohio U.S.A. **36** D2 41 30N 82 58W
Port-de-Paix Haiti **67** J3 19 56N 72 52W
Port Elizabeth New Jersey U.S.A. **64** F2 39 19N 74 59W
Port Elizabeth Republic of South Africa **107** K1 33 58S 25 36E
Port Gentil Gabon **106** G7 0 40S 8 50E
Port Hacking *b.* Australia **111** G1 34 04S 151 07E
Port Hacking Point Australia **111** G1 34 05S 151 10E
Port Harcourt Nigeria **106** G8 4 43N 7 05E
Port Hedland Australia **110** B5 20 24S 118 36E
Port Huron Michigan U.S.A. **63** J5 42 59N 82 28W
Portile de Fier *(Iron Gate) gorge* Europe **81** D2 44 00N 22 00E
Portimaõ Portugal **77** A2 37 08N 8 32W
Port Island Hong Kong U.K. **98** D3 22 30N 114 21E
Port Jackson *b.* Australia **111** H2 33 51S 151 15E
Port Jervis *tn.* New York U.S.A. **65** F4 41 22N 74 40W
Port Kaituma Guyana **68** F14 7 44N 59 53W
Portland Australia **110** G2 38 21S 141 38E
Portland Maine U.S.A. **63** L5 43 41N 70 18W
Portland Michigan U.S.A. **36** B3 42 52N 84 53W
Portland Oregon U.S.A. **62** B6 45 32N 122 40W
Portland Canal *sd.* Alaska U.S.A. **42** B3 55 00N 130 10W
Portland Point Jamaica **67** Q7 17 42N 77 11W
Portlaoise Irish Republic **78** D5 53 02N 7 17W
Port Lincoln Australia **110** F3 34 43S 135 49E
Port Macquarie Australia **110** I3 31 28S 152 25E
Port Maria Jamaica **67** R8 18 22N 76 54W
Port Matilda *tn.* Pennsylvania U.S.A. **64** B3 40 47N 78 04W
Port Morant Jamaica **67** R7 17 53N 76 20W
Port Moresby Papua New Guinea **110** H8 9 30S 147 07E
Port Nolloth Republic of South Africa **107** I2 29 17S 16 51E
Port Norris *tn.* New Jersey U.S.A. **64** E2 39 15N 75 02W
Porto *(Oporto)* Portugal **77** A3 41 09N 8 37W
Pôrto Alegre Brazil **69** G6 30 03S 51 10W
Porto Amboim Angola **107** H5 10 47S 13 43E
Portobelo Panama **67** Y2 9 33N 79 37W
Port of Spain Trinidad and Tobago **66** S10 10 38N 61 31W
Pôrto Grande Brazil **68** G13 0 43N 51 23W
Porto Novo Benin **106** F9 6 30N 2 47E
Porto-Vecchio Corsica **77** D3 41 35N 9 16E
Pôrto Velho Brazil **68** E11 8 45S 63 54W
Portoviejo Ecuador **68** A12 1 07S 80 28W
Port Pirie Australia **110** F3 33 11S 138 01E
Port Royal Jamaica **67** R7 17 55N 76 52W
Port Said *(Bûr Sa'îd)* Egypt **107** S4 31 17N 32 18E
Port Sudan Sudan **92** E2 19 38N 37 07E
Portsmouth England **78** J2 50 48N 1 05W
Portsmouth New Hampshire U.S.A. **65** K6 43 03N 70 47W
Portsmouth Rhode Island U.S.A. **65** J4 41 00N 71 00W
Portsmouth Virginia U.S.A. **63** K4 36 50N 76 20W
Porttipahdan tekojärvi *l.* Finland **79** F4 68 15N 26 00E
PORTUGAL **77** A3
Port Washington New York U.S.A. **50** D2 40 50N 73 41W
Porus Jamaica **67** Q8 18 02N 77 25W
Posadas Argentina **69** F7 27 27S 55 50W
Potenza Italy **81** C3 40 38N 15 48E
Poti Georgia **90** E3 42 11N 41 41E
Potiskum Nigeria **106** H10 11 40N 11 03E
Po Toi Island Hong Kong U.K. **98** C1 22 10N 114 10E
Potomac River Maryland U.S.A. **64** C2 39 10N 77 30W
Potosí Bolivia **68** D9 19 34S 65 45W
Potsdam Germany **83** D2 52 24N 13 04E
Potsdam *bor.* Germany **83** F2 52 41N 13 25E
Potter's Bar England **82** C3 51 42N 0 11W
Pottstown Pennsylvania U.S.A. **64** E3 40 15N 75 38W
Pottsville Pennsylvania U.S.A. **64** D3 40 41N 76 1W
Poughkeepsie New York U.S.A. **65** G4 41 43N 73 56W
Poverty Bay New Zealand **111** C3 38 40S 178 00E
Powell, Lake U.S.A. **62** D4 37 00N 110 00W
Powers Lake *tn.* North Dakota U.S.A. **40** C1 48 35N 102 39W
Poza Rica Mexico **66** E4 20 34N 97 26W
Poznań Poland **80** C5 52 25N 16 53E
Pradesh *admin.* India **95** E5 26 00N 81 00E
Prague *see* Praha
Praha *(Prague)* Czechoslovakia **80** B5 50 06N 14 26E
Prairie Dog Town Fork *r.* U.S.A. **62** F3 34 00N 101 00W
Prato Italy **81** B3 43 53N 11 06E
Pratt Kansas U.S.A. **62** G4 37 40N 98 45W
Přeau Trinidad and Tobago **66** T9 10 12N 61 19W
Prenzlauer Berg Germany **83** F2 52 33N 13 25E
Prerov Czechoslovakia **80** C4 49 28N 17 30E
Prescott Arizona U.S.A. **62** D3 34 34N 112 28W
Presidencia Roque Sáenz Peña Argentina **69** E7 6 45S 60 30W
Presidente Prudente Brazil **69** G8 22 09S 51 24W
Presidio California U.S.A. **49** B3 37 47N 122 28W
Prešov Czechoslovakia **80** D4 49 00N 21 10E
Presque Isle Maine U.S.A. **33** C2 46 42N 68 01W
Preston England **78** I5 53 46N 2 42W
Pretoria Republic of South Africa **107** K2 25 45E 28 12E
Prettyboy Reservoir Maryland U.S.A. **64** D2 39 38N 76 45W
Préveza Greece **81** D2 38 59N 20 45E
Příbham Czechoslovakia **80** B4 49 42N 14 01E
Price Utah U.S.A. **62** D4 39 35N 110 49W
Price *r.* Utah U.S.A. **62** D4 39 00N 110 00W
Prieska Republic of South Africa **107** J2 29 40S 22 45E
Priest Lake Idaho U.S.A. **43** E1 49 45N 116 50W
Priestly Mountain Maine U.S.A. **37** R7 46 34N 69 23W
Priest River *tn.* Idaho U.S.A. **43** E1 48 11N 116 55W
Prijedor Bosnia-Herzegovina **81** C3 45 00N 16 41E
Prilep Yugoslavia **81** D3 41 20N 21 32E
Prince Edward Island Indian Ocean **112** C2 46 30S 37 20E
Prince of Wales Island Alaska U.S.A. **42** B3 56 00N 132 00W
Princes Town Trinidad and Tobago **66** T9 10 16N 61 23W
Princeton New Jersey U.S.A. **65** F3 40 21N 74 40W
Prince William Sound Alaska U.S.A. **10** F5 61 00N 147 30W
Príncipe *i.* Gulf of Guinea **106** G8 1 37N 7 27E
Prinzapolca Nicaragua **67** H2 13 19N 83 35W
Pripet Marshes *see* Poles'ye Pripyat'
Pripyat' *r.* Belarus/Ukraine **90** B5 52 00N 30 00E
Prispansko ezero *l.* Europe **81** D3 41 00N 21 00E
Priština Serbia Yugoslavia **81** D3 42 39N 21 20E
Prizren Serbia Yugoslavia **81** D3 42 12N 20 43E
Probolinggo Indonesia **99** E2 7 45S 113 09E
Proddatur India **95** D2 14 45N 78 34E
Progres *r.s.* Antarctica **117** 69 24S 76 24E
Progreso Honduras **66** G3 15 20N 87 50W
Progreso Mexico **66** G4 21 20N 89 40W
Prokhladnyy Russia **90** E3 43 46N 44 03E
Prokop'yevsk Russia **91** O5 53 55N 86 45E
Prome Myanmar **96** J2 18 50N 95 14E
Propriá Brazil **68** J10 10 15S 36 51W
Prospect Heights Illinois U.S.A. **53** A3 42 04N 87 55W
Providence Rhode Island U.S.A. **65** J4 41 50N 71 28W
Providence, Cape New Zealand **111** A1 46 01S 166 28E
Provideniya Russia **89** U8 64 30N 73 11W
Provincetown Massachusetts U.S.A. **65** K5 42 04N 70 11W
Provo Utah U.S.A. **62** D5 40 15N 111 40W
Prudhoe Bay *tn.* Alaska U.S.A. **44** B4 70 05N 148 20W
Prutul *(Prut) r.* Romania **81** E4 47 00N 28 00E
Pruzków Poland **80** D5 52 10N 20 47E
Prýdek-Místek Czechoslovakia **80** C4 49 42N 18 20E
Przemyśl Poland **80** D4 49 48N 22 48E
Przheval'sk Kirgyzstan **91** M3 42 31N 78 22E
Pskov Russia **90** B6 57 48N 28 26E
Ptich' Belarus **90** B5 52 15N 28 49E
Ptich' *r.* Belarus **90** B5 53 00N 28 00E
Pucallpa Peru **68** C11 8 21S 74 33W
Pudasjärvi Finland **79** F4 65 25N 26 50E
Pueblo Colorado U.S.A. **62** F4 38 17N 104 38W
Puerta Eugenia *c.* Mexico **66** A5 27 50N 115 05W
Puerto Aisén Chile **69** C3 45 27S 72 58W
Puerto Armuelles Panama **67** H1 8 19N 82 51W
Puerto Ayacucho Venezuela **68** D14 5 39N 67 32W
Puerto Barrios Guatemala **66** G3 15 41N 88 32W
Puerto Berrio Colombia **68** C14 6 28N 74 28W
Puerto Cabello Venezuela **68** D15 10 29N 68 02W
Puerto Cabezas Nicaragua **67** H2 14 0N 83 24W
Puerto Carreño Colombia **68** D14 6 08N 69 27W
Puerto Cortés Honduras **66** G3 15 50N 87 55W
Puerto Cumarebo Venezuela **67** K2 11 31N 69 30W
Puerto de Morelos Mexico **67** G4 20 49N 86 52W
Puerto La Cruz Venezuela **68** E15 10 14N 64 40W
Puertollano Spain **77** B2 38 41N 4 07W
Puerto Maldonado Peru **68** D10 12 37S 69 11W
Puerto Mexico *see* Coatzacoalcos
Puerto Montt Chile **69** C4 41 28S 73 00W
Puerto Natales Chile **69** C2 51 41S 72 15W
Puerto Peñasco Mexico **66** B6 31 20N 113 35W
Puerto Pilón Panama **67** Y2 9 21N 79 48W
Puerto Princesa The Philippines **99** F5 9 46N 118 45E
PUERTO RICO **67** K3
Puerto Rico Trench Atlantic Ocean **113** B9 21 00N 65 00W
Puerto Santa Cruz Argentina **69** D2 50 03S 68 35W
Puerto Vallarta Mexico **66** C4 20 36N 105 15W
Pui O Hong Kong U.K. **98** A1 22 15N 113 58E
Pukekohe New Zealand **111** B3 37 12S 174 56E
Pula Croatia **81** B3 44 52N 13 52E
Pulacoyo Bolivia **68** D8 20 25S 66 41W
Pulau Dolak *i.* Indonesia **110** F8 8 00S 138 00E
Pulau Pulau Batu *is.* Indonesia **99** B3 0 20S 98 00E
Pu-li Taiwan **98** G6 23 58N 120 55E
Pulkkila Finland **79** F3 64 16N 25 50E
Pullman Washington U.S.A. **62** C6 46 46N 117 09W
Puncak Jaya *mt.* Indonesia **110** F9 4 05S 137 09E
Pune India **95** C3 18 34N 73 58E
Punjab *admin.* India **95** D6 30 40N 75 30E
Puno Peru **68** C9 15 53S 70 03W
Punta Alta Argentina **69** E5 38 50S 62 00W
Punta Arenas Chile **69** C2 53 10S 70 56W
Punta del Mono *c.* Nicaragua **67** H2 11 36N 83 37W
Punta Galera *c.* Ecuador **68** A13 0 49N 80 03W
Punta Gallinas *c.* Colombia **68** C15 12 27N 71 44W
Punta Gorda Belize **66** G3 16 10N 88 45W
Punta Manzanillo *c.* Panama **67** Y2 9 37N 79 36W
Punta Negra *c.* Peru **68** A11 6 06S 81 09W
Punta Peñas *c.* Venezuela **66** S10 10 45N 61 51W
Puntarenas Costa Rica **67** H2 10 00N 84 50W
Punto Fijo Venezuela **68** C15 11 50N 70 16W
Punxsutawney Pennsylvania U.S.A. **64** B3 40 57N 78 59W
Puquio Peru **68** C10 14 44S 74 07W
Pur *r.* Russia **89** J9 66 30N 77 30E
Puri India **95** F3 19 49N 85 54E
Purisma Creek California U.S.A. **49** B1 37 24N 122 24W
Purley England **82** C2 51 21N 0 07W
Purnia India **95** F5 25 47N 87 28E
Pursat Cambodia **99** C6 12 27N 103 40E
Purus *r.* Brazil **68** E11 7 00S 65 00W
Puruvesi *l.* Finland **79** F3 61 50N 29 30E
Pusa India **94** L4 28 38N 77 10E
Pusan South Korea **96** P6 35 05N 129 02E
Pushkin Russia **90** C6 59 43N 30 22E
Pu-tai Taiwan **98** G6 23 21N 120 11E
Putao Myanmar **95** H5 27 22N 97 27E
Putian China **98** E8 25 32N 119 02E
Putnam Connecticut U.S.A. **65** J4 41 55N 71 54W
Putney Vermont U.S.A. **65** H5 42 58N 72 35W
Putoran Mountains Russia **89** L9 68 00N 95 00E
Puttalam Sri Lanka **95** D1 8 02N 79 50E
Putumayo *r.* Colombia/Peru **68** C12 2 30S 72 30W
Puulavesi *l.* Finland **79** F3 61 50N 26 40E
Pyasina *r.* Russia **89** K10 71 00N 90 00E
Pyatigorsk Russia **90** E3 44 04N 43 06E
Pyhäjärvi Finland **79** F3 63 41N 26 00E
Pyhäjärvi *l.* Finland **79** E3 61 00N 22 20E
Pyhäjärvi *l.* Finland/Russia **79** F3 61 50N 30 00E
Pyinmana Myanmar **99** B7 19 45N 96 12E
Pymatuning Lake *res.* Ohio/ Pennsylvania U.S.A. **36** F2 41 35N 80 30W
Pyŏngyang North Korea **97** P6 39 00N 125 47E
Pyramid Lake Nevada U.S.A. **62** C5 40 00N 119 00W
Pyramids *hist. site* Egypt **92** D4 29 50N 30 50E
Pyrénées *(Pirineos) mts.* France/Spain **77** B3/C3 42 50N 0 30E
Pysht Washington U.S.A. **42** H4 48 10N 124 08W
Pytäselkä *l.* Finland **79** F3 62 0N 29 30E

Q

Qaidam Basin *see* Qaidam Pendi
Qaidam Pendi (Qaidam Basin) China **96** H6/J6 37 30N 94 00E
Qamdo China **95** H6 31 11N 97 18E
Qanâ el Manzala *can.* Egypt **107** R4 31 21N 31 56E
Qasr-e-Shīrīn Iraq **93** G5 34 32N 45 35E
Qasr Farâfra Egypt **106** K13 27 03N 28 00E
QATAR **93** H4
Qatar Peninsula Middle East **84** 25 00N 53 00E
Qatrāna Jordan **92** P10 31 14N 36 03E
Qattara Depression Egypt **106** K13 24 00N 27 30E
Qazvīn Iran **93** G6 36 16N 50 00E
Qena Egypt **92** D4 26 08N 32 42E
Qeqertarsuaq (Godhavn) Greenland **45** V4 69 18N 53 40W
Qezi'ot Israel **92** O10 30 53N 34 28E
Qiemo China **96** G6 38 08N 85 33E
Qila Saifullah Pakistan **94** B6 30 42N 68 30E
Qilian Shan *mts.* China **97** J6 39 00N 98 00E
Qingdao China **97** O6 36 04N 120 22E
Qinghai Hu *l.* China **97** J6 37 00N 100 00E
Qinghe China **101** G2 40 01N 116 20E
Qingjiang China **97** N5 33 35N 119 02E
Qinhuangdao China **97** N6 39 55N 119 37E
Qin Ling *mts.* China **97** J6 34 00N 107 30E
Qionghai China **97** M2 19 17N 110 30E
Qiqihar China **97** O8 47 23N 124 00E
Qogir Feng *see* K2
Qom Iran **93** H5 34 39N 50 57E
Qomisheh Iran **93** H5 32 01N 51 55E
Quabbin Reservoir Massachusetts U.S.A. **65** H5 42 20N 72 20W
Quakertown Pennsylvania U.S.A. **64** E3 40 27N 75 20W
Quang Ngai Vietnam **99** L2 15 09N 108 50E
Quang Tri Vietnam **97** L2 16 46N 107 11E
Quantock Hills England **78** H3 51 05N 3 15W
Quanzhou China **97** N3 24 53N 118 36E
Quarry Bay *tn.* Hong Kong U.K. **98** C1 22 17N 114 13E
Queanbeyan Australia **110** H2 35 24N 149 17E
Queen Mary Reservoir England **82** B2 51 25N 0 27W
Queen Maud Land *geog. reg.* Antarctica **117** 73 00S 10 00E
Queens New York U.S.A. **50** C1 40 44N 73 54W
Queensland *state* Australia **110** G5 23 00S 143 00E
Queenstown Australia **110** H1 42 07S 145 33E
Queenstown New Zealand **111** A2 45 03S 168 41E
Quelimane Mozambique **107** M4 17 53S 36 51E
Quelpart *see* Cheju do
Quemahoning Reservoir Pennsylvania U.S.A. **64** B3 40 10N 79 00W
Que Que *see* Kwekwe
Querétaro Mexico **66** D4 20 38N 100 23W
Quetta Pakistan **94** B6 30 15N 67 00E
Quezaltenango Guatemala **66** F2 14 50N 91 30W
Quezon City The Philippines **99** G6 14 39N 121 02E
Quibala Angola **107** H5 10 48S 14 59E
Quibdó Colombia **68** B14 5 40N 76 38W
Quiberon France **77** B4 47 29N 3 07W
Quilá Mexico **66** C4 24 26N 107 11W
Quillacollo Bolivia **68** D9 17 26S 66 16W
Quilon India **95** D1 8 53N 76 38E
Quilpie Australia **110** G4 26 35S 144 14E
Quimper France **77** B4 48 00N 4 06W
Quincy Illinois U.S.A. **63** H4 39 55N 91 22W
Quincy Massachusetts U.S.A. **52** B2 42 17N 71 00W
Quinebaug River Connecticut U.S.A. **65** H4 41 30N 72 00W
Qui Nhon Vietnam **99** D6 13 47N 109 11E
Quito Ecuador **68** B12 0 14S 78 30W
Quixadá Brazil **68** J12 4 57S 39 04W
Qus Egypt **92** D4 25 53N 32 48E
Quseir Egypt **92** D4 26 04N 34 15E

R
Raahe Finland **79** E3 64 42N 24 30E
Raas Caseyr *(Guardafui, Cape)* Somalia **106** P10 11 50N 51 16E
Raba Indonesia **99** F2 8 27S 118 45E
Rabat-Salé Morocco **106** D14 34 02N 6 51W
Rabaul Papua New Guinea **110** I9 4 13S 152 11E
Rach Gia Vietnam **99** D5 9 55N 105 05E
Racibórz Poland **80** C5 50 05N 18 10E
Radford Virginia U.S.A. **63** J4 37 07N 80 34W
Radlett England **82** B3 51 41N 0 19W
Radlinski, Mount Antarctica **117** 82 30S 105 00W
Radom Poland **80** D5 51 26N 21 10E
Radom Sudan **106** J9 9 58N 24 53E
Radomsko Poland **80** C5 51 04N 19 25E
Raeside, Lake Australia **110** C4 29 00S 122 00E
Rafah Egypt **92** O10 31 18N 34 15E
Rafsanjān Iran **93** I5 30 25N 56 00E
Ragusa Italy **81** B2 36 56N 14 44E
Rahimyar Khan Pakistan **94** B5 28 22N 70 20E
Rahnsdorf Germany **83** G1 52 26N 13 42E
Raichur India **95** D3 16 15N 77 20E
Raigarh India **95** E4 21 53N 83 28E
Rainbow Park Illinois U.S.A. **53** B2 41 45N 87 32W
Rainham England **82** D3 51 31N 0 12E
Rainier, Mount Washington U.S.A. **62** B6 46 52N 121 45W
Raipur India **95** E4 21 16N 81 42E
Raisin, River Michigan U.S.A. **36** C2 41 55N 83 40W
Rajahmundry India **95** E3 17 01N 81 52E
Rajapalaiyam India **95** D1 9 26N 77 36E
Rājasthan *admin.* India **95** C5 26 30N 73 00E
Rajkot India **95** C4 21 18N 70 53E
Rajpur India **94** K1 22 25N 88 25E
Rajshahi Bangladesh **95** F4 24 24N 88 40E
Raleigh North Carolina U.S.A. **63** K4 35 46N 78 39W
Ralik Chain *is.* Pacific Ocean **114** G8 7 30N 167 30E
Ramat Gan Israel **92** O11 32 04N 34 48E
Ramos Brazil **69** P2 22 51S 43 16W
Rampur India **95** D5 28 50N 79 05E
Rampur India **95** D6 31 26N 77 37E
Ramree *i.* Myanmar **96** H2 9 00N 93 30E
Ramtha Jordan **92** O11 32 34N 36 00E
Rancagua Chile **69** C6 34 10S 70 45W
Ranchi India **95** F4 23 22N 85 20E
Randers Denmark **80** B6 56 28N 10 03E
Randolph New York U.S.A. **64** B5 42 10N 78 59W
Randwick Australia **111** G2 33 50S 151 14E
Rangeley Maine U.S.A. **37** Q5 44 58N 70 40W
Rangiora New Zealand **111** B2 43 18S 172 38E
Rangoon *(Yangon)* Myanmar **96** J2 16 47N 96 10E
Rangpur Bangladesh **95** F5 25 45N 89 21E
Rangsdorf Germany **83** F1 52 16N 13 26E
Rani Bagh India **94** L4 28 41N 77 06E
Raniganj India **95** F4 23 35N 87 07E
Rann of Kachchh *geog. reg.* India/Pakistan **94** B4/C4 24 00N 69 00E
Rapid City South Dakota U.S.A. **62** F5 44 06N 103 14W
Ras al Ḥadd *c.* Oman **93** I3 22 31N 59 45E
Râs Banâs *c.* Egypt **92** E3 23 58N 35 50E
Ras Dashen Terara *mt.* Ethiopia **92** E1 13 15N 38 27E
Râs el Barr Egypt **107** R5 31 32N 31 42E
Râs el 'Ish Egypt **107** S4 31 07N 32 18E
Ras Fartak *c.* Yemen Republic **93** H2 15 20N 52 12E
Râs Ghârib Egypt **92** N9 28 22N 33 04E
Rasht Iran **93** G6 37 18N 49 38E
Raşiţa Romania **81** D4 45 16N 21 55E
Râs Kasar *c.* Sudan **92** E2 18 02N 38 33E
Ras Lanuf Libya **106** I14 30 31N 18 34E
Ra's Madrakah *c.* Oman **93** I2 18 58N 57 50E
Râs Muhammad *c.* Egypt **92** O8 27 44N 34 15E
Ras Nouadhibou *(Cap Blanc) c.* Mauritania **106** B12 20 53N 17 01W
Rasto *geog. reg.* Sweden **79** E4 68 40N 21 00E
Ratak Chain *is.* Pacific Ocean **114** H9 10 00N 172 30E
Rat Buri Thailand **99** B6 13 30N 99 50E
Rathlin Island Northern Ireland **78** E7 55 20N 6 10W
Ratingen Germany **76** H2 51 18N 6 50E
Ratlam India **95** D4 23 18N 75 06E
Ratnapura Sri Lanka **95** E1 6 41N 80 25E
Ratno Ukraine **80** D5 51 40N 24 32E
Raton New Mexico U.S.A. **62** F4 36 54N 104 27W
Raukumara *mt.* New Zealand **111** C3 37 45N 178 09E
Raukumara Range *mts.* New Zealand **111** C3 39 00S 178 00E
Rauma Finland **79** E3 61 09N 21 30E
Raurkela India **95** E4 22 16N 85 01E
Ravenna Italy **81** B3 44 25N 12 12E
Ravensburg Germany **77** D4 47 47N 9 37E
Ravensthorpe Australia **110** C3 33 34S 120 01E
Ravi *r.* Pakistan **95** C6 31 00N 73 00E
Rawalpindi Pakistan **95** C6 33 40N 73 08E
Rawlins Wyoming U.S.A. **62** E5 41 46N 107 16W
Rawson Argentina **69** E4 43 15S 65 06W
Ray North Dakota U.S.A. **40** C1 48 22N 103 11W
Raymondville Texas U.S.A. **63** G2 26 30N 97 48W
Raystown Lake Pennsylvania U.S.A. **64** B3 40 20N 78 15W
Razgrad Bulgaria **81** E3 43 31N 26 33E
Reading England **78** K3 51 28N 0 59W
Reading Pennsylvania U.S.A. **64** E3 40 20N 75 55W
Rebun-tō *i.* Japan **100** D4 45 25N 141 04E
Recherche, Archipelago *is.* Australia **110** C2 35 00S 122 50E
Recife Brazil **68** J11 8 06S 34 53W
Recklinghausen Germany **76** J3 51 37N 7 11E
Reconquista Argentina **69** F7 29 08S 59 38W
Recovery Glacier Antarctica **117** 81 00S 25 00W
Red Bank New Jersey U.S.A. **65** F3 40 21N 74 04W
Redbridge *bor.* Greater London England **82** D3 51 34N 0 05E
Redhead Trinidad and Tobago **66** U10 10 44N 60 58W
Redhill England **82** C1 51 14N 0 11W
Redon France **77** B4 47 39N 2 05W
Redondo Beach *tn.* California U.S.A. **51** A2 33 51N 118 24W
Red River U.S.A. **63** H3 32 00N 93 00W
Red Sea Middle East **92** D4/F1 27 00N 35 00E
Red Sea Hills Africa **102** 27 00N 33 00E
Red Wing Minnesota U.S.A. **63** H5 44 33N 92 31W
Redwood City California U.S.A. **49** B1 37 28N 122 15W
Redwood Regional Park California U.S.A. **49** C3 37 49N 122 10W
Reed City Michigan U.S.A. **36** A4 43 54N 85 31W
Reedsport Oregon U.S.A. **62** B5 43 42N 124 05W
Reedy Glacier Antarctica **117** 85 00S 140 00W
Reefton New Zealand **111** B2 42 05S 171 51E
Regensburg Germany **76** E4 49 01N 12 07E
Reggio di Calabria Italy **81** C2 38 06N 15 39E
Reggio nell'Emilia Italy **81** B3 44 42N 10 37E
Registan *geog. reg.* Afghanistan **93** J5 30 30N 65 00E
Rehovot Israel **92** O10 31 54N 34 46E
Reigate England **82** C1 51 14N 0 13W
Reims France **76** C4 49 15N 4 02E
Reinickendorf Germany **83** F2 52 35N 13 22E
Reinosa Spain **77** B3 43 01N 4 09W
Reisa *r.* Norway **79** E4 69 40N 21 30E
Reisterstown Maryland U.S.A. **64** D2 39 27N 76 51W
Relizane Algeria **77** C2 35 44N 0 35E
Rembang Indonesia **99** E2 6 45S 111 22E
Rennell *i.* Solomon Islands **110** K7 11 45S 160 15E
Rennes France **77** B4 48 06N 1 40W
Renovo Pennsylvania U.S.A. **64** C4 41 20N 77 45W
Rensselaer New York U.S.A. **65** G5 42 37N 73 44W
Republic Washington U.S.A. **43** E1 48 39N 118 45W
REPUBLIC OF SOUTH AFRICA **107** J2
Resistencia Argentina **69** F7 27 28S 59 00W
Réthimnon Greece **81** D2 35 23N 24 28E
Réunion *i.* Indian Ocean **112** E4 21 00S 55 30E
Reus Spain **77** C3 41 10N 1 06E
Reutlingen Germany **76** E4 48 30N 9 13E
Reutov Russia **88** N2 55 46N 37 47E
Revere Massachusetts U.S.A. **52** B2 42 25N 71 02W
Revere Beach Massachusetts U.S.A. **52** C2 42 24N 70 59W
Revesby Australia **111** G2 33 57S 151 01E
Revillagigedo Island Alaska U.S.A. **42** B3 55 30N 131 30W
Rewa India **95** E4 24 32N 81 18E
Reykjanes Ridge Atlantic Ocean **113** E12 57 00N 33 00W
Reykjavík Iceland **79** H6 64 09N 21 58W
Reynosa Mexico **66** E5 26 05N 98 18W
Rēzekne Latvia **79** F2 56 30N 27 22E
Rhein *(Rijn, Rhine) r.*Germany **76** D5 50 30N 7 00E
Rheine Germany **76** D5 52 17N 7 26E
Rhein-Herne-Kanal *can.* Germany **76** H3 51 30N 7 00E
Rheinhausen Germany **76** G2 51 23N 6 41E
Rhine *see* Rhein, Rijn
Rhinelander Wisconsin U.S.A. **35** C2 45 39N 89 23W
Rhode Island *state* U.S.A. **65** J4 41 00N 71 00W
Rhode Island Sound Rhode Island U.S.A. **65** J4 41 00N 71 00W
Rhodes *see* Ródhos
Rhondda Wales **78** H3 51 40N 3 30W
Rhône *r.* France **77** C4 45 00N 4 50E
Rhum *i.* Scotland **78** E9 57 00N 6 20W
Ribble *r.* England **78** I5 53 44N 2 56W
Ribe Denmark **80** A6 55 20N 8 47E
Ribeirão Prêto Brazil **68** H8 21 09S 47 48W
Riberalta Bolivia **68** D10 10 59S 66 06W
Richfield Springs *tn.* New York U.S.A. **64** F5 42 53N 75 00W
Richland Washington U.S.A. **62** C6 46 17N 119 17W
Richmond Australia **110** G5 20 45S 143 05E
Richmond California U.S.A. **49** B3 37 56N 122 20W
Richmond Indiana U.S.A. **63** J4 39 50N 84 51W
Richmond New York U.S.A. **50** B1 40 36N 74 10W
Richmond New Zealand **111** B2 41 20S 173 10E
Richmond Virginia U.S.A. **63** K4 37 34N 77 27W
Richmond Park England **82** B2 51 27N 0 16W
Richmond upon Thames *bor.* Greater London England **82** B2 51 28N 0 19W
Richmond Valley New York U.S.A. **50** B1 40 31N 74 13W
Richmondville New York U.S.A. **65** F5 42 00N 74 00W
Rickmansworth England **82** A3 51 38N 0 29W
Ridgefield Connecticut U.S.A. **65** G4 41 17N 73 30W
Ridgewood New Jersey U.S.A. **50** B2 40 58N 74 08W
Ridgway Pennsylvania U.S.A. **64** B4 41 25N 78 45W
Riesa Germany **76** E5 51 18N 13 18E
Rieti Italy **81** B3 42 24N 12 51E
Rif Mountains Morocco **77** A2 35 00N 5 00W
Riga Latvia **79** E2 56 53N 24 08E
Riga, Gulf of Latvia/Estonia **79** E2 57 30N 23 30E
Rijeka Croatia **81** B4 45 20N 14 27E
Rijn *(Rhein, Rhine) r.* Netherlands **76** D5 52 00N 51 15E
Rimini Italy **81** B3 44 03N 12 34E
Rîmnicu Vîlcea Romania **81** D4 45 06N 24 21E
Ringgold Isles Fiji **114** V16 16 10S 179 50W
Ringkøbing Denmark **80** A6 56 06N 8 15E
Ringkøbing Fjord Denmark **80** A6 56 00N 8 00E
Ringvassøy *i.* Norway **79** D4 69 55N 19 10E
Rio Alto Purus Peru **68** C10 10 30S 72 00W
Rio Amazonas *(Amazon) r.* Brazil **68** G12 2 00S 53 00W
Rio Apaporis *r.* Colombia **68** C13 1 00N 72 30W
Río Apure *r.* Venezuela **68** D14 7 40N 68 00W
Rio Aquidauana *r.* Brazil **68** F9 20 00S 56 00W
Rio Araguaia *r.* Brazil **68** H11 7 20S 49 00W
Río Arauca *r.* Venezuela **68** D14 7 10N 68 30W
Riobamba Ecuador **68** B12 1 44S 78 40W
Río Bermejo Argentina **69** E7 25 00S 61 00W
Rio Branco *r.* Brazil **68** E13 0 00 62 00W
Rio Branco *tn.* Brazil **68** D11 9 59S 67 49W
Río Caqueta *r.* Colombia **68** C12 0 05S 72 30W
Río Caroni *r.* Venezuela **68** E14 7 00N 62 30W
Río Caura *r.* Venezuela **68** E14 6 00N 64 00W
Río Chico *r.* Argentina **69** D3 49 00S 70 00W
Río Chico *r.* Argentina **69** D4 45 00S 67 30W
Río Chubut *r.* Argentina **69** D4 43 30S 67 30W
Rio Claro Trinidad and Tobago **66** T9 10 33N 61 11W
Río Colorado *r.* Argentina **69** D5 37 30S 69 00W
Río Corrientes *r.* Peru **68** B12 2 30S 76 30W
Río Cuarto *tn.* Argentina **69** E6 33 08S 64 20W
Rio de Janeiro *admin.* Brazil **69** I8 22 00S 42 30W
Rio de Janeiro *tn.* Brazil **69** Q2 22 53S 43 17W
Río de la Plata *r.* Uruguay/Argentina **69** F5 35 00S 57 00W
Rio de Para *r.* Brazil **68** H12 1 00S 48 00W
Río Deseado *r.* Argentina **69** D3 47 00S 68 00W
Río Dulce *r.* Argentina **69** E7 29 00S 63 00W
Río Gallegos *tn.* Argentina **69** D2 51 35S 68 10W
Río Grande *r.* Bolivia **68** E9 18 00S 65 00W
Rio Grande *r.* Brazil **68** G8 20 00S 50 00W
Río Grande *r.* Mexico/U.S.A. **66** D5/D6 30 00N 104 00W
Río Grande *tn.* Argentina **69** D2 53 45S 67 46W
Rio Grande *tn.* Brazil **69** G6 32 03S 52 08W
Río Grande *tn.* Mexico **66** D4 23 50N 103 02W
Rio Grande do Norte *admin.* Brazil **68** J11 6 00S 37 00W
Rio Grande do Sul *admin.* Brazil **69** G7 28 00N 52 30W
Rio Grande Rise Atlantic Ocean **113** E3 32 00S 36 00W
Río Guainía *r.* Colombia/Venezuela **68** D13 2 30N 67 30W
Rio Guaporé *r.* Brazil/Bolivia **68** E10 13 00S 62 00W
Río Guarico *r.* Venezuela **67** K1 8 00N 67 30W
Río Guaviare *r.* Colombia **68** C13 3 00N 70 00W
Rio Gurgueia *r.* Brazil **68** I11 9 00S 44 00W
Rio Gurupi *r.* Brazil **68** H12 4 00S 47 00W
Ríohacha Colombia **68** C15 11 34N 72 58W
Rio Hondo *r.* California U.S.A. **51** B3 34 00N 118 07W
Rio Iguaçu *r.* Brazil **69** G7 26 00S 51 00W
Río Inírida *r.* Colombia **68** C13/D13 2 30N 70 00W
Rio Japurá *r.* Brazil **68** D12 2 00S 67 30W
Rio Jari *r.* Brazil **68** G13 2 00N 54 00W
Rio Jequitinhonha *r.* Brazil **68** I9 16 00S 41 00W
Rio Juruá *r.* Brazil **68** D12 4 30S 67 00W
Rio Juruena *r.* Brazil **68** F11 10 00S 57 40W
Rio Madeira *r.* Brazil **68** E11 6 00S 61 30W
Río Madre de Dios *r.* Bolivia **68** D10 12 00S 68 00W
Río Magdalena *r.* Colombia **68** C14 8 00N 73 30W
Río Mamoré *r.* Bolivia **68** E9 15 00S 65 00W
Río Marañón *r.* Peru **68** B12 4 50S 77 30W
Río Meta *r.* Colombia **68** C14 6 00N 71 00W
Río Napo *r.* Peru **68** C12 2 30S 73 30W
Río Negro *r.* Argentina **69** E5 40 00S 65 00W
Rio Negro *r.* Brazil **68** D12 0 05S 67 00W
Río Negro *r.* Uruguay **69** F6 33 00S 57 30W
Río Orinoco *r.* Venezuela **68** E14 8 00N 64 00W
Río Paragua *r.* Venezuela **68** E14 6 00N 63 30W
Río Paraguá *r.* Bolivia **68** E10 14 00S 61 30W
Río Paraguay *r.* Paraguay/Argentina **69** F7 26 30S 58 00W
Rio Paraná *r.* Paraguay/Argentina **69** F7 27 00S 56 00W
Rio Paranaíba *r.* Brazil **68** H8 18 00S 49 00W
Rio Parana Panema *r.* Brazil **69** G8 22 30S 52 00W
Rio Pardo *r.* Brazil **68** J9 15 10S 40 00W
Rio Parnaíba *r.* Brazil **68** I11 7 30S 45 00W
Río Pastaza *r.* Peru **68** B12 2 30S 77 00W
Río Pilcomayo *r.* Paraguay/Argentina **69** F8 24 00S 60 00W
Río Salado *r.* Argentina **69** E7 28 30S 62 30W
Río Salado *r.* Argentina **69** D6 35 00S 66 30W
Rio São Francisco *r.* Brazil **68** J11 8 30S 39 00W
Río San Miguel *r.* Bolivia **68** E9 15 00S 63 30W
Rio Solimões *r.* Brazil **68** D12 3 30S 69 00W
Rio Tapajós *r.* Brazil **68** F11 6 30S 57 00W
Rio Taquari *r.* Brazil **68** F9 18 00S 57 00W
Rio Tefé *r.* Brazil **68** D12 4 30S 65 30W
Rio Teles Pires *r.* Brazil **68** F11 8 00S 57 00W
Rio Tocantins *r.* Brazil **68** H12 3 00S 49 00W
Rio Trombetas *r.* Brazil **68** F13 1 30N 57 00W
Río Ucayali *r.* Peru **68** C11 6 00S 74 00W
Rio Uraricuera *r.* Brazil **68** E13 3 00N 62 30W
Río Uruguay *r.* Uruguay/Argentina **69** F6 32 00S 57 40W
Río Verde *r.* Paraguay **69** F8 23 20S 60 00W
Rio Verde *tn.* Brazil **68** G9 17 50S 50 55W
Río Verde *tn.* Mexico **66** D4 21 58N 100 00W
Río Vuapés *r.* Colombia **68** C13 1 30N 72 00W
Rio Xingu *r.* Brazil **68** G12 2 30S 52 30W
Río Yavari *r.* Peru/Brazil **68** C12 5 00S 72 30W
Rishiri-tō *i.* Japan **100** D4 45 10N 141 20E
Rishra India **94** K2 22 43N 88 19E
Rivera Uruguay **69** F6 30 52S 55 30W
River Cess *tn.* Liberia **106** D9 5 28N 9 32W
River Forest *tn.* Illinois U.S.A. **53** A2 41 54N 87 49W
Riverhead New York U.S.A. **65** H3 40 55N 72 40W
River Rouge *tn.* Michigan U.S.A. **52** E2 42 17N 83 08W
River Rouge Park Michigan U.S.A. **52** E2 42 21N 83 14W
Riverside Illinois U.S.A. **53** A2 41 49N 87 49W
Riverside New Jersey U.S.A. **64** F3 40 02N 74 58W
Riverton New Zealand **111** A1 46 21S 168 02E
Roanne France **77** C4 46 02N 4 05E
Roanoke Virginia U.S.A. **63** K4 37 15N 79 58W
Robbinsville New Jersey U.S.A. **65** F3 40 13N 74 38W
Robert Sibley Regional Park California U.S.A. **49** C3 37 51N 122 11W
Roberts, Point Washington U.S.A. **42** H4 49 00N 123 05W
Robertsport Liberia **106** C9 6 45N 11 22W
Robin's Nest *mt.* Hong Kong U.K. **98** B3 22 33N 114 11E
Roca Alijos *is.* Mexico **115** O10 24 59N 115 49W
Rocas Island Atlantic Ocean **55** 3 50S 33 50W
Roche Harbor Washington U.S.A. **42** H4 48 36N 123 10W
Rochefort France **77** B4 45 57N 0 58W
Rochester Minnesota U.S.A. **63** H5 84 01N 92 27W
Rochester New Hampshire U.S.A. **65** K6 43 18N 70 59W
Rochester New York U.S.A. **64** C6 43 12N 77 37W
Rockall Bank Atlantic Ocean **113** G12 58 00N 15 00W
Rockaway Beach New York U.S.A. **50** C1 40 33N 73 55W
Rockaway Inlet New York U.S.A. **50** C1 40 34N 73 56W
Rockdale Australia **111** G2 33 57S 151 08E
Rockefeller Plateau Antarctica **117** 79 00S 140 00W
Rockford Illinois U.S.A. **63** I5 42 16N 89 06W
Rockford Ohio U.S.A. **36** B1 40 42N 84 40W
Rock Hall Maryland U.S.A. **64** D2 39 08N 76 14W
Rockhampton Australia **110** I5 23 22S 150 32E
Rock Hill tn. South Carolina U.S.A. **63** J3 34 55N 81 01W
Rock Island *tn.* Illinois U.S.A. **63** H5 41 30N 90 34W
Rock Lake *tn.* North Dakota U.S.A. **39** B1 48 49N 99 16W
Rockland Massachusetts U.S.A. **65** K5 42 08N 70 55W
Rockport Washington U.S.A. **42** H4 48 30N 121 38W
Rock Springs *tn.* Wyoming U.S.A. **62** E5 41 35N 109 13W
Rockville Maryland U.S.A. **64** C2 39 05N 77 10W
Rockville Center New York U.S.A. **50** D1 40 40N 73 38W
Rocky Mount *tn.* North Carolina U.S.A. **63** K4 35 56N 77 48W
Rocky Mountains Canada/U.S.A. **10** K4/N1
Rocky Point New York U.S.A. **65** H3 40 57N 72 55W
Rocky Woods Reservation Massachusetts U.S.A. **52** A1 42 13N 71 16W
Rodez France **77** C3 44 21N 2 34E
Ródhos Greece **81** E2 36 26N 28 14E
Ródhos *(Rhodes) i.* Greece **81** E2 36 00N 28 00E
Roding *r.* England **82** D3 51 45N 0 15E
Rodopi Planina *mts.* Bulgaria **81** D3 41 00N 25 00E
Rodrigues *i.* Indian Ocean **112** F5 19 43S 63 26E
Rogers City Michigan U.S.A. **36** C6 45 24N 83 50W
Rokugo *r.* Japan **101** C3 35 31N 139 46E
Rolette North Dakota U.S.A. **39** B1 48 41N 99 50W
Rolla Missouri U.S.A. **63** H4 37 56N 91 55W
Rolla North Dakota U.S.A. **39** B1 48 52N 99 36W
Roma *(Rome)* Italy **81** B3 41 53N 12 30E
Roma Australia **110** H4 26 32S 148 46E
Roman Romania **81** E4 46 56N 26 56E
ROMANIA **81** D4
Rome Georgia U.S.A. **63** I3 34 01N 85 02W
Rome New York U.S.A. **64** E6 43 13N 75 28W
Rome *see* Roma
Romford England **82** D3 51 35N 0 11E
Romney West Virginia U.S.A. **64** B2 39 21N 78 44W
Romulus Michigan U.S.A. **52** D1 42 14N 83 23W
Rona *i.* Scotland **78** F11 59 10N 5 50W
Ronda Spain **77** A2 36 45N 5 10W
Rondônia *admin.* Brazil **68** E10 11 30S 63 00W
Rondonópolis Brazil **68** G9 16 29S 54 37W
Rondout Reservoir New York U.S.A. **65** F4 41 50N 74 30W
Ronne Ice Shelf Antarctica **117** 77 00S 60 00W
Roosevelt Minnesota U.S.A. **39** B1 48 49N 95 06W
Roosevelt Island Antarctica **117** 79 00S 160 00W
Roraima *admin.* Brazil **68** E13 2 30N 62 30W
Rosario Argentina **69** E6 33 00S 60 40W
Rosário Brazil **68** I12 3 00S 44 15W
Rosario Mexico **66** A6 30 20N 115 46W
Rosario Mexico **66** C4 23 00N 105 51W
Rosario Strait Washington U.S.A. **42** H4 48 30N 122 50W
Rosarito Mexico **66** B5 28 38N 114 02W
Roscoff France **76** B4 48 43N 3 59W
Roscommon Michigan U.S.A. **36** B5 44 31N 84 37W
Roseau Dominica **67** L3 15 18N 61 23W
Roseau Minnesota U.S.A. **39** B1 48 51N 95 46W
Roseburg Oregon U.S.A. **62** B5 43 13N 123 21W
Roselle New Jersey U.S.A. **50** A1 40 40N 74 16W
Rosemead California U.S.A. **51** B3 34 03N 118 07W
Rosenheim Germany **76** E4 47 51N 12 09E
Roseville Michigan U.S.A. **52** F2 42 29N 82 05W
Rossano Italy **81** C2 39 35N 16 38E
Ross Ice Shelf Antarctica **117** 80 00S 180 00
Ross Lake Washington U.S.A. **42** H4 48 50N 121 05W
Ross Lake National Recreation Area Washington U.S.A. **42** H4 48 50N 121 00W
Rosslare Irish Republic **78** F4 52 15N 6 22W
Rosso Mauritania **106** A11 16 29N 15 53W
Ross Sea Southern Ocean **117** 75 00S 180 00
Røssvatnet *mt.* Sweden **79** D4 66 00N 15 10E
Rostock Germany **76** E5 54 06N 12 09E
Rostov Russia **90** D6 57 11N 39 23E
Rostov-na-Donu Russia **90** D4 47 15N 39 45E
Roswell New Mexico U.S.A. **62** F3 33 24N 104 33W
Rothera *r.s.* Antarctica **117** 67 34S 68 07W
Rotorua New Zealand **111** C3 38 07S 176 17E
Rotterdam Netherlands **76** C5 51 54N 4 28E
Rotterdam New York U.S.A. **65** G5 42 00N 73 00W
Roubaix France **76** C5 50 42N 3 10E
Rouen France **76** C5 49 26N 1 05E
Rouge, Point Trinidad and Tobago **66** S9 10 09N 61 47W
Rouge, River Michigan U.S.A. **52** E2 42 17N 83 26W
Roulette Pennsylvania U.S.A. **64** B4 41 45N 78 10W
Round Island Hong Kong U.K. **98** C1 22 12N 114 10E
Rovaniemi Finland **79** F4 66 29N 25 40E
Rovigo Italy **81** B4 45 04N 11 47E
Rovno Ukraine **90** B5 50 39N 26 10E
Rovuma *(Ruvuma) r.* Mozambique **107** M5 11 30S 38 00E
Roxas The Philippines **99** G6 11 36N 122 45E
Roxburgh New Zealand **111** A1 45 34N 169 21E
Roxbury Massachusetts U.S.A. **52** B2 42 19N 71 03W
Royal Botanic Gardens England **82** B2 51 28N 0 18W
Royal National Park Australia **111** G1 34 06S 151 06E
Royal Oak Michigan U.S.A. **36** C3 42 31N 83 08W
Royan France **77** B4 45 38N 1 02W
Rtishchevo Russia **90** E5 52 16N 43 45E
Ruaha National Park Tanzania **107** M6 7 00S 35 00E
Ruapehu *mt.* New Zealand **111** C3 39 18S 176 36E
Rub'Al Khālī *d.* Saudi Arabia **93** G2 19 30N 48 00E
Rubtsovsk Russia **90** N5 51 43N 81 11E
Ruby Alaska U.S.A. **10** D5 64 41N 155 35W
Rudnya Russia **90** E5 50 49N 44 35E
Rudnyy Kazakhstan **91** J5 53 00N 63 05E
Rudow Germany **83** F1 52 24N 13 29E
Rudyard Montana U.S.A. **41** C1 48 34N 110 33W
Rueil-Malmaison France **83** A2 48 52N 2 12E
Rufiji *r.* Tanzania **107** M6 7 30S 38 40E
Rugby England **78** J4 52 23N 1 15W
Ruhrort Germany **76** G2 51 27N 6 44E
Ruislip England **82** B3 51 35N 0 25W
Rukwa, Lake Tanzania **107** L6 8 00S 33 00E
Rumoi Japan **100** D3 43 57N 141 40E
Runanga New Zealand **111** B2 42 24S 171 12E
Rungis France **83** B2 48 45N 2 22E
Ruse Bulgaria **81** E3 43 50N 25 59E
Rusk Texas U.S.A. **63** G3 31 49N 95 11W
Russas Brazil **68** J12 4 56N 38 02W
Russell Kansas U.S.A. **62** G4 38 54N 98 51W
Russell New Zealand **111** B3 35 16S 174 10E
RUSSIA *(RUSSIAN FEDERATION)* **90/91** E6/K6
RUSSIAN FEDERATION *see* RUSSIA
Russkaya *r.s.* Antartica **117** 74 46S 136 51W
Rustavi Georgia **90** F3 41 34N 45 03E
Ruston Louisiana U.S.A. **63** H3 32 32N 92 39W
Ruth Nevada U.S.A. **62** D4 39 16N 114 59W
Rutland Vermont U.S.A. **63** L5 43 37N 72 59W
Rutog China **96** E5 33 27N 79 43E
Ruvuma *(Rovuma) r.* Tanzania **107** M5 11 30S 38 00E
Ruwenzori, Mount *mt.* Uganda/Zaïre **102** 0 23N 29 54E
Ruwenzori National Park Rwanda **106** L7 0 30S 29 30E
Ružomberok Czechoslovakia **80** C4 49 04N 19 15E
RWANDA **106** L7
Ryazan' Russia **90** D5 54 37N 39 43E
Rybach'ye Kazakhstan **91** N4 46 27N 81 30E
Rybach'ye *see* Issyk-Kul'
Rybinsk *(Andropov)* Russia **90** D6 58 03N 38 50E
Rybinskoye Vodokhranilishche *(Rybinsk Reservoir)* Russia **90** D6 59 00N 38 00E
Rybinsk Reservoir *see* Rybinskoye Vodokhranilishche
Rybnik Poland **80** C5 50 07N 18 30E
Ryde Australia **111** G2 33 49S 151 06E
Rye New York U.S.A. **50** D2 40 58N 73 41W
Ryukyu Islands *(Nansei-shoto)* Japan **97** P4 27 30N 127 30E
Ryukyu Ridge Pacific Ocean **114** C10 25 50N 128 00E
Ryukyu Trench Pacific Ocean **84** 25 00N 128 00E
Rzeszów Poland **80** D5 50 04N 22 00E
Rzhev Russia **90** C6 56 15N 34 18E

S

Saalfeld Germany 76 E5 50 39N 11 22E
Saarbrücken Germany 76 D4 49 15N 6 58E
Saaremaa *i.* Estonia 79 E2 58 20N 22 00E
Sabadell Spain 77 C3 41 33N 2 07E
Šabac Serbia Yugoslavia 81 C3 44 45N 19 41E
Šabah *state* Malaysia 99 F5 5 00N 117 30E
Sabaloka Cataract *(River Nile)* Sudan 92 D2 16 19N 32 40E
Sabanalarga Colombia 67 J2 10 38N 74 55W
Sabhā Libya 106 H13 27 02N 14 26E
Sabi *r.* Zimbabwe/Mozambique 107 L3 20 30S 33 00E
Sabinas Mexico 66 D5 27 50N 101 09W
Sabinas Hidalgo Mexico 66 D5 26 33N 100 10W
Sabine *r.* U.S.A. 63 H3 30 00N 94 00W
Sabine, Mount Antarctica 117 72 00S 169 00W
Sabkhet el Bardawîl *l.* Egypt 92 N10 31 10N 33 35E
Sable, Cape Florida U.S.A. 63 J2 25 08N 80 07W
Sabor *r.* Portugal 77 A3 41 22N 6 50W
Sabyā Saudi Arabia 92 F2 17 07N 42 39E
Sabzevār Iran 93 I6 36 15N 57 38E
Saclay France 83 A1 48 43N 2 09E
Saco Montana U.S.A. 40 B1 48 27N 107 21W
Sacramento Mountains U.S.A. 62 E3 33 00N 105 00W
Sadar Bazar India 94 L4 28 39N 77 12E
Sadiya India 95 H5 27 49N 95 38E
Sado *r.* Portugal 77 A2 38 15N 8 30W
Sado-shima *i.* Japan 100 C2 38 20N 138 30E
Säffle Sweden 80 B6 59 08N 12 55E
Safi Morocco 106 D14 32 20N 9 17W
Saga Japan 100 B1 33 16N 130 18E
Sagaing Myanmar 95 H4 21 55N 95 56E
Sagami Bay Japan 101 B2 35 15N 139 32E
Sagamihara Japan 100 L2 35 34N 139 22E
Sagami-nada *sea* Japan 100 L1 35 00N 139 30E
Sagami-wan *b.* Japan 100 L2 35 12N 139 20E
Sagar India 95 D4 23 50N 78 44E
Sagavanirktok *r.* Alaska U.S.A. 44 B4 68 00N 149 00W
Sage Creek Montana U.S.A. 41 C1 48 50N 110 50W
Saginaw Michigan U.S.A. 63 J5 43 25N 83 54W
Saginaw Bay Michigan U.S.A. 63 J5 44 00N 84 00W
Sagua la Grande Cuba 67 H4 22 48N 80 06W
Sagunto Spain 77 B2 39 40N 0 17W
Sahara Desert North Africa 106 D12
Saharanpur India 95 D5 29 58N 77 33E
Sahiwal Pakistan 95 C6 30 41N 73 11E
Sahuaripa Mexico 66 C5 29 00N 109 13W
Sahuayo Mexico 66 D4 20 05N 102 42W
Saïda Algeria 77 C1 34 50N 0 10E
Saïda *(Sidon)* Lebanon 92 O11 33 32N 35 22E
Saidpur Bangladesh 95 F5 25 48N 89 00E
Saikhoa Ghat India 95 H5 27 46N 95 38E
Sai Kung Hong Kong U.K. 98 C2 22 23N 114 16E
Saimaa *l.* Finland 79 F3 61 15N 27 45E
St. Abb's Head *c.* Scotland 78 I7 55 55N 2 09W
St. Albans England 78 K3 51 46N 0 21W
St. Albans Vermont U.S.A. 33 B1 44 49N 73 07W
St. Andrews Scotland 78 I8 56 20N 2 48W
St. Ann's Bay *tn.* Jamaica 67 Q8 18 26N 77 12W
St. Augustine Florida U.S.A. 63 J2 29 54N 81 19W
St. Bees Head *c.* England 78 H6 54 31N 3 39W
St-Brieuc France 76 B4 48 31N 2 45W
St. Clair, Lake Canada/U.S.A. 36 D3 42 30N 82 40W
St. Clair Shores Michigan U.S.A. 52 F2 42 29N 82 53W
St-Cloud France 83 A2 48 51N 2 11E
St.Cloud Minnesota U.S.A. 63 H6 45 34N 94 10W
St. Croix *i.* West Indies 67 L3 22 45N 65 00W
St. Croix *r.* North America 63 H6 46 00N 93 00W
St. Croix Falls *tn.* Wisconsin U.S.A. 35 B2 45 25N 92 38W
St. Cyr-l'École France 83 A2 48 47N 2 03E
St. David's Head *c.* Wales 78 F3 51 55N 5 19W
St-Denis France 83 B2 48 57N 2 22E
St.-Dié France 76 D4 48 17N 6 57E
St.-Dizier France 76 C4 48 38N 4 58E
Saint Elias, Mount Canada/U.S.A. 44 C3 60 14N 140 50W
Saint Elias Mountains Canada/U.S.A. 44 D3 60 30N 140 00W
Saintes France 77 B4 45 44N 0 38W
St.-Étienne France 77 C4 45 26N 4 23E
St. Francis *r.* U.S.A. 63 H4 35 00N 90 00W
St. Francis, Cape Republic of South Africa 102 34 13S 24 51E
St. Gallen Switzerland 77 D4 47 25N 9 23E
St.-Gaudens France 77 C3 43 07N 0 44E
St.-Germain-en-Laye France 83 A2 48 54N 2 04E
St. George New York U.S.A. 50 B1 40 48N 74 06W
St. George's Grenada 67 L2 12 04N 61 44W
St. George's Channel British Isles 78 E3 52 00N 6 00W
St. Helena *i.* Atlantic Ocean 113 H5 15 58S 5 43W
St. Helena Bay Republic of South Africa 107 I1 32 00S 17 30E
St. Helens England 78 I5 53 28N 2 44W
St. Helier Jersey Channel Islands 78 I6 49 12N 2 07W
St. Ignace Michigan U.S.A. 63 J6 45 53N 84 44W
St. Ives Australia 111 G3 33 44S 151 10E
St. John North Dakota U.S.A. 39 B1 48 58N 99 41W
Saint John *r.* North America 63 M6 46 00N 69 00W
St. John's Antigua & Barbuda 67 L3 17 08N 61 50W
St. Johns Michigan U.S.A. 36 B4 43 01N 84 31W
St. Joseph Missouri U.S.A. 63 B1 39 45N 94 51W
St Joseph Trinidad and Tobago 66 T10 10 39N 61 25W
St Joseph Trinidad and Tobago 66 U9 10 17N 60 25W
St. Joseph River U.S.A. 36 B2 41 12N 85 00W
St. Kilda *i.* Scotland 78 C9 57 49N 8 34W
ST. KITTS-NEVIS 67 L3
St. Laurent French Guiana 68 G14 5 29N 54 03W
St. Lawrence Island Alaska U.S.A. 10 B5 63 15N 169 50W
St. Lawrence Seaway Canada/U.S.A. 37 L/M5 44 38N 48 34W
St-Lô France 76 B4 49 07N 1 05W
St. Louis Missouri U.S.A. 63 H4 38 40N 90 15W
St. Louis Senegal 106 A11 16 01N 16 30W
St. Louis River Minnesota U.S.A. 35 B2 47 00N 92 45W
ST. LUCIA 67 L2
St.-Malo France 76 B4 48 39N 2 00W
St-Mandé France 83 B2 48 50N 2 26E
St. Mary Montana U.S.A. 41 C1 48 44N 113 25W
St. Marys Pennsylvania U.S.A. 64 B4 41 27N 78 35W
St. Marys River U.S.A. 36 B1 40 50N 84 55W
St. Maur France 83 B2 48 48N 2 30E
St. Moritz Switzerland 77 D4 46 30N 9 51E
St.-Nazaire France 77 B4 47 17N 2 12W
St.-Omer France 76 C5 50 45N 2 15E
St. Ouen France 83 A3 49 03N 2 07E
St. Paul Rocks Atlantic Ocean 113 F7 0 23N 29 23W
St. Peter Port Guernsey Channel Islands 78 I6 49 27N 3 32W
Saint Petersburg Florida U.S.A. 63 J2 27 45N 82 40W
St. Petersburg *(Leningrad, Sankt-Peterburg)* Russia 90 C6 59 55N 30 25E
Saint-Pierre & Miquelon *is.* Atlantic Ocean 11 X2 47 00N 56 20W
St. Pölten Austria 81 C4 48 13N 15 37E
St.-Quentin France 76 C4 49 51N 3 17E
St. Remy France 83 A1 48 42N 2 04E
St. Thomas *i.* West Indies 67 K3 18 00N 65 30W
St.-Tropez France 77 D3 43 16N 6 39E
St. Vincent *i.* St. Vincent and The Grenadines 67 L2 13 15N 61 12W
ST. VINCENT AND THE GRENADINES 67 L2
Saipan Northern Marianas 114 E9 15 12N 145 43E
Saitama *pref.* Japan 100 L3 36 00N 139 30E
Sai Ying Pun Hong Kong U.K. 98 B1 22 17N 114 08E
Sakai Japan 100 C1 34 35N 135 28E
Sākākah Saudi Arabia 92 F4 29 59N 40 12E
Sakakawea, Lake North Dakota U.S.A. 62 F6 48 00N 103 00W
Sakarya *r.* Turkey 92 D6 40 05N 30 15E
Sakata Japan 100 C2 38 55N 139 51E
Sakhalin *i.* Russia 89 Q6 50 00N 143 00E
Sakhalin Bay Russia 89 Q6 54 00N 141 00E
Sakura Japan 100 M2 35 43N 140 13E
Sakurai Japan 100 G1 34 54N 135 12E
Sala Sweden 80 C6 59 55N 16 38E
Salālah Oman 93 H2 17 00N 54 04E
Salamanca Mexico 66 D4 20 34N 101 12W
Salamanca New York U.S.A. 64 B5 42 11N 78 43W
Salamanca Spain 77 A3 40 58N 5 40W
Salavat Russia 91 H5 53 22N 55 50E
Sala y Gomez *i.* Pacific Ocean 115 P5 26 28S 105 28W
Saldus Latvia 79 E2 56 38N 22 30E
Salekhard Russia 89 I9 66 33N 66 35E
Salem India 95 D2 11 38N 78 08E
Salem Massachusetts U.S.A. 52 C3 42 32N 70 53W
Salem New Jersey U.S.A. 64 E2 39 35N 75 28W
Salem Oregon U.S.A. 62 B5 44 57N 123 01W
Salerno Italy 81 B3 40 40N 14 46E
Salgótarján Hungary 81 C4 49 05N 19 47E
Salgueiro Brazil 68 J11 8 04S 39 05W
Salihli Turkey 80 E2 38 29N 28 08E
Salima Malawi 107 L5 13 45S 34 29E
Salina Kansas U.S.A. 63 G4 38 53N 97 36W
Salinas Ecuador 68 A12 2 15S 80 58W
Salinas Grandes *l.* Argentina 69 D6/E7 30 00S 65 00W
Saline Michigan U.S.A. 36 C3 42 12N 83 46W
Salisbury England 78 J3 51 05N 1 48W
Salisbury Maryland U.S.A. 63 K4 38 22N 75 37W
Salisbury North Carolina U.S.A. 63 J4 35 20N 80 30W
Salisbury Plain England 78 J3 51 10N 1 55W
Salmon Idaho U.S.A. 62 D6 45 11N 113 55W
Salmon *r.* Idaho U.S.A. 62 C6 45 00N 116 00W
Salmon River Mountains Idaho U.S.A. 62 C6 45 00N 115 00W
Salo Finland 79 E3 60 23N 23 10E
Salonta Romania 81 D4 46 49N 21 40E
Salpausselka *geog. reg.* Finland 79 F3 61 40N 26 00E
Salt Jordan 92 O11 32 03N 35 44E
Salt *r.* Arizona U.S.A. 62 D3 34 00N 110 00W
Salta Argentina 69 D8 24 46S 65 28W
Salt Creek Illinois U.S.A. 53 A2 41 52N 87 57W
Saltdal Norway 79 D4 67 06N 15 25E
Salten *geog. reg.* Norway 79 D4 67 05N 15 00E
Salt Fork *r.* Texas U.S.A. 62 F3 33 00N 101 00W
Salt Fork *r.* Texas/Oklahoma U.S.A. 62 F4 35 00N 100 00W
Saltillo Mexico 66 D5 25 30N 101 00W
Salt Lake *tn.* India 94 K2 22 35N 88 23E
Salt Lake City Utah U.S.A. 62 D5 40 45N 111 55W
Salto Uruguay 69 F6 31 27S 57 50W
Salvador Brazil 68 J10 12 58S 38 29W
Salween *(Nu Jiang)* *r.* Myanmar 97 J3 21 00N 98 30E
Salybia Trinidad and Tobago 66 T10 10 42N 61 02W
Salzburg Austria 81 B4 47 48N 13 03E
Salzgitter Germany 76 E5 52 13N 10 20E
Samani Japan 100 D3 42 07N 142 57E
Samar *i.* The Philippines 99 G6 12 30N 125 00E
Samara *r.* Russia 90 G5 52 30N 53 00E
Samara *(Kuybyshev)* Russia 90 G5 53 10N 50 10E
Samara *(Kuybyshevskoye)* **Vodokhranilishche** *res.* Russia 90 F5/6 55 00N 45 00E
Samarinda Indonesia 99 F3 0 30S 117 09E
Samarkand Uzbekistan 91 K2 39 40N 66 57E
Sāmarrā' Iraq 92 F5 34 13N 43 52E
Sambalpur India 95 E4 21 28N 84 04E
Sambor Ukraine 80 D4 49 31N 23 10E
Sámos *i.* Greece 81 E2 37 00N 26 00E
Samothráki *i.* Greece 81 E3 40 00N 25 00E
Samsun Turkey 92 E7 41 17N 36 22E
San Mali 106 D10 13 21N 4 57W
San'ā Yemen Republic 92 F2 15 23N 44 14E
Sanae *r.s.* Antarctica 117 70 18S 02 25E
Sanaga *r.* Cameroon 106 H8 4 30N 12 20E
Sanak Islands Alaska U.S.A. 10 C3 54 26N 162 40W
Sanandaj Iran 93 G6 35 18N 47 01E
San Andreas Fault California U.S.A. 49 B1 37 28N 122 18W
San Andreas Lake California U.S.A. 49 B2 37 36N 122 25W
San Andrés Tuxtla Mexico 66 E3 18 28N 95 15W
San Angelo Texas U.S.A. 62 F3 31 28N 100 28W
San Antonio Chile 69 C6 33 35S 71 39W
San Antonio Texas U.S.A. 62 G2 29 25N 98 30W
San Antonio *r.* Texas U.S.A. 63 G2 29 00N 97 00W
San Antonio Oeste Argentina 69 E4 40 45S 64 58W
San Bernado Chile 69 C6 33 37S 70 45W
San Bruno California U.S.A. 49 B2 37 33N 122 24W
San Bruno Mountain California U.S.A. 49 B2 37 41N 122 26W
San Carlos California U.S.A. 49 B2 37 30N 122 16W
San Carlos The Philippines 99 G6 10 30N 123 29E
San Carlos The Philippines 99 G7 15 59N 120 22E
San Carlos Venezuela 68 D14 9 39N 68 35W
San Carlos de Bariloche Argentina 69 C4 41 11S 71 23W
San Carlos del Zulia Venezuela 68 C14 9 01N 71 58W
San-chung Taiwan 98 H8 25 04N 121 29E
San Clemente Island U.S.A. 62 C3 32 55N 118 30W
San Cristóbal Argentina 69 E6 30 20S 61 14W
San Cristóbal Mexico 66 F3 16 45N 92 40W
San Cristobal Venezuela 68 C14 7 46N 72 15W
San Cristobal *i.* Solomon Islands 110 K7 11 00S 162 00E
Sanda Japan 100 G1 34 54N 135 12E
Sandakan Malaysia 99 F5 5 52N 118 04E
Sanday *i.* Scotland 78 I11 59 15N 2 30W
Sandefjord Norway 80 B6 59 00N 10 15E
Sandoway Myanmar 95 G3 18 28N 94 20E
Sandpoint Idaho U.S.A. 43 E1 48 17N 116 34W
Sandpoint *tn.* Idaho U.S.A. 62 C6 48 17N 116 34W
Sandusky Michigan U.S.A. 36 D4 43 56N 82 50W
Sandusky Ohio U.S.A. 36 D2 41 27N 85 42W
Sandusky Bay Ohio U.S.A. 36 D2 41 30N 82 50W
Sandusky River Ohio U.S.A. 36 C1 41 00N 83 15W
Sandviken Sweden 80 C7 60 38N 16 50E
Sandy River Maine U.S.A. 37 Q5 44 45N 70 12W
San Felipe Mexico 66 B6 31 03N 114 52W
San Felipe Venezuela 68 D15 10 25N 68 40W
San Feliú de Guixols Spain 77 C3 41 47N 3 02E
San Fernando California U.S.A. 51 A1 34 17N 118 27W
San Fernando Mexico 66 A5 29 59N 115 10W
San Fernando Spain 77 A2 36 28N 6 12W
San Fernando Trinidad and Tobago 66 T10 10 16N 61 28W
San Fernando de Apure Venezuela 68 D14 7 53N 67 15W
Sanford Florida U.S.A. 63 J2 28 49N 81 17W
San Francique Trinidad and Tobago 66 S9 10 05N 61 39W
San Francisco Argentina 69 E6 31 29S 62 06W
San Francisco Dominican Republic 67 J3 19 19N 70 15W
San Francisco Bay California U.S.A. 49 B2 37 40N 122 18W
San Francisco Bay National Wildlife Refuge California U.S.A. 49 C2 37 31N 122 05W
San Francisco County California U.S.A. 49 B3 37 55N 122 25W
San Francisco del Oro Mexico 66 C5 26 52N 105 50W
San Francisco State Fish and Game Refuge California U.S.A. 49 B2 37 34N 122 26W
San Gabriel California U.S.A. 51 B3 34 06N 118 06W
San Gabriel Mountains California U.S.A. 51 B4 34 18N 118 05W
San Gabriel Reservoir California U.S.A. 51 C3 34 12N 117 52W
San Gabriel River California U.S.A. 51 B2 33 58N 118 06W
Sangar Russia 89 O8 64 02N 127 30E
Sangha *r.* Africa 106 I8 2 00N 17 00E
Sangli India 95 C3 16 55N 74 37E
Sangre de Cristo Mountains New Mexico U.S.A. 62 E4 37 00N 105 00W
Sangre Grande Trinidad and Tobago 66 T10 10 35N 61 08W
San Javier Bolivia 68 E9 16 22S 62 38W
San José Costa Rica 67 H1 9 59N 84 04W
San José Uruguay 69 F6 34 27S 56 40W
San José del Cabo Mexico 66 C4 23 01N 109 40W
San Juan Argentina 69 D6 31 33S 68 31W
San Juán Peru 68 B9 15 22S 75 07W
San Juan Puerto Rico 67 K3 18 29N 66 08W
San Juan Trinidad and Tobago 66 T10 10 39N 61 27W
San Juan *r.* U.S.A. 62 D4 37 00N 110 00W
San Juan de los Morros Venezuela 67 K1 9 53N 67 23W
San Juan Islands Washington U.S.A. 42 H4 48 30N 123 00W
San Juan Mountains Colorado U.S.A. 62 E4 37 50N 107 50W
San Julián Argentina 69 D3 49 17S 67 45W
Sänkrāil India 94 J2 22 33N 88 14E
Sankt-Peterburg *see* St. Petersburg
Sankuru *r.* Zaïre 107 J7 4 00S 23 30E
San Leandro California U.S.A. 49 C2 37 43N 122 10W
San Lorenzo California U.S.A. 49 C2 37 41N 122 08W
Sanlúcar de Barrameda Spain 77 A2 36 46N 6 21W
San Lucas Mexico 66 C4 22 50N 109 52W
San Luis Argentina 69 D6 33 20S 66 23W
San Luis Potosí Mexico 66 D4 22 10N 101 00W
San Marcos Texas U.S.A. 63 G2 29 54N 97 57W
San Mateo California U.S.A. 49 B2 37 33N 122 22W
San Mateo County California U.S.A. 49 C2 37 35N 122 12W
Sanmenxia China 97 M5 34 46N 111 17E
San Miguel El Salvador 66 G2 13 28N 88 10W
San Miguel de Tucumán Argentina 69 D7 26 47S 65 15W
Sanming China 97 N4 26 16N 117 35E
Sannan Japan 100 G2 35 05N 135 03E
San Pablo California U.S.A. 49 B3 37 58N 122 21W
San Pablo The Philippines 99 G6 14 03N 121 19E
San Pablo Creek California U.S.A. 49 B3 37 58N 122 20W
San Pablo Reservoir California U.S.A. 49 C3 37 56N 122 14W
San Pedro Argentina 69 E8 24 12S 64 55W
San Pedro California U.S.A. 51 A2 33 45N 118 19W
San Pedro Côte d'Ivoire 106 D9 4 45N 6 37W
San Pedro Dominican Republic 67 K3 18 30N 69 18W
San Pedro Bay California U.S.A. 51 B1 33 43N 118 12W
San Pedro Channel California U.S.A. 51 A1 33 43N 118 22W
San Pedro de las Colonias Mexico 66 D5 25 50N 102 59W
San Pedro Sula Honduras 66 G3 15 26N 88 01W
San Quentin California U.S.A. 49 A3 37 56N 122 30W
San Rafael Argentina 69 D6 34 35S 68 24W
San Rafael California U.S.A. 49 B3 37 58N 122 30W
San Rafael Bay California U.S.A. 49 B3 37 56N 122 29W
San Remo Italy 81 A3 43 48N 7 46E
San Salvador El Salvador 66 G2 13 40N 89 10W
San Salvador *i.* The Bahamas 67 J4 24 00N 74 32W
San Salvador de Jujuy Argentina 69 D8 24 10S 65 48W
San Sebastián Spain 77 B3 43 19N 1 59W
San Severo Italy 81 C3 41 41N 15 23E
Santa Ana Bolivia 68 D10 13 46S 65 37W
Santa Ana California U.S.A. 51 C2 33 44N 117 54W
Santa Ana El Salvador 66 G2 14 00N 89 31W
Santa Ana River California U.S.A. 51 C2 33 46N 117 54W
Santa Barbara Mexico 66 C5 26 48N 105 50W
Santa Catarina *admin.* Brazil 69 G7 27 00S 51 00W
Santa Clara Cuba 67 I4 22 25S 79 58W
Santa Clara County California U.S.A. 49 C1 37 23N 122 11W
Santa Cruz Bolivia 68 E9 17 50S 63 10W
Santa Cruz Canary Islands 106 B13 28 28N 16 15W
Santa Cruz Jamaica 67 Q8 18 03N 77 43W
Santa Cruz *r.* Argentina 69 D2 50 00S 70 00W
Santa Cruz Islands Solomon Islands 110 L7 11 00S 167 00E
Santa Cruz Mountains California U.S.A. 49 B1 37 28N 122 23W
Santa Fé Argentina 69 E6 31 35S 60 50W
Santa Fe New Mexico U.S.A. 62 E4 35 41N 105 57W
Santa Isabel *i.* Solomon Islands 110 J8 7 30S 158 30E
Santa Maria Brazil 69 G7 29 45S 53 40W
Santa Marta Colombia 68 C15 11 18N 74 10W
Santa Monica California U.S.A. 51 A3 34 00N 118 25W
Santa Monica Mountains California U.S.A. 51 A3 33 07N 118 27W
Santana do Livramento Brazil 69 F6 30 52S 55 30W
Santander Colombia 68 B13 3 00N 76 25W
Santander Spain 77 B3 43 28N 3 48W
Sant'Antioco Italy 81 A2 39 04N 8 27E
Santarém Brazil 68 G12 2 26S 54 41W
Santarém Portugal 77 A2 39 14N 8 40W
Santa Rosa Argentina 69 E5 36 37S 64 17W
Santa Rosa Honduras 66 G2 14 48N 88 43W
Santa Rosa New Mexico U.S.A. 62 F3 34 56N 104 42W
Santa Rosalia Mexico 66 B5 27 20N 112 20W
Santa Teresa Brazil 69 Q2 22 57S 43 12W
Santiago Chile 69 C6 33 30S 70 40W
Santiago Dominican Republic 67 J3 19 30N 70 42W
Santiago Panama 67 H1 8 08N 80 59W
Santiago de Compostela Spain 77 A3 42 52N 8 33W
Santiago de Cuba Cuba 67 I4 20 00N 75 49W
Santiago del Estero Argentina 69 E7 27 47S 64 15W
Santiago Ixcuintla Mexico 66 C4 21 50N 105 11W
San Tin Hong Kong U.K. 98 B3 22 30N 114 04E
Santi Nagar India 94 L4 28 40N 77 10E
Santo Andre Brazil 69 H8 23 39S 46 29W
Santo Domingo Dominican Republic 67 K3 18 30N 69 57W
Santos Brazil 69 H8 23 56S 46 22W
San Uk Ha Hong Kong U.K. 98 C3 22 30N 114 14E
San Vicente El Salvador 66 G2 13 38N 88 42W
São Bernardo do Campo Brazil 69 H8 23 45S 46 34W
São Borja Brazil 69 F7 28 35S 56 01W
São Cristovão Brazil 69 Q2 22 54S 43 14W
São Gonçalo Brazil 69 Q2 22 48S 43 03W
São João de Meriti Brazil 69 P2 22 47S 43 22W
São João de Meriti *r.* Brazil 69 P2 22 48S 43 20W
São José Brazil 69 H7 27 35S 48 40W
São José do Rio Prêto Brazil 68 H8 20 50S 49 20W
São José dos Campos Brazil 69 H8 23 07S 45 52W
São Luís Brazil 68 I12 2 34S 44 16W
Saône *r.* France 77 C4 46 28N 4 55E
São Paulo *admin.* Brazil 68 G8/H8 21 30S 50 00W
São Paulo Brazil 69 H8 23 33S 46 39W
São Paulo de Olivença Brazil 68 D12 3 34S 68 55W
São Tomé *i.* Gulf of Guinea 106 G8 0 25N 6 35E
SÃO TOMÉ AND PRINCIPE 106 G8
São Vicente Brazil 69 H8 23 57S 46 23W
Sapporo Japan 100 D3 43 05N 141 21E
Saqqez Iran 93 G6 36 14N 46 15E
Sarajevo Bosnia-Herzegovina 81 C3 43 52N 18 26E
Sarakhs Iran 93 J6 36 32N 61 07E
Saransk Russia 90 F5 54 12N 45 10E
Sarapui *r.* Brazil 69 P3 22 44S 43 17W
Sarapul Russia 91 G6 56 30N 53 49E
Sarasota Florida U.S.A. 63 J2 27 20N 82 32W
Sarata Ukraine 81 E4 46 00N 29 40E
Saratoga Springs *tn.* New York U.S.A. 65 G6 43 04N 73 47W
Saratov Russia 90 F5 51 30N 45 55E
Saravan Iran 93 J4 27 25N 62 17E
Sarawak *state* Malaysia 99 E4 2 30N 112 30E
Sarcelles France 83 B2 48 59N 2 22E
Sardegna *(Sardinia)* *i.* Italy 81 A3 40 00N 9 00E
Sardindida Plain Kenya 106 M8/N8 2 00N 40 00E
Sardinia *see* Sardegna
Sar-e Pol Afghanistan 93 K6 36 13N 65 55E
Sargasso Sea Atlantic Ocean 113 B9 27 00N 66 00W
Sargeant Barbados 66 V12 13 05N 59 35W
Sargodha Pakistan 95 C6 32 01N 72 40E
Sarh Chad 106 I9 9 08N 18 22E
Sarīr Calanscio *d.* Libya 106 J13 26 00N 22 00E
Sark *i.* Channel Islands British Isles 78 I6 49 26N 2 22W
Sarles North Dakota U.S.A. 39 B1 48 58N 99 00W
Sarmiento Argentina 69 D3 45 38S 69 08W
Sarny Ukraine 80 E5 51 21N 26 31E
Saronikós Kólpos *g.* Greece 81 D2 38 00N 23 00E
Sarpsborg Norway 79 C2 59 17N 11 06E
Sarrebourg France 76 D4 48 43N 7 03E
Sarreguemines France 76 D4 49 06N 6 55E
Sartène Corsica 77 D3 41 37N 8 58E
Sartrouville France 83 A2 48 56N 2 11E
Sary-Ishikotrau *d.* Kazakhstan 91 M4 45 00N 77 00E
Sarysu *r.* Kazakhstan 91 K4 47 00N 67 30E
Sasayama Japan 100 G2 35 03N 135 12E
Sasebo Japan 100 A1 33 10N 129 42E
Sassandra Côte d'Ivoire 106 D9 4 58N 6 08W
Sassandra *r.* Côte d'Ivoire 106 D9 5 50N 6 55W
Sassari Italy 81 A3 40 43N 8 34E
Sassnitz Germany 76 E5 54 32N 13 40E
Satlayev *(Nikol'skiy)* Kazakhstan 91 K4 47 54N 67 25E
Satna India 95 E4 24 33N 80 50E
Satpura Range *mts.* India 95 C4/D4 21 40N 75 00E
Sattahip Thailand 99 C6 12 36N 100 56E
Satu Mare Romania 81 D4 47 48N 22 52E
SAUDI ARABIA 92 F3
Saugus Massachusetts U.S.A. 52 B2 42 27N 71 00W
Saurimo Angola 107 J6 9 39S 20 24E
Sausalito California U.S.A. 49 B3 37 51N 122 30W
Savannah Georgia U.S.A. 63 J3 32 04N 81 07W
Savannah *r.* U.S.A. 63 J3 33 00N 82 00W
Savannakhet Laos 97 L2 16 34N 104 45E
Savanna la Mar Jamaica 67 P8 18 13N 78 08W
Savona Italy 81 A3 44 18N 8 28E
Sawahlunto Indonesia 99 C3 0 41S 100 52E
Sawankhalok Thailand 97 J2 17 19N 99 50E
Sawara Japan 100 M2 35 52N 140 31E
Sawpit Canyon Reservoir California U.S.A. 51 B3 34 10N 117 59W
Sawu Sea Indonesia 99 G2 9 30S 122 00E
Sayanogorsk Russia 91 P5 53 00N 91 26E

Sayano-Shushenskoye Vodokhranilishche *res.* Russia **91** P5 52 00N 92 00E
[illegible]
Saylac Somalia **106** N9 11 21N 43 30E
Saynshand Mongolia **97** L8 44 58N 111 10E
Sayre Pennsylvania U.S.A. **64** D4 41 58N 76 03W
Say'ūn Yemen Republic **93** G2 15 59N 48 44E
Scafell Pike *mt.* England **78** H6 54 27N 3 14W
Scandinavia *geog. reg.* Europe **70** 65 00N 15 00E
Scarborough England **78** K6 54 17N 0 24W
Scarsdale New York U.S.A. **50** C2 40 59N 73 49W
Sceaux France **83** B2 48 46N 2 18E
Scheldt Estuary Europe **70** 51 30N 3 30E
Schenectady New York U.S.A. **65** G5 42 48N 73 57W
Schildow Germany **83** F2 52 40N 13 21E
Schoharie New York U.S.A. **65** F5 42 40N 74 20W
Schoharie Creek New York U.S.A. **65** F5 42 40N 74 20W
Schöneberg Germany **83** F1 52 24N 13 22E
Schöneiche Germany **83** G1 52 28N 13 43E
Schönwalde Germany **83** E2 52 41N 13 27E
Schönwalde Germany **83** F2 52 43N 13 26E
Schulzendorf Germany **83** G1 52 20N 13 34E
Schuykill River Pennsylvania U.S.A. **64** D3 40 40N 76 00W
Schwäbisch Alb *mts.* Germany **76** D4 48 00N 9 00E
Schwanebeck Germany **83** F2 52 40N 13 27E
Schwarzwald *(Black Forest) mts.* Germany **76** D4 47 00N 8 00E
Schweinfurt Germany **76** E5 50 03N 10 16E
Schwerin Germany **76** E5 53 38N 11 25E
Schwielowsee *l.* Germany **83** D1 52 19N 1257E
Scilly, Isles of England **78** E1 49 56N 6 20W
Scituate Reservoir Rhode Island U.S.A. **65** J4 41 00N 71 00W
Scobey Montana U.S.A. **40** B1 48 48N 105 28W
Scoresbysund *tn.* Greenland **116** 70 30N 22 00W
Scotia Ridge Antarctica **113** C1 53 00S 50 00W
Scotia Sea Antarctica **113** C1 56 30N 50 00W
Scotland Pennsylvania U.S.A. **64** C3 40 03N 77 35W
Scotland United Kingdom **78**
Scott Base *r.s.* Antarctica **117** 77 51S 166 45E
Scott Island Southern Ocean **114** H1 66 35S 180 00
Scottsbluff Nebraska U.S.A. **62** F5 41 52N 103 40W
Scranton Pennsylvania U.S.A. **64** E4 41 25N 75 40W
Scunthorpe England **78** K5 53 35N 0 39W
Sealdah India **94** K2 22 32N 88 22E
Sea of Azov Russia/Ukraine **90** D4 46 00N 37 00E
Searsville Lake California U.S.A. **49** C1 37 24N 122 14W
Seattle Washington U.S.A. **62** B6 47 35N 122 20W
Sebewaing Michigan U.S.A. **36** C4 43 44N 83 26W
Sebisseb *r.* Algeria **77** C2 35 30N 4 00E
Seboomook Lake Maine U.S.A. **37** R6 45 55N 69 50W
Sebkra Sidi El Hani *salt l.* Tunisia **81** B2 35 30N 10 00E
Sedalia Missouri U.S.A. **63** H4 38 42N 93 15W
Sedan France **76** C4 49 42N 4 57E
Seddinsee *l.* Germany **83** G1 52 23N 13 42E
Sedro Woolley Washington U.S.A. **42** H4 48 30N 122 15W
Ségou Mali **106** D10 13 28N 6 18W
Segovia Spain **77** B3 40 57N 4 07W
Segre *r.* Spain **77** C3 42 00N 1 10E
Segura *r.* Spain **77** B2 38 00N 1 00W
Seine *r.* France **76** C4 49 15N 1 15E
Seki Japan **100** H2 35 30N 136 54E
Sekiu Washington U.S.A. **42** H4 48 15N 124 19W
Sekondi Takoradi Ghana **106** E9 4 59N 1 43W
Selat Sunda *sd.* Indonesia **99** D2 6 00S 106 00E
Seldovia Alaska U.S.A. **10** E4 59 29N 151 45W
Selemdzha *r.* Russia **89** P6 52 30N 132 00E
Selenga *(Selenge) r.* Russia/Mongolia **97** L9 51 00N 106 00E
Selenge *(Selenga) r.* Mongolia/Russia **97** K8 49 00N 102 00E
Selety *r.* Russia **91** L5 52 50N 73 00E
Selima Oasis Sudan **106** K12 21 22N 29 19E
Selma Alabama U.S.A. **63** I3 32 24N 87 01W
Selsingrove Pennsylvania U.S.A. **64** D3 40 48N 76 53W
Selvas *geog. reg.* South America **55** 7 00S 65 00W
Semarang Indonesia **99** E2 6 58S 110 29E
Semenovskoye Russia **88** M1 55 39N 37 32E
Seminoe Reservoir Wyoming U.S.A. **62** E5 42 00N 106 00W
Seminole Oklahoma U.S.A. **63** G4 35 15N 96 40W
Semiozernoye Kazakhstan **91** J5 52 22N 64 06E
Semipalatinsk Kazakhstan **91** N5 50 26N 80 16E
Semnān Iran **93** H6 35 30N 53 25E
Sendai Japan **100** B1 31 50N 130 17E
Sendai Japan **100** D2 38 16N 140 52E
Seneca Falls tn. New York U.S.A. **64** D5 42 57N 76 47W
Seneca Lake New York U.S.A. **64** D5 42 30N 76 55W
SENEGAL **106** C10
Sénégal *r.* Senegal/Mauritania **106** A11 16 45N 14 45W
Senhor do Bonfim Brazil **68** I10 10 28S 40 11W
Senja *i.* Norway **79** D4 69 15N 17 20E
Sennar Sudan **92** D1 13 31N 33 38E
Sennar Dam Sudan **92** D1 13 20N 33 45E
Senobe Japan **100** G2 35 09N 135 25E
Sens France **76** C4 48 12N 3 18E
Sentinel Range *mts.* Antarctica **117** 78 00S 87 00W
Senyavin Islands Pacific Ocean **114** G8 7 00N 161 30E
Seoul *see* Sŏul
Sepik *r.* Papua New Guinea **110** G9 4 00S 142 30E
Sequoia National Park California U.S.A. **66** A7 36 30N 118 30W
Seram *i.* Indonesia **99** H3 2 50S 129 00E
Seram Sea Indonesia **99** H3/I3 2 30S 130 00E
Serang Indonesia **99** D2 6 07S 106 09E
Serbia *admin.* Yugoslavia **81**
Serdan Mexico **66** C5 28 40N 105 57W
Seremban Malaysia **99** C4 2 42N 101 54E
Serengeti National Park Tanzania **106** L7 2 30S 35 00E
Sergiev Posad *(Zagorsk)* Russia **90** D6 56 20N 38 10E
Sergino Russia **91** K7 62 30N 65 40E
Sergipe *admin.* Brazil **68** J10 11 00S 38 00W
Seria Brunei **99** E4 4 39N 114 23E
Serian Malaysia **99** E4 1 10N 110 35E
Serov Russia **91** J6 59 42N 60 32E
Serpukhov Russia **90** D5 54 53N 37 25E
Serra Brazil **68** I9 20 06S 40 16W
Serra do Mar *mts.* Brazil **69** H7 27 30S 49 00W
Serra do Navio Brazil **68** G13 1 00N 52 05W
Sérrai Greece **81** D3 41 03N 2 33E
Serrania de Cuenca *mts.* Spain **77** B3 40 30N 2 15W
Serra Tumucumaque *mts.* Brazil **68** F13/G13 2 00N 55 00W
Setagaya Japan **101** B3 35 37N 139 38E
Sete Lagoas Brazil **68** [illegible]
Sete Pontes Brazil **69** Q2 22 51S 43 04W
Setesdal *geog. reg.* Norway **79** B2 59 30N 7 10E
Sétif Algeria **106** G15 36 11N 5 24E
Setit *r.* Sudan **92** E1 14 20N 36 15E
Seto Japan **100** J2 35 14N 137 06E
Seto-Naikai *sd.* Japan **100** B1 34 00N 132 30E
Settat Morocco **106** D14 33 04N 7 37W
Setúbal Portugal **77** A2 38 31N 8 54W
Sevastopol' Ukraine **90** C3 44 36N 33 31E
Sevenoaks England **82** D2 51 16N 0 12E
Severn *r.* England/Wales **78** I4 52 30N 2 30 W
Severna Park Maryland U.S.A. **64** D2 39 00N 76 00W
Severnaya *(North)* **Donets** *r.* Russia/Ukraine **88** F5 49 00N 37 00E
Severnaya *(North)* **Dvina** *r.* Russia **88** G8 63 00N 43 00E
Severnaya Sos'va *r.* Russia **91** J7 62 30N 62 00E
Severnaya Zemlya *(North Land) is.* Russia **89** L12 80 00N 95 00E
Severodonetsk Ukraine **90** D4 48 58N 38 29E
Severodvinsk Russia **88** F8 64 35N 39 50E
Sevier *r.* Utah U.S.A. **62** D4 39 00N 113 00W
Sevilla *(Seville)* Spain **77** A2 37 24N 5 59W
Seville *see* Sevilla
Sèvres France **83** A2 48 49N 2 13E
Seward Alaska U.S.A. **10** F5 60 05N 149 34W
Seward Peninsula Alaska U.S.A. **10** B6 65 20N 165 00W
SEYCHELLES **112** 4 30S 55 30E
Seychelles Ridge Indian Ocean **112** E6/F5
Seym *r.* Russia/Ukraine **90** C5 51 00N 34 00E
Seymchan Russia **89** R8 62 54N 152 26E
Sfax Tunisia **106** H14 34 45N 10 43E
Sfîntu Gheorghe Romania **81** E4 45 51N 25 48E
's-Gravenhage *(Den Haag, The Hague)* Netherlands **76** C5 52 05N 4 16E
Sha Chau *i.* Hong Kong U.K. **98** A2 22 21N 113 53E
Shache China **96** E6 38 27N 77 16E
Shackleton Ice Shelf Antarctica **117** 66 00S 100 00E
Shackleton Range *mts.* Antarctica **117** 81 00S 20 00W
Shaftesbury Vermont U.S.A. **65** G5 42 59N 73 13W
Shah Alam Malaysia **99** C4 3 02N 101 31E
Shahdara India **94** M4 28 40N 77 17E
Shahdol India **95** E4 23 19N 81 26E
Shahjahanpur India **95** D5 27 53N 79 55E
Shakhty Russia **90** E4 47 43N 40 16E
Shaki Nigeria **106** F9 8 39N 3 25E
Sha Lo Wan Hong Kong U.K. **98** A1 22 17N 113 54E
Sham Chung Hong Kong U.K. **98** C2 22 28N 114 17E
Sham Chun River Hong Kong U.K. **98** B3 22 30N 114 00E
Shamokin Pennsylvania U.S.A. **64** D3 40 46N 76 35W
Sham Shek Tsuen Hong Kong U.K. **98** A1 22 17N 113 53E
Sham Shui Po Hong Kong U.K. **98** B1 22 20N 114 09E
Sham Tseng Hong Kong U.K. **98** B2 22 22N 114 03E
Shandong Bandao *p.* China **84** 37 30N 120 00E
Shanghai China **97** O5 31 06N 121 22E
Shangqiu China **97** N5 34 27N 115 07E
Shangrao China **97** N4 28 28N 117 54E
Shangshui China **97** M5 33 36N 114 38E
Shannon *r.* Irish Republic **78** C4 53 30N 9 00W
Shannon, Lake Washington U.S.A. **42** H4 48 35N 121 45W
Shantou China **97** N3 23 23N 116 39E
Shanyao China **98** E8 25 07N 118 44E
Shaoguan China **97** M3 24 54N 113 33E
Shaoxing China **97** O5 30 02N 120 35E
Shaoyang China **97** M4 27 10N 111 25E
Shaqrā' Saudi Arabia **93** G4 25 18N 45 15E
Sharon Massachusetts U.S.A. **65** J5 42 08N 71 11W
Sharon Pennsylvania U.S.A. **63** J5 41 16N 80 30W
Sharp Island Hong Kong U.K. **98** C2 22 22N 114 17E
Sharp Park California U.S.A. **49** B2 37 40N 122 30W
Sharp Peak Hong Kong U.K. **98** D2 22 26N 114 22E
Shashi China **97** M5 30 16N 112 20E
Sha Tau Kok Hong Kong U.K. **98** B3 22 33N 114 13E
Sha Tin Hong Kong U.K. **98** C2 22 22N 114 10E
Shatsky Rise Pacific Ocean **114** G11 34 00N 160 00E
Shau Kei Wan Hong Kong U.K. **98** C1 22 16N 114 13E
Shebelē *r.* Ethiopia/Somalia **106** N9 6 00N 44 00E
Sheberghān Afghanistan **93** K6 36 41N 65 45E
Sheboygan Wisconsin U.S.A. **63** I5 43 46N 87 44W
Sheenjek *r.* Alaska U.S.A. **44** C4 67 30N 149 30W
Sheffield England **78** J5 53 23N 1 30W
Sheffield Massachusetts U.S.A. **65** G5 42 00N 73 00W
Sheffield Pennsylvania U.S.A. **64** A4 41 43N 79 03W
Shek Kip Mei Hong Kong U.K. **98** C2 22 20N 114 10E
Shek Kong Hong Kong U.K. **98** B2 22 26N 114 06E
Shek Kwu Chau *i.* Hong Kong U.K. **98** A1 22 12N 113 59E
Shek O Hong Kong U.K. **98** C1 22 14N 114 15E
Shek Pik Hong Kong U.K. **98** A1 22 13N 113 53E
Shek Pik Reservoir Hong Kong U.K. **98** A1 22 14N 113 54E
Shek Uk Shan *mt.* Hong Kong U.K. **98** C2 22 26N 114 18E
Shek Wu Hui Hong Kong U.K. **98** B3 22 30N 114 07E
Shelby Montana U.S.A. **62** D6 48 30N 111 52W
Shelekhov Bay Russia **89** R8 60 00N 157 00E
Shelikof Strait Alaska U.S.A. **10** E4 57 30N 155 00W
Shell Lake *tn.* Wisconsin U.S.A. **35** B2 45 44N 91 56W
Shelter Island Hong Kong U.K. **98** C1 22 19N 114 19E
Shelton Connecticut U.S.A. **65** G4 41 19N 73 06W
Shenandoah Iowa U.S.A. **63** G5 40 48N 95 22W
Shenandoah Pennsylvania U.S.A. **64** D3 40 49N 76 11W
Shenandoah Mountains U.S.A. **64** B2 39 15N 78 45W
Shenandoah National Park Virginia U.S.A. **64** B1 38 50N 78 15W
Shenyang China **97** N7 41 50N 123 26E
Shenzhen China **97** M3 22 31N 114 08E
Sheoraphuli India **94** K3 22 46N 88 20E
Shepetovka Ukraine **80** E5 50 12N 27 01E
Sherburne New York U.S.A. **64** E5 42 41N 75 30W
Sheridan Wyoming U.S.A. **62** E5 44 48N 106 57W
's-Hertogenbosch Netherlands **76** D5 51 41N 5 19E
Sherwood North Dakota U.S.A. **40** C1 48 58N 101 38W
Shetland Islands Scotland **78** J12 60 00N 1 15W
Sheung Shui Hong Kong U.K. **98** B3 22 31N 114 07E
Shevchenko Kazakhstan **90** G3 43 37N 51 11E
Shiawassee River Michigan U.S.A. **36** B4 43 05N 84 12W
Shibuya Japan **101** B3 35 39N 139 42E
Shickshinny Pennsylvania U.S.A. **64** D4 41 30N 76 00W
[illegible]
Shiga *pref.* Japan **100** H2 35 10N 136 07E
Shihezi China **96** G7 44 19N 86 10E
Shijiazhuang China **97** M6 38 04N 114 28E
Shikarpur Pakistan **94** B5 27 58N 68 42E
Shikoku *i.* Japan **100** B1 33 40N 134 00E
Shikotan *i.* Japan **100** E3 43 47N 148 45E
Shiliguri India **95** F5 26 42N 88 30E
Shilka *r.* Russia **89** N6 52 30N 117 30E
Shillong India **95** G5 25 34N 91 53E
Shiloh New Jersey U.S.A. **64** E2 39 28N 75 18W
Shima-hantō *p.* Japan **100** H1 34 25N 136 30E
Shimizu Japan **100** C2 35 01N 138 29E
Shimoga India **95** D2 13 56N 75 31E
Shimonita Japan **100** K3 36 12N 138 47E
Shimonoseki Japan **100** B1 33 59N 130 58E
Shimotsuma Japan **100** L3 36 10N 139 58E
Shinagawa Japan **101** B3 35 37N 139 44E
Shinagawa Bay Japan **101** C3 35 56N 139 50E
Shinano *r.* Japan **100** C2 37 40N 139 00E
Shīndand Afghanistan **93** J5 33 16N 62 05E
Shinglehouse Pennsylvania U.S.A. **64** B4 41 58N 78 11W
Shingū Japan **100** C1 33 42N 136 00E
Shinjō Japan **100** D2 38 45N 140 18E
Shinjuku Japan **101** B3 35 41N 139 42E
Shinyanga Tanzania **107** L7 3 40S 33 25E
Shiono-misaki *c.* Japan **100** C1 33 28N 135 47E
Shipki Pass India **95** D6 31 50N 78 50E
Shirakawa Japan **100** D2 37 07N 140 11E
Shiraoi Japan **100** D3 42 34N 141 19E
Shīrāz Iran **93** H4 29 38N 52 34E
Shiretoko-misaki *c.* Japan **100** E3 44 24N 145 20E
Shishmaref Alaska U.S.A. **10** B6 66 15N 166 11W
Shivaji Park *tn.* India **94** L4 28 40N 77 07E
Shizuishan China **97** L6 39 04N 106 22E
Shizuoka Japan **100** C1 34 59N 138 24E
Shizuoka *pref.* Japan **100** K2 35 10N 138 50E
Shkodër Albania **81** C3 42 03N 19 01E
Shomolu Nigeria **107** V3 6 34N 3 26E
Shreveport Louisiana U.S.A. **63** H3 32 30N 93 46W
Shrewsbury England **78** I4 52 43N 2 45W
Shrewsbury Massachusetts U.S.A. **65** J5 42 18N 71 43W
Shrirampur India **94** K3 22 45N 88 21E
Shuangliao China **97** N7 43 30N 123 29E
Shuangyashan China **97** Q8 46 42N 131 20E
Shuen Wan Hong Kong U.K. **98** C2 22 28N 114 12E
Shui Tau Hong Kong U.K. **98** B2 22 27N 114 04E
Shuksan, Mount Washington U.S.A. **42** H4 48 50N 121 36W
Shumagin Islands Alaska U.S.A. **10** D4 55 00N 159 00W
Shumen Bulgaria **81** E3 43 17N 26 55E
Shunde China **97** M3 22 50N 113 16E
Shuqrā Yemen Republic **93** G1 13 23N 45 44E
Shwebo Myanmar **96** J3 24 26N 97 05E
Shyamnagar India **94** K3 22 50N 88 24E
Sialkot Pakistan **95** C6 32 29N 74 35E
Siauliai Lithuania **80** D8 55 51N 23 20E
Šibenik Croatia **81** C3 43 45N 15 55E
Sibi Pakistan **94** B5 29 31N 67 54E
Sibiti Congo **107** H7 3 40S 13 24E
Sibiu Romania **81** D4 45 46N 24 09E
Sibolga Indonesia **99** B4 1 42N 98 48E
Sibpur India **94** K2 22 34N 88 19E
Sibu Malaysia **99** E4 2 18N 111 49E
Sibut Central African Republic **106** I9 5 46N 19 06E
Sichuan Basin *see* Sichuan Pendi
Sichuan Pendi *(Sichuan Basin)* China **97** K5/L5 32 00N 107 00E
Sicilian Channel Mediterranean Sea **81** B2 37 00N 12 00E
Sicily *i.* Italy **81** B2 37 00N 14 00E
Sicuani Peru **68** C10 14 21S 71 13W
Sidcup England **82** D2 51 26N 0 07E
Sidi Barrani Egypt **106** K14 31 38N 25 58E
Sidi Bel Abbès Algeria **106** E15 35 15N 0 39W
Sidi Ifni Morocco **106** C13 29 24N 10 12W
Sidlaw Hills Scotland **78** H8 56 30N 3 10W
Sidney New York U.S.A. **64** E5 42 19N 75 24W
Sidney Lanier, Lake Georgia U.S.A. **63** J3 34 00N 84 00W
Sidon *see* Saïda
Siedlce Poland **80** D5 52 10N 22 18E
Siemensstadt Germany **83** E2 52 33N 13 14E
Siena Italy **81** B3 43 19N 11 19E
SIERRA LEONE **106** C9
Sierra Blanca *tn.* Texas U.S.A. **62** E3 31 10N 105 22W
Sierra de Maracaju *mts.* Brazil **68** F8/G9 20 00S 55 00W
Sierra de Perija *mts.* Colombia/Venezuela **67** I1/2 10 00N 73 00W
Sierra dos Parecis *hills* Brazil **55** 7 00S 60 00W
Sierra Madre del Sur *mts.* Mexico **66** D3/E3 17 30N 100 00W
Sierra Madre Occidental *mts.* Mexico **66** C5/D4 26 00N 107 00W
Sierra Madre Oriental *mts.* Mexico **66** D5 E4 23 30N 100 00W
Sierra Morena *mts.* Spain **77** A2/B2 38 05N 5 50W
Sierra Nevada *mts.* Spain **77** B2 37 00N 3 20W
Sierra Nevada *mts.* U.S.A. **62** C4 37 00N 119 00W
Sierras de Córdoba *mts.* Argentina **69** D6/E6 32 30S 65 00W
Sighetu Marmaţiei Romania **81** D4 47 56N 23 53E
Sighişoara Romania **81** D4 46 12N 24 48E
Siglufjördur Iceland **79** I7 66 09N 18 55W
Signy *r.s.* South Orkney Islands **117** 60 43S 45 36W
Sigüenza Spain **77** B3 41 04N 2 38W
Siguiri Guinea **106** D10 11 28N 9 07W
Sikar India **95** D5 27 33N 75 12E
Sikasso Mali **106** D10 11 18N 5 38W
Sikhote-Alin' *mts.* Russia **89** P5 45 00N 137 00E
Sikkim *admin.* India **95** F5 27 30N 88 30E
Sil *r.* Spain **77** A3 42 25N 7 05W
Silchar India **95** G4 24 49N 92 47E
Silifke Turkey **92** D6 36 22N 33 57E
Siling Co *l.* China **95** F6 31 45N 88 50E
Silistra Bulgaria **81** E3 44 06N 27 17E
Siljan *l.* Sweden **79** D3 60 55N 14 50E
Silkeborg Denmark **80** A6 56 10N 9 39E
Šilute Lithuania **80** D6 55 18N 21 30E
Silver Bay *tn.* Minnesota U.S.A. **35** B2 47 15N 91 17W
Silver City New Mexico U.S.A. **62** E3 32 47N 108 16W
Silver Creek New York U.S.A. **38** C1 42 32N 79 10W
Silver Lake Reservoir California U.S.A. **51** A3 34 05N 118 16W
Silver Spring *tn.* Maryland U.S.A. **64** C2 39 00N 77 01W
Silves Portugal **77** A2 37 11N 8 26W
Simanggang Malaysia **99** E4 1 10N 111 32E
Simeuluë *i.* Indonesia **99** B4 2 40N 96 00E
Simferopol' Ukraine **90** C3 44 57N 34 05E
Simla India **95** D6 31 07N 77 09E
Simpson Desert Australia **110** F5 24 30S 137 30E
Simsbury Connecticut U.S.A. **65** H4 41 53N 72 48W
Sinai *p.* Egypt **92** N9 29 15N 34 00E
Sinai, Mount *see* Gebel Mûsa
Sincelejo Colombia **68** B14 9 17N 75 23W
Sind *geog. reg.* Pakistan **94** A6 26 20N 68 40E
Sines Portugal **77** A2 37 58N 8 52W
SINGAPORE **99** C4
Singaraja Indonesia **99** F2 8 06S 115 07E
Singatoko Fiji **114** T15 18 10S 177 30E
Sing Bori Thailand **97** K1 14 56N 100 21E
Sinkiang Uighur Autonomous Region *see* Xinjiang Uygur Zizhiqu
Sinop Turkey **92** E7 42 02N 35 09E
Sintra Portugal **77** A2 38 48N 9 22W
Sinŭiju North Korea **97** O7 40 04N 124 25E
Sioux City Iowa U.S.A. **63** G5 42 30N 96 28W
Sioux Falls *tn.* South Dakota U.S.A. **63** G5 43 34N 96 42W
Siparia Trinidad and Tobago **66** S9 10 08N 61 31W
Siping China **97** O7 43 15N 124 25E
Siple, Mount Antarctica **117** 73 25S 122 50W
Sira *r.* Norway **79** B2 58 50N 6 40E
Siracusa Italy **81** C2 37 04N 15 18E
Siret *r.* Romania **81** E4 47 00N 26 00E
Sirte *see* Surt
Sirte Desert Libya **106** I14 30 00N 16 00E
Sirte, Gulf of Libya **106** I14 31 00N 17 00E
Sisak Croatia **81** C4 45 30N 16 22E
Sisophon Cambodia **99** C6 13 37N 102 58E
Sisteron France **77** D3 44 16N 5 56E
Sitka Alaska U.S.A. **42** A3 57 05N 135 20W
Sitka Sound Alaska U.S.A. **42** A3 57 00N 135 50W
Sittwe Myanmar **96** H3 20 09N 92 55E
Sivas Turkey **92** E6 39 44N 37 01E
Siwa Egypt **106** K13 29 11N 25 31E
Sjaelland *i.* Denmark **80** B6 55 15N 11 30E
Skadarsko ezero *l.* Europe **81** C3 42 00N 19 00E
Skagen Denmark **80** B6 57 44N 10 37E
Skagerrak *sd.* Norway/Denmark **79** B2 57 30N 8 00E
Skagit River Washington U.S.A. **42** H4 48 40N 121 15W
Skagway Alaska U.S.A. **42** A3 59 23N 135 20W
Skåne *geog. reg.* Sweden **70** 56 00N 14 00E
Skaneateles New York U.S.A. **64** D5 42 57N 76 27W
Skaneateles Lake New York U.S.A. **64** D5 42 00N 76 00W
Skegness England **78** L5 53 10N 0 21E
Skelleftea Sweden **79** E3 64 45N 21 00E
Skellefte älv *r.* Sweden **79** D4 65 30N 19 00E
Skien Norway **79** B2 59 14N 9 37E
Skierniewice Poland **80** D5 51 58N 20 10E
Skikda Algeria **106** G15 36 53N 6 54E
Skiros *i.* Greece **81** D2 39 00N 24 00E
Skive Denmark **80** A6 56 34N 9 02E
Skokie Illinois U.S.A. **53** B3 42 02N 87 44W
Skokie River Illinois U.S.A. **53** A3 42 15N 87 51W
Skopje Macedonia Yugoslavia **81** D3 42 00N 21 28E
Skövde Sweden **79** C2 58 24N 13 52E
Skovorodino Russia **89** O6 54 00N 123 53E
Skowhegan Maine U.S.A. **37** R5 44 46N 69 44W
Skye *i.* Scotland **78** E9 57 20N 6 15W
Slaney *r.* Irish Republic **78** E4 52 30N 6 35W
Slatina Romania **81** D3 44 26N 24 22E
Slavonski Brod Croatia **81** C4 45 09N 18 02E
Slavyansk Ukraine **90** D4 48 51N 37 36E
Slessor Glacier Antarctica **117** 79 00S 22 00W
Slieve Donard *mt.* Northern Ireland **78** E6 54 11N 5 55W
Sligo Irish Republic **78** C6 54 17N 8 28W
Sliven Bulgaria **81** E3 42 40N 26 19E
Slonim Belarus **80** E5 53 05N 25 21E
Slough England **82** A2 51 31N 0 36W
Slovakia *admin.* Czechoslovakia **80** C4/D4
SLOVENIA **81** B4/C4
Słubice Poland **63** B2 52 20N 14 35E
Sluch' *r.* Ukraine **90** B5 50 00N 27 00E
Słupsk Poland **80** C5 54 28N 17 00E
Slutsk Belarus **80** E5 53 02N 27 31E
Slyne Head *c.* Irish Republic **78** A5 53 25N 10 10W
Smederevo Serbia Yugoslavia **81** D3 44 40N 20 56E
Smethport Pennsylvania U.S.A. **64** B4 41 48N 78 26W
Smoky Hills Kansas U.S.A. **62** G4 39 00N 100 00W
Smøla *i.* Norway **79** B3 63 25N 8 00E
Smolensk Russia **90** C5 54 49N 32 04E
Smolyan Bulgaria **81** D3 41 34N 24 42E
Smyrna Delaware U.S.A. **64** E2 39 18N 75 37W
Snaefell *mt.* Isle of Man British Isles **78** G6 54 16N 4 28W
Snake *r.* U.S.A. **62** C6 47 00N 118 00W
Snake River Plain U.S.A. **62** D5 43 00N 114 00W
Snowdon *mt.* Wales **78** G5 53 04N 4 05W
Snowy Mountains Australia **110** H2 36 50S 147 00E
Snyder Texas U.S.A. **62** F3 32 43N 100 54W
Soar *r.* England **78** J4 52 40N 1 20W
Soa-Siu Indonesia **99** H4 0 40N 127 30E
Sobat *r.* Sudan **106** L9 8 00N 33 00E
Sobral Brazil **68** I12 3 45S 40 20W
Sochi Russia **90** D3 43 35N 39 46E
Society Islands Pacific Ocean **115** K6 16 30S 153 00W
Socotra *i.* Yemen Republic **93** H1 12 05N 54 10E
Sodankylä Finland **79** F4 67 26N 26 35E
Söderhamn Sweden **79** D3 61 19N 17 10E
Södertälje Sweden **79** D2 59 11N 17 39E
Sodo Ethiopia **106** M9 6 49N 37 41E
Sodus New York U.S.A. **64** C6 43 14N 77 04W
Sofiya Bulgaria **81** D3 42 40N 23 18E
Sogamoso Colombia **68** C14 5 43N 72 56W
Sognefjorden *fj.* Norway **79** B3 61 05N 5 30E
Sohâg Egypt **92** D4 26 33N 31 42E
Soissons France **76** C4 49 23N 3 20E
Sok Kwu Wan Hong Kong U.K. **98** B1 22 13N 114 08E
Sokodé Togo **106** F9 8 59N 1 11E
Soko Islands Hong Kong U.K. **98** A1 22 10N 113 54E
Sokoto Nigeria **106** G10 13 02N 5 15E
So Kwun Wat Tsuen Hong Kong U.K. **98** B2 22 23N 114 00E

Solander, Cape Australia **111** G1 34 01S 151 14E
Solāpur India **95** D3 17 43N 75 56E
Soligorsk Belarus **80** E5 52 50N 27 32E
Solihull England **78** J4 52 25N 1 45W
Solikamsk Russia **91** H6 59 40N 56 45E
Sol'-Iletsk Russia **91** G5 51 09N 55 00E
Sollefteå Sweden **79** D3 63 09N 17 15E
Sóller Balearic Islands **77** C2 39 46N 2 42E
Solntsevo Russia **88** L1 55 36N 37 25E
Sologne *geog. reg.* France **77** C4 47 35N 1 47E
SOLOMON ISLANDS 110 J/K8
Solomon Sea Papua New Guinea **110** I8 7 30S 152 00E
Solothurn Switzerland **77** D4 47 13N 7 32E
Soltau Germany **76** D5 52 59N 9 50E
Solway Firth *est.* Scotland/England **78** H6 54 40N 3 40W
SOMALIA 106 O8/9
Somali Basin Indian Ocean **112** E7 5 00N 55 00E
Sombor Serbia Yugoslavia **81** C4 45 46N 19 09E
Sombrerete Mexico **66** D4 23 38N 103 40W
Somerset Massachusetts U.S.A. **65** J4 41 47N 71 08W
Somerset Reservoir Vermont U.S.A. **65** G6 43 00N 72 57W
Somerville Massachusetts U.S.A. **52** B2 42 24N 71 07W
Somerville New Jersey U.S.A. **65** F3 40 34N 74 36W
Somme *r.* France **76** C5 50 00N 1 45E
Sommen *l.* Sweden **79** D2 58 05N 15 15E
Somoto Nicaragua **67** G2 13 29N 86 36W
Son *r.* India **95** E4 24 00N 81 00E
Sonarpur India **94** K1 22 26N 88 26E
Sønderborg Denmark **80** A5 54 55N 9 48E
Søndre Strømfjord *see* Kangerlussuaq
Songea Tanzania **107** M5 10 42S 35 39E
Songhua Jiang *r.* China **97** P8 46 30N 128 00E
Sŏngjin North Korea **97** P7 40 41N 129 12E
Songkhla Thailand **99** C5 7 12N 100 35E
Song-koi *r.* Vietnam **99** C8 22 00N 105 00E
Sonoita Mexico **66** B6 31 53N 112 52W
Sonsonate El Salvador **66** G2 13 43N 89 44W
Sopot Poland **80** C5 54 27N 18 31E
Sopron Hungary **81** C4 47 40N 16 35E
Soria Spain **77** B3 41 46N 2 28W
Sorocaba Brazil **69** H8 23 30S 47 32W
Sorong Indonesia **99** I3 0 50S 131 17E
Soroti Uganda **106** L8 1 42N 33 37E
Sørøya *i.* Norway **79** E5 70 35N 22 30E
Sorraia *r.* Portugal **77** A2 38 55N 9 30W
Sosnowiec Poland **80** C5 50 16N 19 07E
Souillac France **77** C3 44 53N 1 29E
Souk Ahras Algeria **77** D2 36 14N 8 00E
Sŏul *(Seoul)* South Korea **97** P6 37 32N 127 00E
Soûr *(Tyre)* Lebanon **92** O11 33 16N 35 12E
Souris River Canada/U.S.A. **39** A1 49 30N 100 50W
Sousse Tunisia **106** H15 35 50N 10 38E
Southall England **82** B3 51 31N 0 23W
Southampton England **78** J2 50 55N 1 25W
Southampton New York U.S.A. **65** H3 40 54N 72 24W
South Andaman *i.* Andaman Islands **95** G2 11 30N 93 00E
South Australia *state* Australia **110** E4/F4
South Australian Basin Indian Ocean **112** L3 38 00S 125 00E
South Bend Indiana U.S.A. **63** I5 41 40N 86 15W
South Branch Potomac River Maryland/West Virginia U.S.A. **64** B2 39 30N 78 30W
Southbridge Massachusetts U.S.A. **65** H5 42 05N 72 02W
Southbury Connecticut U.S.A. **65** G4 41 28N 73 13W
South Carolina *state* U.S.A. **63** J3 34 00N 81 00W
South China Sea South East Asia **99** E6/E7 15 00N 115 00E
South Dakota *state* U.S.A. **62** F5 45 00N 102 00W
South Downs *hills* England **78** K2 50 50N 0 30W
Southeast Indian Basin Indian Ocean **112** J3 32 00S 108 00E
Southeast Indian Ridge Indian Ocean **112** H2/J2
South East Pacific Basin Pacific Ocean **115** Q2 53 00S 95 00W
Southend-on-Sea England **78** L3 51 33N 0 43E
Southern Alps *mts.* New Zealand **111** B2 43 30S 170 00E
Southern Honshu Ridge Pacific Ocean **114** E10 25 50N 142 30E
Southern Ocean 114/115
Southern Uplands Scotland **78** G7/I7
South Esk *r.* Scotland **78** I8 56 40N 2 55W
Southfield Michigan U.S.A. **52** D2 42 28N 83 16W
South Fiji Basin Pacific Ocean **114** H5 25 00S 176 50E
South Fork Shenandoah River Maryland/Virgina U.S.A. **64** C2 39 00N 78 05W
South Gate California U.S.A. **51** B2 33 56N 118 11W
Southgate Michigan U.S.A. **52** E1 42 11N 83 11W
South Georgia *i.* South Atlantic Ocean **113** E1 54 00S 36 30W
South Head Australia **111** H2 33 50S 151 17E
South Island New Zealand **111** A2 43 00S 169 00E
SOUTH KOREA 97 P6
South Loup *r.* Nebraska U.S.A. **62** G5 42 00N 99 00W
South Negril Point *c.* Jamaica **67** P8 18 16N 78 22W
South Ockenden England **82** E3 51 32N 0 18E
South Orkney Islands Southern Ocean **117** 60 00S 45 00W
South Park Pennsylvania U.S.A. **53** D1 40 19N 80 00W
South Platte *r.* U.S.A. **62** F5 41 00N 103 00W
South Point Barbados **66** V12 13 02N 59 32W
South Pole Antarctica **117** 90 00S
Southport England **78** H5 53 39N 3 01W
South River *tn.* New Jersey U.S.A. **65** F3 40 26N 74 23W
South Sandwich Trench Southern Ocean **113** F1 55 00S 30 00W
South San Francisco California U.S.A. **49** B2 37 30N 122 15W
South Shetland Islands Southern Ocean **69** E0 62 00S 60 00W
South Sioux City Nebraska U.S.A. **63** G5 42 28N 96 24W
South Suburbs *(Behala)* India **94** K1 22 28N 88 18E
South Uist *i.* Scotland **78** D9 57 20N 7 15W
Southwark *bor.* England **82** C3 51 30N 0 06W
Southwest Cape New Zealand **111** A1 47 17S 167 29E
Southwest Indian Ridge Indian Ocean **112** D2/E3 40 00S 50 00E
South West Pacific Basin Pacific Ocean **115** K4 35 00S 155 00W
Southwick Massachusetts U.S.A. **65** H5 42 03N 72 46W
South Yarmouth Massachusetts U.S.A. **65** K4 41 40N 70 12W
Sovetsk Russia **90** A6 55 02N 21 50E
Sovetskaya Gavan' Russia **89** Q5 48 57N 140 16E
Sozh *r.* Belarus **90** C5 53 00N 30 00E
SPAIN 77 A2
Spandau Germany **83** E2 52 32N 13 13E
Spanish Town Jamaica **67** R7 17 59N 76 58W
Sparks Nevada U.S.A. **62** C4 39 34N 119 46W
Spartanburg South Carolina U.S.A. **63** J3 34 56N 81 57W
Spárti Greece **81** D2 37 05N 22 25E
Spassk-Dal'niy Russia **89** P4 44 37N 132 37E
Spasskoye Kazakhstan **91** K5 52 07N 68 32E
Speightstown Barbados **66** V12 13 15N 59 39W
Spencer Iowa U.S.A. **63** G5 43 08N 95 08W
Spencer Gulf Australia **110** F3 34 00S 137 00E
Spencerport New York U.S.A. **64** C6 43 12N 77 46W
Spey *r.* Scotland **78** H9 57 00N 4 30W
Spitsbergen *i.* Arctic Ocean **88** D1 79 00N 15 00E
Spittal an der Drau Austria **81** B4 46 48N 13 30E
Split Croatia **81** C3 43 31N 16 28E
Spokane Washington U.S.A. **62** C6 47 40N 117 25W
Spoleto Italy **81** B3 42 44N 12 44E
Spot Pond Massachusetts U.S.A. **52** B2 42 27N 71 06W
Spratly Islands South China Sea **99** E6 F5 10 00N 115 00E
Spree *r.* Germany **83** G1 52 27N 13 32E
Springbok Republic of South Africa **107** I2 29 44S 17 56E
Springfield Illinois U.S.A. **63** J4 39 49N 89 39W
Springfield Massachusetts U.S.A. **64** H5 42 07N 72 35W
Springfield Missouri U.S.A. **63** H4 37 11N 93 19W
Springfield Ohio U.S.A. **63** J5 39 55N 83 48W
Springfield Oregon U.S.A. **62** B5 44 03N 123 01W
Springfield Vermont U.S.A. **65** H6 43 18N 72 29W
Springfield West Virginia U.S.A. **64** B2 39 26N 78 43W
Springsure Australia **110** H5 24 09S 148 04E
Springville New York U.S.A. **64** B5 42 31N 78 41W
Spurn Head *c.* England **78** L5 53 36N 0 07E
Spy Pond Massachusetts U.S.A. **52** B2 42 24N 71 09W
Sredinnyy Range *mts.* Russia **89** R7 57 00N 158 00E
Srednekolymsk Russia **89** R9 67 27N 153 35E
Sretensk Russia **89** N6 52 15N 117 52E
Srikakulam India **95** E3 18 19N 84 00E
SRI LANKA 95 E1
Srinagar Kashmir **95** C6 34 08N 74 50E
Staaken Germany **83** E2 52 32N 13 06E
Stafford England **78** I4 52 48N 2 07W
Stafford Springs Connecticut U.S.A. **65** H4 41 57N 72 17W
Stahnsdorf Germany **83** E1 52 23N 13 13E
Staines England **82** B2 51 26N 0 30W
Stakhanov Ukraine **90** D4 48 34N 38 40E
Stamford Connecticut U.S.A. **65** G4 41 03N 73 32W
Standish Michigan U.S.A. **36** C4 43 59N 83 58W
Stanhope New Jersey U.S.A. **65** F3 40 55N 74 43W
Stanley Falkland Islands **69** F2 51 45S 57 56W
Stanley North Dakota U.S.A. **40** C1 48 21N 102 23W
Stanovoy Range *mts.* Russia **89** O7 56 00N 122 30E
Stara Planina *mts.* Europe **81** D3 43 00N 23 00E
Stara Zagora Bulgaria **81** E3 42 25N 25 37E
Stargard Szczeciński Poland **80** C5 53 21N 15 01E
Starogard Gdański Poland **80** C5 53 58N 18 30E
Start Point *c.* England **78** H2 50 13N 3 38W
Staryy Oskol Russia **90** D5 51 20N 37 50E
State College Pennsylvania U.S.A. **64** C3 40 48N 77 52W
Staten Island New York U.S.A. **50** B1 40 35N 74 10W
Staunton Virginia U.S.A. **63** K4 38 10N 79 05W
Stavanger Norway **79** B2 58 58N 5 45E
Stavropol' Russia **90** E4 45 03N 41 59E
Stebbins Alaska U.S.A. **10** C5 63 32N 162 20W
Steenstrup Glacier Greenland **11** X8 75 00N 56 00W
Steep Island Hong Kong U.K. **98** C1 22 16N 114 18E
Steglitz Germany **83** F1 52 27N 13 19E
Stehekin Washington U.S.A. **42** H4 48 20N 120 40W
Stendal Germany **76** E5 52 36N 11 52E
Stephen Minnesota U.S.A. **39** B1 48 28N 96 52W
Stephens Passage Alaska U.S.A. **42** B3 58 00N 134 00W
Stepney England **82** C3 51 31N 0 04W
Step' Shaidara *geog. reg.* Kazakhstan **91** K3 40 00N 65 00E
Sterkrade Germany **76** H3 51 31N 6 52E
Sterling Colorada U.S.A. **62** F5 40 37N 103 13W
Sterlitamak Russia **91** H5 53 40N 55 59E
Steubenville Ohio U.S.A. **63** J5 40 22N 80 39W
Stewart Island New Zealand **111** A1 47 30S 168 00E
Steyr Austria **81** B4 48 04N 14 25E
Stickney Illinois U.S.A. **53** A2 41 49N 87 46W
Stikine River Canada/U.S.A. **42** C3 57 00N 132 00W
Stillaguamish River Washington U.S.A. **42** H4 48 17N 121 55W
Stirling Scotland **78** H8 56 07N 3 57W
Štip Macedonia Yugoslavia **81** D3 41 44N 22 12E
Stockbridge Massachusetts U.S.A. **65** G5 42 17N 73 20W
Stockholm Sweden **79** D2 59 20N 18 05E
Stockport England **78** I5 53 25N 2 10W
Stockton-on-Tees England **78** J6 54 34N 1 19W
Stoke-on-Trent England **78** I5 53 00N 2 10W
Stokhod *r.* Ukraine **90** B5 51 30N 25 00E
Stone Canyon Reservoir California U.S.A. **51** A3 34 07N 118 27W
Stonecutters Island Hong Kong U.K. **98** B1 22 18N 114 08E
Stoneham Massachusetts U.S.A. **52** B2 42 27N 71 06W
Stony Brook New York U.S.A. **65** G3 40 56N 73 08W
Stony Brook Reservation Massachusetts U.S.A. **52** B2 42 16N 71 08W
Stony Creek Illinois U.S.A. **53** B1 41 41N 87 44W
Stony Tunguska *see* Podkamennaya Tunguska
Stora Lulevattern *l.* Sweden **79** D4 67 20N 19 00E
Stördal Norway **79** C3 63 18N 11 48E
Støren Norway **79** C3 63 03N 10 16E
Stornoway Scotland **78** E10 58 12N 6 23W
Storsjön *l.* Sweden **79** C3 63 10N 14 10E
Storuman Sweden **79** D4 65 05N 17 10E
Stoughton Massachusetts U.S.A. **65** J5 42 8N 71 05W
Stour *r.* England **78** L4 51 10N 1 10E
Straits of Florida *sd.* Florida U.S.A. **63** J1 25 00N 80 00W
StranraerScotland **78** F6 54 55N 5 02W
Strasbourg France **76** D4 48 35N 7 45E
Stratford Connecticut U.S.A. **65** G4 41 12N 73 08W
Strathfield Australia **111** G2 33 52S 151 06E
Strathmere New Jersey U.S.A. **65** F2 39 12N 74 39W
Straubing Germany **76** E4 48 53N 12 35E
Streatham England **82** C2 51 26N 0 07W
Stretto di Messina *sd.* Italy **81** C2 38 00N 15 00E
Strimón *r.* Greece **81** D3 41 00N 23 00E
Strogino Russia **88** L2 55 49N 37 26E
Stromboli *mt.* Italy **81** C2 38 48N 15 15E
Stronsay *i.* Scotland **78** I11 59 07N 2 37W
Stroudsburg Pennsylvania U.S.A. **64** E3 41 00N 75 11W
Struma *r.* Bulgaria **81** D3 42 00N 23 00E
Stryy Ukraine **80** D4 49 16N 23 51E
Stuart Highway *rd.* Australia **110** E5/E6 20 00S 135 00E
Stung Treng Cambodia **99** D6 13 31N 105 59E
Sturt Creek *r.* Australia **110** D6 18 00S 127 30E
Stuttgart Germany **76** D4 48 47N 9 12E
Stykkishólmur Iceland **79** H7 65 05N 22 44W
Styr' *r.* Ukraine **80** E5 51 00N 25 00E
Su-ao Taiwan **98** H7 24 33N 121 48E
Suakin Sudan **92** E2 19 08N 37 17E
Subotica Serbia Yugoslavia **81** C4 46 04N 19 41E
Suceava Romania **81** E4 47 37N 26 18E
Suck *r.* Irish Republic **78** C5 53 40N 8 30W
Sucre Bolivia **68** D9 19 05S 65 15W
Sucy-en-Brie France **83** C2 48 46N 2 31E
SUDAN 106 K10
Sudd *swamp* Africa **102** 7 00N 30 00E
Sudety Reseniky *mts.* Czechoslovakia/Poland **80** C5 50 40N 16 00E
Sudr Egypt **92** N9 29 40N 32 42E
Sue *r.* Sudan **106** K9 7 00N 28 00E
Suez *see* El Suweis
Suez Canal *(Qanâ el Suweis)* Egypt **107** S4 31 30N 32 20E
Suez, Gulf of Egypt **107** T1 29 56N 32 32E
Suffolk County Massachusetts U.S.A. **52** B2 42 20N 71 09W
Sugar Loaf *see* Pao de Açúcar
Sugarloaf Mountain Maine U.S.A. **37** Q6 45 02N 70 18W
Sugar Notch Pennsylvania U.S.A. **64** E4 41 12N 75 55W
Suginami Japan **101** B3 35 41N 139 40E
Sühbaatar Mongolia **97** L9 50 10N 106 14E
Suiattle River Washington U.S.A. **42** H4 48 17N 121 15W
Suir *r.* Irish Republic **78** D4 52 15N 7 05W
Suita Japan **100** G1 34 46N 135 32E
Sukabumi Indonesia **99** D2 6 55S 106 50E
Sukhona *r.* Russia **90** E7 60 00N 40 00E
Sukhumi Georgia **90** E3 43 01N 41 01E
Sukkertoppen Greenland **45** V4 65 25N 53 00W
Sukkur Pakistan **94** B5 27 42N 68 54E
Sulaiman Range *mts.* Pakistan **94** B5/C6 30 00N 70 00E
Sulawesi *(Celebes) i.* Indonesia **99** F3/G3 2 30S 120 30E
Sulaymānīyah Iraq **93** G6 35 32N 45 27E
Sullana Peru **68** A12 4 52S 80 39W
Sultanpur India **95** E5 26 15N 82 04E
Sulu Archipelago *is.* The Philippines **99** G5 5 30N 121 00E
Sulu Sea Malaysia/The Philippines **99** F5/G5 8 00N 120 00E
Sumas Washington U.S.A. **42** H4 49 00N 122 16W
Sumatera *i.* Indonesia **99** B4/C3 1 00N 101 00E
Sumba *i.* Indonesia **99** F2/G2 10 00S 120 00E
Sumbawa *i.* Indonesia **99** F2 8 00S 117 30E
Sumburgh Head *c.* Scotland **78** J12 59 51N 1 16W
Sumgait Azerbaijan **90** F3 40 35N 49 38E
Sumida Japan **101** C3 35 42N 139 49E
Summit Illinois U.S.A. **53** A2 41 46N 87 49W
Sumner Strait Alaska U.S.A. **42** B3 56 30N 133 30W
Sumoto Japan **100** F1 34 20N 134 53E
Sumy Ukraine **90** C5 50 55N 34 49E
Sunapee New Hampshire U.S.A. **65** H6 43 22N 72 05W
Sunapee Lake New Hampshire U.S.A. **65** H6 43 20N 72 03W
Sunburst Montana U.S.A. **41** C1 48 54N 111 55W
Sunbury England **82** B2 51 24N 0 25W
Sunbury Pennsylvania U.S.A. **64** D3 40 52N 76 47W
Sunch'ŏn South Korea **97** P5 34 56N 127 28E
Suncook New Hampshire U.S.A. **65** J6 43 07N 71 27W
Sundarbans *geog. reg.* Southern Asia **84** 23 00N 90 00E
Sunderland England **78** J6 54 55N 1 23W
Sunderland Massachusetts U.S.A. **65** H5 42 28N 72 35W
Sundsvall Sweden **79** D3 62 22N 17 20E
Sung Kong *i.* Hong Kong U.K. **98** C1 22 11N 114 17E
Sunland California U.S.A. **51** A4 34 15N 118 17W
Sunset Beach *tn.* California U.S.A. **51** B1 33 43N 118 04W
Sunset Peak Hong Kong U.K. **98** A1 22 15N 113 57E
Sunshine Island Hong Kong U.K. **98** B1 22 16N 114 03E
Suntar Russia **88** N8 62 10N 117 35E
Sunyani Ghana **106** E9 7 22N 2 18W
Suō-nada *b.* Japan **100** B1 33 50N 131 30E
Superior Wisconsin U.S.A. **63** H6 46 42N 92 05W
Superior, Lake Canada/U.S.A. **35** B2 48 00N 88 00W
Sūr Oman **93** I3 22 34N 59 32E
Sura *r.* Russia **90** F6 55 00N 46 30E
Surabaya Indonesia **99** E2 7 14S 112 45E
Surakarta Indonesia **99** E2 7 32S 110 50E
Surat India **95** C4 21 10N 72 54E
Surat Thani Thailand **99** B5 9 09N 99 20E
Surendranagar India **95** C4 22 44N 71 43E
Surgut Russia **91** L7 61 13N 73 20E
SURINAM 68 F13
Surrey *co.* England **82** D2 51 15N 0 00E
Surt *(Sirte)* Libya **106** I14 31 13N 16 35E
Surui *r.* Brazil **69** Q3 22 40S 43 08W
Surulere Nigeria **107** V3 6 30N 3 25E
Susitna *r.* Alaska U.S.A. **10** E5 62 10N 150 15W
Susono Japan **100** K2 35 11N 138 50E
Susquehanna Pennsylvania U.S.A. **64** E4 41 56N 75 38W
Susquehanna River U.S.A. **64** D2 40 00N 76 30W
Sussex New Jersey U.S.A. **65** F4 41 12N 74 36W
Susuman Russia **89** Q8 62 46N 148 08E
Sutherland Australia **111** G1 34 02S 151 03E
Sutlej *r.* Pakistan **95** C6 30 00N 73 00E
Sutton *bor.* Greater London England **82** C2 51 22N 0 12W
Suva Fiji **114** U15 18 08S 178 25E
Suvasvesi *i.* Finland **79** F3 62 40N 28 10E
Suzhou China **97** O5 31 21N 120 40E
Suzuka Japan **100** F1 34 52N 136 37E
Suzuka-sanmyaku *mts.* Japan **100** H2 35 00N 136 20E
Suzu-misaki *c.* Japan **100** C2 37 30N 137 21E
Sverdlovsk Ukraine **90** D4 48 05N 39 37E
Svobodnyy Russia **89** O6 51 24N 128 05E
Swale *r.* England **78** J6 54 15N 1 30W
Swampscott Massachusetts U.S.A. **52** C2 42 28N 70 55W
Swanley England **82** D2 51 24N 0 12E
Swansea Wales **78** H3 51 38N 3 57W
Swanton Ohio U.S.A. **36** C2 41 36N 83 54W
Swanton Vermont U.S.A. **37** N5 44 56N 73 08W
SWAZILAND 107 L2
SWEDEN 79 C2
Swedesboro New Jersey U.S.A. **64** E2 39 45N 75 18W
Sweetgrass Montana U.S.A. **41** C1 48 59N 111 58W
Sweetwater *tn.* Texas U.S.A. **62** F3 32 27N 100 25W
Swellendam Republic of South Africa **107** J1 34 01S 20 26E
Swiebodzin Poland **80** C5 52 15N 15 31E
Swindon England **78** J3 51 34N 1 47W
Swinoujście Poland **80** B5 53 55N 14 18E
SWITZERLAND 77 D4
Sydney Australia **110** I3 33 55S 151 10E
Syktyvkar Russia **90** G7 61 42N 50 45E
Sylhet Bangladesh **95** G4 24 53N 91 51E
Syowa *r.s.* Antarctica **117** 69 00S 39 35E
Syracuse New York U.S.A. **64** D6 43 03N 76 10W
Syr-Dar'ya *r.* Asia **91** L3 42 00N 72 30E
SYRIA 92 E6
Syrian Desert Middle East **92** E5 32 30N 39 20E
Syzran' Russia **90** F5 53 10N 48 29E
Szczecin Poland **80** B5 53 25N 14 32E
Szczecinek Poland **80** C5 53 42N 16 41E
Szeged Hungary **81** D4 46 15N 20 09E
Székesfehérvár Hungary **81** C4 47 11N 18 22E
Szolnok Hungary **81** D4 47 10N 20 10E
Szombathely Hungary **81** C4 47 14N 16 38E

T

Tabaquite Trinidad and Tobago **66** T9 10 23N 61 18W
Tabas Iran **93** I5 33 37N 56 54E
Table Rock Lake Missouri U.S.A. **63** H4 36 38N 93 17W
Tábor Czechoslovakia **80** B4 49 25N 14 39E
Tabora Tanzania **107** L7 5 01S 32 48E
Tabrīz Iran **93** G5 38 05N 46 18E
Tabuaaran Island Kiribati **115** K8 4 00N 158 10W
Tabūk Saudi Arabia **92** E4 28 33N 36 36E
Ta-chia Taiwan **98** G7 24 20N 120 34E
Tachikawa Japan **100** L2 35 42N 139 28E
Tacloban The Philippines **99** G6 11 15N 125 01E
Tacna Peru **69** C9 18 00S 70 15W
Tacoma Washington U.S.A. **62** B6 47 16N 122 30W
Tadmur Syria **92** E5 34 40N 38 10E
Taegu South Korea **97** P6 35 52N 128 36E
Taejŏn South Korea **97** P6 36 20N 127 26E
Tafila Jordan **92** O10 30 52N 35 36E
Tafna *r.* Algeria **77** B2 35 00N 2 00W
Taganrog Russia **90** D4 47 14N 38 55E
Tagus *see* Tejo
Tahara Japan **100** J1 34 40N 137 18E
Tahat, Mount Algeria **106** G12 23 18N 5 33E
Tahiti *i.* French Polynesia **115** L6 17 30S 148 30W
Tahoe, Lake U.S.A. **62** C4 39 00N 120 00W
Tahoua Niger **106** G10 14 57N 5 19E
Tahta Egypt **92** D4 26 47N 31 31E
Tai'an China **97** N6 36 15N 117 10E
T'ai-chung Taiwan **98** G7 24 09N 124 40E
Tai Lam Chung Hong Kong U.K. **98** B2 22 22N 114 01E
Tai Lam Chung Reservoir Hong Kong U.K. **98** B2 22 23N 114 01E
Tai Long Hong Kong U.K. **98** D2 22 25N 114 22E
Tai Long Wan *b.* Hong Kong U.K. **98** D2 22 20N 114 20E
Tai Mei Tuk Hong Kong U.K. **98** C2 22 28N 114 14E
Tai Mo Shan *mt.* Hong Kong U.K. **98** B2 22 25N 114 07E
Tai Mong Tsai Hong Kong U.K. **98** C2 22 23N 114 18E
T'ai-nan Taiwan **98** G5 23 01N 120 14E
Tai O Hong Kong U.K. **98** A1 22 15N 113 52E
T'ai-pei Taiwan **98** H8 25 05N 121 32E
Tai Po Hong Kong U.K. **98** C2 22 27N 114 10E
Tai Shui Hang Hong Kong U.K. **98** B1 22 17N 114 01E
Tai Tam Reservoir Hong Kong U.K. **98** C1 22 15N 114 12E
Tai Tam Wan *b.* Hong Kong U.K. **98** C1 22 13N 114 13E
Tai Tan Hong Kong U.K. **98** C2 22 26N 114 19E
Taitō Japan **101** C3 35 43N 139 48E
Tai To Yan *mt.* Hong Kong U.K. **98** B2 22 25N 114 07E
T'ai-tung Taiwan **98** H5 22 43N 121 10E
Tai Wai Hong Kong U.K. **98** C2 22 23N 114 10E
TAIWAN 98 H5
Taiwan Strait Taiwan/China **98** F7 24 00N 119 30E
Tai Wan Tau Hong Kong U.K. **98** C1 22 17N 114 17E
Taiyuan China **97** M6 37 50N 112 30E
Ta'izz Yemen Republic **92** F1 13 35N 44 02E
TAJIKISTAN 91 K2/L2
Tajimi Japan **100** J2 35 22N 137 10E
Tajo *(Tejo) r.* Spain/Portugal **77** A2 40 30N 2 00W
Tajo *r.* Spain **77** B3 40 45N 2 00W
Tak Thailand **99** B7 16 51N 99 08E
Takahama Japan **100** G2 35 30N 135 32E
Takamatsu Japan **100** B1 34 20N 134 01E
Takaoka Japan **100** C2 36 47N 137 00E
Takapuna New Zealand **111** B3 36 48S 174 47E
Takarazuka Japan **100** G1 34 49N 135 19E
Takasago Japan **100** F1 34 45N 134 46E
Takasaki Japan **100** C2 36 20N 139 00E
Takatsu Japan **101** B3 35 35N 139 37E
Takatsuki Japan **100** G1 34 52N 135 36E
Takayama Japan **100** C2 36 09N 137 16E
Takefu Japan **100** C2 35 54N 136 10E
Takeo Cambodia **99** C6 11 00N 104 46E
Takeshita Japan **101** B3 35 33N 139 32E
Taku Inlet Alaska U.S.A. **42** B3 58 30N 134 00W
Ta Ku Ling Hong Kong U.K. **98** C2 22 21N 114 15E
Talara Peru **68** A12 4 38S 81 18W
Talavera del la Reina Spain **77** B2 39 58N 4 50W
Talbot, Cape Australia **110** D7 13 49S 126 42E
Talca Chile **69** C5 35 28S 71 40W

Talcahuano Chile **69** C5 36 40S 73 10W
Taldy-Kurgan Kazakhstan **91** M4 45 02N 78 23E
Tallahassee Florida U.S.A. **63** J3 30 26N 84 19W
Tallinn Estonia **79** E2 59 22N 24 48E
Tall Kalakh Syria **92** P12 34 45N 36 17E
Tal'menka Russia **91** N5 53 50N 83 36E
Talodi Sudan **106** L10 10 40N 30 25E
Talparo Trinidad and Tobago **66** T10 10 30N 61 16W
Taltal Chile **69** C7 25 26S 70 33W
Tama *r.* Japan **101** B3 35 40N 139 30E
Tamabo Range *mts.* Malaysia **99** F4 4 00N 115 30E
Tamale Ghana **106** E9 9 26N 0 49W
Ta-ma-li Taiwan **98** H5 22 37N 121 00E
Tamanrasset Algeria **106** G12 22 50N 5 28E
Tamaqua Pennsylvania U.S.A. **64** E3 40 47 75 58W
Tamar *r.* England **78** G2 50 35N 4 15W
Tambov Russia **90** E5 52 44N 41 28E
Tambre *r.* Spain **77** A3 42 55N 8 50W
Tâmega *r.* Portugal **77** A3 41 40N 7 45W
Tamil Nadu *admin.* India **95** D2 12 00N 78 30E
Tampa Florida U.S.A. **63** J2 27 58N 82 38W
Tampere Finland **79** E3 61 32N 23 45E
Tampico Mexico **66** E4 22 18N 97 52W
Tamworth Australia **110** I3 31 07S 150 57E
Tana *r.* Kenya **106** M7 1 00S 39 50E
Tanabe Japan **100** C1 33 43N 135 22E
Tanafjord *fj.* Norway **79** F5 71 00N 28 15E
Tanahmerah Indonesia **110** G8 6 08N 140 18E
Tana, Lake Ethiopia **106** M10 12 20N 37 20E
Tanana Alaska U.S.A. **10** E6 65 11N 152 10W
Tanana *r.* Alaska U.S.A. **10** G5 63 00N 143 00W
Tananarive *see* Antananarivo
Tanashi Japan **101** B3 35 43N 139 31E
Tandil Argentina **69** F5 37 18S 59 10W
Tanezrouft *geog. reg.* Algeria **106** E12 24 00N 0 30W
Tanga Tanzania **107** M6 5 07S 39 05E
Tanganyika, Lake East Africa **107** L6 7 00S 30 00E
Tanger *(Tangiers)* Morocco **106** D15 35 48N 5 45W
Tanggula Shan *mts.* China **96** H5 32 30N 92 30E
Tangra Yumco *l.* China **95** F6 31 00N 86 15E
Tangshan China **97** N6 39 37N 118 05E
Tanjungkarang Telukbetung Indonesia **99** D2 5 22S 105 18E
Tan Kwai Tsuen Hong Kong U.K. **98** A2 22 25N 113 59E
Tanna *i.* Vanuatu **110** L6 19 30S 169 00E
Tanna Ola *mts.* Russia **91** P5 51 00N 92 30E
Tanout Niger **106** G10 15 05N 8 50E
Tan-shui Taiwan **98** H8 25 13N 121 29E
Tan-shui Ho *r.* Taiwan **98** H7 24 40N 121 20E
Tanta Egypt **92** D5 30 48N 31 00E
TANZANIA **107** L6
Taolañaro Madagascar **107** O2 25 01S 47 00E
T'ao-yüan Taiwan **98** H8 25 00N 121 15E
Tapa Estonia **79** F2 59 16N 25 50E
Tapachula Mexico **66** F2 14 54N 92 15W
Tāpi *r.* India **95** D4 21 30N 76 30E
Tappi-zaki *c.* Japan **100** D3 41 14N 140 21E
Tapti *r.* India **95** C4 21 30N 74 30E
Tapuaenuku *mt.* New Zealand **111** B2 42 00S 173 39E
Taquara Brazil **69** P2 22 55S 43 22W
Tara *r.* Russia **91** M6 56 30N 76 00E
Tarābulus *(Tripoli)* Libya **106** H14 32 54N 13 11E
Tarakan Indonesia **99** F4 3 20N 117 38E
Taranto Italy **81** C3 40 28N 17 15E
Tarapoto Peru **68** B11 6 31S 76 23W
Tararua Range *mts.* New Zealand **111** C2 41 00S 175 30E
Tarauacá Brazil **68** C11 8 06SW 70 45W
Tarawa Kiribati **114** H8 1 30N 173 00E
Tarazona Spain **77** B3 41 54N 1 44W
Tarbes France **77** C3 43 14N 0 05E
Taree Australia **110** I3 31 45S 152 26E
Tarfaya Morocco **106** C13 27 58N 12 55W
Tarija Bolivia **68** E8 21 33S 64 45W
Tarim Basin *see* Tarim Pendi
Tarim He *r.* China **96** F7 41 00N 82 00E
Tarim Pendi *(Tarim Basin)* China **96** F6/G6 39 00N 84 00E
Tarko-Sale Russia **89** J8 64 55N 77 50E
Tarkwa Ghana **106** E9 5 16N 1 59W
Tarn *r.* France **77** C3 44 05N 1 40E
Tarnobrzeg Poland **80** D5 50 35N 21 40E
Tarnów Poland **80** D4 50 01N 20 59E
Taroko National Park Taiwan **98** H7 24 15N 121 30E
Taroom Australia **110** H4 25 39S 149 50E
Tarragona Spain **77** C3 41 07N 1 15E
Tarrasa Spain **77** C3 41 34N 2 00E
Tarrytown Connecticut U.S.A. **65** G4 41 00N 73 00W
Tarsus Turkey **92** D6 36 25N 34 52E
Tartary, Gulf of Russia **89** Q5/Q6 50 00N 141 00E
Tartu Estonia **79** F2 58 20N 26 44E
Tartus Syria **92** E5 34 55N 35 52E
Tashkent Uzbekistan **91** K3 41 16N 69 13E
Tashuaz Turkmenistan **91** H3 41 49N 59 58E
Tasman Basin Pacific Ocean **114** F3 46 00S 154 00E
Tasman Bay New Zealand **111** B2 41 00S 173 20E
Tasmania *state* Australia **110** H1 43 00S 147 00E
Tasman Mountains New Zealand **111** B2 41 20S 172 30E
Tasman Plateau Southern Ocean **114** E3 48 00S 147 00E
Tasman Sea Pacific Ocean **114** F4 40 00S 155 00E
Tassili N'Ajjer *mts.* Algeria **106** G13 26 00N 6 20W
Tatabánya Hungary **81** C4 47 31N 18 25E
Tatarsk Russia **90** C5 54 15N 31 34E
Tatarsk Russia **91** M6 55 14N 76 00E
Tatebayashi Japan **100** L3 36 14N 139 30E
Tate's Cairn *mt.* Hong Kong U.K. **98** C2 22 21N 114 13E
Tateyama Japan **100** L1 34 59N 139 50E
Tatry *mts.* Poland **80** C4 49 00N 20 00E
Tauern *mts.* Europe **70** 47 30N 12 00E
Taumarunui New Zealand **111** C3 38 53S 175 16E
Taunton Massachusetts U.S.A. **65** J4 41 54N 71 06W
Taunton England **78** H3 51 01N 3 06W
Taupo New Zealand **111** C3 38 42S 176 06E
Taupo, Lake New Zealand **111** C3 38 50S 175 55E
Tauranga New Zealand **111** C3 37 42S 176 11E
Tauva Fiji **114** T16 17 31S 177 53E
Tavda *r.* Russia **91** J6 58 00N 64 00E
Taverny France **83** A3 49 01N 2 13E
Taveuni *i.* Fiji **114** U16 16 40S 180 00
Tavira Portugal **77** A2 37 07N 7 39W
Tavoy Myanmar **99** B6 14 02N 98 12E
Taw *r.* England **78** H2 50 58N 3 55W
Tawas City Michigan U.S.A. **36** C5 44 16N 83 33W
Tawau Malaysia **99** F4 4 16N 117 54E
T'a-wu Taiwan **98** G5 22 17N 120 54E
Tay *r.* Scotland **78** H8 56 30N 3 25W
Taylor Michigan U.S.A. **52** D1 42 14N 83 16W
Tayma' Saudi Arabia **92** E4 27 37N 38 30E
Taymyr Peninsula Russia **89** L11/M10 75 00N 100 00E
Tayshet Russia **89** L7 55 56N 98 01E
Taz *r.* Russia **89** K9 67 00N 82 00E
Taza Morocco **106** E14 34 16N 4 01W
Tbilisi Georgia **90** E3 41 43N 44 48E
Tchibanga Gabon **106** H7 2 49S 11 00E
Tczew Poland **80** C5 54 05N 18 46E
Te Anua, Lake New Zealand **111** A1 45 30S 168 00E
Te Aroha New Zealand **111** C3 37 32S 175 43E
Te Awamutu New Zealand **111** C3 38 00S 175 20E
Tébessa Algeria **106** G15 35 21N 8 06E
Tecuci Romania **81** E4 45 50N 27 27E
Tecumseh Michigan U.S.A. **36** C3 42 01N 83 56W
Tedzhen *r.* Turkmenistan/Iran **91** J2 37 00N 61 00E
Tees *r.* England **78** J6 54 30N 1 25W
Tefé Brazil **68** E12 3 24S 64 45W
Tegal Indonesia **99** D2 6 52S 109 07E
Tegel Germany **83** E2 52 36N 13 17E
Tegeler See *l.* Germany **83** E2 52 35N 13 00E
Tegucigalpa Honduras **66** G2 14 05N 87 14W
Tehrān Iran **93** H6 35 40N 51 26E
Tehuacán Mexico **66** E3 18 30N 97 26W
Tehuantepec Mexico **66** E3 16 21N 95 13W
Teifi *r.* Wales **78** G4 52 03N 4 15W
Tejo *(Tagus, Tajo) r.* Portugal **77** A2 39 30N 8 15W
Tekapo, Lake New Zealand **111** B2 43 30S 170 30E
Tekezē *r.* Ethiopia **92** E1 13 48N 38 05E
Tekirdağ Turkey **80** E3 40 59N 27 31E
Te Kuiti New Zealand **111** C3 38 20S 175 10E
Tel *r.* India **95** E4 20 30N 83 30E
Tela Honduras **66** G3 15 46N 87 25W
Tel Aviv-Yafo Israel **92** O11 32 05N 34 46E
Telemark *geog. reg.* Norway **79** B2 59 42N 8 00E
Telford England **78** I4 52 42N 2 28W
Teller Alaska U.S.A. **10** B6 65 12N 166 23W
Teltow Germany **83** F1 52 24N 13 16E
Teltowkanal *can.* Germany **83** E1 52 23N 13 10E
Teluk Bone *b.* Indonesia **99** G3 4 00S 121 00E
Teluk Cenderawisih *b.* Indonesia **110** F9 2 30S 135 30E
Teluk Tomini *b.* Indonesia **99** G3 1 00S 121 00E
Tema Ghana **106** E9 5 41N 0 00
Teme *r.* England **78** I4 52 15N 2 25W
Temirtau Kazakhstan **91** L5 50 05N 72 55E
Tempelhof Germany **83** F1 52 28N 13 23E
Tempio Pausania Italy **81** A3 40 54N 9 07E
Temple Texas U.S.A. **63** G3 31 06N 97 22W
Temple City California U.S.A. **51** B3 34 06N 118 02W
Temuco Chile **69** C5 38 45S 72 40W
Temuka New Zealand **111** B2 44 12S 171 16E
Tenali India **95** E3 16 13N 80 36E
Ten Degree Channel Andaman Islands/Nicobar Islands **95** G1 10 00N 93 00E
Tenerife *i.* Canary Islands **106** B13 28 15N 16 35W
Tennant Creek *tn.* Australia **110** E6 19 31S 134 15E
Tennessee *r.* U.S.A. **63** I4 35 00N 88 00W
Tennessee *state* U.S.A. **63** I4 35 00N 87 00W
Tenojoki *r.* Finland/Norway **79** F4 69 50N 26 10E
Tenri Japan **100** G1 34 36N 135 49E
Teófilo Otôni Brazil **68** I9 17 52S 41 31W
Tepatitlán Mexico **66** D4 20 50N 102 46W
Tépeji Mexico **66** E3 19 55N 99 21W
Tepic Mexico **66** D4 21 30N 104 51W
Ter *r.* Spain **77** C3 41 55N 2 30E
Teramo Italy **81** B3 42 40N 13 43E
Teresina Brazil **68** I11 5 09S 42 46W
Termez Uzbekistan **91** K2 37 15N 67 15E
Termim Imerese Italy **81** B2 27 59N 13 42E
Ternate Indonesia **99** H4 0 48N 127 23E
Terni Italy **81** B3 42 34N 12 39E
Ternopol' Ukraine **90** B4 49 35N 25 39E
Terpeniya Bay Russia **89** Q5 48 00N 144 00E
Terracina Italy **81** B3 41 17N 13 15E
Terre Haute Indiana U.S.A. **63** I4 39 27N 87 24W
Terrey Hills Australia **111** G3 33 41S 151 14E
Teruel Spain **77** B3 40 21N 1 06W
Teseney Ethiopia **92** E2 15 10N 36 48E
Teshio Japan **100** D3 44 53N 141 46E
Test *r.* England **78** J3 51 05N 1 30W
Testa del Gargano *c.* Italy **81** C3 41 00N 16 00E
Teterev *r.* Ukraine **80** E5 50 00N 29 00E
Tétouan Morocco **106** D15 35 34N 5 22W
Tetovo Macedonia Yugoslavia **81** D3 42 00N 20 59E
Texarkana Arkansas U.S.A. **63** H3 33 28N 94 02W
Texas *state* U.S.A. **62** F3 31 00N 100 00W
Texoma, Lake U.S.A. **63** G3 34 00N 97 00W
THAILAND **99** C7
Thailand, Gulf of South East Asia **99** C6 12 00N 101 30E
Thakhek Laos **99** C7 17 22N 104 50E
Thames New Zealand **111** C3 37 08S 175 35E
Thames *r.* England **78** K3 51 30N 0 20W
Thane India **95** C3 19 14N 73 02E
Thanh Hoa Vietnam **99** D7 19 49N 105 48E
Thanjavur India **95** D2 10 46N 79 09E
Thar Desert India **95** C5 27 30N 72 00E
Thásos *i.* Greece **81** D3 40 00N 24 00E
Thayetmyo Myanmar **99** B7 19 20N 95 10E
Thebes *hist. site* Egypt **92** D4 25 41N 32 40E
The Bronx New York U.S.A. **50** C2 40 50N 73 55W
The Brothers *is.* Hong Kong U.K. **98** A2 22 20N 113 58E
The Crane Barbados **66** W12 13 06N 59 25W
The Dalles Oregon U.S.A. **62** B6 45 36N 121 10W
The Everglades *swamp* Florida U.S.A. **63** J2 26 00N 81 00W
The Loop Illinois U.S.A. **53** B2 41 53N 87 36W
Thermaïkós Kólpos *g.* Greece **81** D3 40 00N 22 50E
Thermopolis Wyoming U.S.A. **62** E5 43 39N 108 12W
Thessaloníki Greece **81** D3 40 38N 22 58E
Thiais France **83** B2 48 45N 2 24E
Thief Lake Minnesota U.S.A. **39** B1 48 30N 95 40W
Thief River Falls *tn.* Minnesota U.S.A. **63** G6 48 12N 96 48W
Thiers France **77** C4 45 51N 3 33E
Thiès Senegal **106** B10 14 49N 16 52W
Thimphu Bhutan **95** F5 27 32N 89 43E
Thingangyun Myanmar **96** J2 16 10N 96 10W
Thionville France **76** D4 49 22N 6 11E
Thira *i.* Greece **81** E2 36 00N 25 00E
Thisted Denmark **80** A6 56 58N 8 42E
Thithia *i.* Fiji **114** V16 17 45S 179 20W
Thívai Greece **81** D2 38 19N 23 19E
Thomasville Georgia U.S.A. **63** J3 30 50N 83 59W
Thompson Island Massachusetts U.S.A. **52** B2 42 20N 71 01W
Thompsonville Connecticut U.S.A. **65** H4 42 00N 72 36W
Thomson *r.* Australia **110** G5 24 00S 143 30E
Thornapple River Michigan U.S.A. **36** A3 42 38N 85 15W
Thousand Islands Canada/U.S.A. **35** E1 44 20N 76 10W
Three Kings Island New Zealand **111** B4 34 00S 172 30E
Three Mile Bay *tn.* New York U.S.A. **35** E1 44 04N 76 12W
Three Points, Cape Ghana **106** E9 4 43N 2 06W
Three Rivers Massachusetts U.S.A. **65** H5 42 11N 72 22W
Thule Greenland **45** S6 77 30N 69 00W
Thun Switzerland **77** D4 46 46N 7 38E
Thunder Bay Michigan U.S.A. **36** C5 45 00N 83 25W
Thüringer Wald *hills* Germany **76** E5 50 00N 10 00E
Thurmont Maryland U.S.A. **64** C2 39 00N 77 00W
Thurso Scotland **78** H10 58 35N 3 32W
Thurso *r.* Scotland **78** H10 58 15N 3 35W
Tianjin China **97** N6 39 08N 117 12E
Tianshui China **97** L5 34 25N 105 58E
Tiaret Algeria **77** C2 35 20N 1 20E
Tiber *r.* Italy **81** B3 42 00N 12 00E
Tiberias Israel **92** O11 32 48N 35 32E
Tiberias, Lake *(Sea of Galilee) l.* Israel **92** O11 32 45N 35 30E
Tibesti *mts.* Chad **106** I12 21 00N 17 00E
Tibet Autonomous Region *see* Xizang Zizhiqu
Tibet, Plateau of Asia **84** 33 00N 90 00E
Tiburon California U.S.A. **49** B3 37 53N 122 27W
Tiburón *i.* Mexico **66** B5 28 30N 112 30W
Ticul Mexico **66** G4 20 22N 89 31W
Tien Shan *(Tyan-Shan') mts.* China/Kirgyzstan **89** J4 41 00N 76 00E
Tierra Blanca Mexico **66** E3 18 28N 96 21W
Tierra del Fuego *see* Isla Grande de Tierra del Fuego
Tietar *r.* Spain **77** A3 40 07N 5 15W
Tiffany Mountain Washington U.S.A. **42** J4 48 41N 119 56W
Tiffin Ohio U.S.A. **36** C2 41 07N 83 11W
Tigris *r.* Iraq **93** G5 32 00N 46 00E
Tijuana Mexico **66** A6 32 29N 117 10W
Tijuca Brazil **69** P2 22 56S 43 16W
Tikhoretsk Russia **90** E4 45 52N 40 07E
Tikrīt Iraq **92** F5 34 36N 43 42E
Tiksi Russia **89** O10 71 40N 128 45E
Tilak Nagar India **94** L4 28 38N 77 07E
Tilburg Netherlands **76** D5 51 34N 5 05E
Tilden National Park California U.S.A. **49** B3 37 55N 122 15W
Timaru New Zealand **111** B2 44 23S 171 14E
Timbira *r.* Brazil **69** Q3 22 40S 43 12W
Timișoara Romania **81** D4 45 45N 21 15E
Timișul *r.* Romania/Yugoslavia **81** D4 45 00N 21 00E
Timor *i.* Indonesia **99** G2/H2 9 00S 125 00E
Timor Sea Australia/Indonesia **99** H1/H2 10 00S 128 00E
Timsâh, Lake *see* Bahra el Timsâh
Tindouf Algeria **106** D13 27 42N 8 10W
Tinos *i.* Greece **81** E2 37 00N 25 00E
Tioga North Dakota U.S.A. **40** C1 48 26N 102 57W
Tionesta Pennsylvania U.S.A. **36** G2 41 31N 79 30W
Tionesta Lake Pennsylvania U.S.A. **36** G2 41 30N 79 30W
Tioughnioga River New York U.S.A. **64** D5 42 00N 76 00W
Tiranë Albania **81** C3 41 20N 19 49E
Tiraspol' Moldova **90** B4 46 50N 29 38E
Tir'at el Ismâ'iliya *can.* Egypt **107** R3 30 32N 31 48E
Tir'at el Mansûriya Egypt **107** R4 31 12N 31 38E
Tiraz Mountains Namibia **107** I2 25 30S 16 30E
Tiree *i.* Scotland **78** E8 56 30N 6 55W
Tîrgoviste Romania **81** E3 44 56N 25 27E
Tîrgu Jiu Romania **81** D4 45 03N 23 18E
Tîrgu Mures Romania **81** D4 46 33N 24 34E
Tirso *r.* Italy **81** A2 40 00N 9 00E
Tiruchchirāppalli India **95** D2 10 50N 78 41E
Tirunelveli India **95** D1 8 45N 77 43E
Tirupati India **95** D2 13 39N 79 25E
Tiruppur India **95** D2 11 05N 77 20E
Tisza *r.* Hungary/Yugoslavia **81** D4 46 00N 20 00E
Titāgarh India **94** K2 22 44N 88 22E
Titograd Montenegro Yugoslavia **81** C3 42 28N 19 17E
Titova Mitrovica Serbia Yugoslavia **81** D3 42 54N 20 52E
Titovo Uzice Serbia Yugoslavia **81** C3 43 52N 19 50E
Titov Veles Macedonia Yugoslavia **81** D3 41 43N 21 49E
Tittabawassee River Michigan U.S.A. **36** B4 43 50N 84 25W
Titusville Pennsylvania U.S.A. **36** G2 41 37N 79 42W
Tiu Chung Chau *i.* Hong Kong U.K. **98** C2 22 20N 114 19E
Tiu Keng Leng Hong Kong U.K. **98** C1 22 18N 114 15E
Tiverton Rhode Island U.S.A. **65** J4 41 38N 71 13W
Tivoli Italy **81** B3 41 58N 12 48E
Tizimím Mexico **66** G4 21 10N 88 09W
Tizi Ouzou Algeria **106** F15 36 44N 4 05E
Tiznit Morocco **106** D13 29 43N 9 44W
Tlemcen Algeria **106** E14 34 53N 1 21W
Toamasina Madagascar **107** O4 18 10S 49 23E
Toba Japan **100** H1 34 29N 136 51E
Tobago *i.* Trinidad and Tobago **67** L2 11 15N 60 40W
Tobi-shima *i.* Japan **100** C2 39 12N 139 32E
Tobol *r.* Russia **91** J5 54 00N 64 00E
Tobol'sk Russia **91** K6 58 15N 68 12E
Tobyhanna Pennsylvania U.S.A. **64** E4 41 11N 75 25W
Tochigi *pref.* Japan **100** L3 36 20N 139 40E
Toco Trinidad and Tobago **66** U10 10 49N 60 57W
Tocopilla Chile **69** C8 22 05S 70 10W
Togane Japan **100** M2 35 34N 140 22E
TOGO **106** F9
Tok Alaska U.S.A. **44** C3 63 00N 143 00W
Tokelua Islands Pacific Ocean **114** I7 9 00S 168 00W
Toki Japan **100** J2 35 25N 137 12E
Tokoname Japan **100** H1 34 50N 136 50E
Tokorozawa Japan **101** A4 35 47N 139 28E
Tokrau *r.* Kazakhstan **91** M4 48 00N 75 00E
Tokushima Japan **100** B1 34 03N 134 34E
Tokuyama Japan **100** B1 34 03N 131 48E
Tōkyō Japan **100** L2 35 40N 139 45E
Tōkyō *pref.* Japan **100** L2 35 35N 139 40E
Tokyo Bay *(Tōkyō-wan)* Japan **101** C2 35 25N 139 45E
Tōkyō-wan *(Tokyo Bay) b.* Japan **100** L2 35 30N 139 50E
Tolbukhin *see* Dobrich
Toledo Ohio U.S.A. **63** J5 41 40N 83 35W
Toledo Spain **77** B2 39 52N 4 02W
Toliara Madagascar **107** N3 23 20S 43 41E
Tollygunge India **94** K2 22 30N 88 19E
Tolo Channel Hong Kong U.K. **98** C2 22 28N 114 17E
Tolo Harbour Hong Kong U.K. **98** C2 22 26N 114 14E
Tolosa Spain **77** B3 43 09N 2 04W
Toluca Mexico **66** E3 19 20N 99 40W
Tol'yatti Russia **90** F5 53 32N 49 24E
Tom' *r.* Russia **91** O6 55 00N 86 00E
Tomaniivi *mt.* Fiji **114** U16 17 37S 178 01E
Tomar Portugal **77** A2 39 36N 8 25W
Tomaszów Mazowiecka Poland **80** C5 51 33N 20 00E
Tomatlán Mexico **66** C3 19 54N 105 18W
Tombigbee *r.* U.S.A. **63** I3 32 00N 88 00W
Tombouctou *(Timbuktu)* Mali **106** E11 16 49N 2 59W
Tombua Angola **107** H4 15 49S 11 53E
Tomioka Japan **100** K3 36 14N 138 45E
Tomogashima-suido *sd.* Japan **100** F1 34 15N 134 00E
Tomokomai Japan **100** D3 42 39N 141 33E
Tom Price, Mount Australia **110** B5 22 49S 117 51E
Tomsk Russia **91** O6 56 30N 85 05E
Toms River *r.* New Jersey U.S.A. **65** F2 39 00N 74 00W
Tonala Mexico **66** F3 16 08N 93 41W
Tonasket Washington U.S.A. **43** E1 48 42N 119 28W
Tonawanda New York U.S.A. **64** B6 43 00N 78 00W
Tonawanda Channel New York U.S.A. **38** D2 43 04N 78 56W
Tonawanda Creek New York U.S.A. **64** B6 43 00N 78 00W
Tone-gawa *r.* Japan **100** M2 35 51N 140 09E
TONGA **114** I5
Tong'an China **98** E7 24 43N 118 07E
Tonga Trench Pacific Ocean **114** I5 20 00S 173 00W
Tongchuan China **97** L6 35 05N 109 02E
Tong Fuk Hong Kong U.K. **98** A1 22 14N 113 56E
Tonghai China **97** K3 24 07N 104 45E
Tonghua China **97** P7 41 42N 125 45E
Tongking, Gulf of Vietnam/China **97** L2 19 00N 107 00E
Tongling China **97** N5 30 58N 117 48E
Tonle Sap *l.* Cambodia **99** C6 13 00N 104 00E
Tonpah Nevada U.S.A. **62** C4 38 05N 117 15W
Tønsberg Norway **79** C2 59 16N 10 25E
Tooele Utah U.S.A. **62** D5 40 32N 112 18W
Toowoomba Australia **110** I4 27 35S 151 54E
Topeka Kansas U.S.A. **63** G4 39 02N 95 41W
Torbali Turkey **80** E2 38 07N 27 08E
Torbay England **78** H2 50 27N 3 30W
Tordesillas Spain **77** A3 41 30N 5 00W
Toride Japan **100** M2 35 54N 140 07E
Torino *(Turin)* Italy **81** A4 45 04N 7 40E
Tormes *r.* Spain **77** A3 41 03N 5 58W
Torne älv *r.* Sweden **79** E4 67 03N 23 02E
Torne-träsk *l.* Sweden **79** D4 68 14N 19 40E
Tornio Finland **79** E4 65 50N 24 10E
Tororo Uganda **106** L8 0 42N 34 12E
Toros Dağlari *mts.* Turkey **92** D6 37 10N 33 10E
Torrance California U.S.A. **51** A2 33 50N 118 20W
Torre del Greco Italy **81** B3 40 46N 14 22E
Torrelavega Spain **77** B3 43 21N 4 03W
Torrens, Lake Australia **110** F3 31 00S 137 50E
Torreón Mexico **66** D5 25 34N 103 25W
Torres Strait Australia **110** G7/G8 10 00S 142 30E
Torrington Connecticut U.S.A. **65** G4 41 48N 73 08W
Tortosa Spain **77** C3 40 49N 0 31E
Torún Poland **80** C5 53 01N 18 35E
Tosa-wan *b.* Japan **100** B1 33 20N 133 40E
Toshima Japan **101** B3 35 43N 139 41E
Totoya *i.* Fiji **114** V15 18 56S 179 50W
Totsuka Japan **101** B2 35 23N 139 32E
Tottori Japan **100** B2 35 32N 134 12E
Touggourt Algeria **106** G14 33 08N 6 04E
Tou-liu Taiwan **98** G6 23 42N 120 32E
Toulon France **77** D3 43 07N 5 55E
Toulouse France **77** C3 43 33N 1 24E
Toungoo Myanmar **99** B7 18 57N 96 26E
Tournai Belgium **76** C5 50 36N 3 24E
Tours France **77** C4 47 23N 0 42E
Towanda Pennsylvania U.S.A. **64** D4 41 46N 76 27W
Tower Hamlets *bor.* Greater London England **82** C3 51 30N 0 02W
Towner North Dakota U.S.A. **39** A1 48 20N 100 24W
Townsville Australia **110** H6 19 13S 146 48E
Towson Maryland U.S.A. **64** D2 39 25N 76 36W
Toyama Japan **100** C2 36 42N 137 14E
Toyoake Japan **100** H2 35 02N 136 55E
Toyohashi Japan **100** J1 34 46N 137 22E
Toyokawa Japan **100** J1 34 47N 137 24E
Toyonaka Japan **100** G1 34 48N 135 36E
Toyooka Japan **100** F2 35 35N 134 48E
Toyota Japan **100** J2 35 05N 137 09E
Tozeur Tunisia **106** G14 33 55N 8 07E
Trabzona Turkey **92** E7 41 00N 39 43E
Tralee Irish Republic **78** B4 52 16N 9 42W
Tranäs Sweden **80** B6 58 03N 15 00E
Transvaal *province* Republic of South Africa **107** K3 24 30S 28 00E
Trápani Italy **81** B2 38 02N 12 32E
Traverse City Michigan U.S.A. **63** I5 44 46N 85 38W
Travers, Mount New Zealand **111** B2 42 01S 172 47E

Treinta-y-Tres Uruguay **69** G6 33 16S 54 17W
Trelew Chile **69** D4 43 13S 65 15W
Trelleborg Sweden **80** B6 55 22N 13 10E
Tremplinersee *l.* Germany **83** E1 52 21N 13 02E
Trencín Czechoslovakia **80** C4 48 53N 18 00E
Trenque Lauquen Argentina **69** E5 35 56S 62 43W
Trent *r.* England **78** K5 53 10N 0 50W
Trento Italy **81** B4 46 04N 11 08E
Trenton New Jersey U.S.A. **65** F3 40 15N 74 43W
Treptow Germany **83** F1 52 29N 13 27E
Tres Arroyos Argentina **69** E5 38 26S 60 17W
Três Lagoas Brazil **68** G8 20 46S 51 43W
Treviso Italy **81** B4 45 40N 12 15E
Trichu India **95** D2 10 32N 76 14E
Trieste Italy **81** B4 45 39N 13 47E
Trikkala Greece **81** D2 39 33N 21 46E
Trincomalee Sri Lanka **95** E1 8 34N 81 13E
Trindade *i.* Atlantic Ocean **113** F4 20 30S 29 20W
Trinidad Bolivia **68** E10 14 46S 64 50W
Trinidad Colorado U.S.A. **62** F4 37 11N 104 31W
Trinidad Cuba **67** H4 21 48N 80 00W
Trinidad *i.* Trinidad and Tobago **66** T9 11 00N 61 30W
TRINIDAD AND TOBAGO 67 L2
Trinity *r.* U.S.A. **63** G3 32 00N 96 00W
Trinity Hills Trinidad and Tobago **66** T9 10 07N 61 07W
Trinity Islands Alaska U.S.A. **10** E4 56 45N 154 15W
Trípoli *see* *Tarābulus*
Trípolis Greece **81** D2 37 31N 22 22E
Tripura Mizoram *admin.* India **95** G4 23 40N 92 30E
Tristan da Cunha *i.* Atlantic Ocean **113** G3 37 15S 12 30W
Trivandrum India **95** D1 8 30N 76 57E
Trnava Czechoslovakia **81** C4 48 23N 17 35E
Troitsk Russia **91** J5 54 08N 61 33E
Troitsko Pechorsk Russia **91** H7 62 40N 56 08E
Trollhättan Sweden **79** C2 58 17N 12 20E
Trollheimen *mts.* Norway **79** B3 63 00N 9 00E
Tromsø Norway **79** D4 69 42N 19 00E
Trondheim Norway **79** C3 63 36N 10 23E
Trondheimsfjorden *fj.* Norway **79** C3 63 40N 10 30E
Trouville France **76** C4 49 22N 0 05E
Troy Alabama U.S.A. **63** I3 31 49N 86 00W
Troy Montana U.S.A. **43** E1 48 28N 115 55W
Troy New York U.S.A. **65** G5 42 43N 73 43W
Troy *hist. site* Turkey **92** C6 39 55N 26 17E
Troyes France **76** C4 48 18N 4 05E
Trujillo Peru **68** B11 8 06S 79 00W
Trujillo Spain **77** A2 39 28N 5 53W
Trujillo Venezuela **68** C14 9 20N 70 38W
Truk Islands Caroline Islands **114** F8 7 30N 152 30E
Trumansburg New York U.S.A. **64** D5 42 32N 76 40W
Truro England **78** F2 50 16N 5 03W
Tsavo National Park Kenya **106** M7 3 30S 38 00E
Tselinograd Kazakhstan **91** L5 51 10N 71 28E
Tseung Kwan O Hong Kong U.K. **98** C1 22 19N 114 14E
Tshane Botswana **107** J3 24 05S 21 54E
Tshuapa *r.* Zaïre **106** J7 1 00S 23 00E
Tsimlyanskoye Vodokhranilishche *res.* Russia **90** E4 47 30N 43 00E
Tsin Shui Wan Hong Kong U.K. **98** C1 22 14N 114 12E
Tsing Chau Tsai Hong Kong U.K. **98** B2 22 20N 114 02E
Tsing Yi Hong Kong U.K. **98** B2 22 21N 114 06E
Tsing Yi *i.* Hong Kong U.K. **98** B2 22 10N 114 00E
Tsu Japan **100** H1 34 41N 136 30E
Tsuchiura Japan **100** M3 36 05N 140 11E
Tsuen Wan Hong Kong U.K. **98** B2 22 22N 114 06E
Tsugaru-kaikyō *sd.* Japan **100** D3 41 30N 140 30E
Tsumeb Namibia **107** I4 19 13S 17 42E
Tsuna Japan **100** F1 34 26N 134 53E
Tsunashima Japan **101** B3 35 13N 139 38E
Tsuruga Japan **100** C2 35 40N 136 05E
Tsurugi-zaki Japan **100** L2 35 08N 139 37E
Tsuruoka Japan **100** C2 38 42N 139 50E
Tsushima Japan **100** H2 35 11N 136 45E
Tsushima *i.* Japan **100** A1 34 30N 129 20E
Tsuyama Japan **100** B2 35 04N 134 01E
Tsz Wan Shan Hong Kong U.K. **98** C2 22 21N 114 12E
Tua *r.* Portugal **77** A3 41 20N 7 30W
Tuamotu Archipelago *is.* Pacific Ocean **115** M6 1500S 145 00W
Tuamotu Ridge Pacific Ocean **115** L6 19 00S 144 00W
Tuapse Russia **90** D3 44 06N 39 50E
Tuba *r.* Russia **91** P5 54 00N 94 00E
Tübingen Germany **76** D4 48 32N 9 04E
Tubruq Libya **106** J14 32 05N 23 59E
Tubuai Islands Pacific Ocean **115** L5 23 23S 149 27W
Tucheng Taiwan **98** H7 24 52N 121 49E
Tuckerton New Jersey U.S.A. **65** F2 39 36N 74 20W
Tucson Arizona U.S.A. **62** D3 32 15N 110 57W
Tucumcari New Mexico U.S.A. **62** F4 35 11N 103 44W
Tucupita Venezuela **68** E14 9 02N 62 04W
Tucuruí Brazil **68** H12 3 42S 49 44W
Tudela Spain **77** B3 42 04N 1 37W
Tuen Mun Hong Kong U.K. **98** A2 22 23N 113 57E
Tujunga California U.S.A. **51** A3 34 14N 118 16W
Tukums Latvia **79** E2 56 58N 23 10E
Tula Mexico **66** E4 20 01N 99 21W
Tula Mexico **66** E4 23 00N 99 41W
Tula Russia **90** D5 54 11N 37 38E
Tulcán Ecuador **68** B3 0 50N 77 48W
Tulcea Romania **81** E4 45 10N 28 50E
Tulkarm Jordan **92** O11 32 19N 35 02E
Tulle France **77** C4 45 16N 1 46E
Tulsa Oklahoma U.S.A. **63** G4 36 07N 95 58W
Tuluá Colombia **68** B13 4 05N 76 12W
Tulun Russia **89** M6 54 32N 100 35E
Tumaco Colombia **68** B13 1 51N 78 46W
Tumbes Peru **68** A12 3 37S 80 27W
Tumkur India **95** D2 13 20N 77 06E
Tunapuna Trinidad and Tobago **66** T10 10 38N 61 23W
Tunduru Tanzania **107** M5 11 08S 27 21E
Tundzha *r.* Bulgaria **81** E3 42 00N 25 00E
Tungabhadra *r.* India **95** D3 16 00N 77 00E
Tung-chiang Taiwan **98** G5 22 26N 120 30E
Tung Chung Hong Kong U.K. **98** A1 22 17N 113 56E
Tung Lung Chau *i.* Hong Kong U.K. **98** C1 22 15N 114 17E
Tunis Tunisia **106** H15 36 50N 10 13E
TUNISIA 106 G14
Tunja Colombia **68** C14 5 33N 73 23W
Tunkhannock Pennsylvania U.S.A. **64** E4 41 00N 75 00W
Tunnsjøen *l.* Norway **79** C3 64 45N 13 25E
Tupelo Mississippi U.S.A. **63** I3 34 15N 88 43W
Tupiza Bolivia **68** D8 21 27S 65 45W
Túquerres Colombia **68** B13 1 06N 77 37W
Tura Russia **89** M8 64 20N 100 17E
Tura *r.* Russia **91** J6 58 00N 63 00E
Turbotville Pennsylvania U.S.A. **64** D4 41 00N 76 00W
Turda Romania **81** D4 46 35N 23 50E
Turfan Depression *see* Turpan
Turgay *r.* Kazakhstan **91** J4 49 00N 63 00E
Turgutlu Turkey **80** E2 38 30N 27 43E
Turia *r.* Spain **77** B2 39 45N 0 55W
Turin *see* Torino
Turkana, Lake Ethiopia/Kenya **106** M8 4 00N 36 00E
Turkestan Kazakhstan **91** K3 43 17N 68 16E
TURKEY 92 D6
Turkish Republic of Northern Cyprus Cyprus **92** D6 35 20N 33 30E
TURKMENIA *see* TURKMENISTAN
TURKMENISTAN 91 H3/J3
Turks and Caicos Islands West Indies **67** J4 21 30N 72 00W
Turks Island Passage *sd.* West Indies **67** J4 21 30N 71 30W
Turku Finland **79** E3 60 27N 22 15E
Turner Montana U.S.A. **41** D1 48 50N 108 26W
Turnu Măgurele Romania **81** D3 43 44N 24 53E
Turpan *(Turfan Depression)* China **96** G7 42 55N 89 06E
Turramurra Australia **111** G3 33 44S 151 07E
Turukhansk Russia **89** K9 65 49N 88 00E
Tuscaloosa Alabama U.S.A. **63** I3 33 12N 87 33W
Tushino Russia **88** L2 55 52N 37 26E
Tuticorin India **95** D1 8 48N 78 10E
Tuttlingen Germany **76** D4 47 59N 8 49E
TUVALU 114 H7
Tuxpan Mexico **66** C4 21 58N 105 20W
Tuxpan Mexico **66** E4 20 58N 97 23W
Tuxtla Gutierrez Mexico **66** F3 16 45N 93 09W
Túy Spain **77** A3 42 03N 8 39W
Tuz Gölü *l.* Turkey **92** D6 38 40N 33 35E
Tuzla Bosnia-Herzegovina **81** C3 44 33N 18 41E
Tver' *(Kalinin)* Russia **90** D6 56 49N 35 57E
Tweed *r.* Scotland/England **78** I7 55 45N 2 10W
Twin Falls *tn.* Idaho U.S.A. **62** D5 42 34N 114 30W
Twin Peaks California U.S.A. **49** B3 37 45N 122 26W
Twin Rivers *tn.* New Jersey U.S.A. **65** F3 40 17N 74 31W
Twisp Washington U.S.A. **42** H4 48 22N 120 08W
Twisp River Washington U.S.A. **42** H4 48 25N 120 30W
Two Harbors Minnesota U.S.A. **35** B2 47 02N 91 40W
Two Medicine River Montana U.S.A. **41** C1 48 30N 113 05W
Tyan-Shan' *(Tien Shan) mts.* Kirgyzstan/China **89** J4 41 00N 76 00E
Tyler Texas U.S.A. **63** G3 32 22N 95 18W
Tym *r.* Russia **91** N7 60 00N 84 00E
Tynda Russia **89** O7 55 10N 124 35E
Tyne *r.* England **78** J7 55 00N 1 50W
Tynset Norway **79** C3 62 17N 10 47E
Tyre *see* Soûr
Tyrone New York U.S.A. **64** C5 42 22N 77 05W
Tyrone Pennsylvania U.S.A. **64** B3 40 41N 78 15W
Tyrrhenian Sea Europe **81** B3 40 00N 12 00E
Tyumen' Russia **91** K6 57 11N 65 29E
Tyung *r.* Russia **89** N8 65 00N 119 00E
Tywi *r.* Wales **78** H3 51 53N 3 35W

U

Uaupés Brazil **68** D12 0 07S 67 05W
Ubagan *r.* Russia **91** K5 54 00N 65 00E
Ubangi *r.* Central African Republic/Zaïre **106** I8 4 00N 18 00E
Ube Japan **100** B1 33 57N 131 16E
Uberaba Brazil **68** H9 19 47S 47 57W
Uberlândia Brazil **68** H9 18 57S 48 17W
Ubly Michigan U.S.A. **36** D4 43 44N 82 58W
Ubon Ratchathani Thailand **99** D7 15 15N 104 50E
Ubundu Zaïre **106** K7 0 24S 25 30E
Uchiura-wan *b.* Japan **100** D3 42 30N 140 40E
Uda *r.* Russia **89** P6 54 00N 134 00E
Udaipur India **95** C4 24 36N 73 47E
Uddevalla Sweden **80** B6 58 20N 11 56E
Uddjaur *l.* Sweden **79** D4 65 55N 17 50E
Udgir India **95** D3 18 26N 77 11E
Udine Italy **81** B4 46 04N 13 14E
Udon Thani Thailand **99** C7 17 25N 102 45E
Ueda Japan **100** C2 36 27N 138 13E
Uele *r.* Zaïre **106** K8 4 00N 27 00E
Uelen Russia **89** U9 66 13N 169 48W
Uelzen Germany **76** E5 52 58N 10 34E
Ueno Japan **100** H1 34 45N 136 08E
Ufa Russia **91** H5 54 45N 55 58E
Ufa *r.* Russia **91** H6 55 30N 56 30E
Ugab *r.* Namibia **107** I3 21 00S 15 00E
UGANDA 106 L8
Ugra *r.* Russia **90** C5 54 30N 34 00E
Uinta Mountains Utah U.S.A. **62** D5 40 00N 111 00W
Uitenhage Republic of South Africa **107** K1 33 46S 25 25E
Uji Japan **100** G1 34 54N 135 48E
Ujjain India **95** D4 23 11N 75 50E
Ujung Pandang Indonesia **99** F2 5 09S 119 28E
Ukhta Russia **91** G7 63 33N 53 44E
Ukmerge Lithuania **80** D6 55 14N 24 49E
UKRAINE 90 A5/D5
Ulaanbaatar *(Ulan Bator)* Mongolia **97** L8 47 54N 106 52E
Ulaangom Mongolia **96** H8 49 59N 92 00E
Ulan Bator *see* Ulaanbaatar
Ulan-Ude Russia **89** M6 51 55N 107 40E
Ulhasnagar India **95** C3 19 15N 73 08E
Uliastay Mongolia **96** J8 47 42N 96 52E
Ullapool Scotland **78** F9 57 54N 5 10W
Ulm Germany **76** E4 48 24N 10 00E
Uluberiya India **94** J1 22 28N 88 07E
Ulungur Hu *l.* China **96** G8 47 10N 87 10E
Ulutau *mts.* Kazakhstan **91** K4 49 00N 67 00E
Ul'yanovsk Russia **90** F5 54 19N 48 22E
Uman' Ukraine **90** C4 48 45N 30 10E
Umanak Fjord Greenland **11** Y7 71 00N 52 00W
Umbagog Lake Maine/New Hampshire U.S.A. **37** P5 44 45N 71 00W
Umeå Sweden **79** E3 63 50N 20 15E
Ume älv *r.* Sweden **79** D3 64 45N 18 20E
Umiat Alaska U.S.A. **44** A4 69 25N 152 20W
Umm as Samīm *geog. reg.* Oman **93** I3 22 10N 56 00E
Umm Ruwaba Sudan **106** L10 12 50N 31 20E
Umtata Republic of South Africa **107** K1 31 35S 28 47E
Umuarama Brazil **69** G8 23 43S 52 57W
Una *r.* Bosnia-Herzegovina/Croatia **81** C4 45 15N 16 15E
Unalakleet Alaska U.S.A. **10** C5 63 52N 160 50W
'Unayzah Saudi Arabia **92** F4 26 06N 43 58E
UN Buffer Zone Cyprus **92** D6 35 00N 33 30E
Union New Jersey U.S.A. **50** B1 40 42N 74 14W
Union City California U.S.A. **49** C2 37 36N 122 02W
Union City New Jersey U.S.A. **50** B2 40 45N 74 01W
Union City Pennsylvania U.S.A. **36** G2 41 56N 79 51W
Union City Reservoir Pennsylvania U.S.A. **36** G2 42 00N 79 50W
Union of Soviet Socialist Republics *now* ARMENIA, AZERBAIJAN, BELARUS, ESTONIA, GEORGIA, KAZAKHSTAN, KIRGYZSTAN, LATVIA, LITHUANIA, MOLDOVA, RUSSIA, TAJIKISTAN, TURKMENISTAN, UKRAINE,UZBEKISTAN,
Uniontown Pennsylvania U.S.A. **63** K4 39 54N 79 44W
Unionville Michigan U.S.A. **36** C4 43 41N 83 29W
UNITED ARAB EMIRATES *(U.A.E.)* **93** H3
UNITED KINGDOM *(U.K.)* **78**
UNITED STATES OF AMERICA *(U.S.A.)* **62/63**
Unst *i.* Scotland **78** K12 60 45N 0 55W
Unuk *r.* Alaska U.S.A. **42** B3 56 00N 131 00W
Unzha *r.* Russia **90** E6 58 00N 44 00E
Uparnavik Greenland **11** X7 72 40N 56 05W
Upata Venezuela **68** E14 8 02N 62 25W
Upham North Dakota U.S.A. **39** A1 48 36N 100 44W
Upington Republic of South Africa **107** J2 28 28S 21 14E
Upolu Point Hawaiian Islands **115** Z18 20 16N 155 52W
Upper Bay New Jersey/New York U.S.A. **50** B1 40 40N 74 03W
Upper Crystal Springs Reservoir California U.S.A. **49** B1 37 30N 122 20W
Upper Hutt New Zealand **111** C2 41 06S 175 06E
Upper Lough Erne *l.* Ireland **78** D6 54 15N 7 30W
Upper Manzanilla Trinidad and Tobago **66** T10 10 32N 61 03W
Upper Red Lake Minnesota U.S.A. **63** H6 48 04N 94 48W
Upper Rouge Creek Michigan U.S.A. **52** D2 42 11N 83 18W
Upper Sandusky Ohio U.S.A. **36** C1 40 48N 83 17W
Upper San Leandro Reservoir California U.S.A. **49** C3 37 46N 122 06W
Uppland Sweden **80** C6 59 30N 18 15E
Uppsala Sweden **79** D2 59 55N 17 38E
Ur *hist. site* Iraq **93** G5 30 56N 46 08E
Uraga Japan **101** B1 35 14N 139 43E
Uraga-suidō *sd.* Japan **100** L2 35 10N 139 45E
Urakawa Japan **100** D3 42 10N 142 46E
Ural *r.* Russia **90** G4 50 00N 52 00E
Ural Mountains Russia **91** H4 H7
Ural'sk Kazakhstan **90** G5 51 19N 51 20E
Urawa Japan **100** L2 35 52N 139 40E
Ure *r.* England **78** J5 54 20N 1 40W
Urengoy Russia **89** J9 65 59N 78 30E
Urfa Turkey **92** E6 37 08N 38 45E
Urgench Uzbekistan **91** J3 41 35N 60 41E
Urmia, Lake *see* Daryacheh-ye Orumiyeh
Urmston Road *sd.* Hong Kong U.K. **98** A2 22 22N 113 54E
Uroševac Yugoslavia **81** D3 42 21N 21 09E
Urubamba Peru **68** C10 13 20S 72 07W
Uruguaiana Brazil **69** F7 29 45S 57 05W
URUGUAY 69 F6
Ürümqi China **96** G7 43 43N 87 38E
Uryasu Japan **101** C3 35 39N 139 54E
Urziceni Romania **81** E3 44 43N 26 39E
U.S.A. *see* UNITED STATES OF AMERICA
Usa *r.* Russia **89** H9 66 00N 57 00E
Usan South Korea **97** P6 35 32N 129 21E
Ushiku Japan **100** M2 35 59N 140 10E
Ushuaia Argentina **69** D2 54 48S 68 19W
Usinsk Russia **88** H9 65 57N 57 27E
Usküdar Turkey **92** C7 41 02N 29 02E
Usol'ye-Sibirskoye Russia **89** M6 52 48N 103 40E
Uspenskiy Kazakhstan **91** L4 48 41N 72 43E
Ussuri *(Wusul Jiang) r.* Russia **89** P5 47 00N 134 00E
Ussuriysk Russia **89** P4 43 48N 131 59E
U.S.S.R. *see* Union of Soviet Socialist Republics
Ustica *i.* Italy **81** B2 38 00N 13 00E
Ustinov *see* Izhevsk
Ust'-Kamchatsk Russia **89** S7 56 14N 162 28E
Ust'-Kamenogorsk Kazakhstan **91** N5 50 00N 82 40E
Ust'-Kut Russia **89** M7 56 48N 105 42E
Ústí nad Labem Czechoslovakia **80** B5 50 40N 14 02E
Ust'-Ilimsk Russia **89** M7 58 03N 102 39E
Ust'-Nera Russia **89** Q8 64 35N 143 14E
Ust'Maya Russia **89** P8 60 25N 134 28E
Ust'Olenëk Russia **89** N10 72 59N 119 57E
Ust-Urt Plateau Kazakhstan/Uzbekistan **91** H3 44 00N 57 00E
Usulután El Salvador **66** G2 13 20N 88 25W
Utah *state* U.S.A. **62** D4 39 00N 112 00W
Utah Lake Utah U.S.A. **62** D5 40 10N 111 50W
Utica New York U.S.A. **64** E6 43 06N 75 15W
Utrecht Netherlands **76** D5 52 05N 5 07E
Utrera Spain **77** A2 37 10N 5 47W
Utsunomiya Japan **100** C2 36 33N 139 52E
Uttar *admin.* India **95** E4 27 00N 80 00E
Uttaradit Thailand **99** C7 17 38N 100 05E
Uttarpāra-Kotrung India **94** K2 22 39N 88 20E
Uummannaq *see* Dundas
Uvalde Texas U.S.A. **62** G2 29 14N 99 49W
Uvinza Tanzania **107** L6 5 08S 30 23E
Uvs Nuur *l.* Mongolia **96** H9 50 10N 92 30E
Uwajima Japan **100** B1 33 13N 132 32E
Uxbridge England **82** B3 51 33N 0 30W
Uyuni Bolivia **68** D8 20 28S 66 47W
Uza *r.* Russia **90** F5 52 30N 45 30E
UZBEKISTAN 91 J3
Uzhgorod Ukraine **90** A4 48 39N 22 15E

V

Vaal *r.* Republic of South Africa **107** K2 27 30S 25 30E
Vaasa Finland **79** E3 63 06N 21 36E
Vác Hungary **81** C4 47 46N 19 08E
Vadodara India **95** C4 22 19N 73 14E
Vaga *r.* Russia **90** E7 62 00N 43 00E
Váh *r.* Czechoslovakia **81** C4 48 00N 18 00E
Vail New Jersey U.S.A. **64** F3 40 59N 75 01W
Vakh *r.* Russia **91** N7 61 30N 80 00E
Vakhsh *r.* Tajikistan **91** K2 37 30N 68 30E
Valdai Hills Russia **90** C6 57 00N 32 30E
Valdepeñas Spain **77** B2 38 46N 3 24W
Valdés, Peninsula Argentina **69** E4 42 30S 63 00W
Valdivia Chile **69** C5 39 46S 73 15W
Valdosta Georgia U.S.A. **63** J3 30 51N 83 51W
Valdres *geog. reg.* Norway **79** B3 60 55N 8 40E
Valença Brazil **68** J10 13 22S 39 06W
Valence France **77** C3 44 56N 4 54E
Valencia Spain **77** B2 39 29N 0 24W
Valencia Trinidad and Tobago **66** T10 10 39N 61 12W
Valencia Venezuela **68** D15 10 14N 67 59W
Valencia, Gulf of Spain **77** C2 39 30N 0 20E
Valenciennes France **76** C5 50 22N 3 32E
Valera Venezuela **68** C14 9 21N 70 38W
Valga Estonia **79** F2 57 44N 26 00E
Valier Montana U.S.A. **41** C1 48 19N 112 14W
Valjevo Yugoslavia **81** C3 44 16N 19 56E
Valladolid Mexico **66** G4 20 40N 88 11W
Valladolid Spain **77** B3 41 39N 4 45W
Valle de la Pascua Venezuela **68** D14 9 15N 66 00W
Valledupar Colombia **68** C15 10 31N 73 16W
Valle Grande Bolivia **68** E9 18 30S 64 06W
Vallenar Chile **69** C7 28 36S 70 45W
Valletta Malta **81** B2 35 54N 14 32E
Valley *tn.* Barbados **66** V12 13 07N 59 35W
Valley Stream *tn.* New York U.S.A. **50** D1 40 39N 73 42W
Valmiera Latvia **79** F2 57 32N 25 29E
Valparaíso Chile **69** C6 33 05S 71 40W
Van Turkey **92** F6 38 28N 43 20E
Van Buren Maine U.S.A. **31** A2 47 10N 67 59W
Vancouver Washington U.S.A. **62** B6 45 38N 122 40W
Vänern *l.* Sweden **79** C2 59 00N 13 30E
Vänersborg Sweden **80** B6 58 23N 12 19E
Van Etten New York U.S.A. **64** D5 42 13N 76 33W
Van Gölü *l.* Turkey **92** F6 38 33N 42 46E
Vanna *i.* Norway **79** D5 70 05N 19 50E
Vännäs Sweden **79** D3 63 56N 19 50E
Vannes France **77** B4 47 40N 2 44W
Van Norman Lake California U.S.A. **51** A4 34 17N 118 28W
Vantaa Finland **79** E3 60 20N 24 50E
Vanua Levu *i.* Fiji **114** U16 16 20S 179 00E
Vanua Levu Barrier Reef Fiji **114** U16 17 10S 179 00E
Vanua Mbalavu *i.* Fiji **114** V16 17 15S 178 55W
VANUATU 110 L6
Vanves France **83** B2 48 49N 2 17E
Van Wert Ohio U.S.A. **36** B1 40 53N 84 36W
Var *r.* France **77** D3 43 55N 6 55E
Varanasi India **95** E5 25 20N 83 00E
Varangerfjorden *fj.* Norway **79** G4 70 00N 30 00E
Varangerhalvøya *p.* Norway **79** F5 70 22N 29 40E
Varaždin Croatia **81** C4 46 18N 16 21E
Varberg Sweden **80** B6 57 06N 12 15E
Vardar *r.* Greece **81** D3 41 30N 20 15E
Vardø Norway **79** G5 70 22N 31 06E
Varkhaus Finland **79** F3 62 20N 27 50E
Varna Bulgaria **81** E3 43 12N 27 57E
Värnamo Sweden **80** B6 57 11N 14 03E
Várzea Grande Brazil **68** I11 6 32S 42 05W
Väsby Sweden **80** C6 56 13N 12 37E
Vaslui Romania **81** E4 46 37N 27 46E
Vassar Michigan U.S.A. **36** C4 43 23N 83 33W
Västerås Sweden **79** D2 59 36N 16 32E
Västerdalälven *r.* Sweden **79** C3 61 15N 18 10E
Västervik Sweden **79** D2 57 45N 16 40E
Vasyugan *r.* Russia **89** J7 59 00N 77 00E
Vatnajökull *ice cap* Iceland **79** I6 64 30N 17 00W
Vättern *l.* Sweden **79** C2 58 20N 14 20E
Vatulele *i.* Fiji **114** T15 18 30S 177 38E
Vaucresson France **83** A2 48 51N 2 08E
Växjö Sweden **79** C2 56 52N 14 50E
Vaygach *i.* Russia **89** H10 70 00N 59 00E
Vega *i.* Norway **79** C4 65 38N 11 52E
Vejle Denmark **80** A6 55 43N 9 33E
Velbert Germany **76** J2 51 22N 7 03E
Velebit *mts.* Croatia **81** C3 44 00N 15 00E
Velikaya *r.* Russia **90** B6 57 00N 28 45E
Velikiye-Luki Russia **90** C6 56 19N 30 31E
Veliko Tŭrnovo Bulgaria **81** E3 43 04N 25 39E
Vellore India **95** D2 12 56N 79 09E
Velten Germany **83** E2 52 42N 13 12E
Venézia Italy **81** B4 45 26N 12 20E
VENEZUELA 68 D14
Venezuelan Basin Caribbean Sea **113** B8 15 00N 65 00W
Venta *r.* Latvia/Lithuania **79** E2 56 05N 21 50E
Ventspils Latvia **79** E2 57 22N 21 31E
Ver *r.* England **82** B3 51 43N 0 21W
Veracruz Mexico **66** E3 19 11N 96 10W
Veraval India **94** C4 20 53N 70 28E
Vercelli Italy **81** A4 45 19N 8 26E
Verde *r.* Arizona U.S.A. **62** D3 34 00N 112 00W
Verdun-sur-Meuse France **76** D4 49 10N 5 24E
Vereeniging Republic of South Africa **107** K2 26 41S 27 56E
Verin Spain **77** A3 41 55N 7 26W
Verkhoyansk Russia **89** P9 67 35N 133 25E
Verkhoyansk Range *mts.* Russia **89** O9-P8 65 00N 130 00E
Vermilion Ohio U.S.A. **36** D2 41 24N 82 21W
Vermillion Lake Minnesota U.S.A. **35** B2 42 48N 96 55W
Vermillion Range Minnesota U.S.A. **35** B2 48 00N 91 30W
Vermont *state* U.S.A **63** L5
Vernon Texas U.S.A. **62** G3 34 10N 99 19W
Véroia Greece **81** D3 40 32N 22 11E
Verona Italy **81** B4 45 26N 11 00E
Verrières France **83** B1 48 44N 2 16E

Versailles France 83 A2 48 48N 2 07E
Verviers Belgium 76 D5 50 36N 5 52E
Vestfjorden fj. Norway 79 C4 68 00N 14 50E
Vestmannaeyjar is. Iceland 79 H6 63 28N 20 30W
Vesuvio mt. Italy 81 B3 40 49N 14 26E
Vesuvius see Vesuvio
Vetlanda Sweden 79 D2 57 26N 15 05E
Viangchan (Vientiane) Laos 97 K2 17 59N 102 38E
Viano do Castelo Portugal 77 A3 41 41N 8 50W
Viar r. Spain 77 A2 37 45N 5 50W
Viborg Denmark 80 A6 56 28N 9 25E
Vicecomodoro Marambio r.s. Antarctica 117 64 14S 56 38W
Vicente Guerrero Mexico 66 A6 30 48N 116 00W
Vicenza Italy 81 B4 45 33N 11 32E
Vichy France 77 C4 46 07N 3 25E
Vicksburg Mississippi U.S.A. 63 H3 32 21N 90 51W
Victoria Chile 69 C5 38 20S 72 30W
Victoria Hong Kong U.K. 98 B1 22 16N 114 03E
Victoria Texas U.S.A. 63 G2 28 49N 97 01W
Victoria r. Australia 110 E6 131 30S 17 00S
Victoria state Australia 110 G2/H2
Victoria Falls Zambia/Zimbabwe 107 K4 17 55S 25 51E
Victoria Harbour Hong Kong U.K. 98 C1 22 21N 114 00E
Victoria Island tn. Nigeria 107 W3 6 21N 3 31E
Victoria, Lake East Africa 106 L7 2 00S 33 00E
Victoria Land geog. reg. Antarctica 117 75 00S 157 00E
Victoria Peak Hong Kong U.K. 98 B1 22 17N 114 10E
Victoria West Republic of South Africa 107 J1 31 25S 23 08E
Vidin Bulgaria 81 D3 44 00N 22 50E
Viedma Argentina 69 E4 40 45S 63 00W
Vienna Virginia U.S.A. 64 C1 38 56N 77 17W
Vienna see Wien
Vienne France 77 C4 45 32N 4 54E
Vientiane (Viangchan) Laos 97 K2 17 59N 102 38E
Vierzon France 77 C4 47 14N 2 03E
VIETNAM 99 D6/8
Vigia Brazil 68 H12 0 50S 48 07W
Vigo Spain 77 A3 42 15N 8 44W
Vijayawada India 95 E3 16 34N 80 40E
Vijosë r. Albania 81 D3 40 30N 20 00E
Vikna l. Norway 79 C3 64 55N 10 55E
Vila Vanuatu 110 L6 17 45S 168 18E
Vila Nova de Gaia Portugal 77 A3 41 08N 8 37W
Vila Pedro Brazil 69 P2 22 49S 43 20W
Vila Real Portugal 77 A3 41 17N 7 45W
Vila Velha Brazil 68 I8 20 23S 40 18W
Vilhelmina Sweden 79 D3 64 38N 16 40E
Vilhena Brazil 68 J10 12 40S 60 08W
Villa Constitución Mexico 66 B5 25 05N 111 45W
Villahermosa Mexico 66 F3 18 00N 92 53W
Villa María Argentina 69 E6 32 25S 63 15W
Villa Montes Bolivia 68 E8 21 15S 63 30W
Villanueva Mexico 66 D4 22 24N 102 53W
Villarica Chile 69 C5 39 15S 72 15W
Villarrobledo Spain 77 B2 39 16N 2 36W
Villa Unión Argentina 69 D7 29 27S 62 46W
Villa Unión Mexico 66 C4 23 10N 106 12W
Villavicencio Colombia 68 C13 4 09N 73 38W
Villefranche-sur-Saône France 77 C4 46 00N 4 43E
Villejuif France 83 B2 48 47N 2 23E
Villeneuve St. Georges France 83 B1 48 43N 2 27E
Villeneuve-sur-Lot France 77 C3 44 25N 0 43E
Villeparisis France 83 C2 48 56N 2 37E
Villeurbanne France 77 D4 45 46N 4 54E
Vilnius Lithuania 80 E5 54 40N 25 19E
Vilnya r. Lithuania 80 D5 54 00N 25 00E
Vilyuy r. Russia 89 O8 64 00N 123 00E
Vilyuysk Russia 89 O8 63 46N 121 35E
Viña del Mar Chile 69 C6 33 02S 71 35W
Vinaroz Spain 77 C3 40 29N 0 28E
Vincennes France 83 B2 48 51N 2 27E
Vincennes Indiana U.S.A. 63 I4 38 42N 87 30W
Vindelälven r. Sweden 79 D4 65 15N 18 15E
Vindhya Range mts. India 95 C4 23 00N 75 00E
Vineland New Jersey U.S.A. 64 E2 39 29N 75 02W
Vineyard Sound Massachusetts U.S.A. 65 K4 41 30N 70 40W
Vinh Vietnam 99 D7 18 42N 105 41E
Vinkovci Croatia 81 C4 45 16N 18 49E
Vinnitsa Ukraine 90 B4 49 11N 28 30E
Vipiteno Italy 81 B4 46 54N 11 27E
Virgin r. U.S.A. 62 D4 37 00N 114 00W
Virginia Minnesota U.S.A. 63 H6 47 30N 92 28W
Virginia state U.S.A. 63 K4 38 00N 77 00W
Virginia Beach tn. Virginia U.S.A. 63 K4 36 51N 75 59W
Virgin Islands West Indies 67 L3 18 00N 64 30W
Virovitica Croatia 81 C4 45 50N 17 25E
Vis i. Croatia 68 C3 43 00N 16 00E
Visby Sweden 79 D2 57 32N 18 15E
Viseu Portugal 77 A3 40 40N 7 55W
Vishakhapatnam India 95 E3 17 42N 83 24E
Vitebsk Belarus 90 C6 55 10N 30 14E
Viterbo Italy 81 B3 42 24N 12 06E
Vitichi Bolivia 68 D8 20 14S 65 22W
Viti Levu i. Fiji 114 T15 18 10S 177 55E
Vitim Russia 89 N7 59 28N 112 35E
Vitim r. Russia 89 N7 58 00N 113 00E
Vitória Brazil 68 I8 20 20S 40 18W
Vitoria Spain 77 B3 42 51N 2 40W
Vitória da Conquista Brazil 68 I10 14 53S 40 52W
Vitry-le-François France 76 C4 48 44N 4 36E
Vitry-sur-Seine France 83 B2 48 47N 2 24E
Vityaz Trench Pacific Ocean 114 G7 9 30S 170 00E
Vivi r. Russia 89 L9 61 00N 96 00E
Vize i. Russia 89 J11 79 30N 77 00E
Vizianagaram India 95 E3 18 07N 83 30E
Vladikavkaz (Ordzhonikidze) Russia 90 F3 43 02N 44 43E
Vladimir Russia 90 E6 56 08N 40 25E
Vladimir Volynskiy Ukraine 80 D5 50 51N 24 19E
Vladivostok Russia 89 P4 43 09N 131 53E
Vlissingen Netherlands 76 C5 51 27N 3 35E
Vlorë Albania 81 C3 40 29N 19 29E
Vltava r. Czechoslovakia 81 B4 49 00N 14 00E
Vokhma r. Russia 90 F6 58 00N 45 30E
Volga r. Russia 90 F4 47 30N 46 30E
Volgodonsk Russia 90 E4 47 35N 42 08E
Volgograd Russia 90 E4 48 45N 44 30E
Volgogradskoye Vodokhranilishche res. Russia 90 F4 50 00N 45 30E
Volkhov r. Russia 90 C6 59 00N 31 30E
Vologda Russia 90 D6 59 10N 39 55E
Vólos Greece 81 D2 39 22N 22 57E
Vol'sk Russia 90 F5 52 04N 47 22E
Volta Redonda Brazil 69 I8 22 31S 44 05W
Volta, Lake Ghana 106 E9 7 30N 0 30W
Volturno r. Italy 81 B3 41 00N 14 00E
Volzhskiy Russia 90 E4 48 48N 44 45E
Vopnafjördur Iceland 79 J7 65 46N 14 50W
Vorίai Sporadhes is. Greece 81 D2 39 00N 24 00E
Vorkuta Russia 89 I9 67 27N 64 00E
Vorna r. Russia 90 E5 52 00N 42 30E
Voronezh Russia 90 D5 51 40N 39 13E
Voroshilovgrad see Lugansk
Vørterkaka Nunatak mt. Antarctica 117 71 45S 32 00E
Võrtsjärv l. Estonia 79 F2 58 15N 26 10E
Võru Estonia 79 F2 57 46N 26 52E
Vosges mts. France 76-77 C4 48 10N 6 50E
Voss Norway 79 B3 60 38N 6 25E
Vostochnyy Russia 89 P4 42 52N 132 56E
Vostok r.s. Antarctica 117 78 27S 106 51E
Votkinsk Russia 91 G6 57 00N 54 00E
Votkinskoye Vodokhranilishche res. Russia 91 H6 57 00N 55 30E
Vouga r. Portugal 77 A3 40 45N 8 15W
Voxnan Sweden 79 D3 61 22N 15 39E
Vrangelya (Wrangel) i. Russia 89 T10 61 30N 180 00
Vranje Yugoslavia 81 D3 42 33N 21 54E
Vratsa Bulgaria 81 D3 43 12N 23 32E
Vrbas r. Bosnia-Herzegovina 81 C3 44 00N 17 00E
Vršac Yugoslavia 81 D4 45 07N 21 19E
Vryburg Republic of South Africa 107 J2 26 57S 24 44E
Vukovar Croatia 81 C4 45 19N 19 01E
Vunisea Fiji 114 U15 19 04S 178 09E
Vung Tau Vietnam 99 D6 10 21N 107 04E
Vyatka r. Russia 90 F6 58 00N 49 00E
Vyaz'ma Russia 90 C6 55 12N 34 17E
Vyborg Russia 90 B7 60 45N 28 41E
Vychegda r. Russia 90 F7 62 00N 48 00E
Vyshniy-Volochek Russia 90 C6 57 34N 34 23E

W

Wabash r. North America 63 I4 38 00N 87 30W
Wachusett Reservoir Massachusetts U.S.A. 65 J5 42 23 71 45W
Waco Texas U.S.A. 63 G3 31 33N 97 10W
Wadayama Japan 100 F2 35 22N 134 49E
W.D. Boyce Regional Park Pennsylvania U.S.A. 53 E1 40 27N 79 28W
Waddeneilanden (West Frisian Islands) Netherlands 76 C5 53 25N 5 15E
Waddenzee sea Netherlands 76 C5 53 15N 5 15E
Wadi al Masi lah r. Yemen Republic 93 H2 16 00N 50 00E
Wadi Araba r. Israel 92 O10 30 30N 35 10E
Wadi el'Arish r. Egypt 92 N10 30 05N 33 50E
Wâdi el Gafra Egypt 107 R2 30 16N 31 46E
Wadi Halfa Sudan 92 D3 21 55N 31 20E
Wad Medani Sudan 92 D1 14 24N 33 30E
Waesch, Mount Antarctica 117 77 00S 127 30W
Wagga Wagga Australia 110 H2 35 07S 147 24E
Wagin Australia 110 B3 33 20S 117 15E
Waglan Island Hong Kong U.K. 98 C1 22 10N 114 18E
Wah Pakistan 95 C6 33 50N 72 44E
Waha Libya 106 J13 28 10N 19 57E
Wahiawa Hawaiian Islands 115 X18 21 35N 158 05W
Wahpeton North Dakota U.S.A. 63 G6 46 16N 96 36W
Waialua Hawaiian Islands 115 X18 21 35N 158 08W
Waigeo i. Indonesia 99 I3 0 00 131 00E
Waihi New Zealand 111 C3 37 22S 175 51E
Waikaremoana, Lake New Zealand 111 C3 38 50S 178 40E
Waikato New Zealand 111 C3 38 00S 175 30E
Wailuku Hawaiian Islands 115 Y18 20 54N 156 30W
Waimate New Zealand 111 B2 44 45S 171 03E
Wainwright Alaska U.S.A. 10 D7 70 39N 160 10W
Waipawa New Zealand 111 C3 39 48S 176 36E
Wairoa New Zealand 111 C3 39 03S 177 25E
Waitaki r. New Zealand 111 B2 44 30S 170 30E
Waitara New Zealand 111 B3 38 59S 174 13E
Wajima Japan 100 C2 37 23N 136 53E
Wajir Kenya 106 N8 1 46N 40 05E
Wakasa-wan b. Japan 100 C2 35 40N 135 30E
Wakatipu, Lake New Zealand 111 A1 45 00S 168 50E
Wakayama Japan 100 G1 34 12N 135 10E
Wakayama pref. Japan 100 G1 34 13N 135 20E
Wake Island Pacific Ocean 114 G10 19 18N 166 36E
Wakefield Massachusetts U.S.A. 52 B3 42 29N 71 04W
Wakefield Rhode Island U.S.A. 65 J4 41 26N 71 30W
Wakkanai Japan 100 D4 45 26N 141 43E
Wako Japan 101 B4 35 46N 139 37E
Wałbrzych Poland 80 C5 50 48N 16 19E
Walden Pond Massachusetts U.S.A. 52 C3 42 30N 70 45W
Walden Pond Reservation Massachusetts U.S.A. 52 A2 42 26N 71 26W
Wales Alaska U.S.A. 100 B6 65 38N 168 09W
Wales United Kingdom 78
Walhalla North Dakota U.S.A. 39 B1 48 57N 97 54W
Walker Lake Nevada U.S.A. 62 C4 38 40N 118 43W
Wallaroo Australia 110 F3 33 57S 137 36E
Walla Walla Washington U.S.A. 62 C6 46 05N 118 18W
Wallingford Connecticut U.S.A. 65 H4 41 28N 72 49W
Walnut Creek California U.S.A. 49 C3 37 53N 122 03W
Walnut Creek tn. California U.S.A. 49 C3 37 55N 122 03W
Walsall England 78 J4 52 35N 1 58W
Walsenburg Colorado U.S.A. 62 F4 37 36N 104 48W
Walsum Germany 76 G3 51 32N 6 41E
Waltham Massachusetts U.S.A. 52 B2 42 23N 71 14W
Waltham Forest bor. Greater London England 82 C3 51 36N 0 00
Walthamstow England 82 C3 51 34N 0 01W
Walton-on-Thames England 82 B2 51 24N 0 25W
Waltrop Germany 76 K3 51 37N 7 25E
Walvis Bay tn. Namibia 107 H3 22 59S 14 31E
Walvis Ridge Atlantic Ocean 113 I14 30 00S 3 00E
Walyevo Fiji 114 V16 17 35S 179 58W
Wamba r. Zaïre 107 I6 6 30S 17 30E
Wanaka, Lake New Zealand 111 A2 44 30S 169 00E
Wandsworth bor. Greater London England 82 C2 51 27N 0 11W
Wanganui New Zealand 111 C3 39 56S 175 02E
Wanganui r. New Zealand 111 C3 39 30S 175 00E
Wangaratta Australia 110 H2 36 22S 146 20E
Wang Chau i. Hong Kong U.K. 98 D1 22 20N 114 22E
Wang Toi Shan Hong Kong U.K. 98 B2 22 26N 114 05E
Wanheim Germany 76 H2 51 23N 6 45E
Wanne-Eickel Germany 76 J3 51 31N 7 09E
Wannsee Germany 83 E1 52 24N 13 09E
Wanstead England 82 D3 51 34N 0 02E
Wanxian China 97 L5 30 54N 108 20E
Wappingers Falls tn. New York U.S.A. 65 G4 41 36N 73 55W
Warangal India 95 D3 18 00N 79 35E
Ware River Massachusetts U.S.A. 65 H5 42 15N 72 20W
Warnow r. Germany 63 B2 53 00N 12 00E
Warrego r. Australia 110 H4 27 30S 146 00E
Warren Michigan U.S.A. 52 E2 42 30N 83 02W
Warren Ohio U.S.A. 36 F2 41 15N 80 49W
Warren Pennsylvania U.S.A. 64 A4 41 52N 79 09W
Warrnambool Australia 110 G2 38 23S 142 03E
Warroad Minnesota U.S.A. 39 B1 48 54N 95 20W
Warsaw see Warszawa
Warszawa (Warsaw) Poland 80 D5 52 15N 21 00E
Warta r. Poland 80 C5 52 00N 17 00E
Waruha r. India 95 D4 20 30N 79 00E
Warwick Australia 110 I4 28 12S 152 00E
Warwick New York U.S.A. 65 F4 41 15N 74 21W
Warwick Rhode Island U.S.A. 65 J4 41 42N 71 23W
Washburn Wisconsin U.S.A. 35 B2 46 41N 90 53W
Washington state U.S.A. 62 B6 47 00N 120 00W
Washington County Pennsylvania U.S.A. 53 D1 40 18N 80 06W
Washington Crossing Pennsylvania U.S.A. 64 F3 40 17N 74 53W
Washington D.C. District of Columbia U.S.A. 64 C1 38 55N 77 00W
Washington Park Illinois U.S.A. 53 B2 41 48N 87 37W
Wash, The b. England 78 L4 52 55N 0 10E
Watampone Indonesia 99 G3 4 33S 120 20E
Waterbury Connecticut U.S.A. 65 G4 41 33NB 73 03W
Waterfall Australia 111 G1 34 08S 151 00E
Waterford Irish Republic 78 D4 52 15N 7 06W
Waterford New York U.S.A. 65 G5 42 46N 73 42W
Waterloo Iowa U.S.A. 63 H5 42 30N 92 20W
Waterloo New York U.S.A. 64 D5 42 55N 76 53W
Waterloo Trinidad and Tobago 66 T9 10 28N 61 28W
Watersmeet Michigan U.S.A. 35 C2 46 28N 89 10W
Watertown Connecticut U.S.A. 65 G4 41 32N 73 08W
Watertown Massachusetts U.S.A. 52 B2 42 21N 71 11W
Watertown New York U.S.A. 63 K5 43 57N 75 56W
Watertown South Dakota U.S.A. 63 G5 44 54N 97 08W
Waterville Maine U.S.A. 63 M5 44 34N 69 41W
Waterville New York U.S.A. 64 E5 42 55N 75 24W
Waterville Ohio U.S.A. 36 C2 41 29N 83 44W
Watford Hertfordshire England 82 B3 51 39N 0 24W
Watkins Glen New York U.S.A. 64 D5 42 23N 76 53W
Wattenscheid Germany 76 J2 51 27N 7 07E
Wau Papua New Guinea 110 H8 7 22S 146 40E
Wau Sudan 106 K9 7 40N 28 04E
Waukegan Illinois U.S.A. 63 I5 42 21N 87 52W
Waukesha Wisconsin U.S.A. 63 I5 43 01N 88 14W
Wausau Wisconsin U.S.A. 63 I5 44 58N 89 40W
Waveney r. England 78 M4 52 30N 1 30E
Waverly New York U.S.A. 64 D5 42 01N 76 33W
Waycross Georgia U.S.A. 63 J3 31 12N 82 22W
Wayland Massachusetts U.S.A. 52 A2 42 22N 71 22W
Wayland New York U.S.A. 64 C5 42 33N 77 36W
Wayne Michigan U.S.A. 52 D2 42 16N 83 26W
Wayne New Jersey U.S.A. 50 A2 40 55N 74 15W
Wayne County Michigan U.S.A. 52 F2 42 11N 82 26W
Waynesboro Pennsylvania U.S.A. 64 C2 39 45N 77 36W
Weald, The geog. reg. England 78 L3 51 05N 0 25E
Wear r. Durham England 78 J6 54 40N 1 50W
Webster Massachusetts U.S.A. 65 J5 42 04N 71 53W
Webster New York U.S.A. 64 C6 43 13N 77 27W
Weddell Sea Southern Ocean 117 71 00S 40 00W
Wedding Germany 83 F2 52 33N 13 21E
Weedville Pennsylvania U.S.A. 64 B4 41 17N 78 30W
Weiden Germany 76 E4 49 40N 12 10E
Weifang China 97 N6 36 44N 119 10E
Weigelstown Pennsylvania U.S.A. 64 D2 39 59N 76 47W
Wei He r. China 97 L5 34 00N 106 00E
Weimar Germany 76 E5 50 59N 11 20E
Weipa Australia 110 G7 12 35S 141 56E
Weirton West Virginia U.S.A. 63 J5 40 24N 80 37W
Weissenfels Germany 76 E5 51 12N 11 58E
Wejherowo Poland 80 C5 54 36N 18 12E
Welland r. England 78 K4 52 50N 0 00
Wellesly Massachusetts U.S.A. 52 A2 42 18N 71 18W
Wellesley Islands Australia 110 F6 16 30S 139 00E
Wellfleet Massachusetts U.S.A. 65 K4 41 56N 70 01W
Wellington Kansas U.S.A. 63 G4 37 17N 97 25W
Wellington New Zealand 111 B2 41 17S 174 47E
Wellington Ohio U.S.A. 36 D2 41 11N 82 13W
Wells Maine U.S.A. 65 K6 43 20N 70 35W
Wellsboro Pennsylvania U.S.A. 64 C4 41 45N 77 18W
Wellsford New Zealand 111 B3 36 16S 174 32E
Wellsville New York U.S.A. 64 C5 42 07N 77 56W
Wels Austria 81 B4 48 10N 14 02E
Wembley England 82 B3 51 33N 0 18W
Wensum r. England 78 M4 52 45N 1 10E
Wenyu He r. China 101 H2 40 02N 116 32E
Wenzhou China 97 N4 28 02N 120 40E
Werder Germany 83 D1 52 23N 12 56E
Wernersville Pennsylvania U.S.A. 64 D3 40 19N 76 06W
Wertach r. Germany 76 H1 48 00N 10 00E
Weser r. Germany 76 D5 53 00N 8 00E
West Antarctica geog. reg. Antarctica 117 80 00S 120 00W
West Australian Basin Indian Ocean 112 I4 J5 20 00S 100 00E
West Bank territory Israel 92 O11 32 00N 35 00E
West Bengal admin. India 95 F4 22 00N 88 00E
West Branch Michigan U.S.A. 36 B5 44 16N 84 14W
West Branch Delaware River r. New York U.S.A. 64 E5 42 15N 75 00W
West Branch Susquehanna River Pennsylvania U.S.A. 64 B4 41 00N 78 00W
Westby Montana U.S.A. 40 C1 48 32N 104 06W
West Caroline Basin Pacific Ocean 114 D8 3 00N 136 00E
Westchester Illinois U.S.A. 53 A2 41 50N 87 53W
West Chester Pennsylvania U.S.A. 64 E2 39 58N 75 37W
West Covina California U.S.A. 51 C3 34 04N 117 56W
West Dvina see Zap Dvina
Westerly Rhode Island U.S.A. 65 J4 41 22N 71 50W
Western Australia state Australia 110 C4/C5 25 00S 117 00E
Western Desert Egypt 102 30 00N 30 00E
Western Ghats mts. India 95 C3/C2 15 30N 74 00E
WESTERN SAHARA 106 C12
WESTERN SAMOA 114/115 I6
Western Sayan mts. Russia 91 O5 52 30N 92 30E
Western Springs Illinois U.S.A. 53 A2 41 48N 87 54W
Western Yamuna Canal India 94 L4 28 40N 77 08E
Westerwald geog. reg. Germany 76 D5 50 00N 8 00E
West European Basin Atlantic Ocean 113 G11 47 00N 18 00W
West Falkland i. Falkland Islands 69 E2/F2 51 00S 60 40W
Westfield Massachusetts U.S.A. 65 H5 42 07N 72 45W
West Frisian Islands see Waddeneilanden
West Grand Lake Maine U.S.A. 31 A2 45 15N 68 00W
West Ham England 82 D3 51 32N 0 01E
Westhope North Dakota U.S.A. 39 A1 48 56N 101 02W
West Hurley New York U.S.A. 65 F4 41 59N 74 06W
West Ice Shelf Antarctica 117 66 00S 85 00E
West Indies is. Caribbean Sea 67 J4/K4 22 00N 69 00W
West Kingsdown Kent England 82 D2 51 20N 0 16E
Westlake Ohio U.S.A. 36 E2 41 25N 81 54W
West Lamma Channel Hong Kong U.K. 98 B1 22 10N 114 00E
Westland Michigan U.S.A. 52 D2 42 18N 83 25W
West Los Angeles California U.S.A. 51 A3 34 02N 118 25W
West Marianas Basin Pacific Ocean 114 D9 16 00N 137 30E
West Memphis Arkansas U.S.A. 63 A4 35 09N 90 11W
Westminster California U.S.A. 51 C2 33 45N 117 59W
Westminster Maryland U.S.A. 64 C2 39 35N 77 00W
Westminster bor. England 82 C2 51 30N 0 09W
Westmoreland County Pennsylvania U.S.A. 53 E1 40 18N 79 48W
Weston Massachusetts U.S.A. 52 A2 42 21N 71 18W
West Palm Beach tn. Florida U.S.A. 63 J2 26 42N 80 05W
West Plains tn. Missouri U.S.A. 63 H4 36 44N 91 51W
West Point tn. New York U.S.A. 65 G4 41 23N 73 58W
Westport Connecticut U.S.A. 65 G4 41 09N 73 22W
Westport Irish Republic 78 B5 53 48N 9 32W
Westray i. Scotland 78 I11 59 18N 3 00W
West Rift Valley Africa 102 0 00 30 00E
West Scotia Basin Southern Ocean 117 58 00S 52 00W
West Siberian Lowland Russia 91 L7 M6 60 00N 75 00E
West Springfield Massachusetts U.S.A. 65 H5 42 06N 72 38W
West View Pennsylvania U.S.A. 53 D2 40 32N 80 03W
West Virginia state U.S.A. 63 J4 39 00N 81 00W
West Winfield New York U.S.A. 64 E5 42 53N 75 16W
Wetar i. Indonesia 99 H2 7 30S 126 30E
Wewak Papua New Guinea 110 G9 3 35S 143 35E
Wexford Irish Republic 78 E4 52 20N 6 27W
Wey r. England 82 B2 51 18N 0 30W
Weybridge England 82 B2 51 22N 0 28W
Weymouth England 78 I2 50 37N 2 25W
Weymouth Massachusetts U.S.A. 52 C1 42 14N 71 58W
Whakatane New Zealand 111 C3 37 56S 177 00E
Whangarei New Zealand 111 B3 35 43S 174 20E
Wharfe r. England 78 53 50N 1 50W
Wharton Basin Indian Ocean 112 I5 J5 15 00S 100 00E
Whatcom, Lake Washington U.S.A. 42 H4 48 40N 122 20W
Wheeler Lake Alabama U.S.A. 63 I3 34 00N 87 00W
Wheeling West Virginia U.S.A. 63 J5 40 05N 80 43W
Whidbey Island Washington U.S.A. 42 H4 48 20N 122 40W
White r. U.S.A. 63 H4 35 00N 92 00W
Whitefish Montana U.S.A. 43 F1 48 25N 114 21W
Whitefish Bay Michigan U.S.A./Ontario Canada 36 B7 46 40N 84 45W
Whitehaven England 78 H6 54 33N 3 35W
White Nile see Bahr el Abiad
White Nile see Bahr el Jebel
White Nile Dam Sudan 92 D2 14 18N 32 30E
White Oak Park Pennsylvania U.S.A. 53 E1 40 20N 79 48W
White Plains New York U.S.A. 65 G4 41 02N 73 46W
White Sea Russia 88 F9 66 00N 37 30E
White Volta r. Ghana 106 E10 9 30N 1 30W
Whitewater tn. Montana U.S.A. 40 B1 48 46N 107 38W
Whitewater Creek Montana U.S.A./Canada 40 B1 48 50N 107 40W
Whiting Illinois U.S.A. 53 C1 41 41N 87 32W
Whitmans Ponds Massachusetts U.S.A. 52 C1 42 05N 70 55W
Whitney Point tn. New York U.S.A. 64 E5 42 20N 75 58W
Whitney Point Lake New York U.S.A. 64 E5 42 20N 76 00W
Whitney Woods Reservoir Massachusetts U.S.A. 52 C1 42 14N 70 52W
Whittier California U.S.A. 51 B2 33 58N 118 02W
Whyalla Australia 110 F3 33 04S 137 34E
Wichita Kansas U.S.A. 63 G4 37 43N 97 20W
Wichita r. Texas U.S.A. 62 F3 33 00N 100 00W
Wichita Falls tn. Texas U.S.A. 62 G3 33 55N 98 30W
Wick Higland Scotland 78 H10 58 26N 3 06W
Wickliffe Ohio U.S.A. 36 E2 41 38N 81 25W
Wicklow Mountains Irish Republic 78 E5 53 00N 6 20W
Wien (Vienna) Austria 81 C4 48 13N 16 22E
Wiener Neustadt Austria 81 C4 47 49N 16 15E
Wieprz r. Poland 80 D5 51 00N 23 00E
Wiesbaden Germany 76 D5 50 05N 8 15E
Wiessensee l. Germany 83 F2 52 35N 13 28E
Wigan England 78 I5 53 33N 2 38W
Wilcox Pennsylvania U.S.A. 64 B4 41 36N 78 40W
Wildau Germany 83 G1 52 18N 13 38E
Wildcat Canyon Regional Park California U.S.A. 49 B3 37 57N 122 17W
Wildcat Creek California U.S.A. 49 B3 37 57N 122 19W
Wildrose North Dakota U.S.A. 40 C1 48 39N 103 11W
Wildwood New Jersey U.S.A. 65 F1 38 59N 74 49W
Wilhelmshaven Germany 76 D5 53 32N 8 07E
Wilkes-Barre Pennsylvania U.S.A. 64 E4 41 15N 75 50W
Wilkes Land geog. reg. Antarctica 117 68 00S 120 00E
Wilkinsburg Pennsylvania U.S.A. 53 E1 40 27N 79 53W
Willard New York U.S.A. 64 D5 42 38N 76 50W
Will County Illinois U.S.A. 53 A1 41 38N 87 59W

Willemstad Curaçao **67** K2 12 12N 68 56W
Willesden England **82** C3 51 33N 0 14W
Williams Minnesota U.S.A. **39** C1 48 47N 94 56W
Williamsport Pennsylvania U.S.A. **64** C4 41 16N 77 03W
Williamstown New Jersey U.S.A. **64** F2 39 41N 74 59W
Willimantic Connecticut U.S.A. **65** H4 41 43N 72 12W
Williston North Dakota U.S.A. **62** F6 48 09N 103 39W
Willoughby Hills Ohio U.S.A. **36** E2 41 35N 81 29W
Willow Creek Montana U.S.A. **41** C1 48 55N 111 30W
Willow Grove Pennsylvania U.S.A. **64** E3 40 08N 75 7W
Willow River Michigan U.S.A. **36** D4 43 50N 82 58W
Willow Springs *tn.* Missouri U.S.A. **63** H4 36 59N 91 59W
Willmar Minnesota U.S.A. **63** G6 45 06N 95 03W
Wilmersdorf Germany **83** F1 52 28N 13 16E
Wilmette Illinois U.S.A. **53** A3 42 04N 87 43W
Wilmington Delaware U.S.A. **64** E2 39 46N 75 31W
Wilmington North Carolina U.S.A. **63** K3 34 14N 77 55W
Wilmington Vermont U.S.A. **65** H5 42 52N 72 53W
Wilson North Carolina U.S.A. **63** K4 35 43N 77 56W
Wiluna Australia **110** C4 26 37S 120 12E
Wimbledon England **82** C2 51 25N 0 13W
Winchendon Massachusetts U.S.A. **65** H5 42 41N 72 04W
Winchester England **78** J3 51 04N 1 19W
Winchester Massachusetts U.S.A. **52** B2 42 26N 71 08W
Winchester New Hampshire U.S.A. **65** H5 42 46N 72 24W
Winchester Virginia U.S.A. **64** B2 39 11N 78 12W
Windber Pennsylvania U.S.A. **64** B3 40 16N 78 51W
Windhoek Namibia **107** I3 22 34S 17 06E
Wind River Ranges *mts.* Wyoming U.S.A. **62** E5 43 00N 109 00W
Windsor England **82** A2 51 29N 0 38W
Windsor Connecticut U.S.A. **65** H4 41 52N 72 38W
Windsor Locks Connecticut U.S.A. **65** H4 41 56N 72 37W
Windward Islands Lesser Antilles **67** L2 12 30N 62 00W
Windward Passage *sd.* Cuba/Haiti **67** J3/J4 20 00N 73 00W
Winnemucca Nevada U.S.A. **62** C5 40 58N 117 45W
Winnetka Illinois U.S.A. **53** B3 42 06N 87 46W
Winona Minnesota U.S.A. **63** H5 44 02N 91 37W
Winslow Arizona U.S.A. **62** D4 35 01N 110 43W
Winsted Connecticut U.S.A. **65** G4 41 55N 73 04W
Winston-Salem North Carolina U.S.A. **63** J4 36 05N 80 18W
Winterthur Switzerland **77** D4 47 30N 8 45E
Winthrop Massachusetts U.S.A. **52** C2 42 23N 70 59W
Winthrop Washington U.S.A. **42** H4 48 29N 120 11W
Winton Australia **110** G5 22 22S 143 00E
Wisconsin *state* U.S.A. **63** H6 45 00N 90 00W
Wisconsin River Wisconsin U.S.A. **63** H6 4500N 90 00W
Wisła *r.* Poland **80** C5 53 00N 19 00E
Wisłok *r.* Poland **80** D5 50 00N 22 00E
Wismar Germany **76** E5 53 54N 11 28E
Witham *r.* England **78** K5 53 05N 0 10W
Witten Germany **76** K2 51 25N 7 19E
Wittenberg Germany **76** E5 51 53N 12 39E
Wittenberge Germany **76** E5 52 59N 11 45E
Włocławek Poland **80** C5 52 39N 19 01E
Woburn Massachusetts U.S.A. **52** B2 42 27N 71 09W
Woking England **82** A2 51 20N 0 34W
Wolcott New York U.S.A. **64** D6 43 14N 76 51W
Wolf Lake State Park and Conservation Indiana U.S.A. **53** C1 41 40N 87 30W
Wolfsberg Austria **81** B4 46 50N 14 50E
Wolfsburg Germany **76** E5 52 27N 10 49E
Wollongong Australia **110** I3 34 25S 150 52E
Wolverton England **78** I4 52 04N 0 50W
Wompah Australia **110** G4 29 04S 142 05E
Wompatuck State Park Massachusetts U.S.A. **52** C1 42 12N 70 52W
Wong Chuk Hang Hong Kong U.K. **98** C1 22 15N 114 10E
Wong Chuk Yuen Hong Kong U.K. **98** B2 22 26N 114 06E
Wŏnju South Korea **97** P6 37 24N 127 52E
Wŏnsan North Korea **97** P6 39 07N 127 26E
Woodbine New Jersey U.S.A. **64** F2 39 14N 74 49W
Woodbridge New Jersey U.S.A. **50** A1 40 33N 74 16W
Woodbury Connecticut U.S.A. **65** G4 41 32N 73 12W
Woodbury New Jersey U.S.A. **64** E2 39 50N 75 09W
Woodford England **82** D3 51 37N 0 02E
Woodlark Island Papua New Guinea **110** I8 9 00S 152 30E
Woodport New Jersey U.S.A. **65** F3 40 59N 74 37W
Woodside California U.S.A. **49** B1 37 26N 122 15W
Woods, Lake of the Canada/USA **34** B2 49 00N 94 00W
Woodstock Virginia U.S.A. **64** B1 38 55N 78 31W
Woodstown New Jersey U.S.A. **64** E2 39 39N 75 19W
Woodville New Zealand **111** C2 40 20S 175 54E
Woodward Oklahoma U.S.A. **62** G4 36 26N 99 25W
Woollahra Australia **111** H2 33 53S 151 15E
Woolwich England **82** D2 51 29N 0 04E
Woonsocket Rhode Island U.S.A. **65** J5 42 00N 71 30W
Wooster Ohio U.S.A. **36** E1 40 46N 81 57W
Worcester England **78** I4 52 11N 2 13W
Worcester Massachusetts U.S.A. **65** J5 42 17N 71 48W
Worcester New York U.S.A. **65** F5 42 36N 74 44W
Worcester Republic of South Africa **107** I1 33 39S 19 26E
Workington England **78** H6 54 39N 3 33W
Worland Wyoming U.S.A. **62** E5 44 01N 107 58W
Woronora Reservoir Australia **111** F1 34 07S 150 56E
Woronora River Australia **111** G1 34 07S 151 00E
Worth Illinois U.S.A. **53** A1 41 40N 87 48W
Worthing Barbados **66** V12 13 05N 59 35W
Worthing England **78** K2 50 48N 0 23W
Worthington Minnesota U.S.A. **63** G5 43 37N 95 36W
Wrangell Alaska U.S.A. **42** B3 56 28N 132 23W
Wrangell Island Alaska U.S.A. **42** B3 56 25N 132 05W
Wrangell Mountains Alaska U.S.A. **44** C3 62 00N 143 00W
Wrangell St. Elias National Park Alaska U.S.A. **44** C3 63 00N 143 00W
Wrath, Cape Scotland **78** G10 58 37N 5 01W
Wrexham Wales **78** H5 53 03N 3 00W
Wright Peak Antarctica **117** 73 15S 94 00W
Wrights Corners New York U.S.A. **64** B6 43 12N 78 40W
Wrightsville Pennsylvania U.S.A. **64** D3 40 02N 76 3W
Wrocław Poland **80** C5 51 05N 17 00E
Wuhai China **97** L6 39 40N 106 40E
Wuhan China **97** M5 30 35N 114 19E
Wuhu China **97** N5 31 23N 118 25E
Wukari Nigeria **106** G9 7 49N 9 49E
Wuppertal Germany **76** D5 51 15N 7 10E
Wurtsboro New York U.S.A. **65** F4 41 33N 74 29W
Würzburg Germany **76** E4 49 48N 9 57E
Wusul Jiang *(Ussuri) r.* China **97** Q8 47 00N 134 00E
Wutongqiao China **97** K4 29 21N 103 48E
Wuxi China **97** N5 31 35N 120 19E
Wuyi Shan *mts.* China **97** N4 26 00N 116 30E
Wuzhou China **97** M3 23 30N 111 21E
Wyandotte Michigan U.S.A. **52** E1 42 11N 83 10W
Wye *r.* England **78** H4 1 58N 2 35W
Wyndham Australia **110** D6 15 30S 128 09E
Wyoming *state* U.S.A. **62** E5 43 00N 108 00W

X

Xaafuun Somalia **106** P10 10 27N 51 15E
Xaidulla China **95** D7 36 27N 77 46E
Xam Nua Laos **97** K3 20 25N 103 50W
Xánthi Greece **81** D3 41 07N 24 56E
Xiaguan China **97** K4 25 33N 100 09E
Xiamen China **97** N3 24 28N 118 05E
Xi'an China **97** L5 34 16N 108 54E
Xiangfan China **97** M5 32 05N 112 03E
Xiangtan China **97** M4 27 48N 112 55E
Xianyang China **97** L5 34 22N 108 42E
Xianyou China **98** E8 25 23N 118 40E
Xieng Khouang Laos **99** C7 19 21N 103 23E
Xigaze China **96** G4 29 18N 88 50E
Xi Jiang *r.* China **97** M3 23 30N 111 00E
Xingtai China **96** M6 37 08N 114 29E
Xining China **97** K6 36 35N 101 55E
Xinjiang Uygur Zizhiqu *(Sinkiang Uighur Autonomous Region) admin.* China **96** F6/G7 41 00N 85 00E
Xinjin China **97** O6 39 25N 121 58E
Xiqing Shan *mts.* China **97** K5 34 00N 102 30E
Xizang Zizhiqu *(Tibet Autonomous Region) admin.* China **96** F5/G5 33 30N 85 00E
Xizhuang China **101** G1 39 51N 116 20E
Xochimiko Mexico **66** E3 19 08N 99 09W
Xuanhua China **97** N7 40 36N 115 01E
Xuchang China **97** M5 34 03N 113 48E
Xuwen China **97** M3 20 25N 110 08E
Xuzhou China **97** N5 34 17N 117 18E

Y

Yaba Nigeria **107** V3 6 29N 3 27E
Yablonovy Range *mts.* Russia **89** M6/N6 51 30N 110 00E
Yakima *r.* Washington U.S.A. **62** B6 47 00N 120 00W
Yakutat Alaska U.S.A. **42** A3 59 29N 139 49W
Yakutat Bay Alaska U.S.A. **42** A3 59 50N 140 00W
Yakutsk Russia **89** O8 62 10N 129 50E
Yalu *r.* China/North Korea **97** P7 42 00N 127 00E
Yamagata Japan **100** D2 38 16N 140 19E
Yamaguchi Japan **100** B1 34 10N 131 28E
Yamal Peninsula Russia **89** I10/J10 72 00N 70 00E
Yamanashi *pref.* Japan **100** K2 35 40N 138 48E
Yamato Japan **101** A2 35 29N 139 27E
Yamato-takada Japan **100** G1 34 31N 135 43E
Yambol Bulgaria **81** E3 42 28N 26 30E
Yamburg Russia **89** J9 68 19N 77 09E
Yamoussoukro Côte d'Ivoire **106** D9 6 50N 5 20W
Yamuna *r.* India **94** L4 28 43N 17 13E
Yamunanagar India **95** D6 30 07N 77 17E
Yana *r.* Russia **89** P9 69 00N 135 00E
Yanbu'al Baçr Saudi Arabia **92** E3 24 07N 38 04E
Yancheng China **97** O5 33 23N 120 10E
Yangon *see* Rangoon
Yangquan China **97** M6 37 52N 113 29E
Yangtse *see* Jinsha Jiang or Chang Jiang
Yanji China **97** P7 42 52N 129 32E
Yanjing China **97** J4 29 01N 98 38E
Yankton South Dakota U.S.A. **63** G5 42 53N 97 24W
Yantai China **97** O6 37 30N 121 22E
Yao Japan **100** C1 34 36N 135 37E
Yaotsu Japan **100** J2 35 29N 137 10E
Yaoundé Cameroon **106** H8 3 51N 11 31E
Yap Islands Pacific Ocean **114** D8 9 30N 138 09E
Yap Trench Pacific Ocean **114** D8 10 00N 139 00E
Yaqui *r.* Mexico **66** C5 28 00N 109 50W
Yaritagua Venezuela **67** K2 10 05N 69 07W
Yarkant He *r.* China **89** J3 36 00N 76 00E
Yarlung Zangbo Jiang *(Tsangpo) r.* China **96** H4 29 00N 92 30E
Yaroslavl' Russia **89** F7 57 34N 39 52E
Yarumal Colombia **68** B14 6 59N 75 25W
Yasawa *i.* Fiji **114** T16 16 50S 177 30E
Yasawa Group *is.* Fiji **114** T16 17 00S 177 40E
Yatsushiro Japan **100** B1 32 32N 130 35E
Yau Ma Tei Hong Kong U.K. **98** C1 22 18N 114 10E
Yau Tong Hong Kong U.K. **98** C1 22 18N 114 14E
Yawatahama Japan **100** B1 33 27N 132 24E
Ya Xian China **97** L2 37 10N 119 55E
Yazd Iran **93** H5 31 54N 54 22E
Yazoo *r.* Mississippi U.S.A. **63** H3 33 00N 90 00W
Ye Myanmar **97** J2 15 15N 97 50E
Yekaterinburg *(Sverdlovsk)* Russia **91** J6 56 52N 60 35E
Yelets Russia **90** D5 52 35N 38 30E
Yell *i.* Shetland Islands Scotland **78** J12 60 35N 1 10W
Yellow Sea *(Huang Hai)* China **97** O6 35 30N 122 30E
Yellowstone *r.* U.S.A. **62** E6 46 00N 108 00W
Yellowstone Lake Wyoming U.S.A. **62** D5 44 30N 110 20W
Yellowstone National Park Wyoming U.S.A. **62** D5 44 00N 11 30W
YEMEN REPUBLIC **92** F2
Yenakiyevo Ukraine **90** D4 48 14N 38 15E
Yenisey *r.* Russia **89** K8 65 00N 85 00E
Yenisey, Gulf of Russia **89** J10/K10 72 30N 80 00E
Yeniseysk Russia **91** P6 58 27N 92 13E
Yeppoon Australia **110** I5 23 05S 150 42E
Yerba Buena Island California U.S.A. **49** B3 37 48N 122 21W
Yerevan Armenia **90** E3 40 10N 44 31E
Yermolayevo Russia **91** H5 52 46N 55 54E
Yerres *r.* France **83** C1 48 40N 2 36E
Yesil *r.* Turkey **92** E7 41 00N 36 25E
Yeu Myanmar **95** H4 22 49N 95 26E
Yevpatoriya Ukraine **90** C4 45 12N 33 20E
Ye Xian China **97** N6 37 10N 119 55E
Yiannitsá Greece **81** D3 40 46N 22 24E
Yibin China **97** K4 28 42N 104 30E
Yichang China **97** M5 30 46N 111 20E
Yinchuan China **97** L6 38 30N 106 19E
Yingkou China **97** O7 40 40N 122 17E
Ying Pun Hong Kong U.K. **98** B2 22 28N 114 06E
Yining China **96** F7 43 50N 81 28E
Yirga 'Alem Ethiopia **106** M9 6 48N 38 22E
Yiyang China **97** M4 28 39N 112 10E
Yoakum Texas U.S.A. **63** G2 29 18N 97 20W
Yogyakarta Indonesia **99** E2 7 48S 110 24E
Yoichi Japan **100** D3 43 14N 140 47E
Yōka Japan **100** F2 35 25N 134 40E
Yokadouma Cameroon **106** I8 3 26N 15 06E
Yōkaichi Japan **100** H2 35 05N 136 11E
Yōkaichiba Japan **100** M2 35 40N 140 30E
Yokkaichi Japan **100** H1 34 58N 136 38E
Yokohama Japan **101** B2 35 27N 139 38E
Yokosuka Japan **100** L2 35 18N 139 39E
Yokote Japan **100** D2 39 20N 140 31E
Yola Nigeria **106** H9 9 14N 12 32E
Yonago Japan **100** B2 35 27N 133 20E
Yonaguni *i.* Japan **98** J7 24 29N 123 00E
Yongchun China **98** E8 25 18N 118 13E
Yonkers New York U.S.A. **50** C2 40 56N 73 52W
Yonne *r.* France **77** C4 48 00N 3 15E
Yorii Japan **100** L3 36 07N 139 12E
York England **78** J5 53 58N 1 05W
York Maine U.S.A. **65** K6 43 00N 70 00W
York Pennsylvania U.S.A. **63** K4 39 57N 76 44W
York, Cape Australia **110** G7 10 42S 142 32E
Yorkshire Wolds hills England **78** K6 54 00N 0 45W
Yoshino-Kumano National Park Japan **100** H1 34 15N 136 00E
Yoshkar-Ola Russia **90** F6 56 38N 47 52E
Yŏsu South Korea **97** P5 34 50N 127 30E
Youghal Irish Republic **78** D3 51 51N 7 50W
You Jiang *r.* China **97** L3 23 30N 107 00E
Younghiogheny River Pennsylvania U.S.A. **53** E1 40 19N 79 51W
Youngstown New York U.S.A. **38** C2 43 14N 79 01W
Youngstown Ohio U.S.A. **63** J5 41 05N 80 40W
Youngsville Pennsylvania U.S.A. **36** G2 41 52N 79 22W
Ypsilanti Michigan U.S.A. **36** C3 42 15N 83 36W
Yser *see* Ijzer
Ystad Sweden **80** B6 55 25N 13 50E
Ytterhogdal Sweden **79** C3 623 10N 14 55E
Yuan Jiang *r.* Asia **84** 30 00N 112 00E
Yüan-li Taiwan **98** G7 24 29N 120 40E
Yüan-lin Taiwan **98** G6 23 57N 120 33E
Yūbari Japan **100** D3 43 04N 141 59E
Yucatan *p.* Mexico **66** G3 19 00N 89 00W
Yucatan Basin Caribbean Sea **115** R9 20 00N 85 00W
Yuci China **97** M6 37 40N 112 44E
Yuen Long Hong Kong U.K. **98** B2 22 26N 114 02E
Yugawara Japan **100** L2 35 09N 139 06E
YUGOSLAVIA **81** C3
Yukagir Plateau Russia **89** R9 66 30N 156 00E
Yü-kitka *l.* Finland **79** F4 66 15N 28 30E
Yukon Delta Alaska U.S.A. **10** C5 62 45N 164 00W
Yukon Flats National Wildlife Refuge Alaska U.S.A. **44** B4 66 30N 147 30W
Yukon River Canada/U.S.A. **44** D3 63 00N 138 50W
Yü-li Taiwan **98** H6 23 22N 121 20E
Yuma Arizona U.S.A. **62** D3 32 40N 114 39W
Yumen China **96** J6 39 54N 97 43E
Yun *(Grand Canal)* China **101** H1 39 54N 116 33E
Yung Shue Wan Hong Kong U.K. **98** B1 22 13N 114 06E
Yung-kang Taiwan **98** G5 23 00N 120 15E
Yura-gawa *r.* Japan **100** G2 35 20N 135 08E
Yurimaguas Peru **68** B11 5 54S 76 07W
Yü Shan *mt.* Taiwan **98** G6 23 25N 120 52E
Yü Shan National Park Taiwan **98** H6 23 15N 121 00E
Yushu China **95** H6 33 06N 96 48E
Yü-weng Tao *i.* Taiwan **98** F6 23 36N 119 30E
Yuzhno-Sakhalinsk Russia **89** Q5 46 58N 142 45E
Yuzhnyy Bug *r.* Ukraine **90** C4 48 00N 30 00E
Yverdon Switzerland **77** D4 46 47N 6 38E
Yvetot France **76** C4 49 37N 0 45E

Z

Zaanstad Netherlands **76** C5 52 27N 4 49E
Zābol Iran **93** J5 31 00N 61 32E
Zabrze Poland **80** C5 50 18N 18 47E
Zacapa Guatemala **66** G3 15 00N 89 30E
Zacatecas Mexico **66** D4 22 48N 102 33W
Zacatecoluca El Salvador **66** G2 13 29N 88 51W
Zadar Croatia **81** C3 44 07N 15 14E
Zafra Spain **77** A2 38 25N 6 25W
Zagań Poland **80** C5 51 37N 15 20E
Zagazig Egypt **92** D5 30 36N 31 30E
Zagorsk *see* Sergiev Posad
Zagreb *(Agram)* Croatia **81** C4 45 48N 15 58E
Zagros Mountains Iran **93** G5 32 45N 48 50E
Zāhedān Iran **93** J4 29 32N 60 54E
Zahlé Lebanon **92** O11 33 50N 35 55E
ZAÏRE **106** J7
Zaïre *(Congo) r.* Zaïre **106** I7 2 00S 17 00E
Zákinthos *i.* Greece **81** D2 38 00N 20 00E
Zakopane Poland **80** C5 49 17N 19 54E
Zalaegerszeg Hungary **81** C4 46 53N 16 51E
Zal'u Romania **81** D4 47 10N 23 04E
Zaliv Kara Bogaz Gol *b.* Turkmenistan **90/1** H4 41 30N 53 30E
Zaltan Libya **106** I13 28 15N 19 52E
Zambeze *(Zambesi) r.* Mozambique **107** L4 16 00S 34 00E
Zambezi *(Zambeze) r.* Zambia/Zimbabwe **107** J4 16 00S 23 00E
Zambezi Zambia **107** J5 13 33S 23 08E
ZAMBIA **107** K5
Zamboanga The Philippines **99** G5 6 55N 122 05E
Zamora Spain **77** A3 41 30N 5 45W
Zamość Poland **80** D5 50 43N 23 15E
Zanderij Surinam **68** F14 5 26N 55 14W
Zanesville Ohio U.S.A. **63** J4 39 55N 82 02W
Zanjan Iran **93** G6 36 40N 48 30E
Zanthus Australia **110** C3 31 01S 123 32E
Zanzibar Tanzania **107** M6 6 10S 39 12E
Zanzibar *i.* Tanzania **107** M6 6 10S 39 13E
Zaozhuang China **97** N5 34 53N 117 38E
Zapadnaya *(West)* **Dvina** *r.* Latvia **79** E2 56 45N 24 30E
Zaporozh'ye Ukraine **90** D4 47 50N 35 10E
Zaporozhye Ukraine **90** D4 47 50N 35 10E
Zaragoza Spain **77** B3 41 39N 0 54W
Zarand Iran **93** I5 30 50N 56 35E
Zaraza Venezuela **68** D14 9 23N 65 20W
Zarembo Island Alaska U.S.A. **42** B3 56 30N 132 50W
Zargun *mt.* Pakistan **94** B6 30 15N 67 11E
Zaria Nigeria **106** G10 11 01N 7 44E
Zarqa Jordan **92** P11 32 04N 36 05E
Zaysan Kazakhstan **91** N4 47 30N 84 57E
Zefat Israel **92** O11 32 57N 35 27E
Zehlendorf Germany **83** F1 52 26N 13 15E
Zell-am-See *tn.* Austria **81** B4 47 19N 12 47E
Zemlya Frantsa-Iosifa *(Franz Josef Land) is.* Russia **89** G12-I12 80 00N 50 00E
Zenica Bosnia-Herzegovina **81** C3 44 11N 17 53E
Zepernick Germany **83** G2 52 41N 13 31E
Zernsdorf Germany **83** G1 52 17N 13 42E
Zeya Russia **89** O6 53 48N 127 14E
Zeya *r.* Russia **89** O6 53 00N 127 30E
Zêzere *r.* Portugal **77** A2 39 50N 8 05W
Zgierz Poland **80** C5 51 52N 19 25E
Zgorzelec Poland **80** C5 51 10N 15 00E
Zhandov *see* Mariupol
Zhangjiakou China **97** M7 40 51N 114 59E
Zhangzhou China **97** N2 24 31N 117 40E
Zhanjiang China **97** M3 21 10N 110 20E
Zharma Kazakhstan **91** N4 48 50N 80 50E
Zhdanov *see* Mariupol
Zhengzhou China **97** M5 34 45N 113 38E
Zhenjiang China **97** N5 32 08N 119 30E
Zhigansk Russia **89** O9 66 48N 123 27E
Zhitomir Ukraine **90** B5 50 18N 28 40E
Zhlobin Belarus **90** B5 52 50N 30 00E
Zhmerinka Ukraine **90** B4 49 00N 28 02E
Zhob Pakistan **94** B6 31 30N 69 30E
Zhonghai *l.* China **101** G1 39 56N 116 22E
Zhuzhou China **97** M4 27 53N 113 07E
Zibo China **97** N6 36 51N 118 01E
Zielona Góra Poland **80** C5 51 57N 15 30E
Zigong China **97** K4 29 25N 104 47E
Ziguinchor Senegal **106** B10 12 35N 16 20W
ZIMBABWE **107** K4
Zinder Nigeria **106** G10 13 46N 8 58E
Ziqudukou China **96** J5 33 03N 95 51E
Zlatoust Russia **91** H6 55 10N 59 38E
Zlúi *(Gottwaldov)* Czechoslovakia **80** C4 49 14N 17 40E
Znojmo Czechoslovakia **80** C4 48 52N 16 04E
Zolochev *Ukraine* **80** D4 49 49N 24 53E
Zomba Malawi **107** M4 15 22S 35 22E
Zouar Chad **106** I12 20 30N 16 30E
Zouérate Mauritania **106** C12 22 44N 12 21W
Zrenjanin Yugoslavia **81** D4 45 22N 20 23E
Zuethener See *l.* Germany **83** G1 52 20N 13 40E
Zújar *r.* Spain **77** A2 38 35N 5 30W
Zunyi China **97** L4 27 35N 106 48E
Zürich Switzerland **77** D4 47 23N 8 33E
Zushi Japan **101** B2 35 17N 139 35E
Zvishavane Zimbabwe **107** L3 20 20S 30 02E
Zwickau Germany **76** E5 50 43N 12 30E
Zwolle Netherlands **76** D5 52 31N 6 06E
Zyardów Poland **80** D5 52 02N 20 28E
Zyryanka Russia **89** R9 65 42N 150 49E
Zyryanovsk Kazakhstan **91** N4 49 45N 84 16E

Land

1. Land and Freshwater Area

PROVINCE OR TERRITORY	LAND (km²)	FRESHWATER (km²)	TOTAL (km²)
Newfoundland	371 690	34 030	405 720
Prince Edward Island	5 660	–	5 660
Nova Scotia	52 840	2 650	55 490
New Brunswick	72 090	1 350	73 440
Quebec	1 356 790	183 890	1 540 680
Ontario	891 190	177 390	1 068 580
Manitoba	548 360	101 590	649 950
Saskatchewan	570 700	81 630	652 330
Alberta	644 390	16 800	661 190
British Columbia	929 730	18 070	947 800
Yukon	478 970	4 480	483 450
Northwest Territories	3 293 020	133 300	3 426 320
Canada	**9 215 430**	**755 180**	**9 970 610**

SOURCE: *Canada Year Book 1992*.

2. Primary Land Cover in Canada

LAND COVER CLASS	PREDOMINANT COVER IN THE CLASS	AREA[a] (km², 000s)	% CANADA TOTAL[b]
Forest and taiga	Closed canopy forest and/or open stands of trees with secondary occurrences of wetland, barren land, or others	4 456	45
Tundra/sparse vegetation	Well-vegetated to sparsely vegetated or barren land, mostly in arctic or alpine environments	2 303	23
Wetland	Treed and non-treed fens, bogs, swamps, marshes, shallow open water, and coastal and shore marshes	1 244	12
Freshwater	Lakes, rivers, streams, and reservoirs	755	8
Cropland	Fenced land (including cropland and pasture land), hedge rows, farms, and orchards	658	6
Rangeland	Generally nonfenced pasture land, grazing land; includes natural grassland that is not necessarily used for agriculture	203	2
Ice/snow	Permanent ice and snow fields (glaciers, ice caps)	272	3
Built-up	Urban and industrial land	79	1
Total		**9 970**	**100**

[a]Includes the area of all land and freshwater. [b]Rounded to the nearest percent. NOTE: Data for this table are derived from satellite imagery and may deviate slightly from other sources of data.
SOURCE: Energy, Mines and Resources Canada (1989). From *The State of Canada's Environment*, published by the authority of the Minister of the Environment and the Minister of Supply and Services Canada, 1991.

3. Land Activity in Canada

LAND ACTIVITY CLASS	PREDOMINANT ACTIVITY IN THE CLASS	AREA (km², 000s)[a]	% CANADA TOTAL[b]
Forestry	Active forest harvesting or potential for future harvesting	2 440	24
Recreation and conservation	Recreation and conservation within national, provincial, and territorial parks, wildlife reserves, sanctuaries, etc.	708	7
Agriculture	Agriculture on improved farmland (cropland, improved pasture, summerfallow) and unimproved farmland	678	7
Urban/industrial	Residential and industrial activities of urban environments	72[c]	1
Other activities	Includes hunting and trapping, mining, energy developments, and transportation	6 072	61
Total		**9 970**	**100**

[a] Includes the area of land and freshwater. [b]Rounded to the nearest percent. [c] Includes only the 25 major metropolitan areas.
SOURCE: Environment Canada (1985). From *The State of Canada's Environment*, published by the authority of the Minister of the Environment and the Minister of Supply and Services Canada, 1991.

Population

4. Total Population Growth, 1851 to 1991

CENSUS YEAR	POPULATION (000)	AVERAGE ANNUAL RATE OF POPULATION GROWTH (%)
1851	2 436.3	—
1861	3 229.6	2.9
1871	3 689.3	1.3
1881	4 324.8	1.6
1891	4 833.2	1.1
1901	5 371.3	1.1
1911	7 206.6	3.0
1921	8 787.9	2.0
1931	10 376.8	1.7
1941	11 506.7	1.0
1951[1]	14 009.4	1.7
1961	18 238.2	2.5
1971	21 568.3	1.5
1981	24 343.2	1.1
1991[2]	27 296.9	1.5

[1]Newfoundland included for the first time.
[2]1991 Census
SOURCE: *Canada Year Book 1992*. and 1991 Census

5. Population Growth, 1961 to 1991, and Population Density, 1991

PROVINCE OR TERRITORY	1961	1971	1981	1991[1]	POPULATION DENSITY/KM² 1991
Newfoundland	457 853	522 104	567 181	568 474	1.4
Prince Edward Island	104 629	111 641	122 506	129 765	22.9
Nova Scotia	737 007	788 960	847 882	899 942	16.2
New Brunswick	597 936	634 557	696 403	723 900	9.9
Quebec	5 259 211	6 027 764	6 438 403	6 895 963	4.5
Ontario	6 236 092	7 703 106	8 625 107	10 084 885	9.4
Manitoba	921 686	988 247	1 026 241	1 091 942	1.7
Saskatchewan	925 181	926 242	968 313	988 928	1.5
Alberta	1 331 944	1 627 874	2 237 724	2 545 553	3.8
British Columbia	1 629 082	2 184 021	2 744 467	3 282 061	3.5
Yukon	14 628	18 388	23 153	27 797	0.06
Northwest Territories	22 998	34 807	45 741	57 649	0.02
Canada	**18 238 247**	**21 568 310**	**24 343 181**	**27 296 859**	**2.7**

SOURCE: *Canada Year Book*, various years; 1991 Census, *A National Overview*, Statistics Canada, April 1992.

6. Births, Deaths, and Migration Rates, 1990, and Infant Mortality and Life Expectancy, 1989

DEMOGRAPHIC CATEGORY	NFLD	PEI	NS	NB	QUE	ONT	MAN	SASK	ALTA	BC	YUKON	NWT	CANADA
BirthRate/1000	12.8	14.4	14.1	13.6	14.1	15.2	16.0	16.6	17.5	14.2	19.4	27.6	**15.0**
Death Rate/1000	6.5	8.5	8.5	7.6	7.2	7.4	8.3	8.2	5.6	7.4	4.6	3.9	**7.3**
Immigration Rate/1000	1.0	1.3	1.7	1.1	5.9	11.5	6.1	2.4	7.6	9.1	3.2	1.5	**8.0**
Emigration Rate/1000	0.4	0.4	0.4	1.0	0.7	1.9	1.6	0.8	2.3	1.6	1.4	0.9	**1.4**
Interprovincial In-migration/1000	17.2	23.7	24.2	22.9	4.9	9.6	18.3	20.3	31.4	28.3	99.8	72.7	**14.7**
Interprovincial Out-migration/1000	25.2	35.3	24.6	23.5	6.3	10.5	26.4	35.7	27.9	15.3	94.3	82.1	**14.7**
Infant Mortality/1000	8.2	6.2	5.8	7.1	6.8	6.8	6.6	8.0	7.5	8.2	4.2	16.2	**7.1**
Life Expectancy M	73.3	72.9	72.6	73.3	72.7	74.0	73.6	74.3	74.3	74.4	n.a.	n.a.	**73.6**
at birth (in years) F	79.4	81.1	79.7	80.3	80.3	80.2	80.5	81.3	80.7	80.8	n.a.	n.a.	**80.3**

n.a.—not available
SOURCE: *Quarterly Demographic Statistics*, Oct.–Dec. 1990, April 1991, Statistics Canada, and *Report on the Demographic Situation in Canada 1991*, Statistics Canada, Dec. 1991.

7. Population by First Language, 1981 and 1986

OFFICIAL LANGUAGE	1981[1]		1986	
	NUMBER	%	NUMBER	%
English	14 684 365	60.3	15 334 085	60.6
French	6 127 530	25.2	6 159 740	24.3
NON-OFFICIAL LANGUAGE				
Aboriginal	150 235	0.6	138 060	0.5
Italian	499 920	2.1	455 820	1.8
Portuguese	159 295	0.7	153 985	0.6
Spanish	64 575	0.3	83 130	0.3
German[2]	485 375	2.0	438 680	1.7
Yiddish	27 945	0.1	22 665	0.1
Dutch	136 500	0.6	123 670	0.5
Ukrainian	258 575	1.1	208 415	0.8
Russian	28 525	0.1	24 860	0.1
Polish	116 095	0.5	123 120	0.5
Finnish	31 130	0.1	25 770	0.1
Hungarian	77 630	0.3	69 000	0.3
Greek	116 835	0.5	110 350	0.4
Arabic[3]	44 425	0.2	40 665	0.2
Punjabi	49 670	0.2	63 640	0.3
Chinese	212 785	0.9	266 560	1.1
Vietnamese	28 325	0.1	41 560	0.2
Tagalog (Filipino)	36 195	0.1	42 420	0.2
Other Languages	409 270	1.7	428 205	1.7
Sub-total Single Response	23 745 200	97.5	24 354 390	96.2
Multiple Response	597 980	2.5	954 940	3.8
Canada[4]	**24 343 180**	**100.0**	**25 309 330**	**100.0**

[1]Since multiple responses are shown in this table, the 1981 data do not correspond to those previously released.
[2]Includes Alsacians in 1986.
[3]Includes Maltese in 1981.
[4]The figures for 1986 exclude the population on 136 incompletely enumerated Native reserves and settlements. The total population on these reserves was estimated to be about 45 000 in 1986.
SOURCE: *Canada Year Book 1988*.

8. Components of Population Growth, 1960 to 1990

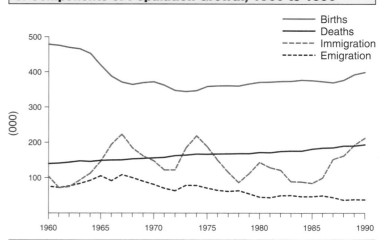

Legend: —— Births, —— Deaths, - - - Immigration, - - - Emigration

SOURCE: Statistics Canada, Demography Division.

9. Percentage of People Who Are Bilingual (English and French), 1971 and 1986

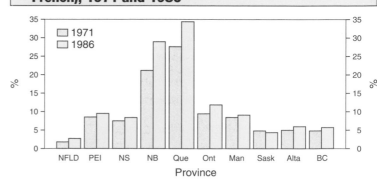

Legend: ☐ 1971, ☐ 1986

Province: NFLD, PEI, NS, NB, Que, Ont, Man, Sask, Alta, BC

SOURCE: Statistics Canada, *Market Research Handbook*, 1991

10. Population of Census Metropolitan Areas, 1961 to 1991

CENSUS METROPOLITAN AREA	km²	1961	1971	1981[1,2]	1991[3]
Calgary	5 056	279 062	403 319	625 966	754 033
Chicoutimi-Jonquière	1 723	127 616	133 703	158 229	160 928
Edmonton	11 397	359 821	495 702	740 882	839 924
Halifax	2 508	193 353	222 637	277 727	320 501
Hamilton	1 358	401 071	498 523	542 095	599 760
Kitchener	824	154 864	226 846	287 801	356 421
London	2 105	226 669	286 011	326 817	381 522
Montreal	3 509	2 215 627	2 743 208	2 862 286	3 127 242
Oshawa	894	—	120 318[1]	186 446	240 104
Ottawa-Hull	5 138	457 038	602 510	743 821	920 857
Quebec	3 150	379 067	480 502	583 820	645 550
Regina	3 422	113 749	140 734	173 226	191 692
Saint John	2 905	98 083	106 744	121 012	124 981
St. Catharines-Niagara	1 400	257 796	303 429	342 645	364 552
St. John's	1 130	106 666	131 814	154 835	171 859
Saskatoon	4 749	95 564	126 449	175 058	210 023
Sherbrooke	916	—	—	125 183	139 194
Sudbury	2 612	127 446	155 424	156 121	157 613
Thunder Bay	2 203	102 085	112 093	121 948	124 427
Toronto	5 614	1 919 409	2 628 043	3 130 392	3 893 046
Trois-Rivières	872	—	—	125 343	136 303
Vancouver	2 786	826 798	1 082 352	1 268 183	1 602 502
Victoria	1 951	155 763	195 800	241 450	287 897
Windsor	862	217 215	258 643	250 885	262 075
Winnipeg	3 295	476 543	540 262	592 061	652 354

—not applicable
[1]Adjusted due to boundary changes
[2]Based on 1986 Census Metropolitan Area
[3]1991 Census.
SOURCE: *Canada Year Book 1988 and 1992*; Statistics Canada, *Canada's Population From Ocean to Ocean*, Cat. No. 98-120.

11. Population by Ethnic Origin, 1986

PROVINCE OR TERRITORY	BRITISH	FRENCH	DUTCH	GERMAN	ITALIAN	ABORIGINAL PEOPLES	POLISH	SCANDINAVIAN	UKRAINIAN	OTHER SINGLE ORIGINS	MULTIPLE ORIGINS	TOTAL
Newfoundland	449 760	11 315	400	1 155	235	3 825	200	265	105	96 745	93 725	564 005
Total % Distribution	79.7	2.0	0.1	0.2	—	0.7	—	—	—	17.2	16.6	100.0
Prince Edward Island	59 275	11 135	1 275	540	75	415	100	135	65	52 075	50 980	125 090
Total % Distribution	47.4	8.9	1.0	0.4	0.1	0.3	0.1	0.1	0.1	41.6	40.8	100.0
Nova Scotia	417 685	52 905	9 320	21 205	2 260	5 960	1 845	1 230	1 435	350 305	328 245	864 150
Total % Distribution	48.3	6.1	1.1	2.5	0.3	0.7	0.2	0.1	0.2	40.5	38.0	100.0
New Brunswick	251 315	232 575	2 895	3 755	865	3 880	380	1 215	490	204 485	197 505	701 855
Total % Distribution	35.8	33.1	0.4	0.5	0.1	0.6	0.1	0.2	0.1	29.1	28.1	100.0
Quebec	319 550	5 015 565	6 365	26 785	163 875	49 320	18 835	2 540	12 220	839 430	444 480	6 454 485
Total % Distribution	5.0	77.7	0.1	0.4	2.5	0.8	0.3	—	0.2	13.0	6.9	100.0
Ontario	2 912 830	531 575	171 155	285 155	461 375	55 560	117 580	26 755	109 705	4 329 480	3 049 065	9 001 170
Total % Distribution	32.4	5.9	1.9	3.2	5.1	0.6	1.3	0.3	1.2	48.1	33.9	100.0
Manitoba	224 375	55 725	27 875	96 165	8 225	55 415	22 015	14 835	79 940	464 750	367 740	1 049 320
Total % Distribution	21.4	5.3	2.7	9.2	0.8	5.3	2.1	1.4	7.6	44.3	35.0	100.0
Saskatchewan	222 120	33 540	13 020	128 850	1 950	55 645	13 325	24 895	60 550	442 805	391 950	996 700
Total % Distribution	22.3	3.4	1.3	12.9	0.2	5.6	1.3	2.5	6.1	44.4	39.3	100.0
Alberta	592 345	77 585	55 920	182 865	23 635	51 665	28 505	46 525	106 760	1 174 460	950 330	2 340 265
Total % Distribution	25.3	3.3	2.4	7.8	1.0	2.2	1.2	2.0	4.6	50.2	40.6	100.0
British Columbia	871 075	68 965	62 945	148 280	46 755	61 125	19 305	52 565	48 195	1 470 375	1 089 775	2 849 585
Total % Distribution	30.6	2.4	2.2	5.2	1.6	2.1	0.7	1.8	1.7	51.6	38.2	100.0
Yukon	5 370	775	350	880	75	3 275	80	445	345	11 765	10 505	23 360
Total % Distribution	23.0	3.3	1.5	3.8	0.3	14.0	0.3	1.9	1.5	50.4	45.0	100.0
Northwest Territories	7 015	1 510	240	1 085	255	27 175	100	305	395	13 940	12 045	52 020
Total % Distribution	13.5	2.9	0.5	2.1	0.5	52.2	0.2	0.6	0.8	26.8	23.2	100.0
Canada	**6 332 725**	**6 093 165**	**351 765**	**896 715**	**709 590**	**373 265**	**222 260**	**171 715**	**420 210**	**9 450 595**	**6 986 345**	**25 022 005**
Total % Distribution	**25.3**	**24.4**	**1.4**	**3.6**	**2.8**	**1.5**	**0.9**	**0.7**	**1.7**	**37.8**	**27.9**	**100.0**

SOURCE: Statistics Canada, *Ethnicity, Immigration and Citizenship*, Cat. No. 93-109, 1986 Census of Canada.

188

12. Percentage of Population in Urban Areas, 1851 to 1991

PROVINCE	1851	1871	1891	1911	1931	1951	1971	1991
Newfoundland	—	—	—	—	—	43.3	57.2	53.6
Prince Edward Island	—	9.4	13.1	16.0	19.5	25.1	38.3	39.9
Nova Scotia	7.5	8.3	19.4	36.7	46.6	54.5	56.7	53.5
New Brunswick	14.0	17.6	19.9	26.7	35.4	42.8	56.9	47.7
Quebec	14.9	19.9	28.6	44.5	59.5	66.8	80.6	77.6
Ontario	14.0	20.6	35.0	49.5	63.1	72.5	82.4	81.8
Manitoba	—	—	23.3	39.3	45.2	56.0	69.5	72.1
Saskatchewan	—	—	—	16.1	20.3	30.4	53.0	63.0
Alberta	—	—	—	29.4	31.8	47.6	73.5	79.8
British Columbia	—	9.0	42.6	50.9	62.3	68.6	75.7	80.4
Canada	**13.1**	**18.3**	**29.8**	**41.8**	**52.5**	**62.4**	**76.1**	**76.6**

SOURCE: *Urban Development in Canada* by Leroy O. Stone, *1961 Census Monograph*; 1971 Census of Canada; 1991 Census of Canada.

13. Native Population, 1986

PROVINCE OR TERRITORY	NATIVE INDIAN	MÉTIS	INUIT	TOTAL[1]
Newfoundland	4.7	1.4	4.1	9.6
Prince Edward Island	1.1	0.2	0.03	1.3
Nova Scotia	13.1	1.1	0.3	14.2
New Brunswick	8.7	0.8	0.2	9.4
Quebec	68.6	11.4	7.4	80.9
Ontario	150.7	18.3	3.0	167.4
Manitoba	56.0	33.3	0.7	85.2
Saskatchewan	55.2	25.7	0.2	77.7
Alberta	69.0	40.1	1.1	103.9
British Columbia	112.8	15.3	1.0	126.6
Yukon	4.8	0.2	0.07	5.0
Northwest Territories	9.4	3.8	18.4	30.5
Canada	**554.1**	**151.6**	**36.5**	**711.7**

POPULATION (000s)

[1]Totals do not add up because some individuals are identified as having more than one Native origin.
SOURCE: 1986 Census of Canada.

14. Registered Indian Population On and Off Reserve, 1991

PROVINCE OR TERRITORY	ON RESERVE	% CHANGE 1986-1991	OFF RESERVE	% CHANGE 1986-1991
Atlantic Provinces	12 752	14.6	7 337	62.9
Quebec	35 693	15.0	14 320	80.8
Ontario	65 537	18.5	52 903	69.3
Manitoba	48 979	18.8	27 229	67.2
Saskatchewan	47 972	23.8	32 750	50.2
Alberta	42 032	20.0	25 209	84.3
British Columbia	49 530	21.2	40 098	55.9
Yukon	3 500	42.1	3 124	74.9
Northwest Territories	10 278	22.4	2 218	218.7
Canada	**316 273**	**19.7**	**205 188**	**66.0**

SOURCE: *1966–1988: Indian Register; 1991-2001: Population Projections of Registered Indians, 1987 to 2011, Preliminary Report*, Department of Indian Affairs and Northern Development, 1989.

15. Numbers of Immigrants and Immigration Rates, Canada,1944-1990

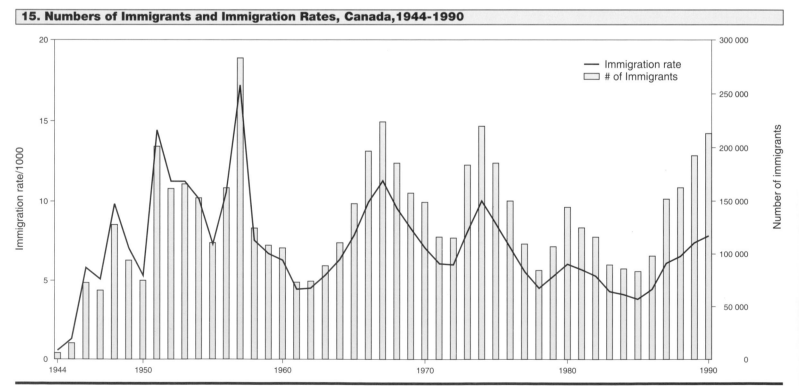

SOURCE: Employment and Immigration Canada, 1990.

16. Population, by Sex and Age Group, 1990

SEX AND AGE	PROVINCE OR TERRITORY												
	CANADA	NFLD	PEI	NS	NB	QUE (000)	ONT	MAN	SASK	ALTA	BC	YUKON	NWT
Male	**13 104.2**	**285.7**	**64.4**	**437.8**	**357.1**	**3 312.6**	**4 785.0**	**537.4**	**498.0**	**1 237.2**	**1 547.6**	**13.6**	**27.9**
0-4	961.7	19.8	5.0	31.1	25.1	221.7	351.9	43.0	42.5	107.1	109.9	1.3	3.4
5-9	949.1	22.7	5.0	30.8	26.0	231.2	336.4	40.7	41.3	100.6	110.3	1.2	2.9
10-14	938.0	25.7	5.2	31.8	27.9	243.7	325.0	39.3	39.9	91.5	104.5	1.0	2.5
15-19	953.8	27.6	5.3	34.8	29.8	228.8	347.0	41.3	37.4	92.4	105.9	1.0	2.4
20-24	1 016.6	26.3	5.1	36.0	29.4	251.2	376.1	42.3	36.5	98.3	111.8	0.9	2.7
25-29	1 190.4	23.5	5.6	40.3	31.2	306.9	444.8	48.4	41.7	116.0	127.9	1.4	2.8
30-34	1 182.2	23.1	5.3	37.9	30.6	310.4	426.8	46.4	41.6	122.6	133.6	1.5	2.6
35-39	1 082.7	22.9	4.8	34.6	28.9	284.0	386.0	41.5	37.7	108.5	130.2	1.4	2.2
40-44	988.4	21.1	4.6	32.6	27.0	259.2	361.3	36.7	31.0	90.1	121.5	1.2	2.0
45-49	775.9	15.3	3.4	25.0	20.2	212.2	284.2	28.4	24.2	67.2	93.8	0.9	1.3
50-54	636.2	12.3	3.0	20.5	16.2	167.2	238.9	23.9	21.4	54.2	77.2	0.6	0.9
55-59	599.5	11.1	2.7	18.9	14.6	156.3	226.3	23.0	21.4	49.9	74.1	0.5	0.7
60-64	555.3	10.0	2.5	17.1	13.8	142.2	211.5	22.3	20.9	43.5	70.5	0.4	0.5
65-69	475.6	8.6	2.3	15.9	12.8	116.9	180.7	20.4	19.2	34.8	63.5	0.2	0.4
70-74	339.2	7.0	1.9	13.0	9.9	80.3	122.4	15.9	16.1	25.4	47.0	0.1	0.2
75 +	459.6	8.7	2.8	17.5	13.7	100.5	165.7	23.8	25.2	35.2	66.0	0.1	0.2
Female	**13 479.8**	**287.3**	**65.9**	**453.8**	**366.8**	**3 449.7**	**4 946.2**	**552.6**	**502.3**	**1 232.6**	**1 584.1**	**12.3**	**26.2**
0-4	917.9	18.9	4.9	29.9	23.5	211.3	334.6	41.0	40.7	103.1	105.3	1.2	3.5
5-9	902.8	22.1	4.8	29.8	24.9	219.3	320.1	38.4	39.7	95.0	104.8	1.0	2.8
10-14	890.4	24.2	4.9	30.4	26.5	230.0	309.7	37.7	38.0	86.4	99.2	0.9	2.4
15-19	906.6	26.2	4.8	33.0	28.6	217.6	329.2	39.1	35.7	88.3	100.9	1.0	2.4
20-24	981.6	25.7	5.0	34.3	28.2	242.6	362.9	40.2	34.7	95.7	108.8	0.9	2.5
25-29	1 190.8	24.2	5.5	40.1	31.3	304.7	444.7	47.7	41.5	117.1	129.8	1.3	2.8
30-34	1 197.4	24.2	5.4	38.8	31.3	314.7	433.7	45.5	41.0	120.0	139.2	1.4	2.5
35-39	1 101.3	23.6	4.9	35.7	29.8	289.2	399.6	42.1	36.3	104.9	131.9	1.3	2.0
40-44	993.2	21.0	4.7	32.8	26.8	263.1	367.1	36.9	30.5	87.6	120.1	1.1	1.6
45-49	772.9	14.8	3.3	25.1	19.6	214.9	284.1	28.4	24.2	64.7	92.1	0.6	1.0
50-54	639.3	11.9	2.9	20.6	16.2	172.5	240.8	24.2	21.2	52.6	75.2	0.4	0.8
55-59	610.1	10.6	2.6	19.6	15.3	167.0	229.8	23.5	21.2	48.1	71.3	0.4	0.7
60-64	597.8	10.3	2.6	19.1	15.2	161.2	226.8	23.9	21.7	43.9	72.4	0.3	0.5
65-69	566.7	8.9	2.6	19.0	15.0	144.1	217.0	24.8	21.4	39.7	73.7	0.2	0.3
70-74	442.1	8.0	2.4	16.8	12.5	111.2	159.7	20.3	19.4	31.7	59.9	0.1	0.2
75 +	768.5	12.8	4.5	28.9	22.1	186.3	286.3	38.7	35.2	53.8	99.4	0.1	0.2

SOURCE: *Post-censal Annual Estimates of Population by Marital Status, Age, Sex, and Components of Growth for Canada and the Provinces.* 1 June Cat. No. 91-210, Annual. *Market Research Handbook, Statistics Canada,* 1991, Cat. No. 63-224.

17. Immigrant Population by Place of Birth, 1970 to 1990

COUNTRY OR REGION	1970	1975	1980	1985	1990
Great Britain	23 688	29 454	16 445	3 998	6 701
Portugal	8 594	9 158	4 222	917	5 396
Italy	8 659	4 919	1 873	733	1 058
Poland	1 403	1 191	1 395	3 642	16 446
Total Europe	**75 006**	**68 733**	**40 210**	**18 530**	**50 059**
Philippines	3 305	7 688	6 147	3 183	12 492
India	7 089	13 401	9 531	4 517	12 513
Hong Kong	2 250	6 438	3 874	5 121	22 789
China	3 397	6 235	8 965	5 166	13 971
Total Asia	**23 682**	**52 024**	**73 026**	**39 438**	**112 854**
United States	20 859	16 729	8 098	5 614	4 995
Caribbean	13 371	18 790	7 515	6 240	11 721
Africa	4 017	11 715	5 383	3 912	13 691
Australasia	3 462	1 574	1 215	399	714
South America	4 506	13 102	5 381	4 273	8 544
Oceania	—	2 675	944	612	1 671
Total	**147 713**	**187 881**	**143 117**	**84 302**	**212 166**

SOURCE: Statistics Canada, *Report on the Demographic Situation in Canada 1990: Current Demographic Analysis*, Dec. 1991, Cat. No. 91-209E.

18. Employment, Unemployment, and Participation Rates[1], 1989

PROVINCE	POPULATION (000)	LABOUR FORCE (000)	EMPLOYED (000)	UNEMPLOYED (000)	PARTICIPATION RATE (%)
Newfoundland	571	239	201	38	55.7
Prince Edward Island	130	65	54	11	65.0
Nova Scotia	898	414	373	41	61.2
New Brunswick	726	325	284	41	59.5
Quebec	6 812	3 342	3 031	311	64.0
Ontario	9 840	5 213	4 949	264	69.8
Manitoba	1 093	539	498	41	67.0
Saskatchewan	995	482	446	36	66.2
Alberta	2 501	1 308	1 214	94	72.4
British Columbia	3 186	1 579	1 435	144	66.8
Canada	**26 833**	**13 504**	**12 486**	**1 018**	**67.0**

[1]The participation rate is the percentage of the population (over 15 years of age) in the labour force and includes both employed and unemployed.   SOURCE: Statistics Canada.

19. Employees by Industry, 1989

PROVINCE OR TERRITORY	INDUSTRY (000)									
	FORESTRY	MINING	MANUFACTURING	TRANSPORTATION AND COMMUNICATION	CONSTRUCTION	TRADE	FINANCE, INSURANCE AND REAL ESTATE	SERVICES	PUBLIC ADMINISTRATION	TOTAL
Newfoundland	1.4	3.4	17.8	14.5	6.3	29.5	5.4	51.3	18.1	**147.7**
Prince Edward Island	—	—	3.7	3.1	2.1	6.7	1.5	14.3	5.2	**36.6**
Nova Scotia	2.2	4.1	40.1	24.3	16.3	57.0	15.9	108.5	29.3	**297.6**
New Brunswick	3.8	3.2	35.5	21.5	12.2	42.7	9.7	76.6	19.4	**224.6**
Quebec	14.6	17.5	530.4	204.5	118.3	457.9	145.0	888.7	167.7	**2 544.5**
Ontario	9.5	28.9	978.9	307.7	224.1	749.5	292.3	1424.8	253.2	**4 268.9**
Manitoba	0.9	4.4	56.7	44.6	13.2	68.9	25.3	145.1	29.1	**388.3**
Saskatchewan	0.9	8.2	22.6	29.2	12.4	61.1	19.6	121.0	26.5	**301.4**
Alberta	2.4	63.9	85.8	90.2	53.3	181.5	54.9	366.2	72.2	**970.5**
British Columbia, Yukon, and Northwest Territories	23.6	14.5	164.2	111.2	57.5	208.1	75.7	424.9	73.9	**1 159.2**

SOURCE: Statistics Canada, *Market Research Handbook, 1991*, Ottawa, 1990.

20. Geographic Distribution of the Population, 1986

SELECTED PARALLELS OF LATITUDE	POPULATION	%
South of 49°	17 827 382	70.4
Between 49° and 54°	6 898 501	27.3
Between 54° and 60°	505 222	2.0
North of 60°	78 226	0.3
SELECTED DISTANCES NORTH OF CANADA-USA BORDER		
0 - 150 km	18 218 596	72.0
151 - 300 km	3 394 247	13.4
301 - 600 km	2 630 864	10.4
Over 600 km	1 065 624	4.2
Total Canadian Population	**25 354 064**	**100.0**

SOURCE: 1986 Census of Canada, *Canada's Population From Ocean to Ocean*, Minister of Supply and Services Canada, 1989.

Agriculture

21. Net Income and Cash Receipts from Farming

PROVINCE	CASH RECEIPTS ($000 000)		NET INCOME[1] ($000 000)	
	1983	1989	1983	1989
Newfoundland	34.8	57.9	4.5	11.3
Prince Edward Island	172.3	256.1	25.4	77.8
Nova Scotia	236.0	315.1	26.4	71.5
New Brunswick	199.8	272.1	30.8	65.6
Quebec	2 710.1	3 648.9	484.9	917.6
Ontario	4 989.9	5 662.5	810.7	941.2
Manitoba	1 797.6	2 101.7	215.2	295.3
Saskatchewan	4 026.1	4 474.8	702.9	760.1
Alberta	3 750.8	4 509.4	412.4	782.6
British Columbia	914.9	1 163.9	38.1	175.7
Canada	**18 832.3**	**22 462.4**	**2 751.4**	**4 099.0**

[1]Income excludes the value of inventory change.
SOURCE: Statistics Canada, *Agriculture Economic Statistics*, June 1990.

22. Number of Farms and Average Size, 1901 to 1991

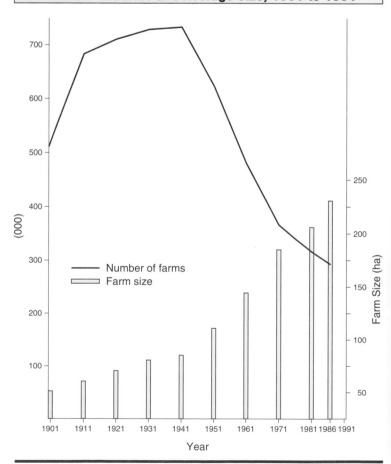

SOURCE: Statistics Canada

23. Agricultural Land Use, 1986

PROVINCE	FARMLAND AREA (000 ha)	% CHANGE 1971–1986	% CLASSED AS CLASS 1, 2, or 3	NUMBER OF FARMS	AVERAGE FARM SIZE (CHANGE 1971–1986)	CROPLAND AREA (000 ha)	SUMMER FALLOW AREA (000 ha)	WOODLAND AREA (000 ha)
Newfoundland	36.6	44.1	0.005	652	56 (+131 %)	4.9	0.4	5.2
Prince Edward Island	272.4	−13.1	71.2	2 838	96 (+39 %)	156.5	2.7	61.2
Nova Scotia	416.5	−22.6	20.7	4 284	97 (+9 %)	109.5	3.9	200.8
New Brunswick	409.0	−24.5	17.9	3 556	115 (+16 %)	129.5	4.3	184.4
Quebec	3 638.8	−16.8	1.4	41 350	88 (+23 %)	1 744.4	31.8	1 029.6
Ontario	5 646.6	−12.6	6.8	72 392	76 (+13.9 %)	3 458.0	80.3	587.5
Manitoba	7 740.2	0.6	8.0	27 350	283 (+29 %)	4 519.3	509.2	124.2
Saskatchewan	26 599.4	1.0	25.0	63 483	419 (+23 %)	13 325.8	5 661.6	152.7
Alberta	20 655.3	3.1	16.2	57 697	358 (+12 %)	9 162.5	2 123.7	288.8
British Columbia	2 411.1	2.2	1.0	19 135	126 (−1.2 %)	570.8	81.2	154.5
Canada	**67 825.8**	**−1.2**	**4.6**	**293 618**	**231 (23 %)**	**33 181.2**	**8 499.0**	**2 789.0**

NOTE: Information about the territories is excluded because of the small number of farms. SOURCE: Statistics Canada, *Human Activity and the Environment, 1991*.

24. Census Farms with Sales of $2500 or More, by Product Type, 1986

PROVINCE	DAIRY	CATTLE	HOGS	POULTRY	WHEAT	SMALL GRAINS (EXCLUDING WHEAT FARMS)	FIELD CROPS, OTHER THAN SMALL GRAINS	FRUITS AND VEGETABLES	MISCELLANEOUS SPECIALTY	MIXED FARMS LIVESTOCK COMBINATION	MIXED FARMS OTHER COMBINATIONS[1]	TOTAL
Newfoundland	68	45	17	54	—	—	13	94	75	12	37	**415**
Prince Edward Island	584	652	221	28	4	90	474	60	149	127	69	**2 458**
Nova Scotia	698	979	132	127	1	62	45	457	481	42	146	**3 170**
New Brunswick	631	739	125	96	7	62	384	252	313	45	122	**2 776**
Quebec	15 906	5 763	2 749	893	217	2 922	771	2 250	4 051	382	1 256	**37 160**
Ontario	11 028	17 160	4 840	1 643	733	13 693	1 988	4 089	4 203	1 653	2 223	**63 253**
Manitoba	1 412	4 682	1 111	356	6 272	8 758	415	100	731	615	810	**25 262**
Saskatchewan	881	7 866	906	166	30 968	16 942	285	36	609	1 064	1 086	**60 809**
Alberta	1 828	17 110	1 635	533	8 504	15 403	1 187	119	1 944	1 399	2 081	**51 743**
British Columbia	1 150	4 266	290	752	151	663	356	2 920	1 893	238	1 020	**13 699**
Canada	34 186	59 262	12 026	4 648	46 857	58 595	5 918	10 377	14 449	5 577	8 850	**260 745**

[1]In 1986, "field crops combination". SOURCE: *Canada Year Book 1992.*

25. Livestock Facts

PROVINCE	NUMBER OF CATTLE (000 head) JULY 1990	NUMBER OF PIGS (000 head) JULY 1990	NUMBER OF SHEEP AND LAMBS (000 head) JULY 1990	POULTRY PRODUCTION (tonnes) JULY 1989	TURKEY PRODUCTION (tonnes) JULY 1989	EGG PRODUCTION (000 doz.) 1989	MILK AND CREAM PRODUCTION (000 kL) 1989
Newfoundland	9	16	7	6 927	—	8 136	—
Prince Edward Island	97	117	5	1 471	24	2 862	99
Nova Scotia	128	135	34	19 421	3 132	19 185	175
New Brunswick	105	84	10	15 016	2 047	10 675	134
Quebec	1 413	2 975	118	169 909	27 407	82 499	2 873
Ontario	2 250	3 181	215	195 041	52 238	181 409	2 454
Manitoba	1 075	1 240	24	25 659	9 002	54 956	302
Saskatoon	2 160	790	56	17 358	4 734	19 682	225
Alberta	4 310	1 760	233	47 985	9 850	38 248	585
British Columbia	740	234	58	66 477	11 998	59 298	494
TOTAL	**12 287**	**10 532**	**759**	**565 264**	**120 432**	**476 950**	**7 341**[1]

[1]As of October 1988, Nfld data are excluded from Canada total for reasons of confidentiality. SOURCE: *Canada Year Book 1992.*

26. Wheat Statistics, 1983 to 1991

	1983[1]	1984	1985	1986	1987	1988	1989	1990	1991
Carryover from Previous Crop Year (000 t)	9 983	9 190	7 598	8 569	12 731	7 305	5 032	6 442	10 472
Production (000 t)	26 505	21 199	24 252	31 378	25 992	15 996	24 334	32 709	31 904
Total Supply (000 t)	36 448	30 389	31 850	39 947	38 723	23 301	29 366	39 151	42 191
Exports (000 t)	21 765	17 542	17 683	20 783	23 519	12 413	17 418	21 913	n.a.
Domestic Use (000 t)	5 534	5 250	5 598	6 433	7 899	5 856	5 581	6 766	n.a.
Carryover at the End of the Crop Year (000 t)	9 189	7 598	8 569	12 731	7 305	5 032	6 442	10 472	n.a.
Final Price ($/t)	194	186	160	130	134	197	172	135	n.a.

[1]The crop year begins 1 July 1983 and ends 30 June 1984. n.a.—not available SOURCE: *Canada Year Book*, various years; The Canadian Wheat Board *Annual Reports*.

27. World Wheat Production, 1981 and 1990

COUNTRY	1981	1990
		(000 000 t)
Argentina	8.3	11.4
Australia	16.4	15.1
Canada	24.8	32.7
China	59.6	98.2
European Community	58.0	84.6
India	36.3	49.7
Soviet Union[1]	81.1	108.0
Turkey	17.0	20.0
United States	75.8	74.5

[1]The Soviet Union was dissolved in 1991. Data for Russia and the other independent countries that were formed after dissolution are not available for the years prior to 1992.
SOURCE: *The Canadian Wheat Board Annual Report, 1990–1991.*

28. World Wheat Imports and Exports, 1981 and 1990

	IMPORTS (000 000 t)	
COUNTRY	1981	1990
Soviet Union[1]	19.6	14.5
China	13.2	9.6
Egypt	6.0	6.0
Japan	5.6	5.5
Iran	1.4	4.1
Brazil	4.6	2.8
Republic of Korea	1.9	4.1
Algeria	2.3	3.5
Iraq	1.6	0.2
Poland	3.8	0.3
Indonesia	1.5	2.0
Bangladesh	1.2	1.4
World Total	**100.7**	**90.6**

	EXPORTS (000 000 t)	
COUNTRY	1981	1990
Argentina	4.3	5.1
Australia	11.4	11.9
Canada	28.5	21.9
European Community	13.9	18.5
United States	48.8	28.3
World Total	**100.7**	**90.6**

[1]The Soviet Union was dissolved in 1991. Data for Russia and the other independent countries that were formed after dissolution are not available for the years prior to 1992.
SOURCE: *The Canadian Wheat Board Annual Report, 1990–1991.*

29. Canadian Wheat Exports, 1980, 1985, and 1990

COUNTRY OR REGION	1980[1]	1985	1990
		(000 t)	
Western Europe	**2 347**	**1 298**	**935**
Great Britain	1 409	633	281
Italy	765	240	320
Eastern Europe	**5 129**	**6 285**	**7 228**
Soviet Union[2]	3 971	6 019	7 228
Africa	**901**	**934**	**2 047**
South Africa	n.a.	55	554
Middle East	**674**	**1 608**	**1 556**
Iran	96	41	1 419
Asia	**4 467**	**4 672**	**7 328**
China	2 879	2 780	2 923
Japan	1 381	1 323	1 393
South Korea	n.a.	n.a.	1 258
North and South America	**2 049**	**2 275**	**2 818**
United States	n.a.	159	660
Total	**15 569**	**17 114**	**21 913**

[1]The crop year extends from 1 July 1980 to 30 June 1981.
[2]The Soviet Union was dissolved in 1991. Data for Russia and the other independent countries that were formed after dissolution are not available for the years prior to 1992.
n.a.—not available
SOURCE: *The Canadian Wheat Board Annual Report, 1990–1991.*

30. Farm Cash Receipts, 1990 ($000 000)

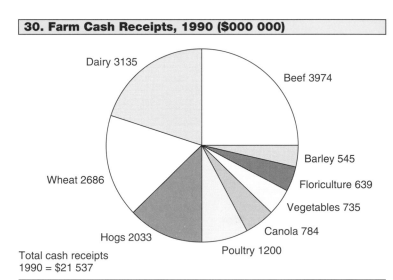

Dairy 3135
Beef 3974
Barley 545
Floriculture 639
Vegetables 735
Canola 784
Poultry 1200
Hogs 2033
Wheat 2686

Total cash receipts
1990 = $21 537

SOURCE: Statistics Canada, *Canadian Economic Observer,* June 1991.

31. Area and Production of Major Field Crops, Various Years

FIELD CROP AND PROVINCE[1]	AREA (000 ha)				TOTAL PRODUCTION (000 t)			
	AVERAGE 1945–49	AVERAGE 1963–67	1974	1990	AVERAGE 1945–49	AVERAGE 1963–67	1974	1990
Wheat	**9 823**	**11 630**	**9 391**	**14 063**	**9 873**	**18 473**	**14 220**	**31 009**
Quebec	5	9	24	55	6	16	42	170
Ontario								
Winter	248	159	168	304	493	433	519	1 301
Spring	16	8	4	20	22	14	8	54
Manitoba	968	1 324	1 200	2 198	1 306	2 145	1 715	5 851
Saskatchewan	5 775	7 575	6 160	8 288	5 035	11 523	8 872	16 847
Alberta	2 766	2 509	1 800	3 136	2 939	4 262	2 994	6 614
British Columbia	42	44	28	51	71	74	52	136
Oats	**4 605**	**3 284**	**2 442**	**1 517**	**5 034**	**5 773**	**3 929**	**3 546**
Prince Edward Island	44	35	20	10	63	67	43	24
New Brunswick	71	32	20	12	95	53	35	25
Quebec	550	430	250	115	508	654	367	315
Ontario	601	547	198	117	876	1 118	361	287

FIELD CROP AND PROVINCE[1]	AREA (000 ha)				TOTAL PRODUCTION (000 t)			
	AVERAGE 1945–49	AVERAGE 1963–67	1974	1990	AVERAGE 1945–49	AVERAGE 1963–67	1974	1990
Manitoba	584	633	480	182	756	1 046	663	432
Saskatchewan	1 634	718	760	405	1 481	1 258	1 157	833
Alberta	1 058	849	680	627	1 157	1 505	1 234	1 511
British Columbia	37	28	26	41	70	51	54	102
Barley	**2 628**	**2 670**	**4 600**	**4 590**	**3 074**	**5 042**	**8 585**	**13 232**
Prince Edward Island	2	5	8	29	4	12	23	78
New Brunswick	4	2	4	13	7	4	10	39
Quebec	34	6	21	162	41	13	36	530
Ontario	94	79	136	198	163	195	337	638
Manitoba	706	282	720	627	914	501	1 154	1 981
Saskatchewan	942	775	1 600	1 416	936	1 463	2 787	3 701
Alberta	835	1 462	2 040	2 084	980	2 761	4 093	6 096
British Columbia	8	57	68	55	16	91	139	150
Soybeans	**29**	**103**	**178**	**504**	**41**	**202**	**300**	**1 259**
Ontario	29	103	178	486	41	202	300	1 211
Quebec	—	—	—	18	—	—	—	48
Mixed Grains	**490**	**646**	**724**	**391**	**999**	**1 726**	**1 831**	**1 051**
Prince Edward Island	19	19	30	21	43	56	99	59
Quebec	76	40	50	30	112	90	106	90
Ontario	366	320	328	190	804	998	993	541
Manitoba	7	61	80	32	11	129	136	78
Saskatchewan	5	49	80	32	6	103	145	67
Alberta	13	148	148	81	17	328	331	204
Flaxseed	**466**	**713**	**600**	**721**	**241**	**518**	**363**	**899**
Manitoba	180	397	300	324	108	263	180	419
Saskatchewan	210	177	220	344	85	136	119	406
Alberta	58	122	80	53	35	102	64	74
Canola/Rapeseed	**16**	**468**	**1 304**	**2 630**	**673**	**430**	**1 200**	**3 257**
Ontario	—	—	—	20	—	—	—	43
Manitoba	—	47	200	384	—	41	193	499
Saskatchewan	16	192	600	1 133	673	195	544	1 406
Alberta	—	229	480	1 052	—	194	442	1 270
British Columbia	—	—	—	41	—	—	—	39
Shelled Corn	**98**	**291**	**584**	**1 003**	**280**	**1 468**	**2 589**	**6 846**
Quebec	—	—	66	260	—	—	293	1 730
Ontario	92	286	516	704	273	1 450	2 291	4 953
Manitoba	5	2	2	34	8	4	5	142
Potatoes	**167**	**118**	**112**	**117**	**1 801**	**2 183**	**2 427**	**2 929**
Prince Edward Island	18	18	18	30	272	403	467	850
New Brunswick	24	23	23	20	396	551	608	567
Quebec	47	29	21	18	406	389	382	385
Ontario	37	20	17	13	363	427	368	365
Manitoba	8	9	14	19	64	119	222	352
Alberta	—	—	—	10	—	—	—	278
Tame Hay	**4 214**	**5 121**	**5 355**	**5 976**	**15 176**	**21 368**	**23 604**	**33 112**
Prince Edward Island	88	72	51	56	302	296	204	290
Nova Scotia	161	90	60	69	634	429	288	435
New Brunswick	214	100	64	71	678	430	251	417
Quebec	1 584	1 345	1 070	991	5 013	5 495	4 518	7 000
Ontario	1 348	1 354	1 080	1 032	5 559	6 701	5 733	7 439
Manitoba	130	407	500	668	504	1 571	2 177	3 084
Saskatchewan	192	467	800	850	617	1 579	2 903	2 722
Alberta	376	1 114	1 480	1 882	1 243	3 949	6 078	9 525
British Columbia	121	174	250	352	624	917	1 451	2 177
Fodder Corn	**162**	**212**	**419**	**233**	**3 183**	**5 594**	**10 043**	**7 734**
Quebec	28	26	64	53	549	705	1 855	1 800
Ontario	123	166	336	150	2 531	4 579	7 697	5 080
Manitoba	6	15	11	12	53	213	190	272
British Columbia	2	2	7	11	38	77	299	354

[1]Only provinces with over 10 000 ha in 1990 in a particular crop are listed.   —means not applicable.   SOURCE: *Canada Year Book 1961, 1970–71, 1975,* and *1992.*

Forestry and Fishing

32. Areas of Land, Forest Land, and Productive Forest Land

PROVINCE OR TERRITORY	TOTAL AREA (000 000 ha)	AREA OF FOREST LAND (000 000 ha)	AREA OF PRODUCTIVE FOREST LAND (000 000 ha)	WOOD VOLUME (000 000 m)	FOREST FIRE LOSSES AS A % OF PRODUCTIVE FOREST LAND (AVG. ANNUAL %, LATE 1980s)
Newfoundland	40.6	22.5	11.2	525	0.3
Prince Edward Island	0.6	0.3	0.3	26	0.04
Nova Scotia	5.5	4.0	3.9	244	0.01
New Brunswick	7.3	6.3	6.1	571	1.9
Quebec	154.1	94.0	54.8	4 225	1.2
Ontario	106.9	80.7	38.3	3 529	0.7
Manitoba	65.0	34.9	14.9	680	8.8
Saskatchewan	65.2	23.7	15.9	905	1.6
Alberta	66.1	37.7	25.4	2 656	0.03
British Columbia	94.8	60.3	51.1	8 867	0.05
Yukon	48.3	27.4	7.6	480	1.9
Northwest Territories	342.6	61.4	14.3	446	2.4
Canada	**997.1**	**453.3**	**243.7**	**23 154**	**1.2**

SOURCE: Statistics Canada, *Canadian Forestry Statistics*, 1987.

33. Volume of Wood, by Age Class

PROVINCE OR TERRITORY	REGENERATION	IMMATURE	MATURE	OVERMATURE	UNEVEN-AGED	UNDETERMINED	TOTAL	VOLUME OF WOOD CUT 1986
				(000 000 m³)				
Newfoundland	—	—	123	122	—	280	525	2.4
Prince Edward Island	—	—	—	—	—	26	26	0.5
Nova Scotia	1	147	79	3	15	—	244	3.9
New Brunswick	—	210	344	17	1	—	571	8.7
Quebec	119	734	2 167	—	18	1 187	4 225	38.1
Ontario	1	930	1 465	1 132	1	—	3 529	30.2
Manitoba	—	390	246	43	—	—	680	1.7
Saskatchewan	9	443	165	163	—	125	905	3.5
Alberta	1	716	1 330	608	—	—	2 656	10.4
British Columbia	9	1 604	7 226	28	—	—	8 867	77.5
Yukon	—	308	172	—	—	—	480	} 0.2
Northwest Territories	—	144	301	1	—	—	446	
Total	**140**	**5 625**	**13 619**	**2 117**	**34**	**1 618**	**23 154**	**177.1**

SOURCE: Statistics Canada, *Canadian Forestry Statistics*, 1987.

34. Wood Industries Manufacturing Activity, 1986

PROVINCE	SAWMILLS	OTHER WOOD	PULP AND PAPER	OTHER PAPER	TOTAL
			($000 000)		
Newfoundland	4.6	3.2	141.7	6.3	155.8
Prince Edward Island	0.8	6.6	—	—	7.4
Nova Scotia	40.5	29.3	232.7	26.5	329.0
New Brunswick	91.7	63.9	426.6	13.6	595.8
Quebec	652.1	632.0	2 547.3	551.6	4 383.0
Ontario	323.2	767.9	1 680.2	1 109.6	3 880.9
Manitoba	8.7	78.8	80.3	43.5	211.3
Saskatchewan	21.4	36.7	62.3	10.3	130.7
Alberta	145.2	168.3	108.2	77.7	499.4
British Columbia	1 927.5	520.7	1 694.4	104.7	4 247.3
Total	**3 215.7**	**2 307.4**	**6 973.7**	**1 943.8**	**14 440.6**

SOURCE: *Canada Year Book 1990*.

35. Quantity and Value of Sea and Inland Fish Landed and Persons Employed in Fishing, 1972 and 1986

PROVINCE OR TERRITORY	QUANTITY (t)		VALUE ($000)		PERSONS EMPLOYED FISHING	
	1972	1986	1972	1986	1972	1986
Newfoundland	295 135	515 464	35 723	209 603	14 452	27 075
Prince Edward Island	25 780	45 802	9 540	62 154	3 210	4 462
Nova Scotia	286 856	450 720	66 375	422 738	11 735	14 859
New Brunswick	162 144	143 033	19 923	88 167	5 161	7 784
Quebec	83 210	91 190	11 138	100 163	5 843	6 528
Ontario	19 589	25 180	8 119	46 317	2 097	1 837
Manitoba	11 101	12 143	4 523	20 564	1 827	} 5 850
Saskatchewan	4 864	3 789	1 634	3 968	1 800	
Alberta	2 202	1 613	727	1 891	1 547	
British Columbia	153 060	225 738	75 128	401 959	9 902	20 033
Yukon and Northwest Territories	1 625	1 530	866	1 406	201	n.a.
Totals	**1 045 566**	**1 516 202**	**233 696**	**1 358 930**	**57 775**	**88 428**

n.a.—not available.   SOURCE: *Canada Year Book 1992.*

36. Landings of Chief Commercial Fish, 1990[1]

SPECIES	ATLANTIC COAST		PACIFIC COAST		CANADA	
	Quantity (t)	Value ($000)	Quantity (t)	Value ($000)	Quantity (t)	Value ($000)
Total groundfish	**634 061**	**375 782**	**130 991**	**73 009**	**765 052**	**448 791**
Cod	381 819	239 398	5 502	2 902	387 321	242 300
Haddock	21 346	23 094	—	—	21 346	23 094
Redfish	80 326	22 006	23 380	14 343	103 706	36 349
Halibut	2 135	9 769	4 715	19 688	6 850	29 457
Flatfishes	71 515	37 184	5 926	4 364	77 441	41 548
Turbot	18 888	13 000	1 948	447	20 836	13 447
Pollock	36 819	19 381	545	143	37 364	19 524
Hake	13 087	6 981	79 890	10 982	92 977	17 963
Cusk	3 481	2 183	—	—	3 481	2 183
Catfish	1 516	397	—	—	1 516	397
Other	3 129	2 389	9 085	20 140	12 214	22 529
Total pelagic and other finfish	**370 474**	**77 367**	**139 068**	**299 955**	**509 542**	**377 322**
Herring	255 187	37 508	40 228	74 400	295 415	111 908
Mackerel	14 680	4 081	—	—	14 680	4 081
Tuna	466	6 715	272	837	738	7 552
Alewife	6 331	1 501	—	—	6 331	1 501
Eel	284	1 240	—	—	284	1 240
Salmon	515	2 286	95 271	223 470	95 786	225 756
Skate	98	6	132	23	230	29
Smelt	695	511	—	—	695	511
Capelin	89 787	17 546	—	—	89 787	17 546
Other	2 431	5 973	3 165	1 225	5 596	7 198
Total shellfish	**208 838**	**447 705**	**15 068**	**34 898**	**223 906**	**482 603**
Clams	18 914	14 089	6 227	14 405	25 141	28 494
Oyster	3 200	7 300	3 856	3 200	7 056	10 500
Scallop	80 029	96 264	68	315	80 097	96 579
Squid	3 851	1 003	47	51	3 898	1 054
Lobster	44 963	222 303	—	—	44 963	222 303
Shrimp	27 819	53 120	2 422	7 767	30 241	60 887
Crab	26 062	49 326	2 060	8 441	28 122	57 767
Other	4 000	4 300	388	719	4 388	5 019
Miscellaneous items	**—**	**6 082**	**—**	**4 089**	**—**	**10 171**
Total seafisheries	**1 213 373**	**906 936**	**285 127**	**411 951**	**1 498 500**	**1 318 887**
Inland fisheries					**45 000[2]**	**82 000**
Grand total—Canada					**1 543 500**	**1 400 887**

[1]Preliminary estimates (data underestimate the final catch).   [2]Main species by value include smelt, yellow pickerel, perch, and whitefish.
SOURCE: Department of Fisheries and Oceans

Mining

37. Production of Leading Minerals, 1991ₚ ($000)

MINERAL	NFLD	PEI	NOVA SCOTIA	NEW BRUNSWICK	QUEBEC	ONTARIO	MANITOBA	SASKAT-CHEWAN	ALBERTA	BRITISH COLUMBIA	YUKON	NWT	TOTAL CANADA
Petroleum, crude	—	—	—	—	—	36 437	92 104	1 259 208	8 783 753	261 685	—	196 276	10 629 463
Natural gas	—	—	—	—	—	45 506	—	307 031	4 306 480	519 276	—	12 692	5 190 985
Gold	x	—	—	x	692 376	1 025 635	33 289	38 458	453	248 694	67 097	220 742	2 355 325
Natural gas by-products	—	—	—	—	—	—	830	12 272	2 044 095	65 205	—	3 055	2 125 457
Copper	—	—	x	27 535	299 268	723 187	154 598	x	—	895 110	—	—	2 101 168
Coal	—	—	238 000	34 200	—	—	—	95 300	541 100	997 300	—	—	1 905 900
Nickel	—	—	—	—	—	1 237 668	590 567	—	—	—	—	—	1 828 235
Zinc	—	—	x	212 529	143 727	276 536	98 364	x	—	154 205	178 340	279 002	1 350 970
Iron ore	737 704	—	—	—	x	x	—	—	—	3 095	—	—	1 307 888
Potash (K₂O)	—	—	—	x	—	—	—	x	—	—	—	—	918 994
Cement	x	—	x	—	142 330	388 543	x	x	x	x	—	—	816 802
Sand and gravel	11 701	2 453	15 045	14 387	83 022	209 649	35 203	17 597	106 584	120 708	6 883	8 160	631 391
Stone	5 015	—	23 576	18 398	206 173	222 374	7 948	—	2 892	22 725	—	3 735	512 837
Uranium (U)	—	—	—	—	—	165 000	—	307 074	—	—	—	—	472 074
Asbestos	4 023	—	—	—	223 150	—	—	—	—	47 362	—	—	274 535
Salt	—	—	x	x	x	142 614	—	26 759	15 410	—	—	—	258 585
Sulphur, elemental	—	—	—	—	—	153	—	3 032	200 269	40 650	—	—	244 104
Lead	—	—	x	50 225	—	x	2 096	—	—	42 191	81 036	26 724	203 864
Lime	—	—	—	x	x	103 550	7 199	—	20 488	—	x	—	186 287
Silver	x	—	x	22 869	22 159	44 070	7 022	x	—	73 240	12 856	2 876	185 261
Platinum group	—	—	—	—	—	x	x	—	—	—	—	—	141 790
Clay products	x	—	x	x	x	85 279	x	x	x	14 015	—	—	139 411
Peat	69	—	x	26 934	38 892	—	x	x	14 237	—	—	—	91 675
Sulphur in smelter gas	566	—	144	6 547	16 756	44 115	345	—	—	4 924	—	3 195	76 592
Gypsum	x	—	52 342	—	—	13 900	x	—	—	—	x	—	74 315
Total all minerals	793 306	2 453	444 627	617 008	2 934 229	5 062 151	1 107 794	2 852 043	16 147 718	3 749 999	346 215	756 705	34 814 247

ₚ Preliminary;–Nil; x Confidential.
Note: Certain minerals are not included in the leading minerals due to confidentiality constraints. Confidential values are included in totals. Numbers may not add to totals due to rounding.
SOURCE: Energy, Mines and Resources Canada; Statistics Canada.

38. Canada's World Role as a Producer of Certain Important Minerals, 1990[1]

MINERAL	RANK OF FIVE LEADING COUNTRIES (% of World Total)				
	1	2	3	4	5
Uranium (U concentrates)	**Canada 27.7**	Australia 11.2	United States 10.8	Namibia 10.1	France 8.9
Zinc (mine production)	**Canada 16.4**	Australia 12.7	Soviet Union[2] 11.9	China 8.5	Peru 8.0
Gypsum	United States 15.2	**Canada 9.0**	Iran 8.2	China 8.2	Japan 6.5
Potash (K₂O equivalent)	Soviet Union 33.1	**Canada 25.5**	East Germany[3] 9.7	West Germany 8.0	United States 6.0
Nickel (mine production)	Soviet Union 30.0	**Canada 21.0**	New Caledonia 9.1	Australia 7.2	Indonesia 5.8
Asbestos	Soviet Union 61.1	**Canada 17.2**	Brazil 4.8	Zimbabwe 4.5	China 3.9
Molybdenum (Mo content)	United States 55.8	Chile 12.5	**Canada 11.0**	Soviet Union 10.0	Mexico 3.6
Platinum group metals (mine production)	South Africa 48.3	Soviet Union 43.6	**Canada 3.9**	United States 2.7	Japan 0.8
Sulphur, elemental	United States 26.3	Soviet Union 16.3	**Canada 15.1**	Poland 11.4	Mexico 5.5
Aluminum (primary metal)	United States 22.3	Soviet Union 12.1	**Canada 8.6**	Australia 6.8	Brazil 5.1
Cobalt (mine production)	Zaire 40.6	Zambia 19.6	Soviet Union 9.7	**Canada 8.8**	Cuba 6.5
Titanium concentrates (ilmenite)	Australia 30.8	Norway 15.0	South Africa 13.1	**Canada 12.7**	Malaysia 8.4
Copper (mine production)	Chile 17.6	United States 17.6	Soviet Union 10.0	**Canada 8.8**	Zambia 5.5
Silver (mine production)	Mexico 16.3	United States 13.9	Peru 11.4	**Canada 9.6**	Soviet Union 8.8
Lead (mine production)	Australia 16.9	United States 14.9	Soviet Union 14.7	China 9.5	**Canada 7.2**
Cadmium (refined production)	Japan 12.3	Soviet Union 12.0	Belgium 9.8	United States 8.4	**Canada 7.4**
Gold (refined production)	South Africa 29.7	United States 14.3	Soviet Union 12.3	Australia 12.0	**Canada 8.3**

[1]Preliminary data.
[2]The Soviet Union was dissolved in 1991. Data for Russia and the other independent countries that were formed after dissolution are not available for the years prior to 1992.
[3]East and West Germany were reunited in October 1990.
SOURCE: Energy, Mines and Resources Canada, *1992 Canadian Minerals Yearbook.*

Energy

39. Coal, Supply and Demand

	1960	1970	1980	1991
			(10⁶ t)	
Supply				
Production	10.0	15.1	36.7	71.1
Imports	11.5	18.0	15.6	12.4
Total Supply	**21.5**	**33.1**	**52.3**	**83.5**
Demand				
Domestic	20.4	25.7	37.3	49.4
Exports	0.9	4.3	15.3	34.1
Total Demand	**21.3**	**30.0**	**52.6**	**83.5**

Inc. bituminous, sub-bituminous, and lignite.
SOURCE: Statistics Canada, *Coal and Coke Statistics*, Cat. No. 45-002.

40. Electricity Consumption by Sector, 1960 to 1990

	1960	1970	1980	1990*
SECTOR		(GW.h)		
Residential	20 397 (19)	43 431 (21)	92 440 (27)	133 327 (29)
Commercial	12 632 (12)	44 068 (22)	75 912 (21)	107 092 (23)
Industrial	66 353 (60)	98 450 (49)	142 247 (42)	190 903 (41)
Line Losses**	9 920 (9)	16 388 (8)	32 469 (10)	34 295 (7)
Total	**109 304 (100)**	**202 337 (100)**	**340 068 (100)**	**465 617 (100)**

¹Preliminary data.
²Losses during transmission, distribution, and unallocated energy.
Figures in parentheses are percentage shares.
SOURCE: Statistics Canada, *Electric Power Statistics, Volume II*, Cat. No. 57-202.

41. Electricity, Supply and Demand

(10⁹ kW/h)	1960	1970	1980	1991
Supply				
Production	114.0	204.7	367.3	489.2
Imports	1.0	3.2	2.9	6.2
Total Supply	**115.0**	**207.9**	**370.2**	**495.4**
Demand				
Domestic	109.0	202.3	239.9	470.8
Exports	6.0	5.6	30.3	24.6
Total Demand	**115.0**	**207.9**	**370.2**	**495.4**

SOURCE: Statistics Canada, *Electric Power Statistics*, Cat. No. 57-202.

42. Marketable Natural Gas, Supply and Demand

(10⁹ m³)	1960	1970	1980	1991
Supply				
Production	12.5	52.9	69.8	105.2
Imports	0.2	0.3	5.6	0.3
Total Supply	**12.7**	**53.2**	**75.4**	**105.5**
Demand				
Domestic	9.4	29.5	43.3	54.8
Exports	3.1	22.1	22.6	47.6
Total Demand	**12.5**	**51.6**	**75.4**	**102.4**

SOURCE: Statistics Canada, *Crude Petroleum and Natural Gas Production*, Cat. No. 26-006.

43. Petroleum, Supply and Demand

(10⁶ m³)	1960	1970	1980	1991
Supply				
Production	36.5	80.2	89.5	96.7
Imports	21.2	33.1	32.2	31.5
Total Supply	**57.7**	**113.3**	**121.7**	**128.2**
Demand				
Domestic	46.8	74.3	109.8	84.4
Exports	10.7	38.9	11.9	44.2
Total Demand	**57.5**	**113.2**	**121.7**	**128.6**

SOURCE.: Statistics Canada, *Refined Petroleum Products*, Cat. No. 45-004.

44. Installed Electrical Generating Capacity by Fuel Type and Region, 1960, 1970, 1975, and 1990

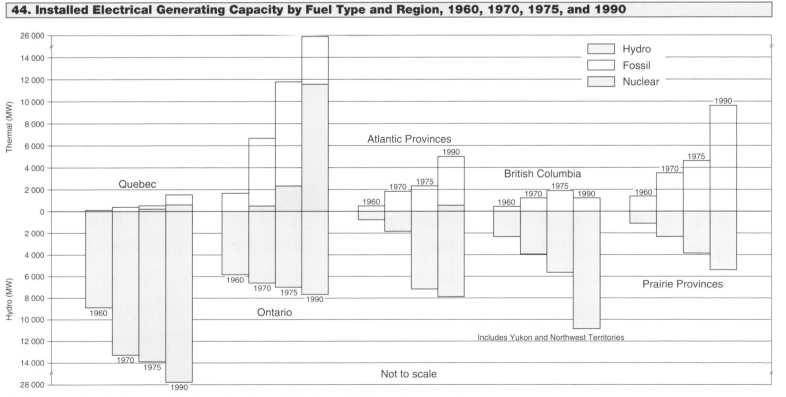

Electrical capacity in the Yukon and Northwest Territories (MW): Fossil 189, Hydro 135, Nuclear 0

SOURCE: Department of Energy, Mines and Resources Canada, *Electrical Power in Canada*, 1975, 1990

45. Crude Oil and Equivalent Remaining Established Reserves, 1990

	PROVINCE OR REGION										
	BRITISH COLUMBIA	ALBERTA	SASKATCHEWAN	MANITOBA	ONTARIO	EASTERN CANADA	MAINLAND TERRITORIES[2]	MACKENZIE DELTA-BEAUFORT SEA[1]	ARCTIC ISLANDS[1]	EASTCOAST OFFSHORE[2]	CANADA
			(000 m³)								
CRUDE OIL											
Remaining reserves as at 12-31-1989	18 490	582 531	111 909	8 349	1 324	5	22 734	53 950	101	138 600	937 993
Gross additions	1 034	65	16 186	726	339	—	—	—	—	—	18 350
Total crude oil	**19 524**	**582 596**	**128 095**	**9 075**	**1 663**	**5**	**22 734**	**53 950**	**101**	**138 600**	**956 343**
1990 net production[3]	1 958	52 391	11 199	724	249	—	1 841	—	24	—	68 386
Remaining reserves as at 12-31-1990	17 566	530 205	116 896	8 351	1 414	5	20 893	53 950	77	136 600	887 957
Net change in reserves during 1990	–924	–52 326	4 987	2	90	—	–1 841	—	–24	—	–50 036
PENTANES PLUS											
Remaining reserves[1] as at 12-31-1989	4 260	114 157	498	26	—	—	357	11 671	6 617	—	137 586
Gross additions	–13	1 747	31	—	—	—	–9	—	—	—	1 756
Total pentanes plus	**4 247**	**115 904**	**529**	**26**	**—**	**—**	**348**	**11 671**	**6 617**	**—**	**139 342**
1990 net production[3]	223	6 268	26	2	—	—	21	—	—	—	6 540
Remaining reserves as at 12-31-1990	4 024	109 636	503	24	—	—	327	11 671	6 617	—	132 802
Net change in reserves during 1990	–236	–4 521	5	–2	—	—	–30	—	—	—	–4 784
Total crude oil and equivalent	**21 590**	**639 841**	**117 399**	**8 375**	**1 414**	**5**	**21 220**	**65 621**	**6 694**	**138 600**	**1 020 759**

[1]As with all other areas, reserves for frontier areas are carried in accordance with the definition of established reserves. However, reserves for frontier areas are only shown when a threshold volume has been determined to exist.
[2]Crude oil reserves were booked for the eastcoast offshore for the first time in year-end 1981 reserves.
[3]Preliminary estimate.
SOURCE: Canadian Petroleum Association. (excludes oil sands reserves).

46. Marketable Natural Gas Remaining Established Reserves, 1990

	PROVINCE OR REGION									
	BRITISH COLUMBIA	ALBERTA	SASKATCHEWAN	MANITOBA	ONTARIO	EASTERN CANADA	MAINLAND TERRITORIES[1]	ARCTIC ISLANDS[1]	EASTCOAST OFFSHORE[2]	CANADA
			(000 000 m³)							
Remaining reserves as at 12-31-1989	218 393	1 705 559	74 791	—	17 529	90	10 987	298 730	406 370	2 732 449
Gross additions	16 857	74 069	8 539	—	172	—	—	—	—	99 637
Total natural gas	**235 250**	**1 779 628**	**83 330**	**—**	**17 701**	**90**	**10 987**	**298 730**	**406 370**	**2 832 086**
Net change in underground storage	—	—	—	—	—	—	—	—	—	—
1990 net production[3]	11 612	89 744	4 450	—	798	18	74	—	—	106 696
Remaining reserves at 12-31-1990	223 638	1 689 884	78 880	—	16 903	72	10 913	298 730	406 370	2 725 390
Non-associated	214 484	1 411 564	76 236	—	16 903	67	10 802	274 430	377 040	2 381 526
Associated	9 154	278 320	2 644	—	—	5	111	24 300	29 330	343 864
Dissolved	—	—	—	—	—	—	—	—	—	—
Underground storage	—	—	—	—	—	—	—	—	—	—
Net change in reserves during 1990	5 245	–15 675	4 089	—	–626	–18	–74	—	—	–7 059

[1]As with all other areas, reserves for frontier areas are carried in accordance with the definition of established reserves. However, reserves for frontier areas are only shown when a threshold volume has been determined to exist.
[2]Crude oil reserves were booked for the eastcoast offshore for the first time in year-end 1981 reserves.
[3]Preliminary estimate.
SOURCE: Canadian Petroleum Association.

47. Electricity Production and Consumption, 1960 to 1990

PROVINCE OR TERRITORY	1960		1970		1980		1990	
	PRODUCTION	CONSUMPTION	PRODUCTION	CONSUMPTION	PRODUCTION	CONSUMPTION	PRODUCTION	CONSUMPTION
		(GW.h)		(GW.h)		(GW.h)		(GW.h)
Newfoundland	1 512	1 427	4 854	4 770	46 374	8 545	36 813	10 650
Prince Edward Island	79	79	250	250	127	518	81	752
Nova Scotia	1 814	1 733	3 511	3 706	6 868	6 814	9 430	9 678
New Brunswick	1 738	1 684	5 142	4 221	9 323	8 838	16 665	13 173
Quebec	50 433	44 002	75 877	69 730	97 917	118 254	135 458	157 308
Ontario	35 815	37 157	63 857	69 488	110 283	106 509	129 343	142 818
Manitoba	3 742	4 021	8 449	8 601	19 468	13 927	20 149	17 450
Saskatchewan	2 204	2 124	6 011	5 402	9 204	9 827	13 540	13 589
Alberta	3 443	3 472	10 035	9 880	23 451	23 172	42 874	42 041
British Columbia	13 409	13 413	26 209	25 761	43 416	42 789	60 662	57 206
Yukon	89	89	224	220	381	381	480	480
Northwest Territories	100	100	304	308	494	494	472	472
Canada	**114 378**	**109 304**	**204 723**	**202 337**	**367 306**	**340 068**	**465 967**	**465 617**

SOURCE: Statistics Canada, *Electrical Power Statistics, Vol. II*, Cat. No. 57-202.

48. Electrical Energy Production by Fuel Type, 1990

PROVINCE OR TERRITORY	FUEL TYPE						
	COAL	OIL	NATURAL GAS	NUCLEAR	HYDRO	OTHER	TOTAL
				(GW.h)			
Newfoundland	0	1 881	0	0	34 932	0	36 813
Prince Edward Island	107	81	0	0	0	0	188
Nova Scotia	5 680	2 470	0	0	1 150	130	9 430
New Brunswick	1 140	6 293	0	5 338	3 484	303	16 558
Quebec	0	1 908	0	4 146	129 404	0	135 458
Ontario	26 352	1 087	2 000	59 353	40 225	326	129 343
Manitoba	345	5	8	0	19 747	44	20 149
Saskatchewan	8 623	14	507	0	4 220	176	13 540
Alberta	35 195	0	5 123	0	2 060	496	42 874
British Columbia	0	688	1 569	0	57 245	1 160	60 662
Yukon	0	57	0	0	423	0	480
Northwest Territories	0	215	0	0	257	0	472
Canada	**77 442**	**14 699**	**9 207**	**68 837**	**293 147**	**2 635**	**465 967**

SOURCE: Statistics Canada, *Electric Power Statistics, Vol. II*, Cat. No. 57-202.

Manufacturing

49. Summary Statistics, Annual Census of Manufacturers, 1965–1988

YEAR	NUMBER OF ESTABLISHMENTS[1]	PRODUCTION AND RELATED WORKERS			COST OF FUEL AND ELECTRICITY ($000)	COST OF MATERIALS AND SUPPLIES USED ($000)	VALUE OF SHIPMENTS OF GOODS OF OWN MANUFACTURE ($000)	VALUE ADDED ($000)
		NUMBER	WORK HOURS PAID (000)	WAGES ($000)				
1965	33 310	1 115 892	2 384 002	5 012 345	675 641	18 622 213	33 889 425	14 927 764
1970	31 928	1 167 063	2 450 058	7 232 256	903 264	25 699 999	46 380 935	20 047 801
1975	30 100	1 271 786	2 613 062	12 699 228	1 805 398	51 177 942	88 427 031	36 105 457
1980	35 495	1 346 187	2 780 203	22 162 309	4 448 859	99 897 576	168 058 662	65 851 774
1984	36 464	1 240 816	2 583 486	28 294 553	7 306 383	136 133 629	230 070 091	88 667 660
1988	40 262	1 474 738	3 089 681	38 890 576	7 362 810	166 534 406	298 210 479	125 175 167

[1]The increase in the number of establishments between 1975 and 1980 was largely a result of the addition of 4 962 small establishments by improved coverage.
SOURCE: *Canada Year Book 1976-77, 1992*.

50. Value of Shipments of Goods of Own Manufacture, by Industry Group, 1988 ($000 000)

INDUSTRY GROUP	PROVINCE OR TERRITORY											
	NFLD	PEI	NS	NB	QUE	ONT	MAN	SASK	ALTA	BC	YUKON AND NWT	CANADA
Food	799.7	266.0	1 265.1	1 127.8	9 027.0	14 826.1	1 640.3	985.8	4 113.1	2 928.6	—	37 159.5
Beverage	[1]	[1]	144.8	173.0	1 527.6	2 708.1	174.4	117.9	417.5	471.5	—	5 865.4
Tobacco Products	—	—	—	—	[1]	[1]	—	—	—	—	—	1 778.6
Rubber Products	—	—	[1]	[1]	1 454.9	[1]	[1]	[1]	[1]	[1]	—	2 694.7
Plastic Products	[1]	[1]	64.2	64.0	1 469.5	3 390.0	184.9	47.4	289.6	371.4	—	5 893.1
Leather and Allied Products	[1]	—	0.5	[1]	533.9	641.4	40.9	6.0	23.3	[1]	—	1 293.3
Primary Textile	—	[1]	[1]	[1]	1 687.5	1338.5	[1]	—	[1]	20.3	—	3 173.3
Textile Products	[1]	[1]	100.1	[1]	1 629.1	1 460.0	53.0	12.5	65.6	82.5	—	3 411.0
Clothing	[1]	[1]	49.9	15.7	4 062.1	1 812.3	338.2	15.0	140.0	221.6	—	6 656.7
Wood	29.2	14.1	159.8	497.6	3 613.5	2 906.0	220.5	151.9	797.7	6 931.9	—	15 322.2
Furniture and Fixture	0.9	—	18.8	20.7	1 438.4	2 571.4	153.8	10.6	217.4	187.8	—	4 619.7
Paper and Allied Products	[1]	[1]	661.8	1 643.5	8 122.6	7 906.4	322.9	[1]	631.0	5 728.1	—	25 661.1
Printing, Publishing, and Allied	45.1	16.5	146.1	96.3	3 315.0	6 638.0	452.2	203.4	733.9	879.4	—	12 525.7
Primary Metal	[1]	—	[1]	[1]	7465.6	11 903.4	512.4	[1]	1 089.7	1 241.9	—	22 715.4
Fabricated Metal Products	25.0	13.5	113.2	183.5	4 085.7	10 948.1	428.9	145.9	954.9	1 156.8	—	18 055.8
Machinery	1.7	11.5	39.4	69.8	1 667.6	6 162.4	430.7	175.7	761.4	692.3	—	10 012.3
Transportation Equipment	[1]	18.5	368.4	[1]	6 302.5	42 304.7	652.7	98.8	227.5	972.1	—	51 718.1
Electrical and Electronic Products	[1]	[1]	119.0	50.7	4 843.4	11 707.7	514.7	184.6	344.3	407.3	—	18 191.7
Non-metallic Mineral Products	51.6	4.4	105.2	108.5	1 837.5	4 159.2	199.4	99.5	629.7	608.5	—	7 803.6
Petroleum and Coal Products	[1]	—	[1]	[1]	2 700.2	5 376.2	[1]	[1]	2 876.4	1 473.5	[1]	14 938.9
Chemical and Chemical Products	90.5	22.4	58.3	103.1	5 132.6	12 571.0	229.1	164.0	3 442.6	814.6	—	22 628.0
Other Manufacturing	4.1	6.1	[1]	[1]	[1]	[1]	76.9	28.0	229.9	259.1	[1]	6 092.3
All Manufacturing Industries	**1 726.0**	**391.7**	**5 455.7**	**5 627.7**	**73 750.6**	**157 540.2**	**6 671.0**	**3 380.1**	**18 100.5**	**25 510.1**	**57.0**	**298 210.5**

—not applicable   [1]Confidential.   SOURCE: *Canada Year Book, 1992*.

51. Principal Statistics on Manufacturing Industries, 1987

PROVINCE OR TERRITORY	NUMBER OF ESTABLISHMENTS	NUMBER OF EMPLOYEES	SALARIES AND WAGES	COST OF FUEL AND ELECTRICITY	COST OF MATERIALS, SUPPLIES, AND GOODS FOR RESALE	VALUE OF SHIPMENTS AND OTHER REVENUE	VALUE ADDED
				($000)			
Newfoundland	318	18 627	397 423	97 528	1 181 306	2 056 117	786 407
Prince Edward Island	135	3 530	60 698	7 579	276 838	416 915	137 727
Nova Scotia	761	37 715	904 984	155 234	3 528 073	5 629 641	1 977 995
New Brunswick	691	32 424	838 345	253 059	3 715 621	6 018 550	2 092 485
Quebec	11 183	520 459	13 443 485	2 067 000	40 411 645	72 608 303	30 287 556
Ontario	15 109	956 400	27 488 737	3 007 220	109 362 283	174 700 261	62 452 655
Manitoba	1 186	54 031	1 284 561	165 220	3 904 361	6 992 457	2 910 052
Saskatchewan	810	19 772	516 865	110 302	2 050 042	3 522 989	1 371 214
Alberta	2 590	78 220	2 278 685	438 604	11 275 650	17 242 833	5 538 627
British Columbia	3 969	142 512	4 610 679	751 600	13 450 792	24 805 204	10 708 896
Yukon and Northwest Territories	38	328	7 785	795	30 233	56 249	25 959
Canada	**36 790**	**1 864 018**	**51 832 248**	**7 054 140**	**189 186 844**	**314 049 518**	**118 289 573**

SOURCE: Statistics Canada, *Market Research Handbook*, 1991.

Transportation

52. St. Lawrence Seaway Traffic by Classification and Direction, 1990

MONTREAL-LAKE ONTARIO SECTION

COMMODITIES	UPBOUND (000 t)	SOURCES AND DESTINATIONS OF UPBOUND COMMODITIES (%)	DOWNBOUND (000 t)	SOURCES AND DESTINATIONS OF DOWNBOUND COMMODITIES (%)
Wheat	—	—	9 276.2	Can→Can 76 US→Can 10 US→For 10
Corn	—	—	1 206.0	US→Can 48 US→For 37 Can→Can 13
Barley	2.4	Can→Can 100	1 122.9	US→Can 54 Can→Can 25 US→For 21
Soybeans	—	—	272.9	US→For 86 Can→For 14
Flaxseed	—	—	165.7	Can→For 100
Total Agricultural Products	**6.5**		**12 426.9**	
Bituminous Coal	—		489.4	US→Can 91 Can→Can 5 US→For 4
Coke	—		946.2	US→Can 54 US→For 33 Can→Can 10
Iron Ore	11 518.6	Can→US 53 Can→Can 47	9.2	US→Can 100
Aluminium Ore and Concentrates	178.3	For→Can 87 For→US 8 Can→Can 5	—	
Clay and Bentonite	5.9	For→US 100	223.7	US→Can 63 US→For 37
Stone and Gravel	—	—	715.5	Can→Can 73 US→Can 27
Salt	368.7	Can→Can 100	815.1	Can→Can 77 US→Can 23
Total Mine Products	**13 072.9**		**3 470.2**	
Gasoline	37.7	Can→Can 51 For→Can 42 US→Can 5	109.6	Can→Can 78 Can→For 22
Fuel Oil	262.8	Can→Can 39 Can→US 41 For→Can 10	627.8	Can→Can 93 Can→US 6
Chemicals	370.2	For→Can 52 US→Can 30 Can→US 5	446.8	Can→For 59 Can→Can 30 Can→US 11
Sodium Production	13.1	US→Can 91	92.2	Can→Can 100
Iron and Steel Production	2 683.4	For→Can 14 For→US 86	924.1	Can→For 67 US→For 31
Sugar	266.1	For→Can 100	—	
Scrap Iron and Steel	0.8	For→US 97	232.8	US→For 58 Can→For 29 Can→Can 13
Total Manufactures[1]	**4 567.9**		**3 047.0**	
Grand Total (000 t)	**17 647.2**		**19 008.7**	
($000)	**21 286.2**		**15 683.6**	
WELLAND CANAL SECTION				
Wheat	—	—	9 366.4	Can→Can 77 US→Can 10 US→For 10
Corn	—	—	1 392.7	US→Can 53 US→For 32 Can→Can 13
Barley	—	—	1 125.3	US→Can 54 Can→Can 25 US→For 21
Soybeans	—	—	364.8	US→For 64 US→Can 23 Can→For 10
Flaxseed	—	—	165.7	Can→For 100
Total Agricultural Products	**0.2**		**12 801.2**	
Bituminous Coal	—	—	6 266.0	US→Can 99
Coke	106.2	Can→US 100	930.8	US→Can 57 US→For 33 Can→Can 8
Iron Ore	6 448.9	Can→US 95 Can→Can 4	1 034.1	US→Can 100
Aluminium Ore and Concentrates	178.3	For→Can 87 For→US 8 Can→Can 5	—	—
Clay and Bentonite	5.9	For→US 100	223.7	US→Can 63 US→For 37
Stone, Gravel, and Sand	820.4	Can→US 98	1 175.5	Can→Can 65 US→Can 35
Salt	—	—	1 513.2	Can→Can 50 US→Can 47 Can→US 3
Total Mine Products	**7 866.5**		**11 724.0**	

WELLAND CANAL SECTION (Continued)

Gasoline	25.4	Can→Can 63 Can→US 37	198.6	US→Can 99 US→For 1	
Fuel Oils	106.2	Can→Can 39 Can→US 47 For→Can 14	832.5	US→Can 57 US→For 33 Can→Can 8	
Chemicals	144.2	For→Can 47 For→US 34 Can→US 12	540.6	Can→For 47 Can→Can 38 Can→US 14	
Sodium Products	—	—	87.5	Can→Can 100	
Iron and Steel Production	2 390.0	For→US 97 For→Can 3	440.6	US→For 64 Can→For 34	
Cement	399.0	Can→US 86 Can→Can 14	8.3	Can→US 59	
Scrap Iron and Steel	217.5	Can→Can 54 Can→US 46	151.6	US→For 89 Can→For 11	
Total Manufactures[1]	**4 094.8**		**2 842.8**		
Grand Total (000 t)	**11 961.5**		**27 436.4**		
($000)	**12 190.2**		**19 561.2**		

[1]Includes unclassified cargoes.
SOURCE: *The St. Lawrence Seaway Traffic Report—1990 Navigation Season*, St. Lawrence Seaway Authority (Ottawa) and the Saint Lawrence Seaway Development Corporation (Washington).

53. Canadian Travel Balance of Trade ($000 000)

YEAR	RECEIPTS	PAYMENTS	BALANCE
1930	180	92	88
1935	117	64	53
1940	105	43	62
1945	166	83	83
1950	275	226	49
1955	328	449	−121
1960	420	627	−207
1965	747	796	−49
1970	1 234	1 460	−226
1975	1 815	2 542	−727
1980	3 349	4 577	−1 228
1981	3 760	4 876	−1 116
1982	3 724	5 008	−1 284
1983	3 841	6 045	−2 204
1984	4 416	6 542	−2 126
1985	5 006	7 110	−2 104
1986	6 333	7 499	−1 166
1987	6 299	8 828	−2 529
1988	6 894	9 631	−2 737
1989	7 232	10 708	−3 476
1990[1]	7 437	11 961	−4 524

[1]Preliminary.
SOURCE: Statistics Canada

54. Vessels and Tonnage Handled by Canada Ports Corporation, 1989

PORT	NUMBER OF VESSEL ARRIVALS	CARGO HANDLED (000 t)	GRAIN ELEVATOR SHIPMENTS (000 t)
St. John's	979	977	—
Halifax	2 163	16 784	457
Saint John	1 518	14 702	90
Belledune	39	393	—
Sept-Îles	696	23 302	—
Chicoutimi	94	484	—
Baie-des-Ha! Ha!	206	3 857	—
Quebec	952	15 668	1 813
Trois-Rivières	488	1 584	428
Montreal	2 431	20 423	1 209
Prescott	23	289	239
Port Colborne	—	45	108
Churchill	26	320	292
Vancouver	9 409	64 025	9 624
Prince Rupert	1 705	11 332	3 475
Total	**20 729**	**174 185**	**17 735**

SOURCE: *Canada Year Book, 1992.*

55. Where Canadians Travel (000)[1]

COUNTRY OR REGION	1980	1985	1989
Total Visits	**27 402**	**28 118**	**39 006**
United States	**24 594**	**23 886**	**33 969**
California	826	763	1 047
Florida	1 482	1 536	2 234
Maine	1 098	974	1 333
Michigan	2 099	2 052	2 549
New Hampshire	778	708	942
New York	3 623	3 700	5 299
Ohio	815	757	1 067
Pennsylvania	873	867	1 331
Vermont	1 273	1 189	1 506
Washington	1 833	1 642	2 388
Europe	**1 591**	**2 578**	**2 764**
Austria	75	130	122
Belgium	74	107	129
Denmark	28	29	51
France	205	377	380
West Germany	169	259	293
Greece	38	72	61
Ireland	29	53	58
Italy	105	190	169
Netherlands	120	187	231
Portugal	35	62	82
Spain	39	98	87
Switzerland	117	200	175
United Kingdom	446	644	667
Yugoslavia	13	25	41
Caribbean	**621**	**776**	**929**
Bahamas	125	100	103
Barbados	110	87	64
Bermuda	42	40	62
Cuba	33	60	68
Dominican Republic	n.a.	n.a.	186
Jamaica	70	77	96
Central America	**236**	**290**	**514**
Mexico	220	264	475
Asia	**159**	**274**	**382**
Hong Kong	24	53	75
Japan	27	47	52
Australasia[2]	**66**	**108**	**131**
Africa	**66**	**86**	**100**
South America	**56**	**108**	**204**

[1]Includes visits which lasted less than one day.
[2]Includes islands in the Pacific, Indian, and Atlantic Oceans.
n.a.—not available.
SOURCE: Statistics Canada.

56. Principal Seaway Ports[1], 1990

CANADA

(000 t)[2]	UP	DOWN
Hamilton	10 621.1	1 165.4
Port Cartier	2 948.6	3 014.9
Montreal	2 727.2	276.8
Baie Comeau	2 761.8	3.6
Quebec City	2 143.3	1 210.7
Toronto	1 275.4	83.1
Pointe Noire	258.7	5 082.2
Sarnia	118.1	1 259.6
Sept Îles	616.1	2 211.1
Thunder Bay	9.0	7 991.2
	31 352.1	**28 779.0**

UNITED STATES

(000 t)	UP	DOWN
Indiana-Burns Harbor	2 682.7	514.0
Cleveland	2 402.8	547.8
Detroit	1 763.5	489.5
Chicago	1 014.9	444.8
Ashtabula	832.4	1 643.7
Conneaut	48.2	1 288.4
Duluth-Superior	131.3	3 730.0
Sandusky	—	1 955.2
Toledo	279.2	2 378.7
	11 746.5	**15 245.3**

[1]Includes all ports or installations within 20 km radius of the main harbour.
[2]Figures are limited to cargo volumes moved through the seaway lock structures.
SOURCE: *The St. Lawrence Seaway Traffic Report—1990 Navigation Season*, St. Lawrence Seaway Authority (Ottawa) and the Saint Lawrence Seaway Development Corporation (Washington).

Trade

57. Principal Commodities, Imported, 1991

	($000 000)
Food, Feed, Beverages, and Tobacco	**8 268.3**
Fruits and vegetables	1 965.2
Crude Materials, Inedible	**7 709.8**
Crude petroleum	4 416.4
Fabricated Materials, Inedible	**24 888.6**
Plastics and Chemicals	8 284.4
End Products, Inedible	**90 423.9**
Passenger autos	11 660.4
Trucks and other motor vehicles	3 687.0
Motor vehicle parts	15 792.8
Industrial and agricultural machinery	11 123.1
Apparel and footwear	3 460.9
Total	**134 323.2**

SOURCE: Statistics Canada, *Summary of Canadian International Trade*, Cat. No. 65-001.

58. Principal Commodities, Exported, 1991

	($000 000)
Food, Feed, Beverages, and Tobacco	**11 336.4**
Wheat and wheat flour	4 021.1
Fish and fish products	2 447.4
Crude Materials, Inedible	**18 495.2**
Crude petroleum	5 880.9
Natural gas	3 421.3
Metal ores (iron, copper, zinc)	4 443.3
Coal	1 582.7
Fabricated Materials, Inedible	**44 882.6**
Forestry products	18 995.7
Metals and alloys	12 738.3
End Products, Inedible	**64 032.3**
Passenger autos	16 287.4
Trucks and other vehicles	7 778.6
Motor vehicle parts	7 985.1
Aircraft and other transport equipment	6 708.1
Total	**141 701.2**

SOURCE: Statistics Canada, *Summary of Canadian International Trade*, Cat. No. 65-001.

59. Imports To Canada, Principal Nations, 1987, 1989, and 1991

COUNTRY	1987	1989	1991
		($000 000)	
United States	76 716	88 017	86 235
Japan	8 351	9 571	10 249
Great Britain	4 276	4 562	4 182
Germany	3 649	3 709	3 734
South Korea	1 912	2 441	2 110
Taiwan	2 166	2 351	2 212
France	1 590	2 019	2 670
Italy	1 793	2 015	1 792
Mexico	1 165	1 704	2 574
China	812	1 182	1 852
Hong Kong	1 097	1 160	1 021
Brazil	858	1 129	706
All countries	**116 238**	**135 033**	**135 284**

[1]Figures for 1987 and 1989 do not include the former East Germany.
SOURCE: Statistics Canada, *Imports by Countries*, Cat. No. 65-006.

60. Exports From Canada, Principal Nations, 1987, 1989, and 1991

COUNTRY	1987	1989	1991
		($000 000)	
United States	91 756	98 548	103 449
Japan	7 036	8 803	7 111
Great Britain	2 850	3 441	2 920
Germany[1]	1 515	1 801	2 125
South Korea	1 167	1 645	1 861
Netherlands	1 021	1 534	1 655
Belgium	1 123	1 398	1 073
France	1 037	1 268	1 350
China	1 432	1 120	1 849
Italy	843	1 099	1 017
Hong Kong	480	1 050	817
Australia	689	1 031	628
All countries	**121 462**	**134 511**	**138 079**

[1]Figures for 1987 and 1989 do not include the former East Germany.
SOURCE: Statistics Canada, *Exports by Countries*, Cat. No. 65-003.

The Economy

61. Gross Domestic Product at Factor Cost, by Industry[1], 1970 to 1989

INDUSTRY	1970	1980	1989
Agricultural and Related Services	2.9	2.1	1.6
Fishing	0.3	0.2	0.2
Forestry	0.8	0.6	0.6
Mining	6.4	4.1	3.5
Manufacturing	19.7	17.7	16.8
Construction	6.2	5.7	5.8
Trade	10.5	9.6	10.6
Finance, Insurance, and Real Estate	12.3	13.4	14.1
Transportation, Communications, and Utilities	9.1	10.1	10.5
Community, Business, and Personal Services	20.2	20.2	20.0
Public Administration	7.5	6.7	5.8

[1]Based on per cent of Canada's GDP.
SOURCE: *Canada Year Book 1992.*

64. Gross Domestic Product at Market Prices[1], 1970 to 1989

PROVINCE OR TERRITORY	1970	1980	1989
Newfoundland	1.4	1.3	1.3
Prince Edward Island	0.3	0.3	0.3
Nova Scotia	2.5	2.0	2.5
New Brunswick	1.9	1.6	1.9
Quebec	25.5	23.3	23.6
Ontario	42.0	37.1	41.5
Manitoba	4.2	3.6	3.5
Saskatchewan	3.4	4.0	3.1
Alberta	8.0	13.9	10.3
British Columbia	10.6	12.4	11.5
Yukon and Northwest Territories	0.3	0.4	0.4

[1]Based on per cent of Canada's GDP.
SOURCE: *Canada Year Book 1992.*

62. National Finances, 1970 to 1991

YEAR	REVENUE	EXPENDITURE ($ 000 000)	SURPLUS/ DEFICIT	GROSS DEBT
1970-1971	15 364	16 002	(638)[1]	35 250
1975-1976	32 354	37 464	(5 110)	55 889
1980-1981	53 796	67 829	(14 033)	113 170
1985-1986	83 060	116 911	(33 851)	249 452
1990-1991	127 067	155 502	(28 435)	408 483

[1]( ) indicates a negative value.
SOURCE: Statistics Canada, *Canadian Economic Observer*, June 1991.

63. Inflation Rates, 1915 to 1990

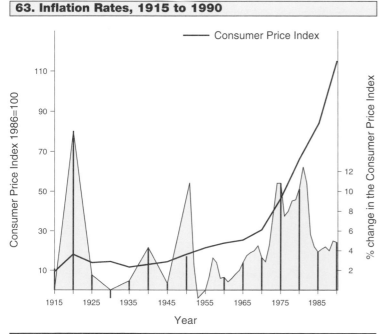

NOTE: Prior to 1950, data was compiled every five years. Since 1950, data has been compiled annually.

65. Canadian Balance of International Payments, All Countries, Current Account, 1987 to 1989

ITEM	1987	1988	1989	% CHANGE 1989/1988
	($000 000)			
Current Receipts				
Merchandise Exports	126 120	137 294	138 934	1.2
Non-merchandise Services				
Total Services	18 316	19 982	20 470	2.4
Travel	6 299	6 894	7 091	2.9
Freight and Shipping	4 740	5 065	5 365	5.9
Business Services	6 126	6 678	6 852	2.6
Government Transactions	680	636	669	5.2
Other Services	471	708	493	–30.4
Investment Income	7 061	10 867	7 661	–29.5
Transfers	5 429	7 935	8 722	9.9
Total Non-merchandise Receipts	30 806	38 784	36 853	–5.0
Total Receipts	**156 926**	**176 078**	**175 788**	**–0.2**
Current Payments				
Merchandise Imports	114 767	127 486	134 255	5.3
Non-merchandise Services				
Total Services	24 586	25 964	27 528	6.0
Travel	8 828	9 631	10 589	9.9
Freight and Shipping	4 817	4 614	4 708	2.0
Business Services	9 397	10 111	10 543	4.3
Government Transactions	1 185	1 232	1 293	5.0
Other Services	358	376	395	5.1
Investment Income	23 580	29 279	30 023	2.5
Transfers	3 353	3 665	3 640	–0.7
Total Non-merchandise Payments	51 519	58 908	61 191	3.9
Total Payments	**166 286**	**186 394**	**195 446**	**4.9**
Balances				
Merchandise	+11 353	+9 808	+4 679	–52.3
Non-merchandise	–20 713	–20 124	–24 338	—
Total Current	**–9 360**	**–10 316**	**–19 659**	**—**

SOURCE: Statistics Canada, *Quarterly Estimates of the Canadian Balance of International Payments, Fourth Quarter*, Cat. No. 67-001.

Conservation and Pollution

66. Ecozone Biophysical Characteristics[1]

ECOZONE	LANDFORMS	VEGETATION	SOILS AND SURFACE MATERIALS	CLIMATE
Atlantic Maritime	Hills and coastal plains	Mixed broadleaf and conifer stands	Acid and well-weathered soils (podzols) and soils with clay-rich sublayers (luvisols), moraine, marine bottom soils, and rock debris	Cool to cold winters, mild summers, moderate to heavy precipitation
Mixed-Wood Plain	Plains, some interior hills	Mixed broadleaf and conifer stands	Temperate region soils with clay-rich sublayers (luvisols), marine bottom soils, moraine, rock	Cool to cold winters, warm to hot summers, moderate precipitation
Boreal Shield	Plains, uplands, interior hills, many lakes and streams	Conifer and broadleaf boreal stands	Acid and well-weathered soils (podzols), lake bottom soils, moraine, rock	Cold winters, warm to hot summers, moderate precipitation
Prairie	Plains, some foothills	Short and mixed grasslands, aspen parkland	Organically rich, relatively fertile grassland soils (chernozems), moraine, and lake bottom materials	Cold winters, hot summers minimal precipitation
Boreal Plain	Plains, some foothills	Conifer and broadleaf boreal stands	Temperate region soils with clay-rich sublayers (luvisols), moraine and lake bottom materials	Cold winters, warm summers, moderate precipitation
Montane Cordillera	Mountainous highlands, interior plains	Mixed vegetation, conifer stands to sage brush	Temperate region soils with clay-rich sublayers (luvisols), soils with minimal weathering (brunisols), moraine, rock, rock debris	Cool to cold winters, warm to hot summers, and in lee areas, moist in montane areas
Pacific Maritime	Mountainous highlands, some coastal plains	Coastal western and mountain hemlock	Acid and well-weathered soils (podzols), moraine, rock, rock debris	Mild winters, mild summers, heavy precipitation, especially in fall and winter
Boreal Cordillera	Mountainous highlands, some hills and plains	Boreal, some alpine tundra and open woodland	Soils with minimal weathering (brunisols), moraine, rock	Cold winters, mild summers, minimal precipitation in lee areas, moist in montane areas
Tundra Cordillera	Mountainous highlands	Alpine and arctic tundra	Soils with minimal weathering (brunisols), frozen soils (cryosols), moraine, rock	Very cold winters, cool summers, minimal precipitation
Taiga Plain	Plains, some foothills	Open woodland, shrublands, and wetlands	Soils with minimal weathering (brunisols), some frozen soils (cryosols), organic materials, moraine	Cold winters, mild to warm summers, moderate precipitation
Taiga Shield	Plains, uplands, some interior hills, many lakes and streams	Open woodlands, some arctic tundra and lichen heath	Soils with minimal weathering (brunisols), acid and well-weathered soils (podzols), some frozen soils (cryosols), moraine, rock	Cold winters, warm summers, moderate precipitation
Hudson Bay Plain	Plains	Wetland, arctic tundra, and some conifer stands	Organic soils, sea bottom and beach materials	Cold winters, mild summers, minimal precipitation
Southern Arctic	Plains, some interior hills	Shrub/herb/heath arctic tundra	Frozen soils (cryosols), moraine rock, marine bottom sediments	Cold winters, cool summers, minimal precipitation
Northern Arctic	Plains and hills	Herb-lichen arctic tundra	Frozen soils (cryosols), moraine, rock, marine bottom sediments	Very cold winters, cool summers, minimal precipitation
Arctic Cordillera	Mountainous highlands	Largely non-vegetated, some shrub/herb arctic tundra	Frozen soils (cryosols), rock, rock debris, ice	Very cold winters, cool to cold summers, minimal precipitation

This list is meant to be illustrative only and is not a comprehensive presentation of the characteristics of these areas.
SOURCE: Environment Canada, Lands Directorate. *Terrestrial Ecozones of Canada*, by E. Wiken, unpublished working paper, August, 1983.

67. Conservation Lands and Waters, Area and Number of Reserves

PROVINCE OR TERRITORY	NATIONAL PARKS	NATIONAL WILDLIFE AREAS, MIGRATORY BIRD SANCTUARIES	PROVINCIAL/ TERRITORIAL PARKS	PROVINCIAL/ TERRITORIAL WILDLIFE AREAS	PROVINCIAL/ TERRITORIAL WILDERNESS AREAS	PROVINCIAL/ TERRITORIAL ECOLOGICAL RESERVES	OTHER PROVINCIAL/ TERRITORIAL RESERVES	AREA OF PROVINCE/ TERRITORY	% OF PROVINCE/ TERRITORY RESERVED	TOTAL AREA OF RESERVES WITH NO LOGGING, MINING, OR SPORT HUNTING[1]	% OF PROVINCE/ TERRITORY RESERVED WITH NO LOGGING, MINING, OR SPORT HUNTING
					TOTAL AREA IN KM² / NUMBER OF RESERVES						
British Columbia	6 302 / 6	54 / 15	52 337 / 387	177 / 6	1 315 / 1	1 558 / 120	—	948 596	6.5	22 685	2.4
Alberta	54 085 / 4.8	145 / 7	1 365 / 106	680 / 8	5 607 / 4	185 / 10	309 / 114	661 185	9.4	56 420	8.5[2]
Saskatchewan	4 781 / 2	827 / 23	9 081 / 31	18 848 / 1 662	—	8 / 1	769 / 298	651 900	5.1	6 289	1.0
Manitoba	2 976 / 1	1 / 2	14 314 / 60	30 658 / 74	—	178 / 9	15 666 / 5	650 087	9.8	3 189	0.5
Ontario	2 171 / 5	443 / 23	56 273 / 217	9 240 / 45	618 / 37	—	539 / 323	1 068 582	6.5	24 249	2.2
Quebec	935 / 3	661 / 42	4 000 / 16	67 000 / 16	—	484 / 21	537 / 1	1 540 680	4.8	5 956	0.4
New Brunswick	445 / 2	62 / 7	217 / 49	3 219 / 19	—	—	1 / 3	73 436	5.4	663	0.9
Nova Scotia	1 332 / 2	66 / 15	131 / 107	1 396 / 25	—	1 / 2	3 / 4	55 491	5.3	1 387	2.5
Prince Edward Island	26 / 1	1 / 1	42 / 67	29 / 5	—	—	—	5 657	1.7	97	1.7
Newfoundland	2 338 / 2	9 / 1	235 / 75	—	1 070 / 1	23 / 6	—	404 517	0.9	2 597	0.6

PROVINCE OR TERRITORY	NATIONAL PARKS	NATIONAL WILDLIFE AREAS, MIGRATORY BIRD SANCTUARIES	PROVINCIAL/ TERRITORIAL PARKS	PROVINCIAL/ TERRITORIAL WILDLIFE AREAS	PROVINCIAL/ TERRITORIAL WILDERNESS AREAS	PROVINCIAL/ TERRITORIAL ECOLOGICAL RESERVES	OTHER PROVINCIAL/ TERRITORIAL RESERVES	AREA OF PROVINCE/ TERRITORY	% OF PROVINCE/ TERRITORY RESERVED	TOTAL AREA OF RESERVES WITH NO LOGGING, MINING, OR SPORT HUNTING[1]	% OF PROVINCE/ TERRITORY RESERVED WITH NO LOGGING, MINING, OR SPORT HUNTING
Yukon	32 183 / 2		114 / 1	5 918 / 2	—	—	—	482 515	7.9	32 273	6.7
Northwest Territories	74 698 / 3.2	113 405 / 15	130 / 44	26 464 / 3	—	—	—	3 379 684	6.4	98 658	2.9
Canada	182 272 / 34	115 674 / 151	138 239 / 1 160	163 629 / 1 865	8 680 / 43	2 437 / 169	17 824 / 748	9 922 330	6.3	254 463	2.6

[1]Not including hunting by aboriginal people under treaty or land claim settlements.
[2]Two-thirds of this area is accounted for by the Alberta portion of Wood Buffalo National Park.
SOURCE: Reprinted with permission from *Endangered Spaces: The Future for Canada's Wilderness*, Monte Hummel, ed., published by Key Porter Books Limited, Toronto, Ontario. Copyright © 1989 Monte Hummel.

68. Major Air Pollutants for Selected Canadian Cities

CITY	SULPHUR DIOXIDE (PPB)	NITROGEN DIOXIDE (PPB)	OZONE (PPB, 1 HOUR)	CARBON MONOXIDE (PPB, 1 HOUR)	TOTAL SUSPENDED PARTICLES (UG/M)
MAXIMUM ACCEPTABLE CONCENTRATION	23	53	82	13	70
MAXIMUM DESIRABLE CONCENTRATION	11	23	50	5	60
Toronto	5.1	26	100	3	65
Montreal	7.1	27	85	3	40
Vancouver	6	25	58	4.8	36
Ottawa	4.5	28	45	2.5	43
Edmonton	3	24	60	3.6	46
Calgary	3	28	55	4.0	54
Winnipeg	1.5	17	80	2	46
Quebec City	5	31	70	3	*
Hamilton	12	25	110	2	83
St. Catharines-Niagara Falls	6	21	60	2	55
London	6	22	100	2	57
Kitchener	3	25	80	3	60
Halifax	11	12	65	2	35
Victoria	nm	nm	nm	nm	33
Windsor	8	28	100	2	54
Oshawa	6	24	110	3	55
Saskatoon	0.0	15	60	1	31
Regina	*	14	60	3	39
St. John's, Nfld.	8	nm	90	3	31
Chicoutimi-Jonquière	nm	nm	nm	nm	nm
Sudbury	8	11	80	1	36
Sherbrooke	nm	nm	nm	nm	46
Trois-Rivières	8	nm	nm	nm	46
Kingston	nm	nm	nm	nm	
Thunder Bay	0.0	12	70	nm	37
Saint John, N.B.	10	*	70	2	32
Sydney, N.S.	2	nm	nm	nm	41
Fredericton	nm	nm	nm	nm	30
Charlottetown	2	nm	nm	nm	22
Whitehorse	nm	nm	nm	nm	32
Yellowknife	nm	nm	nm	nm	63
Dorset	2	19	138*m	nm	19

* insufficient data collected   nm – not measured   *M – based on absolute maximum ozone peak (other measurements use 99.9 percentile, but this was not available for Dorset)   *Based on city average.
SOURCE: T. Furmancyk, Environment Canada, Regulatory Affairs and Program Integration Branch, in *The State of Canada's Environment*, published by the Minister of the Environment and the Minister of Supply and Services Canada, 1991.

Climate

69. Average Daily Temperature (°C)

STATION	JAN	FEB	MAR	APR	MAY	JUNE	JULY	AUG	SEPT	OCT	NOV	DEC	ANNUAL
Goose Bay	−17.3	−15.5	−9.2	−1.8	5.1	10.9	15.5	14.2	9.0	2.5	−4.0	−13.4	−0.3
St. John's West	−4.0	−4.6	−2.0	1.8	6.4	11.3	15.8	15.6	11.8	7.3	3.3	−1.4	5.1
Charlottetown	−7.2	−7.5	−3.0	2.7	9.2	14.8	18.8	18.4	14.0	8.6	3.1	−3.6	5.7
Halifax	−5.8	−6.0	−1.7	3.6	9.4	14.7	18.3	18.1	13.8	8.5	3.2	−3.0	6.1
Saint John	−8.2	−7.7	−2.6	3.2	9.1	13.8	16.9	16.7	12.7	7.5	2.1	−5.0	4.9
Kuujjuarapik	−22.8	−23.1	−17.5	−7.1	1.2	6.3	10.2	10.6	7.2	2.1	−5.0	−16.6	−4.5
Quebec	−12.4	−11.0	−4.6	3.3	10.8	16.3	19.1	17.6	12.5	6.5	−0.5	−9.1	4.0
Sept-Îles	−14.6	−13.0	−6.8	0.0	5.9	11.6	15.2	14.2	9.2	3.4	−2.7	−11.0	0.9
Montreal	−10.3	−8.8	−2.4	5.7	12.9	18.0	20.8	19.4	14.5	8.3	1.6	−6.9	6.1
Ottawa	−10.7	−9.2	−2.6	5.9	13.0	18.1	20.8	19.4	14.7	8.3	1.5	−7.2	6.0
Thunder Bay	−15.0	−12.8	−5.6	2.7	9.0	13.9	17.7	16.4	11.2	5.4	−2.6	−11.3	2.4
Toronto	−4.5	−3.8	1.0	7.5	13.8	18.9	22.1	21.1	16.9	10.7	4.9	−1.5	8.9
Windsor	−5.0	−3.9	1.7	8.1	14.4	19.7	22.4	21.3	17.4	10.9	4.7	−1.9	9.1
The Pas	−21.4	−17.5	−10.0	0.5	8.7	14.8	17.7	16.4	9.9	3.5	−7.7	−18.0	−0.3
Winnipeg	−18.3	−15.1	−7.0	3.8	11.6	16.9	19.8	18.3	12.4	5.7	−4.7	−14.6	2.4
Churchill	−26.9	−25.4	−20.2	−10.0	−1.1	6.1	11.8	11.3	5.5	−1.4	−12.5	−22.7	−7.1
Regina	−16.5	−12.9	−6.0	4.1	11.4	16.4	19.1	18.1	11.6	5.1	−5.1	−13.6	2.6
Saskatoon	−17.5	−13.9	−7.0	3.9	11.5	16.2	18.6	17.4	11.2	4.8	−6.0	−14.7	2.0
Calgary	−9.6	−6.3	−2.5	4.1	9.7	14.0	16.4	15.7	10.6	5.7	−3.0	−8.3	3.9
Edmonton	−14.2	−10.8	−5.4	3.7	10.3	14.2	16.0	15.0	9.9	4.6	−5.7	−12.2	2.1
Penticton	−2.0	0.7	4.5	8.7	13.3	17.6	20.3	19.9	14.7	8.7	3.2	−1.1	9.0
Vancouver	3.0	4.7	6.3	8.8	12.1	15.2	17.2	17.4	14.3	10.0	6.0	3.5	9.9
Prince Rupert	0.8	2.5	3.7	5.5	8.4	10.9	12.9	13.3	11.3	8.0	3.8	1.7	6.9
Alert	−31.9	−33.6	−33.1	−25.1	−11.6	−1.0	3.4	1.0	−9.7	−19.5	−27.0	−29.5	−18.1
Inuvik	−28.8	−28.5	−24.1	−14.1	−0.7	10.6	13.8	10.5	3.3	−8.2	−21.5	−26.1	−9.5
Yellowknife	−27.9	−24.5	−18.5	−6.2	5.0	13.1	16.5	14.1	6.7	−1.4	−14.8	−24.1	−5.2
Whitehorse	−18.7	−13.1	−7.2	0.3	6.6	11.6	14.0	12.3	7.3	0.7	−10.0	−15.9	−1.0
Resolute	−32.0	−33.0	−31.2	−23.5	−11.0	−0.6	4.0	1.9	−5.0	−15.2	−24.3	−29.0	−16.6

70. Average Monthly Precipitation (mm)

STATION	JAN	FEB	MAR	APR	MAY	JUNE	JULY	AUG	SEPT	OCT	NOV	DEC	ANNUAL
Goose Bay	64.9	57.0	68.6	57.1	66.4	100.9	119.4	98.3	90.6	78.8	79.9	77.6	959.5
St. John's West	179.4	154.9	146.3	124.5	107.0	93.5	77.8	113.8	117.0	149.0	152.8	163.5	1579.5
Charlottetown	97.1	82.3	83.1	88.3	94.2	87.5	78.5	90.1	91.9	112.4	115.0	116.7	1137.1
Halifax	146.9	119.1	122.6	124.4	110.5	98.4	96.8	109.6	94.9	128.9	154.4	167.0	1473.5
Saint John	128.3	102.6	109.9	109.7	123.1	104.8	103.7	103.0	111.3	122.5	146.2	167.6	1432.8
Kuujjuarapik	28.1	21.1	21.1	25.1	36.4	57.3	72.7	89.0	93.6	73.3	62.1	35.1	614.9
Quebec	90.0	74.4	85.0	75.5	99.9	110.2	118.5	119.6	123.7	96.0	106.1	108.9	1207.7
Sept-Îles	86.8	68.9	80.9	93.4	96.3	92.4	90.8	99.6	111.5	100.8	99.6	107.0	1127.9
Montreal	63.3	56.4	67.6	74.8	68.3	82.5	85.6	100.3	86.5	75.4	93.4	85.6	939.7
Ottawa	50.8	49.7	56.6	64.8	76.8	84.3	86.5	87.8	83.6	74.7	81.0	72.9	869.5
Thunder Bay	32.4	25.6	40.9	47.1	69.3	84.0	79.9	88.5	86.4	60.9	49.4	39.3	703.5
Toronto	55.2	52.6	65.2	65.4	68.0	67.0	71.0	82.5	76.2	63.3	76.1	76.5	818.9
Windsor	50.3	53.7	72.0	80.3	75.7	97.0	85.3	85.7	86.7	57.9	75.4	81.6	901.6
The Pas	16.6	15.1	21.0	26.2	33.6	63.1	69.1	65.0	58.3	37.5	26.6	19.8	451.9
Winnipeg	19.3	14.8	23.1	35.9	59.8	83.8	72.0	75.3	51.3	29.5	21.2	18.6	504.5
Churchill	17.3	12.8	18.3	22.6	30.5	44.5	50.7	60.5	52.6	46.5	35.5	19.7	411.6
Regina	14.7	13.0	16.5	20.4	50.8	67.3	58.9	40.0	34.4	20.3	11.7	15.9	364.0
Saskatoon	15.9	12.9	16.0	19.7	44.2	63.4	58.0	36.8	32.1	16.9	14.1	17.2	347.2
Calgary	12.2	9.9	14.7	25.1	52.9	76.9	69.9	48.7	48.1	15.5	11.6	13.2	398.8
Edmonton	22.9	15.5	15.9	21.8	42.8	76.1	101.0	69.5	47.5	17.7	16.0	19.2	465.8
Penticton	27.3	20.6	20.4	25.8	33.0	34.4	23.3	28.4	23.0	15.7	24.3	32.1	308.5
Vancouver	149.8	123.6	108.8	75.4	61.7	45.7	36.1	38.1	64.4	115.3	169.9	178.5	1167.4
Prince Rupert	250.8	216.5	188.2	181.0	142.0	119.5	112.9	162.8	244.7	378.9	284.4	269.8	2551.6
Alert	7.8	5.2	6.8	9.4	9.9	12.7	25.0	23.8	24.3	13.2	8.8	7.4	154.2
Inuvik	15.6	11.1	10.8	12.6	19.1	22.2	34.1	43.9	24.2	29.6	17.5	16.8	257.4
Yellowknife	14.9	12.6	10.6	10.3	16.6	23.3	35.2	41.7	28.8	34.8	23.9	14.7	267.3
Whitehorse	16.9	11.9	12.1	8.3	14.4	31.2	38.5	39.3	35.2	23.0	18.9	18.9	268.8
Resolute	3.5	3.2	4.7	6.2	8.3	12.7	23.4	31.5	22.8	13.1	5.7	4.6	139.6

SOURCE: Average Daily Temperature and Average Monthly Precipitation statistics are from Environment Canada, Atmospheric Environment Service. These statistics for the 1961-1990 period are from a preliminary draft.

71. Annual Average "Number of Days with" and Bright Sunshine Hours for Selected Weather Stations

STATION	WINDS (>63 km/h)	HAIL[4]	THUNDER[5]	FOG[6]	FREEZING TEMPER- ATURES[7]	FREEZING PRECIP- ITATION[8]	RAIN[9]	SNOW[10]	BRIGHT SUNSHINE[3] (HOURS)
Goose Bay	1	*	9	14	215	13	102	97	1 564.9
St. John's	23	*	3	124	176	38	156	88	1 497.4
Charlottetown	6	*	9	47	169	17	124	68	1 818.4
Halifax	3	*	9	122	163	19	125	64	1 885.0
Saint John	6	*	11	106	173	12	124	59	1 865.3
Kuujjuarapik	3	*	6	45	243	10	83	100	1 497.8
Quebec	*	*	24	35	180	15	115	73	1 851.7
Sept-Îles	9	*	7	51	206	8	93	72	1 990.6
Montreal	1	*	25	20	155	13	114	62	2 054.0
Ottawa	*	*	24	35	165	16	107	62	2 008.5
Thunder Bay	*	*	26	38	204	8	88	61	2 202.8
Toronto	*	*	27	35	155	10	99	47	2 045.4
Windsor	2	*	33	37	136	9	105	45	n/a
The Pas	*	*	23	15	209	12	65	73	2 167.5
Winnipeg	1	3	27	20	195	12	72	57	2 321.4
Churchill	11	*	7	48	258	19	58	100	1 827.9
Regina	9	1	23	29	204	14	59	58	2 331.1
Saskatoon	*	*	19	25	202	9	57	59	2 449.7
Calgary	6	3	25	22	201	5	58	62	2 314.4
Edmonton	*	3	22	17	185	8	70	59	2 263.7
Penticton	*	*	12	1	129	1	78	29	2 032.2
Vancouver	*	*	6	45	55	1	156	15	1 919.6
Prince Rupert	4	8	2	37	107	0	218	35	1 224.1
Alert	10	0	0	46	338	5	10	93	1 767.4
Inuvik	*	*	1	24	267	6	36	99	1 898.8
Yellowknife	*	*	5	21	226	13	46	82	2 276.6
Whitehorse	*	*	6	16	224	1	52	120	1 843.8
Resolute	25	0	*	62	324	13	20	82	1 505.1

*denotes a value less than 0.5 (but no zero).
[1]Average, mean, or normal refer to the value of the particular element averaged over the period from 1951-1980.
[2]A "day with" is counted once per day regardless of the number of individual occurrences of that phenomenon that day.
[3]Bright sunshine is reported in hours and tenths.
[4]Hail is a piece of ice with a diameter of 5 mm or more.
[5]Thunder is reported when thunder is heard or lightning or hail is seen.
[6]Fog is a suspension of small water droplets in air that reduces the horizontal visibility at eye level to less than 1 km.
[7]Freezing temperature is a temperature below 0°C.
[8]Freezing precipitation is rain or drizzle of any quantity that freezes on impact.
[9]Rain is a measurable amount of liquid water (rain, showers, or drizzle) equal to or greater than 0.2 mm.
[10]Snow is a measurable amount of solid precipitation (snow, snow grains, ice crystals, or ice and snow pellets) equal to or greater than 0.2 cm.
SOURCE: Environment Canada. *The Climates of Canada*. David Phillips. Supply and Services Canada. Ottawa, 1990; Environment Canada, Atmospheric Environment Service. *Canadian Climate Normals*; Environment Canada, Atmospheric Environment Service. *Principal Station Data*.

Trade

($000 000)

COUNTRY, REGION, OR AREA	IMPORTS		EXPORTS	
	1970	1989	1970	1989
Canada	13 360	114 004	16 119	116 037
USA	42 833	493 195	43 246	363 812
Central and South America	18 380	102 005	16 633	121 315
Europe	148 448	1 360 253	136 127	1 318 800
Eastern Europe (including former USSR)	31 704	202 076	30 969	195 560
Africa	15 166	77 048	14 897	70 801
Asia	48 900	719 899	47 872	786 380
Oceania	7 096	55 703	6 312	46 819
Total Developing Economies	61 992	681 827	59 359	697 983
Total Developed Economies	237 772	2 248 556	223 130	2 126 653
World[1]	331 468	3 132 459	313 457	3 020 295

[1]World total equals the sum of "Developed economies," "Developing economies," and "Eastern Europe," including the former USSR.
SOURCE: United Nations, *1989 International Trade Statistics Yearbook*, Vol. 1, New York, 1991.

73. Imports and Exports by Economic Category and Industrial Origin, 1989

COUNTRY	% IMPORTS BY COMMODITY							% EXPORTS BY COMMODITY							
	FOOD PRODUCTS	UNPROCESSED RESOURCES	ENERGY RESOURCES	MACHINERY	TRANSPORT EQUIPMENT	CONSUMER GOODS	OTHERS	AGRICULTURAL PRODUCTS	MINERALS	FOOD BEVERAGES TOBACCO	TEXTILES	WOOD PAPER	CHEMICALS	PROCESSED METALS	OTHER MANUFACTURING
USA	5.4	20.0	11.3	21.2	19.8	19.5	2.7	8.6	2.5	4.9	2.1	4.2	13.5	54.5	9.8
Germany (West)	9.3	31.7	7.2	17.6	12.5	17.0	2.5	1.1	0.8	4.2	5.6	3.5	14.8	65.7	2.5
Japan	13.6	36.9	20.6	10.2	4.2	13.3	1.2	0.3	0.2	0.5	2.3	0.7	8.5	84.5	2.9
UK	8.8	29.6	5.1	22.5	14.6	14.0	1.6	2.0	6.8	5.7	3.8	2.7	17.3	54.9	4.0
France	8.9	32.9	8.7	20.3	13.4	15.7	0.1	6.7	0.6	10.5	6.4	3.5	18.1	51.3	2.8
Italy	11.4	37.0	11.7	17.3	12.7	9.6	0.3	2.2	0.4	4.5	18.2	2.5	12.5	55.9	3.8
USSR (former)	Not available														
Canada	5.3	21.9	4.6	25.0	28.2	12.4	2.6	6.0	10.7	2.9	0.9	17.2	8.3	51.2	2.9
Netherlands	10.8	32.2	9.9	19.6	10.8	15.8	0.9	8.0	3.0	16.1	4.2	3.6	25.3	35.1	4.7
Belgium/Luxembourg	8.6	41.3	7.6	13.2	11.5	12.0	5.7	2.7	8.1	7.9	7.1	3.6	20.0	45.5	5.0
Spain	8.8	30.6	11.6	21.9	16.8	10.2	0.0	10.0	1.0	6.7	7.5	4.0	17.0	52.0	1.7
Hong Kong	6.5	38.6	2.4	19.0	2.8	30.3	0.5	2.3	1.4	2.8	34.1	1.9	8.6	38.1	10.7
South Korea	3.9	43.8	12.4	30.8	5.3	3.6	0.3	2.9	0.2	1.4	30.9	1.0	7.5	52.1	4.0
China	Not available														
Switzerland	5.6	34.6	3.9	20.8	11.4	22.9	0.7	0.5	5.0	2.7	5.6	2.7	23.1	53.3	7.0
Singapore	5.4	25.1	13.8	32.6	8.3	13.3	1.5	4.7	0.4	3.9	5.1	2.7	23.4	57.5	2.4
Sweden	5.3	27.9	7.5	25.0	15.8	17.3	1.1	0.8	1.5	1.7	2.0	19.4	11.2	61.7	1.5
Australia	4.1	24.8	4.9	27.3	18.2	16.0	4.7	21.5	20.4	11.7	2.9	0.7	5.1	18.5	19.2
Austria	4.8	32.5	5.6	23.4	14.0	19.7	0.1	1.4	0.5	2.7	9.3	11.8	13.3	57.8	3.2
Denmark	9.5	35.5	7.0	19.4	10.8	15.2	2.7	9.8	1.4	21.5	5.0	3.7	12.8	39.8	6.1
Thailand (1987)	4.2	41.9	13.3	25.0	7.4	3.8	4.4	22.6	4.8	22.3	21.5	2.1	4.1	17.0	5.5
Finland	4.6	29.9	9.8	25.6	15.0	14.4	0.8	1.5	0.5	1.8	3.7	39.8	8.8	43.3	0.7
Mexico	13.2	37.1	3.8	27.3	6.3	11.4	0.7	9.8	34.6	3.3	2.6	1.8	9.8	37.2	0.9
Malaysia	9.0	33.0	5.3	39.2	6.2	7.0	0.3	20.2	15.3	12.6	5.6	6.3	4.6	34.0	1.4
Saudi Arabia	14.2	22.4	0.3	14.7	16.4	25.2	6.9	1.3	84.9	—	—	—	—	9.1	4.7
India (1987)	8.2	40.8	19.1	18.7	3.5	1.6	8.1	17.0	21.0	5.3	34.0	0.3	9.6	9.9	2.9
OTHER PACIFIC RIM COUNTRIES															
Indonesia	6.0	45.2	7.3	30.3	8.4	2.3	0.4	13.2	38.0	3.9	10.3	16.7	7.4	10.0	0.7
Philippines	7.3	35.9	13.1	15.0	5.1	2.6	20.9	11.2	5.8	12.2	8.0	5.1	6.2	18.7	32.8
New Zealand	6.7	29.7	5.7	21.8	19.2	16.2	0.7	17.4	1.4	37.5	10.6	7.7	6.9	16.7	1.9
Pakistan (1988)	14.8	35.0	14.1	24.6	7.6	3.5	0.3	22.1	0.5	9.9	61.4	0.1	1.1	2.8	2.2
Chile (1988)	4.0	32.1	12.1	27.0	14.0	8.6	2.1	15.2	12.8	11.3	0.8	8.9	3.7	46.6	0.8
Colombia	7.0	45.8	3.6	24.4	13.4	3.6	2.1	45.0	22.3	3.6	8.4	2.3	9.9	6.8	1.6
Bangladesh (1987)	29.4	36.0	13.6	11.7	5.5	3.3	0.4	24.1	0.0	1.1	70.8	0.2	1.6	1.9	0.4
Ecuador	8.0	44.8	4.1	23.6	12.3	6.6	0.6	42.0	44.0	6.0	0.5	0.9	5.3	1.1	0.2
Peru (1987)	16.6	38.5	4.0	25.8	9.4	5.3	0.1	10.2	25.0	14.4	10.7	0.2	17.3	20.1	2.1
Papua New Guinea (1987)	14.2	23.1	10.8	23.8	15.3	11.3	1.6	35.6	57.2	4.8	0.0	0.3	0.4	0.9	0.7
Panama	14.3	33.3	16.5	9.1	8.6	18.2	0.1	63.9	0.0	14.3	10.1	2.1	6.0	3.0	0.6
New Caledonia (1983)	20.8	16.5	22.9	9.2	11.0	19.6	0.1	0.7	15.7	0.9	0.1	0.2	0.5	70.9	11.0

SOURCE: United Nations, *1989 International Trade Statistics Yearbook*, Vol. 1, New York, 1991.

74. Imports and Exports, Principal Nations and Pacific Rim 1989

COUNTRY	($000 000 000) IMPORTS/EXPORTS	% IMPORTS/EXPORTS							
		OCEANIA	AFRICA	CANADA	EUROPE (EX. USSR)	LATIN AMERICA	ASIA (EX. USSR)	USA	USSR (FORMER)
USA	493.2/363.2	1.2/2.7	3.1/2.1	18.0/12.3	21.5/27.1	10.6/10.7	43.9/31.6	—	0.2/1.2
Germany (West)	269.9/342.4	0.7/0.8	3.0/2.7	0.8/0.8	67.9/74.7	2.7/1.5	15.1/9.9	7.5/7.3	1.7/1.8
Japan	210.8/275.2	6.5/3.6	2.0/1.9	4.0/2.5	16.3/20.7	3.8/1.9	42.3/32.9	23.4/34.1	1.3/1.1
UK	197.7/152.5	1.2/2.3	2.1/3.6	1.8/2.3	65.7/59.6	1.4/1.0	15.4/15.6	10.8/13.1	0.7/0.7
France	192.5/178.9	0.8/1.0	4.9/7.4	0.7/0.9	68.7/70.3	2.0/1.4	11.9/9.7	7.6/6.6	1.4/1.0
Italy	152.9/138.5	0.8/1.0	6.9/4.8	0.7/1.1	70.0/69.0	2.6/1.7	10.5/11.1	5.6/8.6	2.4/1.8
USSR (former)	114.6/109.2	1.0/0.0	1.2/1.4	0.6/—	72.9/70.0	1.5/0.2	13.2/13.6	4.0/0.8	—
Canada	114.0/116.0	0.6/1.0	0.9/0.8	—	13.8/10.0	2.9/1.3	14.6/11.7	65.4/74.2	0.1/0.5
Netherlands	104.3/107.9	0.4/0.5	2.6/2.3	0.8/0.6	70.3/77.9	2.2/0.6	12.5/5.0	8.3/4.1	1.3/0.5
Belgium/Luxembourg	99.7/101.3	0.7/0.4	4.6/2.5	0.6/0.4	78.1/80.6	1.6/0.6	8.3/9.0	4.6/4.8	1.2/0.5
Spain	71.4/44.5	0.6/0.5	6.4/4.6	0.5/0.9	63.6/72.4	4.5/2.7	13.0/7.6	9.1/7.4	1.8/0.9
Hong Kong	72.2/73.1	1.2/2.2	0.8/1.5	0.5/2.1	12.5/18.3	1.0/0.6	75.4/48.7	8.3/25.3	0.1/0.1
South Korea	61.5/62.4	4.4/2.1	0.8/2.0	2.7/3.0	12.4/14.0	2.3/1.5	45.1/40.4	25.9/33.2	—
China	58.6/51.6	3.0/0.9	0.7/1.4	1.8/0.8	21.3/13.2	3.7/0.5	47.9/69.7	13.3/8.4	3.6/3.5
Switzerland	58.2/51.6	0.2/1.0	1.8/2.1	0.4/0.9	79.1/66.0	0.8/2.2	9.5/17.2	6.4/8.9	0.4/1.1
Singapore	52.2/44.7	1.9/4.2	0.9/1.9	0.5/0.9	15.1/15.3	1.0/0.6	62.9/52.5	17.1/23.4	0.3/0.4
Sweden	48.9/51.5	0.5/1.5	0.4/1.8	0.8/1.6	74.1/74.3	1.6/1.4	12.0/8.7	8.2/9.3	1.6/0.7
Australia	40.0/36.7	4.5/7.5	0.4/1.7	2.4/1.4	26.9/16.9	1.5/0.9	41.3/56.5	22.7/11.2	0.1/2.4
Austria	38.9/32.4	0.1/0.5	2.2/1.8	0.5/1.0	80.6/83.0	1.0/0.6	10.0/6.9	3.6/3.5	1.7/2.7
Denmark	26.7/28.1	0.2/0.7	0.9/1.8	0.4/0.6	74.5/73.0	1.6/0.7	11.2/9.5	6.3/5.0	0.8/0.9
Thailand	25.8/20.1	2.1/2.1	1.5/3.5	1.3/1.8	20.1/23.4	1.9/0.1	58.7/47.6	13.6/20.1	0.3/0.4
Finland	24.6/23.3	0.4/1.3	0.5/1.6	0.9/1.4	66.0/64.5	1.5/0.9	11.9/7.3	6.3/6.4	11.1/14.4
Mexico	23.6/22.8	0.5/0.2	0.3/0.4	1.6/1.2	15.5/12.2	3.0/3.2	6.6/8.0	70.4/70.0	0.0/0.2
Malaysia	22.5/25.1	5.3/2.7	0.5/0.7	1.3/0.8	15.1/15.6	1.7/0.8	57.8/61.4	17.9/17.4	0.3/0.6
Saudi Arabia	21.2/28.4	1.2/1.5	1.3/0.7	0.1/—	41.0/45.9	1.5/2.3	35.2/45.9	18.2/26.0	0.1/—
India	19.9/15.7	2.5/1.3	3.0/2.4	1.3/1.0	39.1/31.5	2.2/0.1	33.1/28.2	9.0/18.6	5.2/12.5
OTHER PACIFIC RIM COUNTRIES									
Indonesia	16.4/22.2	6.3/2.1	1.2/1.0	1.9/0.5	19.5/11.4	2.6/0.2	53.7/68.3	13.6/16.0	0.3/0.5
Philippines	10.7/7.7	5.1/2.4	1.1/0.3	1.0/1.5	14.6/18.4	2.0/1.0	54.6/40.7	21.2/35.7	0.4/0.3
New Zealand	9.0/9.0	21.6/22.0	0.4/0.8	2.0/1.7	22.8/19.5	1.3/2.0	34.5/36.5	16.8/13.2	0.2/2.0
Pakistan	7.1/4.6	2.2/1.9	1.1/4.3	1.5/1.6	31.8/34.9	1.2/0.1	48.7/44.1	13.0/11.2	0.4/2.0
Chile	6.7/8.2	0.5/0.5	4.5/0.7	2.3/0.6	27.1/42.4	28.7/13.0	14.6/23.1	21.2/18.3	0.3/—
Colombia	5.0/5.7	0.3/0.1	0.0/1.3	3.6/1.2	26.0/34.2	18.7/11.1	12.1/7.0	36.2/39.3	0.2/0.3
Bangladesh	3.5/1.3	1.7/1.6	1.6/5.7	5.7/2.1	18.7/30.0	0.8/0.9	61.2/24.7	9.1/31.9	1.2/3.1
Ecuador	1.9/2.4	0.7/0.4	1.9/0.5	2.3/0.2	26.3/9.8	20.7/13.3	11.7/5.4	33.9/60.6	0.3/0.2
Peru	1.8/3.6	2.4/0.2	1.3/0.6	2.2/0.7	28.6/14.7	31.5/7.3	7.4/12.3	25.9/16.1	0.1/0.9
Papua New Guinea	1.3/1.3	46.4/7.4	0.1/0.0	2.1/0.0	8.9/33.4	0.5/0.0	33.5/56.2	8.0/2.7	0.0/0.0
Panama	1.0/0.3	0.7/0.0	0.2/0.1	0.6/1.2	10.8/28.0	17.4/4.1	9.6/1.1	38.4/46.1	0.0/0.0
New Caledonia	0.8/0.7	10.3/5.2	0.0/0.0	0.0/0.0	64.6/65.6	0.0/0.0	12.9/22.3	4.9/6.6	0.0/0.0

SOURCE: United Nations, *1989 International Trade Statistics Yearbook*, Vol. 1, New York, 1991.

Demographics

REGION OR COUNTRY	POPULATION ESTIMATE MID-1992 (MILLIONS)	BIRTH RATE (PER 1 000 POP.)	DEATH RATE (PER 1 000 POP.)	NATURAL INCREASE (ANNUAL, %)	POPULATION "DOUBLING TIME" IN YEARS (AT CURRENT RATE)	POPULATION PROJECTED TO 2025 (MILLIONS)	INFANT MORTALITY RATE[a]	TOTAL FERTILITY RATE[b]	% POPULATION UNDER AGE 15/65 +	LIFE EXPECTANCY AT BIRTH MALE/FEMALE (YEARS)	URBAN POPULATION (%)	ADULT LITERACY MALE/FEMALE OR COMBINED 1985-1990	PER CAPITA GNP, 1990 (US$)	HUMAN DEVELOPMENT INDEX (HDI), 1992
WORLD	5 420	26	9	1.7	41	8 545	68	3.3	33/ 6	63/67	43	—	3 790	—
MORE DEVELOPED	1 224	14	9	0.5	148	1 392	18	1.9	21/12	71/78	73	—	17 900	—
LESS DEVELOPED	4 196	30	9	2.0	34	7 153	75	3.8	36/ 4	61/64	34	—	810	—
LESS DEVELOPED (EXCL. CHINA)	3 031	33	10	2.3	30	5 562	84	4.4	39/ 4	58/61	37	—	1 000	—
AFRICA	654	43	14	3.0	23	1 540	99	6.1	45/ 3	52/55	30	—	630	—
Northern Africa	147	35	8	2.6	27	274	72	4.8	42/ 4	59/62	43	—	1 070	—
Algeria	26.0	35	7	2.4	28	47.1	61	4.9	44/ 4	65/67	50	70/46	2 060	0.533
Egypt	55.7	32	7	2.4	28	103.1	73	4.4	41/ 4	58/61	45	63/34	600	0.385
Libya	4.5	37	7	3.0	23	9.3	64	5.2	50/ 2	65/70	76	75/50	—	0.659
Morocco	26.2	33	8	2.4	29	43.9	73	4.2	41/ 4	62/65	46	61/38	950	0.429
Sudan	26.5	45	14	3.1	22	57.3	87	6.5	46/ 2	52/53	20	43/12	—	0.157
Tunisia	8.4	27	6	2.1	33	13.4	44	3.4	38/ 5	65/66	53	62	1 420	0.582
Western Africa	182	47	17	3.0	23	449	111	6.7	46/ 3	48/50	23	—	410	—
Benin	5.0	49	19	3.1	23	12.8	88	7.1	46/ 3	45/49	39	32/16	360	0.111
Burkina Faso	9.6	50	17	3.3	21	26.0	121	7.2	48/ 4	51/52	18	28/ 9	330	0.074
Cape Verde	0.4	41	8	3.3	21	0.9	41	5.4	45/ 5	59/63	33	48	890	0.437
Côte d'Ivoire	13.0	50	14	3.6	19	39.3	92	7.4	48/ 3	52/55	43	67/40	730	0.289
Gambia	0.9	46	21	2.6	27	2.4	138	6.3	44/ 3	42/46	22	25	260	0.083
Ghana	16.0	44	13	3.2	22	35.4	86	6.4	45/ 3	52/56	32	70/51	390	0.310
Guinea	7.8	47	22	2.5	28	16.1	148	6.1	44/ 3	40/44	22	35/13	480	0.052
Guinea-Bissau	1.0	43	23	2.0	35	1.9	151	5.8	41/ 4	40/43	27	50/24	180	0.088
Liberia	2.8	47	15	3.2	22	8.3	144	6.8	46/ 4	53/56	44	50/29	—	0.227
Mali	8.5	52	22	3.0	23	21.7	113	7.3	47/ 4	43/46	22	41/24	270	0.081
Mauritania	2.1	46	18	2.8	25	5.0	122	6.5	44/ 3	46/49	41	47/21	500	0.141
Niger	8.3	52	20	3.2	22	24.3	124	7.1	49/ 3	43/46	15	40/17	310	0.078
Nigeria	90.1	46	16	3.0	23	216.2	114	6.5	45/ 2	48/49	16	62/40	370	0.241
Senegal	7.9	45	17	2.8	25	17.4	84	6.3	46/ 3	47/49	37	52/25	710	0.178
Sierra Leone	4.4	48	23	2.6	27	10.2	147	6.5	44/ 3	41/44	30	31/11	240	0.062
Togo	3.8	50	13	3.7	19	11.3	99	7.2	49/ 2	53/57	24	56/31	410	0.218
Eastern Africa	206	47	15	3.2	22	528	110	7.0	47/ 3	50/53	19	—	230	—
Burundi	5.8	47	15	3.2	21	14.9	111	7.0	46/ 3	50/54	5	61/40	210	0.165
Comoros	0.5	48	12	3.5	20	1.4	89	7.1	48/ 3	54/58	26	15	480	0.269
Djibouti	0.4	46	17	2.9	24	1.1	117	6.6	45/ 3	46/49	79	20	—	0.084
Ethiopia	54.3	47	20	2.8	25	140.2	139	7.5	46/ 3	46/48	12	—	120	0.173
Kenya	26.2	45	9	3.7	19	62.3	62	6.7	49/ 2	59/63	22	80/59	370	0.366
Madagascar	11.9	45	13	3.2	22	31.7	115	6.6	47/ 3	53/56	23	88/73	230	0.325
Malawi	8.7	53	18	3.5	20	23.1	137	7.7	48/ 3	48/50	15	41	200	0.166
Mauritius	1.1	21	7	1.5	48	1.4	20.4	2.2	30/ 5	65/72	41	83	2 250	0.793
Mozambique	16.6	45	18	2.7	26	35.6	136	6.3	44/ 3	46/49	23	45/21	80	0.153
Reunion	0.6	24	6	1.8	38	0.9	13	2.3	33/ 5	67/75	62	—	—	—
Rwanda	7.7	51	16	3.4	20	23.2	117	8.0	48/ 3	48/51	7	64/37	310	0.186
Somalia	8.3	49	19	2.9	24	17.8	127	6.6	46/ 3	44/48	24	27/ 9	150	0.088
Tanzania	27.4	50	15	3.5	20	77.9	105	7.1	48/ 3	49/54	21	93/88	120	0.268
Uganda	17.5	52	15	3.7	19	49.6	96	7.4	49/ 2	50/52	10	62/35	220	0.192
Zambia	8.4	51	13	3.8	18	24.2	76	7.2	49/ 2	51/54	49	81/65	420	0.315
Zimbabwe	10.3	41	10	3.1	22	22.6	61	5.6	45/ 3	58/61	26	74/60	640	0.397
Middle Africa	72	45	15	3.0	23	182	97	6.1	44/ 3	49/53	38	—	460	—
Angola	8.9	47	19	2.8	25	21.6	132	6.4	45/ 3	42/46	26	56/29	—	0.169
Cameroon	12.7	44	12	3.2	22	36.3	85	6.4	46/ 3	54/59	42	66/43	940	0.313

211

REGION OR COUNTRY	POPULATION ESTIMATE MID-1992 (MILLIONS)	BIRTH RATE (PER 1 000 POP.)	DEATH RATE (PER 1 000 POP.)	NATURAL INCREASE (ANNUAL, %)	POPULATION "DOUBLING TIME" IN YEARS (AT CURRENT RATE)	POPULATION PROJECTED TO 2025 (MILLIONS)	INFANT MORTALITY RATE[a]	TOTAL FERTILITY RATE[b]	% POPULATION UNDER AGE 15/65 +	LIFE EXPECTANCY AT BIRTH MALE/FEMALE (YEARS)	URBAN POPULATION (%)	ADULT LITERACY MALE/FEMALE OR COMBINED 1985-1990	PER CAPITA GNP, 1990 (US$)	HUMAN DEVELOPMENT INDEX (HDI), 1992
Central African Republic	3.2	44	18	2.6	27	6.9	141	5.6	42/ 3	45/48	43	52/25	390	0.159
Chad	5.2	44	19	2.5	28	10.3	127	5.8	43/ 4	45/47	30	42/18	190	0.088
Congo	2.4	43	14	2.9	24	5.5	114	5.8	45/ 3	52/55	41	70/44	1 010	0.372
Equatorial Guinea	0.4	43	16	2.6	26	0.8	112	5.5	43/ 4	48/52	28	40	330	0.163
Gabon	1.1	41	16	2.5	28	1.8	99	5.2	33/ 6	51/54	43	74/49	3 220	0.545
Zaïre	37.9	46	14	3.1	22	98.2	83	6.1	43/ 4	50/54	40	84/61	230	0.262
Southern Africa	**47**	**35**	**8**	**2.7**	**26**	**106**	**57**	**4.6**	**40/ 4**	**60/66**	**52**	—	**2 390**	—
Botswana	1.4	40	9	3.1	23	3.3	45	4.8	45/ 3	55/62	24	84/65	2 040	0.534
Lesotho	1.9	41	12	2.9	24	4.4	95	5.8	43/ 4	53/62	19	—	470	0.423
Namibia	1.5	43	11	3.1	22	4.1	102	5.9	46/ 3	59/61	27	—	—	0.295
South Africa	41.7	34	8	2.6	26	92.0	52	4.5	40/ 4	61/67	56	—	2 520	0.674
Swaziland	0.8	44	12	3.2	22	2.2	101	6.2	46/ 3	51/59	23	—	820	0.458
ASIA	**3 207**	**26**	**9**	**1.8**	**39**	**4 998**	**68**	**3.2**	**33/ 5**	**63/66**	**31**	—	**1 680**	—
ASIA (EXCL. CHINA)	**2 042**	**30**	**10**	**2.0**	**34**	**3 407**	**81**	**3.9**	**36/ 4**	**60/63**	**34**	—	**2 520**	—
Western Asia	**139**	**36**	**8**	**2.8**	**24**	**313**	**63**	**4.7**	**41/ 4**	**64/68**	**62**	—	—	—
Bahrain	0.5	27	3	2.4	29	1.0	20	3.9	35/ 2	70/74	81	79/63	—	0.790
Cyprus	0.7	19	9	1.1	66	0.9	11	2.4	26/10	74/78	62	93/85	8 040	0.912
Iraq	18.2	45	8	3.7	19	51.9	67	7.0	45/ 3	66/68	73	70/49	—	0.589
Israel	5.2	21	6	1.5	45	8.0	8.7	2.9	31/ 9	75/78	91	79	10 970	0.939
Jordan	3.6	39	5	3.4	20	9.2	39	5.6	48/ 3	69/73	70	89/70	1 240	0.586
Kuwait	1.4	32	2	3.0	23	4.6	16	4.4	45/ 1	72/76	—	77/67	—	0.815
Lebanon	3.4	28	7	2.1	33	6.1	46	3.7	40/ 5	66/70	84	88/73	—	0.561
Oman	1.6	42	7	3.5	20	4.9	44	6.7	47/ 3	64/68	11	—	—	0.598
Qatar	0.5	27	2	2.5	28	0.9	26	4.5	28/ 1	69/74	90	40	15 860	0.802
Saudi Arabia	16.1	42	7	3.5	20	47.1	65	7.1	45/ 3	63/66	77	52	—	0.687
Syria	13.7	45	7	3.8	18	38.7	48	7.1	49/ 4	64/66	50	78/51	990	0.665
Turkey	59.2	29	7	2.2	32	98.1	59	3.6	35/ 4	64/69	59	90/71	1 630	0.671
United Arab Emirates	2.5	31	3	2.8	25	6.6	25	4.9	35/ 1	69/73	78	58/38	19 860	0.740
Yemen	10.4	51	17	3.5	20	29.9	124	7.5	49/ 3	48/51	25	47/21	—	0.232
Southern Asia	**1 231**	**33**	**11**	**2.2**	**31**	**2 151**	**95**	**4.3**	**38/ 4**	**58/58**	**26**	—	**440**	—
Afghanistan	16.9	48	22	2.6	27	48.5	172	6.9	46/ 4	41/42	18	44/14	—	0.065
Bangladesh	111.4	37	13	2.4	29	211.6	120	4.9	44/ 3	54/53	14	47/22	200	0.185
Bhutan	0.7	39	19	2.0	35	1.4	142	5.9	39/ 4	46/49	13	51/25	190	0.146
India	882.6	30	10	2.0	34	1 383.1	91	3.9	36/ 4	58/59	26	62/34	350	0.297
Iran	59.7	41	8	3.3	21	159.2	43	6.1	46/ 3	63/66	54	65/43	2 450	0.547
Nepal	19.9	42	17	2.5	28	40.8	112	6.1	42/ 3	50/50	8	38/13	170	0.168
Pakistan	121.7	44	13	3.1	23	281.4	109	6.1	44/ 4	56/57	28	47/21	380	0.305
Sri Lanka	17.6	21	6	1.5	46	24.0	19.4	2.4	35/ 4	68/73	22	93/84	470	0.651
Southeast Asia	**451**	**28**	**8**	**1.9**	**36**	**696**	**61**	**3.4**	**37/ 4**	**60/64**	**29**	—	—	—
Cambodia	9.1	38	16	2.2	32	13.4	127	4.5	36/ 3	47/50	13	48/22	—	0.178
Indonesia	184.5	26	8	1.7	40	278.2	70	3.0	37/ 4	58/63	31	84/62	560	0.491
Laos	4.4	46	17	2.9	24	9.8	112	6.8	44/ 4	48/51	16	—	200	0.240
Malaysia	18.7	30	5	2.5	27	34.9	29	3.6	37/ 4	69/73	35	87/70	2 340	0.789
Myanmar (Burma)	42.5	30	11	1.9	36	69.9	72	3.9	37/ 4	58/60	24	89/72	—	0.385
Philippines	63.7	32	7	2.4	28	100.8	54	4.1	39/ 4	63/66	43	90/90	730	0.600
Singapore	2.8	19	5	1.4	51	3.3	6.7	1.8	23/ 6	72/77	100	87	12 310	0.848
Thailand	56.3	20	6	1.4	48	76.4	39	2.4	34/ 4	64/69	18	96/90	1 420	0.685
Viet Nam	69.2	30	8	2.2	31	108.2	45	4.0	39/ 5	62/66	20	92/84	—	0.464
East Asia	**1 386**	**19**	**7**	**1.2**	**57**	**1 839**	**32**	**2.1**	**27/ 6**	**69/73**	**34**	—	**2 910**	—

REGION OR COUNTRY	POPULATION ESTIMATE MID-1992 (MILLIONS)	BIRTH RATE (PER 1 000 POP.)	DEATH RATE (PER 1 000 POP.)	NATURAL INCREASE (ANNUAL, %)	POPULATION "DOUBLING TIME" IN YEARS (AT CURRENT RATE)	POPULATION PROJECTED TO 2025 (MILLIONS)	INFANT MORTALITY RATE[a]	TOTAL FERTILITY RATE[b]	% POPULATION UNDER AGE 15/65 +	LIFE EXPECTANCY AT BIRTH MALE/FEMALE (YEARS)	URBAN POPULATION (%)	ADULT LITERACY MALE/FEMALE OR COMBINED 1985-1990	PER CAPITA GNP, 1990 (US$)	HUMAN DEVELOPMENT INDEX (HDI), 1992
China	1 165.8	20	7	1.3	53	1 590.8	34	2.2	28/ 6	68/71	26	84/62	370	0.612
Hong Kong	5.7	12	5	0.7	99	6.2	6.7	1.2	21/ 9	75/80	—	75	11 540	0.913
Japan	124.4	10	7	0.3	217	124.1	4.6	1.5	18/13	76/82	77	99/99	25 430	0.981
Korea, North	22.2	24	6	1.9	37	32.1	31	2.5	29/ 4	66/72	64	95	—	0.654
Korea, South	44.3	16	6	1.1	65	54.8	15	1.6	26/ 5	67/75	74	99/94	5 400	0.871
Mongolia	2.3	36	8	2.8	25	4.6	64	4.6	44/ 4	62/67	42	—	—	0.574
NORTH AMERICA	**283**	**16**	**8**	**0.8**	**89**	**363**	**9**	**2.0**	**21/12**	**72/79**	**75**	**—**	**21 580**	**—**
Canada	27.4	15	7	0.8	89	35.0	7.1	1.8	21/11	73/80	78	99	20 450	0.982
United States	255.6	16	9	0.8	89	327.5	9.0	2.0	22/13	72/79	75	99	21 700	0.976
LATIN AMERICA	**453**	**28**	**7**	**2.1**	**34**	**729**	**54**	**3.4**	**36/ 5**	**64/70**	**70**	**—**	**2 170**	**—**
Central America	**118**	**31**	**6**	**2.5**	**28**	**204**	**50**	**4.1**	**40/ 4**	**65/71**	**64**	**—**	**2 170**	**—**
Costa Rica	3.2	27	4	2.4	29	5.6	15.3	3.3	36/ 5	75/79	45	93/93	1 910	0.842
El Salvador	5.6	36	8	2.9	24	9.6	55	4.6	44/ 4	61/68	48	76/70	1 100	0.498
Guatemala	9.7	39	7	3.1	22	21.6	61	5.2	45/ 3	60/65	39	63/47	900	0.485
Honduras	5.5	40	8	3.2	22	11.5	69	5.6	46/ 3	62/66	44	76/71	590	0.473
Mexico	87.7	29	6	2.3	30	143.3	47	3.8	38/ 4	66/72	71	90/85	2 490	0.804
Nicaragua	4.1	38	8	3.1	23	8.2	61	5.0	47/ 4	59/65	57	78/78	—	0.496
Panama	2.4	24	5	1.9	37	3.7	21	2.9	35/ 5	71/75	53	88/88	1 830	0.731
Caribbean	**35**	**26**	**8**	**1.8**	**38**	**49**	**54**	**3.1**	**33/ 7**	**67/71**	**58**	**—**	**—**	**—**
Barbados	0.3	16	9	0.7	102	0.3	9.0	1.8	25/11	70/76	32	99/99	6 540	—
Cuba	10.8	18	6	1.1	62	12.9	11.1	1.9	23/ 9	74/78	73	95/93	—	0.732
Dominican Republic	7.5	30	7	2.3	30	11.4	61	3.6	39/ 3	66/69	58	85/82	820	0.595
Haiti	6.4	45	16	2.9	24	12.3	106	6.0	45/ 4	53/56	29	—	370	0.276
Jamaica	2.5	25	5	2.0	35	3.6	17	2.6	34/ 8	71/75	51	98/99	1 510	0.722
Martinique	0.4	18	6	1.2	59	0.5	9	2.0	22/ 9	74/81	82	—	—	—
Trinidad and Tobago	1.3	21	7	1.4	50	1.7	10.2	2.5	34/ 5	67/73	64	96/94	3 470	0.876
South America	**300**	**26**	**7**	**1.9**	**36**	**476**	**56**	**3.2**	**35/ 5**	**64/70**	**74**	**—**	**2 180**	**—**
Argentina	33.1	21	8	1.2	56	45.5	25.7	2.7	30/ 9	66/73	86	96/95	2 370	0.833
Bolivia	7.8	36	10	2.7	26	14.2	89	4.9	41/ 4	58/64	51	63	620	0.394
Brazil	150.8	26	7	1.9	37	237.2	69	3.1	35/ 5	62/68	74	83/80	2 680	0.739
Chile	13.6	23	6	1.8	39	19.8	17.1	2.7	31/ 6	71/76	85	94/93	1 940	0.863
Colombia	34.3	26	6	2.0	35	54.2	37	2.9	36/ 4	68/73	68	88/86	1 240	0.758
Ecuador	10.0	31	7	2.4	29	17.9	57	3.8	41/ 4	65/69	55	88/84	960	0.641
Guyana	0.8	25	7	1.8	39	1.2	52	2.6	33/ 4	61/67	35	97/94	370	0.539
Paraguay	4.5	34	7	2.7	25	9.2	34	4.7	40/ 4	65/69	43	92/88	1 110	0.637
Peru	22.5	31	9	2.2	32	37.4	76	4.0	39/ 4	60/63	70	92/79	1 160	0.600
Suriname	0.4	26	6	2.0	34	0.7	31	2.8	34/ 4	67/72	48	93/92	3 050	0.749
Uruguay	3.1	18	10	0.8	83	3.7	20.4	2.4	26/12	68/75	89	97/96	2 560	0.880
Venezuela	18.9	30	5	2.5	27	34.6	24.2	3.6	38/ 4	67/73	84	87/90	2 560	0.824
EUROPE	**511**	**12**	**10**	**0.2**	**338**	**516**	**11**	**1.6**	**20/14**	**71/78**	**75**	**—**	**12 990**	**—**
Northern Europe	**93**	**14**	**11**	**0.3**	**242**	**97**	**9**	**1.9**	**19/15**	**72/79**	**83**	**—**	**17 930**	**—**
Denmark	5.2	13	12	0.1	753	4.8	7.5	1.7	17/16	72/78	85	99	22 090	0.953
Estonia	1.6	14	12	0.2	365	1.8	25	2.0	22/11	66/75	71	—	—	—
Finland	5.0	13	10	0.3	224	4.8	5.8	1.8	19/13	71/79	62	100	26 070	0.953
Iceland	0.3	19	7	1.2	58	0.3	5.9	2.3	26/11	75/80	90	99	21 150	0.958
Ireland	3.5	15	9	0.6	122	3.3	8.0	2.2	27/11	71/77	56	99	9 550	0.921
Latvia	2.7	14	13	0.1	630	3.0	19	2.0	21/12	65/75	71	—	—	—
Lithuania	3.7	15	11	0.4	158	4.4	18	2.0	23/11	67/76	69	—	—	—
Norway	4.3	14	11	0.4	193	4.7	6.9	1.9	19/16	73/80	71	100	23 120	0.978

REGION OR COUNTRY	POPULATION ESTIMATE MID-1992 (MILLIONS)	BIRTH RATE (PER 1 000 POP.)	DEATH RATE (PER 1 000 POP.)	NATURAL INCREASE (ANNUAL, %)	POPULATION "DOUBLING TIME" IN YEARS (AT CURRENT RATE)	POPULATION PROJECTED TO 2025 (MILLIONS)	INFANT MORTALITY RATE[a]	TOTAL FERTILITY RATE[b]	% POPULATION UNDER AGE 15/65 +	LIFE EXPECTANCY AT BIRTH MALE/FEMALE (YEARS)	URBAN POPULATION (%)	ADULT LITERACY MALE/FEMALE OR COMBINED 1985-1990	PER CAPITA GNP, 1990 (US$)	HUMAN DEVELOPMENT INDEX (HDI), 1992
Sweden	8.7	14	11	0.3	210	9.0	6.0	2.1	18/18	75/80	83	99	23 860	0.976
United Kingdom	57.8	14	11	0.3	257	61.0	7.9	1.8	19/16	73/79	90	99	16 070	0.962
Western Europe	**178**	**12**	**10**	**0.2**	**398**	**174**	**7**	**1.6**	**18/14**	**73/79**	**82**	—	—	—
Austria	7.9	12	11	0.1	495	8.2	7.4	1.5	17/15	73/79	55	98	19 240	0.950
Belgium	10.0	13	11	0.2	347	9.3	7.9	1.6	18/15	72/79	95	98	15 440	0.950
France	56.9	13	9	0.4	169	58.6	7.3	1.8	20/14	73/81	73	99	19 480	0.969
Germany	80.6	11	11	−0.1	(—)	73.7	7.5	1.4	16/15	72/78	90	99	—	0.955
Luxembourg	0.4	13	10	0.3	239	0.4	7.4	1.6	17/13	71/78	78	100	28 770	0.929
Netherlands	15.2	13	9	0.5	147	16.7	6.8	1.6	18/13	74/80	89	99	17 330	0.968
Switzerland	6.9	13	10	0.3	231	6.9	6.8	1.6	16/15	74/81	60	99	32 790	0.977
Eastern Europe	**96**	**13**	**11**	**0.2**	**369**	**103**	**17**	**1.9**	**23/11**	**67/75**	**63**	—	**2 080**	—
Bulgaria	8.9	12	12	−0.0	(—)	8.6	14.8	1.7	20/13	68/75	68	95	2 210	0.865
Czechoslovakia	15.7	14	12	0.2	347	17.2	11.3	2.0	23/12	68/75	76	99	3 140	0.897
Hungary	10.3	12	14	−0.2	(—)	10.4	15.4	1.8	20/14	65/74	63	99	2 780	0.893
Poland	38.4	14	11	0.4	187	42.7	15.9	2.0	25/10	67/76	61	98	1 700	0.874
Romania	23.2	12	11	0.1	578	24.4	25.7	1.6	23/11	67/73	54	98	1 640	0.733
Southern Europe	**144**	**11**	**9**	**0.2**	**344**	**141**	**12**	**1.5**	**20/13**	**72/79**	**68**	—	**12 860**	—
Albania	3.3	25	6	1.9	36	4.5	30.8	3.0	33/ 5	70/76	36	75	—	0.791
Bosnia-Hercegovina[e]	4.2	14	6	0.8	90	4.3	15.2	1.7	28/ 6	69/75	36	—	—	—
Croatia[e]	4.6	12	11	0.1	1 386	4.8	10.0	1.7	21/12	68/76	51	—	—	—
Greece	10.3	10	9	0.1	990	10.0	10.0	1.5	19/14	73/78	58	98/99	6 000	0.791
Italy	58.0	10	9	0.1	1 386	51.9	8.6	1.3	17/14	73/80	72	98/96	16 850	0.901
Macedonia[e]	1.9	17	7	1.0	70	2.3	35.3	2.1	29/ 7	70/74	54	—	—	—
Malta	0.4	15	8	0.7	92	0.4	11.3	2.0	23/11	74/78	85	83	6 630	0.922
Portugal	10.5	11	10	0.1	533	10.5	11.0	1.4	21/13	71/78	30	89/82	4 890	0.854
Slovenia[e]	1.9	13	10	0.3	267	2.2	8.9	1.6	23/11	69/77	49	—	—	—
Spain	38.6	10	9	0.2	433	39.3	7.6	1.3	20/13	73/80	91	97/93	10 920	0.916
Yugoslavia[f]	10.0	15	9	0.5	131	11.0	24.4	2.1	24/ 9	69/74	47	97/88	—	0.857
FORMER USSR[d]	**284**	**17**	**10**	**0.7**	**104**	**362**	**39**	**2.2**	**26/ 9**	**65/74**	**66**	**99**	—	—
Armenia	3.5	24	7	1.8	40	5.0	35	2.9	30/ 5	69/75	68	—	—	—
Azerbaijan	7.1	26	6	2.0	36	11.4	45	2.7	33/ 5	67/74	53	—	—	—
Belarus	10.3	14	11	0.3	217	11.5	20	1.9	23/10	67/76	67	—	—	—
Georgia	5.5	17	9	0.9	80	6.5	33	2.2	25/ 9	68/76	56	—	—	—
Kazakhstan	16.9	22	8	1.4	50	26.8	44	2.7	32/ 6	64/73	58	—	—	—
Kyrgyzstan	4.5	29	7	2.2	31	8.7	35	3.7	37/ 5	64/72	38	—	—	—
Moldova	4.4	18	10	0.8	88	5.8	35	2.3	28/ 8	66/72	48	—	—	—
Russia	149.3	14	11	0.2	301	170.7	30	1.9	23/10	64/75	74	—	—	—
Tajikistan	5.5	38	6	3.2	22	12.2	73	5.0	43/ 4	67/72	31	—	—	—
Turkmenistan	3.9	34	7	2.7	26	6.8	93	4.2	41/ 4	62/68	45	—	—	—
Ukraine	52.1	13	12	0.1	1 155	52.9	22	1.9	22/12	66/75	68	—	—	—
Uzbekistan	21.3	33	6	2.7	25	43.1	64	4.0	41/ 4	66/72	40	—	—	—
OCEANIA	**28**	**20**	**8**	**1.2**	**57**	**39**	**33**	**2.6**	**26/ 9**	**69/75**	**71**	—	**13 190**	—
Australia	17.8	15	7	0.8	83	23.9	8.0	1.9	22/11	73/80	85	99	17 080	0.971
Fiji	0.8	27	7	2.0	35	1.1	20	3.1	38/ 3	62/60	39	80	1 770	0.713
New Zealand	3.4	18	8	1.0	71	4.0	7.6	2.1	23/11	72/78	84	99	12 680	0.947
Papua-New Guinea	3.9	34	11	2.3	31	7.3	99	5.4	40/ 3	53/55	13	32	860	0.321
Solomon Islands	0.4	41	5	3.6	20	0.8	32	6.3	47/ 3	60/61	9	60	580	—

[a]Infant deaths per 1000 live births.
[b]Average number of children born to a woman during her lifetime.
[c]The Human Development Index (HDI) is a measure of human development calculated using life expectancy, educational attainment, and per capita income. The scale ranges from 0 (low) to 1 (high).
[d]Estonia, Latvia, and Lithuania are shown under Northern Europe.
[e]Former republics of Yugoslavia.
[f]On 27 April 1992, Serbia and Montenegro formed a new state, the Federal Republic of Yugoslavia.
—indicates data unavailable or inapplicable.
(—) indicates countries where the natural increase is negative.

Definitions

Mid-1992 Population: Estimates are based on a recent census or on official national data or on UN, US Census Bureau, or World Bank projections. The effects of refugee movements, large numbers of foreign workers, and population shifts due to contemporary political events are taken into account to the extent possible.

Birth and Death Rates: These rates are often referred to as "crude rates" since they do not take a population's age structure into account. Thus, crude death rates in more developed countries, with a relatively large proportion of older persons, are often higher than those in less developed countries.

Rate of Natural Increase (RNI): Birth rate minus the death rate, implying the annual rate of population growth without regard for migration. Expressed as a percentage.

Population "Doubling Time": The number of years until the population will double assuming a *constant* rate of natural increase (RNI). Based upon the *unrounded* RNI, this column provides an indication of potential growth associated with a given RNI. It is not intended to forecast the actual doubling of any population.

Population in 2025: Population projections are based on reasonable assumptions on the future course of fertility, mortality, and migration. Projections are based on official country projections, or on series issued by the UN, the US Bureau of the Census, World Bank, or PRB projections.

Infant Mortality Rate: The annual number of deaths of infants under age one year per 1000 live births. Rates shown with decimals are completely registered national statistics, while those without are estimates from sources cited above. Rates shown in italics are based upon less than 50 annual infant deaths and, as a result, are subject to considerable yearly variability.

Total Fertility Rate (TFR): The average number of children a woman will have assuming that current age-specific birth rates will remain constant throughout her childbearing years (usually considered to be ages 15-49).

Population Under Age 15/Age 65+: The percentage of the total population in those age groups, often considered the "dependent ages."

Note

This table lists all geopolitical entities with populations of 150 000 or more and all members of the UN. These include sovereign states, dependencies, overseas departments, and some territories whose status or boundaries may be undetermined or in dispute. *More developed countries*, following the UN classification, comprise all of Europe and North America, plus Australia, Japan, New Zealand, and the former USSR. All other regions are classified as *less developed*.

Sources: The Human Development Index was compiled by the United Nations Development Program, *Human Development Report 1992*, (New York: Oxford University Press, 1992); Adult Literacy data are from the United Nations Development Program, *Human Development Report 1991* (New York: Oxford University Press, 1991); all other data is from the *1992 World Population Data Sheet*, Population Reference Bureau, 1875 Connecticut Avenue NW, Suite 520, Washington, DC 20009.

pyright Oxford University Press (Canada) 1992. All rights reserved—no
of this book may be reproduced in any form without written permission of the
sher. Photocopying or reproducing mechanically in any other way parts of
book without the permission of the publisher is an infringement of the
right law.

ps copyright Oxford University Press.

rd University Press, 70 Wynford Drive, Don Mills, Ontario M3C 1J9

nto   Oxford   New York   Delhi   Bombay   Calcutta   Madras   Karachi
a Lumpur   Singapore   Hong Kong   Tokyo   Nairobi   Dar es Salaam
e Town   Melbourne   Auckland   Madrid

associated companies in

n   Ibadan

book is printed on permanent (acid-free) paper ⊗

rd is a trademark of Oxford University Press.

adian Cataloguing in Publication Data

rd University Press (Canada)
nadian Oxford school atlas

d.
l 0-19-540895-0 (school ed.)
l 0-19-540897-7 (trade ed.)

lases, Canadian.   2.   Canada—Maps.
anford, Quentin H.   II.   Title.

?1.084 1992   912   C02-093438-2

edition 1957
nd edition 1963
 edition 1972
:h edition 1977
edition 1985
 edition 1992

ed and bound in Canada by D.W. Friesen

4 5 6 7   98 97 96 95 94 93

Acknowledgements

The publisher would like to thank the following for their assistance in the preparation of this atlas:

Agriculture Canada; Alberta Recreation and Parks; British Columbia Environment and Land Use Committee Secretariat; British Columbia Ministry of Lands and Parks; The British Petroleum Company p.l.c.; The Canadian Wheat Board; The City of Calgary; The City of Edmonton, Planning and Development Department; The City of Halifax, Development and Planning Department; The City of Winnipeg, Department of Environmental Planning; Communauté Urbaine de Montréal; Energy, Mines and Resources Canada, Distribution Section, Mineral Policy Sector, Secretariat for Geographic Names, and Surveys, Mapping and Remote Sensing Sector; Environment Canada, Lands Directorate; Hydro Québec; Manitoba Hydro; The Mining Association of Canada; The National Transportation Agency of Canada, Rail Rationalization Directorate; Nova Scotia Department of Municipal Affairs, Community Planning Division; Ontario Ministry of Natural Resources; Regional Municipality of Ottawa-Carleton; Dr. Marie Sanderson, University of Waterloo; Statistics Canada (Donald Dubreuil).

Credits

Front and back cover: Baum & Angus/Masterfile

Landsat images of Southwestern British Columbia; the Fraser River; Calgary, Alberta; Lake Huron and western Lake Erie; southern Nova Scotia; and Toronto courtesy of the Canada Centre for Remote Sensing, Energy, Mines and Resources Canada.

Satellite images of the Mackenzie Delta and the Canadian Shield courtesy of Radarsat International Inc.

Canadian Government statistics and maps are reproduced/adapted with permission of the Minister of Industry, Science, and Technology 1992. Information provided through the cooperation of Statistics Canada.

Maps   pages 120-121 Smith, Hurley, and Briden, *Phaneroxoic Paleocontinental World Maps* (Cambridge University Press) page 124 Lean, Hinrichsen, and Mardham, *WWF Atlas of the Environment* (Arrow Books) page 127 (Tropical Deforestation) Collins, *The Last Rainforest* (Oxford University Press); Collins, Sayer, and Whitmore, *The Conservation Atlas of Tropical Forests* (Simon and Schuster); *The WWF Atlas of the Environment* (Oil Spills) World Resources Institute, *World Resources, 1990-1991* (Oxford University Press); Seager, *The State of the Earth Atlas* (Unwin Hyman); *WWF Atlas of the Environment* pages 128-129 (Global Warming) *World Resources 1990-1991*; (Past and Future Temperatures) Hansen, "Global Climate Changes," *Journal of Geophysics Research*, Vol. 93, No. D-8 (1988); (Ozone Depletion) *The State of the Earth Atlas*; (Air Pollution) *World Resources, 1990-1991*, Global Environment Monitoring System, WHO/UN Environment Program, and Monitoring and Assessment Research Centre, London; (Acid Rain) US Environmental Protection Agency; *The Climates of Canada* (Ministry of Supply and Services Canada) pages 130-131 (Fresh Water) United Nations, *Human Development Report, 1991* (Oxford University Press); UNICEF, *The State of the World's Children, 1991* (Oxford University Press); World Bank, *World Development Report, 1992* (Oxford University Press); *World Resources, 1990-1991*; (Protected Areas) *World Resources, 1990-1991*; Greenpeace; the World Wildlife Fund; (Nuclear) Greenpeace; World Nuclear Directory; David Lowry, Nuclear Verification Unit, Open University; Vipin Gupta, Imperial College, London; (Military/Refugees) *Human Development Report, 1991*; *State of the Earth Atlas*; *World Resources, 1990-1991* pages 132-133 World Population Profile; Population Reference Bureau; *World Development Report, 1991* pages 134-135 *Human Development Report, 1991*; *State of the World's Children, 1991* pages 136-137 *Human Development Report, 1991*; *World Resources, 1990-1991*; *World Development Report, 1992* pages 140-141 and 143 *BP Annual Review, 1991*; *Europa Yearbook*.

Notes to Countries and Regions of the World Statistical Data

The table lists all geopolitical entities with populations of 150 000 or more and all members of the UN, including sovereign states, dependencies, overseas departments, and territories whose status or boundaries may be in dispute.

Populations are estimates based on a recent census or on official national data or on UN, US Census Bureau, or World Bank projections and provided by the Population Reference Bureau in the *1992 World Population Data Sheet*. For some smaller places, estimates are earlier than 1992.

More statistical data on the principal countries of the world can be found on pages 210 to 213.

Source: *1992 World Population Data Sheet*, Population Reference Bureau, 1875 Connecticut Avenue SW, Suite 520, Washington, DC 20009; and *The Statesman's Year-Book, 1991-1992*, Brian Hunter, ed., (New York: Macmillan, 1991).

Glossary

Ákra	cape (Greek)	Ling	mountain range (Chinese)
Älv	river (Swedish)	Llyn	lake (Welsh)
Bahia	bay (Spanish)	-misaki	cape (Japanese)
Bahr	stream (Arabic)	Mont	mountain (French)
Baie	bay (French)	Montagne	mountain (French)
Bugt	bay (Danish)	Monts	mountains (French)
Cabo	cape (Portuguese; Spanish)	Monti	mountains (Italian)
Cap	cape (French)	More	sea (Russian)
Capo	cape (Italian)	Muang	city (Thai)
Cerro	hill (Spanish)	Mys	cape (Russian)
Chaîne	mountain range (French)	-nada	gulf; sea (Japanese)
Chapada	hills (Portuguese)	-nama	cape (Japanese)
Chott	salt lake (Arabic)	Ostrova	islands (Russian)
Co	lake (Chinese)	Ozero	lake (Russian)
Collines	hills (French)	Pergunungan	mountain range (Indonesian)
Cordillera	mountain range (Spanish)	Pendi	basin (Chinese)
Costa	coast (Spanish)	Pic	summit (French; Spanish)
Côte	coast (French)	Pico	summit (Spanish)
-dake	peak (Japanese)	Pik	summit (Russian)
Danau	lake (Indonesian)	Planalto	plateau (Portuguese)
Dao	island (Chinese)	Planina	mountain range
Dasht	desert (Persian; Urdu)		(Bulgarian; Serbo-Croat)
Djebel	mountain (Arabic)	Poluostrov	peninsula (Russian)
Do	island (Korean; Vietnamese)	Puerto	port (Spanish)
Embalse	reservoir (Spanish)	Pulau-pulau	islands (Indonesian)
Erg	dunes (Arabic)	Puncak	mountain (Indonesian)
Estrecho	strait (Spanish)	Punta	cape (Italian; Spanish)
Estreito	strait (Portuguese)	Ras; Râs	cape (Arabic)
Gebel	mountain (Arabic)	Ra's	cape (Persian)
Golfe	gulf; bay (French)	Rio	river (Portuguese)
Golfo	gulf; bay (Italian; Spanish)	Rio	river (Spanish)
Göiü	lake (Turkish)	Rivière	river (French)
Gora	mountain (Russian)	Rubha	cape (Gaelic)
Gunto	islands (Japanese)	-saki	cape (Japanese)
Gunung	mountain (Indonesian; Malay)	Salina	salt pan (Spanish)
Hafen	harbour (German)	-san	mountain (Japanese)
Hai	sea (Chinese)	-sanchi	mountains (Japanese)
Ho	river (Chinese)	-sanmyaku	mountain range (Japanese)
Hu	lake (Chinese)	Sebkra	salt pan (Arabic)
Île; Isle	island (French)	See	lake (German)
Ilha	island (Portuguese)	Selat	strait (Indonesian)
Inseln	islands (German)	Seto	strait (Japanese)
Isla	island (Spanish)	Shan	mountains (Chinese)
Istmo	isthmus (Spanish)	-shima	island (Japanese)
Jabal; Jebel	mountain (Arabic)	-shotō	islands (Japanese)
Jezero	lake (Serbo-Croat)	Sierra	mountain range (Spanish)
Jezioro	lake (Polish)	Song	river (Vietnamese)
Jiang	river (Chinese)	-suidō	strait (Japanese)
-jima	island (Japanese)	Tassili	plateau (Berber)
-kaikyō	strait (Japanese)	Tau	island (Chinese)
Kamen'	rock (Russian)	Teluk	bay (Indonesian)
Kap	cape (Danish)	-tō	island (Japanese)
Kepulauan	islands (Indonesian)	Tonle	lake (Cambodian)
-ko	lake (Japanese)	-wan	bay (Japanese)
Lac	lake (French)	-zaki	cape (Japanese)
Lago	lake (Italian; Portuguese; Spanish)	Zaliv	bay (Russian)
Laguna	lagoon (Spanish)		